Lecture Notes in Computer Science

Lecture Notes in Computer Science

Lecture Notes in Computer Science

Edited by G. Goos and J. Hartmanis

88

Mathematical Foundations of Computer Science 1980

Proceedings of the 9th Symposium
Held in Rydzyna, Poland, September 1–5, 1980

Edited by P. Dembiński

Springer-Verlag
Berlin Heidelberg New York 1980

Editor

P. Dembiński
Institute of Computer Science, Polish Academy of Sciences
P.O. Box 22
00-901 Warsaw PKiN
Poland

AMS Subject Classifications (1970): 68CXX, 68BXX
CR Subject Classifications (1974): 4.2, 4.3, 5.2

ISBN 3-540-10027-X Springer-Verlag Berlin Heidelberg New York
ISBN 0-387-10027-X Springer-Verlag New York Heidelberg Berlin

Printing and binding: Beltz Offsetdruck, Hemsbach/Bergstr.
2145/3140-543210

FOREWORD

The nineth symposium on Mathematical Foundations of Computer Science /MFCS'80/ was preceded by similar symposia held alternately in Poland /every even year/ and Czechoslovakia /every odd year/.

This volume contains 7 invited papers and 46 short communications, selected from 108 papers submitted to the symposium.

The program committee of MFCS'80 consisted of: J.W. de Bakker, J. Bečvář, D. Bjørner, A. Blikle, R.M. Burstall, P. Dembiński /chairman/, H. Ehrig, J. Gruska, V.E. Kotov, P. Lauer, K. Lautenbach, A. Mazurkiewicz, U. Montanari, J.W. Thatcher, J. Winkowski.

Special thanks are due to the members of the program committee for their hard work and to the following referees who helped in evaluating submitted papers: V.N. Agafonov, K.R. Apt, E. Astesiano, R.J. Back, L. Banachowski, W.M. Bartol, W. Baytel, J. Bergstra, A. Bonuccelli, H. Bollmann, A. Brandstadt, L.V. Chernobrod, L. Czaja, P. Degano, M.I. Dekhtiar, P. van Emde Boas, J.A. Goguen, M. Grabowski, P. Hajek, D. Harel, I. Havel, I.M. Havel, G. Iazeolla, T. Imieliński, K. Indenmark, V.E. Itkin, R. Janicki, B. Konikowska, E. Konrad, V.V. Korneev, D. Kozen, I. Kramosil, H.J. Kreowski, W. Kwasowiec, K. Lautemann, J. van Leeuwen, J. Leszczyłowski, W. Lipski, B. Mahr, J. Małuszyński, D. Mandrioli, A. Martelli, A. Marzollo, K. Mehlhorn, R. Milner, C. Montangero, J. Morávek, V.A. Nepomniaschy, J.F. Nilsson, P. Padawitz, L. Pagli, G. Patcolla, N. Pippenger, G. Plotkin, S. Pretu, P. Pudlak, S. Radziszowski, G. Riedewald, B.K. Rosen, A. Salwicki, V.Y. Sazonov, G. Schmeltz, D. Siefkes, M.B. Smyth, I. Staiger, P.H. Starke, A. Tarlecki, C. Thanos, P.S. Thiagarajan, J.V. Tucker, M.K. Valiev, P. Wachtel-Chrząstowski, W. Wadge, E.G. Wagner, K. Wagner, G. Wechsung, A. Wieczorek, A. Wnuk, S. Žak.

The Symposium is being organized by the Institute of Computer Science of the Polish Academy of Sciences. The main part of the organizational work has been done by: A. Blikle, P. Dembiński, E. Gąsiorowska-Wirpszo, C. Góral, J. Małuszyński /symposium chairman/, B. Martyniak, A. Mazurkiewicz, J. Winkowski.

The organizers are much indebted to all those who contributed to the program of the Symposium. Finally, the help of Springer-Verlag in the timely publication of this volume is highly appreciated.

Piotr Dembiński

Warsaw, May 1980

CONTENTS

*

For technical reasons the contribution by H.J. Genrich, K. Lautenbach and P.S. Thiagarajan had to be placed at the end of this volume.

FORMAL DESCRIPTION OF PROGRAMMING CONCEPTS
A Software Engineering Viewpoint

Dines Bjørner*
Department of Computer Science
Technical University of Denmark
DK-2800-Lyngby, Denmark

In this paper we outline, partially motivate, and cursorily exemplify a planned book on ABSTRACT SOFTWARE ARCHITECTURES - and Programming Systems Design. The current au= thor is presently writing this book. In reporting on its didactics, i.e. its founda= tional theses, its techniques and contents, we explore one view of the profession of software engineering. As part of this view we advocate, in particular, a formal, ma= thematics-based software development method. One may also view this paper as a sharp= ly contrasting replique to current preferred subjects when researching, present-day methods of teaching, and especially the prevalent practising of computer science and software engineering.

Foundation

The main bases of the book, and hence of the advocated method, are two= fold. (I)** We advocate abstract software specification methods based on denotational semantics -- as "tempered" by the main ideas of algebraic semantics. And (II) we pursue formal steps of realization of abstractly specified software in terms of complementing techniques of object-, or data structure-, refinement and operation decomposition; the latter in terms mostly of sound program transformation schemes. We regard (I) to belong to the realm of "Formal Description of Programming Concepts", & (II) to belong to "Programming Methodology".

First Theses

The main THESIS is here (I) that the mastery of a not so large number of reasonably orthogonal programming concepts, and (II) that fluency in the use of a somewhat large(r) catalogue of sound object refinement and program transformation techniques, forms the common basis for (I) archi= tecting-, respectively (II) implementing- seemingly diverse software sy= stems. Examples of systems are: (I) Programming Languages, and (II) in= terpreters & compilers; (I) data base languages, and (II) their data ba= se management systems; (I) operating system command & control languages, and (II) their kernel-, nucleus-, supervisor- and i/o systems; etc..

Thus we believe in teaching abstract, functional programming [Burge,Hender= son,Gordon](I) software specification principles, and (II) formal program derivation methods -- before we teach university students the subject- oriented areas listed at the end of the last paragraph, and preferably also before we teach them the use of commercial languages such as FOR=

** Subsequent recurrent uses of (I) and (II) are interrelated, i.e. refer to first use.

* Written while at the Dept.of Comp.Sci.,University of Kiel, Federal Republic of Germany.

TRAN and PASCAL.

A derivative THESIS is that the software engineering profession needs the distinct, separately educated professions of (I) Software Architects, (II) Program Design Engineers, and -- Coders. Analogous to divisions found in e.g. civil (building) engineering.

Structure of Paper

The structure of this paper follows the planned structure of the book.

Structure of Book

The aim of the book is to advance primarily (I) the concepts and spe= cification techniques of software architectures; secondarily (II) the principles of systematic program realization; and -- only as an illustra= tion -- their application to specific subject areas. The book according= ly has three major parts: A-B-C.

Writing, publishing & studying just part (A) alone constitutes quite a substantial undertaking. The THESIS is that by going all out -- i.e. by combining architecture with design, while subsequently showing general applicability -- a proof will be convincingly demonstrated: only then will abstract specifications readily be accepted.

PART A: ABSTRACTION PRINCIPLES

The central subject of this part is the study of programming concepts, techniques for their formalization, and the study of their properties. However, before we can embark on that subject, the software architect 'in spe' must, it is firmly believed, be lead through two intermediate stages of schooling.

GROUP α : Foundations

At the foundation of any architecting of any software system, i.e. any language, there are the (natural language) notions of semiotics, being the "linguistic sum" of syntax, semantics & pragmatics. CHAPTER 0 is therefore devoted to a C.W.Morris-, R.Karnap-like view of semiotics, & to a G.Frege, B.Russell, W.W.Quine, A.Church etc. view of names & their denotation, propositions & predicates as denoting classes, and of func= tion abstraction - the mere beginnings of a λ-algebra, which in later chapters, is more fully explained, and where the Scott-Strachey λ-nota= tion is also introduced.

In order to proceed into GROUP β we also dispense with non computer science-, i.e. ordinary discrete mathematics and the barest of a nota= tional system. CHAPTERS 1 & 2 therefore surveys Logic, Set Theory, A= rithmetic, Graphs - Relations - Functions (incl. more on the λ-algebra) and Algebra; respectively an Applicative style meta-language permitting recursive definitions of e.g. sets, relations and functions, yet without properly explaining what such definitions mean. That comes later.

GROUP β: Abstraction Techniques

The purpose of this group is threfold: (i) to introduce further notational constructs in conjunction with the additional abstract data types of tuples (A^*, A^+), finitely constructed maps ($A \underset{m}{\rightarrow} B$), and 'trees', i.e. (anonymous: *(C1 C2 ... CM)* or named: *A :: B1 B2 ... BN*) cartesian product constructed Domains; (ii) to apply these -- thus illustrating principles of Representational- & Operational Abstraction; and (iii) to outline the basic components of abstract models.

Operations on objects can be either implicitly or explicitly abstracted. An implicit definition of function F consists of three parts:

i   *type: pre-F: A → BOOL*   *pre-F(a) = $P_i(a)$*

o   *type: post-F: A B → BOOL*   *post-F(a,b) = $P_o(a,b)$*

f   *type: F: A ⥲ B*

Uniqueness of definition of F is expressed by:

io $(\forall a \in A)(pre\text{-}F(a) \supset (\exists! b \in B)(post\text{-}F(a,b)))$

u $(\forall a \in A, b \in B)(pre\text{-}F(a) \wedge post\text{-}F(a,b) \supset F(a)=b)$

An explicit function definition consists of just the function F definition:

fd   *type: F: A ⥲ B*   *F(a) = (...)*

Example:

f   *type: G: $(A \underset{m}{\rightarrow} B\text{-set}) \rightarrow (A \underset{m}{\rightarrow} B)\text{-set}$*

i   *type: pre-G: $(A \underset{m}{\rightarrow} B\text{-set}) \rightarrow BOOL$*

o   *type: post-G: $(A \underset{m}{\rightarrow} B\text{-set})\ (A \underset{m}{\rightarrow} B)\text{-set} \rightarrow BOOL$*

i $pre\text{-}G(x) \triangleq (\forall bs \in \underline{rng}\, x)(bs \neq \{\})$ $pre\text{-}S(bs) = bs \neq \{\}$

$post\text{-}S(bs,b) = b \in bs$

o $post\text{-}G(x,y) = (\forall f \in y)(\underline{dom} f = \underline{dom} x) \wedge (\{\underline{rng} f \mid f \in y\} = \{\{S(x(a)) \mid a \in \underline{dom} x\} \mid S \in B\text{-set} \rightarrow B\})$

fd $G(x) = \underline{if}\ x = [\,]\ \underline{then}\ \{[\,]\}\ \underline{else}\ \{[a \rightarrow b] \cup f \mid a \in \underline{dom} x \wedge b \in x(a) \wedge f \in G(x \setminus \{a\})\}$

The input map from a's to sets of b's is converted into a set of maps from a's to b's such that every 'pairing' of a with b in some input, for all a's of the input is found in the output.

End - of - Example

CHAPTER 3 is based on the THESIS that a vast majority, if not all, composite concepts can be representationally abstracted by means of the four (five) composite abstract data type objects of sets (*-set*), tuples (*,+), maps ($\underset{m}{\rightarrow}$) (, λ-functions) and trees (*(...)*, *::*); and operationally abstracted either directly by the primitive operations defined on ob=

jects of these data types, or by simple functions (F,G,...) defined in terms of thereof. This thesis, we believe, has been supported by quite a number of abstract models of non-trivial architectures (PL/I [Bekić], ALGOL 60 [Henhapl], CHILL [Haff80] ,ADA [DDC80] ,PASCAL/R [Lamersdorf], SEQUEL/SQL [Hansen], PRTV/IS1 [Hansal], IMS [Bjørner80b], etc.). The the= sis is at some variance with the algebraic semantics school of thought. Here one does not basically presuppose any given abstract data types. The restrict, derive, enrich etc. operations of CLEAR [Burstall] howe= ver point to a consolidation of the two views. For each of the data ty= pes we establish a set of 'laws'. These expresses properties of the ob= jects of the data types. Given an abstract model one can now use these laws to prove asserted properties of the definitions using the data ty= pes. Although system specifications, it is argued, should most transpa= rently express such properties, rather than how they are effected, laws enabling further properties to be validated are often found useful. It is, in fact, a THESIS that formality of specifications means just this: facilitation of proofs that the specified systems further possesses o= therwise not explicitly stated properties.

In CHAPTER 4 we (1) first round up the bits & pieces already introduced in order to frame the semantic notion of Domains, and the syntactic no= tions of Domain Expressions & Domain Equations, in short: Abstract Syn= tax. Then (2) we very briefly review the Scott theory of (recursively) defined Domains -- relying otherwise on references to [Stoy77] & [Stoy80]. Finally (3) we can state what is so abstract about abstract syntax: na= mely the algebraic semantics idea of initiality [ADJ,Goguen].

The main components of a constructive definition are these three: (a) the Semantic Domain equations, (b) the Syntactic Domain equations, and (c) the definition of semantic Meaning, or Elaboration Functions. The latter ascribe meaning to syntactic objects in the form of semantic ob= jects. Subcomponents of specifications are: defined data type Invariant- & Well-Formedness Functions which specify run-time, respectively sta= tically satisfiable, respectively checkable context constraints, respect= ively -conditions that semantic, respectively syntactic objects satis= fies, respectively must satisfy. The notion of a, or the State, and the careful specification of its Domain is also introduced & emphasized in CHAPTER 5. In gently leading the reader to an understanding of the back= ground and motivation for these components, a bit more notational appa= ratus is introduced -- most significantly the 'imperative' constructs. This enables us to illustrate the stylistic techniques of Applicative vs. Imperative Specifications; Denotational vs. Computational (or Me= chanical/Operational) Semantics; and Hierarchical vs. Configurational

-- i.e. Top-Down vs. Bottom-Up -- Understanding (construction &/or do= cumentation) of Systems.

The THESIS of GROUP β is that these three pairs of contrasting specifi= cation styles, together with the complementing pair of Representational & Operational Abstraction, cover a complete set of abstraction princip= les, the conscious and judicious uses of which are a prerequisite for producing good specifications.

The distinction between Applicative-, or Functional-, and Imperative-Programming (being merely that of not using, respectively employing de= clared, assignable (updateable) variables) is here considered purely pragmatic. Thus examples will tend to emphasize their common foundation & interchangeability, rather than differences. After all: the imperati= ve forms of the meta-language, and hence of any system being abstract= ly modelled, will be defined applicatively -- with reference to the λ-no= tation. The THESIS here is that "the more abstract, i.e. specification-oriented: the more applicative -- the more concrete, realization-orien= ted: the more imperative".

The distinction between Denotational- and Computational Semantics can perhaps best be phrased as follows: If a semantics definition, Ψ, of a composite construct: "c1,c2,...,cn" can be defined as a function, F, of the semantics of its immediate constituent constructs, ci for $1 \leq i \leq n$, i.e. if:

$$\Psi(\text{"}c1,c2,\ldots,cn\text{"}) \;=\; F(\Psi(\text{"}c1\text{"}),\Psi(\text{"}c2\text{"}),\ldots,\Psi(\text{"}cn\text{"}))$$

then the definition, Ψ, is Denotational; otherwise it is Computational! Really two things are involved here: a 'denotation' and an 'algebra' principle . In the former one sets out to find the meaning of each i= dentifier of a formal text. The algebra principle is then to combine these meanings using the kind of unique homomorphism alluded to in the above schema. The contrast between Denotational- & Computational Seman= tics is also a contrast between the nature of the state concept used in respective models. In the Denotational Semantics, the state, roughly speaking, is composed from a few functional objects; whereas in the Com= putational model it usually consists of many (more), non-functional ob= jects. The THESIS is here: "the more abstract, i.e. specification-ori= ented: the more Denotational -- the more concrete, realization-oriented: the more Computational a definition is".

The distinction between Hierarchical- and Configurational Understanding is more troublesome -- but still we find it indispensible. The THESIS is here: "the more a-priori understanding the architecture Developer, respectively the User/Reader, already has of the subject area of the architecture to be defined, respectively defined, the more Top-Down, Hierarchically the Architect can proceed constructing, respectively present, the architecture definition. Vice-versa: the more experimental, concept-breaking & new concept-forming the architecture subject appears, the more Bottom-Up, Configurationally the Definer must proceed construct= ing, respectively present, the architecture. Observe that a definition thus may be "X"-developed and "Y" presented, where X is either Top-Down or Bottom-Up, and Y likewise. Today, 1980, it seems that defining, and presenting definitions of ("ordinary") programming languages, can be done Hierarchically. That for command & control languages of (and) ope= rating systems, especially when "geared" to new machine concepts, it must be done Configurationally. For the Data Base area we find ourselves somewhere between the two "extremes". That is: our taxonomic understand= ing of programming language linguistics is strong, and of operating sy= stems it is (very) weak. (It is in this sense that we do not find the title of [Brinch Hansen] appropriate: we are not presented with archi= tectures, but with very high level, and one may grant elegant to beau= tiful, designs.)

GROUP γ: Formal Description of Programming Concepts

The concepts that we cover are intended to form a complete, linguistic taxonomy of the totality of software systems! In our endeavour to apply the kind of semantic analyses upon which the book, and the method, rests, and of which the book is otherwise full of examples of, we have yet to find notions which do not fall within the subject concepts. These are: Binding, Types, Variables, Statically- & Dynamically specified Elabora= tion Orders, Scope - Visibility & Referability, Functions, Deterministic- vs. Non-Deterministic State Transitions -- i.e. Sequentiality vs. Concur= rency, and hence Processes. A meaningful treatment of some of these con= cepts require prior familiarity with other concepts. The first THESIS of this group is that the above concepts suffice, and that they enjoy some partial orderings w.r.t. "being defined in terms of" -- exemplified e.g. by the above linear ordering.

CHAPTER 6 deals with the constituents of the concept of Type. These are indirectly illustrated by the below example. The THESIS here is that the same ideas re-appear in other than just programming languages, and thus that their proper decomposition is also important when designing e.g. operating-, data base management- and office automation system langua= ges.

EXAMPLE: Type System

The example is most typical of a PASCAL/CHILL/ADA like Language:

Concrete Schema:

```
program
  types: ti = integer,
         tb = boolean,
         te = enum(q1,q2,q3)
  vars:  vi = 3 type ti,
         vb = true type tb,
         ve = q2 type te
  expr: if (vi<1 ∧ ~vb) ∨ (ve ∈ te)
         then vb
         else vi=2
end
```

Abstract Syntax - Programs, Syntactic Domains

```
1  Prgr   :: TypDef VarDef Expr
2  VarDef  = Id →m (VAL Tnm)
3  Expr    = Var|Prefix|Infix|Cond|VAL
4  Var    :: Id
5  Prefix :: MOp Expr
6  Infix  :: Expr DOp Expr
7  Cond   :: Expr Expr Expr
8  MOp     = NOT|MINUS|..
9  DOp     = ADD|AND|EQ|MBR|..
```

Abstract Syntax - Type Definitions, Syntactic Domains

```
10 TypDef  = Tnm →m Type                  Type Definitions
11 Type    = ScaTyp | CompTyp             Type Expressions
12 ScaTyp  = IntgTyp | BoolTyp | EnumTyp  Scalar Type Expressions
13 IntgTyp :: INTG                        Integers
14 BoolTyp :: BOOL                        Booleans
15 EnumTyp :: TOKEN-set                   Enumerated ('Set') Types
16 CompTyp = RecTyp | ArrTyp              Composite Type
17 RecTyp  :: Snm →m (Tnm|ScaTyp)         Record ('Structure') Types
18 ArrTyp  :: (INTG INTG)+ (Tnm|ScaTyp)   Array Types
```

Statically Decidable (Type Definition) Well-Formedness Context Condition Functions

```
19 is-wf-TypDef(td) = (∀tnm ∈ dom td)(is-wf-Type(td(tnm))(tnm,td)

20 is-wf-Type(t)(tnm,td) =
21   cases t: mk-RecTyp(rtp)      → (∀t∈rng rtp)(iswfTnmType(t,tnm,td),
22            mk-ArrTyp(bl,etp)   → (∀(l,u)∈elems bl)(l<u) ∧ iswfTnmType(etp,tnm,td),
23            T                   → true
24   type: Type → (Tnm TypDef → BOOL)

25 iswfTnmType(t,tnm,td) = is-Tnm(t)⊃((t ∈ dom td)∧ (tnm ~∈ Names(t,td)))
26   type: (Tnm|ScaTyp) Tnm TypDef → BOOL

27 Names(t,td) = (cases td(t): mk-RecTyp(rtp) → union{Names(r,td)|r∈rng rtp∧is-Tnm(r)}
28                             mk-ArrTyp(,t') → (is-Tnm(t') → Names(t',td),T → {}),
29                             T              → {})∪{t}
30   type: Tnm TypDef → Tnm-set
31   pre:  is-wf-Type(td(t))(t,td)
```

Modes are Types, Mode Expressions are Type Expression with no Type Names

```
32 Mode   = ScaTyp | CompMd            36 ConMd(tnm,td)=
33 CompMd = RecMd | ArrMd              37   cases td(tnm):
34 RecMd  :: Snm →m Mode               38     mk-RecTyp(rtp)
35 ArrMd  :: (INTG INTG)+ Mode         39       →mk-RecMd([s↦m|s∈domrtp∧
                                       40          (let t=rtp(s) in
                                       41           is-Tnm(t) → m=ConMd(t,td),
                                       42           T         → m=t) ]),
                                       43     mk-ArrTyp(bl,t)
                                       44       →mk-ArrMd(bl,is-Tnm(t) → ConMd(t,td),T→t),
                                       45     T → td(tnm)
                                       46   type: Tnm TypDef → Mode
```

Values - Semantic Domains

```
47 VAL     = ScaVAL | CompVAL
48 ScaVAL  = IntgVAL|BoolVAL|...
49 IntgVAL :: INTG
50 BoolVAL :: BOOL
51 EnumVAL :: TOKEN EnumTyp
52 CompVAL = RecVAL | ArrVAL
53 RecVAL  :: Snm →m VAL
54 ArrVAL  :: INTG+ → VAL
```

Space(indices) is set of all indices spanning entire space from lower to upper bounds in all dimensions.

Invariant (VALue) Context Constraint Function

```
55 is-wf-VAL(v)=
56   cases v:
57     mk-EnumVAL(t,mk-EnumTyp(ts)) → t∈ts,
58     mk-ArrVAL(arr) → dom arr = Space(dom arr) ∧
59                      (∀v1,v2 ∈ rng arr)((is-wf-VAL(v1)∧
60                      (xMd(v1) = xMd(v2))),
61     mk-RecVAL(rec) → (∀v1 ∈ rng rec)( is-wf-VAL(v)),
62     T              → true
```

VALue to Mode Relationship

```
xMd(v) = cases v: mk-EnumVAL(t,etp) → etp,
                  mk-RecVAL(rec)  → mk-RecMd([s→xMd(rec(s)) | s ∈ dom rec]),
                  mk-ArrVAL(arr)  → (let bl = <(li,ui) | il ∈ dom arr: 1≤i≤len il ∧
                                          (li,ui) = (min,max){il[i] | il ∈ dom arr }:
                                       v' ∈ rng arr in
                                     mk-ArrMd(bl,xMd(v'))),
                  mk-IntgVAL(i)   → mk-IntgTyp(INTG),
                  mk-BoolVAL(b)   → mk-BoolTyp(BOOL)
```

Mode to VALue Relationship - Mode Expressions Denote VALue Classes

```
MDen(md) =
  cases md:
    mk-IntgTyp(INTG)   → {mk-IntgVAL(i) | i ∈ INTG},
    mk-BoolTyp(BOOL)   → {mk-BoolVAL(b) | b ∈ BOOL},
    mk-EnumTyp(ets)    → {mk-EnumVAL(e,md) | e ∈ ets},
    mk-RecMd(rm)       →  (let map = [s→MDen(rm(s)) | s ∈ dom rm] in
                           {mk-RecVAL(rec) | rec ∈ G(map)} )   G defined in Group β
    mk-ArrMd(bl,md')   → { mk-ArrVAL([il→v | il ∈ H(bl) ∧ v ∈ vs]) | vs ⊆ MDen(md')}
```

Auxiliary Function (H) Definition

```
type: H: (INTG INTG)+ → INTG+-set
H(bl) = if bl = <> then {<>} else (let (l,u)=hd bl in {<i>⌢t | l≤i≤u ∧ t ∈ H(tl bl)})
```

Program Well-Formedness - The notion of Dictionaries - Strong Typing

```
is-wf-Prgr(td,vd,e)=
   is-wf-TypDef(td)
  ∧(let tdict = [tnm→ConMd(tnm,td) | tnm ∈ dom td ] in
    is-wf-VarDef(vd,tdict)
   ∧(let vdict = [id→md | id ∈ dom vd: ( ,tnm)=vd(id) ∧ md = tdict(tnm)] in
     is-wf-Expr(e,vdict)))

is-wf-VarDef(vd,tdict)=
   (∀(v,tn) ∈ rng vd)( tn ∈ dom dict ∧ is-wf-VAL(v) ∧ (xMd(v) = tdict(tn)))

Etcetera, etcetera, ... .
```

End - of - Exampl

Already when illustrating aspects of the type concept are we given a fai number of examples of 'similarities' between Syntactic- & Semantic Domai equations, and of structures a various functions defined between, or on, these. This enables us to bring the underlying Homomorphisms into focus. The THESIS is, throughout, that we first bring examples of hopefully goo styles of definitions, and then explain, with reference to algebra, what it is that makes the styles good.

CHAPTER 7 first disposes of the mathematical notion of a variable, which denotes a VALue, and then goes on, to treat, at great length, the ordi= nary programming language notion of variable: something which denotes a STоraGe LOCation, whose VALue can be updated. Different languages per= mit different kinds of updates, including passing of LOCations and the keeping of LOCations as VALues. This leads to the presentation of a var= iety of Storage Models.

EXAMPLE: Storage Models [Bekič70,Løvengreen]

Environments record association between variable names (i.e. Identifiers) and their denoted Locations, Storages record the association between LOCations and VALues.

Common Domains

1	*LOC*	= *ScaLOC* | *StructLOC*	4	*VAL*	= *ScaVAL* | *StructVAL*
2	*ScaLOC*	= *TOKEN*	5	*ScaVAL*	= *INTG* | *BOOL* | *CHAR*
3	*StructLOC*	= $Index \underset{m}{\rightarrow} LOC$	6	*StructVAL*	= $Index \underset{m}{\rightarrow} VAL$
7	*Index*	= *ScaVAL* | *Id*	8	*VarLOC*	:: $LOC\ Index^{+}$

Model I: Assignments only to, incl. Passing of at most, Scalar LOCations (ALGOL60)

9	*ENV*	= $Id \underset{m}{\rightarrow} LOC$	10	*STG*	= $ScaLOC \underset{m}{\rightarrow} ScaVAL$

The notion of a Variable LOCation is then required.

Model II: Assignment to, incl. Passing of, arbitrary SubLOCations (PL/I,CHILL)

11	*ENV*	= $Id \underset{m}{\rightarrow} LOC$	12	*STG*	= $LOC \underset{m}{\rightarrow} VAL$

Level-1 LOCations are those explicitly allocated, SubLOCations form a subset of LOC.

Model III: Assignment to arbitrary (Sub-)LOCations, Passing only of Level-1 LOCations

13	*ENV*	= $Id \underset{m}{\rightarrow} elemLOC$	14	*STG*	= $elemLOC \underset{m}{\rightarrow} VAL$

elementary LOCations are just TOKENs, elemLOC may be VALues. PASCAL, ADA.

End - of - Examples.

CHAPTERS 8 - 9 deal with the concepts of (primarily statement) sequencing, incl. GOTOs. Both applicative & imperative, abstract models, and models based both on the *exit* [Jones78,Bjørner80c], and continuation semantics will be covered. Thus these chapters deals with some syntactic means of designating some elaboration orders, while CHAPTERS 11-12-14 -- in addition to other notions -- deals with other elaboration orders and their designation.

□ □ □ □ □

The above should have given some taste for the theses of PART A, and the style of examples it carries. Place does not permit us to detail all aspects here, so we hasten to present our ideas on "Programming Methodology".

PART B: PROGRAM DESIGN PRINCIPLES

The main purpose of this part is to show general directions for the implementation of programs from their specification. Thereby part B forms a bridge between parts A & C. Part B is, at this time, not intended to present a comprehensive introduction to all aspects of correct program design techniques.

We focus on what is considered the basic two sides of program realization: Data Structure- & Algorithm implementation. We do so by establishing two catalogues: one for sound object refinements, another for sound operation transformations. In this part we also present a number of techniques for proving programs, including object refinements and operation decompositions correct. The THESIS of part B, as also reflected by the above split of the program realization subject, is that program implementation first should proceed from abstractions, and then evolve, in stages, and on the basis of sound refinements & transformations -- and only where existing catalogues do not suggest applicable such refinements &/or transformations, should the designer become involved in actual, detailed proofs of correctness. Another THESIS of this part is that in so stepwise developing a program, from asbtractions, through decreasingly abstract, increasingly concrete realizations, the designer is documenting all design decisions [Sintzhoff] through the refinement & transformations adopted, through the carefully stated correctness theorems, and through either the formal proof, or informal argument of correctness of these theorems. Again another THESIS of this part is that in each step of realization there is a main design decision, and that this decision is either object refinement, or is algorithm (= logic + control [Kowalski]) transformation. We most readily acknowledge that not all program realization today is, nor in the future will become, so seemingly 'mechanical', catalogue-driven, as apparently suggested above. But it is a THESIS that more & more of what we do today can be paraphrased in terms of such catalogues. Hence this part emphasizes that aspect -- leaving it to other monographs & textbooks to present the other, remaining sides of the program realization story.

CHAPTER 18 outlines through a tiny example the basic parts of the Development Method (see below). CHAPTERS 19 - 20 then attempts to establish the abovementioned catalogues. Since more has been published on the algorithm transformation aspects [Burstall & Darlington,Munich,Arsac] ,and since regrettably little has been published on object refinement [Jones 79,Bjørner78,Jones80] we shall bring more novel material in this area. Thus we present a thorough introduction to 'abstraction'[Hoare72] ,or retrieval-, to data structure invariant functions, and to theories of (refined) data types -- thus extending the set of 'laws' first introduced in chapter 3. Remaining CHAPTERS, 21 - 22, presents proof techniques, respectively a number of extensively annotated 'case' development stories.

<u>EXAMPLE</u>: <u>Realization of Abstract MAPs in terms of Binary Trees</u>

<u>The Abstraction</u>: <u>MAP Objects and Application</u>

1 $X0 = A \underset{m}{\rightarrow} B$ 2 $\underline{is\text{-}wf}\text{-}X0(x0) = \underline{true}$ 3 $x0(a) = apply0(x0,a)$

-- where, for simplicity, it is assumed that: $\underline{pre}\text{-}apply0(a) = a \in \underline{dom}\, x0$

<u>First Realization Step</u>: <u>Object Refinement</u>

4 $X1 = [BT1]$ 5 $BT :: X1\ A\ B\ X1$

Assuming an ordering, $\prec$, on the A Domain:

```
is-wf-X1(x1) = (t=nil) → (let mk-BT1(lt,a,,rt) = x1 in
                          (∀la∈xas(lt))(la≺a)∧(∀ra∈xas(rt))(a≺ra)
                          ∧is-wf-BT1(lt) ∧ is-wf-BT1(rt))
   type: X1 → BOOL

xas(t) = ((t=nil) → {},T → (let mk-BT1(lt,a,,rt) = t in xas(lt)∪{a}∪xas(rt)))
   type: X1 → A-set
```

Retrieval- or Abstraction - Function:

```
retr-X0(x1) = cases x1: nil → [], mk-BT1(lt,a,b,rt) → [a→b]∪retr-X0(lt)∪retr-X0(rt)
   type: X1 → X0
   pre:  is-wf-X1(x1)
```

Operation Decomposition - 1st Level Realization of the 'apply' operation:

```
apply1(x1,a) = (let mk-BT1(lt,a',b,rt) = x1 in
               a≺a' → apply1(lt,a),a≻a' → apply1(rt,a),a=a' → b)
   type: X1 A → B
   pre:  a ∈ xas(x1) ∧ is-wf-X1(x1)
```

Second Realization Step: Object Refinement - Embedding Binary Tree in Linked Structure

```
X2    ::  s-root:[Ptr]  TREE                      TREE  =  Ptr →m NODE2
NODE2 ::  s-left:[Ptr]  A B  s-right:[Ptr]        Ptr   =  TOKEN

is-wf-X2(mk-X2(p,t))=(trap exit with false in
                      let ps = xps(p,t){} in
                      ((ps≠domt) → exit,T → (let as = xas2(p,t) in true)))

xps(p,t)(ps) = ((p=nil)→{},(p∉domt)→ exit,T → (let mk-NODE2(lp,,,rp)=t(p) in
                                              let lps = xps(lp,t)(ps∪{p}) in
                                              let rps = xps(rp,t)(ps∪{p}) in
                                              ((lps∩rps≠{})∨(p∈lps∪rps)→exit,
                                              T → lps∪{p}∪rps )))
   type: [Ptr]  TREE → (Ptr-set → Ptr-set)

xas2(p,t) = ((p=nil) →{},T → (let mk-NODE2(lp,a,,rp) = t(p) in
                             let las = xas2(lp,t),
                                 ras = xas2(rp,t) in
                             ((∃la∈las)(a≺la)∨(∃ra∈ras)(ra≺a)) → exit,
                             T                                  → las∪{a}∪ras))
   type: [Ptr]  TREE → A-set
```

Retrieval Function:

```
retr-X1(mk-X2(p,t))=((p=nil) → nil,T → (let mk-NODE2(lp,a,b,rp) = t(p) in
                                        let lt = retr-X1(lp,t), rt = retr-X1(rp,t) in
                                        mk-BT1(lt,a,b,rt))
   type: X2 → X1
   pre:  is-wf-X2(mk-X2(p,t))
```

Operation Decomposition - 2nd Level Realization of the 'apply' Operation

```
apply2( a ,mk-X2(p,t)) = (let mk-NODE2(lp,a',b,rp) = t(p) in
                          a≺a' → apply 2(a,mk-X2(lp,t)),
                          a = a' → b,
                          a'≻a → apply2(a,mk-X (rp,t)))
   type: A  X2 → B
   comm: initial call of apply2 satifies: pre: is-wf-X2(mk-X2(p,t))
   pre:  a ∈ xas2(p,t)
```

Third Realization Step: Applicative to Imperative Program Transformation

```
dcl a := a type A, t := t type TREE, r := root type [Ptr]

Σ = (a →m A) ∪ (t →m TREE) ∪ (r →m Ptr )
```

Retrieval Function:

```
retr-X2() = mk-X2(cr,ct)
  type:  → X2
```

Operation Transformation: 3rd Level Realization of the 'apply' Function

```
apply3(p) = (def mk-NODE2(lp,a,b,rp) : (ct)(p);
               if ca=a then b else apply3(if ca a then lp else rp))
  type:  Ptr → (Σ → B)
  pre:   ca ∈ xas2(p,ct)

apply3'(mk-NODE2(lp,a,b,rp)) =
  if ca=a then b else apply3'(if ca<a then (ct)(lp) else (ct)(rp))
  type: Ptr → (Σ → B)
  pre:  ca ∈ xas2(lp,ct) ∪ {a} ∪ xas2(rp,ct)
```

Fourth Realization Step: Recursion Removal - Algorithm Transformation

```
F(x) = if B then R else F(y)                       Recursive
                                                    Schema 'equiv=
while B do x := y; return R                         alent to Iter=
                                                    ative Loop.
((lp,a',b',rp) := (ct)(cp);
while ca ≠ ca' do                                   Realization of
     (lp,a',b',rp) := if ca < ca' then (ct)(clp) else (ct)(crp);   'apply' func=
cb')                                                tion, 4th Lvl.
```

Fifth Realization Step: Object Refinement - Dynamic Data Structures

Instead of the t variable, being explicitly declared, we now dynamically allocate *NODE2* objects as *NODE5* objects:

```
NODE5 ::  s-lp:[refNODE5]  A  B  s-rp:[refNODE5]

Σ     =   (r →m refNODE5) ∪ (a →m A) ∪ (refNODE5 →m NODE5) ∪ (p →m refNODE5)

(r := cp;
 while ca < c(r·s-A) do
     r := if ca < c(r·s-A) then c(r·s-lp) else c(r·s-rp);
 c(r·s-B))
```

The p variable 'points' to root, r 'running' pointer to searched Node.

End - of - Example.

Not all objects of (Domain Equation) Specified Domains, *B*, are appro= priate in the sense of being well-formed. That is: Domain equations, especially when representing concretization of more abstract ideas, de= fine too much. Hence an *is-wf-B* predicate (total) function, *type*: $B \to BOOL$ is defined which specifies which objects are appropriate, or represen= tative of objects encountered. Operation *F*, *type*: $A \to B$, usually yields i.e. are intended to produce such well-formed objects. The stepwise development of a more abstract function *Fi* on more abstract Domains *Xi* and *Yi* into a more concrete operation *Fi'* on more concrete, refin= ed Domains *Xi'* and *Yi'* , is subject to the following kind of object consistency, and operation correctness criteria: [Jones 80]

1 $(\forall xi \in Xi, yi \in Yi)(\textit{is-wf-Xi}(xi) \supset (\exists xi' \in Xi')(xi = \textit{retr-Xi}(xi')) \wedge (\textit{is-wf-Yi}(yi) \supset (\exists yi' \in Yi')(yi = \textit{retr-Yi}(yi'))$

2 $(\forall xi' \in Xi', \ldots)(\textit{is-wf-Xi'}(xi') \supset (\exists xi \in Xi)(xi = \textit{retr-Xi}(xi') \wedge \textit{is-wf-Xi}(\textit{retr-Xi}(xi')) \wedge (\ldots)$

3 $(\forall xi' \in Xi')(\textit{is-wf-Xi'}(xi') \wedge \textit{pre-Fi}(\textit{retr-Xi}(xi')) \supset \textit{pre-Fi'}(xi')$

4 $(\forall xi' \in Xi')(\textit{is-wf-Xi'}(xi') \wedge \textit{pre-Fi'}(xi') \wedge \textit{post-Fi'}(xi', Fi'(xi')) \supset \textit{post-Fi}(\textit{retr-Xi}(xi'), \textit{retr-Yi}(Fi'(xi')))$

PART C: APPLICATIONS

The central subject of this part is now the applcation of the ideas of parts A & B to specific, primarily Systems Software, respectively Sys= tems Programming Areas. The THESIS, to repeat, is that very similar ab= straction, respectively implementation techniques can be used across the entire spectrum of otherwise classically distinct software & programming areas.

AREA I: PROGRAMMING LANGUAGES & THEIR PROCESSORS: INTERPRETERS AND COMPILERS.

The THESIS of this rather large section is basically the following: Be= fore one embarks on e.g. a compiler development project it is crucially important that precise specifications exists of the source language [Be= kič74,Haff80,Henhapl78,DDC80], the target language, the interfaces between the desired compiler and its host (e.g. operating & i/o - file) system, and the (run-time) interfaces between the compiled, executing programs and the target (e.g. operating & i/o - file) system. Needless to say,we always find this elementary and obvious requirement completely neglected & totally disregarded. The next step of (e.g. compiler) development is then (1) the construction of a formal compiling algorithm, i.e. a com= plete specification which,independent of any particular compiler struct= ure, to each construct of the source language defines exactly which code of the target language to be generated; and (2), for the case of paral= lel process languages, like CHILL [Haff80] and ADA [DDC80], the specifica= tion of the centralized, or the distributed, kernels for handling short-, medium- & long-term scheduling of processes.

References [Bjørner77a,Bjørner77b,Bjørner79] outlines general techniques for the isolated modelling of specific programming language constructs, and for the stepwise development of compiling algorithms. References [DDC80] applies and extends these to ADA.

The formal denotational static semantics specification of the compile-time checkable context conditions that programs must satisfy, and the likewise formal compiling algorithm specification then constitutes the complete specification for the compiler. Now general techniques, like those outlined in part B, in addition to the traditional techniques for the mechanical construction of lexical scanners and error correcting syntax analyzers are used in the construction of the compiler itself. This part we pursue from compiler specifications alone, i.e. essential= ly without having to know what the source- and target languages are! Again we find that too many compiler developments do not properly sepa= rate these two issues: the compiler i/o function, and its implementation.

AREA II: DATA BASE MODELS & THEIR PROCESSORS: DATA BASE MANAGEMENT SYSTEMS [Bjørner80d]

The THESIS of this section is best expressed in the following belief: Data Base Models are so very similar in their linguistic composition to Programming Languages, that just as Interpreters & Compilers are re= alizations of Programming Languages, so Data Base Management Systems are realizations of Data Base Models; and just as one constructs Programs, in some language and executes them on a Programming Language Processor, so does one construct Data Bases and embeds them in a Data Base Manage= ment System.

The central theme of this area are the three most dominant models and their realization. The models are: the Relational-, the Hierarchical-, and the Network- Data Base Models, or Data Base Languages. Examples of corresponding Data Base Management Systems are: SYSTEM/R [Astrahan], IMS [IBM] and e.g. the Data Base Management Systems based on the [CODASYL/DB TG]. For each of the three models we therefore divide our treatment in two major sections: abstractions and realizations, i.e. Data Base Models and Data Base Management Systems. Within the abstraction section we fur= ther subdivide into two subsections: first abstracting the Data Part, then abstracting the related operations (Queries, DL/I, DML, ...). We can phrase, as a THESIS of our approach to covering this area that in Data Bases the language designer emphasizes first architecting extensive= ly interrelated and sometimes highly complex data structures of the data part, then 'matching' these intricate objects with suitably abstracted operations. "Surprisingly" we find, however, that whereas the Relation= al Data Model is quite simple, its corresponding operations are very high level (i.e. to us Abstract); and that whereas both the Hierarchical and Network Data Models are quite complex, their corresponding operations are rather simple - so-called "record-at-a-time" transaction-oriented. Our treatment will, in its abstract sections, therefore suggest which higher-order abstracted operations originators of the basic ideas of Hierarchical- & Network- Data Base Models might have had in mind. Cor= respondingly we take the reverse viewpoint when dealing with Relational operations: now, in the realization section decomposing these into tuple-at-a-time operations.

Our coverage of the Data Base area, especially the stepwise development into Data Base Management Systems, exemplifies a more general THESIS of the book, and hence of how we would prefer architects to unfold systems architectures. Some systems are necessarily complex. To avoid making them unncessarily complex we start with a simplified architecture -- i.e. we lie (sometimes: quite) a bit. Then we carefully introduce further desired properties of our architecture, as the result of refining its Semantic Domains and of transforming its elaboration functions. Some of the added features transpires as the result of resource-efficiency considerations. In steps we lie, less and less. The limit of all our lies becomes the truth! Not only is it good for engineering, but also for users of the system. Once fundamental, but idealized, simplified notions are grasped, one can more easily stomach more detailed and in= volved 'features'.

EXAMPLE: Abstractions of the Data Part of Data Base Models.

The Relational Data Model:

1 $\quad RDB = (Rnm \underset{m}{\rightarrow} (Fnm \underset{m}{\rightarrow} VAL)\text{-}\underline{set})$ $\qquad$ 2 $\quad is\text{-}wf\text{-}RDB(rdb) = (\forall t1, t2\ rdb)(\underline{dom}\,t1 = \underline{dom}\,t2)$

Annotation: The Relational Data Base consists of a(n unordered) number of named Rela= tions. Each Relation is a(n unordered) set of Tuples. A Tuple consist of an unordered set of distinctly named Fields. All tuples of a Relation have the same fields.

The Hierarchical Data Model:

3 $\quad HDB = (Fid \underset{m}{\rightarrow} SEGM^{+})$ $\qquad$ 4 $\quad SEGM :: (Snm\ INTG)\ (Snm \underset{m}{\rightarrow} VAL)\ HDB$

Annotation: The Hierarchical Data Base consists of a number of named Files. Each File consists of a sequence of Segments. Each Segment has three parts: a Sequence Field, whose value is always an Integer; some other, distinctly named Fields; and a possib= ly null number of named Files, i.e. a Hierarchical Data Base itself. The latter is what 'produces' the hierarchy, and leads to our recursive Domain definition. We omit well-formedness explications.

The Network Data Model:

5 $\quad NDB :: (Fid \underset{m}{\rightarrow} R\text{-}\underline{set})\ \ (Sid \underset{m}{\rightarrow} SET)$

6 $\quad SET = SET11 \mid SET1n' \mid SET1n'' \mid SETmn' \mid SETmn''$

7 $\quad SET11 :: Fid\ \ Fid\ \ (R \underset{m}{\rightarrow} R\text{-}\underline{set})$

8 $\quad SET1n' :: Fid\ \ (R \underset{m}{\rightarrow} (Fid\ \ R\text{-}\underline{set}))$

9 $\quad SET1n'' :: Fid\ \ (R \underset{m}{\rightarrow} (Fid \underset{m}{\rightarrow} R\text{-}\underline{set}))$

10 $\quad SETmn' :: (Fid\ R) \underset{m}{\rightarrow} (Fid\ \ R\text{-}\underline{set})$

11 $\quad SETmn'' :: (Fid\ R) \underset{m}{\rightarrow} (Fid \underset{m}{\rightarrow} R\text{-}\underline{set})$

Annotation: A Network Da= Base consists of two pts.: A number of identified Fi= les, and a number of iden= tified Relations, called Sets. A File consists of an unordered collection of Records. Sets 'connect' Records of one file with sets of Records of other Files. Many such are possib= le: Either (7) only records in two files are related, the owner and the member Files. Or (8) a Record of an owner File is connected to Records of a member File, while ano= ther Record, of the same owner File is related to Records of another member File. Or (9) Records of an owner File is related to records of several, distinct member Files. Finally (10-11) a 'set' may connect records from different owner Files with Records in one (10) or more (11) member Files. The Fid's mentioned in 7-11 identify owner & mem= ber Files: the first Fid the owner, the second the member File. We omit constraints.

EXAMPLE: Concretizations of the Data Part of Some Data Base Models

The Hierarchical Model:

1 $\quad HSAM = (Fid\ \ SEGM1^{+})^{*}$ $\qquad$ 2 $\quad SEGM1 = ((Snm\ INTG)\ (Snm\ VAL)^{*}\ HSAM)$

Annotation: In the Hierarchical Sequential Access Method, HSAM, identified Files are ordered.

3 $\quad \underline{retr}\text{-}HDB(fsl) = [fid \rightarrow \langle \underline{retr}\text{-}SEGM(sl[i]) \mid 1 \leq i \leq \underline{len}\ sl \rangle \mid (fid, sl) \in \underline{elems}\ fsl]$

4 *retr-SEGM(mk-SEGM1(sf,fl,hsam)) = mk-SEGM(sf,[f↦v | (f,v)∈elems fl],retr-HSAM(hsam))*

Annotation: The retrieval function relates HDBs to HSAMs.

5 *HDAM* = $(Fid \underset{m}{\rightarrow} Ptr)$

6 *STG* = $(Ptr \underset{m}{\rightarrow} SEGM2)$

7 *SEGM2* :: $(Snm\ INTG)\ (Snm \underset{m}{\rightarrow} VAL)\ [Ptr]\ PTR$

8 *PTR* = *NxtSegmPtr | SiblPtr | ParentPtr*

Annotation: In a Hierarchical Di= rect Acces Method Segments are in= dividually allocated Storage, and pointed to. A Segment therefore contains an optional Pointer to a first (left-to-right) child, and to either the next segment, to a first segment in a sibling (File), or to its parent. The three PTR Domains are otherwise disjoint(ed).

The CODASYL/DBTG Network Model

9 *DBTG* :: $(Fid \underset{m}{\rightarrow} FILE)\ (Sid \underset{m}{\rightarrow} SET111)$

10 *FILE* = $rPtr \underset{m}{\rightarrow} R$

11 *SET111* :: *s-own:Fid s-1st:[oPtr]* $(oPtr \underset{m}{\rightarrow} OWN)$ *s-mbr:Fid* $(mPtr \underset{m}{\rightarrow} MBR)$

12 *OWN* :: *rPtr mPtr [oPtr]*

13 *MBR* :: *rPtr (mPtr | oPtr)*

Annotation: The CODASYL Network Data Base consists of identified Files and 'Sets', where we only treat the simple (1:1) sets. A File is a map from record Pointers to Records. A Set has 5 parts: names of the owner and member Files, a Pointer to a first owner Pointer-Record, and two maps: from owner- & member Pointers to respectively ow= ner & member Pointer-Records. These point to Records, as well as to next owner and member Pointer-Records. We omit rather tricky context constraints, and retrievals!

End - of - Example.

AREA III: COMMAND & CONTROL LANGUAGES -- AND THEIR OPERATING SYSTEMS

A main THESIS of this, the last, major, area & subject of the book, is, in accordance with previous analogies, to view an operating system as a processor for a usually parallel programming language. This Command & Control Language has some (traditionally) unusual (!) data types. An= other THESIS is the lack of a well-defined taxonomy, or linguistics of such operating systems. A final THESIS of our treatment of this area is that we can only properly understand the totality of all aspects of op= erating systems, by viewing them as the composition of a usually fixed number of system-related processes with a usually dynamically varying number of user-related processes, such that these processes share no resources. As a consequence of this distributed & disjointed process view we presently feel content with CSP [Hoare78,Folkjær] and BA/CBL [Mil= ner] (Communicating Sequential Processes, respectively Behaviour Algebra/ Concurrent Behaviour Language) like abstractions of such systems. In CHAPTER 14 we treat(ed) both the aspects of Concurrency, through the abstraction technique of Petri-nets & Path-Expressions, and the notion of Communication and Synchronization. In Part Cs Area III we almost ex= clusively make use of the latter kind of expression tools.

EXAMPLE: Abstraction & Design of a Low Level File Handler

The example is inspired by [Abrial] who credits it to C.A.R.Hoare. Our treatment is different from that of [Abrial] in two aspects: We start with an abstraction, and then design; and our notational system, as well as the way we compose the definition takes the form exemplified above. We believe the first difference to be important, while the the latter is 'only syntax'.

Informal specification: A File System consists of a number of Files, each distinctly identified. A File consists of a number of Pages, each distinctly identified. The o= perations of Create, Kill, Put & Get are defined on the File System. Create establish= es a new File, Kill deletes it. Put writes a possibly new Page onto a File, Get reads a Page of a File.

```
1   SYSTEM    =  Fid →m (Pid →m PAGE)                    Semantic Domains
2   Fid,Pid   =  TOKEN
3   PAGE      =  ...
4   Cmd       =  Create | Kill | Put | Get                Syntactic Domains
5   Create    :: Fid
6   Kill      :: Fid
7   Put       :: Fid Pid PAGE
8   Get       :: Fid Pid
9   elab-Cmd(cmd)(sys) =                                  Elaboration Function
10     cases cmd:
11        mk-Create(fid)      → if fid ∈ dom sys
12                                then undefined
13                                else sys + [fid → []],
14        mk-Kill(fid)        → sys \ {fid},
15        mk-Put(fid,pid,pg)  → if fid ~∈ dom sys
16                                then undefined
17                                else if pid ∈ dom(sys(fid))
18                                        then sys + [fid → sys(fid) + [pid → pg]]
19                                        else sys + [fid → sys(fid) ∪ [pid → pg]],
20        mk-Get(fid,pid)     → if fid ~∈ dom sys ∨ pid ~∈ dom(sys(fid))
21                                then undefined
22                                else (sys(fid))(pid)
23  type: Cmd → (SYSTEM ⥲ (SYSTEM | PAGE))
```

No invariant- or static context constraints need(ed) be defined. In the above we have chosen to distinguish between writing (19) and updating (18) a page. We also left un= specified what a Page is. The chosen abstraction is not necessarily a 'highest' level abstraction: the notion of page seems to be realization-oriented. Be that as it may.

In preparation for a Disk / Main Storage realization of the File System we now introduce the notion of Page Names, being 'realizations' of Page Identifiers, and hence of a Fi= le Directory mapping Page Identifiers to Page Names. File Directories are Named, and a master Catalogue records the File Identifier to Directory Name association. Our System now consists of a Catalogue, distinctly named Directories, and distinctly named Pages.

```
24  SYSTEM1  ::  CTLG   (Dnm →m DIR)   (Pnm →m PAGE)
25  CTLG     =   Fid →m Dnm
26  DIR      =   Pid →m Pnm
27  is-wf-SYSTEM1(mk-SYSTEM1(ctlg,dirs,pgs))=
28     (rng ctlg = dom dirs) ∧ (union { dirs(dn) | dn ∈ dom dirs } = dom pgs)
29  retr-SYSTEM(mk-SYSTEM1(ctlg,dirs,pgs))=
30     [fid → [pid → pg | pid ∈ dom dirs(ctlg(fid)) ∧ pg = pgs(dirs(ctlg(fid)))] | fid ∈ dom ctlg]
```

where we presently omit rewriting the Elaboration Function.

The storage hierarchy of our computer system consists of a Main Storage and a Disk.To speed up access to Pages of Files 'currently' being operated upon we keep 'copies' of the master Catalogue and some File Directories in Storage. It is thus that we intro= duce the notions of Opening & Closing Files. In the next level model we also 'think' of the Catalogue & the Directories being Page-like, i.e. we think of Storage and Disk being maps from various kinds of Names to either a Catalogue, Directories or Pages. The Directories 'copied' into Storage are directly named by their File Identifier. The Catalogue is extended to contain an entry designating itself.

```
31   SYSTEM2  ::  STG2  DISK2
32   STG2      =  (master →m CTLG2)  ∪ (Fid →m DIR)
33   DISK2     =  (catalog →m CTLG2) ∪ (Dnm →m DIR) ∪ (Pnm →m PAGE)
34   CTLG2     =  (MASTER →m catalog) ∪ CTLG
```

The operations of Open and Close copy a Directory from Disk into Storage, respective=ly from Storage to Disk deleting the copy in Storage. The operations of Create and Kill 'updates' the Storage copy of the Catalogue only: Create by 'adding' a new entry, Kill by 'removing' such an entry. The entry designate a Directory which is not yet 'filled' in. The operation of Put obtains a 'fresh' Page upon which the data is writ=ten. You will observe that the above operation 'semantics' has been designed with the following two notions in mind: avoiding, as far as possible, accesses to Disks, and enabling restarts in the event of crashes. Since manipulations are mostly restricted to Storage copies of system tables, and since writes are on new pages, the Storage and the Disk'copies'of system tables (Catalogue & Directories) do not remain identic=al. In the event of a system crash the Disk copies can be restored, thus 'rolling' the system 'back' to an earlier, 'consistent' state. It is thus we introduce our final notions of Checkpointing the system: i.e. of forcing, at operator determined intervals, the system into consistent states. For the purposes of space allocation (on Disk) we keep, in storage, a map recording all 'free' Directory & Page Tables. For the purpos=es of Checkpointing we also record which Files have been 'restored'.

```
35   SYSTEM3  ::  STG3  DISK2
36   STG3      =  STG2 ∪ (free →m (Dnm|Pnm)-set) ∪ (saved →m Fid-set)

37   is-wf-SYSTEM3(mk-SYSTEM3(stg,dsk))=
38        (master ∈ domstg) ∧ (free ∈ domstg) ∧ (saved ∈ domstg)  ∧ (catalog ∈ domdsk)
39      ∧ (stg(master) = dsk(catalog))
40      ∧ (let ctlg = (stg(master))∖{MASTER} in  (rngctlg = (dsk|Dnm)∖stg(free)))
41      ∧ (rng(stg|Fid) ⊂ rng(dsk|Dnm))
42      ∧ (union{rngm | m ∈ rng(dsk|Dnm)} = ((dsk|Pnm)∖stg(free))
43      ∧ (dom(dsk∖{catalog}) = (rng(dsk(catalog)|Fnm)
44                                ∪ union{rngm | m ∈ rng(dsk|Dnm)} ∪ stg(free)))
45      ∧ ...
```

The above well-formedness predicate expresses the conditions which must be satisfied for a state to be consistent, i.e. right after successful Checkpointing. Between such Checkpoints the equalities of lines 40 (rightmost) and 43 are to be replaced by set inclusion: ⊆.

```
46   Cmd'      =  Cmd | Open | Close | ChkF | ChkC
47   Open     ::  Fid
48   Close    ::  Fid
49   ChkF     ::
50   ChkC     ::

51   int-Create(mk-Create(fid))(mk-SYSTEM3(stg,dsk))=
52       if (fid ∈ dom(stg(master))) ∨ ((stg(free)|Dnm)={})
53          then undefined
54          else (let dnm ∈ stg(free)|Dnm in
55                mk-SYSTEM3(stg + [master → stg(master) ∪ [fid → dnm]]
56                                + [free → stg(free)∖{dnm} ],
57                           dsk))
58   type: Create → (SYSTEM3 ⥲ SYSTEM3)

59   int-Kill(mk-Kill(fid))(mk-SYSTEM3(stg,dsk))=
60       if fid ∈ dom(stg(master)∖dom(stg|Fnm)
61          then mk-SYSTEM3(stg + [master → stg(master)∖{fid}],dsk)
62          else undefined
63   type: Kill → (SYSTEM3 ⥲ SYSTEM3)
```

Only Closed files (60) may be Killed.

```
int-Close(mk-Close(fid))(mk-SYSTEM3(stg,dsk))=
    if (fid∈domstg) ∧ (stg(free)|Dnm ≠ {})
       then (let dnm∈stg(free)|Dnm in
             mk-SYSTEM3((stg + [master→stg(master) + [fid→dnm]]
                              + [free→stg(free)∖{dnm}])∖{fid},
                        dsk + [dnm→stg(fid)]))
       else undefined
type: Close → (SYSTEM3 ⥲ SYSTEM3)

int-Put(mk-Put(fid,pid,pg))(mk-SYSTEM3(stg,dsk))=
    if (fid∈domstg) ∧ (pid∈dom(stg(fid))) ∧ (stg(free)|Pnm ≠ {})
       then (let pnm∈stg(free)|Pnm in
             mk-SYSTEM3(stg + [fid→stg(fid) + [pid→pnm],free→stg(free)∖{pnm}],
                        dsk + [pnm→pg]))
       else undefined
type: Put → (SYSTEM3 ⥲ SYSTEM3)

int-ChkF(mk-ChkF())(mk-SYSTEM3(stg,dsk))=
    if dom(stg|Fnm)∖stg(saved) ≠ {}
       then (let fid∈dom(stg|Fnm)∖stg(saved) in
             if stg(free)|Dnm ≠ {}
                then (let dnm∈stg(free)|Dnm in
                      let stg' = [master→stg(master) + [fid→dnm]] +
                                 [saved→stg(saved)∖{fid}],
                          dsk' = [dnm→stg(fid)]                       in
                      mk-SYSTEM3(stg+stg',dsk+dsk'))
                else undefined)
       else mk-SYSTEM3(stg,dsk)
type: ChkF → (SYSTEM3 ⥲ SYSTEM3)
```

Etcetera, etcetera. End - of - Examples.

□ □ □ □ □

CONCLUSION

Behind the book, the outline & theses of which have been given above, lies the following, rather strongly stated belief: We are teaching and pursuing Computer Science & Software Engineering in altogether the wrong way today! It is wrong to introduce Computer Science & Software Engineering students at Universities to computing by teaching them im= perative languages like FORTRAN or Pascal. Mathematics-, Natural Science-, and other (than Computer/Software) engineering students have not been, and are not being, lead astray, and away, but strictly, and effectively on towards the core of their subjects when spending at least their first year, and usually more, studying, but not applying, theories. We should be able to do likewise. First expose students to the Art of Abstraction and to the Craft of Architecting. Then to the Engineering of Implementa= tion and Craft of Programming. The same sequence of activities should be pursued in Software Development. The vast resources today spent on testing, integrating & maintaining software must be redirected into Ar= chitecting and the many, useful steps of Design. Computer Science Theory needs focus far more attention on 'Formal Description of Programming Con= cepts', and on 'Programming Methodology' than we see done today.

REFERENCES & BIBLIOGRAPHY

[Abrial] J.R.Abrial:"A Low Level File Handler Design",Oxford Univ.Comp.Lab.,PRG, April 1980.

[ADJ] J.A.Goguen,J.W.Thatcher,E.G.Wagner & J.B.Wright:"An Initial Algebra Ap= proach to the Specification,Correctness & Implementation of Abstract Da= ta Types",in 'Current Trends in Programming Methodology' "Data Structur= ing",ed.R.Yeh,Prentice-Hall,1978.

[Arsac] J.R.Arsac:"Syntactic Source to Source Transforms and Program Manipula= tion",CACM,vol.22,No.1,1979,pp 43-54.

[Bekič70] H.Bekič & K.Walk:"Formalization of Storage Properties",in:'Formal Seman= tics of Algorithmic Languages',ed.E.Engeler,Springer-Verlag,LN in Math., vol.188,1971.

[Bekič74] H.Bekič,D.Bjørner,W,Henhapl,C.B.Jones & P.Lucas:"A Formal Definition of a PL/I Subset",IBM Techn.Rpt.TR25.139,IBM Vienna Lab.,Austria,1974.

[Bjørner77a] D.Bjørner:"Programming Languages:Linguistics & Semantics",in:European ACM Int'l.Comp.Symp.,North Holland,1977,pp 521-536.

[Bjørner77b] ---------:"Programming Languages:Formal Development of Interpreters and Compilers",ibid,pp 1-21.

[Bjørner78] ---------:"The Vienna Development Method:Software Abstraction & Program Synthesis",in:'Math.Stud.in Inform.Proc.',eds.E.Blum et al.,Springer-Verlag,LNCS75,1979.

[Bjørner78'] --------- & C.B.Jones:"The Vienna Development Method:The Meta-Language", (eds.),Springer-Verlag,LNCS61,1978. D.Bjørner:"Programming in the Meta-Language - A Tutorial" pp 24-217,& 'Software Abstr.Principles',pp 337-374.

[Bjørner79] ---------:"The Systematic Development of a Compiling Algorithm",in'State of the Art of Compiling',eds.Amirchahy & Neel,IRIA Publ.,1979.

[Bjørner80a] ---------:"Abstract Software Specifications" (ed.),Springer-Verlag,LNCS 86,1980 -- this volume is referred to below.

[Bjørner80b] --------- et al.:"A Formal Model of Abstractions & Realizations of IMS", Techn.Rept.,Comp.Sci.Dept.,Techn.Univ.of Denmark,1979-1980.

[Bjørner80c] ---------:"Experiments in Block-Structured GOTO-Modelling:Exits vs.Con= tinuations",in [Bjørner80a],pp 216-247.

[Bjørner80d] ---------:"Formalization of Data Base Models",in [Bjørner80a],pp 144-215.

[Bjørner80e] ---------:"A Multi-Micro-Processor Ring Implementation of a CSP-like Language for Parallel Programming",Techn.Note,Dept.Comp.Sci.,Techn.Univ. of Denmark,1980 -- see also:[Folkjær].

[Brinch Hansen] P.Brinch Hansen:"The Architecture of Concurrent Programs",Prentice-Hall, 1977.

[Burge] H.Burge:"Recursive Programming Techniques",'Systems Programming Series', Addison-Wesley,1975.

[Burstall] R.Burstall & J.Goguen:"The Semantics of CLEAR:A Specification Language", in [Bjørner80a],pp 292-332.

[DDC80] DDC80/2-3-5:D.Bjørner & O.Oest:"The DDC ADA Compiler Project Development Method",DDC80/11:H.H.Løvengreen et al.:"A Formal Model of ADA Storage", DDC80/13:O.Dommergaard:"The Design,and a Formal Definition,of a Virtual (A-Code) Machine for ADA",DDC80/14:O.Oest & J.Storbank:"Systematic Deriv= ation of an A-Code Compiling Algorithm from a Denotational Semantics of ADA",DDC80/15:H.H.Løvengreen & P.Folkjær:"Formal Models of ADA Tasking & Tasking Primitives",1980.DDC:Danish Datamatics Centre,Techn.Univ.Denmark.

[Darlington] J.Darlington:"A Synthesis of Several Sorting Algorithms",Acta Informati= ca,vol.11,pp 1-30,1978.

[Folkjær] P.Folkjær & D.Bjørner:"A Formal Model of a Generalized CSP-like Langu= age",Proc.IFIP80 World Congress,Melbourne,Oct.1980,North-Holland,1980.

[Gordon] M.Gordon,R.Milner,C.Wadsworth:"Edinburgh LCF",Springer-Verlag,LNCS78,1980.

[Henderson] P.Henderson:"Functional Programming:Application & Implementation",Pren= tice-Hall Int'l.,1980.

[Haff80] P.Haff,D.Bjørner et al.:"The Formal CCITT Definition of CHILL",to be publ.as CCITT Recommendation Z200,Geneva,Switzerland,1980.

[Hansal] A.Hansal:"A Formal Definition of a Relational Data Base System",IBM UK Sci.Ctr.,Techn.Rpt. UKSC 0080, June 1976.

[Hansen] K.W.Hansen:"Abstraction & Realization of SQL",M.Sc.Thesis,Dept.Comp.Sci., Techn.Univ.Denmark,1979.

[Goguen] J.Goguen:"Some Ideas in Algebraic Semantics",Naropa Inst.,Boulder,Co., UCLA Dept.Comp.Sci.,Los Angeles,Calif.,USA,1978.

[Hoare72] C.A.R.Hoare:"Proof of Correctness of Data Representation",Acta Informa= tica,vol.1,pp 271-281,1972.

[Hoare78] -----------:"Communicating Sequential Processes",CACM,vol.21,Aug.78,no.8, pp 666-677,1978.

[Jones78] C.B.Jones:"Denotational Semantics of GOTO: An Exit Formulation and its relation to Continuations",in Bjørner78' ,pp 278-304,1978.

[Jones79] ---------:"Constructing a Theory of a Data Structure as an Aid to Pro= gram Development",Acta Informatica,vol.11,pp 119-137,1979.

[Jones80] ---------:"Software Development:A Rigorous Approach",Prentice-Hall Int'l., 1980.

[Jones80'] ---------:"Models of Programming Language Concepts",in [Bjørner80a],pp 100-143,1980.

[Kowalski] Kowalski:"Algorithm = Logic + Control",CACM,vol.22,no.8,Aug.,pp 424 436, 1978.

[Lamersdorf] W.Lamersdorf & D.Bjørner:"A Formal Specification of PASCAL/R - A Relation= al Data Type extension of PASCAL",Techn.Rpt.Depts.Comp.Sci.:Techn.Univ. of Denmark & Hamburg Univ.,Germany,1979.

[Løvengreen] H.H.Løvengreen:"Varieties of Storage Models",Techn.Note,Dept.Comp.Sci., Techn.Univ.of Denmark,April 1980.

[Milner] R.Milner:"Algebraic Concurrency / Concurrent Behaviour Language / Behav= iour Algebra",Lect.Notes,Dept.Comp.Sci.,Århus Univ.,Denmark,Fall 1979, subm.for publ.:Springer-V erlag,LNCS(?),1980(?).

[Munich] F.L.Bauer & M.Broy (eds.):"Program Construction",Springer-Verlag,LNCS 69,1979.

[Sintzhoff] M.Sintzhoff:"Suggestions for Composing & Specifying Program Design De= cisions",in '4th Int'l.Colloq.on "Programming"',Springer-Verlag,LNCS83, April 1980,Paris.

[Stoy77] J.E.Stoy:"Denotational Semantics:The Scott-Strachey Approach to Program= ming Language Theory",MIT Press,1977.

[Stoy80] --------:"Foundations of Denotational Semantics",in [Bjørner80],pp 43- 99,1980.

[Henhapl] W.Henhapl & C.B.Jones:"A Formal Definition of ALGOL60 as Described in the 1975 Modified Report",in [Bjørner78'],pp 305-336,1978.

ELECTRONIC CATEGORY THEORY

R.M. Burstall
Dept. of Computer Science
University of Edinburgh
Edinburgh EH9 3JZ
Scotland

Abstract This paper describes some experiments in using algebraic and categorical ideas to write programs. In particular a program to compute colimits in a category given coproducts and coequalisers has been written, also one to 'lift' such colimits to comma categories. The discussion is informal and aims to show how categorical concepts can be painlessly realised in computational practice.

Introduction

If we can have electronic music, why not electronic category theory? 'Music has charms to soothe the savage breast', said Congreve. Has category theory less charm? Can we not make the electrons dance to a categorical tune?

This paper records some experiments in converting algebraic and categorical constructions into programs. The examples from universal algebra, sketched briefly, go back over a dozen years, those from category theory, particularly concerned with colimits, go back only three. The algebraic ones seemed at the time a useful way to attack tasks which then concerned me in a systematic manner, using general functions which might be reused on another occasion. They gave a good mathematically meaningful structure to the programs. The categorical examples were undertaken to educate myself and get a better understanding of the techniques Joseph Goguen and I were using to formulate the semantics of Clear, a specification language which we were designing. They involved colimits, which are of some general interest in view of their use (specifically pushouts) by Ehrig, Pfender and Schneider [1973] for graph grammars and by Ehrig et al [1977] for general rewriting systems. This paper does not assume knowledge of category theory beyond the basic ideas of category and functor; colimits will be explained. Arbib and Manes [1975] or MacLane [1971] are useful textbooks.

The rather general and abstract functions which were programmed can be seen as a further move in the direction of encapsulating the iterative/recursive parts of a program in a few general functions, for example LISP 'mapcar', APL '/' and other such operators advocated by Backus [1978], also CLU and ALPHARD iterators. These general functions suffice to perform non-trivial programming tasks when given as parameters suitable functions, usually combined into structures as algebras or categories. Ideally a repertoire of such general functions should allow one to construct many programs without writing any more recursions or iterations, just simple expressions. To write such general functions we need the ability to pass around functions (closures) as arguments and make data structures out of them. The language should be typeless, like LISP, or have the ability to handle parametric types.

In writing these categorical style programs I have noticed a great deal of coherence in the functions one writes; there seems to be a tight discipline. In particular I have noticed sometimes that two functions are the object and morphism parts respectively of a functor; or that several functions are related as part of an adjoint situation: unit, counit and bijection. An adjunction also includes a data type. Such 'clusters' of functions and types have a mathematical cohesiveness and rationale lacking in the apparently ad hoc clusters and modules which we usually encounter. There seems to be a possibility of categorically structured programming.

I am most grateful to my postgraduate students, David Rydeheard and Don Sannella, who have completed, typed in and debugged the colimit programs which I wrote in HOPE [Burstall, MacQueen, Sannella 1980]. Their skilled and timely assistance made it possible to write this paper. The language HOPE itself is largely due to the efforts of David MacQueen, with the help of Michael Levy and Don Sannella. My work on colimits grew out of Joseph Goguen's work on systems with Susanna Ginali, and his work with me on Clear. Gordon Plotkin has provided much stimulus and has a number of sophisticated ideas about categorical programming.

What follows is preliminary and unfinished. I hope an invited paper may be taken as a suitable occasion for bringing up rather speculative ideas.

Programs embodying concepts of universal algebra

My interest in using algebraic ideas in programming goes back to work with Peter Landin, who first interested me in universal algebra and category theory [Burstall and Landin 1969]. We developed an algebraic formulation of a simple compiler which translated expressions into reverse polish machine code. In 1968 I programmed this method in POP-2 [Burstall, Collins and Popplestone 1971], a local LISP-like language. The main function 'extend' was one which took a signature Σ and a Σ-algebra A and extended a given function f:S->A to a homomorphic function f :W (S)->A where W(S) is the Σ-word algebra on S (the free Σ-algebra on S). It is not hard to write 'extend' as a functional in a LISP-like language, once you realise that an algebra is just a list (or record) whose components are functions. One can start with non-word algebras provided that the construction operations have inverses (decomposition functions). Klaeren [1980] has recently explored the use of such functionals or 'schemes', calling them 'Structural Recursion'. Thatcher, Wagner and Wright [1979] have applied similar algebraic techniques to a more serious compiler. The 'extend' function is quite general; by giving it particular arguments it specialises to LISP 'mapcar and with other arguments to APL '/'. Indeed it may be seen as a general example of the kind of functional advocated by Backus [1978].

Let us look at 'extend' specialised to the particular case of monoids. The free monoid is not a word algebra but obeys the identity and associativity equations. Monoid 'extend' is a good example because it specialises to LISP 'mapcar' and to APL '/'; also it is simpler than the extend for arbitrary Σ-algebras. Now the free monoid on X, X*, that is the algebra of X-strings, is characterised by the unique extension, for any monoid M, of any f to an f* which makes the triangle below commute. η_X is the injection of X into X* (unit string of x).

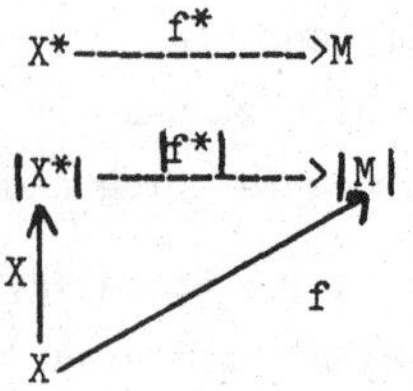

Thus if X is the set of natural numbers, f is squaring and M is the monoid of numbers with 0 and +, then f* is the sum of squares of a list of numbers. Now the extension function 'extend_m' takes M and f as parameters and gives f*. In the program the monoid M is represented by a pair (ident,mult) where ident: $|M|$ and mult: $|M|^2 \to |M|$. The monoid X* is represented by several functions used in 'extend.m'. Writing X* for $|X^*|$ for brevity, they are

empty: X* - the identity, the empty string
concat: X^{*2}->X* - the multiplication, string concatenation
is_empty: X*->truthvalue - is equal to empty
deconcat: X*->X^{*2} - inverse of concat
wrap: X->X* - η_X, unitstring
unwrap: X*->X - inverse of wrap
is_basic: X*->truthvalue - is in image of wrap

Note that deconcat given non-empty, non-basic strings must produce shorter strings but is otherwise an arbitrary inverse.

Now we define extend_m in recursive, ISWIM-like, notation thus:-

```
extend_m(ident,mult)f = fstar where rec
                          fstar(s) = if is_basic s then f(unwrap s)
                                     if is_empty s then ident
                                     else let s1,s2 = deconcat s in
                                          mult(fstar s1,fstar s2)
```

<u>Examples</u> extend_m(0,+) square (1,2,5,10) = $1^2+2^2+5^2+10^2$ = 130
extend_m(1,×)(λx.x+1)(2,5,10) = 3×6×11 = 198
extend_m(true,and) even (2,4,7) = true and true and false = false

We might use LISP lists to represent X*, with empty = NIL, concat = APPEND, wrap x = (CONS x NIL), deconcat s = ((CONS(CAR s)NIL),(CDR s)) etc. We have mapcar g = extend(nil,concat) wrap   (M is X* itself).

For APL '/' we have slash mult = extend(identof(mult),mult)wrap.
(Here identof gives the identity, e.g. identof(+)=0, by table lookup, thus for example slash+(1,2,3) = 1+2+3 or +/(1,2,3) in APL).

The general case of extension with respect to a free Σ-algebra, given Σ, is not much harder to program. We can represent the terms of the free Σ-algebra as being either a basic generating element or a pair consisting of an operator in Σ and a list of terms. The general term decomposition function is then straightforward. The target algebra is a map from operators in Σ to functions.

I used this extend technique again in 1969 for a program I wrote with Sylvia Weir [Burstall, Collins and Popplestone 1971, POP-2 Library program 'Quizzing Machine']. This was a simple computer-aided instruction program which generated sentences in English, German and Finnish from terms in an abstract syntax; it could also generate sums of increasing difficulty. The program used the 'extend' function for a general algebra to convert the terms in the abstract syntax to their homomorphic images in various algebras whose carriers were strings of words and numbers.

Another general algebraic funct on which is not hard to program is the closure of a subset of the carrier of an algebra. Here the parameters are just the algebra (i.e. its operations) and the subset. The closure is computed by taking the given set S_0 and applying each n-ary operator to each n-tuple in S_0^n; the results are collected to make S_1. We do the same to S_1 to get S_2, and so on until $S_{i+1}=S_i$. We may distinguish new elements in $S_{i+1}-S_i$ from old ones in S_i and not reapply operators to old tuples in S_{i+1}^n, thus avoiding some duplication. Closure operations are common in search algorithms, e.g. theorem proving. I used this closure function in a program for generating all automata satisfying some given input/output data [Perryman 1970]. I used it again later, generalised to many-sorted algebras, in a program to match relational structures in a picture processing problem [Barrow, Ambler and Burstall 1972]; here the operations of the algebra took matches already found and generated new ones. In both these programs the general closure function did a lot of the work, yielding a neat and well-structured program.

Computing colimits

I became interested in the problem of computing colimits of diagrams in a category when I began working with Joseph Goguen on the semantics of Clear, a specification language which we had designed together [Burstall and Goguen 1977]. At Goguen's suggestion we were using colimits to express the sharing structure of complex theories and operations on them. This grew out of his earlier work with Susanna Ginali on a categorical approach to general systems [Goguen and Ginali 1978]. Our work on Clear semantics has recently been published [Burstall and Goguen 1980]; it combines the categorical approach with denotational semantics.

Since the concept of colimit was rather new to me and abstract, I felt that I might understand it better if I coded it up and ran a few examples. I thought that this might also shed some light on an eventual implementation of Clear. Using the first order applicative language NPL [Burstall 1977], developed for transformation work with Darlington, I wrote a program to compute the colimit of a finite diagram in the category of finite sets. To understand this program let us review, briefly and informally, the underlying concepts.

First a diagram in a category $\underline{\underline{K}}$ is just a graph G with a function f_o from nodes of G to $\underline{\underline{K}}$-objects and a function f_m from edges of G to $\underline{\underline{K}}$-morphisms. For example the following is a diagram in $\underline{\underline{Set}}$

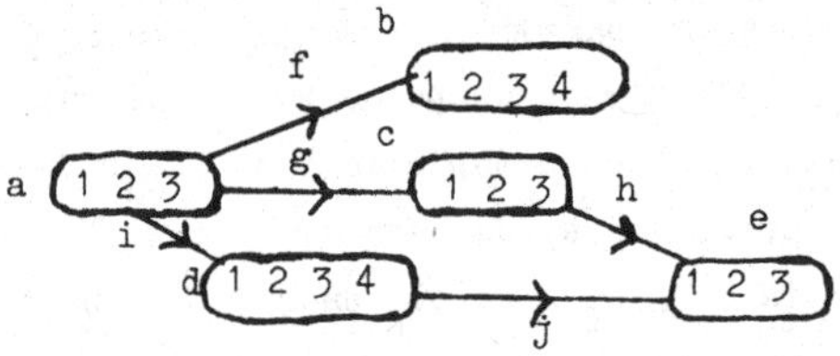

f	g	h	i	j
11	13	13	11	11
23	22	21	22	21
34	31	31	33	33
				43

Here G has nodes a,b,c,d,e and f_o maps them to the indicated sets of numbers. G has edges f,g,h,i,j and f_m maps them to the functions shown in the tables.

Now a cone on a diagram $\langle G, f_o, f_m\rangle$ is a $\underline{\underline{K}}$-object, γ, the apex, and a function Γ which assigns to each node n of G a $\underline{\underline{K}}$-morphism $\Gamma(n): f_o(n) \to \gamma$, that is from the object at node n of the diagram to the apex such that for each edge e: m -> n in G the following triangle commutes

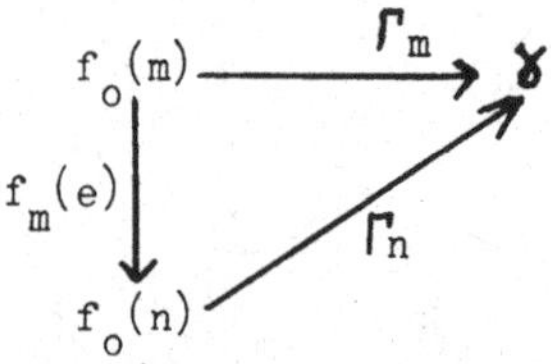

For example here is a cone on the above diagram

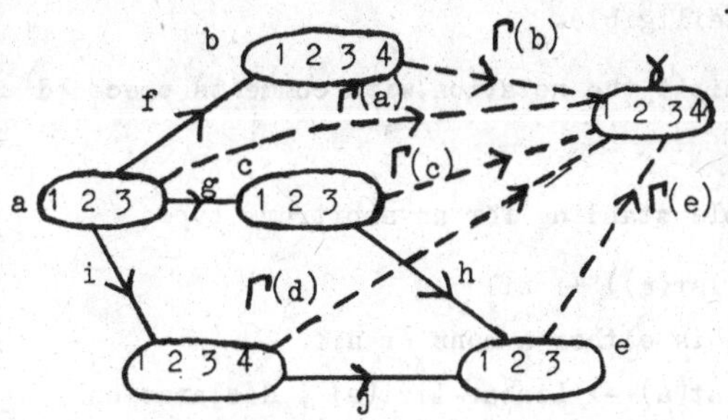

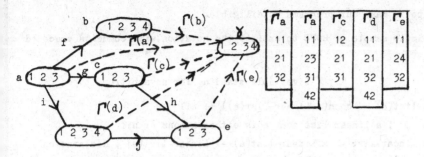

Γ_a	Γ_a	Γ_c	Γ_d	Γ_e
11	11	12	11	11
21	23	21	21	24
32	31	31	32	32
	42		42	

Now the colimit of a diagram is a prince among cones; to be more precise, it is a cone $\langle \gamma, \Gamma \rangle$ on the diagram such that for any other cone $\langle \gamma', \Gamma' \rangle$ on the same diagram there is a unique morphism $u: \gamma \to \gamma'$ such that for each node n the following triangle commutes

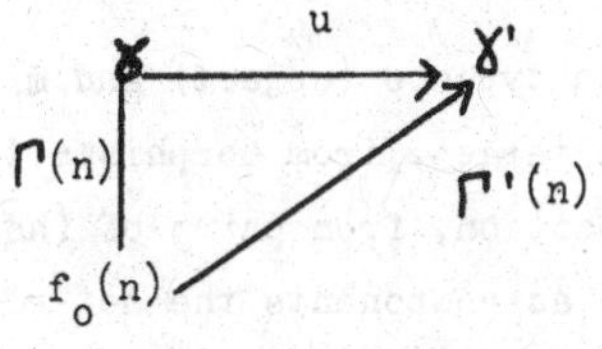

Pictorially we have two cones thus

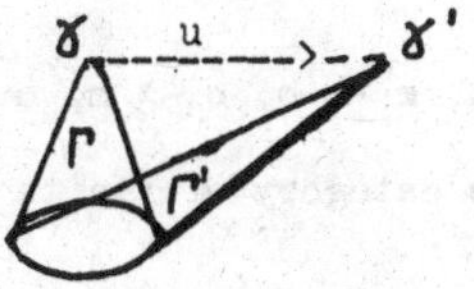

In fact the cone given in the example above is the colimit of the diagram. Its defining property, the existence of a unique morphism, is called a universal property. In the category Set it means that the colimit set has an element representing each element of each node set, with no superfluous elements, also that two elements in node sets only get the same representative if the maps along the edges of the diagrams make this necessary (since f maps 1_a to 1_b these must get the same representative if the cone triangle on f is to commute).

I coded up these notions in NPL in 1977. Recently with the able and energetic assistance of David Rydeheard and Don Sannella, postgraduate students at Edinburgh, I have rewritten the programs in HOPE [Burstall, MacQueen and Sannella 1980] an improved version of NPL which permits higher order functions taking functions as arguments. Rydeheard and Sannella entered these programs on the DEC-10 system and debugged them; it took them a couple of weeks. The HOPE colimit program, unlike the previous NPL one, works for arbitrary categories, not just Set, provided of course that we can represent their objects and morphisms finitely on the machine. To attain this generality we need either functions as parameters to functions (LISP with FUNARG) or parameterised modules (ADA); CLU allows both. HOPE is a strongly typed applicative language with auxiliary definitions and pattern-matched function calls; this helps to make our programs intelligible.

Here is a very simple sample of HOPE to exhibit the notation, with comments preceded by '!'.

```
typevar a                      ! variable standing for an arbitrary type

data Linear-list(a) == cons(a,Linear-list(a)) ++ nil
                ! a linear list over a is either a cons or nil
dec append: Linear-list(a) × Linear-list(a) -> Linear-list(a) ! declaration
--- append(nil,L) <= L                              ! definition,case nil
--- append(cons(x,M),L) <= cons(x,append(M,L)) ! definition,case cons
```

We will build up data types for category, graph, diagram and cone. Capitalised identifiers will be type constructors, like Linear-List, lower case identifiers will be data element constructors, like cons (we often use the same name).

A <u>category</u> is a data object with types o (object) and m (morphism). Its components are four functions: source and target, from morphisms to objects, identity, from objects to morphisms, and composition, from pairs of (adjacent) morphisms to morphisms. (We do not include as components the set of objects or the set of morphisms). Note that Cat constructs types, and cat constructs data objects.

```
typevar o,m
data Cat(o,m) == cat(m -> o, m -> o, o -> m, m × m -> m)
```

For example we may construct the category of finite sets thus, assuming a data-type set.

```
typevar A
data Set_mor(A) == set_mor(Set(A),A->A,Set(A))
          ! set morphisms are triples consisting of two sets (source and target)
            and a function between them
dec source,target: Set_mor(A) -> Set(A)
dec identity: Set(A) -> Set_mor(A)
dec comp: Set_mor(A) × Set_mor(A) -> Set_mor(A)

--- source(set_mor(a,f,b)) <= a
--- target(set_mor(a,f,b)) <= b
--- identity(a) <= set_mor(a,lambda x => x,a)
--- comp(set_mor(a,f,b),set_mor(b1,g,c))
          <= set_mor(a,lambda x => g(f(x)),c) if b = b1)
             else error

dec cat_of_sets: Cat(Set(a),Set_mor(a))
  ! declares cat_of_sets to be a constant of type category,with objects sets
      and morphisms set morphisms
--- cat_of_sets <= cat(source,target,identity,comp)
```

In fact we put all this in a module and only export from the module the constant cat_of_sets; it contains all we need. We would have proceeded differently, and perhaps more elegantly, if parameterised modules had been available in HOPE; we plan to provide them in the future. Other particular categories such as partially ordered sets or the category of graphs and their structure preserving maps may be coded up similarly. However we shall see below that some of these can be constructed systematically from the category of sets.

To define diagrams we first define graphs, taking nodes and edges to be numbers for convenience. A graph has a node set, an edge set and a function assigning to each edge its source and target nodes.

```
data Graph == graph(set num, set num, num -> (num × num)
data Diagram(o,m) == diagram(Graph, (num -> o), (num -> m))
```

We need a few functions for manipulating graphs and diagrams; we omit these and pass on to cones. A cone on a diagram is an object and a function from nodes to morphisms

```
data Cone(o,m) == cone(o,num -> m)
```

Now colimits can be analysed in terms of simpler concepts: initial objects, coproducts and coequalisers.

An object a in a category is <u>initial</u> if for each object a' there is a unique morphism f: a -> a'. For example the empty set is initial in <u>Set</u>, the category of sets. In fact the initial object is the colimit of the empty diagram.

The <u>coproduct</u> of a pair of objects a and b is an object c together with a pair of morphisms f: a -> c and g: b -> c such that for any object c' with morphisms f': a -> c', g': b -> c' there is a unique fill-in morphism u: c -> c' such that f.u = f' and g.u = g'.

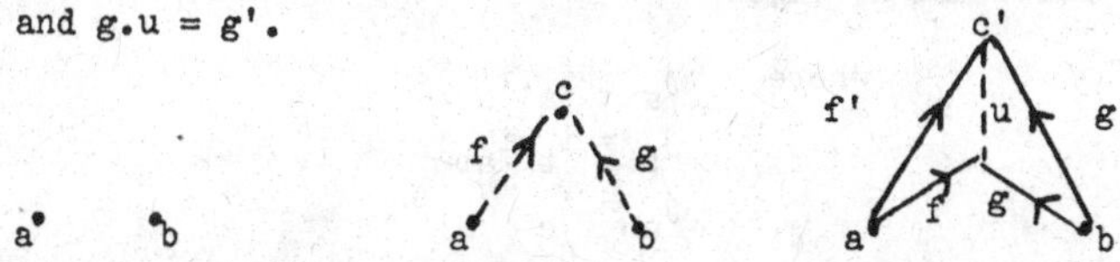

For example the coproduct of a pair of sets is their disjoint union with two injections. In fact the coproduct is the colimit of a diagram with just two nodes.

The <u>coequaliser</u> of a pair of morphisms f: a -> b and g: a -> b is an object c with a morphism h: b -> c such that f.h = g.h, and for any object c' with h': b -> c' such that f.h' = g.h' there is a unique fill-in morphism u: c -> c' such that h.u = h'.

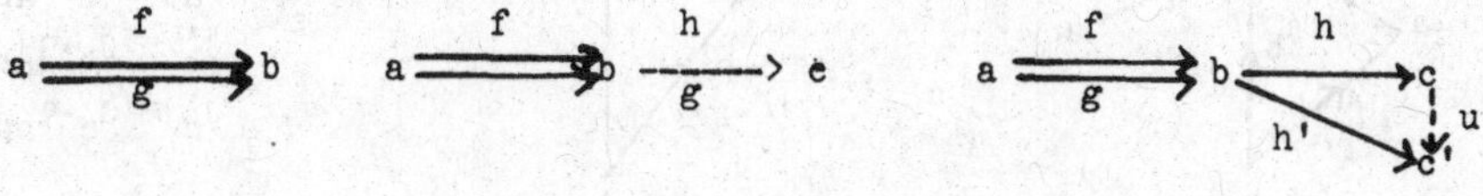

For example the coequaliser of two functions f and g between sets a and b is the quotient set of b by the equivalence induced by $f(x) \equiv g(x)$ for each $x \in a$, together with the function taking each element of b to its equivalence class. In fact the coequaliser is the colimit of a diagram with just two edges and two nodes.

We see from the above that if a category has colimits for all finite diagrams then it has initial objects, coproducts and coequalisers. Conversely if a category has initial objects, coproducts and coequalisers it may be shown to have colimits for all finite diagrams. What is more this is proved by constructing the colimit, and hence it gives us a means to <u>compute</u> the colimit.

The basic idea of the construction (and hence of the computation) is to deal first with the nodes of the diagram, using the coproduct operation to combine the corresponding objects. We then deal with the edges, using the coequaliser operation to successively quotient the result of the coproduct combination. An example will illustrate this. Consider the diagram

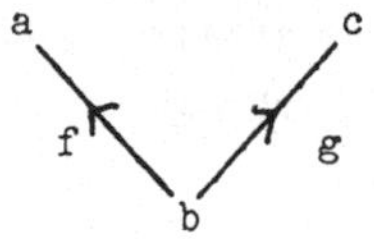

We coproduct a successively with b and c

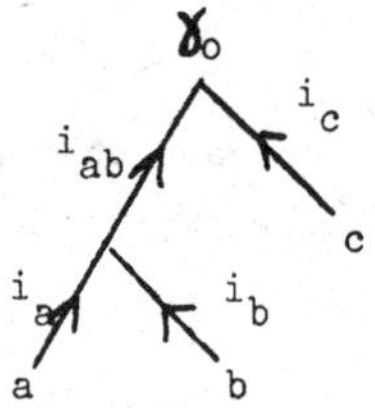

γ_0 has a morphism from each of a, b and c; indeed it is the apex of a cone on the diagram with nodes a, b and c and no edges

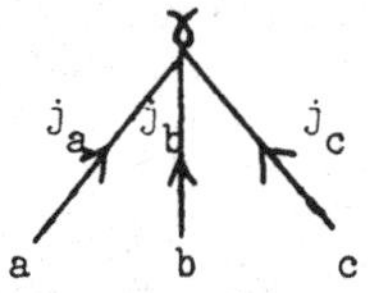

where $j_a = i_a . i_{ab}$
$j_b = i_b . i_{ab}$
$j_c = i_c$

But we must now take account of the edges. First we quotient with respect to f by coequalising j_b with $f.j_a$.

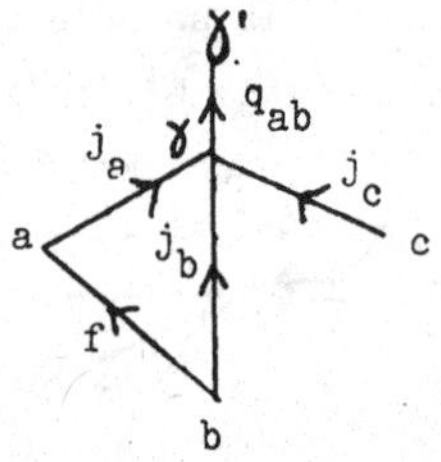

that is

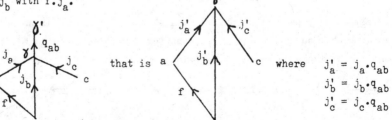

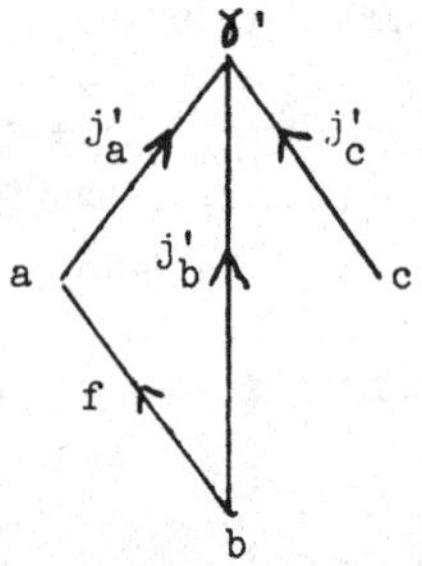

where $j'_a = j_a . q_{ab}$
$j'_b = j_b . q_{ab}$
$j'_c = j_c . q_{ab}$

Now we do this again with respect to g, coequalising j'_b with $g.j'_c$.

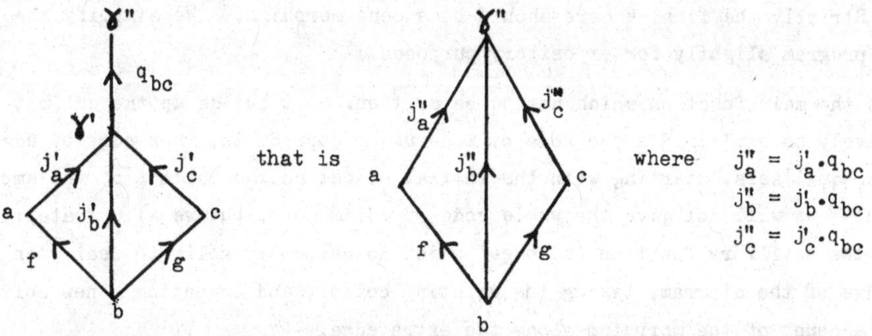

This gives the required colimit cone. We have only given the construction, but the proof that this is the colimit is straightforward.

How do we turn all this category theory into a HOPE program? How do we represent initial objects, coproducts and coequalisers?

An <u>initial object constant</u> in the HOPE program is a pair consisting of (i) an object (a) and (ii) a function from objects (a') to morphisms (f:a->a'). Thus its type is

    o × (o->m)

A <u>coproduct function</u> in the HOPE program is a function from pairs of objects (a,b) to pairs consisting of (i) an object and two morphisms (c, f:a->c, g:b->c) and (ii) a function assigning to any other such triple (c', f':a->c', g':b->c') a morphism (u:c->c'). Thus its type is

    o×o -> (o×m×m) × (o×m×m->m)

A <u>coequaliser function</u> in the HOPE program is a function from pairs of morphisms (f,g:a->b) to pairs consisting of (i) an object and a morphism (c, h:b->c) and (iii) a function assigning to any other such pair (c',h':b->c') a morphism (u:c->c'). Thus its type is

    m×m -> (o×m) × (o×m->m)

Now we can define a cocomplete category as a data structure consisting of a category, an initial object constant, a coproduct function and a coequaliser function

```
data C_cat(o,m) == c_cat(Cat(o,m),o×(o->m),
                         o×o -> (o×m×m) × (o×m×m->m),
                         m×m -> (o×m) × (o×m-> m))
```

We define a cone as an object and a function from nodes to morphisms, thus

```
data Cone(o,m) == cone(o,num->m)
```

We want a function to compute the colimit of any diagram, this colimit being a cone together with a function to compute its fill-in morphism to any other given cone (we call this pair a 'colimiting cone')

```
dec colim:C_cat(o,m) ->
        (Diagram(o,m) -> Cone(o,m) × (Cone(o,m) -> m))
```

(Note Strictly the final m here should be a cone morphism. We simplify the actual program slightly for expository purposes.)

This is the main function which has to be written. It builds up the colimit recursively as explained above node by node using coproducts, then edge by edge using coequalisers, starting with the initial object as the colimit of the empty diagram. We will not give the whole code of colim here, but we illustrate it by giving the auxiliary function 'addedge' which is called by colim to deal with the next edge of the diagram, taking the existing colimit and computing a new colimit taking account of the morphism along the extra edge.

```
dec addedge:C_cat(o,m) ->
            ((Cone(o,m) × (Cone(o,m)->m)) × (num×m×num)
             -> Cone(o,m) × (Cone(o,m)->m))
```

For any cocomplete category K this gives a function taking (i) a colimiting cone, C, and (ii) a morphism connecting a pair of nodes, (m,f,n), and produces a colimiting cone C'. If C is the colimit of diagram D then C' is the colimit of D extended by an extra edge associated with morphism f from node m to node n. We get this new cone by coequalising Γ(m) and f. Γ(n) as explained previously. The definition of addedge in HOPE (simplified slightly from our actual program) is

```
--- addedge(c_cat(cat(s,t,id,comp),init,coprod,coeq)) <=
      lambda (cone(a,gamma),cone_univ),(m,f,n) =>
          let(b,g),coeq_univ ==
                  coeq(gamma(m),comp(f,gamma(n))) in
          let new_cone == cone(b,lambda i => comp(gamma(i),g)) in
          let new_cone_univ ==
                lambda cone1 =>
                     let u == cone_univ(cone1) in
                     let cone(a1,gamma1) == cone1 in
                         coeq_univ(a1,u)
              in
              (new_cone,new_cone_univ)
```

Impenetrable? A couple of diagrams will help.

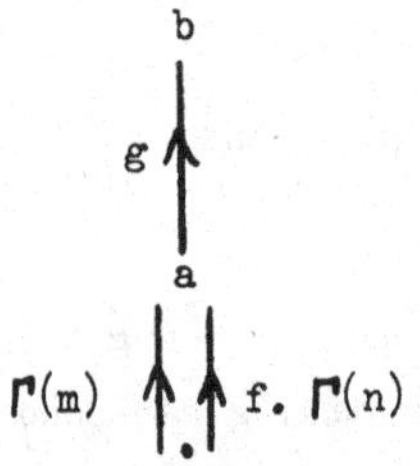

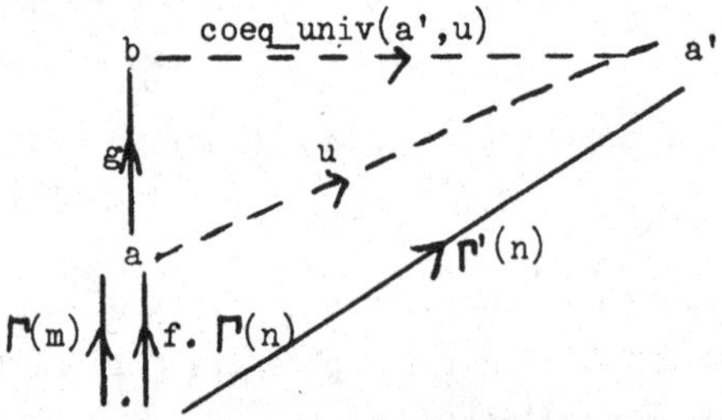

Once you get the idea it is rather easy to translate such categorical constructions into code. The syntax analyser and typechecker catch minor slips and categorical

discipline tends to prevent logical errors. I hope it is fairly obvious how the main colim function uses this addedge function to build up the colimit of a diagram.

To test the colim function we may try it on the category of finite sets. For this we must code up the initial object, coproduct and coequaliser for finite sets. The general function colim can then be given these and will compute colimits of diagrams in Set. This is quite straightforward. We would like to do it for an arbitrary set, say sets of 'a' where a is a type variable. How can we ensure that the coproduct of two sets of elements of type a is a set of elements of type a? We must use not sets of a's but of tagged a's. Thus

```
data Tagged(a) == just(a) ++ pink(Tagged(a)) ++ blue(Tagged(a))
```

Now, using s*f to mean the set of all f(x) for $x \in s$, the coproduct of two sets of tagged a's, s and t, is

```
let u == s*pink ∪ t*blue in
   (u,set_mor(s,pink,u),set_mor(s,blue,u))
```

where set_mor constructs set morphisms.

Note. Later in dealing with graphs as a comma category we will need products of sets so we add to the definition of Tagged(a)

```
... ++ pair(Tagged(a),Tagged(a))
```

Comma categories

When I wrote the original colimit program in NPL in 1977, I first tested it on sets. I then decided to try it on the category of graphs and their morphisms (functions from nodes to nodes and edges to edges which preserve the graph structure). This meant coding up coproducts and coequalisers for graphs. The task was tedious but straightforward once I notice that the existing coproduct and coequaliser programs could be used to help. I wrote most of the program although I did not test it. Some time later Goguen pointed out in connection with our work on Clear semantics that the category of graphs could be constructed from the category of sets by the standard 'comma category' construction [MacLane 1977]; he also pointed out that this construction preserves colimits [Goguen and Burstall 1978]. I realised that this was a computational shortcut. It was no accident that coproducts in Set had been useful for coproducts in Graph. You can code up the general comma category construction and also the construction of colimits in the resulting category. Rydeheard and Sannella have now done this in HOPE and we can compute colimits of diagrams in Graph. (I should say that this is now a big interpreted program and runs very slowly on our DEC-10)

This is not the place to exhibit the detailed code, but let me give you the ideas. Consider first a category K and a fixed object a in K. Now the morphisms from a themselves form a category, say (a,K). The new objects are K-morphisms f:a->b for some b, and the new morphisms between f:a->b and f':a->b are K-morphisms h such that the following commutes.

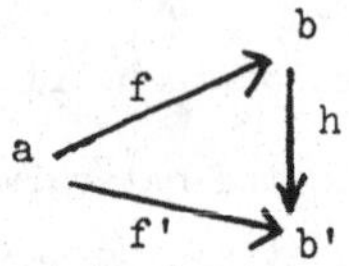

We have constructed the category (a,K) from K. It is not hard to see that given a diagram in (a,K) we can find its colimit in (a,K) by using the colimits in K. An example would be the simple diagram of two nodes

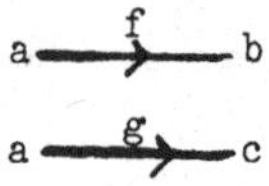

Its colimit (i.e. the coproduct) is formed by taking the colimit in K of

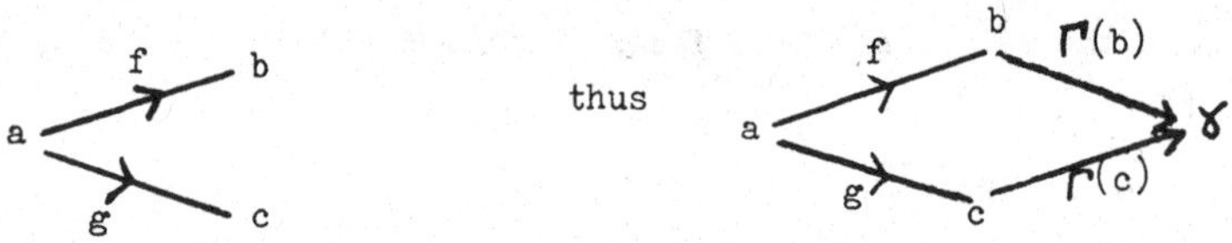

Now the colimit (coproduct) object in (a,K) is f. Γ(b):a-> γ (= g.Γ(c)) and the cone morphisms are Γ(b) and Γ(c). This construction can easily be generalised to any diagram.

But we can do grander things in similar style. Let K and L be categories and F:L->K a functor. Define a new category, say (K,F) whose objects are triples

(a,h,b)

where a is a K-object, b an L-object and h:a->F(b) is a K-morphism. The morphisms of (K,F) are pairs consisting of a K-morphism and an L-morphism. Thus (i,j):(a,h,b) -> (a',h',b') in (K,F) just if the following commutes

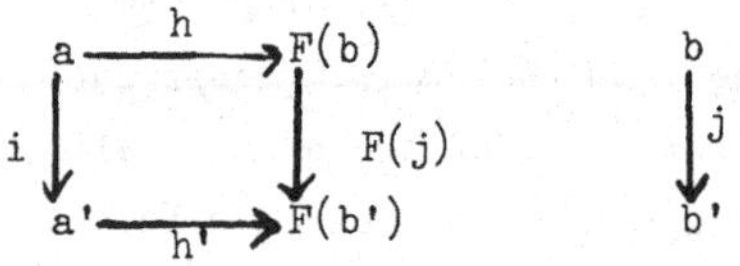

Example 1 We can construct the category of graphs from the category of sets in this way. **A graph is a set of edges, a set of nodes and a function from edges to** pairs of nodes (source and target of the edge). So take K and L both to be Set and let F be the product functor ×, F(S) = S×S. Now Graph = (Set,×)

Example 2 We can similarly construct the category of signatures. A signature is a set Σ of operators, a set S or sorts and a function from Σ to S*×S (argument sorts and result sort of each operator). So take K and L both to be Set and F to be the functor F(S) = S*×S (with the obvious effect on morphisms). Now (Set,F) is the category of signatures.

Now if K and L have colimits then so does (K,F) [Goguen and Burstall 1978]; F does not even have to preserve colimits. The construction of colimits in (K,F) from those in K and L is quite straightforward. (We do it directly rather than via coproducts and coequalisers as in Goguen and Burstall [1978].) The following diagram gives the idea of the proof, and of the program. It is a diagram in the category of diagrams, considering a cone as a diagram morphism from its base to the constant diagram with all nodes going to object γ . D is a diagram in (K,F), and D_K and D_L are its K and L projections. D_{mor} is the morphism part of D considered as a morphism of diagrams. $F(D_L)$ is the functor F applied to the whole diagram D_L. The colimit object in (K,F) is (γ_K,u,γ_L) where u is the fill-in from colimit γ_K.

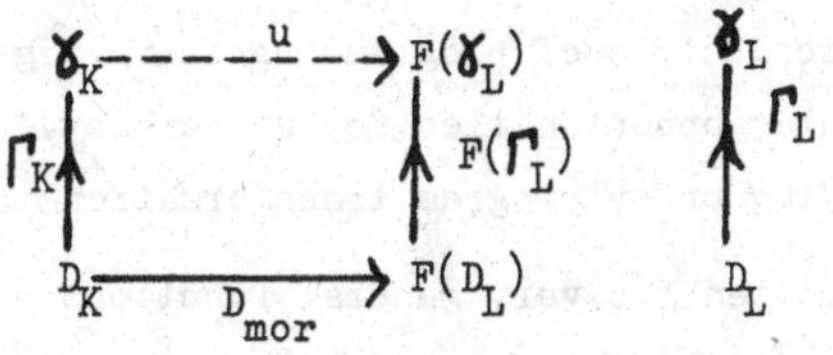

There is a still more general comma category construction [MacLane 1971] with three categories K, L and M and two functors F:K->L and G:M->L. Thus

$$K \xrightarrow{\ F\ } L \xleftarrow{\ G\ } M$$

The objects are triples (a,h:F(a) -> G(b),b) and morphisms are pairs (i:a->a', j:b->b') such that the following square commutes

$$
\begin{array}{ccc}
a & F(a) \xrightarrow{\ h\ } G(b') & b \\
i\downarrow & F(i)\downarrow \qquad \downarrow G(j) & \downarrow j \\
a' & F(a') \xrightarrow{\ h'\ } G(b) & b'
\end{array}
$$

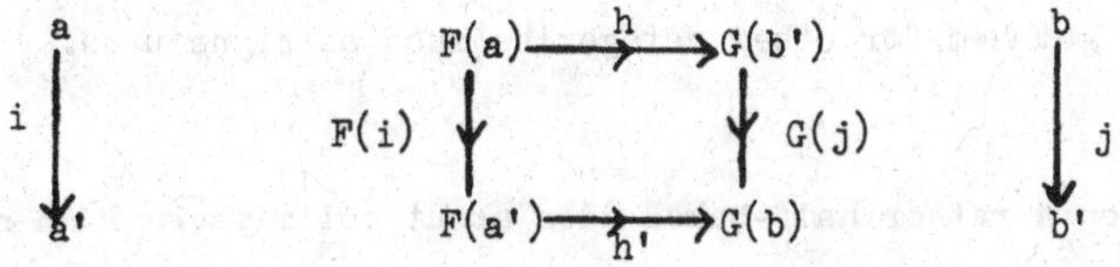

An example is the category of indexed sets. The two previous kinds of comma category are special cases taking F and G to be special functors, constant or identity. If K and L are co-complete and F preserves colimits then we can compute colimits for the comma category, known as (F,G), [Goguen and Burstall 1978].

Now Rydeheard and Sannella have coded up this construction in HOPE for (K,F) style comma categories, writing a function to lift the colimits in K and L to colimits in (K,F). We first define functors as a data type, then morphisms of the comma category, then a function to produce the comma category, i.e. its source, target, identity and composition.

```
data Functor(o,m,o1,m1) == functor(o->o1,m->m1)
data Fcomma_mor(o,m,o1,m1) == fcomma_mor(oxmxo1,mxm1,oxmxo1)
dec functor_comma_cat:(Cat(o,m)xCat(o1,m1)xFunctor(o1,m1,o,m)
                        ->Cat(oxmxo1,Fcomma_mor(o,m,o1,m1))
```

We omit the definition of functor_comma_cat; it is straightforward. The main function lift_colimit given any pair of categories with a functor between them takes a diagram in the resulting comma category to its colimit. Its declaration is as follows (we abbreviate o×m×o1 to O and Fcomma_mor(o,m,o1,m1) to M)

```
dec lift_colimit:C_cat(o,m)×C_cat(o1,m1)×Functor(o1,m1,o,m)
              ->(Diagram(O,M)->(Cone(O,M)×(Cone(O,M)->M)))
```

The definition is about 20 lines of code which we omit; the style is similar to the definition of addedge given above. We hope to publish a more detailed account elsewhere. The program has been tested by using it to obtain the colimit of a very simple diagram in Graph. Because HOPE is interpreted in POP-2 and our initial implementation is slow and space-consuming, even trivial examples take a very long time. The categorical style of programming is very general and doesn't take advantage of particular opportunities for efficiency. How much improvement could be obtained by recoding or by program transformation is an open question.

To sum up we have written two very general functions

(i) getting colimit from initial object, coproduct and coequaliser
(ii) lifting colimits to comma categories.

We have also written several particular functions for Set

(i) initial object, coproduct and coequaliser
(ii) product functor.

This enables us to compute colimits for diagrams of sets and graphs. With little extra effort we could get them for other categories such as signatures.

Colimit recursion

I would like to mention a rather half-baked idea about colimits. I am not sure of the details and have not worked properly through an example. Nevertheless I think the idea might be useful. Suppose we have categories K and L and want to compute some functor F:K->L which is co-continuous (preserves colimits). Now a K object, a, may be decomposable into a diagram, D, in K of which it is the colimit. We can then find F(a) (to within isomorphism) by computing colim(F(D)). But F(a') where a' is an object in D can be computed in a similar manner. Of course the recursion must stop on some elementary indecomposable K objects. However to compute F(D) we need to compute F for K morphisms, so we also need to decompose a K-morphism $f:a_1 \to a_2$ into a morphism of diagrams $\emptyset:D_1 \to D_2$ where D_1 is the decomposition of a_1 and D_2 that of a_2. In short we need a functor decomp:K->Diagrams(K) such that decomp∘colim is naturally equivalent to the identity functor, and such that decomp eventually produces diagrams using only some base set of elementary objects and morphisms for which we can compute F directly.

An example would be some cocontinuous functor from the category of graphs. We can easily decompose a graph G into the pushout of three subgraphs, say G is the pushout of $G_1 \xleftarrow{f_1} G_3 \xrightarrow{f_2} G_2$ where G_3 is the graph showing the nodes and edges shared by G_1 and G_2. This method, say colimit recursion, has some interest because normally 'divide and conquer' methods, e.g. recursion whose argument is an element of an initial algebra, divide the problem into two or more distinct pieces whereas colimit recursion would allow arbitrary sharing.

Possible applications are

(i) the narcissistic one of computing the colimit of a diagram, since colimit is itself a cocontinuous functor and we can easily express a diagram as the colimit of a diagram of smaller diagrams (this is an alternative to the method given earlier; we wanted to program this alternative but time was too short).

(ii) shortest path in a graph where the functor takes graphs with length-labelled edges to metrics over their nodes; the category of metrics having objects maps from pairs of nodes to reals which form a metric space and morphisms maps f from nodes to nodes such that $d_{fifj} \leq d_{ij}$. (But this is a guess. I have not had time to check the details.)

Colimit recursion has some promise as by choosing nice decompositions we might get good 'divide and conquer' techniques suitable for parallel implementation. But beware this is all speculative and not worked out!

Another example, of a related nature, is a program I once wrote for matching relational structures in picture processing and robotics [Barrow, Ambler and Burstall 1972]. In the appendix to that paper the program is described in categorical terms, although without benefit of colimits of which I was then ignorant; indeed the code in POP-2 faithfully mirrored this description. The idea is that each structure to be recognised is decomposed into a related set of substructures, which in turn are decomposed further. • The program first matches the smallest structures against the given target structure, combines successful matches to get matches for structures in the next level up of the hierarchy, and so on. The decomposition could well have been as described above with each structure being the colimit of its decomposition. At any rate this has interest as a program embodying categorical concepts which performs a practically interesting task.

Conclusions

I hope I have shown that ideas from universal algebra and category theory can actually be applied to programming itself as a means of imparting a coherent and rigorous structure to some non-numerical programs. This contrasts with the usual applications to the theory of computation. Possible benefits may be

(1) Enabling the average computer scientist to acquire understanding of categorical concepts by connecting them closely with computation.

(2) Examples of mathematically well-structured programs in which functions

reflect important mathematical constructions.

(3) The ability to encapsulate the hard part of a number of different programs in a few very general functionals - ideally writing the particular programs requires no other recursion or iteration just supplying a few suitable lambda expressions. The functionals might admit parallel implementation.

Whether or not any of the expected benefits accrue the enterprise is certainly a stimulating and entertaining one and I hope there is room in our subject for some intellectual forays irrespective of practical benefits.

Acknowledgements

I have already acknowledged my indebtedness to D. Rydeheard and D. Sannella, also to D. MacQueen and M. Levy. My algebraic education, such as it is, is due to P. Landin, J. Thatcher, J. Goguen, M. Arbib and G. Plotkin. D. Rydeheard has provided categorical stimulus, and I. Nemeti encouraged me when I presented the earlier colimit program at the Banach Institute in 1978. Eleanor Kerse has provided superb typing help. Our work has been supported by the Science Research Council. My thanks go to the MFCS Committee for the invitation which stimulated this paper.

References

Arbib, M. and Manes, E. (1975) Arrows, Structures and Functors. Academic Press: New York.

Backus, J. (1978) Can programming be liberated from the von Neumann style? A functional style and its algebra of programs. CACM, 21, 8, 613-641.

Barrow, H., Ambler, A.P. and Burstall, R.M. (1972) Some techniques for recognising structures in pictures. Proc. of the International Conference on Frontiers of Pattern Recognition (ed. S. Watanabe), Honolulu, Hawaii. Academic Press: New York, pp. 1-29.

Burstall, R.M. (1977) Design considerations for a functional programming language, in Proc. of Infotech State of the Art Conference "The Software Revolution", Copenhagen, pp. 45-57.

Burstall, R.M., Collins, J.S. and Popplestone, R.J. (1971) Programming in POP-2. (A revision of POP-2 Papers, Edinburgh: University Press, 1968.) Edinburgh: University Press.

Burstall, R.M. and Goguen, J.A. (1977) Putting theories together to make specifications, in Proc. of Fifth International Joint Conference on Artificial Intelligence, Boston, pp. 1045-1058. (From Comp. Sci. Dept., Carnegie-Mellon Univ.)

Burstall, R.M. and Goguen, J.A. (1980) The semantics of CLEAR, a specification language, in Proc. of Advanced Course on Abstract Software Specifications, Copenhagen (1970). Lecture Notes in Computer Science. Berlin: Springer-Verlag (in press).

Burstall, R.M. and Landin, P.J. (1969) Programs and their proofs: an algebraic approach. Machine Intelligence 4 (eds. B. Meltzer and D. Michie) Edinburgh: University Press, pp. 17-44.

Burstall, R.M., MacQueen, D.B. and Sannella, D.T. (1980) HOPE: an experimental applicative language. Research Report, Dept. of Computer Science, University of Edinburgh.

Ehrig, H., Kreowski, H-J., Maggiolo-Schettini, A., Rosen, B. and Winkowski, J. (1977) Deriving structures from structures. Research Report, IBM Research Center, Computer Sc ence Dept., Yorktown Heights, N.Y.

Ehrig, H., Pfender, M. and Schneider, H. (1973) Graph grammars: an algebraic approach. Proc. 14th Ann. IEEE Symp. on Switching and Automata Theory, pp. 167-180.

Goguen, J.A. and Burstall, R.M. (1978) Some fundamental properties of algebraic theories: a tool for semantics of computation. DAI Research Report No. 53, Dept. of Artificial Intelligence, University of Edinburgh. (Revised version to appear shortly from Edinburgh University Computer Science Dept.)

Goguen, J.A. and Ginali, S. (1978) A categorical approach to general systems. In Applied General Systems Research (ed. G. Klir) Plenum, pp. 257-270.

Klaeren, H. (1980) An abstract software specification technique based on structural recursion. SIGPLAN Notices, 15, 3, 28-34.

MacLane, S. (1971) Categories for the Working Mathematician. Springer-Verlag.

Perryman, G. (1970) Discovering the structure of an automaton from partial information. M.Sc. thesis. Dept. of Artificial Intelligence, University of Edinburgh.

Thatcher, J., Wagner, E. and Wright, J. (1979) More advice on structuring compilers and proving them correct. Research Report RC 7588, IBM Research Center, Computer Science Dept., Yorktown Heights, N.Y.

AN ESSAY ABOUT RESEARCH ON SPARSE NP COMPLETE SETS

J. Hartmanis and S. R. Mahaney
Department of Computer Science
Cornell University
Ithaca, New York 14853

Abstract

The purpose of this paper is to review the origins and motivation for the conjecture that sparse NP complete sets do not exist (unless P = NP) and to describe the development of the ideas and techniques which led to the recent solution of this conjecture.

1. Introduction

The research in theoretical computer science and computational complexity theory has been strongly influenced by the study of such feasibly computable families of languages as P, NP and PTAPE. This research has revealed deep and unsuspected connections between different classes of problems and it has provided completely new means for classifying the computational complexity of problems. Furthermore, this work has raised a set of interesting new research problems and created an unprecedented consensus about what problems have to be solved before real understanding of the complexity of computations can be achieved.

In the research on feasible computations the central role has been played by the families of deterministic and nondeterministic polynomial time computable languages, P and NP, respectively [AHU, C, GJ, K]. In particular, the NP complete languages have been studied intensively and virtually hundreds of natural NP complete problems have been found in many different areas of applications [AHU, GJ]. Though we do not yet know whether P ≠ NP, we accept today a proof that a problem is NP complete as convincing evidence that the problem is not polynomial time computable (and therefore not feasibly computable); a proof that a problem is complete for PTAPE is viewed as even stronger evidence that the problem is not feasibly computable (even though there is no proof that P ≠ NP ≠ PTAPE).

As part of the general study of similarities among NP complete problems it was conjectured by Berman and Hartmanis, for reasons given in the next section, that all NP complete problems are isomorphic under polynomial time mappings and therefore there could not exist (sparse) NP complete sets with considerably fewer elements than the known classic complete problems (e.g. SAT, CLIQUE, etc. [BH]).

When the conjecture was first formulated in 1975, the understanding of NP complete problems was more limited and several energetic frontal assaults on this problem failed. As a matter of fact, the problem looked quite hopeless after a considerable initial effort to solve it. Fortunately, during the next five years a number of different people in Europe and America contributed a set of ideas and techniques which recently led to an elegant solution of this problem by S. Mahaney of Cornell University [M].

The purpose of this paper is to describe the origins of the sparseness conjecture about NP complete sets, to relate the information flow about this problem and to describe the development of the crucial ideas that finally led to the proof that if sparse NP complete sets exist, then P = NP [M].

We believe that this is an interesting and easily understandable development in the study of NP complete problems and that there are some lessons to be learned about computer science research from the way this tantalizing problem was solved.

Furthermore, it is hoped that these results may provide a new impetus for work on the main conjecture that all NP complete sets are p-isomorphic.

2. Preliminaries and the Sparseness Conjecture

Let P and NP denote, respectively, the families of languages accepted by deterministic and nondeterministic Turing machines in polynomial time.

A language C is said to be NP complete if C is in NP and if for any other language B in NP there exists a polynomial time computable function f such that

$$x \in B \Leftrightarrow f(x) \in C.$$

The importance of the family of languages P stems from the fact that they provide a reasonable model for the feasibly computable problems. The family NP contains many important practical problems and a large number of problems from different areas of applications in computer science and mathematics have been shown to be complete for NP [AHU, C, BJ, K]. Since today it is widely conjectured that $P \neq NP$, the NP complete problems are believed not to be solvable in polynomial time. Currently one of the most fascinating problems in theoretical computer science is to understand better the structure of feasibly computable problems and, in particular, to resolve the P = NP question. For an extensive study of P and NP see [AHU, GJ].

A close study of the classic NP complete sets, such as SAT, the satisfiable Boolean formulas in conjunctive normal form, HAM, graphs with Hamiltonian circuits, or CLIQUE, graphs with cliques of specified size, revealed that they are very similar in a strong technical sense [BH]. Not only can they be reduced to each other, they are actually isomorphic under polynomial time mappings as defined below:

Two languages A and B, $A \subseteq \Sigma^*$ and $B \subseteq \Gamma^*$, are p-isomorphic iff there exists a bijection $f: \Sigma^* \to \Gamma^*$ (i.e. a one-to-one and onto mapping) such that

1. f and f^{-1} are polynomial time computable,
2. f is a reduction of A to B and f^{-1} is a reduction of B to A.

Further study revealed that all the "known" NP complete sets are p-isomorphic and that one could formulate (after a number of technical lemmas) a very simple condition for NP complete sets to be p-isomorphic to SAT in terms of two padding functions [BH].

__Theorem 1__: An NP complete set B is p-isomorphic to SAT iff there exists two polynomial time computable functions D and S such that

1. $(\forall x,y)\ [D(x,y) \in B \Leftrightarrow x \in B]$

2. $(\forall x,y)\ [S \circ D(x,y) = y]$.

All the known NP complete sets have these padding functions and in most cases they are easy to find. A good example is SAT, for which y can easily be encoded in any given formula in terms of new variables which do not change the satisfiability of the formula [BH].

From these studies grew the conviction that all NP complete sets are p-isomorphic and this conjecture was explicitly stated in [BH].

Clearly, if all NP complete sets are p-isomorphic then they all must be infinite and therefore P ≠ NP. Thus it was realized that this conjecture may be very hard to prove, but the possibility was left open that it may be easier to disprove it. One way of disproving the p-isomorphism conjecture is suggested by the fact that p-isomorphic sets have quite similar densities. To make this precise we define sparseness below:

A set B, $B \subseteq \Sigma^*$ is said to be __sparse__ if there exists a polynomial p(n) such that

$$| B \cap (\epsilon + \Sigma)^n | \le p(n).$$

Thus p(n) bounds the number of elements in B up to size n.

It is easily seen that SAT and other known NP complete sets are not sparse (any set possessing the padding functions D and S is not sparse) and that a sparse set cannot be p-isomorphic to SAT. These considerations lead to the conjecture [BH] that there do not exist sparse NP complete sets (unless P = NP). In particular, it was conjectured that no set over a single letter alphabet say $B \subseteq a^*$, can be NP complete.

It is interesting to note that the p-isomorphism conjecture quickly leads to the sparse set conjecture and then to the innocuous looking conjecture that no language on a single letter alphabet could be NP complete. We return to this last conjecture in the next section, it was the first to be solved.

A more indirect motivation for the p-isomorphism conjecture comes from the suggested analogy between recursive and recursively enumerable languages and P and NP as their feasibly computable counterparts. This analogy becomes particularly intrigueing and suggestive when it is extended to the Kleene Hierarchy and the polynomial time hierarchy [S]. The NP complete sets correspond in this analogy to the r.e. complete sets, which are known to be the same as the creative sets and they are all recursively isomorphic. This suggests that by analogy the NP complete sets should be p-isomorphic, as conjectured in [BH].

Lastly, a sparse NP complete set would imply that the necessary information to solve NP problems can be condensed in a sparse set. In other words, the sparse set could be computed and then used as a polynomially long oracle tape to solve other NP complete problems. At the time of stating the sparseness conjecture this looked very unlikely, and now we know that it is not possible unless P = NP. For related results discussing the consequences of the existence of polynomial size circuits for the recognition of SAT, see [KL].

3. Sparse Ranges and SLA Languages

The p-isomorphism and sparseness conjecture and the more specialized conjecture that no language on a single letter alphabet can be NP complete received a fairly wide exposure at conferences and journal publications in the United States and Europe [BH, HB1, HB2]. Unfortunately, in spite of different attempts, no progress was made on this problem for several years and it started to look like an interesting problem about NP complete sets which was not likely to be solved in the near future.

The situation changed suddenly when Piotr Berman from Poland submitted a paper "Relationships Between Density and Deterministic Complexity of NP-Complete Languages" to ICALP '78. In this paper, motivated by the sparseness conjecture, P. Berman considered the consequences of P-time reductions with sparse range, particularly NP complete subsets of a^*. One of the authors was on the program committee for ICALP '78 and the paper, which in its first version was not easy to understand, was studied at Cornell with great interest. After some effort, with the help of S. Fortune, we convinced ourselves that indeed P. Berman's result was correct. In retrospect it is surprising how elegant and simple P. Berman's proof is and why so many other people who had thought about this problem missed it.

The paper was, as it amply deserved, accepted for ICALP '78 and received considerable attention. Unfortunately, P. Berman did not attend ICALP '78 himself and the paper was read at the conference by Ron Book, who had also worked on single letter alphabet languages [BWSD].

We state P. Berman's Theorem below and outline a proof:

Theorem 2: a) If there is a P-time reduction with sparse range for an NP complete set, then P = NP.

b) If there is an NP complete subset of a^*, then P = NP.

Note carefully that P. Berman's hypothesis of part a) is that there is a reduction g so that $|\{g(x) : |x| \leq n\}|$ is polynomially bounded. Though his proof used CLIQUE as an NP complete problem, we will consider the SAT problem in our outline of the proof. Part b), of course, is immediate from part a).

Proof: Let g be a p-time reduction of SAT to a sparse range. We outline an algorithm to determine if a boolean formula $F(x_1,\ldots,x_n)$, is satisfiable (and if so, finds an assignment). The algorithm will search part of a binary tree of self-reductions of F. The root is $F(x_1,\ldots,x_n)$. Each node will correspond to F with certain variables instantiated by 0 or 1 as follows: if $F(b_1,\ldots,b_{i-1},x_i,\ldots,x_n)$ is at a node, then its offspring will be

$$F(b_1,\ldots,b_{i-1},0,x_{i+1},\ldots,x_n)$$

and

$$F(b_1,\ldots,b_{i-1},1,x_{i+1},\ldots,x_n).$$

We construct the tree depth first, computing a label g(F) at each formula F encountered. The algorithm determines that certain formulas, F, correspond to unsatisfiable formulas and their labels, g(F), are marked as follows: a leaf with formula 0 (i.e. FALSE) is marked unsatisfiable; if both offspring of a node are marked unsatisfiable then the label at that node is marked unsatisfiable also. When a label is marked unsatisfiable other nodes occurring with the same label are similarly marked.

A careful analysis shows that whenever a bottom-most node is selected, then either a satisfying assignment is found or a new value g(F) is marked unsatisfiable in examining the next n nodes of the tree. Thus, the running time is polynomial in the size of $F(x_1,\dots,x_n)$.

QED

A close inspection of this proof shows that no explicit use has been made of the fact that the set A is in NP. Thus we have actually proved:

<u>Corollary</u> 3: If SAT can be reduced to a sparse set, then P = NP.

Even more fully formalized, P. Berman's proof is quite simple, but it provided the first important step in the solution of the sparseness conjecture. We believe that in the solution of this problem interaction between different groups played an important role and that a solution of even a highly specialized conjecture, like the sparse range case, provided the necessary impetus for further work.

4. <u>No Sparse CO-NP Complete Sets</u>.

In the attempt to understand P. Berman's proof of the single letter case, Steve Fortune, who at that time was a graduate student at Cornell, noticed that in Berman's proof the negative answers yielded valuable information. When a formula F is found to be unsatisfiable, its label g(F) is marked; one never has to explore beneath any other node of the tree with the same label value. Furthermore, such negative answers can be found only polynomially often before the possible values from $g(\text{SAT}^c)$ are exhausted.

This insight lead S. Fortune to a proof that the complete sets in CO-NP cannot be reduced to sparse sets, if P ≠ NP [F].

<u>Theorem 4</u>: If a CO-NP complete set can be reduced to a sparse set S, then P = NP.

<u>Proof</u>: Applying the same tree search method as before, observe that only negative answers are propogated up the tree by conjunctive self-reducibility (i.e., a node is not satisfiable if and only if both sons are not satisfiable). Since only the negative answers are used to prune the tree search, the polynomial running time is preserved under this weaker hypothesis.

QED

For a casual observer of theoretical computer science research the above result may look artificial since it does not answer the sparseness question, but instead solves a strange new problem about complete sparse sets for CO-NP. On the other hand, this was a critical step, as will be seen, in the solution of the general sparseness conjecture for NP complete sets.

5. <u>The Census Function</u>

Early in 1980, while working on his Ph.D. dissertation under Juris Hartmanis at Cornell, Steve Mahaney observed that if the exact number of elements in a sparse NP complete set can be computed in polynomial time, then some very interesting consequences followed, as stated below [HM].

For a set S let the <u>census</u> function C_S be defined by

$$C_S(n) = | S \cap (\epsilon+\Sigma)^n | \quad .$$

Mahaney's observation leads to the following result.

<u>Theorem 5</u>: If there exists a sparse NP complete set S with a polynomial time computable census function, C_S, then

$$NP = CO\text{-}NP.$$

<u>Proof</u>: We will show that under the hypothesis we can recognize the complement of S in nondeterministic polynomial time. Since S^c is complete for CO-NP this guarantees that NP = CO-NP.

Given a string w, compute the census function $C_S(|w|)=k$. Using a nondeterministic polynomial time machine guess k different sequences $w_1, w_2, \ldots, w_k$, such that $|w_i| \leq |n|$, for $i=1,2,\ldots,k$ and verify that they all are in S using the NP recognizer of S. If the guessing and verification succeeds then w is in S^c iff $w \neq w_i$, $i=1,2,\ldots,k$. Thus, S^c is in NP and therefore NP = CO-NP.

QED

Combining the above result with Fortune's theorem we get the following.

<u>Corollary 6</u>: If there exists a sparse NP complete set, S, with a polynomial time computable census function then P = NP.

<u>Proof</u>: From the previous theorem, under the hypothesis of the corollary, we get that NP = CO-NP. But then every set complete for NP is complete for CO-NP and then, because S is a sparse complete set for CO-NP, by Fortune's result we get that P = NP.

QED

Again, the assumption that we have a sparse NP complete set with an easily computable census function may appear like imposing unnatural and restrictive conditions just to be able to derive a result. Surprisingly, the careful exploitation of the census functions lead a step closer to the solution of the sparseness conjecture.

6. Solution of the Sparseness Conjecture

During the spring of 1980 Karp and Lipton made available to us a draft of their forthcoming SIGACT paper "Some Connections Between Nonuniform and Uniform Complexity Classes" [KL]. This paper investigates the consequences of having "advice functions" (or oracles) which give values that depend only on the length of the input to be decided. Karp and Lipton develop uniform algorithms that utilize the existence, but not the easy computability, of such advice.

Two results in that paper are relevant to the sparseness conjecture. The first considers the consequence of having a Turing reduction of SAT to a sparse set or, equivalently, the existence of polynomial size circuits to solve NP (see Discussion below). The second result considered advice functions that yield only O(log(n)) bits of advice for inputs of size n.

__Theorem 7__: Suppose h(.) is an advice function for NP satisfying

1. for some c, | h(n) | ≤ c log(n), and
2. there is a deterministic polynomial time algorithm using c log(n) bits of advice that correctly decides SAT with advice h(.).

Then P = NP.

The proof of this theorem shows that all potential values of the c log(n) bits can be examined and the correct answer determined uniformly in polynomial time.

The deciphering of the Karp and Lipton paper, though it did not deal directly with the sparseness conjecture, suggested to Mahaney a new approach to the sparseness conjecture which combined the previously developed methods and led to its solution.

The intuitive link between Theorem 7 and the sparseness conjecture is found in the census results (Theorem 5 and Corollary 6). The unnatural hypothesis of the census results was that the census function, $C_S(n)$, was easily computable. Instead, observing that $C_S(n)$ is bounded by a polynomial, we see that the census may be written in O(log(n)) bits. The census results suggest a method to construct an algorithm that uniformly tries potential values of the census.

The essence of Mahaney's idea is to apply a census-like method (without knowing the exact census) to a sparse NP complete set to construct a p-time reduction of a CO-NP set to the sparse set, and then to use a Berman-Fortune depth first search method to solve SAT. The lack of knowledge about the census function is overcome by trying all of the polynomially many values for the census function and proving that the incorrect values can either be detected or that they cannot give a wrong answer.

In the proof below the ignorance about the census function is overcome by constructing a pseudo-complement of the sparse NP complete set S. The pseudo-complement incorporates guesses about what the corresponding census is and it is used to construct the desired sparse set of labels for the depth first search.

The outline of the proof below is as follows: We first give an NP recognizer for the "pseudo-complement" of the sparse set S. A reduction of this set to the sparse set S is used to provide the sparse set of labels for SAT^c; however, the certain computation of this set of labels requires knowing the census of S. Finally, the depth first search is modified to determine satisfiability of a formula (without exact knowledge of how to generate the sparse set of labels for SAT^c).

For the following discussion let $S \subset (0,1)^*$ be a sparse complete set for NP. Let M_S be a nondeterministic polynomial time recognizer of S and let

$$C_S(n) = | S \cap (\epsilon+\Sigma)^n | \le p(n)$$

where $C_S(.)$ is the true census function of S, and p(.) is a polynomial that bounds the size of the census.

We begin by constructing a Turing machine to recognize the pseudo-complement of S in nondeterministic polynomial time. Inputs include a padding $\#^n$ and an integer k which is a possible value of $C_S(n)$. Define the non-deterministic recognizer M by the following procedure:

$M(\#^n, s, k)$:

Check $|s| \le n$; otherwise reject.

Check $k \le p(n)$; otherwise reject.

Guess $s_1, \ldots, s_k$ so that

i. for all i, $|s_i| \le n$.

ii. for all i and j, $i \ne j \Rightarrow s_i \ne s_j$.

iii. for all i, check that s_i is accepted by M_S, the recognizer of S.

iv. check that for all i, $s \ne s_i$.

<u>Lemma 8</u>: Let $|s| \le n$ and $k \le p(n)$. Then on input $(\#^n, s, k)$ the machine M will:

1. accept if $k < c(n)$;

2. reject if $k > c(n)$; and

3. if $k = C_S(n)$, then M accepts if and only if M_S rejects s.

__Proof of Lemma__: We show part 3. If M accepts, then it will have enumerated the elements of S up to size n, verified that they belong to S, and shown that s is distinct from these elements. Since k is the true census, M accepts if and only if s is not in S.

QED

Intuitively, for $k = C_S(n)$, M is a recognizer of S complement. Moreover, M accepts its language in non-deterministic polynomial time (the input $\#^n$ is a padding to ensure this).

We will require labelling functions for pruning tree searches. The following discussion shows how to construct such functions from the sparse set S and many-one reductions of L(M).

Since M is an NP machine and S is NP complete, there is a p-time many-one reduction

$$g:L(M) \to S$$

so that for some monotonic polynomial q(.), inputs to M of size n are reduced to strings of size at most q(n) (cf. [C] and [K]). Similarly, for the NP-complete problem SAT, there is a P-time many-one reduction

$$f:SAT \to S$$

and a monotonic polynomial r(.) bounding the increase in size.

Let F of size m be a formula to be decided and let $n = r(m)$. Then any formula F' occurring in the tree of all self reductions will have size $\leq$ m and f(F') will have size at most n. Regarding k as a possible value for $C_S(n)$, we define

$$L_{n,k}(F') = g(\#^n, f(F'), k)$$

which will be the labelling function.

__Lemma 9__: Let F be a formula of size m and let $n = r(m)$. Furthermore, let k =

$C_S(n)$ be the true census. Then the function

$$L_{n,k}(F')$$

for formulas F' of size at most m satisfies:

1. F' is not satisfiable if and only if $L_{n,k}(F)$ is in S;

2. The unsatisfiable formulas of size at most m are mapped by $L_{n,k}$ to at most

$$p(q(2n+c\log(n))) \leq p(q(3n))$$

distinct strings of S where c is a constant depending only on p(.).

Proof: Part 1 is immediate from Theorem 5. For part 2 observe that $2n+c\log(n) \leq 3n$ is a bound on the size of $(\#^n, f(F'), k)$. Applying p o q gives an upper bound on the census of strings that the triple could map to.

QED

We now know that a suitable labelling function exists for $k = C_S(n)$; but we do not know $C_S(n)$, the true census! The algorithm in the following theorem shows how we can try $L_{n,k}$ for all $k \leq p(n)$.

Theorem 10: If NP has a sparse complete set, then P = NP.

Proof: We give a deterministic procedure to recognize SAT. Let F be a formula of size m. Apply the following algorithm:

```
begin
For k = 0 to p(r(m)) do
    Execute the depth first search algorithm using
        labelling function: L_{n,k}(F')
        at each node F' encountered in the pruned search tree.
    If a satisfying assignment is found,
        then halt; F is satisfiable.
    If a tree search visits more than
        m + m * p(q(3 r(m))) internal nodes,
        then halt the search for this k.
    end;
F is not satisfiable;
end
```

The algorithm clearly runs in polynomial time since the loop is executed at most p(r(m)) times and each iteration of the loop visits a polynomially bounded in m number of nodes.

The correctness of the algorithm is established in the following result.

Lemma 11: If F is satisfiable, then for $k = C_S(r(m))$ the search will find a satisfying assignment.

Proof: By Theorem 5, this k gives a labelling function that maps the unsatisfiable formulas of size at most m to a polynomially bounded set. Fortune shows that the depth first search will find a satisfying assignment visiting at most

$$m + m * p(q(3r(m)))$$

internal nodes.

QED

It is interesting to note here that we have not computed the census: a satisfying assignment could be found with any number of k's; similarly, if no satisfying assignment exists, many of the trees could be searched but the tree with k =

$C_S(r(m))$ is not distinguished.

The method of conducting many tree searches is parallelled in the uniform algorithm technique by Karp and Lipton [KL]. They show that if NP could be accepted in P with log( ) advice, then P = NP. The census function might be compared to a log( )-advisor to the polynomial information in the set S.

It is not necessary to assume an NP recognizer for the sparse set: just that S is NP-hard.

Lemma 12: If S is sparse and NP-hard, then there is a set S# that is sparse, NP complete, and has a P-time reduction: SAT --> S# that is length increasing.

Proof: Let f: SAT → S be a p-time reduction and let # be a new symbol. Define f#: SAT → S# by

$$f\#(F) = f(F)\#^p$$

where $p = \max\{0, |f(F)| - |F|\}$. Clearly S# is sparse. The mapping f# reduces SAT to S#. Membership of s in S# is verified by guessing a satisfiable formula that maps to s and verifying satisfiability.

QED

Corollary 13: If NP is sparse reducible, then P = NP.

7. Discussion

Although the isomorphism results [BH] are the direct ancestors of the work discussed here, the concept of sparseness has another motivation as stated in the Introduction: Can a "sparse amount of information" be used to solve NP problems in polynomial time? The approach here assumes the information is given as a many-one reduction to a sparse set.

For Turing reductions, the information is given as a sparse oracle set. A. Meyer has shown that a sparse oracle for NP is equivalent to the existence of polynomial size circuits to solve NP [BH]. The recent work by Karp, Lipton and Sipser [KL] has shown that if NP has polynomial size circuits, then the polynomial time hierarchy [S] collapses to Σ_2^P. Their result is weaker than Theorem 10, but it also has a weaker hypothesis. It is an interesting open problem to determine if polynomial size circuits for NP implies P = NP.

Similarly, now that we know that sparse NP complete sets cannot exist unless P $\neq$ NP, it would be interesting to determine whether there can exist sparse sets in NP - P. By Ladner's result [L] we know that if P $\neq$ NP then there exist incomplete sets in NP - P; the proof of this result does not yield sparse sets and we have not found a way to modify it to yield sparse sets.

For a related study of the structure of NP complete sets, see [LLR]. In this paper Landweber, Lipton, and Robertson explore the possibility of having large gaps in NP complete sets.

Finally, it is hoped that the success in solving the sparseness conjecture will initiate a new attack on the p-isomorphism conjecture for NP complete sets.

In conclusion, it is interesting to see how many people have directly or indirectly worked and contributed to the solution of the sparseness conjecture, among them, referenced in this paper are L. Berman, P. Berman, R. Book, D. Dobkin, S. Fortune, J. Hartmanis, R. Karp, L. Landweber, R. Lipton, S. Mahaney, A. Meyer, M. Patterson, E. Robertson, A. Selman, M. Sipser, and C. Wrathall.

References

[AHU] Aho, A.V., Hopcroft, J.E., and Ullman, J.D., The Design and Analysis of Computer Algorithms, Addison-Wesley (1974).

[B] Berman, P. "Relationship Between Density and Deterministic Complexity of NP-Complete Languages," Fifth Int. Colloquium on Automata, Languages and Programming, Italy (July 1978), Springer-Verlag Lecture Notes in Computer Science Vol. 62, pp. 63-71.

[BH] Berman, L. and Hartmanis, J., "On Isomorphisms and Density of NP and Other Complete Sets," SIAM J. Comput., 6 (1977), pp. 305-322. See also Proceedings 8th Annual ACM Symposium on Theory of Computing, (1976) pp. 30-40.

[BWSD] Book, R., Wrathall, C., Selman, A., and Dobkin, D., "Inclusion Complete Tally Languages and the Hartmanis-Berman Conjecture."

[C] Cook, S.A., "The Complexity of Theorem Proving Procedures," Proc. 3rd Annual ACM Symposium on Theory of Computing, (1977) pp. 151-158.

[F] Fortune, S., "A Note on Sparse Complete Sets," SIAM J. Comput., (1979), pp. 431-433.

[GJ] Garey, M.R., and Johnson, D.S., "Computers and Intractability, A Guide to the Theory of NP-Completeness," W.H. Freeman and Co., San Francisco, 1979.

[HB1] Hartmanis, J., and Berman, L., "On Polynomial Time Isomorphisms of Complete Sets," Theoretical Computer Science, 3rd GI Conference, March, 1977, Lecture Notes in Computer Science, Vol. 48, Springer-Verlag, Heidelberg, pp. 1-15.

[HB2] Hartmanis, J., and Berman, L., "On Polynomial Time Isomorphisms of Some New Complete Sets," J. of Computer and System Sciences, Vol. 16 (1978), pp. 418-422.

[HM] Hartmanis, J., and Mahaney, S.R., "On Census Complexity and Sparseness of NP-Complete Sets," Department of Computer Science, Cornell University, Technical Report TR 80-416 (April 1980).

[K] Karp, R., "Reducibility Among Combinatorial Problems," in Complexity of Computer Computations (R.E. Miller and J.W. Thatcher, eds.), Plenum, New York (1972).

[KL] Karp, R.M., and Lipton, R.J., "Some Connections between Nonuniform and Uniform Complexity Classes," Proc. 12th ACM Symposium on Theory of Computing, (May 1980).

[L] Ladner, R.E., "On the Structure of Polynomial Time Reducibility," J. Assoc. Computing Machinery, Vol. 22 (1975), pp. 155-171.

[LLR] Landweber, L.H., Lipton, R.J., and Robertson, E.L., "On the Structure of Sets in NP and Other Complexity Classes," Computer Science Tech. Report 342 (December 1978), University of Wisconsin-Madison.

[M] Mahaney, S.R., "Sparse Complete Sets for NP: Solution of a Conjecture by Berman and Hartmanis," Department of Computer Science, Cornell University, Technical Report TR 80-417 (April 1980).

[MP] Patterson, M, and Meyer, A.R., "With What Frequency are Apparently Intractable Problems Difficult?", Laboratory for Computer Science, M.I.T. Tech. Report., February 1979.

[S] Stockmeyer, L.J., "The Polynomial-Time Hierarchy," Theoretical Computer Science Vol. 3, (1977), pp. 1-22.

Some Theoretical Aspects of Applicative Multiprocessing

Robert M. Keller[1]

Department of Computer Science
University of Utah
Salt Lake City, Utah 84112

INTRODUCTION

Distributed computing systems, in which computational load is shared among many asynchronously-communicating processor and memory units, form the basis of an area of crucial importance, due to the pragmatic necessity of such systems, as well as the many interesting theoretical questions raised by them. The problem of intellectually managing computations on such systems has lead some researchers to seriously consider the value of so-called "applicative" languages as the central means for describing and effecting such computations.

By "applicative", we of course mean that the underlying basis of computation is conceptualized in terms of **application of functions** to data objects to form new data objects, in contrast to a conceptualization in terms of **assignments** which change the **state** of a collection of data objects. Thus the term "applicative multiprocessing", which seems to have first appeared in [Friedman and Wise 78], is here used to denote systems consisting of multiple computation units with the intention of describing all, or a significant part, of the computational aspects of such systems through an applicative language.

We intend to mention a number of theoretical questions, along with their practical motivations, which have arisen in connection with the design of a specific type of applicative multiprocessing system, called AMPS [Keller, Lindstrom, and Patil 79]. Although there are undoubtedly many other equally important questions which are not mentioned here, either for lack of space or because they have not yet

---

[1]This material is based upon work supported by the National Science Foundation under Grant MCS-77-09369 A01.

categorized into one of the following areas:

1. Comparison of expressiveness of applicative languages

2. Language proof methods

3. Comparative complexity of problem solutions expressed in applicative languages

4. Resource management within applicative languages

5. Proofs of implementation of applicative languages and systems

6. Processor management issues

7. Storage management issues

During the course of the paper, I hope to touch on examples of the above categories, particularly as they appear to give rise to interesting theoretical questions. Unfortunately (or fortunately, depending on whether one is playing the role of implementor or theorist), the set of such questions seems to significantly outnumber the set of answers.

A SPECIFIC CONCRETE MODEL

I have found the AMPS system useful as a model on which to base discussion of concepts and draw comparisons. Accordingly, I shall describely very briefly the key ideas in this system.

AMPS is a distributed multiprocessing system in which the internal program representation is essentially a coded directed graph. This graph is called a **function graph** because the nodes represent functions over data types (in the sense of [Scott 76]). The domain objects of data types may be variously thought of as trees, dags, streams, or nested tuples of values, where a component of a data object may be shared in storage by other objects. The graphs which are executed by the AMPS machine are members of a language of graphs called FGL (Function Graph Language). The germinal ideas for this language appeared in [Keller 77].

Figure 1 shows an example of an FGL graph. The caption describes the intended function of the graph. The method of operation is to create a stream of trees, each of which corresponds to some sub-tree of the original tree. The function **passatom** acts as a filter, allowing only atoms to pass into the output stream, whereas **passnonatom** acts as a filter allowing only non-atoms to pass.

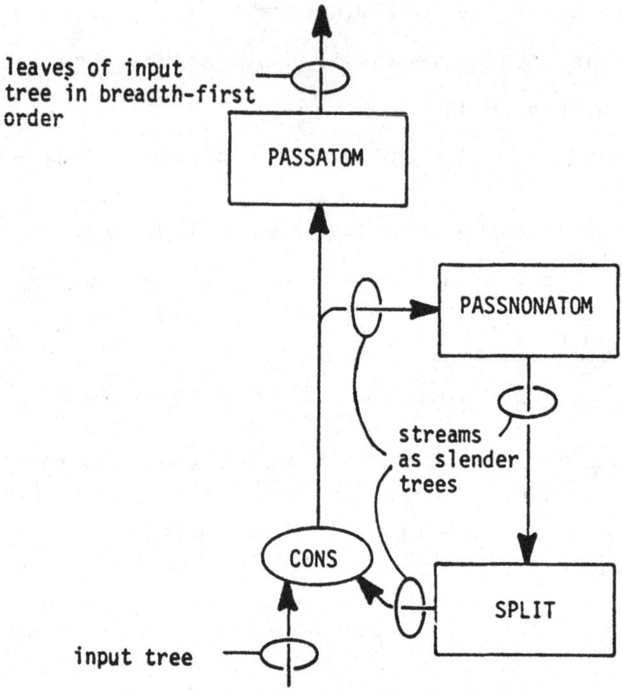

Figure 1: An FGL graph which outputs a stream of atoms which are the leaves of the input tree as they occur in breadth-first order.

A textual form of FGL is available ([Keller, et al. 80]). Because of limited space in which to present graphs, we present in Figure 2 the entire text of the function **breadthf** from Figure 1. The textual form can be considered to be an "equational" representation (cf. [O'Donnell 77]).

Since the basic model contains no notion of a writable object (although certain adulterations of the model do), there are no problems arising from concurrent "updating" of an object. On the other hand, the computation can proceed incrementally, so that data objects are being constructed at the same time they are being used. If a function needs to use a component which has not yet been computed, it simply waits (without busy waiting) until the component has been computed. Such waiting mechanisms are built into the basic

```
function breadthf t
imports(atoms, aux)
result  atoms aux t

function aux t
imports(split, nonatoms)
result  cons(t, split nonatoms aux t)

function atoms x
result  if null x
          then nil()
          else if atom car x
                 then cons(car x, atoms cdr x)
                 else atoms cdr x

function nonatoms x
result  if null x
          then nil()
          else if atom car x
                 then nonatoms cdr x
                 else cons(car x, nonatoms cdr x)

function split x
result  if null x
          then nil()
          else cons(car car x, cons(cdr car x, split cdr x))
```

Figure 2: The complete textual FGL representation for the function of Figure 1.

machine structure and are implicit in the language without further concern of the programmer.

The AMPS system works on what could be called a "task" basis, as opposed to a "process" basis. That is, processing proceeds by execution of atomic entities called "tasks", which correspond to evaluation of simple functions, data transfer operations, and storage allocation and reclamation operations. In contrast to process-based architectures, there is no notion of sequential process nor process state fundamental to the operation of the system. On the other hand, the equivalent of a system of cooperating, intercommunicating sequential processes can easily be constructed.

Communication channels are simply represented by an arc having a stream as its data type. In contrast with the pipe idea of Unix [Balzer 71, Ritchie and Thompson 75], which is restricted to sending a stream of characters, in FGL any objects can be sent in a stream, e.g. atoms, functions, other streams, etc. in any mixture.

To **represent sequential behavior** as in a sequential process, "tail recursion" is used, since there are no built-in iterative constructs. With programming experience, avoidance of such built-in constructs results in much clearer specifications based on recursion. Of course, a wide variety of iterative constructs may be constructed from the basic recursion mechanism.

COMPARISON OF EXPRESSIVENESS OF APPLICATIVE LANGUAGES

FGL resembles the "simple language for parallel programming" of [Kahn 74], except that it includes the richer data structuring primitives of Lisp, which allow Kahn's one-level streams to effectively be extended to streams with streams as components, etc. to any number of levels. Also provided is the capability to treat any function as a data value, as can be done in the untyped lambda calculus [Church 41], for example.

The cons of Lisp has been extended in FGL to allow arbitrarily-many arguments, instead of just two. When accompanied by an accessing function which exploits the indexing capability of the underlying computer memory, this extension allows a powerful array-like capability. Furthermore, such an array may be used as an argument wherever a function with integer domain could be used (in that A[i] is viewed as array A applied to argument i), achieving an extremely useful program development device.

Our cons does not evaluate its arguments in the sense of [Friedman and Wise 76] and [Henderson and Morris 78]. We call such a function a "lenient" function, as opposed to its "strict" counterparts, which are found in most Lisp implementations.

Lenient functions, because of their lack of forced synchronization, provide opportunities for exploitation of concurrency. On the other hand, we rely on strict functions for the generation of the current tasks. Any function which requires all of its arguments will automatically cause the creation of tasks to evaluate those arguments concurrently. The programmer may artificially introduce strict functions to enhance the degree of concurrency during execution. Other types of control are available through similar introductions of other types of functions, to allow tailoring execution somewhat in the spirit of [Schwarz 77].

One concept which has been found extremely useful is that of an "applicative loop". By this we mean that our function graphs are permitted to be cyclic. Such a loop is visible in the graph of Figure 1 and in the function aux of its textual representation in Figure 2. This was also allowed in the language of [Kahn 74], but without motivating examples being presented. Meanwhile, [Keller 77] showed that such loops were always eliminable, at the expense of adding extra recursions. However, we also commented then that such eliminations may be at the expense of storage efficiency. Later, [Kahn and MacQueen 76] used the idea in their coroutine-based language, which we conjecture can be syntactically translated into FGL. (We make the same claim for Lucid [Ashcroft and Wadge 77]).

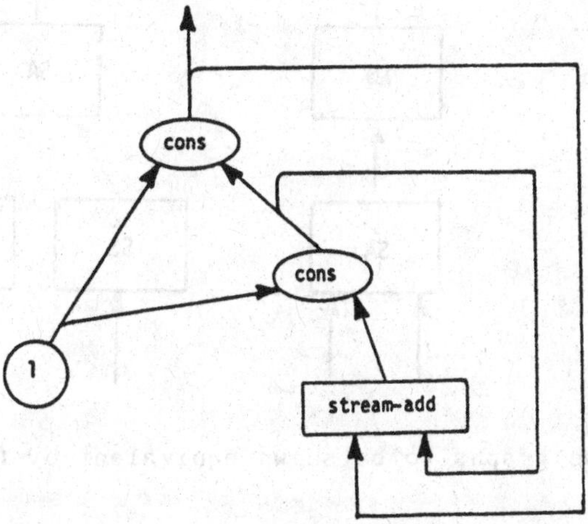

Figure 3: FGL graph resulting in the Fibonacci stream

Since the early implementations of our language, we have found the applicative loop notion virtually indispensible in constructing efficient well-structured applicative programs. Not only does it eliminate a lurking exponential storage in many examples, but it also provides for the program to be isomorphic to certain real-world models, such as digital filters and certain varieties of world models (cf. [Forrester 73]). An example is in the linear time Fibonacci stream generator shown in Figure 3.

Theoretically, it seems that applicative loops could always be provided by replacing a cyclic structure by a unary self-referential function generating it, which only gets evaluated once, but this appears to add an unnecessary step, as the cyclic structures themselves present no implementation difficulties (other than for reference-counting, which is discussed later).

Although the loop elimination theorem [Keller 77] is trivial to verify for functional programs, [Giordano 80] shows that it does not work for programs with indeterminate operators. Translation questions in the latter context present a wide assortment of open problems.

LANGUAGE PROOF METHODS

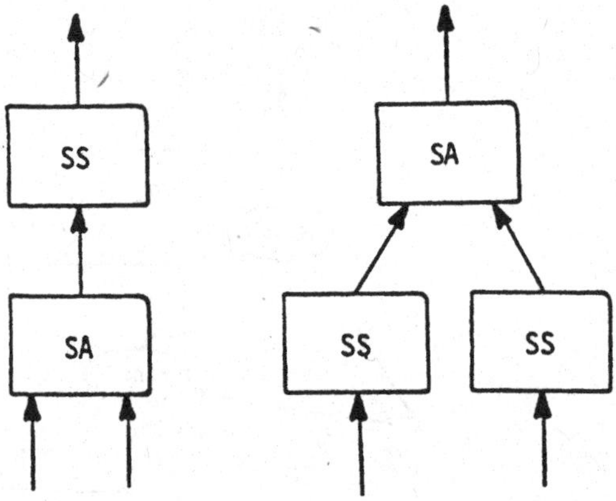

Figure 4: Two graphs to be shown equivalent by fixed-point induction

The use of operators such as (lenient) cons to construct mathematically infinite streams enhances the motivation for study of induction methods, such as **fixed point induction** (cf. [Manna and Vuillemin 72]), and the trade-offs with other induction methods (cf. [Keller 80b]). At the same time, the use of lenient operators creates some annoyances in constructing such proofs. Consider, for example, proving the equivalence of the two functions shown in Figure 4, where the functions inside the boxes are defined by the following equations:

SA(x, y) = cons((car x) + (car y), SA(cdr x, cdr y))

SS(x) = cons(car x, SA(cdr x, SS(x)))

Thus SA adds two streams together point-wise (the same function is called "stream-add" in Figure 3), while SS produces the stream of partial sums of its argument stream (using an applicative loop).

Suppose we wish to prove the following:

Theorem: For all infinite streams x, y,

SS(SA(x,y)) = SA(SS(x), SS(y))

It would seem that fixed point induction would be ideal for this equivalence proof. To wit, SS is the least fixed point H of the equation

```
H(x) = cons(car x, SA(cdr x, H(x)))
```

with respect to the more-or-less obvious ordering among functions on streams. Use of fixed point induction to prove equivalence of the two functions in Figure 4 would require proofs of

(i) ?(SA(x, y)) = SA(?(x), ?(y)), where ? denotes the function which produces the empty stream.

(ii) For all functions H, if H(SA(x, y)) = SA(H(x), H(y)), then

```
cons(car SA(x, y), SA(cdr SA(x, y), H(SA(x, y)))) =
        SA(cons(car x, SA(cdr x, H(x))),
           cons(car y, SA(cdr y, H(y))))
```

Although the induction step is valid, the basis of the induction unfortunately fails due to the lenient operator cons, since cons(?, ?) ≠ ? in the most natural implementation. In order to make the proof work, we have to introduce some means of ignoring the "slack" between the two basis functions, such as temporarily "re-defining" cons to make the proof work. We currently see no way of overcoming such difficulties with finesse.

Another interesting proof technique enters when we consider various adulterations of pure functionality. The desire to do so comes in the interest of efficiency improvements for various computations. Such improvements seem to require indeterminate operators. This can be proved by considering the distinctions between programs which use no indeterminate operators and those that do.

It can be shown (cf. [Keller 78b]) that programs which use no indeterminate operators are necessarily determinate in the "stream sense", i.e. that they determine a unique function from input streams to output streams, independent of system timings which occur during their execution, so long as a type of "finite-delay" property is insured. By appealing to the observation that some phenomena observable in programs with the aforementioned improved efficiency must result from operators not determinate in the stream sense, the necessity is established for indeterminate operators for certain types of efficiency improvement. Of course, this necessity is not one of a sense of computability, as it is it easy to establish that the even most primitive of applicative languages is Turing universal.

An example which may be used to demonstrate the distinction between operators which are stream determinate and those which are not is alpha-beta tree pruning. There it is possible to exploit parallel processors by evaluating several sub-trees concurrently. However, the method relies on the presence of a "cell" at the parent node which is constantly being updated with the best value found so far in the sub-trees. The sequence of values which are read from this cell are obviously time-dependent. Thus the desired behavior is not obtainable through the use of stream determinate operators alone.

An interesting proof paradigm arises out of the desire to include indeterminate operators. It is applicable in the case of programs which are determinate in some weaker sense. Exactly what we mean by a weaker sense has only been partially formalized, and we give a brief account of such a formalization.

It is not difficult to see that the same technique which gives us the determinacy of an interconnection of determinate stream-based functions readily generalizes to functions based on other data objects, so long as the set of such objects forms a "data type" in a sense similar to that of [Scott 76] and so long as the primitive functions are "continuous" over that data type. One use of this generalization is that the same underlying "concrete" objects which arise in machine execution of the program may admit to interpretations as more than one data type, as the latter entails an ordering relation, in addition to the domain of the data type.

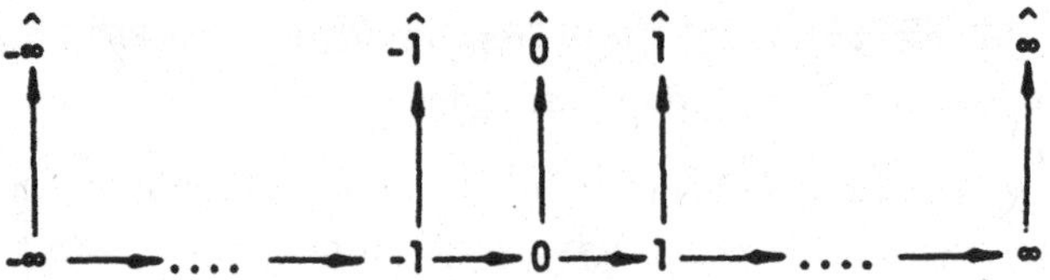

Figure 5: A useful non-flat ordering of the integers

We have some freedom in chosing the ordering so that the functions of interest become continuous on the chosen data type. In [Keller 78a] for example, we showed that a program which is not determinate with respect to an input/output stream becomes determinate if we are willing to relax than the implied sequencing and view the streams as bags. A more involved example appears in [Keller 78b], where we use an ordering more akin to the numeric ordering of the integers (see

Figure 5), rather than the usual flat ordering, to prove determinacy of a program with cell-like operators which are not determinate in the stream sense.

In the course of the latter proof, it was necessary to devise "constrained trajectories" for the data values, as the operators apparently could not be made continuous on their (unconstrained) domains. This suggests that a set of assertion-like techniques can be devised for dealing with such trajectories. The exactly scope of application of the above techniques remains for future investigation. Equally interesting seem to be issues concerning the possible ways of expressing such data-type assumptions in a mechanizable proof language.

COMPARATIVE COMPLEXITY OF PROBLEM SOLUTIONS

The most obvious shortcoming in strict adherence to applicative languages is that certain accepted programming techniques seem to be very difficult to achieve in the applicative context. In the previous section we vaguely alluded to such techniques, most of which involve in-situ modification of data structures. Of course, if parallel processing is present, such modifications cannot be allowed in any programming context without additional mechanisms which provide for careful control of potentially concurrent modifications. This is indeed one of the advantages of an applicative languages: such controls are provided without requiring thought by the programmer. However, as mentioned, this control appears to sacrifice certain techniques upon which programmers have come to rely.

To my knowledge, there has been no study of how expensive (in terms of additional time and space) the unavailability of in-situ modification is. Such a study would likely go into trade-offs in storage representations and could even get involved in storage reclamation. For example, if a reference-count scheme is being used, then an object being referenced by a task and having a reference count value of one could obviously be modified in place, since no other task could now or subsequently have reference to that same object.

A preliminary and very limited-scope discussion of data structure trade-offs is presented in [Keller 80a], wherein a list structure scheme differing from that of Lisp is proposed. This scheme involves combination of lists through a constructor external to the lists

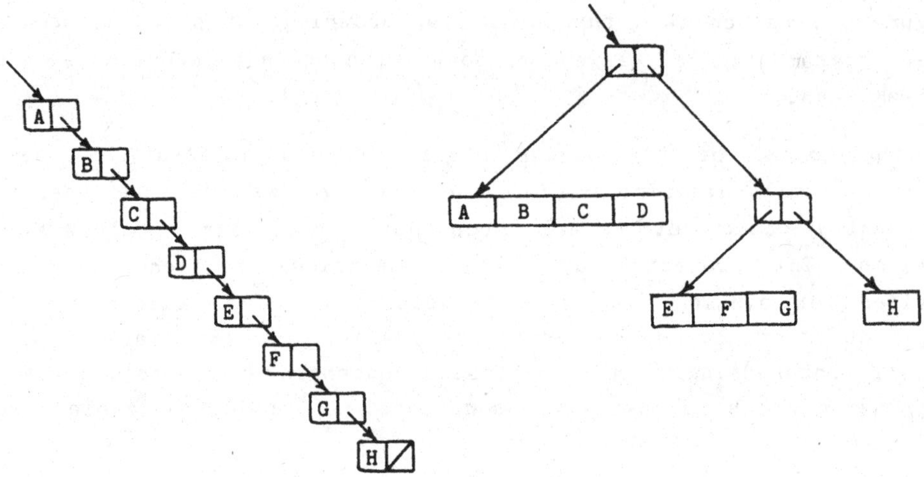

Figure 6: Two distinct schemes for list representation

themselves, as opposed to the familiar links (see Figure 6). The claimed advantages of the scheme are better exploitation of memory-space contiguity, for advantage in space as well as time, better uniformity in the way in which data objects can be combined, and greater ease in application of divide/conquer strategies, as would occur in exploiting concurrent processors.

RESOURCE MANAGEMENT WITHIN APPLICATIVE LANGUAGES

Efficiency issues can arise even if one stays entirely in the applicative context. For example, suppose two functions are known to require huge amounts of system resource (e.g. intermediate memory) to compute. It is possible to introduce constructs which explicitly order the computation of the two functions, but in some cases this may be overly restrictive: The need for the functions' values may arise in an unpredictable order. Thus some form of resource control primitive seems necessary to provide mutual exclusion of the functions' computations.

Similar primitives would be desired for controlling concurrent access to in-situ modified data, etc. One way of representing the above effects, all of which will be lumped into the term **resource management**, is to consider conceptually "overlaying" the function graph with a superstructure describing exclusion relations, etc. Conceptualized in Figure 7 is a situation in which the relative ordering of requests for f and g is unpredictable, but both f and g require such large amounts of resources to make it desirable to

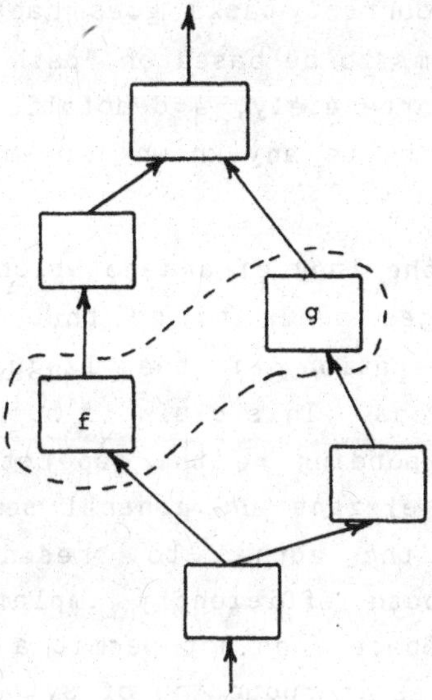

Figure 7: Conceptual overlay for resource management

exclude their simultaneous computation.

In the case of a purely applicative underlying program, such a superstructure need be provided only after the program is fully developed.

In considering the implementation of such an overlay, it was found that the implementation could be achieved with minimal conceptual additions by inserting in the data arcs what might be called "clamps". Such clamps allow other functions to control the demand for values of functions attached to those arcs. We soon saw that it was possible to introduce the generality of "sentinel-like" resource management [Keller 78c], a scheme which resembles others currently being introduced [Hoare 78, Ichbiah, et al. 79] but excludes the possibility of internal non-determinism to provide flexible, yet full and easily comprehended programmer control.

Unfortunately, sentinel-like management schemes do not possess the aspects of applicative languages which allow decomposition into succinct denotationally-defined units. What seems to be more desirable is an "expression-based" means of resource management, which could be syntactically translated into a sentinel-like scheme. The history of such "regular-like" expressions for expressing communication among concurrent tasks goes back to [Petri 66]. The most popular example seems to be based on "path expressions" [Campbell and Habermann 74]. Unfortunately, a denotational semantics for path expressions which conforms to any known implementation has yet to be presented.

Part of the reason for the lack of a denotational semantics for these expression-based languages seems to be that the most natural, yet fully general, interpretation of the language yields impossibly inefficient implementations. This claim is supported by on-going work [Jayaraman 80]. In responding to the gap between desired efficient implementation and both elegant and general semantics, work is under way by Jayaraman and the author to present a variant of path expressions which is both efficiently implementable, yet free of semantic ambiguities. Space does not permit a full exposition of the idea here, but it involves introduction of symbols into the expression indicating when it is possible to "commit" to a feasible sub-path of the expression.

PROOFS OF IMPLEMENTATION OF APPLICATIVE LANGUAGES AND SYSTEMS

Another interesting area involves the level below the use of applicative languages, i.e. the **implementation** of such languages. Proofs have been sketched for the correctness of languages having some aspects of FGL (cf. [Friedman and Wise 76], [Henderson and Morris 76], [O'Donnell 77]), but these proofs have not dealt with issues which arises in multiprocessor systems.

In [Keller and Lindstrom 80a], we attempt a proof of the correctness of the basic AMPS evaluator (by "basic", we mean without resource management primitives, etc.). We desired to include certain pragmatic aspects in our machine model, namely "forwarding" of data values throughout the system, boundedness of the number of certain stored pointer values, assurance of the finite-delay property, etc. We found it convenient to introduce an **intermediate level** language for purposes of the proof, even though such a language played no role in the conception or implementation of the machine itself.

The proof is perhaps interesting because it relates the top level fixed-point semantics of FGL to the operational semantics of the machine language by going through the intermediate level. The construction of the relevant mappings is reminiscent of the method of

[Hoare 72], but also includes an argument for the finite-delay property. The intermediate level has a more "machine-oriented" fixed point semantics because of the introduction of reference values not present in FGL, but is still based on a graphical formalism. Additionally, the concept of demand flow is introduced at this level.

PROCESSOR MANAGEMENT ISSUES

The architecture as proposed in [Keller, Lindstrom, and Patil 79] includes a mechanism to automatically balance the computational load across available hardware units. So far, this idea has not been fully proven, either theoretically or through sufficiently detailed simulation, due to lack of time on the part of the investigators. It does, however, seem to present a rich source of theoretical questions, including some requiring stochastic or operational modeling techniques. Related to this issue are some of the complexity questions discussed earlier. Indeed, it seems that investigators in the area of complexity theory could profitably address such issues which arise when problems have to be mapped to a specific class of parallel machine models. A sampling can be seen in the work of [Savitch and Stimson 79].

STORAGE MANAGEMENT ISSUES

Storage management in multi-processing systems is one problem which has made the rounds among verification theorists (e.g. [Dijkstra, et al. 78]). To date, most attention seems to have been devoted to garbage collection. However, the alternative of "reference counting" holds high intuitive appeal for use in distributed systems, as reference counts seem inherently "more distributable" and are less likely to cause a significant delay in the computational process.

No quantitative comparison between these schemes has been made in the context of interest. Reference counting is often dismissed as not offering reclamation of cyclic data structures. In certain applicative languages, such structures might never exist, but we have already hailed the use of applicative loops in FGL, which indeed are cyclic and sometimes yield unreclaimed residues. But there are alternatives. One is to use reference counting as the main means of reclamation, turning to garbage collection when things get really tight. Additionally, empirical evidence shows that the unreclaimed residual structures are not as pervasive as one might initially believe, and that the behavior of such structures is predictable from examination of the program structure to some extent.

Furthermore, the reference counting scheme being used on the experimental (simulation) version of AMPS is a **two-level** one (see [Nori 79]), in which large units of storage have reference counts distinct from smaller units inside them. Indications are that this scheme is generalizable to three levels, wherein additional counts are maintained for **strong components** of the program graph. Since such components are relatively invariant over the lifetime of a computation, the three-level scheme should allow reclamation of all garbage. Proofs of the reference counting schemes are still being developed.

CONCLUSIONS

We have described several aspects of languages and systems for "applicative" multiprocessing, including some solved and some unsolved problems. From a theoretical point of view, the combination of distributed processing and applicative languages seems to provided an extremely interesting and varied array of topics for future investigation. There seems to be little doubt that this combination will have a significant impact on future uses of computers, as well as theories relating to these uses.

REFERENCES

[Ashcroft and Wadge 77] E.A. Ashcroft and W.W. Wadge. Lucid, a nonprocedural language with iteration. CACM, 20, 7, 519-526 (July 1977).

[Balzer 71] R.M. Balzer. Ports - A method for dynamic interprogram communication and job control. AFIPS Proc. 38, 485-489 (Spring 1971).

[Campbell and Habermann 74] R.H. Campbell and A.N. Habermann. The specification of process synchronization by path expressions in Gelenbe and Kaiser (eds.) Operating Systems, Springer Lecture Notes in Computer Science, 16, 89-102 (1974).

[Church 1941] A. Church. The calculi of lambda-conversion. Princeton University Press (1941).

[Dijkstra, et al. 78] E.W. Dijkstra, et al. On-the-fly garbage collection: An exercise in cooperation. CACM, 21, 11, 966-975 (Nov. 1978).

[Forrester 73] J. W. Forrester. World dynamics. Wright-Allen

Press (1973).

[Friedman and Wise 76] D.P. Friedman and D.S. Wise. CONS should not evaluate its arguments. in Michaelson and Milner (eds.), Automata, Languages, and Programming, 257-284, Edinburgh University Press (1976).

[Friedman and Wise 78] D.P. Friedman and D.S. Wise. The impact of applicative programming on multiprocessing. IEEE Trans. on Computers, C-27, 4, 289-296 (April 1978).

[Giordano 80] J.V. Giordano. A transformation for parallel programs with indeterminate operators. UC Irvine Dataflow Architecture Project Note No. 46 (Feb. 1980).

[Henderson and Morris 76] P. Henderson and J.H. Morris, Jr. A lazy evaluator. Proc. Third ACM Conference on Principles of Programming Languages, 95-103 (1976).

[Hoare 72] C.A.R. Hoare. Proof of correctness of data representations. Acta Informatica, 1, 271-281 (1972).

[Hoare 78] C.A.R. Hoare. Communicating sequential processes. CACM, 21, 8, 666-677 (Aug. 1978).

[Ichbiah, et al. 79] J.D. Ichbiah, et al. Rationale for the design of the ADA programming language. Sigplan notices, 14, 6, Part B (June 1979).

[Jayaraman 80] B. Jayaraman. Resource control in a demand-driven data-flow model. University of Utah, Dept. of Computer Science, PhD dissertation proposal (May 1980).

[Kahn 74] G. Kahn. The semantics of a simple language for parallel programming. Proc. IFIP '74, 471-475 (1974).

[Kahn and MacQueen 76] G. Kahn and D. MacQueen. Coroutines and networks of parallel processes. Proc. IFIP '77, 993-998 (1977).

[Keller 77] R.M. Keller. Semantics of parallel program graphs. University of Utah, Dept. of Computer Science, Tech. Rept. UUCS-77-110 (July 1977).

[Keller 78a] R.M. Keller. Denotational models for parallel programs with indeterminate operators. In E.J. Neuhold (ed.), Formal description of programming concepts, 337-366, North-Holland (1978).

[Keller 78b] R.M. Keller. An approach to determinacy proofs. University of Utah, Dept. of Computer Science, Tech. Rept. UUCS-78-102 (March 1978).

[Keller 78c] R.M. Keller. Sentinels: A concept for multiprocess coordination. University of Utah, Dept. of Computer Science, Tech. Rept. UUCS-78-104 (June 1978).

[Keller, Lindstrom, and Patil 79] R.M. Keller, G. Lindstrom, and S. Patil. A loosely-coupled applicative multi-processing system. AFIPS Proc. (June 1979).

[Keller, Lindstrom, and Patil 80] R.M. Keller, G. Lindstrom, and S. Patil. Data-flow concepts for hardware design. Digest of papers, IEEE Compcon 80, 105-111 (Feb. 1980).

[Keller 80a] Divide and CONCer: Data structuring aspects of applicative multiprocessing. Manuscript submitted for publication (March 1980).

[Keller 80b] Semantics and applications of function graphs. Manuscript submitted for publication (March 1980).

[Keller and Lindstrom 80a] R.M. Keller and G. Lindstrom. Hierarchical analysis of a distributed evaluator. Manuscript submitted for publication (March 1980).

[Keller and Lindstrom 80b] R.M. Keller and G. Lindstrom. Programming paradigms in a graph-based Lisp extension. Manuscript submitted for publication (March 1980).

[Keller, et al. 80] FGL Programmer's guide. Internal memorandum, Dept. of Computer Science, University of Utah (March 1980).

[Manna and Vuillemin 72] Z. Manna and J. Vuillemin. Fixpoint approach to the theory of computation. CACM, 15, 7, 528-536 (July 1972).

[Nori 79] A.K. Nori. A storage reclamation scheme for AMPS. M.S. Thesis, Dept. of Computer Science, University of Utah (Dec. 1979).

[O'Donnell 77] M. O'Donnell. Computing in systems described by equations. Lecture Notes in Computer Science, 58 (1977).

[Petri 66] C.A. Petri. Communication with automata. Supplement 1 to Tech. Rept. RADC-TR-65-377. Griffiss Air Force Base, New York (1966).

[Ritchie and Thompson 75] D.M. Ritchie and K. Thompson. The Unix time-sharing system. CACM, 17, 7, 365-381 (July 1975).

[Savitch and Stimson 79] W.J. Savitch and M.J. Stimson. Time bounded random access machines with parallel processing. JACM, 26, 1, 103-118 (Jan. 1979).

[Scott 76] D. Scott. Data types as lattices. SIAM J. Comp., 5, 3, 522-587 (Sept. 1976).

[Schwarz 77] J. Schwarz. Using annotations to make recursion equations behave. Res. Rept. 43, Dept. of Artificial Intelligence, University of Edinburgh (Sept. 1977).

ON SOME DISCRETE OPTIMIZATION PROBLEMS IN MASS STORAGE SYSTEMS

by

C. K. Wong

IBM T. J. Watson Research Center
P. O. Box 218
Yorktown Heights, NY 10598
U.S.A.

1. INTRODUCTION

In this paper, we are concerned mainly with the problem of minimizing expected read/write head movement in one-dimensional and two-dimensional mass storage systems. We shall use the terms linear and one-dimensional interchangeably. Tape is the prototypical linear storage medium but, when minimization of head movement in a disk is of interest, it is useful to view the cylinders as forming a linear storage [1, Ch. 5], [2-4]. In the case of a linear storage, the head movement is measured by the familiar Euclidean metric. Recently, due to the storage requirement of large data base systems, more attention has been given to two-dimensional mass storage systems. Depending on the system, we may have different access mechanisms. Consequently, the head movement may be measured by other metrics. Currently, in addition to the Euclidean (L_2) metric, the rectilinear (L_1) and maximum (L_∞) metrics are also appropriate measures [5-8]. These non-Euclidean metrics make the minimization problem more interesting and in the meantime more difficult.

In general, consider a set of records $R_1,\ldots,R_n$, with independent access probabilities (or relative access frequencies) $p_1,\ldots,p_n$ ($\sum_{i=1}^{n} p_i=1$). Our basic objective function to be minimized is the expected distance traveled by the head from one record to another:

$$D = \sum_{i,j} p_i\, p_j\, d(i,j) \tag{1}$$

where $d(i,j)$ denotes the distance between R_i and R_j and it depends on the arrangement of records as well as on the metric.

We shall represent a linear storage by the real line and records will be allocated on integral points $0, \pm 1, \pm 2, \ldots$ only. Thus, if records R_i, R_j are situated at points ξ, η, then

$$d(i,j) = d_2(\xi,\eta) = |\xi-\eta|,$$

where d_2 signifies the use of the Euclidean metric.

For a two-dimensional storage, we shall represent it by a plane with records located at points with integral coordinates only. In general, we consider the following metrics:

Let $\xi = (x, y)$, $\eta = (u, v)$ be two points in the plane. The L_p metric is defined as follows:

$$d_p(\xi, \eta) = (|x-u|^p + |y-v|^p)^{1/p}, \ 1 \leq p \leq \infty.$$

By $p = \infty$, we mean

$$d_\infty(\xi, \eta) = \max(|x-u|, |y-v|).$$

We are mainly interested in L_1, L_2, L_∞ metrics.

The problems discussed in this paper can be summarized as follows:

A. Linear storage.

Problem 1. Give records $R_1, \ldots, R_n$ with access probabilities $p_1, \ldots, p_n$, we want to find an arrangement of records such that (1) is minimized.

Problem 2. Two-level version of Problem 1. Given records $R_1, R_2, \ldots, R_{mk}$ with access probabilities $p_1, \ldots, p_{mk}$, we want to first partition them into m pages of k records each. Each page now has access probability q_j which is the sum of the k access probabilities in the page. Now consider the placement of pages in linear storage, i.e. Problem 1 with pages instead of records. Thus, we have a two-level problem: partition and arrangement.

Problem 3. Dynamic version of Problem 1. In Problems 1 and 2, we assume that the records, and hence their relative access frequencies are known before their placement in the linear storage. Here we consider a stiuation where the records come in one by one and they have to be placed in the storage immediately. After all n records are placed, we then know their relative frequencies and we can compute (1). Under some statistical assumptions about the relative frequencies, what is the best placement strategy to minimize (1)? This problem is motivated by the space allocation problem for the minidisks of users of VM/370. As each user logs on, space for his minidisk must be obtained on the online disks immediately.

Problem 4. Batched processing version of Problem 1. Previously, we assume that requests to records are processed sequentially, i.e. one request at a time on the first-come-first-served basis. Here we consider the accessing of batched requests, i.e. we process a fixed number (a batch) of requests at a time. Our objective is to minimize expected distance traveled by the read/write head for a batch. Two problems are involved here. First, for a given arrangement of the records, what is a good scheduling algorithm for the head movement? Second, what is a good arrangement of the records?

B. Two-dimensional storage.

Problem 5. Two-dimensional version of Problem 1. Here we consider all three metrics L_1, L_2, and L_∞. Given reocrds $R_1, R_2, \ldots, R_n$ with access probabilities $p_1, p_2, \ldots, p_n$, we want to find an arrangement of records such that (1) is minimized. Now $d(i,j) = d_p(\xi,\eta)$ is the distance between records under L_p metric and we are mainly interested in the cases when $p = 1, 2, \infty$.

Problem 6. Batched processing version of Problem 5. As in Problem 4, we consider the processing of a fixed number (a batch) of requests at a time. The two questions mentioned in Problem 4 are present here, except they become more complex.

We shall outline some solutions to these problems and shall give proper references to them. As in many discrete optimization problems, in general it is either difficult or too time-consuming to compute an optimal solution. In that case, we shall present near-optimal solutions.

Clearly, many open problems remain, especially in the two-dimensional case. Further research is needed.

2. ONE-DIMENSIONAL RECORD ARRANGEMENT (PROBLEM 1)

The general statement is as follows: Given positive numbers $p_1, p_2, \ldots, p_n$, place them on the integral points of the real line such that $D = \sum_{i,j} p_i\, p_j\, d(i,j)$ is minimized, where $d(i,j)$ is the Euclidean distance between the locations of p_i and p_j.

This problem was solved in a classical mathematical work by Hardy-Littlewood-Pólya [9]. The solution is simply to place the largest p_i and then repetitively to place the next largest p_i alternating between the position immediately to the left (right) of those already placed and the position immediately to the right (left). For example, if $p_1 \geq p_2 \geq \ldots \geq p_n$, then an optimal placement is depicted in Fig. 1. This arrangement will be referred to as the <u>organ-pipe arrangement</u>. A proof of this result can also be found in [10].

3. PARTITION AND ARRANGEMENT (PROBLEM 2)

Given positive numbers $p_1, \ldots, p_{mk}$, we want to first partition them into m groups of k numbers each, let their group sums be $q_1, \ldots, q_m$. Then place these m numbers on the integral points of the real line such that $D = \sum_{i,j} q_i\, q_j\, d(i,j)$ is minimized.

The solution is as follows: Assume $p_1 \geq p_2 \geq \ldots \geq p_{mk}$. Then place the first k numbers in one group, the second k numbers in another group, and so on. We then obtain a m-vector $\underline{q}_0 = (q_1, \ldots, q_m)$ with $q_1 \geq q_2 \geq \ldots \geq q_m$. Application of the organ-pipe arrangement to these $q_1, \ldots, q_m$ yields an optimal solution. The proof depends on the notion of vector majorization and a powerful theorem by Schur. [11-15].

<u>Definition</u>. If $\underline{v} = (v_1, \ldots, v_m)$ and $\underline{u} = (u_1, \ldots, u_m)$ are such that $v_1 \geq \ldots \geq v_m$, $u_1 \geq \ldots \geq u_m$ and $\sum_{i=1}^{k} v_i \geq \sum_{i=1}^{k} u_i$, $k = 1,2,\ldots,m-1$, $\sum_{i=1}^{m} v_i = \sum_{i=1}^{m} u_i$, then $\underline{v}$ is said to majorize $\underline{u}$, in symbol, $\underline{u} < \underline{v}$.

<u>Definition</u>. A real-valued function of m real variables $\phi = \phi(x_1, \ldots, x_m)$ is said to be a <u>Schur function</u> if

$$(x_i - x_j)\left(\frac{\partial\phi}{\partial x_i} - \frac{\partial\phi}{\partial x_j}\right) \geq 0 \quad \text{for all } i,j.$$

Theorem. (Schur) If $\phi(x_1,...,x_m)$ is a Schur function and if $\underline{u}<\underline{v}$, then $\phi(v_1,...,v_m) \geq \phi(u_1,...,u_m)$.

Note that given $p_1 \geq p_2 \geq ... \geq p_{mk}$, among all possible partitions into m groups, the vector $\underline{q}_0$ obtained by our algorithm majorizes all other resulting vectors. Thus, it remains only to show that $-D$ is a Schur function of $q_1, q_2, ..., q_m$. The proof is given in details in part 3 of [15].

4. DYNAMIC PLACEMENT (PROBLEM 3)

As mentioned in Problem 1, given a set of records with probabilities p_1, $p_2,...,p_n$, the organ-pipe arrangement minimizes (1). We now consider the problem that not all records (and their probabilities) are known before hand, but rather they come in one by one and they have to be placed as soon as they come in. The objective is still the minimization of (1). This problem is motivated by the space allocation problem for the minidisks of users of VM/370 [4]. As each user logs on, space for his minidisk must be obtained on the on-line disks. For each user it is possible to estimate his activity based on accounting information from past usage of the system. But since it is in general not possible to know exactly who will log on at a given time, relative frequency of access is not known prior to the allocation of individual disks. We assume that a sequence of users $\{u_t\}$, $1 \leq t \leq n$, arrive at the system at distinct points in time. Associated with each user, u_t, is a frequency of use, f_t. The f_t's are assumed to be independent, identically distributed random variables. We further assume that f_t is uniformly distributed on the interval (0,1]. Each user is allocated a vacant space, i, in a linear store where locations have been numbered as in Fig. 2.

After complete allocation of all users, user u_t will have relative frequency $f_t / \sum_{t=1}^{n} f_t$ and the expected access time is $D = \sum_{ij} \frac{f_i f_j}{(\Sigma f_i)^2} d(i,j)$ where f_i now corresponds to the user at location i and d(i,j) is the distance between locations i and j (as labelled in Fig. 2).

We propose the following dynamic allocation algorithm: Partition the interval (0,1] into n subintervals: $(0, \frac{1}{n}], (\frac{1}{n}, \frac{2}{n}], \ldots, (\frac{n-1}{n}, 1]$. If the frequency f_1 of the first user u_1 belongs to the j-th subinterval, allocate location j to this user. We now partition the interval (0,1] into (n-1) subintervals: $(0, \frac{1}{n-1}], (\frac{1}{n-1}, \frac{2}{n-1}], \ldots, (\frac{n-2}{n-1}, 1]$. If f_2 of the second user belongs to the k-th subinterval, allocat the k-th smallest labelled location among the remaining (n-1) locations to this user, and so on. Let D_h donote the expected access time by this algorithm and D_o that by the organ-pipe placement if all frequencies are known before hand. Of course, $D_o \leq D_h$. But surprisingly, the average values $\overline{D_o}$, $\overline{D_h}$ over all possible samples $\{f_t\}$, $1 \leq t \leq n$, from the distribution are asymptotically the same (as n tends to infinity). Thus, for n large, the dynamic allocation algorithm is nearly optimal. In fact, computation shows that

$$\overline{D_o} = \frac{7}{30} \quad n + 0(1)$$

and

$$\overline{D_h} = \frac{7}{30} \quad n + a \ln n + 0(1),$$

where a is a small constant.

For comparison, if we do not use any intelligent allocation algorithm at all, but rather assign space to the users randomly, then the average value of the expected access time will be

$$\overline{D_r} = \frac{n}{3} + 0(1).$$

Thus, the dynamic allocation algorithm indeed brings forth some improvement. Detailed derivation is given in [4].

5. BATCHED PROCESSING (PROBLEM 4)

In all previous problems it is assumed that requests to records are processed sequentially, i.e. one request at a time on the first-come-first-served basis.

Here we shall consider the accessing of batched requests, i.e. we process a fixed number (a batch) of b requests at a time. We make the same assumption as in Problem 1, namely, consecutive accesses are independent and the frequencies are known. Our objective is to minimize the expected distance traveled by the read/write head for a batch.

Two problems arise immediately. First, for a given arrangement of the records, what is a good scheduling algorithm (or rule for short) for the head movement? Second, what is a good arrangement of the records?

Here we address ourselves primarily to the first problem since we believe that the organ-pipe arrangement is the best arrangement for most reasonable rules. In fact, we can prove this for the two simple rules discussed later.

Let the locations of a linear storage be labeled 1,2,...,n from left to right. We use a row n-vector to represent the arrangement of records, e.g. $(R_1,...,R_n)$ means record R_i is at location i for all i. Let p_i be the access probability of record R_i for i = 1,2,...,n. Then $\sum_{i=1}^{n} p_i = 1$. At time t, b requests are generated (with repetitions allowed) according to these probabilities. Let $L_1 \leq L_2 \cdots \leq L_b$, $1 \leq L_i \leq n$, be the b locations where the requests are made. From now on L_1, L_b will be referred to as the <u>left</u> and <u>right extremes</u> respectively and will be written as L and R. Suppose the current head location is x, $1 \leq x \leq n$. A <u>rule</u> specifies the order in which the head goes through $L_1, L_2, ..., L_b$, starting from x. The head stops when all locations have been visited. Let the stopping location be y. y will be the starting location for the next batch, i.e. for time t + 1. Let d(x,y) denote the distance traveled by the head from x to y, whose expected value is our <u>cost</u>. Here we are only interested in rules whose cost has a definite value. For example, rules whose behavior can be modeled by a Markov chain. A more formal definition of rules will be given later. Our objective is to find rules with as small a cost as possible.

Several simple rules immediately suggest themselves: Leftist rule. From the current head location x, move to the left extreme L, then sweep across to the right extreme R, and stop.

A Rightist rule can be similarly defined. That is, the head moves to the right extreme first and then sweep to the left extreme.

Alternating rule. When the time t is odd, use Leftist rule, otherwise use Rightist rule.

Let $COST_L$, $COST_R$, $COST_A$ be the cost functions of the Leftist, Rightist and Alternating rules respectively. Also, define

$$\lambda_i = \text{Prob}(L \geq i) = \left(\sum_{j=1}^{n} p_i\right)^b$$

$$\rho_i = \text{Prob}(R \leq i) = \left(\sum_{j=1}^{i} p_i\right)^b$$

By symmetry, $COST_L = COST_R$. It can be shown that

$$COST_L = 2\sum_{i=1}^{n-1}(1-\lambda_{i+1})(1-\rho_i)$$

$$COST_A = \sum_{i=1}^{n-1} (1 - \rho_i^2 - \lambda_{i+1}^2)$$

and that $COST_L$ ($COST_R$), $COST_A$ are all minimized when the record arrangement is the organ-pipe arrangement.

Based on these results, it can be further shown that

(1) $COST_A \leq COST_L = COST_R$

for any record arangement.

(2) $C_{min} \leq C_A \leq 2 \cdot C_{min}$,

where C_{min} is the smallest possible cost among all rules and all record arrangements; C_A is $COST_A$ when the organ-pipe arrangement is used.

Therefore the Alternating rule is better than the Leftist or Rightist rule and is never more than twice larger than the minimum.

A slightly more complicated but intuitively appealing rule is the following.

Nearest rule. From the current head location, move to the closer of the two extremes, then sweep across to the other extreme and stop. In case of tie, choose either extreme. However, unlike the previous rules we are unable to obtain closed-form expression for its cost $COST_N$ because it is difficult to calculate the probability that the head will be at a given position after accessing a batch.

The head position can be described by a Markov chain where the i-th state (i=1,...,n) corresponds to having the head at location i. It is not difficult to write down the transition matrix $[p_{xy}]$, where p_{xy} = Prob (head ends up at y | head starts at x). But solving for the steady state distribution $(s_1,...,s_n)$ symbolically is difficult and $COST_N = \sum_{i=1}^{n-1}(1 - \lambda_{i+1} - \rho_i) + \sum_{i=1}^{n} \sum_{u \le r} s_i \cdot \text{Prob}(L = u, R = r) \cdot \min(|i-u|, |i-r|)$.

Numerical computations were carried out for several standard record access probability distributions. For all cases, $COST_N \le COST_A$. However, one can construct a distribution such that this is not true. Also, it is not known if the organ-pipe arrangement minimizes $COST_N$.

All the previous rules are simple to execute, but their costs are not optimal. Next, we present a procedure to calculate an optimal rule for a given record arrangement. The amount of computation depends on the arrangement and the access probabilites. We follow the idea of "discret dynamic programming" developed by Blackwell [16].

The situation in discrete dynamic programming is as follows: we are given a system with T states (labeled 1,...,T). At any time, the system is in exactly one state. At intervals of time, we are required to choose any one of a given set of A actions (labeled 1,...,A) to be performed. The cost of performing action a in state t is given by c(t,a). (We will assume all costs are non-negative.) After an action is performed, the system moves to a new state. The probability that action a will cause the system to move from state t to t' is denoted by

$p(t \rightarrow t' \mid a)$. A decision function, f is a function from $\{1,...,T\}$ into $\{1,...,A\}$ where $f(t)$ specifies that action to be performed in state t. A policy $\pi = (f_1, f_2,...,)$ is a sequence of decision functions where f_i is used to determine the i-th decision.

The correspndence between this terminology and the original problem should be clear: a state corresponds to an ordered triple (x, ℓ, r) where x is the current head position and ℓ and r are the extremes of the current batch. There are only two actions: one for moving to the left extreme first, then sweeping across to the right and another for moving right first. (Note that when we apply an action in a given state, only the x of the next state is determined; ℓ and r are chosen probabilistically.) The correspondence for costs and probabilities follow directly.

It can be shown that for our case an optimal rule is a uniform rule, i.e. a rule consisting of one decision function only, which is used to access all batches. This is intuitively clear since the batches are independent and each batch will have an infinite number following, there is no intuitive justification for using different decision functions for accessing two different batches.

The procedure for calculating an optimal rule starts with an arbitrary rule (we choose the Nearest rule) and iteratively improves it. At each iteration we assume the current rule will be used to access all batches except the first and then calculate the best rule for accessing the first batch. It can be shown that the asymptotic cost for this rule is less than or equal to that for the original rule. This new rule is then used on the next iteration, and we continue iterating until the new rule and the current rule are identical. The procedure for calculating an optimal rule is given below.

1. Make the Nearest rule the "current" rule.
2. Calculate $f_B(x)$ (the cost of accessing B batches with the head starting at psition x) for the "current" rule. $f_B(x)$ is iteratively calculated for B = 1,2,... using the formula

   $f_0(x) = 0$

   $f_B(x) = \sum_{\ell,r} \text{Prob}(L = \ell, R = r) \cdot \delta(x,\ell,r)$

where

$$\delta(x,\ell,r) = \begin{cases} |x-\ell| + (r-\ell) + f_{B-1}(r) & \text{if the current rule goes to } \ell \text{ first with the head at x and extremes } \ell \text{ and r} \\ |x-r| + (r-\ell) + f_{B-1}(\ell) & \text{if it goes to r first.} \end{cases}$$

The calculation continues until we reach a B such that $f_B(x) - f_{B-1}(x)$ is nearly constant with respect to x.

3. Calculate the "new" rule as follows:

For each x, ℓ and r, if

$$|x-r| - |x-\ell| + \lim_{B\to\infty}[f_B(\ell) - f_B(r)] < 0$$

the "new" rule should move to the right extreme first with head at x and extremes ℓ and r. If this quantity is non-negative, the rule should move left first. (Note that $\lim_{B\to\infty}[f_B(\ell) - f_B(r)]$ is closely approximated by $f_B(\ell) - f_B(r)$ for some large B.)

4. If the new rule is the same as the current rule, stop. This rule is an optimal rule. Otherwise set the "current rule" to be the "new rule" and go to step 2.

Details are given in [2].

6. TWO-DIMENSIONAL RECORD ARRANGEMENT (PROBLEM 5)

Here we consider a two-dimensional version of Problem 1. The metrics of interest are L_1, L_2, L_∞. Let R^2_1 and R^2_∞ denote the plane with L_1 and L_∞ respectively. Then R^2_1 and R^2_∞ are isometric due to the mapping f: $R^2_\infty \to R^2_1$ defined by $f((x,y)) = ((y+x)/2, (y-x)/2)$. Since this mapping has $\pm 1/2$ as coefficients, any computational problem in one metric is polynomially equivalent to that in the other metric in the sense that any deterministic polynomial time algorithm for the problem in one metric can be applied to solve the same problem in the other metric. Thus, it suffices to consider only one metric [17-18]. Returning to the record arrangement problem, we consider L_2 (Euclidean) metric first. Note that in the present case the optimal solution depends on the values of the access probabilities rather than on their rankings alone as in the one-dimensional case. This is demonstrated in Fig. 3.

We now propose a simple ranking-dependent heuristic which is asymptotically optimal (as n tends to infinity). This heuristic is a generalization of the organ-pipe arrangement in the one-dimensional case, namely, placing the largest p_i at the center and then filling "shells" of points which are equidistant from the center with a set of the next largest p_i. This heuristic will be referred to as the "shell" algorithm.

By considering the continuous analog, it can be shown that

$$D_{shell} \leq D_{optimal} + c,$$

where D_{shell} is the value of $D = \sum_{i,j} p_i \, p_j \, d_2 \, (i,j)$ when the "shell" algorithm is used and $D_{optimal}$ is that of D when the optimal algorithm is used, and c is a constant independent of n. Thus the "shell" algorithm is asymptotically optimal.

However, for L_1 metric, it can be shown that there does not exist any asymptotically optimal ranking-dependent heuristics in general except in the uniform case when $p_i = 1/n$ for all i. In L_2, the "shell" algorithm implies putting the p_i's in decreasing order along concentric circles. In L_1 and for $p_i = 1/n$, to obtain an asymptotically optimal solution, we put the p_i's in decreasing order along concentric symmetric closed curves. In the first quadrant, this curve $v = f(u)$ is given by the following differentio-integral equation:

$$f'(u) \left[\frac{n}{4} - \int_0^u f(x)dx + uf(u)\right] + \int_0^u f(x)dx = 0.$$

By applying the isometry between R^2_∞ and R^2_1 mentioned at the beginning of this section, similar results can be obtained for L_∞ metric. For details, see [5].

7. BATCHED PROCESSING IN TWO-DIMENSIONAL STORAGE (PROBLEM 6)

As in Problem 4, we consider here the minimization of head movement in a two-dimensional storage when a fixed number (a batch) of requests are processed at a time. Because of the dimension of the storage, the problems involved become very complex and only limited results have been obtained. More specifically, given a set of records with known access probabilities, to minimize the head movement (under different metrics), we have the following problems:

(a) How to place the records?

(b) For a single batch of requests, how to schedule the head movement so that it goes through the requested records in minimum distance?

(c) What is an optimal rule to schedule the head movement so that the expected distance traveled by the head for a batch is minimized?

Note that solution to (b) does not necessarily imply a solution to (c). To minimize the expected distance for a batch, we have to consider infinitely many batches and the stopping position of the head for a batch becomes the starting position for the next batch. Therefore, it is important to consider not only the shortest path which the head has to follow but also the starting and stopping positions. (b) is trivial in the one-dimensional case since for a single batch, the Nearest rule is the optimal solution.

When all the record access probabilities are equal, (a) disappears and (b) is equivalent to finding a shortest Hamiltonian path with a fixed starting point in L_1, L_2, and L_∞ metrics. This problem can be shown to be NP-complete. Therefore, heuristics become necessary. Based on the notion of Voronoi diagrams, one can construct minimum spanning trees for n points in 0(n log n) time for all three metrics, where n is the batch size plus 1. Then a depth-first search can be performed starting with the specified point to visit each point once. It can be shown that the distance traveled by the head according to this algorithm is never more than twice the minimum distance. Details are given in [7]. Other problems still remain open.

8. SOME OPEN PROBLEMS

In addition to the problem of extending all the remaining results from the one-dimensional case to the two-dimensional case, we have some other open problems:

(1) Related to Problem 1, instead of independent access probabilities $p_1,\ldots,p_n$, if we assume that they form a first order Markov chain, what will be the optimal placement? Let p_{ij} denote the conditional probability to access record j if record i has just been accessed and let $q_1,\ldots,q_n$ be the stationary probability distribution. Then the counterpart of equation (1) will be $D = \sum_{i,j} q_i\, p_{ij}\, d(i,j)$. Intuitively, one may want to arrange the records alternately according to the ranking of $q_1,\ldots,q_n$. However, it can easily be shown that it is not always optimal. But how does such a heuristic perform?

(2) Related to Problem 2, given mk records with known independent access probabilities, how to allocate them in m linear stores, with capacity k each to minimize expected access time, assuming inter-storage movement takes no time? One obvious algorithm is as follows: Regard the storage system as a $m \times k$ matrix, fill it column by column in an alternating fashion. Clearly, this is not optimal. For example, for $m=2$, $k=3$, the placement in Figure 4a has a smaller expected access time than that in Figure 4b, which results from the alternating algorithm. But how does this algorithm perform?

(3) Can we carry out the same analysis in Problem 3 for more general distributions than the uniform distribution?

(4) Related to Problem 4, we conjecture that the organ-pipe record arrangement will be best for both the Nearest rule and the optimal rule. Is it true?

(5) Related to Problem 5, if instead of an infinite plane, we have an $m \times n$ rectangle and $m \times n$ records, how to place them so that equation (1) is minimized? Some experiments with variations of the "shell" algorithm were performed [6]. They seemed to be very good. But no analytic results were obtained.

(6) There are many remaining questions in Problem 6. Just to name one: Can we generalize the procedure for calculating an optimal rule in Problem 4 to a comparably efficient rule for the two-dimensional case?

REFERENCES

1. E. G. Coffman, Jr. and P. J. Denning, Operating Systems Theory, Prentice-Hall, New Jersey, 1973.
2. J. R. Bitner and C. K. Wong, Optimal and near-optimal scheduling algorithms for batched processing in linear storage, SIAM J. COMPUT, Vol. 8, No. 4, (1979), pp. 479-498.
3. D. D. Grossman and H. F. Silverman, Placement of records on a secondary storage device to minimize access time, J. Assoc. Comput. Mach., 20 (1973), pp. 429-438.
4. A. C. McKellar and C. K. Wong, Dynamic placement of records in linear storage. J. Assoc. Comput. Mach., 25 (1978), pp. 421-434.
5. R. M. Karp, A. C. McKellar, and C. K. Wong, Near-optimal solutions to a 2-dimensional placement problem, SIAM J. Computing, Vol. 4, No. 3, (1975), pp. 271-286.
6. P. C. Yue and C. K. Wong, Near-optimal heuristics for an assignment problem in mass storage. Internat. J. Computer and Information Sciences, Vol. 4, No. 4, (1975), pp. 281-294.
7. D. T. Lee and C. K. Wong, Voronoi diagrams in L_1, (L_∞) metrics with 2-dimensional storage applications, Vol. 9, No. 1, (1980), pp. 200-211.
8. A. K. Chandra, Hsu Chang and C. K. Wong, Two-dimensional magnetic bubble memory, U.S. Patent No. 4,174,538,

(1979).

9. G. H. Hardy, J. E. Littlewood, and G. Pólya, Inequalities, Cambridge University Press, Cambridge, England, 1952.

10. P. P. Bergmans, Minimizing expected travel time on geometrical patterns by optimal probability rearrangements, Information and Control, 20 (1972), pp. 331-350.

11. A. W. Marshall, I. Olkin, and F. Proschan, Monotonicity of ratios of means and other applications of majorization. In Inequalities, Shisha (Ed.), Academic Press, New York, 1967.

12. A. Ostrowski, Sur quelques applications des fonctions conveses et convaves au sens de I. Schur, J. Math. Pures Appl. 31 (1952), pp. 253-292.

13. I. Schur, Uber ein Klasse von Mittlebildungen mit Anwendungen auf die Determinatentheorie. Sitzber. Berl. Math. Ges. 22 (1923), pp. 9-20.

14. C. K. Wong and P. C. Yue, A majorization theorem for the number of distinct outcomes in N independent trials, Discrete Math. 6 (1973), pp. 391-398.

15. P. C. Yue and C. K. Wong, On the optimality of the probability ranking scheme in storage application, J. Assoc. Comput. Mach., 20 (1973), pp. 624-633.

16. D. Blackwell, Discrete Dynamic Programming, Annals of Mathematical Statistics, 33 (1962), pp. 719-726.

17. C. K. Wong and K. C. Chu, Average distances in L_p disks,

SIAM Review, 19 (1977), pp. 320-324.

18. D. Coppersmith, D. T. Lee and C. K. Wong, An elementary proof of non-existence of isometries between L_p^k and L_q^k, IBM J. of Res. Devel., Vol. 23, No. 6, (1979), pp. 696-699.

Abstract Data Types:
A Retrospective and Prospective View

Wm. A. Wulf

Computer Science Department
Carnegie Mellon University
Pittsburgh, Pa.

May 1980

Abstract

This paper presents a retrospective view of the last decade's research in a number of related areas: programming methodology, formal semantics, program specification and verification, and programming languages. The synergistic effect of these threads of research is especially evident in the area called *abstract data types*, and this area is taken as the focus of the paper. After reviewing some of the history and status of the area, some important open problems are identified.

This research was sponsored by the National Science Foundation under Grant MCS77-03883 and by the Defense Advanced Research Projects Agency (DOD), ARPA Order No. 3597, monitored by the Air Force Avionics Laboratory Under Contract F33615-78-C-1551. The views and conclusions contained in this document are those of the author and should not be interpreted as representing the official policies, either expressed or implied, of the National Science Foundation, the Defense Advanced Research Projects Agency, or the US Government.

Abstract Data Types: A Retrospective and Prospective View

1. Introduction

The organizers of this conference have asked me to present a lecture on abstract data types, and to try to both summarize their present state as well as to speculate on the future of research in this dynamic area. Doing so is a tall order! Developments have been rapid and are continuing. Literally hundreds of researchers, spanning many fields in computer science, are involved. Dozens of experimental languages have been designed and implemented. Research on programming methodology and the more formal aspects of semantics, verification, and specification are continuing to impact the area.

Faced with the magnitude of the task, I have not attempted a complete survey; rather, I have merely attempted to cover some of the highlights of the past decade's research and bright spots on the horizon. The result, of course, is a somewhat subjective and possibly parochial view. Nonetheless, I hope it will be useful. I suspect that many, if not most of the attendees of this conference are theoretically inclined. By contrast, I consider myself an engineer and a practitioner -- but one that appreciates the importance of a sound theoretical basis for my work. Thus, I hope the perspective that I can bring to these proceedings is one that will further expand the contacts between the practitioners and the theoreticians.

The decade of the 70's has been, I believe, truely remarkable in terms of the development of concepts and tools to support the construction of high quality software. I shall often use the phrase *abstract data type* in this paper, but actually this is merely a catch phrase. I intend it to connote a confluence of ideas from programming methodology, program specification and verification, formal semantics and programming languages. It is really the synergistic effect of the interplay of these areas, and not merely the manifestation of them in programming languages, that is remarkable -- and hence is really the subject of this lecture. To me, this confluence is most evident in programming languages, and so that will be my focus for the lecture; nonetheless, behind each language issue are the contributions from the other areas -- I trust that will be evident.

2. Some History and Persective

It is, perhaps, worthwhile to *very* briefly recount some of the history that lead us to our present understanding of abstract data types. It's difficult to know where to begin, but perhaps the best place is with the large system debacles of the 60's. Painful as they were, the experiences with these systems lead to the recognition that software construction is a great deal more difficult than had been imagined. The state of affairs as this recognition emerged was expressed well at the two NATO Software Engineering Conferences [24, 3]. As a direct consequence of our experience with these large systems, we finally began to appreciate the intellectual difficulty of the programming task. More importantly, we began to appreciate that the root of the difficulty was our own human inability to deal with the complexity of these systems. This, in turn, lead to the recognition that certain program organizations, certain *structures*, were more intellectually tractable than others.

During the late 60's and early 70's there was a great deal of research aimed at solving the "software crisis" (a term that, fortunately, is not used much anymore). Of special interest to us here were five major threads:

- *Structured control*: Spurred by Dijkstra's famous letter, [6], involuted control flow was identified as one source of intellectual complexity -- and the infamous *goto* was identified as a language mechanism that could be used to construct intellectually intractable programs. This, in turn, lead to research on both alternative control constructs and to the class of programming methodologies typified by "stepwise refinement" [43]. These methodologies advocated beginning with a high-level, abstract, and self-evidently correct program, and refining it through a sequence of successively more concrete program into the final, executable version.

- *Hierarchical decomposition*: Among the simplest, and hence most intellectually manageable program structures are those that are hierarchical -- that is, ones in which the relation between the components of a system can be viewed as a tree. Systems such as THE [7] were constructed using hierarchy as a guiding principle and were demonstrated to have many desirable properties. Later, of course, we came to realize that there is generally more than one relation between the components of a system [31, 32], and hence that a system might be hierarchically structured with respect to some of these while simultaneously not hierarchical with respect to others.

- *Modular decomposition*: In the systems of the 60's, the term *module* often simply meant *compilation unit*. Often, a module was a functional (procedural) unit; data was "passed" from module-to-module with each module performing some specified operations on it. In a long and important series of papers, Parnas changed our view of a module in at least three ways [27, 28, 29, 30, 32, 31]. First, a module is now more often a *data abstraction* rather than a functional one. Second, instead of a large and complex "interface" involving many details of data format, a module has (primarily) a procedural interface that admits of a formal specification, and that is invariant under many changes of implementation. Third, the details of the implementation of a module are *hidden* from its users so that that can be shielded from irrelevant detail. Parnas' research was, and remains primarily methodological; yet this view of program decomposition is the most direct ancestor of the data abstraction facilities of modern programming languages, and is a key to the formal specification and verification of practical programs.

- *Semantics, Verification and Specification*: It is, perhaps, unfair to lump these three important areas under one banner, but they share much in common and it seems appropriate to discuss them together. Beginning about the same time as these other threads of research, *cf* [8], all three areas have made tremendous strides. Only the technology of machine-aided proofs seems to have lagged and to be preventing the routine verification of at least some (important) practical programs. To be sure, important theoretical problems remain, but in little more than a decade we have advanced to the point where the semantics of complete programming languages have been specified (*cf* [12, 21]), and the behavior of non-trivial programs have been both specified and verified (*cf* [26]). London, [20], contains a good survey of much of the material on program verification.

- *Languages*: It seems likely that, whether or not there had been a "software crisis", research on programming languages would have continued; they are the primary notational vehicle of our discipline and, as such, were always of research interest. Several significant trends, however, were altered because of our emerging appreciation of the role of complexity; I shall mention only two. First, there was a turn away from complexity toward simplicity in languages themselves -- and languages such as Pascal [14] appeared. Second, the research on "extensible" languages [34] withered; although many of the concepts of extensible languages survived in the data abstraction languages that we will discuss below. In part this happened because of a series of unsolved technical problems; more important, however, was the recognition that mere syntactic extension provided primarily convenience and did not address the more fundamental issues of complexity.

None of these research threads *by itself*, of course, solved the software crisis -- nor were they likely to. On the other hand, the confluence of the results from these separate areas precipitated the stream of research that I have loosely labeled "abstract data types" -- and that stream embodies aspects of them all.

2.1. The Purpose of Languages

At the risk of being pedantic, and before discussing abstract data types, let's review the *purpose* of programming languages as a basis for evaluating the state of abstract data types relative to that purpose; languages have at least three goals:

- they are design tools, in terms of which humans think about the solution of a problem,

- they are a vehicle for human-to-human communication, and

- they are a vehicle for instructing a computer.

Design tool. Faced with a task, the programmer must determine an overall strategy -- a program structure -- which will accomplish that task. He must choose a structure that will be correct, acceptably efficient, amenable to the inevitable modifications, and so on. The initial stages of this design process are generally best conducted at a relatively abstract level and then slowly refined to a specific implementation. However, designing a program is not unlike other engineering design activity -- it must ultimately be grounded in reality; design must be constrained by practical considerations. Even at the earliest, most abstract stages, the limitations imposed by the available processor, memory, secondary storage, and language must be considered -- even if only to the extent of determining that they are not limiting factors for the task at hand.

As design progresses and becomes more specific, the programming language plays an increasingly significant role. The choice of data structures (e.g., arrays or lists) and algorithms (e.g., recursive or iterative) is affected by both what is conveniently expressible and what is acceptably efficient in the language. Sometimes the design decisions may be consciously considered, but one suspects that the Whorfian hypothesis [42] is operative at this level; Whorf conjectured that language strongly influences both *what* we can think about and *how* we think about it. Thus, one suspects that Fortran programmers seldom, if ever, even consider the possibility of a recursive algorithm or linked-list data structure.

Of particular relevance to the design activity, and closely coopled to the Whorfian hypothesis, are the units into which a language allows a program to be decomposed. All significant programs are too large to be comprehended, or designed, *en masse*. They must be decomposed. They *will* be decomposed in a way supported by the language being used; in traditional languages this means into *compilation units, procedures, blocks*, and *statements*. As we shall see, one of the important developments of the past decade is to provide another -- and probably more important -- unit.

Person-to-person communication. A programming language serves as a communication medium between people in two contexts: (1) after a program is operational and is in the use/modification stage, and (2) in large, multiperson projects. In both contexts, one's ability to read and understand a fragment of program text is more important than the ability to write the same fragment. To understand a program requires that you first understand what it is intended to do. Programming languages, however, tend to focus on how something is to be done rather than on what was intended to be accomplished. Thus, one's ability to infer the latter from the former is crucial. A language's direct inclusion of central concepts is a major factor in making this inference; it is easier, for example, to recognize a de-queueing operation in a language which includes queues than to infer that a sequence of operations on integer arrays, say in APL, achieves the same effect.

The observation above alludes to one of the major tensions in all language design efforts -- a tension directly related to the limitations of the human mind. Should a language contain every conceivably useful construct, or should it be complete but relatively spartan? In the former case the language will usually contain a construct that is "just right" for the problem at hand, but the language itself will be big -- probably too big for any individual to be facile with all of it. In the latter case the language itself will be small enough to be grasped in its entirety, but almost every program will necessarily have to bootstrap itself to the point where a given problem solution can be stated succinctly.

Instructing the computer. A program, if it is to be useful, must be executed on a real computer. This is the practical rule against which a program must ultimately be measured, and was the initial goal of programming languages. Although no longer the only goal, it remains an important one. It manifests itself primarily as a constraint on language design -- it must be possible for programs written in the language to be executed with reasonable space and time efficiency. It also manifests itself, however, in the need to supply painstaking detail, correctly. This need is the root of the potential for unmanageable complexity.

The need to make the implementation of a language acceptably efficient reveals another basic tension in language design. This tension may be loosely described as existing between "generality" and "efficiency", although in some ways that description belies the subtlety of the problem. "More general" does not always imply "less efficient"; quite the opposite is often the case. Usually difficult and unexpected efficiency problems do not arise because of a single language feature, no matter how general it is. Rather, they arise as a result of the interaction of several features.[1] Choosing the proper balance between the generality of individual features and the cost of their interaction is what has often turned out to be more difficult than expected, and what has often been done badly.

3. Abstract Data Types

Beginning in the early 70's, a number of researchers recognized the potential of the idea, pioneered in the Simula *class* [5], of providing direct language support for Parnas-like modules. Although I have said that it is actually the synergy between language and the other disciplines that I wish to talk about -- it seems most natural to do so in the context of the language developments. Thus, in this section I will focus on these linguistic mechanisms.

3.1. Properties of Data Abstraction Languages

In a brief paper, especially one that is to be both retrospective and prospective, it is hopeless to try to cover all the languages that have incorporated a data abstraction facility. The list of such languages is well known; a few that the interested reader might wish to explore further are Ada [13], Alphard [46], CLU [18], Concurrent Pascal [2], Euclid [16], Gypsy [1], Mesa [9], and Modula [44]. Here, however, we will take a meta view and examine only major similarities and differences between these and other languages of the genre. The major similarities arise from a shared set of premises and goals, for example:

- Abstraction is *the* issue. To control complexity, the programmer must be able to ignore detail and work with a simplified, or *abstract* model of a system component. Well done, this can avoid the exponential growth of complexity with program size -- reducing it to, at most, linear growth and, at best, no growth at all.

- The abstractions used to design a program *must* be retained in the program text. Program maintenance costs more than development -- often by large factors. Thus, purely methodological approaches such as stepwise refinement, while important, are flawed in that the intermediate abstractions are lost in the final program.

---

[1] It is popularly believed, for example, that recursive procedures are inefficient. As implemented in most Algol and PL/1 systems, they are! However, the need for that inefficiency arises primarily because of an interaction with block structure; without block structure, recursion can be extremely efficient.

- Separation of specification and implementation. The specification of a component must *be* its abstraction; this should be all that a user of the component needs to know about it. The implementation of the component is a separate concern and may be done by a different person. In Parnas' terms, the implementation should be *hidden* from the user. Language should support this separation (and this hiding).

- A type is *not* a data structure; it is, rather a set of values *plus* a set of operations that together completely characterize the behavior of objects of that type (*cf*, [22]). In short, the notion of *type* in programming languages ought to correspond closely -- if not exactly -- with the mathematical notion of a hetrogeneous algebra.

- The *module*, in Parnas' sense, is a convenient and practical unit of program specification and verification; they are not too large to be handled by current and expected verification technology. Moreover, experience suggests that there is a high degree of correlation between understandability (by humans) and specifyability/verifyability.

Given the similarity of goals and premises, coupled with the model of Simula as a starting point, it is not surprising that the resulting languages share a number of common characteristics and mechanisms. Among these are:

- An *encapsulation* mechanism: Roughly speaking, these are simply a means for better control over *scope* -- or the *visibility* of names. In one form or another, they provide a means for selectively *importing* names from the enclosing environment and *exporting* others to it. In Ada, for example, the encapsulation mechanism is called a *package*; in Modula, Euclid and others it is called a *module*; in Alphard it is called a *form*; and, in CLU it is called a *cluster*.

  Whatever the name, the intent is similar -- it allows the system designer to control (some of) the dependencies between the components of the system being constructed. Not all dependencies, or *assumptions* in Parnas' terminology, can be expressed as names, of course -- but many important ones can. Of special interest are those involving control of access to the representation of an abstract type (see below). This, in turn, allows the programmer to ensure the invariant properties of the type.

- A *type* definition mechanism: These are generally evolved forms of the style of type definition present in Pascal (or *mode* definitions in Algol 68) -- with one important exception. In cooperation with the encapsulation mechanism, they provide a means for exporting the type (name) without disclosing its representation. Thus, users may declare variables of that type -- but they cannot manipulate its representation directly. They are forced to invoke operations provided by the encapsulation to do that; thus "information hiding", of a particular kind at any rate, is enforced.

- An *operator* definition mechanism: An operator definition is both syntactically and semantically similar to the familiar *procedure* and *function* definitions of traditional languages. Again, however, in conjunction with the encapsulation mechanism, they can be used to define type-specific operators. Thus, what is exported from the encapsulation is close to the mathematical notion of type -- a set of values together with a set of operations defined on them. A particular case of this is evident in the notion of *overloading* of operator names.

  Much is gained in the simplicity and coherence of a language if user-defined, abstract, data types behave as much like the base, or *built-in* ones as possible. It would be abhorrent if, for example, a different syntax were needed to declare variables of an abstract type[2]. A particular case of symmetry with the built-in types arises in the matter of infix operators. The built-in operators are *overloaded* in the sense that, for example, " + " operates on both integers and reals. Permitting further overloading, as in defining " + " on *complex*, is one of the ways that the data abstraction languages have borrowed from the research on extensible languages -- and have thereby reduced the complexity with which the programmer must deal.

There are other mechanisms that appear in some, but not all of the data abstraction languages. They are common enough, and bear strongly enough on the subject, that they warrant mention. Among these are:

- *Generics*: The notion of *parameterization* is familiar from procedural abstractions; it allows one to define a computation that works over an unspecified set of data and thus substantially increases the utility of the algorithm. Typically, however, parameters of procedures have been limited to naming data items and their values. A *generic* definition is simply a parameterized one -- but the class of parameters is extended to include (abstract) types, procedures, and other non-data objects of the language. Moreover, the class of entities that can be so parameterized is also extended -- to include, for example, type definitions, entire encapsulations, and so on. This facility, for example, allows for the definition of the abstract type *stack* to be parameterized with the type of objects to be stored in it.

- *Control Abstractions*: Procedures provide computational abstractions; abstract data types provide data abstractions. There is, however, at least one other kind of abstraction that appears in some of the data abstraction languages. Called *generators* in Alphard [35] and *iterators* in CLU [19], these abstractions serve to define looping control over the elements of an abstract type. Thus, in Alphard, for example, the user may write

  for *x* **from** *InSet(S)* **do** *<stmt>* **od**.

  The effect will be to perform the *<stmt>* (once) for each element of the set *S*; the generator *InSet* is defined by the encapsulation that defines sets. While generators (iterators) are only one example that might be classified as a control abstraction, they are an important special case and we will have more to say about them later.

- *Other Operators*: Some of the data abstraction languages permit the user to specify the implementation of operations that have often been thought of as solely within the domain of the base language. These include assignment, initialization and "finalization" actions on allocation and deallocation of a variable, storage allocation, scheduling (of asynchronous tasks), and so on Permitting such specifications is both semantically subtle and may violate one's intuitive notions about the "safety" of a language. We will also say more about this later.

- *Formal Specification, Verification, and Definition*: Some of the data abstraction languages have considered verification as an explicit goal -- and, to varying degrees have

---

[2] No one, so far as I know has proposed such a thing; I merely used this as an extreme example of what one should *not* do.

- provided a formal semantic definition of the language,
- included specific facilities and notation for formally specifying the properties of the entities being defined, and
- provided a specific verification methodology to accompany the language and specification technique.

Much of the data abstraction specific work in this area is grounded in the work by Hoare [11], but there is a host of additional work, including [46, 10, 33, 17, 38] and others.

Finally, there are a number of issues, some quite fundamental, on which the extant languages take rather different positions. There are literally dozens of languages that have included some form of data abstraction facility; it should not be surprising that they differ in significant ways. Even ignoring issues of taste and aesthetics, a language designer can weight the various purposes of a language differently. Moreover, a language must be coherent; small differences in a single, key concept can be amplified into large overall differences in the process of making all the pieces fit smoothly. Looking at some of the small differences -- the original and more fundamental ones -- can go a long way toward characterizing the current state of research in this area. A few of the differences are[3]:

- *Details of the basic notion of type*: Despite the attraction of equating the notion of type in a programming language with that of its counterpart in mathematics -- types in programming languages serve a number of pragmatic functions that are irrelevant in pure mathematics, and so the notions differ. Based on one's perception of the importance of these various functions, and perhaps on one's sense of aesthetics, the linguistic notion can take different forms. Are types parameterized or not? Is "name equivalence" or "structural equivalence" a better model? In what ways, if at all, are the "base types" of the language allowed to have properties not shared by user-defined types; can user types, for example, (re)define literals? Do the base types, as well as the user defined ones, possess mathematical properties such as associativity and commutativity?
- *Object vs. Variable model*: The concept of a "variable" -- an object that can assume different values at different times does not exist (directly) in mathematics[4]. Languages such as CLU have been faithful to this notion by viewing objects (values) as *immutable*; most other languages have taken the more traditional -- and possibly more efficient -- view of variables as containers that hold values of some type, and that these values many be altered during execution.
- *Identification of type with encapsulation instance*: In Alphard, each encapsulation (*form*) defines precisely one type; it is, in effect, a type definition and the name of the encapsulation is the name of the type. Most other languages have separated the two concepts -- thus, for example, allowing two or more types to share information about their representations.

---

[3] These are not all equally important and the order of the list is random.

[4] Except, perhaps, through the circumlocution of *functionals*.

- *Separation of specification and implementation*: Ada and Alphard have enforced a textual separation of specification and implementation, most other languages have not. While there may be sound methodological arguments for this separation, enforcing it introduces a certain amount of redundant text (as well as complicating the implementation -- although that should not be a major concern).

- *The role of generics and parameterization*: Generic definitions add substantial expressive power to a language. In most languages they have been added to achieve (only) that added power; in a few, however (e.g., in the preliminary version of Ada), they have been used as the primary parameterization facility for non-procedural abstractions. In most languages, for technical (i.e., efficiency) reasons, generics have been treated as a compile-time parameterization facility; but, again, in a few the notion of type has been promoted to a "first-class" object of the language and generics have run-time semantics (and cost).

- *Closed vs. open scopes*: The familiar Algol 60 scope rules have been termed *open*. A closed scope is one that does not automatically inherit names from its enclosing environment. Some languages, such as Ada, have adopted a default open scope for encapsulations; others, such as Alphard and Euclid, have adopted closed scopes as the default.

- *Generic instantiation*: Given a generic definition facility -- and specifically one that provides only compile-time parameterization -- should the user be required to explicitly create an instance of the definition, or should mention of its name together with a suitable set of actual parameters be sufficient? In very pragmatic terms, given a generic definition of stacks that is parameterized by the type of the stack element, must one say

  ```
  type IntStack is Stack(integer);
  var I: IntStack;
  ```

  or is it sufficient to say

  ```
  var S: Stack(integer);
  ```

  In the latter case, what are the interaction with the notion of type equivalence?

- *Concurrency*: Many of the data abstraction languages, like most of their predecessors, have ignored the issue of concurrency. Concurrent Pascal, Gypsy, Modula, and Ada have not -- each has provided a facility with which the programmer can specify asynchronous tasks as well as their synchronization and communication. It seems inevitable that this kind of facility will become increasingly important in routine programming. Given that concurrent programs are potentially even more complex than sequential ones -- providing appropriate support is correspondingly important. Each of the languages mentioned above, however, takes quite a different view of how this facility should mesh with the other abstraction facilities of the language, and data abstraction in particular.

- *Mapping to/from the underlying representation of a type*: In reality, of course, during execution a value of a type is always represented in its primitive form -- that is, a collection of bits. At the language level, however, it is sometimes necessary to treat the value as if it were either its abstract type or its representation type. The details of how this is done may seem like a niggling detail since the transformation is always null at run-time; it is merely "syntactic sugar". Often, however, the form of this mapping is indicative of the underlying model of type in the language and how user-defined abstract types relates to it.

There are also differences that do not always show up at the language level. One such, for example, is the preferred form of specification. The Alphard group, for example, prefers abstract modeling while the CLU group seems to prefer algebraic axions. Another, more important difference is related to the designer's notion of safety -- and hence what is permitted to be (re)defined; I will have more to say about this later.

3.2. Summary of Status

Obviously, a great deal has been written about abstract data types -- the linguistic facilities to support them, their specification and their verification. Also, a substantial number of languages have been designed and to some extent used, although it is vaguely disturbing that there isn't a larger body of experience on which to proceed -- especially in light of the fact that at least one of these languages, Ada, is destined for widespread use. The wide variety of approaches mentioned above, and the subtle but important ways that they can interact, can only intensify our disquiet.

Nonetheless, this author at least, feels an enormous confidence and enthusiasm about the status of the developments that have surrounded abstract data types. Relative to the purposes of languages discussed earlier, they seem to be better design tools and better vehicles for person-to-person communication than anything available to date. They are, perhaps, not as expressive as some of the "very high level" languages such as SETL -- but they do not have the efficiency problems of these languages either. With the exception of generics and tasking, the data abstraction languages pose only minor problems beyond conventional compiler technology.

To each the full potential of the abstract data type concept, however, I feel that a number of major problems remain. Some of these have barely been touched upon, and are the subject of the next section.

4. The Next Problems

My crystal ball is, of course, no better than anyone else's. However, my personal list of the next set of important problems in the abstract data type area is:

- Specification and verification of properties other than functional correctness.
- Exploitation of the similarity of abstract data types to the "objects" of object-oriented, capability-based operating systems.
- Solving a number of technical problems affecting the efficiency of generics and tasking.
- Developing the technology of program specification and verification into a usable tool.

- Incorporating concurrency and exception handling more smoothly into the abstract data type model.
- Exploiting the similarity of abstract data type languages and data base systems.
- Extending the class of abstractions that can be expressed by a richer notion of transformation than can be captured with (generic) parameterization.
- Relaxing the strict notion of invariant currently needed in verification of abstract data types and, in particular, recognizing that not all operations may be applied at all points in the life of an object.
- Exploiting the abstract data type model to permit the relaxation of many preemptive assumptions that have traditionally been made in the design and implementation of programming languages.

I will try to expand on a few of these points below.

Specification/Verification of "other" properties: To date we have been primarily concerned with the specification and verification of "functional correctness" defined in a fairly narrow sense. We have ignored, for example, the issues of correctness that arise because of finite-precision arithmetic; this kind of correctness is extremely important in many systems. There are properties of programs that have nothing to do with correctness, however, that we also need to be able to specify and verify. A program, like any other engineering product, has performance goals as well as functional ones. To be useful a program must execute with acceptable efficiency and in acceptable space limitations. A program must also respond in an acceptable manner to incorrect or illegal input, and to failing hardware.

I am hard pressed to decide whether I would prefer to ride on an airplane whose avionics had been verified, but was too slow to react in an emergency -- or to ride in the same plane if its avionics had known bugs, but could react swiftly enough. Both alternatives seem bad. Similarly, I am not impressed by the notion of a computer that controls a nuclear reactor and whose program has been verified *unless* you can assure me of *precisely* how the system will behave under virtually any hardware malfunction. A controller that will sometimes retract all control rods because of a hardware failure is no better than one that will do the same thing -- with the same probability -- because of a program bug. Hardware does fail; indeed, it fails with probability 1.0!

We are beginning to see some beginning of these kinds of specifications of performance (*cf* [40, 36]), security (*cf* [26, 39]), and reliability (*cf* [41]). These are small beginnings, however, and there is a great deal to be done and to be learned.

Similarity to capability-based operating systems: A *capability* is merely a reference to an object, but it carries some additional information -- namely the operations that may legally be applied to that object through that particular reference. The objects named through capabilities are typed, and protection is stated in terms of (dis)allowing type-specific operations to be applied. In systems such as Hydra [45], new types, along with their associated operations and protections, can be easily defined. In retrospect, it seems reasonable to view such systems as the run-time support for an (unspecified) data abstraction language.

There appears to be much to be gained on both the language and operating system fronts by a merger of these ideas. In particular, the operating systems interfaces have not always been an ideal match to the needs of a programming language -- and systems would benefit from the more formal and mature perspective of the language community in that area. On the other hand, protection facilities allow us to express constraints on the dynamic behavior of programs and thus to make stronger assertions about them -- thus aiding verification. Some of these ideas have been explored, *cf* [23, 15], but not in the depth warranted. In particular, none of the latest data abstraction languages seem to have recognized this missed opportunity.

Developing specification and verification technology: The theoretical bases for these is far better established than are the practical technologies necessary for their application. It is still far to difficult to precisely define an abstract data type -- let alone prove that its implementation satisfies this specification.

Incorporating tasking and exceptions: Exceptions, in the sense of the PL/1 "on condition" have been a stepchild of language design -- especially academically centered design. There is, in fact, no universally accepted agreement on what the term means -- are exceptions unexpected errors (as, for example, a subscript out of bounds), or are they rare but expected events (as, for example, an end-of-file)? Because they have been handled in rather unstructured ways in older systems and languages, and possibly because of an attitude that "errors should not happen in a correct program" (a silly position when the error may be due to hardware malfunction), relatively little has been done to provide structured means for handling exceptional conditions.

As we move into the next decade, however, will are going to see many more distributed systems, and many more systems with high reliability requirements. The data abstraction paradigm seems ideally suited to dealing with both these issues, although only the concurrency issues have received much attention. The encapsulation boundary, however, is an ideal firewall for preventing the propagation of failures -- just as it is an ideal synchronization boundry (as in *monitors*, [2]). Moreover, the conceptual issues involved in handling exceptions are not dissimilar from those of concurrency -- particularly if one can forget all about traditional facilities for handling them. One can hope that a unified mechanism, integrated with data abstraction, will emerge one of these days. One can also hope that this unified mechanism will admit of the same precision of specification and verification as the more well-developed features of languages.

Relaxing the notion of invariant: Many of the techniques for specifying and verifying the properties of an abstract data type are descended from the sentinel paper by Hoare, [11]. These involve, among other things, the specification of an invariant property -- a property that holds for all objects of the (abstract) type and at all times when the objects exist. This is such a strong requirement that, in practice, it often forces the invariant to be very weak.

To see why this is so, consider the abstract type *file*, with operations *open, close, read*, and *write* defined on it. We know that the only legal sequences of invocations of these operations are those described by the regular expression

```
(open (read | write)* close)*.
```

That is, reads and writes can only be applied to open files. Indeed, to me as a programmer, the only really interesting periods in the life of a file variable is when it is open; it has almost no interesting properties when it is closed. Unfortunately, the invariant must hold at *all* points in the life of such an object; since not much can be said about closed files, not much can be said, at all.

What is needed, of course, is a better way to relate properties of a type to this allowed histories of objects of that type. Path expressions, as in [4], are one way to express the allowed histories; there may be others. The pressing need, however, is to better exploit this information in the specification and verification of programs.

Relaxing pre-emptive assumptions: This subject is one that I feel strongly about, and a more complete discussion may be found in [37]. Many decisions, mostly of a relatively low level, are pre-empted in traditional language definitions or their implementations. Examples include the representations of arrays and other base types, synchronization and scheduling, storage allocation and heap management, and iteration control. For the most part, the pre-empted decisions are made well *on the average*, and making them relieves the programmer from concern over irrelevant detail. However, in special cases the programmer knows a great deal more about his specific application that the language designer/implementor possibly can, and the default decisions are wrong. Alas, current language gives him no way to override the pre-empted decisions. In such cases the programmer may be forced to ill-structured circumlocutions to achieve a desired, and necessary effect.

As a simple example, I have often observed Fortran programs in which two triangular matrices were stored in the same array -- with one of them transposed so that it could use the "top half" of the array. In at least some of these cases the program would not have fit into core if this had not been done, so, messy as it is, it was necessary. The blame for this awkward program structure lies with Fortran -- which neither gave the programmer a direct base type for triangular arrays nor provided him a means for defining them. Most other languages have similar limitations; the blame is not with Fortran alone. Nor is the problem limited to arrays; similar examples exist for other data structures and for control.

In general, whenever a language designer makes a pre-emptive decision he violates one of the most basic tenets of good programming methodology -- namely, that decisions should be postponed until there is the maximal amount of information available to make them wisely; each such decision ought to be encapsulated (hidden) in a manner that allows its implementation to be changed. Language design/implementation time is just about as early, rather than as late, as one can imagine, and there is a paucity of information available with which to make a good engineering choice.

The mechanisms of data abstraction provide the means for avoiding the dilatory effects of such decisions while preserving the beneficial effects of having defaults for them. To date these languages have not been defined this way except in some special cases -- but one can imagine a language whose semantics are defined relative to those of a set of (abstract) types. A default set of types can be provided to supply the familiar functionality of conventional languages -- but these types need not have special status. Thus, the user could define new types with different properties to replace them.

The *generators* of Alphard and *iterators* of CLU are examples of the sort of thing I have in mind; however, let's consider a simple example of this design approach from quite a different domain. The RED candidate for Ada [25] defined a data type *DataLock* (essentially a mutex semaphore) and a **region** statement. Informally, the operations on *DataLocks* were *Lock* and *UnLock* with semantics similar to Dijkstra's *P* and *V* on boolean (mutex) semaphores. The form and semantics of the **region** statement are illustrated by the following example:

```
var L: DataLock;
. . .
region L do . . . end region
```

The **region** statement implicitly performs a *Lock* on *L* before executing its body and guarantees that it will perform an *UnLock* on *L* on *any* exit from the body[5].

RED did not, however, demand that the variable mentioned in the **region** statement (*L* above) be of the pre-defined type, *DataLock*. Rather, the language merely defined that the **region** statement guaranteed to invoke *Lock(L)* and *UnLock(L)* at the appropriate places -- and defined what the semantics of these operations had to be. The pre-defined type *DataLock* satisfied these semantics and thus made the **region** statement immediately useful, but the user was free to define another type that satisfied these specifications and use it with the **region** statement. Doing so gave the programmer control over, for example, scheduling and resource allocation decisions that would

[5] This guarantee includes exits caused by exceptions that are not handled by the body, return, exit, and goto statements in the body, abnormal terminations of the task in which the body is executing, and so on.

normally have been pre-empted by the implementation. At the same time, the language *did* predefine *DataLocks* so that the programmer who did not need more elaborate facilities or policies needn't be concerned with defining them.

Given a reasonable specification and verification technology, this approach to language design is just as "safe" as the current pre-emptive one, and will lead to better structured, more efficient programs.

5. Closing Remarks

Programming is, in my opinion, an engineering discipline. Like other engineering, it is concerned with the production of artifacts of great practical utility. Like other engineering there are criteria by which we can distinguish good products from poor ones -- principally these are that the product must perform its intended function reliably and cost-effectively. Also, like other engineering, good programming must be based on good science and mathematics; it must have a sound theoretical underpinning.

The most encouraging thing to me about the last decade is the synergy between methodology, theory and languages. We have seen a trend toward providing the underpinning that is needed. Inded, it seems that much of that underpinning exists, if, perhaps, only in skelatal form.

The trend is not complete, of course. Present technology will not "solve" the software crisis -- if only because our aspirations seem to grow faster than the technology to fulfil them. Especially pressing, it seems to me, is the need to carry forward the work on specifications and verification -- to make them practical tools. (In my own research on Alphard, and using it on various examples, there is no question that the most difficult task was the specification of the properties of various abstractions.) Equally pressing is the need to make progress on the specification and verification of the "other" important properties such as performance and reliability.

Nonetheless, based on current and projected technology, I cannot help but feel an enormous enthusiasm. I believe that programming in 1990 will be *qualitatively* different than it is today -- different in a much deeper sense than today's is from that of 1970, or even 1960. This enthusiasm arises not from a single development or area, but rather from the confluence of ideas from the various area. We *have* embarked upon a course that leads to a scientific and mathematical basis for program engineering.

References

1. Allen L. Ambler, Donald I. Good, James C. Browne, Wilhelm F. Burger, Richard M. Cohen, Charles G. Hoch, Robert E. Wells. "Gypsy: A Language for Specification and Implementation of Verifiable Programs." *ACM SIGPLAN Notices 12*, 3 (March 1977).

2. Per Brinch Hansen. "The Programming Language Concurrent Pascal." *IEEE Transactions on Software Engineering SE-1* (June 1975).

3. J. N. Buxton and B. Randell (eds). *Software Engineering Techniques.* NATO, 1970. Report on a Conference Sponsored by the NATO Science Committee, Rome, Italy, 27th to 31st October 1969

4. R. H. Campbell and A. N. Habermann. The Specification of Process Synchronization by Path Expressions. Lecture Notes in Computer Science 16, 1974.

5. O.-J. Dahl. Simula 67 Common Base Language. Norwegian Computing Center, Oslo, 1968.

6. Edsger W. Dijkstra. "Goto Statement Considered Harmful." *Communications of the ACM 11*, 3 (March 1968).

7. Edsger W. Dijkstra. "The Structure of the 'THE' Multiprogramming System." *Communications of the ACM 11*, 3 (May 1968).

8. R. W. Floyd. Assigning Meanings to Programs. Proceedings of the Symposium in Applied Mathematics, American Mathematical Society, 1967, pp. 19-32.

9. Charles M. Geschke, James H. Morris Jr., and Edwin H. Satterthwaite. "Early Experience with Mesa." *Communications of the ACM 20*, 8 (August 1977).

10. John V. Guttag, Ellis Horowitz and David R. Musser. "Abstract Data Types and Software Validation." *Communications of the ACM 21*, 12 (December 1978).

11. C. A. R. Hoare. "Proof of Correctness of Data Representations." *Acta Informatica 1*, 4 (1972).

12. C. A. R. Hoare and N. Wirth. "An Axiomatic Definition of the Programming Language Pascal." *Acta Informatica 2*, 4 (1973).

13. J. D. Ichbiah, et al. "Preliminary ADA Reference Manual." *ACM SIGPLAN Notices 14*, 6A (June 1979).

14. Kathleen Jensen and Niklaus Wirth. *Pascal User Manual and Report.* Springer-Verlag, 1974.

15. A. K. Jones and B. H. Liskov. "A Language Extension for Controlling Access to Shared Data." *IEEE Transactions on Software Engineering SE-2*, 4 (December 1976), 277-285.

16. B. W. Lampson, J. J. Horning, R. L. London, J. G. Mitchell and G. J. Popek. "Report on the Programming Language Euclid." *ACM SIGPLAN Notices 12*, 2 (February 1977).

17. Barbara H. Liskov and Stephen N. Zilles. "Specification Techniques for Data Abstractions." *IEEE Transactions on Software Engineering SE-1* (March 1975).

18. Barbara Liskov, Alan Snyder, Russell Atkinson and Craig Schaffert. "Abstraction Mechanisms in CLU." *Communications of the ACM 20*, 8 (August 1977).

19. B. Liskov, E. Moss, C. Schaffert, R. Scheifler and A. Snyder. *The CLU Reference Manual.* Laboratory for Computer Science, Massachusetts Institute of Technology, 1978. *Computation Structures Group Memo* No. 161.

20. R. L. London. A View of Program Verification. Proceedings of the International Conference on Reliable Software, April, 1975, pp. 534-545.

21. R. L. London, J. V. Guttag, J. J. Horning, B. W. Lampson, J. G. Mitchell, and G.J. Popek. "Proof Rules for the Programming Language Euclid." *Acta Informatica 10*, 1 (1978), 1-26.

22. J. H. Morris. Types Are Not Sets. Proceedings of the ACM Symposium on Principles of Programming Languages, ACM, 1973, pp. 120-124.

23. J. H. Morris. "Protection in Programming Languages." *Communications of the ACM 16* (January 1973).

24. Peter Naur and Brian Randell (eds). *Software Engineering.* NATO, 1969. Report on a Conference Sponsored by the NATO Science Committee, Garmisch, Germany, 7th to 11th October 1968

25. J. Nestor and M. Van Deusen. *RED Language Reference Manual.* Intermetrics, Inc., 1979.

26. Peter G. Neumann, Robert S. Boyer, Richard J. Feiertag, Karl N. Levitt and Lawrence Robinson. A Provably Secure Operating System: The System, its Applications, and Proofs. Tech. Rept. 4332 Final Report, SRI International Project, February, 1977.

27. David L. Parnas. Information Distribution Aspects of Design Methodology. Proceedings of IFIP Congress, IFIP, 1971, pp. 26-30. Booklet TA-3.

28. David L. Parnas. "On the Criteria to be Used in Decomposing Systems into Modules." *Communications of the ACM 15*, 12 (December 1972).

29. David L. Parnas. "A Technique for Software Module Specification with Examples." *Communications of the ACM 15* (May 1972).

30. D. L. Parnas, J. E. Shore and Elliott. On the Need for Fewer Restrictions in Changing Compile-time Environments. NRL Report 7847, Naval Research Lab, November, 1974.

31. David L. Parnas. Some Hypotheses about the "Uses" Hierarchy for Operating Systems. Technische Hochschule Darmstadteich Informatik, 1976.

32. David Parnas. On a Buzzword, Hierarchical Structure. Proceedings of the IFIP Congress, August, 1974.

33. O. Roubine and L. Robinson. *Special (SPECIfications and Assertion Language): Reference Manual.* SRI International Memo, 1976.

34. S. A. Schuman, Ed. "Proceedings of the International Symposium on Extensible Languages." *ACM SIGPLAN Notices 6* (December 1971).

35. Mary Shaw, Wm. A. Wulf and Ralph L. London. "Abstraction and Verification in Alphard: Defining and Specifying Iteration and Generators." *Communications of the ACM 20*, 8 (August 1977).

36. Mary Shaw. A Formal System for Specifying and Verifying Program Performance. Tech. Rept. CMU-CS-79-129, Carnegie-Mellon University, June, 1979.

37. Mary Shaw and Wm. A. Wulf. "Toward Relaxing Assumptions in Languages and Their Implementations." *SIGPLAN Notices 13*, 3 (March 1980), 45-61.

38. J. Spitzen and B. Wegbreit. "The verification and synthesis of data structures." *Acta Informatica 4* (1975).

39. Bruce J. Walker, Richard A. Kemmerer, and Gerald J. Popek. "Specification and Verificaton of the UCLA Security Kernel." *Communications of the ACM 23*, 2 (Feburary 1980).

40. Ben Wegbreit. "Verifying Program Performance." *Journal of the ACM 23*, 4 (October 1976).

41. John H. Wensley, Leslie Lamport, Milton W. Green, Karl N. Levitt, P. M. Melliar-Smith, Robert E. Shostak, and Charles B. Weinstock. "SIFT: Design and Analysis of a Fault-tolerant Computer for Aircraft Control." *Proceedings of the IEEE 66*, 10 (October 1978), 1240-1255.

42. B. L. Whorf. A linguistic consideration of thinking in primitive communities. In *Language, Thought, and Reality*, MIT Press, Cambridge, Massachusetts, 1956.

43. Niklaus Wirth. "Program Development by Stepwise Refinement." *Communications of the ACM 14*, 4 (April 1971).

44. Niklaus Wirth. "Modula: A Language for Modular Programming." *Software -- Practice and Experience 7*, 1 (January 1977).

45. W. Wulf, E. Cohen, W. Corwin, A. Jones, R. Levin, C. Pierson and F. Rollack. "Hydra: The Kernel of a Multiprocessor Operating System." *Communications of the ACM 17* (June 1974).

46. Wm. A. Wulf, Ralph L. London and Mary Shaw. "An Introduction to the Construction and Verification of Alphard Programs." *IEEE Transactions on Software Engineering SE-2*, 4 (December 1976).

CONTROLLING BEHAVIOURS OF SYSTEMS :
SOME BASIC CONCEPTS AND SOME APPLICATIONS

A. ARNOLD, Laboratoire d'Informatique, Université de Poitiers
M. NIVAT, LITP, Université de Paris VII and CNRS

ABSTRACT

We define observable systems and controls of these systems as a way to restrict their set of behaviours. Some applications to the deadlock problem are given.

INTRODUCTION

In [4] Nivat studied the classical problem of synchronizing the behaviours of a set of concurrent processes. He proved that for rational processes, synchronizing behaviours as well as avoiding deadlock could be achieved by the mean of an overall automaton which controls the evolution of the system.

This notion of control of a system appears to be general enough to be applied successfully to other systems than the rational ones, provided an adequate definition of concepts involved in this approach.

Obviously the most general notion of a (discrete dynamic) system is simply a set of configurations and a set of transitions between configurations with conditions on configurations for firing transitions (see [3] for a similar notion). We refine this general notion by adding the natural hypothesis that the firing condition does not depend on the whole configuration but only on a part of it, the "visible part", for example the state and the read symbol in "states-and-tapes-machines", thus we define observable systems as having this property.

The control of such a system is a kind of automaton which takes into account the visible part of a configuration and also some stored information about the behaviour of the system which led it into this configuration to forbid, at this point, some firable transitions. The behaviours of a system obeying a control constitue a subset of the set of behaviours of the system.

The general problem of controlling a system is thus to design a control such that the controlled behaviours of the system are the behaviours of the system having the expected property (synchronized, non deadlocking, etc.). We prove in this paper that, roughly speaking, there exists a least control which allows all the behaviours in a given set (but maybe others), and we apply this general result to some synchronization and deadlock problems.

Of course the applications mentioned in this paper are just examples and many other problems can be fruitfully treated with this approach.

This paper contains four parts. The observable systems are defined in the first one and the controls in the second one. In the third one we construct controls which upperly approach a given set of behaviours. In the last one we deal with three examples of systems : the rational processes (Nivat [4]), the generalized sequentiel mappings and the nets of processes defined by Kahn [2] (see also [1]). For saving room, all results are given without proofs. These proofs can be found in an extended version of this paper available as Research Report n° 3, Laboratoire d'Informatique, Université de Poitiers.

1. OBSERVABLE SYSTEMS

The behaviours of systems we are looking at are sequences of actions, or transitions, each of them modifying the state, or configuration, of the object of this action. Here is the formal definition of a system.

Definition 1.1 A *system* is a quadruple $<C,C_o,T,\delta>$ where

C is the set of *configurations* ;

$C_o \subset C$ is the set of *initial configurations* ;

T is a set of partial functions from C into C, the *transitions* of the system ;

δ is a mapping from C into $\mathcal{P}(T)$, the *firing function*, such that $\forall c \in C$, $\forall t \in \delta(c)$, t(c) is defined ; the set $\delta(c)$ is the set of transitions *firable* in the configuration c.

Definition 1.2 A finite word $c_o t_1 c_1 \ldots t_n c_n$ in $C(TC)^*$ is a *finite behaviour* of the system $\mathcal{S}$ iff

$c_o \in C_o$ and for $i = 1,\ldots,n$ $t_i \in \delta(c_{i-1})$ and $c_i = t_i(c_{i-1})$. An infinite word $c_o t_1 c_1 \ldots t_n c_n \ldots$ in $C(TC)^\omega$ is an *infinite behaviour* of $\mathcal{S}$ if, for any n, $c_o t_1 c_1 \ldots t_n c_n$ is a finite behaviour.

We denote by $B(\mathcal{S})$ (resp. $B^\omega(\mathcal{S})$, $B^\infty(\mathcal{S})$) the set of finite (resp. infinite, finite and infinite) behaviours of $\mathcal{S}$.

Example A.1 Let $G = <\Xi, X, \xi_o, P>$ a regular grammar. Derivations in this grammar can be seen as behaviours in the following system.

Let $\mathcal{S}_G$ be the system having (i) $(\{stop\} \cup \Xi) \times X^*$ as set of configurations, (ii) (ξ_o, Λ) as unique initial configuration, (iii) $\{t_p / p \in P\}$ as set of transitions where $t_{\xi \to x\xi'}(\xi'',u)$ = if $\xi = \xi''$ then (ξ', ux) else undefined and $t_{\xi \to x}(\xi',u)$ = if $\xi = \xi'$ then $(stop, ux)$ else undefined , (iv) the function δ defined by $\delta(c) = \{t_p / t_p(c)$ is defined$\}$ as firing function.

<u>*Example B.1*</u> Let τ be the gsm $<X, Y, Q, q_o, R>$ and $X^\infty = X^* \cup X^\omega$ the set of finite and infinite words on X. With this gsm we associate the following system $\mathcal{S}_\tau$:

configurations : $X^\infty \times Q \times Y^*$;

initial configurations : $X^\infty \times \{q_o\} \times \{\Lambda\}$;

transitions : $\{t_r / r \in R\}$ with $t_{(q,x \to v,q')}(u,q'',w)$ = if $q = q''$ and $u = xu'$ then (u',q',w) else undefined

firing function : $\delta(c) = \{t_r / t_r(c)$ is defined$\}$

These two examples share a common property : for any configuration c, the set $\delta(c)$ of firable transitions depends only on a part of the configuration, namely the first component of the configuration for $\mathcal{S}_G$ and the second component and the first letter of the first component for $\mathcal{S}_\tau$.

We name this part the *visible part* of the configuration ; hence the following definition.

<u>*Definition 1.3*</u> An *observable system* $\mathcal{S}$ is a tuple $<C, C_o, T, \delta, V, \psi>$ where $<C, C_o, T, \delta>$ is a system ; V is the set of *visible parts* of configurations ; $\psi : C \to V$, the *observation mapping*, associates with every configuration its visible part ; such that $\forall c, c' \in C$, $\psi(c) = \psi(c')$ implies $\delta(c) = \delta(c')$. Hence the set $\delta(c)$ depends only on $\psi(c)$ and sometimes we shall denote by $\delta(v)$, for $v \in V$, the common value $\delta(c)$ of δ on the configurations c such that $\psi(c) = v$.

<u>*Example A.2*</u> The system $\mathcal{S}_G$ defined in example A.1 becomes observable by adding $\Xi \cup \{stop\}$ as set of visible parts and by defining the observation mapping by $\psi(\xi, u) = \xi$. It is obvious that $t_p(\xi, u)$ and $t_p(\xi', u')$ are both defined if and only if $\xi = \xi'$, that is $\psi(\xi, u) = \psi(\xi', u)$. Hence $\psi(c) = \psi(c')$ iff $\delta(c) = \delta(c')$.

<u>*Example B.2*</u> The set of visible parts of the system $\mathcal{S}_\tau$ is $(X \cup \{\Lambda\}) \times Q$ and the observation mapping is defined by $\psi(\Lambda,q,v) = (\Lambda,q)$ and $\psi(xu,q,v) = (x,q)$.

Then we have also $\delta(c) = \delta(c')$ iff $\psi(c) = \psi(c')$ and the system $\mathcal{S}_\tau$ is observable.

But now it appears a difference between the observable systems $\mathcal{S}_G$ and $\mathcal{S}_\tau$ of examples A2 and B2. If a transition t is applied to a configuration c, the visible part $\psi(t(c))$ of the resulting configuration depends only on t and on the visible part of c ; this istrue for $\mathcal{S}_G$ but false for $\mathcal{S}_\tau$ as we shall see later. An observable system like $\mathcal{S}_G$ will be said fully observable.

<u>*Definition 1.4*</u> An observable system $\mathcal{S}$ is *fully observable* if the following property holds :

$$\forall c,c' \in C,\ \psi(c) = \psi(c') \Rightarrow \forall t \in \delta(c) = \delta(c'),\ \psi(t(c)) = \psi(t(c')).$$

Example A.3 Let $c = (\xi,u)$ and $c' = (\xi',u')$ be two configurations in C. Let us assume that $\psi(c) = \psi(c')$; hence $\xi = \xi'$. Each firable transition t has either the form $t_{\xi\to x\xi''}$ and then $t(c) = (\xi'',ux)$, $t(c') = (\xi'',u'x)$ and $\psi(t(c)) = \psi(t(c')) = \xi''$, or $t_\xi = t_{\xi\to x}$ and then $t(c) = (stop,ux)$, $t(c') = (stop,u'x)$ and $\psi(t(c) = \psi(t(c')) = stop$. It follows that $\mathcal{S}_G$ is fully observable.

Example B.3 Let us consider the two configurations $c = (xy,q,w)$ and $c' = (xy',q,w')$ with $y \neq y'$, such that $\psi(c) = \psi(c') = (x,q)$, and let $t = t_{(q,x\to z,q')}$ a firable transition. We get $t(c) = (y,q',zw)$, $t(c') = (y',q',zw')$, hence $\psi(t(c)) = (y,q') \neq (y',q') = \psi(t(c'))$ and $\mathcal{S}_T$ is not fully observable.

2. CONTROL OF AN OBSERVABLE SYSTEM

Intuitively we can see a control as a mechanism seeing the visible part of configurations and, according to its own state, restricts the set of firable transitions. Formally we ignore the way the control is realized ; it is only a way to forbid some behaviours.

Definition 2.1 The control $\mathcal{C}$ of an observable system $\mathcal{S} = \langle C,C_o,T,\delta,V,\psi\rangle$ is a triple $\langle Q,q_*,\lambda,\gamma\rangle$ where Q is the set of states of the control, $q_* \in Q$ is the initial state, $\lambda : Q \times V \to \mathcal{P}(T)$, $\gamma : Q \times V \times T \to Q$, such that $\forall q \in Q$, $v \in V$, $\lambda(q,v) \subset \delta(v)$.

Definition 2.2 Two controls $\langle Q,q_*,\lambda,\gamma\rangle$ and $\langle Q',q'_*,\lambda',\gamma'\rangle$ of the same system $\mathcal{S}$ are *similar* if $Q = Q'$, $q_* = q'_*$ and $\gamma = \gamma'$. The set of similar controls are ordered by $\langle Q,q_*,\lambda,\gamma\rangle \leq \langle Q,q_*,\lambda',\gamma\rangle$ iff $\forall q \in Q$, $\forall v \in V$, $\lambda(q,v) \subseteq \lambda'(q,v)$.

Definition 2.3 Let $\mathcal{S}$ be an observable system and $\mathcal{C}$ be a control of $\mathcal{S}$. For $q \in Q$ and $v \in V$ we define the set $B(\mathcal{C},q,v)$ of finite behaviours of $\mathcal{S}$ by $c_o t_1 c_1 \ldots t_n c_n \in B(\mathcal{C},q,v)$ iff $c_o \in C_o$ and there exists a sequence $q_o,\ldots,q_n$ such that $q_o = q_*, q_n = q, v = \psi(c_n)$ and for $i = 1,\ldots,n$, $t_i \in \lambda(q_{i-1}, \psi(c_{i-1}))$, $c_i = t_i(c_{i-1})$ and $q_i = \gamma(q_{i-1}, \psi(c_{i-1}),t_i)$.

The set $B(\mathcal{C}) = \bigcup_{q\in Q, v\in V} B(\mathcal{C},q,v)$ is the set of all finite *controlled behaviours*. It is obvious from the definitions that $B(\mathcal{C}) \subset B(\mathcal{S})$. We define also, as in definition 1.2 the sets $B^\omega(\mathcal{C})$ and $B^\infty(\mathcal{C})$ of infinite and finite or infinite controlled behaviours. We have also $B^\omega(\mathcal{C}) \subset B^\infty(\mathcal{S})$ and $B^\infty(\mathcal{C}) \subset B^\infty(\mathcal{S})$.

The following proposition is a straightforward consequence of the previous definitions.

Proposition 2.4 *Let $\mathcal{C}$ and $\mathcal{C}'$ be two similar controls of the same system. If $\mathcal{C} \subseteq \mathcal{C}'$ then for any $q \in Q$, $v \in V$, $B(\mathcal{C},q,v) \subseteq B(\mathcal{C}',q,v)$.*

Definition 2.5 Two controls $\mathcal{C}$ and $\mathcal{C}'$ are *equivalent* if $B(\mathcal{C}) = B(\mathcal{C}')$; they are *ω-equivalent* if $B^{\omega}(\mathcal{C}) = B^{\omega}(\mathcal{C}')$. A control $\mathcal{C}$ of an observable system $\mathcal{S}$ is *complete* if $B(\mathcal{C}) = B(\mathcal{S})$ and *ω-complete* if $B^{\omega}(\mathcal{C}) = B^{\omega}(\mathcal{S})$. Of course every complete control is ω-complete and two equivalent controls are ω-equivalent.

We exhibit now two canonical complete controls of an observable system.

Let $\mathcal{S}$ be an observable system. Let $\mathcal{S}_{max}$ be the control $<\{q\}\ q,\lambda_{max},\gamma_{max}>$ with $\lambda_{max}(q,v) = \delta(v)$ and $\gamma_{max}(q,v,t) = q$.

(*Remark* - For this control we shall ignore the state q and thus the mapping γ).

Let $\mathcal{S}_{min}$ be the control $<(VT)^*,\Lambda,\lambda_{min},\gamma_{min}>$ with $\lambda_{min}(u,v) = \delta(v)$ and $\gamma_{min}(u,v,t) = uvt$.

Clearly these two controls are complete since the state of the control is never used to restrict theset of firable transitions. This kind of control exists, whatever is the set of states.

Proposition 2.6 *For any control $\mathcal{C}$ of an observable system $\mathcal{S}$ there exists a complete control $\mathcal{C}'$ similar to $\mathcal{S}$.*

To end this section we give a result which justifies the notations $\mathcal{S}_{min}$ and $\mathcal{S}_{max}$ for two canonical complete controls defined above.

From the definition of a finite controlled behaviour, it comes that every behaviour belongs to at most one set $B(\mathcal{C},q,v)$; hence if $\mathcal{C}$ is complete, this allows to define an equivalence relation, denoted by $\equiv_{\mathcal{C}}$, on $B(\mathcal{S}) = B(\mathcal{C})$. We denote by ≤ the classical order on equivalence relations = $\equiv_1 \leq \equiv_2$ iff $\forall x,y\ x \equiv_1 y \Rightarrow x \equiv_2 y$.

Proposition 2.7 *For any complete control $\mathcal{C}$ of $\mathcal{S}$, we have* $\equiv_{\mathcal{S}_{min}} \leq \equiv_{\mathcal{C}} \leq \equiv_{\mathcal{S}_{max}}$

3. CORE OF A CONTROL

Let $B(\mathcal{C})$ the set of controlled behaviours of a control $\mathcal{C}$ of an observable system $\mathcal{S}$ and let A be any subset of $B(\mathcal{C})$. We want to define a new control $\mathcal{C}'$ of $\mathcal{S}$ such that $B(\mathcal{C}')$ is as close as possible to A.

Let us give two instances of this problem borrowed from [4].

If A is the set of behaviours obeying a synchronization condition, to find $\mathcal{C}'$ amounts to solve a synchronization problem ; if A is the set of behaviours that are the beginning of infinite behaviours, to find $\mathcal{C}'$ amounts to solve a deadlock problem.

If we want to have some chance to get $\mathcal{C}'$ such that $B(\mathcal{C}')$ is exactly A, surely A has to be prefix, in the sense defined below ; moreover since the behaviours reduced to a single initial configuration cannot be forbidden by a control, we must have $A \cap C = C$

Definition 3.1 Let A be a subset of $C(TC)^*$. A is *admissible* iff (i) $A \cap C = C_o$ and (ii) A is *prefix*, i.e $\forall c_o t_1 \ldots c_{n-1} t_n c_n \in A$, $c_o t_1 \ldots c_{n-1} \in A$.

But even if A is admissible, a control $\mathcal{C}'$ such that $B(\mathcal{C}') = A$ can not to exist. Thus we seek for $\mathcal{C}'$ such that $B(\mathcal{C}')$ is either the greatest set of controlled behaviou included in A or the least set of controlled behaviours containing A. We are interest only in set of controlled behaviours containing A for the following reason.

Let $\mathcal{C}_1 = \langle Q, q_o, \lambda_1, \gamma \rangle$ and $\mathcal{C}_2 = \langle Q, q_o, \lambda_2, \gamma \rangle$ be two similar controls. We define the controls $\mathcal{C}_1 \cap \mathcal{C}_2$ (resp $\mathcal{C}_1 \cap \mathcal{C}_2$) similar to $\mathcal{C}_1$ and $\mathcal{C}_2$ by setting $\lambda_1 \cap \lambda_2(q,v) = \lambda_1(q,v) \cap \lambda_2(q$ (resp $\lambda_1 \cup \lambda_2(q,v) = \lambda_1(q,v) \cup \lambda_2(q,v)$).

Then we can easily prove that $B(\mathcal{C}_1 \cap \mathcal{C}_2) = B(\mathcal{C}_1) \cap B(\mathcal{C}_2)$ but we can prove only the inclusion $B(\mathcal{C}_1) \cup B(\mathcal{C}_2) \subset B(\mathcal{C}_1 \cup \mathcal{C}_2)$, thus we are not sure that the greatest set of controlled behaviours included in A does exist.

Definition 3.2 Let $\mathcal{C} = \langle Q, q_o, \lambda, \gamma \rangle$ be a control of an observable system $\mathcal{S} = \langle C, C_o, T, \delta, V, \psi \rangle$ and A be an admissible subset of $B(\mathcal{C})$.

The A-*core* of $\mathcal{C}$ is the control $\overline{\mathcal{C}}_A = \langle Q, q_o, \overline{\lambda}_A, \gamma \rangle$, similar to $\mathcal{C}$, where $\overline{\lambda}_A(q,v) = \{t \in \lambda(q,v) / \exists\, dc \in A \cap B(\mathcal{C},q,v)$ such that $dctt(c) \in A\}$

The following result shows that $\overline{\mathcal{C}}_A$ has the expected property.

Proposition 3.3 *Let $\mathcal{C}$ be a control and A an admissible subset of $B(\mathcal{C})$. Then the following assertions hold :*

(i) $A \subset B(\overline{\mathcal{C}}_A)$

(ii) $\forall \mathcal{C}'$ *similar to* $\mathcal{C}$, $A \subset B(\mathcal{C}') \Rightarrow B(\overline{\mathcal{C}}_A) \subset B(\mathcal{C}')$

Now we give a characterization of those admissible subsets A such that $A = B(\overline{\mathcal{C}}_A)$

Definition 3.4 An admissible subset A of $B(\mathcal{C})$ is $\mathcal{C}$-*congruent* if $\forall dc, d'c' \in A, dc \equiv_{\mathcal{C}} d'c'$ implies $\forall t \in T, dctt(c) \in A$ iff $d'c'tt(c') \in A$.

Proposition 3.5 *Let* A *be an admissible subset of* $B(\mathcal{C})$. $A = B(\overline{\mathcal{C}}_A)$ *iff* A *is* $\mathcal{C}$-*congrue*

The next result amounts to say that the A-core of a control depends only on its similarity type.

Proposition 3.6 *Let $\mathcal{C}$ and $\mathcal{C}'$ be two similar controls and* A *an admissible subset of* $B(\mathcal{C}) \cap B(\mathcal{C}')$ *then* $\overline{\mathcal{C}}_A = \overline{\mathcal{C}}'_A$

From this result and from proposition 2.6 we can always assume that every A-core is the A-core of a complete control.

Proposition 3.7 Let $\mathcal{C}$ and $\mathcal{C}'$ be two complete controls of $\mathcal{S}$ and A be an admissible subset of $B(\mathcal{S})$. If $\equiv_{\mathcal{C}} \leq \equiv_{\mathcal{C}'}$, then $B(\overline{\mathcal{C}}_A) \subset B(\overline{\mathcal{C}}'_A)$.

As a consequence of thisproposition and of propositions 3.6, 2.6 and 2.7 we get

Proposition 3.8 For any control $\mathcal{C}$ of $\mathcal{S}$ and any admissible subset A of $B(\mathcal{C})$ we have $B(\overline{\mathcal{S}}_{min,A}) \subset B(\overline{\mathcal{C}}_A) \subset B(\overline{\mathcal{S}}_{max,A})$.

In case A is $\mathcal{S}_{max}$-congruent we get from propositions 3.5 and 3.8 that $B(\overline{\mathcal{C}}_A) = A$ for any control $\mathcal{C}$. This happens when the fact that the behaviour dc belongs to A depends only on the visible part of the last configuration c.

Proposition 3.9 Let $\mathcal{S}$ be fully observable. If A is an admissible subset of $B(\mathcal{S})$ such that $\forall dc, d'c' \in C(TC)^*, \psi(c) = \psi(c') \Rightarrow (dc \in A \Leftrightarrow d'c' \in A)$, then $B(\overline{\mathcal{C}}_A) = A$ for any control $\mathcal{C}$ of $\mathcal{S}$ such that $B(\mathcal{C}) \supset A$.

4. SOME APPLICATIONS

4.1 The synchronization and deadlock problems for rational processes

In [4] Nivat defined rational processes as finite-state automaton recognizing a prefix rational subset of X^*, the free monoïd generated by the alphabet X. The process is Y-synchronized, with Y a proper subset of X, if it cannot recognize words not in Y^*. It is deadlock-free if every finite behaviour is the beginning of an infinite one.

This can be restated in the formalism of the present paper.

A rational process is a system $\mathcal{S}$ like the one defined in example A.1. With the visible parts defined in example A.2 it becomes a fully observable system.

A behaviour $b = c_o t_1 c_1 \ldots t_n c_n$ is Y-synchronized if every $c_i \in \Xi \times Y^* \subset \Xi \times X^* = C$. It is easy to see that the set A of Y-synchronized behaviours is an admissible subset of $B(\mathcal{S})$. Moreover A is $\mathcal{S}_{max}$-congruent : let dc and d'c' in A be $\mathcal{S}_{max}$-equivalent ; this implies that $c = (\xi,u)$, $c' = (\xi,u')$ with $u, u' \in Y^*$; if $dctt(c) \in A$, then $t(c) = (\xi',uy)$ with $\xi' \in \Xi \cup \{stop\}$ and $y \in Y$; hence $t(c') = (\xi',u'y)$ and $d'c'tt(c') \in A$.

By proposition 3.5 we get $B(\overline{\mathcal{S}}_{max,A}) = A$. It remains to construct $\overline{\mathcal{S}}_{max,A}$. $\mathcal{S}_{max}$ is the control $<\{q\},q,\lambda,\gamma>$ defined by $\lambda(q,\xi) = \{t_{\xi\to x\xi'}, t_{\xi\to x}\}$ and $\gamma(q,\xi,t) = q$.

By definition of $\overline{\lambda}_A$ and of ψ, $t_{\xi\to x\xi'}$ (resp $t_{\xi\to x}$) $\in \overline{\lambda}_A$ iff $\exists$ dc with $c = (\xi,u)$ and $u \in Y^*$ such that $dctt(c) \in A$, which is equivalent to $x \in Y$.

Now let F be the set of behaviours of $\mathcal{S}$ which are the beginning of infinite behaviours of $\mathcal{S}$ and H be the set of behaviours of $\mathcal{S}$ controlled by $\mathcal{C} = \overline{\mathcal{S}}_{max,A}$ which are also the beginning of infinite controlled behaviours. Both sets F and H are admissible.

It is easy to prove that a behaviour dc, with $c = (\xi,u)$, is in F (resp. H) iff there exists a word u in X^* (resp. Y^*) of length greater than the cardinal of Ξ such that ξ can be derived in $u\xi'$, in the grammar G (cf the proof of the pumping lemma for rational languages). The set of such ξ(denoted respectively by Ξ_F and Ξ_H) is effectively constructible.

Then let dc and d'c' be two behaviours in F (resp in H), $\mathcal{S}_{max}$-congruent. We have $\psi(c) = \psi(c') \in \Xi_F$ (resp Ξ_H) and dctt(c)$\in$F (resp H) iff $t = t_{\xi\to x\xi'}$ with $\xi' \in \Xi_F$ (resp $\xi' \in \Xi_H$ and $x \in Y$) ; in this case d'c'tt(c') is also in F (resp H). Hence F and H are $\mathcal{S}_{max}$-congruent.

Therefore $F = B(\overline{\mathcal{S}}_{max,F})$ and $H = B(\overline{\mathcal{C}}_H) = B(\overline{\mathcal{S}}_{max,H})$, where these cores are defined respectively by $\lambda(q,\xi) = \{t_{\xi\to x\xi'}/\xi,\xi'\Xi\epsilon_F$ and $\lambda(q,\xi) = \{t_{\xi\to x\xi'}/\xi,\xi' \in \Xi_H, x \in Y\}$.

4.2 The deadlock problem for gsm

In examples B.1 et B.2 we defined a gsm as an observable system $\mathcal{S}$. Let A be the set of behaviours of $\mathcal{S}$ which are the beginnings of infinite behaviours. Clearly A is an admissible subset of $B(\mathcal{S})$.

For any complete control $\mathcal{C}$ of $\mathcal{S}$, included $\mathcal{S}_{min}$ and $\mathcal{S}_{max}$, we can construct a A-core $\overline{\mathcal{C}}_A$ and we get, from propositions 3.3 and 3.8, $A \subset B(\overline{\mathcal{S}}_{min,A}) \subset B(\overline{\mathcal{C}}_A) \subset B(\overline{\mathcal{S}}_{max,A})$.

First we show on an example that A is not $\mathcal{S}_{min}$-congruent ; thus, by proposition 3.5, $A \neq B(\overline{\mathcal{S}}_{min,A})$ and then $A \neq B(\overline{\mathcal{C}}_A)$ for any control $\mathcal{C}$ such that $A \subset B(\mathcal{C})$.

Example 4.1 Let $X = \{a,b\}$, $S = \{s_o,s_1\}$, $R = \{r_1,r_2,r_3\}$ with $r_1 = s_a,a \to a,s_o$; $r_2 = s_o,a \to a,s_1$; $r_3 = s_1,b \to b,s_1$; and τ be the gsm $\langle X,X,S,s_o,R\rangle$.

The system $\mathcal{S} = \langle C,C_o,T,\delta,V,\psi\rangle$ associated with it is defined like in example B.1 - B.2. Let $\mathcal{S}_{min}$ be its complete control defined in section 2.

Let us consider, for any positive integer n, the two infinite behaviours $b = c_o t_1 c_1 t_2 c_2 \ldots$ and $b' = c'_o t'_1 c'_1 t'_2 c'_2 \ldots$ with

- $\forall i \geq 1$, $t_i = t_{r_1}$ and $c_i = (a^\omega, s_o, a^i)$
- $\forall i$, $1 \leq i \leq n$, $t'_i = t_{r_1}$ and $c'_i = (a^{n+1-i}b^\omega, s_o, a^i)$
- $t'_{n+1} = t_{r_2}$ and $c'_{n+1} = (b^\omega, s_1, a^{n+1})$
- $\forall i > n+1$, $t'_i = t_{r_3}$ and $c'_i = (b^\omega, s_1, a^{n+1}b^{i-n-1})$

Let now $b_n = c_o t_1 \ldots t_n c_n$ and $b'_n = c'_o t'_1 \ldots t'_n c'_n$. Clearly b_n and b'_n are both in A and b_n is $\mathcal{S}_{min}$-equivalent to b'_n.

But $b_n t_{r_1} t_{r_1}(c_n) = b_n t_n c_{n+1}$ is obviously in A while $b'_n t_{r_1} t_{r_1}(c'_n)$ is not since $t_{r_1}(c'_n) = (b^\omega, s_o, a^{n+1})$ and no transition is firable in this configuration. Nevertheless we can prove that in this special case, the A-core is independant of the similarity type of the control.

Proposition 4.2 *For any complete control* $\mathcal{B}$ *of* $\mathcal{S}$, $B(\overline{\mathcal{B}}_A) = B(\mathcal{S}_{max,A})$.

The construction of the A-core of $\mathcal{S}_{max}$ is effective as a consequence of a further result.

Let k be the cardinal of $V = S \times X$ and let $\overline{S}$ be the subset of S such that $s \in \overline{S}$ iff there exist a word u of length k+1 and a behaviour $c_o t_1 c_1 \ldots t_k c_k$ with $c_o = (u,s,\Lambda)$. Clearly the construction of $\overline{S}$ is effective.

Proposition 4.3 *Let* $dc \in B(\mathcal{S})$ *with* $c = (u,s,v)$. *Then* $dc \in B(\mathcal{S}_{max,A})$ *iff* $s \in \overline{S}$.

The construction of the A-core of $\mathcal{S}$ is now very simple : it suffices to set

$\overline{\lambda}_A(q,v) = \{t_{sx \to vs'} \in \lambda(q,v) = \delta(v)/s, s' \in \overline{S}\}$.

4.3 The deadlock problem for net of processes

In [1] are studied operational and denotational semantics of nets of processes similar to those defined by Kahn [2] . To avoid cumbersome notations we restrict ourselves to the following simple case to which every net can be reduced in some sense (cf [1]) and which therefore captures the essence of the problem.

Let τ be a non-erasing gsm with two input words, that is $\tau = \langle X,S,s_o,R \rangle$ where X is an alphabet, S a set of state (possibly infinite), s_o the initial state, R a set of rules of the form $s,x,x' \to v,s'$ with $s, s' \in S, x,x' \in X, v \in X^*$.

The net we consider is obtained by connecting the output of τ to one of the inputs and we choose a finite word $u_o \in X^*$ which will be always on this looping line in initial configurations.

The observable system $\mathcal{S} = \langle C,C_o,T,\delta,V,\psi \rangle$ associated with this net is defined by $C = X^* \times S \times X^\infty$; $C_o = \{u_o\} \times \{s_o\} \times X^\infty$; $T = \{t_r / r \in R\}$ with $t_{sxx' \to vs'}(xu,s,x'w) = (uv,s',w)$; $V = (X \cup \{\Lambda\}) \times S \times (X \cup \{\Lambda\})$ and $\psi(u,s,w) = (u',s,w')$ with $u' = \Lambda$ if $u = \Lambda$ and x if u = xu" ; and similarly for w'.

We are still interested in the set A of finite behaviours which are the beginnings of infinite ones. But here, unlike the previous case, A-cores of different controls are different, as shown by the following example.

Example 4.4 Let $X = \{a,b\}$, $S = \{s_o,s_1,s_2\}$ and let $\mathcal{S}$ be the system defined by $C_o = \{a\} \times \{s_o\} \times X^\infty$, and $T = \{t_1,t_2,t_3,t_4,t_5\}$ are the transitions respectively associated with the rules $r_1 : s_o,a,a \to ab, s_1$; $r_2 : s_1,a,b \to a,s_1$; $r_3 : s_1,a,b \to a,s_2$; $r_4 : s_1,b,b \to a,s_1$; $r_5 : s_2,a,a \to a,s_2$. Let now $c_o = (a,s_o,ab^3a^\omega)$; $c_1 = (ab,s_1,b^3a^\omega)$; $c_2 = (ba,s_1,b^2a^\omega)$; $c_3 = (aa,s_1,ba^\omega)$; $c_4 = (aa,s_1,a^\omega)$.

Then $c_o t_1 c_1 t_2 c_2 t_4 c_3 t_3 c_4 t_5 c_4 t_5 c_4 t_5 c_4$ ... is an infinite behaviour.

Now let $B(\mathcal{S}_{max,A})$ the A-core of the control $\mathcal{S}_{max}$. The following behaviours are are in A and then are also in $B(\mathcal{S}_{max,A})$: $c_o, c_o t_1 c_1, c_o t_1 c_1 t_2 c_2 t_4 c_3, c_o t_1 c_1 t_2 c_2 t_4 c_3 t_3 c_4$. Hence, abbreviating $\bar{\lambda}_{max,A}(v)$ in $\bar{\lambda}(v)$, we get $t_1 \in \bar{\lambda}(\psi(c_o)) = \bar{\lambda}(a,s_o,a)$ and $t_3 \in \bar{\lambda}(\psi(c_3)) = \bar{\lambda}(a,s_1,b) = \bar{\lambda}(\psi(c_1))$.

Therefore $c_o t_1 c_1 t_3 c_2'$ is in $B(\mathcal{S}_{max,A})$ with $c_2' = t_3(c_1) = (ba, s_2 b^2 a^\omega)$ and this behaviour is deadlocked since $\delta(\psi(c_2')) = \delta(b,s_2,b) = \emptyset$.

Nevertheless this deadlock can be avoided if we remember that after firing t_1, b will be the second letter on the first input ; it suffices to forbid as second transitions, those which reach a state s which cannot read b on its firt input ; here these states are s_o and s_2, then t_3 is forbidden as second transition.

This is the reason why we introduce the following complete control.

Let $\mathcal{C} = \langle Q, q_*, \lambda, \gamma \rangle$ the complete control of $\mathcal{S}$ defined by $Q = X^+$, $q_* = u_o$, $\lambda(xu,(x,s,x')) = \delta(x,s,x') = \{t_{s,x,x' \to w,s'} / w \in X^*, s' \in S\}$ and $\gamma(xu,(x,s,x'),t_{s,x,x' \to w,s'}) = u$

In fact it is very easy to prove inductively that the state q reached by the control at the end of a controlled behaviour is exactly the first component of the last configuration, that is the word on the first input in this configuration.

Up to now we don't know a characterization of A, like those given for the two previous examples which allows an explicit construction of the A-core of $\mathcal{C}$. But we can prove that this A-core is the best we can expect.

<u>*Proposition 4.5*</u> *Let* $\mathcal{C}$ *be the control defined above. Then* $B(\bar{\mathcal{C}}_A) = B(\bar{\mathcal{S}}_{min,A})$.

REFERENCES

1. A. Arnold. Sémantique des processus communicants. Rapport de Recherche n° 1, Laboratoire d'Informatique, Université de Poitiers (1979).

2. G. Kahn. The semantics of a simple language for parallel processing. Proc. IFIP Congress (1974).

3. R.M. Keller. Formal verification of parallel programs. Comm. Assoc. Comput. Mach. (1976) 371-384.

4. M. Nivat. On the synchronization of processes. Rapport LITP n° 79-34, Université de Paris VII (1979).

CONCEPTUAL RELATIONS BETWEEN DATABASES

TRANSFORMED UNDER JOIN AND PROJECTION

G. Ausiello, C. Batini, M.Moscarini
CSSCCA - CNR
and Istituto di Automatica
Università di Roma, Italy

ABSTRACT

The concept of equivalence among data bases is defined in terms of ability of two data bases of providing the same answer to equal (or corresponding) queries and of allowing equal (or corresponding) updates. After discussing some basic properties of the concepts introduced, the case in which conceptual relations (inclusion or equivalence) among data bases may be proved by means of transformations based on projections and joins is examined in detail.

1. INTRODUCTION AND MOTIVATION

The motivation for research on different kinds of relations that may be established among different Data Bases according to their conceptual content are various and relevant; such a research field is indeed related to different topics:

1) Design of conceptual schemata [3]
2) Data translation, file integration and data base restructuring [12]
3) Comparisons between different data models [4]
4) Comparisons between different schemata in the same data model [3]
5) Consistency of different schemata [5]
6) Comparisons and mappings between static and behavioural properties of data [5]
7) Mappings in a DBMS architecture [13]

Among the different conceptual relations that we aim to study equivalence plays a central role.

An intuitive definition of equivalence was first given in [10]: "Two data bases are equivalent if they represent the same set of facts about a certain piece of world".

In [2],[3] the concept of equivalence is considered with respect to pairs of data bases obtained one from the other by decomposition operators and on which the only definable integrity constraints are functional dependencies.

In this paper we want to generalize the concept of equivalence to data bases in which, in principle, any kind of integrity constraint can be defined.

In particular in § 2 we give the basic definitions of the various concepts of conceptual inclusion and of conceptual equivalence among data bases; furthermore we consider examples and basic properties; in § 3 we show under what conditions equivalence may be proved between data bases obtained by means of relational operations JOIN and PROJECTION.

2. BASIC DEFINITIONS AND EXAMPLES

As we already stated in the introduction, throughout this paper we will study inclusion and equivalence of data bases with respect to conceptual content, by referring to a specific data model, precisely the n-ary relational model([6] , [7] , [8]).

In order to introduce the basic concepts and in order to prove properties of these concepts we should first define what languages are used for expressing queries and integrity constraints. Actually we do not need to make explicit what languages we are referring to and to specify their syntax and semantics. In the following, we will realize that inclusion and equivalence relations among data bases may depend on the choice of these languages and, for example, it is clear that conceptual relations which can be established in the presence of "complete" query languages do not necessarily hold when we only allow restricted subsets of queries.

DEFINITION 2.1. <u>A data base schema</u> (dbs) is a 6-tuple

- $S = \langle A, R, Dom, Rel, V_S, V_D \rangle$ where:
- A is a finite set of names of <u>attributes</u> $\{A_1, A_2, \dots A_n\}$;
- R is an m-tuple of names of <u>relations</u> $\langle R1, R2, \dots Rm \rangle$;
- Dom is a function that associates to every attribute Ai, $1 \leq i \leq n$ a domain of values Di;
- Rel: $R \longrightarrow A^+$ is a function that associates to every relation name Rj, $1 \leq j \leq m$, a set of names of attributes $(A_{j1}, \dots, A_{jh_j})$;
- V_S is the set of <u>static constraints</u> (e.g. functional dependencies);
- V_D is the set of <u>dynamic constraints</u>.

With the notation $Rj(A_{j1}, \dots, A_{jh_j})$ we mean that $Rel\ (Rj) = \langle A_{j1}, \dots, A_{jh_j} \rangle$

<u>DEFINITION 2.2</u>

a) <u>Tuple of a relation</u> $Rj(A_{j1}, \dots A_{jh_j})$ is a set of pairs

$\{A_{j1} : x_{j1}, \dots, A_{jh_j} : x_{jh_j}\}$ such that

$\forall i \quad x_{ji} \in Dom\ (A_{ji})$.

b) <u>Instance of a relation</u> $Rj\ (A_{j1}, \dots A_{jh_j})$ is a set of tuples of relation Rj.

In the following we denote an instance of R with $\bar{R}j$.

c) <u>Instance of a dbs</u> S with relation names $\langle R1, \dots, Rm \rangle$ is an m-tuple $i = \langle \bar{R}1, \dots \bar{R}m \rangle$ where $\bar{R}j$ is an instance of $Rj(A_{j1}, \dots, A_{jh_j})$ for every $1 \leq j \leq m$.

Notice that we do not take into account undefined values (see for instance [11]).

DEFINITION 2.3. A <u>data base</u> (DB) is a triple DB = $\langle S, I, T\rangle$ where:

- S is a dbs.
- I is the set of all instances of S that satisfy the static constraints,
- T is the set of all pairs $\langle i_1, i_2\rangle$ where $i_1, i_2 \in$ I and the transition from i_1 to i_2 satisfies the dynamic constraints.

EXAMPLE 2.1. Let us consider the DB of employees and their salaries PAYROLL = $\langle \bar{S}, \bar{I}, \bar{T}\rangle$ where

- $\bar{S} = (\bar{A}, \bar{R}, \overline{Dom}, \overline{Rel}, \bar{V}_S, \bar{V}_D)$ whose unique relation is

Employee (Emp , Salary) and $\overline{Dom}$ (Emp) = "set of integers from 00001 to 99999".

$\overline{Dom}$(Salary) = "set of integers from 10^6 to 10^8"

$\bar{V}_S$ = "Every employee has exactly one salary" (this constraint is a functional dependency and corresponds to usual notation Emp# $\longrightarrow$ Salary

$\bar{V}_D$ = "In every transition the salary of every employee must not decrease",

- $\bar{I}$ is the set of instances that satisfy the functional dependency,
- $\bar{T}$ is the set of transitions (pairs of instances) that satisfy the dynamic constraint.

With the following definitions we introduce the basic concepts of inclusion and equivalence of data bases with respect to their conceptual content.

First of all we define the syntactical inclusion between instances of relations, then we define the (conceptual) inclusion between instances of DBs and finally we define the (conceptual) inclusion and equivalence between DBs

DEFINITION 2.4. Let $\bar{R}1$ and $\bar{R}2$ be two instances of relations. We say that $\bar{R}1 \subseteq \bar{R}2$ ($\bar{R}_1$ is syntactically included in $\bar{R}2$) if for every tuple $t \in \bar{R}1$, there exists $t' \in \bar{R}2$ where t is a subset of t'.

DEFINITION 2.5. Let the following DBs be given: DB1 = $\langle$S1, I1, T1$\rangle$ where S1 = $\langle A, \langle R1, \ldots Rn\rangle, Dom, Rel, V_S, V_D\rangle$ and DB2 = $= \langle$S2, I2, T2$\rangle$

and let $i_1 \in$ I1, $i_2 \in$ I2 be two instances. We say that $i_1 = \langle \bar{R}_1, \ldots \bar{R}_n\rangle$ is <u>included</u> in i_2 ($i_1 \leq i_2$) (with respect to the query language Q) if:

a) - there is a function f : $Q \longrightarrow Q$ such that

$$(\forall q)\ (q \in Q \Rightarrow q(i_1) \subseteq f(q)(i_2))$$

(alternatively:

b) - there is $\bar{f} = < f_1, \ldots, f_m >$ $f_i \in Q$ such that:

$$(\forall i)((1 \leq i \leq m) \Rightarrow (\bar{R}_i \subseteq f_i(i_2)))$$

where symbol $\Rightarrow$ denotes logical implication.

We denote this property by $i_1 \propto \bar{f}(i_2)$.

Definition 2.5.a. assumes as inclusion criterion the existence of a transformation of queries over the first instance into queries over the second instance in such a way that the second answer provides at least the same information as the first one.

Definition 2.5.b. assumes as inclusion criterion the existence of a transformation of the second instance into a new instance that provides at least the same information as the first one.

Both the definitions reduce conceptual content comparisons among instances to set theoretical comparisons.

THEOREM 2.1: Definition 2.5.a $\equiv$ Definition 2.5.b.

Proof

a. Definition 2.5.a $\Rightarrow$ Definition 2.5.b
From definition 2.5.a we may state that:

$$\forall i((1 \leq i \leq n) \Rightarrow (q_i(i_1) \subseteq f(q_i)(i_2)))$$

where $q_i(i_1) = I(Ri) = Ri$

and I is the identity query.

So, function $\bar{f}$ in definition 2.5.b is just

$$\bar{f} = < f(q_1), \ldots, f(q_n) > .$$

b. Definition 2.5.b $\Rightarrow$ Definition 2.5.a.

If definition 2.5.b holds we may simply derive function f of definition 2.5.a as the composition of $\bar{f}$ with query q.

In the following we assume for inclusion among instances definition 2.5.b.

DEFINITION 2.6. Let the following DBs be given:

DB1 = < S1, I1, T1 > and DB2 = < S2, I2, T2 > and let $i_1 \in$ I1 and $i_2 \in$ I2 be two instances: we say that i_1 is equivalent to i_2 ($i_1 \equiv i_2$) (with respect to the query language Q) if $i_1 \leq i_2$ and $i_2 \leq i_1$.

Finally we want to remark that even in the same DB there may be different instances which are nevertheless equivalent.

PROPOSITION 2.1. Given a DB DB1 = < S1,I1,T1 > and given $i_1, i_2 \in I1$ $i_1 \equiv i_2$ does not imply $i_1 = i_2$.

PROOF. Let us suppose that S1 contains the following relations:

R1 (Social-Security-No, Salary)
R2 (Emp #, Salary)
R3 (Social-Security-No, Emp #)

with the following constraints:

1) Emp # ⟶ Salary
2) Social-Security-No ⟶ Salary
3) Social-Security-No ⟶ Emp #
4) Emp # ⟶ Social-Security-No
5) In every instance of the DB, for every employee the salary is stored either in $\overline{R1}$ or in $\overline{R2}$ but not necessarily in both.

Clearly there may be two instances which are exactly the same except for the fact that in one of them the salary of "JONES" is stored in R1 while in the other is stored in $\overline{R2}$. In both we have the social security number of "JONES" in R3. Clearly the two instances are equivalent but not identical.

The same situation arises in all cases in which more than one access path is available for some attribute and only in some simple cases suitable integrity constraints may impose that the equivalence of instances implies their identity.

DEFINITION 2.7. Let DB1 and DB2 be as in definition 2.5 and let $i_1 \in I1$ and $i_2 \in I2$ be two instances. We say that:

a) i_1 is <u>strongly included</u> in i_2 ($i_1 \lessapprox i_2$) (with respect to the query language Q) if there is $\bar{f} = < f_1, \dots f_n >$ where $f_i \in Q$ such that $(\forall i)((1 \leq i \leq n) \Rightarrow (\bar{R}i = f_i(i_2)))$ (we denote this fact by $i_1 \propto\!\in \bar{f}(i_2)$)
b) i_1 is <u>strongly equivalent</u> to i_2 ($i_1 \approxeq i_2$) if $i_1 \lessapprox i_2$ and $i_2 \lessapprox i_1$.

Now we may introduce the basic definitions.

DEFINITION 2.8. Let DB1 = < S1, I1, T1 > and DB2 = < S2, I2, T2 > be two DBs .

a) we say that DB1 <u>is weakly included</u> in DB2 (DB1 ≤ DB2) if $\exists \bar{f} \in \bar{Q}$ such that for every instance $i_1 \in I1$ there exists an instance $i_2 \in I2$ such that
   - $i_1 \propto\!\subset \bar{f}(i_2)$
   - for every transition $< i_1, i_1' > \in T1$, there exists a corresponding transition $< i_2, i_2' > \in T2$ such that $i_1' \propto\!\subset \bar{f}(i_2')$;
b) we say that DB1 is <u>weakly equivalent</u> to DB2 (DB1 ≡ DB2) if DB1 ≤ DB2 and DB2 ≤ DB1.

Definition 2.8.b is allowed by the fact that queries are monotonous functions over instances and hence the weak inclusion is a partial order. Analogously we have:

DEFINITION 2.9. Let DB1 = < S1, I1, T1 > and DB2 = <S2, I2, T2> be two DBs; we say that:

a) DB1 is <u>strongly included</u> in DB2 (DB1 $\precsim$ DB2) if there exist $\bar{f}$, $\bar{f}'$ $\in$ Q such that for every instance $i_1 \in$ I1 there exists an instance $i_2 \in$ I2 such that

- $i_1 \propto \bar{f}(i_2)$ and $i_2 \propto \bar{f}'(i_1)$

- for every transition $\langle i_1, i_1' \rangle \in$ T1 there exists a corresponding transition $\langle i_2, i_2' \rangle \in T_2$ such that $i_1' \propto \bar{f}(i_2')$ and $i_2' \propto \bar{f}(i_1')$

b) DB1 is <u>strongly equivalent</u> to DB2 (DB1 $\approx$ DB2) if DB1 $\precsim$ DB2 and

DB2 $\precsim$ DB1

Notice that pairs of DBs exist such that in definition 2.9 of strong inclusion i_1 and i_2 are such that $\bar{f}(i_2)$ properly incluses i_1 and $\bar{f}(i_1)$ properly includes i_2.

<u>Example 2.1</u>

Consider DB1 = <S1, I1, T1> and DB2 = < S2, I2, T2> where:

- S1 contains the relations

  R1 (A, B, C, D)

  R2 (E, F)

  R3 (F, G, H)

  with the following constraints:

  C1) A $\longrightarrow$ B;

  C2) B, C $\longrightarrow$ D;

  C3) E $\longrightarrow$ F;

  C4) F, G $\longrightarrow$ H

  C5) For every instance of the DB, <u>Proj</u> [$\bar{R2}$; F] = <u>Proj</u> [$\bar{R3}$; F] (with Proj [$\bar{R}$; X] we mean the Projection of a relation R over a list of attributes X).

- S2 contains the relations

  R1' (A, B)
  R2' (B, C, D)
  R3' (E, F, G, H)

  with constraints C1, C2, C3, C4 and:

  C6) For every instance of the DB, <u>Proj</u> [$\bar{R1}$'; B] = <u>Proj</u> [$\bar{R2}$'; B].

$\bar{f}$ and $\bar{f}'$ in definition 2.9 are the following:

$\bar{f} = \langle$ <u>Join</u> $[\overline{R1'}, \overline{R2'}; B]$, <u>Proj</u> $[\overline{R3'}; E, F]$, <u>Proj</u> $[\overline{R3'}; F, G, H] \rangle$
(with <u>Join</u> [R1, R2; X] we mean the natural join of relations R1 and R2 on the common set of attributes X).

$\bar{f}' = \langle$ <u>Proj</u> $[\overline{R1}; A, B]$, <u>Proj</u> $[\overline{R1}; B, C, D]$, <u>Join</u> $[\overline{R2}, \overline{R3}; F] \rangle$

Now, given the instance i_1 of I1:

R1

A	B	C	D
a_1	b_1	c_1	d_1
a_2	b_1	c_2	d_2

R2

E	F
e_1	f_1
e_2	f_1

R3

F	G	H
f_1	g_1	h_1
f_1	g_2	h_2

an instance i_2 that ensures strong inclusion is the following (notice that the method is of general applicability):

R1'

A	B
a_1	b_1
a_2	b_1

R2'

B	C	D
b_1	c_1	d_1
b_1	c_2	d_2

R3'

E	F	G	H
e_1	f_1	g_1	h_1
e_2	f_1	g_2	h_2

It may be easily seen that i_1 is properly included in $\bar{f}(i_2)$ and i_2 is properly included in $\bar{f}'(i_1)$.

DEFINITION 2.10. Let DB1 = $\langle$S1, I1, T1$\rangle$ and DB2 = $\langle$S2, I2, T2$\rangle$ be two data bases. We say that:

a) DB1 is <u>very strongly included</u> in DB2 (DB1 $\sqsubset$ DB2) if there exist $\bar{f}, \bar{f}' \in \bar{Q}$ such that for every instance $i_1 \in$ I1 there exists an instance $i_2 \in$ I2 such that
   - $i_1 \Subset \bar{f}(i_2)$ and $i_2 \Subset \bar{f}'(i_1)$
   - for every transition $\langle i_1, i_1' \rangle \in$ T1 there exists a corresponding transition $\langle i_2, i_2' \rangle \in$ T2 such that $i_1' \Subset \bar{f}(i_2')$ and $i_2' \Subset \bar{f}'(i_1')$;

b) DB1 is <u>very strongly equivalent</u> to DB2 (DB1 $\sqsubseteq$ DB2) if DB1 $\sqsubset$ DB2 and DB2 $\sqsubset$ DB1.

<u>Example 2.2</u>

As an example of various possible conceptual relations among DBs we consider two DBs DB1 and DB2 whose schemata are the following:

- S1 contains the relations:

Anagraphic-Employee (Emp # , Sex, Age)
Income (Emp # , Gross-Salary)
with $V_{S1} = \{Emp\# \longrightarrow Sex, Age, Gross\text{-}Salary\}$

- S2 contains the relations:

Employee (Emp # , Sex, Age, Gross-Salary)
with $V_{S2} = \{Emp\# \longrightarrow Sex, Age, Gross\text{-}Salary\}$

In this case DB1 $\leq$ DB2 and DB2 $\leq$ DB1: so they are weakly equivalent. Notice that while, given an instance i_2 of DB2, an instance i_1 of DB1 exists from which i_2 can be exactly computed, in the instances of DB1 in general the two sets of employees do not coincide and so the "corresponding" instances of DB2 necessarily are conceptually richer.

So DB2 $\sqsubset$ DB1 but DB1 $\not\sqsubset$ DB2.

If we enrich V_{S1} with the constraint:

<u>Proj</u> [Anagraphic-Employee; Emp #] = Proj [Income; Emp #] then DB1 $\sqsubset$ DB2 and so the two DBs are very strongly equivalent.

In the second example we simply hint at the kind of results that we may prove if we allow a more powerful query language.

<u>Example 2.3.a</u>

In this case:

- S1 contains the relation Income (Emp # , Gross-Salary) with $V_{S1} = \{Emp\# \longrightarrow Gross\text{-}Salary\}$
- S2 contains the relation Income (Emp # , Net-Salary, Tax) with $V_{S2} = \{Emp\# \longrightarrow Net\text{-}Salary, Tax\}$

If we have a sufficiently powerful query language and the auxiliary constraint Gross-Salary = Net-Salary + Tax we may show that DB1 $\sqsubset$ DB2.

<u>Example 2.3.b</u>

As in example a) but in S1 the relation is

Income (Emp # , Gross-Salary, Tax)

in this case DB1 $\sqsubsetneq$ DB2.

In [1] we prove that:

1) DB1 $\lesssim$ DB2 $\Rightarrow$ DB1 $\leq$ DB2
2) DB1 $\leq$ DB2 $\not\Rightarrow$ DB1 $\lesssim$ DB2
3) DB1 $\lesssim$ DB2 $\not\Rightarrow$ DB1 $\equiv$ DB2
4) DB1 $\equiv$ DB2 $\not\Rightarrow$ DB1 $\underset{\sim}{\equiv}$ DB2.
5) There exist two data bases DB1 and DB2 such that DB1 $\equiv$ DB2 but for no pair of instances $i_1 \in I_1$ and $i_2 \in I_2$ it is true that $i_1 \equiv i_2$.

In the proofs we assume as query language a language whose operators are Proj and Join previously defined.

We can now state within the same query language the following properties (notice that in DBs considered as counterexamples V_D is empty and so conditions on transitions in definitions 2.8, 2.9, 2.10 are trivially verified);

Proposition 2.1

1) DB1 $\sqsubset$ DB2 $\Rightarrow$ DB1 $\lessapprox$ DB2

2) DB1 $\not\lessapprox$ DB2 $\not\Rightarrow$ DB1 $\sqsubset$ DB2

Proof

1) Trivial
2) Consider now two DBs DB1 and DB2 such that:

- S1 contains R1 (Student # , Teacher # , Course # , Grade) with $V_{S1} = \{$Teacher # $\longrightarrow$ Course # ; Student # , Course # $\longrightarrow$ Grade$\}$

- S2 contains R2 (Student # , Course # , Grade) and R_3 (Teacher # , Course #) with $V_{S2} = V_{S1}$

Step 2.1 DB1 $\lessapprox$ DB2

Let $\bar{f}$, $\bar{f}'$ in definition 2.9 be

$\bar{f}' = \langle$ Proj $[R_1$; Student # , Course # , Grade$]$,
Proj $[R_1$; Teacher # , Course #$]\rangle$

$\bar{f} = \langle$ Join $[$R2, R3; Course$]\rangle$

Given $i_1 = \langle \bar{R}1 \rangle$ the instance $i_2 \in$ I2 such that $i_1 \propto \bar{f}(i_2)$ and $i_2 \propto \bar{f}'(i_1)$ is

$i_2 = \langle$ Proj $[\bar{R}1$; Student # , Course # , Grade$]$,
Proj $[\bar{R}1$; Teacher # , Course #$]\rangle$

Step 2.2 DB1 $\not\sqsubset$ DB2

An instance $i_1 \in$ I1 may be obtained from an instance $i_2 \in$ I2 only by a Join operator. Because of the lack of the lossless join property, equality conditions in definition 2.10 cannot, in general, be achieved.

QED

Proposition 2.2 DB1 $\sqsubset$ DB2 $\not\Rightarrow$ DB1 $\approx$ DB2

Proof Consider DB1 and DB2 such that:

- S1 contains R1 (Employee, Age, Address) with $V_{S1} = \{$ Employee $\longrightarrow$ Age, Address$\}$

- S2 contains R2 (Employee,Age) and R3 (Employee, Address) with $V_{S2} = \{$Employee $\longrightarrow$ Age, Address$\}$

Step 1 DB1 $\sqsubset$ DB2

Let $\bar{f}$, $\bar{f}'$in definition 2.10 be

$$\bar{f}' = \langle \underline{Proj}\ [R1;\ Employee,\ Age]\ ;\ \underline{Proj}\ [R1;\ Employee,\ Address] \rangle$$

$$\bar{f} = \langle \underline{Join}\ [R2,\ R3;\ Employee] \rangle$$

Given $i_1 = \langle \bar{R1} \rangle$ the instance $i_2 \in I_2$ such that $i_1 \propto\!\!\in \bar{f}\ (i_2)$ and $i_2 \propto\!\!\in \bar{f}'\ (i_1)$ is

$$i_2 = \langle \underline{Proj}\ [\bar{R1};\ Employee,\ Age],\ \underline{Proj}\ [\bar{R1};\ Employee,\ Address] \rangle$$

Step 2 DB1 $\not\succeq$ DB2 (i.e. DB2 $\not\preceq$ DB1)

Let $i_2 \in I_2$ be an instance that contains different sets of Employees in $\bar{R1}$ and $\bar{R2}$; in every $i_1 \in$ I1 such that $i_2 \propto\!\!\subset \bar{f}'\ (i_1)$ dummy values must be assigned to a certain number of Ages and Addresses, values that can never be reconstructed.

Proposition 2.3.

$$DB1 \ \eqsim\ DB2 \ \not\Rightarrow\ DB1 \ \subseteq\ DB2$$

Proof

The two DBs of example 2.1 are strongly equivalent. But, because of the lack of the lossless join property, equality conditions in definition 2.10 cannot, in general, be achieved.

The previous properties show the adecuacy of the given definitions.

3. EQUIVALENCE BETWEEN CLASSES OF DATA BASES

In this section, we want to state inclusion and equivalence conditions for particular classes of DBs.

Such properties may be proved by finding transformations between databases obtained by composition of operators of a query language.

In [1] we studied in detail the class of DBs in which inclusion and equivalence conditions among DBs may be proved by means of transformations based on restriction and union.

Recently in the literature (see [9] , [14]) the importance of such transformations, has been recognized. Another kind of transformations, concerning Join and Projection operations has been, on the contrary, deeply examined (see [2] , [3]).

We want in the following to show that, given two DBs obtained one from the other by transformations in which Join and Projection operations are used, various kinds of conceptual relations can be defined over the two DBs , according to semantic properties (i.e. set of constraints) the two DBs satisfy.

In the following we assume as query language a language with the two operators Proj [R; X] , Join [R; X] we have defined in section 2

In the proofs we do not verify the correspondence of transitions because of the lack of dynamic constraints.

THEOREM 3.1 - Let DB1 = <S1, I1, T1> and DB2 = <S2, I2, T2> where

- S1 contains

  R(X)

  $V_{S1} = FD_1$ (the set of functional dependencies in R(X))

- S2 contains

  R1 (X1), R2(X2)

  where $X1 \cup X2 = X$ and $X1 \cap X2 = X12 \neq \emptyset$

  $V_{S2} = FD_2$ (the set of functional dependencies in R1(X1) and R2(X2)).

Let FD_1^+ and FD_2^+ be respectively the closure of FD_1 and FD_2 [3].

If

α. $FD_1^+ \supseteq FD_2^+$

then DB1 $\underset{\sim}{\angle}$ DB2.

<u>Proof</u>

Let $\bar{f}$ and $\bar{f}'$ in definition 2.9 be:

$\bar{f} = \langle f_1 \rangle$ when $f_1(i_2)$ = <u>Join</u> $[\overline{R1}, \overline{R2}; X12]$

$\bar{f}' = \langle \bar{f}_1', f_2' \rangle$ where f_1' = <u>Proj</u> $[\bar{R}; X1]$

f_2' = <u>Proj</u> $[\bar{R}; X2]$

<u>Step 1</u> $\forall i_1 \in I_1 \; \exists \, i_2 \in I2 \; (i_1 \propto \bar{f}(i_2) \wedge i_2 \propto \bar{f}'(i_1))$

Given $i_1 = \langle \bar{R} \rangle$ let $i_2 = \langle \overline{R1}, \overline{R2} \rangle$ where $\bar{R}i$ = Proj $[\bar{R}, Xi]$

<u>Step 1.1</u> $i_2 \in I_2$.

Trivial, for the hypothesis $FD_1^+ \supseteq FD_2^+$.

<u>Step 1.2</u> $i_1 \propto \bar{f}(i_2)$.

In fact:

$\bar{R} \subseteq$ <u>Join</u> [<u>Proj</u> $[\bar{R}, X1]$, <u>Proj</u> $[\bar{R}, X2]$; X12] = <u>Join</u> $[\bar{R}1, \bar{R}2; X12]$

<u>Step 1.3</u> $i_2 \propto \bar{f}'(i_1)$.

Trivial.

THEOREM 3.2 - Let DB1 and DB2 be as in theorem 3.1. Furthermore, let the following properties hold:

β. $FD2^+ \supseteq FD1^+$

γ. for every instance $\langle \bar{R}1, \bar{R}2 \rangle \in I_2$ <u>Proj</u> $[\bar{R}1, X12]$ = <u>Proj</u> $[\bar{R}2, X12]$

Then DB2 $=$ DB1 and DB1 $\underset{\sim}{\neq}$ DB2.

Proof

Step 1 DB2 $\sqsubset$ DB1.

Let $\bar{f}$ and $\bar{f}'$ be as in proof of theorem 3.1.

Step 1.1 $\forall i_2 \in I_2 \; \exists i_1 \in I1 \; (i_1 \propto\!\equiv \bar{f}(i_2) \wedge i_2 \propto\!\equiv \bar{f}'(i_1))$

Given $i_2 \in I_2$ let $i_1 = \langle \bar{R} \rangle$ when $\bar{R} = \underline{\text{Join}}\,[\bar{R}1, \bar{R}2;\ X12]$.

Step 1.1.1 $i_1 \in I1$

Trivial for hypothesis β.

Step 1.1.2. $i_2 = \bar{f}'(i_1)$

In general

$$\bar{R}1 \supseteq \underline{\text{Proj}}\,[\underline{\text{Join}}\,[\bar{R}1, \bar{R}2;\ X12];\ X1]$$
$$\bar{R}2 \supseteq \underline{\text{Proj}}\,[\underline{\text{Join}}\,[\bar{R}1, \bar{R}2;\ X12];\ X2]$$

Because of hypothesis γ no tuple of $\bar{R}1$ and $\bar{R}2$can be lost in the transformation.

Step 2 DB1 $\approxeq$ DB2

Trivial from theorem 3.1 and Step 1.

THEOREM 3.3 - Let DB1 and DB2 be as in theorem 3.1. Furthermore let hypothesis α of theorem 3.2 and:

δ. $X12 \longrightarrow X1 \vee X12 \longrightarrow X2$ holds both in FD_1^+ and in FD_2^+ then DB1 $\sqsubset$ DB2.

Proof

Let $\bar{f}$ and $\bar{f}'$ be as in proof of theorem 3.1.

Step 1 $\forall i_1 \in I_1 \exists i_2 \in I_2 \; (i_1 \propto\!\equiv \bar{f}(i_2) \wedge i_2 \propto\!\equiv \bar{f}(i_1))$

Given $i_1 = \langle \bar{R} \rangle$ let $i_2 = \langle \bar{R}1, \bar{R}2 \rangle$, where $\bar{R}i = \underline{\text{Proj}}\,[\bar{R}, Xi]$

Step 1.1 $i_2 \in I_2$

Trivial for the hypothesis α.

Step 1.2 $i_1 \propto\!\equiv \bar{f}(i_2)$

For hypothesis γ it follows

$$\bar{R} = \underline{\text{Join}}\,[\underline{\text{Proj}}\,[\bar{R}, X1], \underline{\text{Proj}}\,[\bar{R}, X2];\ X12] = \underline{\text{Join}}\,[\bar{R}1, \bar{R}2;\ X12]$$

Step 1.3 $i_2 \propto\!\equiv \bar{f}'(i_1)$

Trivial.

COROLLARY 3.1 Let DB1 and DB2 be as in theorem 3.1. Furthermore let $\alpha, \beta, \gamma, \delta$ hold. Then DB1 $\equiv$ DB2.

Finally, we want to compare definitions of inclusion and equivalence given in section 2 with definitions Rep 2, Rep 3, Rep 4 of equivalence among databases given in [3] by Beeri, Bernstein and Goodman.

First of all we have to notice that both in this paper and in Beeri's paper only "vertical decompositions" are considered (i.e. decompositions obtained by Proj and Join operators). Secondly, Beeri assumes universal relation assumption, while in this paper a more general approach is followed.

In Table 1 a comparison is made between Beeri's definitions and Theorems 3.1. ÷ 3.4.

implies	our definitions	definitions in 3
$\alpha \wedge \beta \wedge \gamma$	DB1 $\approx$ DB2 $\wedge$ DB2 $\sqsubset$ DB1	Rep 2
$\alpha \wedge \delta \wedge \gamma$	DB1 $\sqsubset$ DB2	Rep 3
$\alpha \wedge \beta \wedge \delta \wedge \gamma$	DB1 $\sqsubseteq$ DB2	Rep 4

Table 1

4. CONCLUSIONS

In this paper our aim was to put the basis for a theory of conceptual comparisons between DBs.

We have defined several conceptual relations between DBs and shown their adequacy to represent typical situations of the real world.

It is our opinion that the concepts we have introduced on one side unify various aspects of relational theory and on the other side allow to begin a constructive research of the concept of "conceptual content" in data base theory.

A data base is defined in [7] as a set of time varying relations. So, to compare the conceptual content of DBs it is necessary to compare both their ability to represent reality and their ability to represent the evolution of reality. And the only way to investigate systematically such a research field is to formally define the set of integrity constraints that express the semantic properties of reality modeled by DBs in a suitable language.

In the future, we will aim, once defined a formalism to express integrity constraints, to go deeper in the systematization of properties of algebraic transformations and generalize such research to more general kind of transformations. Furthermore we want to investigate properties of new kind of conceptual relations between DBs like for instance the "maximal common conceptual content" between DBs that could be useful in studying the problems of file integration.

Finally we want to remark that in any case our ultimate goal is to give a contribution to foundations of theory of relations and we feel that the concept of equivalence of data bases takes certainly a relevant role in such a theory.

References

[1] G. Ausiello, C. Batini, M. Moscarini- On the equivalence among data base schemata - International Conference on Data Bases. Aberdeen, July 1980.

[2] C. Beeri, A.O. Mendelzon, Y. Sagiv, J.D. Ullman - Equivalence of Relational Data base Schemes - Technical Report # 252, Princeton University (1978).

[3] P. Bernstein, C. Beeri, N. Goodman - A Sophisticate's introduction to DB Normalization Theory - Proc. Conf. Very Large Data Bases - Berlin (1978).

[4] M. Borkin - Data Model Equivalence - Proc. Conf. Very Large Data Bases - Berlin (1978).

[5] M. Brodie - Specification and Verification of DB Semantic Integrity Constraints - Tecn. Rep. University of Toronto (1978).

[6] E.F. Codd - Further Normalization on the Data base Relational Model in Data Base Systems - Prentice Hall (1972).

[7] E.F. Codd - A relational Model of Data for Large Shared data banks- CACM June 1970.

[8] E.F. Codd - Relational Completness of Data Base Sublanguages - in Data Base Systems - Prentice Hall (1972).

[9] R. Fagin - Normal Forms and Relational Database Operators.SIGMOD 1979.

[10] W.C. Mc Gee - A contribution to the Study of Data Equivalence - DB Management, Cargese (1974).

[11] W. Lipski - On Semantic issues connected with Incomplete Information Databases. ACM TODS 4,3,1979.

[12] S. Navathe, J. Fry - Restructuring for Large DB: Three Levels of Abstraction - ACM TODBS (1976).

[13] P. Paolini - An Alternative Structure for DBMS - Proc. Conf. Very Large Data Bases - Berlin (1978).

[14] E. Sciore - Improving Semantic Specification in a Relational Database - SIGMOD, 1979.

THE WEIGHTED SPERNER'S SET PROBLEM

X. Berenguer, J. Diaz

Facultat d'Informàtica
Universitat Politècnica de Barcelona
Barcelona, Spain

Abstract

A polynomial time bounded algorithm is presented for solving the Weighted Sperner's Set Problem, that is, the problem of computing an independent Set of maximal weight on a weighted partially ordered set.

1. Introduction

Given a poset $(P, \geqslant)$ with a weight function associated to each of its elements, $w: P \rightarrow Z^{+}$, the Weighted Sperner's Set Problem consists of finding an independent set (or a "stable set") of P with maximal weight (the weight of a set is the sum of the weight of its members).

When $\forall p \in P$, $w(p)=1$ we are faced with the problem of finding an independent set of maximal cardinality, usually named as "maximal unrelated set" or "maximal Dillworth set". A polynomial time bounded algorithm to solve this problem is sketched at /3/. In this work it is shown that, in general, the problem can be solved with time complexity $O(n^3)$, where $n = |P|$.

As background reading for the basic concepts of this paper, see /4/ and /5/.

An independent set I of a graph G is a subset of vertices of G such that any pair of points in I forms an arc which is not an arc of G. A vertex cover W is a subset of vertices of G such that for each arc of G at least one of its endpoints belongs to W. A minimal vertex cover (MVC) W is a vertex cover such that if $v \in W$ and $W' = W - \{v\}$, then W' is not a vetex cover of G. A minimal weight vertex cover (MWVC) of a weighted graph is a vertex cover with minimal weight. A maximal weight independent set of a weighted graph is an independent set with maximal weight. (A weighted graph is a graph with weights on its vertices).

2. Relation between Weighted Sperner's Set and Max-Flow

The following lemmas are clear:

Lemma 1: In any weighted graph, the complement of a MWVC is a Maximal Weight Independent Set.

Lemma 2: In any weighted graph, any MWVC is also a MVC.

A weighted poset $(P,\geq)$ can be represented by a digraph $P(V,A)$, where $V = P$ with same weights and $\forall v_i, v_j \in V$, $(v_i,v_j) \in A$ iff $v_i \geq v_j$ (here and below arcs are directed: when we write (v,y) we mean $(\overrightarrow{v,y})$). We shall use indistinctly $(P,\geq)$ and $P(V,A)$.

Given a weighted poset $P(V,A)$ the Associated Bipartite Weighted Graph $B(V^A,V^B,E)$ is the Bipartite Graph defined by:

i) $V^A = V$, $V^B = V$.

ii) $E = \{(v_i^a, v_j^b) \mid v_i^a \in V^A, v_j^b \in V^B \text{ s.t. } v_i \geq v_j \text{ in } P(V,A)\}$.

iii) Assign the same weights in V^A and V^B as the corresponding weights in V.

Lemma 3: A vertex cover W in B is minimal iff W is also a minimal vertex cover in $P(V,A)$.

Proof: If $W=\{v_{i_1}^a, v_{i_2}^a, \ldots\ldots, v_{j_1}^b, v_{j_2}^b, \ldots\}$ is a MVC in B, we must prove that all vertices in W are distinct (i.e. all indexes $i_1, i_2, \ldots$ are different from the $j_1, j_2, \ldots$

Suppose not, i.e. there exists some i_k and some j_e such that $i_k = j_e$ and therefore $v_{i_k}^a \equiv v_{j_e}^b$. By the definition of a MVC it exists at least one arc $(v_{i_k}^a, y)$ with $y \in V^B$ such that $y \notin W$, and also some arc $(z, v_{j_e}^b)$ with $z \in V^A$ such that $z \notin W$. If $v_{i_k}^a \equiv v_{j_e}^b$, by the transitivity of B (inherited from P), $v_{i_k}^a \geq y$ and $z \geq v_{i_k}^a$ implies $y \leq z$, which will be an arc with endpoints not covered by any node in W, but this will be against the hypothesis that W be a MVC.

Now we must prove that a MVC in $P(V,A)$ is also a MVC in B. Let W a MVC in P. Split W in the following way:

$$W^A = \{v^a \mid v^a \in W \text{ and } \exists y \in V-W \text{ s.t. } v \geq y,\ y \notin W\}$$
$$W^B = \{v^b \mid v^b \in W \text{ and } \exists z \in V-W \text{ s.t. } v \leq z,\ z \notin W\}.$$

If we take W^A as a subset of V^A and W^B as a subset of V^B then $W^A \cup W^B$ forms a MVC in B.

From lemma 2 and lemma 3, it follows:

Corollary: Given a poset $P(V,A)$ and its associated weighted bipartite graph $B(V^A,V^B,E)$, W is a MWVC in P iff W is a MWVC in B.

We define now the Associated Flow Graph $B_f(V_f^A,V_f^B,E_f)$ of the Associated Weighted Bipartite Graph $B(V^A,V^B,E)$ by introducing two distinguished nodes s,t and making:

i) $V_f^A = V^A \cup \{s\}$, $V_f^B = V^B \cup \{t\}$.

ii) $E_f = E \cup \{(s,v_i^a) \mid v_i^a \in V^A\} \cup \{(v_j^b,t) \mid v_j^b \in V^B\}$.

iii) To the arcs of B_f the following capacities are assigned:

$\forall e \in E,\ c(e) = \infty$

$\forall e_i \in \{(s,v_i^a),\ v_i^a \in V^A\},\ c(e_i) = w(v_i^a)$

$\forall e_j \in \{(v_j^b,t),\ v_j^b \in V^B\},\ c(e_j) = w(v_j^b)$.

Exemple : Here it is an example to clarify the previously defined associated graphs to $(P,\geqslant)$: Be $P = \{v_1,v_2,v_3,v_4\}$, $v_1 \geqslant v_2$, $v_1 \geqslant v_3$, $v_2 \geqslant v_4$, $v_3 \geqslant v_4$, and $w(v_1)=3$, $w(v_2)=2$, $w(v_3)=5$ and $w(v_4)=1$. In the figures, numbers between parenthesis indicate weights.

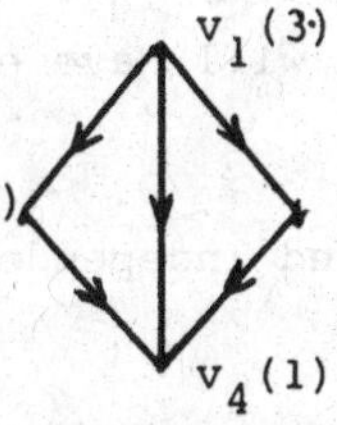

$P(V,A)$

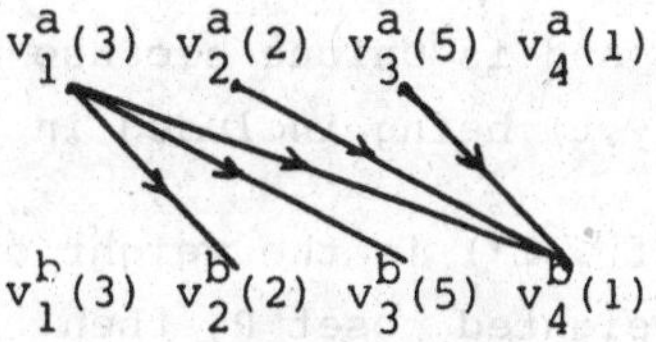

$B(V^A,V^B,E)$

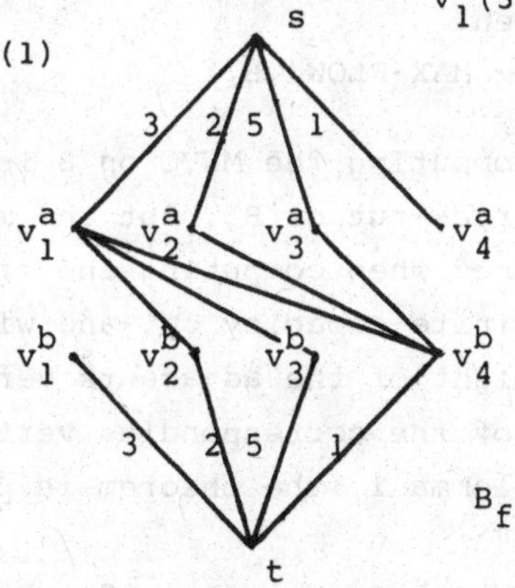

$B_f(V_f^A,V_f^B,E_f)$

Let $\mathcal{R}$ the set of all finite-capacity cuts in B_f (a cut is a minimal subset of arcs which covers all the paths between s and t). A vertex-cut C_R associated to $R \in \mathcal{R}$ is defined as

$$C_R = \{v \mid v \in V_f^A \text{ and } (s,v) \in R\} \cup \{v \mid v \in V_f^B \text{ and } (v,t) \in R\}$$

<u>Lemma 4</u>: A set C_R is a vertex-cut iff it is a MVC of B.

Let $\mathcal{G}_{\mathcal{R}}$ the set of all vertex-cuts associated to all $R \in \mathcal{R}$. As previously defined, $C_R \in \mathcal{G}_{\mathcal{R}}$ will be a vertex cover on B, because it does not exist an arc $(v,y) \in E$ not covered by C_R, otherwise it would exist a path (s,v,y,t) not covered by the arcs of R.

Now let us see that any $C_R \in \mathcal{G}_{\mathcal{R}}$ is a MVC of B.

Suppose not, and let $v \in C_R$ be some vertex of B which can be thrown away without changing the condition of C_R to be a vertex cover.
If $v \in V^A$ it will exist an arc $(v,y) \in E$ with $y \in C_R$, for that it must exist an arc $(y,t) \in C_R$. But in this case the path (s,v,y,t) will be covered two times and R will be not a (minimal) cut. If $v \in V^B$ an analogous reasoning can be applied.

Now let us see that any MVC in B, W, has an unique associated (finite-capacity) cut.

Construct this cut as follows:

$$R = \left\{ (s,v) \mid v \in W \text{ and } v \in V^A \right\} \cup \left\{ (v,t) \mid v \in W \text{ and } v \in V^B \right\}.$$

R is a cut and is unique because any path (s,v,y,t) will have either (s,v) or (y,t) being included in R.

<u>Theorem</u>: If $w(I^*)$ is the weight of a Maximal Weighted Independent Set I^* on a weighted poset P, then

$$w(I^*) = \sum_{\forall v \in P} w(v) - \text{MAX-FLOW } (B_f)$$

Proof: From lemmas 2 and 4, computing the MWVC on B is equivalent to compute a minimal weighted vertex-cut on B_f. But the minimal weighted vertex-cut on B_f can be obtained when computing the minimum capacitated cut on B_f (which will be a finite-capacity cut and with capacity exactly equal to the total weight of the adjacents vertices of their arcs, i.e., the total weight of the corresponding vertex-cut). From the min-cut max-flow theorem and lemma 1, the theorem is proved.

3. Algorithm for solving the Weighted Sperner's Set Problem

From the previous theorem, here it is an algorithm for solving the Weighted Sperner's Set Problem:

1) Given the poset $(P, \geqslant)$ (or P(V,A)), construct $B(V^A,V^B,E)$ and $B_f(V_f^A,V_f^B,E_f)$.

2) Find a max-flow on B_f using, for instance, Dinic-Karzanov algorithm /2/. This will give us a min-cut and so a MWVC, W, in B.
3) W will be too a MWVC in P. Find the complement I = V - W in P. The set I will be the desired Maximal Weight Independent Set.

Note that as Dinic-Karzanov algorithm is bounded by $O(n^3)$, the complexity of the whole algorithm will be also bounded by $O(n^3)$. And the Weighted Sperner's Set Problem belongs to the class $\mathcal{P}$.

4. Comments

Lemma 4 works on any weighted bipartite graph, so a polynomial time bounded solution for the MWVC (and the Maximal Weight Independent Set) in these graphs has been presented.

The authors, together with L.H. Harper, have generalised the techniques presented here for solving the "Sperner-Erdös problem", that is, the problem of computing the k-independent set of maximal weight on a weighted poset /1/.

5. References

/1/ Berenguer X., Diaz J., Harper L.H. "A solution to the Sperner-Erdös Problem", manuscript in preparation.
/2/ Even S. "The Max Flow Algorithm of Dinic and Karzanov: an exposition" MIT/LCS/TM-80 (1976).
/3/ Golumbic M.C. "Algorithmic Graph Theory and Perfect Graphs", Academic Press, N.Y. (1980).
/4/ Lawler E. "Combinatorial Optimization: Networks and Matroids", Hold Rinehart and Winston, N.Y. (1976).
/5/ Rota G.C., Harper L.H. "Matching theory: an introduction", in Advances in Probability, vol. 1, pp. 171-215, N.Y. (1971).

Proof of a Concurrent Program Finding Euler Paths

by

E. Best
Computing Laboratory
University of Newcastle upon Tyne
England

Abstract

A concurrent program finding Euler paths in a graph is described, proved and analysed. The importance of atomic actions is particularly stressed.

1 Introduction

In the present paper we discuss a moderately complex concurrent program and its proof. The program had been conceived as an exercise in parallel programming, and in particular it had been the author's wish to test the feasibility of an experimental concurrent programming language constructed from guarded commands and atomic actions - the same language as has been used in [DIJ78] and in [DLM78]. In the event this language (particularly the atomic action feature) proved appropriate.

The problem to be solved is to find an Euler path in an undirected graph. Our solution provides for separate processes residing at the nodes of the graph and for the interaction between processes by means of atomic actions, via the edges of the graph. We describe first the program and then the proof in terms of invariants and termination conditions. Thus, in style (though not perhaps in elegance) our solution resembles work previously reported in [DIJ78] and in [DLM78].

The concept of an atomic action is vital to our proof insofar as we prove the invariants of the program by considering atomic actions in isolation from each other. The special property of atomic actions which allows us to consider them as separate units is that all executions of atomic actions are required to be interference-free. The reader is referred to [BES80] for a formal characterisation of interference-freeness in terms of occurrence graphs. For the purposes of the present paper we take it that atomic actions occur interference-freely and can therefore be treated as separate units in the proof.

We now describe the problem in detail. We consider an undirected, connected graph with N vertices and M edges. We use as an example the following graph in which N=4 and M=5:

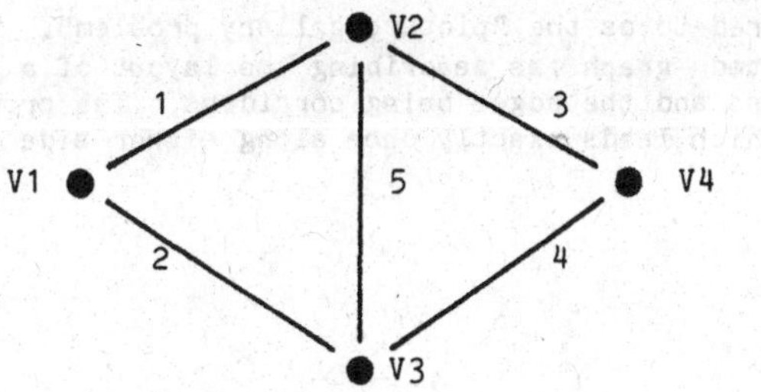

Figure 1

For each undirected edge j ($1 \leq j \leq M$) we introduce two opposed directed edges j and -j:

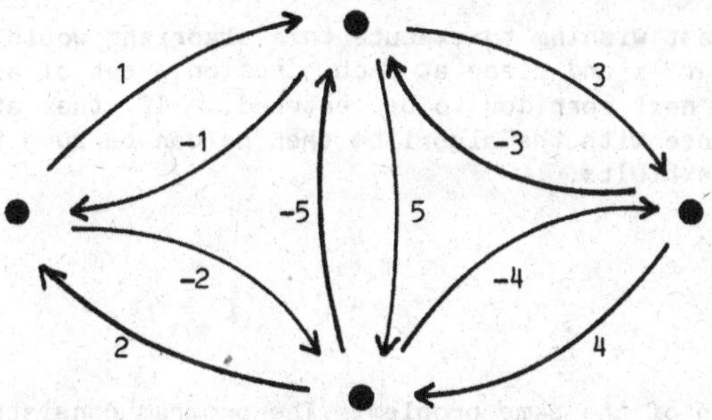

Figure 2

The problem is to find a single directed cycle which contains all directed edges, each edge exactly once; in other words, an Euler path. This problem is solvable because each vertex has the same number of incoming and outgoing edges. There are in general many possible solutions. The following Figure shows one possible solution for our example graph:

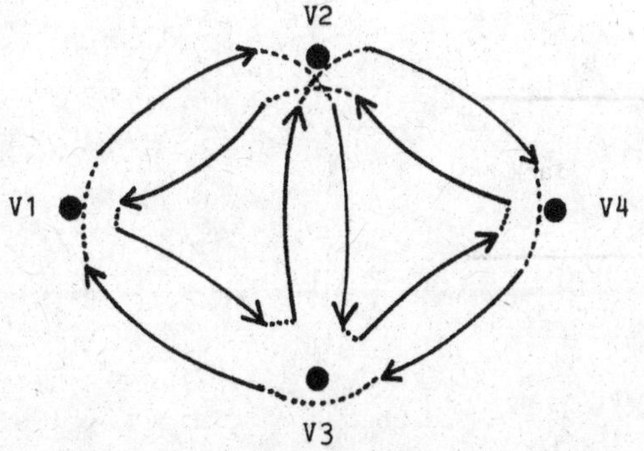

Figure 3

This problem has often been referred to as the "picture gallery problem". We can think of the underlying undirected graph as describing the layout of a picture gallery, the vertices being junctions and the edges being corridors. The problem is to find a route for the visitors which leads exactly once along either side of each corridor.

2 Sequential Solution

In [ORE62] a sequential solution is described as follows: "Beginning at an arbitrary vertex one follows a path, marking each edge as one passes with the direction in which it has been traversed. When one arrives at some vertex for the first time the entering edge is marked especially. When one reaches a vertex one always follows next an edge which either has not previously been traversed, or, if it has, then only in the opposite direction. However, the entering edge should be followed only as a last resort when there are no other edges available".

In a picture gallery, an attendant wishing to execute this algorithm would have to choose an arbitrary initial vertex and place at each junction a set of signposts which indicate to the visitor the next corridor to be entered. If the attendant sets these signposts in accordance with the algorithm then he can be sure that the visitors will be able to see all exhibits.

3 Concurrent Solution

We present a concurrent solution of the same problem. The program consists of N components, one for each vertex. We first describe the algorithm informally and thereafter we give the program.

Assume that there is an attendant at each junction of the picture gallery. Each attendant is responsible for the placing of the signposts at his junction. He may use the light in the corridors to signal the fact that visitors might come along a corridor. Initially all corridors are dark. An attendant waits for some corridor leading to his junction to light up. Then he undertakes some action. Given, for example, the following situation:

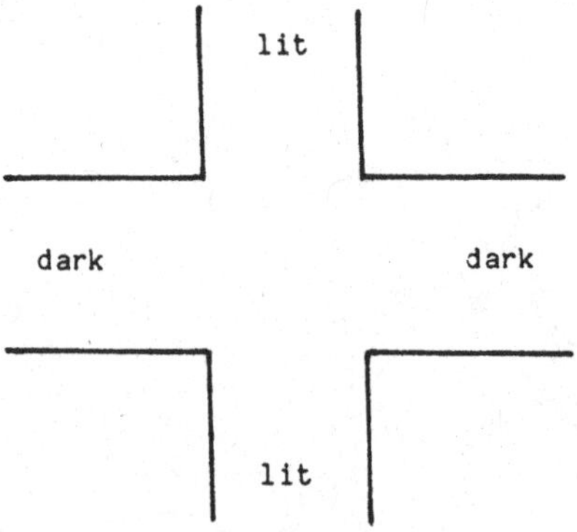

Figure 4

In our solution the attendant responsible for this junction arbitrarily selects a lit corridor and assumes that the visitors are going to enter his junction from this corridor. He considers it to be his task to lead them back into the same corridor after having exhausted all dark corridors.

Suppose that he selects the bottom corridor of Figure 4. He then places his signposts so that the visitors are led to the two dark corridors but also so that any visitors coming through the other lit corridor are immediately turned back. Of course, he has himself to light up the two previously dark corridors:

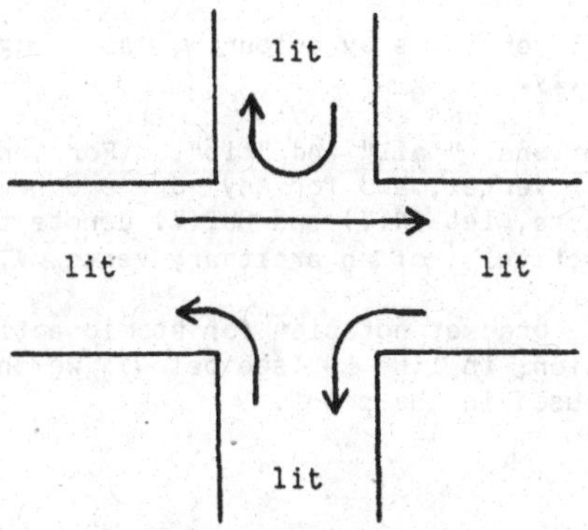

Figure 5

We now give the program implementing this strategy. We assume that initially there is a special corridor, say the "entrance", which is lit already. The entrance is represented by an edge dangling at an arbitrary vertex. We shall also define a function "suc" which gives for each directed edge its successor edge. Thus, suc is a permutation (a bijection) on the set of directed edges. The cycle which will be a result of the program will be contained in suc. Initially we assume that suc contains the adjacent edges of a vertex in some cyclic order. Thus, suc contains implicitly the incidence matrix of the graph.

Let us, for example, assume that the "entrance" edge is appended to the vertex V2. A possible initial configuration is shown in Figure 6 where the function suc is represented by dotted lines:

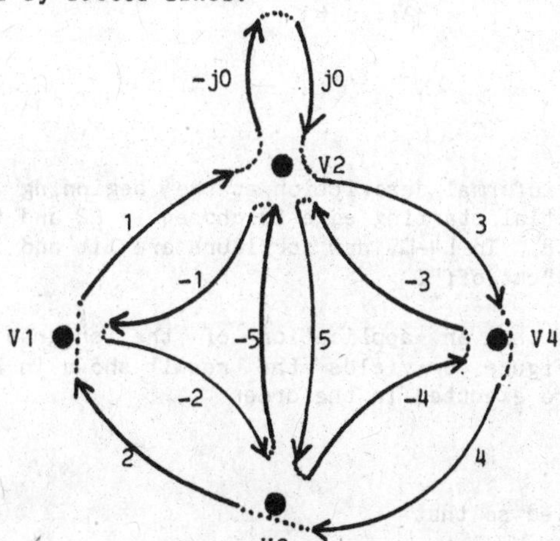

Figure 6 (an initial configuration)

We use the fixed names j0 and -j0 for the two directed edges corresponding to the "entrance". The suc of an incoming edge of a vertex gives the next outgoing edge of that vertex. For example, suc(j0)=3, suc(-3)=5, suc(-5)=-1 and suc(1)=-j0 enumerates all edges incident to V2.

The "lighting" of a corridor will be represented by the colouring of the edges. We define a function

col: edges --> {B,W}

and represent the initial darkness of all corridors by colouring all edges black; that is, col(e)=B for all edges e initially.

We introduce two further constant functions, "tail" and "tip". For any edge e other than j0, tail(e) denotes its tail vertex, and for any edge e other than -j0, tip(e) denotes its tip vertex. Furthermore, let IN(V) and OUT(V) denote the sets of incoming edges and outgoing edges, respectively, of an arbitrary vertex V.

We now give the program using the angle bracket notation for atomic actions. Each component contains only one atomic action, in line L4 (see below); we shall see in section 4 how this atomic action can be used in the proof.

<u>Initialisation</u>:

```
        col(j0) := W;
```

<u>Vertex V</u>:

```
L1      await ∃ f∈IN(V): col(f)=W then
L2      begin "choose an arbitrary f∈IN(V) with col(f)=W";
                  {f is a local constant}
L3            j1:=f; j2:=suc(j1);
                  {j1,j2 are local variables}
L4            do j2≠-f --> if <col(-j2)=B --> col(j2):=W>;
L5                                             j1:=-j2;
                                                 j2:=suc(j1);
L6                           [] col(-j2)=W --> suc(j1):=suc(-j2);
L7                                             suc(-j2):=j2;
L8                                             j2:=suc(j1)
                             fi
              od
        end.
```

This algorithm corresponds to the informal description at the beginning of this section. At each vertex, an initial starting edge is chosen in L2 and the other adjacent edges are traversed in L3-L8. In L4-L5 new corridors are lit and in L6-L8, corridors which are already lit are "cut off".

The reader is encouraged to verify that an application of the program to the initial configuration shown in Figure 6 yields the result shown in Figure 7, provided that the vertex programs are executed in the order

V2;V3;V1;V4

and the choices in line L2 are settled so that

f[V2]=j0, f[V3]=5, f[V1]=2, f[V4]=-4.

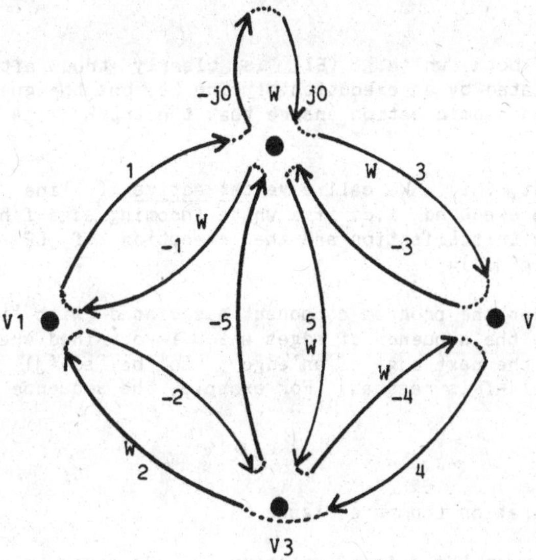

Figure 7 (a final configuration)

4 Proof of the Concurrent Solution

It would be nice to devise the proof in such a way that it reflects the structure of the program, i.e. its being partitioned into N component programs co-ordinated via the atomic action in line L4. This is what we shall attempt to do in this section.

Notice the regularities within a vertex program. For example, f denotes a constant incoming white edge of V (line L2), and j1, j2 and -j2 always point to an incoming, outgoing and incoming edge of V, respectively. Thus individual program components access the "suc" just of incoming rather than of outgoing edges (lines L5-L8). Hence the variable suc can be partitioned into local parts so that programs are disjoint over suc. Two programs may exclude each other over the variable "col" in line L4. Nevertheless, each program no more than reads the colour of an <u>incoming</u> edge and changes the colour of an <u>outgoing</u> edge. Notice also that an edge, once white remains white.

Hopefully these regularities can be exploited in the proof. Our plan for the proof is the following. For each program component we establish a separate invariant, (LI), which can be proved locally. For each possible program interaction, i.e. for each edge, we establish another invariant, (EI). Finally we prove a global invariant, (GI), which captures the global behaviour of the program. From the invariants we derive appropriate termination conditions. Our ultimate goal is to prove the following termination condition:

(T) $\forall e,e' \in E: e \leq e'$,

where E denotes the set of edges and $e \leq e'$ if e=e' or if there is a suc-chain from e to e', i.e. if e' = suc(...suc(e)...).

We start with the edge invariant (EI) because it is the simplest one and because we need it in the proof of the local invariant.

(EI) $\forall$e ∈ E: col(e) = B or col(-e) = B.

In words, no two opposite edges are both white. (EI) is clearly true after initialisation. It could only be violated by an execution of line L4, but the guard "col(-j2)=B" and the fact that L4 is an atomic action ensure that the truth of L4 is preserved.

Let us now define the local invariant, (LI). We call a vertex active if line L2 of its associated program has been executed, i.e. if a white incoming edge f has been fixed. In our example, after the initialisation and the execution of L2 of tip(j0) the latter is active with f[tip(j0)]=j0.

We fix an active vertex V and consider the program component associated with it. We define the orbit around V to be the sequence of edges which is obtained when, starting with the edge f, one defines the next edge of an edge j to be suc(j) if j ∈ IN(V) and -j if j ∈ OUT(V), until -f is reached. For example, the sequence of edges

(j0,3,-3,5,-5,-1,1,-j0)

is the orbit of tip(j0) after initialisation (compare Figure 6).

During the execution of a vertex program the pair of pointers (j1,j2) moves along the orbit from f=j1 initially to j2=-f finally, so that at all times the relation j2=suc(j1) is maintained. During the execution the orbit may change but j1 and j2 are always part of it. Thus the orbit has the general invariant form

(f,...,j1,j2,...,-f)

which includes the special cases f=j1 and j2=-f. For our local invariant we split the orbit into two disjoint subsequences, (f,...,j1) and (j2,...,-f), and we prove two separate invariants, (LI1) and (LI2), one for each subsequence.

(LI1) $\forall$e ∈ OUT(V): col(e)=W <=> e is in (f,...,j1)
(LI2) $\forall$e ∈ OUT(V): col(e)=B <=> e is in (j2,...,-f) or e=suc(-e).

(LI1) states that the first part of the orbit contains exactly all white outgoing edges of V (and their opposites). (LI2) states that black outgoing edges e either are in the second part of the orbit, or satisfy e=suc(-e); and vice versa.

Before commencing the proof of the invariants (LI1) and (LI2) we remark that it is indeed possible to prove them locally: no outside interference can affect their truth. For the orbit is defined in terms of the "suc" of incoming edges and the invariants mention the colouring of outgoing edges. As we have seen at the beginning of this section, both can be changed only locally.

(LI1) is clearly true initially: there are no white outgoing edges when f=j1. On the other hand, (LI2) is also satisfied initially because we have defined our initial configuration such that all outgoing edges and their opposites are in the orbit.

In order to prove the invariance of (LI1) and (LI2) we take advantage of the fact that they can be proved locally. Let us first consider lines L4-L5. While L4 may temporarily destroy the validity of both (LI1) and (LI2), L5 immediately restores their validity (we do not even need the guard of L4 in order to see this). Because of the locality property we are justified in regarding L4-L5 as a single "local atomic action" and it suffices to establish the invariance of (LI1) and (LI2) over L4-L5 as a whole.

The same is true for L6-L8. L6-L8 have the overall effect of transforming the orbit as follows:

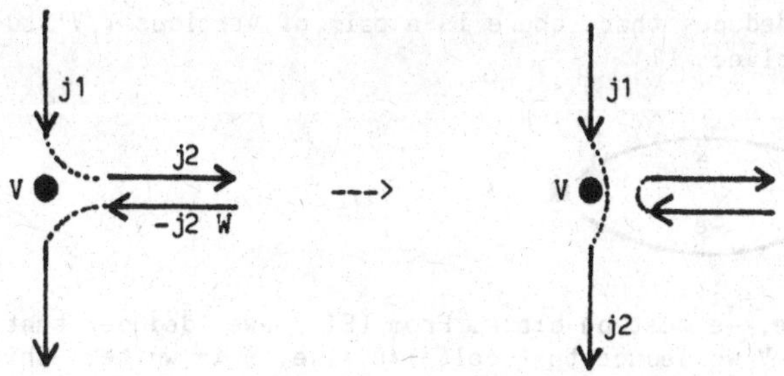

i.e. to "cut off" a white incoming edge. The guard of L6 in conjunction with (EI) implies that col(j2)=B and because L7 establishes j2=suc(-j2), i.e. the last term of (LI2), the truth of both (LI1) and (LI2) is preserved by L6-L8 as a whole. This completes the proof of the invariance of (LI1) and (LI2).

From (LI1), (LI2) and the loop termination condition "j2=-f" we can derive the following two local termination conditions:

(LT1) $\forall$e ∈ OUT(V): col(e)=W <=> e≠-f <u>and</u> e is in the orbit of V
(LT2) $\forall$e ∈ OUT(V): col(e)=B <=> e=-f <u>or</u> e=suc(-e).

Finally we define the global invariant (GI). Again we split (GI) into two parts, (GI1) and (GI2). Note that (LI) and (LT) are only defined for active vertices. Thus we have to prove that on termination all vertices are active. We use (GI1) for this purpose. In (GI2) we capture the fact that vertices become activated in a tree-like fashion.

We introduce an <u>activation ordering</u> of vertices by calling a vertex V an <u>activator</u> of another vertex V' if there is an edge e ∈ OUT(V) with e=f[V']. We call a vertex V an <u>ancestor</u> of V' (or V' a <u>descendant</u> of V) if either V=V' or V precedes V' in the activation ordering.

We prove the truth of

(GI1) Either all vertices are active or there are two neighbouring vertices one of which is active while the other is not.
(GI2) The set of active vertices and the activation ordering form a directed tree with root tip(j0).

(GI1) and (GI2) are both true after the initialisation, and both remain true because the graph is connected and because f is a local constant.

Next we show that upon termination (GI1) and (GI2) respectively reduce to the following:

(GT1) All vertices are active.
(GT2) The set of vertices and the activation ordering form a directed tree with root tip(j0).

(GT2) follows immediately from (GI2) and (GT1). For the purpose of proving (GT1) we found it necessary to establish a further edge invariant, (EI'):

(EI') $\forall$e ∈ E: if tail(e) is active and e=suc(-e) then col(-e)=W.

(EI') is true upon activation of tail(e) and it remains true because of the guard of L6 and because an edge, once white remains white.

To prove (GT1), suppose that not all of the vertices are active upon termination.

Then from (GI1) we deduce that there is a pair of vertices V,V' such that V is active and V' is not active:

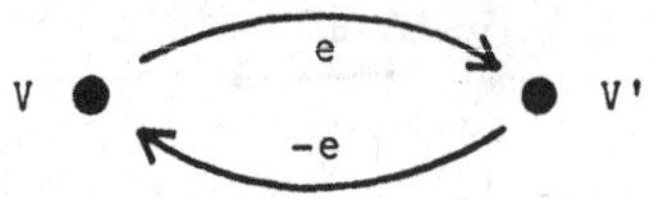

Because V' is not active, -e must be black. From (EI') we deduce that e≠suc(-e). From (LT2) applied to V we deduce that col(e)≠B, i.e. e is white. This means that the condition in line L1 is satisfied for V' and that V' will become active after a while (assuming, of course, finite delay once the condition is satisfied). This proves (GT1).

We can now also prove the following edge termination condition:

(ET) $\forall$e: col(e)=B <=> col(-e)=W.

For suppose there is a pair (e,-e) of black edges on termination. Then (LT2) applied to both tail(e) and tip(e) (both are active according to (GT1)!) implies suc(e)=-e and suc(-e)=e which is excluded by (EI'). (ET) then follows from (EI).

We prove (T) using (LT), (GT) and (ET). First we state (T) in a form which makes it more amenable to an induction argument:

(T') For any vertex V there is a suc-chain from f[V] to -f[V] which leads through all white outgoing edges of all descendants of V, and their opposites.

(T) follows immediately from (T'), (GT) and (ET). For consider (T') in the special case V=tip(j0). By (GT), all vertices are descendants of V and by (ET), all edges are included in the suc-chain from j0 to -j0 which exists by (T').

We prove (T') by induction over the activation tree.

Base: Consider a leaf vertex V. This means that no outgoing white edge e of V equals f[tip(e)]. By (EI) we have col(-e)=B for such edges, and by (LT2) applied to tip(e), suc(e)=-e. Hence the orbit of V is a suc-chain from f[V] to -f[V] which by (LT1) contains all white outgoing edges and, by definition, also their opposites.

Induction step: Consider an arbitrary vertex V. If a white outgoing edge equals f[tip(e)] then we can apply the induction hypothesis. Otherwise we apply the same argument as above.

5 Performance Considerations

Both for the sequential program of section 2 and the concurrent program of section 3 we shall estimate the execution times, Tseq and Tcon, respectively, relative to the number of vertices N and the number of edges M. Note first that

$$N-1 \leq M \leq N(N-1)/2$$

because the graph is connected. In other words, M varies from being of the order of N to being of the order of N^2, or

$$O(N) \leq M \leq O(N^2).$$

The execution time of the sequential program is linear in M because each edge is traversed twice. Hence

$Tseq = O(M)$ and $O(N) \leq Tseq \leq O(N^2)$.

For the execution time of the concurrent algorithm we have to make some intermediate estimates. Since each vertex program consists of two parts, a delay and an actual execution, we have to estimate (1) the average execution time t, (2) the average delay time d and (3) the total average time of a vertex program.

(1) $t = O(M/N)$ because t varies as A, the average number of edges adjacent to a vertex, and $A = 2M/N$.

(2) d depends on D, the average distance between two vertices of the graph. D is not independent of A; it is suggested that the product DA varies at most as N. Each vertex program has to wait until, on the average, each other vertex on the shortest path starting with the initial vertex has completed half a turn. Therefore d varies as DA/2, that is, $d \leq O(N)$.

(3) The average total time of a vertex program, <u>Tave</u>, is the sum of d and t, i.e.

$$Tave = d + t \leq O(N + M/N),$$

in which the first term is dominant, i.e.

$$Tave \leq O(N).$$

Tave gives the time we have to wait from starting the program until completion of an average vertex program, and this time varies linearly with N (the influence of M is balanced out between d and t). Because maximal distances in a graph also vary as N/A, this is also the time we have to wait until <u>all</u> vertex programs are completed. In other words:

$$Tcon = O(Tave) \leq O(N).$$

That is, concurrency gives us an algorithm which is time-linear in N rather than in M. Thus the algorithm represents a speed up by a factor of up to N if of the order of N processors rather than a single one are used.

Finally we estimate the time needed by a sequential simulation of the concurrent program, <u>Tsim</u>. We could simulate the program by maintaining a queue of vertices, the head of the queue indicating which vertex program is to be executed next. The time taken would then be the time taken by going round each vertex once, i.e.

$$Tsim = O(NA) = O(M).$$

Thus a sequential simulation of the concurrent program takes roughly the same time as the sequential program. In other words, the concurrent program is not by any reasonable standard significantly slower than the sequential program. In the remainder of this section we shall show that the former is however more general than the latter.

Consider the cycle shown in Figure 7 and notice that it could not have been generated by the sequential algorithm given in section 2, due to the two "loops" at both vertex V1 and V4. On the other hand it is easy to see that for each application of the sequential algorithm there is an initial configuration and application of the concurrent algorithm resulting in the same cycle.

Thus the concurrent program is more general than the sequential one. On the other hand it is not fully general. For example, the cycle shown in Figure 3 cannot be generated by the concurrent program, whatever the initial configuration (and a fortiori, neither by the sequential program). This is because the concurrent program necessarily generates a certain number of edges e with suc(e)=-e but there are no such edges in Figure 3.

6 Concluding Remarks

The author is aware that neither the proof presented in section 4 nor its justification are overwhelmingly elegant and can most certainly be improved. Perhaps it is even possible to generalise the program simultaneously, so that cycles such as the one shown in Figure 3 are included as potential results of the algorithm. However, even though the proof is lenghty and inelegant, the author would not consider it too complicated. Rather, it appears that the pattern of the proof quite naturally matches the pattern of the program and that its length is simply due to the fact that it captures various details not "visible" in the program but certainly intended by the programmer. The proof should thus be regarded as a welcome complementary explanation of the program. Considering the inherent complexity of even modest concurrent programs, it is very likely that such proofs will increasingly become a necessity of programming.

As to the language used, the author believes that the provision of guarded commands with atomic actions is well worth further consideration. It can be hoped that the semantics of such a concurrent language can be formally defined along the lines of the predicate transformer formalism of [DIJ76]. Indeed, the idea behind this formalism is to associate with each program a function describing its input/output behaviour. Since, as the author has argued in [BES80], atomic actions are just those portions of a program which admit such a characterisation in input/output terms, it may be possible to adapt the predicate transformer formalism accordingly.

Such a language seems attractive from a practical point of view, not just because "nice" parallel programs have been written in it. Also, being a means of structuring the actions (as opposed to the data) of a program, the atomic action feature suggests itself for the purposes of program structuring and program proving, as has been seen above.

In the experimental language we used, atomic actions are "divorced" from the "wait" command, in contradistinction to some earlier proposals (for example, the "await" clause of [OWG76]). It seems natural to separate these two different concepts: sometimes one does not wish to care which one of two competing atomic actions "occurs first". Again, a case in point is the above program.

Structuring by means of atomic actions should, in the opinion of the author, be thought of as complementary to structuring by means of variables. Contrary to the assumption of [DLM78], the author believes that atomic actions should be allowed to be nested. However the author has not yet experienced a case in which the nesting of atomic actions is actually necessary. A more thorough discussion of such matters is beyond the scope of this paper which has been written in the first place as a contribution to our basic experience with concurrent programming.

Acknowledgements

The proof presented in section 4 is a result of the joint efforts of Graham Wood and the author. This research has been supported by the Science Research Council of Great Britain.

References

[BES80] Best, E.: Atomicity of Activities. In: Proceedings of the Advanced Course in General Net Theory, Springer Lecture Notes in Computer Science, to appear in 1980.

[DIJ76] Dijkstra, E.W.: A Discipline of Programming. Prentice Hall 1976.

[DIJ78] Dijkstra, E.W.: Finding the Correctness Proof of a Concurrent Program. Proc. of the Koninklijke Nederlandse Akademie van Wetenschappen, Amsterdam, Series A, Vol. 81(2), June 1978.

[DLM78] Dijkstra, E.W., Lamport, L., Martin, A.J., Scholten, C.S. and Steffens, E.F.M.: On-the-Fly Garbage Collection: An Exercise in Co-operation. CACM 21/11, November 1978, pp. 966-975.

[ORE62] Ore, O.: Theory of Graphs. American Mathematical Society, Colloquium Publications, Vol. XXXVIII, Rhode Island 1962.

[OWG76] Owicki, S. and Gries, D.: An Axiomatic Proof Technique for Parallel Programs I. Acta Informatica 6/1976, pp. 319-340.

A THEORETICAL BASIS FOR THE SYSTEMATIC PROOF METHOD

Wolfgang Bibel
Technische Universität München

Abstract. All redundancies are removed from derivations in a Gentzen-like formal system of first-order logic. The resulting skeleton derivations are characterized in terms of the formulas to be derived. This provides the formal basis for a powerful proof procedure developed earlier by the author.

INTRODUCTION. Much evidence has been accumulated in the last few years that automated theorem proving (ATP) has applications far beyond of mathematics, its original field of interest. In particular, it has become obvious that a powerful theorem proving system of some kind is of crucial importance for a further automation of the program construction process, both from a theoretical [22;13;18;etc.] as well as a more practical point of view [17;8;etc.].

More than ten years ago the author began to develop a general theorem proving method. It was called the *systematic* method since the proof search is done in a more systematic, less redundant way than in the popular resolution methods. It may be characterized mainly by the following six distinguished features.
(i) A minimal number of instances of the given set F of (generalized) clauses has to be considered (for any "spanning set of connections"), in order to obtain a proof.
(ii) No transformation into any normal form of the given formula F is required (hence full use of antiprenexing can be built in easily, e.g.).
(iii) No Skolem functions are required, i.e. only the terms originally in F have to be unified (in a special way).
(iv) The proof search is performed on the given formula (rather than on thousands of mostly redundant clauses).
(v) No factoring is required.
(vi) A detected proof can easily be transformed into a natural, immediately comprehensible deduction of F.

Since there exists only a preliminary [3] and a more informal [9] description the purpose of the present paper is the development of a mathematically rigorous, formal basis for this method. Specifically, the first two sections provide the definitions w.r.t. the formal system by which the notion of a theorem is characterized. It is derived from Schütte's [24], hence from Gentzen's [12] system for first-order logic, tailored to the needs of theorem proving. Any derivation in such a system is a terribly redundant construct. In section 3 all that redundancy is eliminated providing the concept of a *skeleton* (derivation). It is amazing how little one needs in order to uniquely determine a derivation modulo certain irrelevancies (cf. the figures 2 and 7!) It is then easy to characterize skeletons, encoding derivations of a given formula F, in terms of F which provides the main results (4.2 - 4.4) of this paper and the basis from which a proof procedure as that described in [9] can be easily obtained (see section 4).

However, the results are subject to the following two restrictions. Function symbols are allowed of arity zero only. This restriction does not at all affect the essence of the method; it can be easily removed as described in section 5 and, hopefully, makes the paper more easily readable. The second restriction to theorems of *degree* 1 [3;9] is not really a restriction from a theoretical point of view (see the well-known result of lemma 2.3). It is relevant from a practical point of view, however, since (2.3) again introduces redundancy. The generalization to arbitrary degrees without recourse to (2.3) is postponed to a future paper and is indicated only briefly in section 5. It will result in a general proof procedure potentially matched by none of the popular methods w.r.t. efficiency, according to the arguments given in section 5. For the expert the features (i) through (v) by themselves should already indicate an extremely powerful method.

Earlier and closely related (but, of course, less advanced) work was carried out by Prawitz [20], Maslow [19], and Herbrand [14]. More recently, Andrews has developed his method of general matings [1;2] which upon closer inspection reveals many similarities with the systematic method although it has not the features (i) and (iii) above and sofar is subject to the second restriction as well. In fact, to the best knowledge of this author feature (i), which is a consequence of the special notion "unifiable" in this paper (see 4.1.iii), is accomplished by no other existing method. W.r.t. the resolution methods it has been shown in [6;7] that they can be easily modelled in the author's approach and thus are not so different, after all (but more redundant and less "systematic").

1. THE LANGUAGE. This section introduces the formulas, their structure, paths, and (spanning) sets of connections.

The first-order language is built upon an alphabet consisting of a denumerable set V of *variables* (denoted by $x,y,z,\ldots$), a denumerable set C of (functional) *constants* (denoted by $a,b,c,\ldots$), a denumerable set P of *predicate symbols* (denoted by $P,Q,R,\ldots$), the logical symbols $\neg,\wedge,\vee,\forall,\exists$, and of the comma and parentheses. The notations (including $\wedge,\vee$) are also used with indices. Each constant c, or predicate P, has an arity $\alpha(c)\geq 0$, or $\alpha(P)\geq 0$.

The set T of *terms* (denoted by $s,t,\ldots$) includes V and with any n terms $t_1,\ldots,t_n$ also the term $at_1\ldots t_n$ for any constant with $n=\alpha(a)$.

1.1.D.*) Inductive definition of the set F of *formulas* (denoted by $F,G,\ldots$) and of their *formula trees*.

a. $Pt_1\ldots t_n$ and $\neg Pt_1\ldots t_n$ (for $n=\alpha(P)$) are literals (denoted by $K,L,\ldots$), the simplest kind of formulas. Their formula tree consists of a single node labelled with the literal.

b. If F is a formula, and if $\mathbb{X}$ denotes $\forall$ or $\exists$, and $z_1,\ldots,z_n$, $n\geq 1$, de-

---

*) D.,T.,L.,C. abbreviate Definition, Theorem, Lemma, Corollary.

note (pairwise different) constants of arity zero or variables, resp., which do not occur bounded in F, then $\mathbb{X} z_1 \ldots z_n F$ is a formula in which the $z_1,\ldots,z_n$ are called *bounded* and for which the formula tree consists of a new node labelled with $z_1,\ldots,z_n$ and the formula tree of F as its subtree.

c. If $F_1,\ldots,F_m$, $m \geq 2$, are formulas with pairwise disjoint sets of bounded constants and variables, and with no *free* i.e. non-bounded, constant or variable in F_i occurring bounded in F_j, $1 \leq i,j \leq m$, further if $*$ denotes $\wedge$ or $\vee$ then $*(F_1,\ldots,F_m)$ is a formula, and its formula tree consists of a new node k (as root) labelled with $*$ and the formula trees of $F_1,\ldots,F_m$ is subtrees of k. $\square$

Apparently, this is the usual concept of a formula except for some minor variations which provide technical improvements. For example, $\wedge$ and $\vee$ are allowed to bind more than 2 arguments and are used in prefix notation (but for sake of readability infix notation will often be used as well). Also, negation is allowed only (once) in literals since it can easily be defined by $\neg F := \bar{F}$, where $\bar{F}$ is obtained from F by substituting $Pt_1 \ldots t_n, \neg Pt_1 \ldots t_n, \wedge, \vee, \forall, \exists, c$, and x by $\neg Pt_1 \ldots t_n$, $Pt_1 \ldots t_n, \vee, \wedge, \exists, \forall, x$, and c, respectively (with a little care for x,c which stand for bounded variables and constants). $\rightarrow$, $\leftrightarrow$, etc. can then be defined as usual.

Since there is an obvious 1-1-correspondence between formulas and their trees, they will not be distinguished carefully. The tree-ordering, denoted by $<_F$ or shortly $<$, among the nodes in the tree (root $<$ any other node) or among correspondent positions in the formula induces an ordering relation among occurrences of conjunction and disjunction symbols, of bounded constants and variables, and of literals which will also be denoted by $<_F$ or $<$. For example, $<$ for the formula $\forall a(\exists x(Pax \vee \neg Qa) \wedge R \wedge \exists yz(Pyz \wedge Qa))$ is illustrated in figure 1.

Where required, an arbitrary denotation of the nodes in such a formula tree, hence of positions in the formula, is assumed. If k denotes such a position in a formula F then Huet's notation $F_{|k}$ is used [16] to denote the *subformula* in F at position k (which is represented by the subtree with root k). E.g., if the nodes labelled by $Pax, \neg Qa, yz$ in the tree of formula F in figure 1 are denoted by $k = 1,2,3$, then $F_{|k}$ is Pax, $\neg Qa$, $\exists yz(Pyz \wedge Qa)$, respectively.

1.2.D. For a formula F a *path* p through F is a set of such positions in F defined inductively as follows, according to the structure of F.

a. For a literal at position k the path is $\{k\}$.

b. For a formula $\vee(F_1,\ldots,F_n)$ and for any path p_i through F_i, $i = 1,\ldots,n$, $\bigcup_{i=1}^{n} p_i$ is a path through F.

c. For a formula $\wedge(F_1,\ldots,F_n)$ any path through F_i is a path through F, $i = 1,\ldots,n$.

d. For a formula $\mathbb{X} z_1 \ldots z_n F_o$ any path through F_o is a path through F.

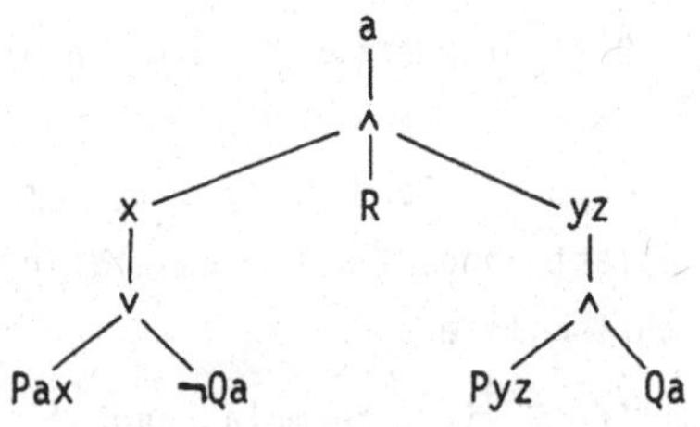

Figure 1. A formula tree

Any such path p determines a set $\tilde{p}$ of literals given by $\{L | L = F_{|k}$ for some $k \in p\}$ which also will be called a *path* through F. ▯

This definition generalizes the concept, which has been introduced formally for propositional logic in [5, definition 1.3]. The only paths through the formula of figure 1 are {Pax,¬Qa}, {R}, {Pyz}, {Qa}.

1.3.D. A *connection* in F is an unordered pair (k,k') of positions k,k' in F such that $F_{|k} = Pt_1 \ldots t_n$ and $F_{|k'} = \neg Pt'_1 \ldots t'_n$. Again, also the unordered pair $(Pt_1 \ldots t_n, \neg Pt'_1 \ldots t'_n)$ will be called a *connection*. A set A of connections in F is called *spanning* if each path through F *contains* a connection from A, i.e. two literals $Pt_1 \ldots t_n$, $\neg Pt'_1 \ldots t'_n$ such that $(Pt_1 \ldots t_n, \neg Pt'_1 \ldots t'_n) \in A$. ▯

For the "ground case", i.e. for formulas F without any quantifiers and variables, it is easy to see that F is tautology iff there exists a spanning set of connections in F [6,theorem 1.3 and lemma 2.2]. This syntactic characterization of the set of valid formulas does not require any rewriting of (parts of) the given formula as all other syntactic methods (like resolution or inverse Gentzen-systems, etc.) do. Hence, a proof method based on this characterization should be less redundant. In fact, for such a method, which has been described in [9;4] and slightly improved in [7], it is proved in [7] that it is less redundant and consequently more efficient than other popular methods.

If one could "lift" this result to the first-order level without sacrificing its essential point ("no rewriting required") then an even more significant improvement might be expected since the ground case (inherent in the general case) is but one source of redundancy among others. This paper solves exactly this for a restricted first-order level.

2. THE FORMAL SYSTEM.

This section introduces a formal system which characterizes the subset *S* of theorems in F.

2.1.D. Inductive definition of the *derivable* formulas or *theorems*, i.e. of a unary relation ⊢ (read "is derivable") on F, of the *derivation trees* and the *reduced derivation trees* for theorems. In the following the G_j are (possibly empty) formulas, $j = 1,2,3$, and all occurring formulas are assumed to be well-formed according to (1.1).

a. $\vdash G_1 \vee Pt_1 \ldots t_n \vee G_2 \vee \neg Pt_1 \ldots t_n \vee G_3$, the *axioms*. The (reduced) derivation tree consists of a single node labelled with the axiom (with the unordered pair (k,k')*) where k,k' denote the positions of $Pt_1 \ldots t_n$ and $\neg Pt_1 \ldots t_n$, resp., in the axiom).

b. If $\vdash G_1 \vee F_i \vee G_2$, $i = 1,\ldots,n$; then $\vdash G_1 \vee \wedge(F_1,\ldots,F_n) \vee G_2$. The (reduced) derivation tree consists of a new node k, as root, labelled with the *conclusion* (with ∧), and the (reduced) derivation trees of the *premises* as subtrees of k.

*) Of course, one could allow also more than one such pair as label.

c. If $\vdash G_1 \vee F \vee G_2$ then $\vdash G_1 \vee \forall c_1 \ldots c_n F \vee G_2$, where c_i must not occur in G_j, $i = 1,\ldots,n$, $j = 1,2$. The (reduced) derivation tree consists of a new node labelled with the conclusion (with $c_1 \ldots c_n$) and the (reduced) derivation tree of the premise as its subtree.

d. If $\vdash G_1 \vee \exists x_1 \ldots x_n F \vee F^{t_1 \ldots t_n}_{x_1 \ldots x_n} \vee G_2$ then $\vdash G_1 \vee \exists x_1 \ldots x_n F \vee G_2$, where $F^{t_1 \ldots t_n}_{x_1 \ldots x_n}$ denotes the formula obtained from F by substituting each occurrance of x_i by t_i, $i = 1,\ldots,n$. The (reduced) derivation tree consists of a new node labelled with the conclusion (with the substitutions $(x_1,t_1)\ldots(x_n,t_n)$) and the (reduced) derivation tree of the premise as its subtrees.

In the cases b,c,d it is assumed that the denotations of corresponding positions in the premise(s) and the conclusion are identical. ▯

This formal system of first-order logic differs only slightly from one developed by Schütte from Gentzen's system. Hence for its consistency and completeness the reader may be referred to [24] (or to [4]). From $\vdash$ a *restricted* relation $\vdash'$ is obtained by cancelling the subformula $\exists x_1 \ldots x_n F$ in the premise of (2.1.d). Figure 2 gives an example of a derivation tree in this restricted system for the formula $\forall abcd(\exists x(\exists y Payx \wedge \exists z Pbzx) \vee (\exists u \neg Puuc \wedge \exists v \neg Pvbd))$, abbreviated by T within this paper. Note that for the same derivation in the unrestricted system additional space of approximately 10 times the length of T would have been required. For comparison figure 3 shows the reduced derivation tree

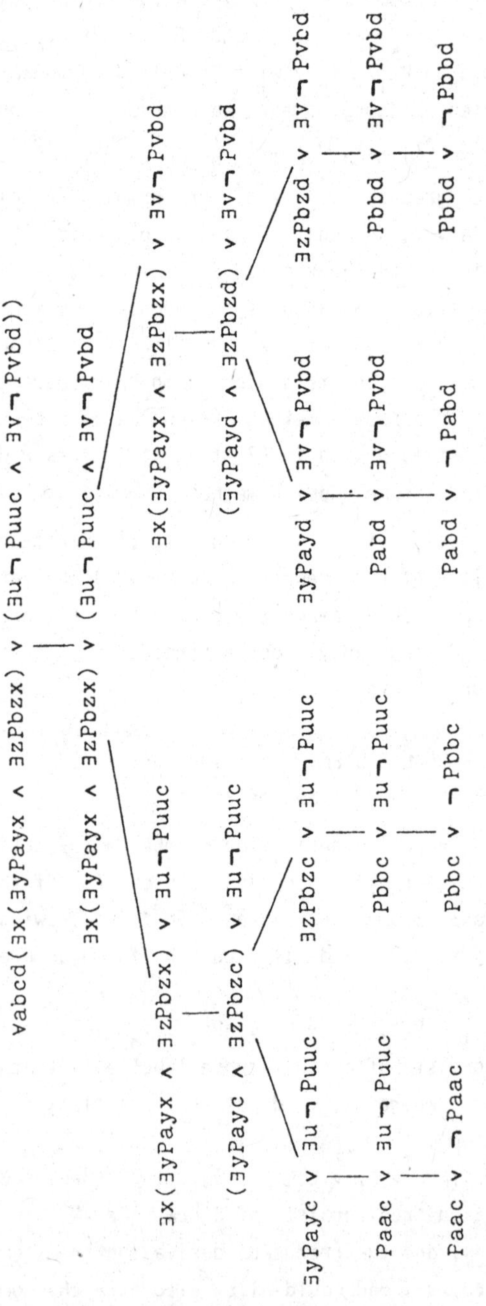

Figure 2. A derivation tree for theorem T (w.r.t. $\vdash'$)

for T which clearly is the same for both systems, in general. Yet, the following lemma notices that both concepts encode the same amount of information. Of course, logicians do not mind about such a redundancy, computer memory (and human patience) do, however.

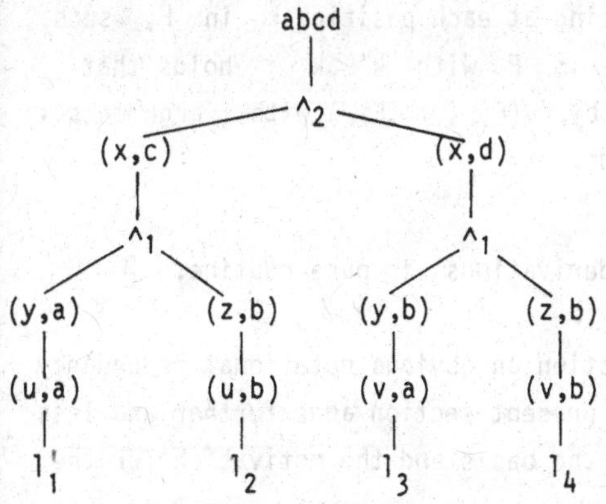

Figure 3. Reduced derivation tree for the theorem

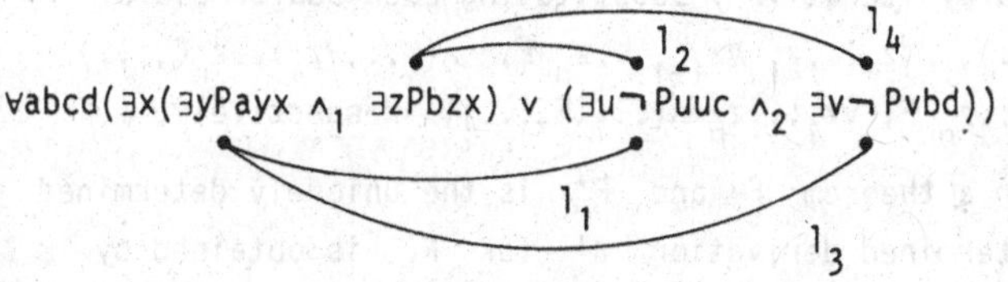

Definition (2.1) implicitly defines a function DERIV in an inductive way which relates a reduced derivation tree for a formula F with a (uniquely determined) derivation tree for F. The inverse of DERIV is not necessarily a function since an axiom may contain more than one pair of *complementary* [5] literals.

2.2.L. If Δ_F is a derivation tree for a theorem F and $\delta_F \in \mathrm{DERIV}^{-1}(\Delta_F)$ then $\mathrm{DERIV}(\delta_F) = \Delta_F$. DERIV can be computed in time linear in the *size* of (i.e. number of symbols in) Δ_F.

The proof (by induction on the *length* - i.e. the number of nodes in the longest branch - of Δ_F) follows immediately from (2.1). ▯

On the basis of this lemma we may assume from now on that "derivation tree", or shortly "derivation", means "reduced derivation tree" (if not explicitly stated otherwise). The tree-ordering, denoted by $<_\delta$, or shortly $<$, among the nodes in such a tree δ induces an ordering relation among occurrences of conjunction symbols, bounded constants, bounded variables (via the substitutions in which they occur), and connections from the derived theorem which will also be denoted by $<_\delta$ or $<$. For a derivation of T this is already illustrated in figure 3.

In the next section the discussion will be restricted to the restricted system $\vdash'$ with constants of arity zero only, for reasons mentioned in the introduction. The restriction to $\vdash'$ means that only theorems of *degree* ≤ 1 [3] are considered. In terms of this paper the *degree of a derivation* δ_F is the maximal number of occurrences of a variable in a branch of δ_F, where the maximum is taken over all branches of δ_F and all bounded variables in F. The *degree of a theorem* F is the minimum of the degrees of all derivations for F. $\vdash_i F$ is used to express that F is a theorem of degree i, $i \geq 0$. Obviously, $\vdash_1 = \vdash'$ and $\bigcup_{i=0}^{\infty} \vdash_i = \vdash$. Let

F^i be obtained from a formula F by substituting at each position k in F, such that (i) $F_{|k} = \exists x_1 \ldots x_n G$, and (ii) for no k' in F with $k' < k$ it holds that $F_{|k'} = \exists y_1 \ldots y_m G'$, the subformula $F_{|k}$ in F by $v(F_{|k}, \ldots, F_{|k})$ with i arguments. With these definitions the following lemma holds.

2.3.L. $\vdash_i F$ iff $\vdash' F^i$.
The proof (by induction on the lengths of the derivations) is pure routine. □

3. ELIMINATING REDUNDANCY. In the previous section an obvious notational redundancy has been eliminated from derivation trees. The present section adds further and less trivial steps in the same direction, providing the basis and the motivation for the main result of this paper.

In the first step, formulas and derivations will be normalized in the following sense. A formula F is *normalized* by iteratively substituting each subformula of the form $\ast(\ldots, \ast(F_{i+1}, \ldots, F_j), \ldots)$, $\forall\!\!\!\exists z_1 \ldots z_i \, \forall\!\!\!\exists z_{i+1} \ldots z_n \, F$, $\wedge(\ldots, \forall z_1 \ldots z_n F, \ldots)$ by $\ast(\ldots, F_{i+1}, \ldots, F_j, \ldots)$, $\forall\!\!\!\exists z_1 \ldots z_n \, F$, $\forall z_1 \ldots z_n \wedge(\ldots, F, \ldots)$, respectively.

3.1.L. If δ is a derivation for a theorem F and F' is the uniquely determined normalized F then a uniquely determined derivation δ' for F' is obtained by contracting or exchanging corresponding pairs of immediately succeeding nodes in an obvious way. The size of δ' is not greater than that of δ and the degrees are equal.
The proof (by induction on the length of δ) is trivial. □

A derivation δ of a theorem F is *normalized* by constructing δ' for the normalized F according to (3.1) and by iteratively substituting for each pair of immediately succeeding nodes $\S \prec \S'$ a single node labelled with $\S, \S'$ whenever $\S$ and $\S'$ both are conjunctions, constants, or variables, respectively. For example, the normalized version of the derivation in figure 3 is given in figure 4, which illustrates that normalization drops the unimportant information whether the derivation rules are applied, e.g., first to $\exists y \ldots$ and then to $\exists u \ldots$, or in opposite order; hence figure 4 in fact represents 16 different derivations.

This suggests defining an equivalence class $[\tilde{\delta}_F]_{\underset{\sim}{n}}$ of derivations of F for each normalized derivation $\tilde{\delta}_F$ of a normalized F; each member of $[\tilde{\delta}_F]_{\underset{\sim}{n}}$ is obtained from $\tilde{\delta}_F$ by substituting each node with more than one label set $\S_1, \ldots, \S_n$, $n \geq 2$, by a sequence $\S_{\pi 1} \prec \cdots \prec \S_{\pi n}$ of nodes, for some permutation π.

3.2.L. If $\tilde{\delta}_F$ is the uniquely determined normalized derivation obtained from δ_F then $\delta_F \in [\tilde{\delta}_F]_{\underset{\sim}{n}}$ and all members in $[\tilde{\delta}_F]_{\underset{\sim}{n}}$ are derivations of F having equal size and degree.
The proof (by induction on the length of $\tilde{\delta}_F$) is trivial.

For the rest of this section the discussion is now confined to the restricted system

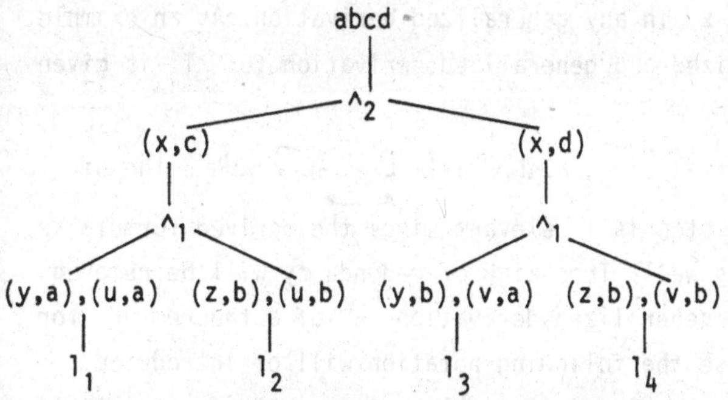

Figure 4. Normalized derivation for the theorem from figure 3

$\vdash'$ with constants of arity zero only. $\prec$, as we now know, encodes the information for any one out of a class of equivalent derivations for a theorem F; but it still does this in a redundant way since (i) the substitutions at "variable nodes" can be determined by the connections of the derivation (again with a completely irrelevant loss of information), (ii) in general the derivation contains irrelevant steps, and (iii) $\prec$ partially coincides with $<$. This is made more precise in the next three lemmas.

For a derivation δ_F of a theorem F the *generalized* derivation $\tilde{\delta}_F$ is obtained from δ_F by replacing any label (x,a) in δ_F by $(x,\sigma x)$ where the substitution σ is determined as follows. If $l_i = (P_i t_{i1} \ldots t_{in_i}, \neg P_i t'_{i1} \ldots t'_{in_i})$ denote exactly those connections in δ such that $x \prec l_i$, $i = 1,\ldots,m$, then σ is the *most general unifier* (e.g. see [21]), shortly mgu, of $\bigcup_{i=1}^{m} \bigcup_{j=1}^{n_i} \{<t_{ij}, t'_{ij}>\}$, the *unificand* of $\{l_1,\ldots,l_m\}$.

This again suggests to define an equivalence class $[\tilde{\delta}_F]_{\underset{\sim}{s}}$ of derivations of F for each generalized derivation $\tilde{\delta}_F$; each member of $[\tilde{\delta}_F]_{\underset{\sim}{s}}$ is obtained as follows and is called an *instance* of $\tilde{\delta}_F$. Let $y_1,\ldots,y_m$ denote those (pairwise different) variables such that (x,y_i) is in $\tilde{\delta}_F$ for some x. Then each label (x,y_i) is replaced by (x,b) for any constant b such that b is not a constant in F. See figure 5 for an example.

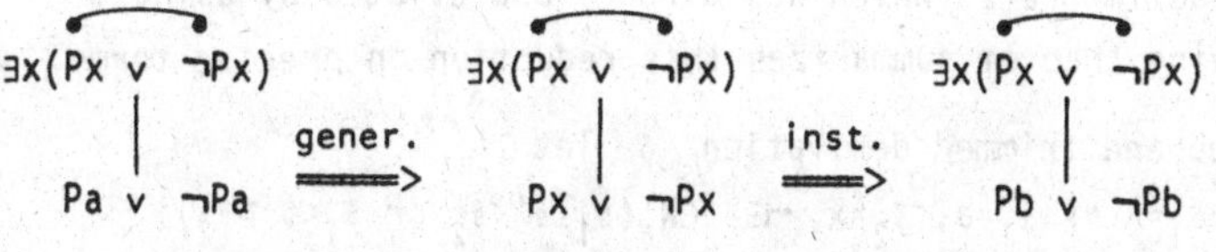

Figure 5. Generalization and instantiation of a derivation

3.3.L. If $\tilde{\delta}_F$ is the generalized derivation obtained from δ_F then $\delta_F \in [\tilde{\delta}_F]_{\underset{\sim}{s}}$ and all members in $[\tilde{\delta}_F]_{\underset{\sim}{s}}$ are derivations of F having equal size and degree. The proof (by induction on the length of δ_F) is obvious. (Note that the notion of an instance has to be extended for the induction to include the substitution of a variable x free in F by a constant b which does not occur in F.) □

According to this lemma the passage from a derivation δ_F to its generalized form $\tilde{\delta}_F$ implies only an irrelevant loss of information. Moreover, σ in any label $(x,\sigma x)$ in $\tilde{\delta}_F$ is uniquely determined by F and $\prec$. Hence, $(x,\sigma x)$ can be re-

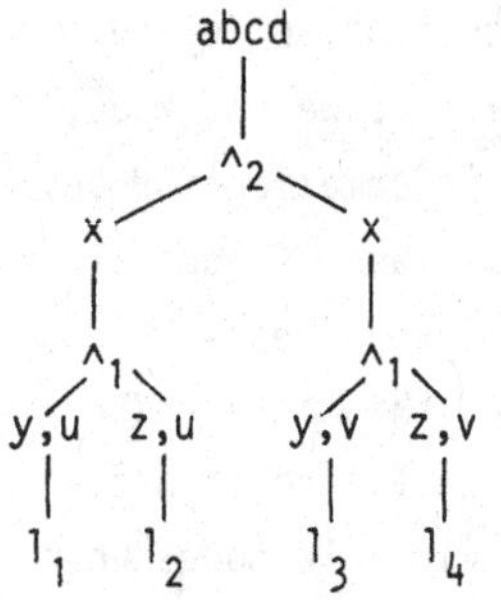

Figure 6. Normalized and generalized derivation of the theorem from figure 3

placed by x in any generalized derivation. As an example, the normalized and generalized derivation for T is given in figure 6.

In the derivation $L \vee \neg L \vee Pa \vdash L \vee \neg L \vee \forall a Pa$ the single derivation step is irrelevant since the derived formula is an axiom as well. This kind of redundancy will be removed now. For a generalized derivation δ of a theorem F for that purpose the following notation will be introduced. S_δ, or simply S, denotes the spanning set of connections. W_δ, or simply W, denotes the set of occurrences of labels in δ which are not connections. W_F denotes the set of occurrences of labels in the formula tree F which are not literals or disjunction symbols. $W_\delta \subseteq W_F$ holds when the positions are disregarded (an inaccuracy which is dissolved by the context and which allows simplified notation).

The *trimmed* derivation $\tilde{\delta}$ is obtained from δ by deleting in δ any label $\S \in W_\delta$ - and then any node without label - such that for no $l=(k_1,k_2)\in S$, $\S<k_i$ for some $i=1,2$,. The equivalence class $[\tilde{\delta}]_{\underset{\sim}{t}}$ is the set of all derivations of F for which trimming yields $\tilde{\delta}$.

3.4.L. If $\tilde{\delta}$ is obtained from δ by trimming then $\tilde{\delta}$ is a uniquely determined derivation with size and degree less or equal to that of δ.
The proof (by induction on the length of δ) is trivial. □

A substantial subset of $<_\delta$ is uniquely determined by $<_F$. For instance, for the theorem T of this section with its labels $S=\{l_1,l_2,l_3,l_4\}$, the whole derivation given in figure 6 is uniquely determined by $<_T$ and $\{\wedge_2 < x, \wedge_1 < u, \wedge_1 < v\}$ which is illustrated in figure 7. Note that figure 7 together with T and S encodes essentially the same information as figure 2 (which was already abbreviated by using $\vdash'$ rather than $\vdash$). The following theorem summarizes this reduction in precise terms.

For a normalized, generalized and trimmed derivation δ let
$\lessdot := \{(\S_1,\S_2)\in W_\delta \times W_\delta \mid \S_1<\S_2,\ \S_1=\wedge \text{ or } \S_1=a,\ \S_2=x,\ \neg\exists \S'\in W_\delta(\S_1 \leqq \S' < \S_2 \text{ or } \S_1 < \S' \leqq \S_2)\}$.
$\S=a$, e.g., has the obvious meaning "some constant a occurs at position $\S$". For instance, figure 7 shows $\lessdot$ for the derivation of T in figure 6. The triple $(F,S_\delta,\lessdot_\delta)$ will be called a *skeleton derivation* or shortly a *skeleton*. Finally, let $\sim$ denote the equivalence relation obtained by taking the transitive closure w.r.t. $\underset{\sim}{n}$, $\underset{\sim}{s}$, $\underset{\sim}{t}$ for given δ_F.

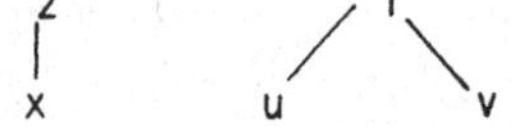

Figure 7. The skeleton derivation for the theorem from figure 3

3.5.T.a. An arbitrary derivation δ of degree ≤ 1 of a normalized theorem F with S_δ uniquely determines a skeleton $(F,S_\delta,\lessdot_\delta)$.

b. If $\bar{\delta}=(F,S,\prec)$ is such a skeleton of such a derivation δ then δ is uniquely determined by $\bar{\delta}$ modulo $\sim$ and can be computed from $\bar{\delta}$ in time linear in the size of δ.

Proof. The first part follows immediately from the definitions and the lemmas (2.2, 3.2-3.4). For the second part a derivation $\tilde{\delta}$ is defined in the following inductive way which turns out to be the normalized, generalized and trimmed version of δ.

Inductive definition of $\tilde{\delta}$ for $(F,S,\prec)$. It may be assumed that F is of the form $v(F_1,\ldots,F_n,F_{n+1},\ldots,F_m)$ by allowing $m=n=1$. Let $\S_j$ denote the labels from W_F at the root of F_j, $j\in\{1,\ldots,m\}$. Among those let $\S_i$ denote those such that $\S_i<k$ for some $l=(k,k')\in S$, $i=1,\ldots,n$.

1. If $n=0$ then $\tilde{\delta}$ consists of one node labelled with S.
2. If all $\S_i$ are of the same kind, either variables or constants, i.e. $F_i=\forall z_{i1}\ldots z_{in_i}F_i'$, and if δ' is the derivation tree for $v(F_1',\ldots,F_n',F_{n+1},\ldots F_m)$ then $\tilde{\delta}$ has a root labelled with $\bigcup_{i=1}^{n} z_{i}\ldots z_{in_i}$ with δ' as subtree.
3. If all $\S_i$ are conjunctions $\wedge(F_{i1},\ldots,F_{in_i})$ then both S and $\prec$ naturally can be separated into S_{ij} and $\prec_{ij}$; hence, by induction, δ_{ij} are determined by $(v(F_{ij},F_{n+1},\ldots,F_m),S_{ij},\prec_{ij})$; $\tilde{\delta}$ has its root labelled with $\S_1\ldots\S_n$ with the subtrees δ_{ij}, $j=1,\ldots,n_i$, $i=1,\ldots,n$.
4. For the remaining case let $\S,\S'\in\{\S_i|i=1,\ldots,n\}=:Q$ such that $\S$ and $\S'$ are of a different kind. Then $\prec$ determines a subset $\emptyset\neq Q_o\subset Q$ with labels of the same kind only such that $\S_o<\bar{\S}_o$ for any $\S_o\in Q_o$, $\bar{\S}_o\in Q\setminus Q_o$, as will be shown in (i),(ii).
(i) $\S=\wedge$ or $\S=a$, $\S'=x$: if $\S\prec\S'$ then $\S<\S'$ else $\S'<\S$.
(ii) $\S=\wedge$, $\S'=a$: if there is $\S''=x\in Q$, and if $\S<\S''<\S'$ by (i) then $\S<\S'$ by transitivity, otherwise if $\S''<\S,\S''<\S'$ then only $\S''$ is a candidate for Q_o; in all 3 remaining cases $\S'<\S$ by transitivity or normality. Q_o apparently determines a subset $\{F_1',\ldots,F_{n'}'\}\subseteq\{F_1,\ldots,F_n\}$ for which now either step 2 or 3 applies.

The linearity of this process is obvious. On the basis of the lemmas (2.2,3.2-3.4) it is also obvious that $\tilde{\delta}$ is the uniquely determined normalized, generalized and trimmed derivation obtained from δ, and that from $\tilde{\delta}$ an instance in the original system can be obtained in linear time. □

4. A CHARACTERIZATION OF SKELETONS AND APPLICATIONS FOR ATP. It has been shown in the previous section that skeletons uniquely determine derivations except for irrelevances. They have been defined in terms of derivations. In order to show that they are of practical importance w.r.t. theorem proving it is necessary to characterize them in terms of structural properties of formulas. This will be accomplished in the following theorem.

As before let F denote any formula without function symbols with a spanning set S of connections. As throughout this paper it may be assumed that each path through F contains *exactly* one connection which is achieved by cancelling superfluous ones. Let U_S, shortly U, denote the unificand of S (see before 3.3). In analogy to the definition of $\lessdot_\delta$ before (3.5) an ordering $\lessdot \in W_F \times W_F$ will be called a *skeleton ordering* iff $\S_1 \lessdot \S_2$ implies $\S_1=\wedge$ or $\S_1=a$, $\S_2=x$, and ($\S_1 \overset{\lessdot}{=} \S' < \S_2$ or $\S_1 < \S' \overset{\lessdot}{=} \S_2$) for no $\S' \in W_F$. $\lessdot$ *induces* a derivation-like structure, hence a tree-ordering $<$, determined by the inductive definition given in the proof of 3.5.

4.1.D. Let $l=(k_o,k_1)\in S$.
(i) $V_l := \{\S \in W_F \mid \S=\wedge,\ \S<k_j$ for some $j=0,1\}$.
(ii) $U|l := U \setminus \overline{U|l}$, where $\langle x_o,x_1\rangle \in \overline{U|l}$ iff there exists an $\S \in V_l$ such that x_i was taken from a literal at position k, where k_j,k occur in different subtrees of $\S$ w.r.t. $<$, and $\S < x_{i+1\,(\mathrm{mod}\,2)}$, for some $i,j=0,1$.
(iii) U is called *unifiable* w.r.t. $\lessdot$ iff there exists a mgu for each U_l, $l\in S$, such that $x=a$ implies $a<x$. □

For instance, if $\lessdot$ is chosen from figure 7 for T, the theorem shown in figure 3 with $S=\{l_1,\dots,l_4\}$, then $<$ induced by $\lessdot$ is given in figure 6. What is then $U|l_1$, say? All pairs in $U_{l_1}=\{\langle a,u\rangle,\langle y,u\rangle,\langle x,c\rangle\}$ are contained in $U|l_1$ since obviously (ii) cannot be satisfied. Considering U_{l_2}, in $\langle b,u\rangle$ it is b and $\wedge_1$ which fulfil the condition imposed on x_i and $\S$, resp., in (ii); since for $x_{i+1\,(\mathrm{mod}\,2)}$ which here is u, $\wedge_1<u$ holds, it follows that $\langle b,u\rangle$ is not in $U|l_1$. Proceeding in that way it turns out that $U|l = U_{l_1}\cup\{\langle x,c\rangle,\langle a,v\rangle\}$ for which obviously an mgu exists. Similarly for $U|l_i$, $i=2,3,4$. The idea behind this definition becomes clear by a look at any of figures 2,3,4 where the reader can and should notice that u may have two different associated constants a and b occurring in two different subtrees of $\wedge_1$ because $\wedge_1<u$. Any known kind of splitting is a special case of this definition.- The condition in (iii) takes care of the condition on c in (2.1.c).

4.2.T. For any F,S, and $\lessdot$, $(F,S,\lessdot)$ is a skeleton iff U_S is unifiable w.r.t. $\lessdot$.
The proof for the only-if-part is trivial with (3.5.b). Conversely it is obvious, that $\tilde{\delta}$ defined for $\lessdot$ as in the proof of (3.5) is in fact a derivation of F. □

4.3.C. $\vdash_1 F$ iff U_S is unifiable for some spanning set S of connections and for some skeleton ordering $\lessdot$ for F.

4.4.C. If for F a spanning set S of connections and a skeleton ordering $\lessdot$ has been determined such that U_S is unifiable w.r.t. $\lessdot$ then a Gentzen-like derivation δ can be computed from $(F,S,\lessdot)$ in time linear in the size of δ.*)

These results have obvious applications for theorem proving. For degree 1 formulas according to (4.3) only S and $\lessdot$ have to be determined. A procedure doing exact-

*) In a recent paper on "Transforming matings into natural deduction proofs" (Proc. CADE-5, Springer, 1980) P. Andrews has an analog result w.r.t. his matings

ly this has been described in [9]. It uses an algorithm for determining S which does not require F to be given in or transformed into any normal form. This algorithm has been improved to one defined in [7], which, as has been proved in [7], is less redundant, hence more efficient than a number of well-known methods.

The determination of S and $\lessdot$ will not be performed separately. Rather, for the connection l determined in each step of (4.1) it will be checked whether U_l can be added to U obtained sofar without destroying unifiability; if this is not the case possible candidates for extending $\lessdot$ obtained sofar are determined from F which retain the unifiability of $\overline{U \cup U_l}$. This iterated process starts with an empty S and $\lessdot$, and terminates as soon as S becomes spanning. It has to consider backtracking to other such candidates upon failure later on in order to preserve the strong completeness property expressed by (4.3). Under certain circumstances, however, one might prefer a weakening of this property by pruning the backtracking process in a strategical way, and still would retain the essential advantages of this method.

For instance, after selection of l_1 and determining U_{l_1} for the example T above this process would then consider l_3. However, $U_{l_1} \cup U_{l_3}$ is not unifiable with $\lessdot = \emptyset$ since $y=a, x=c$ are in conflict with $y=b, x=d$. The only candidate for extension of $\lessdot$ in order to resolve this conflict is $\wedge_2 \lessdot x$. Therefore the process proceeds now with $S=\{l_1, l_3\}$, $U=U_{l_1} \cup \{\langle a,v \rangle\}$, and $\lessdot = \{(\wedge_2, x)\}$. For more details on these algorithmic aspects see [9].

If the reader prefers he may consider each step of this process as the application of a new proof rule, $(F,S,\lessdot) \vdash (F, S\cup l, \lessdot \cup \lessdot')$, where l is the added connection and $\lessdot'$ the extension of $\lessdot$. Note how easily structure sharing can be implemented for this rule!

5. PROSPECTUS. The restriction to formulas without variables imposed on the previous 2 sections can be easily removed by a straightforward generalization. This includes the applications of a general unification algorithm. For that purpose Huet's algorithm [15] is particularly appropriate since his relation $\rightarrow$ defined in CYCLE on p. 5-46 in [15] for a Skolem function F (in his notation) plays exactly the same role as the relation $>$ in the present paper restricted to variables and constants. Hence extending $<$ on arbitrary terms according to Huet's definition of $\rightarrow$ essentially is all which needs to be done in this matter.

An efficient way to remove the restriction on formulas of degree 1 requires more investment, however. In particular, one has to consider different instances of positions k in a formula F with $x<k$ for some x and an appropriate generalization of the concepts "spanning set of connections" and "unifiable". The "father-grandfather" formula $\forall u \exists a Fau \wedge \forall xyz(Fzy \wedge Fyx \rightarrow GFzx) \rightarrow \forall b \exists v GFvb$ which is of degree 2 may

illustrate this. The unificand determined by the 3 connections is not unifiable in the sense of the previous section unless the process notices that it may consider 2 independent copies of Fau according to definition (2.1.d). As shown in the picture these copies have not to be created explicitly but only indicated by simply numbering the positions in the connections and taken care of in the definition of "unifiable". This example also demonstrates that the implication sign might be easily retained in the formula by appropriately adapting the definitions of this paper.

The alert reader who is familiar with the contents of [6;7] will see that such a generalized systematic method may simulate any popular ATP method like those mentioned in [7] such that each connection to be considered in the process of the previous section, generalized as indicated above, corresponds to at least one single resolution step, e.g.. That is to say this method would not be worse than those ones.

In fact it would be strikingly better, not only because of the enormous representational advantage (storage is required for exactly one copy of the formula and for $S, U_S, \prec$) but also because there are theorems for which the number of connections to be considered is even strictly smaller than the number of resolution steps. One such theorem is the formula $\exists xyzw(Payxw \wedge Pbzxw) \vee \exists uvs(\neg Puucs \wedge \neg Pvbds)$ which is a variant of T considered in the previous sections, and which, like T, after anti-prenexing, requires 4 links to be considered. For resolution this slight change of T makes a difference, however, increasing the number of steps beyond 4. Such a situation arises for arbitrarily many theorems with the difference growing arbitrarily high (see [9] for some more details).

Acknowledgements. I thank W.W. Bledsoe, K.M. Hörnig and R. Kowalski for careful reading and/or discussions of the paper, and A. Bußmann for the excellent typescript.

REFERENCES

[1] P.B. Andrews, Refutations by matings, IEEE Transactions on Computer C-*25* (1976) 801-807.

[2] P.B. Andrews, Theorem Proving via General Matings, Journal of the ACM (to appear).

[3] W. Bibel, An approach to a systematic theorem proving procedure in first-order logic, Computing *12* (1974) 43-55.

[4] W. Bibel, Maschinelles Beweisen, Jahrbuch Überblicke Mathematik (Bibliographisches Institut, Mannheim, 1976) 115-142.

[5] W. Bibel, Tautology testing with a generalized matrix reduction method, Theoretical Computer Science *8* (1979), 31-44.

[6] W. Bibel, On matrices with connections, Bericht *79*, Universität Karlsruhe (1979), submitted to JACM.

[7] W. Bibel, A comparative study of several proof procedures, Proc. AISB-80 (1980).

[8] W. Bibel, Syntax-directed, semantics-supported program synthesis, Artificial Intelligence Journal (to appear).

[9] W. Bibel and J. Schreiber, Proof search in a Gentzen-like system of first-order logic, Proc. Int. Computing Symposium (North-Holland, Amsterdam, 1975) 205-212.

Also contained in: W. Bibel, Programmieren in der Sprache der Prädikatenlogik, Habilitationsarbeit (abgelehnt), Technische Universität München (1975).

[10] W.W. Bledsoe, Non-resolution theorem proving, Artificial Intelligence *9* (1977) 1-35.

[11] J. Friedrich, Ein systematischer Algorithmus zum Beweisen von Theoremen in einem Prädikatenkalkül erster Ordnung, Diplomarbeit, Techn. Univ. München (1973).

[12] G. Gentzen, Untersuchungen über das logische Schließen I, Mathemat. Zeitschrift *39*, (1935) 176-210.

[13] C.A. Goad, Proofs as descriptions of programs, Proc. CADE-5, Springer (to appear).

[14] J. Herbrand, Recherches sur la Theorie de la Demonstration, Travaux de la Societe des Sciences et des Lettres de Varsovie, Classe III sciences mathematiques et physiques, *33* (1930).

[15] G. Huet, Résolution d'équations dans des languages d'ordres 1,2,...,ω, Thèse de doctorat d'état, Université Paris VII (1976).

[16] G. Huet, Confluent Reductions: Abstract Properties and Applications to Term Rewriting Systems, Rapport Laboria n° 250, IRIA-LABORIA, Domaine de Voluceau, 78150 Le Chesnay, France (1977).

[17] R. Kowalski, Algorithm = logic + control, Comm. of the ACM *22* (1979) 424-436.

[18] Z. Manna, R. Waldinger, A deductive approach to program synthesis, Proc. IJCAI-79 (1979) 542-551.

[19] S.J. Maslow, The inverse method for establishing deducibility for logical calculi, Proc. Steklov Inst. Math. *98* (1968).

[20] D. Prawitz, An improved proof procedure, Theoria *26* (1960) 102-139.

[21] J.A. Robinson, Logic: form and function, Edinburgh University Press (1979).

[22] M. Sato, Towards a mathematical theory of program synthesis, Proc. IJCAI-79 (1979) 757-762.

[23] J. Schreiber, Vergleichende qualitative und quantitative Untersuchungen von Beweisverfahren, Bericht Nr. 7411, Technische Universität München (1974).

[24] K. Schütte, Proof theory, Springer Verlag (Berlin, 1977).

Consistent Semantics for a Data Flow Language*

J. Dean Brock

Laboratory for Computer Science

Massachusetts Institute of Technology

Cambridge, Massachusetts 02139 USA

1. Introduction

Recent attempts to design programming languages for specifying concurrent computation, and, consequently, recent attempts to semantically characterize concurrent computation, have been "hardware-driven." Programming languages have made the transition from modeling a single serial von Neumann process and its memory; to modeling several processes sharing a memory; to modeling several communicating processes, each with its own memory. Concurrent programming concepts, such as Hoare's [9] *communicating sequential processes* and Brinch Hansen's [4] *distributed processes*, may be forgiven their semantic complexity, since they introduce abstraction to the very important application area of real-time systems presently dominated by *ad hoc* machine language programming, and since most real-time systems are inherently non-determinate and time-dependent and therefore beyond straightforward semantic description. However, there are many semantically "simple" application areas, such as numerical simulation, in which any performance benefits that could be gained using concurrency are overwhelmed by the programming cost of partitioning tasks among several communicating processes. This partitioning task would be immense on envisioned computer architectures exploiting the advantages of VLSI technology by incorporating thousands of very small processing elements. Consequently, it is imperative that models of concurrent computation other than variations of the von Neumann model be investigated. The data flow model of computation [6] is one such model.

A data flow program may be translated into a data flow graph in which the grain of concurrency appears at the level of elementary program operations instead of procedures consisting of several program statements. Furthermore, data flow programming languages are applicative languages, and, consequently, share with applicative languages elegance of semantic characterization and ease of program verification.

In this paper we will examine the data flow model of computation and define ADFL, an Applicative Data Flow Language. Additionally, the denotational and operational semantics of ADFL will be given and shown to be consistent. Scott's [11] fixpoint theory will be used to specify the denotational semantics. The operational semantics are given by a two step process. One step corresponds to the translation of programs into data flow graphs, while the other corresponds to the execution of the resulting graphs. The result of graph execution is derived using Kahn's [10] fixpoint theory of communicating processes.

The denotational and operational semantics of ADFL are not equivalent. The denotational semantics specify that expression evaluation must terminate to yield results and that, if expression evaluation terminates, all

*This research was supported by the National Science Foundation under contract 7915255-MCS and the Department of Energy under contract DE-AC02-79ER10473.

subexpression evaluations terminate. However, in data flow, and many other models of concurrent computation, a computation may produce results even if some internal computations do not terminate. The characterization of such computations contributes much to the complexity of the operational semantics of ADFL. Consequently, the simpler denotational semantics are the more useful in tasks such as program verification. The proof of consistency assures those using the simpler semantics that the two semantic theories agree on all "denotationally" terminating expression evaluations.

1.1 The Data Flow Model of Computation

The program schema of the data flow model of computation is the *data flow graph*, a directed graph whose nodes are called *operators*. Each operator has labeled input and output ports, and graph links are directed from operator input ports to operator output ports. Graphs, like operators, have input and output ports. The unlinked operator ports within a graph are the ports of the graph itself.

The execution of a data flow graph can be interpreted within Kahn's [10] fixpoint theory by viewing the operators as parallel programs and the links as channels for program (operator) communication. Because graph operators correspond to elementary program operators, they are exceeding simple parallel "programs." For most operators, execution consists of a repetition of *firings*. Operators are *enabled* for firing by the presence of input values. In firing, an operator accepts values at its input ports and produces results at its output ports. The following program of Kahn's parallel programming language implements the data flow + operator:

```
Process plus(integer in I1, I2; integer out O) ;
 Repeat Begin Integer T ;
  Comment : the order of the wait invocations is irrelevant ;
  T := wait(I1) + wait(I2) ;
  send T on O ;
 End ;
```

The data flow graph and parse tree representation of elementary expressions are very similar. The graph representing an application of + to two arguments is formed by linking the output ports of the graphs computing the two arguments to the input ports of a + operator. The data flow graph for the simple expression:

x*x + y*y

is illustrated in Figure 1. Note that the graph input ports are labeled by the free variables of the expression. If a free variable occurs more than once, a copy operator (represented in the figure by a solid black dot) is used to distribute the

---

Figure 1. A Sample Data Flow Program

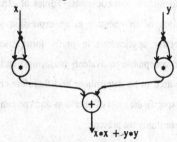

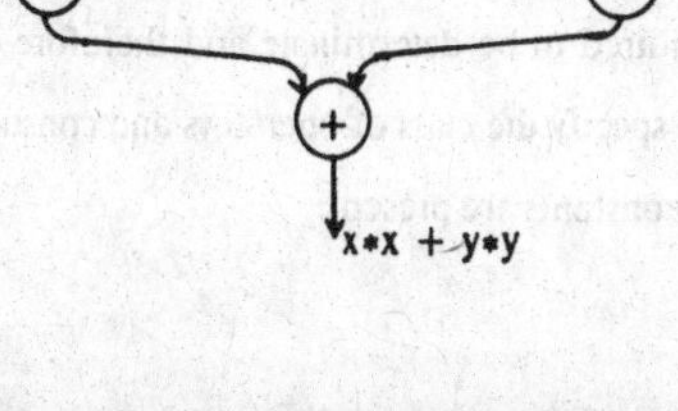

variable. The data flow graph implementations of other commonly used programming constructs will be discussed in Section 3.

There are two prerequisites to the practical use of data flow computation: (1), a machine which executes data flow graphs; and (2), a programming language which can be translated into data flow graphs. Preliminary data flow machine designs have been made by Dennis and Misunas [8] and Arvind and Gostelow [2]. Within these machines, a data flow graph is distributed over a network of processing elements. These elements operate concurrently, constrained only by the operational dependencies of the graph. Thus, a very efficient utilization of the machine's resources appears possible.

Data flow programming languages resemble conventional languages restricted to those features whose ease of translation does not depend on the state of a computation being a single, easily manipulated entity. Because the "state" of a data flow graph is distributed for concurrency, *goto*'s, expressions with side effects, and multiple assignments to the same variable are difficult to represent. Since these "features" are generally avoided in structured programming, their absence from data flow languages is little reason for lament.

The "First Version of a Data Flow Language" by Dennis [6] was a rudimentary ALGOL-like language. Most data flow language are statement-oriented languages given an applicative flavor by imposing the *single-assignment* rule: Programs are syntactically restricted to guarantee that each variable would be assigned only one value during the program's execution. The languages of Weng [13] and Arvind, Gostelow, and Plouffe [3], in addition to having the expressive power of ALGOL, facilitate the programming of networks of communicating processes, such as co-routines and operating systems.

1.2 ADFL - An Applicative Data Flow Language

ADFL, Applicative Data Flow Language, is a simplification of VAL, the Value-oriented Algorithmic Language developed by Ackerman and Dennis [1]. A BNF specification of the syntax of ADFL follows:

exp ::= *id* | *const* | *oper*(*exp*) | *exp* , *exp* | **let** *idlist* = *exp* **in** *exp* **end** |
  if *exp* **then** *exp* **else** *exp* **end** | **for** *idlist* = *exp* **do** *iterbody* **end**

iterbody ::= *exp* | **iter**(*exp*) | **let** *idlist* = *exp* **in** *iterbody* **end** |
  if *exp* **then** *iterbody* **else** *iterbody* **end**

id ::= ... programming language identifiers ...

idlist ::= *id* { , *id* }

const ::= ... programming language constants ...

oper ::= ... programming language operators ...

The most elementary expressions of ADFL are identifiers and constants. Tuples of expressions are also expressions. One such expression is "x, 5". The application of an operator to an expression is an expression. Although, the BNF specification only provides for operator applications in prefix form, such as "+(x, 5)"; applications in infix form, such as "x + 5", are considered acceptable equivalents (sugarings) and will be used in example ADFL programs. All operators of ADFL are required to be determinate and therefore characterizable by mathematical functions. We will not attempt to completely specify the class of operators and constants. It is assumed that at least the usual arithmetic and boolean operators and constants are present.

Since ADFL is applicative, it provides for the binding, rather than the assignment, of identifiers. Evaluation of the binding expression:

let y, z = x + 5, 6 **in** y * z **end**

implies the evaluation of "y * z" with y equal to "x + 5" and z equal to 6. The result of binding is local: the values of y and z outside the binding expression are unchanged.

ADFL contains a conventional conditional expression, but has an unusual iteration expression. The evaluation of the iteration expression:

for *idlist* = *exp* **do** *iterbody* **end**

is accomplished by first binding the *iteration identifiers*, the elements of *idlist*, to the values of *exp*. Note from the BNF specification of *iterbody*, that the evaluation of the *iteration body* will ultimately result in either an expression or the "application" of a special operator iter to an expression. This application to iter is actually a tail recursive call of the iteration body with the iteration identifiers bound to the "arguments" of iter. The iteration is terminated when the evaluation of the iteration body results in an ordinary, non-iter, expression. The value of this expression is returned as the value of the iteration expression. The following iteration expression computes the factorial of n:

```
for i, y = n, 1 do
    if i > 1 then iter(i - 1, y * i) else y end
end
```

In conventional languages execution exceptions, such as divide by zero errors, are generally handled by program interrupts. This solution is inappropriate for data flow since there is no control flow to interrupt. In ADFL execution exceptions are handled by generating special error values. A detailed specification of the class of error values and the results of operator application to error values is given in the documentation of VAL [1].

2. $\mathcal{E}$: The Denotational Semantics of ADFL

ADFL has a simple denotational characterization, similar to those given by Scott [11] and by Tennent [12] for other applicative languages. Before proceeding, we briefly review some of the notations and concepts of fixpoint theory.

Notation: Given a set A with partial ordering $\sqsubseteq$, the least upper bound of a subset E of A is denoted $\sqcap E$, and the *limit*, $\sqcap \{x_1, x_2, ...\}$, of an increasing sequence $x_1 \sqsubseteq x_2 \sqsubseteq ...$ of A is denoted $\sqcap x_i$.

Definition: A *domain* is a partially ordered set A with a least element, usually denoted $\perp$, such that every increasing sequence of A has a limit.

Definitions: A function F from domain A to domain B is *continuous* if, for every increasing sequence $x_1 \sqsubseteq x_2 \sqsubseteq ...$, $F(\sqcap x_i) = \sqcap F(x_i)$. Every continuous function F is also *monotonic*, that is, $x \sqsubseteq y$ implies $F(x) \sqsubseteq F(y)$.

Definition and Theorem: Given domains A and B, the *product* domain $A \times B$, populated by the elements of the Cartesian product of A and B and ordered so that $(x_1, y_1) \sqsubseteq (x_2, y_2)$ if and only if $x_1 \sqsubseteq x_2$ and $y_1 \sqsubseteq y_2$, and the *function* domain $A \rightarrow B$, populated by the continuous functions from A to B and ordered so that $F \sqsubseteq G$ if and only if $F(x) \sqsubseteq G(x)$ for all elements x of A, are domains.

Definition and Theorem: Given a continuous function F of $A \rightarrow A$, the *least fixpoint* (solution) to the equation

$F(x) = x$

exists and it denoted $\mathbf{Y}(F)$. Furthermore, letting F^n denote the function formed by composing F with itself n times:

$\mathbf{Y}(F) = \sqcap F^i(\perp)$

Let V be the set of all values of ADFL, $V^{\star}$ be the set of all tuples of values, and $V^{\star}_{\perp}$ be the *discrete* value domain formed by adjoining to $V^{\star}$ a least element $\perp$. $V^{\star}_{\perp}$ is ordered discreetly, that is, for all elements x and y of $V^{\star}_{\perp}$, $x \sqsubseteq y$ if and only if $\perp = x$ or $x = y$. The five semantic categories of ADFL, constants, operators, identifiers, expressions, and iteration bodies, will be denoted, respectively, **Const**, **Oper**, **Id**, **Exp**, and **Iterbody**. The semantic function $\mathcal{I}$ maps ADFL constants and operators into their interpretations. The interpretation $\mathcal{I}[\![const]\!]$ of a constant *const* is an element of $V^{\star}$. $\mathcal{I}[\![oper]\!]$ is the usual arithmetic or Boolean function associated with *oper*, extended to $V^{\star}_{\perp}$ by defining applications of $\mathcal{I}[\![oper]\!]$ to tuples inappropriate in type to map into special error values. For example:

$\mathcal{I}[\![+]\!](x, y) = x + y$, if x and y are integer values
$\mathcal{I}[\![\wedge]\!](x, y) = x \wedge y$, if x and y are boolean values

A complete specification of $\mathcal{I}$ will not be given here. However, the denotational interpretation of operators is required to be *strict* in the following sense: $\mathcal{I}[\![oper]\!](x) = \perp$ if and only if $x = \perp$. Because $\perp$ will correspond to the result of a non-terminating computation, this strictness requirement insures that an application of *oper* to an expression terminates if and only if the expression terminates. In addition, this requirement insures that $\mathcal{I}[\![oper]\!]$ is continuous.

Because ADFL is applicative, its expressions may be denotationally characterized by a function mapping each *environment*, association of identifiers and values, into the tuple of values returned by expression evaluation within that environment. Let U, the environments of ADFL, be $\mathbf{Id} \to V$, the continuous functions from Id to V. The semantic function $\mathcal{E}$ is the expression evaluation function of ADFL. $\mathcal{E}$, a member of $\mathbf{Exp} \to U \to V^{\star}_{\perp}$, maps (in curried notation) expressions and environments into tuples of values. In the specification of $\mathcal{E}$, expressions which a compiler could declare "invalid" are ignored. Such expressions are invalid either because they contain instances in which an unbound (uninitialized) identifier could be evaluated or instances in which an operator could be applied to an expression of inappropriate arity.

The specification of $\mathcal{E}$ for expressions without iteration is trivial. Evaluation of an identifier yields the value of the identifier within the current environment, evaluation of a constant yields $\mathcal{I}[\![const]\!]$, and evaluation of an operator application is accomplished by applying $\mathcal{I}[\![oper]\!]$ to the values of the argument expression.

$\mathcal{E}[\![id]\!]\rho = \rho[\![id]\!]$
$\mathcal{E}[\![const]\!]\rho = \mathcal{I}[\![const]\!]$
$\mathcal{E}[\![oper(exp)]\!]\rho = \mathcal{I}[\![oper]\!](\mathcal{E}[\![exp]\!]\rho)$

Let $\Vert_s$ denote the strict concatenation operator over elements of $V^{\star}_{\perp}$. That is, for tuples x and y of $V^{\star}$, $x \Vert_s y$ is $x \Vert y$, the concatenation of x and y, and $x \Vert_s \perp$ and $\perp \Vert_s y$ are both $\perp$. Using the strict concatenation operator, we define the value of a tuple of expressions to be $\perp$ if one of its component expressions is $\perp$.

$\mathcal{E}[\![exp_1, exp_2]\!]\rho = \mathcal{E}[\![exp_1]\!]\rho \Vert_s \mathcal{E}[\![exp_2]\!]\rho$

The updated environment resulting from binding the values of a tuple x to successive identifiers of a list *idlist* in environment ρ is denoted $\rho[idlist/x]$. Our denotational specification requires the binding expression and the conditional expression to be strict. The *precedes* function $\Rightarrow$ and the *condition* function $\rightarrow$ enforce strictness.

$\perp \Rightarrow y = \perp$
$x \Rightarrow y = y$, if $x \neq \perp$

$\mathcal{E}[\![\mathbf{let}\ idlist = exp_1\ \mathbf{in}\ exp_2\ \mathbf{end}]\!]\rho = \mathcal{E}[\![exp_1]\!]\rho \Rightarrow \mathcal{E}[\![exp_2]\!]\rho[idlist/\mathcal{E}[\![exp_1]\!]\rho]$

$\perp \rightarrow x, y = \perp$
true $\rightarrow x, y = x$
false $\rightarrow x, y = y$
$z \rightarrow x, y =$ ... some error value ..., if $z \notin \{\perp, \text{true}, \text{false}\}$
$\mathcal{E}[\![\text{if } exp_1 \text{ then } exp_2 \text{ else } exp_3 \text{ end}]\!]\rho = \mathcal{E}[\![exp_1]\!]\rho \rightarrow \mathcal{E}[\![exp_2]\!]\rho, \mathcal{E}[\![exp_3]\!]\rho$

Evaluation of the iteration expression "let *idlist* = *exp* in *iterbody* end" could be specified by considering *iterbody* to be a recursive procedure, with name iter and parameters *idlist*. However, for the proof of consistency, it is more convenient to view the iteration body as returning a tuple with a tag indicating whether or not iteration is to be continued or terminated. To do so, we extend tuples from their mathematical foundation as functions whose domain is a subset of the integers to functions with arbitrary domains. Note that environments are such tuples. The tag of the tuple x returned by the iteration body is appropriately denoted x_{tag}. Additionally, this tuple has either I components $x_{I1}, x_{I2}, \ldots$, denoted x_I, or R components $x_{R1}, x_{R2}, \ldots$, denoted x_R. A true tag requests continued iteration with the I components bound to the iteration identifiers. A false tag requests return of the R components as the result of the iteration expression.

The iteration body evaluation function $\mathcal{E}_I$ of Iterbody $\rightarrow$ U $\rightarrow V_\perp^\star$ is defined like $\mathcal{E}$. In the definition of $\mathcal{E}_I$, in imitation of the environment updating notation, the tuple x with a true tag and I components x_I is denoted $\Lambda[\text{tag/true}][I/x_I]$. Similarly, the tuple x with a false tag and R components x_R is denoted $\Lambda[\text{tag/false}][R/x_R]$.

$\mathcal{E}_I[\![exp]\!]\rho = \mathcal{E}[\![exp]\!]\rho \Rightarrow \Lambda[\text{tag/false}][R/\mathcal{E}[\![exp]\!]\rho]$
$\mathcal{E}_I[\![\text{iter}(exp)]\!]\rho = \mathcal{E}[\![exp]\!]\rho \Rightarrow \Lambda[\text{tag/true}][I/\mathcal{E}[\![exp]\!]\rho]$
$\mathcal{E}_I[\![\text{let } idlist = exp \text{ in } iterbody \text{ end}]\!]\rho = \mathcal{E}[\![exp]\!]\rho \Rightarrow \mathcal{E}_I[\![iterbody]\!]\rho[idlist/\mathcal{E}[\![exp]\!]\rho]$
$\mathcal{E}_I[\![\text{if } exp \text{ then } iterbody_1 \text{ else } iterbody_2 \text{ end}]\!]\rho = \mathcal{E}[\![exp]\!]\rho \rightarrow \mathcal{E}[\![iterbody_1]\!]\rho, \mathcal{E}[\![iterbody_2]\!]\rho$

The least fixpoint operator **Y** is used to specify the iteration performed during evaluation of an iteration expression:

$$\mathcal{E}[\![\text{for } idlist = exp \text{ do } iterbody \text{ end}]\!]\rho = \mathbf{Y}(\lambda F.\, \lambda x.\, x \Rightarrow (\mathcal{E}_I[\![iterbody]\!]\rho[idlist/x])_{tag} \rightarrow F((\mathcal{E}_I[\![iterbody]\!]\rho[idlist/x])_I), (\mathcal{E}_I[\![iterbody]\!]\rho[idlist/x])_R)\mathcal{E}[\![exp]\!]\rho$$

That is, each iteration is an evaluation of the iteration body with the iteration identifiers bound to some x and yields the tuple $\mathcal{E}_I[\![iterbody]\!]\rho[idlist/x]$. If the tuple has a true tag, its I components are bound to the iteration identifiers and iteration is resumed. If the tuple has a false tag, its R components are returned as the result of the iteration. The iteration identifiers are bound to $\mathcal{E}[\![exp]\!]\rho$ on the first iteration. If the iteration never terminates, evaluation is defined to "yield" $\perp$. The following easily proven lemma will be used in Section 4 to prove the consistency of the denotational and operational semantics of ADFL.

Lemma: If $\mathcal{E}[\![\text{for } idlist = exp \text{ do } iterbody \text{ end}]\!]\rho$ does not equal $\perp$, then there exists a sequence $\rho_1, \ldots, \rho_n$ such that for all i between 1 and n-1:

$\rho_1 = \rho[idlist/\mathcal{E}[\![exp]\!]\rho]$
$\rho_{i+1} = \rho_i[idlist/(\mathcal{E}_I[\![iterbody]\!]\rho_i)_I]$
$(\mathcal{E}_I[\![iterbody]\!]\rho_i)_{tag} = \text{true}$
$(\mathcal{E}_I[\![iterbody]\!]\rho_n)_{tag} = \text{false}$
$(\mathcal{E}_I[\![iterbody]\!]\rho_n)_R = \mathcal{E}[\![\text{for } idlist = exp \text{ do } iterbody \text{ end}]\!]\rho$

3. $\mathcal{O} \circ \mathcal{T}$: The Operational Semantics of ADFL

The operational semantics of an ADFL expression are a formal characterization of the behavior of the expression's data flow graph. The translation algorithm $\mathcal{T}$ is the "compiler" of ADFL. It maps expressions into their data flow graph implementations. The semantic function $\mathcal{O}$ maps graphs into functions representing their input-output behavior. $\mathcal{O} \circ \mathcal{T}$, the composition of these functions, is the operational semantics of ADFL.

In this section emphasis will be placed on the operational semantics of iteration expressions. In Section 4, the consistency of the denotational and operational semantics of ADFL will be proven using the productions of the BNF specification of ADFL as the inductive structure. Recall that, in the specification of the denotational semantics, the least fixpoint operator was used for only one production, that of the iteration expression. Likewise, in the specification of the translation algorithm, cyclic data flow graphs will be constructed for only one production, that of the iteration expression. Consequently, the iteration expression is the difficult and interesting case of the consistency proof, thus justifying our emphasis. Readers interested in a more detailed description of the operational semantics of ADFL may consult previous work of the author [5].

$\mathcal{T}$ maps expressions and $\mathcal{T}_I$ maps iteration bodies into their data flow graph implementations. The implementation of an expression or iteration body has an input port for each free variable of the expression or iteration body and, if needed, an input port trigger for enabling constants. An expression graph has an output port, labeled by an integer, for each value returned by evaluation of *exp*. Recall the domain of the tuple $\mathcal{E}[\![\mathit{iterbody}]\!]\rho$. An iteration body graph has an output port tag for the tag; a set of **I** output port for results to be re-iterated; and a set of **R** output ports for results to be returned.

The semantic function $\mathcal{O}$ mapping data flow graphs into their operational characterization is defined using Kahn's [10] theory of parallel computation, which we briefly review.

Definition: The *history* of an operator or graph port is the sequence, possibly infinite, of values received or transmitted at that port during a data flow computation.

Theorem: Let V^{ω} denote the set of histories of data flow values. If V^{ω} is ordered so that $X \sqsubseteq Y$ if and only if X is a prefix of Y, then V^{ω} is a domain whose least element is the empty history ε.

Definition: The operational semantics of a data flow operator o are given by a continuous *history function* $\mathcal{O}[\![o]\!]$ mapping input history tuples into output history tuples. For each input history tuple X, representing the history of values received at the input ports of o, the output history tuple $\mathcal{O}[\![o]\!](X)$ represents the history of values produced at the output ports of o in response to X.

Note: Not all operators may be characterized by history functions. In particular, only determinate operators which for each input history tuple have only one possible output history tuple may be characterized thusly. Since only determinate operators are used to construct graph implementations of ADFL expressions, the history function characterization is adequate for describing the operational semantics of ADFL.

The result of graph execution is defined to be the least fixpoint (solution) to a set of simultaneous equations, inferred from the history functions of the graph operators, whose variables represent the histories transmitted through the graph links.

In the remainder of this section, we will give a recursive definition of $\mathcal{O} \circ \mathcal{T}$ derived from fixpoint theory but will omit many details of the derivation. Also, the operational characterization of many ADFL expressions will be justified more by the actions of their data flow executions than by the structure of their data flow graph implementations. Readers desiring more detail knowledge of graph implementations should consult Brock [5],

Dennis [6], or Weng [13].

Note that the range and domain of $\mathcal{O}\circ\mathcal{T}[\![exp]\!]$ differ from the range and domain of $\mathcal{E}[\![exp]\!]$. $\mathcal{O}\circ\mathcal{T}[\![exp]\!]$ maps *history* environments, which are functions from identifiers to histories, into output history tuples. Viewed operationally, identifiers of ADFL are bound to histories of values.

The expression graphs, other than those for conditional and iterative expressions, have simple operational characterizations. Evaluation of an identifier yields the history to which the identifier is bound.

$$\mathcal{O}\circ\mathcal{T}[\![id]\!]\mathrm{P} = \mathrm{P}[\![id]\!]$$

The data flow graphs $\mathcal{T}[\![const]\!]$ and $\mathcal{T}[\![oper(exp)]\!]$ contain the data flow operators *const* and *oper*. The operator *const* has a single input port, labeled trigger, and produces $\mathcal{I}[\![const]\!]$ whenever it receives the input value trigger. Whenever, the operator *oper* receives an input tuple x, it produces $\mathcal{I}[\![oper]\!](\mathrm{x})$.

$$\mathcal{O}\circ\mathcal{T}[\![const]\!]\mathrm{P} = \mathcal{O}[\![const]\!](\mathrm{P}[\![\mathrm{trigger}]\!])$$
$$\mathcal{O}\circ\mathcal{T}[\![oper(exp)]\!]\mathrm{P} = \mathcal{O}[\![oper]\!](\mathcal{O}\circ\mathcal{T}[\![exp]\!]\mathrm{P})$$

The denotational and operational semantics of ADFL differ in in their treatment of tuple expressions and binding expressions. The denotational semantics use the strict tuple concatenation operator $\Vert_s$ and strict identifier binding. The operational semantics use the usual tuple concatenation operator, $\Vert$, and non-strict identifier binding.

$$\mathcal{O}\circ\mathcal{T}[\![exp_1, exp_2]\!]\mathrm{P} = \mathcal{O}\circ\mathcal{T}[\![exp_1]\!]\mathrm{P} \Vert \mathcal{O}\circ\mathcal{T}[\![exp_2]\!]\mathrm{P}$$
$$\mathcal{O}\circ\mathcal{T}[\![\mathbf{let}\ idlist = exp_1\ \mathbf{in}\ exp_2\ \mathbf{end}]\!]\mathrm{P} = \mathcal{O}\circ\mathcal{T}[\![exp_2]\!]\mathrm{P}[idlist/\mathcal{O}\circ\mathcal{T}[\![exp_1]\!]\mathrm{P}]$$

$\mathcal{T}[\![\mathbf{if}\ exp_1\ \mathbf{then}\ exp_2\ \mathbf{else}\ exp_3\ \mathbf{end}]\!]$, illustrated in Figure 2, contains a predicate subgraph $\mathcal{T}[\![exp_1]\!]$, a then expression subgraph $\mathcal{T}[\![e{\cdot}p_2]\!]$, a else expression subgraph $\mathcal{T}[\![exp_3]\!]$, and several *gates*. Each input value of the then expression must pass through a T gate and each input value of the else expression must pass through a F gate. The T gate has a control input port, a data input port, and a data output port. Each control value determines whether or not a data value may pass through the gate. If a true control value is received, a data value is absorbed and passed through the data output port. If a false control value is received, a data value is absorbed but not passed. In the F gate the sense of the control value is reversed. The output ports of the then expression subgraph and the else expression subgraph are paired by label, and each pair is joined by a M gate. The M gate has a control input port, two data input

---

Figure 2. $\mathcal{T}[\![\mathbf{if}\ exp_1\ \mathbf{then}\ exp_2\ \mathbf{else}\ exp_3\ \mathbf{end}]\!]$

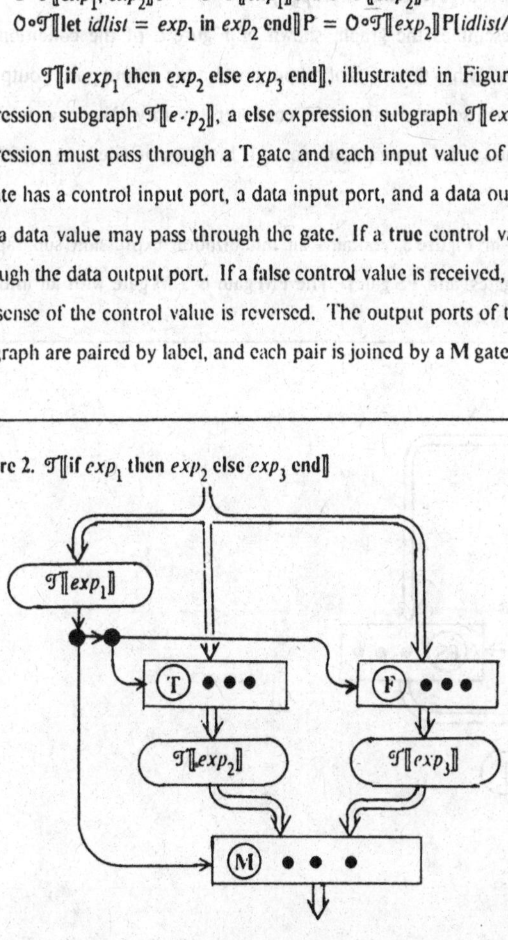

ports, and a data output port. The control value determines which data value is passed through the gate. Connecting the control input ports of all these gates to the output of the predicate graph insures that the predicate can enable the execution of and select the results of the appropriate subexpression.

Let $\underline{T}$ be the composite history function of all the T gates used to implement the conditional expression. $\underline{T}$ maps a control history and a history environment into a history environment.

$$\underline{T}(X, P)[\![id]\!] = \mathcal{O}[\![T]\!](X, P[\![id]\!])$$

With $\underline{F}$ and $\underline{M}$ denoting similar composite history functions, the operational semantics of the conditional expression may be expressed as:

$$\begin{aligned}\mathcal{O}\circ\mathcal{T}[\![\textbf{if } exp_1 \textbf{ then } exp_2 \textbf{ else } exp_3 \textbf{ end}]\!]P = \underline{M}(&\mathcal{O}\circ\mathcal{T}[\![exp_1]\!]P,\\ &\mathcal{O}\circ\mathcal{T}[\![exp_2]\!](\underline{T}(\mathcal{O}\circ\mathcal{T}[\![exp_1]\!]P, P)),\\ &\mathcal{O}\circ\mathcal{T}[\![exp_3]\!](\underline{F}(\mathcal{O}\circ\mathcal{T}[\![exp_1]\!]P, P)))\end{aligned}$$

The operational semantics of iteration bodies are a straightforward extension of the denotational semantics of iteration bodies and the operational semantics of expressions and will be discussed before the more onerous iteration expression is examined. Again, except for the conditional iteration body, the semantic equations are simple.

$$\mathcal{O}\circ\mathcal{T}_I[\![exp]\!]P = \Lambda[\text{tag}/\mathcal{O}\circ\mathcal{T}[\![\text{false}]\!]P][R/\mathcal{O}\circ\mathcal{T}[\![exp]\!]P]$$

$$\mathcal{O}\circ\mathcal{T}_I[\![\text{iter}(exp)]\!]P = \Lambda[\text{tag}/\mathcal{O}\circ\mathcal{T}[\![\text{true}]\!]P][I/\mathcal{O}\circ\mathcal{T}[\![exp]\!]P]$$

$$\mathcal{O}\circ\mathcal{T}_I[\![\textbf{let } idlist = exp \textbf{ in } iterbody \textbf{ end}]\!]P = \mathcal{O}\circ\mathcal{T}_I[\![iterbody]\!]P[idlist/\mathcal{O}\circ\mathcal{T}[\![exp]\!]P]$$

The graph $\mathcal{T}[\![\textbf{if } exp \textbf{ then } iterbody_1 \textbf{ else } iterbody_2 \textbf{ end}]\!]$ resembles the graph, shown in Figure 2, of the conditional expression. However, because the conditional iteration body has three sets of output ports, a tag output port, I output ports and R output ports it has three sets of M gates, each set receiving a different control history. We leave to the most particular the wearisome task of defining the three appropriate control histories needed to specify $\mathcal{O}\circ\mathcal{T}[\![\textbf{if } exp \textbf{ then } iterbody_1 \textbf{ else } iterbody_2 \textbf{ end}]\!]P$.

$\mathcal{T}[\![\textbf{for } idlist = exp \textbf{ do } iterbody \textbf{ end}]\!]$, illustrated in Figure 3, contains an initialization expression subgraph $\mathcal{T}[\![exp]\!]$, an iteration body subgraph $\mathcal{T}_I[\![iterbody]\!]$, FM gates, and FS gates. The FM gate is a M gate with an initial

---

Figure 3. $\mathcal{T}[\![\textbf{for } idlist = exp \textbf{ do } iterbody \textbf{ end}]\!]$

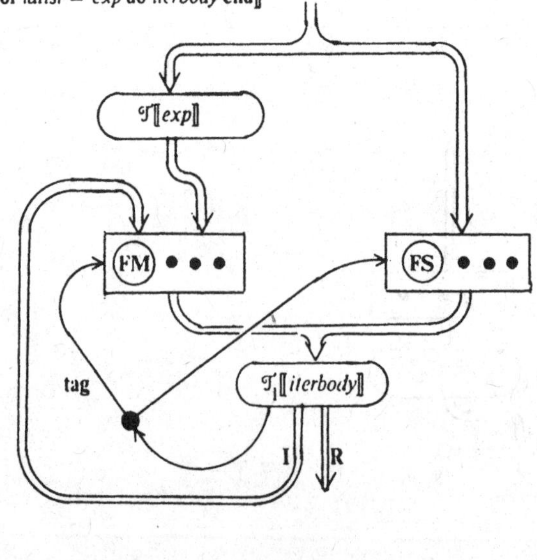

false control input. The FM gates select, under control of the tag values of the iteration body, either the outputs of the initialization expression or the R outputs of the iteration body. The selected values are sent to the iteration body input ports labeled by the iteration variables. The other iteration body inputs pass through FS gates. The FS gate absorbs, produces, and stores its data value whenever it receives a false control value. It produces its stored value, without absorbing a data value, whenever it receives a true control value. The FS gate has an initial false control value. Succeeding control values are the tag values of the iteration body. Thus, the FS gates store new values only when a "new" execution of the iteration body commences.

Let $\underline{\text{FMS}}^{idlist}$ be the composite history function of the FM and FS gates. $\underline{\text{FMS}}^{idlist}$ maps a quadruple consisting of the iteration body tag output, the iteration body I outputs, the initialization expression outputs, and the iteration expression history environment into the history environment input to the iteration body.

$$\underline{\text{FMS}}^{idlist}(X, Y, Z, \text{P})[\![id]\!] = \mathcal{O}[\![\text{FM}]\!](X, Y_i, Z_i), \text{ if } id \text{ is the } i\text{-th element of } idlist$$
$$= \mathcal{O}[\![\text{FS}]\!](X, \text{P}[\![id]\!]), \text{ if } id \text{ is not an element of } idlist$$

The operational characterization of the iteration expression is obtained by deriving the least fixpoint to an equation constraining the outputs of the iteration body subgraph.

$$\mathcal{O}\circ\mathcal{T}_I[\![\textbf{for } idlist = exp \textbf{ do } iterbody \textbf{ end}]\!]\text{P} = (\text{Y}(\lambda X.\, \mathcal{O}\circ\mathcal{T}_I[\![iterbody]\!](\underline{\text{FMS}}^{idlist}(X_{tag}, X_I, \mathcal{O}\circ\mathcal{T}[\![exp]\!]\text{P}, \text{P}))))_R$$

The operational semantics of ADFL are certainly more complicated than the denotational. Furthermore, this complexity is not entirely the fault of our presentation, but rather largely the fault of the unusual conditions in which graphs containing non-terminating computations may produce results. Consider the following ADFL expressions with one free variable i:

for j = i do if j = 0 then iter(j) else j end end

which we abbreviate *DZ(i)*, for its evaluation diverges on zero values of i, and:

let k = *DZ(i)* in if i = 0 then 0 else k end end

which we abbreviate *IDZ(i)*, for its evaluation internally diverges on zero values of i. That is, when i is zero, although *DZ(i)* diverges, $\mathcal{T}[\![IDZ(i)]\!]$, the graph implementation *IDZ(i)*, "ignores" this internal divergence and yields zero. However, the ability to ignore divergence is limited. For example, if $\mathcal{T}[\![IDZ(i)]\!]$ receives the input sequence $0 \cdot 1$ as values of i, it will produce the output sequence 0. The second output cannot be produced until *DZ(i)* terminates its "computation" of the first output. Consequently, the ADFL expression:

for i = 0 do
if *IDZ(i)* = 0 then iter(1) else i end
end

does not terminate, although it would if *IDZ(i)* freely ignored internal divergence.

The preceding example illustrates the intrinsic complexity of the operational semantics of ADFL and demonstrates the need for the simpler denotational semantics. In the next section, we will prove the consistency of the operational and denotational semantics.

4. The Consistency of ADFL

The operational and denotational characterizations of ADFL are consistent if they agree on all expression and iteration body evaluations defined to be non-terminating by the denotational semantics. We believe that it is quite reasonable to expect VAL programmers to only consider expressions which denotationally terminate to be correct. Expressions which terminate operationally, but not denotationally, waste resources in unnecessary computation.

Formally, the consistency requirement may be stated as:

$$\mathcal{E}[\![exp]\!]\rho \neq \perp \text{ implies } \mathcal{O}\circ\mathcal{T}[\![exp]\!]\rho = \mathcal{E}[\![exp]\!]\rho\text{, and}$$
$$\mathcal{E}_I[\![iterbody]\!]\rho \neq \perp \text{ implies } \mathcal{O}\circ\mathcal{T}_I[\![iterbody]\!]\rho = \mathcal{E}_I[\![iterbody]\!]\rho$$

To prove, by induction on the syntax of ADFL, the consistency requirement, a stronger consistency requirement is needed for the induction hypothesis, namely:

Given a sequence $\rho_1, \ldots, \rho_n$ of environments such that, for all i, $\mathcal{E}[\![exp]\!]\rho_i \neq \perp$:

$$\mathcal{O}\circ\mathcal{T}[\![exp]\!]\rho_1 \bullet \ldots \bullet \rho_n = \mathcal{E}[\![exp]\!]\rho_1 \bullet \ldots \bullet \mathcal{E}[\![exp]\!]\rho_n$$

Similarly, if, for all i, $\mathcal{E}_I[\![iterbody]\!]\rho \neq \perp$:

$$\mathcal{O}\circ\mathcal{T}_I[\![iterbody]\!]\rho_1 \bullet \ldots \bullet \rho_n = \mathcal{E}_I[\![iterbody]\!]\rho_1 \bullet \ldots \bullet \mathcal{E}_I[\![iterbody]\!]\rho_n$$

The proof of consistency is straightforward, but often tedious, for all BNF productions except the iteration expression, the only expression semantically characterized with the least fixpoint operator. For the simpler productions, the weaker consistency requirement easily implies the stronger. We will sample the inductive proofs of the simpler productions by proving the weaker consistency requirement for the binding expression.

Let ρ be an environment such that:

$$\mathcal{E}[\![\textbf{let } idlist = exp_1 \textbf{ in } exp_2 \textbf{ end}]\!]\rho \neq \perp.$$

The strictness of the denotational specification of the binding expression implies that $\mathcal{E}[\![exp_2]\!]\rho \neq \perp$. Consequently, using the weaker consistency requirement as the induction hypothesis, we know that:

$$\mathcal{O}\circ\mathcal{T}[\![exp_2]\!]\rho = \mathcal{E}[\![exp_2]\!]\rho$$

With successive applications of the definition of $\mathcal{O}\circ\mathcal{T}$, the weaker consistency requirement, the preceding equality, and the definition of $\mathcal{E}$, the desired case is proven.

$$\begin{aligned}\mathcal{O}\circ\mathcal{T}[\![\textbf{let } idlist = exp_1 \textbf{ in } exp_2 \textbf{ end}]\!]\rho &= \mathcal{O}\circ\mathcal{T}[\![exp_2]\!]\rho[idlist/\mathcal{O}\circ\mathcal{T}[\![exp_1]\!]\rho] \\ &= \mathcal{E}[\![exp_2]\!]\rho[idlist/\mathcal{O}\circ\mathcal{T}[\![exp_1]\!]\rho] \\ &= \mathcal{E}[\![exp_2]\!]\rho[idlist/\mathcal{E}[\![exp_1]\!]\rho] \\ &= \mathcal{E}[\![\textbf{let } idlist = exp_1 \textbf{ in } exp_2 \textbf{ end}]\!]\rho\end{aligned}$$

Now we shall show how the stronger consistency requirement, used as an induction hypothesis, implies that the weaker consistency requirement holds for iteration bodies. Let ρ be an environment such that:

$$\mathcal{E}[\![\textbf{for } idlist = exp \textbf{ do } iterbody \textbf{ end}]\!]\rho \neq \perp$$

From, the lemma stated at the end of Section 2, we know that there exists a sequence $\rho_1, \ldots, \rho_n$ such that for all i between 1 and n-1:

$$\rho_1 = \rho[idlist/\mathcal{E}[\![exp]\!]\rho]$$
$$\rho_{i+1} = \rho_i[idlist/(\mathcal{E}_I[\![iterbody]\!]\rho_i)_I]$$
$$(\mathcal{E}_I[\![iterbody]\!]\rho_i)_{tag} = \mathbf{true}$$
$$(\mathcal{E}_I[\![iterbody]\!]\rho_n)_{tag} = \mathbf{false}$$
$$(\mathcal{E}_I[\![iterbody]\!]\rho_n)_R = \mathcal{E}[\![\mathbf{for}\ idlist = exp\ \mathbf{do}\ iterbody\ \mathbf{end}]\!]\rho$$

Recall the operational characterization of the iteration body. Let F be the iteration evaluation function:

$$F = \lambda X.\ \mathcal{O}\circ\mathcal{T}_I[\![iterbody]\!](\underline{\mathrm{FMS}}^{idlist}(X_{tag}, X_I, \mathcal{O}\circ\mathcal{T}[\![exp]\!]\rho, \rho))$$

Consequently:

$$\mathcal{O}\circ\mathcal{T}[\![\mathbf{for}\ idlist = exp\ \mathbf{do}\ iterbody\ \mathbf{end}]\!]\rho = \mathrm{Y}(F)_R = (\sqcap F^i(\perp))_R$$

By induction on i, we may prove that:

$$F^i(\perp) = \mathcal{E}_I[\![iterbody]\!]\rho_1 \cdot ... \cdot \mathcal{E}_I[\![iterbody]\!]\rho_i = \mathcal{O}\circ\mathcal{T}_I[\![iterbody]\!]\rho_1 \cdot ... \cdot \rho_i,\ \text{if } i \leq n$$
$$F^i(\perp) = \mathcal{E}_I[\![iterbody]\!]\rho_1 \cdot ... \cdot \mathcal{E}_I[\![iterbody]\!]\rho_n = \mathcal{O}\circ\mathcal{T}_I[\![iterbody]\!]\rho_1 \cdot ... \cdot \rho_n,\ \text{if } i \geq n$$

For $i = 1$, we prove with successive applications of the definition of $F^1(\perp)$, the consistency requirement, the definition of $\underline{\mathrm{FMS}}^{idlist}$ (recall its initial false control value), the definition of ρ_1, and the consistency requirement that:

$$\begin{aligned} F^1(\perp) &= \mathcal{O}\circ\mathcal{T}_I[\![iterbody]\!](\underline{\mathrm{FMS}}^{idlist}(\varepsilon, \varepsilon, \mathcal{O}\circ\mathcal{T}[\![exp]\!]\rho, \rho)) \\ &= \mathcal{O}\circ\mathcal{T}_I[\![iterbody]\!](\underline{\mathrm{FMS}}^{idlist}(\varepsilon, \varepsilon, \mathcal{E}[\![exp]\!]\rho, \rho)) \\ &= \mathcal{O}\circ\mathcal{T}_I[\![iterbody]\!]\rho[idlist/\mathcal{E}[\![exp]\!]\rho] \\ &= \mathcal{O}\circ\mathcal{T}_I[\![iterbody]\!]\rho_1 \\ &= \mathcal{E}_I[\![iterbody]\!]\rho_1 \end{aligned}$$

For $i < n$, the induction hypothesis and the lemma of Section 2 imply that:

$$F^i(\perp)_{tag} = (\mathcal{E}_I[\![iterbody]\!]\rho_1)_{tag} \cdot ... \cdot (\mathcal{E}_I[\![iterbody]\!]\rho_i)_{tag} = \mathbf{true}^i$$

By successive applications of the definition of ρ_i, the induction hypothesis, the definition of $\underline{\mathrm{FMS}}^{idlist}$, and the preceding equality, we may conclude that:

$$\begin{aligned} \rho_1 \cdot ... \cdot \rho_{i+1} &= \rho \cdot ... \cdot \rho\ [idlist/\mathcal{E}[\![exp]\!]\rho \cdot (\mathcal{E}_I[\![iterbody]\!]\rho_1)_I \cdot ... \cdot (\mathcal{E}_I[\![iterbody]\!]\rho_i)_I] \\ &= \rho \cdot ... \cdot \rho\ [idlist/\mathcal{E}[\![exp]\!]\rho \cdot F^i(\perp)_I] \\ &= \underline{\mathrm{FMS}}^{idlist}(\mathbf{true}^i, F^i(\perp)_I, \mathcal{E}[\![exp]\!]\rho, \rho) \\ &= \underline{\mathrm{FMS}}^{idlist}(F^i(\perp)_{tag}, F^i(\perp)_I, \mathcal{O}\circ\mathcal{T}[\![exp]\!]\rho, \rho) \end{aligned}$$

The definition of $F^{i+1}(\perp)$, the preceding equality, and the consistency requirement imply that:

$$\begin{aligned} F^{i+1}(\perp) &= \mathcal{O}\circ\mathcal{T}_I[\![iterbody]\!](\underline{\mathrm{FMS}}^{idlist}(F^i(\perp)_{tag}, F^i(\perp)_I, \mathcal{O}\circ\mathcal{T}[\![exp]\!]\rho, \rho)) \\ &= \mathcal{O}\circ\mathcal{T}_I[\![iterbody]\!]\rho_1 \cdot ... \cdot \rho_{i+1} \\ &= \mathcal{E}_I[\![iterbody]\!]\rho_1 \cdot ... \cdot \mathcal{E}_I[\![iterbody]\!]\rho_{i+1} \end{aligned}$$

Similarly, for $i \geq n$:

$$\begin{aligned} F^{i+1}(\perp) &= \mathcal{O}\circ\mathcal{T}_I[\![iterbody]\!](\underline{\mathrm{FMS}}^{idlist}(F^i(\perp)_{tag}, F^i(\perp)_I, \mathcal{O}\circ\mathcal{T}[\![exp]\!]\rho, \rho)) \\ &= \mathcal{O}\circ\mathcal{T}_I[\![iterbody]\!](\underline{\mathrm{FMS}}^{idlist}(\mathbf{true}^{n-1} \cdot \mathbf{false}, F^i(\perp)_I, \mathcal{E}[\![exp]\!]\rho, \rho)) \\ &= \mathcal{O}\circ\mathcal{T}_I[\![iterbody]\!]\rho_1 \cdot ... \cdot \rho_n \\ &= \mathcal{E}_I[\![iterbody]\!]\rho_1 \cdot ... \cdot \mathcal{E}_I[\![iterbody]\!]\rho_n \end{aligned}$$

Therefore, the above definitions of ρ_i and F imply:

$$\begin{aligned} \mathcal{O}\circ\mathcal{T}[\![\mathbf{for}\ idlist = exp\ \mathbf{do}\ iterbody\ \mathbf{end}]\!]\mathrm{P} = \mathrm{Y}(F)_R = (\sqcap F^i(\perp))_R &= (\mathcal{E}_I[\![iterbody]\!]\rho_1 \cdot ... \cdot \mathcal{E}_I[\![iterbody]\!]\rho_n)_R \\ &= \mathcal{E}[\![\mathbf{for}\ idlist = exp\ \mathbf{in}\ iterbody\ \mathbf{end}]\!]\rho \end{aligned}$$

This proof can be extended to the stronger consistency requirement by observing that the control input $\mathbf{true}^{n-1} \cdot \mathbf{false}$ of $\underline{\mathrm{FMS}}^{idlist}$ has reset $\underline{\mathrm{FMS}}^{idlist}$ to its original state of waiting for inputs from outside the iteration expression. That extension completes the inductive proof of semantic consistency.

5. Summary

We have defined ADFL, an Applicative Data Flow Language, given its denotational semantics, thus demonstrating its simplicity, given its operational semantics, thus demonstrating its concurrency, and proven the consistency of the two semantic definitions.

This research is best extended by extension of the data flow language. Procedures are an obvious, and easy, addition to the language. The addition of constructs for programming real-time systems is a difficult, though rewarding, extension. In the data flow language of Weng [13], program identifiers may have *streams* (histories) as values. Interprocess communication, similar to that observed in real-time systems, is accomplished by the passing of streams. Dennis [7] has defined a stream operator which non-determinately merges two input stream and has used it to specify the inherently non-determinate airline reservation system. While the non-determinacy of this language limits the simplicity of its semantic characterization, the elevation of process communication and synchronization to the level of passed parameters results in programs which are easier to comprehend and verify.

6. References

[1] Ackerman, W. B., and J. B. Dennis, *VAL -- A Value-Oriented Algorithmic Language: Preliminary Reference Manual*, Computation Structures Group, Laboratory for Computer Science (TR-218), MIT, Cambridge, Massachusetts, June 1979.

[2] Arvind, and K. P. Gostelow, "A Computer Capable of Exchanging Processors for Time", *Information Processing 77: Proceedings of IFIP Congress 77* (B. Gilchrist, Ed.), August 1977, 849-853.

[3] Arvind, K. P. Gostelow, and W. Plouffe, "Indeterminacy, Monitors and Dataflow", *Proceedings of the Sixth ACM Symposium on Operating Systems Principles, Operating Systems Review 11*, 5(November 1977), 159-169.

[4] Brinch Hansen, P., "Distributed Processes: A Concurrent Programming Concept," *Communications of the ACM 21*, 11(November 1978), 934-941.

[5] Brock, J. D., *Operational Semantics of a Data Flow Language*, Laboratory for Computer Science (TM-120), MIT, Cambridge, Massachusetts, December 1978.

[6] Dennis, J. B., "First Version of a Data Flow Procedure Language", *Programming Symposium: Proceedings, Colleque sur la Programmation* (B. Robinet, Ed.), *Lecture Notes in Computer Science 19*, 362-376.

[7] Dennis, J. B., "A Language Design for Structured Concurrency", *Design and Implementation of Programming Languages: Proceedings of a DoD Sponsored Workshop* (J. H. Williams and D. A. Fisher, Eds.), *Lecture Notes in Computer Science 54*, October 1976.

[8] Dennis, J. B., and D. P. Misunas, "A Preliminary Architecture for a Basic Data-Flow Processor", *The Second Annual Symposium on Computer Architecture: Conference Proceedings*, January 1975, 126-132.

[9] Hoare, C. A. R., "Communicating Sequential Processes", *Communications of the ACM 21*, 8(August 1978), 666-677.

[10] Kahn, G., "The Semantics of a Simple Language for Parallel Programming", *Information Processing 74: Proceedings of the IFIP Congress 74*, August 1974, 471-475.

[11] Scott, D. S., "Data Types as Lattices", *SIAM Journal of Computing 5*, 3(September 1976), 522-587.

[12] Tennent, R. D., "The Denotational Semantics of Programming Languages", *Communications of the ACM 19*, 8(August 1976), 437-453.

[13] Weng, K.-S., *Stream-Oriented Computation in Recursive Data Flow Schemas*, Laboratory for Computer Science (TM-68), MIT, Cambridge, Massachusetts, October 1975.

ANALOG PROCESSES

Luca Cardelli

Department of Computer Science
University of Edinburgh
J.C.M.B., The King's Buildings
Edinburgh EH9 3JZ

Introduction

We intend to study systems of communicating processes in which processes interact with each other in a continuous asynchronous fashion, as do planets around a star. Such processes cannot be considered "computing agents" as they just behave instant by instant according to laws which are not "computations" in any mechanical sense. Their interactions are not instantaneous synchronous communications, but rather a continuous flow of information which does not fit in the message passing paradigm. These systems develop in continuous time and their interactions are often expressed in terms of continuous values. More importantly, their behaviour cannot be fully understood by forcing them into a discrete environment, as a whole range of interesting phenomena is then lost.

Asynchronous electronic circuits will be used as a source of interesting examples, and we shall be able to model and analyse puzzling behaviours like asynchronous feedbacks, metastable states, arbitration and indeterminacy. All these phenomena will be explained in terms of a single principle, which simply forbids the existence of null-delay feedback loops. This also shows that these complex real-world behaviours can be described by just assuming concurrency in continuous time, and do not necessarely depend on other features of the physical universe, like relativistic or quantum mechanic effects.

Analog Processes

A *signal* is a value varying in continuous time, and an *analog process* is a transformation of signals, for example:

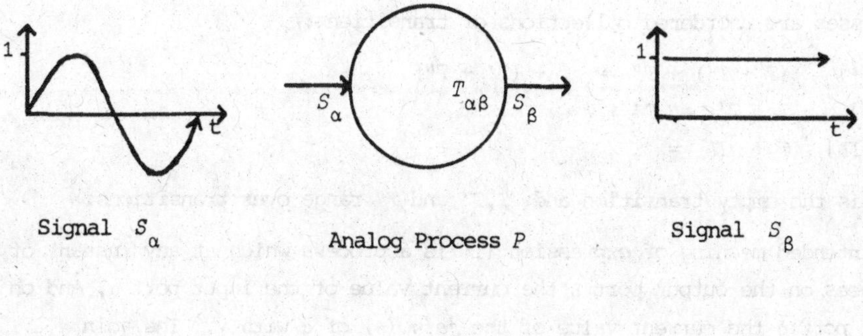

Signal S_α Analog Process P Signal S_β

The signals above can be expressed as functions of time:

$$S_\alpha(t) = \sin t \qquad\qquad S_\beta(t) = 1$$

and the process P transforming S_α into S_β can be described by a single *transition* $T_{\alpha\beta}$ which could be in this case:

$$T_{\alpha\beta}(s)(t) = s(t) - \sin t + 1$$

In fact, applying $T_{\alpha\beta}$ to S_α we get S_β:

$$\begin{aligned} T_{\alpha\beta}(S_\alpha) &= \lambda t.\ S_\alpha(t) - \sin t + 1 \\ &= \lambda t.\ \sin t - \sin t + 1 \\ &= \lambda t.\ 1 \\ &= S_\beta \end{aligned}$$

In general a process will consist of several transitions, and systems will comprise several connected processes.

An algebra of analog processes

A *process* is described by a collection of *transitions* $M \to \beta$, where the term M is the *signal* produced by the transition, and β is the *output port* of the transition. The signal M is an expression of some of the *input ports* of the process. Here is an example of the syntax we shall use to talk about processes:

$$(\alpha \to \beta) + ((\alpha \uplus \gamma) \to \delta)$$

For clarity we shall sometimes prefix processes with their input ports, although this is not strictly necessary as the input ports of a process will always coincide with the free variables of the signal parts of the transitions:

$$\alpha\ \gamma:\ \alpha \to \beta \ + \ \alpha \uplus \gamma \to \delta \qquad (1)$$

this is a process with input ports α,γ and output ports β,δ (parenthesis have been omitted).

The intended behaviour of processes will be explained by algebraic laws. We will only be concerned with the most interesting laws and we shall not try to present a complete set of equations. The following three laws express the fact that processes are unordered collections of transitions:

$$[{+}{+}] \qquad (T + T') + T'' = T + (T' + T'')$$

$$[+] \qquad T + T' = T' + T$$

$$[NIL] \qquad T + NIL = T$$

where NIL is the empty transition and T,T' and T'' range over transitions.

The intended meaning of expression (1) is a process which at any instant of time produces on the output port β the current value of the input port α, and on the output port δ the current value of the *join* ($\uplus$) of α with γ. The join operation represent the simultaneous presence of two signals on the same "line", and its exact meaning is left unspecified, except that the join operation must exist for every pair of signals (of the same type) and it must satisfy:

[⊎⊎] $(M \uplus N) \uplus P \;=\; M \uplus (N \uplus P)$

[⊎] $M \uplus N \;=\; N \uplus M$

For example, for boolean-valued signals s_1, s_2 we might define $s_1 \uplus s_2$ to be at any instant of time a boolean *or*, i.e.: $(s_1 \uplus s_2)(t) = s_1(t)$ *or* $s_2(t)$.

The existence of a constant $\dot{-}$ (*nosignal*) is also assumed; it relates to join as follows:

[$\dot{-}$] $M \uplus \dot{-} \;=\; M$

In the previous boolean example we can define nosignal as the signal constantly *false*, i.e.: $\dot{-}(t) = false$. The join operation is also used in the following law, which accounts for the presence of repeated output ports:

[⊎+] $M \rightarrow \beta \;+\; N \rightarrow \beta \;=\; M \uplus N \rightarrow \beta$

Now we will define some basic operations on processes, together with their algebraic laws.

COMPOSITION. The composition of two processes P and Q is written $P|Q$. The output ports of P are linked to the homonymous input ports of Q, and the output ports of Q are linked to the homonymous input ports of P; the idea being that signals flow through these connections from one process to the other. We have the following rules for composition:

[||] $(P \mid Q) \mid R \;=\; P \mid (Q \mid R)$

[|] $P \mid Q \;=\; Q \mid P$

[|+] $(\sum_{i\in I} T_i) \mid (\sum_{j\in J} T_j) \;=\; \sum_{k\in I\cup J} T_k$
where I and J are disjoint sets of indexes

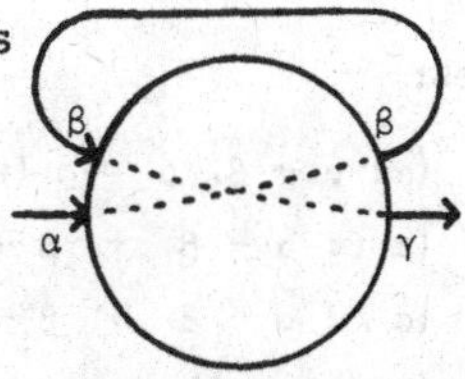

An example of the law [|+] is:

$(\alpha\!: \alpha \rightarrow \beta) \mid (\beta\!: \beta \rightarrow \gamma) \;=\; \alpha\,\beta\!: \alpha \rightarrow \beta \;+\; \beta \rightarrow \gamma$

Note that composition may introduce loops of signals (β being both an input and an output port) and indeed such loops may be present in the first place. We will come later to the exact semantics of such situations; for the moment it will be intended that a looping signal overwrites itself by a join operation.

RESTRICTION. The restriction $P\backslash\alpha$ of P cancels α from the input and output ports of P, making communication via α impossible. We have:

[\] $P\backslash\alpha \;=\; P$ if $\alpha \notin$ ports(P)

[\\] $P\backslash\alpha\backslash\beta \;=\; P\backslash\beta\backslash\alpha$

$[\backslash|]$ $(P \mid Q)\backslash\alpha = P\backslash\alpha \mid Q\backslash\alpha$
if not $((\alpha \in \text{input-ports}(P)$ *and* $\alpha \in \text{output-ports}(Q))$ *or*
$(\alpha \in \text{output-ports}(P)$ *and* $\alpha \in \text{input-ports}(Q))$

Now we need a law to distribute \ over +, and at first sight this could be:

$$(\textstyle\sum_{i\in I} T_i)\backslash\alpha = \sum_{i\in I}(T_i\backslash\alpha)$$
$$(M \to \alpha)\backslash\alpha = NIL$$
$$(\ldots \alpha \ldots \to \beta)\backslash\alpha = \ldots \dot{-} \ldots \to \beta$$

Unfortunately this does not work well in the case:

$$(\alpha\colon M \to \alpha \quad + \quad \alpha \to \beta)\backslash\alpha = \dot{-} \to \beta$$

In fact we want to interpret \ as a hiding operator, which should not change the inner behaviour of the process. The result we want to get is, at least:

$$(M \to \alpha \quad + \quad \alpha \to \beta)\backslash\alpha = M \to \beta$$

But even this is not enought in the case that M is an expression $M[\alpha]$ of α itself, e.g. when we have a loop over the restriction variable whose result is exported through another output port (in this case β). To solve this problem we need to introduce recursively defined signals $(\mu\alpha.\ M)$:

$[\mu]$ $\mu\alpha.\ M = \mu\beta.\ M[\beta/\alpha]$

$[\mu\mu]$ $\mu\alpha.\ M = M[\mu\alpha.\ M/\alpha]$

Then the law for restriction is:

$[\backslash+]$ $(\sum_{i\in I} T_i)\backslash\alpha = \sum_{j\in J} T'_j$
where $J = \{i\in I\colon T_i = M_i \to \alpha_i$ *and* $\alpha_i \neq \alpha\}$
and $T'_j = T_j[\mu\alpha.\ N/\alpha]$
with N = the join of all the M_i such that $T_i = M_i \to \alpha_i$
is in $\sum_{i\in I} T_i$ and $\alpha_i = \alpha$ (and $N = \dot{-}$ if no such M_i exists)

Examples:

$$(\alpha\colon \alpha \to \beta)\backslash\alpha = (\mu\alpha.\ \dot{-}) \to \beta = \dot{-} \to \beta$$
$$(\alpha\ \beta\colon \alpha \to \beta \quad + \quad \beta \to \gamma)\backslash\beta = \alpha\colon \alpha \to \gamma$$
$$(\alpha\ \beta\colon \alpha \to \beta \quad + \quad \beta \to \alpha)\backslash\beta = \alpha\colon \alpha \to \alpha$$
$$(\alpha\colon \alpha \to \alpha)\backslash\alpha = NIL$$
$$(\alpha\colon \alpha \to \alpha \quad + \quad \alpha \to \beta)\backslash\alpha = (\mu\alpha.\ \alpha) \to \beta$$

The important point in this definition is that looping situations are somehow hidden or preserved, but never "unfolded" by $\backslash\alpha$.

RELABELLING. The relabelling $P\langle\alpha_1/\beta_1;\ \ldots\ ;\ \alpha_n/\beta_n\rangle$ is the process obtained from P simulataneously substituting the (input and/or output) ports $\alpha_1 \ldots \alpha_n$ by $\beta_1 \ldots \beta_n$. A relabelling $\langle R\rangle = \langle\alpha_i/\beta_i\rangle$ is a bijection $R\colon L \to L$ over the ports L of P, i.e. β_i are all and only the ports of P, and α_i are distinct port names. Dummy substitutions will be omitted, so that $<> = <\alpha_i/\alpha_i>$.

$$[<>] \quad P<> \;=\; P$$

$$[<><>] \quad P<R><S> \;=\; P<S \circ R>$$

$$[<>\backslash] \quad (P\backslash\alpha)<R> \;=\; (P<R;\ \beta/\alpha>)\backslash\beta$$

$$\text{if } \alpha \in \text{ports}(P) \text{ and } \beta \notin \text{range}(R)$$

$$[<>|] \quad (P|Q)<R> \;=\; (P<R'>)\,|\,(Q<R''>)$$

$$\text{where } R' = R \text{ restricted to ports}(P)$$
$$\text{and } \quad R'' = R \text{ restricted to ports}(Q)$$

To distribute $<R>$ over $+$ we actually perform a (metasyntactical) substitution:

$$[<>+] \quad (\textstyle\sum_{i\in I} T_i)<\alpha_j/\beta_j> \;=\; \sum_{i\in I}(T_i[\alpha_j/\beta_j])$$

Ex:

$$(\alpha\ \beta\colon \alpha \to \beta \;+\; \beta \to \alpha)<\alpha/\beta;\ \beta/\alpha> \;=\; \beta\ \alpha\colon \beta \to \alpha \;+\; \alpha \to \beta$$

The algebraic laws we have so far presented form what we will call an *analog algebra*. These laws can be grouped into two categories: external laws (relating $|$, $\backslash\alpha$ and $<R>$: [||], [|], [\], [\\], [\|], [<>], [<><>], [<>\] and [<>|]) concerning the syntesis of processes from simpler processes, and internal laws (all the others) concerning the inner structure of processes. The external laws hold for Milner's *flow algebras* [Milner 79]. Flow algebras are extended in [Milner 78] by a set of internal laws for communicating processes, and are then called *behaviour algebras*. Our internal laws are quite different from Milner's ones, but they seem to fit very well in the general framework of flow algebras, even if the meaning of $|$, $\backslash\alpha$ and $<R>$ is radically different.

A denotational model

In the rest of this paper we will study a particular analog algebra, built within the denotational semantics framework. This will allow us to study the exact meaning of processes just by computing their semantics and observing their input-output behaviour. The denotational semantics will also prove useful in discussing some tricky situations like feedbacks and recursive signals. Unfortunately we do not have space for full details and we shall only try to sketch the main ideas.

Processes are collections of transitions; in particular a process with n inputs is an association of labels (the output ports) to transitions with n inputs:

$$P_n \;=\; L \to T_n$$

where P_n, L and T_n are semantic domains (complete partial orders): L is the flat domain of port labels, T_n is the domain of transitions with n inputs, and P_n is the domain of processes with n inputs. The domain P will also denote (the disjoint union of) the domains P_n for any n.

A transition with n inputs is a function taking n input signals (each labelled with its input ports) and producing an output signal:

$$T_n = S_L^n \rightarrow S$$

where S_L^n is some domain of unordered labelled n-tuples of signals.

Signals are functions from time to a domain of values. We can have several types of signals, like boolean signals, real signals etc.

$$S = K \rightarrow V$$

where K is the flat domain of positive real numbers, and V is some data domain admitting a constant $\phi \in V$ and an (infix) operation $\cup$: $V \times V \rightarrow V$ such that the properties $[\uplus\uplus]$, $[\uplus]$ and $[\dot{-}]$ hold by defining:

$$\dot{-}(t) = \phi \qquad\qquad s_1(t) \cup s_2(t) = s_1 \uplus s_2$$

for all $t \in K$ and $s_1, s_2 \in S$.

We need some notation for elements in these domains; λ-notation will be used for signals $s \in S = K \rightarrow V$. Elements of S_L^n will be denoted by expressions like:

$$[\alpha_1 : s_1; \ \ldots \ ; \alpha_n : s_n] \qquad \text{with } \alpha_1 \ldots \alpha_n \in L, \ s_1 \ldots s_n \in S$$

which are meant to be unordered tuples of labelled signals $\alpha_i : s_i$ with the additional property:

$$[\ \ldots \ \alpha : s'; \ \alpha : s'' \ \ldots \ ] = [\ \ldots \ \alpha : s' \uplus s'' \ \ldots \ ]$$

and operations:

$$[\alpha_i : s_i] \backslash \alpha = [\alpha_j : s_j] \qquad \text{with } i \in I, \ j \in J \text{ and } J = \{ i \in I \mid \alpha_i \neq \alpha \}$$
$$[\alpha_i : s_i].\alpha = \uplus\{ s_k \mid \alpha_k = \alpha \} \qquad (\text{where } \uplus\{\} = \dot{-})$$
$$[\alpha_i : s_i] \uplus [\alpha'_j : s'_j] = [\alpha_i : s_i; \ \alpha'_j : s'_j] \ .$$

Elements of $T_n = S_L^n \rightarrow S$ of the form:

$$\lambda x. \ \ldots \ x.\alpha_1 \ \ldots \ x.\alpha_n \ \ldots \qquad\qquad (\alpha_1 \ldots \alpha_n \in L)$$

will be abbreviated (with a change of font) as:

$$\lambda[a_1 \ldots a_n]. \ \ldots \ a_1 \ \ldots \ a_n \ \ldots$$

where $[a_1 \ldots a_n]$ is an unordered tuple of variables. Notice that this notation allows for unordered application by label names, as in:

$$(\lambda[a_1 \ a_2]. \ a_1 * a_2)[\alpha_2 : 3; \ \alpha_1 : 5] = 5*3$$

Finally, processes $p \in P_n = L \to T_n$ of the form:

$$\lambda x.\ (x{=}\alpha_1) \Rightarrow t_1\ ;\ \ldots\ ;\ (x{=}\alpha_n) \Rightarrow t_n\ ;\ (\lambda[\,].\ \dot{-})$$

will be abbreviated as:

$$\{t_1 \to \alpha_1;\ \ldots\ ;\ t_n \to \alpha_n\}$$

There are three semantic evaluation functions:

$\mathcal{T}$: terms × vars → T	for term expressions
$\mathcal{S}$: signals × ports → S	for signal expressions
$\mathcal{P}$: processes × ports → P	for process expressions

with two kinds of environments: vars = Ide → V; ports = L → S.

We shall first discuss the semantics of process expressions, then the semantics of signal expressions, giving the syntax at the same time. We shall not treat the semantics of terms, as term expressions will always have an evident meaning.

The following is the semantics of a very simple process, consisting of a single transition:

$$\mathcal{P}[\![\alpha_i\colon S \to \beta]\!]\sigma =$$
$$Y\ \lambda P.\ \{\lambda[a_i].\ \mathcal{S}[\![S]\!]\sigma[a_i \uplus P(\beta)[\alpha_i{:}a_i]/\alpha_i] \to \beta\}$$

The fixpoint and the join operation are needed just in case β is equal to one of the α_i, i.e. when there is a feedback. Otherwise the previous expression reduces simply to:

$$\{\lambda[a_i].\ \mathcal{S}[\![S]\!]\sigma[a_i/\alpha_i]\}$$

In case of a feedback, say $\alpha_3{=}\beta$, the input to α_3 is a_3 (the input to processor P) joined to what comes out of β, which is $P(\beta)[\alpha_i{:}a_i]$. In fact $P(\beta)$ is the transition associated with β, which receives as input the same input of the process: $[\alpha_i{:}a_i]$.

The same idea is used in giving the semantics of composition, in which the component processes may feed each other in complex ways:

$$\begin{aligned} p|q\ =\ & \text{let } p = \{s_i \to \gamma_i\} \\ & \text{and } q = \{r_j \to \delta_j\} \text{ in} \\ & \text{let } s_i = \lambda[a_h].\ M_i \\ & \text{and } r_j = \lambda[b_k].\ N_j \text{ in} \\ Y\ \lambda R.\ & \{\lambda[a_h b_k].\ p(\gamma_i)[\alpha_h{:}a_h \uplus R(\alpha_h)[\alpha_h{:}a_h;\ \beta_k{:}b_k]] \to \gamma_i\} \\ \uplus\ & \{\lambda[a_h b_k].\ q(\delta_j)[\beta_k{:}b_k \uplus R(\beta_k)[\alpha_h{:}a_h;\ \beta_k{:}b_k]] \to \delta_j\} \end{aligned}$$

This composition is commutative ([|] holds); to prove associativity ([||]) we had to assume absorption of $\uplus$, i.e. $s \uplus s = s$ (which also implies $P|P = P$).

The other laws of analog algebras are easily verified, if we complete the definition of P by the following equations:

$$\mathsf{P}[\![T_1 + \ldots + T_n]\!]\sigma \;=\; \mathsf{P}[\![T_1]\!]\sigma \mid \ldots \mid \mathsf{P}[\![T_n]\!]\sigma$$

$$\mathsf{P}[\![P\backslash\alpha]\!]\sigma \;=\; \lambda\beta.\ \lambda x.\ \beta{=}\alpha \Rightarrow \dot{-}\ ;\ (\mathsf{P}[\![P]\!]\sigma)(\beta)(x \uplus [\alpha{:}\dot{-}])$$

$$\begin{aligned}\mathsf{P}[\![P\langle\beta_i/\alpha_i\rangle]\!]\sigma \;=\;& \text{let } p = \mathsf{P}[\![P]\!]\sigma \\ & \text{in } \lambda\gamma.\ \lambda[b_i].\ \gamma{=}\beta_1 \Rightarrow p(\alpha_1)[\alpha_i{:}b_i]\ ;\ \ldots\ ; \\ & \qquad\qquad\quad \gamma{=}\beta_n \Rightarrow p(\alpha_n)[\alpha_i{:}b_i]\ ;\ \dot{-}\end{aligned}$$

We pass now to consider signals; a simple way to specify them is to describe their value at any instant of time, using a sort of λ-notation:

$$\mathsf{S}[\![@t.V]\!]\sigma \;=\; \lambda a.\ \mathsf{T}[\![V]\!]\varepsilon[a/t] \qquad (\varepsilon \text{ is the empty environment})$$

for example @t. 3*sin t. We have the equivalences $\dot{-} = @t.\ \phi$ and $a \uplus b = @t.\ a(t) \cup b(t)$. The notation $\hat{}V$ will be used as an abbreviation of $@t.\ V$, when t is not a free variable in V, like in $\hat{}3 = @t.\ 3$.

Signals can also be defined by recursion:

$$\mathsf{S}[\![\mu s.\ S]\!]\sigma \;=\; Y\ \lambda a.\ \mathsf{S}[\![S]\!]\sigma[a/s]$$

like in $\mu s.\ @t.\ t{<}1 \Rightarrow \phi\ ;\ s(t-1) \equiv \dot{-}$. Two other useful abbreviations are conditional signals and delays:

$$S \Rightarrow S'\ ;\ S'' \;=\; @t.\ S(t) \Rightarrow S'(t)\ ;\ S''(t)$$

$$S'\ \Delta\ S'' \;=\; @t.\ t{<}S''(t) \Rightarrow \phi\ ;\ S'(t-S''(t))$$

A simple example of delay is $S\ \Delta\ \hat{}3$ which is the signal S constantly delayed by 3 units of time, yielding ϕ during the first three units of time. This notation also allows us to express variable delays.

Notice that the @-notation has too big an expressive power, being able for example to define a signal in terms of the "future" of another signal (or even of itself), but we might impose syntactic restriction to avoid that, leaving Δ as a primitive.

Unfeasibility

Great care has been put into the definition of the algebraic laws and of the denotational semantics, in order to be able to treat circularities; so let us see how it works. The simplest example of a feedback can be found in the following *fast loop* process:

$\alpha{:}\ \alpha \rightarrow \alpha$

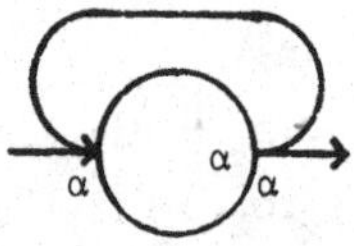

This process has an input port α, whose input is mixed to the output coming from the output port α. The tricky point is that this process has no internal delay, and the output at any instant t depends on the input at the same instant t, which depends again on the output at time t. Computing the semantics:

$$\mathbb{P}[\![\alpha: \alpha \to \alpha]\!]\sigma$$

$$= \gamma\ \lambda P.\ \{\lambda[a].\ \mathbb{S}[\![\alpha]\!]\sigma[a \uplus P(\alpha)[\alpha:a]/\alpha] \to \alpha\}$$

$$= \gamma\ \lambda P.\ \{\lambda[a].\ a \uplus P(\alpha)[\alpha:a] \to \alpha\} =_{def} p$$

It is not immediatly clear what p does, but we can try to understand its behaviour by applying some input. We first extract the transition we are interested in (there is only one in this case) applying the output port α:

$$p(\alpha) = \lambda[a].\ a \uplus p(\alpha)[\alpha:a]$$

then we apply an input signal to see what is the response of the transition; we choose to apply nosignal:

$$p(\alpha)[\alpha:\dot{-}] = \dot{-} \uplus p(\alpha)[\alpha:\dot{-}] = p(\alpha)[\alpha:\dot{-}] = \perp$$

the result is $\perp$: it happens that the output of the fast loop is $\perp$ for any input, if we assume $\uplus$ to be strict in both its arguments.

Here we have a first example of a clearly "unfeasible" process, which is semantically mapped to undefined. We can also see that a *slow loop* is not mapped to $\perp$ and is perfectly well-defined:

$$\mathbb{P}[\![\alpha: \alpha\ \Delta\ \hat{}1 \to \alpha]\!]\sigma$$

$$= \gamma\ \lambda P.\ \{\lambda[a].\ \lambda t.\ t<1 \Rightarrow \phi\ ;\ (a \uplus P(\alpha)[\alpha:a])(t-1) \to \alpha\} =_{def} p$$

$$p(\alpha)[\alpha:\dot{-}] = \lambda t.\ t<1 \Rightarrow \phi\ ;\ (p(\alpha)[\alpha:\dot{-}])(t-1) = \dot{-}$$

There are also processes whose output signals are only partially undefined; an example is the *zeno loop*:

$$\alpha: \alpha\ \Delta\ (@t.\ t<1 \Rightarrow 1-t\ ;\ 0) \to \alpha$$

this is a feedback loop which increases its speed, and at a finite point in time reaches an infinite speed (i.e. a zero delay). The output of the zeno loop for a nosignal input is $\lambda t.\ t<1 \Rightarrow \phi\ ;\ \perp$.

As a general principle, the output of a feedback loop is defined as long as the delay in the loop is greater than zero. This may look trivial, but feedback loops appear in almost any interesting process, and this simple fact has several intriguing consequences. We are going now to look at some of these.

Unexpressibility

We have seen that we can express several physically unfeasible processes. This suggests that our formalism has too big an expressive power, and we might try to impose some constraints in order to exclude unwanted processes. However it would be wrong to think that we can express anything we like.

In particular there are several processes which cannot be exactly expressed, and yet admit approximations up to an arbitrary degree of accuracy. We shall call such unexpressible processes *perfect*, and *imperfect* their expressible approximations.

Consider for example the following (*naive*) *memory cell*.

$$\alpha\ \beta:\ \alpha \uplus \beta\ \Delta\ \hat{}1 \rightarrow \beta$$

To work properly as a (write once) memory cell, this process must receive a *set* impulse of length 1 on α. Then this impulse gets into the loop and is "remembered". This memory cell presents two main defects: it will not work properly (i) if the set impulse is longer than 1, or (ii) if the set impulse is shorter than 1. We can solve the first problem by the following (*improved*) *memory cell*:

$$\alpha\ \beta:\ (\alpha = \dot{-} \Rightarrow \alpha\ ;\ \beta)\ \Delta\ \hat{}1 \rightarrow \beta$$

This process will cut off its α line after having received a signal different from $\dot{-}$ for 1 unit of time. But the second problem still remains; if the α signal differs from $\dot{-}$ for less then one unit of time, the output β is not constant. The same problem occurs when the set impulse changes its value during the setting time. Then a varying signal is recorded into the feedback loop, and the output of the memory cell oscillates: we get a (quench free) *metastable state*.

In effect what we really want is a *perfect memory cell* which stores constantly the value of an instantaneous setting spike, so that there can be no indeterminacy due to fluctuations of the input signal. Notice that starting from our improved memory cell we can get better and better approximations to a perfect cell, simply by reducing the delay in the feedback loop. Unfortunatly if we reduce the delay to zero, we do not get a perfect storage device, but only an undefined output. Hence (conjecture) there is no expression denoting a perfect memory cell (which yet exists inside our semantic domains) because there seems to be no way to define a storing device without the use of feedbacks.

Therefore, expressible memory cells are imperfect. It is important to notice that many useful processes have memory cells (or their equivalent) as basic building blocks, and such processes must take into account this imperfection and are likely to be themselves imperfect. In general an imperfect process works "correctly" under some classes of input signals, but in certain critical circumstances there is no way to guarantee its intended operation.

Indeterminacy

Consider the problem of designing a process which determines the time of occurrence of an event, or which measures the the value of a signal when some event (e.g. "measure it now") occurs. First we must agree on a definition of *determining* or *measuring*, and a sensible one seems to be *storing constantly for an unlimited amount of time*. We will not go into the details of such design because it is very similar to the problem of producing a perfect memory cell. In fact it is not difficult to see that perfect determination is impossible, just because perfect storage devices are unfeasible.

A well known case of indeterminacy is *arbitration*, where a device attempts to *determine* which of two events arrives first. A simple way of implementing an arbiter is to use a *decider* and a memory cell. The decider tells at any instant whether the first, the second or both signals are arriving, and the memory cell tries to remember the first decision of the decider. But memory cells are imperfect and so are arbiters based on memory cells. If the two signals arrive too close, the decider changes its decision while the cell is storing it, and the output of the cell is unstable. An alternative way of building an arbiter is by using two *detectors* to determine the time of occurrence of two events, and then compare these times. But it can be shown that detectors are imperfect, and so are arbiters built in this way.

In general the order or coincidence in time of two events cannot be determined. The order cannot be determined when the signals are too close, and the coincidence cannot be determined when the simultaneous signals are too short.

Flip-flops

In this last section we analyse a particular analog process, showing how its detailed behaviour can be derived from its semantics:

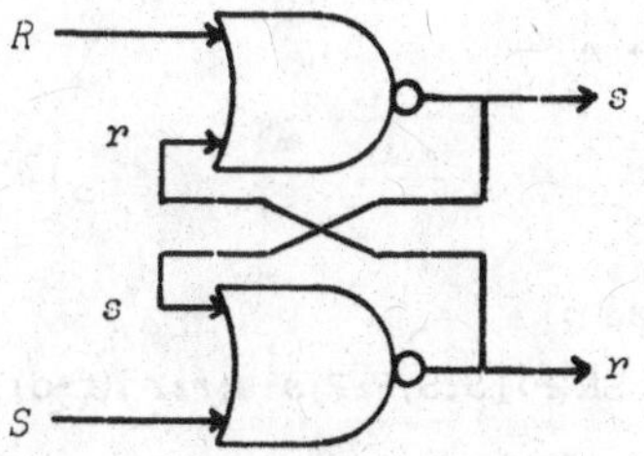

ϕ = *false*

υ = or

This is an *SR flip-flop*. In its *steady state condition* we have the following values on the ports:

$$R = S = s = false; \qquad r = true$$

Starting from this condition and applying a *set* pulse to the port S we get

s = *true* and r = *false*. Another set pulse has no effect. Then applying a *reset* pulse to the port R we change the output back to s = *false* and r = *true*. Another reset pulse has no effect. Applying both a set and a reset signal, the output signals oscillate between *true* and *false*, and this is called a *metastable state*. The actual behaviour of a real flip-flop in a metastable state can be rather different from the one described above. We believe it can be modelled by introducing some "quench", but here we shall not undertake this analysis.

The SR can be synthetized from smaller components:

$$OR = in1\ in2\text{: } (in1 \text{ or } in2)\ \Delta\ \hat{}\text{d}' \rightarrow out$$

$$NOT = in\text{: } (\text{not } in)\ \Delta\ \hat{}\text{d}'' \rightarrow out$$

$$OR1 = OR\langle R/in1;r/in2;w1/out\rangle$$

$$OR2 = OR\langle S/in1;s/in2;w2/out\rangle$$

$$NOT1 = NOT\langle w1/in;s/out\rangle$$

$$NOT2 = NOT\langle w2/in;r/out\rangle$$

$$SR = (OR1 \mid NOT1 \mid OR2 \mid NOT2)\backslash w1\backslash w2$$

It is an easy exercise to show that this is equivalent to:

$$SR = S\ R\ s\ r\text{: not}(R \text{ or } r)\ \Delta\ \hat{}\text{d} \rightarrow s \ + \ \text{not}(S \text{ or } s)\ \Delta\ \hat{}\text{d} \rightarrow r$$

where d=d'+d". Unfortunatly if we try to switch on the flip-flop without supplying any signal (i.e. supplying *false* on all inputs) we immediatly get a metastable state. This happens because starting with *false* on all the inputs, we are not in the steady state condition. To enforce a well defined start, we supply *true* to r for the first d seconds. At that time the signal from S reaches r and the system is ready to work. Hence we redefine:

$$\begin{aligned} SR = {} & S\ R\ s\ r\text{:} \\ & \text{not}(R \text{ or } r)\ \Delta\ \hat{}\text{d} \rightarrow s \ + \\ & (\text{not}(S \text{ or } s)\ \Delta\ \hat{}\text{d})\ \uplus\ (@\text{t. t<d}) \rightarrow r \end{aligned}$$

Computing the semantics:

$$\begin{aligned} \text{SR} &= \mathcal{P}[\![SR]\!]\sigma \\ &= \text{Y}\ \lambda\text{SR. }\{\lambda[\text{S R s r}].\ \lambda\text{t. t<d} \Rightarrow \textit{false}\ ; \\ &\qquad\qquad \text{not(R(t-d) or r(t-d) or SR}(r)[S\text{:S};R\text{:R};s\text{:s};r\text{:r}]\text{(t-d))} \rightarrow s; \\ &\qquad \lambda[\text{S R s r}].\ \lambda\text{t. t<d} \Rightarrow \textit{true}\ ; \\ &\qquad\qquad \text{not(S(t-d) or s(t-d) or SR}(s)[S\text{:S};R\text{:R};s\text{:s};r\text{:r}]\text{(t-d))} \rightarrow r\} \end{aligned}$$

and extracting the output transitions:

$$\mathrm{SR}(s) \;=\; \gamma\ \lambda T.\ \lambda[S\ R\ s\ r].\ \lambda t.\ t<d \Rightarrow \mathit{false}\ ;$$
$$\mathrm{not}(R(t-d) \text{ or } r(t-d) \text{ or }$$
$$(t<2d \Rightarrow \mathit{true}\ ;$$
$$\mathrm{not}(S(t-2d) \text{ or } s(t-2d) \text{ or }$$
$$T[S{:}S; R{:}R; s{:}s; r{:}r](t-2d)))$$

$$\mathrm{SR}(r) \;=\; \ldots$$

We look at the output signals in absence of input:

$$\mathrm{SR}(s)[S{:}\dot{-}; R{:}\dot{-}; s{:}\dot{-}; r{:}\dot{-}] \;=\; \gamma\ \lambda S.\ \lambda t.\ t<2d \Rightarrow \mathit{false}\ ;\ S(t-2d)$$
$$= \lambda t.\ \mathit{false}$$

$$\mathrm{SR}(r)[S{:}\dot{-}; R{:}\dot{-}; s{:}\dot{-}; r{:}\dot{-}] \;=\; \lambda t.\ \mathit{true}$$

This means that for $S=\hat{}\mathit{false}$, $R=\hat{}\mathit{false}$ we obtain $s=\hat{}\mathit{false}$, $r=\hat{}\mathit{true}$; we are in the steady state condition. Now we supply a pulse ($\lambda t.\ t<\pi$) of an unspecified length π:

$$\mathrm{SR}(s)[S{:}(\lambda t.\ t<\pi); R{:}\dot{-}; s{:}\dot{-}; r{:}\dot{-}] \;=$$
$$\gamma\ \lambda S.\ \lambda t.\ t<2d \Rightarrow \mathit{false}\ ;\ t<2d+\pi \Rightarrow \mathit{true}\ ;\ S(t-2d)$$

There are two cases: (i) the length of the set pulse is $\pi \geq 2d$; then the flip-flop is properly set (the expression above reduces to $\lambda t.\ t<2d \Rightarrow \mathit{false}\ ;\ \mathit{true}$) or (ii) the length of the set pulse is $\pi<2d$; then the flip-flop is in a metastable state and the output signal oscillates between *true* and *false*.

Acknowledgements

Milner's papers on concurrent behaviours have been of inspiration and guide to this work. Robin Milner and Gordon Plotkin also contributed with discussion to the clarification and refinement of several points. I had encouraging talks with Matthew Hennessy at the very beginning of this research, which has been carried out under a scholarship from the Italian National Research Council.

References

[MacQueen 79] D. B. MacQueen, "Models for Distributed Computing", Report 351, IRIA-Laboria, April 1979.

[Milner 78] R. Milner, "Synthesis of Communicating Behaviour", 7th Symposium on Mathematical Foundations of Computer Science, Zakopane, Poland, 1978.

[Milner 79] R. Milner, "Flowgraphs and Flow Algebras", J.ACM, vol 26, n 4, Oct 1979, pp. 794-818.

AN EXTENDED POLYMORPHIC TYPE SYSTEM FOR APPLICATIVE LANGUAGES

Mario Coppo

Istituto di Scienza dell'Informazione
Università di Torino
Corso Massimo D'Azeglio, 42
10125 TORINO (ITALY)

Abstract

This paper deals with the problem of finding a type system for programming languages, which allows the greatest generality in the definition of polymorphic procedures. The type system introduced in this paper can be seen as an extension of the one proposed in /MLN/ (which is implemented in the language ML).
The rules for type assignement are given and their semantic correctness is proved. Moreover, some results about the semantic characterization of typed terms are proved.

1. INTRODUCTION

In recent years there has been a substantial agreement on the great advantages of using languages with type constraints for improving both programming style (/GG/) and program reliability (/GAM/). An the other hand, a widely experimented class of programming languages, especially structure-processing ones (like LISP, SNOBOL), have shown the utility of defining procedures suitable to work on a wide variety of objects (for example, the operator "CAR" in LISP requires only that its argument be a list, but it does not matter what kind of objects are its elements). From this point of view, languages like ALGOL 68, in which each procedures must declare explicity the types of its parameters, are completely inadequate.

An intermediate approach is that of these programming languages (for example CLU (/LS/) or RUSSEL (/DD/)) in which the type specifications of a procedure can contain also occurrences of type variables, which are considered as parameters of the procedure itself. The semantic correctness of this way of considering types has been proved, even if from different points of view, by Reynolds (/RAY/) and Donahue (/DON/) which proved this result for an applicative language (similar to the one used in this paper) with an operator of abstraction on types. However, the fact of considering types as parameters may, in some cases, complicate the programs and increase the difficulty of defining the semantics of the language.

A different way of considering type variables is given by the language ML (/GMW/), where the notion of "polymorphic" type is introduced. A polymorphic type, in fact, does not contain any parameter but it represents the class of all types that can be obtained by replacing its variables by arbitrary ground types. For example (using standard notations), in ML, a function like $F \equiv \lambda fx.f(x)$ possesses type $(\alpha \to \beta) \to \alpha \to \beta$ (where α , β are type variables). This means that F possesses the types (int → int) → int → int, (bool → bool) → bool → bool and many others. In this way, we can apply F to a wide class of arguments but we can also detect (at compile-time) uncorrect applications as for example (F 3) 3 (since F has no type which allows this application).

This research was supported by C.N.R. - G.N.A.S.I.

The semantics of polymorphic types can be studied in a simple way. In fact, a polymorphic type, aś a basic one, can be interpreted as a set of values.

In ML, moreover, types need not to be defined explicity by the programmer, but they can be inferred at compile-time by a (static) typechecker which is able to find the "must general" type which can be assigned to a given function or constant. An introduction to the type system of ML is given in /MLN/.

The type system of ML, however, is not yet completely adequate. As Milner points out (/MLN/) (and we will prove in this paper) there are many applications (of a function to its arguments), which are correct from a semantic point of view but are not allowed by the type constraints of ML. As a consequence, there are many functions, which are semantically meaningful, to which a type cannot be given. The simplest case is represented by the operator of auto-application delta $\equiv \lambda$ x.xx. It has no type but if we apply it, for example, to the function twice $\equiv \lambda$ x. f (f x) it gives (as it is easy to verify) the function λ f x. f (f (f (f x))) which is well-defined and has a type in ML.

The aim of this paper is to introduce and prove the semantic correctness of a type system in which it is possible to assign a type to many functions that have no type in ML (for example delta) and to prove correct many applications which are not allowed in ML. The essential feature of our system is the introduction of a most powerful operation for type formation (called sequencing) which allows different types to be assigned to the same variable in its different occurrencies. For example, in the case of λ x.xx, if we assume that x has <u>both</u> type $\alpha \rightarrow \beta$ <u>and</u> type α , we can deduce that xx has type β . We can express this by writing that λ x.xx has type $(\alpha \rightarrow \beta,\ \alpha) \rightarrow \beta$, where $(\alpha \rightarrow \beta,\ \alpha)$ is a new object that we call a sequence of types. The introduction of sequences is the main difference between our type system and the one of ML. It also eliminates the need for the introduction of "generic" type variable (/MLN/.

Our system is derived from a type assignment system for terms of the λ-calculus (/CD/) which generalizes the theory of functionality of Curry (/CF/) (which ispired also the type system of ML).

We shall describe our system on a sample applicative language (Exp) quite similar to the one used in /MLN/ (which can be seen as a subset of ML). We shall introduce Exp, together with its denotational semantics, in section 2. In section 3 we will introduce types and give their semantics. In section 4 we give the rules for type assignment and prove its correctness with respect to the denotational semantics of Exp (this proof extends to our system an analogous result of /MLN/). Although (as in /MLN/) we will not be able to give a sufficient semantic condition to characterize the typed terms of Exp (syntactical ones are given in section 4), in section 5 we will prove some properties which will give some insight into this problem.

We will not deal, in this paper, with type checking since we are concerned essentially with the semantics of types. We shall discuss briefly this problem in the conclusion.

2. THE LANGUAGE AND ITS SEMANTICS

The languages Exp is essentially a λ-calculus with some constants, an "if then else" construct and a fixpoint operator. To simplify exposition we shall choose as basic functions and domains the ones utilized in the language PCF of Plotkin (/PTK1/), this choice being indifferent for our purposes.

The constant objects of the language are the booleans constants TT and FF, the numerals $\underline{0}$, $\underline{1}$, ... and the constants suc, pred, Δ [1] which represent standard functions on natural numbers.

Let V be a set of formal variables. The set of terms of Exp is defined by the following syntax, where e ranges over terms:

e →	TT | FF | $\underline{0}$ | $\underline{1}$ | ... | suc | pred | Δ .	
	x | y | z | ...	x, y, z,... ∈ V
	λ x.e	(abstraction)
	(e e)	(application)
	if e then e else e	(conditional)
	μ x.e	(least fixpoint)

We shall use, in writing terms, the usual conventions of λ-calculus (for ex., $\lambda x_1 \lambda x_2.e$ stands for $\lambda x_1.(\lambda x_2.e)$ and $e_1\, e_2\, e_3$ for $(e_1\, e_2)\, e_3$). Moreover, we will take from λ-calculus the usual definitions of bound and free occurrences of a variable in a term (here we intend also μx as a variable binding) and the definition of substitution denoted by $e_1[e_2/x]$. The notion of subterm of a term is straightforward from the syntax of Exp.

Some typical constructs of ML can be translated very simply in exp. For example, let x = e_1 in e_2 is equivalent to $(\lambda x.e_2)\, e_1$.

We give now a "typeless" denotational semantics of Exp. We build our value domain D as a complete partial order (c.p.o.) starting from a given set of basic c.p.o.s plus a special one-value domain W = {error} which represents an error condition. We take as basic domains, besides W, the flat c.p.o.s B (boolean values) and N (natural numbers). We define D as the domain which satisfies the equation

$$D = W + B + N + [D \to D]$$

where + indicates the separated sum of c.p.o.s while $[D \to D]$ represents the c.p.o. of all continuous functions from D to D. The solution of this equation, up to isomorphism, is known to exist (/PTK2/). To simplify notations, we shall identify, for all costituents V of D, an element $d \in V$ with its image in D.

Let's shortly recall some usual notations (/STY/). $\perp$ is the least element of D while $\perp_B$ and $\perp_N$ are the least elements of their respective subdomains. If V represents one of the domains W, B, N or $[D \to D]$ and $d \in D$ then EV is the function : $D \to B$ defined as

$$d\,E\,V = \begin{cases} \perp_B & \text{if } d = \perp \\ tt & \text{if } d \in V \\ ff & \text{otherwise} \end{cases}$$

where we assume $B = \{\perp_B, tt, ff\}$. d E V stands for E V(d). If $d \in B$ and $d_1, d_2 \in D$ then:

$$d \to d_1, d_2 = \begin{cases} \perp & \text{if } d = \perp_B \\ d_1 & \text{if } d = tt \\ d_2 & \text{if } d = ff \end{cases}$$

We assume $+ : N \times N \to N$ and $\delta : N \to B$ be two strict functions (/STY/), with obvious meaning. An environment η is a function $\eta : V \to D$ which associates a value in D to all

(1) We will write sometimes x = 0 for Δ x

variables. $\eta [\![x]\!]$ represents the value of η for x. $\eta [v/x] = \eta'$ is identical with η except that $\eta' [\![x]\!] = v$. If e is a term then $[\![e]\!]_\eta$ represents the value of e in the environment η.

<u>Definition 1</u> - Denotational semantics of Exp

a) $[\![TT]\!]_\eta = tt \in B$, $[\![FF]\!]_\eta = ff \in B$, $[\![\underline{n}]\!]_\eta = n \in N$ $(0 \leq n)$

b) $[\![suc]\!]_\eta = \lambda d.d \; E \; N \rightarrow d + 1, error$

c) $[\![pred]\!]_\eta \quad \lambda d.d \; E \; N \rightarrow (\delta (d) \rightarrow \perp, d - 1), error$

d) $[\![\Delta]\!]_\eta = \lambda d.d \; E \; N \rightarrow (\delta (d) \rightarrow tt, ff), error$

e) $[\![x]\!]_\eta = \eta [\![x]\!]$

f) $[\![e_1 \, e_2]\!]_\eta = v_1 E [D \rightarrow D] \rightarrow (v_2 E \{ error \} \rightarrow error, v_1(v_2)), error$ where $v_i = [\![e_i]\!]_\eta$ for $i = 1,2$

g) $[\![\text{if } e_1 \text{ then } e_2 \text{ else } e_3]\!]_\eta \quad v.EB \rightarrow (v_1 \rightarrow v_2, v_3), error$ where $v_i \quad [\![e_i]\!]_\eta$ for $i \quad 1, 2, 3$

h) $[\![\lambda x.e]\!]_\eta = \lambda d. [\![e]\!]_{\eta [d/x]}$

k) $[\![\mu x.e]\!]_\eta = Y(\lambda d. [\![e]\!]_{\eta [d/x]})$
where $Y = \bigsqcup_n \{ \lambda f.f^n(\perp) \}$ is the least fixpoint operator of D.

Let's observe that we have $[\![e]\!]_\eta \neq$ error iff all subterms of e have values different from error. This corresponds, to a call-by-value evaluation strategy.

3. SYNTAX AND SEMANTICS OF TYPES

The set T of types is defined from a set of basic types (in our case the types B and N) and a denumerable set of type variables (which we will indicate by $\alpha, \beta, \gamma, \delta$ ...). Because of the simplicity of Exp, the only operator we need for type construction is the operator $\rightarrow$ which expresses functionality (we will avoid to write it explicitly to shorten notation). σ, τ will range over arbitrary types.

The syntax of types is the following

a) each basic type and each type variable is a type.

b) if $\sigma_1, ..., \sigma_n, \tau$ $(n \geqslant 1)$ are types then $(\sigma_1, ..., \sigma_n)\tau$ is a type

$(\sigma_1, ..., \sigma_n)\tau$ is an abbreviation for $(\sigma_1, ..., \sigma_n) \rightarrow \tau$. We call $(\sigma_1, ..., \sigma_n)$ a <u>sequence</u> and we will briefly indicate it by $(\bar{\sigma})$. If $(\sigma_1, ..., \sigma_n)$ is a sequence we say that σ_i $(1 \leqslant i \leqslant n)$ is <u>contained</u> in it. As we shall see, sequences can be considered as sets of types (their meaning, in fact, is independent of order and multiplicity). However, we prefer not calling them sets because of their syntactic character.

The fact of considering sequences instead of single types in rule b) is the main difference between our type system and the one of /MLN/. Our set of types, moreover, properly includes that of /MLN/.

A <u>monotype</u> is a type which does not contain occurrences of type variables. Otherwise (i.e. if it contains at least one occurrence of a type variables) we call it a <u>polytype</u>. We shall use $\varphi, \psi, ...$ to indicate monotypes.

We now associate to each type σ (or sequence $(\bar{\sigma})$) a subdomain of D and we shall write d: σ (d: $(\bar{\sigma})$) to indicate that d (d $\in$ D) belongs to the domain associated to σ (or $(\bar{\sigma})$). We shall make no formal distinction between a type or sequence and its associated subdomain (this being clear from the context).

The semantics of types is suggested by their natural interpretation. We give first the semantics of monotypes and sequences of monotypes. Let v be an arbitrary value in D.

1) $v : B$ iff $v = \perp$ or v is a value in B
2) $v : N$ iff $v = \perp$ or v is a value in N
3) $v : (\phi_1, \dots, \phi_n)$ iff $v : \phi_i$ for all $1 \leq i \leq n$
4) $v : (\phi_1, \dots, \phi_n)\psi$ iff either $v = \perp$ or, for all v': $(\phi_1, \dots, \phi_n)$ $v(v') : \psi$

From point 3) it is clear that a sequence of types can be interpreted as the intersection of all types contained in it. So there are, in our system, types which represent some subdomains of D which are not interpretations of any type of ML.

As in /MLN/, we interpret a polytype as the intersection of all the monotypes that are instances of it.

As usual a <u>substitution</u> s is a set of pairs (α_i, σ_i) $(0 \leq i)$ where α_i are type variables and σ_i arbitrary types. s(τ) is the type obtained by replacing each occurrence of the variables α_i in τ by σ_i $(0 \leq i)$. We say that σ is an <u>instance</u> of τ $(\sigma < \tau)$ iff there is a substitution s such that $\sigma = s(\tau)$. $<$ is, obviously, a reflexive and transitive relation. For example (N) N $< (\alpha)\alpha < (\alpha)\beta$

Now we are able to define formally the interpretation of a polytype σ .

- $v : \sigma$ iff $v : \phi$ for all monotypes ϕ such that $\phi < \sigma$

We will need some properties of types.

A subset X of a c.p.o. D is said to be <u>downward closed</u> iff:

-- $v \in X$ and $v \sqsubseteq v'$ (1) implies $v' \in X$

and <u>directed complete</u> iff:

-- for each directed subset X' of X, $\sqcup X' \in X$

<u>Lemma 1</u>. for all types σ , the domain associated with σ is downward closed and directed complete.

<u>Lemma 2</u> - If $v : \sigma$ and $\tau < \sigma$ then $v : \tau$

<u>Lemma 3</u> - If $v : (\sigma)\tau$ and $v' : (\sigma)$ then $v(v') : \tau$

The proof of Lemma 1 for monotypes is by a straightforward induction on the (syntactic) structure of types. The generalization to polytypes is immediate. Lemmas 2 and 3 are trivially true for monotypes and generalize immediatly to polytypes.

---

(1) $\sqsubseteq$ represents the partial order relation on D.

4. TYPE ASSIGNMENT AND ITS PROPERTIES

We will give a set of syntactic conditions under which we can say that a term possesses a type. We could formalize these rules in a classical deduction system as in /CD/ but we prefer a more intuitive (although formally correct) formulation, as in /MLN/. We will use also a similar (but not identical) terminology.

To simplify the next definitions, we shall consider only terms in which no bound variable has the same name of a free one (unambiguity condition). This is not restrictive since it is obvious that terms can be considered modulo a re-naming of bound variables. We will, so, consider, for example, λ x.x(λ y.y) instead of λ x.x(λ x.x).

Let a prefix p be a sequence of variables in which each variable occurs only once. We write p.x to indicate the prefix obtained by concatenating x to p. A prefix, obviously, may be empty.

A prefixed expression (p.e.) $p \mid e$ is the association of an expression e and a prefix p which contains (at least) all the variables free in e.

A typing of a p.e. $p \mid e$ is an assignment of a sequence to each variable in p and of a type to e. We will write $\bar{p}$ to indicate a typed prefix and e_σ to indicate that type σ is assigned to e. $x_{(\bar{\sigma})}$ indicates the association of the sequence $(\bar{\sigma})$ to the variable x.

In /MLN/, in a typed expression, a type is assigned to each subterm of e. In our case, because of rule c) of definition 2, this is not possible.

If $\bar{p} \mid e_\sigma$ is a typed p.e., seq(p,x) the sequence associated to x in p.

Definition 2 - A typed p.e. is well-typed (w.t.) (1) iff it satisfies the following conditions.

a) if k is a constant $\bar{p} \mid k_\sigma$ is w. t. iff σ is the natural monotype of k (i.e. N for each numeral, B for each boolean constant, (N)N for suc and pred, (N)B for Δ).

b) $\bar{p} \mid x_\sigma$ is w.t. iff σ is contained in seq(p,x)

c) $\bar{p} \mid (e_1 e_2)_\tau$ is w.t. iff there exists a sequence $(\sigma_1, \dots, \sigma_n)$ such that $\bar{p} \mid (e_1)_{(\sigma_1, \dots, \sigma_n)\tau}$ and $\bar{p} \mid (e_2)_{\sigma_i}$ (for all $1 \leq i \leq n$) are w.t.

d) $\bar{p} \mid (\text{if } e_1 \text{ then } e_2 \text{ else } e_3)_\tau$ is w.t. iff $\bar{p} \mid (e_1)_B$, $\bar{p} \mid (e_2)_\tau$ and $\bar{p} \mid (e_3)_\tau$ are w.t.

e) p $(\lambda\, x.e)_\tau$ is w.t. iff $\tau \equiv (\bar{\sigma})\rho$ and $\bar{p}.x_{(\bar{\sigma})} \mid e_\rho$ is w.t.

f) p $(\mu\, x.e)_\tau$ is w.t. iff $\bar{p}.x_{(\tau)} \mid e_\tau$ is w.t.

For example, $\mid ((\lambda\, x.xx)\, \lambda\, y.y)_{(a)a}$ is w. t. (from c)) since:

$x_{(((\beta)\beta)(a)a,\, (\beta)\beta)} \mid x_{((\beta)\beta)(a)a}$ is w.t. (from b))

$x_{(((\beta)\beta)(a)a,\, (\beta)\beta)} \mid x_{(\beta)\beta}$ " " (from b))

$x_{(((\beta)\beta)(a)a,\, (\beta)\beta)} \mid (xx)_{(a)a}$ " " (from e))

$\mid (\lambda\, x.xx)_{(((\beta)\beta)(a)a,\, (\beta)\beta)(a)a}$ " " (from e))

$\mid (\lambda\, y.y)_{((\beta)\beta)(a)a}$ and $\mid (\lambda\, y.y)_{(\beta)\beta}$ are well-typed.

---

(1) Another way of expressing that $\bar{p} \mid e_\sigma$ is w.t. is to say that e possesses type σ under typed prefix p. In this case we could write, in a notation similar to the one of /CF/, $\vec{p} \vdash \sigma\ e$.

Let's observe that we did not need the introduction of "generic" variables as in /MLN/. The introduction of sequences, in fact, makes them useless. Moreover, our system extends properly the one of ML: i.e. if $\bar{p} \mid e_\tau$ is w.t. according to /MLN/ then it is w.t. also according to definition 2.

Let s be an arbitrary substitution. If $\bar{p}$ is a typed prefix then $s(\bar{p})$ is that typed prefix obtained by applying s to all sequences assigned to the variables of p. Moreover $s(\bar{p} \mid e_\tau) = s(\bar{p}) \mid e_{s(\tau)}$

It is easy, following a standard technique (/CDV/), to prove the following lemma.

Lemma 4 - If $\bar{p} \mid e_\tau$ is w.t. and s is an arbitrary substitution then $s(\bar{p} \mid e_\tau)$ is w.t.

Now we can prove the correctness of the typing rules with respect to Definition 1. Let η be an environment and $\bar{p}$ a typed prefix. We say that η respects $\bar{p}$ iff for all variables x which occur in p $\eta[\![x]\!]$: seq (p,x)

Theorem 1: Let $\bar{p} \mid e_\tau$ be a w.t. p.e.. Then, for all environments η which respect $\bar{p}$, $[\![e]\!]_\eta : \tau$

Proof: by structural induction on e. The property is obvious if e is a constant (from point a) of definition 2) and if e is a variable (from point b) of definition 2 and the interpretation of sequencies).

If $e \equiv (e_1 e_2)$ then, by definition, there exists a sequence $(\sigma_1, \dots, \sigma_n)$ such that $\bar{p} \mid (e_1)_{(\sigma_1,\dots,\sigma_n)\tau}$ and $\bar{p} \mid (e_2)_{\sigma_i}$ for $1 \leq i \leq n$ are w. t. and by inductive hypothesis, satisfy the teorem. Then $[\![e_2]\!]_\eta : (\sigma_1, \dots, \sigma_n)$ and, by definition 1 and Lemma 3 $[\![e_1 e_2]\!]_\eta = ([\![e_1]\!]_\eta)[\![e_2]\!]_\eta : \tau$

If $e \equiv \lambda x.e'$ then, by definition 2 e), $\tau \equiv (\bar{\sigma})\rho$ and $\bar{p}.x_{(\bar{\sigma})} \mid e'_\rho$ is w.t. To prove $[\![e]\!]_\eta : (\bar{\sigma})\rho$ we must prove $[\![e]\!]_\eta : (\bar{\phi})\psi$ for all $(\bar{\phi})\psi < (\sigma)\rho$. Let s be a substitution such that $(\bar{\phi})\psi = s((\bar{\sigma})\rho)$ and let $\bar{p}' = s(\bar{p})$. Then $\bar{p}' \mid e_{(\bar{\phi})\psi}$ is w.t. (by Lemma 4) and this implies (Definition 2 e)) that $\bar{p}'.x_{(\bar{\phi})} \mid e'_\psi$ is w.t. Now for all v : $(\bar{\phi})$ and all η which respects $\bar{p}$ we have, from Lemma 2, that $\eta[v/x]$ respects $\bar{p}'.x_{(\bar{\phi})}$ and, by inductive hypothesis, $[\![e]\!]_{\eta[v/x]} : \psi$. Then, we have immediately $[\![\lambda x.e']\!]_\eta : (\bar{\phi})\psi$

If $e \equiv$ x.e' then, by definition 2 f), there exists a type τ such that $\bar{p}.x_{(\tau)} \mid e_\tau$ is w. t. It is well known that $[\![e]\!]_\eta = \bigsqcup_i \{v_i\}$ where $v_0 = \perp$ and $v_{i+1} = [\![e]\!]_{\eta[v_i/x]}$

Now, obviously, $v_0 : \tau$ and, by inductive hypothesis, $v_{i+1} : \tau$ whenever $v_i : \tau$ (since $\eta[v_i/x]$ respects $\bar{p}.x_{(\tau)}$). Then $v_i : \tau$ for all i and the result follows immediately from Lemma 1.

If $e \equiv$ if e_1 then e_2 else e_3 the proof is trivial.

As an immediate corollary of theorem 1 we have that a typed term has a denotation different from error. In fact the value error does not belong to any type.

5. SOME PROPERTIES OF TYPED TERMS

The converse of Theorem 1 is not true i.e. $[\![e]\!]_\eta : \tau$ for all η which respects $\bar{p}$ does not imply that $\bar{p} \mid e_\tau$ is w.t. In this section we will prove some properties of typed terms that can help to understand what terms can be typed.

We firsly define a relation of reducibility between terms which can be seen as a partial definition of an operational semantics for Exp.

Definition 3

i) Let e be a term. A redex in e is a subterm of e of the kind:

- $(\lambda x.e)e'$ (λ -redex)
- (if e_1 then e_2 else e_3)e (if-redex)

which reduce, respectively, to

- $e\,[e'/x]$
- if e_1 then (e_2 e) else (e_3 e)

ii) $e \rightarrow e'$ if e' differs from e for the reduction of a redex

In the redexes $(\lambda x.e)e'$ and (if e_1 then e_2 else e_3)e we call $\lambda x.e$ or if e_1 then e_2 else e_3 the rand of the redex.

As usual $\rightarrow^*$ is the symmetric and transitive closure of $\rightarrow$. It is easy to verify (/HIN1/) that $\rightarrow^*$ possesses the Church-Rosser property. Let's notice that we have avoided, in definition 3, to consider μ x.e as a redex (which should reduce to e $[\mu\, x.e/x]$, as suggested by the interpretation of μ x as a fixpoint operator). Moreover, it is obvious that it may be necessary, to respect the unambiguity condition, to consider the reduction of a redex of the shape $(\lambda x.e)e'$ modulo a re-naming of bound variables.

We can prove that, under very weak conditions, types are preserved by the relation $\rightarrow^*$ in both directions.

Lemma 5 - Let e be a redex and $\bar{p}\,|\,e_\tau$ a w.t. p.e.. If $e \rightarrow e'$ then $\bar{p}\,|\,e'_\tau$ is w.t.

Lemma 6 - Let e be a redex such that $e \rightarrow e'$ and $\bar{p}\,|\,e'_\tau$ a w.t. p.e.. Then:

i) if e is an if-redex, then $\bar{p}\,|\,e_\tau$ is w.t.

ii) if $e \equiv (\lambda x.e_1)e_2$ is a λ -redex then $\bar{p}\,|\,e_\tau$ is w.t. iff there exists at least one type σ and one typed prefix $\bar{q}$ such that $\bar{q}\,|\,(e_2)_\sigma$ is w.t..

If $e \equiv (\lambda x.e_1)e_2$ the proofs of Lemmas 5 and 6 are given (although in a slightly different formalism) by Lemmas 1 and 3 of /CD/. In the other case the proof is trivial.

The condition of Lemma 6 ii) is very weak. It is not satisfied only in the case that x does not occur in e_1 and e_2 has no type with respect to any typed prefix (it is surely satisfied, with $\bar{p} = \bar{q}$, if x occurs at least once in e). In other words it fails only in the case of a term which reduces to a typed one by erasing some untyped subterm.

Theorem 2 - Let $\bar{p}\,|\,e_\tau$ be a w.t. p.e.

i) if $e \rightarrow^* e'$ then $\bar{p}\,|\,e'_\tau$ is w.t.

ii) if $e' \rightarrow^* e$ then $\bar{p}\,|\,e'_\tau$ is w.t. iff all λ-redexes contracted to obtain e from e' satisfy the condition of Lemma 6 ii).

In the system of /MLN/ theorem 2i) holds, but a result similar to the one of Theorem 2 ii) can be proved only under much heavier conditions.

For example, let K $\equiv \lambda$ xy.x and twice $\equiv \lambda$ fx.f(fx). It is easy to verify that, in our system, K has type $(\alpha)(\beta)\alpha$ (as in ML) and twice has type $((\alpha)\beta,(\beta)\gamma)(\alpha)\gamma$. So we can assign type $(\alpha)(\beta)(\gamma)\alpha$ to twice (K). Moreover, twice (K) $\rightarrow^*$ λ xuv.x. In ML we can assign type $(\alpha)(\beta)(\gamma)\alpha$ to λ xuv.x but not to twice (K).

Theorem 2 confirms that we would not obtain any substantial improvement by adding to the sintax of Exp terms like "let x = e_1 in e_2". In fact, this expression has the same type as $(\lambda x.e_2)e_1$.

On the other hand in evaluations which involve the fixpoint operator, it may happen that a term with no type produces a term which has a type. Let's consider, for example, the following two terms (1):

$e_1 \equiv \mu f.\lambda n \lambda y.$ if n = o then yy else yy(f(n-1)y)

$e_2 \equiv \mu f.\lambda n \lambda y.$ if n = o then y else f(n-1)yy

It is easy to see that $(e_1)(N)(\alpha,(\alpha)\beta,(\alpha)(\beta)\beta)\beta$ is w.t. while e_2 has no type (in fact, by definition 1, to give a type to e_2 there must exist a type τ and three sequences $(\bar{\sigma}_1)$ $(\bar{\sigma}_2)$ and $(\bar{\sigma}_3)$ such that $(N)(\bar{\sigma}_1)\tau = (N)(\bar{\sigma}_2)(\bar{\sigma}_3)\tau$: this is clearly impossible). We have

$$e_1\ \underline{n} = \lambda y.\underbrace{yy(yy(\dots(yy)).)}_{n\ \text{times}} =_{\text{def}} e_{1,n}$$

and

$$e_2\ \underline{n} = \lambda y.\underbrace{y \dots y}_{n\ \text{times}} =_{\text{def}} e_{2,n}$$

It is easy to see that, for all n, $e_{1,n}$ has type $(\alpha,(\alpha)\beta,(\alpha)(\beta)\beta)\beta$ while $e_{2,n}$ has type $((\alpha_1)\dots(\alpha_n)\beta,\alpha_1,\dots,\alpha_n)\beta$, but there exists no type τ such that $e_{2,n}$ possesses type τ for all n.

We can prove another property of typed terms. Let's define a term to be in $\rightarrow$ normal form ($\rightarrow$ n.f.) iff it is irreducible with respect to $\rightarrow$.

Theorem 3 - If e is a term such that $\bar{p}\,|\,e_\tau$ is w.t. for some typed prefix $\bar{p}$ and type τ then e has a $\rightarrow$ n.f.

Proof Hint - The proof of this theorem can be given with the same technique used to prove Lemma 2 and Theorem 2 of /CD/. We must first define the height of a redex r in e as the maximum number of symbols of the types assigned to the rator of r in the proof (following definition 2) of the well typing of $\bar{p}\,|\,e_\tau$. The measure of a typed expression is the pair of integers defined by the maximum height of rators of redexes in e and the number of redexes of e which have this height.

It is not difficult to show that, for all e not in $\rightarrow$ n.f., there exists a redex (in the case of a λ-redex) or a finite "chain" of redexes (in the case of if-redexes) whose contraction transforms e in a term e' (which is still typed by Lemma 5) whose measure is lower then that of e (according to the usual lexicographic ordering of pairs of integers). This property allows us to prove the theorem by a simple transfinite induction.

The meaning of theorem 3 is that, in a typed term, the condition of non-termination can be controlled only by the fixpoint operator. Obviously, theorem 3 holds also for the type system of /MLN/ (this has been proved almost completely in /MR/).

(1) Let's notice that both e_1 and e_2 do not have a type in /ML/.

On the other hand, it is well know that the fixpoint operator can be represented also by the term Y ≡ $\lambda f.(\lambda x.f(xx))(\lambda x.f(xx))$ which, having no normal form, does not possess a type (by Theorem 3). It is easy to see, however, that $[\![Y]\!]_\eta : ((a)a)a$ (for all η).Then, also non-terminating programs which do not contain the μ -operator can be semantically well-typed (but not syntactically, by Theorem 3).

6. CONCLUSION

The language Exp is very simple. It is easy, however, to extend the type system presented in this paper by adjoining (as in ML) (primitive) type operators for cartesian products, list forming, etc.

As pointed out by Milner (/MLN/), each term e of ML which has a type, has also a "most general" type τ , in the sense that all other types which can be given to e can be obtained as instances of τ . Moreover, there exists an algorithm to find, for each term e, its most general type (a formal proof of this is given for pure λ -calculus in /BY/).

With a simple extension of the results of /CDV/ we can prove that, in our system too, for each term e of Exp, there exists a type τ which is the "most general" for e in the sense that all other types of e can be generated from this one. But, as proved in /CDV/, with the only operation of substitution we can generate only a subset of the types that can be assigned to e. To generate all such types we need, besides substitution, another (effective) operation which is called "expansion" in /CDV/. Moreover, from theorems 2 and 3 it is easy to prove that it is only semi-decidable if a term of Exp possesses a type (in fact, on the contrary, it should be decidable the property of having normal form terms of the λ- I-calculus). This proves that an extension to our system of the algorithm $\mathcal{W}$ of /MLN/ is not possible. We suppose, however, that the design of a type cheking algorithm for a satisfactory (although not complete) implementation of our system should be possible.

REFERENCES

/BJ/ C. Ben-Yelles
"Type assignment in the lambda-calculus: Syntax and Semantics", P.h.D. thesis, University of Wales (1979)

/CD/ M. Coppo, M. Dezani-Ciancaglini.
"An extension of Basic Functionality theory for λ -calculus", Internal report, University of Turin. To appear in "Notre Dame Journal of Formal Logic"

/CDV/ M. Coppo, M. Dezani-Ciancaglini, B. Venneri.
"Principal Type Schemes and calculus Semantics" Internal report, University of Turin. To appear in: To H.B. Curry, Essays on Combinatory Logic, Lambda-calculus and Formalism, eds. R. Hindley and J.P. Seldin, Academic Press (1980).

/CF/ H.B. Curry, R.Feys
"Combinatory Logic I", North-Holland (1958)

/DD/ A. Demers, J. Donahue
"Report on the Programming Language Russel", TR79-371, Computer Science Department, Cornell University (1979)

/DON/ J. Donahue
"On the Semantics of data types", TR77-311, Computer Science Department, Cornell University (1977)

/GAM/ J.D. Gammon
"An Experimental Evaluation of Data Type Conventions", Comm. ACM 20,8 (1977) 584-595

/GG/ D. Gries and N. Gehani
"Some ideas on data types in high-level languages", Camm. ACM. 20,6 (1977).

/GMW/ M.J. Gordon, A.J. Milner, C.P. Wadsworth
"Edimburgh LCF", Lecture notes in Computer Science, n. 78.

/HIN1/ R. Hindley
"An abstract Church-Rosser Theorem II: applications", Journal of Symbolic Logic, 39, 1 (1974), 1-21.

/LS/ B. Liskov, A. Snyder
"Abstraction Mechanisms in CLU", Camm. ACM. 20,3 (1977), 564-583

/MLN/ R. Milner
"A theory of type polymorphism in programming", Journ. Comp. and Syst. Science 17,3 (1978), 348-375.

/MR/ J. H. Morris
"Lambda-calculus models of programming languages", Ph.D.Thesis, MAC-TR-57, MIT (1968)

/PTK1/ G. Plotkin,
"LCF considered as a programming language", J. Theoret. Comput. Sci. 5,3 (1977) 522-537

/PTK2/ G. Plotkin
"T_ω as a Universal Domain", J. Comput. System Sci. 17,2 (1978), 209-236.

/REY/ J.C. Reynolds
"Towards a theory of type structure", Lecture Notes in Computer Science n. 12, 408-425

/STY/ J. Stoy
"Denotational Semantics", MIT Press (1977)

A CRITERION OF UNDECIDABILITY OF ALGORITHMIC THEORIES

Wiktor Dańko

University of Warsaw, Division Białystok

Akademicka 2, 15-267 Białystok, Poland

1. Introduction.

This paper presents some methods of examining the problems of decidability and undecidability of algorithmic theories. By an algorithmic theory we shall mean a formalized theory based on the language and consequence operation of algorithmic logic [1,8] . The language of algorithmic logic contains all formulas of first order logic, programs algorithms and formulas describing properties of programs which may be realized in arbitrary structures of suitable signatures .

By means of algorithmic formulas we can express properties of structures which are not expressible in first order logic. For instance we can express that the characteristic of a field is finite using the formula describing the fact that the algorithm

x := 1 ; while x $\neq$ 0 do x := x + 1

halts.

Thus we can talk over algorithmic theory of fields of finite characteristic, algorithmic theory of fields of characteristic zero and others algorithmic theories of abstract structures e.g. Archimedean ordered fields.

Algorithmic arithmetic of natural numbers is based only on the notion of the successor function (see [8] for example). This theory characterizes categorically the standard model of natural numbers and the set of its theorems is hyperarithmetical.

Algorithmic theories of fields of rational and complex numbers were investigated in works of A.Kreczmar [5,6] . The properties of algorithms realized in these fields were examined in [5] from the point of view of recursion theory and degrees of undecidability and arithmetical classes of algorithmic properties like halting property, correctness were established.

First theories of data structures based on algorithmic logic contains the paper of L.Banachowski [2] . Algorithmic theories of stacks and dictionaries were formulated in the works of A.Salwicki [10,11].

All theories mentioned above are hyperarithmetical except theories of dictionaries and fields of finite characteristic. The set of theorems of theory of dictionaries is in Π_1^0 (compare [11]). The following questions arise in a natural way:

- is the theory of dictionaries decidable ?
- are there decidable algorithmic theories ? are they nontrivial ?

Criterion formulated in this paper can be used in order to answer negatively first question and it shows that this theory is in $\Pi_1^0 - \Sigma_1^0$. By the application of this criterion we are able to assert undecidability of algorithmic theory of finite fields, theories of data structures like dictionaries, storage management system and others theories of structures with finite universes. To prove this criterion we make use of some facts concerning the decidability and undecidability of first order theories. In particular we use result of Matijasevič [7].

Let us note that in the case of dynamic logic DL [4] every theory T based on the deductive system given in [4] and specific axioms of T is undecidable because the set of logical axioms of DL contains all sentences true in the system of narural numbers.

The second question has positive answer. For example algorithmic theory of two element Boolean algebra is decidable (compare M.Grabowski [3]).

In third section of this paper we prove that every decidable algorithmic theory admits elimination of iteration quantifiers. The proofs of the criterion and the above fact make essential use of the completeness theorem for algorithmic logic [1,8] completeness is understood as in the first order predicate calculus .

At the end of this paper we give examples of decidable algorithmic theoties. In general they are simple. However there are decidable algorithmic theories with infinite models.

2. Algorithmic logic and its semantics, basic denotations and lemmas.

First we recall some notions concerning the system of algorithmic logic. The alphabet of a language L of algorithmic logic contains the sets V, V_o, P, Φ of individual variables, propositional variables, predicates and functors respectively.

The sets T, F_o of terms and open formulas are defined as usually. The set S of substitutions is the set of all expressions of the form $x := \omega$ where x is an individual variable and ω is a term or x is a propositional variable and ω is an open formula.

The set Pr of programs (algorithms) is the least set of expressions containing all substitutions and such that:

if K, M are in Pr and γ is an open formula then

<u>begin</u> <u>end</u>

<u>begin</u> K ; M <u>end</u>

<u>if</u> γ <u>then</u> K <u>else</u> M

<u>while</u> γ <u>do</u> K

are in Pr .

If M is empty program i.e. M is of the form <u>begin</u> <u>end</u> then we shall write <u>if</u> γ <u>then</u> K instead of <u>if</u> γ <u>then</u> K <u>else</u> M .

Let A be a structure for the language L . Let K be a program from L and let v be a valuation of variables. By $K_A(v)$ we shall denote the valuation of variables after execution of the program K ($K_A(v)$ can be undefined).

Let K be a program and let α be a formula. The logical value of the formula $K\alpha$ is defined as follows

$$K\alpha_A(v) = \begin{cases} 1 & \text{if the valuation } v' = K_A(v) \text{ is defined} \\ & \text{and } \alpha_A(v') = 1 \\ 0 & \text{otherwise} \end{cases}$$

The meaning of iteration quantifiers is as follows:

$$\bigcup K\alpha_A(v) = \sup_{i \in N} K^i\alpha_A(v)$$

N denotes the set of natural numbers

$$\bigcap K\alpha_A(v) = \inf_{i \in N} K^i\alpha_A(v)$$

where K^i denotes the composition of i times of the program K . The meaning of classical quantifiers is known.

We recall that by an algorithmic theory T we mean the system $\langle L, C, Ax \rangle$ where L is a language of algorithmic logic, Ax is the set of formulas from L called nonlogical or specific axioms of T and C denotes the consequence operation defined as in [1] . The fact that α belongs to the set C(Ax) we shall denote $T \vdash \alpha$.

Let ω be an expression from L and let $\bar{x} = (x_1,\ldots,x_n)$ be the sequence of all variables occurring in ω . We shall often write $\omega(x_1,\ldots,x_n)$ instead of ω .

Let $\omega(x_1,\ldots,x_n)$ be an expression from L and let $\bar{x} = (x_1,\ldots,x_n)$, $\bar{y} = (y_1,\ldots,y_n)$ be sequences of different variables. By $\omega(y_1,\ldots,y_n)$ we shall denote the expression obtained from ω after replacing all occurrences of x_i by y_i for $i = 1,\dots,n$.

Let $M(x_1,\dots,x_p)$ be a program of the form while γ do K . Let $\alpha_{M,n}(x_1,\dots,x_p)$ denote the formula $\gamma \wedge K\gamma \wedge \dots \wedge K^{n-1}\gamma \wedge \wedge K^n(\neg\gamma)$ for natural $n>0$ and let $\alpha_{M,o}$ denote the formula $\neg\gamma$. It is easy to notice that

> $\alpha_{M,n}(\bar{x})_A(v) = \mathbb{1}$ if and only if the program M ends computation after n executions of the subprogram K (with initial valuation v)

Let v be a valuation. In the case when the valuation $M_A(v)$ is defined we shall denote by $number_M(v(x_1),\dots, v(x_p))$ the number of executions of the subprogram K in the computation of the program M with the initial valuation v . The sequence $v(x_1),\dots, v(x_p)$ will be often denote by $v(\bar{x})$ and we shall often write $number(x_1,\dots,x_p)$ or $number(\bar{x})$ instead of $number_M(v(x_1),\dots, v(x_p))$ if it does not lead to any confusion.

Now, we introduce two formulas describing some properties of programs which are essential for further considerations.

Let $M(x_1,\dots,x_p)$ be a program such as described above and let $\bar{x} = (x_1,\dots,x_p)$, $\bar{y} = (y_1,\dots,y_p)$, $\bar{z} = (z_1,\dots,z_p)$ be sequences of different variables. Let us denote by $Add_M(\bar{x}, \bar{y}, \bar{z})$ the formula $M(\bar{x})\mathbb{1} \wedge M(\bar{y})\mathbb{1} \wedge M(\bar{z})\mathbb{1} \wedge P(\neg\gamma(\bar{x}) \wedge \neg\gamma(\bar{y}) \wedge \wedge \neg\gamma(\bar{z}))$ where P denotes the following program

```
begin
    while γ(x̄) ∧ γ(z̄) do
        begin K(x̄) ; K(z̄) end ;
    if ¬γ(x̄) then
        while γ(ȳ) ∧ γ(z̄) do
            begin K(ȳ) ; K(z̄) end
end
```

We recall that the formula of the form $N(\bar{x})\mathbb{1}$ where N is a program describes the halting property of the program $N(\bar{x})$. If a program is loop- free (without " while ") then its halting formula is equivalent to an open formula.

Lemma 1

$Add_M(\bar{x}, \bar{y}, \bar{z})_A(v) = 1$ if and only if the computations of programs $M(\bar{x})$, $M(\bar{y})$, $M(\bar{z})$ with the initial valuation v are finite and $number_M(v(\bar{x})) + number_M(v(\bar{y})) = number_M(v(\bar{z}))$.

The proof is omitted.

Remark 1

Let A be a structure for L and let $M(\bar{x})$ be a program of the form <u>while</u> γ <u>do</u> K. If $\exists \bar{x}\, \alpha_{M,n}(\bar{x})_A(v) = 1$ then for all natural k less than n $\exists \bar{x}\, \alpha_{M,k}(\bar{x})_A(v) = 1$.

Remark 1 can be written as

$A \models \exists \bar{x}\, \alpha_{M,n}(\bar{x})$ implies $A \models \exists \bar{x}\, \alpha_{M,k}(\bar{x})$ for $k \leqslant n$.

The expression $\exists \bar{x}$ is an abbreviation for $\exists x_1 \ldots \exists x_p$.

Corollary 1

Let A be a structure for L and let $M(\bar{x})$ be a program of the form <u>while</u> γ <u>do</u> K. Let v be a valuation such that $number_M(v(\bar{x})) = m$, $number_M(v(\bar{y})) = n$. If for some $k \geqslant m + n$ $A \models \exists \bar{x}\, \alpha_{M,k}(\bar{x})$ then $\exists \bar{z}\, Add_M(\bar{x}, \bar{y}, \bar{z})_A(v) = 1$. In particular $A \models \exists \bar{x}\, \alpha_{M,m+n}(\bar{x})$ implies $\exists \bar{z}\, Add_M(\bar{x}, \bar{y}, \bar{z})_A(v) = 1$.

Let $M(x_1,\ldots,x_p)$ be a program of the form <u>while</u> γ <u>do</u> K and let $\bar{x} = (x_1,\ldots,x_p)$, $\bar{y} = (y_1,\ldots,y_p)$, $\bar{z} = (z_1,\ldots,z_p)$ be sequences of different variables. Let us denote by $Mult_M(\bar{x}, \bar{y}, \bar{z})$ the formula

$$M(\bar{x})1 \wedge M(\bar{y})1 \wedge M(\bar{z})1 \wedge R(\neg\gamma(\bar{x}) \wedge \neg\gamma(\bar{t}) \wedge \wedge \neg\gamma(\bar{z}))$$

where R denotes the following program

<u>begin</u>

<u>while</u> $\gamma(\bar{x}) \wedge \gamma(\bar{z})$ <u>do</u>

<u>begin</u>

$t_1 := y_1$; . . . ; $t_p := y_p$;

$\underline{\text{while}}\ \gamma(\bar{t}) \wedge \gamma(\bar{z})\ \underline{\text{do}}$

$\underline{\text{begin}}\ K(\bar{t})\ ;\ K(\bar{z})\ \underline{\text{end}}\ ;$

$\underline{\text{if}}\ -\gamma(\bar{t})\ \underline{\text{then}}\ K(\bar{x})$

$\underline{\text{end}}$

$\underline{\text{end}}$

Lemma 2

$Mult_M(\bar{x}, \bar{y}, \bar{z})_A(v) = \mathbb{1}$ if and only if the computations of programs $M(\bar{x})$, $M(\bar{y})$, $M(\bar{z})$ with the initial valuation v are finite and $number_{M(\bar{x})}(v(\bar{x})) \times number_{M(\bar{y})}(v(\bar{y})) = number_{M(\bar{z})}(v(\bar{z}))$.

The proof is omitted.

Corollary 2

Let A be a structure for L and let $M(\bar{x})$ be a program of the form $\underline{\text{while}}\ \gamma\ \underline{\text{do}}\ K$. Let v be a valuation such that $number(v(\bar{x})) = m$, $number(v(\bar{y})) = n$. If for some $k \geqslant m \times n$ $A \models \exists \bar{x}\, \alpha_{M,k}(\bar{x})$ then $\exists \bar{z}\, Mult_M(\bar{x}, \bar{y}, \bar{z})_A(v) = \mathbb{1}$. In particular $A \models \exists \bar{x}\, \alpha_{M, m\times n}(\bar{x})$ implies $\exists \bar{z}\, Mult_M(\bar{x}, \bar{y}, \bar{z})_A(v) = \mathbb{1}$.

2. Undecidable algorithmic theories

In this section we shall be concerned with the problem of undecidability in algorithmic logic.

Let us consider the structure $\mathcal{N} = \langle N, 0, 1, +, \times, = \rangle$ of natural numbers. Let us define the relations add , mult as follows

$$add(i,j,k) \Leftrightarrow i + j = k$$

$$mult(i,j,k) \Leftrightarrow i \times j = k$$

Let $p_1(i_1,\dots,i_r)$, $p_2(i_1,\dots,i_r)$ be two polynomials with natural coeficients. Let $\{c_1,\dots,c_s\}$ be the set of all coeficients of polynomials p_1 , p_2 . By $\psi'(p_1,p_2)$ we shall denote the formula obtained from the formula $p_1 = p_2$ by replacing all occurrences of a constant c_n by a variable k_n for $n = 1,\dots,s$. By $\psi''(p_1,p_2)$ we shall denote the formula $\psi'(p_1,p_2) \wedge k_1 = c_1 \wedge \dots \wedge k_s = c_s$.

Let us eliminate the functor symbols $+$, $\times$ by means of the predicates add , mult . The formula $\psi(p_1,p_2)$ obtained in such way contains some additional variables.

Example

Let $p_1(i_1, i_2)$, $p_2(i_1, i_2)$ denote polynomials $2 \times i_1 \times i_2$, $i_1 \times i_1 + 3$ respectively. Then formulas $\psi'(p_1,p_2)$, $\psi''(p_1,p_2)$ and $\psi(p_1,p_2)$ are as follows :

$\psi'(p_1,p_2)$: $k_1 \times i_1 \times i_2 = i_1 \times i_1 + k_2$

$\psi''(p_1,p_2)$: $k_1 \times i_1 \times i_2 = i_1 \times i_1 + k_2 \wedge k_1 = 2 \wedge k_2 = 3$

$\psi(p_1,p_2)$: $\exists j_1 \exists j_2 \exists j_3 \exists j_4$ $mult(i_1,i_2,j_1) \wedge mult(k_1,j_1,j_2) \wedge mult(i_1,i_1,j_3) \wedge add(j_3,k_2,j_4) \wedge j_2 = j_4 \wedge k_1 = 2 \wedge k_2 = 3$

Let $p_1(i_1,\dots,i_r)$, $p_2(i_1,\dots,i_r)$ be two polynomials and let $\psi(p_1,p_2)(i_1,\dots,i_r, k_1,\dots,k_s, j_1,\dots,j_t)$ be formula defined above. Let $M(x_1,\dots,x_p)$ be a program of the form <u>while</u> γ <u>do</u> K . We define an algorithmic formula associated with the polynomials p_1 , p_2 and the program M .

Let $\bar{x}_1,\dots,\bar{x}_r$, $\bar{z}_1,\dots,\bar{z}_s$, $\bar{y}_1,\dots,\bar{y}_t$ be p-element sequences of different variables. We shall say that the variable i_n and the sequence $\bar{x}_n$ are compatibile for $n = 1,\dots,r$ and similarly for variables k_n , j_n . Let us denote by $Tr[M, p_1, p_2]$ the formula obtained from the formula $\psi(p_1,p_2)$ after replacing :

- every subformula of the form $add(i,j,k)$ by formula $Add_M(\bar{x}, \bar{y}, \bar{z})$ where i,j,k and $\bar{x}$, $\bar{y}$, $\bar{z}$ are compatibile respectively
- every subformula of the form $mult(i,j,k)$ by formula $Mult_M(\bar{x}, \bar{y}, \bar{z})$ where i,j,k and $\bar{x}$, $\bar{y}$, $\bar{z}$ are compatibile respectively
- every subformula of the form $k = c$ where c is a coeficient by $\alpha_{M,c}(\bar{z})$ where k and $\bar{z}$ are compatibile
- every expression of the form $\exists j$ by $\exists y_1 \dots \exists y_p$ where j and $(y_1,\dots,y_p)$ are compatibile

The following lemmas are immediate consequences of Lemmas 1,2 and Corollaries 1,2 .

Lemma 3

Let $p_1(i_1,\dots,i_r)$, $p_2(i_1,\dots,i_r)$ be two polynomials. Let A be a structure for L and let $M(x_1,\dots,x_p)$ be a program of the form <u>while</u> γ <u>do</u> K .

If $Tr[M, p_1, p_2](\bar{x}_1,\dots,\bar{x}_r, \bar{z}_1,\dots,\bar{z}_s, \bar{y}_1,\dots,\bar{y}_t)_A(v) = 1$ then the numbers $number_M(v(\bar{x}_1))$, . . . , $number_M(v(\bar{y}_t))$ are defined, $number_M(v(\bar{z}_n)) = c_n$ for $n = 1,\dots,s$ and

$$p_1(m_1, \dots, m_r) = p_2(m_1, \dots, m_r)$$

where m_n denotes $number_M(v(\bar{x}_n))$, $n = 1,\dots,r$.

Lemma 4

Let $p_1(i_1,\dots,i_r)$, $p_2(i_1,\dots,i_r)$ be two polynomials and let $m_1, \dots, m_r$ be a sequence of natural numbers such that

$$p_1(m_1, \dots, m_r) = p_2(m_1, \dots, m_r)$$

Let A be a structure for L and let $M(x_1,\dots,x_p)$ be a program of the form <u>while</u> γ <u>do</u> K . Let v be a valuation of variables such that $number_M(v(\bar{x}_n)) = m_n$ for $n = 1,\dots,r$. Then

$$A \models \exists \bar{x}\, \alpha_{M,k}(\bar{x}) \quad \text{where } k \geqslant p_1(m_1,\dots,m_r)$$

implies

$$Tr[M, p_1, p_2](\bar{x}_1,\dots,\bar{x}_r, \bar{z}_1,\dots,\bar{z}_s, \bar{y}_1,\dots,\bar{y}_t)_A(v) = 1$$

Now, we formulate the criterion of undecidability of algorithmic theories . The proof of this criterion is based on Lemmas 1,2,3,4 and result of Matijasevič [7] . However, it can be carried out without the use of result of Matijasevič (compare Trachtenbrot [14]).

Theorem 1

Let $T = \langle L, C, Ax \rangle$ be an algorithmic theory such that for some program $M(x_1, \dots, x_p)$ of the form <u>while</u> γ <u>do</u> K the theory $T_n = \langle L, C, Ax \cup \{\exists x_1 \dots \exists x_p\, \alpha_{M,n}(x_1,\dots,x_p)\} \rangle$ is consistent for every natural number n .

Then the theory T is undecidable. Moreover, it is at least in Π^0_1.

Proof.

Using preceding Lemmas we can prove the equivalence formulated below :

Let $p_1(i_1,\dots,i_r)$, $p_2(i_1,\dots,i_r)$ be polynomials and let $m_1, \dots, m_w$ where $w < r$ be a sequence of natural numbers. Let $M\,x$ be a program of the form while γ do K . We recall the meaning of the formula $\alpha_{M,n}(\bar{x})$: the logical value of this formula is true if and only if the program M ends computation after n executions of the subprogram K . Let $M(x_1,\dots,x_p)$ be a program such as in Th. 1. The following equivalence holds :

$$\mathcal{N} \models \neg \exists j_{w+1} \dots \exists j_r \; p_1(m_1,\dots,m_w, j_{w+1},\dots,j_r) = \\ = p_2(m_1,\dots,m_w, j_{w+1},\dots,j_r)$$

if and only if

for every model A of the theory T

$$A \models \neg \exists \bar{x}_1 \dots \exists \bar{x}_w \exists \bar{x}_{w+1} \dots \exists \bar{x}_r \; Tr[M, p_1, p_2](\bar{x}_1, \dots,\bar{x}_w, \bar{x}_{w+1},\dots,\bar{x}_r, \bar{z}_1,\dots,\bar{z}_s, \bar{y}_1,\dots,\bar{y}_t) \wedge \\ \wedge \alpha_{M,m_1}(\bar{x}_1) \wedge \dots \wedge \alpha_{M,m_w}(\bar{x}_w)$$

We omit the proof of the above equivalence.

Let T be a theory satisfying the assumptions of Theorem 1 and let M be such a program. Let us suppose that theory T is decidable. Then for every formula α from the language of T we can decide whether α is theorem of T or not. But in virtue of the above formulated equivalence this means that we can decide whether the formula

$$\exists j_{w+1} \dots \exists j_r \; p_1(m_1,\dots,m_w, j_{w+1},\dots,j_r) = p_2(m_1,\dots,m_w, j_{w+1}, \dots,j_r)$$

is true in the structure of natural numbers or not. This contradicts the result of Matijasevič [7] :

for every recursively enumerable relation $R(m_1, \dots, m_w)$ there are polynomials $p_1(j_1,\dots,j_w, j_{w+1},\dots,j_r)$, $p_2(j_1,\dots,j_w, j_{w+1}, \dots,j_r)$ such that

$$R(m_1, \dots, m_w) \Leftrightarrow \exists j_{w+1} \dots \exists j_r \; p_1(m_1,\dots,m_w, j_{w+1},\dots \\ \dots,j_r) = p_2(m_1,\dots,m_w,j_{w+1},\dots,j_r)$$

Thus undecidability of theory T is proved.

3. Decidable algorithmic theories.

In this section we shall consider the case when theory T is undecidable. We shall assume that the language L of theory T contains two argument predicate = and the set of axioms of theory T contains the set of axioms for equality.

Lemma 5

Let T be a decidable theory with equality and let $K(x_1,\dots,x_p)$ be a loop-free without "while" program. Then there is a natural number n_o such that for every model A of theory T and for every valuation of variables v the sequence of valuations

$$v\ ,\ K_A(v)\ ,\ K^2{}_A(v)\ ,\ \dots$$

contains at most n_o different valuations.

Proof.

Let us suppose that for every natural number n there is a model A of theory T and a valuation v such that the valuations

$$v\ ,\ v_1 = K_A(v)\ ,\ \dots\ ,\ v_n = K^n{}_A(v)$$

are different. Let v' be a valuation satisfying

$$v'(x_i) = v(x_i) \quad \text{for } i = 1,\dots,p$$
$$v'(y_i) = v_n(x_i) \quad \text{for } i = 1,\dots,p$$

Let us consider the following program $M(x_1,\dots,x_p, y_1,\dots,y_p)$

$$\underline{\text{while}}\ \neg\, x_1 = y_1 \wedge \dots \wedge \neg\, x_p = y_p\ \underline{\text{do}}\ K\ .$$

Let us notice that the number of executions of the subprogram K in the computation of the program M with initial valuation v' is equal to n. Thus the theory $T_n = \langle L, C, Ax \cup \{\exists x_1 \dots \exists x_p \exists y_1 \dots \exists y_p\ \alpha_{M,n}(x_1,\dots,x_p, y_1,\dots,y_p)$ is consistent for every number n what contradicts Theorem 1 .

In an analogous way we can prove

Lemma 6

Let T be a decidable theory with equality. Let K be a loop-free program. There is a number n_o such that for every formula β from the language of theory T

$$T \vdash \bigcap K\beta \Leftrightarrow (\beta \wedge K\beta \wedge \dots \wedge K^{n_o}\beta)$$

and

$$T \vdash \bigcup K\beta \Leftrightarrow (\beta \vee K\beta \vee \dots \vee K^{n_o}\beta).$$

We recall that an algorithmic formula α is in the normal form if it is of the form $Q_1 \dots Q_n \delta$ where $n \geqslant 0$, δ is an open formula and every expression Q_i is of one of the forms $\exists x$, $\forall x$, $s\bigcup K$, $s\bigcap K$ where K is a loop-free program and s denotes a sequence (may be empty) of substitutions.

In [1] it is proved that for every formula α there is a formula β in the normal form such that $\alpha \Leftrightarrow \beta$ is a tautology of algorithmic logic. This fact is essential to proving the following

Lemma 7

Let T be a decidable theory with equality. Then for every formula α from the language of theory T there is a first order formula α^{o} such that $T \vdash \alpha \Leftrightarrow \alpha^{o}$

The proof of this lemma proceeds by induction on the number of quantifiers in the normal form of formula α.

This lemma can be strengthened as follows :

Theorem 2

Let $T = \langle L, C, Ax \rangle$ be a decidable algorithmic theory with equality. There is a theory $T^{o} = \langle L, C, Ax^{o} \rangle$ such that Ax^{o} is a set of first order formulas and such that for every formula α of the language L

(i) $T \vdash \alpha$ if and only if $T^{o} \vdash \alpha$

The idea of the proof.

Let us denote by Ax^{o} the set of all first order formulas which are theorems of theory T. It is sufficient to prove that

$$T \vdash \alpha \quad \text{implies} \quad T^{o} \vdash \alpha$$

We can assume that α is in the normal form $Q_1 \ldots Q_r \delta$. Let $It(\alpha)$ denote the number of iteration quantifiers occurring in the sequence $Q_1 \ldots Q_r$.

The proof of (i) proceeds by induction on the number $It(\alpha)$. We illustrate our method of reasoning in the case when Q_1 is of the form $s \bigcap K$. Let us denote by β the formula $Q_2 \ldots Q_r \delta$. From Lemma 7 it follows that there is a first order formula β^{o} such that $T \vdash \beta \Leftrightarrow \beta^{o}$. In virtue of theorem of replacing [1] we have

$$T \vdash s \bigcap K \beta \Leftrightarrow s \bigcap K \beta^{o} \quad \text{and consequently}$$

$$T \vdash \alpha \Leftrightarrow s \bigcap K \beta^{o} .$$

In virtue of Lemma 6 there is a number n_o such that

$$T \vdash s \bigcap K \beta \Leftrightarrow s (\beta \wedge K\beta \wedge \ldots \wedge K^{n_o}\beta)$$

$$T \vdash s \bigcap K \beta^{o} \Leftrightarrow s (\beta^{o} \wedge K\beta^{o} \wedge \ldots \wedge K^{n_o}\beta^{o})$$

Let us denote by α_o the formula $s(\beta^o \wedge K\beta^o \wedge \ldots \wedge K^{n_o}\beta^o)$ This formula is equivalent to some first order formula because K is loop-free.

Since $T \vdash \alpha$ then $T \vdash \alpha_o$ and $T \vdash \alpha_o \Rightarrow sK^i\beta^o$ for all natural numbers i . In virtue of inductive assumption we have $T^o \vdash \alpha_o \Rightarrow sK^i\beta^o$ for every natural number i . Using the ω - rule of inference $\dfrac{\{\alpha \Rightarrow sM^i\beta\}_{i\in N}}{\alpha \Rightarrow s\bigcap M\beta}$ we obtain $T^o \vdash \alpha_o \Rightarrow s\bigcap K\beta^o$ and consequently $T^o \vdash s\bigcap K\beta^o$.

To prove $T^o \vdash s\bigcap K\beta$ it is sufficient to note that $T^o \vdash \beta \Leftrightarrow \beta^o$ because $It(\beta \Rightarrow \beta^o) = It(\beta^o \Rightarrow \beta) = It(\beta)$. This ends the proof of inductive step.

4. Examples.

First, we give examples of undecidable theories. The undecidability of these theories immediately follows from Theorem 1 .

1. Algorithmic arithmetic of natural numbers.

Let s denotes the successor function. The set of axioms consists of the axioms for identity and the following axioms :

$$\neg s(x) = 0$$

$$s(x) = s(y) \Rightarrow x = y$$

$$[y := 0]\bigcup[y := s(y)]\ x = y$$

As we have mentioned above the undecidability of this theory follows from Theorem 1 . It is sufficient to take as the program M the program <u>begin</u> y := 0 ; <u>while</u> ¬ x = y <u>do</u> y := s(y) <u>end</u> . The undecidability of this theory was proved earlier A.Salwicki. He also proved that this theory characterizes categorically the standard model of natural numbers (compare [8]).

2. Algorithmic theory of fields of characteristic zero.

The set of axioms of this theory consists of the set of axioms of fields and of the following axiom

$$[y := 1]\bigcap[y := y + 1]\ \neg y = 0$$

The following program M satisfies the assumptions of Theorem 1 :

<u>begin</u> y := 1 ; <u>while</u> ¬ y = x <u>do</u> y := y + 1 <u>end</u>

3. Algorithmic theory of fields of finite characteristic.

The set of axioms of this theory consists of the axioms of fields and the axiom

$[y := 1] \bigcup [y := y + 1] \quad y = 0$

The program M is the same as in the point 2 .

4. Algorithmic theory of rings $Z_m = \langle \{0,1,\ldots,m-1\}, +_m, \times_m, 0, 1, = \rangle$

This theory is obtained from the theory of rings by adding the axioms

$[y := 0] \bigcup [y := y +_m 1] \quad y = x$

$[y := 1] \bigcup [y := y +_m 1] \quad y = 0$

To prove undecidability of this theory it is sufficient consider the program given in the point 2.

By an analogous way we prove undecidability of

5. Algorithmic theory of stacks [10] .

6. Algorithmic theory of dictionaries [11] .
This theory is in Π^0_1 .

Now, we give examples of decidable algorithmic theories.

7. Algorithmic theory of two element Boolean algebra [3] .
The proof of decidability of this theory is contained in quoted paper of M.Grabowski [3] .

8. The same idea can be used to prove that every theory of a finite structure is decidable. Thus, for example, for every fixed number m the theory of the structure Z_m is decidable.

9. In a similar way we can prove decidability of the following theory S_n with one functor f based on the set of axioms for equality and the following axioms

$x = f(x) \vee x = f(f(x)) \vee \ldots \vee x = f^n(x)$

$f(x) = f(y) \Longrightarrow x = y$

The theory S_n has infinite models.

10. Let T be a first order theory based on the set of axioms Ax . Let P, Φ be the sets of functors and predicates of the language L of the theory T. Let L_{alg} be an algorithmic language with the sets of functors Φ and predicates P . By T_{alg} we shall denote the algorithmic theory $\langle L_{alg}, C, Ax \rangle$. One can prove that the following implication holds :

If the set of functors of the language of a first order theory is empty and T is a decidable theory then the algorithmic theory T_{alg} is decidable.

Let us note that in algorithmic logic functors cannot be eliminated by predicates contrary to first order logic where for every theory T the theory T′ obtained from T by elimination of functor symbols is interpretable in T and vice versa.

Let T denotes the first order theory of successor function. Then both theories T, T′ are decidable. The theory T'_{alg} is decidable. However the theory T_{alg} is undecidable what proves the above formulated fact.

References.

[1] L.Banachowski, Investigations of properties of programs by means of extended algorithmic logic, Fundamenta Informaticae,I, 1977

[2] L.Banachowski, An axiomatic approach to the theory of data structures, Bull.Acad.Pol.Sci.Sèr.Math.Astr. Phys. 23, 1975 , 315-323

[3] M.Grabowski, The set of tautologies of zero order algorithmic logic is decidable, Bull.Acad.Pol.Sci.Sèr.Math. Astr.Phys. 20, 1972 , 575-582

[4] D.Harel, A.R.Meyer, V.R.Pratt, Computability and completeness in logic of programs, Proc. 9th Ann. ACM Symp. on Theory of Computing, 261-268

[5] A.Kreczmar, Effectivity problems of algorithmic logic, Fundamenta Informaticae I, 1977 , 19-32

[6] A.Kreczmar, Programmability in fields, Fundamenta Informaticae I, 1977 , 195-230

[7] J.Matijasevič, Recursively enumerable relations are diophanic, Reports of Academy of Science of USSR 191, 279-282

[8] G.Mirkowska, Algorithmic logic and its applications in program theory, Fundamenta Informaticae I, 1977 , 1-17, 147-167

[9] H.Rasiowa, R.Sikorski, Mathematics of metamathematics, PWN, Warszawa 1963

[10] A.Salwicki, On algorithmic theory of stacks, CC PAS Reports

[11] A.Salwicki, On algorithmic theory of dictionaries, Fundamenta Informaticae ,to appear

[12] A.Salwicki, Programmability and recursiveness, Dissertationes Mathematicae, to appear

[13] A.Tarski, A decision method for elementary algebra and geometry, RAND Corporation, Santa Monica, Calif. 1948

[14] B.A.Trachtenbrot, There is no algorithm for deciding the validity of formulas in finite structures, Reports of Academy of Science of USSR, 70 , 569-572

ON FINDING THE OPTIMAL ACCESS PATH TO RESOLVE A RELATIONAL DATA BASE QUERY

P. Degano, A. Lomanto
Istituto di Scienze della Informazione, Università degli Studi
C/so Italia, 40 - 56100 Pisa

F. Sirovich(*)
Istituto di Elaborazione della Informazione - C.N.R.
Via S. Maria, 46 - 56100 Pisa

Abstract.

The paper presents a formal model to specify a data base, a query and the access path which must be followed to obtain the ansewer. The model is based on the problem reduction hypergraphs, for which an admissible and optimal search algorithm is known. An effective method is given to map the data base and the query into a problem reduction hypergraph, which the known search algorithm can be applied to. The optimal solution to the problem reduction hypergraph provides an optimal (and possibly parallel) program to obtain the answer to the given query. Since the model allows to determine the correct answer, if any, without modifications of the data base nor requiring further information, it is an improvement over the models presented in the literature.

1. Introduction.

The widespread application of computer science to the management of large systems and the identification of the data bases as components of the data information systems contributed both to the adoption of general purpose data base management systems and to progressive increase of the data bases sizes. Consequently, the cost of accessing the data base is becoming a substantial one, especially when a service to casual users must be provided, possibly in addition to the conventional support to stable application programs.
Since casual users cannot be requested to be aware of the logical organization of the data base, the queries are declaratively frased in terms of input-output relationships, with no attention to the procedural artifacts involved with answering them. Moreover, high level data manipulation languages tend to make available to the application programmer this kind of non-procedural query statements in order to enhance the data base independence of the applicative program. Obviously, the procedural artifacts must be

---

This work has been partially supported by G.R.I.S.-C.N.R., under grant n. 7900830.07

(*) Present address: Olivetti-DRAS, Via Jervis 77, 10125 Ivrea.

filled in, possibly minimizing the overall cost of resolving the query. Thus the problem is to find a data base access path with minimal cost which answers the given query.
Carlson and Kaplan /CK/ present a formal definition for access paths in relational data bases, based on the composition of functional and inverted functional dependence accesses, projections and attribute comparisons. In the model of /CK/ all access paths can be derived and checked for conditional acceptability, i.e. a test on the paths is performed to determine whether the provided answer may include illegitimate values.
We present here a formal definition to specify relational data base accesses and a query. We give a definition of access path which is more general than the one in /CK/ namely we are able to provide a query resolution in cases in which Carlson and Kaplan require the data base to be restructured. Moreover, we provide an algorithm to find the optimal access path since an optimal search algorithm is known for the formalism used in the model.
Section 2 provides a few background definitions on relational data bases and the hypergraph formalism used in the model. In Section 3 we give the model for the data base accesses and the access paths. The problem of the conditional acceptable paths is faced in Section 4, where we provide a refined definition and resolve a wider class of queries.

2. Background.

2.1. Relational Data Model.

A good introduction to the subject can be found in /TL/ along with a supportive bibliography.
The relational data model is a formal model for representing both the relationships among the characteristics of the objects recorded in a data base, and the associations between them.
Consider a set of domains S1,S2,...,Sn (not necessarily distinct). A relation R is a subset of the Cartesian product S1xS2x...xSn. Note that data base relations differ from mathematical relations since they are time-varying.
An n-ary relation can be represented as a table, whose columns are called attributes and whose rows correspond to n-tuples belonging to the relation. Every attribute is uniquely identified by a role name, which specifies the role played by the domain on which the attribute takes value. In the sequel we will assume that identical role names are given to attributes iff they play identical roles in (possibly) different relations.
A key K of a relation R is a subset of attributes of R with the following time-independent properties:
- In each tuple of R the value of K uniquely identifies that tuple;
- No attribute in K can be discarded without destroying the above property.

An attribute is called prime if it partecipates in a key of R. Otherwise an attribute is called nonprime.
Let A,B,C be attributes of R. B is (time-independent) functionally dependent on A (A--> B) iff all the tuples of R which take a given values on A present a unique value on B, i.e. the tuples of R define a time-varying mapping from A to B. C is transitively dependent on A iff A--> B and B--> C. Let

A1,...,An--> B(*), and let B functionally depend in the same way on A1,...,Am where m<n, then B is partially dependent on A1,...,An. If no such m exists, then B is fully dependent on A1,...,An.
A relation is in First Normal Form (1NF) if every attribute is based on domains consisting of simple values. A relation is in Second Normal Form (2NF) if it is in 1NF and each nonprime attribute is fully dependent on every key. A relation is in Third Normal Form (3NF) if it is in 2NF and no nonprime attribute is transitively dependent on any key. In the following we will consider only relations in 3NF, since algorithms are given to transform any set of relations into a equivalent 3NF set of relations.
The access to the data is supplied by a data language in which the user can express his query. The answer to a query is a relation itself. The language supplies relational operators which allow a user to construct new relations from existing ones.
We briefly describe the most important relational operators in terms of the relational algebra.
Let r= r1,...,rn and s= s1,...,sm be tuples, the concatenation of r with s is the (n+m)-tuple defined by $r\hat{\ }s$= r1,...,rn,s1,...,sm .
Let R be a relation, r ε R a tuple, D1,...,Dn the domains of R: then
1. r.Di designates the i-the component of r;
2. if A ε D1,...,Dn , then
2.1. r.A is a tuple containing only those components specified by A;
2.2. R.A= r.A:r ε R (projection).
Let Θ be one of the conditional operators $<, \leq, >, \geq, =, \neq$, v be a literal value, A and B attributes of R, then
R.A Θ v= r:r ε R & (r.A Θ v) (restriction);
R.A Θ B= r:r ε R & (r.A Θ r.B) (selection).
Two sets of attributes A,B are compatible if they are of the same degree and the corresponding domains are of the same data type.
Let A and B be compatible sets of attributes of relations R and S respectively, then
R.A Θ S.B= r^s:r ε R & sεS & (r.A Θ s.B) (Θ -join).
The user can express queries of the following form SELECT O WHERE I Θ v where O denotes a collection of "output" attributes, I denotes an "input" attribute, Θ is a conditional operator and v is a literal value.
Whenever an attribute name (in O or I) occurs in more than one relation, the user is requested to specify the intended relation. This is the standard approach to avoid ambiguity problems.

2.2. Problem Reduction Hypergraphs.

We will briefly describe a model for problems solving in Artificial Intelligence which is based on non-independent problem reduction /LS1,LS2/. We propose the same model to formally specify a data base and a query and to find the optimal access path to answer the query.

(*) The extension of functional dependence on a set of attributes is immediate.

A problem solving task is defined as a set of problems D and a finite set of reduction operators F. Set D must contain two distinct elements S and T denoting the "starting problem" and the "terminal (trivially solved) problem" respectively. Each reduction operator fi maps an n-tuple of problems d1,..., dn into an m-tuple e1,...,em, and it is represented by the production fi: d1,...,dn--> e1,...,em. The problems dj (j=1,...,n) and ek (k=1,...,m) are called fi-input and fi-output problems respectively.
A problem solving task can be represented by a problem reduction hypergraph (prh) H which is defined as a finite directed hypergraph (*) whose nodes are in one-to-one direct correspondence with (and labelled by) the elements of D and whose arcs are in one-to-one correspondence with (and labelled by) the elements of F.
An arc labelled fi can be graphically represented by a special node whose input arcs come from the nodes labelled by the fi-initial problems and whose output arcs lead to fi-final problems.
Figure 1 represents the problem solving task and the corresponding prh.

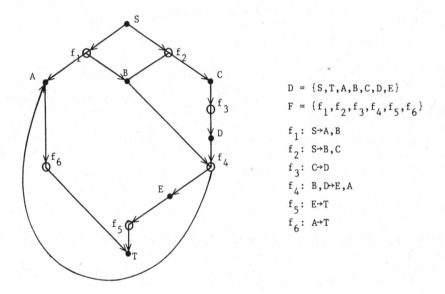

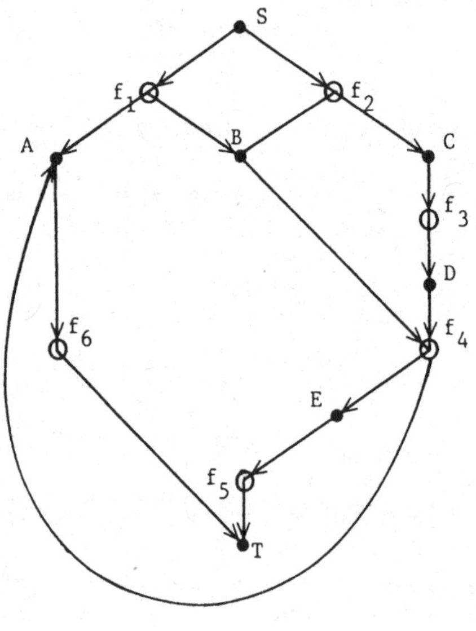

D = {S,T,A,B,C,D,E}

F = $\{f_1,f_2,f_3,f_4,f_5,f_6\}$

f_1: S→A,B

f_2: S→B,C

f_3: C→D

f_4: B,D→E,A

f_5: E→T

f_6: A→T

Fig. 1 A problem solving task and the corresponding hypergraph.

(*) A finite hypergraph /BE/ is a pair H=(N,E), where N is a finite set of nodes, and E is a set of subset (arcs) of N. A finite directed hypergraph is a pair H=(N,E), where N is a finite set of nodes, and E is a set, such that each element (directed arc) ai is an ordered pair (Ii,Oi) of subsets of N. The elements of Ii and of Oi are called respectively initial and final nodes of ai.

Prh's are searched in order to find solutions, to show how the starting problem S can be solved by reducing it to the trivially solved problem T. Solutions are defined over the (generally infinite) hypertree H' associated to the prh H, which is obtained by unfolding H, i.e. by recursively duplicating the output arcs of those nodes having more than one input arc, starting from the node labelled by S.

A potential solution (ps) of H is a subtree of H' which is rooted in S and is obtained by applying the given productions. In other words, a ps is a sort of derivation hypertree of the type 0 grammar ({T},D,S,F) /LS2/ corresponding to the productions in F. A solution to H is any ps such that all its leaf nodes are labelled by T.

Depending on the problem described by the prh H, non-negative costs may be associated to arcs which obviously express the costs associated to the reduction operators which label the arcs. The cost of a (potential) solution is defined as the sum of the costs associated to the arcs occurring in the (potential) solution.

A search algorithm (Ao) which finds in the minimal number of steps the optimal solution is given in /LS2/. It has been shown that Ao is NP-complete. The optimal solution is obtained by unfolding H in an orderly way. At any step, Ao expands the ps with minimal cost, according to the (non-negative) costs associated to the arcs of H. It is easy to show that the obtained solution, if any, is optimal, since the costs associated to ps's never decrease.

Figure 2 shows all the ps's of the prh in Figure 1. The ps c9 is the (only) solution.

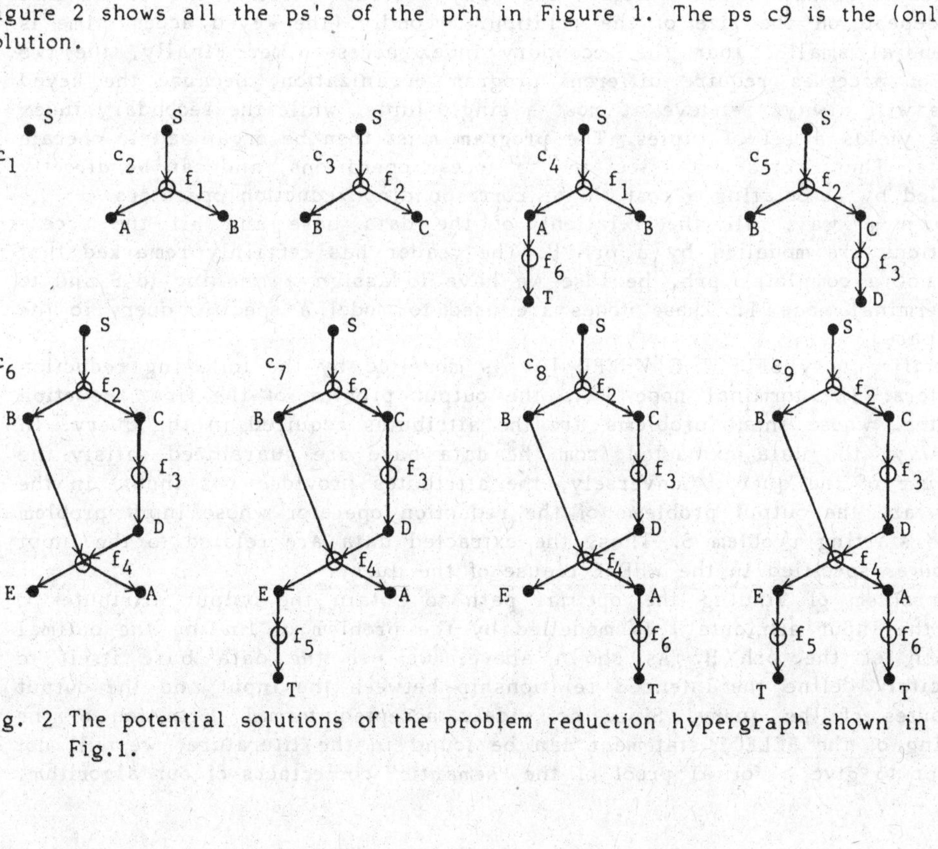

Fig. 2 The potential solutions of the problem reduction hypergraph shown in Fig.1.

3. Formal model for the access path problem.

We will now show how the problem of finding the optimal access (if any) to a given query can be casted as the problem of finding an optimal solution for a given prh. Obviously the prh will model both the data base and the given query.

The 3NF relational data base will consists of a set of relations. Each relation attribute corresponds to a non-terminal node of H. With the exception of S there is no other non-terminal node in H.

A specific data base provides a well defined set of primitive access operators to the existing relations, namely keyed accesses and secondary index accesses. A keyed access guarantees that a single relation tuple is retrieved by providing one value for the relation key. The keyed access corresponds to follow a functional dependence. Such an access is modelled by a reduction operator whose input problems are the attributes belonging to the key and whose output problems are all the attributes belonging to the relation. The secondary index access guarantees that a subset of the relation tuples is retrieved (generally by means of one or more inverted files) by providing one value for the relation secondary index. Secondary index access corresponds to follow inverted (generally non bijective) functional dependences. Such an access is analogously modelled by a reduction operator whose input problems are the attributes of the secondary index and whose output problems are all the relation attributes.

The access operators are different for many reasons. Firstly, the access time may depend on the size of the relation. Secondly, the keyed access time is in general smaller than the secondary index access time. Finally, the two kind of accesses require different program organization, because the keyed access will always retrieve at most a single tuple, while the secondary index access yields a set of tuples. The program must then be organized to operate on sets. Thus, costs are associated to access operations, and can be directly modelled by associating a cost to the corresponding reduction operators.

In such a way, all the relations of the data base and all the access operations are modelled by a prh H. The reader has certainly remarked that H is not a complete prh, because we have to assign a meaning to S and to the terminal node T. These nodes are used to model a specific query to the data base.

A specific query SELECT O WHERE Iθv is modelled by the following reduction operators. The terminal node T is the output problem of the first reduction operator, whose input problems are the attributes required in the query. In this way, the data extracted from the data base are guaranteed satisfy the O clause of the query. Conversely, the attributes provided (as input) in the query are the output problems of the reduction operator whose input problem is the starting problem S. Thus, the extracted data are related to the input attributes specified in the WHERE clause of the query.

The problem of finding the optimal path to obtain the output attributes O from the input attribute I is modelled by the problem of finding the optimal solution of the prh H. As shown above, we use the data base itself to implicitely define the intended relationship between the input and the output attributes of the query. Since no widely accepted formal definition of the meaning of the SELECT statement can be found in the literature, we will not attempt to give a formal proof of the "semantic" correctness of our algorithm.

The admissible and optimal algorithm Ao /LS2/ can be used to find the solution. One minor modification is needed, which actually simplifies Ao. Namely, a ps to a hypergraph H is defined to be a solution iff at least one of its leaf nodes is labelled by T.

Example 1:
We have a data base consisting of the following relations and associated operations (this example is taken from /CK/ and only those relations relevant to the present case are reported here).

Relation PR(Part#,Purchase_Req#,PR_Q,Job#,Empl#)
The key is (Part#,Purchase_Req#), secondary index is (Purchase_Req#).

Relation PO(Purchase_Ord#,Empl_Ord#,Supplier,Job#)
The key is (Purchase_Ord#), the secondary index is (Job#).

Relation POI (Purchase_Ord#,Part#,PO_Q,Delivery_Date)
The key is (Purchase_Ord#,Part#), the secondary index is (Part#).

Thus, the available reduction operators are
KPR: Part#,Purchase_Req#--> Part#,Purchase_Req#,PR_Q,Job#, Empl#
SPR: Purchase_Req#--> Part#,Purchase_Req#,PR_Q,Job#,Empl#

KPO: Purchase_Ord#--> Purchase_Ord#,Empl_Ord#,Supplier,Job#
SPO: Job#--> Purchase_Ord#,Empl_Ord#,Supplier,Job#

KPOI: Purschase_Ord#,Part#-->Purchase_Ord#,Part#,PO_Q, Delivery_Date
SPOI: Part#-->Purchase_Ord#,Part#,PO_Q,Delivery_Date

Now suppose the query is
SELECT Part#,Delivery_Date WHERE Purschase_Req= v
The query is modelled by the reduction operators
QI: S--> Purchase_Req#
QO: Part#,Delivery_Date--> T
According to the provided costs we do not show here, the optimal solution is show in the following Figure 3.

The prh solution must be translated into a program to search the data base for the query answer. The search program transforms relations until the answer relation is obtained. The application of the QI reduction operator is translated into the generation of the relation defined by the WHERE clause I Θ v. This clause may actually specify any operation provided by the Data Base Management System, e.g. it may be a SELECT statement itself /CB/. This is the place where other tecniques for query optimization, such as those in /HA, ES, KL/, can be profitably integrated with the present technique. The application of QI can be seen as an input operation which provides to the program the input relation. The relation is then transformed by executing the access operations corresponding to the reduction operator occurring into the solution hypertree. A new relation is built, in which the input attributes to the reduction operator are substituted by the output attributes. Note that if no projection operators are applied, as in our example, the arity of the working relation is always increasing . Once that the optimal solution has been determined, the size of the working relations can be minimized by

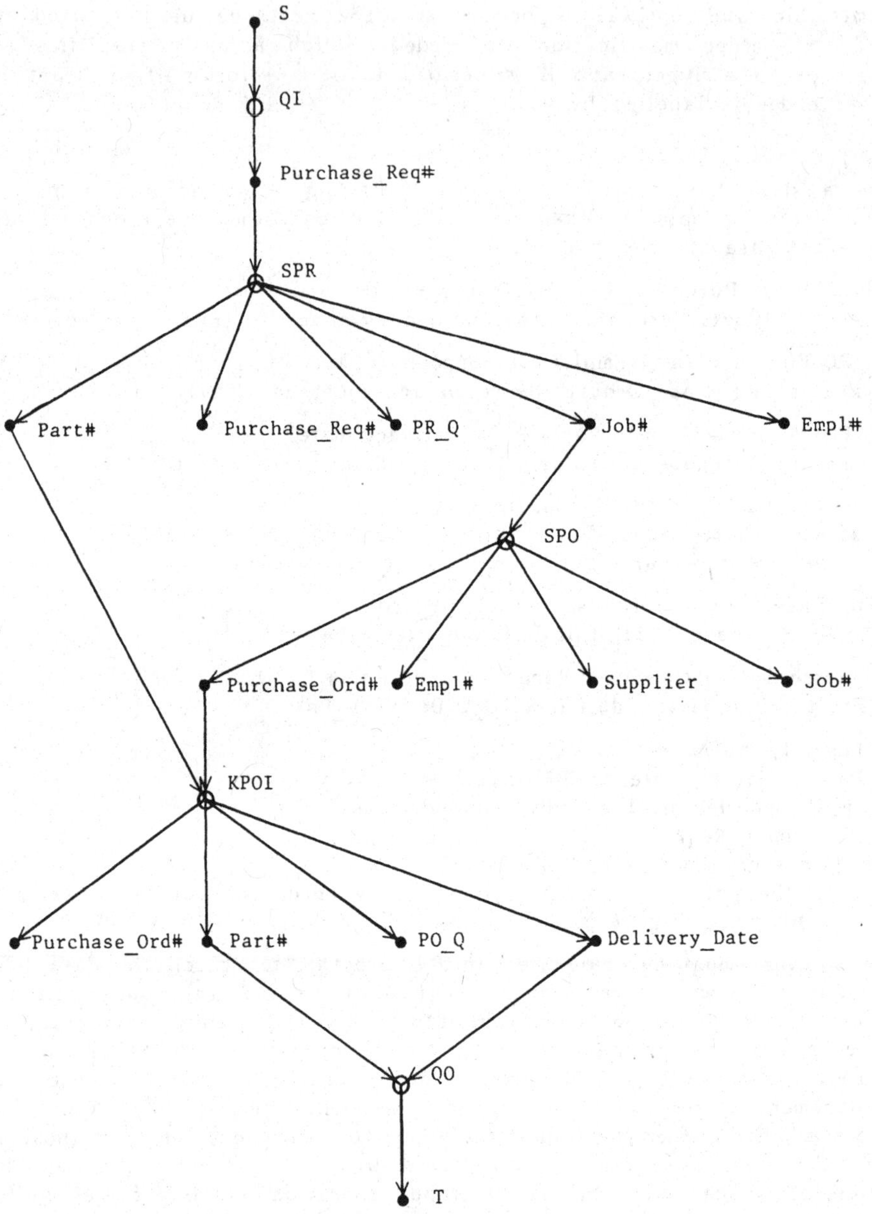

Fig. 3 The hypertree corresponding to the access path to resolve the query of Example 1.

introducing the necessary projection operations during the solution translation. The application of QO is translated into a projection to the output relation defined by the O clause of the query statement.
Note that, since the solution is a hypertree, two or more reduction operators may be applied in parallel, thus exploiting concurrent computing environments. This opportunity is not provided by any of the access path models suggested in the literature.

4. The problem of conditionally acceptable solutions.

It is well known that, when secondary index accesses are used, an incorrect relation can be obtained which strictly contains the required answer relation. Access paths which may provide such kind of incorrect answers are called conditionally acceptable /CK/. For example, suppose that the query is
SELECT Part#,Delivery_date WHERE Purchase_Req# = v, and that the access path is obtained by using the secondary index Part# to the POI relation. The hypertree corresponding to the access path is shown in the following Figure 4. The answer relation may contain illegitimate tuples (see /CK/ for a numerical instantiation of this example) since the working relation, from which the answer is projected, is obtained by concatenation of successive secondary index accesses. These accesses follow inverse functional (generally non bijective) dependence, hence the combination of at least two function inversions possibly produces inconsistent tuples. The values of some attributes are consistent, because they may have been obtained through functional dependencies and at most one function inversion (e.g. Part# in the example). Inconsistent attribute values combination can be filtered out by using them to access a relation through a key together with at least one of the consistent attributes. Thus, acceptable access paths can be obtained by combining acceptable and conditionally acceptable access sub-paths. This is exactly what was done in the Example 1, where the inconsistent values of Purchase_Ord# are filtered by key accessing the relation POI together with the consistent attribute value of Part#.
The filtering method described above can simply be casted in the algorithm Ao. In fact, only the following slight modification to the definition of solution to a hypergraph H is needed. A solution to H is any ps such that at least one of its nodes is labelled by T and no non-filtered combination of at least two functional inversion reduction operator occurs.
Note that the last condition is tested after a ps with a node labelled by T has been generated. If the test succedes, the solution is obtained. Otherwise, the ps is discarded (and eventually be recorded to derive a "conditional" answer if no "acceptable" answer can be found).
When the above modified definition of solution is adopted, the algorithm Ao finds the optimal correct access path and the correct access path, and consequently the correct answer, if any. The obtained solution is still optimal, because the costs of any ps (including the discarded one) are ordered by increasing costs. With the above modification, Ao possibly finds the optimal solution in a number of steps which is not minimal. In practice, however the cost of functional inversions, which can invalidate a solution, is very high, thus discarded solutions are not likely to be generated.

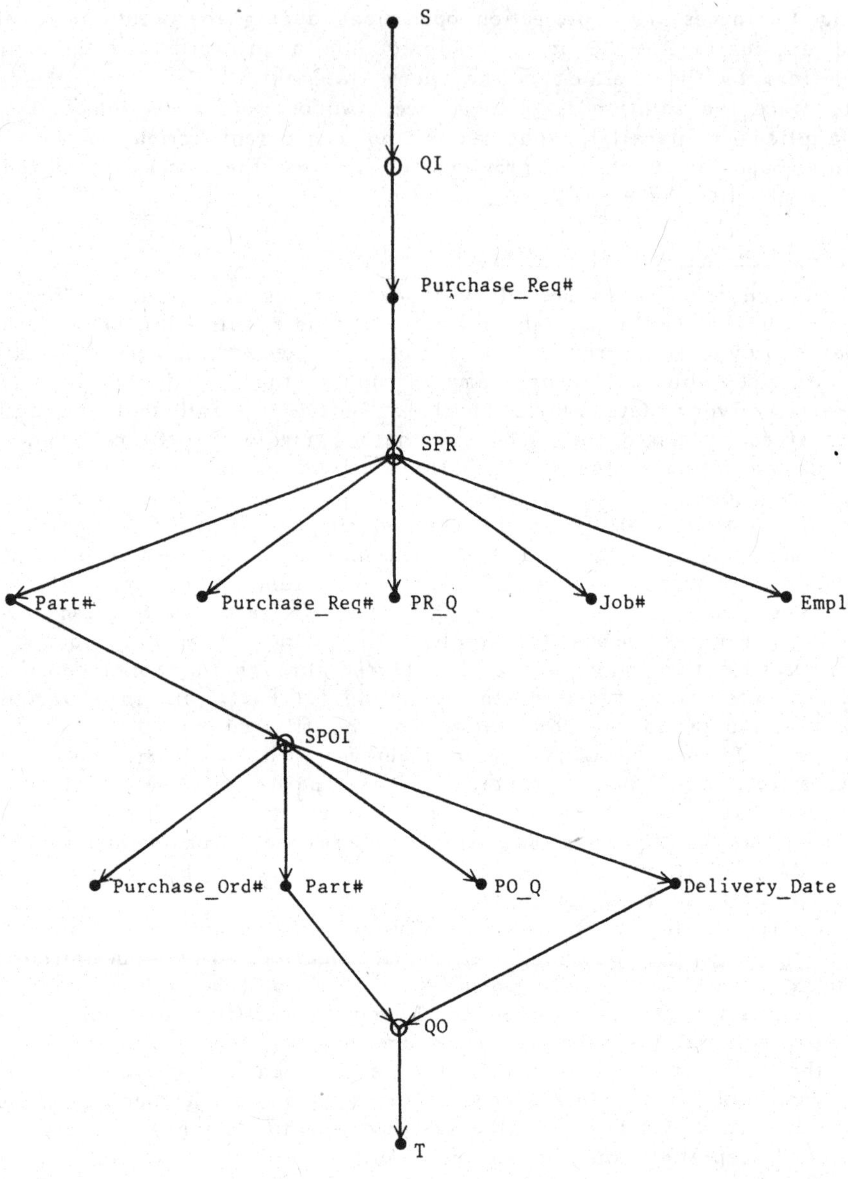

Fig. 4 A hypertree corresponding to a conditionally acceptable access path to resolve the query of Example 1.

It is worth noting that the method we present here improves over that method presented in /CK/, which in some situations requires to modify the structure of the data base. As an example, Carlson and Kaplan require the introduction of a new relation to correctly answer the query of Example 1, even if it can be correctly resolved, as shown by Figure 3, by the data base as it is.

5. Concluding remarks.

We presented a model, based on problem reduction hypergraphs, which formalizes the notion of access path for a given query to a relational data base.

Firstly, a partial prh is obtained once and for all by translating the given data base and the operations available on it. Then, the prh is completed by modelling a sepcific query, which determines the staring problem (the conditions the answer should satisfy) and the terminal problems (the answer required). The searching algorithm Ao is applied to the resulting prh, and the optimal access path is obtained which the correct answer can be derived from.

Remarkably enough, the resulting optimal access path can be translated into a (possibly parallel) program which accesses the data base and processes the query.

Moreover, the model provides the means to obtain the optimal access path, if any, without modifying the data base nor requiring additional information from the user.

The proposed model does not require any limitation on the data base. An obvious limitation only is required on the costs associated to the access operations, namely they must be non-negative.

We envision two possible applications of the optimal access path method. When queries from a casual user must be serviced, the method provides minimal cost answer program which fully exploit the available data base access organization. It is our feeling that it is unrealistic to modify a data base organization in order to optimally answer a query from a casual user. On the other hand, the costs associated to the reduction operators can be periodically updated by the data base administrator in order to reflect changes that might have been occurred into the data base access organization. The search algorithm can be used to provide optimal query answer for the application programs.

Finally, optimal access path method can be exploited when the data base access organization is to be designed to optimally comply with a predefined set of queries. In such a case as this, all the logically possible problem reduction operators must be provided to the search algorithm which thus suggests the most effective access operations. Obviously, the search space is (exponentially) greater in this application, and the availability of an optimal search algorithm is a major advantage.

References.

/CK/ Carlson, C.R., and Kaplan, R.S. A generalized access path model and its application to a relational data base system. Proc. ACM-SIGMOD Int. Conf. on Management of Data 1976, Washington, D.C., USA, pp. 143-154.

/TL/ Tsichritzis, D.C., and Lochovski, F.H. Data Base Management Systems. Academic Press, New York (1977).

/LS1/ Levi, G., and Sirovich, F. A problem reduction model for non independent subproblems. Proc. 4th Int. Joint Conf. on Artif. Intel. 1975, Tbilisi, GSSR, USSR, pp. 340-344.

/LS2/ Levi, G., and Sirovich, F. Generalized And/Or graphs. Artificial Intelligence, 7 (1976), pp. 243-259.

/BE/ Berge, C. Graphes et Hypergraphes. Dunod, Paris (1970).

/CB/ Chamberlin, D.D., and Boyce, R.F. SEQUEL: A structured English query language, Proc. ACM-SIGMOD Workshop on Data Description, Access and Control 1974, pp. 249-264.

/HA/ Hanani, M.Z. An optimal evaluation of boolean expressions in an online query system, CACM 20, 5 (1977), pp. 344-347.

/ES/ Eisner, M.J., and Severance, D.G. Mathematical techniques for efficient record segmentation in large shared data bases, J. ACM 23, 4 (1976), pp. 619-635.

/KL/ Klar, P. Conditional answer in question-answering systems, 6th Proc. Int. Conf. on Artif. Intel. (1979). Tokyo.

COMPOUND ALGEBRAIC IMPLEMENTATIONS: AN APPROACH TO STEPWISE REFINEMENT OF SOFTWARE SYSTEMS

H. Ehrig
H.-J. Kreowski
B. Mahr
P. Padawitz
Technische Universität Berlin, Germany

ABSTRACT

A precise mathematical approach to stepwise refinement of software systems is given within the framework of algebraic specifications. Since our new concept for the implementation of abstract data types - recently introduced in another paper - corresponds to a single refinement step, the composition problem for algebraic implementations is studied in this paper. It is shown that in general algebraic implementations are not closed under composition unless we have the special case of "persistent implementations". For other types of implementations sufficient consistency conditions are given to achieve closure under composition. These results can be extended to compound algebraic implementations which are syntactically defined to be sequences of (weak) implementations according to the idea of stepwise refinement of software systems.

1. INTRODUCTION

The idea of stepwise refinement of structured programs and software systems was introduced by Dijkstra /Dij 72/ and Wirth /Wir 71/. Guttag /Gut 76/ and Guttag, Horowitz, Musser /GHM 78/ have shown how to use algebraic specifications for stepwise refinement of a symbol table specification. The foundations for a strict mathematical theory of algebraic specifications, however, was given by Goguen, Thatcher and Wagner /GTW 78/. This paper included already a first algebraic approach to the implementation of abstract data types. Other algebraic approaches were given by Goguen-Nourani /GN 78/, Ehrich /Eh 78 a+b/, Wand /Wa 77/, Lehmann-Smyth /LS 77/ and in our own paper /EKP 78/. In /EKP 79/ we have introduced a new concept with strict distinction between syntactical and semantical level and correctness of an implementation. Moreover, we were able to show in /EKP 79/ that all other algebraic approaches mentioned above more or less turn out to be special cases of our new concept. This concept is reviewed in Section 2. From the software engineering point of view an implementation of abstract data type ADT0 by an abstract data type ADT1 is nothing else but a refinement step. Hence it makes sense to study stepwise

refinement via several steps. Actually we are able to define the composition of implementations IMPL1 of ADT0 by ADT1 and IMPL2 of ADT1 by ADT2 leading to a weak composite implementation IMPL3 of ADT0 by ADT2.
Surprisingly it turns out that the composition is not necessarily a correct implementation. A counterexample shows that certain side effects may violate consistency. But we are able to give sufficient conditions for the correctness of composition for different types of implementations. Especially for "persistent implementations" the additional consistency condition can be avoided. Note that our composition concept is different from that of Ehrich and avoids the difficulties mentioned in /Eh 78a/. The composition of strong implementations is also used in our paper /EM 80/ on complexity of implementations to show a desirable composition property for relative complexity measures.
According to the idea of stepwise refinement a compound algebraic implementation is syntactically defined as a sequence of (strong) implementations. The semantics is that of the n-fold composition such that correctness criteria can be derived from those of the composition. While all these constructions and results are given in Section 3 a 4-step example of a compound implementation is sketched in Section 4. Our notion of a compound algebraic implementation developed so far corresponds to a vertical refinement procedure without considering a horizontal structuring of the specifications. Such a horizontal structuring concept is given in Burstall and Goguen's algebraic specification language CLEAR /BG 77 + 80/. The simplest case of a horizontal structuring is the disjoint union of specifications which corresponds to a special case of the combine concept in CLEAR. It is easy to see that at least this simple horizontal structuring can be extended to the concept of parallel composition of implementations which is compatible with (sequential) composition considered above. Using both types of composition algebraic implementation schemes - closely related to our algebraic specification schemes in /EKW 78/ - can be defined corresponding to a tree structured refinement strategy in contrast to the linear structure of compound algebraic implementations. These ideas are only sketched in Section 4 and will be studied in a forthcoming paper together with other horizontal structuring concepts. For some more detail concerning the present version we refer to our technical report version /EKMP 80/ which also contains a detailed 4-step compound implementation with correctness proof.
Finally let us note that this paper was also inspired by a draft paper /BG 79/ by Burstall and Goguen introducing the idea of horizontal and vertical refinement of data structures. They propose that the vertical structure should correspond to suitable theory morphisms which may turn out to be similar to persistent implementations in our approach.

ACKNOWLEDGEMENTS

For several fruitful discussions concerning algebraic specifications and implementations having a major influence on our concepts in this paper we are grateful to the ADJ-group, H.-D. Ehrich, C. Floyd (incl. the software engineering group at TU Berlin), and H. Weber. Thanks also to H. Barnewitz for excellent typing.

2. ALGEBRAIC SPECIFICATIONS AND IMPLEMENTATIONS

In the algebraic framework proposed by ADJ /GTW 78/ a specification SPEC=$\langle S,\Sigma,E\rangle$ of an abstract data type consists of sorts S, operation symbols (or short operations) Σ and equations E. Sorts denote data domains, operations declare data access and manipulation facilities and equations determine the effect of the operations. The semantics of a specification SPEC is defined by the corresponding quotient term algebra T_{SPEC} (or any isomorphic algebra initial in the category of all SPEC-algebras). In the terminology of universal algebra a specification is an equational presentation of T_{SPEC}. There are several good reasons widely discussed in /GTW 78/ to consider any initial algebra T_{SPEC} as an abstract data type and vice versa. Data correspond to elements of the algebra and operations of an abstract data type to those of an algebra.

2.1 GENERAL ASSUMPTIONS

Let us assume that we have two specifications SPEC0 and SPEC1 together with a common subspecification SPEC which can be considered as common parameter part of SPEC0 and SPEC1. Hence we assume to have the following algebraic specifications

$$SPEC0=SPEC+\langle S0,\Sigma 0,E0\rangle$$
$$SPEC1=SPEC+\langle S1,\Sigma 1,E1\rangle$$
$$SPEC=\langle S,\Sigma,E\rangle$$

where the former ones are combinations in the following sense:

SPEC+$\langle S0,\Sigma 0,E0\rangle$ is called <u>combination</u> if SPEC=$\langle S,\Sigma,E\rangle$ and SPEC0=$\langle S+S0,\Sigma+\Sigma 0,E+E0\rangle$ are algebraic specifications (where + stands for disjoint union), but $\langle S0,\Sigma 0,E0\rangle$ is not assumed to be an algebraic specification. That means the operations in $\Sigma 0$ may use sorts belonging to S+S0 and the equations E0 may use operations of $\Sigma+\Sigma 0$. Due to the intention that SPEC is a common parameter part we assume that SPEC0 and SPEC1 are both extensions of SPEC:

$$(T_{SPEC0})_{SPEC}\cong T_{SPEC}\cong(T_{SPEC1})_{SPEC}$$

where A_{SPEC} is the restriction of an algebra A to sorts and operations of SPEC.

Now we are able to give the general definition of an implementation of SPEC0 by SPEC1 including general devices $\langle\Sigma SORT,ESORT\rangle$ and hidden parts $\langle SHID,\Sigma HID,EHID\rangle$. For first reading $\Sigma SORT$ may be restricted to copy operations $c:s1\longrightarrow s0$ for $s1\in S1$, $s0\in S0$, and ESORT,SHID,ΣHID,EHID may be empty such that the only relevant part is EOP, the operations implementing equations, defining $\Sigma 0$-operations in terms of $\Sigma+\Sigma 1$-operations. Note, that the hidden part, which is only implicit in /EKP 79/, is necessary to define the composition of implementations.

2.2 DEFINITION (implementation)

Given specifications SPEC0 and SPEC1 as above, an implementation, written IMPL:SPEC1 $\Rightarrow$ SPEC0, of SPEC0 by SPEC1 is a 6-tuple

IMPL=(ΣSORT,ESORT,EOP,SHID,ΣHID,EHID):SPEC1 $\Rightarrow$ SPEC0

consisting of

ΣSORT, a set of sorts implementing operations,

ESORT, a set of sorts implementing equations,

EOP, a set of operations implementing equations,

SHID,ΣHID,EHID, sets of hidden sorts, hidden operations and hidden equations respectively

such that the following syntactical and semantical requirements are satisfied:

SYNTACTICAL REQUIREMENTS:

DEVIMPL:=<S+S1,$\emptyset$,$\emptyset$>+<S0+SHID,ΣSORT,ESORT>,

SORTIMPL:=SPEC1+<S0+SHID,ΣSORT,ESORT>, and

OPIMPL:=(SORTIMPL+<$\emptyset$,ΣHID,EHID>)+<$\emptyset$,Σ0,EOP>

are combinations, called device of the implementation, sort implementation and operation implementation level respectively.

SEMANTICAL CONSTRUCTION:

The semantical construction is the composition of the following three steps:

$$T_{SPEC1} \xrightarrow{\text{SYNTHESIS}} T_{OPIMPL} \xrightarrow{\text{RESTRICTION}} REP_{IMPL} \xrightarrow{\text{IDENTIFICATION}} S_{IMPL}$$

REP_{IMPL}, called representation of the implementation, is the restriction of T_{OPIMPL} generated by (Σ+Σ0)-operations, i.e. REP_{IMPL}=image(eval-0) where eval-0 is the unique term evaluation eval-0:$T_{\Sigma+\Sigma 0} \rightarrow (T_{OPIMPL})_{\Sigma+\Sigma 0}$; S_{IMPL}, called semantical algebra of the implementation, is the quotient of REP_{IMPL} by the congruence generated by the E0-equations, i.e. $S_{IMPL}=REP_{IMPL}/\equiv_{E0}$.

SEMANTICAL REQUIREMENTS (CORRECTNESS):

1. type protection: SORTIMPL is an extension of SPEC1, i.e. $(T_{SORTIMPL})_{SPEC1} \cong T_{SPEC1}$

2. Σ0-completeness: Σ+Σ0-terms in OPIMPL can be reduced to Σ+Σ1+ΣSORT-terms, i.e. eval-0$(T_{\Sigma+\Sigma 0}) \subseteq$ eval-1$(T_{\Sigma+\Sigma 1+\Sigma SORT})$ where eval-1 is the term evaluation eval-1:$T_{\Sigma+\Sigma 1+\Sigma SORT} \rightarrow (T_{OPIMPL})_{\Sigma+\Sigma 1+\Sigma SORT}$

3. RI-correctness: The semantical algebra of the implementation is isomorphic to T_{SPEC0} , i.e. $S_{IMPL} \cong T_{SPEC0}$.

If only the syntactical requirements are considered IMPL:SPEC1 $\Rightarrow$ SPEC0 is called weak implementation.

For the interpretation of our implementation concept we refer to /EKP 79/.

2.3 EXAMPLE

An implementation IMPL1=(ΣSORT1,ESORT1,EOP1,SHID1,ΣHID1,EHID1) of SPEC0=pset(nat1) by SPEC1=set(nat1) is given in the long version /EKMP 80/ of this paper. The specification pset(nat1) specifies the data type powerset of finite subsets of natural numbers together with the well-known powerset operations empty, singleton, union, intersection, difference and the boolean operation is-element, while set(nat1) specifies sets of natural numbers with operations create, insert, delete and the boolean operations is-member and is-empty. In the implementation IMPL1 ΣSORT1 consists of a copy operation c:set$\rightarrow$ pset, ΣHID1 contains an if-then-else operation for pset with the well-known equations in EHID1, the essential part of the implementation is given in EOP1 where the powerset operations are defined in terms of the set operations e.g.

$$\{n\}=c(INSERT(n,CREATE))$$
$$c(s)\cup c(INSERT(n,s'))=c(INSERT(n,s))\cup c(s')$$

2.4 DEFINITION (strong and persistent implementation)

A weak implementation IMPL:SPEC1$\Rightarrow$ SPEC0 is called strong implementation if the following strong semantical requirements 1.-3. are satisfied:

STRONG SEMANTICAL REQUIREMENTS:

1. strong type protection: DEVIMPL is a persistent extension of $\langle S+S1,\emptyset,\emptyset\rangle$, i.e. for all S+S1-algebras A we have $F(A)_{S+S1}\cong A$ where F(A) is the DEVIMPL-algebra freely generated by A.

2. strong Σ0-completeness: $\Sigma+\Sigma 0$-terms in OPIMPL can be reduced using EOP,EHID and ESORT-equations only (but not E and E1) to $\Sigma+\Sigma 1+\Sigma SORT$-terms, i.e. for all $t0\in T_{\Sigma+\Sigma 0}$ there is $t1\in T_{\Sigma+\Sigma 1+\Sigma SORT}$ such that $t0\equiv_{EOP+EHID+ESORT} t1$.

3. RI-correctness: (as in 2.2)

A strong implementation is called persistent if we have:

4. persistent Σ0-completeness: OPIMPL'=OPIMPL$\setminus$(E+E1) is a persistent enrichment of SORTIMPL'=SORTIMPL$\setminus$(E+E1), i.e. for all SORTIMPL'-algebras A we have $F(A)_{SORTIMPL'}\cong A$ where F(A) is the OPIMPL'-algebra freely generated by A.

The relationship between all the different notions will be shown now:

2.5 PROPOSITION

Given a weak implementation IMPL:SPEC1$\Rightarrow$ SPEC0 we have:

1. strong type protection implies type protection.
2. If EOP and EHID are derivor equations for Σ0 and ΣHID (i.e. for each $\sigma\in\Sigma 0+\Sigma HID$ there is only one equation with left hand side $\sigma(x_1,\ldots,x_n)$ and the right hand side is using only $\Sigma+\Sigma 1+\Sigma SORT$-operations) then we have persistent Σ0-completeness.
3. persistent Σ0-completeness implies strong Σ0-completeness and OPIMPL persistent extension of SORTIMPL. Each of the latter ones implies Σ0-completeness.
4. RI-correctness is equivalent to the existence of a $(\Sigma+\Sigma 0)$-homomorphism $rep:REP_{IMPL}\rightarrow T_{SPEC0}$ and also equivalent to the condition that OPIMPL is consistent with respect to SPEC0, i.e. for all $t,t'\in T_{\Sigma+\Sigma 0}$ we have

$t \equiv_{E(OPIMPL)} t'$ implies $t \equiv_{E(SPECO)} t'$

where E(SPEC) are the equations of the specification SPEC. Moreover the characterization remains true if REP_{IMPL} is replaced by R(A) for some OPIMPL-algebra A where R(A) is the restriction of A to (Σ+ΣO)-generated data (see 2.2) and only the existence of such an A is assumed.

5. We have the following strict hierarchy: persistent implementation ⟹ strong implementation ⟹ implementation ⟹ weak implementation.

Proof: We will use the following lemma which is a corollary of the main theorem in /EKTWW 79/.

PERSISTENCY-LEMMA: Let SPECi=SPEC1+<Si,Σi,Ei> for i=2,3 where S2 and S3 as well as Σ2 and Σ3 are pairwise disjoint. Moreover let SPEC4=SPEC2+<S3,Σ3,E3> = =SPEC3+<S2,Σ2,E2>. If SPEC2 is a persistent extension of SPEC1 then also SPEC4 is a persistent extension of SPEC3.

Now we are going to prove conditions 1.-5. of our proposition:

1. <S+S1,∅,∅> ⊆ DEVIMPL persistent implies by the persistency lemma SPEC1 ⊆ SORTIMPL persistent and hence type protection.

2. It is well-known and easy to check that derived operations define persistent extensions.

3. Persistent ΣO-completeness implies that OPIMPL is a persistent extension of SORTIMPL by the persistency lemma. This implies the enrichment property and especially ΣO-completeness (see /EKP 78/). Moreover we have strong ΣO-completeness because SORTIMPL' ⊆ OPIMPL' is enrichment where (E+E1)-equations are not involved.

4. The first part of the equivalence is shown in /EKP 79/ where $REP_{IMPL}=R(T_{OPIMPL})$. To show the equivalence with arbitrary OPIMPL-algebra A instead of T_{OPIMPL} let us assume that we have $h: R(A) \longrightarrow T_{SPECO}$. Since restriction R is a functor we also have a (Σ+ΣO)-homomorphism $R(f): R(T_{OPIMPL}) \longrightarrow R(A)$ where f is uniquely defined by initiality of T_{OPIMPL}. Hence the composition $h \bullet R(f): REP_{IMPL} \rightarrow T_{SPECO}$ is a (Σ+ΣO)-homomorphism showing RI-correctness by the first part of the equivalence.

5. Follows from 1.-3. and the fact that the implications in 1. and 3. are strict. Actually it is easy to find examples for operations implementing equations which are not persistent but strong (see Example 2.3) and enrichments where the equations of the base specification are needed. A weak implementation which is not an implementation will be given in Section 3.

Remark: Strong type protection means that <S+S1,∅,∅> ⊆ DEVIMPL is a parameterized specification in the sense of /TWW 79/ and /EKTWW 79/. This assumption will be crucial for the implementation of parameterized data types to be studied elsewhere.

3. COMPOSITION AND COMPOUND IMPLEMENTATIONS

In this section we will study the composition of different kinds of implementations. The difficult part to show is that the composition satisfies the corresponding semantical requirements. Actually there are counterexamples showing that the composition of implementations (resp. strong implementations) is not RI-correct in general. But we are able to give sufficient consistency conditions implying RI-correctness. Persistent implementations, however, are closed under composition. Unfortunately most of the interesting implementations (see Section 4) are not persistent. Finally we study compound implementations - corresponding to iterated compositions. A detailed example is discussed in Section 4.

3.1 DEFINITION (composition of implementations)

Given weak implementations IMPL2:SPEC2⟹ SPEC1 and IMPL1:SPEC1⟹ SPEC0 with SPECi=SPEC+<Si,Σi,Ei> (i=0,1,2) and IMPLi=(ΣSORTi,ESORTi,EOPi,SHIDi,ΣHIDi,EHIDi) for i=1,2, then the weak composition (resp. strong composition)

IMPL(1,2)=IMPL1∘IMPL2:SPEC2⟹SPEC0

is defined by

ΣSORT(1,2)=ΣSORT1+ΣSORT2

ESORT(1,2)=ESORT1+ESORT2

EOP(1,2)=EOP1+EOP2

SHID(1,2)=SHID1+SHID2+S1

ΣHID(1,2)=ΣHID1+ΣHID2+Σ1

$$\text{EHID}(1,2)=\begin{cases}\text{EHID1+EHID2+E1} & \text{weak composition}\\ \text{EHID1+EHID2} & \text{strong composition}\end{cases}$$

Convention: If not specified otherwise we will take the weak composition for weak implementations and implementations and the strong composition for strong or persistent implementations. In these cases we may omit the prefixes weak resp. strong.

Remark: We will show that the composition of weak (resp. persistent) implementations is again weak (resp. persistent). But composition closure is not true in general for implementations and strong implementations.

3.2 COUNTEREXAMPLES

1. First we give an example of two implementations such that the weak composition is not RI-correct.

Let SPEC0 = bool

S0: sorts: bool

Σ0: opns: TRUE,FALSE: → bool

SPEC1 = 2 elements

S1: sorts: 2

Σ1: opns: ZERO: → 2

NEXT: 2 → 2

E1: eqns: $\text{NEXT}(x)=\text{NEXT}^2(x)$

SPEC2 = empty

IMPL2: SPEC2⟹ SPEC1 defined by

ΣSORT2: 0: → 2   ESORT2: SP(x)=x   EOP2: ZERO=0

S,P: 2 → 2   PS(x)=x   NEXT(x)=S(x)

IMPL1: SPEC1⟹ SPEC0 defined by

ΣSORT1: c: 2 → bool EOP1: TRUE=c(ZERO)   FALSE=c(NEXT(ZERO))

Since E(OPIMPL(1,2))=EOP2+E1+EOP1+ESORT2 we have

$$(T_{OPIMPL(1,2)})_{2} \cong \{0\} \cong (T_{OPIMPL(1,2)})_{bool}$$

This implies $S_{IMPL(1,2)} \cong \{0\} \not\cong \{TRUE,FALSE\} = T_{SPEC0}$ such that IMPL(1,2) is not RI-correct although IMPL1 and IMPL2 are RI-correct implementations.

2. In the counterexample above E1 is responsible for additional identifications. But those identifications can also be caused by EOP2+EOP1 only. Take for example E1=∅ and add $c(NEXT(x))=c(NEXT^2(x))$ to EOP1 in the equations above where IMPL1 and IMPL2 are still RI-correct implementations. Hence we have a strong composition of strong implementations which is not RI-correct.

Now we will give sufficient conditions for the correctness of weak and strong composition of implementations in Theorem 3.3 and 3.4 respectively.

3.3 THEOREM (correctness of weak composition)

Implementations are closed under weak composition provided that they are strongly type protecting and one of the CONSISTENCY CONDITIONS below is satisfied. In more detail we have: Given weak implementations IMPL2:SPEC2⟹ SPEC1 and IMPL1:SPEC1⟹SPEC0 then the weak composition IMPL(1,2):SPEC2⟹SPEC0 is a strongly type protecting implementation if the following conditions 1-3 are satisfied.

1. IMPL1 and IMPL2 are strongly type protecting.
2. IMPL1 and IMPL2 are Σ0- resp. Σ1-complete.
3. IMPL1 is RI-correct and one of the following consistency conditions is valid:

CONSISTENCY CONDITION

OPIMPL(1,2) is consistent with respect to OPIMPL1, i.e. for all $t,t' \in T_{\Sigma(OPIMPL1)}$ we have $t \equiv_{E(OPIMPL(1,2))} t'$ implies $t \equiv_{E(OPIMPL1)} t'$

SEMANTICAL CONSISTENCY CONDITION

There is an OPIMPL(1,2)-algebra A and a Σ(OPIMPL1)-homomorphism $h: R(A) \to T_{OPIMPL1}$ where R(A) is the restriction of A generated by Σ(OPIMPL1)-operations (see restriction construction in 2.2).

Remarks:

1. We use the assumption that IMPL1 and IMPL2 are strongly type protecting because type protection is not preserved by weak (or strong) composition in general. For a counterexample consider SO={so}, S1={s1}, S=∅, Σ+Σ1=∅, ΣSORT1={c1:s1→so, r1:so→ s1}, ESORT1=∅, SPEC2=nat, ΣSORT2={c2:nat→ s1, r2:s1→ nat}, and ESORT2={r2(c2(x))=x} such that SPEC1⊆ SORTIMPL1 is a (non persistent) extension, SPEC2⊆ SORTIMPL2 is a persistent extension, but SPEC2⊆ SORTIMPL(1,2) is not extension because ESORT1=∅.

2. Summarizing the properties of weak composition we have

a) all syntactical requirements are preserved,

b) ΣO/1-completeness is preserved,

c) strong (resp. persistent) ΣO/1-completeness is preserved (Corollary of Theorem 3.4.),

d) type protection is not preserved in general (see Remark 1. above),

e) strong type protection is preserved,

f) RI-correctness is not preserved in general (see Counterexample 3.2.1.).

<u>Proof:</u> The proof will be given in three steps showing strong type protection, ΣO-completeness and RI-correctness of IMPL(1,2) in part 1,2 and 3 respectively.

<u>Part1: STRONG TYPE PROTECTION OF IMPL(1,2)</u>

We have to show that $\langle S+S2,\emptyset,\emptyset\rangle \subseteq$ DEVIMPL(1,2) is persistent. Since IMPL2 and IMPL1 are implementations we know that $\langle S+S2,\emptyset,\emptyset\rangle \subseteq \langle S+S2+S1+SHID2,\Sigma SORT2,ESORT2\rangle$=DEVIMPL2 and $\langle S+S1,\emptyset,\emptyset\rangle \subseteq \langle S+S1+SO+SHID1,\Sigma SORT1,ESORT1\rangle$=DEVIMPL1 are persistent. Since DEVIMPL2=$\langle S+S1,\emptyset,\emptyset\rangle + \langle S2+SHID2,\Sigma SORT2,ESORT2\rangle$ the PERSISTENCY LEMMA in 2.5 implies that DEVIMPL2$\subseteq \langle S+S1+SO+SHID1+S2+SHID2,\Sigma SORT1+\Sigma SORT2,ESORT1+ESORT2\rangle$=DEVIMPL(1,2) is persistent. Moreover the composition of persistent extensions is persistent (see /EKTWW 79/) so that also $\langle S+S2,\emptyset,\emptyset\rangle \subseteq$ DEVIMPL(1,2) is persistent.

<u>Part2: ΣO-completeness of IMPL(1,2)</u>

It suffices to show that each $(\Sigma+\Sigma O)$-term tO can be reduced via OPIMPL(1,2)-equations to a Σ(SORTIMPL(1,2))-term t2. By ΣO-completeness of IMPL1 we can reduce tO via OPIMPL1-equations to a $(\Sigma+\Sigma 1+\Sigma SORT1)$-term t1. Moreover t1 can be assumed to be $(\Sigma+\Sigma 1)$-normal, i.e. all the maximal subterms t1j (j=1,...,m) of sorts in S+S1 are $(\Sigma+\Sigma 1)$-terms, because SPEC1$\subseteq$ SORTIMPL1 is an extension. Each of the t1j (j=1,...,m) can be reduced to a $(\Sigma+\Sigma 2+\Sigma SORT2)$-term via OPIMPL2-equations because IMPL2 is Σ1-complete. Hence t1 can be reduced via OPIMPL(1,2)-equations to a term t2 where each subterm t1j of t1 is replaced by t2j (j=1,...,m).

<u>Part3: RI-correctness of IMPL(1,2)</u>

The CONSISTENCY CONDITION together with RI-correctness of IMPL1 implies directly RI-correctness of IMPL(1,2). The SEMANTICAL CONSISTENCY CONDITION and initiality of $T_{OPIMPL1}$ implies that $T_{OPIMPL1} \to R(A)$ and hence also $T_{OPIMPL1} \to A_{OPIMPL1}$ is injective. Since the last morphism is equal to

$T_{OPIMPL1} \to (T_{OPIMPL(1,2)})_{OPIMPL1} \to A_{OPIMPL1}$, its first one is injective, too, which is equivalent to our CONSISTENCY CONDITION and we are done.

□

3.4 <u>THEOREM (correctness of strong composition)</u>

Persistent implementations are closed under strong composition. The same is true for strong implementations provided that one of the CONSISTENCY CONDITIONS in 3.3 applied to strong composition is satisfied.

<u>Remark:</u> Summarizing the properties of strong composition we have

a) all syntactical requirements are preserved,

b) Σ0/1-completeness is not preserved in general (see proof of Prop. 2.5.5),

c) strong (resp. persistent) Σ0/1-completeness is preserved,

d) type protection is not preserved in general (see Remark 1 of Theorem 3.3),

e) strong type protection is preserved,

f) RI-correctness is not preserved in general (see Counterexample 3.2.2).

<u>Proof:</u> The denotation of Theorem 3.3 is used with IMPL3:=IMPL(1,2).

<u>Part1: STRONG TYPE PROTECTION OF IMPL3</u> (same as part 1 of 3.3)

<u>Part2: STRONG RESP. PERSISTENT Σ0-COMPLETENESS OF IMPL3</u>

If IMPL1 and IMPL2 are strong Σ0-complete, part 2 of the proof of Theorem 3.3 can be used to show that also IMPL3 is strong Σ0-complete: Actually E+E1 can be avoided in the first and E+E2 in the second step by strong Σ0-completeness of IMPL1 and IMPL2 respectively, hence E+E1+E2 can be avoided in the complete reduction sequence. If IMPL1 and IMPL2 are persistent Σ0-complete we conclude from the PERSISTENCY LEMMA (see Proof of 2.5) that persistency of SORTIMPL2'$\subseteq$ OPIMPL2' implies persistency of SORTIMPL3'$\subseteq$ SORTIMPL3'+AUX2 with AUX2=$\langle\emptyset,\Sigma1+\Sigma HID2,EOP2+EHID2\rangle$. On the other hand persistency of SORTIMPL1'$\subseteq$ OPIMPL1' implies persistency of SORTIMPL1'+AUX1$\subseteq$OPIMPL1'+ +AUX1 with AUX1=$\langle S2+SHID2,\Sigma2+\Sigma SORT2+\Sigma HID2,ESORT2+EOP2+EHID2\rangle$. But SORTIMPL1'+AUX1= =SORTIMPL3'+AUX2 and OPIMPL1'+AUX1=OPIMPL3' implies that the composition SORTIMPL3'$\subseteq$ OPIMPL3' is persistent. Hence IMPL3 is persistent Σ0-complete.

<u>Part3: RI-CORRECTNESS OF IMPL3</u>

First we consider the case of strong implementations. If IMPL1 is RI-correct and we have the SEMANTICAL CONSISTENCY CONDITION then we have an OPIMPL3-algebra A and a homomorphism $h:R(A)\rightarrow T_{OPIMPL1}$. Since R is a functor we have a Σ(OPIMPL1)-homomorphism $R(g):R(T_{OPIMPL3})\rightarrow R(A)$ where $g:T_{OPIMPL3}\rightarrow A$ is the initial homomorphism. Similar to the proof of Prop. 2.5.4 the existence of the composition $h\cdot R(g):R(T_{OPIMPL3})\rightarrow T_{OPIMPL1}$ implies the CONSISTENCY CONDITION. The CONSISTENCY CONDITION together with RI-correctness of IMPL1 (see 2.5.4) implies RI-correctness of IMPL3. It remains to show RI-correctness of IMPL3 in the case of persistent implementations IMPL1 and IMPL2 without using additional conditions. Given $\Sigma+\Sigma$0-terms t0 and t0' which are E(OPIMPL3)-equivalent we have by strong Σ0-completeness (see 2.5.3) transformations t0$\Rightarrow$ t1$\Rightarrow$ t2 and t0'$\Rightarrow$ t1'$\Rightarrow$ t2' where t1,t1' are $\Sigma+\Sigma$1-normal $\Sigma+\Sigma1+\Sigma$SORT1-terms (see proof of Thm. 3.3 part 2) and t2,t2' are $\Sigma+\Sigma2+\Sigma$SORT2-normal $\Sigma+\Sigma2+\Sigma SORT2+\Sigma$SORT1-terms. Moreover the E(OPIMPL2)-transformations t1$\Rightarrow$t2 and t1'$\Rightarrow$ t2' can be restricted to transformations of $\Sigma+\Sigma$1-terms. E(OPIMPL3)-equivalence of t0 and t0' implies E(OPIMPL3)-equivalence of t2 and t2'. Now consistency of SORTIMPL3$\subseteq$ OPIMPL3 (which follows from persistent Σ0-completeness of IMPL3 in step 2 of this proof) implies E(SORTIMPL3)-equivalence of t2 and t2'. From the syntax of DEVIMPL1 it is clear that the equations ESORT1 can only be applied to ΣSORT1-operations. Hence ESORT1-transformations are independent of E(OPIMPL2)-transformations and can be shifted to the left. Hence we obtain a transformation sequence

*) $t0 \Rightarrow t1 \Rightarrow \bar{\bar{t1}} \Rightarrow \bar{\bar{t2}} \Rightarrow t2' \Rightarrow t1' \Rightarrow t0'$ where $t1 \Rightarrow \bar{\bar{t1}}$ corresponds to the ESORT1-transformations in the E(SORTIMPL3)-sequence $t2 \Rightarrow t2'$. Only the subsequence $\bar{\bar{t2}} \Rightarrow t2'$ of (E+E2+ESORT2)-transformations in $t2 \Rightarrow t2'$ is left, and $\bar{\bar{t1}} \Rightarrow \bar{\bar{t2}}$ corresponds to $t1 \Rightarrow t2$. Now $\bar{\bar{t1}} \Rightarrow \bar{\bar{t2}} \Rightarrow t2' \Rightarrow t1'$ is an E(OPIMPL2)-transformation which can be restricted to a transformation of $\Sigma+\Sigma1$-terms and the remaining transformations in (*) are E(OPIMPL1)-transformations. RI-correctness of IMPL2 allows to reduce the E(OPIMPL2)-transformations to (E+E1)-transformations. Hence the sequence (*) can be transformed to an E(OPIMPL1)-transformation which implies E(SPEC0)-equivalence of t0 and t0' by RI-correctness of IMPL1.

□

Now we are going to study compound implementations. Similar to Definition 2.2 we assume to have specifications $SPECi=SPEC+\langle Si,\Sigma i,Ei\rangle$ such that SPECi is extension of SPEC for i=0,...,n.

3.5 DEFINITION (compound implementation)

A compound implementation COMPIMPL is a sequence COMPIMPL=(IMPL1,...,IMPLn) of weak implementations IMPLi:SPECi$\Rightarrow$SPEC(i-1) for some n≥1 and i=1,...,n such that the composition IMPL(1,...,n)=IMPL1∘IMPL2∘...∘IMPLn is an implementation. The sequence of weak implementations is called syntax and the semantical construction and semantical algebra of the composition IMPL(1,...,n) is called semantics of the compound implementation respectively. A compound implementation COMPIMPL is called weak, strong and persistent if the composition IMPL(1,...,n) is a weak, strong and persistent implementation respectively.

Remark: The weak and the strong composition of weak implementations is associative because + (disjoint union) is associative. Hence we are able to write the n-fold composition without brackets. Weak and strong composition are used for weak and strong or persistent compound implementations respectively:

INTERPRETATION:

Since each implementation IMPLi:SPECi$\Rightarrow$SPEC(i-1) corresponds to a refinement of SPEC(i-1) by SPECi a compound implementation corresponds to a stepwise refinement of specification SPEC0 by SPEC1 up to SPECn. In principle it is possible to end up with a specification SPECn of an actual programming language. It is important to note that the stepwise refinement procedure corresponds to the sequence of specifications and implementations and - at least concerning the syntax - not to the composite implementation IMPL(1,...,n) of SPEC0 by SPECn because all the intermediate steps would be lost. Concerning the semantics and correctness, however, only that of the composition IMPL(1,...,n) seems to be important.

As Corollary of Theorem 3.3 and 3.4 we obtain the following correctness conditions for compound implementations.

3.6 COROLLARY (correctness of compound implementations)

Each sequence COMPIMPL=(IMPLi)i=1,...,n of weak implementations IMPLi:SPECi$\Rightarrow$SPEC(i-1) is already a weak compound implementation. Moreover we have that COMPIMPL is a

1. compound implementation, if all the IMPLi are strongly type protecting and Σ(i-1)-complete and if the weak composition IMPL(1,...,n) is RI-correct. Sufficient for this RI-correctness is each of the following GLOBAL CONSISTENCY CONDITIONS together with RI-correctness of IMPL1.

GLOBAL CONSISTENCY CONDITION

OPIMPL(1,...,n) is consistent with respect to OPIMPL1 (see 3.3.3)

GLOBAL SEMANTICAL CONSISTENCY CONDITION

There is an OPIMPL(1,...n)-algebra A and a Σ(OPIMPL1)-homomorphism h:R(A)$\rightarrow$ $T_{OPIMPL1}$ where R(A) is the restriction of A generated by Σ(OPIMPL1)-operations.

2. strong compound implementation, if all the IMPLi are strongly type protecting and strongly Σ(i-1)-complete and if the strong composition IMPL(1,...,n) is RI-correct. Sufficient for this RI-correctness is each of the GLOBAL CONSISTENCY CONDITIONS above together with RI-correctness of IMPL1 where, however, OPIMPL(1,...,n) corresponds to strong composition now.

3. persistent compound implementation, if all the IMPLi are persistent implementations.

Proof: Most of the proof follows by induction from Theorem 3.3 and 3.4. Only for RI-correctness in the case of implementations and strong implementations IMPL(1,..,n) is considered to be the 1-step composition of IMPL1 and IMPL(2,..,n) where again Theorem 3.3 and 3.4 can be applied.

□

4. TOWARDS STEPWISE REFINEMENT OF SOFTWARE SYSTEMS

In this section we sketch a 4-step strong compound implementation of pset(nat1) (powersets of natural numbers) by a subset small lisp of LISP. Moreover we give some basic ideas of algebraic implementation schemes corresponding to a tree structured refinement strategy of software systems.

4.1 EXAMPLE

In Example 2.3 we have sketched an implementation IMPL1:set(nat1)$\Rightarrow$ pset(nat1) where the powerset operations are implemented by elementary set operations like insert and delete in set(nat1). The next step IMPL2 is to implement the set operations by hash operations where sets are represented as hashtables with specification hash(nat1). In a third step hashtables can be implemented by strings and arrays with string entries leading to an implementation IMPL3:string(nat1)$\Rightarrow$ hash(nat1). Finally string(nat1) can be implemented in a subset small lisp of LISP which becomes an implementation IMPL4:small lisp $\Rightarrow$ string(nat1). An explicit construction of all these steps is given in our long version /EKMP 80/ where also the correctness of the first three steps of the corresponding 4-step strong compound implementation

pset(nat1) $\xLeftarrow{IMPL1}$ set(nat1) $\xLeftarrow{IMPL2}$ hash(nat1) $\xLeftarrow{IMPL3}$ string(nat1) $\xLeftarrow{IMPL4}$ small lisp of powerset operations in small lisp is shown using Thm. 3.6. (The last step has not been verified because small lisp is only incompletely specified without error handling.) In the composition IMPL(1,2,3):string(nat1)⟹ pset(nat1) all components of the implementation - including hidden sorts, hidden operations and hidden equations-are nontrivial.

Up to now we have only considered the vertical structure of stepwise refinement. Starting with an abstract data type ADT0 of specification SPEC0 we are - in principle - able to give a sequence of refinements ADTi of specification SPECi for i=1,...,n such that ADTn corresponds to an actual programming language with algebraic specification SPECn. In general, however, it is not advisable to specify an actual software system in terms of a single (unstructured) algebraic specification SPEC0. What we would need is something like a horizontal structure of SPEC0 and of the subsequent specifications SPEC1,...,SPECn. Such a horizontal structure is proposed by the algebraic specification language CLEAR /BG 77/ for example. The simplest case of a horizontal structure is the disjoint union of specifications. This leads to parallel composition of implementations which can be defined componentwise. It turns out that the parallel composition of two (correct) implementations is again correct and that (sequential) composition is compatible with parallel composition (see Lemma 5.2 in /EKMP 80/). Using both types of composition we would be able to define algebraic implementation schemes corresponding to a tree structured refinement strategy in contrast to the linear structure of compound algebraic implementations. Instead of a formal definition we will only give an illustrating example:

4.2 EXAMPLE (algebraic implementation scheme)

Consider the following tree scheme where each node is colored with an algebraic specification and each bunch of edges is colored with an implementation of the source specification by the combination of all the target specifications

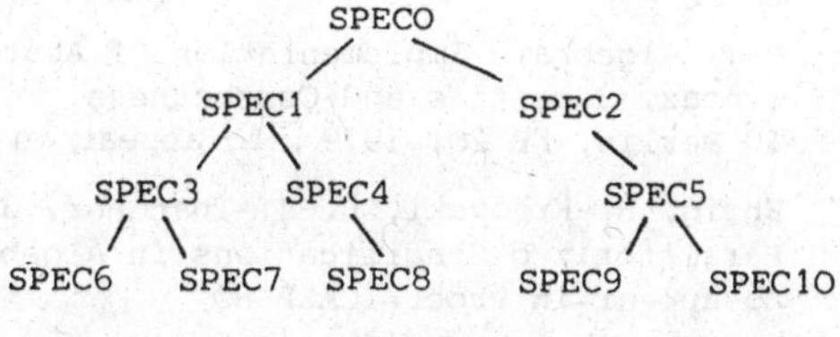

IMPL0: SPEC1+SPEC2⟹ SPEC0, IMPL1: SPEC3+SPEC4⟹ SPEC1, IMPL2: SPEC5⟹ SPEC2, IMPL3: SPEC6+SPEC7⟹ SPEC3, IMPL4: SPEC8⟹ SPEC4, IMPL5: SPEC9+SPEC10⟹ SPEC5.
The semantics of this algebraic implementation scheme is the semantics of the following compound implementation COMPIMPL=(IMPL0,IMPL1+IMPL2,IMPL3+IMPL4+IMPL5) or that of the following "equivalent" compound implementation having the same semantics COMPIMPL'=(IMPL0,IMPL1∘(IMPL3+IMPL4)+IMPL2∘IMPL5).

Example 4.2 shows how a tree structured stepwise refinement of software systems may be considered within our concept. The advantage of such a design is that each subtree can be considered as a separate smaller software system and that the semantics of the complete system is independent of the order they are combined as far as they are syntactically well-defined.

So far this is more or less an immediate consequence of Section 3. More interesting than disjoint union is the case of procedures (/BG 77 + 80/) or parameterizations (/TWW 79/, /EKTWW 80/) as horizontal structuring principle. The compatibility of these concepts with stepwise refinement will be studied in a forthcoming paper. This seems also to be one of the main problems which have to be tackled in the system CAT sketched by Burstall and Goguen in /BG 79/.

5. REFERENCES

/BG 77/ Burstall, R.M.-Goguen, J.A.: Putting Theories together to Make Specifications, Proc. Int.Conf. Artificial Intelligence, Boston, 1977

/BG 79/ --: CAT, a System for the Structured Elaboration of Correct Programs from Structured Specifications, Preliminary Draft, 1979

/BG 80/ --: Semantics of CLEAR, a specification language, Proc. 1979 Copenhagen Winter School on Abstract Software Specif., 1980

/Dij 72/ Dijkstra, E.W.: Notes on Structured Programming, in: Structured Programming, C.A.R. Hoare, Ed.,Academic Press, New York, 1972

/Eh 78a/ Ehrich, H.D.: Extensions and Implementations of Abstract Data Type Specifications, Proc.Conf.MFCS'78,Zakopane,Springer Lect. Not. in Comp. Sci. 64, 1978, 155-163

/Eh 78b/ --: On the Theory of Specification, Implementation and Parametrization of Abstract Data Types, Forschungsbericht Univ. Dortmund, 1978

/EKMP 80/ Ehrig, H.-Kreowski,H.-J.-Mahr,B.-Padawitz,P.: Compound Algebraic Implementations: An Approach to Stepwise Refinement of Software Systems (long version), Forschungsbericht Nr. 80-04, TU Berlin, FB 20, 1980

/EKP 78/ Ehrig, H.-Kreowski, H.-J.-Padawitz,P.: Stepwise Specification and Implementation of Abstract Data Types, Proc. ICALP'78, Udine, Springer Lect. Notes in Comp. Sci. 62, 1978, 205-226.

/EKP 79/ --: Algebraic Implementation of Abstract Data Types: Concept, Syntax, Semantics and Correctness, Forschungsbericht Nr. 79-23, TU Berlin, FB 20, 1979 , to appear in Proc. ICALP'80.

/EKTWW 80/ Ehrig, H.-Kreowski, H.-J.-Thatcher, J.-Wagner,E.-Wright,J.: Parameterized Specifications in Algebraic Specification Languages, to appear in Proc. ICALP'80

/EKW 78/ Ehrig, H.- Kreowski, H.-J.-Weber, H.: Algebraic Specification Schemes for Data Base Systems, Proc.4. Int.Conf. on Very Large Data Bases, Berlin, 1978

/EM 80/ Ehrig, H. - Mahr, B.: Complexity of Implementations on the Level of Algebraic Specifications, Proc. 12.SIGACT Symp. on Theory of Computing, Los Angeles, 1980

/GN 78/ Goguen, J.A. - Nourani, F.: Some Algebraic Techniques for Proving Correctness of Data Type Implementation, Extended Abstract, Comp. Sci. Dept.,UCLA, Los Angeles, 1978

REFERENCES (cont'd)

/GTW 78/ Goguen, J.A.-Thatcher, J.W.-Wagner, E.G.: An Initial Algebra Approach to the Specification, Correctness and Implementation of Abstract Data Types, in: Current Trends in Programming Methodology, IV: Data Structuring (R.Yeh,Ed.),Prentice Hall, New Jersey, 1978, 80-144

/Gut 76/ Guttag, J.V.: Abstract Data Types and the Development of Data Structures, Supplement to Proc. Conf. on Data Abstraction, Definition, and Structure, SIGPLAN Notices 8, March 1976

/GHM 78/ Guttag, J.V.-Horowitz, E.-Musser, D.R.: Abstract Data Types and Software Validation, Comm. ACM, Vol. 21, No. 12, 1978, 1048-1063

/LS 77/ Lehmann, D.H.-Smyth, M.B.: Data Types, Univ. of Warwick, Dept. of Comp. Sci., Report No. 19, 1977, and Proc. 18th IEEE Symp. on Found. of Computing, Providence, R.I., Nov. 77, 7-12

/TWW 79/ Thatcher, J.W.-Wagner, E.G.-Wright, J.B.: Data Type Specification: Parameterization and the Power of Specification Techniques, Proc. 10. SIGACT Symp. on Theory of Computing, San Diego, 1978, 119-132; revised version in IBM Research Report RC 7757, 1979

/Wa 77/ Wand, M.: Final Algebra Semantics and Data Type Extensions, Indiana Univ., Comp. Sci. Dept., Technical Report No. 65, 1977

/Wir 71/ Wirth, N.: Program Development by Stepwise Refinement, Comm. ACM, Vol.14, No.4, 1971, 221-227

On And/Or Schemes

David Harel†

IBM Thomas J. Watson Research Center
Yorktown Heights, New York 10598

Abstract: A computational model, based on and/or subgoaling, is described. It is shown that various models of computation, such as recursive program schemes, decision trees and combinational networks, are naturally embedded in the and/or language. These observations pose some interesting questions for further research. As a first result in the metatheory of and/or schemes, we prove a normal form theorem showing that with the addition of "auxiliary variables", every and/or scheme is strongly equivalent to one with "and/or depth" equal to 1.

I. Introduction

In [H1], a programming/specification language was introduced and it was therein argued to be useful for specifying and verifying large programs. The purpose of this paper is to present this language (independently of [H1]) to the theoretically oriented reader, accompanied by (i) some observations and thoughts regarding its relationships with other models of computation and its possible theoretical usefulness, and (ii) a technical result concerning a normal form for schemes in the language.

The language is based on the idea of describing the solution to a computational problem over some primitive operations and tests as an and/or subgoaling tree. In such a tree (or scheme, as we shall call it) one associates with each node u the goal of producing some output values out_u from some input values in_u (much as with a gate in a Boolean network one associates the goal of producing the value in the output wire from those in the input ones). If u is not a leaf, the offspring of u represent the decomposition of that goal into subgoals. If u is an *or*-node (resp. *and*-node) the goal(s) associated with one (resp. both) of these offspring has (resp. have) to be achieved for its own goal to be achieved. To an edge of the tree one can optionally attach a *test*, the falsity of which prevents the goal associated with its outgoing node from being attempted. A leaf can be of one of two kinds: a *primitive* leaf, i.e., one corresponding to a primitive, known operation (like a gate in network), and a *call* leaf, the goal associated with which is that associated with some other particular node elsewhere in the tree. Thus, primitive leaves act somewhat like assignment statements in a programming language, call leaves like procedure calls, *or*-nodes like nondeterministic choice (or deterministic conditionals when appropriate tests are present), and *and*-nodes like sequential or parallel execution of subprograms. Accordingly, we shall exhibit a natural correspondence between a subclass of the and/or schemes and conventional (recursive) program schemes.

This though, is only one way of viewing these schemes. The other involves combinational networks and decision trees. We shall argue that call-free *and*-schemes (i.e. no *or*-nodes) correspond to networks, while call-free *or*-schemes correspond to decision trees. The way in which combinations of these are allowed in this language provides what seems to be a natural tool for describing certain kinds of algorithms.

Furthermore, the well-known notion of *uniformity*, a necessary restriction when families of networks are to be regarded as solutions to computational problems (see Borodin [B], Pippenger [P] and Ruzzo [R]), is considered. Our main observation here concerns the ability of and/or schemes to provide a finite description of certain "uniform" families of networks with the appealing property that "unwinding" the scheme sufficiently for fixed n and pruning unnecessary parts (resulting in a call-free scheme), leaves one with precisely the network for n-size inputs.

Section IV consists of a technical result concerning a certain measure of "textual" complexity of and/or schemes. We define the *and/or depth* of a scheme to be the maximal number of alternations of *and*- and *or*-nodes from the root to a leaf. The question of whether every program can be brought to fixed and/or depth is posed (it being similar in spirit to the question concerning the depth of the nesting of loops in *while*-programs). It is shown that with the addition of some trivial "auxiliary machinery" (much like the

† Current address: Department of Applied Mathematics, Weizmann Institute of Science, Rehovot, Israel.

addition of Boolean variables in the above analogue), every and/or scheme has an equivalent "conjunctive" normal form with and/or depth 1. This result can be viewed as providing a kind of interpreter, or an operational semantics, for and/or schemes.

Section II can be skipped by the reader familiar with [H1]. Sections III and IV are mutually independent.

II. And/Or Schemes

We assume we are given fixed sets Σ, Δ and Π, of *variable*, *action* and *test* symbols, respectively. (Note: If x and y are elements of Σ^*, i.e., finite tuples of variables, we will use, throughout the paper, multi-set-theoretic terminology such as $x \subset y$ and $x = \phi$, which are to be understood to refer to the "unordered" versions of x and y. It might help the reader to have Figure 1 in mind when reading the following definition.)

An *and/or scheme* is a finite binary tree labelled in such a way as to satisfy the following:

(1) Each node u is labelled with a 4-tuple of the form $(\delta_u, lab_u, in_u, out_u)$, where $\delta_u \in \{\wedge, \vee\}$, $lab_u \in \Delta$, $in_u, out_u \in \Sigma^*$, and $in_u \cap out_u = \phi$. If $\delta_u = \wedge$ (resp. $\vee$), u is said to be an *and*-node (resp. *or*-node). Pictorially, as in Figure 1, we draw δ_u below u and format the rest of the 4-tuple thus: $out_u = lab_u\,(in_u)$.

(2) Each edge e is labelled with a pair $(test_e, arg_e)$, formatted $test_e(arg_e)$, where $test_e \in \Pi$ and if, say, $e = (u, u')$, then $arg_e \subset in_u$.

(3) For an *or*-node u with offspring u' and u'', $(in_{u'} \cup in_{u''}) \subset in_u$ and $out_u \subset (out_{u'} \cap out_{u''})$.

(4) For an *and*-node u with offspring u' and u'', $out_u \subset (out_{u'} \cup out_{u''})$ and $out_{u'} \cap out_{u''} = \phi$. Furthermore, one of the following two situations holds:

  (4.1) $in_{u'} \subset in_u$ and $in_{u''} \subset in_u$, or

  (4.2) $in_{u'} \subset in_u$ but $in_{u''} - in_u \neq \phi$ and $(in_{u''} - in_u) \subset out_{u'}$.

  (This is without loss of generality; the dual, with u' and u'' interchanged, is allowed.)

In case (4.1) the *and*-node u is called a *concurrent* node, and in case (4.2) a *sequential* one.

(5) Say that two nodes u and u' are *similar* if $lab_u = lab_{u'}$. Then, no two internal nodes (i.e., non-leaves) are similar. Furthermore, a leaf ℓ which is similar to the internal node u is said to be a *call* leaf, and we say that ℓ *calls* u. A leaf which is not a call leaf is said to be *primitive*. For every two similar nodes u and u' (of which, of course, at least one must be a leaf), $|in_u| = |in_{u'}|$ and $|out_u| = |out_{u'}|$.

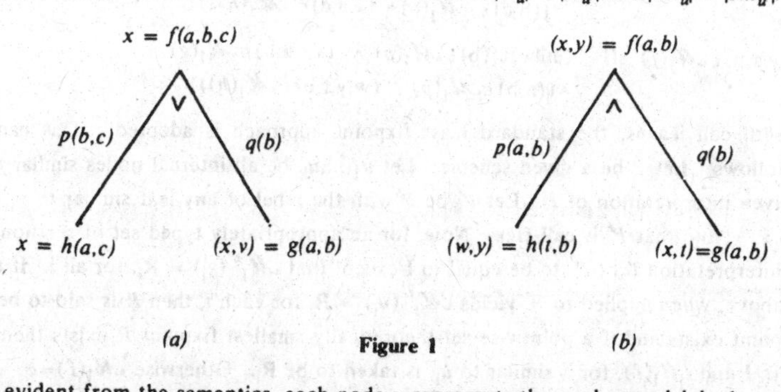

(a) **Figure 1** (b)

As will become evident from the semantics, each node u represents the goal named lab_u (a name we will also be using to denote the subtree rooted at u) which is to "receive" its inputs, in_u, and "produce" and "hand up" its outputs, out_u. The inputs are received by u either from the "outside" (if u happens to be the root of the tree), or from its parent and possibly also from its *and*-sibling (as in (4.2)). The outputs are handed up either to the "outside" (if u is the root), or to its parent and possibly to its *and*-sibling An (internal) *and*-node u achieves the goal of producing out_u from in_u (i.e., the goal lab_u) by its offspring each achieving their own subgoal, either independently or in sequence, and an *or*-node u achieves lab_u by one of its offspring achieving its subgoal.

However, the attempt at achieving any subgoal is dependent upon the test on the corresponding incoming edge being true of its arguments. This particularly makes sense with the offspring of an *or*-node, where tests can restrict the possible choice of a subgoal to be achieved. By convention, omission of a test from an edge will indicate the fixed test which is always true. For a leaf ℓ, we can disregard δ_ℓ, which plays no role in the sequel.

The primitive leaves are, in effect, the assumed-to-be-known operations (like functions in a flowchart or gates in a network) to which the interpretation will assign meaning. A call leaf represents a "procedure call" to the internal node similar to it, allowing as a special case a call to a node, the subtree of which includes the leaf itself -- i.e., a recursive call. Notice the particularly important requirement that $in_u \cap out_u = \phi$, for every u.

The meaning of an and/or scheme P is given relative to an interpretation I and is denoted $\mathcal{M}_I(P)$. I consists of a finite set of domains and appropriate interpretations for each of the primitive operations and tests. In order to describe this precisely, one assumes that I associates a domain with each variable of Σ appearing in P , in such a way that similar nodes are of the same *type*. For example, if u and u' are labelled $(x_1,x_2) = f(x_3,x_4)$ and $(x_5,x_2) = f(x_6,x_7)$ respectively, and if domain D_i is associated with x_i for $1 \leq i \leq 4$, then to qualify as an interpretation of P , I must associate D_1 , D_3 and D_4 with x_5 , x_6 and x_7, respectively. The type of u (and u') will then be $D_1 \times D_2 \times D_3 \times D_4$. An analogous requirement is adopted for the tests on "similar" edges. The interpretation I assigns a relation of the appropriate type to each action symbol in Δ labelling a primitive leaf in P , and a predicate of the appropriate type to each test symbol in Π labelling an edge in P. Above, if $R \subset D_1 \times D_2 \times D_3 \times D_4$ is assigned by I to f , we write $\mathcal{M}_I(f) = R$. Similarly, for an edge labelled with $p(x_1,x_2)$, we might have $\mathcal{M}_I(p) = R' \subset D_1 \times D_2$. We sometimes use $\mathcal{M}_I(u)$ synonymously with $\mathcal{M}_I(f)$.

Given an interpretation I of P , the meaning function $\mathcal{M}_I$ is extended upwards in the tree to provide meanings for all nodes of P as follows; $\mathcal{M}_I(P)$ is then defined to be $\mathcal{M}_I(r)$, where r is the root of P. The extension of $\mathcal{M}_I$ is achieved by a rather standard combination of least-fixpoint semantics for the call leaves and a simple propagation up *and*- and *or*-nodes. The latter takes the general form

$$u \text{ behaves iff } \quad (\exists \text{ locals})((u' \text{ test true} \wedge u' \text{ behaves})\ \delta_u\ (u'' \text{ test true} \wedge u'' \text{ behaves}))$$

where u' and u'' are the offspring of the "δ_u-node" u. For example, here is how the simple nodes of Figure 1 are assigned meaning assuming the meaning of their offspring has already been given.

(a) $\quad (x,a,b,c) \in \mathcal{M}_I(f)$ iff $\quad (\exists v)(((b) \in \mathcal{M}_I(q) \wedge (x,v,a,b) \in \mathcal{M}_I(g)) \vee ((b,c) \in \mathcal{M}_I(p) \wedge (x,a,c) \in \mathcal{M}_I(h)))$

(b) $\quad (x,y,a,b) \in \mathcal{M}_I(f)$ iff $\quad (\exists t \exists w)(((b) \in \mathcal{M}_I(q) \wedge (x,t,a,b) \in \mathcal{M}_I(g)) \wedge ((a,b) \in \mathcal{M}_I(p) \wedge (w,y,t,b) \in \mathcal{M}_I(h)))$

In order to deal with call leaves, the standard least fixpoint approach is adopted. This can be informally described here as follows: Let P be a given scheme. Let $u_1,\ldots,u_k$ be all internal nodes similar to call leaves in P, and let I be a given interpretation of P. Let P' be P with the label of any leaf similar to u_i replaced by the new action symbol g_i. Note that P' is call-free. Now, for an appropriately typed set of relations $R = R_1,\ldots,R_k$ we can define the interpretation I$'$ of P' to be equal to I except that $\mathcal{M}_I'(g_i) = R_i$, for all i. If the propogation process described above, when applied to P' yields $\mathcal{M}_I'(u_i) = R_i$ for each i, then R is said to be a *fixpoint* of P in I. If such a fixpoint exists and if a pointwise set-theoretically smallest fixpoint R exists then R is called the *least fixpoint* of P in I and $\mathcal{M}_I(\ell)$, for ℓ similar to u_i, is taken to be R_i. Otherwise $\mathcal{M}_I(\ell)=\phi$. More details on least fixpoints can be found in work of Scott, Park, etc.

As a simple example of an and/or scheme, consider the scheme P of Fig. 2. Let the domain of interpretation I be N, the set of natural numbers. Let $c()$ be the constant 1, $p(n)$ iff $n=0$, $t(n+1)=n$, $h(n,m)=nm$, and $id(n)=n$. Then, $\mathcal{M}_I(P) = \mathcal{M}_I(f) = \{(n!,n) \mid n \in N\}$. Similarly, let the domain of J be A^* for some set A, $c()=\Lambda$, the empty string, $p(s)$ iff $s=\Lambda$, $t(as)=s$ for $a \in A$ and $s \in A^*$, $h(as,s')=as'$, and $id(s)=s$. Then, $\mathcal{M}_J(P) = \{(s^R,s) \mid s \in A^*\}$, where s^R is the reverse of the string s. (See [M, pp.244-246].) Ways of proving such "correctness" properties of schemes are discussed in [H1].

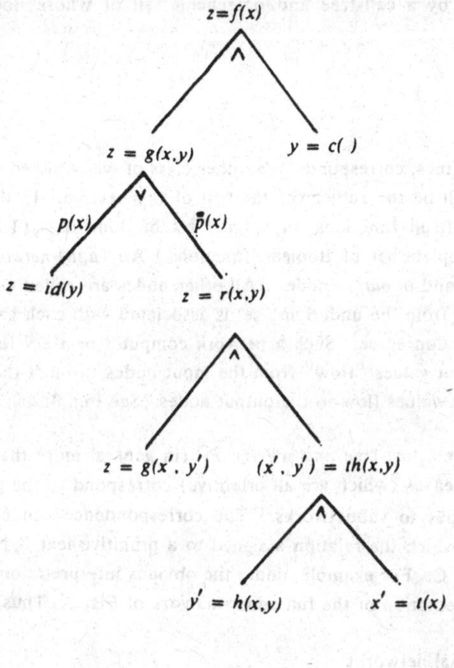

Figure 2

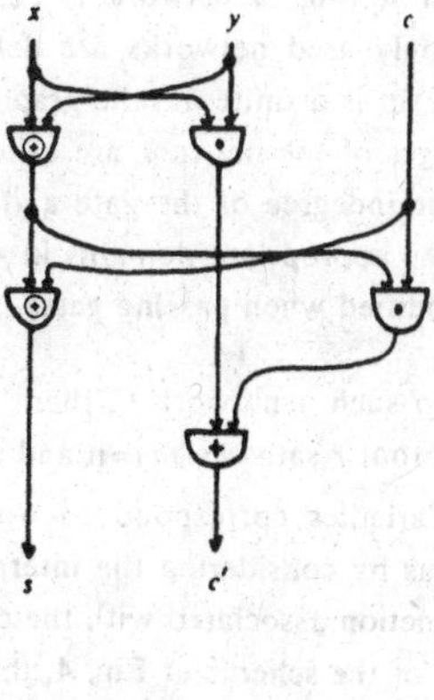

Figure 3

III. Relationship with Other Formalisms

First, we establish the correspondence between conventional uninterpreted program schemes and a subset of the class of and/or schemes. For definiteness, we adopt the formalism of *recursion schemes* in Greibach [G, pp. 7-3 to 7-6]. These are deterministic, mutually recursive schemes which are more powerful than regular (flowchart) schemes, and represent one way of modelling recursive programs.

Referring the reader to [G] for details, we recall here that for a recursion scheme S with "initial equation" $F_0(x_1,...,x_n)$, the fact that S terminates on input $\bar{a} = (a_1,...,a_n)$ under interpretation I, is denoted by $val(S,I,\bar{a})\downarrow = b$ and its (unique) final value is b. Now, define an interpretation I to be *reasonable* if for each test symbol $p \in \Pi$ there is a symbol in Π, denoted $\bar{p}$, which is interpreted by I as the complement (negation) of $\mathcal{M}_I(p)$. Assuming that the "variables", "predicate letters" and "function letters" of [G] are included, respectively, in Σ, Π and Δ, we have:

Lemma: For any recursion scheme S with initial equation $F_0(x_1,...,x_n)$, there is an and/or scheme P_S with root labelled $y = F_0(x_1,..., x_n)$ such that for any reasonable interpretation I of S and values $\bar{a} = (a_1,...,a_n)$ and b in the appropriate domains, $(S,I,\bar{a})\downarrow = b$ iff $(b,\bar{a}) \in \mathcal{M}_I(P_S)$.

The proof is straightforward, and involves constructing a subtree for each equation in the recursion scheme. These are then attached to an *or*-root with false tests (except for the initial equation). The resulting P_S is a simple and/or scheme in which the *or*-nodes are deterministic and the leaves single-valued. Thus,

Observation 1: Deterministic, sequential and/or schemes = recursion schemes.

Our next observation concerns decision trees, such as binary sorting trees which sort by comparisons. The computation process (see e.g. Knuth [K]) involves selecting a path down a (binary) tree, based on the outcome of certain tests applied along the way. When a leaf is reached, a single operation associated with that leaf is carried out. Clearly, such a tree can be modelled by a call-free and/or scheme, all of whose nodes are *or*-nodes.

Observation 2: Call-free *or* - schemes = decision trees.

Interestingly, the dual sublanguage, call-free *and*-trees, corresponds to another class of well-studied objects, namely combinational networks or circuits. These will be the subject of the rest of this section. In the most general setting, a network is defined over a set of fixed functions on a fixed set of domains. (The most commonly used networks are defined over some complete set of Boolean functions.) An (n,m)-*network* over such a set is a finite acyclic graph with n *input* nodes and m *output* nodes. All other nodes are called *gates* and the edges of the network are called *wires*. A function from the underlying set is associated with each gate such that the indegree of the gate and the arity of the function agree. Such a network computes m n-ary functions over the appropriate domains in the obvious way; input values "flow" from the input nodes through the wires, get modified when passing gates, and finally the output values flow to the output nodes. See Fig. 3.

To such a network C there corresponds a call-free, test-free *and*-scheme P_C (in general more than one), whose root r satisfies $|in_r|=n$ and $|out_r|=m$, and whose leaves (which are all primitive) correspond to the gates of C. Variables correspond to wires, and internal nodes to subnetworks. The correspondence can be made rigorous by considering the interpretation I of P_C in which the relation assigned to a primitive leaf is precisely the function associated with the corresponding gate in C. For example, under the obvious interpretation for the leaves of the scheme of Fig. 4, that scheme is a representation of the full adder network of Fig. 3. Thus,

Observation 3: Call-free *and* - schemes = combinational networks.

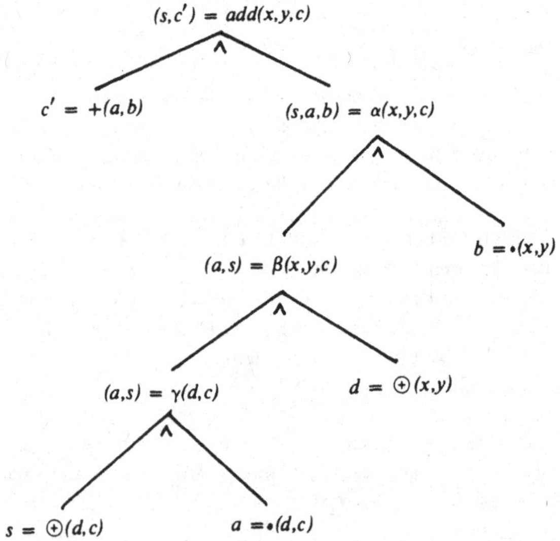

Figure 4

Our reason for drawing the analogies between decision trees and networks on the one hand and certain kinds of and/or schemes on the other, is not merely to provide notational variants for these formalisms. For one, there are functions, whose evaluation is naturally described by a *mixture* of these two formalisms, say by starting out with a network computation, at the end of which, based on an output value, one of a number of further networks is selected. For example, shortest path algorithms, network flow etc., where backtracking is a prominent feature. Although usually (if the base set of primitive functions allowed in the network is "complete" in an appropriate sense) the function is describable in pure network form too, it lends itself more naturally to a description involving an *or*-node inside the network -- that is, a call-free and/or scheme.

These ideas can be pushed a step further, to the description of *uniform families* of networks, and possibly of decision trees too. Consider adding n-bit binary numbers using a network. The problem with this is that for each n there is a different network C_n for achieving the goal. Thus, we are led into considering a family $C=(C_1,C_2,...)$ of networks as a solution to the computational problem at hand. As pointed out by Borodin [B], this suggestion makes no computational sense unless the family C is required to be "*uniform*". Researchers interested (as was Borodin) in comparing the computational power of "universal" models of computation, such as Turing machines, with "finite function" models, such as networks, are forced into formalizing this notion of uniformity. The various definitions which have been proposed [B,P,R] involve requiring the existence of a machine which, on appropriate input including n, constructs all or some of C_n in some moderate amount of time or space. For example, the definition of Borodin and Cook (see [R]) requires the existence of a DTM which on input 1^n outputs a description of C_n, and operates within space the logarithm of the number of gates in C_n (log the *size* of C_n). While these suggestions give rise to interesting comparative results, one gets the feeling that, at least pragmatically, "uniformness" should be more structured and disciplined.

Consider the aforementioned problem of adding n-bit numbers. The obvious solution, in which C_n consists of n appropriately linked copies of the full adder of Fig. 3, has a very simple structure. One would expect to be able to describe the family $\{C_n\}$ by some kind of finite "*while*-loop". Nevertheless, the only such description that seems to come to mind involves, like the Turing machine of Borodin and Cook, a "program" which outputs a *description* of the family. The question arises as to whether there is a structured language in which there is a finite object that, on input n, does not *construct* C_n but rather *is itself* C_n. Such an object could then be said to *be* the network solution to the binary addition problem, and its structure would presumably reflect the iterative character of the family of binary adders. To be slightly more specific, we are interested in the possibility of describing a "uniform" family of networks $C=(C_1,C_2,...)$ by a finite syntactic "program", which has the property that if its "loops" are unwinded indefinitely and then, for fixed n, its parts which are unreachable by inputs of length n are removed, what remains is precisely the network C_n.

Indeed, we argue that one such language is that of and/or schemes. In Fig. 5 we have an and/or scheme which represents the family of networks for binary addition in the following sense: If I is the interpretation described below then $\mathcal{M}_I(\textit{bin-add}) = \{(X+Y,X,Y) \mid X,Y \in \{0,1\}^*; |X|=|Y|\}$, where + is binary addition. Let $B=\{0,1\}^*$. In I, variables X,Y,Z and their primed versions range over B^*, variables c,x,y,z and theirs range over B, $\mathcal{M}_I(\textit{strip}) = \{(x,y,X,Y,\ xX,yY) \mid x,y \in B;\ X,Y \in B^*\}$, $\mathcal{M}_I(\textit{attach}) = \{(zZ,z,Z) \mid z \in B,\ Z \in B^*\}$, $\mathcal{M}_I(\textit{empty}) = \{\Lambda\}$, $\mathcal{M}_I(\textit{not-empty}) = \{X \mid X \neq \Lambda\}$, and the other primitive leaves act like in Fig. 4, with 0 and Λ standing for themselves. Note how the obvious structure is reflected in, essentially, the "*while*-loop" of *bin-add*, and that it has the unwinding property discussed above.

Many more complex families of networks are described in the literature (see, for example, [Pe], [PF] and [LF]). In most cases the iterative or recursive definition of C_n using, say, copies of $C_{n/2}$, is given simply by a diagram. In the corresponding and/or scheme, the use of $C_{n/2}$ will be modelled by a recursive call with a shorter input. The advantages of a formal, structured description such as ours over diagrams which are structured but not formal or over Turing machines which are formal but not structured, should be clear. Not the least of these is the possibility of using known methods to prove properties of the described networks, much like proving the correctness of conventional programs. Proving the "partial correctness" of *bin-add*, i.e., that $\mathcal{M}_I$ behaves as claimed above, involves a simple Floyd-Hoare proof using an invariant assertion attached to the node and leaf labelled *proc*. Details of the method of proof can be found in [H1]. Note that the properties provable by such methods include analyzing the complexity (say, the size or depth) of such networks, besides proving their correctness. In most of the literature we have seen, both correctness and complexity are proved by induction on the structure of the diagrams, and hence can be formalized as indicated above.

We might remark here that hardware designers have also confronted the problem of describing structured families of networks, and our model might be helpful in their endevours as well. See for example Section III of [HN].

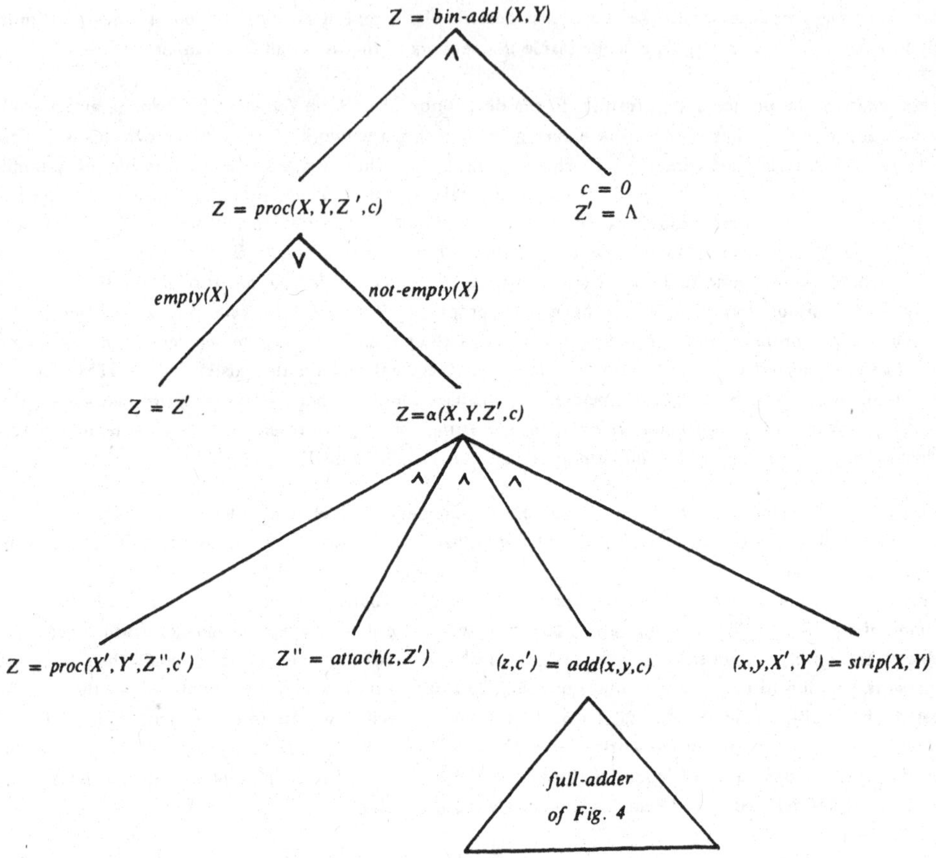

(The 4-ary node α is an abbreviation in the spirit of Section IV.)

Figure 5

Notice that schemes representing uniform families of networks have two kinds of primitive leaves. The actions of one correspond to the gates in the original network; those of the other, which we might term *cable operations*, involve manipulating "cables" of wires. In the case of Fig. 5 we *strip* a wire from a cable, and *attach* a wire to a cable. In all the examples of networks we have found in the literature, the cable operations involved were extremely simple. In fact, they were always computable by a finite automaton. This observation, points to the fact that, in practice, uniformity really requires no more than our naive *structured uniformity*. Moreover, it raises the question of whether some or all of the notions suggested in [B,S,P,R] can be reduced to structured uniformity. In other words, can one show, for example, that a family of networks is logspace-uniform (Borodin and Cook) iff it is describable as a certain kind of and/or scheme with, say, logspace-computable cable operations? Hence,

Observation 4: And/or schemes can express families of combinational networks encountered in practice.

Question: Can and/or schemes express all uniform families of combinational networks?

We briefly mention two additional lines of possible further work. One involves families of decision trees. A simple case would be the family of sort trees, and a more complex one would be the median algorithm of

[SPP], which is essentially a description of a family of decision trees. It is not clear what is a good way to describe such families in a disciplined, structured fashion, as we have done for families of networks.

Second, one might attempt to define and investigate "alternating transducers", i.e., to find an appropriate parallel model of computing (rather than accepting) machines, suited for analyzing the complexity of parallel function computation. It would seem that such a model would have to incorporate some kind of *and* states in which the outcome of one computation is taken as the input of the next, and hence would come very close to the and/or scheme model.

IV. A Normal Form for And/Or Schemes.

Various measures of the *textual* complexity of certain classes of programs have been proposed recently. These measures, which have little or nothing to do with *computational* complexity, do say something about how complicated the *description* of an algorithm is in a certain language. Besides the obvious, suitably formalized measure of the size of the program, examples of such measures are the depth of the nesting of loops, the "cyclomatic number" of the graph underlying a flowchart, and the "normal number" of such a graph. See e.g. [Mc, My, Ha, EM, Cu]. Some of these measures have the property that they can be reduced to a constant for all programs, if some trivial auxiliary machinery, such as a finite number of Boolean variables, is allowed. See [H2] for a detailed discussion of this phenomenon in the context of the loop-depth measure. (Note that if one adds enough such machinery so as to allow the construction of a universal program and encodings for all other programs, all textual measures reduce to a constant.) These results, although in a sense trivializing the suggested concept as a measure of inherent complexity, usually give some insight into the operational behavior of the program in question; the proof (see [Co,H2]) that every flowchart can be written as a *while* program with one loop (with additional Boolean variables) is a good example, supplying in effect an interpreter for simulating the computation of the flowchart.

In this section we propose a textual measure, defined for and/or schemes, and prove that it too possesses the aforementioned property; every and/or scheme *P* is equivalent to a normal form scheme *P'* of complexity 1 with additional "Boolean variables". The measure, the and/or depth, is analogous to the alternation depth of alternating Turing machines [CKS] and the alternating quantifier depth of formulae in various formal logics. The proof can be viewed as supplying a kind of interpreter for executing and/or schemes on sequential machines.

Define the *and/or depth* of an and/or scheme *P* to be the maximal number of alternations of *and*- an *or*-nodes along paths from the root to a leaf. Intuitively, we are counting the number of times we had to alternate when splitting a goal into two subgoals in the description of *P*, between the case in which both of these, and that in which one of these, were to be achieved in order to achieve the goal. A scheme is said to be in *normal form* if its and/or depth is 1 and its root is an *and*-node.

Note that, as in [H1], one can often abbreviate a sequence of (binary) nodes of the same and/or "gender" by one k-ary node simply by eliminating the internal nodes and grouping the leaves under the common ancestor. (This can be done whenever a called node does not disappear as a result.) In the *or*-case the resulting tree can be thought of as a k-ary (in general nondeterministic) *case* statement, as in [D], and in the *and*-case as a mixture of sequencing and parallelism suggested by the partial ordering on the leaves induced by their *in* and *out* lists. With this in mind, our normal form programs will have the general form:

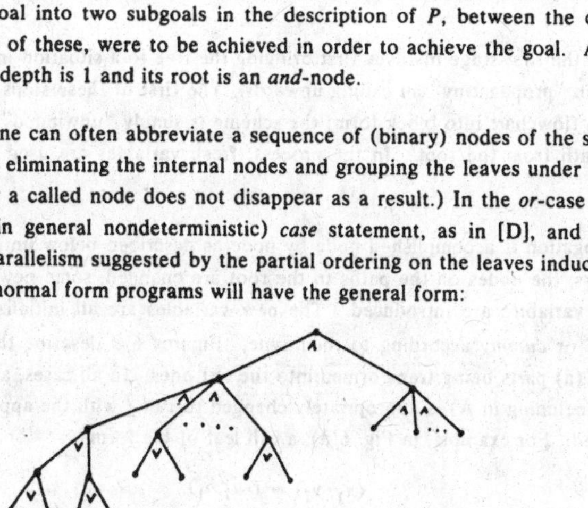

The auxiliary machinery we will be needing will manifest itself in three additional mild restrictions on the interpretations we will be considering in the sequel. An interpretation I is said to be *agreeable* if it is reasonable (i.e., supports negations of tests) and if:

(1) For each domain in I there is an action symbol in Δ which is interpreted in I as the (unary) identity over D.

(2) For each domain in I there is an action symbol in Δ which is interpreted in I as some element of D.

(3) There is some domain in I with two distinct elements, definable by two action symbols in Δ and distinguishable by a test symbol in Π.

In other words, besides negations of tests, we want (1) identity functions for "copying" values, (2) "dummy" values for handing over unimportant information, and (3) "Boolean" variables, i.e., the ability to mark a yes/no situation and later test it. In most real cases, though, all these are "built in" for free. We use *id*(), *dummy*, T , F , =T?, and =F? to stand, respectively for these. For example, in any agreeable interpretation I, a primitive leaf labelled $y = id(x)$ is interpreted as $\{(a,a) \mid a \in D\}$, where I associates D with both x and y. Similarly for the others.

Two and/or schemes P and P' with roots r and r' are said to be *compatible* if $|in_r| = |in_{r'}|$ and $|out_r| = |out_{r'}|$. They are *equivalent* if they are compatible and if for every agreeable interpretation I providing meanings for all primitives and tests in both P and P' , $\mathcal{M}_I(P) = \mathcal{M}_I(P')$.

Theorem: For every and/or scheme P there exists an equivalent scheme P' in normal form.

Proof: The proof consists of three stages. In the first, we show how the structure of the calls in any given scheme P can be changed in an equivalence-preserving manner, so that all call leaves call one designated node corresponding to the root of P. This is very much like showing that every (mutually) recursive program is equivalent to one with one procedure calling itself (see e.g. [C]), and can be visualized in the following way, where arrows denote calling:

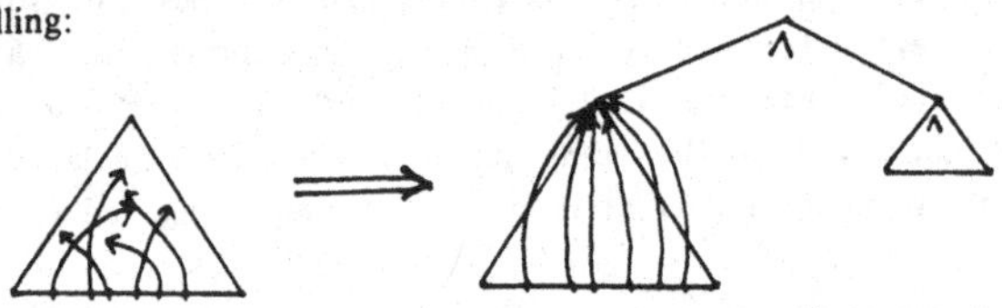

The subtree on the far right is a call-tree *and*-tree which we name the "initialization tree". The second stage consists of proving the theorem for call-free schemes, and the third combines the first and second to prove the theorem.

(1) The proof of the first stage involves first bringing the tree to a situation in which call leaves call their ancestors only, and then "propagating" all calling upwards. The first of these steps is very similar to Engeler's [E] transformation of a flowchart into block form; the scheme is simply "unwinded" sufficiently so that all calls are to nodes on the path from the root. In the process, fresh variables are used when parts of the tree are duplicated.

The upward propogation is accomplished node by node as described below until all calls are to the root of the tree. In the process, the nodes on the paths to the root are changed, some new leaves are added, and new Boolean and auxiliary variables are introduced. The new variables are all initialized at the start, i.e., in the initialization tree, to F or *dummy* according to their type. Figures 6-8 describe the propogation in the three possible situations, the (a) parts being transformed into the (b) ones. In all cases, any call leaf to the original f elsewhere in the tree (including in A) is appropriately changed to call $\hat{f}$ with the appropriate initialization of the new variables if required. For example, in Fig. 6(a), a call leaf of the form

$$(x_1, y_1) = f(a_1, b_1)$$

is replaced by the subtree

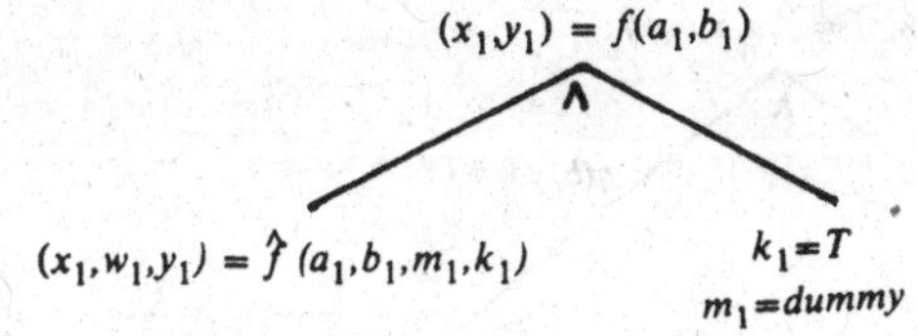

The reader should be able to see why, e.g., the transformation in Fig. 6 works: initially k=F so that p and q govern the node as in (a). If, in this case, $\hat{g}$ is reached, g is carried out - again, as in (a). When h is reached A is executed, and upon reaching one of the $\hat{h}$ leaves k' is set to T, a' to *dummy* and $\hat{f}$ is called. Now k=T, a = *dummy* and $m = t'$. In this case $\hat{g}$ is forced to be reached first but now all that happens is that h gets executed with $t=m=t'$, i.e., its correct argument as in (a). Here one can prove

$$(x,y,a,b) \in \mathcal{M}_I(f) \text{ iff } (\exists w)\ (\forall m)\ (x,w,y,a,b,m,F) \in \mathcal{M}_I(\hat{f})$$

The reasoning for Figures 7 and 8 is similar, establishing the equivalence of the resulting scheme to P.

(2) The second stage of the proof involves showing that any *call-free* and/or scheme has an equivalent normal form. One first observes that in such a scheme P there are only a finite number of Herbrand terms to ever be computed. For example, in Fig. 9 these are y, fy, gy, hgy and kgy. Furthermore, with each of these there is associated a finite number of tests which have to be true when applied to various other such terms, before the term itself is computed. (If the computation of the term is naively attempted at the outset without first checking the tests, its value might be undefined, i.e., the relation empty.) For example, in Fig. 9 hgy cannot be computed before rgy and py are checked to be true. One can impose a partial order on all such required terms, in such a way that t_1 precedes t_2 iff t_1 has to be computed before t_2, by virtue of t_1 being a subterm of either t_2 or a test upon which the computation of t_2 depends. This process can be carried out even in the face of the nondeterminism and parallelism involved in the and/or scheme P.

Upon topologically ordering this partially-ordered set of terms in any way, one can then construct the desired normal form for the call-free scheme: it consists of a large *and*-node which, say from the right, considers each term in order; the term is computed if the appropriate tests are true, and, if not, a dummy value is prepared. In either case the outcome value is passed to the left sibling, who considers the next term. When all terms (or dummies) have been computed, the leftmost sibling executes a large *or* to (possibly nondeterministically) determine which of the final values it hands up to its parent, the root, as the result. Fig. 9 transformed into Fig. 10 is a simple example of this construction (which can be reduced somewhat in size at the expense of complicating its explanation).

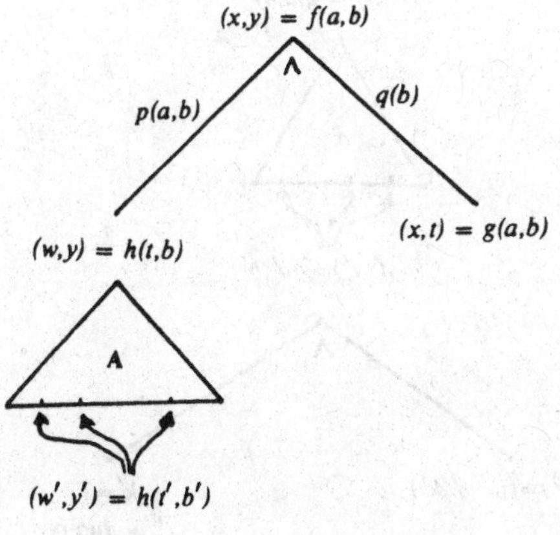

Figure 6(a)

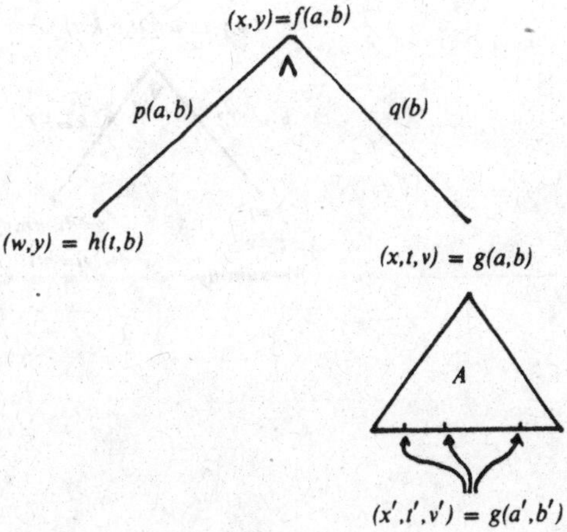

Figure 7(a)

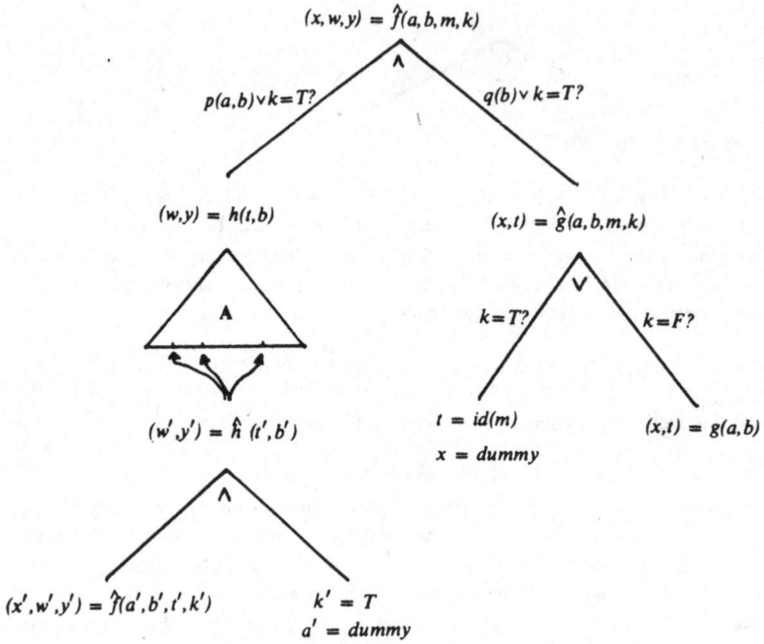

Figure 6(b)

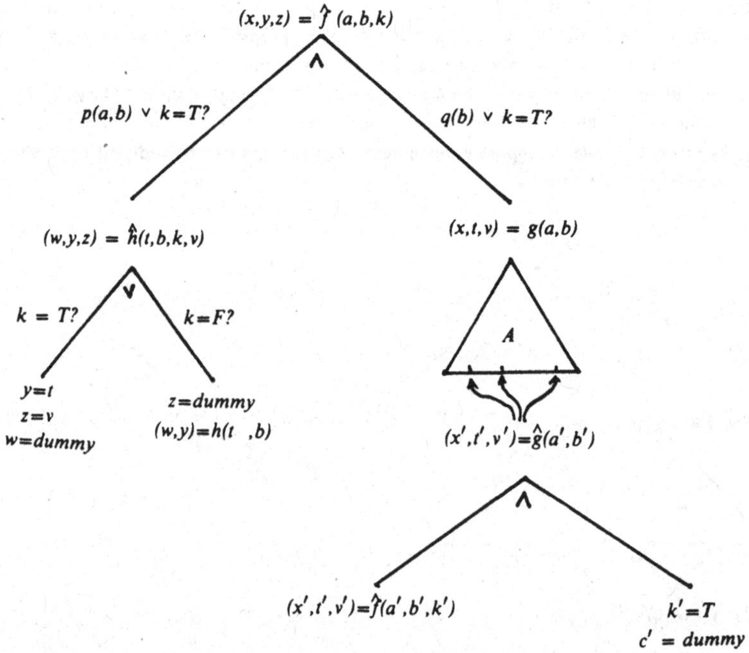

Figure 7(b)

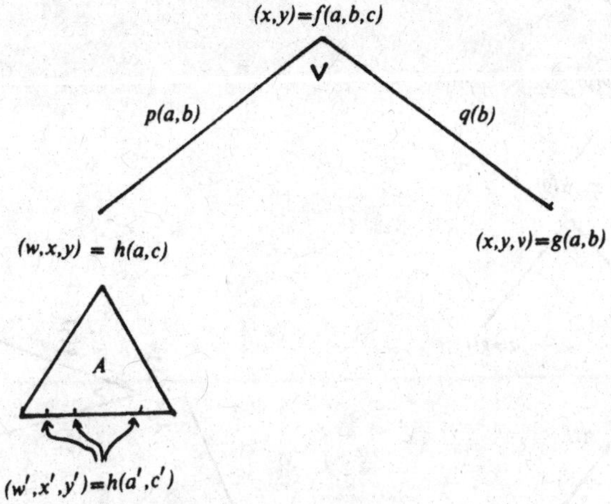

Figure 8(a)

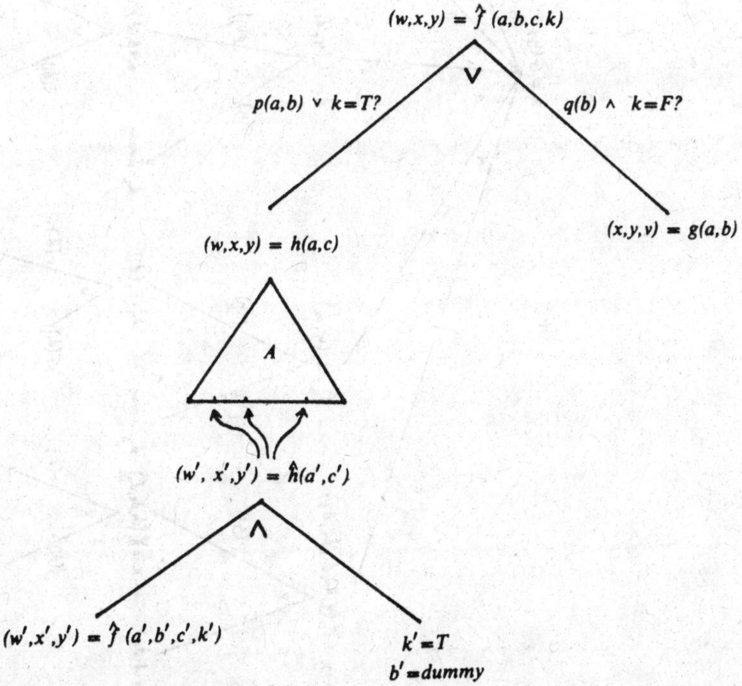

Figure 8(b)

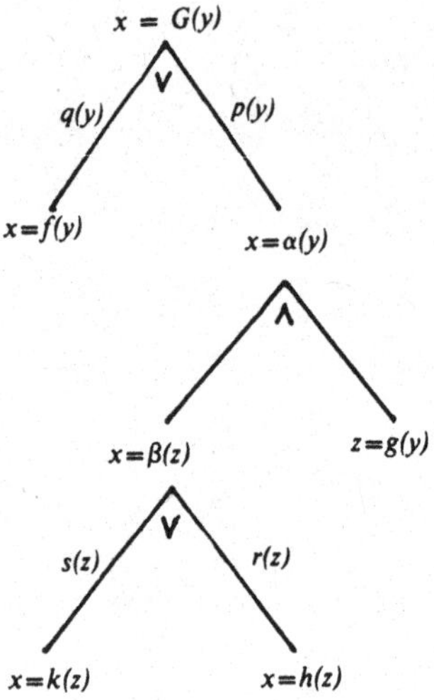

Figure 9

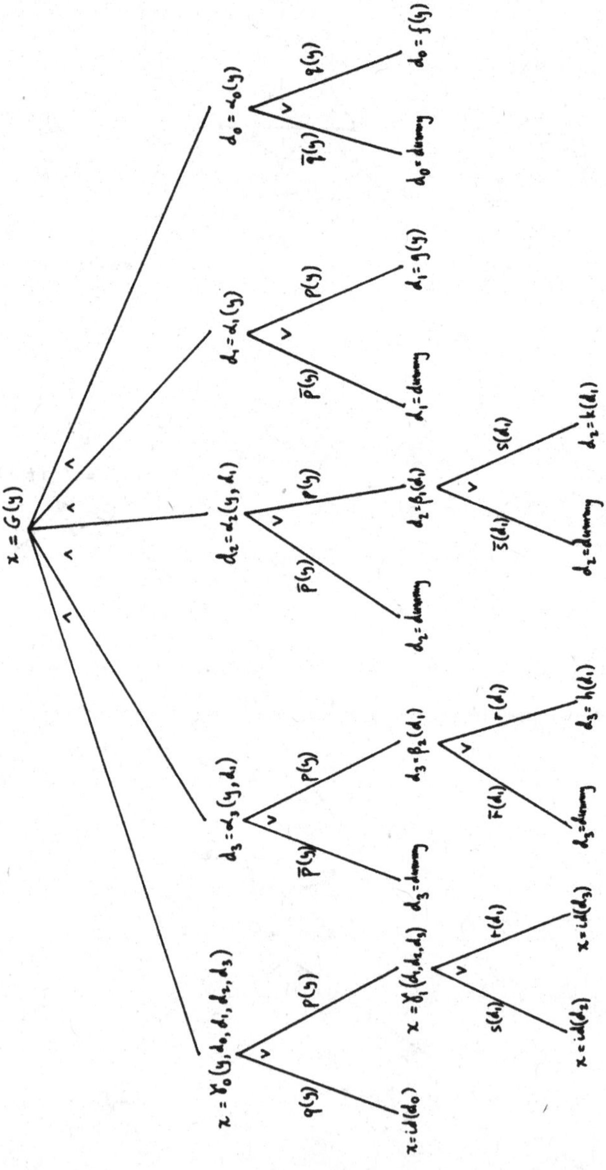

Figure 10

(3) To complete the proof of the theorem, a given scheme P is first converted to "single-procedure" form as in stage one. Then the procedure "body" A (see figure 11) is thought of as having the form B for a new action symbol g. The call-free scheme B is then transformed, as in stage two, into normal form B′. Finally, since B and B′ are equivalent in any (agreeable) interpretation, in particular in ones in which g is assigned the same meaning as f in A, the occurences of g in B′ are replaced by f, and the resulting A′ is attached to its proper place, under the root r. Note that the *and*-root of A′ merges with the *and*'s of the main root r and initialization tree, resulting in overall and/or depth 1. □

As mentioned, the rather operational spirit of the various parts of this proof, and the sequencing of parallelism that occurs in the second stage, result in a normal form with particularly simple structure; all primitive operations are performed in sequence from right to left with occasionally a recursive call to this process itself. The nondeterminism is reduced to the leftmost, final node in which a choice of the term to hand up is made. Thus, the theorem and its proof provide a kind of operational semantics for and/or schemes.

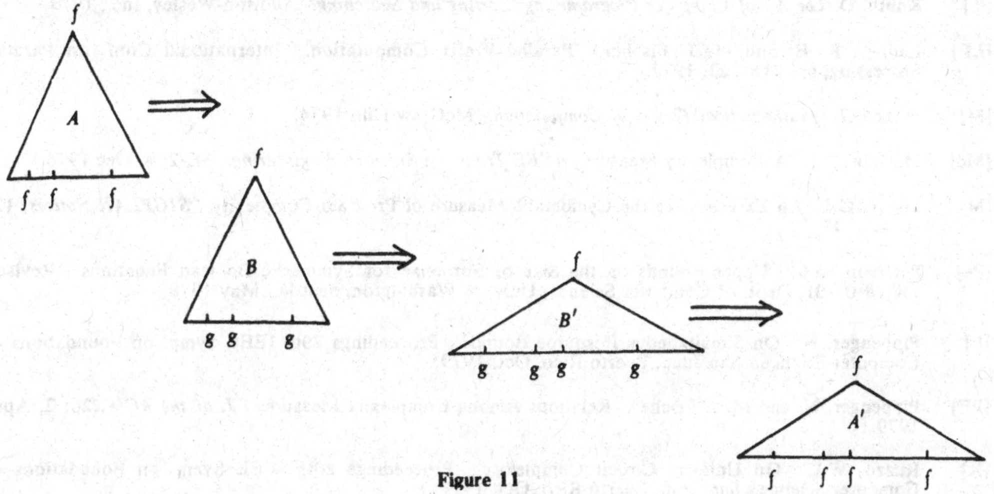

Figure 11

Acknowledgements:

We are deeply indebted to N. Pippenger for many stimulating conversations about the material presented here. In particular his ideas concerning networks and decision trees form the basis of Section III. The cheerful typing assistance of S. Hawkins and M. Cofer is gratefully acknowledged.

VI. References

[B] Borodin, A.B. On Relating Time and Space to Size and Depth. *SIAM J. on Computing*, 6, pp.733-744, 1977.

[C] Chandra, A.K. Degrees of Translatability and Canonical Forms in Program Schemas. Proceedings of the 6th ACM Symp. on Theory of Computing, pp.1-12, 1974.

[Co] Cooper, D.C. Bohm and Jacopini's Reduction of Flow Charts. *Comm. of the ACM*, Vol.10, pp.463,473. Aug.1967.

[CKS] Chandra, A.K. D. Kozen and L. Stockmeyer. Alternation. To appear in *J. of the ACM*.

[Cu] Culik, K. The Cyclomatic Number and the Normal Number of Programs. *SIGPLAN Notices*, 14;4, April 1979.

[D] Dijkstra, E.W. A Discipline of Programming. Prentice-Hall, Inc.. Englewood Cliffs, NJ. 1976.

[EM] Elshoff, J.L. and M. Marcotty. On the Use of the Cyclomatic Number to Measure Program Complexity. *SIGPLAN Notices*, 13;12, Dec. 1978.

[E] Engeler, E. Structure and Meaning of Elementary Programs. *Proc. Symp. on Semantics of Algorithmic Languages*. Lecture Notes in Mathematics, Vol. 188, Springer-Verlag, 1971, pp.89-101.

[G] Greibach, S.A. *Theory of Program Structures: Schemes, Semantics, Verification*. Lecture Notes in Computer Science, Vol.36, Springer-Verlag. 1974.

[Ha] Hansen, W.J. Measurement of Program Complexity by the Pair (Cyclomatic Number, Operator Count). *SIGPLAN Notices*, 13; 3, Mar. 1978.

[H1] Harel, D. And/Or Programs: A New Approach to Structured Programming. *ACM Transactions on Prog. Lang. and Syst.*, Vol.2, No.1, Jan. 1980, pp.1-17.

[H2] Harel, D. On Folk Theorems. *Comm. of the ACM*. 23:7, July 1980.

[HN] Hill, F. J. and Z. Narabi. Extending Second Generation AHPL Software to Accomodate AHPL III. Proceedings IEEE 4th International Symp. on Computer Hardware Description Languages. Palo Alto, CA, Oct. 1979.

[K] Knuth, D. *The Art of Computer Programming: Sorting and Searching*. Addison-Wesley, Inc., 1973.

[LF] Ladner, R. E. and M. J. Fischer. Parallel Prefix Computation. International Conf. on Parallel Processing, pp. 218-223, 1977.

[M] Manna, Z. *Mathematical Theory of Computation*. McGraw Hill, 1974.

[Mc] McCabe, T.J. A Complexity Measure. *IEEE Trans. on Software Engineering*. SE-2; 4, Dec.1976.

[My] Myers, G.J. An Extension to the Cyclomatic Measure of Program Complexity. *SIGPLAN Notices*, 12; 10, Oct. 1977.

[Pe] Peterson, G.L. Upper Bounds on the Size of Formulae for Symmetric Boolean Functions. Revised TR-78-03-01, Dept. of Computer Science, Univ. of Washington, Seattle. May 1978.

[P] Pippenger, N. On Simultaneous Resource Bounds. Proceedings 20th IEEE Symp. on Foundations of Computer Science. San Juan, Puerto Rico, Oct. 1979.

[PF] Pippenger, N. and M. J. Fischer. Relations Among Complexity Measures. *J. of the ACM*, 26; 2, April 1979.

[R] Ruzzo, W.L. On Uniform Circuit Complexity. Proceedings 20th IEEE Symp. on Foundations of Computer Science. San Juan, Puerto Rico, Oct. 1979.

[S] Schnorr, C. P. The Network Complexity and the Turing Maching Complexity of Finite Functions. *Acta Informatica*, 7 pp.95-107 1976.

[SPP] Schonhage, A., M. Paterson and N. Pippenger. Finding the Median. *J. of Comp. and System Sciences*, Vol.13, No.2, Oct. 1976.

A TERM MODEL FOR CCS

M.C.B. Hennessy and G.D. Plotkin

Dept. of Computer Science
University of Edinburgh
Edinburgh EH9 3JZ
Scotland

1. Introduction

In a series of papers [Hen2, Mil1, Mil4–7] Milner and his colleagues have studied a model of parallelism in which concurrent systems communicate by sending and receiving values along lines. Communication is synchronised in that the exchange of values takes place only when the sender and receiver are both ready, and the exchange is considered as a single event; this kind of communication is also found in Hoare's model [Hoa]. In these papers, and particularly in [Mil5], a notation for expressing systems is introduced which (as remarked in [Hen2]) can be considered as a programming language, called here CCS- (Milner's) Calculus of Communicating Systems. More precisely there will be a family of languages incorporating these ideas and in this paper we study one such language.

In sections 2 and 3 we give a formal definition of the syntax of our version of CCS and then give an operational semantics by axiomatising the capabilities of programs to communicate along lines. A number of laws for behaviours were proposed in [Mil5]. A simpler version of these laws, based on a programming language not involving recursion or value passing, was justified and shown complete in [Hen2] by using an operational equivalence relation based on an operational semantics. The initial algebra for these laws then easily gave a denotational semantics for the simple language which was fully abstract with respect to the operational semantics. This meant that, for programs, being operationally equivalent was just the same as having the same denotation.

In section 4 we tentatively propose a certain operational preorder on programs; this seems more appropriate than an equivalence. In section 5 we give a formal proof system for a fragment of our language (excluding recursion but allowing value passing and nonconvergence). This system provides analogues of all the laws in [Hen2,Mil5] as well as adding some unexpected rules, and it is shown sound and complete in Theorem 5.1. In section 6 we give a variant of Milner's behaviour algebras, [Mil5], that enables us to give a denotational semantics for CCS. An initial fully abstract model is obtained in Theorem 6.7 by employing a term model construction based on the so-called behaviourally finite terms and our operational preorder (cf. [Mil3][Ber]). Available models using powerdomains (such as in [Mil1]) are not fully abstract but perhaps such a model could be obtained along the lines of [Hen1].

2. The Syntax of CCS

The syntax is parameterised on certain sets and functions as follows:

1. AVar - a given countably infinite set of arithmetic variables, ranged over by (the metavariable) x.
2. AExp - a given countably infinite set of arithmetic expressions, ranged over by e, and assumed to contain the set, N, of integers.

3. BExp - a given countable set of <u>Boolean expressions</u> ranged over by b, and assumed to contain the set $T = \{tt, ff\}$ of truthvalues.

4. Δ - a given countable set of <u>line names</u> ranged over by α, β and γ.

5. $Proc_k$ (one for each integer k) - a given countably infinite set of <u>procedure names of degree k</u> ranged over by P_k.

In addition it is assumed that all expressions e, b have given finite sets FV(e), FV(b) of <u>free arithmetic variables</u> and that it is possible to <u>substitute</u> arithmetic expressions, e', for arithmetic variables, x, in expressions e,b to obtain expressions $[e'/x]e$, $[e'/x]b$ of the same type. Finally we assume that there are relations $e =_\alpha e'$, $b =_\alpha b'$ of <u>α-conversion</u> in expressions and that free variables, substitution and α-conversion have the usual properties (see [Cur], [Hin']).

Now we can give the main syntactic sets:

6. Ren - the set of <u>renamings</u>, ranged over by S, is the set of finite partial functions from Δ to Δ.

7. Term - the set of <u>terms</u>, ranged over by t, u and v, is given by the grammar:

$$t ::= NIL \mid (t + u) \mid (t \mid u) \mid t[S] \mid (\alpha x.t) \mid \alpha(e,t) \mid (\underline{if}\ b\ \underline{then}\ t\ \underline{else}\ u) \mid P^k(e_1,\ldots,e_k)\ (k \in N)$$

Free variables, substitution and α-equivalence are extended to terms in the evident way, the only new binding operators being the $(\alpha x.—)$.

8. Dec - the set of <u>declarations</u>, ranged over by d, and including all sequences of the form:

$$P^1_{k(1)}(x_{11},\ldots,x_{1k(1)}) \Leftarrow t_1,\ldots,P^l_{k(l)}(x_{l1},\ldots,x_{lk(l)}) \Leftarrow t_l$$

where $l \geq 0$, and $P^1_{k(1)},\ldots,P^l_{k(l)}$ are all different and include any procedure name occurring in any of the t_i, and $FV(t_i)$ is a subset of $\{x_{i1},\ldots,x_{ik(i)}\}$ for $i = 1, k$. In other words we impose the usual restrictions on simultaneous recursive definitions.

9. Prog - the set of <u>programs</u>, ranged over by p, q and r, whose elements have the form:

<u>letrec</u> d <u>in</u> t

where any procedure name occurring in t also occurs in d and where $FV(t) = \emptyset$.

The present version of CCS differs from what is expected in the light of [Mil5] in that integers are the only type of values considered, terms and programs are not sorted on the names of the lines on which they input and on which they output, and restriction and relabelling have been replaced by the more general renaming. Notationally we have replaced $(\alpha?x:t)$ and $(\alpha!e:t)$ by the more neutral $(\alpha x.t)$ and $\alpha(e,t)$; we might also have allowed a more flexible form of procedure definition than the present two-level one. None of these variations should materially affect our results.

3. <u>Operational Semantics</u>

Following the intuitions in [Mil1,Mil4-7] we understand the behaviour of programs in terms of their capabilities. These include the capability to input a value off a line or to output a value on a line or to make some internal communication. Further the recursive definitions allow computation to proceed forever without any communication occurring. For any given program none, one or several of each of these kinds of possibilities may obtain. It is presumably possible to invent an abstract machine with these capabilities, following [Lan, Weg] but we prefer the more direct, if more abstract, method of axiomatising them. This method could be called axiomatic operational semantics and has also been pursued in [Hen1,Hen2].

For the communication capabilities we need the following binary relations:

Input Here we have the relations, $p \xrightarrow{\alpha ?m} q$, (one for each α in Δ and m in N) meaning that program p has the capability of inputting m off α and q represents the remaining capabilities of p after this communication.

Output Here we have the relations, $p \xrightarrow{\alpha !m} q$, (one for each α in Δ and m in N) meaning that program p can output m on α and q represents the rest of p.

Internal Communication Here we have the relation, $p \xrightarrow{\tau} q$, meaning that program p can perform an internal communication and q represents the rest of p. (We do not need any detailed knowledge about which internal communication took place as we intend to treat all the possibilities as indistinguishable.)

For the possibility of infinite computation without communication we axiomatise the property:

Convergence The property, $p \downarrow$, means that program p cannot compute forever without any communication occurring.

To understand programs it is necessary to understand expressions and terms (the latter in the context of declarations). For the first we just assume that any expressions e and b have values $[\![e]\!]$ and $[\![b]\!]$ in, respectively, N and T provided they are closed (have no free variables). For the second we introduce a little axiomatic system. Let Com be the set of communication capabilities where:

$$\text{Com} = \{\alpha ?m \mid \alpha \in \Delta, m \in N\} \cup \{\alpha !m \mid \alpha \in \Delta, m \in N\} \cup \{\tau\}$$

It is ranged over by the variable c. The formulae of our axiomatic system have the form, $t \xrightarrow[d]{c} u$ or $t \downarrow d$ where t and u are closed and where d is the context of declarations in which the communication c is made or the convergence occurs. The rules have the form $F_1, \ldots, F_m \Rightarrow G_1, \ldots, G_n$ $(m \geq 0, n > 0)$ meaning that if $F_1, \ldots, F_m$ are theorems so are $G_1, \ldots, G_n$ (where the F_i and G_j are formulae). The relations that hold are to be just those whose corresponding formulae are provable.

Rules

NULLITY

1. $\Rightarrow (\text{NIL} \downarrow d)$

Although NIL cannot communicate it converges.

AMBIGUITY

1. $t \xrightarrow[d]{c} t' \Rightarrow (t+u) \xrightarrow[d]{c} t',\ (u+t) \xrightarrow[d]{c} t'$

2. $t \downarrow d, u \downarrow d \Rightarrow (t+u) \downarrow d$

The capabilities of (t+u) are those of t and u, with commitment to whichever is exercised.

COMPOSITION

1. $t \xrightarrow[d]{c} t' \Rightarrow (t|u) \xrightarrow[d]{c} (t'|u),\ (u|t) \xrightarrow[d]{c} (u|t')$

2. $t \xrightarrow[d]{\alpha!m} t',\ u \xrightarrow[d]{\alpha?m} u' \Rightarrow (t|u) \xrightarrow[d]{\tau} (t'|u'), (u|t) \xrightarrow[d]{\tau} (u'|t')$

3. $t \downarrow d,\ u \downarrow d \Rightarrow (t|u) \downarrow d$

The capabilities of (t|u) are those of t and u, but without commitment, together with an internal communication. This is handshake or synchronised communication.

RENAMING

1. $t \xrightarrow[d]{\alpha?m} t' \Rightarrow t[S] \xrightarrow[d]{S\alpha?m} t'[S]$ (if S is defined at α)

2. $t \xrightarrow[d]{\alpha!m} t' \Rightarrow t[S] \xrightarrow[d]{S\alpha!m} t'[S]$ (if S is defined at α)

3. $t \xrightarrow[d]{\tau} t' \Rightarrow t[S] \xrightarrow[d]{\tau} t'[S]$

4. $t \downarrow d \Rightarrow t[S] \downarrow d$

Renaming serves to relabel or remove communication capabilities.

INPUT

1. $\Rightarrow (\alpha x.t) \xrightarrow[d]{\alpha?m} [m/x]t,\ (\alpha x.t) \downarrow d$

The term $(\alpha x.t)$ can input any integer off α and the rest is obtained by binding x to m in t.

OUTPUT

1. $\Rightarrow \alpha(e,t) \xrightarrow[d]{\alpha![\![e]\!]} t,\ \alpha(e,t) \downarrow d$

The term $\alpha(e,t)$ can output the value of e on α and t is the rest.

CONDITIONAL

1. $t \xrightarrow[d]{c} t' \Rightarrow$ (if b then t else u) $\xrightarrow[d]{c} t'$ (if $[\![b]\!] = tt$)

2. $u \xrightarrow[d]{c} u' \Rightarrow$ (if b then t else u) $\xrightarrow[d]{c} u'$ (if $[\![b]\!] = ff$)

3. $(t \downarrow d) \Rightarrow$ (if b then t else u) $\downarrow d$ (if $[\![b]\!] = tt$)

4. $(u \downarrow d) \Rightarrow$ (if b then t else u) $\downarrow d$ (if $[\![b]\!] = ff$)

PROCEDURE CALL

1. $[[\![e_1]\!]/x_1]\ldots[[\![e_k]\!]/x_k]t \xrightarrow[d]{c} t' \Rightarrow P^k(e_1,\ldots,e_k) \xrightarrow[d]{c} t'$
(if $P^k(x_1,\ldots,x_k) \Leftarrow t$ is in d)

2. $[[\![e_1]\!]/x_1]\ldots[[\![e_k]\!]/x_k]t \downarrow d \Rightarrow P^k(e_1,\ldots,e_k) \downarrow d$
(if $P^k(x_1,\ldots,x_k) \Leftarrow t$ is in d)

It is now easy to define the behaviour of programs by similar rules:

PROGRAMS

1. $t \xrightarrow[d]{c} t' \Rightarrow$ (*letrec* d *in* t) $\xrightarrow{c}$ (*letrec* d *in* t')
2. $(t\downarrow d) \Rightarrow$ (*letrec* d *in* t)

As in [Hen2] we take the view that internal communication is not observable and so wish to define *observable* communication cpabilities, $p \overset{c}{\Rightarrow} q$, and convergence $p\Downarrow$ by the rules:

OBSERVABLE COMMUNICATION

1. $\Rightarrow (p \overset{\tau}{\Rightarrow} p)$
2. $(p \overset{\tau}{\Rightarrow} p'), (p' \xrightarrow{c} q'), (q' \overset{\tau}{\Rightarrow} q) \Rightarrow (p \overset{c}{\Rightarrow} q)$

Note that this defines $p \overset{\tau}{\Rightarrow} q$ which, unfortunately, does not seem to correspond to anything observable.

OBSERVABLE CONVERGENCE

1. $p\downarrow, q\Downarrow$ (for all q such that $p \xrightarrow{\tau} q$) $\Rightarrow p\Downarrow$

This looks like an infinitary rule but it can be shown that if $p\Downarrow$ then $\{q \mid p \xrightarrow{\tau} q\}$ is finite; $p\Downarrow$ means that p cannot compute forever without an input or output communication occurring.

We will be interested in such properties of programs as are determined by the trees of communication capabilities and convergences issuing from them. The issue of fairness will be neglected; in the present context that might mean ruling out certain infinite branches of the tree as unfair. From the point of view of Petri and his followers ([Pet]) the capabilities correspond to possible events and there is a structure of concurrency and conflict on these events which we are also ignoring.

4. An Operational Preorder for Programs

An operational equivalence relation on a simpler kind, Prog', of programs than ours was introduced in [Hen2]; here we introduce an operational preorder on our kind. It should be admitted that our definition is just something that works, being based on the ideas in [Hen2] and intuitions about powerdomains [Plo,Smy] and Scott-Strachey semantics generally.

In the case of [Hen2] a simpler kind, Com', of communication capabilities was appropriate and there all programs converged. The function, E, on relations on programs was defined by putting, for any p,q in Prog':

$$pE(\sim)q \equiv (\forall c,p'.p \overset{c}{\Rightarrow} p' \supset \exists q'.q \overset{c}{\Rightarrow} q' \wedge p' \sim q') \wedge$$
$$(\forall c,q'.q \overset{c}{\Rightarrow} q' \supset \exists p'.p \overset{c}{\Rightarrow} p' \wedge p' \sim q').$$

Then the operational equivalence relation, $\sim$, was defined as $\bigcap_n \sim_n$ where $\sim_0$ is the universal relation on programs and, for any n, $\sim_{n+1} = E(\sim_n)$. As it happened the communication relations, $\overset{c}{\Rightarrow}$, obeyed the *image finiteness condition* that for all p, the set $\{q \mid p \overset{c}{\Rightarrow} q\}$ is finite; this can be used to prove that $\sim$ is the maximal fixed-point of E.

All this can be understood, to some extent, in terms of an operational <u>difference</u> relation $\#$ on programs, which we take to be generated by the following rules:

I <u>Symmetry</u> $p \# q \Rightarrow q \# p$

II <u>Communication</u> $p \overset{c}{\Rightarrow} p', p' \not\# q'$ (whenever $q \overset{c}{\Rightarrow} q'$) $\Rightarrow p \# q$ (for any c).

The complement of $\#$ is the maximal fixed-point of E and so, by image-finiteness, it must be $\sim$. Image-finiteness ensures the rules are finitary and so differences between programs can somehow be detected from a finite amount of information about their behaviour.

Unfortunately in our case image-finiteness fails. For example consider the program:

$$P_\infty = \underline{\text{letrec}}\ I(y) \Leftarrow (\alpha x.\beta(y,NIL)) + I(y+1)\ \underline{\text{in}}\ I(0)$$

Then $P_\infty \xrightarrow{\alpha ?0} \beta(m,NIL)$ for any integer m. Further we have also the possibility of nonconvergence, which suggests using a preorder, $\sqsubseteq$, instead of an equivalence.

After some experimentation we were led to defining maps, Q^F, on preorders which employed some finiteness ideas (hence the superscript); we hope later to give a properly justified map of this kind. Now, define $p \Downarrow c$ by:

$$p \Downarrow c \text{ iff } p\Downarrow \wedge \forall p'(p \overset{c}{\Rightarrow} p' \supset p' \Downarrow)$$

For any finite subset, F, of Com define a function Q^F on relations over Prog by:

$$\begin{aligned} pQ^F(\sqsubseteq)q \equiv\ & (1).\ (\forall c \in F, p'.p \overset{c}{\Rightarrow} p' \supset \exists q'.q \overset{c}{\Rightarrow} q' \wedge p' \sqsubseteq q') \wedge \\ & (2).\ (\forall c \in F. p\Downarrow c \supset ((a) q \Downarrow c \wedge \\ & \qquad (b) \forall q'.q \overset{c}{\Rightarrow} q' \supset \exists p'.p \overset{c}{\Rightarrow} p' \wedge p' \sqsubseteq q')) \end{aligned}$$

Next take $\sqsubseteq_0^F$ to be the universal relation over Prog and for all n, put $\sqsubseteq_{n+1}^F = Q^F(\sqsubseteq_n^F)$ and define the operational preorder, $\sqsubseteq_O$, by:

$$p \sqsubseteq_O q \text{ iff } \forall F,n.\ p \sqsubseteq_n^F q$$

Following the ideas in [Hen2] we regard p as less than q not just when p is operationally less than q, but when p is less than q in all contexts of possible use. A <u>term context</u> is just a term u[·] with a "hole" in it (a formal definition is omitted); it can be filled in with a term t to give a term u[t] which is of use as part of a program if it is closed. For programs we are also interested in adding extra recursive definitions. We take a <u>program context</u> to be of the form, v[·] = <u>letrec</u> [·], d' <u>in</u> u[·], (where u[·] is a term context); it can be filled in with the program p = <u>letrec</u> d <u>in</u> t to give $v[p] =_{def}$ <u>letrec</u> d,d' <u>in</u> u[t] which is of use if it is a program (this means that u[t] must be closed and there should be no syntactic difficulties with the declarations). The contectual preorder, $\sqsubseteq$, on programs can now be defined:

$$p \sqsubseteq q \text{ iff } \forall r[\cdot].(r[p] \wedge r[q] \text{ are programs}) \supset r[p] \sqsubseteq_O r[q]$$

The slightly awkward notion of program context seems appropriate in the light of the two-level structure of programs.

5. A Proof System

We would have liked here to present a complete proof system characterising the operational preorder on programs; instead we consider a fragment of the language without procedure calls, but with terms for internal communication and nonconvergence. The set, BTerm, of basic terms is given by:

$$t ::= NIL \mid (t+u) \mid (t \mid u) \mid t[S] \mid (\alpha x.t) \mid \alpha(e,t) \mid (\underline{if}\ b\ \underline{then}\ t\ \underline{else}\ u) \mid \tau(t) \mid \Omega$$

For the operational semantics of closed basic terms we define $t \xrightarrow{c} t'$ $(c \in Com)$ and $t\downarrow$. The rules NIL, AMBIGUITY, COMPOSITION, RENAMING, INPUT, OUTPUT, CONDITIONAL are like those for terms, just dropping the component for declarations. The new rules are:

INTERNAL COMMUNICATION

1. $\Rightarrow \tau(t) \xrightarrow{\tau} t$ 2. $\Rightarrow \tau(t)\downarrow$

CONVERGENCE

There are no rules for Ω and so it has no communication behaviour and (unlike NIL) does not converge.

Next $\overset{c}{\Longrightarrow}$, $\Downarrow$ and $\sqsubseteq_0$ on closed basic terms are defined as before. Taking contexts, $v[\cdot]$, as basic terms, with a hole, a natural contextual preorder, $\sqsubseteq$ for open basic terms is:

$$t \sqsubseteq u \text{ iff } \forall v[\cdot], \forall \rho \in AEnv.\ \rho(v[t]) \sqsubseteq_0 \rho(v[u])$$

using the obvious extension of arithmetic environments (note that AEnv = AVar -> N).

The next job is to characterise the operational preorder on basic terms by giving an axiomatic system for proving formulae of the forms $t \sqsubseteq u$ and $t = u$. This continues the work in [Hen2] but because of the variable binding mechanism we follow the usual pattern for λ-calculus systems rather than an algebraic style of giving universally valid equations. However the main difference from [Hen2] is that we need conditional rules, such as VIII 3, and even an infinitary rule, the ω-rule, X.

A few abbreviations will make the presentation of the rule for composition much easier. We write $\sum_{i=1,n} t_i$ for the sum, $(t_1 + (t_2 + \ldots\ t_n \ldots))$. A basic term is atomic iff it has one of the forms, $\alpha x.t$, $\alpha(m,t)$, $\tau(t)$ or Ω. Binary functions, $|_i$, (for i=1,3) on basic terms are defined by:

$$(t \mid_1 u) = \begin{cases} \alpha x.(t' \mid u) & (t = \alpha x.t') \\ \alpha(m, t' \mid u) & (t = \alpha(m,t')) \\ \tau(t' \mid u) & (t = \tau(t')) \\ \Omega & (t = \Omega) \\ NIL & (\text{otherwise}) \end{cases}$$

and $|_2$ is defined symmetrically and,

$$(t\,|_3\,u) = \begin{cases} \tau(([m/x]t')\,|\,u') & (t = \alpha x.t',\ u = \alpha(m,u')) \\ \tau(t'\,|\,[m/x]u') & (t = \alpha(m,t'),\ u = \alpha x.u') \\ \text{NIL} & (\text{otherwise}). \end{cases}$$

Rules

I PARTIAL ORDER

1. $\Rightarrow t \sqsubseteq t$ 2. $t \sqsubseteq u,\ u \sqsubseteq v \Rightarrow t \sqsubseteq v$

3. $t \sqsubseteq u,\ u \sqsubseteq t \Rightarrow t = u$ 4. $t = u \Rightarrow t \sqsubseteq u,\ u \sqsubseteq t$

II SUBSTITUTIVITY

1. $t \sqsubseteq t' \Rightarrow t[S] \sqsubseteq t'[S], (\alpha x.t) \sqsubseteq (\alpha x.t'), \alpha(e,t) \sqsubseteq \alpha(e,t'), \tau(t) \sqsubseteq \tau(t')$
2. $t \sqsubseteq t',\ u \sqsubseteq u' \Rightarrow (t+u) \sqsubseteq (t'+u'), (t|u) \sqsubseteq (t'|u'),$ (if b then t else u) $\sqsubseteq$ (if b then t' else u')
3. $\Rightarrow \alpha(e,t) = \alpha(m,t)$ (if $FV(e) = \emptyset$ and $[\![e]\!] = m$)
4. $\Rightarrow$ (if b then t else u) = (if tr then t else u) (if $FV(b) = \emptyset$ and $[\![b]\!] = tr$)

III AMBIGUITY

1. $\Rightarrow (t + u) + v = t + (u + v)$ 2. $\Rightarrow (t + u) = (u + t)$

3. $\Rightarrow (t + t) = t$ 4. $\Rightarrow (t + \text{NIL}) = t$

IV COMPOSITION

1. $\Rightarrow (\sum_i t_i)\,|\,(\sum_j u_j) = \sum_i t_i\,|_1(\sum_j u_j) + \sum_j(\sum_i t_i)\,|_2 u_j + (\sum_i\sum_j t_i\,|_3 u_j)$ (if all the t_i and u_j are atomic)

V RENAMING

1. $\Rightarrow \text{NIL}[S] = \text{NIL},\ (t + u)[S] = (t[S] + u[S]),\ \tau(t)[S] = \tau(t[S]), \Omega[S] = \Omega$
2. $\Rightarrow (\alpha x.t)[S] = (\beta x.t[S]), \alpha(e,t)[S] = \beta(e,t[S])$ (if $S(\alpha) = \beta$)
3. $\Rightarrow (\alpha x.t)[S] = \text{NIL}, \alpha(e,t)[S] = \text{NIL}$ (if S is not defined at α)

VI α-CONVERSION

1. $\Rightarrow \alpha x.t = \alpha y.[y/x]t$ (if $y \notin FV(t)$)

VII CONDITIONAL

1. $\Rightarrow$ (if tt then t else u) = t, (if ff then t else u) = u

VIII COMMITMENT

1. $\Rightarrow \tau(\tau(t)) = \tau(t),\ t + \tau(t) = \tau(t)$ 2. $\Rightarrow \tau(t + \Omega) = t + \Omega$
3. $\sum_i \tau(t_i) \sqsubseteq \sum_j \tau(u_j) \Rightarrow \sum_i (\alpha x.t_i) \sqsubseteq \sum_j (\alpha x.u_j)$
4. $\sum_i \tau(t_i) \sqsubseteq \sum_j \tau(u_j) \Rightarrow \sum_i \alpha(m,t_i) \sqsubseteq \sum_j \alpha(m,u_j)$

IX OMEGA

1. $\Rightarrow \Omega \sqsubseteq t.$

X ω-RULE

1. $[m/x]t \sqsubseteq [m/x]u$ (all m in N) $\Rightarrow t \sqsubseteq u$

Allowing for the differences in the nature of the proof systems, we have or can derive analogues of all the laws in [Hen2], [Mil4]. An example due to B. Mayoh shows a typical use of the ω-rule in conjunction with VIII 3. To show:

$\alpha x.t + \alpha x.u \sqsubseteq \alpha x.$ (if x=0 then t else u) $+ \alpha x.$ (if x=0 then u else t)

it is enough by VIII 3 to show:

$$\tau t + \tau u \sqsubseteq \tau(\underline{if}\ x{=}0\ \underline{then}\ t\ \underline{else}\ u) + \tau(\underline{if}\ x{=}0\ \underline{then}\ u\ \underline{else}\ t)$$

and by the ω-rule, X, it is enough to show for every m that:

$$\tau t + \tau u \sqsubseteq \tau(\underline{if}\ m{=}0\ \underline{then}\ t\ \underline{else}\ u) + \tau(\underline{if}\ m{=}0\ \underline{then}\ u\ \underline{else}\ t)$$

and that will follow by I, II, VII and III 2 (if $m \neq 0$).

Clearly this proof system is far from providing a complete, practical proof system for programs. It may be possible to make a complete one for programs by adding suitable formulae for programs and handling recursion by a Scott fixed-point rule (like the rules FIXP, INDUCT in [Mil2]). Perhaps one could then eliminate the ω-rule to obtain a finitary relatively complete system (see [Apt]) which could be a first step towards a practical one. In the meantime we have the following completeness theorem showing we have at least characterised $\underset{\approx}{\sqsubseteq}$:

Theorem 5.1 (Completeness) For all basic terms t,u: t $\underset{\approx}{\sqsubseteq}$ u iff t $\sqsubseteq$ u is a theorem of the above axiomatic system.

Hopefully, this result will increase the reader's confidence in our definition of the preorder, $\sqsubseteq$.

6. Natural Interpretations

When constructing term models it clarifies matters if it is known in what sense they are models and so we look for a class (even category) of possible interpretations for CCS. A reasonable choice would be some class of algebras, but the binding operators, (αx.—), present difficulties and we do not follow a strictly algebraic treatment - at least in the usual narrow sense of algebra. What we do is treat the binding operators in a natural way: if terms have type A then for each α we use a function of type (N -> A) -> A to interpret α x.t. Note that this does not amount to the same thing as an algebraic treatment along the lines, say, of the treatment of SAL in [ADJ] - that would result in a wider class of semantics. Much attention has been paid to this kind of problem in the case of the λ-calculus ([Bar], [Hin2], [Obt]).

Our natural interpretations of CCS are ω-continuous algebras with some extra structure; see [ADJ] for a definition of strict ω-complete partial orders (called ω-cpos here), ω-continuous functions, ω-continuous algebras and strict ω-continuous homomorphisms.

Definition 6.1 The one-sorted signature, Σ , has one operator symbol, NIL, of arity 0 and one, [S], of arity one, for each S, and two, + and $|$, of arity two.

Definition 6.2 A natural interpretation, $\mathfrak{A}$, of CCS is an ω-continuous Σ-algebra, A, together with functions:

$In_{\alpha,\mathfrak{A}}$: (N -> A) -> A (one for each α in Δ)
$Out_{\alpha,\mathfrak{A}}$: (N $\times$ A) -> A (one for each α in Δ)

where $In_{\alpha,\mathfrak{A}}$ is ω-continuous (taking N -> A as the ω-cpo of all functions from N to A under the pointwise ordering) and where $Out_{\alpha,\mathfrak{A}}$ is continuous in its second argument.

Definition 6.3 A homomorphism h: $\mathcal{A} \to \mathcal{A}'$ of natural interpretations is a strict ω-continuous homomorphism of the underlying Σ-algebras, A and A', such that for all α in Δ:

1. $\forall f \in (N \to A).h(In_{\alpha,\mathcal{A}}(f)) = In_{\alpha,\mathcal{A}'}(h \circ f)$
2. $\forall m \in N, a \in A.h(Out_{\alpha,\mathcal{A}}(m,a)) = Out_{\alpha,\mathcal{A}'}(m,h(a))$

Natural interpretations are closely related to Milner's behaviour algebras [Mil5]. The differences are:

1. Behaviour algebras allow other value sets than the integers.
2. Certain differences regarding renaming.
3. Natural interpretations have an order structure.
4. Behaviour algebras are many-sorted (on finite subsets of port labels).

The first two differences are trivial, reflecting what we have already discussed: the difference between our definition of CCS and what might be expected from [Mil5]. The third difference is needed for the treatment of recursion (or any linguistic device permitting infinite behaviours). We do not understand the significance of the last difference.

Any natural interpretation, $\mathcal{A}$, of CCS gives rise to a denotational semantics for CCS. There are two kinds of environments, arithmetic and procedural, ranged over by ρ and π, and given by:

AEnv = (A Var -> N) PEnv = $\prod_{k \in \omega} Proc_k \to (N^k \to A)$ respectively. Updating environments and applying environments to expressions is defined as usual; we write K_0 for the trivial arithmetic environment $\lambda m \in N.0$.

The denotational semantics of CCS is now given by three functions all of which are also called $\mathcal{A}$:

$\mathcal{A}$: Term -> (AEnv × PEnv -> A), $\mathcal{A}$: Dec -> PEnv, $\mathcal{A}$: Prog -> A.

For the denotation of terms we just give enough equations to make the rest of the definition obvious:

3. $\mathcal{A}[\![t|u]\!](\rho,\pi) = \mathcal{A}[\![t]\!](\rho,\pi) |_{\mathcal{A}} \mathcal{A}[\![u]\!](\rho,\pi)$
4. $\mathcal{A}[\![\alpha x.t]\!](\rho,\pi) = In_{\alpha,\mathcal{A}}(\lambda m \in N. \mathcal{A}[\![t]\!](\rho[m/x],\pi))$
5. $\mathcal{A}[\![\alpha(e,t)]\!](\rho,\pi) = Out_{\alpha,\mathcal{A}}([\![\rho e]\!], \mathcal{A}[\![t]\!](\rho,\pi))$
6. $$\mathcal{A}[\![b \to t,u]\!](\rho,\pi) = \begin{cases} \mathcal{A}[\![t]\!](\rho,\pi) & ([\![\rho(b)]\!] = tt) \\ \mathcal{A}[\![u]\!](\rho,\pi) & ([\![\rho(b)]\!] = ff) \end{cases}$$
7. $\mathcal{A}[\![P_k(e_1,\dots,e_k)]\!](\rho,\pi) = \pi_k[\![P_k]\!]([\![\rho(e_1)]\!],\dots,[\![\rho(e_k)]\!])$

It is easy to show $\mathcal{A}[\![t]\!](\rho,\pi)$ is ω-continuous in π.

Given a procedure environment, π, any term t defines a function of its free variables and so if $FV(t) \subseteq \{x_1,\dots\dots,x_k\}$ we define:

$$\mathcal{F}[\![t;x_1,\dots,x_k]\!](\pi) = \lambda m_1,\dots,m_k \in N.\ \mathcal{A}[\![t]\!](K_0[m_1/x_1]\dots[m_k/x_k],\pi)$$

Now the denotation of declarations is defined by

$$\mathcal{A}[\![P^1_{k(1)}(x_{11},\dots,x_{1k(1)}) \Leftarrow t_1,\dots,P^1_{k(1)}(x_{11},\dots,x_{1k(1)}) \Leftarrow t_1)]\!]$$
$$= Y(\lambda\pi.[\mathcal{F}[\![t_1;\ x_{11},\dots,x_{1k(1)}]\!](\pi)/P^1_{k1}]\dots[\mathcal{F}[\![t_1;\ x_{11},\dots,x_{1k(1)}]\!](\pi)/P^1_{k(1)}]\pi)$$

Finally the denotation of whole programs is given by:

$$\mathcal{A}[\![\underline{\text{letrec}}\ d\ \underline{\text{in}}\ t]\!] = \mathcal{A}[\![t]\!](K_0, \mathcal{A}[\![d]\!])$$

Definition 6.4 A natural interpretation, $\mathcal{A}$, of CCS is a model for CCS iff for all programs p,q:

$$p \lessapprox q \Rightarrow \mathcal{A}[\![p]\!] \sqsubseteq \mathcal{A}[\![q]\!];$$

a model, $\mathcal{A}$, for CCS is fully abstract iff for all programs p,q:

$$\mathcal{A}[\![p]\!] \sqsubseteq \mathcal{A}[\![q]\!] \Rightarrow p \lessapprox q.$$

Finally, we turn to the construction of a fully abstract term model, $\mathcal{M}$. The idea is to base $\mathcal{M}$ on the completion of a preorder, $\langle F, \lesssim \rangle$ of basic terms. The terms in F will all represent finite behaviours and the preorder will just be $\lessapprox$.

Definition 6.5 The b-finite (behaviourally finite) terms are the least set, F, of closed basic terms, t, such that:
If $\{\langle c,t'\rangle \mid t \overset{c}{\Rightarrow} t' \not\approx \Omega\}$ is finite and also t' is in F whenever $t \overset{c}{\Rightarrow} t'$, for any c, then t is in F.

For example, for any m, α x.(if $x \le m$ then NIL else Ω) is b-finite but (αx.NIL) is not. As we have already remarked, F is a preorder under $\lessapprox$ (restricted to F). Note that the least element of F is Ω. Further NIL is b-finite and so are t[S], (t + u) and (t|u) if t and u are; therefore we can turn F into a Σ-algebra if we define:

$$NIL_F = NIL;\quad [S]_F(t) = t[S];\quad t +_F u = (t + u);\quad t\,|_F\,u = (t|u)$$

and indeed F is even a preordered Σ-algebra in that all the operations are monotonic.

Now M, the underlying continuous Σ-algebra of $\mathcal{M}$, is taken to be the completion by directed ideals of F. Note the natural monotonic $[\cdot]$: F -> M, where $[u] = \{t \mid t \le u\}$. The operations on M are defined in the evident element-wise way so that, for example,

$$X +_M Y = \bigcup\{[u +_F v] \mid u \in X,\ v \in Y\}$$

(By the way, we have used the countability of F in that if F were not countable the correct definition of M would use countably generated directed ideals.)

It remains to define $In_{\alpha,\mathcal{M}}$ and $Out_{\alpha,\mathcal{M}}$. For this purpose we assume from now on that for all m there is a condition, x = m, with one free variable x and the obvious meaning (i.e. $[\![[n/x](x = m)]\!] = tt$ iff n equals m). Now just define for any f: N -> M and X $\in$ M:

$In_{\alpha,\mathfrak{M}}(f) = \bigcup\{[\alpha x.\ \underline{if}\ x = 0\ \underline{then}\ t^{(0)}\ \underline{else} \ldots \underline{else}\ (\underline{\ f}\ x = m\ \underline{then}\ t^{(m)}\ \underline{else}\ \Omega)$
$\ldots\ ]\ |\ m \geq 0,\ t^{(i)} \in f(i)\ (\text{for } i = 0,m)\}$

$Out_{\alpha,\mathfrak{M}}(m,X) = \bigcup\{[\alpha(m,t)]\ |\ t \in X\}$

The closure properties of F ensure these definitions are correct and it is easy to show that $In_{\alpha,\mathfrak{M}}$ and $Out_{\alpha,\mathfrak{M}}$ have the required continuity properties, making $\mathfrak{M}$ a natural interpretation.

Note that the definition of $\mathfrak{M}$ does not use the characterisation of $\sqsubseteq$ presented in section 5. However we do use it to prove:

Theorem 6.7 (Full Abstraction) The natural interpretation, $\mathfrak{M}$, is a fully abstract model of CCS and, indeed, is initial in the category of models of CCS and their homomorphisms.

It is possible to construct other fully abstract models, showing that the second part of this theorem has point; it may also be the case that $\mathfrak{M}$ is initial in a wider class of models including "unnatural" interpretations.

Acknowledgements

This research was carried out with the aid of SRC grant GR/A/75125. We thank R. Milner, K. Apt and the referees for their helpful suggestions.

References

[ADJ] (Goguen, J.A., Thatcher, J.W., Wagner, E.G. and Wright, J.B.) (1977) Initial algebra semantics and continuous algebras. JACM, Vol. 24, No. 1, 68-95.

[Apt] Apt, K.R. (1979) Ten years of Hoare's logic, a survey. To appear.

[Bar] Barendregt, H. (1977) The type-free lambda calculus. Handbook of Mathematical Logic (ed. J. Barwise), pp. 1092-1131, Amsterdam: North Holland.

[Ber] Berry, G. (1979) Modèles Complètement Adéquats et Stables des Lambda-Calculus Typeés. Thèse de doctorat d'état. Université Paris VII.

[Cur] Curry, H.B., Feys, R. and Craig, W. (1968) Combinatory Logic, Volume 1. Amsterdam: North Holland.

[Hen1] Hennessy, M.C.B. and Plotkin, G.D. (1979) Full abstraction for a simple parallel programming language. MFCS '79, Olomouc. Springer-Verlag Lecture Notes in Computer Science, Vol. 74, pp. 108-120.

[Hen2] Hennessy, M.C.B. and Milner, R. (1980) On observing nondeterminism and concurrency. ICALP '80, Noordwijkerhout. Springer Verlag Lecture Notes in Computer Science. To appear.

[Hin1] Hindley, J.R., Lercher, B. and Seldin, J.P. (1972) Introduction to combinatory logic. Cambridge: Cambridge University Press.

[Hin2] Hindley, J.R. and Longo, B. (1978) Lambda calculus models and extensionality. Universita degli Studi di Pisa, Istituto di Scienze dell'Informazione. Note Scientifiche S-78-4.

[Lan] Landin, P.J. (1966) A lambda-calculus approach. Chapter 5. Advances in Programming and Non-Numerical Computation. Pergamon Press.

[Mil1] Milne, G.J. and Milner, R. (1979) Concurrent processes and their syntax. JACM, Vol. 26, No. 2, 302-321.

[Mil2] Milner, R. (1976) Models of LCF. Mathematical Centre Tracts, 82, pp. 49-63. Amsterdam.

[Mil3] Milner, R. (1977) Fully abstract models of typed λ-calculi. Theoretical Computer Science, Vol. 4, 1-22.

[Mil4] Milner, R. (1978) Algebras for communicating systems. Proc. AFCET/SMF Joint Colloquium in Applied Mathematics (Palaiseau, France). Also available as CSR-25-78, Computer Science Department, University of Edinburgh, 1978.

[Mil5] Milner, R. (1978) Synthesis of communicating behaviour. Proc. 7th MFCS Conference, Zakopane, Poland. Springer Verlag Lecture Notes in Computer Science, Vol.64, pp. 71-83. Berlin: Springer Verlag.

[Mil6] Milner, R. (1979) An algebraic theory for synchronisation. Theoretical Computer Science 4th GI Conference, Aachen. Springer Verlag Lecture Notes Computer Science, Vol. 67, pp. 27-35. Berlin: Springer Verlag.

[Mil7] Milner, R. (1979) Flowgraphs and flow algebras. JACM, Vol. 26, No. 4, 794-818.

[Obt] Obtulowicz, A. (1977) Functorial semantics of the type free calculus. Fundamentals of Computation Theory. Springer Verlag Lecture Notes in Computer Science, Vol. 56, pp. 302-207. Berlin: Springer Verlag.

[Pet] Petri, C.A. (1976) Nichtsequentielle Prozesse. Arbeitsberichte des IMMD, Bd. 9, Heft. 8, p.57 ff. Universität Erlangen-Nurnberg. Also Non Sequential Processes, Translation by P. Krause and J. Low. Internal Report GMD-ISF-77-05, Bonn (1977).

[Plo] Plotkin, G.D. (1976) A powerdomain construction. SIAM Journal on Computing, Vol. 5, No. 3, 452-487.

[Smy] Smyth, M. (1978) Powerdomains. JCSS, Vol. 16, No. 1.

[Weg] Wegner, P. (1972) The Vienna definition language. Computing Surveys, Vol. 4, No. 1.

[Hoa] Hoare, C.A.R. (1978) Communicating sequential processes. CACM, Vol. 21, No. 8, 666-677.

A MATHEMATICAL APPROACH TO MULTI-PASS PARSING

Berthold Hoffmann*, Ilse-R. Schmiedecke
TU Berlin, DFG-Projekt EAGLE
Ernst-Reuter-Platz 7, TEL 1808
D - 1000 Berlin 10

Abstract:

Derivations from Two-Level Grammars have been defined only in terms of the infinite context-free grammars that can be generated from them. This fact has proven a severe theoretical obstacle to solving the parsing problem for two-level grammars. So far, partial solutions exist for Van Wijngaarden Grammars, Extended Affix Grammars, and Affix Grammars which allow parsing in a single pass from left to right, because these special cases could be handled without developing a full theory of parsing for two-level grammars.

In this paper, we propose a new theory of Extended Affix Grammar derivations. The key idea is to use a graph grammar for modelling the two-level derivation process. This allows us to give a precise definition of a parse, which applies correctly to any well-formed Extended Affix Grammar. The concept of multi-pass parsing originates from practical compiler design, where parses are organized as a sequence of passes in order to avoid random access to the full parse tree. We demonstrate how this concept can be incorporated into our theoretical framework by means of canonical graph derivations. This allows us not only to establish the adequacy of the multi-pass approach, but can also be used as a complexity measure for Extended Affix Grammars.

Keywords:

Extended Affix Grammars, Graph Grammars, Two-Level Derivations, Parsing, Passes, Pass-Complexity.

0. INTRODUCTION

This paper deals with the problem of parsing two-level grammars, which, in general, require more than one analysis pass.

Two-level grammars have been introduced by A. van Wijngaarden in 1965 [Wij 65] and have become well-known as van Wijngaarden Grammars (W-Grammars, VWGs) through the ALGOL68 report [A68 RR]. After their initial acceptance as a definition tool, mathematical treatment revealed several difficulties and inadequacies, such as their type 0-equivalence [Sin 67], and the undecidability of the cross-reference problem [Kos 74]. Further research lead to restrictions [Bak 72, Gre 74, Deu 75], and even parsing algorithms for restricted classes of VWGs [Weg 78a].

In 1970 C.H.A. Koster suggested to use another kind of two-level grammars, "akin to VWGS" but immediately suited to parsing, for the implementation of ALGOL68; he called them Affix Grammars [Kos 71a]. A compiler compiler for Affix Grammars, called CDL, was

---

*Work supported by the German Research Society (DFG).

soon implemented and is still used with very good results [Kos 71b,CDL 76].

In 1974, D.A. Watt introduced so-called Extended Affix Grammars (EAGs) which are really VWGs restricted such as to have the "neat" properties of Affix Grammars [Wat 75]. He also defined a parsing technique for EAGs, which was implemented in 1976 by H. Franzen and the authors [FHP 76].

However, all three approaches to solving the parsing problem for two-level grammars share one severe restriction: They only apply to grammars for which parsing can be achieved during a single scan over the input. We believe the reason for this restriction is the fact that the properties of such one-pass parses can still be captured by regarding canonical derivations from the infinite context-free grammar which is defined by the two-level grammar. For a more general treatment, however, parsing has to be defined independant of this infinite grammar.

In this paper, such a definition is developed for Extended Affix Grammars. We concentrate on EAGs for two reasons: Firstly, we consider EAGs a useful restriction to VWGs, as they disallow the typically intractible VWG constructions; and secondly there is a realistic perspective of obtaining a generalized parser generator by modifying the existing software.

We proceed in three major steps. Section one contains the problem specification. First, we introduce Extended Affix Grammars; then, the parsing problem is stated, contrasting the general question of decidability to parsability requirements. In section two, the mathematical framework of a general solution to the parsing problem is developed. We first follow Watt's approach [Wat 75] and transform the EAG into an equivalent Affix Grammar. From the Affix Grammar, a graph grammar is obtained, which defines so-called affix-decorated parse trees as an analogue to parse trees for context-free grammars. It is shown that derivation sequences from this graph grammar provide an adequate model for EAG parses (Theorem 2.12). Finally, in section three, practical considerations lead to defining canonical graph derivations to describe pass-structured parsers, and it is shown that such a space efficient multi-pass parse exists for each word of a parsable EAG (Theorem 3.3).

Because of the multitude of definitions and results we need to unfold this theory, theorems are either given without proof, or the proof is just sketched. Readers interested in the details are referred to [HS 80], which is a long version of this paper, containing full proofs.

1. THE PARSING PROBLEM FOR EAGs

Extended Affix Grammars

Extended Affix Grammars (EAGs) should be regarded as restricted VWGs which can be used for parser generation. They were first defined by Watt [Wat 75]. The general definition below hardly restricts VWGs at all; most of the affix grammar properties are imposed on EAGs by means of additional well-formedness conditions which we shall introduce in the next subsection (definition 1.7).

Definition 1.1 An Extended Affix Grammar (EAG) G is a two-level grammar given by G = (AT, ANT, AR, HT, HNT, HR, arity, s, AV, type) such that 1-3 are satisfied.

1. The affix level AL_G = (AT, ANT, AR) is a context-free grammar scheme with alphabets AT (affix terminals), and ANT (affix nonterminals), context-free production rules AR (affix rules), such that for $a \in ANT$, $AL_G(a)$ = (AT, ANT, AR, a) is a context-free grammar with start symbol a.
2. The hyper level (HL_G) is a 7-tuple HL_G = (HT, HNT, HR, arity, s, AV, AT) with
   - four alphabets, HT (hyperterminals), HNT (hyper nonterminals), AV (affix variables), AT (as above),
   - a function arity: HNT $\rightarrow \mathbb{N}$,
   - a start symbol $s \in HNT$ with arity (s) = 0,
   - and a set $HR \subset HN \times (HN \cup HT)^*$ of hyperrules, (written $hn_0 \rightarrow hn_1, \ldots, hn_k$) where HN, the set of hypernotions, is defined as $HN = \{h(s_1, \ldots, s_n) \mid h \in HNT$, n = arity (h), $s_i \in (AV \cup AT)^*$ for $1 \leq i \leq n\}$. The s_i are called the affixes of the hypernotions; they are called affix expressions if they do not consist of a single affix variable.
3. type is a function type: AV $\rightarrow$ ANT. □

Example 1 shows the affix rules and the first few hyperrules of an EAG for a very simple block-structured language, which does not restrict the order of declaration and application of identifiers, but disallows double declaration and the use of undeclared identifiers. The start symbol is "program"; arity is given implicitly by the number of affixes, type by the letter portion of affix variables. The rôle of the three symbol tables is hard to understand without knowing the full example, which is given in [HS 80]: The second list covers the left context and is updated to yield the third one, while the first list covers the entire context.

Example 1: EAG fragment "Exgram"

{a, b}	*L:: nil; L and T.*	{*List of Identifiers*}
{c, d}	*T:: x; x T.*	{*Identifiers*}
{1}	*program: block (nil).*	
{2}	*block (L): 'BEGIN', stmts (L_1, L, L_1), 'END'.*	
{3}	*stmts (L, L_1, L_3): stmt (L, L_1, L_3);*	
{4}	*stmts (L, L_1, L_2), ';', stmt (L, L_2, L_3). ...*	

The most important aspect in which EAGs differ from general VWGs is the structure of the hypernotions: Each hypernotion possesses a "handle" which is not a derivation from the affix level. Thus, a context-free skeleton is immediately apparent from the grammar by simply ignoring the affixes:

Definition 1.2 The underlying context-free grammar of an EAG G, UG(G) is given by

UG(G) = (HT, HNT, HR_u, s) where

- HT, HNT, s are defined as in G
- $HR_u = \{ proj(hn_0) \rightarrow proj(hn_1) \ldots proj(hn_k) \mid hn_0 \rightarrow hn_1 \ldots hn_k \in HR \}$ with

  proj: $(HN \cup HT) \longrightarrow (HNT \cup HT)$ given as $proj(hn) = \begin{cases} hn & \text{if } hn \in HT \\ h & \text{if } hn = h(s_1, \ldots, s_n) \in HN \end{cases}$ □

In fact, we have $L(UG(G)) \supset L(G)$, so that the underlying context-free grammar provides a helpful clue to understanding a language definition. This type of structuring of the grammar into a context-free skeleton with the second level added to its nonterminals is a commom property of parsing-oriented two-level grammars, both Attribute and Affix Grammars [Knu 68, Kas 80]. In contrast to Attribute Grammars, however, a two-level derivation is defined for Affix Grammars and EAGs, which includes the affix evaluation. Similar to VWG derivations, a proto level grammar is obtained from the EAG by uniformly replacing affixes by terminal affixes, and all derivations are based on this infinite context-free grammar.

Definition 1.3 Let G be an EAG as defined in definition 1.1. A uniform replacement in G is a function ur: $AV \rightarrow AT^*$ such that $ur(v) \in L(AL(type(v)))$.

ur^* is the natural extension of ur onto affix expressions $s \in (AV \cup AT)^*$:

let $s = d_1 \ldots d_n$, then

$ur^*(s) = \bar{d}_1 \ldots \bar{d}_n$ such that for $1 \le i \le n$, $\bar{d}_i = \begin{cases} d_i & \text{for } d_i \in AT \\ ur(d_i) & \text{for } d_i \in AV \end{cases}$.

Similarly, $eval_{ur}$ is the natural extension of ur onto hypernotions and hyperrules. □

Definition 1.4 Let G be an EAG as defined in defintion 1.1. The proto level grammar of G, PG(G), is the infinfite context-free grammar PG(G) = (PT, PN, PR, s) where

- PT = HT is its terminal alphabet,
- PN is an infinite "alphabet" of protonotions

  $PN = \{ eval_{ur}(hn) \mid hn \in HN,$ ur is uniform replacement in G$\}$,
- PR is an infinite set of protorules

  $PR = \{ eval_{ur}(hr) \mid hr \in HR,$ ur is uniform replacement in G$\}$,
- s is the common start symbol of G and PG(G).

A derivation in PG(G) is called proto derivation. Instead of rules pr ∈ PR, the steps of a proto derivation may be annotated by pairs (hr, ur) s.t. $eval_{ur}(hr) = pr$; in this case the derivation sequence is called explicit proto derivation. □

Definition 1.5 The language generated by an EAG G is defined as the language generated by its proto level grammar: L(G) = L(PG(G)). □

Example 2: Beginning of a proto derivation in "Exgram"

Rule, uniform replacement	*sentential form*
	program
1	*block(nil)*
2 $L=nil, L_1=nil$ *and x*	*BEGIN stmts(nil and x,nil,nil and x) END*
4 $L=L_3=nil$ *and x,* $L_1=L_2=nil$	*BEGIN stmts(nil and x,nil,nil) ; stmt(nil and x,nil,nil and x) END*
3 $L=nil$ *and x,* $L_1=L_3=nil$	*BEGIN stmt(nil and x,nil,nil) ; stmt(nil and x,nil,nil and x) END*
.	.
.	.

Decidability and Parsabiltiy Properties

In spite of their more lucid structure, general EAGs raise the same problems as VWGs: They are Turing-equivalent, and not even the cross-reference problem [*Kos 74*] is decidable for two arbitrary hypernotions, as this amounts to solving the non-empty intersection problem for context-free languages.

Now, decidability can easily be established by immediately applying the decidability restriction which Wegner gives for "predicative" VWGs [Weg 78b] (c.f. also [Deu 75]). As far as practical parsing is concerned, however, this criterion is not very helpful; for, it is quite restrictive on the grammar, and it does not support any efficient parsing algorithm.

For parsing to be efficient, we want it to be a deterministic algorithm based on the finite EAG, rather than on its infinite proto level grammar. This requires unambiguous grammmars for which the cross-reference problem is efficiently solvable and for which there is an effective procedure for determining the uniform replacement function of each production step.

Well-formed Affix Grammars meet these requirements; we shall introduce similar well-formedness conditions for EAGs to make the parsing problem solvable. But let us first define what we mean by an unambiguous EAG:

Definition 1.6 An EAG G is called unambiguous if it satisfies the following conditions:

1. G is hyperrule determined, i.e. any two explicit proto derivations defining the same proto derivation have the same HR-annotations on their production steps.
2. G is metadetermined, (c.f. [Weg 78b]), i.e. if two explicit proto derivations coincide in their HR-annotations, they also coincide in their ur-annotations.
3. The affix level AL(a) is unambiguous for all a ∈ ANT. □

Notice that hyperrule determinism is closely related to the way in which the context-free skeleton is recognized; therefore, the corresponding grammar restrictions vary with the parsing algorithm. The other two conditions are established by the following well-formedness criteria:

Definition 1.7 A well-formed EAG is a two-level grammar $G' = (G, dom, dir)$ where G is an EAG satisfying the following conditions:

1. For all $a \in ANT$, the affix level grammar AL(a) is unambiguous.

2. There exists a domain function dom: $APOS \longrightarrow ANT$, with $APOS = \{(h,i) \mid h \in HNT, 1 \le i \le arity(h)\}$, such that $HN = \{h(s_1,...,s_n) \mid h \in HNT, n=arity(h)$, and for $1 \le i \le arity(h)$ $dom(h,i) \overset{*}{\Longrightarrow} type^*(s_i)\}$ (where $type^*: (AV \cup AT)^* \longrightarrow (ANT \cup AT)^*$ is the natural extension of type onto affix expressions).

3. There is a direction function dir: $APOS \longrightarrow \{inh, der\}$ which divides the affix positions of a hyperrule $r = h_1(...) \rightarrow t_0h_1(...)t_1...h_n(...)$, where for $0 \le i \le n$, $h_i \in HNT$, $t_i \in HT^*$, into defining positions $DEF(r) = \{(i,j) \mid 0 \le i \le k, (h_i,j) \in APOS$ and (($i=0$ and $dir(h_i,j)=inh$) or ($i>0$ and $dir(h_i,j)=der$)) $\}$ and applied positions $APP(r) = \{(i,j) \mid 0 \le i \le k, (h_i,j) \in APOS, (i,j) \notin DEF(r)\}$, such that if an affix variable v occurs in an applied position in the hyperrule r, v also occurs in at least one defining position in r.

4. The direction function is given such that, for any possible derivation, the affix dependency relation FD, which connects applied occurrences of affix variables to their corresponding defining ones (c.f. [DM 78, Kas 80]) is acyclic. (For the formal definition of FD see [HS 80]). □

Although dom and dir can be determined automatically, we usually give them in the grammar. For the EAG fragment "Exgram", all affix positions have the same domain, "L". Example 3 indicates the direction function by means of arrows: An arrow in front of an affix means "inherited" (inh), behind it, "derived" (der).

Example 3: Direction function for "Exgram"

{1} *program: block (>nil).*

{2} *block (>L): 'BEGIN', stmts (>L₁, >L, L₁>), 'END'.*

{3} *stmts (>L, >L₁, L₃>): stmt (>L, >L₁, L₃>);*

{4} *stmts (>L, >L₁, L₂>), ';', stmt (>L, >L₂, L₃>).*

For EAGs which satisfy conditions 1 and 2, the cross-reference problem is reduced to solving the word problem for a context-free grammar and therefore easily solvable. In particular, if condition 1 is further restricted to, say, LR(k) grammars, this becomes a linear problem, and condition 1 is rendered decidable. It is a well-known result that such a restriction does not reduce the power of a two-level grammar. Conditions 3 and 4 establish metadeterminism, so that altogether we have

Theorem 1.8 A well-formed EAG is unambiguous if it is hyperrule determined. □

Notice that EAG-unambiguity does imply the unambiguity of the proto level grammar, but not of the underlying context-free grammar. This is the major reason why EAG parsing is such an intricate problem.

2. TOWARDS A SOLUTION OF THE EAG PARSING PROBLEM

In his definition of Affix Grammars, Koster differentiates between recognition and parsing [Kos 71a]. In contrast to the mere recognition of a word, a parser must yield some representation of its derivation which can be used in the subsequent translation process. The appropriate data structure for EAGs is the so-called affix decorated parse tree (ADPT). It consists, basically, of the parse tree of the underlying context-free grammar, plus, for each affix position, a derivation tree of its terminal substitution from its domain. It is a collapsed tree, because all occurences of an affix variable in a production are represented by identical subtrees.

In this section, a graph grammar defining the set of ADPTs of an EAG is used as a mathematical model of an EAG parse. The idea is that the graph grammar captures the structural and functional dependencies between affixes; it can therefore be used to model the integrated derivation of the context-free skeleton and the affixes, which is primarily a question of order. We proceed in three steps. First, we follow Watt's one-pass approach, defining the equivalent Affix Grammar of an EAG. Based on this Affix Grammar, the graph grammar and a general EAG parse are defined.

The Affix Grammar AG(G)

The Affix Grammars which we obtain from EAGs are a restricted subclass of the general Affix Grammars defined by Koster [Kos 71]; in particular, they possess only a fixed set of "primitive predicates", and do not have any affix expressions in affix positions. Our well-formedness conditions, on the other hand, are less restrictive because we do not insist on one-pass and LL properties.

Definition 2.1 (Watt) Let G = (AT, ANT, AR, HT, HNT, HR, arity, s, AV, type, dom, dir) be a well-formed EAG. Its related Affix Grammar, AG(G) is defined as AG(G) = (AT, ANT, AR, HT, HNT, Q, HR', arity', s, AV', type', dom', dir', F) where

- AT, ANT, AR, HT, HNT, s are defined as in G,
- Q is a set of primitive predicate symbols $Q = \{synth_z \mid z \in AR\} \cup \{anal_z \mid z \in AR\} \cup \{equal_A \mid A \in ANT\}$ which is disjoint of all alphabets in AG(G),
- arity', dom', dir' are natural extensions of the corresponding EAG mappings onto Q, which, together with the set of control functions $F = \{F_q \mid q \in Q\}$ define the production behaviour of the predicates as mappings of their inherited into their derived affixes:

  Let $z \in AR$ be of the form $A_0 \rightarrow t_0 A_1 t_1 \dots t_{n-1} A_n t_n$, with $A_i \in ANT$, $t_i \in AT^*$, $1 \leq i \leq n$, and let $|z|_{ANT}$ denote the number of affix nonterminals of z, i.e $|z|_{ANT} = n+1$.

  anal$_z$ is a decomposition predicate, mapping an affix nonterminal into its nonterminal substructures, if they correspond to the structure of z:

  $\text{arity}'(anal_z) = |z|_{ANT}$; $\text{dom}'(anal_z, i) = A_{i-1}$;

  $\text{dir}'(anal_z, i) =$ if i=1 then inh else der;

$F_{anal_z} : L(A_0) \longrightarrow L(A_1) \times \ldots \times L(A_n) \cup \{\underline{false}\};$

$F_{anal_z}(x_0) = \underline{if}\ x_0 = t_0x_1t_1 \ldots x_nt_n\ \underline{then}\ (x_1, \ldots, x_n)\ \underline{else}\ \underline{false};$

$\underline{synth_z}$ is the inverse function of $anal_z$:

$arity'(synth_z) = |z|_{ANT};\quad dom'(synth_z, i) = \underline{if}\ i=|z|_{ANT}\ \underline{then}\ A_0\ \underline{else}\ A_i;$

$dir'(synth_z, i) = \underline{if}\ i=|z|_{ANT}\ \underline{then}\ der\ \underline{else}\ inh;$

$F_{synth_z} : L(A_1) \times \ldots \times L(A_n) \longrightarrow L(A_0);$

$F_{synth_z}(x_1, \ldots, x_n) = t_0x_1t_1 \ldots x_nt_n;$

$\underline{equal_A}$, for $A \in ANT$, is a structural comparison predicate between two affixes of domain A:

$arity'(equal_A) = 2;\quad dom'(equal_A, i) = A$ for $i=1,2;\quad dir'(equal_A, i) = inh$ for $i=1,2$

$F_{equal_A} : L(A) \times L(A) \longrightarrow \{\underline{true}, \underline{false}\};$

$F_{equal_A}(x_1, x_2) = \underline{if}\ x_1=x_2\ \underline{then}\ \underline{true}\ \underline{else}\ \underline{false}.$

- HR' is a set of simple hyperrules $HR' \subset HN' \times (HN' \cup QN' \cup HT)^*$ where $HN' = \{h(v_1,\ldots,v_n) \mid h \in HNT,\ n=arity'(h),\ v_i \in AV',\ type'(v_i) = dom'(h,i)\}$ is a set of simple hypernotions, and QN' is a set of simple predicate notions defined analogously for $q(v_1,\ldots,v_n)$, $q \in Q$. HR' is obtained from HR as follows:
  - Let $s \in (AV \cup AT)^*$ be an affix expression occurring in the affix position (h,i) of a hyperrule $r \in HR$. Construct the derivation tree t for $dom(h,i) \overset{*}{\Longrightarrow} type^*(s)$ The elementary trees will be of the form

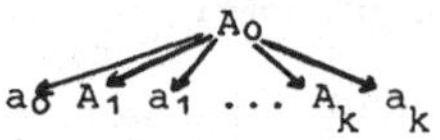

    representing an affix rule $z = A_0 \rightarrow a_0A_1a_1 \ldots A_ka_k$. Associate with each link node A_i a new affix variable V_i with $type'(V_i) = A_i$. For leaf nodes A_i of t, take instead the corresponding variables V_i in s. Construct, for each elementary tree in t, a predicate notion $synth_z(V_1,\ldots,V_k,V_0)$ or $anal_z(V_0,V_1,\ldots,V_k)$. Replace s in r by the variable associated with the root of t. — If (h,i) is an applied affix position in r, concatenate the synth predicates according to a postfix traversal of t, and place them before h in r; otherwise, concatenate the anal predicates in prefix order, and place them behind h in r.
  - Let a variable V occur in two defining positions in r; then one occurrence of V is replaced by a new variable V', and a predicate notion $equal_A(V,V')$ is introduced in r, where $A = type(V) = type'(V')$.
- AV' and type' are extensions of AV and type to include the newly introduced affix variables. □

Our example grammar "Exgram" contains only one non-simple hyperrule, namely rule 1. Example 4 shows its transformation into a simple hyperrule.

<u>Example 4:</u> Transformation of "Exgram" into AG("Exgram")

{a}	*L :: nil.*	======>	*{a'}*	F_{synth_a} *= nil.*
{1}	*program: block (>nil).*		*{1'}*	*program:* $synth_a$ *(L>), block (>L).*

Definition 2.2 (Watt) Let AG(G) be given as in definition 2.1. The proto level grammar of AG(G), PG(AG(G)), is the infinite context-free grammar PG = (PT, PN, PR', s) where
- PT, PN and s are defined as in PG(G) (definition 1.4),
- $PR' = \overline{PR} \cup \overline{QR}$ is an infinite set of protorules,

$\overline{PR} = \{eval_{ur}(hr) \mid hr \in HR'$ and ur is uniform replacement in AG(G)$\}$,

$\overline{QR} = \{q(x_1, \ldots, x_m) \rightarrow \varepsilon \mid q \in Q, (x_1, \ldots, x_m) \in F_q\}$, and ur is defined as in 1.3. □

Definition 2.3 (Watt) The language generated by AG(G) is the language of its proto level grammar: L(AG(G)) = L(PG(AG(G))). □

Theorem 2.4 (Watt) An EAG G and its related Affix Grammar AG(G) define the same language: L(G) = L(AG(G)). □

In fact, the structural coherence between an EAG and its corresponding Affix Grammar is much stronger than stated in theorem 2.4: As intended, the conversion of a well-formed EAG always yields a well-formed Affix Grammar. Somewhat more striking is the observation that, after some standardization on PG(AG(G)), both G and AG(G) have the same proto level grammar.

Affix Grammars possess one important new property compared to EAGs: They do not contain any affix expressions, but only simple affix variables. This allows us to use the variable for identifying an affix during a derivation, even when we do not know its terminal replacement. In the graph grammar below, we shall make use of this fact for the initial representation of affixes in the parse tree: We just represent them by the roots of their derivation trees.

The Graph Grammar GG(G)

Graph grammars are rewriting systems for graphs, i.e. the result of a derivation step is a replacement of one subgraph of a host graph by another one. The work in this paper is founded on the theory of graph grammars according to [Ehr 79]. We only recall the basic definitions here in order to introduce the necessary notation. For further detail, the reader is referred to the survey paper mentioned.

Definition 2.5 (Ehrig) A (labelled) graph G = (E, N, source, target, $label_E$, $label_N$) consists of a set of edges, E, a set of nodes, N, two mappings, source: $E \longrightarrow N$, target: $E \longrightarrow N$, and two labelling maps, $label_E: E \longrightarrow L_E$, $label_N: N \longrightarrow L_N$, where L_E is an alphabet of edge labels, and L_N is an alphabet of node labels.
For simplicity, we often just give one combined map label: $E \cup N \longrightarrow L_E \cup L_N$, provided, E and N are distinct. □

Definition 2.6 (Ehrig) A graph production p is a pair of graph morphisms $p = (B_1 \xleftarrow{'b} K \xrightarrow{b'} B_2)$ where B_1 is called the left hand side, B_2 the right hand side, and K the interface of p.

A direct derivation $G_1 \Longrightarrow G_2$ using the graph production p is obtained by first determining an occurrence of B_1 in G_1, and then replacing B_1 by B_2 using 'b and b'.

A <u>graph grammar</u> is defined as a quadruple, consisting of a label alphabet, a terminal label alphabet, a start graph and a set of graph productions. □

For the graph grammar defining ADPTs, the alphabets are of course defined in terms of the alphabets of the Affix Grammar AG(G), and the productions in terms of its hyper-rules:

<u>Definition 2.7</u> Let G be a well-formed EAG according to 1.1 and 1.6, and let AG(G) be its related Affix Grammar according to 2.1; then GG(G), the <u>related graph grammar</u> of G, is defined as GG(G) = (L, T, S, P) where

- $L = (L_N, L_E)$ is a label alphabet, $L_N = (\overline{HNT} \cup \overline{Q} \cup \overline{HT} \cup \overline{ANT} \cup \overline{AT}) \cup (HNT \cup Q \cup ANT)$, $L_E = \mathbb{N}$;
- $T = (T_N, T_E)$ is a terminal label alphabet, $T_N = (\overline{HNT} \cup \overline{Q} \cup \overline{HT} \cup \overline{ANT} \cup \overline{AT})$, $T_E = \mathbb{N}$;
- S is the start graph, which is a single node v with label(v) = s ∈ HNT;
- P = {gr(hr) | hr ∈ HR'} ∪ {gr(q) | q ∈ Q} is a finite set of graph productions, which are partly labelled in such a way that all graphs derivable from S are labelled. The definition of gr is given further down. □

Although this does not show up in our results and hardly effects the methods, let us remark here that our use of partly labelled graph productions is not quite covered by the theory of graph grammars, but leads us into the theory of structures [ER 79]. This however allows us to regard node labels as pairs (colour(v), mark), where colour: N ⟶ (HNT ∪ Q ∪ HT ∪ ANT ∪ AT) and a missing mark indicates nonterminal labels.

<u>Convention 2.8</u> In the following definition, we shall give P in a graphical representation. B , K, and B are given explicitly, 'b and b' are given implicitly by using the same layout for all three constituent graphs.

The labelling of the nodes is partly represented by the node shapes. We draw a node v

- as a box, if colour(v) ∈ HNT ∪ Q
- as a bar, if colour(v) ∈ HT
- as a circle, if colour(v) ∈ ANT
- as a blot, if colour(v) ∈ AT.

A fat-lined box or circle is used for nonterminal labelling, an unlined node for terminal labelling. Thin linings indicate a free choice between terminal and nonterminal labels.

Hence, the start graph of GG(G) will be drawn as 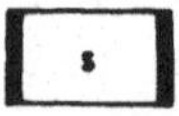

. □

<u>Definition 2.9</u> The function gr: HR' ∪ Q ⟶ P is defined as follows:

- Let, without loss of generality, hr ∈ HR' be of the form
$h_o(V_{o1},\ldots,V_{oi}, V_{o,i+1},\ldots,V_{om_o}) \rightarrow t_1\, h_1(V_{11},\ldots,V_{1m_1}) \ldots h_k(V_{k1},\ldots,V_{km_k})\, t_k$,
with h_o ∈ HNT and $dir(h_o,j)$ = <u>if</u> $1 \leq j \leq i$ <u>then</u> inh <u>else</u> der, h_i ∈ HNT ∪ Q for $1 \leq i \leq k$, t_i ∈ HT for $0 \leq i \leq k$, V_{ij} ∈ AV' and $dom'(h_i,j) = A_{ij}$ for $0 \leq i \leq k$ and $1 \leq j \leq m_i = arity'(h_i)$;

then, gr(hr) is defined by

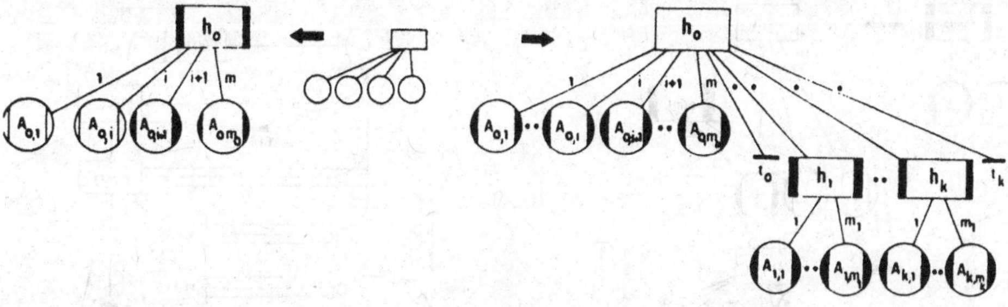

(where the edges marked with a dot are labelled with increasing numbers, starting from m_0+1), with the following modification (elimination of multiple variable nodes, c.f. example 5):

Let $V_{i_1,j_1} = V_{i_2,j_2}$ be affix variables in hr with $(i_1, j_1) \neq (i_2,j_2)$; let e_1,e_2 be the edges in gr(hr) for which for k=1,2, label$(e_k) = j_k$ and colour(source$(e_k)) = h_{i_k}$; if $(i_1,j_1) \in$ DEF(hr), then target(e_2) is eliminated, and e_2 is redirected into target (e_1).

- Let $z \in$ AR be of the form $A_0 \rightarrow a_0A_1a_1...A_ma_m$ with $A_i \in$ ANT, $a_i \in AT^*$ for $0 \leq i \leq m$, then, gr(synth$_z$) is defined by and gr(anal$_z$) is defined by

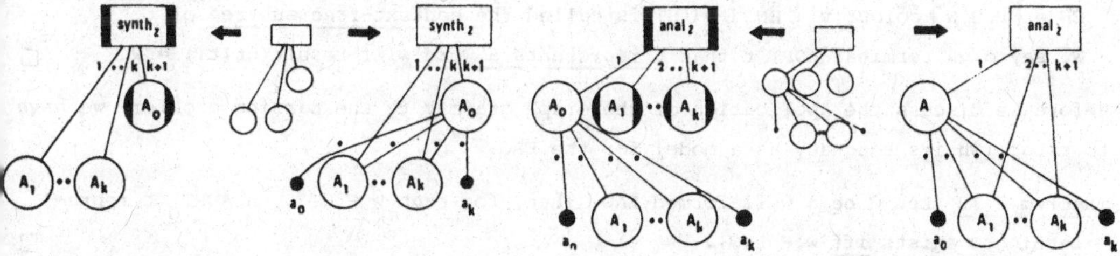

(In both cases, the edges marked with a dot are labelled with increasing numbers, starting from 1.)

- For A $\in$ ANT, gr(equal$_A$) is defined as expected, i.e. it has a terminal derivation only for equal affix graphs; the details are given in [HS 80]. □

Definition 2.10 A graph derived from GG(G) is called Affix Decorated Parse Tree of G, short ADPT$_G$. (If no misunderstanding is possible, the index G is omitted.) □

In example 5, we give the graph productions for hyperrules 3 and 4, and a nonterminal ADPT derived from GG("Exgram"). The interfaces of the graph productions are given implicitly by means of number tags on the nodes of the left and right hand side.

The EAG rules of "Exgram" seem to imply the existence of a great number of different affixes in the ADPT; but the example shows that this impression is quite misleading. The main structure of the ADPT is a context-free parse tree, which in particular contains all terminal symbols of the sentential form it represents.

Example 5: Graph productions and ADPT for "Exgram"

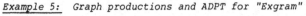

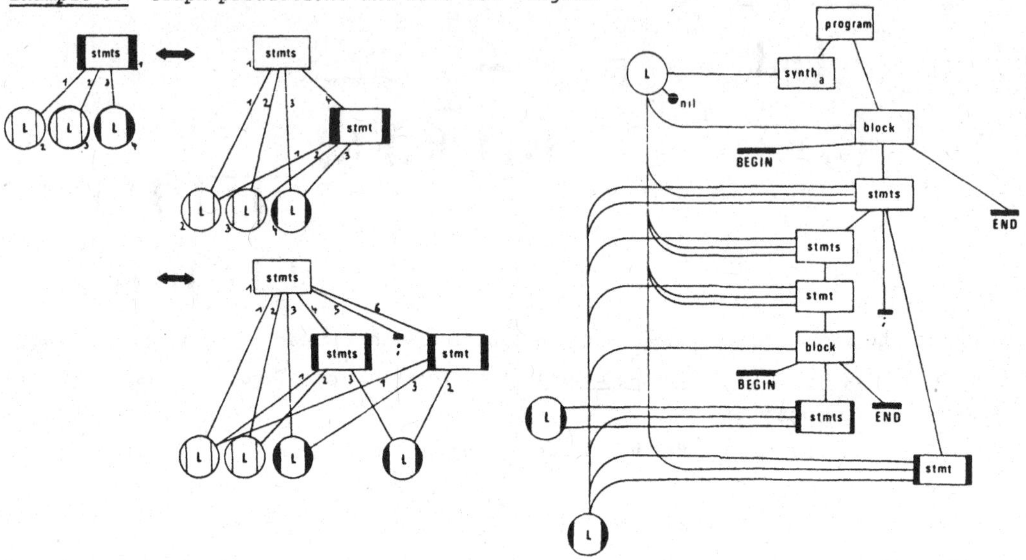

Definition 2.11 Let t = (N, E, source, target, label) be an ADPT derived from GG(G). Then its full subtree ct(t) = (CN, CE, source', target', label) defined by CN = {v ∈ N | colour(v) ∈ HNT ∪ Q ∪ HT} is called the context-free subtree of t. We say of a terminal ADPT t that t represents a word w if result(ct(t)) = w. □

Before we discuss the application of the graph grammar to the parsing problem, we have to establish its adequacy as a model for the EAG:

Theorem 2.12 Let G be a well-formed EAG. Then, for each $w \in HT^*$, an $ADPT_G$ t representing w exists iff w ∈ L(G). □

This theorem is proven by tranforming an ADPT into a proto derivation tree, and by transforming a proto derivation into a graph derivation. The latter step is quite instructive for understanding the significance of the graph grammar: It is impossible to find, for an arbitrary proto derivation, a graph derivation which runs step-by-step in parallel with it. Rather, the proto derivation must first be reordered according to the functional dependecy relation FD. The reason is that graph derivations do not allow for guesses about the ur functions; on the other hand, the re-ordering always succeeds because well-formed EAGs are metadetermined. In conclusion, graph derivations are integrated derivations of both the context-free sekeleton and the affixes.

The Parse of an EAG

Notice the impact of the above theorem: For every derivable word, there is a graph derivation, which integrates the context-free and the affix derivation. Hence, we could use a graph derivation in GG(G) as a model of the derivation in G and be sure that the model is correct. However, a graph parse is not what we want; for we are interested in analysing a string, not a graph. Therefore, let us reconsider the relation between a word and an ADPT representing it.

Theorem 2.13 If G is an unambiguous EAG, then for each word $w \in L(G)$, the ADPT representing w is uniquely defined. □

This means that the relation between EAG ambiguity and the ADPT is the same as between context-free ambiguity and the context-free parse tree. It is therefore adequate to define an EAG parse as follows:

Definition 2.14 A parse of a word $w \in L(G)$, where G is a well-formed EAG, is a graph derivation in GG(G) of an ADPT representing w. □

3. MULTI - PASS PARSING

The parse defined in 2.14 works, i.e. it succeeds iff the parsed word is in the language, and it generates a well-defined parse tree, the ADPT. However, the ADPT is a large data structure, and in general, random access to it is required during a parse. In practical compiler construction, it is a well-known technique to organize the operations on the internal representation of a program - the ADPT in our case - into so-called passes, each of which performs a unidirectional traversal of it. The advantage of this discipline is twofold: The amount of code resident in core is smaller, because passes can be loaded one after another, and the internal representation is accessed sequentially, so that it can be read from a sequential file during processing, and at any time, only a small portion of it has to be kept in primary storage.

This technique is incorporated into our theory by defining, for each parse, an equivalent canonical parse which obeys the above discipline.

Definition 3.1 A pass is a graph derivation $t_1 \rightarrow \ldots \rightarrow t_m$ such that
- in $t_1 \rightarrow t_2$, a production is applied to the first productive node of ct(t) in prefix order;
- for $1 < i < m$, it holds that if in $t_{i-1} \rightarrow t_i$ a production is applied to a node v_1, and in $t_i \rightarrow t_{i+1}$ a production is applied to v_2, then v_2 is the next productive node following v_1 in $ct(t_i)$ in prefix order;
- if in $t_{m-1} \rightarrow t_m$ a production is applied to a node v, then none of the successors of v in $ct(t_m)$ in prefix order is productive. □

Definition 3.2 A multi-pass parse of a word $w \in L(G)$ is a parse of w which is subdivided into passes $p_1, p_2, \ldots, p_n$, with $p_i = t_{i1} \rightarrow t_{i2} \rightarrow \ldots \rightarrow t_{im_i}$ such that
- $t_{im_i} = t_{i+1,1}$ for $1 \leq i \leq n-1$;
- $t_{11} = S$, the start graph of the graph grammar;
- $result(ct(t_{nm_n})) = w$.

n is called the pass-complexity of the parse. □

Theorem 3.3 For every well-formed EAG G and every word $w \in HT^*$, there is a multi-pass parse of w iff $w \in L(G)$.

The multi-pass parse is uniquely defined if G is unambiguous. □

Finally, notice that the pass-complexity of a parse is mainly a property of the grammar, so that it is meanigful to extend the above definition as follows:

Definition 3.4 The pass-complexity of a word w in G is the minimum pass-complexity of all multi-pass parses of w in G. The pass-complexity of the grammar G is the maximum pass-complexity of all words $w \in L(G)$ in G. □

Notice however that the pass-complexity of a grammar is not always defined; for there are cases where the pass-complexity of a word in G is an unbounded function of the word This consideration leads to an important further classification of EAGs, namely into grammars of constant pass complexity, for which such a number exists, and those of unlimited pass-complexity. Grammars of constant pass-complexity are of particular interest, because parsers can be generated from them which do not have to decide at runtime on their iteration behaviour. This topic shall be discussed in a forhtcoming paper; let us only note here that there is an effective procedure for determining the pass-complexity of a grammar and that the class of constant-pass grammars is reasonably large.

4. CONCLUSION

In this paper, we have given a mathematical model for multi-pass parsing of Extended Affix Grammars (EAGs). The motivation of the work presented here is a very practical one: To render two-level grammars a useful, well-defined tool both for the specification and implementation of programming languages. We are therefore aiming at compiler-compilers which process EAGs not only to produce correct translators, but also to assist the understanding of the language definition. The automatic extraction of the underlying context-free language, or a pass-complexity analysis pointing at the complexity raising hyperrules are only two examples for such assistance on various levels.

Numerous practical concepts for compiler generation exist already, some within the project, others are implemented in compiler generators for Attribute Grammars [LB 74, Loh 77, GW 77]. To keep up with our aim, however, we need a sound theoretical foundation of our concepts. Here, we have obtained a principle solution to the general parsing problem. Through its formalization, parsing has been defined for the most general class of EAGs which can be expected to be parsable, namely well-formed EAGs.

Furthermore, the graph grammar approach taken allowed us to formalize a very practical optimization, the pass-structuring of a parse. Other existing optimization concepts, such as the "delay-supply scheme" for EAGs [FHS 78], or pass-complexity reducing grammar transformations, can easily be incorporated in the theory. In the near future, we intend to formalize as many of them as possible in order to prove their correctness and optimization power.

Finally, let us recall that EAGs are really just restricted van Wijngaarden Grammars, and that our approach makes use of a certain class of Affix Grammars. The result given here can therefore be expected to be helpful in overcoming the present one-pass restriction in these other two-level grammars.

REFERENCES:

[A68RR] WIJNGAARDEN v., A. (ed): Revised Report on the Algorithmic Language ALGOL68. Springer-Verlag, Berlin-Heidelberg-New York (1974)

[Bak72] BAKER, John L.: Grammars with Structured Vocabulary: a Model for the ALGOL-68 Definition. Information & Control 20, pp. 351-359 (1972)

[CDL76] DEHOTTAY, J.-P., FEUERHAHN, H., KOSTER, C.H.A., STAHL, H.-M.: Syntaktische Beschreibung von CDL2. Technical Report, Research Group Softwaretechnik, TU Berlin (1976)

[Deu75] DEUSSEN, P.: A Decidability Criterion for van Wijngaarden Grammars. Acta Informatica 5, pp. 355-375 (1975)

[DM78] DEMBINSKI, P., MAŁUSZINSKI, J.: Attribute Grammars and Two-Level Grammars: A Unifying Approach. Proc. of the 7th Symposium on Mathematical Foundations of Computer Science, LNCS 64, Zakopane (1978)

[Ehr79] EHRIG, H.: Introduction to the Algebraic Theory of Graph Grammars. In: Proceedings of the International Workshop on Graph Grammars and their Applications to Computer Science and Biology. Springer, LNCS 73, pp. 1-69 (1979)

[FHP76] FRANZEN, H., HOFFMANN, B., PETERSEN, I.-R.: Ein Parser-Generator für Erweiterte Affix-Grammatiken. Research Report 76-24, FB 20, TU Berlin (1976)

[FHS79] FRANZEN, H., HOFFMANN, B., SCHMIEDECKE, I.-R.: Using Two-Level Language Descriptions for Compiler Construction. In: Tagungsbericht über das "Fachgespräch Compiler-Compiler", Berlin 78, Forschungsbericht TU Darmstadt (1979)

[FH79] FRANZEN, H., HOFFMANN, B.: Automatic Determination of Data Flow in Extended Affix Grammars. Proceedings of the 8th annual GI meeting, Bonn 79, Informatik Fachbericht 19, Springer-Verlag, Berlin-Heidelberg-New York (1979)

[Gre74] GREIBACH, S.A.: Some Restrictions on W-Grammars. In: ACM Proceedings of the 6th STOC, Seattle (1974)

[GW77] GIEGERICH, H., WILHELM, R.: Implementierbarkeit attributierter Grammatiken. In: GI - 7.Jahrestagung, Informatik Fachbericht 10, Springer-Verlag, Berlin-Heidelberg-New York (1977)

[HS80] HOFFMANN, B., SCHMIEDECKE, I.-R.: Multi-Pass Parsing for Two-Level Grammars: A Mathematical Approach. Research Report, FB 20, TU Berlin, May (1980)

[Kas80] KASTENS, U.: Ordered Attributed Grammars. Acta Informatica 13,3, pp. 229-256 March (1980)

[Knu68] KNUTH, D.E.: Semantics of Context-Free Languages. In: Mathematic Systems Theory, 2(2), pp. 125-145 (1968). Correction: 5(1), (1971)

[Kos71a] KOSTER, C.H.A.: Affix Grammars. In: ALGOL-68-Implementation, J.E.L. Peck (ed.), North Holland Publ. Comp., Amsterdam-London, pp. 95-109 (1971)

[Kos71b] KOSTER, C.H.A.: A Compiler Compiler. Technical Report MR 127, Mathematisch Centrum, Amsterdam (1971)

[Kos74] KOSTER, C.H.A.: Two-Level Grammars. In: Proceedings of the Advanced Course on Compiler Construction, Munich, Lecture Notes, Springer-Verlag, Berlin-Heidelberg-New York, pp. 146-156 (1974)

[LB74] LECARME, O., BOCHMANN v., G.: A (truly) Usable and Portable Compiler Writing System. In: Information Processing 1974, pp. 218, North Holland Publ. Comp., Amsterdam (1974)

[Loh77] LOHRO, B.: Semantic Attributes Processing in the System DELTA. In: Methods of Algorithmic Language Implementation, Springer-Verlag, Berlin-Heidelberg-New York, pp. 21-40 (1977)

[Sin67] SINTZOFF, M.: Existence of a van Wijngaarden Syntax for Every Recursive Enumerable Set. Ann. Soc. Scientifique de Bruxelles 81, pp. 115-118 (1967)

[Wat75] WATT, D.A.: Analysis-Oriented Two-Level Grammars. Ph. D. thesis, Glasgow (1974), printed at the Technical University of Berlin (1975)

[Weg78a] WEGNER, L.M.: On Parsing Two-Level Grammars. Bericht 7, Institut für Informationsverarbeitung, TU Graz, March (1978)

[Weg78b] WEGNER, L.M.: Bracketed Two-Level Grammars: A Decidable and Practicable Approach to Language Definitions. Universität Karlsruhe, Institut für Angewandte Informatik und formale Beschreibungsverfahren, Report No. 76, Sept. 1978

[Wij65] WIJNGAARDEN v., A.: Orthogonal Design and Description of Formal Language. Report MR 76, Mathematisch Centrum, Amsterdam (1965)

ABSTRACT IMPLEMENTATION OF ABSTRACT DATA TYPES

Ulrich L. Hupbach
VEB Robotron ZFT, Abt. E4F
DDR 8012 Dresden, PSF 330

1. Introduction

The unabated interest in abstract data types is motivated by its importance for the problems of programming methodology and technology. Languages for algebraic specification of abstract data types BG 77, GT 77, GT 79, EKP 79, HKR 80 are a promising approach for describing a program design before it is programmed. In general, it is very hard to transform such a design in one step into a program of a usual programming language. One would rather translate the complex problem-oriented data types step by step into simpler data types that are closer to the types of the programming language. Only the so translated design will be coded in the language. Therefore, what is needed here is a concept of implementation of one abstract data type by another one in such a way that various steps of an implementation can be composed to the resulting implementation.

In this paper an implementation concept is introduced that describes the implementation of abstract data types in terms of their specifications. The concept is based on the Canon-Specification Method REI 79, HUP 79, HKR 80, HR 80, REI 80 . The specification method and the implementation concept both work for non-parameterized abstract data types as well as for parameterized ones. As main results we prove that

- the implementation concept meets exactly the class of all implementations that are compatible with effective computability of the data type operations and
- there is a universal construction for the composition of implementations.

In this results the introduced concept contrasts with other implementation concepts known from literature GUT 78, ADJ 78, BG 77, GOG 78, EHR 78, BOT 78, EKP 79 .

The implementation concept results from close cooperation with H. Kaphengst and H. Reichel of VEB Robotron, Centre of Research and Development Dresden.
I must thank also the referees of MFCS'80 for their suggestions.

2. The Canon-Specification Method

The Canon-Specification Method has been developed and improved by H. Kaphengst, H. Reichel and this author in the last years KR 71, REI 79, HUP 79, HKR 80, HR 80 . The motivations and basic definitions can be found in the paper REI 80 . Therefore, this section only recapitulates the basic concepts and defines the specification language.

In the Canon-Specification Method parameterized abstract data types are described by specifications which have as their semantics classes of many-sorted equationally partial algebras. For the mathematical description of the necessary classes of algebras the notion of a canon has been introduced. In simple cases a canon defines the isomorphism class of initial algebras. But in order to handle parameterized data types yet more general classes are needed. Many-sorted equationally partial algebras are a generalization of many-sorted algebras KR 71 + 77, REI 79 They allow the partiality of operations to be taken into account in a way different from introducing error values. The equationally partial algebras are motivated by generalizations of computability concepts they render possible. In this paper, except section 4, we restrict ourselves to non-partial algebras, but all concepts can be generalized to equationally partial algebras also.

We assume the algebraic background of ADJ 78, EKTWW 79 .
A (representation of a) many-sorted algebraic <u>theory</u> $\underline{T} = \langle S, \Sigma, E \rangle$ is a triple where $\langle S, \Sigma \rangle$ is a <u>signature</u> with the set S of <u>sorts</u> and the operator domain $\Sigma = (\Sigma_{w,s} \mid w \in S^*, s \in S)$ and E is the set of <u>axioms</u>. The axioms have the form $es_1 \Longrightarrow es_2$ where es_1 and es_2 are sets of equations of Σ-terms.
Some authors call $\underline{T}$ a specification but in our approach a specification is a more general concept and, as a consequence, we need not admit inequalities in the axioms.
The theory $\underline{T}$ characterizes the category $Alg_{\underline{T}}$ of $\underline{T}$-algebras.

If the theory $\underline{T}'$ contains all sorts, operators, and axioms of $\underline{T}$ and the arity of operators in $\underline{T}$ is the same as in $\underline{T}'$ then $\underline{T}'$ is a <u>theory-enlargement</u> of $\underline{T}$, notation: $\underline{T} \subseteq \underline{T}'$. For a $\underline{T}'$-algebra A then $A{\downarrow}\underline{T}$ denotes its $\underline{T}$-part and $f{\downarrow}\underline{T}$ is the $\underline{T}$-part of the $\underline{T}'$-homomorphism f.

A $\underline{T}'$-algebra F is a <u>free</u> $\underline{T}'$-<u>extension</u> of the $\underline{T}$-algebra A if $F{\downarrow}\underline{T} = A$ holds and any $\underline{T}$-homomorphism $f: A \longrightarrow X{\downarrow}\underline{T}$ with a $\underline{T}'$-algebra X can uniquely be extended to a $\underline{T}'$-homomorphism $f^+: F \longrightarrow X$, i.e. $f^+{\downarrow}\underline{T} = f$.

A canon (or initially restricting algebraic theory) is a pair $\underline{\underline{T}} = \langle \underline{T}, \Delta \rangle$ of a theory $\underline{T}$ and a finite set Δ of ordered pairs $\underline{R} \triangleleft \underline{S}$ of sub-theories $\underline{R} \subseteq \underline{S} \subseteq \underline{T}$, the so called initial restrictions of $\underline{\underline{T}}$.
A $\underline{\underline{T}}$-model is a $\underline{T}$-algebra A for which $A \downarrow \underline{S}$ is a free $\underline{S}$-extension of $A \downarrow \underline{R}$ for all $\underline{R} \triangleleft \underline{S} \in \Delta$.

Let $\langle S_1, \Sigma_1 \rangle$ and $\langle S_2, \Sigma_2 \rangle$ be signatures. A pair of mappings $\varphi_S : S_1 \longrightarrow S_2$ $\varphi_\Sigma : \Sigma_1 \longrightarrow \Sigma_2$ is called a signature-morphism $\varphi : \langle S_1, \Sigma_1 \rangle \longrightarrow \langle S_2, \Sigma_2 \rangle$ if it is compatible with arity of operators, i.e. $\sigma : s_1, \dots, s_n \longrightarrow s_o$ implies $\varphi(\sigma) : \varphi(s_1), \dots, \varphi(s_n) \longrightarrow \varphi(s_o)$. Then φ defines a forgetful functor $V_\varphi : Alg_{\langle S_2, \Sigma_2 \rangle} \longrightarrow Alg_{\langle S_1, \Sigma_1 \rangle}$ by $V_\varphi A = ((A_{\varphi_S(s)} \mid s \in S_1), (\varphi_\Sigma(\sigma)_A \mid \sigma \in \Sigma_1))$.

A theory-morphism $\varphi : \langle S_1, \Sigma_1, E_1 \rangle \longrightarrow \langle S_2, \Sigma_2, E_2 \rangle$ is a signature-morphism for which $V_\varphi A$ is a $\langle S_1, \Sigma_1, E_1 \rangle$-algebra for every $\langle S_2, \Sigma_2, E_2 \rangle$-algebra A.
A canon-morphism $\varphi : \langle \underline{T}_1, \Delta_1 \rangle \longrightarrow \langle \underline{T}_2, \Delta_2 \rangle$ is a theory-morphism for which $V_\varphi A$ is a $\langle \underline{T}_1, \Delta_1 \rangle$-model for every $\langle \underline{T}_2, \Delta_2 \rangle$-model A.

The Canon-Specification Language HKR 80 is a language for describing (parameterized) abstract data types by means of a specification, which is a more readable representation of a canon. The semantics of the specification (i.e. the specified abstract data type) is the set of models of the canon. Thus, we consider a (parameterized) abstract data type as the model class of a canon. Especially, a non-parameterized abstract data type is the class of models of a finite totally restricted canon $\underline{\underline{T}}$, that means the class of initial $\underline{T}$-algebras , cf. REI 80 .
The Canon-Specification Language rests on the observation that every canon can be built by means of the following three constructions starting from the empty canon $\underline{\underline{\emptyset}} = \langle \emptyset, \emptyset \rangle$.

(1) req-enlargement :

Let $\underline{\underline{R}} = \langle \underline{R}, \Delta \rangle$ be a canon and let $\langle S, \Sigma, E \rangle$ be a triple (not necessary a theory) such that $\underline{R}' = \underline{R} \cup \langle S, \Sigma, E \rangle$ is a theory-enlargement of $\underline{R}$, then the canon $\underline{\underline{R}}' = \langle \underline{R}', \Delta \rangle$ is a req-enlargement of $\underline{\underline{R}}$.
In the language this is represented in the form

$\underline{\underline{R}}' = \underline{\underline{R}}$ req sorts s_1 ; ... {elements of S}
oprs $\sigma_1 : s_i, \dots, s_k \longrightarrow s_l$; ... {elements of Σ}
axioms for all ... let e_1 ; ... {elements of E}
end

This language statement introduces $\underline{\underline{R}}'$ as the name of the req-enlargement presupposing that $\underline{\underline{R}}$ has already been introduced as a name.

Example: Attribute = req sorts Attr; oprs undef: ⟶ Attr end

(2) def-enlargement :

Let R and R' be as in (1). Then the canon R' = ⟨R', $\Delta \cup \{$R ◁ R'$\}$⟩ is a def-enlargement of R.

Language representation:

```
R' = R  def sorts s1 ; ...
            oprs  σ1: si,..., sk ⟶ sl ; ...
            axioms for all ... let e1 ; ...
        end
```

Example: Bool = def sorts Bool; oprs true, false: ⟶ Bool end

(3) join :

If R = ⟨R, Δ⟩ and S = ⟨S, Γ⟩ are canons such that all operators they have in common posses the same arity in R and S, then the canon R ∪ S = ⟨R ∪ S, $\Delta \cup \Gamma$⟩ is the join of R and S.

As another example we consider

```
Identifier = Bool req  sorts Id
                       oprs  eq : Id, Id ⟶ Bool
                       axioms for all x,y ∈ Id let
                             eq(x,x) = true
                             if eq(x,y) = true then x = y fi
                  end
```

The Identifier-models are Bool-models extended by an arbitrary set with equality operation.

In any of the mentioned language statements one may distinguish a certain sub-canon of the righthand side as a parameter: R'(P) = ... This corresponds to a pair (R', P) of canon and sub-canon. For a canon-morphism φ: P ⟶ A the substitution of A for P delivers a new canon (for more details cf. REI 80).

A slightly modified version of the symbol table data type GUT 75 + 78 should illustrate the language:

```
Sytab = Identifier ∪ Attribute  def sorts  Stab
oprs init: ⟶ Stab                    add: Stab, Id, Attr ⟶ Stab
  enter, leave: Stab ⟶ Stab          retrieve: Stab, Id ⟶ Attr
axioms for all s ∈ Stab; i,j ∈ Id; a ∈ Attr  let
  leave(init) = init ;               retrieve(init,i) = undef
  leave(enter(s)) = s ;              retrieve(enter(s),i) = retrieve(s)
  leave(add(s,i,a)) = leave(s) ;     retrieve(add(s,i,a),i) = a
  if eq(i,j) = false then retrieve(add(s,i,a),j) = retrieve(s,j)  fi
end
```

3. Abstract Implementations

The implementation of a programming language S (source) by a machine-oriented language T (target) in principle is a translation from S into T that maps any S-program onto an equivalent T-program such that a realization of the language T defines a realization of S as well.

Let $\underline{\underline{S}}$ and $\underline{\underline{T}}$ be canons and M an $\underline{\underline{S}}$-model (i.e. a concrete data type). An implementation of M by means of a $\underline{\underline{T}}$-model then must give a $\underline{\underline{T}}$-model N and a rule of how to represent the elements and operations of M by means of elements and operations of N, that means a rule for making M into N. In this sense N is able to do the work of M.

By an abstract implementation of $\underline{\underline{S}}$ by means of $\underline{\underline{T}}$ we understand a uniform (i.e. independent of peculiarities of any model) rule that for any $\underline{\underline{S}}$-model M determines an implementation by means of a $\underline{\underline{T}}$-model in such a way that any computable realization of $\underline{\underline{T}}$ (i.e. a $\underline{\underline{T}}$-model N with effectively computable operations and with carriers that are relative to this operations effectively enumerable) determines a computable realization of $\underline{\underline{S}}$ via this rule. This computability requirement takes into account that only data types with effectively computable operations are of practical value.

Definition 1: An abstract implementation of a canon $\underline{\underline{S}}$ by a canon $\underline{\underline{T}}$ is given by a canon $\underline{\underline{A}}$ ("auxiliary canon") and two canon-morphisms

$\underline{\underline{S}} \xrightarrow{\varphi} \underline{\underline{A}} \xleftarrow{\alpha} \underline{\underline{T}}$ such that

(I) $\underline{\underline{A}}$ is a weak enlargement of $\underline{\underline{T}}$, that means $\underline{\underline{A}}$ is a finite def-enlargement of $\underline{\underline{T}}$ and each $\underline{\underline{T}}$-model has a free $\underline{\underline{A}}$-extension, and α is the inclusion of $\underline{\underline{T}}$ in $\underline{\underline{A}}$;

(II) the sort $\varphi(s)$ is recursive over $\underline{\underline{T}}$ for every sort s of $\underline{\underline{S}}$;

(III) φ respects models, that means for every $\underline{\underline{S}}$-model M there is an $\underline{\underline{A}}$-model A such that $V_\varphi A = M$

Definition 2: Let $\underline{\underline{A}}$ be a weak enlargement of $\underline{\underline{T}}$. A sort s of $\underline{\underline{A}}$ is recursive over $\underline{\underline{T}}$ if there is an $\underline{\underline{A}}$-term τ and a finite $\underline{\underline{A}}$-equation system g both in the variables $x_1:s_1, \ldots, x_n:s_n$ such that

(i) $s_1,\ldots,s_n$ are sorts of $\underline{\underline{T}}$ and

(ii) in any $\underline{\underline{A}}$-model A the interpretation τ_A of the term τ is a one-to-one mapping of the set A_g of solutions of g in A onto A_s .

Of course, the sorts of $\underline{\underline{T}}$ are recursive over $\underline{\underline{T}}$.

Let an abstract implementation $\underline{\underline{S}} \xrightarrow{\varphi} \underline{\underline{A}} \xleftarrow{\alpha} \underline{\underline{T}}$ be given. Then for any

S-model M there is an A-model A and a T-model $N = V_{\alpha} A$. An operation σ_M is represented by the operation $\varphi(\sigma)_A$ which by condition (II) may be treated as a partial function on N. Thus, the abstract implementation for any S-model defines a concrete implementation.

To describe abstract implementations we slightly extend the specification language as shown in the following example. We implement the canon Sytab by the canon Pairstack. A symbol table is to be represented by a stack the entries of which are pairs (identifier,attribute) and marks for beginning of blocks.

```
Pair = Identifier ∪ Attribute  def sorts  Pair
       oprs pair: Id, Attr ——> Pair ;   begin, error: ——> Pair
end

Pairstack = Pair def sorts Stack
   oprs create: ——> Stack ;                   pop: Stack ——> Stack
     push: Stack, Pair ——> Stack ;            top: Stack ——> Pair
   axioms for all s ∈ Stack; p ∈ Pair  let
     pop(create) = create ;                   pop(push(s,d)) = s
     top(create) = error    ;                 top(push(s,d)) = d
   end

implement Sytab in Pairstack by
   sorts Stab' = Stack
   oprs  init': ——> Stack ;                   add': Stack,Id,Attr ——> Stack
     enter', leave': Stack ——> Stack ;        retrieve': Stack,Id ——> Attr
   axioms for all  s ∈ Stack; i,j ∈ Id; a ∈ Attr  let
     init' = create
     enter'(s) = push(s,begin)
     leave'(create) = create
     leave'(push(s,begin)) = s
     leave'(push(s,pair(i,a))) = leave'(s)
     retrieve'(create,i) = undef
     retrieve'(push(s,begin),i) = retrieve'(s,i)
     retrieve'(push(s,pair(i,a)),i) = a
     if eq(i,j)=false then retrieve'(push(s,pair(i,a)),j) =
                                              = retrieve'(s,j)  fi
   end
```

This text defines the canon A and the canon-morphism φ simultaneously.

```
A = Pairstack def  oprs init': ——> Stack; ... {as above} ...
                   axioms ..... {as above} .....
                end
```

$\varphi_S(\text{Stab}) = \text{Stack}$, $\varphi_S(s) = s$ for all other sorts of Sytab

$$\varphi_\Sigma(\sigma) = \begin{cases} \sigma', & \text{for } \sigma = \text{init, enter, leave, add, retrieve} \\ \sigma, & \text{for all other operators of Sytab} \end{cases}$$

The general rule for semantics of this language statement is:
implement S in T by ..... <text> ..... end
defines the canon A = T def ... <text> ... end and the canon-morphism φ that maps any sort s and operator op of S onto the sort s' (or s) and operator op' (or op) of A respectively. There is but one exception: If the sorts-phrase of the <text> contains an "equation" s' = t for a sort s of S and a sort t of T then s' is not introduced as a new sort in A, but it is only another name of the already existing sort t of T.

The correctness proof for an abstract implementation has to verify that

(a) A is a weak enlargement of T, i.e. any T-model has a free A-extension.

(b) φ is a canon-morphism:
- φ is a signature-morphism and for any implication $\mathcal{X}$ of S the implication $\varphi(\mathcal{X})$ is a logical consequence of the axioms of A.
- For any A-model A the S-algebra $V_\varphi A$ is an S-model.

(c) The sorts $\varphi_S(s)$ are recursive over T for all sorts s of S.

(d) For any S-model M there is an A-model A such that $V_\varphi A = M$.

The definition of an implementation concept needs some justification by showing that it meets a set of requirements that, on an intuitive level of reasoning, are constitutive for the notion "implementation".

(1) Any effective realization of the target-specification gives rise to an effective realization of the source-specification.

(2) There is a universal construction for the composition of implementations delivering the resultant implementation.

(3) The implementation of parameterized specifications commutes with parameter substitution.

In the following sections (1) and (2) will be proved for the abstract implementation concept, while (3) that needs a more general treatment of pushouts in the category of canons will be deferred to another paper.

4. Implementations and Computability

To make precise the notion of effective computability we use the concept of numbered sets ERS 73 .
Let $T = \langle S, \Sigma, E \rangle$ be a finitary theory (i.e. S, Σ, E finite) and let

N be a $\underline{T}$-algebra with at most countable carriers. A numbering for N is a family $l = (l_s\colon Nat \longrightarrow N_s \mid s \in S)$ of surjective mappings, where Nat is the set of natural numbers. l is called a strong numbering of N if the sets $\{(x_1,x_2) \mid l_s(x_1) = l_s(x_2)\}$ are recursively enumerable for all sorts s of $\underline{T}$.

A partial mapping $f\colon N_{s_1} \times \dots \times N_{s_n} \longrightarrow N_{s_0}$ $(s_1,\dots,s_n \in S)$ is recursively realizable with respect to l if there is a partial-recursive number function $g\colon Nat^n \longrightarrow Nat$ such that $g(x_1,\dots,x_n)$ has the same domain as $f(l_{s_1}(x_1),\dots, l_{s_n}(x_n))$ and for all $(x_1,\dots,x_n) \in dom(g)$ $f(l_{s_1}(x_1),\dots, l_{s_n}(x_n)) = l_{s_0}(g(x_1,\dots, x_n))$ holds.

Following KAP 80 we define:
A partial mapping $f\colon N_{s_1} \times \dots \times N_{s_n} \longrightarrow N_{s_0}$ is computable relative to N if f is recursively realizable w.r.t. every strong numbering l of N for which all operations of N are recursively realizable.
The set $H \subseteq N_{s_1} \times \dots \times N_{s_n}$ is enumerable relative to N if the set $\{(x_1,\dots,x_n) \mid (l_{s_1}(x_1),\dots,l_{s_n}(x_n)) \in H\}$ is recursively enumerable for every strong numbering l of N for which all operations of N are recursively realizable.

Theorem 1 (KAP 80):

Let $\underline{T}$ be a finitary equationally partial theory, let N be an initial $\underline{T}$-algebra and let f, H as in the above definition.

$\left\{\begin{array}{l} \text{f is computable relative to N} \\ \text{H is enumerable relative to N} \end{array}\right\}$ iff there is a finite theory-enlargement $\underline{R} \supsetneq \underline{T}$ for which N has a free $\underline{R}$-extension F such that $\left\{\begin{array}{l} \text{there is an operator } \sigma\colon s_1,\dots,s_n \longrightarrow s_0 \text{ of } \underline{R} \text{ with } \sigma_F = f \\ \text{there is a finite equation system g on } \underline{R} \text{ with } F_g = H \end{array}\right\}$.

(F_g is the set of solutions of g in F).

This theorem is not true for theories with total operations only, at least in $\underline{R}$ partial operations must be admitted.

The above definitions together with theorem 1 give a precise meaning of computability and relative computability for non-parameterized abstract data types.

Let $\underline{S}$ and $\underline{T}$ be specifications of non-parameterized abstract data types. As stated above, for an abstract implementation of $\underline{S}$ by $\underline{T}$ an effectively computable realization of $\underline{T}$ is expected do deliver an effectively computable realization of $\underline{S}$. In the light of the above definitions we can express the expected property in the form of

Theorem 2: Let $\underline{\underline{S}} \xrightarrow{\varphi} \underline{\underline{A}} \xleftarrow{\alpha} \underline{\underline{T}}$ be an abstract implementation with totally restricted canons $\underline{\underline{S}}$ and $\underline{\underline{T}}$. Then for any $\underline{\underline{T}}$-model N there is an extension of N to an $\underline{\underline{A}}$-model F such that $V_\varphi F$ is an $\underline{\underline{S}}$-model whose operations are computable relative to N and whose carriers are enumerable relative to N.

Proof: Since $\varphi(s)$ is recursive over $\underline{\underline{T}}$ there is an $\underline{\underline{A}}$-term $\tau: s_1,\dots,s_n \longrightarrow \varphi(s)$ and a finite equation system g in variables of sorts $s_1,\dots,s_n$ of $\underline{\underline{T}}$ such that in any $\underline{\underline{A}}$-model A the interpretation $\tau_A: A_g \longrightarrow A_{\varphi(s)}$ of τ is a bijection. Hence, there is an $\underline{\underline{A}}$-model F such that $F_g = F_{\varphi(s)}$ for all sorts s of $\underline{\underline{S}}$, and F is an extension of N if A is.
$F_g \subseteq N_{s_1} \times \dots \times N_{s_n}$ holds because all variables of g belong to sorts of $\underline{\underline{T}}$. Then by theorem 1 $F_{\varphi(s)}$ is enumerable relative to N.
For any operator $\sigma: r_1,\dots,r_n \longrightarrow r_0$ of $\underline{\underline{S}}$ the sets $F_{\varphi(r_i)}$ are subsets of products $N_{s_{i1}} \times \dots \times N_{s_{ik_i}}$, $(0 \leqslant i \leqslant n)$, and hence
$\varphi(\sigma)_F: N_{s_{11}} \times \dots \times N_{s_{nk_n}} \xrightarrow{o} N_{s_{o1}} \times \dots \times N_{s_{ok_o}}$ is a partial mapping on N. An obvious generalization of theorem 1 to tuple-valued functions proves $\varphi(\sigma)_F$ computable relative to N.
end of proof

The other way round, we may ask if every uniform rule for making $\underline{\underline{T}}$-models N into $\underline{\underline{S}}$-models M(N) such that the operations/carriers of M(N) are computable/enumerable relative to N can be described as an abstract implementation. The answer is yes.
Because of relative enumerability of the carriers of M(N) by theorem 1 there is a weak enlargement $\underline{\underline{A}}$ of $\underline{\underline{T}}$ and a free $\underline{\underline{A}}$-extension F of N and to each sort s of $\underline{\underline{S}}$ we can assign a finite equation system g[s] in variables $x_1^s,\dots,x_n^s$ of sorts $s_1,\dots,s_n$ of $\underline{\underline{T}}$ such that $F_{g[s]} = M_s$ holds.
Let $\underline{\underline{A}}^+$ be the enlargement of $\underline{\underline{A}}$ by the new sorts s' and partial(!) operators $rep^s: s_1,\dots,s_n$ iff $g[s] \longrightarrow s'$ for all sorts s of $\underline{\underline{S}}$. (In the terminology of KR 77 g[s] is the definition-condition of rep^s. In every equationally partial $\underline{\underline{A}}^+$-algebra A the domain of rep^s_A is the set $A_{g[s]}$ of solutions of g[s] in A.)
Let $\underline{\underline{A}}^+ = \langle \underline{A}^+, \Delta_{\underline{\underline{A}}} \cup \{\underline{\underline{A}} \triangleleft \underline{\underline{A}}^+\} \rangle$. Then $\underline{\underline{A}}^+$ is a weak enlargement of $\underline{\underline{T}}$ and rep^s_A is a bijective mapping in every $\underline{\underline{A}}^+$-model A. If we extend F by the carriers $F^+_s = F_{g[s]}$ and operations $rep^s_{F^+}$ = identity so we get an $\underline{\underline{A}}^+$-model F^+ that is a free $\underline{\underline{A}}^+$-extension of N.

Applying theorem 1 to the operations of M(N) we get a weak enlargement $\underline{\underline{A}}^{++}$ of $\underline{\underline{A}}^{+}$, which then is also a weak enlargement of $\underline{\underline{T}}$, and a free $\underline{\underline{A}}^{++}$-extension F^{++} of N such that for every operator σ of $\underline{\underline{S}}$ there is an operator σ' of $\underline{\underline{A}}^{++}$ with $\sigma'_{F^{++}} = \sigma_{M(N)}$.

Now, if we interpret "uniform" as "for all $\underline{\underline{T}}$-models the same weak enlargement $\underline{\underline{A}}^{++}$ and the same correspondence $s \longmapsto s'$, $\sigma \longmapsto \sigma'$ " then the proof is accomplished.

5. Composition of Implementations

Let $\overbrace{\underline{\underline{S}} \xrightarrow{\varphi} \underline{\underline{A}} \xleftarrow{\alpha}}^{F} \underline{\underline{T}} \overbrace{\xrightarrow{\psi} \underline{\underline{B}} \xleftarrow{\beta}}^{G} \underline{\underline{R}}$ be two abstract implementations. This data then are expected to define an abstract implementation of $\underline{\underline{S}}$ by $\underline{\underline{R}}$ that is in some sense the composition of F and G. In this section we'll show that such composed implementations can be constructed by means of the pushout in the category of canons.

The existence of a universal construction for the composition of implementations is a non-trivial property and, therefore, confirms a given implementation concept. For the deriver-concept ADJ 78, GCG 78 and the abstract implementation concept of EHR 78 the pushout delivers again an implementation. For EKP 79 the question is open. In EHR 78a a counterexample shows that the pushout in general does'nt deliver an implementation.

<u>Theorem 3:</u> Let $\overbrace{\underline{\underline{S}} \xrightarrow{\varphi} \underline{\underline{A}} \xleftarrow{\alpha}}^{F} \underline{\underline{T}} \overbrace{\xrightarrow{\psi} \underline{\underline{B}} \xleftarrow{\beta}}^{G} \underline{\underline{R}}$ be two abstract implementations. Then in the category of canons a pushout $\underline{\underline{A}} \xrightarrow{\psi'} \underline{\underline{C}} \xleftarrow{\alpha'} \underline{\underline{B}}$ of $\underline{\underline{A}} \xleftarrow{\alpha} \underline{\underline{T}} \xrightarrow{\psi} \underline{\underline{B}}$ exists and $\underline{\underline{S}} \xrightarrow{\varphi \circ \psi'} \underline{\underline{C}} \xleftarrow{\beta \cdot \alpha'} \underline{\underline{R}}$ is an abstract implementation, the composition of F and G.

<u>Proof</u>: (1) Following EHR 78a we define a theory $\underline{\underline{C}}$ and theory-morphisms by pushout diagrams in the category of sets

$$\begin{array}{ccc} \mathrm{sorts}(\underline{\underline{T}}) & \xrightarrow{\psi_S} & \mathrm{sorts}(\underline{\underline{B}}) \\ \downarrow \alpha_S & & \downarrow \alpha'_S \\ \mathrm{sorts}(\underline{\underline{A}}) & \xrightarrow{\psi'_S} & \mathrm{sorts}(\underline{\underline{C}}) \end{array} \qquad \begin{array}{ccc} \mathrm{oprs}(\underline{\underline{T}}) & \xrightarrow{\psi_\Sigma} & \mathrm{oprs}(\underline{\underline{B}}) \\ \downarrow \alpha_\Sigma & & \downarrow \alpha'_\Sigma \\ \mathrm{oprs}(\underline{\underline{A}}) & \xrightarrow{\psi'_\Sigma} & \mathrm{oprs}(\underline{\underline{C}}) \end{array}$$

The axioms of $\underline{\underline{C}}$ are $\psi'(\mathrm{axioms}(\underline{\underline{A}})) \cup \alpha'(\mathrm{axioms}(\underline{\underline{B}}))$.

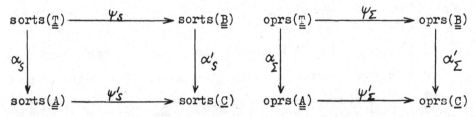

This way we get a pushout in the category of theories and α' is an inclusion since α is.
(In the case of equationally partial theories $\underline{\underline{C}}$ contains some additional axioms.)

(2) Let $\langle Alg_{\underline{A}}, Alg_{\underline{B}} \rangle$ be the subcategory of $Alg_{\underline{A}} \times Alg_{\underline{B}}$ whose objects $\langle A, B \rangle$ and morphisms $\langle f, g \rangle$ satisfy the condition $V_\alpha A = V_\psi B$ and $V_\alpha f = V_\psi g$. Let $\_\dot{\cup}\_ : \langle Alg_{\underline{A}}, Alg_{\underline{B}} \rangle \longrightarrow Alg_{\underline{C}}$ be the functor defined by

$$(A \dot{\cup} B)_s = \begin{cases} A_r & \text{if there is a sort } r \text{ of } \underline{\underline{A}} \text{ such that } s = \psi'(r) \\ B_r & \text{if there is a sort } r \text{ of } \underline{\underline{B}} \text{ such that } s = \alpha'(r) \end{cases}$$

$$\sigma_{A \dot{\cup} B} = \begin{cases} \varrho_A & \text{if there is an operator } \varrho \text{ of } \underline{\underline{A}} \text{ such that } \sigma = \psi'(\varrho) \\ \varrho_B & \text{if there is an operator } \varrho \text{ of } \underline{\underline{B}} \text{ such that } \sigma = \alpha'(\varrho) \end{cases}$$

One easily proves the

Lemma: $\_\dot{\cup}\_$ is an isomorphism.
$A \dot{\cup} B$ is a free $\underline{\underline{C}}$-extension of B if A is a free $\underline{\underline{A}}$-extension of $V_\psi B$.

(3) We set $\underline{\underline{C}} = (\,\underline{C}\,, \Delta_{\underline{\underline{B}}} \cup \{\underline{B} \triangleleft \underline{C}\})$.

(4) Then α' and ψ' are canon-morphisms: For any $\underline{\underline{C}}$-model C, $V_{\alpha'} C = C \downarrow \underline{B}$ is a $\underline{\underline{B}}$ model, and if A is a free $\underline{\underline{A}}$-extension of the $\underline{\underline{T}}$-model $V_\psi V_{\alpha'} C$ so $M = A \dot{\cup} V_{\alpha'} C$ is a free $\underline{\underline{C}}$-extension of $V_{\alpha'} C$. As C is another such extension, there is a $\underline{\underline{C}}$-isomorphism $\iota : M \longrightarrow C$. Hence $V_{\psi'} \iota : A \longrightarrow V_{\psi'} C$ is an $\underline{\underline{A}}$-isomorphism. Since $V_{\psi'} C$ is isomorphic to the $\underline{\underline{A}}$-model A, it must be an $\underline{\underline{A}}$-model for itself.

(5)
$$\begin{array}{ccc} \underline{\underline{T}} & \xrightarrow{\ \psi\ } & \underline{\underline{B}} \\ {\scriptstyle \alpha}\downarrow & & \downarrow{\scriptstyle \alpha'} \\ \underline{\underline{A}} & \xrightarrow{\ \psi'\ } & \underline{\underline{C}} \end{array}$$

is a pushout diagram in the category of canons: If $\underline{\underline{A}} \xrightarrow{\ \mu\ } \underline{\underline{D}} \xleftarrow{\ \nu\ } \underline{\underline{B}}$ are canon-morphisms such that $\alpha \circ \mu = \psi \circ \nu$ holds, then the unique (the diagram is also a pushout for theories) theory-morphism $\gamma : \underline{\underline{C}} \longrightarrow \underline{\underline{D}}$ with $\psi' \circ \gamma = \mu$ and $\alpha' \circ \gamma = \nu$ is also a canon-morphism, because for any $\underline{\underline{D}}$-model D $\quad V_\mu D \dot{\cup} V_\nu D = V_{\psi'} V_\gamma D \dot{\cup} V_{\alpha'} V_\gamma D = V_\gamma D$ is a $\underline{\underline{C}}$-model.

From the lemma it follows that $\underline{\underline{C}}$ is a weak enlargement of $\underline{\underline{B}}$, hence, $\underline{\underline{C}}$ is also a weak enlargement of $\underline{\underline{R}}$.

(6) It is left to prove $\psi'(s)$ recursive over $\underline{\underline{R}}$ for sorts s of $\underline{\underline{A}}$ that are recursive over $\underline{\underline{T}}$. To do so we construct a $\underline{\underline{C}}$-term ϱ' and a finite $\underline{\underline{C}}$-equation system h' such that $\varrho'_C : C_{h'} \longrightarrow C_{\psi'(s)}$ is a bijection in every $\underline{\underline{C}}$-model C.

Let τ be the $\underline{\underline{A}}$-term and g the $\underline{\underline{A}}$-equation system for s both in variables $x_1, \ldots, x_n$ as in definition 2. Extending ψ' to terms and equations we get the $\underline{\underline{C}}$-term $\varrho = \psi'(\tau)$ and the $\underline{\underline{C}}$-equation system $h = \psi'(g)$ both in variables $x_1,\ldots,x_n$ ranging over sorts $\psi'(s_1),\ldots,\psi'(s_n)$ of $\underline{\underline{B}}$. For any $\underline{\underline{C}}$-model C we have $\varrho_C = \tau_{V_{\psi'}C}$ and $C_h = (V_{\psi'}C)_\varepsilon$ and hence $\varrho_C\colon C_h \longrightarrow C_{\psi'(s)}$ is a bijection.

According to presupposition on ψ, the sorts $\psi'(s_i) = \psi(s_i)$, $i = 1\ldots n$ are recursive over $\underline{\underline{R}}$, that means there are $\underline{\underline{B}}$-terms ϱ^i and $\underline{\underline{B}}$-equation systems h_i in variables $x_{i1},\ldots,x_{im_i}$ ranging over sorts $t_{i1},\ldots,t_{im_i}$ of $\underline{\underline{R}}$ such that $\varrho^i{}_B\colon B_{h_i} \longrightarrow B_{\psi'(s_i)}$ is bijective in any $\underline{\underline{B}}$-model B.

Since α' is a weak enlargement, ϱ^i is a $\underline{\underline{C}}$-term as well and $\varrho^i{}_C\colon C_{h_i} \longrightarrow C_{\psi'(s_i)}$ is bijective in every $\underline{\underline{C}}$-model C.

Let h_i^+ denote the $\underline{\underline{C}}$-equation system h_i taken as equation system in variables $x_{11},\ldots,x_{nm_n}$ ranging over sorts $t_{11},\ldots,t_{nm_n}$ of $\underline{\underline{R}}$. Let

$$(\varrho^1,\ldots,\varrho^n)\circ h = \{\langle(\varrho^1,\ldots,\varrho^n)\circ\omega,\ (\varrho^1,\ldots,\varrho^n)\circ\omega'\rangle \mid \langle\omega,\omega'\rangle \in h\}$$

where $(\varrho^1,\ldots,\varrho^n)$ denotes source-tupling. Then $\varrho' = (\varrho^1,\ldots,\varrho^n)\circ\varrho$ is a $\underline{\underline{C}}$-term and $h' = (\varrho^1,\ldots,\varrho^n)\circ h \cup h_1^+ \cup \ldots \cup h_n^+$ is a $\underline{\underline{C}}$-equation system both in variables $x_{11},\ldots, x_{nm_n}$ of sorts $t_{11},\ldots, t_{nm_n}$ of $\underline{\underline{R}}$, and $\varrho'_C\colon C_{h'} \longrightarrow C_{\psi'(s)}$ is bijective for any $\underline{\underline{C}}$-model C.

<u>end of proof</u>

6. Discussion

The main difference between the introduced implementation concept and EHR 78 + 78a, EKP 79, ADJ 78, GOG 78 is the absence of any kind of factorization in our concept. The reason for this is that the class of recursively enumerable sets is not closed under factorization. Thus, if factorization were allowed in our implementation concept then the computability requirement of section 4 could'nt be satisfied.

Another difference stems from the fact that in the framework of total algebras subsets of carriers cannot be specified by means of equation systems, as we do. So we describe the necessary subsets in the weak enlargement $\underline{\underline{T}} \longrightarrow \underline{\underline{A}}$, while EKP 79, ADJ 78, GOG 78 locate subset-formation in the transition $Alg_{\underline{A}} \rightsquigarrow Alg_{\underline{S}}$.

A third difference arises with the condition that all elements of the source data type are to be represented by aggregations of target type elements only (condition (II) in definition 1). We guess that this condition is the reason why in EHR 78 + 78a a one-to-one correspondence between sorts of the auxiliary specification and sorts of the target-specification is required. But in our approach in general we need an overhead of sorts in the auxiliary canon in order to specify a relatively enumerable set.

References

ADJ 78 J.A.Goguen, J.W.Thatcher, E.G.Wagner: An initial algebra approach to the specification, correctness and implementation of abstract data types, in Current trends in programming methodology Vol. IV (ed. R.T.Jeh), Prentice-Hall 1978

BG 77 R.M.Burstall, J.A.Goguen: Putting Theories Together to Make Specifications, 5th Int.Joint Conf.on AI, p.1045-1058, 1977

BOT 78 K.Bothe: Spezifikation und Verifikation abstrakter Datentypen, Akademie der Wissenschaften, ZfR-Informationen 78.11, Berlin1978

EHR 78 H.-D.Ehrich: Extensions and Implementations of Abstract Data Type Specifications, LNCS 64(1978),p.155-164

EHR 78a --: On the Theory of Specification, Implementation and Parametrization of Abstract Data Types, Forschungsbericht, Dortmund 1978

EKP 79 H.Ehrig, H.-J.Kreowski, P.Padawitz: Algebraische Implementierung abstrakter Datentypen, TU Berlin FB Informatik, Bericht Nr. 79-3, 1979

EKTWW 79 H.Ehrig, H.-J.Kreowski, J.Thatcher, E.Wagner, J.Wright: Parameterized Data Types in Algebraic Specification Languages, 7th Int.Colloqu. Automata, Languages and Programming

ERS 73 Ju.L.Ershov: Theorie der Nummerierungen I, Z.math.Logik Grundl. Mathematik 19(1973),p.289 ff

GOG 78 J.Goguen: Some Ideas in Algebraic Semantics, 4th IBM-Japan Symp. on Math. Foundations of Comp. Sci., Kobe, Japan 1978

GT 77 J.A.Goguen, J.Tardo: OBJ-0 Preliminary Users Manual, UCLA, Semantics and Theory of Computation Report No. 10, 1977

GT 79 --: An Introduction to OBJ, UCLA, Los Angeles 1979

GUT 75 J.V.Guttag: The Specification and Application to Programming of Abstract Data Types, Univ.of Toronto, Report CSRG-59, 1975

GUT 78 J.V.Guttag, E.Horowitz, D.R.Musser: Abstract Data Types and Software Validation, CACM 21(1978),p.1048-1064

HKR 80 U.L.Hupbach, H.Kaphengst, H.Reichel: Initial Algebraic Specification of Data Types, Parameterized Data Types and Algorithms, VEB Robotron ZFT, Techn.Report, Dresden 1980

HR 80 U.L.Hupbach, H.Reichel: Abstrakte Spezifikation von Datenbanken und Anfragen an Datenbanken, Problemseminar Datenbanken, Schriftenreihe des Weiterbildungszentr., TU Dresden 1980

HUP 79 U.L.Hupbach: A Uniform Mathematical Framework for Initial Algebraic Specifications, VEB Robotron ZFT, Techn.Report, 1979

KAP 80 H.Kaphengst: Was ist berechenbar für abstrakte Datentypen?, VEB Robotron ZFT, Techn. Report, Dresden 1980

KR 71 H.Kaphengst, H.Reichel: Algebraische Algorithmentheorie, VEB Robotron ZFT, Wiss.Inf.u.Berichte Nr.1 , Dresden 1971

KR 77 H.Kaphengst, H.Reichel: Initial Algebraic Semantics for Non-Contextfree Languages, LNCS 56,p.120-126

REI 79 H.Reichel: Theorie der Äquoide, Dissertation B, Humboldt-Universität Berlin, Sektion Mathematik, 1979

REI 80 --: Initially-Restricting Algebraic Theories, MFCS'80, LNCS (this volume)

PARALLEL ALGORITHMS IN GRAPH THEORY: PLANARITY TESTING
(preliminary version)

Joseph Ja'Ja'
Janos Simon
Department of Computer Science
The Pennsylvania State University
University Park, PA 16802, USA

1. Abstract

We present $O(\log^2 n)$ step parallel algorithms for planarity testing and for finding the triply connected components of a graph. The algorithms use a polynomial number of synchronous processors with shared memory.

2. Introduction

One of the major problems in both theoretical and applied computer science is our lack of knowledge about parallel computation. It is now feasible to build huge conglomerates of processors and they represent the only hope for order of magnitude improvements in computing power in the near future. At the same time, beyond the problems of interconnection, synchronization and reliability of such conglomerates, there is a more basic problem, that is probably the main obstacle to the construction and widespread use of such machines: we have no idea what to do with them. Our algorithms, our formal reasoning, our intuition about computing were all developed for serial models. There are some situations, where tasks that are independent can be done in parallel, but, except in very special cases (sorting, portions of numerical linear algebra, evaluation of arithmetic expressions, linear recurrences, etc. ...[Br], [C], [Ch], [He], [Hi], [P], ...), the use of, say a polynomial number of processors, seems to yield only marginal improvements in the running time of algorithms. Our main objective is to gain a better understanding of parallelism. We would like to have a collection of techniques for obtaining efficient parallel algorithms, and an intuition of how to recognize features that make a problem amenable to efficient parallel solution.

In this paper, we consider a well-known problem in graph theory, namely testing whether a given graph is planar. This problem has linear time serial algorithms [HT], [BK], [Ev], but no obvious parallel algorithm with $o(n)$ running time. We develop two fast parallel algorithms, each of which runs in $O(\log^2 n)$ time. The first algorithm uses $O(n^4)$ processors (which don't add or multiply), the second uses $O(n^{3.29}/\log^2 n)$ arithmetic processors. These results are surprising because the known serial algorithms for this problem, referred to above, seem inherently sequential. We assume here the unbounded synchronous parallel model of computation: we have an unlimited number of processors, each identified by a unique label. These processors have access to a common main memory which contains the data, and the instructions for each processor. We make the assumption that different processors can obtain the content of one memory location at the same time; they may store information into different memory locations simultaneously but no two processors should attempt to change the content of the same memory location at the same time. We further assume that all the processors are synchronous in the sense that if a set of instructions is executed in parallel, then each must be allowed to finish before the next set of instructions is started. The instruction set of each processor does not include multiplication, unless otherwise specified.

Parallel algorithms for several graph problems exist. The following list includes some of the known results in this area. n is the number of nodes and m is the number of edges in the graph.

Problem	Time Bound	# of Processors
Transitive Closure [H]	$O(\log^2 n)$	$O(n^3)$
Connectivity Testing [SJ]	$O(\log^2 n)$	$O(n \log n + m)$
Finding the biconnected components [SJ]	$O(\log^2 n)$	$O(n^3/\log n)$
Finding minimal spanning trees [SJ]	$O(\log^2 n)$	$O(n^2)$
Finding the bridge-connected components [SJ]	$O(\log^2 n)$	$O(n^2 \log n)$
Testing whether G is bipartite	$O(\log^2 n)$	$O(n^2)$
Testing k-connectedness [G2]	$O(\log^2 n \log k)$	$O(n^{k+1})$

Because of well-known results ([HS], [PS], [FW]) our algorithms may also be viewed as space-efficient. Thus, these investigations may shed some light on the $P \stackrel{?}{=} \bigcup_{k \in N} \mathrm{DSPACE}[(\log n)^k]$ question. A companion paper [JS] presents space-efficient versions of these algorithms, with space bounds that exactly match our time bounds (and, therefore are better than the algorithms obtained by simply translating time to space).

Our graph terminology is standard, and uses the notation of [H], [BM]. Special notions and notations will be defined in the text. Due to space restrictions, we do not provide complete proofs in most of the paper: the next section is a relatively detailed exposition of the algorithm for finding triply connected components, but with the proof of well-known results omitted. Section 4 sketches our first planarity algorithm, omitting almost all proofs. Section 5 outlines our second algorithm.

3. Finding the triply connected components of a graph

Since our planarity algorithms assume that the graph is triconnected, we present in this section a fast parallel algorithm to find the triconnected components of a graph. We define the triconnected components of a graph so that the graph is planar if and only if its triconnected components are. We generally follow McLane's definitions [McL1]. Our algorithm finds the triconnected components in $O(\log^2 n)$ time with $O(n^4)$ processors, and can be viewed as a generalization of a technique used in [SJ] to find the biconnected components of a graph. We now proceed to define precisely what we mean by triconnected components of a graph.

Let $G = (V, E)$ be an undirected biconnected graph and let $H_1 = (V_1, E_1)$ and $H_2 = (V_2, E_2)$ be two subgraphs of G. Then $H_1 + H_2$ is defined to be the subgraph $(V_1 \cup V_2, E_1 \cup E_2)$. Let $\{u, v\} \subseteq V$. A split of G at $\{u, v\}$ is a pair of non-empty subgraphs $H_1 = (V_1, E_1)$ and $H_2 = (V_2, E_2)$ such that

$$G = H_1 + H_2, \; E_1 \cap E_2 = \emptyset \text{ and } V_1 \cap V_2 = \{u, v\}.$$

If such a split exists, $\{u, v\}$ is called a separation pair. Corresponding to the split $\langle H_1, H_2 \rangle$, we define the blocks B_1 and B_2 associated with H_1 and H_2 as follows:

$$B_1 = \begin{cases} (V_1, E_1 \cup \{(u, v)\}) & \text{if } H_1 \text{ is not a path} \\ \emptyset & \text{otherwise} \end{cases}$$

$$B_2 = \begin{cases} (V_2, E_2 \cup \{(u, v)\}) & \text{if } H_2 \text{ is not a path} \\ \emptyset & \text{otherwise} \end{cases}$$

(u, v) will be called a virtual edge in this case.

A graph $G = (V, E)$ is triconnected if it is biconnected and has no split. If a biconnected graph $G = (V, E)$ splits into two blocks, then G may be further decomposed by splitting one of these blocks which may happen not to be triply connected. We continue this process (each time ignoring the empty blocks) until no further splitting is possible. These triply connected blocks are called the triply connected components (t.c.c.) of G. We now prove some basic facts about triconnected graphs.

Lemma 3.1: If $G = (V, E)$ is triconnected, then $\deg v \geq 3$, for all $v \in V$.

Lemma 3.2: A graph $G = (V, E)$ is triconnected iff for all pairs $\{v, w\} \subseteq V$, there exist three vertex disjoint paths between v and w.

Theorem 3.3 [McL1]: Every t.c.c. of a graph $G = (V, E)$ is homeomorphic to a maximal triply connected subgraph. Moreover, if $\{A_1, A_2, \ldots, A_m\}$ is a complete set of t.c.c.'s of G, then every maximal triconnected subgraph of G is homeomorphic to one and only one of the A_i's. The t.c.c.'s of G are unique up to a homeomorphism.

Theorem 3.4 [McL1]: A biconnected graph G is planar iff all of its t.c.c.'s are planar.

One way of attempting to find the t.c.c.'s of a graph is to start by removing all separation pairs, find the connected components and try to reconstruct the t.c.c.'s. This approach won't work because a t.c.c. may only have four vertices $\{v_1, v_2, v_3, v_4\}$ such that each pair $\{v_i, v_j\}$, $i \neq j$, is a separation pair. Consider the graph of figure 1.

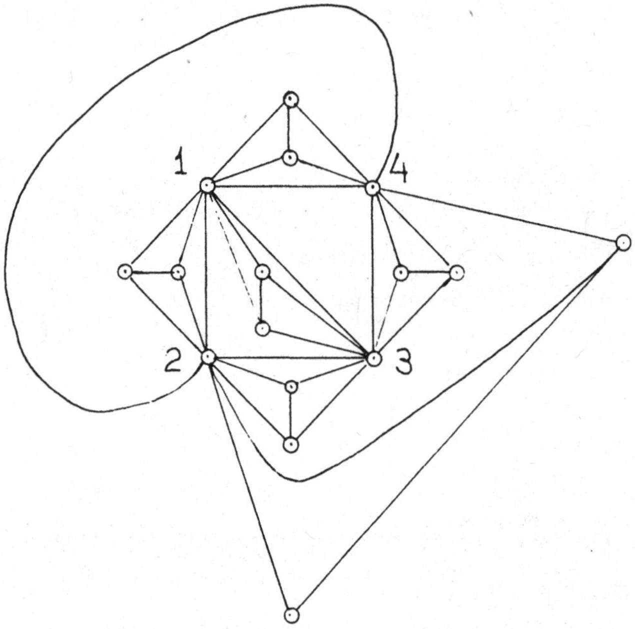

figure 1

{1, 2, 3, 4} is the vertex set of a t.c.c. and yet {1, 2}, {1, 3}, {1, 4}, {2, 3}, {2, 4}, {3, 4} are all separation pairs.

Let $G = (V, E)$ be a biconnected graph;

Define a relation R on $V \times V$ by iRj iff i and j are in a common t.c.c. of G.

<u>Lemma 3.5</u>: iRj iff for all $\{\alpha, \beta\}$ such that $\alpha, \beta \notin \{i, j\}$, $(i, j) \in G^*_{\alpha\beta} = (V_{\alpha\beta}, E^*_{\alpha\beta})$, where $G_{\alpha\beta}$ is the subgraph of G obtained by removing α and β and all edges incident on α or β, and G^* is the reflexive transitive closure of G.

<u>Proof</u>: Let i and j be such that iRj, i.e., i and j are in the same t.c.c. If $(i, j) \in E$, then $(i, j) \in E^*_{\alpha\beta}$ and we are done. Suppose now $(i, j) \notin E$. Then by Menger's Theorem [H], no two points can separate i and j.

The converse follows from Menger's theorem and lemma 3.2. □

It is easy to see that we can construct R in $O(\log^2 n)$ time with $O(n^4)$ processors. We now address the problem of actually determining each t.c.c. of G. Notice that the following holds.

<u>Lemma 3.6</u>: Two t.c.c.'s can intersect in at most two vertices.

It follows that every three vertices in one t.c.c. determines the t.c.c. uniquely. We thus define the following relation T on $V \times V \times V$:

$$(i, j, k) \in T \iff iRj \wedge jRk \wedge iRk$$

Note that since R is <u>not</u> transitive, we need all the three conditions.

We now have the following characterization.

<u>Lemma 3.7</u>: If $(i, j, k) \in T$, then i, j and k belong to the same t.c.c. of G. Moreover, for each $(i, j, k) \in T$, the set

$$V_{ijk} = \{\ell \in V \mid \ell Ri \wedge \ell Rj \wedge \ell Rk\}$$

determines a t.c.c. and, conversely, each t.c.c. of G can be obtained this way.

<u>Proof</u>: The first statement of the lemma is obvious. Now let $\ell \in V_{ijk}$. We prove that ℓ is in the same t.c.c. as i, j and k. Suppose not. Let A_1 be the t.c.c. which contains i, j and k. Then there exists a pair of vertices {u, v} which separate ℓ from i, j and k. Hence one of ℓRi, ℓRj and ℓRk is false.

On the other hand, if a vertex ℓ belongs to the t.c.c. A_1 containing i, j and k, then it is obvious that $\ell \in V_{ijk}$. □

The above lemmas suggest the following algorithm.

<u>Algorithm 3.1</u>

1) Find the set of all separation pairs S_G.
2) For each $\{u, v\} \in S_G$, construct the transitive closure G^*_{uv}.
3) Compute R.
4) Compute T.
5) Find the triply connected components of G using T and R.

<u>Theorem 3.3</u>: The above algorithm correctly finds the triply connected components of a graph $G = (V, E)$. This algorithm can be implemented to run in $O(\log^2 n)$ time with $O(n^4)$ processors.

Proof: The correctness follows directly from Lemma 3.7. The table below gives the running time and the number of processors for each of the steps of the above algorithm.

Step	Time	# of Processors
1	$O(\log^2 n)$	$O(n^4)$
2	$O(\log^2 n)$	$O(n^4)$
3	$O(\log^2 n)$	$O(n^4)$
4	$O(1)$	$O(n^3)$
5	$O(\log^2 n)$	$O(n^3)$. □

4. The first planarity algorithm

In the sequel, unless otherwise noted, we shall always assume graphs to be triconnected. If Y is a set of vertices of a graph G $E(Y)$ is the set of edges of the subgraph induced by Y. Let G be a (triconnected) graph and let T be a spanning tree of G, and let $X \subseteq E(G) - E(T)$. Every edge $a \in X$ defines a unique cycle C_a consisting of a and the unique path in T that joins T's endpoints. Let $F = \{C_a | a \in X\}$. F is a cycle basis.

Let C be a cycle of G, e, f edges of C. Define the equivalence relation $\equiv_c$ by $e \equiv_c f$ iff there is a path in G that includes e and f and has no internal vertices in common with C. The bridges of G relative to C are the subgraphs induced by the edges of the equivalence classes of $E(G) - E(C)$ under $\equiv_c$ (these are the 'connected pieces of G if C is disconnected from G'). C is peripheral if G has a single bridge relative to C. Let F' be a cycle basis of peripheral cycles, and $M = F' \cup \{\sum_{C \in F'} C\}$ (cycles are considered, as usual as vectors in $Z_2^{|E(G)|}$). M is a plane mesh of G if every edge of G appears in exactly two cycles of M. The following is a classical result of McLane's [McL1, BM, H].

Theorem 4.1: G is planar iff it has a plane mesh. The cycles of the plane mesh are the faces in the (unique) embedding of G into the sphere.

Our first algorithm builds a plane mesh or reports that it is impossible to do so. The general strategy is the following: we find a cycle basis. If G is planar, the cycles will be mapped into Jordan curves in a plane embedding. In an embedding bridges will have to be entirely contained in one of the two regions of the plane that the Jordan curve induces. These facts can be stated in a purely combinatorial manner: for every cycle C in the cycle basis and for every edge $e \notin E(C)$ we define a boolean variable $IN(C, e)$. The intended meaning is that $IN(C, e) = 1$ if edge e is mapped to the inside region of the Jordan curve defined by C. We call an assignment of truth values to the variables $\{IN(C, e) | e \notin E(C), C \in F\}$ a <u>pseudo-embedding</u> if the following conditions are met:

a) if e, f belong to the same bridge B, relative to cycle C, then $IN(C, e) \Leftrightarrow IN(C, f)$

b) if $IN(C, e) = 1$ then for every cycle C' such that $e \in E(C')$ and for every edge $f \in [E(C) - E(C')]$ $IN(C', f) = 0$

c) if e, f are edges that belong to bridges B, B' that <u>conflict</u> (see below) relative to cycle C, then $IN(C, e) \Leftrightarrow \neg IN(C, f)$.

The <u>vertices of attachment</u> of bridge B to cycle C are vertices in $V(B) \cup V(C)$. Bridges B and B' <u>conflict</u> relative to cycle C if either

1) there are vertices v_1, v_2, v_3 that are both vertices of attachment of B to C and vertices of attachment of B' to C.

or

2) there are vertices u, v, w, z of V(C) that, in a cyclic ordering of the vertices of V(C) appear in the order above, with u, w vertices of attachment of B to C and v, z vertices of attachment of B' to C.

Note that vertices of attachment, conflicts and pseudo-embeddings are purely combinatorial concepts. We have, however, the following facts: first, every embedding is a pseudo-embedding. This is precisely stated in Lemma 4.2. Before proceeding we need some terminology.

If G is a planar graph and E is an embedding of G into the plane, we use the following notations: if C, C_i, C_j are cycles of G, and if e is an edge of G we denote by Γ_C, Γ_{C_i}, Γ_{C_j} and γ_e respectively the Jordan curves the cycles C, C_i, C_j and the edge e are mapped into, respectively. When C is determined by the context, we drop it as a subscript, to avoid double subscripting, and denote the curves by Γ, Γ_i, Γ_j respectively. The <u>interior</u> of Γ is the bounded domain of the two domains determined by Γ on the plane, the <u>exterior</u> of Γ is the other domain. An edge e (or a cycle D) is <u>inside</u> Γ if the curve γ_e (the closed curve Γ_D) has no points mapped to the exterior of Γ. Similarly, we say that Γ_i is mapped <u>outside</u> Γ if no points of Γ_i are mapped to the interior of Γ.

<u>Lemma 4.2</u>: Let G be a planar graph and E an embedding of G into the plane. Let F be a set of fundamental cycles of G. Assign values to the boolean variables $IN(C, e)$ for all $C \in F$, $e \in E(G) - E(C)$ according to the rule

$$IN(C, e) = 1 \text{ iff } \gamma_e \text{ is inside } \Gamma_C \text{ in } E.$$

Then this assignment is a pseudo-embedding.

For a given planar graph G we say that the pseudo-embedding P obtained from an embedding E as in the lemma above <u>represents</u> the embedding, and that the variables IN(C, e) with the assignments of P <u>have the intended meaning in</u> E. In general, if $C_1, C_2, \ldots, C_k$ are a subset of F, P is a pseudo-embedding and E is an embedding, we say that P restricted to $C_1, C_2, \ldots, C_k$ represents E (or

E is represented by P restricted to $C_1, C_2, \ldots, C_k$) if there is an embedding E' such that P represents E' and the set of edges mapped into the interior of $\Gamma_1, \Gamma_2, \ldots, \Gamma_k$ is the same in E and in E'.

Unfortunately, the converse of Lemma 4.2 is not true: there are pseudo-embeddings that do not represent embeddings. Consider the spanning tree below for K_{33}. The assignment $IN(C, e) = 0$ for all $C \in F$ and all $e \notin E(C)$ is a pseudo-embedding.

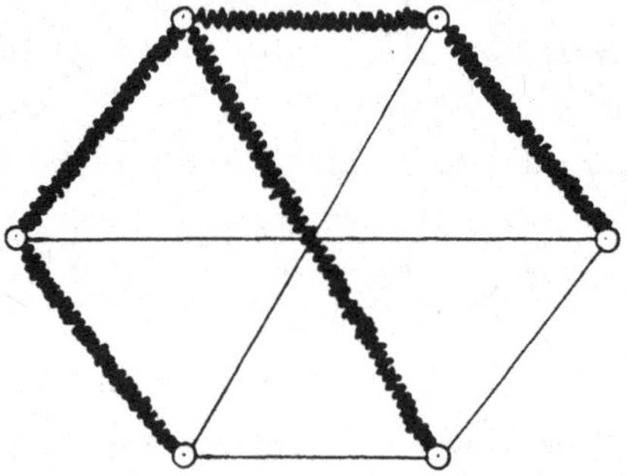

There is, however, a partial converse that we prove later, that enables us to obtain an algorithm: if G is planar every pseudo-embedding represents an embedding (Theorem 4.).

As we shall see, if E is an embedding of a planar graph G, it is easy to obtain from E a plane mesh for G, and the procedure can be stated in terms of the pseudo-embedding P that represents E.

The idea behind our first algorithm is as follows: given G, obtain a pseudo-embedding P of G (if none exists, G is nonplanar). Now, treating P as if it represented an embedding, carry out the procedure that will produce a plane mesh for G if P represents an embedding. Call the resulting set of cycles a pseudo plane mesh. If the pseudo plane mesh is indeed a plane mesh, G is planar. On the other hand, if G is planar then the pseudo plane mesh is in fact a plane mesh. So G is planar iff it has a pseudo-embedding, and the pseudo plane mesh is a plane mesh. In the rest of this section we formalize these notions and prove the facts claimed.

Let $C_1, C_2 \in F$. Define $C_1 \subseteq C_2$ (intended meaning: in the embedding represented by P, Γ_{C_1} lies inside Γ_{C_2}) by

$$C_1 \subseteq C_2 \text{ if } \exists e \in E(C_1) \ IN(C_2, e) = 1.$$

For fundamental cycles (cycles obtained from a spanning tree) $\subseteq$ is well defined (i.e. the definition makes sense - but $\subseteq$ may not have the intended meaning).

Lemma 4.3: Given a cycle $C \epsilon F$, the pseudo-embeddings of G induce a partition F_1, F_2 of $F - \{C\}$, such that for every pseudo-embedding for $i = 1, 2$, $C_1 \epsilon F_i$, $C_2 \epsilon F_i$ imply $C_2 \subseteq C$ iff $C_2 \subseteq C$.

From the proof of Lemma 4.3, we can obtain the

Corollary 4.4: Let G be planar and let C be a cycle of G, $C \epsilon F$. Then the partition above, of the edges in $E(G) - E(C)$ corresponds to the two possible sets of edges that may be mapped into the bounded domain of the plane in plane embeddings of G.

Lemma 4.5: Let G be planar and let $C \epsilon F$. Let P be a pseudo-embedding, and let $\{D_i\}$ be the set of fundamental cycles such that $D_i \subseteq C$ in P. Then there is a plane embedding E of G such that P restricted to $\{C\} \cup \{D_i\}$ represents E. (In other words, the pseudo-embedding P has the intended meaning in the interior of C).

Actually, we get a slightly stronger result: not only are there plane embeddings where P has the intended meaning in the interior of C, but P represents all such embeddings.

The next lemma is a property of plane embeddings. It will be used in the proof of Theorem 4.7.

Lemma 4.6: Let G be planar. Assume G has cycles $C_1, C_2, \ldots, C_k$ and D and a plane embedding E such that

1) in E, for all $1 \leq i \leq j \leq k$ Γ_i lies outside Γ_j and Γ_j lies outside Γ_i

2) for all $1 \leq i \leq k$ Γ_i lies inside Γ_D

3) there is an edge $e \epsilon (E(D) - \bigcup_{i=1}^{k} E(C_i))$

Then there is an embedding E' of G, such that

1) for all $1 \leq i \leq k$, Γ'_i (the image of C_i in E') has in its interior (the images of) exactly the same edges as does the interior of Γ_i

2) for all i Γ'_i lies outside Γ_D.

We are now ready to prove the partial converse to Lemma 4.2, i.e. that for planar graphs every pseudo-embedding represents an embedding.

Theorem 4.7: Let G be a planar graph and P a pseudo-embedding of G. Then there is a plane embedding E, of G, such that P represents E.

Proof: Let F, the set of fundamental cycles of G used in P have k cycles. We give an inductive procedure that yields, at each step, a set $\hat{E}$ of embeddings and a subset S of cycles, such that for every embedding $E \epsilon \hat{E}$, P restricted to the cycles in S represents E, and, moreover, $\hat{E}$ is a collection of all such embeddings. At each step the cardinality of S increases, so the algorithm terminates, since $|F| = k$. We shall prove that $\hat{E}$ is nonempty at each step. This yields the theorem, when $S = F$. At step i we will add a collection of cycles to S in such a way that if $D \in F - S$ then $\neg D \subseteq C$ for $C \in S$ (i.e. the cycles not yet in S are not IN - in the pseudo-embedding P - any cycle in S).

We denote the sets S and $\hat{E}$ at the end of step i by S_i and E_i respectively.

step 0 $S_0 \neq \emptyset$ E_0 = {plane embeddings of G}.

step $i+1$ Choose a cycle C in $F - S_i$ that is maximal with respect to $\subseteq$ - i.e. for all $D \in F$ $\neg C \subseteq D$ in P.

$$S_{i+1} = S_i \cup \{C\} \cup \{D \in (F - S_i) \mid D \subseteq C\}$$

$$E_{i+1} = \{E \in E_i \mid \text{in } E \ \Gamma_i \text{ lies outside } \Gamma_C \text{ for all } C_i \in S\}$$

The construction has the desired properties - we have to show it can be carried out.

a) There is a maximal cycle C in $F - S_i$. By construction, if $C \subseteq D$ for some $D \in S_i$, then $C \in S_i$. Pick a cycle $C_1 \in F - S_i$. If for all $D \in F - S_1$ $\neg C_1 \subseteq D$, pick $C = C_1$, otherwise let C_2 be a cycle such that $C_1 \subseteq C_2$, and continue the procedure with C_2. The procedure either terminates with a cycle C as desired, or we have found a sequence of cycles $C_1, C_2, \ldots, C_e$ with $C_1 \subseteq C_2$, $C_2 \subseteq C_3$, $C_{e-1} \subseteq C_e$, $C_e \subseteq C_1$. But such a sequence contradicts Lemma 4.5: the inside of Γ_e is represented by P in any embedding that maps an edge e with $IN(C_1, e) = 1$ into the interior of Γ_e (such edge must exist, since $C_{e-1} \subseteq C_e$). But in this embedding, by Lemma 4.5, Γ_{e-1} lies inside Γ_e, Γ_{e-2} inside Γ_{e-1}, and hence inside Γ_e, and, finally, Γ_1 lies inside Γ_e. But then, since P restricted to C_1 represents the embedding, $IN(C_1, f) = 0$ for some $f \in E(C_e) - E(C_1)$ and, hence, $\neg C_e \subseteq C_1$.

b) E_{i+1} is nonempty. First note that by construction C is such that all edges of cycles in S have the same value of $IN(C, e)$ in all pseudo-embeddings. By Corollary 4.4, in any embedding of G all these edges are mapped into the same domain, relative to Γ_C. If, for some $E \in E_i$ these edges are mapped into the unbounded region, then we are done: the embedding is represented by P restricted to S_i by induction, P restricted to C represents E and by Lemma 4.5 P restricted to $S_{i+1} - (S_i \cup \{C\})$ also represents E.

So assume $E \in E_i$ but some edge of S_i is mapped to the interior of Γ_C. Then all cycles of S_i are mapped to the interior of Γ_C. By Lemma 4.6, there is an embedding E' in which the interiors Γ'_j of all $C_j \in' S_i$ are the same as in E, but the Γ'_js lie outside Γ'_C. Then P restricted to S_i represents E' (since an edge is mapped inside Γ'_j iff it is mapped inside Γ_j) and hence $E' \in E_i$. But P restricted to S_{i+1} represents E': P restricted to C has the intended meaning by the construction of E', and, by Lemma 4.5, P has the intended meaning for all cycles D in the interior of C.

Finally note that the definition of S_{i+1} ensures that $D \in F - S_{i+1}$ implies $\neg D \subseteq C$ for any $C \in S$, as claimed.

Thus the required embedding can be produced. □

Our planarity algorithm, as explained before, does not attempt to mimic the construction above. We need an additional construction, that, given a pseudo-embedding for a planar graph, finds a plane mesh for it. First we note some properties of plane embeddings.

Let G be a planar graph, F a set of fundamental cycles $E = \{C_i | i = 1, 2, \ldots, n\}$ and E plane embedding of G. Let D_{ij} be the set of peripheral cycles that are mapped to the interior of Γ_i in E. Then

$$C_i = \sum_j D_{ij} \qquad (1)$$

where the sum is the usual sum of cycles [H, BM].

We shall obtain a new cycle basis $\{C_i' | i = 1, 2, \ldots, n\}$ for G, where the C_i' are peripheral. We formalize the following idea: some of the C_i are peripheral. Consider some C_j that (in E) contains only peripheral cycles C_i. Then $C_j' = C_j + \sum_{i \in A} C_i$, with $A = \{i | C_i$ is mapped inside Γ_j by $E\}$ is a peripheral cycle.

More formally, given a pseudo-embedding P, define the relation $C_i < C_j$ (C_j directly surrounds C_i) among cycles of F by

$$C_i < C_j \text{ iff } C_i \subseteq C_j \ \& \ \neg\exists D, D \in F \ \ C_i \subseteq D \ \& \ D \subseteq C_j.$$

Since P represents an embedding, $<$ is an order relation.

For $C_i \in F$ define

$$\text{level}(i) = \begin{cases} 0 & \text{if } \{C_j | C_j < C_i\} = \emptyset \\ k+1 & \text{if } k = \max\{\text{level}(j) | C_j < C_i\} \end{cases}$$

Define $\{C_i' | i = 1, 2, \ldots, n\}$ by

$$C_i' = \begin{cases} C_i & \text{if level}(i) = 0 \\ C_i + \sum'_{C_j \in \text{Int}(i)} C_j & \text{where } \text{Int}(i) = \{C_j | C_j < C_i\} \end{cases}$$

<u>Lemma 4.8</u>: $\{C_i' | i = 1, \ldots, n\}$ is a peripheral cycle basis for G (and, therefore, $\{C_i'\} \cup \{\sum'^{n}_{i=1} C_i'\}$ is a plane mesh for G).

Note that the definition of the C_i' uses only the combinatorial notions of a pseudo-embedding, and the process of computing the C_i' can be carried out for any graph with a pseudo-embedding. If the graph is planar, this yields a peripheral basis and a plane mesh.

These results imply the following efficient parallel algorithm for planarity:

Planar 1 (G)

1. Find a spanning tree T of G, and the corresponding set of fundamental cycles, F.
2. Try to find a pseudo-embedding--if this fails, report G is nonplanar. In more detail,
   2.1. For each $C_i \in F$ find all the bridges B_i of G relative to C_i.
   2.2. For each cycle $C_i \in F$ and for every edge $e \notin E(C_i)$ use a variable $IN(C_i, e)$. Write down the boolean formulas that ensure that conditions 1) 2) and 3) for a pseudo-embedding hold. (Note that this yields a 2-CNF formula).
   2.3. Obtain a satisfying assignment for the formula above. This is a pseudo-embedding. If the formula is unsatisfiable G is nonplanar.
3. Compute the relation $<$ among cycles C_i in F.
4. Obtain the C_i' as in Lemma 6. Let $F' = \{C_i'\} \cup \{\Sigma C_i'\}$.
5. Test whether every edge appears in exactly two cycles of C_i'.

If so, G is planar, otherwise it is nonplanar. □

Theorem 4.9: Planar 1 (G) correctly tests planarity of G. It can be implemented to run in $O(\log^2 n)$ time on $O(n^4)$ processors, where $n = |V(G)|$.

Correctness follows from results of this section. We sketch the time analysis below.

Step 1 can be done in time $O(\log^2 n)$ with $O(n^2)$ processors ([J]).

Step 2.1 is very similar to the connectivity problems in [SJ] or the 3-connected components algorithm in this paper. Every cycle requires $O(n^2)$ processors to find its bridges in $O(\log^2 n)$ time. Since there are at most $O(n)$ cycles (we precede Planar 1 by a procedure that counts the number of vertices and the number of edges and rejects if there are more than $3n - 6$ edges) $O(n^3)$ processors suffice for this step.

Step 2.2 can be done in parallel since conflicts among bridges are easy to detect. The number of processors is $O((\text{number of cycles})^2 \times (\text{number of edges})^2) = O(n^4)$, and the time $O(\log n)$. The number of terms in the 2-CNF formula is at most $O(n^4)$.

Step 2.3 is a 2-CNF satisfiability algorithm, based on merging lists of requirements of truth values induced by partial assignments. There are $O(n^2)$ variables and $O(n^4)$ formulas: $O(\log^2 n)$ time and $O(n^4)$ processors suffice.

Step 3 takes $O(\log n)$ time with $O(n^3)$ processors, as does step 4 (step 4 consists in solving a set of linear recurrences). For step 5 $O(n^2)$ processors and $O(\log n)$ time suffice.

Thus, the whole procedure can be carried out in $O(\log^2 n)$ parallel steps, using $O(n^4)$ processors. □

Corollary 4.10: Planarity testing can be carried out in space $\log^4 n$ by a Turing machine.

This follows by standard simulation of parallel computers [HS, FW] by tape-bounded Turing machines. Actually, we can obtain much sharper results: graph planarity can be tested in $\log^2 n$ space by a Turing machine [JS]. Unfortunately the space-efficient algorithms do not run in polynomial time.

5. The second planarity algorithm

Tutte describes in [T] a method of embedding a triconnected planar graph in the cartesian plane. We sketch the main ideas behind this method.

Let J be a peripheral cycle of a triconnected graph $G = (V, E)$. Let p be the number of vertices of J. Let Q be a p-sided convex polygon in the Euclidean. We view Q as an embedding of J in the Euclidean plane. Let f be a one-one mapping of $V(J)$ onto the set of vertices of Q such that the cyclic order of vertices in J agrees, under f, with the cyclic order of vertices of Q.

Let $V = \{v_1, v_2, \ldots, v_n\}$ be an enumeration of the vertices of V such that $\{v_1, \ldots, v_p\}$ are the vertices of J. We try to extend f to other vertices of G. Let v_i be any vertex and let $A(i)$ be the set of vertices adjacent to v_i. Suppose $f(v_j)$ is defined for each $v_j \epsilon A(i)$. Put a unit mass m_j at each point $f(v_j)$, for each $v_j \epsilon A(i)$. Then $f(v_i)$ is defined to be the centroid of the masses m_j, $v_j \epsilon A(i)$; i.e., if $f(v_\ell) = (x_\ell, y_\ell)$, $1 \leq \ell \leq n$, we have

$$x_i = \frac{x_{j_1} + x_{j_2} + \ldots + x_{j_k}}{k}$$

$$y_i = \frac{y_{j_1} + y_{j_2} + \ldots + y_{j_k}}{k}, \text{ if } A(i) = \{v_{j_1}, \ldots, v_{j_k}\}$$

In order to prove that such an Euclidean embedding is possible if the graph is planar, we define the $n \times n$ matrix $A = (a_{ij})$ such that

$$a_{ij} = \begin{cases} -1 & \text{if } i \neq j \text{ and } G \text{ contains the edge } (v_i, v_j) \\ \deg(i) & \text{if } i = j \\ 0 & \text{otherwise} \end{cases}$$

Consider the solution of the following linear system of equations

$$(*) \quad \begin{aligned} &\sum_{j=1}^{n} a_{ij}x_j = 0 \\ &\sum_{j=1}^{n} a_{ij}y_j = 0, \quad 1 \leq i, j \leq n. \end{aligned}$$

Let (x_i, y_i) be the coordinates of the vertices of Q, $1 \leq i \leq p$. One can prove that the above system has a unique solution with (x_i, y_i) being the centroid of the masses m, $v_j \epsilon A(i)$. The corresponding embedding is called a barycentric representation of G. We now describe the second planarity algorithm.

Planar 2 (G)

1. Find a peripheral cycle C of G with p vertices. Find p cartesian points (x_i, y_i), $1 \le i \le p$, that form a convex polygon in the Euclidean plane.
2. Solve the linear system of equations

$$\sum_{j=1}^{n} a_{ij}x_j = 0$$

$$\sum_{j=1}^{n} a_{ij}y_j = 0, \quad p < i \le n,$$

where $A = (a_{ij})$ is as defined above.
3. For every pair {e, f} of edges of G, write down the equations of the line segments that represent these edges in the embedding of (2) and check that they do not cross. If so G is planar, otherwise, G is nonplanar.

Theorem 5.1: Planar 2(G) correctly checks if a given triconnected graph $G = (V, E)$ is planar and runs in time $O(\log^2 n)$ using $O(n^{3.29}/\log^2 n)$ processors.

Because of space limitation, we refer the reader to the full paper for the proof of Theorem 5.1.

6. Acknowledgement: This research was partially supported by grants MCS 78 27600 and MCS 790 5006 from the National Science Foundation.

Bibliography

[Br] Brent, R. P.: The Parallel Evaluation of General Arithmetic Expressions JACM 21 (1974) 201-206.

[BM] Bondy, J. A. and U. S. R. Murty: Graph Theory with Applications American Elsevier, NY (1977).

[C] Csanky, L.: Fast Parallel Matrix Inversion Algorithms SIAM J. Comput. 5 (1976) 618-623.

[Ch] Chandra, A. K.: Maximal Parallelism in Matrix Multiplication IBM Tech. Rept. RC 6193, Sept. 1976.

[F] Flynn, M. J.: Very High-Speed Computing Systems Proc. IEEE 54 (Dec. 1976) 1901-1909.

[FW] Fortune, S. and J. Wyllie: Parallelism in Random Access Machines Proc. 10th Ann. ACM Symp. Comp. Th. Comp., San Diego, CA (1978) 114-118.

[G1] Goldschlager, C. M.: A Unified Approach to Models of Synchronous Parallel Machines Proc. 10th Ann. ACM Symp. Th. Comp., San Diego, CA (1978) 89-94.

[G2] Goldschlager, L. M.: Synchronous Parallel Computation TR 114 (1977) University of Toronto.

[H] Harary, F.: Graph Theory Addison-Wesley, Reading, Mass. (1969).

[He] Heller, D.: A Survey of Parallel Algorithms in Numerical Linear Algebra SIAM Review 20: 4 (1978) 740-777.

[Hi] Hirschberg, D. S.: Parallel Algorithms for the Transitive Closure and the Connected Components Problems Proc. 8th Ann. ACM Symp. Th. Comp. (1976) 55-57.

[HS] Hartmanis, J. and J. Simon: On the Power of Multiplication in Random Access Machines Proc. 15th SWAT Conf., New Orleans, LA (1974) 13-23.

[J] Ja'Ja', J: Graph Connectivity Problems on Parallel Computers Technical Report CS-78-05, Department of Computer Science, PSU, (Feb. 1978).

[JS] Ja'Ja', J. and J. Simon: Some Space-Efficient Algorithms Proc. 17th Allerton Conference, pp. 677-684, 1979.

[McL1] McLane, S.: A Combinatorial Condition for Planar Graphs Fundamenta Math. 28 (1937) 22-32.

[McL2] McLane, S.: A Structural Characterization of Planar Combinatorial Graphs Duke Math. J. 3 (1937) 46-472.

[P] Preparata, F. P.: Parallelism in Sorting International Conference on Parallel Processing, Belair, Michigan (August 1977).

[PS] Pratt, V. R. and L. J. Stockmeyer: A Characterization of the Power of Vector Machines JCSS 12:2 (1976) 198-221.

[PSa] Preparata, F. P. and D. V. Sarwate: An Improved Parallel Processor Bound in Fast Matrix Inversion IPL 7:3 (1978) 148-150.

[SJ] Savage, C. and J. Ja'Ja': Fast, Efficient Parallel Algorithms for Some Graph Problems, submitted for publication.

[T] Tutte, W. T.: How to Draw a Graph Proc. London Math. Soc. (3) 13 (1963) 743-768.

ON ATOMIC NETS AND CONCURRENCY RELATIONS

Ryszard Janicki

Institute of Mathematics, Warsaw Technical University
Pl. Jedności Robotniczej 1, 00-661 Warszawa/Poland

Introduction.

Petri nets are widely used to model the behaviour of concurrent systems and processes (see [2,4,5,6]). There is a lot of classifications of Petri nets, but the most general seems to be the partition into marked and unmarked nets. Unmarked nets describe the static (or "topological" in the common meaning of this word) aspects of concurrent systems and processes, whereas marked nets describe the dynamic structure of those systems.

An influence of the static unmarked structure of a net on its dynamic properties is one of the problems considered in the paper. The next problem we shall deal with is the partition of nets into indivisible components (atoms). Note that the partition into atoms is one of the basic research methods of science. Usually, this partition depends on what we want to prove about the given system. In this paper by atoms we shall mean nets with "primitive concurrency", and, in particular nets representing sequential systems.

The last problem considered in the paper is the notion and properties of the concurrency relation in the case of nets with cycles.

The paper consists of two parts. In the first part properties of the lattice of unmarked nets are investigated. The second part is devoted to markings, concurrency relations and connections among static and dynamic structures of nets.

It turns out that nets created as the superposition of sequential nets have much properties required from "well defined" concurrent systems.

In the paper we shall use the standard mathematical notation ($|X|$ denote the cardinality of X and so on).

In principle, this paper is the continuation and the complement of [3] , however it can be read independently.

1. A lattice of simple nets.

The simple net defined in [2] is the basic notion of this paper.

For every set X, let left:$X \times X \to X$, right:$X \times X \to X$ be the following functions: $(\forall(x,y)\in X\times X)$ left((x,y))=x, right((x,y))=y.

By a <u>simple net</u> (abbr. <u>s-net</u>) we mean any pair

$$N = (T,P),$$

where: T is a set (of <u>transitions</u>),

$P \subseteq 2^T \times 2^T$ is a relation (also interpreted as a set of <u>places</u>),

$(\forall a\in T)(\exists p,q\in P)\ a\in \mathrm{left}(p) \cap \mathrm{right}(q)$,

$P=\emptyset \iff T=\emptyset$.

We restrict our attention to finite s-nets, and instead of $(\{a_1,\dots,a_n\},\{b_1,\dots,b_m\})\in P$ we shall write $[a_1,\dots,a_n:b_1,\dots,b_n]\in P$. Every s-net N=(T,P) can be graphically represented using the graph:

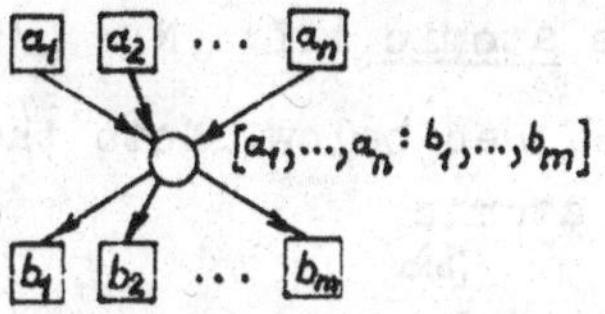

to denote the fact that $[a_1,\dots,a_n:b_1,\dots,b_m]\in P$.

<u>Example 1.1.</u> Let N=(T,P), where T={a,b,c,d,e,f,h},
P = { [∅:a] , [a,f:b,h] , [h:∅] , [c:e] , [b:e] , [b:d] , [d:e] , [e:f] } .
The pair N=(T,P) is a s-net and it can be represented by the following graph.

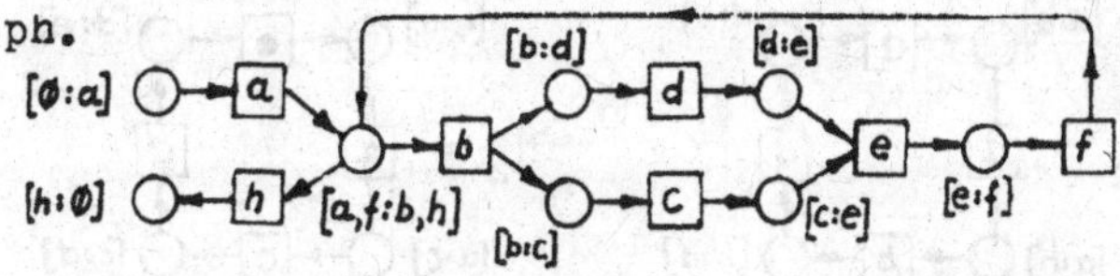

□

In the literature nets are usually defined differently, starting with two disjoint sets of transitions and places, and introducing a flow-relation among them. This approach is luckier in the sense that it makes more easy to handle operation among nets.

Let SNETS denote the family of all finite simple nets.

Let ⊑ be the relation in SNETS defined as follows:

$$N_1=(T_1,P_1) \sqsubseteq N_2=(T_2,P_2) \iff P_1 \subseteq P_2 .$$

Note that ⊑ is a partial order relation and $N_1 \sqsubseteq N_2$ implies $T_1 \subseteq T_2$. Let $\sup\{N_1,N_2\}$, $\inf\{N_1,N_2\}$ denote respectively the least upper bound and the greatest lower bound with respect to the relation ⊑ .

<u>Theorem 1.1.</u>

For every $N_1=(T_1,P_1)$, $N_2=(T_2,P_2) \in$ SNETS:

$$\sup\{N_1,N_2\} = (T_1\cup T_2, P_1\cup P_2),$$

$\inf\{N_1,N_2\}$ = (left(P),P), where P is the maximal set

fulfilling the condition $P \subseteq P_1 \cap P_2$ and left(P)=right(P). ■

Define the following operations: $N_1 \cup N_2 = \sup\{N_1, N_2\}$, $N_1 \cap N_2 = \inf\{N_1, N_2\}$, $\bigcup_{N \in S} N = \sup\{N \mid N \in S\}$, $\bigcap_{N \in S} N = \inf\{N \mid N \in S\}$.

<u>Theorem 1.2.</u>
The algebra (SNETS, ∪, ∩) is a lattice with the greatest lower bound $(\emptyset, \emptyset)$. ■

The lattice (SNETS, ∪, ∩) is not distributive.

A simple net N=(T,P) is said to be an <u>atom</u> iff:

$N \neq (\emptyset,\emptyset)$ & $(N' \sqsubseteq N \implies (N' = N \text{ or } N' = (\emptyset,\emptyset)))$.

For every s-net N, let <u>atoms(N)</u> denote the set of all atoms contained in N, i.e. $\text{atoms}(N) = \{N' \mid N' \sqsubseteq N \text{ \& } N' \text{ is an atom}\}$.

A simple net N is said to be <u>atomic</u> iff: $N = \bigcup\{N' \mid N' \in \text{atoms}(N)\}$.

<u>Example 1.2.</u> Let N, N′ be nets defined below. Note that atoms(N)={N′} and N′≠ N, so the net N is not atomic.

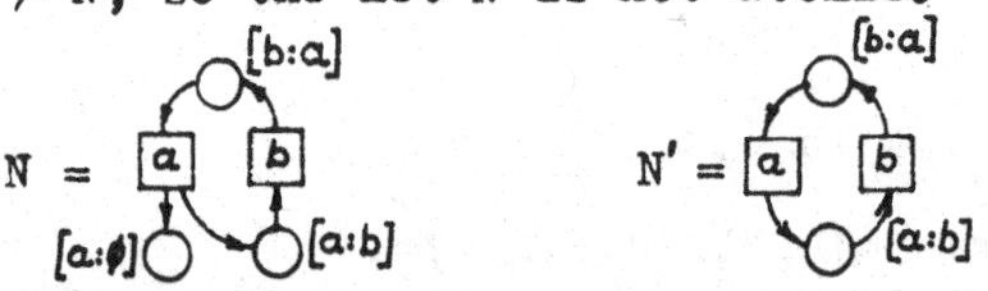

□

<u>Example 1.3.</u> Let N, N_1, N_2 be the following simple nets.

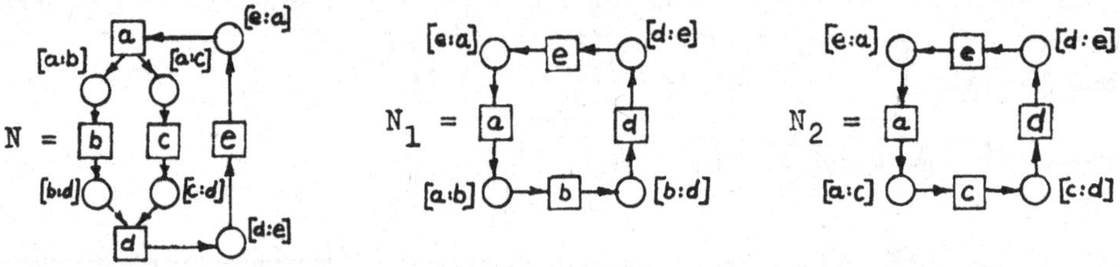

In this case $\text{atoms}(N)=\{N_1,N_2\}$, and $N = N_1 \cup N_2$, thus the net N is atomic □

Let N=(T,P) be a simple net. To simplify the considerations we shall use the following well known notation:

1. $(\forall p \in P)$ $p^\bullet = \text{right}(p)$, ${}^\bullet p = \text{left}(p)$,
2. $(\forall a \in T)$ $a^\bullet = \{p \in P \mid a \in \text{left}(p)\}$, ${}^\bullet a = \{p \in P \mid a \in \text{right}(p)\}$.

Of course, for every $p \in P$, $p = ({}^\bullet p, p^\bullet)$. Note that the above operations are correctly defined for every pair (T,P), where $P \subseteq 2^T \times 2^T$.

<u>Lemma 1.3.</u>
A pair (T,P), where $P \subseteq 2^T \times 2^T$ is a simple net iff:

$(\forall a \in T)$ $a^\bullet \neq \emptyset$ & ${}^\bullet a \neq \emptyset$. ■

Let $F \subseteq T \times P \cup P \times T$ (or F_N if N is not understood) be the following relation: $(\forall x,y \in T \cup P)$ $(x,y) \in F \iff x \in \text{left}(y) \text{ or } y \in \text{right}(x)$.

Note that for every s-net (T,P), the triple (T,P,F) is a standard representation of Petri net (compare [5,6]).

A simple net N is said to be connected iff
$(\forall x,y \in T\cup P) \quad (x,y) \in (F \cup F^{-1})^*$.

Other words, a net is connected if the suitable graph which represents this net is connected.

Theorem 1.4.

Every atom is connected. ■

Now we shall deal with nets representing sequential systems.

A simple net N=(T,P) is said to be elementary iff it is connected and $(\forall a \in T) \quad |{}^{\bullet}a| = |a^{\bullet}| = 1$.

Two nets defined below are examples of elementary nets.

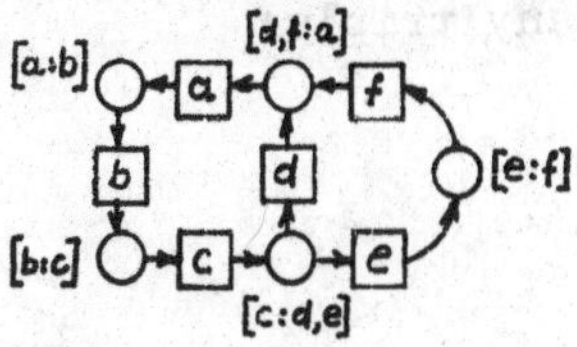

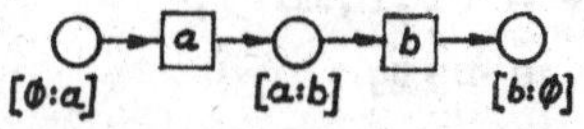

Theorem 1.5.

Every elementary net is an atom. ■

The inverse theorem is not true. An example of the atom which is not elementary is the following simple net.

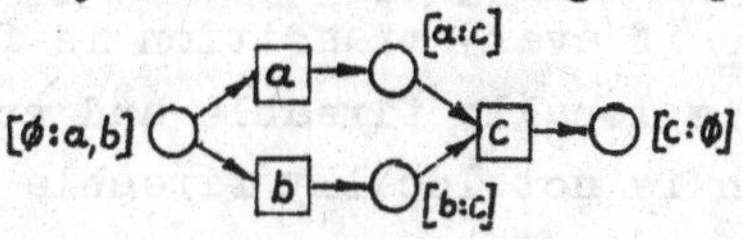

For every s-net N, let $elem(N) = \{N' \mid N' \subseteq N \ \&\ N' \text{ is elementary}\}$.

Note that every elementary net is equivalent with a totally labelled state machine.

The most important class of s-nets is the class of so called proper nets. We shall show in the sequel that proper marked nets have much properties required from well defined concurrent systems.

A s-net N is said to be proper iff $N = \bigcup\{N' \mid N' \in elem(N)\}$.

Corollary 1.6.

A s-net N=(T,P) is proper iff there is a set $\{N_1,\dots,N_m\}$ of elementary nets and $N = N_1 \cup \dots \cup N_m$. ■

Let PNETS denote the family of all proper nets (finite).

Lemma 1.7.

The family PNETS is closed under the operation $\cup$, but it is not closed under the operation $\cap$. ■

2. Markings and concurrency relations.

In this section we aim to show in which way the static structure describes dynamic structure of concurrent systems and vice versa.

Let N=(T,P) be a simple net, and let $Rl \subseteq 2^P \times 2^P$ be the following relation: $(M_1,M_2) \in Rl \Leftrightarrow (\exists a \in T)\ M_1 - {}^\bullet a = M_2 - a^\bullet\ \&\ {}^\bullet a \subseteq M_1\ \&\ a^\bullet \subseteq M_2$.
The relation Rl is called the forward reachability in one step (see [6]). Define $R = (Rl \cup Rl^{-1})^*$. The relation R is called the forward and backward reachability of N (or simply the reachability relation of N). If N is not understood we shall write Rl_N, R_N. Note that R is an equivalence relation. For every $M \in 2^P$, let $[M]_R$ (or simply $[M]$) denote the equivalence class of R containing M.

By a marked simple net (abbr. ms-net) we mean any triple:

$$MN = (T,P,Mar),$$

where: N=(T,P) is a s-net,

$Mar \subseteq 2^P$ is a set of markings of MN,

$Mar = \bigcup \{[M]_{R_N} \mid M \in Mar\}$.

A marked simple net MN=(T,P,Mar) is called compact iff:

$(\forall M \in Mar)\ \ Mar = [M]_{R_N}$.

A transition a T is called fireable iff $(\exists M_1,M_2 \in Mar)\ {}^\bullet a \subseteq M_1,\ a^\bullet \subseteq M_2$.

A ms-net is called locally fireable if every transition is fireable.

A ms-net is called fireable if it is locally fireable and compact. For the example of compact ms-net which is not locally fireable the reader is advised to refer to [3] . Now we introduce the notion of safeness in terms of this paper.

A ms-net MN=(T,P,Mar) is said to be safe iff: $(\forall C \in 2^P)(\forall a \in T)$
$({}^\bullet a \cap C = \emptyset\ \&\ (\exists M \in Mar)\ {}^\bullet a \cup C \subseteq M) \Leftrightarrow (a^\bullet \cap C = \emptyset\ \&\ (\exists M' \in Mar)\ a^\bullet \cup C \subseteq M')$.
It turns out that in the case of elementary nets, safeness defines very regular structure of markings.

Lemma 2.1.
For every ms-net MN=(T,P,Mar), if (T,P) is the elementary net then:

1. MN is safe $\Leftrightarrow$ $Mar = \{\{p\} \mid p \in P\}$,
2. MN is safe $\Rightarrow$ MN is compact and fireable.■

One of the most important notions of the Petri net theory is the notion of concurrency relation (see [1,5,6]). This is the relation that describes which elements can "coexist" and that generates parallelism. Petri has stated ([5]) that a sufficiently comprehensive theory of parallel systems and processes can be established on the basis of that relation.

We are now going to recall and modify some notions and results concerned concurrency-like relations from [1,5] .

Let X be a set, and let $id \subseteq X \times X$ be the identity relation.

A relation $C \subseteq X \times X$ is called the sir-relation (from symmertic and irreflexive) iff:

1. $(\forall a,b \in X)\ (a,b) \in C \iff (b,c) \in C$,
2. $(\forall a,b \in X)\ (a,b) \in C \implies a \neq b$.

Let C be a sir-relation. Define the families of subsets of X: kens(C), $\overline{\text{kens}}$(C) in the following way (compare [5]),

$A \in \text{kens}(C) \iff$ 1. $(\forall a,b \in A)\ (a,b) \in C \cup id$,
2. $(\forall c \notin A)(\exists a \in A)\ (a,c) \notin C$, and

$A \in \overline{\text{kens}}(C) \iff$ 1. $(\forall a,b \in A)\ (a,b) \notin C$,
2. $(\forall c \notin A)(\exists a \in A)\ (a,c) \in C$.

Corollary 2.2.
For every sir-relation $C \subseteq X \times X$, kens(C), $\overline{\text{kens}}$(C) are covers of X.■

We shall now consider some relationship between covers and sir-relations. Let cov be a cover of X, and let $sir(cov) \subseteq X \times X$ be the relation defined as follows:

$(a,b) \in sir(cov) \iff \{A \mid A \in cov\ \&\ a \in A\} \cap \{A \mid A \in cov\ \&\ b \in A\} = \emptyset$.

The relation sir(cov) is called the sir-relation defined by cov.

A sir-relation C is called K-dense (see [1,5]) iff:

$(\forall A \in \text{kens}(C))(\forall B \in \overline{\text{kens}}(C))\quad A \cap B \neq \emptyset$.

A cover cov of X is called minimal iff:

$(\forall A \in cov)\quad cov - \{A\}$ is not a cover of X.

Theorem 2.3. ([1])
For every sir-relation $C \subseteq X \times X$, if $\overline{\text{kens}}$(C) is a minimal cover of X then the relation C is K-dense.■

For more details on the subject of concurrency-like relations, covers , K-densities and so on the reader is advised to refer to [1,5]. Now, we shall show in which way the static structure of the whole net describes its concurrency structure. We shall restrict our attention to proper nets.

2a. Concurrency (coexistency) defined by the whole structure of net.

Let $N=(T,P)$ be a proper simple net. Assume that $elem(N) = \{N_1,\dots,N_m\}$, where $N_i=(T_i,P_i)$ for $i=1,\dots,m$.

Define $cov_P = \{P_1,\dots,P_m\}$. Of course, cov_P is a cover of P.

Let $coex_N \subseteq P \times P$ be the following relation: $coex_N = sir(cov_P)$

Other words: $(a,b) \in coex_N \iff \{P_i \mid a \in P_i\} \cap \{P_i \mid b \in P_i\} = \emptyset$.

The relation $coex_N$ will be called the <u>coexistency defined by the structure of N</u>. This relation describes the concurrent structure defined by N. When N is the net of occurrences (see [5,6]) then $coex_N$ is the concurrency relation from [5] restricted to places and minus identity.

The most imporant laws characterizing connections between the relation $coex_N$ and the dynamic structure of the net N are the following.

<u>Theorem 2.4.</u>

For every proper net $N=(T,P)$:

(1) the triple $(T,P,kens(coex_N))$ is a safe and locally fireable ms-net,

(2) if $coex_N$ is K-dense then $\overline{kens}(coex_N)=cov_P$,

(3) if $(T,P,kens(coex_N))$ is compact then $coex_N$ is K-dense. ■

The above results enable us to introduce the following notions. For every proper net $N=(T,P)$, the markings $kens(coex_N)$ will be called <u>natural</u>, the marked net $(T,P,kens(coex_N))$ will be denoted by the symbol $\dot{N}$ and will be called naturally marked. Generally, a ms-net $MN=(T,P,Mar)$, where $N=(T,P)$ will be called <u>the naturally marked net</u> if N is a proper s-net and $Mar=kens(coex_N)$.

Note that compact and naturally marked nets have very regular properties. This fact justifies the following definition.

A ms-net is called <u>regular</u> iff it is naturally marked and compact. The property $\overline{kens}(coex_N)=cov_P$ requires elucidations. It states that the family of all maximal dependent sets generated by the relation $coex_N$ is equel to that cover which defines this relation. Other words, the decomposition into sequential components given by $coex_N$ is equel to the set of all elementary nets contained in N.

Now we consider a few examples which illustrate results defined above. We shall represent the relation $coex_N$ by means of graphs (see [1]). The line - - - - will be denoted the ralation $coex_N$, and the line —— will be denoted the relation $\overline{coex_N}$-id. In such a representation, $kens(coex_N)$ is the set of all maximal cliques of $coex_N$ and $\overline{kens}(coex_N)$ is the set of all maximal cliques of $\overline{coex_N}$-id.

<u>Example 2.1.</u>

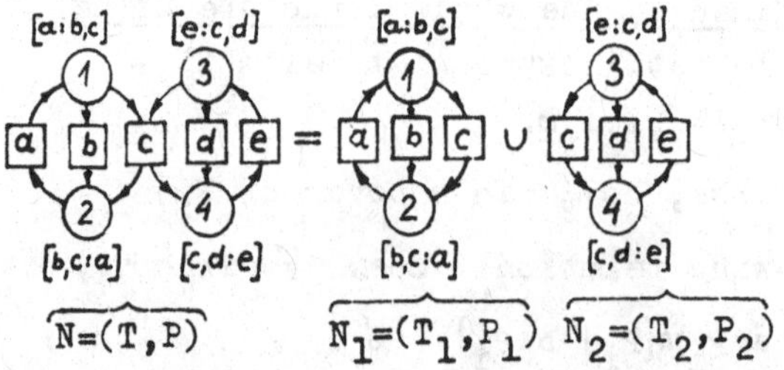

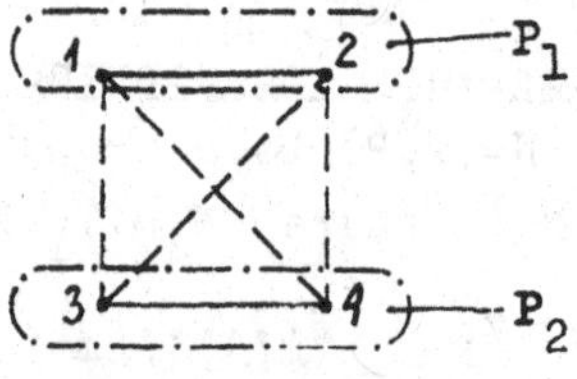

the graph of $coex_N$

Properties of N: $kens(coex_N)=\{\{1,3\},\{1,4\},\{2,3\},\{2,4\}\}$, $\overline{kens}(coex_N)=cov_P=\{P_1,P_2\}=\{\{1,2\},\{3,4\}\}$, $\overline{kens}(coex_N)$ is a minimal cover of P, the relation $coex_N$ is K-dense, and $(T,P,kens(coex_N))$ is compact, safe and fireable. Note also that atoms(N)=elem(N).

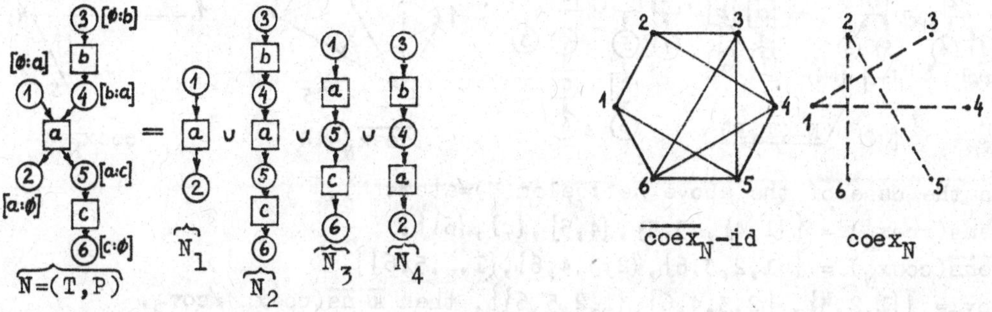

Properties of N: $kens(coex_N)=\{\{1,3\},\{1,4\},\{2,5\},\{2,6\}\}$, atoms(N)=elem(N), $\overline{kens}(coex_N)=cov_P=\{\{1,2\},\{3,4,5,6\},\{1,5,6\},\{3,4,2\}\}$, $\overline{kens}(coex_N)$ <u>is not</u> a minimal cover of P, $coex_N$ is K-dense, and $(T,P,kens(coex_N))$ is compact, safe and fireable.

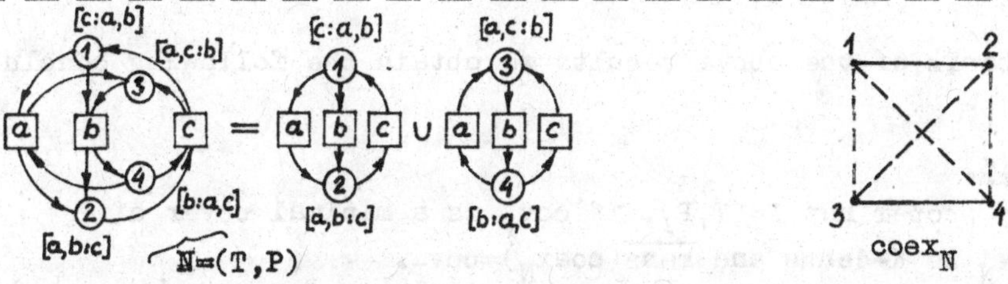

Properties: elem(N)=atoms(N), $kens(coex_N)=\{\{1,3\},\{1,4\},\{2,3\},\{2,4\}\}$, $\overline{kens}(coex_N)=cov_P=\{\{1,2\},\{3,4\}\}$, $\overline{kens}(coex_N)$ is a minimal cover of P, $coex_N$ is K-dense; $(T,P,kens(coex_N))$ is safe and locally fireable but it <u>is not compact</u>. In this case $kens(coex_N)$ consists of two equivalence classes of R_N: $\{\{1,3\},\{2,4\}\}$ and $\{\{1,4\},\{2,3\}\}$.

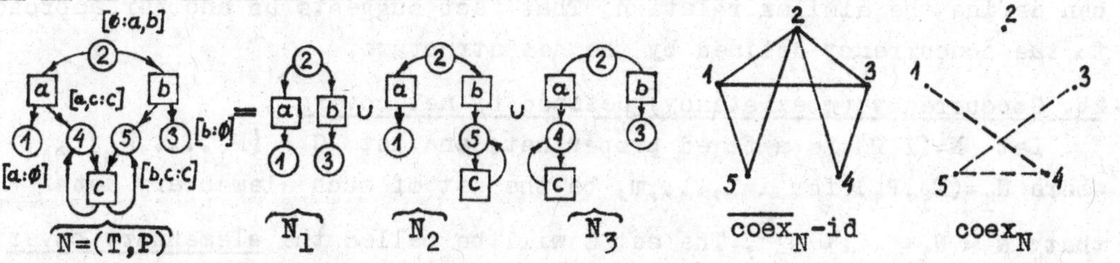

In this case: $elem(N)=\{N_1,N_2,N_3\}\neq atoms(N)$,
$kens(coex_N)=\{\{1,4\},\{3,5\},\{4,5\},\{2\}\}$,
$\overline{kens}(coex_N)=cov_P=\{\{1,2,3\},\{1,2,5\},\{2,3,4\}\}$,
$\overline{kens}(coex_N)$ <u>is not</u> a minimal cover of P;
$coex_N$ <u>is not</u> K-dense, because $\{4,5\}\cap\{1,2,3\}=\emptyset$;

the marked net $(T,P,kens(coex_N))$ is safe and locally fireable, but it <u>is not</u> compact.

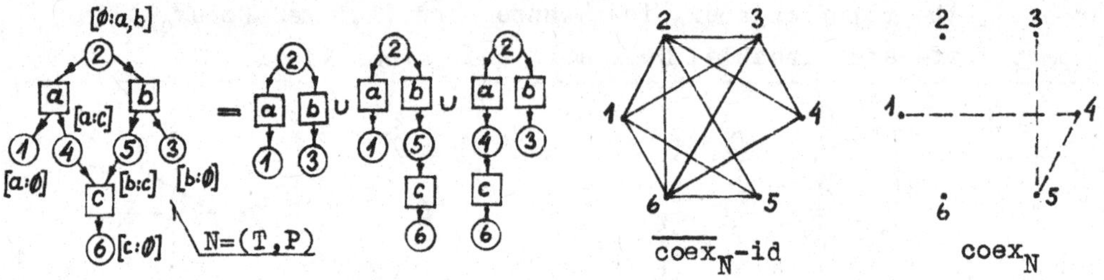

In the case of the above net: $elem(N) \neq atoms(N)$,
$kens(coex_N) = \{\{1,4\},\{3,5\},\{4,5\},\{2\},\{6\}\}$,
$\overline{kens}(coex_N) = \{\{1,2,3,6\},\{2,3,4,6\},\{1,2,5,6\}\}$,
$cov_P = \{\{1,2,3\},\{2,3,4,6\},\{1,2,5,6\}\}$, then $\overline{kens}(coex_N) \neq cov_P$,
the relation $coex_N$ <u>is not</u> K-dense because $\{4,5\} \cap \{1,2,3,6\} = \emptyset$,
$\overline{kens}(coex_N)$ <u>is not</u> a minimal cover of P, and
the marked net $(T,P,kens(coex_N))$ is safe and locally fireable, but it <u>is not</u> compact. ■

On the basis of the above results we obtain the following conclusions.

<u>Corollary 2.5.</u>

1. For every proper net $N=(T,P)$, if cov_P is a minimal cover of P then $coex_N$ is K-dense and $\overline{kens}(coex_N)=cov_P$.
2. For every elementary net $N=(T,P)$: $coex_N=\emptyset$, $kens(coex_N)=\{\{p\} \mid p\in P\}$, and $(T,P,kens(coex_N))$ is the regular marked net. ■

It turns out that $coex_N$ is not the only one concurrency relation defined by the static structure of N. This relation is the concurrency defined by the set elem(N), but every cover of N by elementary nets can define the similar relation. That fact suggests us another approach to the concurrency defined by the net structure.

<u>2b. Concurrency (coexistency) defined by net covers.</u>

Let $N=(T,P)$ be a fixed proper net; and let $C = \{N_1,\dots,N_m\}$, where $N_i=(T_i,P_i)$ for $i=1,\dots,m$, be the set of such elementary nets that: $N = N_1 \cup \dots \cup N_m$. The set C will be called the <u>elementary cover</u> of N (or simply <u>e-cover</u>). Define: $cov_C = \{P_1,\dots,P_m\}$. Note that cov_C is a cover of P and $cov_C \subseteq cov_P$.

Let $coex_C \subseteq P\times P$ be the relation given by: $coex_C = sir(cov_C)$.
Other words: $(a,b)\in coex_C \iff \{P_i \mid P_i\in cov_C \,\&\, a\in P_i\} \cap \{P_i \mid P_i \in cov_C \,\&\, b\in P_i\} = \emptyset$.

The relation $coex_C$ will be called the coexistency defined by the cover C. Note that $coex_N = coex_{elem(N)}$.

Lemma 2.6.

For every proper net N=(T,P) and every elementary cover C of N, the triple $(T,P,kens(coex_C))$ is a safe and locally fireable ms-net.■

Let MN=(T,P,Mar) be a ms-net. A marking M∈Mar is called degenerated iff left(M)=right(M). Other words, the marking M is degenerated when it covers the whole simple net. Usually, the triple $(T,P,kens(coex_C))$ is not compact because $kens(coex_C)$ contains degenerated markings. For every set of markings Mar, let deg(Mar) denotes the family of all degenerated markings.

We set: $kens'(coex_C) = kens(coex_C) - deg(kens(coex_C))$.

We can now extend the notion of K-density, namely:

the relation $coex_C$ is said to be K'-dense iff

$(\forall A \in kens'(coex_C))(\forall B \in kens(coex_C))\ A \cap B \neq \emptyset$.

Of course, if $coex_C$ is K-dense, then it is also K'-dense, but not vice versa.

It turns out that results of Theorem 2.4 hold also in the case of the set $kens'(coex_C)$.

Theorem 2.7.

For every proper net N=(T,P), and every elementary cover C of N:

(1) the triple $(T,P,kens'(coex_C))$ is a safe and locally fireable ms-net,

(2) if $coex_C$ is K'-dense then $\overline{kens(coex_C)} = cov_C$,

(3) if $(T,P,kens'(coex_C))$ is compact then $coex_C$ is K'-dense.■

The above results suggests us the following definitions. For every e-cover C of a proper net N, the family $kens'(coex_C)$ will be called seminatural, and the net $(T,P,kens'(coex_C))$ will be called seminaturally marked. Genarally, a ms-net MN=(T,P,Mar), where N=(T,P) is said to be seminaturally marked if N is proper and there is an e-cover C of N such that $Mar=(T,P,kens'(coex_C))$. We shall now consider the example which illustrates notions defined above.

Example 2.2. Let N=(T,P) be the following simple net.

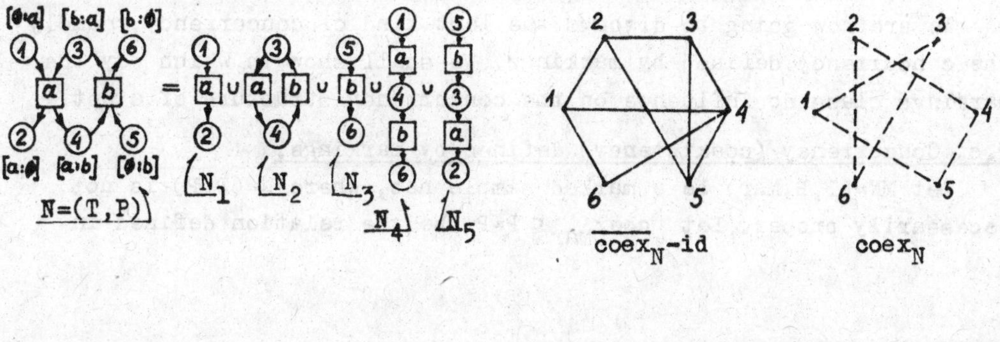

In this case: $\mathrm{elem}(N)=\{N_1,N_2,N_3,N_4,N_5\}=\mathrm{atoms}(N)$,
$\mathrm{kens}(\mathrm{coex}_N)=\{\{1,3\},\{1,5\},\{2,6\},\{2,4\},\{4,5\},\{3,6\}\}$,
$\overline{\mathrm{kens}}(\mathrm{coex}_N)=\mathrm{cov}_P=\{\{1,2\},\{3,4\},\{5,6\},\{1,4,6\},\{2,3,5\}\}$,
the relation coex_C is not K-dense and $(T,P,\mathrm{kens}(\mathrm{coex}_N))$ is not compact.

Let $C=\{N_1,N_2,N_3,N_4\}\subsetneq \mathrm{elem}(N)$. Note that $N=N_1\cup N_2\cup N_3\cup N_4$, then the set C is an elementary cover of N. The graph of coex_C is the following.

Note that: $\mathrm{kens}(\mathrm{coex}_C)=\{\{1,3,5\},\{2,4,5\},\{2,3,6\},\{2,3,5\}\}$,
$\mathrm{deg}(\mathrm{kens}(\mathrm{coex}_C))=\{\{2,3,5\}\}$, $\mathrm{kens}'(\mathrm{coex}_C)=\{\{1,2,5\},\{2,4,5\},\{2,3,6\}\}$,
$\overline{\mathrm{kens}}(\mathrm{coex}_C)=\mathrm{cov}_C=\{\{1,2\},\{3,4\},\{5,6\},\{1,4,6\}\}$; the relation coex_C is not K-dense, but it is K′-dense; the triple $(T,P,\mathrm{kens}(\mathrm{coex}_C))$ is a safe and locally fireable, but not compact ms-net; the triple $(T,P,\mathrm{kens}'(\mathrm{coex}_C))$ is a safe, fireable and compact ms-net. ■

A ms-net MN=(T,P,Mar) will be called <u>semiregular</u> if it is seminaturally marked and compact. Of course, every regular ms-net is also semiregular, but not vice versa. The ms-net $(T,P,\mathrm{kens}'(\mathrm{coex}_C))$ from the above example is semiregular but it is not regular. In order to show when the semiregular net is regular, we must introduce the new notion.

A ms-net MN=(T,P,Mar) is said to be compatible with the elementary structure of N=(T,P) (abbr. <u>e-compatible</u>) iff:

$$(\forall (T_i,P_i)\in \mathrm{elem}(N))(\forall M\in \mathrm{Mar})\quad |M\cap P_i|\le 1.$$

<u>Theorem 2.8.</u>
For every proper net N and every e-cover C of N,
if $(T,P,\mathrm{kens}'(\mathrm{coex}_C))$ is e-compatible then $C=\mathrm{elem}(N)$. ■

<u>Corollary 2.9.</u>
Every seminaturally marked and e-compatible net is naturally marked. ■

We are now going to discuss the last kind of concurrency, namely the concurrency defined by markings. We shall show in which way the markings class do influence on the concurrency structure of a net.

<u>2.c. Concurrency (coexistency) defined by markings.</u>

Let MN=(T,P,Mar) be a marked simple net, where N=(T,P) is not necessarily proper. Let $\mathrm{coex}_{Mar}\subseteq P\times P$ be the relation defined in

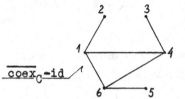

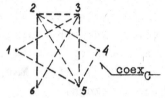

the following way:

$$(\forall p,q\in P)\quad (p,q)\in \mathrm{coex}_{Mar} \iff p\neq q \ \&\ (\exists M\in Mar)\quad \{p,q\}\subseteq M.$$

The relation coex_{Mar} is called the <u>coexistency defined by markings</u>.

The relation coex_{Mar} is called <u>M-dense</u> iff:

$$(\forall M\in Mar)(\forall A\in \overline{\mathrm{kens}}(\mathrm{coex}_{Mar}))\qquad M\cap A\neq\emptyset .$$

If $Mar=\mathrm{kens}(\mathrm{coex}_{Mar})$ (i.e. the net is m-compatible according to [3]) then M-density is obviously equivalent with K-density.

<u>Lemma 2.10.</u>

If coex_{Mar} is M-dense then $Mar\subseteq \mathrm{kens}(\mathrm{coex}_{Mar})$.■

A simple net $N=(T,P)$ is called <u>quasielementary</u> iff:

$$(\forall a\in T)\quad |{}^{\bullet}a| = |a^{\bullet}| = 1.$$

Note that every connected subnet of the quasielementary net is an elementary net. Now we show in which way markings describe the static structure of simple nets.

<u>Theorem 2.11.</u>

For every ms-net $MN=(T,P,Mar)$, if MN is safe, locally fireable and coex_{Mar} is M-dense then for every $A\in\overline{\mathrm{kens}}(\mathrm{coex}_{Mar})$ the pair (left(A),A) /or equivalently (right(A),A)/ is a quasielementary net.■

<u>Corollary 2.12.</u>

For every ms-net $MN=(T,P,Mar)$, if MN is safe, locally fireable and coex_{Mar} is M-dense then (T,P) is a proper net.■

<u>Theorem 2.13.</u>

For every ms-net $MN=(T,P,Mar)$, if MN is safe, compact, fireable and coex_{Mar} is M-dense then for every $A\in\overline{\mathrm{kens}}(\mathrm{coex}_{Mar})$ the pair (left(A),A) /or equivalently (right(A),A)/ is an elementary net.■

Let $\mathrm{kens}'(\mathrm{coex}_{Mar}) = \mathrm{kens}(\mathrm{coex}_{Mar}) - \deg(\mathrm{kens}(\mathrm{coex}_{Mar}))$.

It turns out that the property of semiregularity and the property of regularity can be formulated in terms of the relation coex_{Mar}.

<u>Theorem 2.14.</u>

A ms-net $MN=(T,P,Mar)$ is semiregular $\iff$ it is compact, safe, fireable, the relation coex_{Mar} is M-dense and $Mar=\mathrm{kens}'(\mathrm{coex}_{Mar})$.■

<u>Corollary 2.15.</u>

A ms-net $MN=(T,P,Mar)$ is regular $\iff$ it is compact, safe, fireable, the relation coex_{Mar} is M-dense, $Mar=\mathrm{kens}'(\mathrm{coex}_{Mar})$ and the net is e-compatible.■

Now we consider a few examples which illustrate results defined above.

Example 2.3. Let MN=(T,P,Mar) be the following ms-net.

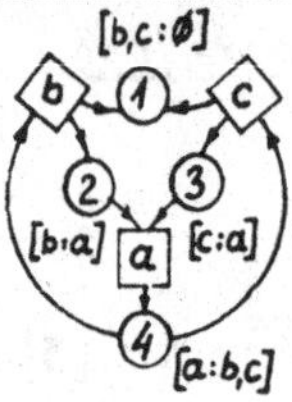

Mar= $\{\{1,2\},\{1,3\},\{2,3\},\{4\}\}$.

N=(T,P)

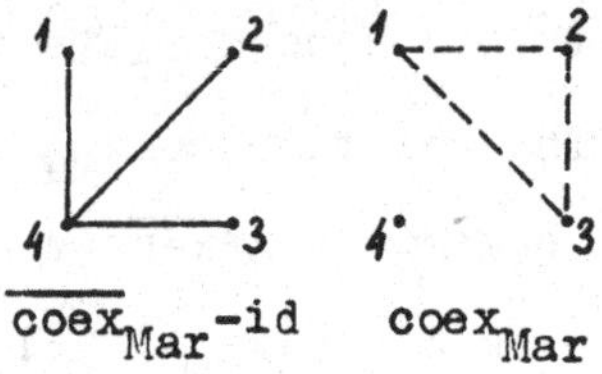

Note that: $\text{kens}(\text{coex}_{Mar})=\{\{1,2,3\},\{4\}\}\not\ni \text{Mar}$, $\overline{\text{kens}}(\text{coex}_{Mar})=\{\{1,4\},\{2,4\},\{3,4\}\}$, the relation coex_{Mar} is K-dense, but it is not M-dense, the ms-net MN is compact, safe and fireable, and the s-net N=(T,P) is not proper.

Let MN=(T,P,Mar) be the ms-net defined below (compare Example 2.2).

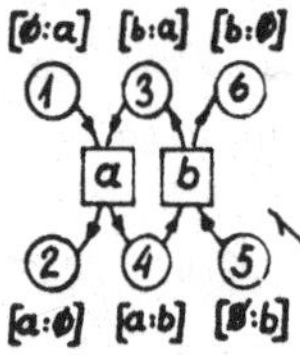

Mar= $\{\{1,3,5\},\{2,4,5\},\{2,3,6\}\}$.

N=(T,P)

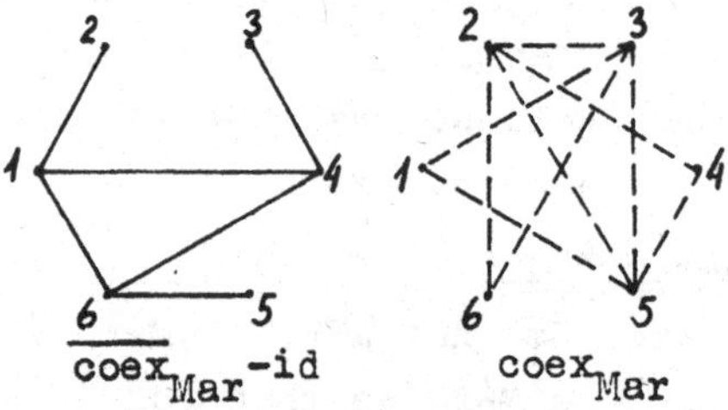

In this case: $\text{kens}(\text{coex}_{Mar})=\{\{1,3,5\},\{2,4,5\},\{2,3,6\},\{2,3,5\}\}$, $\deg(\text{kens}(\text{coex}_{Mar}))=\{\{2,3,5\}\}$, $\text{Mar}=\text{kens}'(\text{coex}_{Mar})\subsetneq \text{kens}(\text{coex}_{Mar})$; the relation coex_{Mar} is not K-dense, but it is M-dense, the ms-net MN is compact, safe and fireable, and the s-net N=(T,P) is proper. The family $\overline{\text{kens}}(\text{coex}_{Mar})$ is of the form $\{\{1,2\},\{3,4\},\{5,6\},\{1,4,6\}\}$ and the family of elementary nets defined by $\overline{\text{kens}}(\text{coex}_{Mar})$ is the following (see Theorem 2.13).

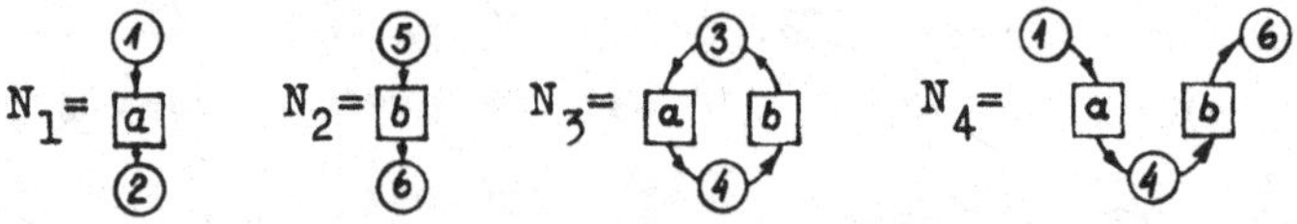

Note that: $N=N_1\cup N_2\cup N_3\cup N_4$, so $\{N_1,N_2,N_3,N_4\}$ is an e-cover of N, and $\{N_1,N_2,N_3,N_4\}\not\subseteq \text{elem}(N)$ (compare Example 2.2).

Let MN=(T,P,Mar) be the following ms-net.

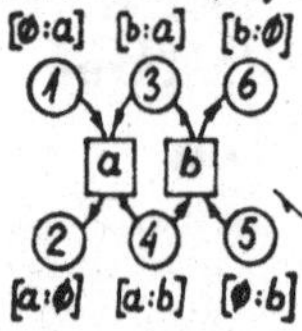

Mar= $\{\{1,3\},\{2,4\},\{4,5\},\{3,6\}\}$.

N=(T,P)

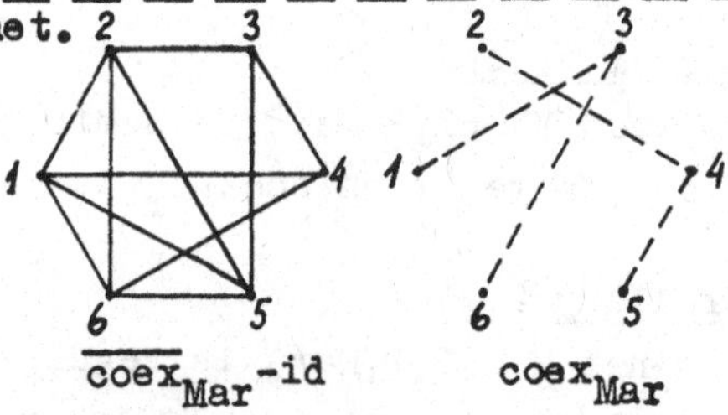

In this case: $\text{kens}(\text{coex}_{Mar})=\text{Mar}$, $\deg(\text{kens}(\text{coex}_{Mar}))=\emptyset$,

$\overline{\text{kens}}(\text{coex}_{Mar}) = \{\{1,2,5,6\},\{2,3,5\},\{1,4,6\},\{3,4\}\}$, the relation coex_{Mar} is K-dense, the ms-net MN is safe and locally fireable, but <u>not compact</u>. The family of quasielementary nets defined by $\overline{\text{kens}}(\text{coex}_{Mar})$ (compare Theorem 2.11) consists of the following nets.

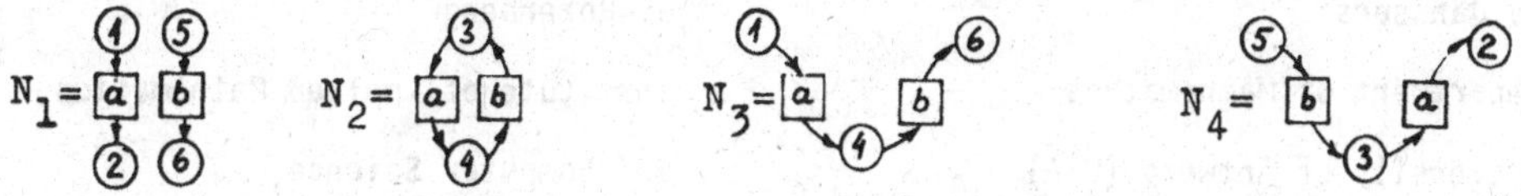

Of course, N=(T,P) is a proper net and $N=N_1 \cup N_2 \cup N_3 \cup N_4$. ■

<u>Conclusion</u>.

We have attempted to present a formalization of decomposition of nets into indivisible sequential components and to investigate different notions of concurrency. We feel that this paper presents a sound foundations for studying the concurrency relation in the case of the whole class of condition/event nets. All proofs will be published soon.

<u>Acknowledgement</u>.

The author wish to thank A.Mazurkiewicz and M.W.Shields for stimulating papers nad discussions, and H.Genrich for essential remarks on the nature of concurrency relation.

<u>References</u>.

[1] Janicki R., <u>A Characterization of Concurrency-like Relations</u>, Lecture Notes in Comp. Sci., vol. 70, Springer-Verlag, 1979, pp. 109-122.

[2] Janicki R., <u>Synthesis of Concurrent Schemes</u>, Lecture Notes in Comp. Sci., vol. 64, Springer-Verlag, 1978, pp.298-307.

[3] Janicki R., <u>An Algebraic Structure of Petri Nets</u>, Proc. of the 4th International Conference on Theory and Practice of Programming, Paris, 1980.

[4] Mazurkiewicz A., <u>Concurrent Program Schemes and Their Interpretations</u>, DAIMI PB-78, Aarhus Univ. Publ., 1977.

[5] Petri C.A., <u>Non-sequential Processes</u>, ISF Report 70-01, GMD, Bonn, 1977.

[6] Petri C.A., <u>Concurrency as a Basis of System Thinking</u>, ISF Report 78-06, GMD Bonn, 1978.

[7] Shields M.W., <u>Adequate Path Expressions</u>, Lecture Notes in Comp. Sci., vol. 70, Springer-Verlag, 1979, pp. 249-265.

NODE-LABEL CONTROLLED GRAPH GRAMMARS

(Extended abstract)

D. Janssens
Department of Mathematics,
University of Antwerp (UIA),
Universiteitsplein 1,
B-2610 Wilrijk,
Belgium

G. Rozenberg
Institute of Applied Mathematics
and Computer Science,
University of Leiden,
Wassenaarseweg 80,
Leiden,
The Netherlands

INTRODUCTION

In recent years the area of graph grammars emerges as one of the basic theoretical tools in various areas of software design and analysis. This is witnessed very well in the collection [CER] and in [NA]. Examples of the use of graph grammars for software specification and analysis are [SC1], [SC2] and, in [CER], [BA], [EL] , [FU] and [PR] , while [WI] and [GT] indicate the use of graph grammars to analyze concurrency.
For a good overview of the area of graph grammars and its applications the reader is referred to survey papers by Ehrig and Nagl in [CER].

Altogether the theory of graph grammars forms a well-motivated area of theoretical computer science. However it is clear that this theory is not yet as rich in results as, e.g., formal (string) language theory. An objective general reason explaining this situation is that graph grammars and languages are intrinsically more difficult to investigate than string grammars and languages. It is perhaps not yet clear which are the central notions of the graph grammar theory, neither do we have enough adequate mathematical means to describe graph languages or derivations in graph grammars. Altogether there is a clear need for further fundamental research in this area. Following this line we introduce a new family of graph grammars and new mathematical tools to analyse it. (A comparison of our techniques with, by now standard, algebraic techniques - as presented in Ehrig's survey in [CER] - is an interesting research topic on its own). The grammars that we introduce are called node-label controlled graph grammars, abbreviated as NLC grammars.

The paper is organized as follows. In Section I NLC grammars and their languages are defined and their position in the general theory of graph grammars is discussed. In Section II various restrictions, extensions and variations of NLC grammars are discussed, while Section III investigates the structure of NLC languages. In Section IV the ability of NLC grammars to generate string languages is considered. In Section V decision problems concerning NLC grammars are presented (most of them are intrinsic to graph grammars in the sense that they concern graph-theoretical properties of NLC languages).

This extended abstract is based on three papers : [JR1] , [JR2] and [JR3]. In the abstract we discuss our basic notions and results in a rather informal way - the formal definitions, as well as the proofs of the results (except for the proof of Theorem 10), can be found in these papers.

I. NODE-LABEL CONTROLLED GRAPH GRAMMARS.

Except for one case (discussed in Section IV) we consider only node-labelled, undirected graphs, shortly called graphs. To establish the basis for the formalism of this paper we give a formal definition of a graph.

Definition. A (node labelled, undirected) graph is a system $H = (V,E,\Sigma,\varphi)$ where

V is a finite nonempty set of nodes,

E is a set of unordered pairs of nodes, called the set of edges,

Σ is a finite nonempty set of labels, and

φ is a function from V into Σ, called the labelling function. ∎

The graph H defined above is called a graph *over* Σ; and we will use V_H to denote the set of nodes of H. If B is a full subgraph of A, then by $A \setminus B$ we will denote the graph obtained from A by removing all the nodes of B together with all the edges, incident to these nodes. A *coding* c is defined to be a letter-to letter function from an alphabet Σ into another alphabet $\overline{\Sigma}$. If H is a graph over Σ then c(H) is the graph which has the same nodes and edges as H, but in which the labels ℓ are replaced by their images $c(\ell)$. The basic notion of this paper is defined as follows.

Definition. A NLC *grammar* is a system $G = (\Sigma, \Delta, P, C, Z)$ where
Σ is a finite nonempty set called the *total alphabet*,
Δ is a nonempty subset of Σ, called the *terminal alphabet*,
P is a set of *productions* of the form (ℓ, D) where $\ell \in \Sigma$ and D is a graph over Σ,
C is a subset of $\Sigma \times \Sigma$, called the *connection relation*, and
Z is a graph over Σ, called the *axiom*. ■

G is used to define a collection of graphs as follows. A *direct derivation step* in G is performed in the following way. Let H be a graph over Σ and let v be a node of H. To rewrite v, a production (ℓ, D) in P is chosen such that ℓ is the label of v in H. We delete v from H, together with all edges incident to v and we replace v by $\overline{D}$ which is an isomorphic copy of D. Then we establish edges between the nodes of $\overline{D}$ and the remaining nodes of H in the following way : if m is a node of $\overline{D}$ with label μ and n is a node of H different from v, and with label ν then an edge between n and m is established if and only if

(1). n was a neighbour of v in H (i.e. there was an edge between n and v in H) and

(2). (μ, ν) is a pair from C.

If $\overline{H}$ is the graph obtained in this way then we write $H \overset{1}{\underset{G}{\Rightarrow}} \overline{H}$. As usual, the relations $\overset{+}{\underset{G}{\Rightarrow}}$ and $\overset{*}{\underset{G}{\Rightarrow}}$ are the transitive and the transitive and reflexive closure of $\overset{1}{\underset{G}{\Rightarrow}}$. The *exhaustive language* of G is defined by $S(G) = \{H \mid Z \overset{*}{\underset{G}{\Rightarrow}} H\}$ while the (terminal) *language* of G is defined by $L(G) = \{H \mid Z \overset{*}{\underset{G}{\Rightarrow}} H$ and H is a graph over $\Delta\}$.

To illustrate the generative power of NLC grammars we now provide two examples. The first one gives a NLC grammar that generates the language of all graphs over a one-label alphabet, the second one defines a grammar that generates the language

consisting of all graphs of the form

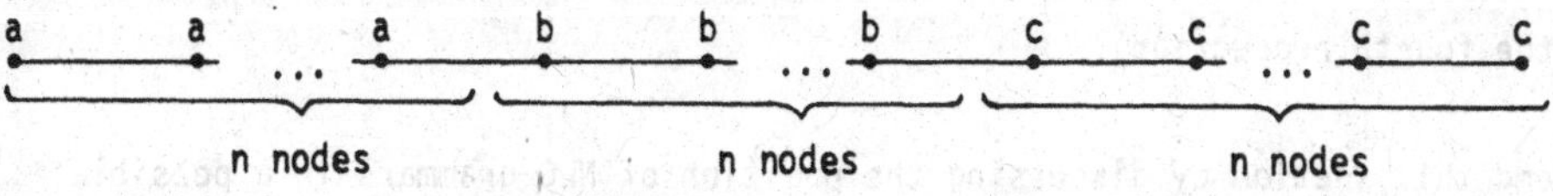

where $n \geqslant 1$.

This language is closely related to the non-contextfree string-language $\{a^n b^n c^n \ n \geqslant 1\}$, and therefore this grammar illustrates why NLC grammars cannot be considered as being "context-free".

Example 1. $G = (\Sigma, \Delta, P, C, Z)$ where

$\Sigma = \{A, \overline{A}\}$

$\Delta = \{A\}$,

$P = \{(A, \overset{A}{\bullet}\!\!-\!\!\!-\!\!\!-\!\!\overset{A}{\bullet}), (A, \overset{\overline{A}}{\bullet}), (\overline{A}, \overset{A}{\bullet}), (A, \overset{A}{\bullet})\}$,

$C = \{(A, \overline{A}), (A, A), (\overline{A}, A)\}$ and

$Z = \overset{A}{\bullet}$. ∎

Example 2. $G = (\Sigma, \Delta, P, C, Z)$ where

$\Sigma = \{a, b, c, S_0, S_1\}$,

$\Delta = \{a, b, c\}$,

$P = \{(S_0, \overset{a}{\bullet}\!\!-\!\!\!\overset{b}{\bullet}\!\!-\!\!\!\overset{c}{\bullet}), (S_0, \overset{a}{\bullet}\,\overset{a}{\bullet}\,\overset{b}{\bullet}\,\overset{S_1}{}\,\overset{c}{\bullet}),$

$(S_1, \overset{a}{\bullet}\!\!\underset{b}{\diagdown}\!\!\overset{S_1 \quad c}{\bullet\!\!-\!\!\!\bullet}), (S_1, \overset{b}{\bullet}\!\!-\!\!\!\overset{c}{\bullet})\}$,

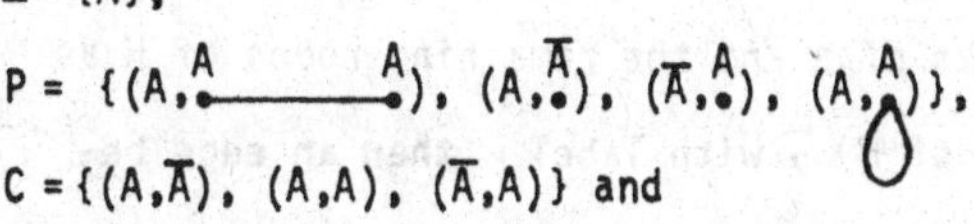

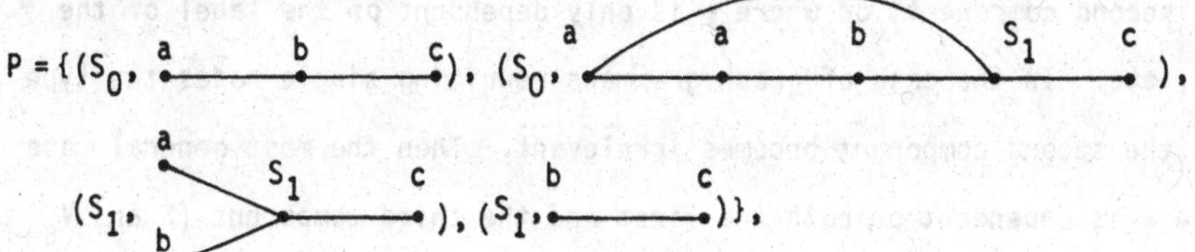

$C = \{(a, a), (b, b), (c, c)\}$, and

$Z = \overset{S_0}{\bullet}$.

We have :

$\overset{S_0}{\bullet} \underset{G}{\rightarrow} \overset{a}{\bullet}\,\overset{a}{\bullet}\,\overset{b}{\bullet}\,\overset{S_1}{}\,\overset{c}{\bullet}$ (applying the 2nd production),

$\underset{G}{\rightarrow} \overset{a}{\bullet}\,\overset{a}{\bullet}\,\overset{a}{\bullet}\,\overset{b}{\bullet}\,\overset{b}{\bullet}\,\overset{S_1}{}\,\overset{c}{\bullet}\,\overset{c}{\bullet}$ (applying the 3rd

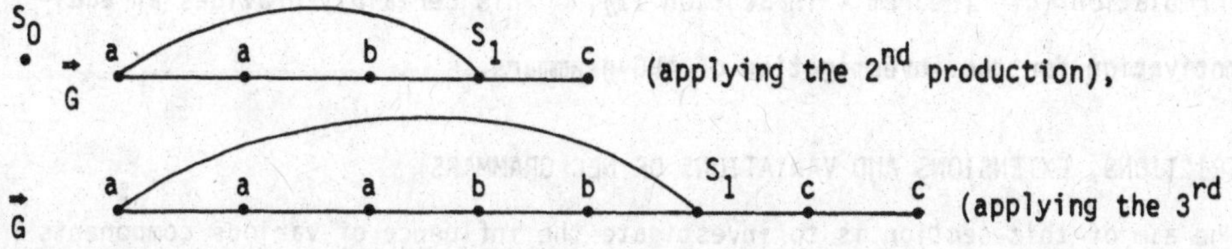

production),

$\underset{G}{\Rightarrow}$ 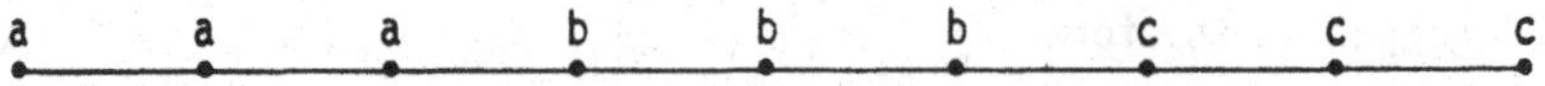

(applying the fourth production). ∎

We end this section by discussing the position of NLC grammars in a possible "general" framework to classify some known and some new ways of defining graph grammars. Extending the approach of [MR] one can define a graph grammar to be a grammar with productions of the form (α,β,ϕ) where α is an arbitrary connected graph (with node set V_α) β is an arbitrary graph (with node set V_β) and ϕ is a boolean function on $\Sigma \times V_\alpha \times V_\beta$. Such a production is then applied to a graph H as follows: if $\bar{\alpha}$ is a full subgraph of H, isomorphic to α, then we delete $\bar{\alpha}$ from H, together with all the edges between nodes of $\bar{\alpha}$ and nodes of the rest of H. Subsequently we replace $\bar{\alpha}$ by β and we establish edges between the nodes of β and the remaining nodes of H as follows : if m is a node of β and n is a node of $H \setminus \bar{\alpha}$ with label ν then an edge between m and n is established if and only if there exist a node $\bar{k}$ in $\bar{\alpha}$, corresponding to a node k in α, such that there is an edge in H between $\bar{k}$ and n and with $\phi(\nu,k,m) = 1$. This approach gives rise to a natural classification of graph grammars by putting restrictions on the function ϕ : e.g., we can consider only productions where ϕ is not dependent on the second component, or where ϕ is only dependent on the label of the second component, etc. In the case of graph grammars rewriting single nodes the type of dependence on the second component becomes irrelevant. Then the most general case is the case where ϕ is dependent on both the first and the third component (Σ and V_β respectively). It can be shown that these grammars are equivalent to grammars in which ϕ is dependent on the first component and on the label of the third component only. It turns out that these grammars are nothing else but NLC grammars in a different formulation (cf. Theorem 4 in Section II). This certainly provides an additional motivation for the investigation of NLC grammars.

II. RESTRICTIONS, EXTENSIONS AND VARIATIONS OF NLC GRAMMARS

The aim of this section is to investigate the influence of various components from the definition of a NLC grammar on the language generating power. Whenever possible, we will at the same time provide normal form results enabling one to prove results about $\mathcal{L}$(NLC) (if XNLC denotes a certain type of graph grammars, then by $\mathcal{L}$(XNLC) we will denote the class of all languages that can be generated by a XNLC grammar). The proofs of the theorems mentioned in this section can be found in [JR2].

According to the tradition of sequential rewriting systems it is natural to consider NLC grammars in which only nodes with nonterminal labels may be rewritten. Such grammars are referred to as NNLC grammars.

Theorem 1. $\mathcal{L}(NNLC) = \mathcal{L}(NLC)$. ■

On the other hand, according to the tradition of parallel rewriting systems it is natural to consider NLC grammars in which every symbol has a production for it. These grammars are called CNLC grammars.

Theorem 2. $\mathcal{L}(CNLC) = \mathcal{L}(NLC)$. ■

To enforce a more "context free" behaviour of a NLC grammar, we can change its definition in such a way that every node of $\overline{D}$ either gets connected to all of the former neighbours of v or to none at all. This can be expressed formally by putting a restriction on the connection relation C : for every label ℓ in Σ we have either $(\{\ell\} \times \Sigma) \cap C = \{\ell\} \times \Sigma$ or $(\{\ell\} \times \Sigma) \cap C = \phi$. The so defined grammars are referred to as CFNLC grammars.

Theorem 3. $\mathcal{L}(CFNLC) \subsetneq \mathcal{L}(NLC)$. ■

A useful programming device is to provide each production with its own connection relation (a production is then of the form $\pi = ((\ell,D); C_\pi))$. Such grammars are referred to as RNLC grammars. (It is instructive to compare RNLC grammars with the grammars studied in [FR]).

Theorem 4. $\mathcal{L}(RNLC) = \mathcal{L}(NLC)$. ■

In a way, somewhat analogous to parallel rewriting systems, one may equip a NLC grammar with several connection relations, where at each direct derivation step, one of those relations is (arbitrarily) chosen. Such grammars are called MNLC grammars.

Theorem 5. $\mathcal{L}(MNLC) = \mathcal{L}(NLC)$. ■

In an effort to strengthen the defining power of NLC grammars it is natural to make them more "context sensitive". A way of achieving this is to introduce productions of the form $\pi = (d,D,K(\pi))$ with $K(\pi)$ being a subset of the total alphabet. Such a production π can be applied to a node v only if for every element k of $K(\pi)$ there is a neighbour of v (in the mother graph) which is labelled by k. The so defined grammars are referred to as CSNLC grammars.

Theorem 6. $\mathcal{L}(\text{NLC}) \subsetneq \mathcal{L}(\text{CSNLC})$. ▪

III. ON THE STRUCTURE OF NLC LANGUAGES

An important direction of research concerning NLC grammars is the search for results describing the combinatorial structure of NLC languages. In particular such results should enable one to prove that various concrete graph languages are not NLC languages. Results in this direction are presented in this section.

Our first task in this section is to provide a mathematical tool especially suited to describe the structure of a NLC language. Such a tool, the $H_{B,\alpha}^{(n)}$ construct, is presented now.

Let H be a graph with node set V and let $B = (B_1, B_2)$ be a pair of subsets of $V \times V$. Then for each positive integer n, $H_B^{(n)}$ is the graph constructed as follows. Let $H_1, H_2, \dots, H_n$ be (disjoint) isomorphic copies of H. Connect the H_i's to each other by adding two kinds of edges : (1). For each $(v, \bar{v})$ in B_1 and for each i with $1 \leq i \leq n-1$, add an edge between the node, corresponding to v in H_i and the node, corresponding to $\bar{v}$ in H_{i+1}. (2). For each $(w, \bar{w})$ in B_2, for each i with $1 \leq i \leq n-1$ and for each j with $i+1 \leq j \leq n$, add an edge between the node, corresponding to w in H_i and the node, corresponding to $\bar{w}$ in H_j. Now let α be a full subgraph of H. Then $H_{B,\alpha}^{(n)}$ is obtained from the graph $H_B^{(n)}$ described above by omitting the subgraphs, corresponding to α in H_1, $H_2, \dots, H_{n-1}$ (together with the edges that connect these subgraphs with the rest of the graph).

As we have said already, the $H_{B,\alpha}^{(n)}$ construct is introduced as a tool to describe the structure of a NLC language. As a matter of fact it is a tool very intrinsic to NLC grammars in the sense that it will not only turn out to be useful to express the structure of NLC languages but also, the $H_{B,\alpha}^{(n)}$ construct itself can be described by a NLC grammar as demonstrated by the following result.

Theorem 7. Let H be a graph over Σ_H with node set V, let B_1 and B_2 be subsets of $V \times V$ and let α be a full subgraph of H. Then there exists a NLC grammar $G = (\Sigma, \Delta, P, C, Z)$ with $\Sigma_H \subseteq \Delta$ and a coding c from Σ into Σ_H such that for each $M \in L(G)$, Z derives

M in n steps implies that c(M) is isomorphic to $H_{B,\alpha}^{(n+1)}$. ■

Now, using the $H_{B,\alpha}^{(n)}$ construct, we can state "the pumping theorem" for NLC languages. Note that, in view of the fact (indicated in previous sections) that NLC grammars posess quite strong "context-dependent" properties, it is not obvious at all that languages in $\mathcal{L}$(NLC) have a "pumping-type" property. A number of "pumping results" for various kinds of graph languages are known (see, e.g., [KR] and [DG]). Still, in our opinion, NLC grammars are perhaps the most "surprising" case where a "pumping" type theorem holds.

Theorem 8. Given a NLC grammar $G = (\Sigma,\Delta,P,C,Z)$, there exists an (effectively computable) integer p with the following property. If M is a graph in S(G) with more than p nodes, then M can be divided into two full subgraphs M' and M", and there exists a full subgraph α of M', sets B_1, B_2 of pairs of nodes from M and a graph M_n, derivable from Z such that

(1). M' has at least 2 and at most p nodes.

(2). M' has at least one node that does not belong to α.

(3). The graph $M \setminus \alpha$ is a full subgraph of M_n.

(4). The graph $M_n \setminus M''$ is of the form $(M')_{B,\alpha}^{(n)}$ where $B = (B_1,B_2)$. Furthermore, if $(M')_{B,\alpha}^{(n)}$ contains copies $K_1,K_2,\ldots,K_{n-1}$ of $M' \setminus \alpha$ (see the Definition of $(M')_{B,\alpha}^{(n)}$) then $K_1 = M' \setminus \alpha$ and if $i > 3$, then there is an edge in M_n between a node x if M" and a node y_i of K_i if and only if there is an edge between x and the node y_3, corresponding to y_i, in K_3. ■

Observe that $M_n \in L(G)$ if $M \in L(G)$. In particular, the above theorem yields the following corollary which enables us to prove that various languages are not NLC languages.

Corollary. Assume that every $H \in L(G)$ is connected and that L(G) is infinite and of bounded degree. Then there exist positive integers m_o,C such that for each integer m with $m > m_o$, there exists a graph M_m in L(G) with diameter bigger than or equal to the number of nodes of M_n divided by C. (The diameter of a graph M is the minimal number n such that between any two nodes of M there exists a path with at most n edges). ■

IV. THE RELATIONSHIP BETWEEN STRING LANGUAGES AND NLC GRAMMARS

From the mathematical point of view graph grammars form a very natural extension of string grammars. Hence it is natural to investigate the power of NLC grammars as string-language generating devices. In other words one would like to know how the string language generating power is influenced by allowing "multidimensional sentential forms". Also in this way one hopes to find "simple" examples of languages positioned in the differences of various language classes within the "NLC-framework".

We start by considering context-free string NLC grammars (abbreviated CFSNLC grammars), that is, CFNLC grammars G which have an "extra" label, $\not\ell$, (that cannot be rewritten by any production) and which have the property that every connected graph of L(G) is of the form $H = \overset{\not\ell}{\bullet} \!-\!\!-\! \overset{\ell_1}{\bullet} \!-\!\!-\! \overset{\ell_2}{\bullet} \!-\!\!-\! \overset{\ell_3}{\bullet} \cdots \overset{\ell_n}{\bullet}$. Clearly, the word $\ell_1\ell_2\ldots\ell_n$ is associated to H in a natural way. Hence, every CFSNLC grammar G defines a string language, which will be denoted by $L_{string}(G)$. The class of all string languages, generated in this way by CFSNLC languages is denoted by $\mathcal{L}_{string}(CFSNLC)$. It turns out that those grammars provide a characterization of regular languages.

<u>Theorem 9</u>. $\mathcal{L}_{string}(CFSNLC) = \mathcal{L}(REG)$. ∎

The reader should note that the context-free restriction in the above theorem is important because example 2 of Section I indicates that otherwise context-sensitive languages can be generated that are not context-free.

A natural next step to consider is a characterization of context-free string languages. It turns out that this step is much more difficult. In order to achieve such a characterization we will consider now CFNLC grammars generating directed graphs. This means that we have to decide how the new parameter- the direction of an edge - influences the use of the connection relation. A natural way to take into account the direction of an edge is to use two connection relations, C_{in} and C_{out}. (Both C_{in} and C_{out} are still assumed to satisfy the "context-free" condition discribed in Section II: for each $\ell \in \Sigma$, either $(\{\ell\} \times \Sigma) \cap C = \{\ell\} \times \Sigma$ or $(\{\ell\} \times \Sigma) \cap C = \phi$). More precisely, if the node v of a graph H is replaced by a daughtergraph $\overline{D}$ in a direct derivation step, if m is a node of $\overline{D}$ labelled by μ and n is a node of H labelled by ν and different from v, then the resulting graph contains an edge (n,m) if and only if H contains an edge (n,v) and if $(\mu,\nu)\in C_{in}$; on the other hand, it contains an edge (m,n) if and only if H contains an edge (v,n) and $(\mu,\nu)\in C_{out}$. The so defined grammars are referred to as DCFNLC grammars. With every DCFNLC grammar G we associate a string $L_{st}(G)$ being the set of words $\ell_1\ell_2\ldots\ell_n$ such that the graph $\overset{\ell_1}{\bullet}\!\longrightarrow\!\overset{\ell_2}{\bullet}\!\longrightarrow\!\overset{\ell_3}{\bullet}\ldots\overset{\ell_n}{\bullet}$ is in L(G). The set of all string languages obtained in this way is denoted as $\mathcal{L}_{st}$(DCFNLC). The following result holds.

Theorem 10. $\mathcal{L}_{st}$(DCFNLC) $=\mathcal{L}$(CF). ∎

We believe that the above result sheds an additional light both on the relationship between graph grammars and string languages and (in comparison with Theorem 9.) on the role that the direction of an edge can play in the generating process of a graph grammar.

Remark. The method of defining string languages (of $\mathcal{L}$(CFSNLC)) in Theorem 9 is different from the approach of Theorem 10 : indeed, in defining CFSNLC grammars we restrict ourselves to grammars G for which every connected graph of L(G) is of the form $\overset{¢}{\bullet}\!\!-\!\!\overset{\ell_1}{\bullet}\!\!-\!\!\overset{\ell_2}{\bullet}\ldots\overset{\ell_n}{\bullet}$, whereas in the case of DCFNLC we simply consider the intersection of the languages with the set of graphs of the form $\overset{\ell_1}{\bullet}\!\longrightarrow\!\overset{\ell_2}{\bullet}\!\longrightarrow\!\bullet\ldots\overset{\ell_n}{\bullet}$. However, it can be shown that Theorem 9 is still true if we define $L_{string}(G)$ for any CFNLC grammar G to be the intersection of L(G) and the set of graphs of the form $\overset{¢}{\bullet}\!\!-\!\!\overset{\ell_1}{\bullet}\!\!-\!\!\overset{\ell_2}{\bullet}\ldots\overset{\ell_n}{\bullet}$.

V. BASIC DECISION PROBLEMS

In this section we turn to several decision problems concerning NLC grammars. As usual, results in this direction are needed to assess the effectiveness of the generation of graph languages by NLC grammars. Our first theorem provides a positive solution to a quite basic decision problem.

Theorem 11. Given an arbitrary NLC grammar $G=(\Sigma,\Delta,P,C,Z)$ and arbitrary labels a,b of Δ, it is decidable whether or not a and b are adjacent in G. ∎

Our second result deals with the standard equivalence problem concerning grammars.

Theorem 12. Given two arbitrary NLC grammars G_1 and G_2, it is undecidable whether or not $L(G_1)=L(G_2)$. ∎

All other decision problems considered in this section are related to graph theoretic properties of NLC languages.

Theorem 13. It is undecidable whether or not, given a NLC grammar G, L(G) contains a totally disconnected graph (A graph is totally disconnected if it has no edges at all). ∎

Theorem 14. It is undecidable whether or not the language of a given NLC grammar contains a planar graph. ∎

Theorem 15. It is undecidable whether or not, given an arbitrary NLC grammar $G = (\Sigma, \Delta, P, C, Z)$ and two arbitrary subsets A,B of Δ, there is a graph H in L(G) such that A is not adjacent to B in H. ∎

Theorem 16. Given an arbitrary NLC grammar G, it is undecidable whether or not S(G) contains a graph H such that the set $\{M | H \overset{*}{\underset{G}{\Rightarrow}} M\}$ is of bounded degree. ∎

Theorem 17. It is undecidable whether or not, for an arbitrary NLC grammar G, L(G) contains a connected graph. ∎

Theorem 18. It is undecidable whether or not, for an arbitrary NLC grammar G, L(G) contains a graph that is not 1-connected. ∎

Theorem 19. It is undecidable whether or not, for an arbitrary NLC grammar G, L(G) contains a hamiltonian graph. ∎

Theorem 20. Given an arbitrary NLC grammar G, it is undecidable whether or not the set of connected graphs in L(G) is of bounded degree. ∎

Theorem 21. It is undecidable whether or not, given two arbitrary NLC grammars G_1 and G_2, the intersection $L(G_1) \cap L(G_2)$ is empty. ∎

Theorem 22. Given an arbitrary NLC grammar $G = (\Sigma, \Delta, P, C, Z)$, and two arbitrary subsets A,B of Δ, it is undecidable whether or not there exist a label a in A, a label b in B and a graph H in L(G) such that there is a path in H from an a-labelled node to a b-labelled node. ∎

A very natural problem from the graph-theoretical point of view is the decidability status of the question : "Given an arbitrary NLC grammar G, is L(G) of bounded degree?" At present, we do not know whether or not this question is decidable. However we can report the following result in this direction. NLC grammars do not allow node erasing. A way to extend NLC grammars by allowing node erasing is to perform an erasing as follows : in rewriting a graph H one "erases" a node v by removing v from H and then establishing an edge between every pair n_1, n_2 of different neighbours of v. Graph grammars, obtained by adding to NLC grammars an erasing mechanism as defined as above are referred to as ΛNLC grammars. For this class of grammars the mentioned decision problem is settled as follows.

Theorem 23. Given an arbitrary ΛNLC grammar G, it is undecidable whether or not L(G) is of bounded degree. ∎

VI. DISCUSSION

This paper presents an effort towards establishing a firm basis for graph grammar theory. It introduces and investigates a new type of graph grammars, called NLC grammars. The underlying embedding mechanism, used in NLC grammars, seems to be very natural - edges connecting the daughter graph with the neighbours of the mother graph are established on the basis of their labels only. Moreover (see Section I), NLC grammars form the most general class to be considered in a classification of graph grammars, based on the approach from [MR], applied to grammars rewriting nodes.

In this paper we have accomplished the following.

(1). We have provided a mathematical tool ($H_{B,\alpha}^{(n)}$ construct) to describe the structure of NLC languages.

(2). We have investigated the combinatorial structure of languages in $\mathcal{L}$(NLC), which resulted in a "pumping-type" theorem for NLC languages.

(3). We have investigated the influence of various parameters of NLC grammars on their language generating power. This resulted in some restrictions and extensions of NLC grammars, as well as in some technically useful normal forms in NLC grammars.

(4). We have investigated the relationship between graph grammars and string grammars by considering NLC grammars (and their extension for directed graphs) as string generators.

(5). We have investigated the "effectiveness" of defining graph languages by NLC grammars by considering several basic decision problems concerning NLC grammars and languages.

Clearly the research presented here forms only the beginning of the theory of NLC grammars. Quite a number of basic theoretical questions (e.g. an "algebraic" description of NLC languages and closure properties of $\mathcal{L}$(NLC)) are still open, and the possibilities for using NLC grammars in various areas of application (as mentioned in the introduction) remain to be investigated.

ACKNOWLEDGEMENT

The second author gratefully acknowledges the financial support of NSF grant number MCS 79-03838.

REFERENCES

[CER] V. Claus, H. Ehrig and G. Rozenberg, Graph-Grammars and Their Application to Computer Science and Biology, Lecture Notes in Computer Science vol. 73, Springer-Verlag, Berlin-Heidelberg-New York, 1979.

[NA] M. Nagl, Graph-Grammatiken, Vieweg und Sohn, Braunschweig, 1979.

[SC1] Schneider, Syntax-directed Description of Incremental Compilers, Lecture Notes in Computer Science vol. 26, 192-201, Springer-Verlag, Berlin 1975.

[SC2] Schneider, Conceptual Data-Base Description Using Graph Grammars, in H. Noltemeier : Graphen, Algorithmen, Datenstrukturen, Applied Computer Science 4, 77-98, Muenchen : Hansen Verlag 1976.

[BA] C. Battini, A. d'Atri, Rewriting Systems as a Tool for Relational Data Base Design, 139-154, in [CER].

[EL] H.D. Ehrich, V.G. Lohberger, Constructing Specifications of Abstract Data Types by replacements, 180-191, in [CER].

[FU] A.L. Furtado, Tranformations of Data Base Structures, 224-236, in [CER].

[PR] T.W. Pratt, Definition of Programming Language Semantics Using Grammars for Hierarchical Graphs, 389-400, in [CER].

[WI] J.C. Wileden, Relationship between Graph Grammars and the Design and Analysis of Concurrent Software, 456-463, in [CER].

[GT] Genrich, Thiagarajan, Bipolar Synchronization Systems, technical report, GMD Bonn, 1979.

[RM] A. Rosenfeld, D. Milgram, Web Automata and Weg Grammars, Machine Intelligence

7, 307-324, 1972.

[JR1] D. Janssens, G. Rozenberg, On the Structure of Node-Label Controlled Graph Languages, Information Sciences, to appear.

[JR2] D. Janssens, G. Rozenberg, Restrictions Extension and Variations of NLC grammars, Information Sciences, to appear.

[JR3] D. Janssens, G. Rozenberg, Decision Problems for Node-Label Controlled Graph Grammars, technical report, UIA Antwerp, 1979.

[FR] R. Franck, A Class of Linearly Parsible Graph Grammars, Acta Informatica 10 (1978), 175-201.

[KR] H.J. Kreowski, A Pumping Lemma for Context-Free Graph Languages, 270-283, in [CER].

[DG] P. Della Vigna, C. Ghezzi, Context-Free Graph Grammars, Information and Control 37, 207-233, 1978.

A method to compare the descriptive power of different types of Petri nets

Kurt Jensen

Computer Science Department
Aarhus University
Ny Munkegade
DK-8000 Aarhus C
Denmark

1. INTRODUCTION

The purpose of this paper is to show how the descriptive power of different types of Petri nets can be compared, without the use of Petri net languages. Moreover the paper proposes an extension of condition/event-nets and it is shown that this extension has the same descriptive power as condition/event-nets.

In many applications the basic Petri net formalism is augmented in different ways. Each of these extensions corresponds to a subclass of the very general "transition systems" defined in [Keller 76]. The descriptive power of such subclasses can be compared by use of formal language theory, where each transition is given a name and the set of possible firing sequences is considered, [Hack 76]. In the present paper it is, however, proposed to compare the descriptive power in a more direct way, which is closely connected to the idea of simulation.

In section 2 we define condition/event-nets and an extension of them called "testing Petri nets". Testing Petri nets were introduced in [Jensen 78], (there they were called "extended Petri nets"), and they have been used to define a formal semantics for a system description language in [Jensen, Kyng & Madsen 79]. Similar primitives are described in [Zuse 79]. The new primitives allow a transition to test some of its conditions without altering their markings.

In section 3 we give a transformation mapping each testing Petri net into a condition/event-net. Moreover we construct a function mapping markings for a testing Petri net into markings for the corresponding condition/event-net. We prove that the transformation satisfies three equations, all of them dealing with reachability.

In section 4 we define "transition systems" (from [Keller 76]) and "simulations" between them. The definition of simulation is directly inspired by the three equations proved for the transformation in section 3. We then prove a close connection between simulation and "strict reduction" (from [Kwong 77]) and this allows us to translate results, obtained for strict reduction by Kwong, to our situation where testing Petri nets are simulated by condition/event-nets. These results show that properties such as existence of a home state, Church-Rosser, non-haltingness and determinacy are preserved by simulation (i.e. the simulated system has the properties iff the simulating system has).

In section 5 we replace transition systems by "named transition systems" (from [Keller 76]) and simulation by "simulation induced by consistent homomorphisms". The latter definition is inspired by "strict reduction induced by homomorphisms" (from [Kwong 77]) and by "consistent" homomorphisms (from [Roucairol & Valk 79]). This allows us to translate a result obtained by Roucairol and Valk concerning liveness.

In section 6 we conclude that the method, used in sections 3, 4 and 5 to compare testing Petri nets and condition/event-nets, can be used to compare other types of Petri nets. We define "equivalence with respect to descriptive power". We discuss how to find the transformations necessary to compare two types of Petri nets, and we give references to papers where such transformations have been sketched.

2. CONDITION/EVENT-NETS AND TESTING PETRI NETS

Definition

A condition/event-net is a 5-tuple CEN = $(P, T, PRE, POST, m_0)$ where

1) P is a set of places
2) T is a set of transitions
3) $P \cap T = \emptyset$, $P \cup T \neq \emptyset$
4) PRE, POST $\in [T \to \mathbb{P}(P)]$ where $[\ldots]$ and $\mathbb{P}$ denote total functions and powersets respectively
5) $\forall t \in T\ [PRE(t) \cap POST(t) = \emptyset]$
6) $m_0 \in [P \to \{0, 1\}]$ is the initial marking.

A marking is a function $m \in [P \to \{0, 1\}]$. A place p is marked iff $m(p) = 1$ and unmarked iff $m(p) = 0$. p is a condition for a transition t iff $p \in COND(t) = PRE(t) \cup POST(t)$. It is a precondition iff $p \in PRE(t)$ and a postcondition iff $p \in POST(t)$.

Functions defined on P or T will in this and the following sections be extended to $\mathbb{P}(P)$ or $\mathbb{P}(T)$ in the usual way. As an example $PRE(X) = \bigcup_{t \in X} PRE(t)$, for all $X \subseteq T$.

Condition/event-nets can be represented as directed graphs with two kinds of nodes. Circles represent places, while squares represent transitions. Each transition has ingoing arcs from its preconditions and outgoing arcs to its postconditions. The initial marking is represented by tokens (solid dots) on the marked places.

Two transitions are independent iff their conditions are disjoint. A nonempty set of mutually independent transitions X has concession (and may fire) in a marking m iff all places in PRE(X) are marked and all places in POST(X) are unmarked. If X fires, a new marking m' is reached where all places in PRE(X) are unmarked and all places in POST(X) are marked. We then say that m' is directly reachable from m, which we write as $m \to m'$ or $m \xrightarrow{X} m'$. The transitive closure of direct reachability is written as $m \xrightarrow{+} m'$ or $m \xrightarrow{X_1 X_2 \ldots X_n} m'$, where $\{X_i \mid i \in 1..n\}$ with

$1 \leq n < \infty$, are the sets of transitions, which are fired to reach m' from m. The transitive and reflexive closure is written as $m \to^* m'$ or $m \xrightarrow{X_1 X_2 \ldots X_n} m'$ with $0 \leq n < \infty$. A marking m is reachable iff $m_0 \to^* m$.

The firing rule can be formalized as follows:

$$m \xrightarrow{X} m'$$
$$\Updownarrow$$
$$\left\{ \begin{array}{ll} X \neq \emptyset & \\ \forall\, t_1, t_2 \in X\ [COND(t_1) \cap COND(t_2) = \emptyset] & \\ \forall\, p \in P & \left[\begin{array}{lll} p \in PRE(X) & \Rightarrow & m(p) = 1 \wedge m'(p) = 0 \\ p \in POST(X) & \Rightarrow & m(p) = 0 \wedge m'(p) = 1 \\ p \notin COND(X) & \Rightarrow & m(p) = m'(p) \end{array} \right] \end{array} \right.$$

Definition

A testing Petri net is a 7-tuple $TPN = (P, T, PRE, POST, TM, TU, m_0)$ where

1) $P, T, PRE, POST$, and m_0 are defined exactly as for condition/event-nets
2) $TM, TU \in [T \to \mathbb{P}(P)]$
3) $\forall\, t \in T$ [PRE(t), POST(t), TM(t), and TU(t) are mutually disjoint].

Now the different definitions for condition/event-nets can be repeated, except that conditions are defined as $COND(t) = PRE(t) \cup POST(t) \cup TM(t) \cup TU(t)$, where TM(t) and TU(t) are testmarked-conditions and testunmarked-conditions respectively. The firing rule has the form:

$$m \xrightarrow{X} m'$$
$$\Updownarrow$$
$$\left\{ \begin{array}{ll} X \neq \emptyset & \\ \forall\, t_1, t_2 \in X\ [COND(t_1) \cap COND(t_2) = \emptyset] & \\ \forall\, p \in P & \left[\begin{array}{lll} p \in PRE(X) & \Rightarrow & m(p) = 1 \wedge m'(p) = 0 \\ p \in POST(X) & \Rightarrow & m(p) = 0 \wedge m'(p) = 1 \\ p \in TM(X) & \Rightarrow & m(p) = 1 \wedge m'(p) = 1 \\ p \in TU(X) & \Rightarrow & m(p) = 0 \wedge m'(p) = 0 \\ p \notin COND(X) & \Rightarrow & m(p) = m'(p) \end{array} \right] \end{array} \right.$$

Testing Petri nets can be represented graphically in the same way as condition/event-nets, except that transitions are connected to their testmarked-conditions by unbroken (undirected) arcs and to testunmarked-conditions by dashed (undirected) arcs.

3. TRANSFORMATION FROM TESTING PETRI NETS TO CONDITION/EVENT-NETS

In this section we define a transformation, which maps each testing Petri net into a condition/event-net with a "similar behaviour". We first define the transformation. Then we give a formal meaning to the term "similar behaviour", and we show that the transformation is consistent with this definition.

Let TPN = (P, T, PRE, POST, TM, TU, m_0) be a testing Petri net. We shall transform TPN into a condition/event-net CEN = (P', T', PRE', POST', m_0').

Transformation A

A straightforward first idea is to split each transition t from TPN into two transitions denoted by f(t) and l(t) and connected by a place c(t). Each subnet in TPN of the form shown in figure 1 is replaced by a condition/event-subnet of the form shown in figure 2, where {...} indicate subsets of conditions.

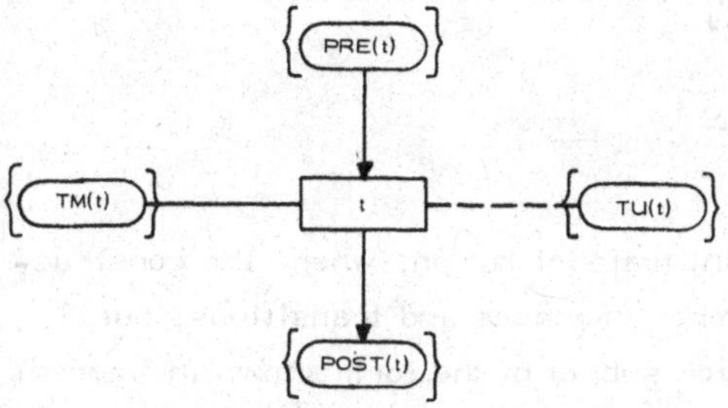

Figure 1

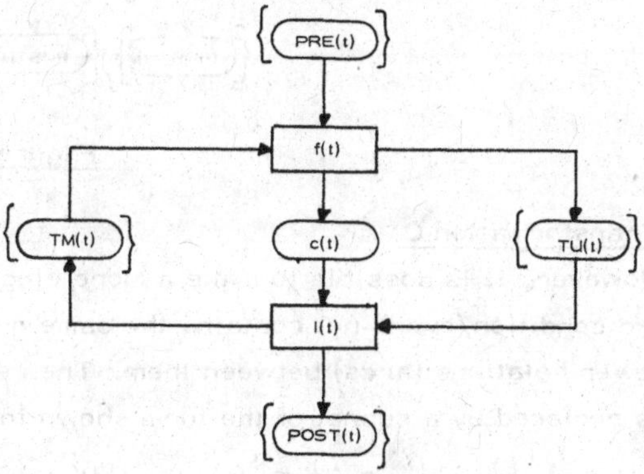

Figure 2

Moreover we define a function h, which maps each marking m of TPN into a marking m' = h(m) of CEN defined by

$$m'(p) = \begin{cases} m(p) & \text{if } p \in P \\ 0 & \text{if } p \in c(T) \end{cases}$$

The initial marking of CEN is $m_0' = h(m_0)$.

Unfortunately, this simple transformation does not yield a condition/event-net with a "similar behaviour" as the original testing Petri net. The problem is that other transitions may change the marking of COND(t) between the firings of f(t) and l(t).

Transformation B

The problem with transformation A can be solved by splitting each place p into two places denoted by p and s(p). s(p) acts as a binary semaphore controlling the use of p. Then each subnet of the form shown in figure 1 is replaced by a subnet of the form shown in figure 3 and m' = h(m) is defined by

$$m'(p) = \begin{cases} m(p) & \text{if } p \in P \\ 0 & \text{if } p \in s(P) \cup c(T) \end{cases}$$

This transformation yields a condition/event-net with a "similar behaviour" as the original testing Petri net.

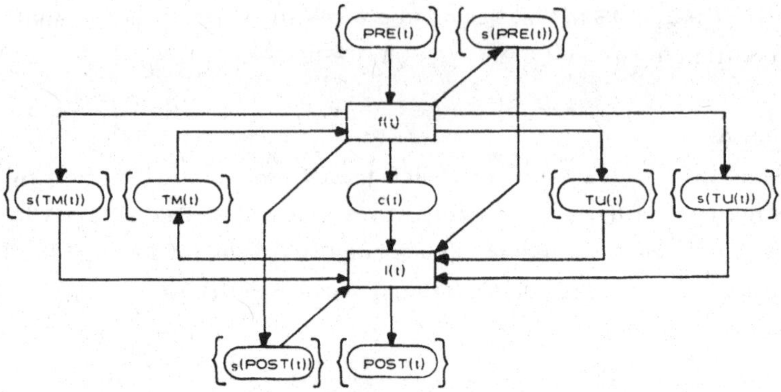

Figure 3

Transformation C

However, it is possible to make a more elegant transformation, where the constructed condition/event-net contains the same number of places and transitions, but fewer relations (arcs) between them. Then each subnet of the form shown in figure 1 is replaced by a subnet of the form shown in figure 4. and $m' = h(m)$ is defined by

$$m'(p) = \begin{cases} m(p') & \text{if } p = a(p') \text{ or } p = b(p') \\ 0 & \text{if } p \in c(T) \end{cases}$$

The initial marking is $m_0' = h(m_0)$.

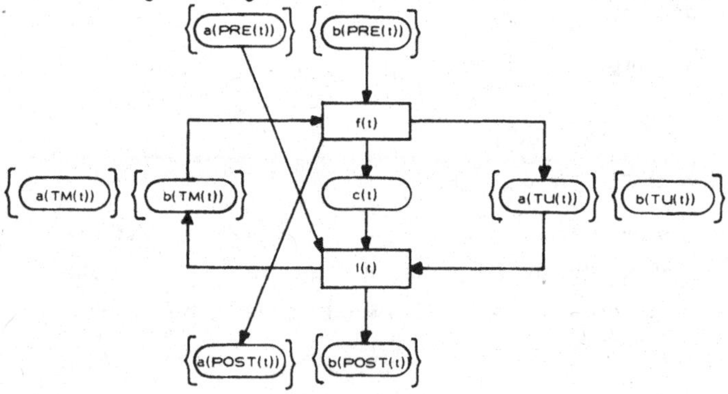

Figure 4

Similar behaviour

What do we mean, when we say that two Petri nets have a "similar behaviour"? To be very informal we mean that they have the same "basic properties". But then we must ask what the "basic properties" are, and the answer to this question depends heavily on the use of the model. The answer could be, that the two nets should have a similar concurrency-relation. For transformation C this could be formalised by proving that two transitions in CEN are concurrent iff the corresponding two transitions in TPN are concurrent. In this paper we shall, however, focus on properties concerning reachability, liveness, home-states, determinacy etc.

Let TPN, CEN and h be defined as in transformation C. By M_{TPN} and M_{CEN} we denote the sets of markings for TPN and CEN, respectively. A marking $m \in M_{CEN}$ is representative iff $m \in h(M_{TPN})$.

Lemma 1 A marking $m \in M_{CEN}$ is representative iff $\forall p \in P\ [m(a(p))=m(b(p))]$ and $\forall t \in T\ [m(c(t))=0]$.

Proof Trivial from definition of h. □

Lemma 2 For all markings $m'' \in M_{CEN}$, reachable from a representative marking, we have $\forall p \in P\ [m''(a(p))=m''(b(p)) + \sum_{t \in A(p)} m''(c(t))]$ where $A(p) = \{t \in T \mid p \in COND(t)\}$.

Proof From figure 4 by the invariant-method described in [Lautenbach 75] or by observing that the property is satisfied by any representative marking and kept invariant by the firing of any set of transitions in CEN. □

Lemma 3 For all markings $m'' \in M_{CEN}$, reachable from a representative marking, we have $\forall t, t' \in T\ [COND(t) \cap COND(t') \neq \emptyset \Rightarrow m''(c(t)) + m''(c(t')) \leq 1]$.

Proof Assume that $p \in COND(t) \cap COND(t')$, then $t, t' \in A(p)$ and we conclude from Lemma 2 that $m''(c(t)) + m''(c(t')) \leq 1$. □

In the proof of the following Theorem 1 we shall exclude infinite concurrency in the sense that we demand each set X of transitions, involved in a single step $m \xrightarrow{X} m'$, to be finite. This assumption will allow us to replace $m \xrightarrow{X} m'$ by a finite sequence of individual transitions $m \xrightarrow{x_1 x_2 \ldots x_n} m'$ where $X = \{x_i \mid 1 \leq i \leq n\}$ and $1 \leq n < \infty$. For a proof of the general situation (allowing infinite concurrency) see [Jensen 78].

Theorem 1 The function $h: M_{TPN} \to M_{CEN}$ is an injection and has the following properties:

(1) $h(m_0) = m_0'$

(2) $\forall m, m' \in M_{TPN}\ [m \xrightarrow[TPN]{+} m' \Leftrightarrow h(m) \xrightarrow[CEN]{+} h(m')]$

(3) $\forall m \in M_{TPN}\ \forall m' \in M_{CEN}\ [h(m) \xrightarrow[CEN]{*} m' \Rightarrow$
$\exists m'' \in M_{TPN}\ [m' \xrightarrow[CEN]{*} h(m'')]]$

Proof Injectivity and equation 1 follows directly from the definition of h, TPN and CEN.

Equation 2 Assume that $m \xrightarrow[TPN]{+} m'$ for two markings $m, m' \in M_{TPN}$. From our exclusion of infinite concurrency this implies the existence of a sequence of transitions $t_1 t_2 \ldots t_r$, with $1 \leq r < \infty$, such that $m \xrightarrow[TPN]{t_1 t_2 \ldots t_r} m'$. Then $h(m) \xrightarrow[CEN]{f(t_1)\ l(t_1)\ f(t_2)\ l(t_2)\ \ldots\ f(t_r)\ l(t_r)} h(m')$.

Next assume that $h(m) \xrightarrow[CEN]{+} h(m')$ and $h(m) \xrightarrow[CEN]{t_1 t_2 \dots t_s} h(m')$ where $1 \leq s < \infty$. We have to prove that $m \xrightarrow[TPN]{+} m'$. The proof is by induction on s:

s = 1: Impossible since firing of only one transition $f(t_1)$ would lead to a marking with $c(t_1)$ marked and by Lemma 1 such a marking cannot be representative.

s = 2: By an argument similar to case s = 1, we conclude that there exists a transition $t \in T$ such that $t_1 = f(t)$ and $t_2 = l(t)$, but then $m \xrightarrow[TPN]{t} m'$.

s > 2: By Lemma 1 all places in c(T) are unmarked in h(m). Thus no transition in l(T) has concession and we conclude that $t_1 = f(t)$ for some $t \in T$. Since c(t) is marked by t_1 and unmarked in $h(m')$, there exists at least one occurrence of l(t) in the sequence $t_2 \dots t_s$. Let t_u with $u \in 2..s$ be the first such occurrence. Let $t' \in T$ be any transition with $COND(t) \cap COND(t') \neq \emptyset$. From Lemma 3 it follows that $c(t')$ is unmarked in all markings between the firings of t_1 and t_u and hence neither $f(t')$ nor $l(t')$ can be contained in $FS = t_2 t_3 \dots t_{u-1}$.

Thus we conclude that no transition in FS has conditions from a(COND(t)) or b(COND(t)), but this means that t_u can be moved just behind t_1 without altering the total effect of the firing sequence:

$$h(m) \xrightarrow[CEN]{t_1 t_u} m'' \xrightarrow[CEN]{t_2 \dots t_{u-1} t_{u+1} \dots t_s} h(m')$$

It is easy to check that $m'' = h(m''')$, where m''' is defined by $m \xrightarrow[TPN]{t} m'''$.

By the inductive hypothesis we then get $m''' \xrightarrow[TPN]{+} m'$ and by transitivity of $\xrightarrow[TPN]{+}$ we conclude $m \xrightarrow[TPN]{+} m'$.

Equation 3 Assume that $h(m) \xrightarrow[CEN]{*} m'$ for two markings $m \in M_{TPN}$ and $m' \in M_{CEN}$. Let $X = \{t \in T \mid m'(c(t)) = 1\}$. From Lemma 2, Lemma 3 and figure 4 it follows that X has concession in m'. Let $m'' \in M_{CEN}$ be the marking reached from m' by firing X in CEN. From figure 4, Lemma 2 and Lemma 1 it follows that m'' is representative. □

In Theorem 1 we showed that h is an injection satisfying three equations. For the moment we will take these equations as our formal definition of similar behaviour. Then Theorem 1 states that transformation C maps each testing Petri net into a condition/event-net with a similar behaviour. In section 4 we shall see that the three equations imply that TPN has a home-state, is Church-Rosser, non-halting or determinate iff CEN has the corresponding property.

4. TRANSITION SYSTEMS, SIMULATION, AND STRICT REDUCTION

In this section we define "transition systems" (from [Keller 76]) and "strict reduction" (from [Kwong 77]). Moreover we shall see that there is a close connection between simulation (defined in the previous section) and strict reduction. This connection allows us to translate Kwong's results to our situation, where testing Petri nets are simulated by condition/event-nets.

<u>Definition (Keller)</u> A <u>transition system</u> is a triple $TS = (Q, \rightarrow, Q^0)$ where

1) Q is a set of <u>states</u>
2) $\rightarrow \subseteq Q \times Q$ is the <u>transition-relation</u>
3) Q^0 is the set of <u>initial states</u>

We shall write $q \rightarrow q'$ for $(q, q') \in \rightarrow$. The transitive closure is denoted by $\rightarrow^+$, the transitive and reflexive closure by $\rightarrow^*$. A state q' is <u>reachable from a state q</u> iff $q \rightarrow^* q'$. The set of all <u>reachable states is</u> $Q^r = \{q \in Q \mid \exists q_0 \in Q^0 [q_0 \rightarrow^* q]\}$.

Let $TS_1 = (Q_1, \xrightarrow[1]{}, Q_1^0)$ and $TS_2 = (Q_2, \xrightarrow[2]{}, Q_2^0)$ be transition systems and $h: Q_1 \rightarrow Q_2$ an injection. Let $h(TS_1)$ denote the transition system defined by $h(TS_1) = (h(Q_1), \xrightarrow[h]{}, h(Q_1^0))$ where $\xrightarrow[h]{}$ is defined by

(*) $\forall q, q' \in Q_1 [q \xrightarrow[1]{} q' \Leftrightarrow h(q) \xrightarrow[h]{} h(q')]$

Q_1^r, Q_2^r and Q_h^r are the set of reachable states for TS_1, TS_2 and $h(TS_1)$, respectively.

The following definition of "simulation" is motivated by the three equations shown for transformation C in Theorem 1 (section 3).

<u>Definition</u> TS_1 is <u>simulated</u> by TS_2 with respect to h iff

(S1) $h(Q_1^0) = Q_2^0$

(S2) $\forall q, q' \in Q_1^r [q \xrightarrow[1]{+} q' \Leftrightarrow h(q) \xrightarrow[2]{+} h(q')]$

(S3) $\forall q \in Q_1^r \forall q' \in Q_2 [h(q) \xrightarrow[2]{*} q' \Rightarrow \exists q'' \in Q_1 [q' \xrightarrow[2]{*} h(q'')]]$

<u>Definition (Kwong)</u> TS_2 <u>strictly reduces</u> to TS_1 iff

(1) $Q_1 \subseteq Q_2$, $Q_1^0 = Q_2^0$

(2) $\forall q_0 \in Q_1^0 \forall q' \in Q_2 [q_0 \xrightarrow[2]{*} q' \Rightarrow \exists q'' \in Q_1 [q' \xrightarrow[2]{*} q'' \wedge q_0 \xrightarrow[1]{*} q'']]$

(3) $\forall q, q' \in Q_1^r [q \xrightarrow[1]{} q' \Rightarrow q \xrightarrow[2]{+} q']$

(4) $\forall q, q' \in Q_1^r [q \xrightarrow[2]{+} q' \Rightarrow q \xrightarrow[1]{+} q']$

<u>Theorem 2</u> TS_1 is simulated by TS_2 with respect to h iff TS_2 strictly reduces to $h(TS_1)$.

<u>Proof</u> TS_1 is simulated by TS_2 iff (S1)-(S3) are satisfied.
TS_2 strictly reduces to $h(TS_1)$ iff

(R1) $h(Q_1) \subseteq Q_2$, $h(Q_1^0) = Q_2^0$

(R2) $\forall h(q_0) \in h(Q_1^0) \forall q' \in Q_2 [h(q_0) \xrightarrow[2]{*} q' \Rightarrow$

$\exists h(q'') \in h(Q_1) [q' \xrightarrow[2]{*} h(q'') \wedge h(q_0) \xrightarrow[h]{*} h(q'')]]$

(R3) $\forall\, h(q), h(q') \in h(Q_1^r)\ [h(q) \underset{h}{\longrightarrow} h(q') \Rightarrow h(q) \underset{2}{\longrightarrow}^{+} h(q')]$

(R4) $\forall\, h(q), h(q') \in h(Q_1^r)\ [h(q) \underset{2}{\longrightarrow}^{+} h(q') \Rightarrow h(q) \underset{h}{\longrightarrow}^{+} h(q')]$

Assume (S1)-(S3)

(R1) follows from the functionality of h and from (S1).

(R2) and (R4) follow from (S2) and (*) in the definition of $h(TS_1)$.

In (R2) the first part, $q' \underset{2}{\longrightarrow}^{*} h(q'')$, follows from (S3). The second part, $h(q_0) \underset{h}{\longrightarrow}^{*} h(q'')$, follows from transitivity of $\underset{2}{\longrightarrow}^{*}$ (used on $h(q_0) \underset{2}{\longrightarrow}^{*} q'$ and $q' \underset{2}{\longrightarrow}^{*} h(q'')$) and from (R4).

Assume (R1)-(R4)

(S1) follows from (R1).

(S2) follows from (R3) and (R4).

(S3) follows from (R2), transitivity of $\underset{2}{\longrightarrow}^{*}$ and (S2). □

From the above proof observe that the second part of (R2) is implied by the first part, transitivity of $\underset{2}{\longrightarrow}^{*}$ and (R4). By a similar argument it can be proved that omission of "$\wedge\, q_0 \underset{1}{\longrightarrow}^{*} q''$" from (2) would yield an equivalent definition of strict reduction.

Let $TS = (Q, \rightarrow, Q^0)$ be a transition system. A state $q \in Q$ is

dead iff there does not exist a state q' such that $q \rightarrow q'$

home iff $q' \rightarrow^{*} q$ for all $q' \in Q^r$

The transition system TS is

non-halting iff all reachable states are non-dead

determinate iff for any $q_0 \in Q^0$ and any $q, q' \in Q$ reachable from q_0

$(\text{dead}(q) \wedge \text{dead}(q')) \Rightarrow (q = q')$

Church-Rosser iff for any $q, q', q'' \in Q^r$

$(q \rightarrow^{*} q' \wedge q \rightarrow^{*} q'') \Rightarrow \exists\, q''' \in Q\ [q' \rightarrow^{*} q''' \wedge q'' \rightarrow^{*} q''']$

Corollary 1 If TS_1 is simulated by TS_2 then TS_1 has a home-state, is Church-Rosser, non-halting or determinate iff TS_2 has the corresponding property.

Proof Theorem 2 and Theorems 4.4, 4.5, 4.6 and 4.7 in [Kwong 77]. □

The basic idea of this (and the following sections) is to consider Petri nets (of different types) as special instances of transition systems. Then Q is the set of all markings, → is direct reachability and Q^0 has only one element, the initial marking.

Now let TPN be a testing Petri net and CEN the condition/event-net constructed from TPN (by transformation C in section 3). Let TPN' and CEN' be the corresponding transition systems. From Theorem 1 it then immediately follows that TPN' is simulated by CEN' and from Corollary 1 we get:

Corollary 2 A testing Petri net has a home state, is Church-Rosser, non-halting or determinate iff the condition/event-net constructed from it has the corresponding property.

In this section we have compared our own definition of simulation (inspired by Theorem 1) with Kwong's definition of strict reduction. It turned out that the two definitions are mathematically equivalent. However, the purpose of the two formalisms is quite different. Kwong uses strict reduction to analyse complicated system descriptions. He starts with a "large" transition system. Then he gradually decreases the number of system states, without altering the basic properties. We use simulation to compare the descriptive power of different types of Petri nets. We start with a "small" transition system corresponding to a description containing some Petri net primitives. Then we translate this description into another set of primitives, and to do this we normally have to enlarge the number of system states. In our situation there is often a nontrivial correspondence between the states in the two transition systems. For this reason we have modified Kwong's definition to make the correspondence between states explicit via the injection h. This is similar to the injection i used in [Roucairol & Valk 79].

5. NAMED TRANSITION SYSTEMS AND SIMULATION INDUCED BY HOMOMORPHISMS

In transformation C (defined in section 3) there is a very close connection between the firing of a transition t in TPN and the firings of f(t) and l(t) in CEN. In the formalisation of simulation (and strict reduction) this connection is not captured, because transition systems do not allow us to attach names to the elements of the transition-relation. To remedy this we define in this section "named transition systems" (from [Keller 76]). Moreover we augment the definition of simulation by adding homomorphisms, which connect the transitions of the two systems.

In Theorem 2 (section 4) we proved a close connection between simulation and strict reduction. A similar connection exists between "simulation induced by homomorphisms" and "strict reduction induced by homomorphisms" (from [Kwong 77], generalised in [Roucairol & Valk 79]). This connection allows us to translate results obtained by Roucairol and Valk.

Definition (Keller) A named transition system is a quadruple $(Q, \Sigma, \rightarrow, Q^0)$ where

1) Q is a set of states
2) Σ is a set of transitions
3) $\rightarrow \subseteq Q \times \Sigma \times Q$ is the transition-relation
4) $Q^0 \subseteq Q$ is the set of initial states.

We shall write $q \xrightarrow{t} q'$ for $(q, t, q') \in \rightarrow$. This represents a single step t transforming q to q'. It is generalised to finite sequences of steps by the following definition, where Σ^* is the set of finite strings over Σ, and Λ the empty string:

For any $q, q' \in Q$

(i) $q \xrightarrow{\Lambda} q' \Leftrightarrow q = q'$

(ii) $\forall y \in \Sigma^* \; \forall t \in \Sigma [q \xrightarrow{yt} q' \Leftrightarrow \exists q'' \in Q [q \xrightarrow{y} q'' \wedge q'' \xrightarrow{t} q']]$

The set of <u>reachable states</u> is defined by $Q^r = \{q \in Q \mid \exists q_0 \in Q \; \exists x \in \Sigma^* [q_0 \xrightarrow{x} q]\}$.

Let $TS_1 = (Q_1, \Sigma_1, \xrightarrow{1}, Q_1^0)$ and $TS_2 = (Q_2, \Sigma_2, \xrightarrow{2}, Q_2^0)$ be named transition systems. $\Sigma^+ = \Sigma^* - \{\Lambda\}$. Let $A_1 : \Sigma_2 \to \mathbb{P}(\Sigma_1) \cup \{\{\Lambda\}\}$ and $A_2 : \Sigma_1 \to \mathbb{P}(\Sigma_2^+)$ be arbitrary functions and $h: Q_1 \to Q_2$ an injection. Q_1^r and Q_2^r are the set of reachable states for TS_1 and TS_2 respectively.

<u>Definition</u> TS_1 is <u>simulated</u> by TS_2 with respect to $<h, A_1, A_2>$ iff

(1) $h(Q_1^0) = Q_2^0$

and extending A_1 and A_2 to homomorphisms in the usual way

(2a) $\forall q, q' \in Q_1^r \; \forall x \in \Sigma_1^+ [q \xrightarrow[1]{x} q' \Rightarrow \exists y \in A_2(x) [h(q) \xrightarrow[2]{y} h(q')]]$

(2b) $\forall q, q' \in Q_1^r \; \forall x \in \Sigma_2^+ [h(q) \xrightarrow[2]{x} h(q') \Rightarrow \exists y \in A_1(x) [q \xrightarrow[1]{y} q' \wedge y \neq \Lambda]]$

(3) $\forall q \in Q_1^r \; \forall q' \in Q_2 \; \forall x \in \Sigma_2^* [h(q) \xrightarrow[2]{x} q' \Rightarrow$
$\exists q'' \in Q_1 \; \exists y \in \Sigma_2^* [q' \xrightarrow[2]{y} h(q'')]]$

With respect to $<A_1, A_2>$ define $\Sigma_2' = \{x \in \Sigma_2 \mid A_1(x) \neq \{\Lambda\}\}$.

<u>Definition (Valk and Roucairol)</u> The homomorphisms $<A_1, A_2>$ are <u>consistent</u> iff

(C1) $\bigcup_{x \in \Sigma_2} A_1(x) \supseteq \Sigma_1$

(C2) $\forall q \in Q_1^r \; \forall x \in \Sigma_2 [\exists y \in A_1(x) [y \text{ fireable in } q] \Rightarrow \forall y \in A_1(x) [y \text{ fireable in } q]]$

(C3) $\forall x \in \Sigma_2' \; \forall y \in \Sigma_2^+ [y \in A_2(A_1(x)) \Rightarrow y \text{ contains } x]$

The definitions above define the range of A_1 and A_2 as powersets. Often we do not need this generality and we have simulations satisfying one or more of the following equations, where the cardinality of a set B is denoted by $|B|$:

(C4) $\forall x \in \Sigma_2 [|A_1(x)| = 1]$

(C5) $\forall x \in \Sigma_1 [|A_2(x)| = 1]$

(C6) $\forall x \in \Sigma_1 [\{x\} = A_1(A_2(x))]$

The simulation defined immediately below (transformation C) satisfies all three equations (C4)-(C6). Two of the transformations sketched in [Jensen 78, 79] satisfy (C4) and (C6), but not (C5). It should be noted that (C4) implies (C2), while (C6) implies (C1).

Simulation induced by consistent homomorphisms is transitive (by functional composition of the involved homomorphisms and injections). This would not be the case if consistent homomorphisms are replaced by <u>strictly consistent</u> homomorphisms as they are defined in [Roucairol & Valk 79].

We again exclude <u>infinite concurrency</u> (see section 4). We can then consider each Petri net (of some type) as a special instance of named transition systems. Then Q is the set of all markings, Σ is the set of transitions, $\rightarrow$ is direct reachability by firing of only one transition, and Q^0 has only one element, the initial marking.

Now let TPN be a testing Petri net and CEN the condition/event-net constructed from TPN (by transformation C in section 3). Let TPN'' and CEN'' be the corresponding named transition systems, with transitions T and $T' = f(T) \cup I(T)$, respectively. Define $A_1: T' \rightarrow \mathbb{P}(T) \cup \{\{\Lambda\}\}$ and $A_2: T \rightarrow \mathbb{P}((T')^+)$ by

$$A_1(t) = \begin{cases} \{t'\} & \text{if } t = f(t') \\ \{\Lambda\} & \text{if } t = I(t') \end{cases} \qquad A_2(t) = \{f(t)\ I(t)\}$$

From these definitions it immediately follows that $<A_1, A_2>$ is consistent. Repeating the proof for Theorem 1, while keeping track of the names attached to fired transitions, we get:

<u>Theorem 3</u> TPN'' is simulated by CEN'' with respect to $<h, A_1, A_2>$. $<A_1, A_2>$ is consistent.

Let $TS = (Q, \Sigma, \rightarrow, Q^0)$ be a named transition system with reachable states Q^r. TS is <u>live</u> iff $\forall q \in Q^r\ \forall x \in \Sigma\ \exists q' \in Q\ \exists y \in \Sigma^*\ [q \xrightarrow{y} q' \wedge x \text{ fireable in } q']$.

Now we can proceed as in section 4. We can define "strict reduction induced by consistent homomorphisms" (from [Kwong 77] and [Roucairol & Valk 79]) and we can relate it to "simulation induced by consistent homomorphisms" (by a Theorem analogous to Theorem 2).

<u>Corollary 3</u> A testing Petri net is live iff the condition/event-net constructed from it is live.

<u>Proof</u> Theorem 3, Theorem 1.2 (a) in [Roucairol & Valk 79] and the fact that each transition $I(t) \in I(T)$ can be fired immediately after the corresponding transition $f(t) \in f(T)$ (cf. the proof for equation 3 in Theorem 1). □

In section 4 we have considered the inverse of transformation C as a "strict reduction". In this section we have considered it as a "strict reduction induced by consistent homomorphisms". It could also be considered as an "algebraic simulation" (from [Milner 71] and [Brand 78]) or as a "contraction" (from [Gourlay, Rounds & Statman 79]).

6. CONCLUSION

In section 2 we defined condition/event-nets and testing Petri nets. In section 3 we gave a transformation mapping testing Petri nets into condition/event-nets, and we proved that this transformation satisfies three equations (Theorem 1). In section 4 we then defined transition systems and simulation between them. The definition of simulation was directly inspired by the three equations proved in Theorem 1. We proved a close connection between simulation and strict reduction (Theorem 2) and this allowed us to translate results obtained for strict reduction to our situation, where testing Petri nets are simulated by condition/event-nets (Corollary 2). In section 5 we replaced transition systems by named transition systems and we replaced simulation by simulation induced by consistent homomorphisms. This allowed us to translate results obtained for strict reduction induced by consistent homomorphisms (Corollary 3).

This approach, described above for testing Petri nets and condition/event-nets, are general enough to be used to compare the descriptive power of other types of Petri nets. We say that a Petri net PN_1 is _simulated_ by another Petri net PN_2 iff the transition system corresponding to PN_1 is simulated by the transition system corresponding to PN_2. The two Petri nets need not be of the same type. An analogous definition is made for _simulation induced by consistent homomorphisms_.

Let A and B be two types of Petri nets. A is _(strongly) not weaker_ than B iff each net in B can be simulated (induced by consistent homomorphisms) by a net in A. A and B are _(strongly) equivalent with respect to descriptive power_ iff A is (strongly) not weaker than B and vice versa. As mentioned earlier simulation (induced by consistent homomorphisms) is transitive and thus (strong) equivalence with respect to descriptive power is an equivalence-relation.

Theorem 4 Condition/event-nets and testing Petri nets are strongly equivalent with respect to descriptive power.

Proof It is trivial that testing Petri nets are strongly not weaker than condition/event-nets. The other direction follows from Theorem 3. □

Having made these formal definitions, an important question arises. Given two types of Petri nets. How do we construct the transformation(s) necessary to compare their descriptive power? The construction-method from section 3 can often be used: Take a single transition together with its conditions and replace this subnet by a simulating subnet of the other type. Do this for each transition.

The method described in this paper has been used to compare the descriptive power of "testing Petri nets" and "hyper Petri nets" and the descriptive power of "place/transition-nets" and "coloured Petri nets". For sketches of the involved transformations see [Jensen 78, 79]. The transformations used there, are simple in the sense that firing of a single transition is simulated by firing only a single transition in the other net. It is the absence of this property, which makes transformation C and the proof of Theorem 1 non-trivial.

Acknowledgments Valuable criticism and comments have been made by Morten Kyng, Antoni Mazurkiewicz, Brian Mayoh, Robin Milner, Mogens Nielsen and Erik Meineche Schmidt.

References

[Brand 78]

Brand, D.: Algebraic simulation between parallel programs. IBM Research Report RC 7206 (June 1978).

[Gourlay, Rounds & Statman 79]

Gourlay, J.S., Rounds, W.C. and Statman, R.: On properties preserved by contractions of concurrent systems. Semantics of Concurrent Computation, Evian 1979, G. Kahn (ed.), Lecture Notes in Computer Science, vol. 70, Springer Verlag 1979, 51-63.

[Hack 76]

Hack, M.: Petri net languages. Technical Report 159, Laboratory for Computer Science, Massachusetts Institute of Technology, March 1976.

[Jensen 78]

Jensen, K.: Extended and hyper Petri nets. DAIMI TR-5, Computer Science Department, Aarhus University, August 1978.

[Jensen, Kyng & Madsen 79]

Jensen, K., Kyng, M. and Madsen, O.L.: Delta semantics defined by Petri nets. DAIMI PB-95, Computer Science Department, Aarhus University, March 1979.

[Jensen 79]

Jensen, K.: Coloured Petri nets and the invariant-method. DAIMI PB-104, Computer Science Department, Aarhus University, October 1979.

[Keller 76]

Keller, R.M.: Formal verification of parallel programs. Comm. ACM 19, 7 (1976), 371-384.

[Kwong 77]

Kwong, Y.S.: On reduction of asynchronous systems. Theoretical Computer Science 5 (1977), 25-50.

[Lautenbach 75]

Lautenbach, K.: Liveness in Petri nets. Interner Bericht ISF-75-02.1, GMD Bonn, July 1975.

[Milner 71]

Milner, R.: An algebraic definition of simulation between programs. Second Int. Joint Conf. on Artificial Intelligence, British Computer Society, 1971, 481-489.

[Roucairol & Valk 79]

Roucairol, G. and Valk, R.: Reductions of nets and parallel programs. Advanced course on general net theory of processes and systems, Hamburg 1979, H. Fuss (ed.), GMD Bonn, 1979. Also to be published by Springer Verlag, 1980. Note, that detailed comments, numbering of Theorems, etc. refer to the revised version from Springer Verlag.

[Zuse 79]

Zuse, K.: Petri-nets from the engineer's viewpoint. Advanced course on general net theory of processes and systems, Hamburg 1979, H. Fuss (ed.), GMD Bonn, 1979. Also to be published by Springer Verlag, 1980.

A SIMPLE CLASS OF ALGORITHMIC SPECIFICATIONS FOR ABSTRACT SOFTWARE MODULES

Herbert A. Klaeren
Lehrstuhl für Informatik II, RWTH Aachen
Büchel 29-31, D-5100 Aachen

1. Introduction

Software modules, considered as combinations of certain sets of data objects, together with sets of operations to be performed thereon, can be described by universal (many-sorted) algebras in a natural way. The problem of abstract software specification can thus be viewed as equivalent to the problem of defining classes of algebras whose operations show a certain common behaviour.

Usually, algebraic specifications are given by triples $\langle S,\Sigma,E \rangle$ where S is a set of sorts, Σ a set of operations over S and E a set of Σ-equations, also called algebraic axioms, explaining the semantics of the operations and their relations to each other. A specification $\langle S,\Sigma,E \rangle$ determines a category $\underline{Alg}_{\Sigma,E}$ of models of this specification, consisting of all S-sorted Σ-algebras which satisfy the equations E. This category contains an initial model $T_{\Sigma,E}$, the so-called abstract software module specified by $\langle S,\Sigma,E \rangle$.

This is in principle a non-constructive approach: there is neither a general procedure which decides whether a certain set of algebraic axioms determines an operation uniquely nor is it possible to give computation rules for the evaluation of operations. Considering implementations of such specifications in real programming languages, however, it is clear that the operations must eventually be described constructively, i.e. by giving an algorithm for their computation. An algorithmic technique for abstract software module specification could thus be helpful.

In writing large specifications, understandability and correctness proofs are facilitated by breaking them up into smaller pieces and developing them step by step from simpler specifications. Enrichments and extensions of specifications [EKP78, GTW76] are thus very important concepts. But here the description of abstract software modules using sets of algebraic axioms shows some deficiencies. The main problem seems to be that with this kind of specification it is not possible to treat certain operations as basic or given, i.e. as operations whose semantics is not influenced by the specification.

Therefore if a specification is extended by some further operations, these are defined by further axioms. However the factorization induced by these new axioms can have unpleasant consequences on previously defined operations or the set of possible data elements. At worst, $T_{\Sigma,E}$ breaks down to a one-element algebra.

We develop a constructive method for abstract definition of recursive operations on arbitrary algebras. This is the definition by structural recursive schemata, a generalization of primitive recursive operations.

Since primitive recursive operations are total, they can serve only for specification of terminating programs. Usually, termination is a very desirable program property which in general is hard to prove. Moreover, specification of operations by structural recursive schemata avoids the enrichment problem mentioned above: since primitive recursive operations of an algebra have effects neither on each other nor on the carrier or the generating basic operations of an algebra, we have a constructive description for a class of extensions of specifications. Considering the fundamental importance of extensions and enrichments of specifications with respect to structured development of specifications, it is particularly significant that at least some of them can be described explicitely and constructively using primitive recursion, in contrast with implicit descriptions, given for example in [EKP78].

2. Decomposition, Structural Recursion

In the following sections, we assume familiarity with the algebraic background of the pertinent literature, e.g. [EKP78, GTW76]. We shall, however, briefly specify some notations.

If $\langle S,\Sigma\rangle$ is a signature, then an S-sorted set A, together with operations F_A for each $F \in \Sigma$, is called a Σ-algebra.

We write A^s for the set of elements of A with a sort $s \in S$ and define $A^w := A^{w_1} \times \ldots \times A^{w_n}$ for $w = w_1 \ldots w_n \in S^*$. We write $\Sigma^{(w,s)}$ for the set of operation symbols in Σ with arity w and coarity s and, similarly,

$$\mathrm{Ops}^{(w,s)}(A) := \{f : A^w \to A^s \mid w \in S^*, s \in S\} .$$

The free Σ-algebra generated by Y is denoted by $T_\Sigma(Y)$; instead of $T_\Sigma(\emptyset)$ we write T_Σ. We think of $T_\Sigma(Y)$ as consisting of variables $x \in Y$ and Σ-Y-terms $Ft_1 \ldots t_n$. If E is a set of Σ-equations, $T_{\Sigma,E}$ denotes the initial algebra in the category of all Σ-algebras satisfying E.

It is well known that in $T_\Sigma(Y)$ we can prove assertions by induction on the structure of terms; furthermore, the freeness property guarantees the unique existence of certain recursively defined operations on $T_\Sigma(Y)$. Both results are based mainly on the unique decomposition of terms in $T_\Sigma(Y)$.

2.1 Definition: Let A be a Σ-algebra generated by Y and let W(A) denote the set of all finite words over A, with empty word ε.

Then a mapping $d : A \to Y \,\dot{\cup}\, (\Sigma \times W(A))$ is called a decomposition of A w.r.t. Y iff for all $a \in A$

$d(a) = (F, b_1 \ldots b_k) \Rightarrow F_A(b_1, \ldots, b_k) = a$ (including the case $k = 0$)

and $d(a) = x \in Y \Rightarrow a = x$.

Define $a \sqsubset_d b$ iff $d(b) = (F, c_1 \ldots c_k)$ and $a = c_i$ for some i . Then d is called a well-founded decomposition iff there is no infinite descending chain $a_o \sqsupset_d a_1 \sqsupset_d a_2 \sqsupset_d \ldots$

Let $<_d$ denote the transitive closure of $\sqsubset_d$.

2.2 Definition: A Y-well-founded Σ-algebra is a Σ-algebra A generated by $Y \subseteq A$ together with a well-founded decomposition d_A w.r.t. Y .

The following two theorems are easy to prove:

2.3 Theorem (Structural Induction): Let A be a Y-well-founded Σ-algebra, P a predicate on A . Then

$$[(\forall a \in A)\ [(\forall\, b <_{d_A} a)\ Pb] \Rightarrow Pa] \Rightarrow (\forall a \in A)\ Pa\ .$$

2.4 Theorem (Recursion Theorem): Let A be a Y-well-founded Σ -algebra, B a Σ-algebra, $f : Y \to B$ a sort-preserving mapping. Then there is a unique mapping $h_f : A \to B$ with the property

$$(\forall a \in A) \quad h_f(a) = \begin{cases} f(a) & \text{for } a \in Y \\ F_B(h_f(c_1), \ldots, h_f(c_k)) & \text{for those} \\ f \in \Sigma,\ c_1, \ldots, c_k \in A \text{ with } & d_A(a) = (F, c_1 \ldots c_k) \end{cases} .$$

If f can be extended to a homomorphism $\hat{f} : A \to B$, then $\hat{f} = h_f$.

Thus, the recursion theorem is a generalization of homomorphic extendability and Y-well-founded algebras have properties very close to those of free algebras. For the rest of this paper we restrict attention to Σ-algebras generated by $\emptyset$. In this case, the unique homomorphism $h_A : T_\Sigma \to A$ is surjective, which implies that each element of A can be referred to by at least one "abstract name" $t \in T_\Sigma$.

2.5 Definition: A Σ-decomposition algebra (Σ-d algebra for short) is a $\emptyset$-well-founded Σ-algebra.

Σ-d algebras have very close relations to the so-called canonical term algebras (CTA's, for short) of [GTW76] .

2.6 Definition: ([GTW76]) A Σ-algebra C is called a canonical Σ-term algebra iff

(i) $C^s \subseteq T_\Sigma^s$ for all $s \in S$

and (ii) $Ft_1 \ldots t_n \in C \Rightarrow (\forall i \in \{1,\ldots,n\})\ t_i \in C$ and

$$F_C(t_1,\ldots,t_n) = Ft_1\ldots t_n \ .$$

2.7 Corollary: Canonical term algebras are Σ-d algebras, where decomposition is given by the unique term decomposition inherited from T_Σ.

2.8 Theorem: ([GTW76], slightly generalized) For every Σ-congruence $\equiv$ on T_Σ there is a CTA C isomorphic to $T_{\Sigma/\equiv}$.

2.9 Theorem: For each Σ-algebra A generated by $\emptyset$ there is a well-founded decomposition d_A of A w.r.t. $\emptyset$.

Proof: It is well known that $A \cong T_{\Sigma/\equiv}$ where $\equiv$ is given by the unique homomorphism $h_A : T_\Sigma \to A$. By 2.8, there is a CTA C with $C \cong T_{\Sigma/\equiv} \cong A$. Let i denote the isomorphism $i : C \to A$ and d_Σ the term decomposition in C inherited from T_Σ. Define

$$d_A(a) := (F, i(t_1)\ldots i(t_k)) \text{ if } a = i(c) \text{ and } d_\Sigma(c) = (F, t_1\ldots t_k)$$

Then d_A is a well-founded decomposition of A w.r.t. $\emptyset$.

The algebras A and C in 2.9 are compatible in the following sense:

2.10 Definition: Let A_o and A_1 be Σ-d algebras, with decompositions d_o, d_1 respectively. If $f : A_o \to A_1$ is a Σ-homomorphism, then A_o and A_1 are called compatible w.r.t. f iff

$$(\forall b \in A_o)\ d_1(f(b)) = (F, a_1\ldots a_k) \Rightarrow d_o(b) = (F, b_1\ldots b_k)$$

and $f(b_i) = a_i$ for all i.

Then we prove:

2.11 Theorem: For each Σ-d algebra A there is a CTA C and an isomorphism $i : C \to A$ such A and C are compatible w.r.t. i.

Proof: By the recursion theorem (2.4), we can define a unique mapping

$$f : A \to T_\Sigma$$

by $\quad f(a) := Ff(b_1)\ldots f(b_k) \quad \text{for} \quad d_A(a) = (F, b_1\ldots b_k)$.

Define $\quad C := \{f(a) \in T_\Sigma \mid a \in A\}$ and, for all $F \in \Sigma^{(w,s)}$, $(t_1,\ldots,t_k) \in C^w$:

$$F_C(t_1,\ldots,t_k) := f(F_A(h_A(t_1),\ldots,h_A(t_k))) \quad .$$

(Remember that h_A is the unique homomorphism $T_\Sigma \to A$) .

Then C is a CTA and $f : A \to C$ an isomorphism. A and C, with term decomposition, are compatible w.r.t. f^{-1} .

The following theorem extends the notion of primitive recursion to arbitrary Σ-d algebras:

2.12 Theorem (Structural Recursion) : Let A be a Σ-decomposition algebra, $v \in S^*$, $s,t \in S$. Let $\Sigma^{(s)} := \bigcup_{w \in S^*} \Sigma^{(w,s)}$.

Then for every $\Sigma^{(s)}$-indexed family g of operations on A such that

$F \in \Sigma^{(w,s)} \Rightarrow g_F \in Ops^{(vwt^k,t)}(A)$, where k is the number of occurrences of s in w ,

there is a unique $h : A^v \times A^s \to A^t$ with the following property: for all $\underline{x} \in A^v$, $y \in A^s$ with

$d_A(y) = (F, z_1\ldots z_r)$, $F \in \Sigma^{(w,s)}$, and for those $i_j \in \{1,\ldots,r\}$ with $w_{i_j} = s$:

$$h(\underline{x},y) = g_F(\underline{x},z_1,\ldots,z_r,h(\underline{x},z_{i_1}),\ldots,h(\underline{x},z_{i_k})) \quad .$$

This result is proved using the recursion theorem (2.4). Note that structural recursion is in principle possible in every algebra generated by $\emptyset$. (2.9).

2.13 : As usual, we define the class of structural recursive operations as the closure of basic operations Σ and projections under composition and structural recursion. This is done by introducing a derived operation alphabet $D(\Sigma)$ which contains (i) the basic operation symbols Σ as constants, (ii) special constant symbols for projections and (iii,iv) operation symbols for substitution and structural recursion of any type. (see [K180] for details). Then a structural recursive schema is an element of the initial algebra $T_{D(\Sigma)}$. By also defining a derived algebra $D(A)$ with carrier $Ops(A)$ for every Σ-d algebra A , we can use initiality to define the semantics of structural recursive schemata, which gives structural recursive operations.

Structural recursive schemata provide a means of specifying structural recursive operations without mentioning decompositions. For the purposes of this paper, however, we shall use a more intuitive notation for structural recursive operations using selector functions:

2.14 Definition: Let A be a Σ-decomposition algebra.

Define $\underline{is} : A \to \Sigma$

by $\underline{is}(a) = F :\Leftrightarrow d_A(a) = (F, b_1 \dots b_k)$.

$\underline{is}$ is called an indicator of A .

For every $F \in \Sigma^{(w,s)}$, define length(w) partial mappings

$$s_i^F : A \dashrightarrow A$$

by
$$s_i^F(a) = \begin{cases} b_i & \text{iff } d_A(a) = (F, b_1 \dots b_k) \\ \text{undefined otherwise} \end{cases}$$

The s_i^F are called F-selectors of A .

Then we can rephrase 2.12 in the following way:

2.15 Theorem: Under the premises of 2.12, there is a unique

$h : A^v \times A^s \to A^t$ with

$$h(\underline{x},y) = g_F(\underline{x}, s_1^F(y), \dots, s_r^F(y), h(\underline{x}, s_{i_1}^F(y)), \dots, h(\underline{x}, s_{i_k}^F(y))) \quad \text{for } F = \underline{is}(y) .$$

In applications, Σ will always be finite. Using the notation of 2.15 and suppressing explicit use of the indicator, we can therefore define h schematically by

$$\begin{aligned} h(\underline{x},y) = \text{CASE } y \text{ OF} \\ F_1 &: g_{F_1}(\underline{x}, s_1^{F_1}(y), \dots, s_{r_1}^{F_1}(y), h(\underline{x}, s_{i_1}^{F_1}(y)), \dots, h(\underline{x}, s_{i_{k_1}}^{F_1}(y))) \\ &\vdots \\ F_n &: g_{F_n}(\underline{x}, s_1^{F_n}(y), \dots, s_{r_n}^{F_n}(y), h(\underline{x}, s_{i_1}^{F_n}(y)), \dots, h(\underline{x}, s_{i_{k_n}}^{F_n}(y))) \\ \text{ESAC} . \end{aligned}$$

Note that this is only a syntactically sugared version of 2.15 .

3. Abstract Software Specifications

3.1 Definition: An abstract software specification is given by $D = \langle S,\Sigma,E;\mathcal{O}\rangle$

where $\langle S,\Sigma\rangle$ is a finite signature,

E is a finite set of Σ-equations and

$\mathcal{O}$ is a finite set of structural recursive schemata.

The elements of Σ are called formal constructors .

An interpretation D is a Σ-decomposition algebra A which satisfies E . An interpretation A induces a set $O \subseteq Ops(a)$ of admissible operations given by the semantics of $\mathcal{O}$.

An interpretation is called a free interpretation iff it is a canonical term algebra isomorphic to $T_{\Sigma,E}$ with decomposition inherited from T_Σ . (Cf. 2.7) .

Of course, equational specifications in the sense of [GTW76, EKP78] are also specifications according to this definition; one could specify the operations in Σ by equations E and then simply set $\mathcal{O} := \Sigma$. In contrast with this procedure, we consider it to be an advantage to have the constructor set Σ as small as possible and to specify as many operations as possible by structural recursion. In particular, E should not be used to define operations, but only for expressing some basic, indispensable properties of formal constructors, such as commutativity, associativity, etc. This gives a simple method of specifying enrichments or extensions [GTW76, EKP78] of specifications, as we shall explain in Section 4 of the present paper. We will, however, first give an example:

3.2 Example: Finite sets of non-negative integers with cardinality:

Let $S = \{nat,set\}$

$\Sigma = \{0^{(\varepsilon,nat)}, suc^{(nat,nat)}, create^{(\varepsilon,set)}, insert^{(set\ nat,set)}\}$

$E = \{insert(insert(s,n),n) = insert(s,n),$

$insert(insert(s,n),m) = insert(insert(s,m),n)\}$

$\mathcal{O} = \{card^{(set,nat)}\}$ where card is defined by

```
card(s) = CASE  s  OF
              create : 0
              insert : suc(card (s_1^insert(s)))
          ESAC
```

Then card really specifies cardinality and $\langle S,\Sigma,E;\mathcal{O}\rangle$ is an enrichment of $\langle S,\Sigma,E;\emptyset\rangle$ in the sense defined in Section 4. This is caused by the well-foundedness of decompositions in all interpretations of this specification because $\underline{is}(s) = insert$ always implies $s = insert(s_1^{insert}(s), s_2^{insert}(s))$ and $s_1^{insert}(s) \neq s$. Compare this to the following equational specification:

Let S, Σ, E as above,

$$\Sigma' := \Sigma \cup \{card^{(set,nat)}\}$$

$$E' := E \cup \{card(create) = 0 ,\; card(insert(s,n)) = suc(card(s))\}$$

Although this seems to be only a syntactic variant of the former specification, it is no correct specification for cardinality since the second equation for card does not take into account the case that s may already be $s = insert(s',n)$ for the same n. Moreover, $\langle S,\Sigma',E'\rangle$ is <u>no</u> enrichment of $\langle S,\Sigma,E\rangle$ (in the sense of [GTW76, EKP78]) since in $T_{\Sigma',E'}$ we have for all $n \geq 1$ $[suc^n(O)] = [suc(O)]$, ([t] denoting the congruence class of $t \in T_\Sigma$). Thus we have a counterexample to a conjecture of [GTW76] which states that adding an operation specified by a "primitive recursive" set of equations to a specification results in an enrichment.

3.3 We note in passing that there is no finite equational specification for card without some "hidden function" [TWW78], e.g. for membership test. This shows that the classes of operations definable by finite sets of equations without hidden functions and of those definable by structural recursion are incomparable since, e.g. the Ackermann function on non-negative integers has a finite equational specification but is not primitive recursive.

One must admit that in example 3.2 the essential point is the well-founded decomposition which every interpretation must posses. In the general case, this decomposition could be considered as some kind of anonymous hidden function. For free interpretations, however, decomposition is a trivial process, since in a canonical Σ-term algebra every term determines its decomposition uniquely. Therefore we will now prove the "Mezei-Wright like" result that in principle it suffices to consider free interpretations (3.5). The abstract software module specified by $\langle S,\Sigma,E;\mathcal{O}\rangle$ is then defined as the Σ-isomorphism class of free interpretations; hence for abstract software modules there is no need to care about decompositions.

On the other hand, if someone implements an abstract software module, we think he should prove that his implementation can be considered as an interpretation of the abstract specification, i.e. contains a Σ-d algebra which satisfies the equations E. To do so, he has to define a decomposition and to show it is well-founded. So decomposition is no hidden function but rather some kind of explanation of the data representation chosen by the implementing programmer. The structural recursive operation definitions can then be implemented automatically, as we shall explain at the end of this paper.

3.4 Lemma: Let A be an interpretation of a specification $\langle S,\Sigma,E;\mathcal{O}\rangle$. Then there is a CTA C isomorphic to $T_{\Sigma,E}$ and an injective mapping $f : A \to C$ such that

(i) $h_A \circ f = id_A$ for the unique $h_A : C \to A$

(ii) C with decomposition inherited from T_Σ and A are compatible w.r.t. f (see 2.10 for definition) .

Proof: For the proof, one first defines $f : A \to T_\Sigma$ as in the proof of 2.11. Then $C' := \{f(a) \mid a \in A\}$ can be extended to a CTA C by an inductive procedure very similar to the existence proof for CTA's in [GTW76] .

3.5 Theorem: Let $D = \langle S,\Sigma,E;\mathcal{O}\rangle$ be a specification, A an interpretation thereof. Then there is a free interpretation C of D and a $D(\Sigma)$-homomorphism $p : D(C) \to D(A)$. (Cf. 2.13).

Remark: Note that this implies commutativity of the diagram

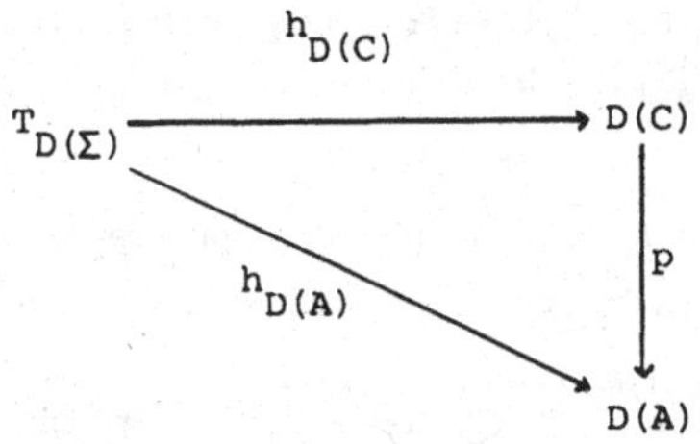

where $h_{D(C)}$, $h_{D(A)}$ are the unique $D(\Sigma)$-homomorphisms. Since these serve for the definition of the semantics $[\![s]\!]^A$, $[\![s]\!]^C$ of a structural recursive schema $s \in T_{D(\Sigma)}$ in A and C , respectively, Theorem 3.5 implies $[\![s]\!]^A = p \circ [\![s]\!]^C$.

Proof: For the proof, define $p : Ops(C) \to Ops(A)$ by

$$\varphi \in Ops^{(w,s)}(C) \quad \mapsto \quad p(\varphi) := h_A \circ \varphi \circ f^w$$

where f is given by 3.4 and f^w is its extension to A^w .
In proving that p is a $D(\Sigma)$-homomorphism, it is essential that A and C are compatible w.r.t. f.

Theorem 3.5 justifies the following definition:

3.6 Definition: The abstract software module specified by $D = \langle S,\Sigma,E;\mathcal{O}\rangle$ is the Σ-isomorphism class of free interpretations of D.

The following definition formalizes correctness of specifications:

3.7 Definition: Let $D = \langle S,\Sigma,E;\mathcal{O}\rangle$ a specification, A an interpretation thereof. The operational algebra A^O of A w.r.t. D is A, regarded as an $\mathcal{O}$-algebra. An $\mathcal{O}$-algebra B is called a functional interpretation of D iff there is a free interpretation C of D such that B is $\mathcal{O}$-isomorphic to the operational algebra C^O.

D is called correct w.r.t. a given $\mathcal{O}$-algebra B iff B is a functional interpretation of C.

4. Morphisms of Specifications

4.1 Definition: A morphism of specifications $f : D_o \to D_1$ for $D_i = \langle S_i,\Sigma_i,E_i;\mathcal{O}_i\rangle$ is a pair $f = (\varphi,\psi)$ with

$$\langle S_o,\Sigma_o,E_o\rangle \xrightarrow{\ \varphi\ } \langle S_1,\Sigma_1,E_1\rangle$$

$$\mathcal{O}_o \xrightarrow{\ \psi\ } \mathcal{O}_1$$

Here, φ is an embedding in Ehrich's [Eh78] category spec of equational specifications; it induces a homomorphism

$\tilde{\varphi} : T_{\Sigma_o,E_o} \to T'_{\Sigma_1,E_1}$ where T'_{Σ_1,E_1} is the reduct of T_{Σ_1,E_1} to sorts and operations coming from $\langle S_o,\Sigma_o\rangle$.

φ is called an extension iff $\tilde{\varphi}$ is an isomorphism; it is called an equivalence iff it is bijecitve and an extension. ψ is simply a mapping between schemes which is semantics-preserving for every pair of free interpretations of D_o and D_1 compatible w.r.t. $\tilde{\varphi}$.

We call f a

structural extension iff φ is an extension,
structural equivalence iff φ is an equivalence,
functional extension iff ψ is injective and a
functional equivalence iff ψ is bijective.

The terminology of [GTW76, EKP78] can be modelled in this context by calling f an extension iff it is both a structural and functional extension and an enrichment iff it is a structural equivalence and a functional extension.

The following theorem is easy to prove:

4.2 Theorem: Let $D_i = \langle S_i, \Sigma_i, E_i; \mathcal{O}_i \rangle$ be specifications, $(i = 0,1)$, $f = (\varphi,\psi) : D_0 \to D_1$ an enrichment. Let A be any interpretation of D_1. Then A is also an interpretation of D_0 and, for all $s \in \mathcal{O}_0$, $[\![s]\!]^A = [\![\psi(s)]\!]^A$.

Hence, our enrichments are always safe, i.e. they preserve the original specification. Safe enrichments are a very useful tool for structured development of large specifications (see [EKP78]) , and our method allows the specification of safe enrichments in an explicit and constructive way, in contrast with the implicit approach of [EKP78]. On the other hand, many possible enrichments are excluded by our method (see 3.3). We are confident, however, that enrichments of specifications turning up in applications can be specified to a large extent using structural recursion.

Another important point is that structural recursive definitions are algorithmic: if h is defined by structural recursion, then we can use its definition as a computation rule in all possible interpretations. Computations will always terminate and give a unique result, though this depends on a decomposition which may in general be a non-effective mapping. In abstract data types, however, which are free interpretations and hence canonical term algebras, decomposition is trivial and in practical cases of implementations the implementing programmer has to program the decomposition as well. Automatic implementation of structural recursive operations is then a straightforward process.

4.3 Example: As an example, we describe an implementation of example 3.2 in PASCAL. Hence, the essential task is the implementation of a Σ-decomposition algebra which satisfies the equations E for Σ,E as in 3.2 . The only creative part, however, is the implementation of the "insert" operation; the rest can be derived automatically from the abstract specification.
We confine ourselves to the implementation of the sort "set" and its constructors; for "nat" with O and suc we can use a subrange type of the standard PASCAL type integer with O and +1.

We begin with

```
type   nat =  O..maxint;
       setind = (iscreate, isinsert);
       set = ↑ setrep;
       setrep = record case ind: setind of
                               iscreate: ;
                               isinsert: (s1:set; s2:nat)
                           end
```

So this implementation will be very close to the abstract software module, the elements of sort "set" being represented as some kind of trees with an operation symbol at the root and, in case of an insert-tree, two subtrees of sort "set" and "nat", respectively. These can be referred to by selectors s1 and s2. Implementation of the constructor create is no problem:

```
function  create:set;
var aux:set;
begin
    new(aux);
    aux ↑.ind := iscreate;
    create := aux
end
```

When implementing the constructor insert, we must make sure that the equations E are satisfied and that there is a well-founded decomposition. To this purpose we use the ordering relation on integers by implementing insert as a recursive procedure which always returns a tree whose s2-branches are in ascending order (viewed from the root). Thus the second axiom is trivially satisfied and it is easy to make the first axiom hold as well.

```
function  insert(s:set; n:nat):set;
var aux:set;
begin
    new (aux);
    aux ↑.ind := isinsert;
    if  s↑.ind = iscreate then begin
                               aux↑.s1 := s;
                               aux↑.s2 := n;
                               insert := aux
                               end
        else if n < s↑.s2 then begin
                               aux↑.s1 := s;
                               aux↑.s2 := n;
                               insert := aux
                               end
        else if n = s↑.s2 then insert = s          (* no change *)
        else if n > s↑.s2 then begin
                               aux↑.s1 := insert(s↑.s1,n);
                               aux↑.s2 := s↑.s2;
                               insert := aux
                               end
end
```

Now it is a straightforward mechanical process to implement the structural recursive definition for card and, of course, all other structural recursive definitions as well:

```
function  card(s:set):nat;
begin
    case  s↑.ind of
       iscreate : card := 0;
       isinsert : card := card(s↑.s1) +1
    end
end
```

For the sake of brevity, we could not comment in this paper on error handling and parameterized specifications; see [Kl 80] for these topics.

References

[Eh78] H.D. Ehrich
Extensions and Implementations of Abstract Data Type Specifications
VIIth MFCS, 1978, Pp. 155-164.

[EKP78] H. Ehrig, H.-J. Kreowski, P. Padawitz
Stepwise Specification and Implementation of Abstract Data Types
Vth ICALP, Udine, 1978 .

[GTW76] J.A. Goguen, J.W. Thatcher, E.G. Wagner
An Initial Algebra Approach to the Specification, Correctness and Implementation of Abstract Data Types
IBM Research Report, RC 6487, 1976 .

[Kl80] H. Klaeren
Eine Klasse von Algebren mit struktureller Rekursion und ihre Anwendung bei der abstrakten Software-Spezifikation
Dissertation, RWTH Aachen, 1980 .

[TWW78] J.W. Thatcher, E.G. Wagner, J.B. Wright
Data Type Specification: Parameterization and the Power of Specification Techniques
10th STOC, 1978 .

INDUCING PATTERNS OF BEHAVIOUR IN DISTRIBUTED SYSTEM PARTS

Norbert Kraft

Horst Wedde

Gesellschaft für Mathematik und Datenverarbeitung mbH Bonn
Postfach 1240

D - 5205 St. Augustin 1
W. Germany

Abstract

For an independent representation of the constraints in distributed system parts the formalism of Loosely Coupled Systems (LCSs) is recalled. The events in these structures are formally derived from symmetrical local restrictions (coupling relations). So the influence on processes in a system part which comes from the interaction with neighbourhood parts can be adequately described by a symmetrical transitional structure (slack of behaviour). A large part of synchronisation constraints can be modelled this way. In order also to represent other types of influence local excitement relations are introduced by means of which we can especially determine directions for processes in the parts and induce forces for processes to leave a given local state. The extended formal system structures are called Interaction Systems (IS). In order to show how the set of standart construction tools can adequately be extended we define an arbitration problem and model a solution by stepwise realizing the wanted interaction.

O. Introduction

The theory of Loosely Coupled Systems (LCSs) has been developed in several aspects and has been presented at several occasions during the last years ([4], [5], [6], [7]). It is a formalism which is solely based on the specification of interaction between distributed system parts. As the event concept in LCSs is derived from the interaction structure (constraints) only we describe the interaction between system parts to be a formally independent aspect of behaviour. The (internal) behavioral structure of the system parts was regarded to be induced by interaction with environmental parts. A formal concept of induced structures was set up in [5] by means of which one can translate interaction structures into corresponding induced internal structures and vice versa. Thus LCSs turned out to be a new modelling and analyzing formalism for solving organizational problems in distributed sytems.

The language of LCSs is based on mutual exclusion relations (coupling relations) as interaction primitives. A large number of synchronization mechanisms can be adequately represented this way ([4], [5]). The internal behaviour structure which may be induced by coupling relations is symmetrical, mainly the slack which is left to the parts under the specified interaction constraints. In order also to induce asymmetrical structures we introduce additional (asymmetrical) interaction primitives in section 1., so-called local excitement relations. They model local influences from one part to another one in such a way that there is a certain equilibrium between the rights of the influencing part and its responsibilities for the influenced part. Although such a principle is often enough not observed - an interrupt e.g. which has not yet been processed can be cancelled by an overlying interrupt: So the influencing state may disappear although the influenced action has not occurred - we found it very helpful for establishing a clean formal concept of induced behavioral structures, including directions of flow and local forces. (Of course there are also good examples for "balanced" interaction relations as mentioned above.)

In order to demonstrate the representational power of our extended tools we formulate a rather complex arbitration problem in DIJKSTRA's style ([1], [2]) and solve it by stepwise realizing the wanted interaction.

1. Interaction Systems

We shall briefly recall some basic notations and properties of LCSs. For more details see [5] or [7].
In order to formalize the interdependence between the components of a real system we do not assume anything about the system parts except that they are in exactly one state or section of activity at any time. We call these states phases. Let B be the (finite) set of parts, P the set of all pases. Our assumption then has the following form:

1.1 $\forall_{b \in B}\ b \subseteq P\ ;\quad \bigcup_{b \in B} b = P\ ;\quad \forall_{b_1, b_2 \in B}\ b_1 \neq b_2 \Longrightarrow b_1 \cap b_2 = \emptyset$

The interdependence between parts b_1 and b_2 is reduced to the mutual exclusion of some of their states (phases), the corresponding relation is denoted by $K\langle b_1 b_2\rangle$ and called coupling relation between b_1 and b_2 . The relation K which contains all pairs of mutual exclusive phases is the union of the $K\langle b_1 b_2\rangle$ and of all relations $K\langle bb\rangle;\ b\in B$ where $(p_1,p_2) \in K\langle bb\rangle$ iff $p_1,p_2 \in b$ and $p_1 \neq p_2$. K is symmetrical. Global system situations are called cases. A case is a subset of phases such that:

1.2 a) $\forall_{b \in B}\ |c \cap b| = 1$; b) $\forall_{p_1, p_2 \in c}\ (p_1,p_2) \notin K$.

The set of all cases is denoted by C.

Elementary events in an LCS are phase transitions in a single part which lead from one case to another one. They are described by a pair $(c_1,c_2);\ c_1,c_2 \in C$ such that $|c_1-c_2| = |c_2-c_1| = 1$. The main axiom is:

1.3 Every event in an LCS is a sequence of elementary ones.

An LCS is then denoted by a quadruple (P,B,C,K). A simple example is found in fig.1 .

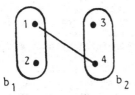

Fig.1

The two parts have two phases each. The coupling relation is represented by the undirected edge between 1 and 4 . The event structure is found in the case graph which has the cases as nodes and the elementary events as (undirected!) edges. We mention briefly that two phase transitions $p_1 \rightarrow q_1$ and $p_2 \rightarrow q_2$ are called concurrent in an initial case c iff each of them may occur in c and $(q_1,q_2) \notin K$. By that, concurrency in LCSs is a basic and local property. It means that two events may occur in an arbitrary order and even simultaneously (compare [5]).

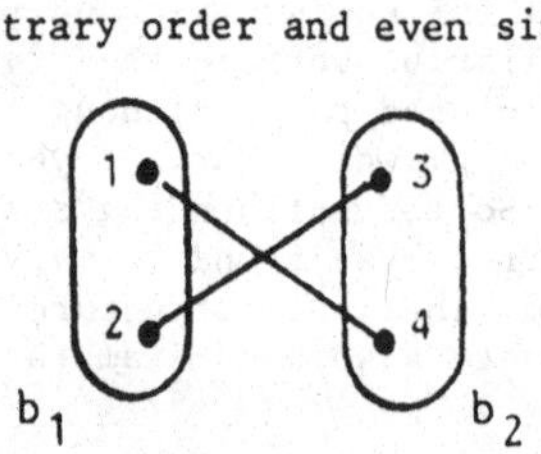

Fig.2

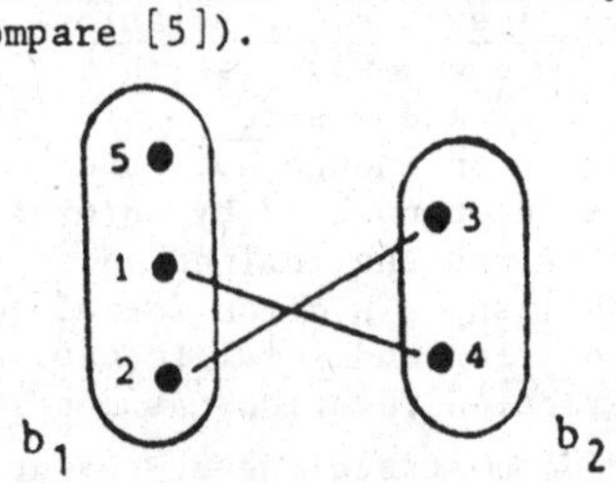

Fig.3

A slack phase with respect to subsystem S is a phase which is not coupled to any phase in a part belonging to S. Starting with the case {1,3} in fig.2 we can see that no event may occur in that situation because there is no elementary event activated. By adding the slack phase 5 (with respect to the subsystem which contains only b_2) as shown in fig.3 we can now pass along the following sequence:
{1,3}, {5,3}, {5,4}, {2,4}.
Thus the slack of b_1 with respect to b_2 was enlarged.
There are, of course, many restrictions involving n parts; $n > 2$ which cannot be expressed by binary restrictions between these parts. If we have e.g. parts b_1, b_2, b_3 with phases p_1, p_2, p_3 as shown in fig.4 we could formulate the following restriction (of a class which is called elementary [5]):

$$1.4 \quad \forall_{c \in C} \; (p_1 \in c \wedge p_2 \in c \implies p_3 \notin c) .$$

This means that p_1, p_2, p_3 cannot belong to a common case. After addition of the part cp as shown in fig.4 exactly the specified restriction holds. For our purpose here

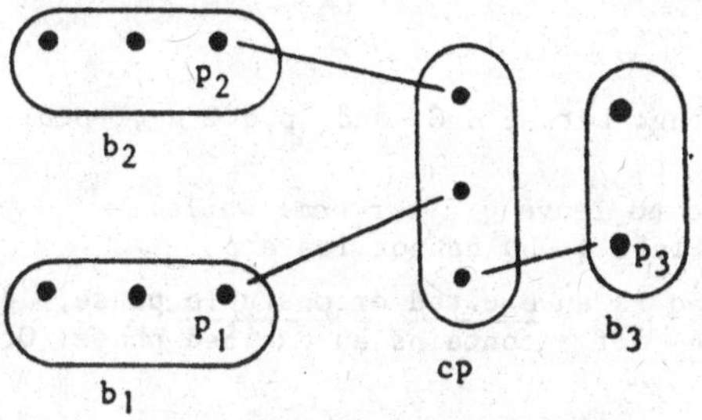

Fig.4

it is important to recall that in the LCS in fig.4 every event may occur which was possible in the previous system and which does not infringe on the restriction which is specified in 1.4 . For more details see e.g. [5] and [7].
In [5] a formal concept had been developed in which the influence on a part b from its environment can be modelled and analyzed. If we want to understand the influence on b_1 in fig.5 which comes from the coupling to b_2 we learn from the case graph of this LCS that e.g. in phase 1 one cannot directly go to 3 (etc. for the phases 2,3,4). Furthermore one can step around in b_1 as indicated by the undirected edges in fig.6 if we assume that certain intermediate steps in b_2 can occasionally be done between two transitions in b_1. As there is no restriction specified about that this is no problem.

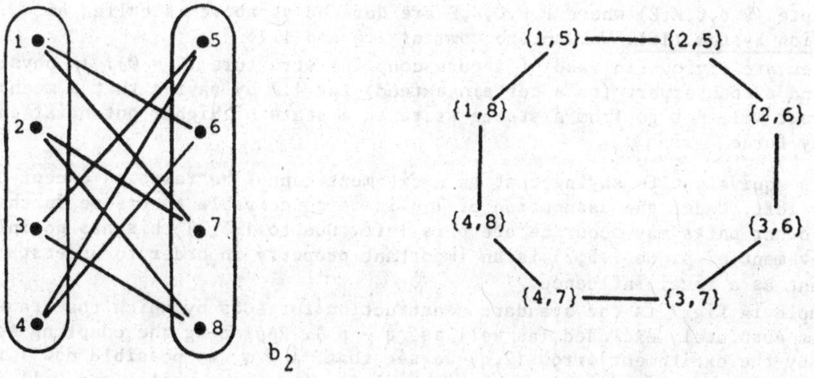

Fig.5

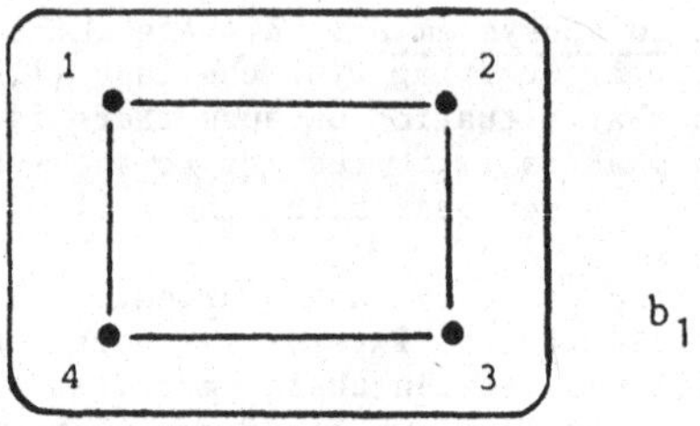

Fig.6

The induced transitional structure in fig.6 is symmetrical. We shall refine these structure by introducing new specification elements.

1.5 For $b_i, b_j \in B$ we regard a relation $E\langle b_i b_j\rangle \subseteq b_i \times b_j$ which we call excitement relation from b_i to b_j.

Let $E := \bigcup_{\substack{b_i, b_j \in B \\ b_i \neq b_j}} E\langle b_i b_j\rangle$.

E has the following meaning: Let $c \in C$ and $p,q \in c$; $p \in b_1$, $q \in b_2$.
If $(p,q) \in E$ then:

1) b_1 is in (local) force to leave q after some while.
2) As long as b_1 has not left q b_2 cannot leave p.

With the notation above q is an excited or unstable phase, p an exciting phase. A case c is called unstable iff c contains an excited phase. Otherwise c is called stable.

As a typical example for such an exciting influence one may think of a job which sends a request for resource allocation. Under normal circumstances the resources will be allocated after some while but as long as this is not done the job has to wait.

In order to get a concept for the global effect of the local excitement relations we formulate two behavioral rules which can be seen as local stability axioms:

1.6 If a part b is forced from outside to leave a given phase p he will do so after some while as long as some other phase in b is free.

1.7 A part b in a phase p will not go to an excited phase by chance, i.e. such a transition will occur either by force or because we explicitly reserve b the right to follow his own interest. Moreover, as long as b can go to a free and stable phase in case it has to leave p b will do so.

A quintuple (P,B,C,K,E) where P,B,C,K,E are defined as above is called an Interaction System (IS). We want to comment 1.6 and 1.7:
Both rules are obvious in case of a pure coupling structure ($E = \emptyset$). In physics we could find a counterpart (to a certain extend) for 1.7 by saying that a mechanical system part will not go from a stable state to a state of higher potential energy except by force.

1.5,2) is equivalent to saying that an excitement cannot be released except the excited phase is left. Under the assumption of 1.6 it is conceivable that some further events in some other parts may occur before p is left. Due to 1.5,2) this has no influence on the excitement of p. So 1.5,2) is an important property in order to understand the excitement as a local influence.
The example in fig.7 is the standart construction for LCSs by which the transition $p \rightarrow q$ is absolutely excluded (as well as $q \rightarrow p$). Replacing the coupling edge between q and 2 by the excitement arrow (2,q) we see that $p \rightarrow q$ is possible now (if we start from the stable case {p,2}) but q has to be left after some while (and will do so due to 1.6). Finally, by reversing the arrow we come to fig.9 in which $p \rightarrow q$ may occur

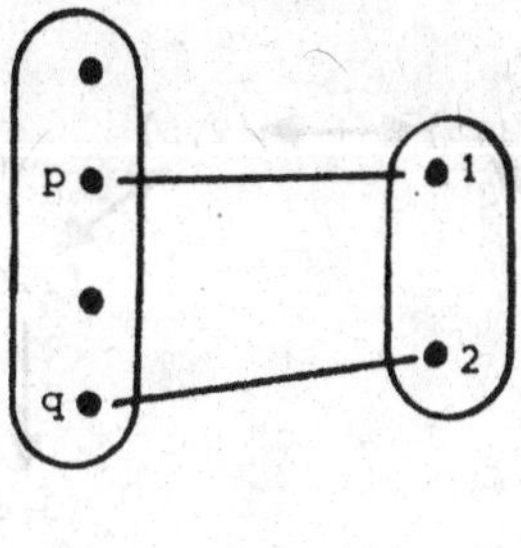

Fig.7

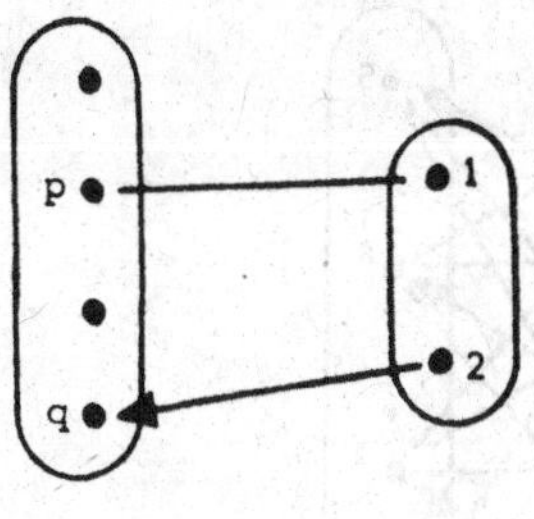

Fig.8

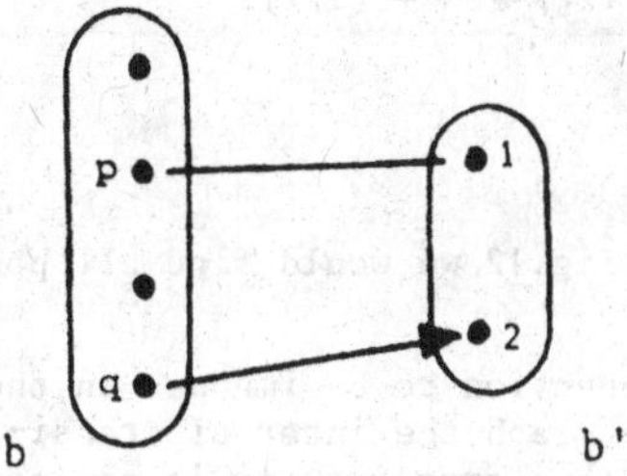

Fig.9

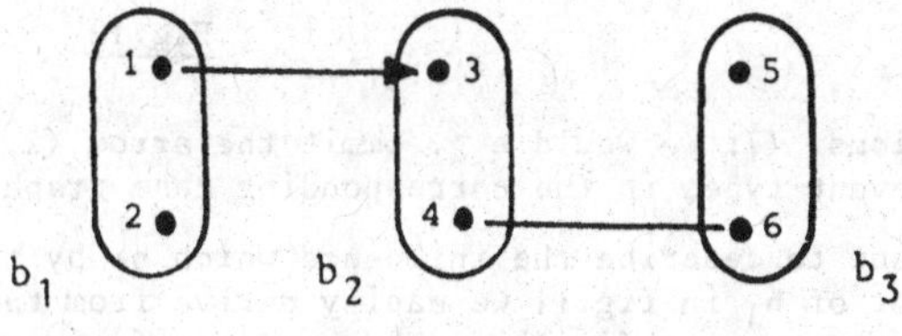

Fig.10

(starting form {p,2}). Afterwards q is exciting 2, and after some while b' will go to 1 . q can be left now but q → p cannot occur. So b can go from p to q - this is not enforced - but it cannot go back directly. - If we start in the case {1,3,6} in fig.10 then b_2 is in force to go to 4 . As 4 is coupled to 6 this cannot happen unless b_3 goes first to 5 . This will be done corresponding to 1.6 . So although there is no arrow between b_2 and b_3 we have an induced force on b_3.

Finally, we shall regard two extensions of the LCS in fig.5 which will be of special interest in section 2. . They are to be found in fig.11 and fig.12, respectively, together with their corresponding (extended) case graphs. If an arrow is crossed in the case graph by a little bar this means that by the corresponding phase transition an excited phase is left, i.e. an excitement is released. If there is a normal arrow from one case to another one then the corresponding phase transition is not enforced but the system cannot go back in this manner. So we have several different types of

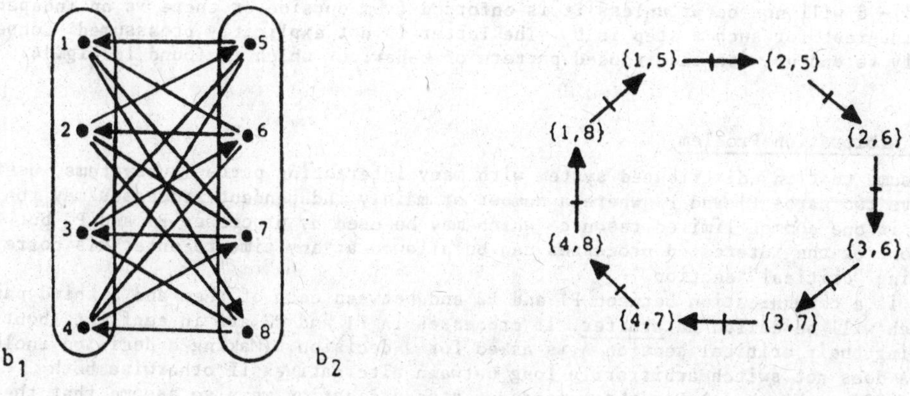

Fig.11

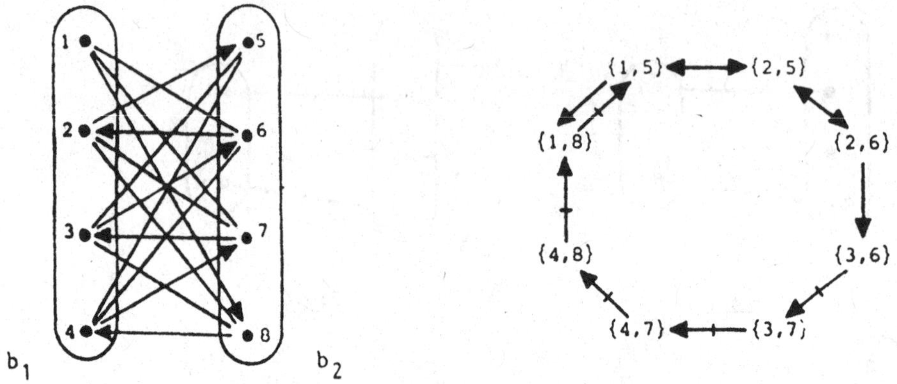

Fig.12

transitions. (If we would e.g. ommit the arrow (2,5) in fig.12 we would find all possible event types in the corresponding case graph.)

If we want to describe the influence which b_2 by its connection to b_1 imposes on the behaviour of b_1 in fig.11 we easily derive from the case graph the internal transitional structure in fig.13 . (The meaning of an arrow with a crossing bar is analogous to that of the corresponding object in the case graph structure in fig.11). Looking

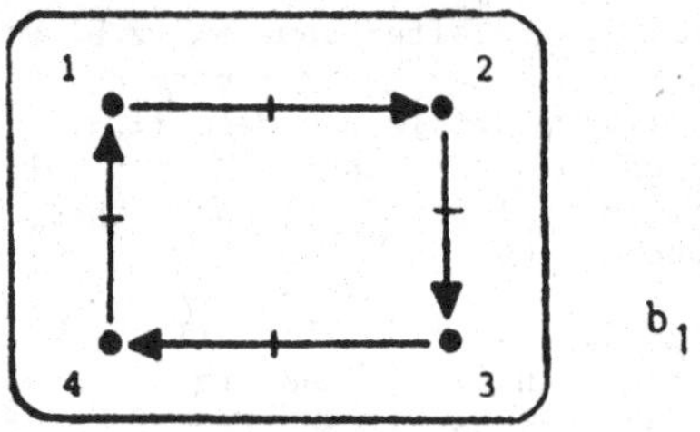

Fig.13

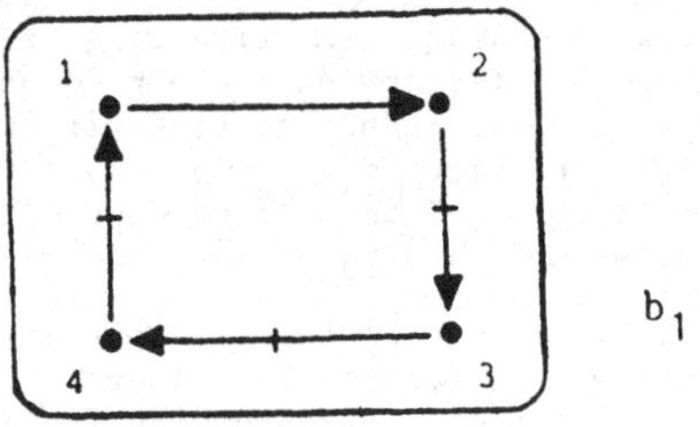

Fig.14

at the case graph in fig.12 we see that b_1 is not forced to execute $1 \rightarrow 2$. $2 \rightarrow 1$ cannot occur directly after $1 \rightarrow 2$ any more. As a consequence of 1.7 we may assume that $5 \rightarrow 8$ will not occur unless it is enforced from outside or there is an independent interest for such a step in b_2. The latter is not explicitly preassumed. Consequently we end up with the induced pattern of behaviour which is found in fig.14.

2. An Arbitration Problem

We assume that in a distributed system with many interacting parts (subsystems, users) we have two parts P1 and P2 where a number of mainly independent processes may run. There is one common limited resource which may be used by processes P1 and P2 but only one of the interested processes can be allowed at any time to enter his corresponding "critical" section.

There is a communication between P1 and P2 and between each of them and a third part A which will be called an arbiter. If processes in P1 and P2 are in conflict about entering their critical section A is asked for a decision. (Making a decision includes that A does not switch arbitrarily long between alternatives if otherwise both P1 and P2 are blocked.) For the purpose of standardization we also assume that the arbiter after a certain time which he is given to make his decision will have chosen an alternative (whether he was really active to reach at one of the alternative positions or not). Besides that, A may do some other work. We may e.g. think of a programmer who uses operating system facilities in an interactive mode.

The cooperation between P1, P2 and A should satisfy the following requirements:

1) There is no assumption on the geographical or timely distance between the parts or on the relative speeds of processes. Also it should be possible that a "fast" process in one of the parts P1 or P2 can pass a "slow" process in the other one if both are on the way to use the common resource.

2) If a process in P1 and a process in P2 have both indicated their interest to enter their critical sections and if both are still outside none of them can enter whithout a decision by A.

3) The decision by A has to be made after a finite time. If A has given permit to one of the processes he cannot change the decision unless the chosen process has entered his critical section. This will be done after some while.

4) As long as at most one process has indicated his interest to enter the critical section A is left free.

5) As long as a process is not involved in the procedure to enter his critical section he is left free.

At first glance it is difficult to see how these requirements influence the structure of a possible solution. But we shall model a suitable Interaction System in several steps. The first is found in fig.15 . P1, P2, and A are represented by one part each. The critical sections for the processes in P1, P2 are given by phase 1 and phase 5, respectively. They exclude each other. We call them <u>critical phases</u>. In the phases

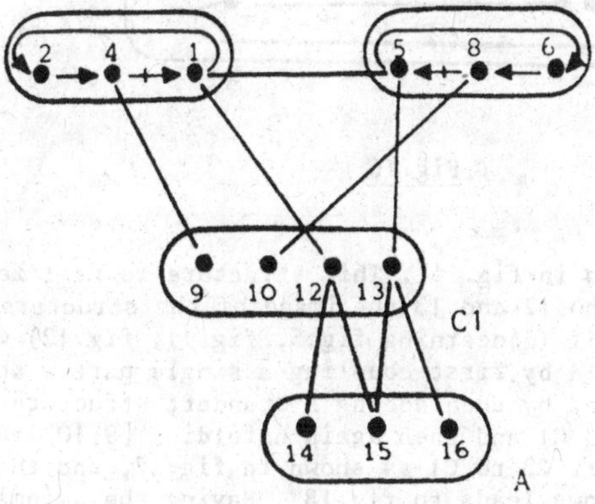

Fig.15

4 and 8 the interested processes are registrated for access to 1 and 5, respectively. They are called <u>registration phases</u>. In 2 and 6 the processes do some other job. They are called <u>remainder phases</u>. The internal transitional structure in P1, P2 is thought to be induced by a suitable interaction with environmental parts. The corresponding construction will be given later. (As there is e.g. no force for P1 to go from 2 to 4 we may assume that a lot of processes may run in P1 which have no interest to enter 1 or 5.) - In phase 14 (16) A keeps the alternative to let P2 (P1) go to the critical phase 5 (1). Phase 15 represents the possible remainder activities of A. We do not provide an internal transitional structure in A because we do not even want to push A into a neutral position (the remainder section).

The first rough idea here is to push C1 out of 9 and 10 when both P1 and P2 are on the way to enter their registration phases. A could no longer be in 15 if he was there before: Otherwise he would block everything. If A is in 14 or 16 C1 will be in 13 or 12, respectively, when P1 and P2 are both registrated. Consequently exactly one of the conflicting processes will have permit to go. 12 and 13 therefore are called permit phases. We may regard C1 as an information transmission facility for the communication between the arbiter and P1, P2 .

The installation of C1 is a simple construction which meets the requirements 1) and 5) only. This "solution" is quite unsatisfactory: Among other things A has no time to make a decision if P1 and P2 are in the registration phases. In order to give A the chance for a real decision we introduce a phase 11 in C1 which is to be a slack phase with respect to A (see 1.) . We want 11 to be passed whenever C1 goes from 8 or 10 to 12 or 13 . Once the arbiter is asked for a decision (in 11) The request should not be removed any more. So we exclude the possibility to go back fromm 11 to 9 or 10.

C1 should step forward from 11 to 12 or 13 in order to occasionally enforce the arbiter to make a decision. As 12 and 13 are understood as permit phases there should be no way back to 11. Altogether we expect, after addition of 11, that C1 has the internal

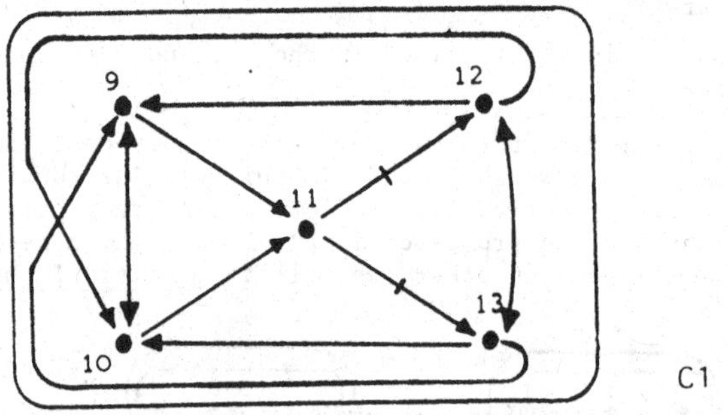

Fig.16

transitional structure as shown in fig.16 . This structure is realized as follows: If we identify 9 and 10 and also 12 and 13 the image of the structure in fig.16 is a cycle. From the discussion in 1. (concerning fig.5, fig.11, fig.12) we recall that such a structure can be realized by first coupling a single part with 3 phases to the given part in a standart way and by then adding a standart structure of excitement arrows. Applying this method to C1 and then again unfolding {9,10} and {12,13} we find that we have coupled a part C2 to C1 as shown in fig.17, and the corresponding addition of the excitement arrows leads to fig.18 . Having the axioms of local stability - 1.6 and 1.7 - in mind it is easy to verify that we in fact induce the desired pattern of behaviour in C2 by our twofold operation.

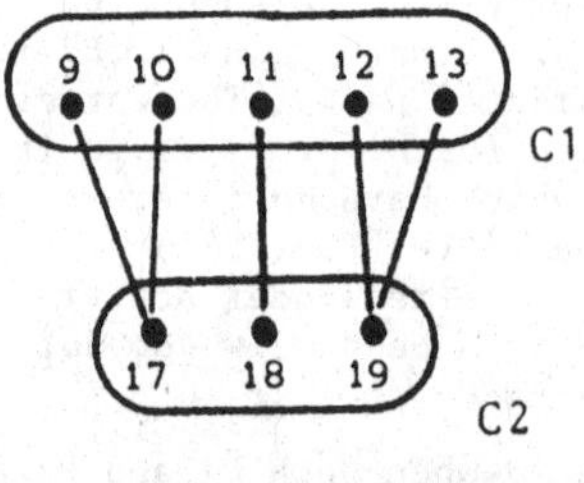

Fig.17

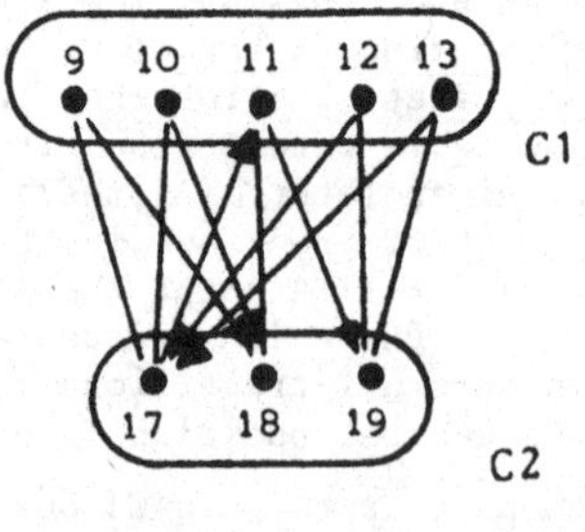

Fig.18

It should be avoided that the conflict between P1 and P2 when both are registrated for access to their critical phases is decided by chance although C1 is in 11 and the arbiter is so in charge for a decision: This could lead to a deadlock. Thus 11 is coupled to 1 and 5 .

The arbiter should be free as long as at least one of the parts P1, P2 is in the remainder phase (requirement 4)). So we couple 11 to 2 and 6 .

The result of these operations are found in fig.19 . The excitement arrows (1,14) and

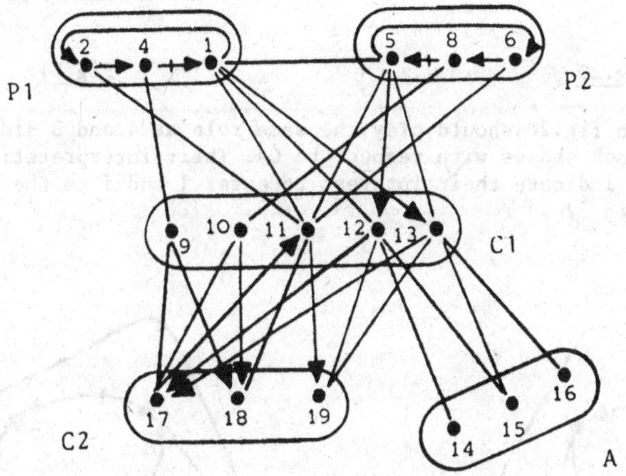

Fig.19

(5,12) which are additionally found there were introduced because we want to take care that C1 goes back to 9 (10) after P1 (P2) had been allowed to go to the critical phase. (In this way also P2 (P1) now would have a chance to go to 5 (1)). The responsibility for this transition in C1 is left to P1 (P2), i.e. P1 (P2) cannot leave 1 (5) unless C1 has left 13 (12).

From fig.19 it can be immedately seen that as long as only one process gets interested to enter the critical section - say P1 is to move from 2 to 4, P2 is in 6 - and if C1 initially is in 9 then C1 cannot come to 11, and so the arbiter is free because 9 and 10 are not coupled to A. As C1 can exploit the slack to go to 10 no deadlock will occur if P1 moves from 2 to 4 even if A is in 15.

As long as C1 is in 12 or 13 - i.e. after A has given permit to P2 or P1,respectively - A cannot do anything.

We summarize that the "solution" in fig.19 already satisfies the requirements 1),2),3),4). 5) is only partially satisfied: Let us assume that P2 is in 8 and that P1 is in 2 . If initially C1 was in 9 and P1 wants to go to 4 this cannot occur because C1 would first have to go to 11 but this cannot happen as P1 is in 2 . So, in contradiction to requirement 5), P1 could not get involved in the procedure to enter 1 .

In order to give P1 (and P2 correspondingly) some slack for a situation like this we split the registration phases 4 and 8 into two phases denoted by 3,4 and 7,8 , respectively. We extend the internal transitional structure as indicated in fig.20 for P1. This structure is realized by connecting P1 (and P2 correspondingly) with a single part as shown in fig.21 . (Compare the discussion in 1. and see fig.14 .)

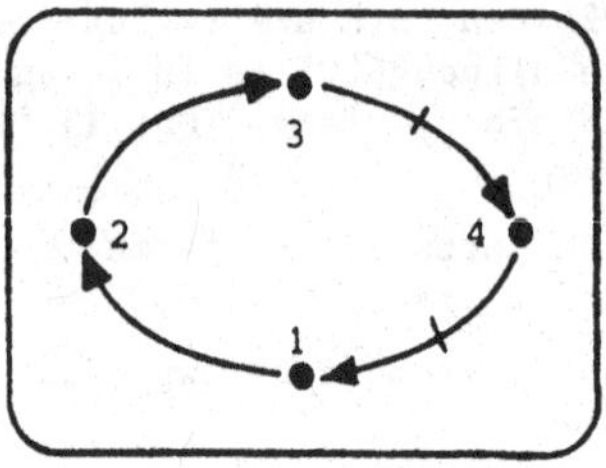

Fig.20

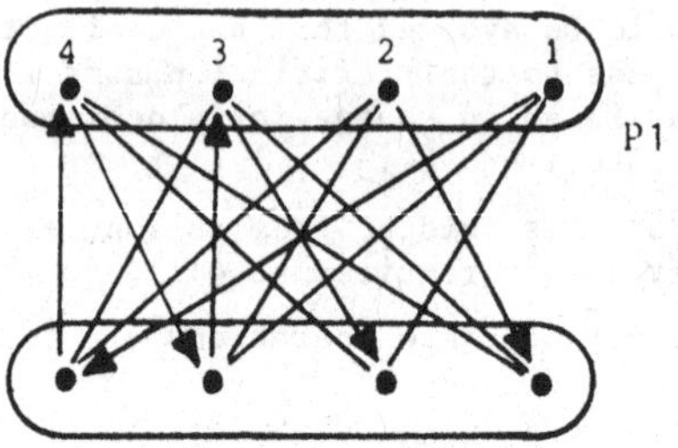

Fig.21

The phases 4 and 8 in fig.20 should play the same role as 4 and 8 did in fig.19 while 3 and 7 are to be slack phases with respect to C1. Their interpretation is that at this point P1 and P2 indicate their interest to enter 1 and 5 to the arbiter. The new construction is in fig.22 .

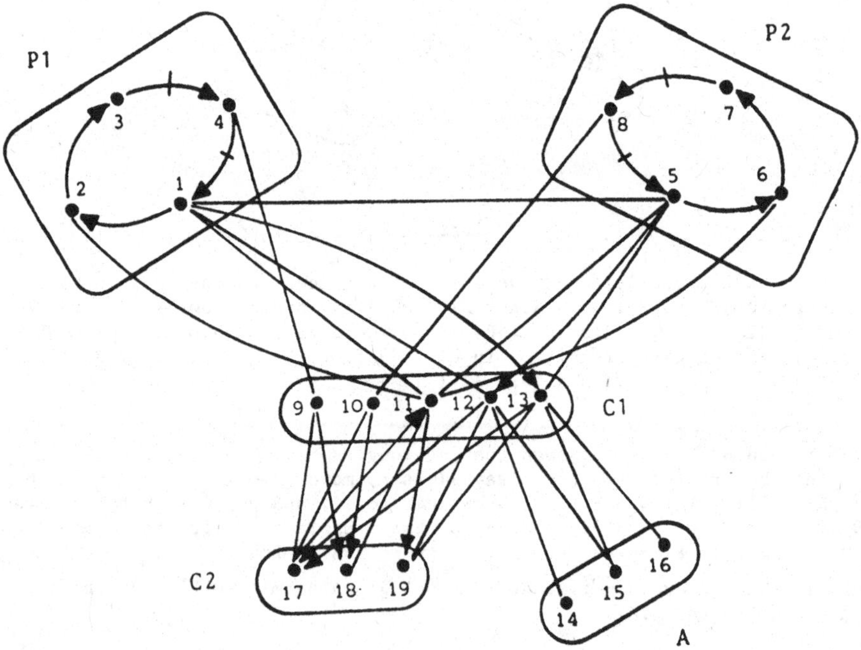

Fig.22

Let P1 be in 3, let P2 be in 7 and C1 in 10 . If P1 is slow relative to P2 the following could happen: 10 → 9, 7 → 8, 8 → 5 . So P2 could enter his critical phase without involving A although both P1 and P2 had indicated their interest to A. This was too "liberal" with respect to P1, P2 . In order to overcome this problem we introduce weak restrictions which are specified as follows:

(*) If P1 (P2) is in 3 (7) and P2 (P1) is in 8 (4) then C1 is in force to leave 9 (10) after some while (and consequently to go to 11), and 8 (4) cannot be left unless either 9 (10) or 3 (7) have been left.

Each of the two restrictions is realized by adding one part - D1 (D2) - to the Interaction System in fig.22 in a way which is shown in fig.23. It should be mentioned

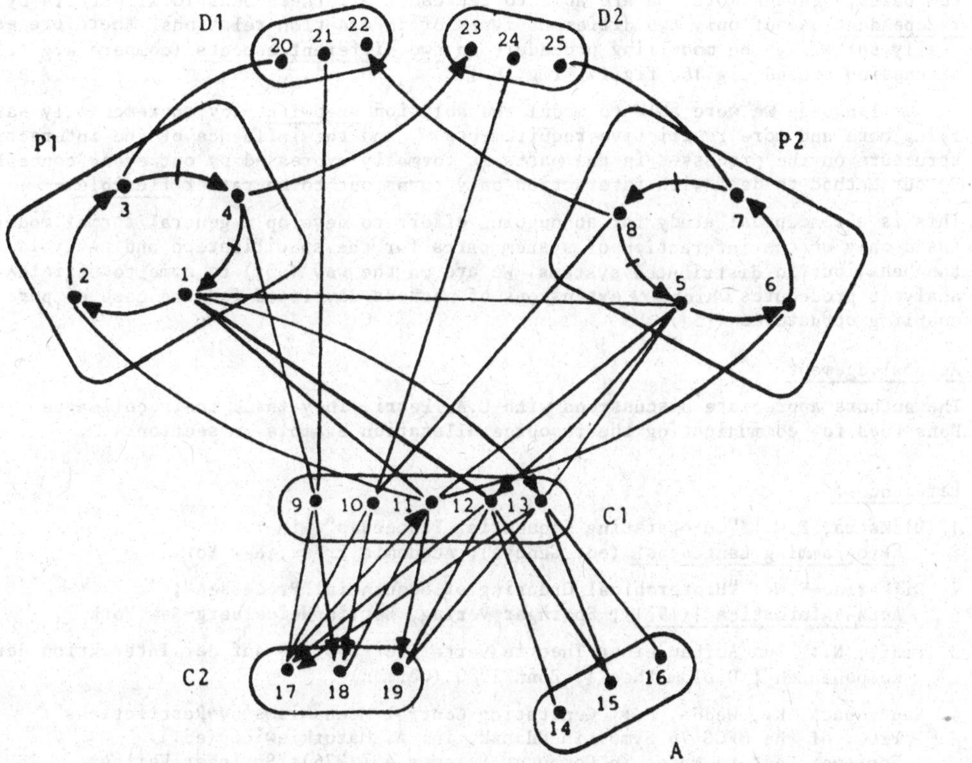

Fig.23

here for short that this construction technique is a slight extension of the installation of elementary restrictions in Loosely Coupled Systems (see the discussion around 1.4 and fig.4). Like in this special case a main property here is that by addition of D1 (D2) to the IS in fig.22 the behaviour of the IS in fig.22 is restricted in the way (and only so far) which is specified in (*).

The IS in fig.23 is a solution of our problem. This comes out without too much difficulty from the discussion in this section if one takes into account that our language of ISs is completely based on local restrictional elements, namely the coupling and excitement relations. So the effect of establishing a restriction by connecting a new part to a given system does not influence the effect of previously established restrictions.

3. Conclusion

In the solution in fig.23 it is left to the interest of the processes and to their direct communication to leave the critical phase 1 or 5, respectively, once one of them has entered it. In a stricter organizational context one could say that each process has to leave the critical phase after some while. This would be easy to arrange here by adding a single arrow each between P1, P2 and the parts which induce their internal structures (fig.21).-

By the requirements which were imposed on the problem solution some process steps were specified to occur by force after some while (requirement 3). Also some directions were excluded. The occurence of some other steps was left to the interest of the involved processes (requirements 4),5)). During the construction procedure it turned out that the language of Interaction Systems is modelled in terms of local structures and based on the assumption of a (partially) independent interest (behaviour) of system parts.- Furthermore, we are able to represent all these behavioral details by independent use of only two different types of interaction relations, therefore especially splitting the modelling procedure in two different aspects (compare e.g. the discussion around fig.16, fig.17, fig.18).

In our language we were able to model the solution stepwise - by incrementally satisfying more and more restrictive requirements -, and the influence of the interaction structure on the processes in the parts is formally expressed by our event concept. So our method to deal with interaction only turns out to be rather flexible.-

This is a conceptual study for an ongoing effort to develop a general formal model based only on the interaction of system parts for the specification and analysis of the behaviour in distributed systems. We are on the way ([3]) to come to efficient analysis procedures which are extensions of methods developed for the case of pure coupling structures ([5]).

Acknowledgement

The authors appreciate discussions with C.A. Petri. They thank their colleague Hans Fuss for communicating the resource allocation example in section 1. .

References:

1. Dijkstra, E.W.: "Co-operating Sequential Processes", in : "Programming Languages" (ed. Genuys); Academic Press, New York

2. Dijkstra, E.W.: "Hierarchical Ordering of Sequential Processes"; Acta Informatica 1(1971); Springer Verlag, Berlin-Heidelberg-New York

3. Kraft, N.: "Zum Aufbau einer Theorie verteilter Systeme auf der Interaktion der Komponenten"; Diplom thesis, Bonn 1980 (German)

4. Lautenbach, K., Wedde, H.: "Generating Control Mechanisms by Restrictions"; Proc. of the MFCS'76 Symp. in Gdansk, in: A. Mazurkiewicz (ed.): Springer Lecture Notes in Computer Science 45(1976); Springer Verlag, Berlin-Heidelberg-New York

5. Maggiolo-Schettini, A., Wedde, H., Winkowski, J.: "Modelling a Solution for a Control Problem in Distributed Systems by Restrictions; Symp. "Semantics of Concurrent Computation" in Evian/France, in: G. Kahn (ed.): Springer Lecture Notes in Computer Science 70(1979); Springer Verlag, Berlin-Heidelberg-New York

6. Wedde, H.: "Lose Kopplung von Systemkomponenten"; Berichte der GMD No. 96, Bonn 1975 (German)

7. Wedde, H., Winkowski, J.: "Determining Processes by Violations"; MFCS'77 Symp. in Tatranska Lomnica, in: Springer Lecture Notes in Computer Science 53(1977); Springer Verlag, Berlin-Heidelberg-New York

VAN WIJNGAARDEN GRAMMARS AS A SPECIAL INFORMATION PROCESSING MODEL

Ingbert Kupka
Fachbereich Informatik
Universität Hamburg

Abstract: Van Wijngaarden grammars can be used for directly constructing problem solutions according to A. van Wijngaarden's nonprocedural problem solving method. The basis for this is the computational power of the grammars as well as their suitability for expressing abstractions and general transformations. A formal analysis of the latter property leads to an approach towards a general information processing model. As an application of this model a state-oriented method of program development is presented.

0. Introduction

The programming concepts of today arose from practical experiences and from the theoretical analysis of algorithms and computability. Information processing is usually considered as a vague idea behind data processing because of the lack of a suitable notion of information in this area. On the other side many problems concerning program development and verification cannot be treated sufficiently with computability theory or formal semantics as fundamentals. Since such problems really refer to handling informations in contrast to handling data, an information-oriented theoretical approach seems to be necessary.

We restrict our considerations about the nature of information and information processing to structural characterizations which are common to the descriptions of real discrete computational processes and try to characterize informations by rules which describe how informations are systematically transformed. The first observation is that the transformational behaviour can be described by rules $A \longrightarrow B$, such that each special transformation $X \longrightarrow Y$ is obtained by consistently specializing A into X and B into Y. A formal foundation of this can be studied in van Wijngaarden's problem solving method. Although it depends on the use of van Wijngaarden grammars, this method is not to be seen in the context of formal languages but in that of programming methodology. Moreover, it is a contribution towards a theoretical foundation of programming methodology.

We analyse the properties of van Wijngaarden grammars which are relevant for our purpose starting with a consideration about their computational power in a narrower sense and proceed with an introduction to van Wijngaarden's method of problem solving by using two-level grammars. The formal principles which are essential for the transformation of information are generalized leading to an approach for a model of information transformations.

1. The computational power of van Wijngaarden grammars

The class of van Wijngaarden languages, i. e. the class of languages generated by some van Wijngaarden grammar, coincides with the class of recursively enumerable sets, cf. Deussen [3]. By application of well-known results of computability theory, see Mal'cev [6], it follows that the range of each partial-recursive function $f: \mathbb{N}^k \longrightarrow \mathbb{N}$ can be produced by some van Wijngaarden grammar. For a direct proof see also Hesse [5]. One can moreover construct special grammars representing computations of the function values, such that starting with a production rule containing representations of the arguments $x_1, \ldots, x_k$ as parameters leads to the production of one word only which represents $f(x_1, \ldots, x_k)$. We call such a grammar a representation of f. In the following we show explicit constructions of representations for partial-recursive functions and take advantage of them for revealing, how the control of the computational process can be expressed. This will immediately lead to the idea of using van Wijngaarden grammars for expressing solutions of information processing problems in general.

Let van Wijngaarden grammars G be represented in the following form, which is similar to formulations used by Deussen [3] and van Wijngaarden [8]:

$$G = \langle V_m, V_o, V_t, R_m, R_h, s_o \rangle ,$$

- V_m a finite set of 'metanotions', the metavocabulary,
- V_o a finite set of characters for building terminal symbols, this set is called the orthovocabulary,
- V_t a set of terminal symbols, $V_t \subset V_o^+$,
- R_m a finite set of context-free metarules, $R_m \subset V_m \times (V_m \cup V_o)^*$,
- R_h a finite set of hyperrules, $R_h \subset (V_m \cup V_o)^+ \times [(V_m \cup V_o)^+]^*$, where words of length $\neq 1$ over $(V_m \cup V_o)^+$ are written with ' , ' as concatenation symbol,
- s_o the start notion, $s_o \in V_o^+$,

with the basic sets being pairwise disjoint.

Let L_M denote the set of elements of V_o^* produced by R_m when starting with $M \in V_m$. The consistent replacement which maps $[(V_m \cup V_o)^+]^*$ partially into $[V_o^+]^*$ by substitution of $M \in V_m$ by $f(M) \in L_M$ is denoted by r_f where f is the partial mapping

$$f : V_m \longrightarrow V_o^*, \quad f(M) \in L_M ,$$

describing the replacements of metanotions. The language produced by G (see [3]) is denoted by $L(G)$. Following van Wijngaarden's notations we combine metarules $\langle M,y_1\rangle$, $\langle M,y_2\rangle$, ..., $\langle M,y_n\rangle$ to one rule with alternatives which is written

$$M :: \ y_1 ; y_2 ; \ldots ; y_n .$$

Hyperrules are written in the form

$$L : R. \quad , L \in (V_m \cup V_o)^+ , \quad R \in [(V_m \cup V_o)^+]^* .$$

If the right-hand-side of each hyperrule is of length 1, i.e. $R \in (V_m \cup V_o)^+$, then the grammar is called a <u>unary grammar</u>.

For the unary grammars constructed in the following we commonly use sets

$$V_m \supset \{N_1, N_2, \ldots, N_z\} \quad \text{for some } z \geq 1,$$

$$V_o = \{a , b , f , i , r , s\} ,$$

$$V_t = \{r , ri , rii , \ldots , ri^k , ri^{k+1} , \ldots\} ,$$

$$R_m \supset \{(N_1 :: \ ; N_1 i.) , (N_2 :: N_1.) , \ldots , (N_z :: N_1.)\}$$

and $s_o = s$.

We construct a representation of a function $g : \mathbb{N}^k \longrightarrow \mathbb{N}$ as follows: Each of the nonterminal symbols N_j, $j = 1, \ldots, z$, produces $\{i\}^*$ and thus can be used for representing a natural number x by i^x. If N_j represents the argument x_j of g, $j = 1, \ldots, k$, then $aN_1aN_2 \ldots aN_kf$ represents the unevaluated expression $g(x_1,x_2, \ldots, x_k)$. We take

$$s : aN_1aN_2 \ldots aN_kf.$$

as start rule and

$$L : rR. \quad , R \in (V_m \cup \{i\})^*,$$

as final rules. The other rules read

$$L : R. \quad , R \in (V_m \cup V_o)^+ ,$$

and the orthosymbol r occurs only at the right-hand-side of final rules. Let $L(G, A)$ denote that subset of $L(G)$ which is obtained when starting with the production rule

$$s : A. \quad , A \in V_o^+ .$$

The grammar G is a representation of the function g if and only if

$$L(G, ai^{x_1} \ldots ai^{x_k}f) = \begin{cases} \{ri^{g(x_1, \ldots, x_k)}\} & \text{if } g(x_1, \ldots, x_k) \text{ is defined} \\ \emptyset & \text{otherwise} . \end{cases}$$

The basic functions

succ : $\mathbb{N} \longrightarrow \mathbb{N}$ (successor),

zero : $\mathbb{N} \longrightarrow \{0\}$,

$proj_j^k$: $\mathbb{N}^k \longrightarrow \mathbb{N}$ (projections)

are represented by unary grammars with the following hyperrules:

<u>succ</u>: s : aN_1f. aN_1f : rN_1i.

<u>zero</u>: s : aN_1f. aN_1f : r.

<u>$proj_j^k$</u>: s : $aN_1aN_2 \ldots . aN_kf$. $aN_1aN_2 \ldots . aN_kf$: rN_j. $(1 \leq j \leq k)$.

From representations for given partial-recursive functions further representations for functions obtained by composition, primitive recursion and minimalization can be constructed systematically as shown in the following. To avoid that illegal results can be obtained by applying composed rules, we exclusively refer to the grammars constructed by this method.

<u>Composition</u>: Let $f_0 : \mathbb{N}^n \longrightarrow \mathbb{N}$, $f_1, \ldots ., f_n : \mathbb{N}^m \longrightarrow \mathbb{N}$ be represented by unary grammars with hyperrules

s : $aN_1aN_2 \ldots . aN_nf$. , resp. s : $aN_1aN_2 \ldots . aN_mf$. ,

L_{ji} : R_{ji}. with $j = 0, 1, \ldots ., n$ indicating f_j and $i = 1, \ldots ., p_j$,

L'_{ji} : rR'_{ji}. , $j = 0, 1, \ldots ., n$, $i = 1, \ldots ., q_j$.

For the representation of g with $g(x_1, \ldots ., x_m) = f_0(f_1(x_1, \ldots ., x_m), \ldots . , f_n(x_1, \ldots ., x_m))$ we use further metarules

A :: ; AaN_1. F :: ; FAf.

The metanotion A denotes an argument string and F denotes a string containing arguments together with the corresponding symbol f indicating function application. The hyperrules are built as follows: The start rule reads

(1) s : $aN_1aN_2 \ldots . aN_mf$.

A further rule generates the formal application of the given functions, i.e. a string corresponding to $f_0(f_1(x_1, \ldots ., x_m), \ldots ., f_n(x_1, \ldots ., x_m))$.

(2) $aN_1aN_2 \ldots . aN_mf$: $a(aN_1 \ldots . aN_mf)^nf$.

Now the context for applying the rules corresponding to f_1 reads

$a \ldots . (aN_1 \ldots . aN_mf)^{n-1}f$

or more general a .... Ff. This leads to the rules

(3) $aL_{1i}Ff$: $aR_{1i}Ff$. $(i = 1, \ldots ., p_1)$

(4) $aL'_{1i}Ff$: $abR'_{1i}Ff$. $(i = 1, \ldots ., q_1)$.

The orthosymbol b indicates intermediate results. To proceed with the evaluation of f_2 we take the rules

(5) $abN_1L_{2i}Ff : abN_1R_{2i}Ff.$ $(i = 1, \ldots, p_2)$

(6) $abN_1L'_{2i}Ff : abN_1bR'_{2i}Ff.$ $(i = 1, \ldots, q_2)$.

Analogously, we build further rules corresponding to f_k, $k = 3, \ldots, n$:

(7) $abN_1 \ldots bN_{k-1}L_{ki}Ff : abN_1 \ldots bN_{k-1}R_{ki}Ff.$ $(i = 1, \ldots, p_k)$

(8) $abN_1 \ldots bN_{k-1}L'_{ki}Ff : abN_1 \ldots bN_{k-1}bR'_{ki}Ff.$ $(i = 1, \ldots, q_k)$.

The final application of f_o is described by

(9) $abN_1 \ldots bN_n f : aN_1 \ldots aN_n f.$

(10) $L_{oi} : R_{oi}.$ $(i = 1, \ldots, p_o)$ (11) $L'_{oi} : rR'_{oi}.$ $(i = 1, \ldots, q_o)$.

The whole grammar controls the computation process such that the evaluation of the arguments of the outer function proceeds from left to right.

<u>Primitive recursion</u>: Let $g : \mathbb{N}^n \longrightarrow \mathbb{N}$ be represented by a grammar with hyperrules

$s : aN_1 \ldots aN_n f.$

$L_{1i} : R_{1i}.$ $(i = 1, \ldots, p_1)$, $L'_{1i} : rR'_{1i}.$ $(i = 1, \ldots, q_1)$,

and correspondingly $g_2 : \mathbb{N}^{n+2} \longrightarrow \mathbb{N}$ by

$s : aN_1 \ldots aN_{n+2}f.$ $L_{2i} : R_{2i}.$ $L'_{2i} : rR'_{2i}.$

Then $h : \mathbb{N}^{n+1} \longrightarrow \mathbb{N}$ defined by

$$h(x_1, \ldots, x_n, 0) = g_1(x_1, \ldots, x_n) ,$$

$$h(x_1, \ldots, x_n, y+1) = g_2(x_1, \ldots, x_n, y, h(x_1, \ldots, x_n, y))$$

is represented by a grammar with the following hyperrules: The start rule reads

(1) $s : aN_1 \ldots aN_{n+1}f.$

The actual information during the computation process consists of the arguments $x_1, \ldots, x_n, x_{n+1}$, the value y, which starts with 0 (right-hand-side of rule (4)) and is increased by 1 as often as g_2 is applied (rule (8)), and of the current value of $h(x_1, \ldots, x_n, y)$. Copies of arguments are generated before the functions g_1 or g_2 are applied. The further rules read

(2) $aN_1 \ldots aN_{n+1}f : bN_1 \ldots bN_{n+1}aN_1 \ldots aN_n f.$

(3) $bN_1 \ldots bN_{n+1}L_{1i} : bN_1 \ldots bN_{n+1}R_{1i}.$ $(i = 1, \ldots, p_1)$

(4) $bN_1 \ldots bN_{n+1}L'_{1i} : bN_1 \ldots bN_{n+1}bbR'_{1i}.$ $(i = 1, \ldots, q_1)$

(5) $bN_1 \ldots bN_{n+1}bN_{n+1}bN_{n+3} : rN_{n+3}.$

(6) $bN_1 \ldots bN_{n+1}bN_{n+2}bN_{n+3} : bN_1 \ldots bN_{n+1}bN_{n+2}aN_1 \ldots aN_n aN_{n+2}aN_{n+3}f.$

(7) $bN_1 \ldots bN_{n+2}L_{2i} : bN_1 \ldots bN_{n+2}R_{2i}.$ $(i = 1, \ldots, p_2)$

(8) $bN_1 \ldots bN_{n+2}L'_{2j} : bN_1 \ldots bN_{n+2}ibR'_{2j}.$ $(j = 1, \ldots, q_2)$.

The rules (2), (3), (4) refer to g_1 , and (6), (7), (8) analogously to g_2 . The

process terminates when $x_{n+1} = y_{n+1}$ is reached (twice N_{n+1} in rule (5)).
Minimalization: Let $g : \mathbb{N}^{n+1} \longrightarrow \mathbb{N}$ be represented by a grammar with rules

$$s : aN_1 \ldots\ldots aN_{n+1}f. \quad L_j : R_j. \quad (j = 1,\ldots\ldots,p), \quad L'_j : rR'_j. \quad (j=1,\ldots\ldots,q).$$

Then $h : \mathbb{N}^n \longrightarrow \mathbb{N}$, $h(x_1, \ldots\ldots, x_n) = \min\{y \mid g(x_1, \ldots\ldots, x_n, y) = 0\}$, is represented by a grammar with the following rules:

(1) $s : aN_1 \ldots\ldots aN_n f.$

(2) $aN_1 \ldots\ldots aN_n f : bN_1 \ldots\ldots bN_n baN_1 \ldots\ldots aN_n af.$

(3) $bN_1 \ldots\ldots bN_n bN_{n+1} L_j : bN_1 \ldots\ldots bN_n bN_{n+1} R_j.$ $\quad (j = 1, \ldots\ldots, p)$

(4) $bN_1 \ldots\ldots bN_n bN_{n+1} L'_j : bN_1 \ldots\ldots bN_n bN_{n+1} bR'_j.$ $\quad (j = 1, \ldots\ldots, q)$

(5) $bN_1 \ldots\ldots bN_{n+1} b : rN_{n+1}.$

(6) $bN_1 \ldots\ldots bN_{n+1} bN_{n+2} i : bN_1 \ldots\ldots bN_{n+1} iaN_1 \ldots\ldots aN_n aN_{n+1} if.$

The rules (3) and (4) refer to the function g. They are applied first after rule (2) and, when the argument y has been increased ($N_{n+1}i$) after (6). Rule (6) can only be applied if the current function value is not zero ($N_{n+2}i$). The terminating rule is (5).

By recursive induction follows that we can construct a unary grammar representation for each partial-recursive function.

2. Van Wijngaarden's problem solving method

We have proven that van Wijngaarden grammars are powerful enough for representing <u>computable functions</u>. In fact, one can also show that each special <u>computation</u> can be described by a van Wijngaarden grammar, such that steps of the computation unambiguously correspond with derivation steps. States of the real or virtual computation device are represented by strings consisting of words over the orthovocabulary. Thus the description method of van Wijngaarden grammars which was originally developed for describing grammars of programming languages, can itself be used directly as a programming language. This idea is due to A. van Wijngaarden. We call this a <u>problem solving method</u> because the whole work of building a formal structure corresponding to the real problem structure, of describing the problem and, if possible, of formulating an algorithmic solution, can be done by applying this method. Its importance results from the following properties:

- Each algorithm can be expressed.
- Nondeterminacy like that of Dijkstra's guarded commands (cf. [4]) can be provided.
- Nonprocedural specifications corresponding to the extended meaning of algorithms as proposed by F.L. Bauer [1] can be expressed.
- There is a close relation between the general structure of information processing and van Wijngaarden grammars based on the formal analogy between abstractions and

metarules and between information transformations and hyperrules.
Here we intend to explain and to emphasize the last property. Some examples shall illustrate the others.
The first example describes the iterative computation of the factorial based upon the representation of natural numbers already used above and without referring to predefined operations. The result is described by symbols of a finite set of terminal symbols. The grammar is not a unary one.

Example 1 : Factorial, iterative

Metavocabulary: $V_m = \{N, N_1, N_2, N_3, N_4, D, X\}$.

Orthovocabulary: $V_o = \{i, n, p, s, 0, 1, 2, 3\}$.

Terminal symbols (elements of V_t):

pO , p1 , which may be externally represented by 'factorial' and 'is',

n , ni , nii , niii , niiii , niiiii , niiiiii , niiiiiii , niiiiiiii , niiiiiiiii, which may be externally represented by 0 , 1, 2 , 3 , 4 , 5 , 6 , 7 , 8 , 9 .

The symbol p3 which indicates multiplication and strings ni^k where $k > 9$ are not considered as terminal symbols.

Metarules:

N :: ; Ni. N_1 :: N. N_2 :: N. N_3 :: N. N_4 :: N. X :: iiiiiiiii.

D :: ; i ; ii ; iii ; iiii ; iiiii ; iiiiii ; iiiiiii ; iiiiiiii ; iiiiiiiii .

Hyperrules:

s : p0 , nN , p1 , Np2 .	(form of the solution)
Np2 : Nnni.	(start of the iteration)
$NnNnN_2$: nN_2.	(finishing the iteration)
NnN_1nN_2 : $NnN_1inN_1inN_2p3n$.	(iteration step introducing multiplication)
$NnN_1nN_2nN_3ip3nN_4$: $NnN_1nN_2nN_3p3nN_2N_4$.	(multiplication step)
$NnN_1nN_2np3N_4$: NnN_1nN_4.	(finishing multiplication)
nXN : ninN. $nNnXN_1$: $nNinN_1$.	(decimal transformation)
nNnD : nN , nD.	(separating digits)

For understanding such rules an insight into the problem structure is necessary. The external readability can be improved using mnemotechniques like in traditional programming languages. One can formulate the main hyperrules like this:

start : factorial , N , is , N fač.

N fac : N fac 0 is 1.

N fac N is I : I.

N fac K is I : N fac K+1 is K+1 times I plus 0.

N fac K is I times L+1 plus M : N fac K is I times L plus IM.

N fac K is I times 0 plus M : N fac K is M.

The next example shows a nondeterministic process with a deterministic result. We omit the explicit definitions of the sets V_m, V_o, V_t .

Example 2 : Multiplying several factors

Metarules:

N :: ; Ni.   N' :: N.   N'' :: N.   F :: ; FnN times .   F' :: F.

Hyperrules:

(1) start : mult F.

(2) mult : ni.   (empty product yields 1)

(3) mult Fn times F' : n.   (one factor is zero, thus the result is zero)

(4) mult Fni times F' : mult FF'   (omitting factors 1)

(5) mult FnN times nN' times F' : mult F product nNnN' plus n times F'.

(6) mult F product nNnN'i plus nN'' times F' : mult F product nNnN' plus nNN''times F'.

(7) mult F product nNn plus nN' times F' : mult FnN' times F'.

(8) mult nN times : nN.   (one factor only)

The rules (5), (6) and (7) describe the preparation, the step-wise execution by addition and the completion of the multiplication of two factors.

Van Wijngaarden's problem solving method provides nonprocedurality in a very natural way: The exact relation between the input data and the result is described, but the way of computing is not determined.

Example 3 : Quadratic equation

We express the solution of $X^2 - NX + N' = 0$ as follows:

Metarules:

N :: ; Ni.   N' :: N.   L :: xx minus N x plus.

Hyperrules:

(1) s : xx minus N x plus N'.

(2) xx minus NN' x plus N times N' : root1 N , root2 N'.

(3) LN : LN' times plus N.

(4) LN times N' plus NN'' : LN times N'i plus N''.

(5) LN times N' plus : LN times N'.

The solution of $X^2 - 3X + 2 = 0$ is represented by the following derivation sequence:

s $\xrightarrow{(1)}$ xx minus iii x plus ii $\xrightarrow{(3)}$ xx minus iii x plus ii times plus ii $\xrightarrow{(4)}$

xx minus iii x plus ii times i plus $\xrightarrow{(5)}$ xx minus iii x plus ii times i $\xrightarrow{(2)}$

root1 ii , root2 i. The success depends on finding a value for N' in rule (3) such that the process terminates. This value must represent a root of the polynomial!
The idea for the construction of this example is very similar to applications of two-level grammars like the description of Fermat's last theorem, see Cleaveland, Uzgalis [2].

Obviously, this method (presented by A. van Wijngaarden, see [8]) offers more than a way of describing algorithms. Motivated by application examples we state the hypothesis that van Wijngaarden's problem solving method is related to information transformations like an algorithmic language is related to algorithms. Hence we try to develop a formal system of information processing guided by the ideas of this method, but generalizing it.

3. An approach towards a general information processing model

Procedural problem solving by means of algorithms consists of combining actions according to so-called control structures like sequencing, branching, repetition and so on. The nonprocedural problem solving method due to van Wijngaarden is based on states instead of actions. Its dynamics is expressed by state transformations. The states occurring in the derivation process correspond with actual information from an application point of view and with states of a machine from the implementation point of view. The program, i.e. the set of rules controlling the process, is a finite set of transformation relations $A_i \longrightarrow B_i$, $i \in I$ with an index set I. A computation then is a process consisting of transformations $X \longrightarrow X'$ such that X is a special case of A_i for some $i \in I$ and X' is the corresponding special case of B_i. In the following we try to define, what 'corresponding special cases' shall be with respect to informations. The relation between the more general state A_i and the special case X is formally described by the union '$\sqsubseteq$' of a transitive, irreflexive relation '$\sqsubset$', the so-called abstraction relation, and the identity relation: $A_i \sqsubseteq X$. This relation can be read as 'The state (-description) A_i is more general than the state (-description) X' or 'The information A_i is part of the information X or equal to X'. We call A_i an abstraction of X and X a specialization of A_i. Furthermore, we assume that X can be obtained from A_i and a mediate information M by applying a function φ which is monotonic in both arguments with respect to the relation '$\sqsubseteq$':

$$X = \varphi(A_i, M).$$

We distinguish basic informations related to the states from metainformations which serve for consistent specializations. The application of a rule $A_i \longrightarrow B_i$ is described as follows: Let X be the actual information related to the state of the computational process. The rule can be applied if X is a specialization of A_i and if a metainformation M can be found such that $X = \varphi(A_i, M)$ and $\varphi(B_i, M)$ exists and can be taken as the next actual information X'.

$$\begin{array}{lccc} \text{rule:} & A_i & \longrightarrow & B_i \\ & | & & | \\ \text{application:} & X = \varphi(A_i, M) & \longrightarrow & X' = \varphi(B_i, M) \end{array}$$

Let the rule be

N times N' plus NN'' : N times N'i plus N''.

Then specializing with the metainformation M, expressed by the mapping

$\{\langle N, ii\rangle, \langle N', i\rangle, \langle N'', i\rangle\}$,

yields

ii times i plus iii : ii times ii plus i.

The formal properties are described more precisely by the following approach towards a structural characterization of information and information processing.

We consider a set with a partial ordering expressing the abstraction relation as the weakest form of an information structure.

Let $\mathfrak{I} = \langle I, \sqsubset \rangle$ be an arbitrary algebraic structure with carrier set I and an irreflexive, transitive binary relation '$\sqsubset$'. We call the elements of I informations and use the notions of abstraction and specialization as explained above.

Two informations X and Y are called consistent (to each other), symbolically $X \sim Y$, if they possess a common specialization. The binary relation is called consistency relation.

If two elements X and Y possess a most special common abstraction, this will be called the intersection of X and Y and is denoted by $X \sqcap Y$.

If two consistent elements X and Y possess a most abstract common specialization, this will be called the union of X and Y and is denoted by $X \sqcup Y$.

$\mathfrak{I}$ is called a full information structure if the following conditions are fulfilled:

i) I contains a most abstract element Ω, i.e. $\Omega \sqsubseteq X$ holds for each $X \in I$.

ii) The intersection $X \sqcap Y$ is defined for arbitrary elements $X, Y \in I$.

iii) The union $X \sqcup Y$ is defined for arbitrary consistent pairs of elements $X, Y \in I$

If a full information structure is extended by adjunction of a most special element and this element is taken as the result of $X \sqcup Y$ for argument pairs being not consistent, then the resulting structure is a lattice. This can be proven directly. For information structures based upon lattices or partial orderings see also Scott [7]. If the lattice is additionally distributive, then the elements can be described by logical formulas with logical disjunction for describing intersections, logical conjunction for unions of consistent elements, TRUE for Ω , but FALSE for no element.

By generalizing the application of unary van Wijngaarden grammars the following information processing model is obtained:

Let $\mathfrak{P} = \langle I_b, I_m, \sqsubset, \varphi \rangle$ be a system with the following properties:

i) $\langle I_b, \sqsubset \rangle$ is an information structure. The elements of I_b are called basic informations. If they possess no further specialization, they are called concrete.

ii) $\langle I_m, \sqsubset \rangle$ is a full information structure. The elements of I_m are called metainformations.

iii) φ is a partial mapping $\varphi : I_b \times I_m \longrightarrow I_b$ expressing specialization in $\langle I_b, \sqsubset \rangle$ as follows:

a) $X \sqsubseteq \varphi(X,M)$, $(X \in I_b,\ M \in I_m)$. M is called a specification for X and, moreover, a minimal specification, if no M' exists with $M' \sqsubset M$ and $\varphi(X,M) = \varphi(X,M')$.

b) Let $X, Y \in I_b$ with $X \sqsubseteq Y$. Then there exists a minimal specification for X such that $\varphi(X,M) = Y$.

c) If $\varphi(Y,M)$ exists and $X \sqsubseteq Y$ holds then also $\varphi(X,M)$ exists and $\varphi(X,M) \sqsubseteq \varphi(Y,M)$ holds.

d) If $M \sim M'$ then $\varphi(X, M \sqcup M') = \varphi(\varphi(X,M),M')$ holds where the left-hand-side is defined if and only if the right-hand-side is defined.

By means of such systems information processing can be described as information transformation according to general rules.

A relation $R \subset I_b \times I_b$ (written with infix symbol $\xrightarrow{R}$) is called a transformation if it is closed under specialization in the following sense:

If $A \xrightarrow{R} B$ holds and $M \in I_m$ is a common specification for A and B, then $\varphi(A,M) \xrightarrow{R} \varphi(B,M)$ holds.

R is additionally called regular, if $A \xrightarrow{R} B$ and $X = \varphi(A,M)$ with a minimal specification $M \in I_m$ implies that M is a specification for B.

A sequential process of information transformation controlled by a transformation R is a finite or infinite sequence

$$X_0 \xrightarrow{R} X_1 \xrightarrow{R} \cdots \xrightarrow{R} X_n \xrightarrow{R} X_{n+1} \xrightarrow{R} \cdots$$

A process is called concrete, if each element of the sequence is concrete.

We are interested in such relations which are finitely generated by some basic relations $A_j \longrightarrow B_j$, $j = 1, \ldots, n$, for some $n \in \mathbb{N}$.

A single step of a concrete process controlled by a regular transformation is performed as follows: Let X be the actual information. Finding its successor X' consists of

i) finding a rule $A_j \longrightarrow B_j$ such that $A_j \sqsubseteq X$;

ii) finding a minimal specification M such that $\varphi(A_j,M) = X$;

iii) specializing B_j by means of M: $Y = \varphi(B_j,M)$;

iv) if Y is not concrete, then finding a minimal specification M_1 such that $\varphi(X,M_1) = X$ and $\varphi(Y,M_1)$ is concrete;

v) specializing Y by means of M_1: $X' = \varphi(Y,M_1)$.

Nondeterminacy can occur independently in the steps i) (like in ex. 2), ii) (e.g. rule (5) of ex. 2) and iv) (e.g. rule (3) of ex. 3).

A unary van Wijngaarden grammar determines a special model of information processing together with a set of basic rules for one transformation. The hypernotions play the role of the basic informations,

$$I_b = (V_m \cup V_o)^* ,$$

with concrete elements belonging to V_o^*. Specialization is defined as consistent replacement of metanotions where the set of metainformations is

$$I_m = \{ f \mid f: V_m \longrightarrow V_o^*, \ f \text{ a partial mapping, } f(N) \in L_N \text{ for each } N \in V_m \} .$$

The mapping φ is defined by

$$\varphi(I,f) = r_f(I), \quad I \in I_b, \quad f \in I_m .$$

(For r_f see sect. 1.) The abstraction relation for metainformations is the set inclusion for the partial mappings. The metarules determine both the full information structure of metainformations and the abstraction relation of the basic informations. The hyperrules define a regular transformation.

We sketch two further applications of the model.
Consider a <u>recursive function definition</u>

$$F(x) = T(F)(x)$$

with a formal expression T. The iterative solution process can be expressed by an information transformation with the basic rule $F \longrightarrow T(F)$ and consists of steps

$$f \xrightarrow{R} T(f)$$

with the additional property $f \subseteq T(f)$. In this case the basic informations are formal expressions, built with functions, and the metainformations are replacements substituting function symbols by functions and function extensions.

In a model with variable-tables as basic informations <u>assignments</u> $x := F(x,y)$ can be expressed as in information transformation based on the rule

$$x = a, \ y = b \longrightarrow x = F(a,b), \ y = b .$$

One can prove that composed statements expressing sequences or branching, for instance, can again be described by information transformations.

4. State-oriented programming as an application of the general model

As main application of the model we present a method of programming and program development which realizes ideas of van Wijngaarden's method in the context of data structures and predefined operations.
The basic informations are state descriptions consisting of strings S and optional boolean expressions B. The strings are built over composed symbols and composed

expressions. All expressions are constructed according to the data structures and predefined operations which are provided. Specialization is performed by substitution and evaluation. A string with a subsequent boolean expression is written in the form

S where B .

S where TRUE means the same as S and S where FALSE is forbidden.
Metainformations are built from datatypes and names like from contextfree languages and metanotions before. The details are illustrated by the following examples.
Like in algorithmic programming we write programs for controlling processes. A program consists of an abstraction part which corresponds to the metarules of a grammar and a set of rules corresponding to the hyperrules.

Example 4 : Greatest common divisor

We declare X , Y as positive integer. The actual informations of the process can be represented by two numbers until the result, one number, is reached. The rules are obtained by writing down what shall happen in any situation. The resulting program reads as follows:

Abstractions
M , N : positive integer.
Rules
M and N where M > N ⟶ M - N and N.
M and N where M < N ⟶ M and N - M.
M and M ⟶ M .

Such a program can be used even if it is incomplete. If the last rule, for example, is omitted, the starting with '24 and 42' would yield the final result '6 and 6' thereby indicating that a rule is lacking. The semantics of such a program can be easily derived from the semantics of the predefined data structures and operations upon them by using the formal properties of the model. We call this kind of programming state-oriented. The following example shows, how program development is facilitated.

Example 5 : Sorting a nonempty array in ascending order

We use as basic abstractions:

A : array [1 : integer] of real. I , K : integer. X : real.

The start information shall be 'start A'. We observe that the subarray with indices [1: 1] is already sorted. This is expressed by the rule

start A ⟶ A sorted 1.

We have to consider the more general case 'A sorted I' and find the rules

A sorted lenght(A) ⟶ ready A.

with 'ready A' as final result and

A sorted I <u>where</u> I < length(A) ⟶ A insert A[I+1] at or below I+1 sorted I+1.

for intermediate steps. Thus we have to treat cases 'A insert X at or below K sorted I'. The next step then depends on conditions to be expressed by boolean expressions. We find three rules:

.... <u>where</u> K = 1 ⟶ A[1 : X] sorted I .

(with A[K : X] as result of assigning X to A[K]),

.... <u>where</u> K > 1, A[K-1] ≤ X ⟶ A[K : X] sorted I.
.... <u>where</u> K > 1, X < A[K-1] ⟶ A[K : A[K-1]] insert X at or below K-1 sorted I.

With some notational abbreviations the whole program reads as follows:

<u>Abstractions</u>
A : <u>array</u> [1 : <u>integer</u>] <u>of</u> <u>real</u>. I, K : <u>integer</u>. X : <u>real</u>.
<u>Rules</u>
start A ⟶ A sorted 1.
A sorted I <u>where</u>
  I = length(A) ⟶ ready A ;
  I < length(A) ⟶ A insert A[I+1] at or below I+1 sorted I+1.
A insert X at or below K sorted I <u>where</u>
  K = 1 ⟶ A[1 : X] sorted I ;
  K > 1, A[K-1] ≤ X ⟶ A[K : X] sorted I ;
  K > 1, X < A[K-1] ⟶ A[K : A[K-1]] insert X at or below K-1 sorted I.

<u>Example 6</u>: Quadratic equation $x^2 + ax + b = 0$

The first program describes a procedural solution:

<u>Abstractions</u>
A , B <u>real</u> .
<u>Rules</u>
A , B ⟶ -A/2 plus root A*A/4 - B .
A plus root B <u>where</u> B ≥ 0 ⟶ solutions A+sqrt(B) , A-sqrt(B) ;
  B < 0 ⟶ no real solutions .

The next program is nondeterministic. For finding a solution, back-tracking is necessary.

<u>Abstractions</u>
A , B , X : <u>real</u>.
<u>Rules</u>
A , B ⟶ A , B try X .
A , B try X <u>where</u> X * X + A * X + B = 0 ⟶ solutions X , -(A+X) .

In the following version a restriction of the choice of metainformation is used for expressing nondeterminacy.

Abstractions

A , B , X : <u>real</u>.

Rules

A , B <u>where</u> X * X + A * X + B = 0 ⟶ solutions X , -(A+X) .

Starting with a state description 'A , B' containing the coefficients of the polynomial the rule can only applied when the solution X is found.

The power of such a language for state-oriented programming is that of van Wijngaarden grammars. Thus one can write nonprocedural and non-executable programs. The programming method can be used for at first developing state-oriented programs and subsequently transforming them to algorithmic programs. Verification of state-oriented programs can be performed by taking advantage of the properties of the formal model.

References

[1] Bauer, F.L.: Algorithms and Algebra, Symposium "Algorithm in Modern Mathematics and Computer Science", Urgench, USSR, September 1979

[2] Cleaveland, J.C., and Uzgalis, R.C.: Grammars for Programming Languages, New York etc., 1977

[3] Deussen, P.: A Decidability Criterion for van Wijngaarden Grammars, Acta Informatica, 5, 353-375, 1975

[4] Dijkstra, E.W.: Guarded Commands, Nondeterminacy and Formal Derivation of Programs, Comm.ACM, 18, 453-457, 1975

[5] Hesse, W.: Vollständige formale Beschreibung von Programmiersprachen mit zweischichtigen Grammatiken, Bericht 7623, TUM, München, 1976

[6] Mal'cev, A.I.: Algorithms and recursive functions, (translated from Russian), Groningen, 1970

[7] Scott, D.: Logic and Programming Languages, Comm.ACM, 19, 634-641, 1976

[8] van Wijngaarden, A.: vW - Grammatiken und konzeptuelle Komplexität, Kolloquium "Rechenanlagen und Anwendungsverfahren", Inst. f. Angew. Math.u. Rechenzentrum d. Univ. Hamburg, Juni 1979 (not published)

APPROACHES TO CONCURRENCY IN B-TREES

Y. S. Kwong and D. Wood

Unit for Computer Science,
McMaster University,
Hamilton, Ontario,
Canada, L8S 4K1.

1. Introduction

The use of B-trees [BM] for the organization of data-bases is now widely accepted. Clearly data-bases need to allow concurrent operations of the type MEMBER, INSERT and DELETE for dictionaries [AHU]. Hence the investigation of how these operations can be efficiently implemented for B-trees in a concurrent environment is an important task. The usual problems associated with any concurrent system will arise, for example process scheduling, correctness, deadlocks, livelocks and integrity. However the structure of the system imposed by the B-trees and its restricted set of operations gives some indication that specific solutions for supporting concurrency in B-trees are possible. Moreover these specific solutions will not only be of practical interest but also give insight into the problems associated with concurrency in general.

In this paper we aim to survey the solutions available at the present time including our own, extract some useful techniques, and discuss some of the many remaining problems.

In Section 2 we detail our assumptions about the processes, data-structures and concurrency control involved in the "solutions" presented. This also means that we define a particular notion of solution. Finally two main types of solution are proposed, which categorize almost all solutions in the literature. These are discussed in Sections 3 and 4. Section 5 discusses the remaining solution and Section 6 is devoted to open problems.

We will <u>not</u> give any solutions here, since they are too voluminous to be presented. The reader is referred to [KW2] for a more detailed presentation.

2. Assumptions and Difficulties

Let us first give the definition of a B-tree [BM] and discuss the two basic means used to represent dictionaries with B-trees.

A <u>B-tree of order m</u> ($m \geq 3$) is a tree which satisfies conditions (i)-(iv).

(i) Each node has at most m sons.

(ii) Each node except for the root node has at least $\lceil m/2 \rceil$ sons.

Work supported under Natural Sciences and Engineering Research Council of Canada Grants, Nos. A-3042 and A-7700.

(iii) The root node has at least two sons.

(iv) All leaves, that is nodes which only have the empty tree as their sons, appear at the same level.

Note that usually an empty tree is called a leaf in the literature, however it is more convenient here to denote what is usually the father-of-leaves level as the leaf level.

A B-tree can be used as a search tree for the dictionary operations [AHU] in one of two ways. Assume we are given n keys K from a totally ordered universe $\mathcal{U}_k$ of keys.

We say that the B-tree T of order m can be used as a <u>(node) search B-tree</u> for K if the total number of sons of the leaves of T = n+1. In this case associate each key in K with a unique node in T such that:

(i) a node with r+1 sons had keys associated with it,

and

(ii) if $p_0 k_1 \ldots p_{r-1} k_r p_r$ represent the r keys at a node and the r+1 subtrees $p_0, \ldots, p_r$ then not only is $k_1 < k_2 < \ldots k_r$ but also: the keys in $p_0 < k_1 <$ keys in $p_1 < k_2 < \ldots < k_r <$ keys in p_r.

We say that the B-tree of order m can be used as a <u>leaf search B-tree</u> (or <u>B*-tree</u>) for K if the total number of sons of the leaves of T = n+q, where q is the number of leaves. In this case associate each key in K with a unique leaf in T such that a leaf with r+1 sons contains r keys and the keys in K can be read in ascending order when traversing the leaves from left to right. The non-leaf nodes are then given routing information according to some routing scheme [KW4].

Both varieties of search B-trees are found in the literature. For example node search B-trees were the original model defined in [BM] and [Kn], whereas leaf search B-trees are defined in [AHU]. Moreover both varieties have been studied from the viewpoint of concurrency for node search B-trees see [S] and [KW2] for example, while for leaf search B-trees see [BS] and [E] for example.

Throughout this paper we assume that the keys and pointers in each node (or page) of a B-tree are stored sequentially; this is called a B-S-tree in [KW1]. Other storage mechanisms for nodes including trees are discussed in [KW1] and the concurrency problem is treated in [KW2] and especially [KW3].

We wish to allow an arbitrary number of processes to operate concurrently on a search B-tree. These processes are assumed to be asynchronous, each of which is progressing at a finite, but undetermined speed and is performing one of the following dictionary operations:

MEMBER (k,T): is k in search B-tree T?

INSERT (k,T): if k is not already present in T then add it to T.

DELETE (k,T): if k is present in T then remove it.

We assume throughout that the original [BM] algorithms are used as a basis for implementing these processes. In supporting concurrency the following basic assumptions about any proposed solution seem to be reasonable:

A1. The integrity of the data and the search B-tree structure must be preserved.

A2. No major modifications of the B-tree structure are allowed.

A3. Implementation details must be invisible.

A2 perhaps requires some further elucidation, namely what is a major as against a minor modification? For the purposes of this paper we assume that the original sequential MEMBER, INSERT and DELETE operations [BM] will operate correctly on the implemented B-tree if it is placed in a sequential environment at any time when any processes acting on it have been completed. If this property holds for a particular modification we say it is minor and otherwise it is major. However more about this later.

To enable us to discuss the problems of allowing concurrent processes on search B-trees we first provide a classification for processes into "readers" and "writers", by considering the three operations in more detail.

A MEMBER process simply reads nodes on some root to leaf path. It does not make either any structural changes to the tree or any changes to the data stored there. Hence we call this a pure reader. An INSERT or DELETE process usually does make these kinds of changes hence we call them both updaters. However the usual implementation [BM] splits them into two distinct sub-processes:

(i) SEARCH (k,T): search for k in T and return the node containing k if it exists.

(ii) RESTRUCTURE (k,u,T): add k to or remove k from leaf u in T and restructure as necessary.

The SEARCH process is essentially the same as MEMBER in that it proceeds on a root to leaf path making no changes to the search B-tree. Hence we call it an updating reader. When an updating reader enters the restructuring process we then call it an updating writer or simply a writer. A writer proceeds along a leaf to root path. A process is called a reader if it is either a pure reader or an updating reader. Thus typically readers progress down the tree and writers progress up the tree.

We also need to define some notion of correctness for readers and writers. First consider readers. The following properties of readers should be clear from their definitions.

Property 1: Any number of readers may read the same node at the same time.

Property 2: It is not necessary to distinguish between pure and updating readers.

Property 3: It is not necessary to prevent overtaking of a reader by another reader on any root to leaf path, that is no ordering need be imposed on readers.

These lead to the following notion of correctness for readers:

A reader searching for a key k is said to be correct provided that:

(i) if k is in the tree and there are no DELETE processes for k (apart from itself), then the reader must find k.

(ii) if k is not in the tree and there are no INSERT processes for k (apart from itself), then k must not be found.

Second consider writers. The notion of correctness for writers is similar to that for readers.

A writer deleting (inserting) a key k is said to be correct provided that:

(i) if k is in the tree (is not in the tree) and there are no other DELETE (INSERT) processes for k, then the writer must remove k (must add k).

(ii) if k is in the tree (is not in the tree) and there are no other INSERT (DELETE) processes for k, then the writer must remove k (must add k).

A trivial technique to ensure these notions of correctness are satisfied is to only allow one process in the tree at any time. This sequentialization certainly provides correctness of implementation but the "degree" of concurrency is severely limited. This is therefore not an attractive solution. We require a solution that allows more than one process within the tree at any moment of time. This leads to a number of difficulties which we will now specify:

Difficulty 1: Two writers must not be allowed to modify a node concurrently.

Difficulty 2: It is dangerous to allow readers at a node which is currently being modified by a writer.

Difficulty 3: It is dangerous to allow readers at the father of a node which a writer is modifying.

Difficulty 4: It is dangerous to allow other writers at the sons of a node which a writer is modifying.

Difficulty 5: Two writers whose restructuring paths have a common section must not be permitted to overtake along the common section.

In [KW2] examples are given which illustrate the effect of ignoring these difficulties. Difficulty 5 displays a significant difference between readers and writers on the same paths. It means that writers must maintain a follow-the-leader (or Indian file) scheme along a common path, whereas readers (Property 3) need not. Each of the difficulties posed above will if ignored lead to either a loss of integrity or a loss of correctness, since readers and or writers may go along wrong paths.

The avoidance of these difficulties implies that some kind of concurrency control is needed. The one we use here is standard in that it consists of three components: locks, a compatibility and convertibility graph and a scheduler.

Each process will normally request a node be locked and only when it is locked may the node be accessed. There will be different types of lock each of which we designate as an α-lock, where α is the type. The request takes the form of:

$$\alpha\text{-lock}(u,\pi)$$

for a process π requesting that node u be π-locked. After finishing with u, π can release the α-lock by $\alpha\text{-unlock}(u,\pi)$. Occasionally it is necessary to change the α-lock to a β-lock. This is written as $\text{convert}(u,\alpha,\beta,\pi)$.

The compatibility and convertibility graph (CCG) specifies a compatibility and convertibility relation which holds among the different lock types. In particular we write:

to indicate that a process π_1 can α-lock a node u and a process π_2 can β-lock node u concurrently, that is α and β are compatible. If the compatibility relation is asymmetric this is represented by a directed edge. Similarly we write

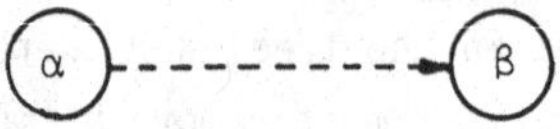

to indicate α may be converted into β by a process.

Finally, the scheduler at each node consists of:

(i) a waiting queue of processes and requests, and

(ii) a fair scheduling discipline for processes waiting in the queue.

When a request, α-lock(u,π), is executed, if α is compatible with the lock types currently at the node, then the request is granted. Otherwise it is entered in the waiting queue at u. When a release, α-unlock(u,π), is executed the α-lock for π is removed from u and some process in the queue at u is granted its request by the scheduler if this is possible. When a convert(u,α,β,π) is executed, if β is compatible with the locks held by other processes currently at the node u then the α-lock for π at u is changed to a β-lock. Otherwise π and the request are entered in the queue at u.

The introduction of concurrency control, while enabling the difficulties posed above to be solved, at the same time introduces its own difficulties.

Difficulty 6: When a node is split into two nodes by an INSERT process, what happens to the processes in the queue at u?

The simplest answer is: only split a node when its associated queue is empty. This is in fact done in a number of the solutions.

Difficulty 7: Deadlock may occur when a writer collides either with a reader or with another writer near the common ancestor node of their restructuring paths.

The problem of a writer colliding with a reader can be avoided by giving them different lock types which are compatible, so that they can slide over each other. The problem of two writers meeting can be avoided by ensuring they are always far enough apart.

The introduction of concurrency control means that we can expand the third assumption into:

A3a: The only assumption about the scheduling discipline for the writing queues should be that it is fair.

A3b: Explicit processing of entries in a waiting queue are not allowed.

We now turn to a classification of the solutions presently available. A particularly important concept which is made much use of is that of a safe node. We say a node in a B-tree of order m is insertion-safe (i-safe) if it has less than m sons, and deletion-safe (d-safe) if it has more than $\lceil m/2 \rceil$ sons. Given a root-to-leaf path in a search B-tree a node on the path is the deepest i-safe (deepest d-safe) node if there is no i-safe (d-safe) node on the path closer to the leaf.

The notion of a deepest safe node u for an updater captures the fact that no structural modifications by that process can propagate above u in a sequential environment. The portion of the path from the deepest safe node to its leaf determined by an updater U is called the <u>scope of U</u>.

We can now classify solutions by means of this concept.

Type I Solutions: The scope of an updater remains invariant during restructuring, which implies that an updater must have its scope locked so that other updaters are excluded.

Type II Solutions: The scope of an updater may be changed during its restructuring phase. Only nodes affected by an updater at each step during restructuring are locked so that other updaters are excluded. These nodes are referred to as the <u>local scope of the updater</u>.

This leaves those solutions which are neither Type I nor Type II. However only one such solution is known to the authors, which is discussed in Section 5.

3. Type I Solutions

A conceptual picture of all Type I solutions is:

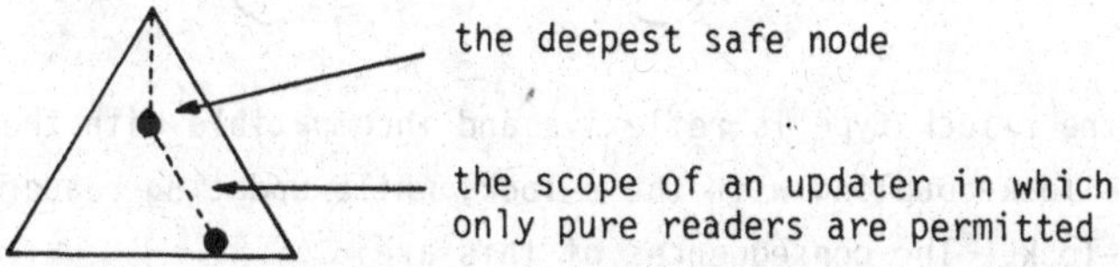

Among ten proposed solutions in the literature, seven of them are Type I.

(1) Samadi and Parr: The solution given by Samadi [S] in 1976 for node search B-trees is the earliest solution available. Independently Parr [P] in 1977 gave a similar solution for leaf search B-trees. In both solutions only one lock type is used, two processes cannot lock the same node simultaneously and there are only the lock and unlock operations available. Thus the lock and unlock can be considered as P and V operations on a binary semaphores; its CCG is:

Two important locking techniques are introduced.

(L1) <u>Scope locking by updaters</u>: An updater first locks the root, then as it continues on its root-to-leaf path it locks nodes. Whenever a safe node is locked, all its ancestors are unlocked.

(L2) <u>Node locking by pure readers</u>: A pure reader first locks the root and then it continues on its root-to-leaf path locking and unlocking nodes. Whenever it has locked a node it unlocks its father.

Two consequences of this locking scheme are:

(a) a total ordering is imposed on all readers sharing a common path, that is overtaking is prevented.

(b) when an updater has locked its scope no other processes can operate on the nodes in the scope or be waiting in the queues of these nodes other than the leading one.

Immediately all the difficulties posed in Section 2 are avoided at the cost of sacrificing Properties 1-3 of readers.

L1 and L2 are in fact special cases of a more general locking technique:

(L3) Lock-coupling principle: A process which has locked a set of nodes N does not unlock all nodes in N until its request to lock another set of nodes M is granted.

Usually M consists of either the descendants or ancestors of the set N, depending on the direction of the process.

(2) Bayer and Schkolnick: In [BS] a solution similar to those of [S] and [P] is proposed for leaf search B-trees. However they use two lock types, r(ead)-locks and e(xclusive)-locks, whose CCG is:

Note that the r-lock type is reflexive and incompatible with the e-lock type. Pure readers use lock-coupling with the r-lock, while updating readers use lock-coupling with the e-lock. The consequences of this are:

(a) more than one pure reader may be simultaneously reading at a node and pure readers can overtake each other.

(b) a total ordering is imposed on updating readers sharing a common path.

(c) an updater "drives off" pure readers from its scope by e-locking its scope starting at its deepest safe node.

(a) and (b) are easily seen and (c) follows because pure readers use r-lock coupling and e- and r-lock types are incompatible. This gives rise to another general locking technique:

(L4) Driving-off principle: Let α and β be two distinct incompatible lock types. Let π_α be a process which uses α-locks and π_β be a process which uses β-locks. If processes π_α and π_β proceed in the same direction and π_α uses a lock coupling technique then π_β can drive off all processes π_α along any path by β-locking the leading node and using the lock-coupling technique along the path.

In this case Property 1 holds for pure readers, Property 2 is sacrificed completely and Property 3 holds for pure readers.

(3) Bayer and Schkolnick: In [BS] a variant of Solution 2 is presented, namely updating readers also use r-locks, except that when a leaf node is found it is e-locked. If it is not safe then updating is repeated using Solution 2.

This variant is based on the observation that leaf nodes are safe most of the time.

(4) Bayer and Schkolnick: Here three lock types are used, read-locks, w(rite)-locks and exclusive-locks, whose CCG is:

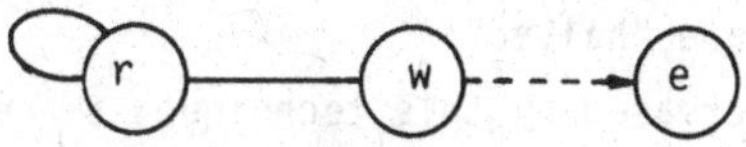

The r-lock type is reflexive and compatible with the w-lock type, which is irreflexive. The e-lock type is incompatible with both r- and w-lock types and a w-lock can be converted to an e-lock.

The solution is similar to Solution 2 except that updating readers use w-locks rather than e-locks. Once an updater has w-locked its scope no other updaters can be present, but pure readers may be present since the r- and w-locks are compatible. Hence before restructuring commences the updater e-locks its scope beginning at its leading node. This drives off the pure readers.

Again Property 3 holds for pure readers except that a pure reader can overtake an updating reader and vice versa, thus providing for a greater degree of concurrency than Solution 2.

(5) Ellis: Ellis [E] proposes a solution for leaf-search B-trees which is a variant of Solution 4. However she does not include DELETE processes. The key idea is:

> Pure readers are allowed to be in the scope of an updater during its restructuring phase as well as during its search phase.

This means that the scope of an updater is never completely e-locked thus causing Difficulties 2, 3 and 6 to resurface. Difficulties 3 and 6 can be avoided at a node u by converting the w-lock at the father of u into an e-lock, which empties the queue at u. This is an application of the technique for driving-off readers. Difficulty 2 is dealt with by using the <u>RW-addition technique</u>:

> The readers and writers at a node are required to proceed in opposite directions. This enables a reader to read a node correctly even when a writer is adding a key and a subtree to the node at the same time.

This is an application of a technique introduced by Lamport [L].

(6) Kwong and Wood: In [KW2] a solution for node search B-trees is proposed, which improves Solutions 4 and 5 by introducing a new restructuring technique called <u>side-branching</u>, discovered also by Kung and Lehman [KL] for binary search-trees. It uses the r-, w- and e-locks of Solution 4 as well as the same CCG.

During the restructuring caused by an INSERT process, nodes which obtain m+1 sons have to be <u>split</u> [BM] into two nodes, and the restructuring is then repeated at the next higher level. <u>Side-branching</u> however carries out the splitting in two passes. In the first pass whenever a split should be made at a node u a new node v is created which is given half of the keys of u (left or right half appropriately) and otherwise u is undisturbed. This is then repeated up the tree until the deepest safe node is met. At this time the "side-branch" is connected to the deepest safe node and then the original path is scanned once more driving off the pure readers and erasing the appropriate halves of the nodes.

Using this scheme means that the side branch is built up completely independently. Secondly the readers are driven off the original path by using lock-coupling with e-locks, while the nodes are "halved".

Thus concurrency is increased by this technique, since the first phase, building the side branch, can be carried out without converting the w-locks to e-locks on the scope. Not only can new pure readers enter the scope even when restructuring has commenced as in Solution 5, but also the number of times a node is e-locked is reduced by a half.

A further improvement over Solution 5 is that DELETE is also included, again using the side-branching technique. The RW-addition technique is used here as well but in an improved form using a repeated-reading technique, for details see [KW2].

4. Type II Solutions

In these solutions the basic idea is to allow other updaters into the scope of an updater. This is done by locking only a bounded number of nodes within its scope at each restructuring step. Hence the deepest safe node of an updater is no longer invariant during the restructuring phase. All Type II solutions are very recent.

(1) Ellis: In [E] a solution is given for leaf search B-trees for which only MEMBER AND INSERT processes are allowed.

Both pure and updating readers use lock coupling with r-locks and hence Properties 1, 2 and 3 are fulfilled completely. When an updating reader becomes a writer it uses lock coupling with w-locks up the tree to lock its local scope. This means that Difficulties 4, 5 and 7 arise once more, in fact they arise in all Type II solutions since writers and readers can appear in each others scope.

Both Difficulties 4 and 5 can be avoided by using the lock-coupling technique and enlarging the local scope of a writer such that interference cannot take place. However deadlock may occur when a reader collides with a writer, since both employ lock-coupling. If the collision occurs above the leaf level deadlock is avoided because r- and w-locks are compatible and readers can be driven down the tree by a writer using e-locks. If the collision occurs at the leaf level, pure readers can still be dealt with, however updating readers cause a deadlock since they need to restructure upwards. Ellis avoids this possibility by having a new lock type for writers at the leaf level and by altering the B-tree structure at the leaves [E]. This is however a major modification in our classification and therefore violates Assumption 2.

(2) Miller and Snyder: In [MS] a solution is given for node search B-trees using three lock types, a(ccess)-locks, p(ioneer)-locks and f(ollower)-locks, the CCG is:

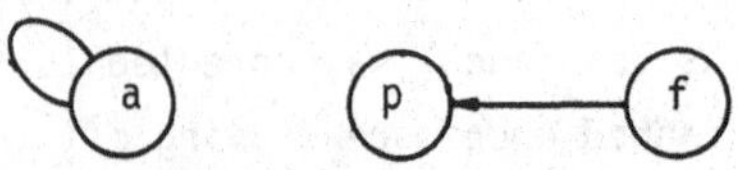

Two main ideas are presented in this solution.

First, readers are decoupled; they search using a-locks, but without the lock-coupling technique. A writer uses lock-coupling with p-locks. Since the a- and p-lock types are incompatible the readers must not use lock-coupling since this would cause deadlocks to occur. However this decoupling prevents the driving-off of readers. Hence [MS] allow explicit queue manipulation, which violates Assumption 3b.

Second, asymmetric locking is introduced. When two writers W_1 and W_2 collide, one of them W_1 say will p-lock the common ancestor, while W_2 must wait. However W_1 may have to modify nodes already held by W_2, therefore [MS] use the f-lock in this situation. W_1 can f-lock any node which is p-locked by W_2, but not vice versa.

One of the major disadvantages of their solution is that although they bound the number of nodes locked by any process at any time, this bound depends on the order of the B-trees. Hence for any large order B-tree (≥ 300 say) the number of nodes locked is completely unacceptable and reduces the "solution" to a pseudo Type I solution in most practical situations.

(3) Lehman and Yao: The solution considered in [LY] for leaf-search B-trees is quite interesting for a number of reasons. No read-locks are used at all, since the need for read-locks is avoided by each process making its own private copy of each node it processes. However this has an effect similar to locking a node.

Their solution also has a constant number of nodes locked at each step of the process; this number is independent of the order of the B-tree. Moreover they avoid the use of father links since each process can remember its path in its private memory. However they introduce right neighbour links, which are useful during node-splitting. In particular Difficulty 3 is avoided by this technique since whenever a node is examined for a particular key k and k is greater than all routing keys in the node then the right neighbour node is also examined. Moreover this is a minor modification according to our classification.

(4) Kwong and Wood: In [KW2] the notion of asymmetric locking introduced by [MS] is used to develop a solution for MEMBER AND INSERT in node search B-trees. The number of nodes locked at each step of a process is a small constant, which is independent of the order of the B-tree. Different and compatible lock types are used for pure and updating readers to avoid deadlocks at the leaf level, their CCG is:

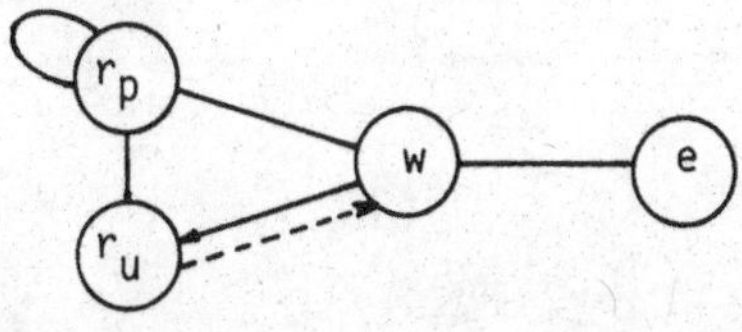

The repeated-reading technique is also used here to avoid exclusive locking of a node.

However this solution while avoiding deadlocks does allow for livelocks.

5. Miscellaneous Solutions

The only solution known to the authors which is neither Type I nor Type II is that proposed by Guibas and Sedgewick [GS] for node-search B-trees. They develop new sequential updating algorithms, which only do a single root-to-leaf scan. Thus it appears they can be adapted to a concurrent environment with little difficulty. Although the one-pass updating algorithm promises much as far as concurrency is concerned, it is not clear that all difficulties are solved. More investigation of the algorithms developed in [GS] needs to be made. Two points noted in [GS] are (a) readers and writers will not interfere provided that they lock a small bounded number of nodes in the B-tree and (b) deletion still causes problems since the key can be interior to the tree.

6. Open Problems

Each of the investigations of concurrency in B-trees presented here discusses either leaf search or node search B-trees, never both. One natural question is: can a solution for a leaf search B-tree easily be transformed into a solution for node search B-trees and vice versa? Although no definitive answer to this question is known, some preliminary work in [KW4] and [KW5] indicates that it depends on the routing scheme used for the leaf search B-trees. If the routing scheme is "clean" then the solutions for node and leaf search trees may be interchangeable as far as MEMBER and INSERT are concerned. In [KW5] it is shown that Type II solutions including DELETE for leaf search B-trees can be obtained, while for node search B-trees it is not clear whether this is possible under Assumptions 1, 2 and 3.

A second problem concerns a proof of correctness of the proposed solutions. Only informal proofs are given in most papers on concurrency in B-trees. Are the techniques introduced in [K1] and [K2] applicable here?

Third, how can solutions be compared? That is when is one solution "better" than another? The notion "degree of concurrency" appears to be one means of comparing the solutions, yet it has no precise definition.

Fourth, [GS] have modified the basic updating algorithms to give a simpler solution, while [LY] have modified the B-tree structure in a uniform way to obtain a reasonable Type II solution. Are there other reasonable modifications to the data structure and/or updating algorithms which will provide extremely simple solutions?

References

[AHU] Aho, A. V., Hopcroft, J. E. and Ullman, J. D. The Design and Analysis of Computer Algorithms. Addison-Wesley, Reading, Mass. (1974).

[BM] Bayer, R. and McCreight, E. Organization and maintenance of large ordered indexes. Acta Informatica 1 (1972), pp. 173-189.

[BS] Bayer, R. and Schkolnick, M. Concurrency of operations on B-trees. Acta Informatica 9 (1977), pp. 1-21.

[E] Ellis, C. S. Concurrent search and insertion in 2-3 trees. Acta Informatica (1980), to appear.

[GS] Guibas, L. J. and Sedgewick, R. A dichromatic framework for balanced trees. Proc. 19th Annual Symposium on Foundation of Computer Science (1978),

[Kn] Knuth, D. E. The Art of Computer Programming, Vol. 3: Sorting and Searching. Addison-Wesley, Reading, Mass. (1973).

[KL] Kung, H. T. and Lehman, P. L. A concurrent database manipulation problem: binary search trees. To appear in ACM Trans. on Database Systems.

[K1] Kwong, Y. S. On reduction of asynchronous systems. Theoretical Computer Science (1977), pp. 25-50.

[K2] Kwong, Y. S. On the absence of livelocks in parallel programs. Proc. International Symposium on Semantics of Concurrent Computation, Lecture Notes in Computer Science 70, Springer-Verlag (1979), pp. 172-190.

[KW1] Kwong, Y. S. and Wood, D. T-trees: a variant of B-trees. Technical Report 78-CS-18, Unit for Computer Science, McMaster University (Nov., 1978).

[KW2] Kwong, Y. S. and Wood, D. Concurrency in B-trees, S-trees and T-trees. Technical Report 79-CS-17, Unit for Computer Science, McMaster University (May, 1979).

[KW3] Kwong, Y. S. and Wood, D. Concurrent operations in large ordered indexes. Proc. 4th Intl. Symposium on Programming, Lecture Notes in Computer Science 83, Springer-Verlag (1980), pp. 207-222.

[KW4] Kwong, Y. S. and Wood, D. On B-trees: routing schemes and concurrency. Proc. 1980 ACM/SIGMOD Intl. Conference on Management of Data (May, 1980).

[KW5] Kwong, Y. S. and Wood, D. A solution to the concurrent deletion problem for B-trees. Technical Report 80-CS-7, Unit for Computer Science, McMaster University (April, 1980).

[LY] Lehman, P. and Yao, S. B. Efficient locking for concurrent operations on B-trees. In preparation.

[MS] Miller, R. E. and Snyder, L. Multiple access to B-trees. Proc. Conference on Information Sciences and Systems (1978).

[P] Parr, J. R. An access method for concurrently sharing a B-tree based indexed sequential file. Technical Report 36, Dept. of Computer Science, University of Western Ontario (April, 1977).

[S] Samadi, B. B-trees in a system with multiple users. Information Processing Letters 5, 4 (1976), pp. 107-112.

ON A SUBCLASS OF PSEUDOPOLYNOMIAL PROBLEMS [1]

BURKHARD MONIEN
UNIVERSITÄT PADERBORN
PADERBORN, WEST - GERMANY

ABSTRACT

A subclass of the class of all pseudopolynomial problems is defined as a family of sets acceptable by some automaton operating with simultaneous time and space bounds. That the class is large enough can be seen in that it contains many (if not all) of the pseudopolynomial problems described in the literature. We study structure preserving reductions within this class and give intuitive reasons (borrowed from our knowledge about space bounded automata) that there exist at least four well known problems which are pairwise not equivalent under these reductions.

1. INTRODUCTION

In this paper we consider problems which are $\mathbb{NP}$-complete but whose complexity depends polynomially on some number defined by the input. We assume that the reader is familiar with the notions $\mathbb{P}$,and $\mathbb{NP}$-complete. Let our reductions " $\leq$ " be those defined by deterministic log-space bounded Turing machines.

Though all $\mathbb{NP}$ - complete problems have the same worst case behaviour up to polynomial transformations, there exist $\mathbb{NP}$ - complete problems which behave numerically well in most applications.

We consider as an example the subset sum problem

$$SUB = \{a_1 ¢ \ldots ¢ a_n ¢ b \mid n,b,a_i \in \mathbb{N},\ 1 \leq i \leq n, \text{ and } \exists\, I \subset \{1, \ldots, n\} : \sum_{i \in I} a_i = b\}$$

where we assume that the numbers a_i, b, $1 \leq i \leq n$, are encoded by their binary notation. SUB is $\mathbb{NP}$-complete ([6]), but on the other hand it is well known that SUB is solved also by a deterministic algorithm working within the time-bound $O(n \cdot b)$. Note that this does not imply that SUB belongs to $\mathbb{P}$, since b grows exponentially with the length of its binary notation.

There have been two approaches to formalize this behaviour: (1) M.R. Garey and D.S. Johnson ([5]) introduce a function Max: {correct encodings} $\to \mathbb{N}$ that associates to the encoding of a problem the largest number occuring in this encoding. They call a problem pseudopolynomial if there exists an algorithm which works for any input w with the time bound $O((|w| + \text{Max}(w))^q)$ for some $q \in \mathbb{N}$.

(2) Paz, Moran ([1o]) and Ausiello et al. ([1]) consider optimization problems. They define the notions "simple" and "p-simple". We will not give their definitions here. If a p-simple optimization problem is replaced by an encoding as a language

---

[1] Some of this work was done while the author visited the department of Mathematics, University of California at Santa Barbara, where it was supported in part by the National Science Foundation under grant MCS 77 - 1136o.

(in the usual way $f(x) = \text{Max}$ is replaced by $\exists x: f(x) \geq D$), then this language is pseudopolynomial with the additional property that the corresponding algorithm is also polynomial in D.

We use in this paper a formalization which generalizes the notion "pseudopolynomial" in the following way: We associate to a problem a function g: {correct encodings} $\to \mathbb{N}$ and we call the problem pseudopolynomial if it can be solved for any input w with the time bound $O((|w| + g(w))^q)$ for some $q \in \mathbb{N}$. Of course, now a problem is pseudopolynomial only in connection with this function g. We get the old notion of "pseudopolynomial" if we take g = Max. (Actually our definition will be still more general by allowing relations instead of functions.)

In order to state this definition formally we consider sets $R \subset X^* \times X^*$ for some alphabet X.

Let $R \subset X^* \times X^*$ be some set and let $f: \mathbb{N} \times \mathbb{N} \to \mathbb{N}$ be some function. We say that R is accepted by a Turing machine (this machine may be deterministic or nondeterministic) within the time bound or space bound, respectively, $f(n,m)$, if M accepts $(u,v) \in X^* \times X^*$ iff $(u,v) \in R$ and if for any $(u,v) \in R$ there exists an accepting computation which needs not more than $f(|u|, |v|)$ steps (or cells, respectively).

<u>Definition</u>: $R \subset X^* \times X^*$ is called pseudopolynomial iff there exists some polynomial p, some $d \in \mathbb{N}$ and some deterministic Turing machine accepting R within the time-bound $p(n+m) \cdot d^m$.

Note that the complexity of accepting a pair (u,v) grows polynomial with the number which is encoded by v. We denote by PP the family of all pseudopolynomial sets.

We define now reductions between sets of pairs in such a way that the number given by the second component grows at most polynomially (that means that the length of the second component grows at most linearly).

<u>Definition</u>: For $R_1, R_2 \in PP$ we say $R_1 \leq_\pi R_2$ if there exist functions $f_1, f_2 \in \text{DSPACE}(\log n)$ such that

(1) $(u,v) \in R_1 \Leftrightarrow (f_1(u,v), f_2(u,v)) \in R_2$

(2) $|f_1(u,v)| \geq |u|$ and $\exists c \in \mathbb{N}: |f_2(u,v)| \leq c \cdot |v|$ $\quad \forall u,v \in X^*$

We use this more general notion of "pseudopolynomial" since:

- under this definition the class PP is closed under $\leq_\pi$ reductions and this allows us to speak about "complete" problems

- there were very good practical reasons to define "pseudopolynomial" in terms of maximum numbers as in [5], since many scheduling and knapsack-like problems are pseudopolynomial in this sense (and in fact all the applied problems we consider in the next section are also pseudopolynomial under the old definition). On the other hand, if we are interested in the structure of $\mathbb{N}$P-complete problems, we may ask whether there are other structural properties than just the maximal number which make a problem behave pseudopolynomially. It is shown in [9] that for graph theory problems the bandwidth of the graph plays the same role as the length of the maximal number does for scheduling problems, i.e. for many graph theory problems the set

$\{(u,v)\ |u$ is an encoding of a graph G with the given property and $v = 0^{f(u)}$, where $f(u)$ = bandwith of the graph encoded by $u\}$ is pseudopolynomial in our sense.

- we will show that there exists a problem which is complete for RPP, the class of restricted pseudopolynomial problems (defined below), and which is pseudopolynomial in the sense of [5]. This means that RPP is just the $\leq_\pi$-closure of a problem which is pseudopolynomial in the old sense.

Definition: $R \subset X^* \times X^*$ is called a restricted pseudopolynomial problem (and the class of all such problems is denoted by RPP) iff there exists some nondeterministic Turing machine accepting R with the space bound $\max\{\log n, m\}$ and the simultaneous time bound $(n+m)^q$ for some $q \in \mathbb{N}$.

This definition implies that for any $R \in$ RPP the language $L_R = \{u \not c\, v \mid (u,v) \in R\}$ belongs to $\mathbb{N}$P. Furthermore the nondeterministic Turing machine accepting R within the space bound $\max\{\log n, m\}$ can be simulated by some deterministic Turing machine accepting R within the time bound $n^q \cdot d^m$ for some $q, d \in \mathbb{N}$.

This implies that RPP $\subset$ PP. Furthermore we note that the deterministic algorithm which simulates the nondeterministic tape bounded Turing machine is a so called "dynamic programming" algorithm. We will see in the next section that RPP contains many of the pseudopolynomial problems studied in the literature. The algorithms which are given in the literature for solving these problems are also "dynamic programming" algorithms reflecting just the behaviour of the corresponding nondeterministic space bounded Turing machine. We feel this observation simplifies the search for pseudopolynomial-time algorithms since it is generally easier to define a space bounded automaton than to construct the corresponding "dynamic programming" algorithm.

It is clear that there exists a close relationship between RPP and the classes of languages defined by nondeterministic Turing machines operating with sublinear space bounds and polynomial time bounds simultaneously. Let us denote by NPTIME SPACE(f) the class of all languages accepted by some nondeterministic Turing machine within polynomial time and simultaneous space bound f. Let us further associate to each $R \in$ PP and to each function $f: \mathbb{N} \to \mathbb{N}$ the language

$L_R(f) = \{u \not c\, v \mid (u,v) \in R$ and $|v| \leq f(|u|)\}$. Then the following theorem holds.

Theorem 1: Let f be any monotonic increasing function which is computable by a deterministic log-space bounded Turing machine and which fulfills $f(n) \geq \log n \quad \forall n \in \mathbb{N}$.

(1) PP and RPP are closed under $\leq_\pi$ reductions

(2) $R_1, R_2 \in$ PP, $R_1 \leq_\pi R_2 \Rightarrow L_{R_1}(f) \leq L_{R_2}(f)$

(3) $R \in$ RPP $\Rightarrow L_R(f) \in$ NPTIMESPACE(f)

(4) R is complete for RPP with respect to $\leq_\pi$

$\Rightarrow L_R(f)$ is complete for $\bigcup_d$ NPTIMESPACE$(f(n^d))$ with respect to $\leq$.

Proof: (1) We have to show that $R_1 \leq_\pi R_2$ and $R_2 \in$ PP(RPP) implies $R_1 \in$ PP(RPP). Suppose $R_1 \leq_\pi R_2$. Then there exist $g_1, g_2 \in$ DSPACE(log n) such that $|g_2(u,v)| \leq c \cdot |v|$ for some $c \in \mathbb{N}$ and $(u,v) \in R_1 \Leftrightarrow (g_1(u,v), g_2(u,v)) \in R_2$. Therefore if $R_2 \in$ PP then there exists a deterministic Turing machine accepting R_1 with the time bound

$(|g_1(u,v)|+|g_2(u,v)|)^q \cdot d^{|g_2(u,v)|} \leq (|u|+|v|)^{\tilde{q}} \cdot \tilde{d}^{|v|}$ for some $q,d,\tilde{q},\tilde{d} \in \mathbb{N}$. If $R_2 \in RPP$ then there exists a nondeterministic Turing machine accepting R_1 with the time bound $(|g_1(u,v)|+|g_2(u,v)|)^q \leq (|u|+|v|)^{\tilde{q}}$ and the space bound $\max\{\log|g_1(u,v)|, |g_2(u,v)|\} \leq \tilde{c}\cdot\max\{\log|u|, |v|\}$. Therefore $R_1 \in PP$ ($R_1 \in RPP$, respectively).

(2) Suppose R_1, $R_2 \in PP$ and $R_1 \leq_\pi R_2$. Then there exist g_1, $g_2 \in DSPACE(\log n)$ such that $|g_1(u,v)| \geq |u|$, $|g_2(u,v)| \leq c\cdot|v|$ for some $c \in \mathbb{N}$ and $(u,v) \in R_1 \Leftrightarrow (g_1(u,v), g_2(u,v)) \in R_2$. If $R_2 = X^* \times X^*$ then also $R_1 = X^* \times X^*$ and obviously $R_1 = R_2$ implies $L_{R_1}(f) = L_{R_2}(f)$. Now suppose $R_2 \neq X^* \times X^*$ and take $(u_o,v_o) \in X^* \times X^* - R_2$. Define g by $g(u \cent v) = (u_o,v_o)$ if $|v| > f(|u|)$ and $g(u \cent v) = g_1(u,v) \cent g_2(u,v)$ otherwise. Then $g \in DSPACE(\log n)$ and $u \cent v \in L_{R_1}(f) \Leftrightarrow (u,v) \in R_1$ and $|v| \leq f(|u|) \Rightarrow (g_1(u,v), g_2(u,v)) \in R_2$ and $|g_2(u,v)| \leq c\cdot|v| \leq c\cdot f(|u|) \leq c\cdot f(g_1(u,v)) \Leftrightarrow g(u \cent v) \in L_{R_2}(f)$. On the other hand, if $g(u \cent v) \in L_{R_2}(f)$ then $(g_1(u,v), g_2(u,v)) \in R_2$ and (because of the definition of g) $|v| \leq f(|u|)$. This implies $u \cent v \in L_{R_1}(f)$. So we have shown that $u \cent v \in L_{R_1}(f) \Leftrightarrow g(u \cent v) \in L_{R_2}(f)$.

(3) Let M be a nondeterministic Turing machine accepting R with the time bound $(n+m)^q$ for some $q \in \mathbb{N}$ and with the space bound $\max\{\log n, m\}$. We define a nondeterministic Turing machine M', accepting $L_R(f)$, in the following way: (i) M' tests whether its input has the form $u \cent v$ with $u,v \in X^*$ and $|v| \leq f(|u|)$; (ii) M' simulates the behaviour of M on (u,v). Clearly M' operates in polynomial time and with the space bound f.

(4) Let L be a language which is complete for $\bigcup_d$ NPTIMESPACE $(f(n^d))$. We can assume that $L \in$ NPTIMESPACE(f). Set $\tilde{R} = \{(u, 0^{f(|u|)}) \mid u \in L\}$.
We want to show that $\tilde{R} \in RPP$. Let M be a nondeterministic Turing machine accepting L within polynomial time and the space bound f. We define a nondeterministic Turing machine M' accepting $\tilde{R}$ in the following way: (i) M' checks whether the input has the form (u,v) with $u \in X^*$ and $v = 0^{f(|u|)}$, (ii) M' simulates the behaviour of M on the string u. Obviously M operates within polynomial time and the space bound $|v|$. Therefore $\tilde{R} \in RPP$ and since R is complete for RPP we get $\tilde{R} \leq_\pi R$. Since f is computable by some deterministic log-space bounded Turing machine, $L \leq L_{\tilde{R}}(f) = \{u \cent 0^{f(|u|)} \mid u \in L\}$ and because of (2) this implies $L \leq L_{\tilde{R}}(f) \leq L_R(f)$. Because of (3) $L_R(f) \in$ NPTIMESPACE(f) and therefore $L_R(f)$ is complete for this class. □

2. REDUCTIONS BETWEEN CONCRETE PROBLEMS

We consider in this section the following problems whose language-encodings are all known to be complete for $\mathbb{N}$P.

(1) subset sum

$$RSUB = \{(a_1 \cent \ldots \cent a_n, b) \mid a_1 \cent \ldots \cent a_n \cent b \in SUB\}$$

(2) partition into k subsets

$$RPAR(k) = \{(a_1 ¢ \dots ¢ a_n, \sum_{i=1}^{n} a_i) \mid \exists\, I_1, \dots, I_k \subset \{1,\dots,n\}: \bigcup_{\nu=1}^{k} I_\nu = \{1,\dots,n\},\ I_\nu \cap I_\mu = \emptyset \text{ for } \nu \neq \mu \text{ and } \sum_{i\in I_\nu} a_i = \sum_{i \in I_\mu} a_i \text{ for all } \nu, \mu \in \{1,\dots,k\}\}$$

(3) multi-processor scheduling on k processors

$$RMPS(k) = \{(a_1 ¢ \dots ¢ a_n, D) \mid \exists\, I_1, \dots, I_k \subset \{1,\dots,n\}: \bigcup_{\nu=1}^{k} I_\nu = \{1,\dots,n\} \text{ and } \sum_{i\in I_\nu} a_i \le D \text{ for all } \nu = 1, \dots, k\}$$

(4) sequencing to minimize tardy task weight

$$RTTW = \{(t_1 ¢ w_1 ¢ d_1 ¢ \dots ¢ t_n ¢ w_n ¢ d_n ¢ W, \max (W, \sum_{i=1}^{n} t_i) \mid \exists \text{ permutation } \sigma: \{1,\dots,n\} \to \{1,\dots,n\} \text{ such that } \sum_{\nu \in I} w_\nu \le W \text{ where } I = \{\nu \mid \sum_{i=1}^{\nu} t_{\sigma(i)} > d_{\sigma(\nu)}\}\}$$

(5) scheduling to minimize weighted mean flow time on k processors

$$RWMFT(k) = \{t_1 ¢ w_1 ¢ \dots ¢ t_n ¢ w_n, W) \mid \exists\, I_1,\dots,I_k \subset \{1,\dots,n\} \text{ and permutations } \sigma_\nu: \{1,\dots, |I_\nu|\} \to I_\nu,\ 1 \le \nu \le k, \text{ such that } \bigcup_{\nu=1}^{k} I_\nu = \{1,\dots,n\} \text{ and } \sum_{\nu=1}^{k} \sum_{i=1}^{|I_\nu|} w_{\sigma_\nu(i)} \sum_{\sigma_\nu(j) \le \sigma_\nu(i)} t_{\sigma_\nu(j)} \le W\}$$

(6) selecting numbers from blocks of length k

$$RSEL(k) = \{(a_1 ¢ \dots ¢ a_{k\cdot n}, b) \mid \exists\, I \subset \{1,\dots,n\} : \sum_{i\in I} a_i = b \text{ and } |I \cap \{a_{i+1},\dots, a_{i+k}\}| = 1 \quad \forall\, i=0, \dots, n-1\}$$

selecting numbers from blocks of arbitrary length

$$RSEL = \{(a_{11} ¢ \dots ¢ a_{1l_1} \# \dots \# a_{n1} ¢ \dots ¢ a_{nl_n}, b) \mid \exists\, j_1,\dots,j_n : 1 \le j_i \le l_i \quad \forall i \text{ and } \sum_{i=1}^{n} a_{ij_i} = b\}$$

(7) solving a linear equation with lower bounds on the subsums

$$RLBS = \{(a_1 ¢ d_1 ¢ \dots ¢ a_n ¢ d_n, b) \mid \exists\, x_1, \dots, x_n \in \{0,1\}: \sum_{i=1}^{n} a_i x_i = b \text{ and } \sum_{i=1}^{j} a_i x_i \ge d_j \quad \forall j = 1,\dots,n\}$$

(8) solving a system of linear equations where the associated matrix $A = (a_{ij})$, $1 \le i \le n$, $1 \le j \le m$, has the form

A = 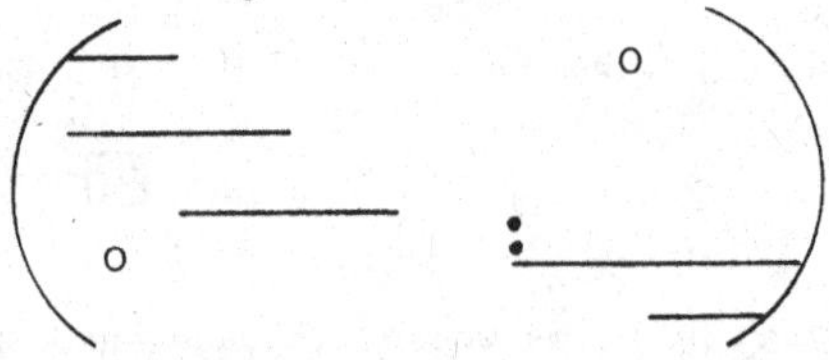

i.e. there exist $d_i \in \mathbb{N}$, $1 \le i \le n+2$, $d_1 \le d_2 \le \dots \le d_{n+2}$, $d_{n+1} = d_{n+2} = n$ such that for all $i=1,\dots,n$: $a_{ij} = 0$ for $j < d_i$ and for $j \ge d_{i+2}$

$$RLSE = \{(a_{11} ¢ a_{12} ¢ \dots ¢ a_{nm} ¢ b_1 ¢ \dots ¢ b_m, \max_i b_i) \mid A = (a_{ij}) \text{ fulfills the above condition, } a_{ij} \in \mathbb{N}, \text{ and } \exists x_1, \dots, x_m \in \{0,1\} \text{ such that } \sum_{j=1}^{m} a_{ij} x_j = b_i \quad \forall i = 1,\dots,n\}$$

(9) looking for a path with nonnegative weights

$$RGAP = \{(E ¢ Z_1 ¢ \dots ¢ Z_n, \max |Z_i|) \mid Z_i \in \mathbb{Z} \ \forall i = 1,\dots,n :$$
$E \subset \{1,\dots,n\} \times \{1,\dots,n\}$ and $(\{1,\dots,n\},E)$ forms an acylic graph;
there exist $r \in \mathbb{N}$ and $k_1, \dots, k_r \in \{1,\dots,n\}$ such
that $k_1 = 1$, $k_r = n$, $(k_i, k_{i+1}) \in E \quad \forall i = 1,\dots,r-1$ and
$$\sum_{\nu=1}^{i} Z_{k_\nu} \geq 0 \quad \forall i = 1,\dots,r-1 \text{ and } \sum_{\nu=1}^{r} Z_{k_\nu} = 0\}$$

(1o) solving a set of quadratic diophantine equations

$$RQDE = \{(a_1 ¢ \dots ¢ a_n ¢ b, d) \mid a_i, b, d \in \mathbb{N};\ \forall i \ \exists x_i, y_i \in \mathbb{N}: a_i x_i^2 + b y_i = d\}$$

We show first that all these problems belong to RPP. Because of theorem 1, (1) and the reductions which will be given in theorem 3 we have only to show:

<u>Theorem 2</u>: RLBS, RLSE, RWMFT(k) $\in$ RPP

<u>Proof</u>: (1) RLBS is accepted by a nondeterministic Turing machine M which scans with its input head the string $a_1 ¢ d_1 ¢ \dots ¢ a_n ¢ d_n$ and which stores on its work tape the sum S of all the a_j which have been chosen up to this point. When M reaches the number a_i it decides whether to set $x_i = 0$ or $x_i = 1$ and it sets $S := S + a_i$ if it has decided to set $x_i = 1$. Afterwards it checks whether $d_i \leq S \leq b$ holds. Having scanned the whole encoding it decides whether $S = b$ holds. Obviously $S \leq b$ holds during the whole computation. Therefore RLBS $\in$ RPP.

(2) In order to solve RLSE a Turing machine has to guess $x_1, \dots, x_m \in \{0,1\}$. Suppose now our machine M is in a configuration where it has to decide whether to set $x_k = 0$ or $x_k = 1$. Instead of storing $x_1,\dots,x_{k-1}$ (which would need too much space) it stores all the information it needs about the sums $\sum_{j=1}^{k-1} a_{ij} x_j$, $1 \leq i \leq n$. Let q be determined by $d_q \leq k < d_{q+1}$. Then because of the structure of A $\sum_{j=1}^{k-1} a_{ij} x_j = 0$ for $i \geq d_{q+1}$ (and therefore these sums need not be stored) and $\sum_{j=1}^{k-1} a_{ij} x_j = \sum_{j=1}^{m} a_{ij} x_j$ for $i \leq d_{q-2}$ and therefore A can only have a solution if $\sum_{j=1}^{k-1} a_{ij} x_j = b_i$ for $1 \leq i \leq d_{q-2}$. M has checked this before it reached our configuration and therefore M has only to store the numbers $y = \sum_{j=1}^{k-1} a_{d_{q-1} j} x_j$, $Z = \sum_{j=1}^{k-1} a_{d_q j} x_j$.

Having decided whether to set $x_k = 0$ or $x_k = 1$ M leaves these numbers unchanged or it changes them to $y := y + a_{d_{q-1} k}$, $Z := Z + a_{d_q k}$. M stops if one of these numbers is larger than $\max_i b_i$. It is obvious that M works with the space bound $\max_i |b_i|$ and therefore RLSE $\in$ RPP.

(3) It is wellknown (see [3]) that if an instance of RWMFT(k) has a solution then there exists also a solution such that $t_{\sigma_\nu(i)} / w_{\sigma_\nu(i)} \leq t_{\sigma_\nu(i+1)} / w_{\sigma_\nu(i+1)}$ holds for all $1 \leq \nu \leq k$ and for all $1 \leq i \leq |I_\nu| - 1$. Set $R_1(k) = \{(t_1 ¢ w_1 ¢ \dots ¢ t_n ¢ w_n, W) \mid (t_1 ¢ w_1 ¢ \dots ¢ t_n ¢ w_n, W) \in$ RWMFT(k) and $t_i / w_i \leq t_{i+1} / w_{i+1} \quad \forall\, 1 \leq i \leq n-1\}$. It is obvious that RWMTF(k) $\leq_\pi R_1(k)$.

We define a nondeterministic Turing machine M accepting $R_1(k)$. Its storage tape is divided into k+1 tracks and when it has to decide on which of the k processors the j-th task has to be performed, then it has already put all the tasks 1,...,j-1 into one of the set I_ν, $1 \le \nu \le k$, and it stores on its k+1 tracks the numbers $y_\nu = \sum_{i \in I_\nu,\, i \le j-1} t_i$, $1 \le \nu \le k$ and $Z = \sum_{\nu=1}^{k} \sum_{i \in I_\nu, i \le j-1} w_i \sum_{p \in I_\nu, p \le i} t_p$. When it decides that the j-th task has to be performed on processor q, $1 \le q \le k$, then it changes these numbers into $y_q := y_q + t_j$, $Z := Z + w_j\, y_q$. At the end M has to decide whether $Z \le W$ holds and it is clear that M can be constructed in such a way that all the numbers stored on its k+1 tracks are bounded by W during its whole computation. Therefore $R_1(k)$ belongs to RPP and because of theorem 1,(1) $\mathrm{RWMFT}(k) \le_\pi R_1(k)$ implies that RWMFT(k) belongs to RPP. □

In the next theorem we state those reductions between these problems which we are able to find. In the next section we will give some intuitive reasons that at least four of these problems are not reducible to each other. This indicates that $\le_\pi$ reductions define a rich structure among the problems belonging to our class RPP.

Theorem 3: RLSE is complete for RPP and there are reductions between the problems (1), ..., (1o) as shown in diagramm 1.

Proof: (1) It was shown in [7] that RLSE is complete for RPP (though a different notation was used in [7]).

(2) It is clear that $R\alpha(k) \le R\alpha(k+1)$ for α = PAR, MPS, WMFT, SEL and for all $k \in \mathbb{N}$ and that $\mathrm{RSEL}(k) \le \mathrm{RSEL}$ for all $k \in \mathbb{N}$. Furthermore RLBS, RQDE, $\mathrm{RWMFT}(k) \le \mathrm{RLSE}$ $\forall k \in \mathbb{N}$, since all these sets belong to RPP and RLSE is complete for RPP.

(3) We want to show $\mathrm{RSUB} \equiv_\pi \mathrm{RPAR}(2)$. $\mathrm{RPAR}(2) \le \mathrm{RSUB}$ holds since $(a_1 ¢ \ldots ¢ a_n, \max_i a_i) \in \mathrm{RPAR}(2)$ iff $\sum_{i=1}^{n} a_i \equiv 0 \bmod 2$ and $(a_1 ¢ \ldots ¢ a_n, \frac{1}{2}\sum_{i=1}^{n} a_i) \in \mathrm{RSUB}$. In order to show $\mathrm{RSUB} \le \mathrm{RPAR}(2)$ we have to consider two cases. Suppose an instance $(a_i ¢ \ldots ¢ a_n, b)$ is given and $\sum_{i=1}^{n} a_i \ge b$. Set $A = \sum_{i=1}^{n} a_i$. If $A \le 2b$ then $(a_1 ¢ \ldots ¢ a_n, b) \in \mathrm{RSUB}$ iff $(a_1 ¢ \ldots ¢ a_n ¢ 2b - A, 2b) \in \mathrm{RPAR}(2)$. If $A \ge 2b$ then $(a_1 ¢ \ldots ¢ a_n, b) \in \mathrm{RSUB}$ iff $(a_1 ¢ \ldots ¢ a_n ¢ A-2b, 2A-2b) \in \mathrm{RPAR}(2)$.

(4) We have to show $\mathrm{RPAR}(k) \equiv_\pi \mathrm{RMPS}(k)$ $\forall k \in \mathbb{N}$. $\mathrm{RPAR}(k) \le \mathrm{RMPS}(k)$ since $(a_1 ¢ \ldots ¢ a_n, \max_i a_i) \in \mathrm{RPAR}(k)$ iff $\sum_{i=1}^{n} a_i \equiv 0 \bmod k$ and $(a_1 ¢ \ldots ¢ a_n, \frac{1}{k}\sum_{i=1}^{n} a_i) \in \mathrm{RMPS}(k)$. In order to show $\mathrm{RMPS}(k) \le \mathrm{RPAR}(k)$ let $(a_1 ¢ \ldots ¢ a_n, D)$ be an instance of the multiprocessor scheduling. Set $E = k \cdot D - \sum_{i=1}^{n} a_i$. Let $p, q \in \mathbb{N}$ be defined by: p is the maximal number such that $k(2^{p+1} - 1) \le E$ and q is the maximal number such that $q \cdot 2^{p+1} \le E - k \cdot (2^{p+1} - 1)$. (Note that $p \le \log_2 E$ and that $q < k$.) Then $(a_1 ¢ \ldots ¢ a_n, D) \in \mathrm{RMPS}(k)$ iff $(a_1 ¢ \ldots ¢ a_n ¢ b_1 ¢ \ldots ¢ b_{k\cdot(p+1)} ¢ c_1 ¢ \ldots ¢ c_q ¢ d, D) \in \mathrm{RPAR}(k)$, where $b_{i \cdot k+\nu} = 2^i$ for $0 \le i \le p$, $1 \le \nu \le k$ and $c_j = 2^{p+1}$ for $1 \le j \le q$ and $d = E - k \cdot (2^{p+1} - 1) - q \cdot 2^{p+1}$.

(5) $\mathrm{RPAR}(k) \le_\pi \mathrm{RSEL}(k)$ since $(a_1 ¢ \ldots ¢ a_n, \max_i a_i) \in \mathrm{RPAR}(k)$ iff $\sum_{i=1}^{n} a_i = 0$ mod k and $(b_1 ¢ \ldots ¢ b_{k \cdot n}, D \cdot \sum_{i=0}^{k-1} A^i) \in \mathrm{SEL}(k)$, where $A = \sum_{i=1}^{n} a_i$ and $D = A/k$ and $b_{k \cdot i+1} = a_{i+1} A^{j-1}$ for $0 \le i \le n-1$, $1 \le j \le k$.

(6) $\mathrm{RPAR}(k) \le_\pi \mathrm{RWMFT}(k)$ was shown in [11] . S.K. Sahni showed that $(a_1 ¢ \ldots ¢ a_n, \max_i a_i) \in \mathrm{RPAR}(2)$ iff $\sum_{i=1}^{n} a_i = 0$ mod 2 and $(a_1 ¢ a_1 ¢ \ldots$

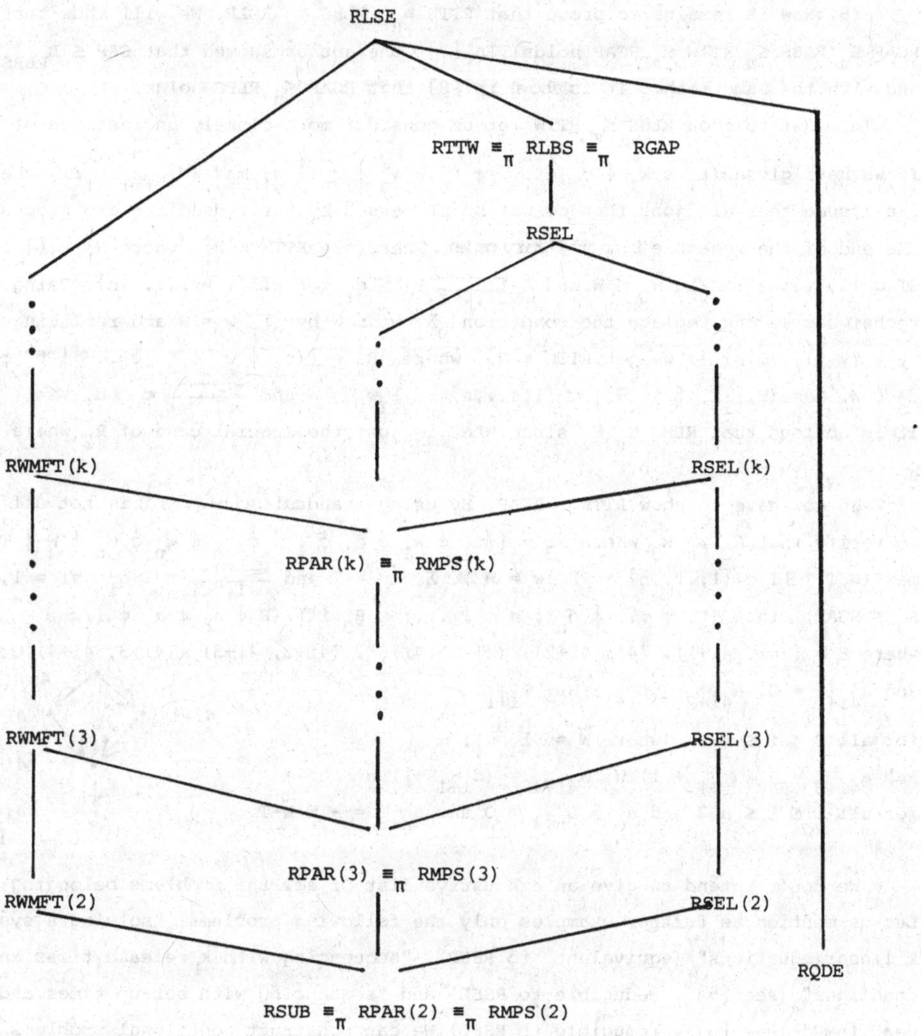

Diagram 1

$..¢\ a_n\ ¢\ a_{n'},\ \frac{1}{2}\sum_{i=1}^{n} a_i^2 + \frac{1}{4}\left(\sum_{i=1}^{n} a_i\right)^2) \in$ RWMFT(2).

(7) In order to show RSEL $\leq_\pi$ RGAP let us first mention that RSEL $\leq_\pi R_1$, where R_1 consists of all those selection problems where all blocks have the same length. (RSEL$\leq_\pi R_1$ holds since we can fill a block up to a given length with one of its elements). Now we have to show $R_1 \leq_\pi$ RGAP and this is true since

$(a_{11}\ ¢ \dots ¢\ a_{1\ell}\ ¢ \dots ¢\ a_{n1}\ ¢ \dots ¢\ a_{n\ell},\ b) \in R_1$ iff $(E\ ¢\ 0\ ¢\ a_{11}\ ¢ \dots ¢\ a_{1\ell}\ ¢\ 0\ ¢ \dots$ $. ¢\ 0\ ¢\ a_{n1}\ ¢ \dots ¢\ a_{n\ell}\ ¢ - b, \dots) \in$ RGAP, where $E \subset \{0,\dots,m\} \times \{0, \dots, m\}$, $m =$ $= n\cdot(\ell+1)$, is defined by $(i,j) \in E \Leftrightarrow$
$1 \leq j - i \leq \ell$ and $[i = k\cdot(\ell+1),$
$0 \leq k < n$ or $j = k\cdot(\ell+1),\ 1 \leq k \leq n]$.

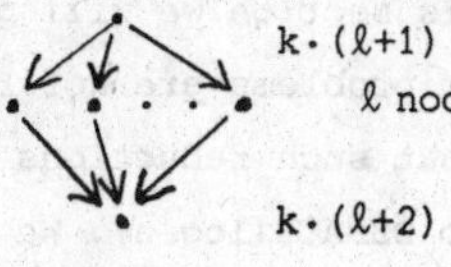

(8) Now it remains to prove that RTTW $\equiv_\pi$ RLBS $\equiv_\pi$ RGAP. We will show that RGAP $\le_\pi$ RLBS $\le_\pi$ RTTW $\le_\pi$ RGAP holds. In [7] the author showed that GAP $\le L_{RLBS}(\log n)$ and with the same method it is shown in [8] that RGAP $\le_\pi$ RLBS holds.

In order to show RLBS $\le_\pi$ RTTW let us consider more closely an instance of RTTW. If we have given $(t_1 \cent w_1 \cent d_1 \cent \ldots \cent t_n \cent w_n \cent d_n \cent W, \max(W, \sum_{i=1}^{n} t_i))$, then we can assume that all jobs that cannot be processed by their deadline are processed at the end of the schedule in an arbitrary order. Therefore RTTW $\equiv R_1$, where $R_1 = \{(\ldots,\ldots) \mid \exists I \subset \{1,\ldots,n\} : \sum_{\nu\in I} w_\nu \le W$ and $\overline{\sum_{\nu\in I,\nu<i}} t_\nu \le d_i$ for all $i = 1,\ldots,n\}$. Using standard techniques we can replace the condition $\sum_{\nu\in I} w_\nu \le W$ by $\sum_{\nu\in I} w_\nu = W$ and replacing finally I by $\{1,\ldots,n\}$ -I we get RTTW $\equiv R_2$, where $R_2 = \{(t_1 \cent w_1 \cent d_1 \cent \ldots \cent t_n \cent w_n \cent d_n \cent W, \max(W, \sum_{i=1}^{n} t_i)) \mid \exists I \subset \{1,\ldots,n\} : \sum_{\nu\in I} w_\nu = W$ and $\overline{\sum_{\nu\in I,\nu<i}} t_\nu > d_i \ \forall i=1,\ldots,n\}$. It is obvious that RLBS $\le_\pi R_2$ since RLBS is just the special case of R_2 where $w_\nu = t_\nu \ \forall \nu = 1, \ldots, n$.

We now have to show RTTW $\le$ RGAP. By using standard techniques it is not difficult to verify that $R_2 \equiv_\pi R_3$ where $R_3 = \{(t_1 \cent w_1 \cent d_1 \cent \ldots \cent t_n \cent w_n \cent d_n \cent W \cent T, \max(W,T) \mid \exists I \subset \{1,\ldots,n\} : \sum_{\nu\in I} w_\nu = W, \sum_{\nu\in I} t_\nu = T$ and $\overline{\sum_{\nu\in I,\nu<i}} t_\nu > d_i \ \forall i = 1,\ldots,n\}$. $R_3 \le$ RGAP, since $(t_1 \cent \ldots \cent d_n \cent W \cent T, \ldots) \in R_3$ iff $(E \cent a_0 \cent a_1 \cent \ldots \cent a_{4n}, \ldots) \in$ RGAP where $E = \{(4i, 4i+1), (4i, 4i+2), (4i+1, 4i+3), (4i+2, 4i+3), (4i+3, 4i+4) \mid 0 \le i \le n-1\}$ and $a_{4i+1} = 0$, $a_{4i+2} = t_{i+1} \cdot \tilde{W} + w_{i+1}$ for all $0 \le i \le n-1$ (where $\tilde{W} = \sum_{i=1}^{n} w_i$) and $a_{4i+3} = -(d_{i+1} + 1)\tilde{W}$, $a_{4i+4} = (d_{i+1} + 1)\tilde{W}$ for all $0 \le i \le n-2$ and $a_0 = a_{n+4} = 0$ and $a_{n+3} = -W \cdot \tilde{W} - T$.

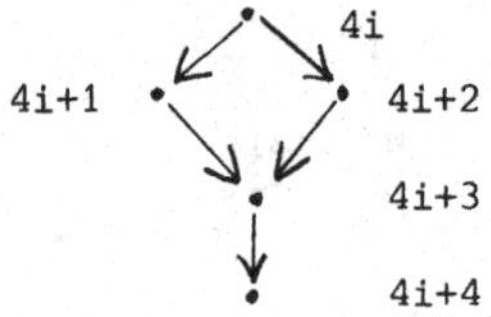

□

We don't intend to give an exhaustive list of all the problems belonging to RPP. Let us mention as further examples only the following problems: "solving a system of k linear equations" (equivalent to RSUB), "sequencing with k_1 release times and k_2 deadlines" (see [5], reducible to RSEL) and "sequencing with set-up times and k deadlines" (see [5], reducible to RSEL). We can construct additional problems which are complete for RPP by making our problems slightly more difficult, e.g. "finding a solution $x_i \in \{0,1\}$ of $\sum_{i=1}^{n} a_i x_i = b$, $\sum_{\nu=1}^{i} c_{j\nu} \ge d_i$ for $j = 1,2,3$ and $1 \le i \le n$" is complete for RPP. In [9] a great number of problems are shown to be complete for RPP just by taking various graph theory problems where the bandwidth of the graph is used as the structural information, e.g. the problem of finding a 3-colouring for a graph is complete for RPP (remember that we consider as inputs pairs $(G, 0^m)$ where m is the bandwidth of G).

3. CONNECTIONS TO SPACE BOUNDED COMPUTATIONS

In this section we will give intuitive reasons to support the conjecture that some of our problems are not reducible to each other. At the moment no method is known to prove that such reductions do not exist. It is an open question whether or not NP is equal to DSPACE(log n). We prove the following lemma:

Lemma 1: Let a be any symbol. If $\mathbb{N}$P=DSPACE(log n) then $R \leq_{\pi} \{(v,\varepsilon) \mid v\varepsilon\{a\}^*\}$ holds for any $R \in$ RPP.

Proof: Suppose $\mathbb{N}$P=DSPACE(log n). Then for any $R \in$ RPP the set $L_R = \{u ¢ v \mid (u, v) \in R\}$ belongs to DSPACE(log n) and $R \leq_{\pi} \tilde{R}$, where $\tilde{R} = \{(u ¢ v,\varepsilon) \mid (u,v) \in R\}$. There exists a function f which is computable by a deterministic log space bounded Turing machine such that $|f(w)| \geq |w|$ and $w \in L_R$ iff $f(w) \in \{a\}^*$. This implies $\tilde{R} \leq_{\pi} \{(v,\varepsilon) \mid v \in \{a\}^*\}$. □

The next lemma gives the basis for our intuitive reasons.

Lemma 2: (1) $L_{RQDE}(\log n) \in$ DSPACE(log n)

(2) There exists a language L_1 which is acceptable by some nondeterministic one-way reversal-bounded counter automaton (for a definition see [2], [8]) such that $L_{RSEL}(\log n) \equiv L_1$.

(3) $L_{RTTW}(\log n)$ is complete for NSPACE(log n).

Proof: (1) In order to solve $a_i x^2 + by = c$ we have only to consider x,y with $x,y \leq c$. This can be done by some deterministic Turing machine with the space bound $|c|$.

(2) Set $L_1 = \{0^{a_{11}} 1 0^{a_{12}} 1 \ldots 1 0^{a_{1\ell_1}} 11 \ldots 11\, 0^{a_{n1}} 1 \ldots 1 0^{a_{n\ell_n}} 111\, 0^b \mid \exists j_1,\ldots,j_n : 1 \leq j_i \leq \ell_i$ such that $\sum_{i=1}^{n} a_{ij_i} = b\}$. Note that the mapping c_1, associating to the binary encoding of a number its unary encoding, is computable by a deterministic Turing machine with a linear space bound and that its inverse mapping c_1^{-1} is computable by a deterministic Turing machine with the space bound log n. Therefore $R_1 \equiv L_{RSEL}(\log n)$ holds. Furthermore we can easily construct a nondeterministic one-way counter automaton M which changes the direction of its counter exactly once and which accepts L_1. M scans with its input head the input string from left to right and it takes from each block i exactly one number a_{ir_i} and adds it to its counter (i.e. while scanning $0^{a_{ir_i}}$ it increases the counter by 1 in each step). After it has reached 111 it starts to decrease the counter and checks whether the number stored by the counter is equal to b.

(3) It was shown in [7] that $L_{RLBS}(\log n)$ is complete for NSPACE(log n) and we showed in theorem 2 that RLBS $\equiv_{\pi}$ RTTW holds. □

We are now ready to state as conjectures that the following reductions do not exist:

Conjecture (1) RSEL is not reducible to RQDE

Conjecture (2) RTTW is not reducible to RSEL

Conjecture (3) RSLE is not reducible to RTTW

Note that because of the reductions given in theorem 1 "RSEL is not reducible to RQDE" implies that also RTTW and RLSE are not reducible to RQDE and that "RTTW is not reducible to RSEL" implies that also RLSE is not reducible to RSEL and that RTTW is not reducible to RMPS(k) for any $k \in \mathbb{N}$.

Reasons: (1) Because of lemma 2 $L_{RQDE}(\log n)$ belongs to DSPACE(log n). Quite a lot of work has been done to show $L_{RSUB}(\log n) \in DSPACE(\log^k n)$ for some $k < 2$. Since these efforts have failed we conjecture that $L_{RSEL}(\log n)$ does not belong to DSPACE $(\log n)$. If this is correct then RSEL $\leq_\pi$ RQDE cannot hold.

(2) Because of lemma 2 RTTW is complete for NSPACE(log n) and there exists a set L_1 which is acceptable by some nondeterministic one-way reversal-bounded counter automaton such that $L_1 \equiv L_{RSEL}(\log n)$. We conjecture that no language acceptable by a reversal bounded counter automaton can be complete for NSPACE(log n). (Note that such an automaton cannot get any information from its storage tape during its computation. It changes its storage tape only by means of its finite memory and only at the end of its computation it asks whether it was able to generate the number 0 in this way). If L_1 is not complete for NSPACE(log n) then RTTW $\leq_\pi$ RSEL cannot hold.

(3) $L_{RTTW}(f)$ is accepted by an automaton which gets from its storage tape only the information whether it is empty or not empty. In the case $f(n) = \log n$ such automata accept languages which are complete for NSPACE(log n). This is true since the number of different storage inscriptions is bounded polynomially in n and we can store the whole flow of information in one string which is bounded polynomially in n (this is just the proof that the graph accessibility problem is complete for NSPACE(log n), [12]). But if $\lim_{n\to\infty} f(n)/\log n = \infty$ then the number of possible storage inscription grows faster than any polynomial in n and therefore this method is not applicable. We believe that for $\lim_{n\to\infty} f(n)/\log n = \infty$ the language $L_{RTTW}(f)$ is not complete for NPTIMESPACE(f) and this implies that RLSE is not reducible to RTTW.

Finally we want to mention that there is annother natural class (let us call this class SPP) such that RPP $\subset$ SPP $\subset$ PP and $R \in SPP \Rightarrow L_R = \{u \not c\, v \mid (u,v) \in R\} \in NP$. R belongs to SPP iff R is accepted by a nondeterministic auxiliary pushdown automaton (see [4])within polynomial time and the simultaneous space bound max $\{\log n, m\}$. All the problems we looked at belonged to RPP. It would be interesting to find a natural problem which seems not to belong to RPP but which belongs to SPP. It would be even more interesting to find a natural problem which is complete for SPP.

Acknowledgement: We want to thank Hal Sudborough and Oliver Vornberger for many helpful discussions and for the careful reading of this manuscript.

References:

1. Ausiello, G., A. Marchetti-Spaccamela and M. Protasi, Toward a unified approach for the classification of NP-complete optimization problems, Proc. Frege-Conference 1979, Jena, GDR
2. Baker, B.S. and R.V. Book, Reversal-bounded multipushdown machines, J. Comp. Syst. Sci. 8(1974), 315-332
3. Conway, R.W., W.L. Maxwell and L.W. Miller, Theory of Scheduling, Addison-Wesley, Reading, Mass., 1967

4. Cook, S.A. Characterizations of Pushdown Machines in Terms of Time-Bounded Computers, J. Ass. Comp. Mach. 18 (1971), 4 - 18

5. Garey, M.R. and D.S. Johnson, "Strong" NP-Completeness Results: Motivation, Examples and Implications, J.Ass. Comp. Mach. 25 (1978), 499 - 5o8

6. Garey, M.R. and D.S. Johnson, Computers and Intractability, A Guide to the Theory of NP-completeness, W.H. Freeman and Company, San Francisco, 1979

7. Monien, B,. Connections between the LBA problem and the knapsack problem, Proc. Frege-Conference 1979, Jena, GDR

8. Monien, B., Scheduling problems and space bounded computations, in preparation

9. Monien, B. and I.H. Sudborough, Bounding the bandwidth of NP-complete problems, in preparation

1o. Paz, A. and S. Moran, Non-deterministic polynomial optimization problems and their approximation, Lecture Notes Comp. Sci. 52, 37o - 379, Springer Verlag Berlin-Heidelberg-New York, 1977

11. Sahni, S.K. Algorithms for Scheduling Independent Tasks, J.Ass. Comp. Mach. 23 (1976), 116 - 127

12 Savitch, W.J., Relationships between nondeterministic and deterministic tape complexities, J. Comp. Syst. Sci. 4(197o), 177 - 192

DECIDABILITY OF REACHABILITY IN PERSISTENT VECTOR REPLACEMENT SYSTEMS

Horst Müller

Universität Erlangen-Nürnberg
Institut für Mathematische Maschinen
und Datenverarbeitung (III)
Martensstraße 3, 8520 Erlangen
Federal Republic of Germany

0. Introduction

Petri Nets have turned out to be a useful model for research of fundamental problems of parallel data processing. Some decidability and complexity questions in this area are settled [1,3]. The fundamental problem of reachability is until now proved decidable only for special classes of Petri Nets resp. equivalent models as vector addition systems (VAS) [2,6]. Sacerdote and Tenney [10] have claimed decidability for the general case but have not as yet provided a rigorous proof. In the known decidable cases semilinearity of the reachability set plays an important part in the proof. Because of the existence of VAS of dimension 6 with a non semilinear reachability set (see [2]) these methods must fail for higher dimensions. Landweber and Robertson [5] have shown semilinearity of the reachability set for persistent Petri nets, but their proof is not constructive and yields therefore no decision procedure for the reachability problem. In this paper we give as a main result an effective construction for a semilinear representation of the reachability set for any persistent vector replacement system (and thus for persistent Petri nets). This yields decidability of reachability, inclusion and equivalence for persistent vector replacement systems. Contrasting to the last inclusion and equivalence are undecidable for the class of arbitrary VAS (Hack [1]).

The construction is based on reachability trees introduced by Karp and Miller [4]. The efficiency of the construction is bad. Because of the existence of sequences of VAS with finite reachability sets not boundable by primitive recursive functions (see Rackoff [9]) the construction needs time and space not boundable by primitive recursive functions. For detailed proofs we refer to [8].

1. Notations and Definitions

Let $\mathbb{Z}$ denote the set of integers, $\mathbb{N}$ denote the set of nonnegative integers. Let $\mathbb{Z}^n(\mathbb{N}^n)$ denote the set of n-tuples of elements of $\mathbb{Z}(\mathbb{N})$ with the usual componentwise defined extension of operations and relations unless otherwise specified. An important exception is the relation $<$ on $\mathbb{N}^n$. $(x_1,\ldots x_n) \leq (y_1,\ldots y_n)$ is defined componentwise by $x_i \leq y_i$ for $i=1,\ldots,n$. But $x < y$ by $x \leq y$ and $x \neq y$, i.e. $x_i \leq y_i$ for $i=1,\ldots,n$ and $x_j \neq y_j$ for some j, $1 \leq j \leq n$. Some simple but important facts about this partial order on $\mathbb{N}^n$ are given in the following Lemma.

Lemma 1.1: a) $<$ is a wellfounded partial order on $\mathbb{N}^n$, i.e. all descending chains are finite.

b) Any set of pairwise incomparable elements of $\mathbb{N}^n$ is finite.

c) Any infinite sequence of pairwise different elements has a strictly increasing subsequence.

d) Any set $S \subseteq \mathbb{N}^n$ has a finite set $\min(S)$ of minimal elements.

Let P be a finite subset of $\mathbb{Z}^n$ and $\alpha|P \to \mathbb{N}$. Using the abreviation

$$\alpha * P = \sum_{p \in P} \alpha(p) \cdot p, \quad \text{define for } C \subseteq \mathbb{N}^n$$

$$\mathcal{L}(C,P) := \{x \mid (\exists c \in C)(\exists \alpha|P \to \mathbb{N})\ x = c + \alpha * p\}.$$

For convenience we write $\mathcal{L}(c,P)$ for $\mathcal{L}(\{c\},P)$.

$$S \text{ is \underline{linear}, iff } (\exists s \in \mathbb{N})(\exists P \subseteq \mathbb{N}^n)(P \text{ finite and } S = \mathcal{L}(s,P)).$$

A set is semilinear, iff it is a finite union of linear sets.

A set S is called effectively semilinear iff there is given an algorithm yielding a representation $S = \cup\{\mathcal{L}(s,P) \mid (s,P) \in I\}$ by computing a finite set $I \subseteq \mathbb{N}^n \times$ set of finite subsets of $\mathbb{N}^n$.

Important for decidability problems is the following

Lemma 1.2: Membership, Inclusion and Equality is decidable for effectively semilinear sets.

Proof: Membership can be decided by solving a system of linear equations. Inclusion (and therefore equality, too) can be expressed by a formula of the theory of addition (Presburger arithmetic) which is decidable (see e.g. [7]).

A <u>vector replacement scheme</u> of dimension n is a finite family $W \mid T \to \mathbb{Z}^n \times \mathbb{Z}^n$ of <u>transitions</u> $W(t)=(u_t, v_t)$ with $u_t \leq v_t$.

A <u>vector replacement system</u> (VRS) is a pair (W,x) of a vector replacement scheme W and an <u>initial vector</u> $x \in \mathbb{N}^n$.

Each transition (u_t, v_t) defines a <u>transitionsrelation</u> $\xrightarrow{t}$ on $\mathbb{N}^n$ by $x \xrightarrow{t} y$ iff $y + u_t \geq 0 \wedge y = x + v_t$.
t is <u>enabled</u> at x iff $x + u_t \geq 0$. These two notions are extended to sequences of transitions in T^* by induction:

$$x \xrightarrow{\Lambda} x (x \in \mathbb{N}^n);\ \Lambda \text{ is enabled at } x \text{ for all } x \in \mathbb{N}^n$$

$$x \xrightarrow{\delta t} y \text{ iff } \exists z (x \xrightarrow{\delta} z \wedge z \xrightarrow{t} y)\quad (\delta \in T^*,\ t \in T)$$

δt is <u>enabled</u> at x iff $\exists z (x \xrightarrow{\delta} z \wedge t$ is enabled at z).

A set or a sequence A of elements of T^* is called <u>enabled</u> at x iff every element of A is enabled at x. The set $L_W(x) := \{\delta \mid \delta$ is enabled at x$\}$ of all finite transitionsequences enabled at x is called the (non-terminal) <u>language</u> of (W,x). The <u>reachability set</u> of (W,x) is the set $R_W(x) := \{y \mid (\exists \delta \in T^*)\ x \xrightarrow{\delta} y\}$. We extend this notion allowing a set M of initial vectors by setting

$$R_W(M) := \{y \mid (\exists\, x \in M)\ y \in R_W(x)\} = \bigcup_{x \in M} R_W(x) \quad (M \subseteq \mathbb{N}^n).$$

If W is known from the context, we omitt the subscript W. Directly from these definitions we have:

<u>Lemma 1.3:</u> a) $M_1 \subseteq M_2 \to R(M_1) \subseteq R(M_2)$

and b) $R(M_1 \cup M_2) = R(M_1) \cup R(M_2) \quad (M_1, M_2 \subseteq \mathbb{N}^n)$

For simplicity let $T = \{1,\ldots,k\}$.

For $\delta \in T^*$ the <u>folding</u> (Parikh-mapping) of δ is a k-dimensional vector fold $(\delta) = (f_1,\ldots,f_k) \in \mathbb{N}^k$ whose i-th component f_i is the number of occurences of i in the sequence δ. Sequences $\delta, \tau \in T^*$ with fold(δ) = fold(τ) are called <u>folding-equivalent</u>.

For $\delta = t_1 \ldots t_{|\delta|} \in T^*$ the <u>displacement</u> is $\mathrm{dis}(\delta) = \mathrm{dis}(t_1 \ldots t_{|\delta|}) =$

$$= \sum_{j=1}^{|\delta|} v_{t_j}.$$

Folding and displacement are monoid homomorphisms and are combined to get the <u>extended Parikh mapping</u> $EPK \mid T^* \to \mathbb{N}^{k+n}$ by EPK(δ) = (fold(δ), dis(δ)).

Easily proven is

Lemma 1.4: $\text{fold}(\delta) = \text{fold}(\tau)$ implies $\text{dis}(\delta) = \text{dis}(\tau)$.

Next let us introduce the difference operation on T^* by

$\delta \dot{-} \Lambda := \delta$

$\delta \dot{-} t :=$ if t in δ then result of deleting the first occurence of t in δ else δ

$\delta \dot{-} (\tau t) := (\delta \dot{-} \tau) \dot{-} t \qquad (\delta, \tau \in T^*, t \in T)$

Some intuitively obvious properties of the difference operation are given.

Lemma 1.5: For all $u, v, w \in T^*$

a) $u \dot{-} vw = u \dot{-} wv$

b) $\text{fold}(v) = \text{fold}(w)$ implies $u \dot{-} v = u \dot{-} w$

c) $\text{fold}(u) \leq \text{fold}(v)$ implies $\text{fold}(v) = \text{fold}(u(v \dot{-} u))$

The proofs are simple exercises on induction.

A vector replacement system (M,x) is persistent iff

$(\forall\, y \in R_W(x))(\forall\, t_1,t_2 \in T)(t_1$ enabled at y and $t_1 \neq t_2$ and t_2 enabled at y implies t_1t_2 enabled at $y)$.

The persistency criterion for Petri nets given by Starke [11] based on work of Landweber and Robertson [4] is easily transferred to the following persistency criterion for VRS.

Lemma 1.6 (Persistency criterion): The VRS (W,x) is persistent iff for every $y \in R_W(x)$ and for every pair δ,τ of finite transition sequences enabled at y the sequence $\delta(\tau \dot{-} \delta)$ is enabled at y.

Short: $\delta,\tau \in L_W(y) \rightarrow \delta(\tau \dot{-} \delta) \in L_W(y)$.

$\delta \in T^*$ is called a period at $x \in \mathbb{N}^n$ iff δ is enabled at x and $\text{dis}(\delta) > 0$. Persistency guarantees transmission of periods at x to vectors y reachable from x in the following sense.

Lemma 1.7: Let (W,x_o) be a persistent VRS and p a period at $x \in R_W(x_o)$. Then for any $y \in R_W(x)$ a period p' at y can be constructed effectively which is folding equivalent to p.

We extend the operation $*$ by

$$\alpha * A := \sum_{i=1}^{m} \alpha_i\, \text{dis}(\delta_i) \text{ for } \alpha \in \mathbb{N}^m \text{ and } A = \langle \delta_1,\ldots,\delta_m \rangle$$

a sequence with $\delta_i \in T^*$ (i=1,...,m) and abbreviate

$\mathcal{L}(x,\{dis(\delta_i) \mid i=1,...,m\})$ by $\mathcal{L}(x,A)$.

Lemma 1.8: Let (W,x) be any (not necessarily persistent) VRS. For any sequence $A = \langle p_1,...,p_m \rangle$ of periods at x holds $\mathcal{L}(x,A) \subseteq R_W(x)$.

Proof by induction on $m = |A|$.

For the following let $A = \langle \delta_1,...,\delta_m \rangle$ be a finite sequence of elements $\delta_i \in T^*$. A is called reduced (relative to EPK) iff not $\exists i, j (i < j$ and $EPK(\delta_i) \leq EPK(\delta_j))$.

2. Results and proof outline for the main theorem

2.1 Main theorem

For any persistent vector replacement system (W,x_o) the reachability set is effectively semilinear.

Outline of proof: For linear sets $\mathcal{L}(x,A)$ of initial vectors (where A is a reduced sequence of periods at x) we construct a set reachability tree SRT(x,A) by modification of the well known Karp/Miller-reachability tree. The tree construction gives a partial representation of the reachability set (compare (4.15),(4.16)):

(2.2) $R_W(\mathcal{L}(x,A)) = \mathcal{L}(C,A) \cup \bigcup\{R_W(\mathcal{L}(x(\xi),A'(\xi))) \mid \xi \text{ jump origin}\}$

C is a finite set and each jump origin ξ is a vertex of the constructed tree leading to a longer sequence of periods $A'(\xi)$ (given by algorithm 4.11). $A'(\xi)$ may be not reduced. Iterating (2.2) directly leads in some cases to infinite computations. By a reduction procedure (theorem 3.2) - for which persistency is essential - we can return to reduced sequences of periods:

(2.3) $R_W(\mathcal{L}(x(\xi),A'(\xi))) = \bigcup\{R_W(\mathcal{L}(y,B)) \mid (y,B) \in I_\xi\}$ with

I_ξ finite and for any $(y,B) \in I_\xi$: B is a reduced sequence of periods at y.

Combining (2.2) and (2.3) we get (theorem 4.14) for some finite sets C and I:

(2.4) $R_W(\mathcal{L}(x,A)) = \mathcal{L}(C,A) \cup \bigcup\{R_W(\mathcal{L}(y,B)) \mid (y,b) \in I\}$ and

for any $(y,B) \in I$: B is a reduced sequence of periods at y.

Starting with $R_W(x_o) = R_W(\mathcal{L}(x_o$, empty sequence$))$ and using (2.4) iteratively we can construct a jump tree (algorithm (5.1)), which is finite because no infinite reduced sequence of periods can exist and which gives the desired representation of $R_W(x_o)$. Section 3,4,5 give details of the reduction, the set reachability tree and the jump tree respectively.

By Lemma 1.2 the main theorem implies:

Corollary 2.5: The reachability problem for persistent vector replacement systems is decidable.

Corollary 2.6: Inclusion resp. equality of the reachability sets of persistent vector replacement systems is decidable.

3. Reduction of periods

3.1 Reduction lemma

Let $A = \langle p_1,\dots,p_m \rangle$ be a sequence of periods at $x \in R_W(x_o)$ and (W,x_o) a persistent VRS. If p_i, p_j are periods with $EPK(p_i) < EPK(p_j)$ and

$$A' := \langle p_1,\dots,p_{j-1},p_j \dot{-} p_i,p_{j+1},\dots,p_m \rangle =: A\begin{bmatrix} p_j \\ p_j \dot{-} p_i \end{bmatrix}$$

then A' is a sequence of periods at $x + dis(p_i)$ and the following equation holds

$$R_W(\mathcal{L}(x,A)) = R_W(\mathcal{L}(x,A-p_i)) \cup R_W(\mathcal{L}(x + dis(p_i), A')).$$

3.2 Reduction-theorem

Let (W,x) be a persistent VRS, A a finite sequence of periods at x and A_{red} the reduced initial segment of A of maximal length. There is effectively constructible a finite set M of pairs (y,B) with

a) B is a reduced sequence of periods at y leaving A_{red} as initial segment and

b) $R_W(\mathcal{L}(x,A)) = \bigcup\{R_W(\mathcal{L}(y,B)) \mid (y,B) \in M\}$.

Proof: We give an algorithm that constructs a tree labelled by pairs $(x(\eta),A(\eta))$ where for any vertex η $A(\eta)$ is a sequence of periods at $x(\eta)$ having A_{red} as an initial segment.

3.3 Algorithm for the reduction tree

Input: W, x, A ;

```
create root;   x(root) := x; A(root) := A;
while ∃η not reduced A(η) do
      choose η with A(η) = <p_1,...,p_m> not reduced and
        EPK(p_i) ≤ EPK(p_j);
      if EPK(p_i) = EPK(p_j) then construct a son labelled (x,A-p_j)
         else construct two sons labelled (x,A-p_j) resp.
              (x + dis(p_i), A[p_j / p_j-p_i])
      fi
                     od
```

This algorithm and the resulting tree have the following properties:

(3.4) $A(\eta)$ is a sequence of periods at $x(\eta)$ having A_{red} as an initial segment.

Proof: Follows directly by tree induction from Lemma 3.1.

(3.5) The algorithm 3.3 terminates with a finite tree.

Proof: To each vertex associate the vector

$(|A(\eta)|, \sum_{p\in A(\eta)} EPK(p)) \in \mathbb{N}^{1+k+n}$. This vector decreases by passing from a vertex to his sons. By Lemma 1.1 (well-foundedness) every path in the tree must have finite length.

(3.6) $R_W(\mathcal{L}(x,A)) = \bigcup\{R_W(\mathcal{L}(x(\eta),A(\eta)))\,|\,\eta$ leaf of the reduction tree$\}$

Proof by repeated application of the reduction lemma.

4. The set reachability tree

In this section we give an algorithm which leads to a partial computation of the reachability set (again in the form of a tree) for a linear set of initial vectors. The computation is stopped when new periods occur. In other words $R_W(\mathcal{L}(x,A))$ is reduced to a finite family of sets of the form $R_W(\mathcal{L}(y,B))$ with a bigger period sequence B.

4.1 Algorithm for the set reachability tree SRT(x,A)

Input: A VRS(W,x), a reduced sequence $A = \langle p_1,\ldots,p_m\rangle$ of periods at x;

```
create root; x(root) := x; type(root) := unfinished; A(root) := A;
while ∃η type(η) = unfinished do
      choose η with type(η) = unfinished;
      if  ∃ξ(ξ ancestor of η and x(ξ) ≤ x(η))
         then if ∃ξ(ξ ancestor of η and x(η) ∈ L(x(ξ),A) )
                 then type(η) := unessential leaf
                 else type(η) := jump leaf fi
```

else for each $t \in T$ do
for each $\alpha \in \min\{\alpha \mid \alpha \in \mathbb{N}^m$ and $x(\eta) + \alpha * A + u_t \geq 0\}$ do
construct a son (η,t,α) of η;
mark the edge from η to (η,t,α) with (t,α);
$x(\eta,t,\alpha) := x(\eta) + \alpha * A + v_t$;
$A(\eta,t,\alpha)$:= sequence of periods at $x(\eta,t,\alpha)$ transmitted by Lemma 1.7 from $A(\eta)$;
$\text{type}(\eta,t,\alpha)$:= unfinished od od;
if η has no son then $\text{type}(\eta)$:= terminal leaf
else $\text{type}(\eta)$:= finished
fi od
output the constructed tree, called SRT(x,A).

In the following we prove some properties of algorithm 4.1, especially termination and properties of the result SRT(x,A).

Lemma 4.2: The set $MM := \min\{\alpha \mid \alpha \in \mathbb{N}^m$ and $x(\eta) + \alpha * A + u_t \geq 0\}$ is computable.

(4.3) Any vertex in the tree SRT(x,A) and in any intermediate tree has only a finite set of sons which are effectively constructible.

(4.4) If $\langle (t_1,\alpha^{(1)}),\dots,(t_r,\alpha^{(r)})\rangle$ is the sequence of edge markings for path from the root to η, then

$$x + \left(\sum_{\rho=1}^{r} \alpha^{(\rho)}\right) * A \xrightarrow{t_1\dots t_r} x(\eta) = x + \sum_{\rho=1}^{r} \alpha^{(\rho)} * A + \text{dis}(t_1\dots t_r).$$

Proof by induction on r.

(4.5) The conditions

(4.5.1) $\exists\xi(\xi$ ancestor of η and $x(\xi) \leq x(\eta))$ and

(4.5.2) $\exists\xi(\xi$ ancestor of η and $x(\xi) \in \mathcal{L}(x(\xi),A))$ are decidable.

Proof: The set of ancestors is finite. For $x(\eta) \in \mathcal{L}(x(\xi),A))$ use Lemma 1.2.

(4.6) The algorithm 4.1 terminates with a finite tree SRT(x,A).

Proof: Suppose algorithm 4.1 does not terminate. Then the constructed tree is infinite and by König's Lemma has an infinite path $\langle \eta_i \mid i \in \mathbb{N}\rangle$ with pairwise different $x(\eta_i)$-values. By Lemma 1.1.c there exist indices j_1, j_2 with $j_1 < j_2$ and $x(\eta_{i_{j_1}}) < x(\eta_{i_{j_2}})$. This contradicts the negation of (4.5.1) which is necessary for non termination.

(4.7) For any vertex η with $\text{type}(\eta)$ = terminal leaf :
$R_w(\mathcal{L}(x(\eta),A)) = \mathcal{L}(x(\eta),A)$

Proof: For terminal leaves the above defined set M is empty. Therefore for any $y \in \mathcal{L}(x(\eta),A)$ no transition is enabled.

(4.8) For any vertex η with type(η) = finished:

$$R_W(\mathcal{L}(x(\eta),A)) = \mathcal{L}(x(\eta),A) \cup \bigcup_{\eta' \text{ son of } \eta} R_W(\mathcal{L}(x(\eta'),A))$$

(4.9) For any vertex η:

type(η) = unessential leaf $\leftrightarrow \exists\xi(\xi$ ancestor of $\eta \wedge x(\eta) \in \mathcal{L}(x(\xi),A))$

and

type(η) = jump leaf $\leftrightarrow (\exists\xi(\xi$ ancestor of $\eta \wedge x(\xi) < x(\eta))$

and $\forall\xi(\xi$ ancestor of $\eta \rightarrow x(\eta) \notin \mathcal{L}(x(\xi),A)))$

Proof by inspection of algorithm 4.1.

For describing new periods some further terminology is needed. We call a pair (ξ,η) of vertices a <u>jump</u> in SRT(x,A) iff type(η) = jump leaf $\wedge$ ξ ancestor of $\eta \wedge x(\xi) < x(\eta)$. If (ξ,η) is a jump, ξ is called a <u>jump origin</u>. ξ is called a <u>minimal jump origin</u> if ξ is a jump origin and on the path from the root to ξ there is no other jump origin.

The preceding properties of SRT(x,A) are true for arbitrary VRS, if we drop the computation of $A(\eta,t,\alpha)$. For the following we have to restrict on persistent VRS.

<u>Lemma 4.10:</u> If (W,x) is persistent, then for any vertex η $A(\eta)$ is a sequence of periods at $x(\eta)$ folding equivalent to A.
Proof by tree induction: A(root) = A is trivial. By Lemma 1.7 the property is transmitted to successors.

For any jump origin ξ we construct a new (not necessarily reduced) sequence of periods $A'(\xi)$ at $x(\xi)$ having a strict initial segment folding equivalent to A.

<u>(4.11) Algorithm for $A'(\xi)$</u>

<u>Input</u> SRT(x,A), ξ jump origin
let jump(ξ) = $\{(\xi,\eta_1),\dots,(\xi,\eta_e)\}$ be the set of jumps originating at ξ;
<u>for</u> <u>any</u> $(\xi,\eta) \in$ jump (ξ) <u>do</u>
let $<(t_1,\alpha^{(1)}),\dots,(t_{n(\xi,\eta)},\alpha^{(n(\xi,\eta))})>$ be the sequence of edge markings on the path from ξ to η in SRT(x,A) and let be p'_i an element of $A(\xi)$ folding equivalent to $p_i (i=1,\dots,m)$;

$$\alpha := \sum_{i=1}^{n(\xi,\eta)} \alpha^{(i)};$$

$p(\xi,\eta) := p'^{\alpha_1}_1 \dots p'^{\alpha_m}_m \quad t_1 \dots t_{n(\xi,\eta)}$ <u>od</u>;

$A'(\xi) := A(\xi) \langle p(\xi,\eta_1),\dots,p(\xi,\eta_e)\rangle$

(4.12) The resulting sequence $A'(\xi)$ is a sequence of periods at $x(\xi)$ having a strict initial segment folding equivalent to A with

(4.13) $R_W(\mathcal{L}(x(\xi),A)) = R_W(\mathcal{L}(x(\xi),A'(\xi)))$.

The constructions in this section are summarized in

<u>Theorem 4.14:</u> Given a persistent n-dim. VRS(W,x_o), a vector $x \in R_W(x_o)$ and a reduced sequence A_x of periods at x there are effectively constructible a finite set $C_x \subseteq \mathbb{N}^n$ and a finite set I_x of pairs (y,B) with

i) $y \in \mathbb{N}^n$

ii) B is a reduced sequence of periods at y with a strict initial segment folding equivalent to A_x and

iii) $R_W(\mathcal{L}(x,A_x)) = \mathcal{L}(C_x,A_x) \cup \bigcup\{R_W(\mathcal{L}(y,B)) \mid (y,B) \in I_x\}$

Proof: By Algorithm 4.1 we construct the set reachability tree $SRT(x,A_x)$. Let $C_x := \{x(\eta) \mid type(\eta) = \text{finished} \wedge$ <u>not</u> $\exists\xi(\xi$ ancestor of $\eta \wedge \xi$ jump origin$)\}$.

By iterated application of (4.8) and the observation that unessential leaves do not contribute new vectors to the reachability set we get

(4.15) $R_W(\mathcal{L}(x,A_x)) = \bigcup\{\mathcal{L}(x(\eta),A_x) \mid type(\eta) \in \{\text{finished, terminal leaf}\}$

$\wedge$ <u>not</u> $\exists\xi(\xi$ ancestor of $\eta \wedge \xi$ jump origin$)\}$

$\cup \bigcup\{R_W(\mathcal{L}(x(\xi),A_x)) \mid \xi \text{ jump origin}\}$

Combining (4.12) with the reduction theorem 3.2 we get for any jump origin ξ a finite set $M(\xi)$ with

(4.16) $R_W(\mathcal{L}(x(\xi),A_x)) = R_W(\mathcal{L}(x(\xi),A'(\xi))) = \bigcup\{R_W(\mathcal{L}(y,B)) \mid (y,B) \in M(\xi)\}$

and

(4.17) $(y,B) \in M(\xi) \rightarrow$ B is a reduced sequence of periods at y having a strict initial segment folding equivalent to A_x.

(4.15) and (4.16) together yield i), ii), iii) in theorem 4.14, if we define

$I_x := \bigcup\{M(\xi) \mid \xi \text{ jump origin in } SRT(x,A_x)\}$.

5. Jump tree and proof of main theorem

For proving the main theorem 2.1 we give an algorithm for constructing a further tree, called jump tree, which yields a finite set I of pairs (x,B) satisfying

i) $x \in \mathbb{N}^n \wedge$ B finite subset of $\mathbb{N}^n$ and

ii) $R_W(x_o) = \bigcup\{\mathcal{L}(x,B) \mid (x,B) \in I\}$.

5.1 Algorithm for the jump tree

Input persistent VRS(W,x_o) of dimension n;
create root; x(root) := x_o;
  C(root) := C_{x_o} {computed in 4.14};
  A(root) := ∅;
  I(root) := I_{x_o} {computed in 4.14};

while ∃η I(η) ≠ ∅ do
    for each (y,B)∈ I(η) do
    construct a son η' = (η,y,B) of η;
    x(η'):= y; C(η') := C_y;
    A(η'):= B; I(η') := I_y od od

Properties of algorithm 5.1 and the constructed tree:

(5.2). For any vertex η: A(η) is a reduced sequence of periods at x(η).

Proof: Trivial for the root. For any other vertex η', son of η,

$(x(\eta'),A(\eta')) = (y,B) \in I(\eta) = I_{x(\eta)}$ we get (5.2) by 4.14ii).

(5.3) ξ ancestor of η → A(η) contains a strict initial segment folding equivalent to A(ξ).

Proof: Follows by induction on the length of the path from ξ to η from 4.14ii).

(5.4) Algorithm 5.1 terminates with a finite tree.

Proof: Suppose 5.1 does not terminate. Because I(η) is finite for any vertex η, any vertex has only finitely many sons and Königs infinity lemma would yield an infinite path $\langle \eta_i \mid i \in \mathbb{N}\rangle$. Let $A(\eta_i) = \langle p_1^{(i)},\dots,p_{n_i}^{(i)}\rangle$ and define $w_i := EPK(p_i^{(i)})$ for $i \neq 0$.

Because of (5.3) we have $n_i \geq i$ and $(\forall j \geq n_i) EPK(p_j^{(i)}) = w_j$.
Because any $A(\eta_i)$ is reduced, we get

$w_i \neq w_j$ if $i \neq j$.

By lemma 1.1c) there must be indices i,j with $i < j \wedge w_i < w_j$. $A(\eta_j)$ reduced yields a contradiction.

(5.5) For any vertex η:

$$R_w(\mathcal{L}(x(\eta),A(\eta)) = \mathcal{L}(C(\eta),A(\eta)) \cup \bigcup \{R_w(\mathcal{L}(x(\eta'),A(\eta'))) \mid \eta' \text{ son of } \eta\}$$

Proof follows directly from 4.14iii). By iterated application of (5.5) we get

(5.6) $R_w(x_o) = \bigcup \{\mathcal{L}(C(\eta),A(\eta)) \mid \eta \text{ vertex in the jump tree}\}$.

To get the main theorem let $I := \{(x(\eta),dis(p)) \mid \eta \text{ vertex in the jump tree} \wedge p \text{ in } A(\eta)\}$.

Addendum (17.4.1980): E. Mayr has announced another proof of the main theorem (to appear in TCS) and a proof for decidability of the reachability problem for general VRS (personal communication).

References

[1] Hack, M.: The equality problem for vector addition systems is undecidable. Theor. Computer Sci. 2 (1976), 77-96

[2] Hopcroft, J. and Pansiot, J.-J.: On the reachability problem for 5-dimensional vector addition systems. Theor. Computer Sci. 8 (1979), 135-159

[3] Jones, N.D.; Landweber, L.H. and Lien, Y.E.: Complexity of some problems in Petri nets. Theor. Computer Sci. 4 (1977), 277-299

[4] Karp, R.M. and Miller, R.E.: Parallel program schemata. J. Comput. System Sci. 3 (1969), 147-195

[5] Landweber, L.H. and Robertson, E.L.: Properties of conflict-free and persistent Petri nets. J. Ass. Computing Machinery 25 (1978), 352-364

[6] Van Leeuwen, J.: A partial solution to the reachability problem for vector addition systems. Sixth Ann. ACM Symp. on the Theory of Computing (1974), 303-309

[7] Machtey, M. and Young, P.: An introduction to the general theory of algorithms. North Holland, New York (1978)

[8] Müller, H.: On the reachability problem for persistent vector replacement systems (to appear)

[9] Rackoff, C.: The covering and boundedness problems for vector addition systems. Theor. Comp. Sci. 6 (1978), 223-231

[10] Sacerdote, G.S. and Tenney, R.L.: The decidability of the reachability problem for vector addition systems. 9th Ann. ACM Symp. on theory of computing (1977), 61-77

[11] Starke, H.P.: Semilinearity and Petri nets. Fundamentals of computation theory 79 (Ed. L. Budach), Akademie-Verlag Berlin (1979), 423-429

Abstract

The reachability problem for persistent vector replacement systems is shown to be decidable by giving an algorithm for constructing a semilinear representation of the reachability set.

GENERALIZED HEAPSORT

Seiichi Okoma

Faculty of Engineering Keio University
Department of Administration Engineering

Kohoku-ku Hiyoshi 3-14-1
Yokohama 223 Japan

1. Introduction

In this paper, effective modification of the Heapsort, its mathematical analysis and its experimental results are discussed. The Heapsort, which was first introduced by J. W. J. Williams[1] and improved by R. W. Floyd[2], represents a binary tree of given data in an array without using explicit pointers. It then performs a tree sort in the array. It is well known as the most efficient sorting algorithm, which does not require memory space other than that for the array. For clarification purposes, We call this sorting method the "Basic Heapsort".

The author proposes a "Generalized Heapsort" which uses a p-ary ($p \geq 2$) tree instead of a binary tree, and shows that sorting time can be experimentally reduced by 20 to 30% compared with the Basic Heapsort by the selection of an appropriate value of p in the Generalized Heapsort. Moreover, precise mathematical formulas are given for the numbers of key comparisons and record moves in sorting execution.

2. Generalized Heapsort

The Basic Heapsort algorithm consists of two phases, "heap creation" and "maximum selection"[3]. Let n records(indicated by "R") stored in internal memory be sorted ascendingly in accordance with the order of the key(indicated by "R[i].K"{key in ith record}) of each record. The first phase creates a heap from a given set of records in a one dimensional array. The heap is defined as a sequence of keys, as follows:

$$R[i].K \geq R[2*i].K$$

and

$$R[i].K \geq R[2*i+1].K$$

for all $1 \leq i \leq n/2$.

After generation of the heap, a binary tree is represented so that R[i] has at most two smaller sons R[2*i] and R[2*i+1]. This is Williams and Floyd's splendid idea which gives a tree in an array without explicit pointers. This process is called "heapifying".

Immediately after the heap creation phase, the maximum selection phase begins. As R[1] is the largest, it is moved to its final position R[n]. After that, the remaining n-1 records are again heapified. This process is iterated until there are no records remaining.

The Generalized Heapsort is an extension of this Basic Heapsort. It uses a p-ary ($p \geq 2$) tree instead of a binary tree. Each R[i] has at most p sons in the heap, as follows:

$$R[p*i-p+2],\ R[p*i-p+3],\ \ldots,\ R[p*i+1].$$

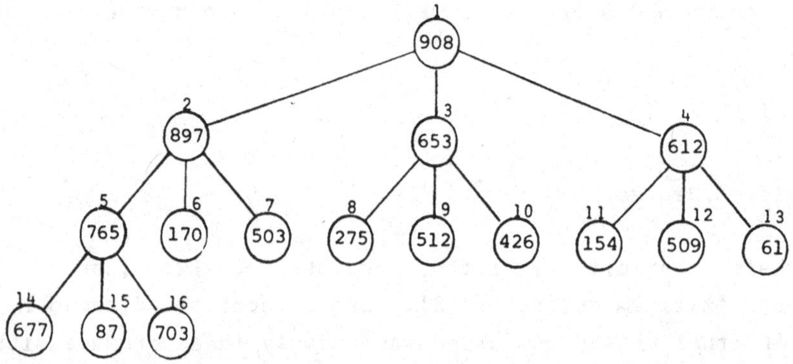

Fig. 1. A heapified tree (p=3)

q	c	m	K_1	K_2	K_3	K_4	K_5	K_6	K_7	K_8	K_9	K_{10}	K_{11}	K_{12}	K_{13}	K_{14}	K_{15}	K_{16}	
0	0	0	503	87	512	61	908	170	897	275	653	426	154	509	612	677	765	703	
5	3	2	503	87	512	61	908	170	897	275	653	426	154	509	612	677	765	703	heap creation
4	6	5	503	87	512	612	908	170	897	275	653	426	154	509	61	677	765	703	
3	9	8	503	87	653	612	908	170	897	275	512	426	154	509	61	677	765	703	
2	15	12	503	908	653	612	765	170	897	275	512	426	154	509	61	677	87	703	
1	21	16	908	897	653	612	765	170	503	275	512	426	154	509	61	677	87	703	
16	29	21	897	765	653	612	703	170	503	275	512	426	154	509	61	677	87	908	maximum selection
15	36	27	765	703	653	612	677	170	503	275	512	426	154	509	61	87	897	908	
14	42	32	703	677	653	612	87	170	503	275	512	426	154	509	61	765	897	908	
13	48	37	677	503	653	612	87	170	61	275	512	426	154	509	703	765	897	908	
12	54	42	653	503	512	612	87	170	61	275	509	426	154	677	703	765	897	908	
11	57	46	612	503	512	154	87	170	61	275	509	426	653	677	703	765	897	908	
10	62	51	512	503	509	154	87	170	61	275	426	612	653	677	703	765	897	908	
9	66	55	509	503	426	154	87	170	61	275	512	612	653	677	703	765	897	908	
8	72	59	503	275	426	154	87	170	61	509	512	612	653	677	703	765	897	908	
7	75	63	426	275	61	154	87	170	503	509	512	612	653	677	703	765	897	908	
6	79	67	275	170	61	154	87	426	503	509	512	612	653	677	703	765	897	908	
5	82	71	170	87	61	154	275	426	503	509	512	612	653	677	703	765	897	908	
4	84	74	154	87	61	170	275	426	503	509	512	612	653	677	703	765	897	908	
3	85	78	87	61	154	170	275	426	503	509	512	612	653	677	703	765	897	908	
2	85	81	61	87	154	170	275	426	503	509	512	612	653	677	703	765	897	908	

q: root position of a tree to be heapified in heap creation, or number of remaining records in maximum selection

c: number of key comparisons

m: number of record moves

Fig. 2. The Generalized Heapsort process (p=3)

```
{  type                                              }
{       element = record                             }
{                 K:key;                             }
{                 body:bodytype                      }
{                 end;                               }
{  var R:array [1..n] of element;                    }
procedure GeneralizedHeapsort(p,n:integer);
   var s:integer; Rtemp:element;
   procedure heapify(left,right:integer);
      label 100; var q,i,j:integer; Ktemp:key;
   begin i:=left; j:=p*i-p+2;
      while j<=right do
         begin for q:=j+1 to min(j+p-1, right) do
                     if R[j].K < R[q].K  then j:=q;
               if Ktemp >= R[j].K then go to 100
                  else begin
                           R[i]:=R[j]; i:=j; j:=p*j-p+2
                       end
         end;
      100: R[i]:=Rtemp
   end{heapify};

begin
   for s:=((n+p-2) div p) downto 1 do
      begin Rtemp:=R[s];
            heapify(s,n)
      end{heap creation};
   for s:=1 to n-1 do
      begin Rtemp:=R[n-s+1];
            R[n-s+1]:=R[1];
            heapify(1,n-s)
      end{maximum selection}
end{Generalized Heapsort};
```

Fig. 3. The Generalized Heapsort algorithm

The Generalized Heapsort consists of two phases just as does the Basic Heapsort. Fig. 1 shows a heapified ternary tree (p=3) at the end of the heap creation phase. The Basic Heapsort adopts the larger son of R[2*i] and R[2*i+1] as the next father. In the Generalized Heapsort, the largest son of R[p*i-p+2], R[p*i-p+3], ..., R[p*i+1] becomes the next father if the son is larger than the father. Fig. 2 shows the two phases when p = 3. Of course, when p = 2, the Generalized Heapsort is reduced to a Basic Heapsort. Fig. 3 shows the algorithm of the Generalized Heapsort. As the height of the p-ary tree becomes lower from $\log_2 n$ to $\log_p n$, the number of the heapifying processes decreases as the height decreases.

3. Mathematical Approach

The efficiency of sorting algorithms is often discussed in terms of the frequency of key comparisons and record moves. Here, C_h and M_h respectively are taken as the numbers of key comparisons and record moves in the heap creation phase. C_m and M_m respectively are taken as the numbers of key comparisons and record moves in the maximum selection phase.

3.1 Number of Comparisons in Heap Creation

For the heap creation phase, first consider jth record. This record has at most p sons from the p*j-P+2th to p*j+1th positions. In order to find the largest of these sons, p-1 key comparisons are required. Then, it is compared with its father, that is, the jth record. Therefore, for the jth family, p key comparisons are executed. If the father is smaller than the largest son, then the largest son becomes the new father. Comparisons continue to search for the largest of the p sons until the largest son becomes smaller than the father or no sons remain. Therefore, if the height of the jth record is represented by i, we need at most

$$i \times p$$

key comparisons in order to heapify a p-ary tree with the root of the jth record.

If the total number of records is n, the highest height h becomes;

$$h = \lfloor \log_p\{(p-1)n-p+2\} \rfloor . \quad (1)$$

The number of records of height $i(1 \le i \le h)$ is at the most;

$$\left\lceil \frac{(p-1)n}{p^{i+1}} \right\rceil$$

thus, the number of key comparisons altogether becomes;

$$C_h = \sum_{1 \le i \le h} \frac{(p-1)n}{p^{i+1}} \times i \times p .$$

This is a simple series summation,

$$C_h = n\left\{\frac{p}{p-1}(1 - \frac{1}{p^h}) - \frac{h}{p^h}\right\} . \quad (2)$$

3.2 Number of Moves in Heap Creation

For height i, the process in which the largest son of the jth father is moved upward is iterated at most i times. In this process, i+2 record moves* are required. Therefore, the number of record moves in heap creation is at the most;

$$\begin{aligned} M_h &= \sum_{1 \le i \le h} \frac{(p-1)n}{p^{i+1}} \times (i + 2) \\ &= n\left\{\frac{1}{p-1}(1 - \frac{1}{p^h}) + \frac{2}{p} - \frac{h+2}{p^{h+1}}\right\} . \end{aligned} \quad (3)$$

---

* For instance, when i=2, 4 moves are performed as follows:

```
temporary:=R[father];
R[father]:=R[son];
R[son]:=R[grandson];
R[grandson]:=temporary;.
```

3.3 Number of Comparisons in Maximum Selection

When j records still remain in the maximum selection phase, as R[1] is the largest, it is moved to the jth position; then the remaining j-1 records are again heapified. The height of the tree, when j records remain, is;

$$h = \left\lfloor \log_p\left\{(p-1)j - p + 2\right\}\right\rfloor .$$

In order to heapify, we iterate the process to find the largest son, i times at the most. Therefore, the number of key comparisons in maximum selection is;

$$C_m = p \times \sum_{1 \leq j \leq n-1} \left\lfloor \log_p\left\{(p-1)j - p + 2\right\}\right\rfloor . \qquad (4)$$

To simplify, let the total number of records be exactly;

$$n = \frac{p^{h+1} - 1}{p - 1} . \qquad (5)$$

This means that the tree is a perfect p-ary tree, that is, each node has exactly p sons, except for the leaves. In this case, formula(5) becomes a summation of the following simple series;

$$C_m = p \times \sum_{0 \leq i \leq h} i \times p^i$$

$$= \frac{p}{p-1}\left\{hp^{h+1} - \frac{p^{h+1} - p}{p - 1}\right\} . \qquad (6)$$

By substituting formula(5), formula(6) becomes;

$$C_m = nph - \frac{p}{p-1}(n - h - 1) . \qquad (7)$$

If the tree is not perfect, the number of comparisons in the maximum selection phase is generally;

$$C_m = nph - \frac{p}{p-1}\left\{\frac{p(p^h - 1)}{p - 1} - h\right\} . \qquad (8)$$

The proof of this is omitted to save space.

3.4 Number of Moves in Maximum Selection

If j records are remain, we perform at most i record shifts, where i is the height of the remaining tree. Therefore,

$$\left\lfloor \log_p \left\{ (p-1)j - p + 2 \right\} \right\rfloor + 3$$

records* are moved. Altogether, the maximum of;

$$M_m = \sum_{1 \leq j \leq n-1} \left[\left\lfloor \log \left\{ (p-1)j - p + 2 \right\} \right\rfloor + 3 \right]$$

moves are performed. In the same manner as above, the number of record moves in the maximum selection phase is;

$$M_m = nh - \frac{1}{p-1}\left\{ \frac{p(p^h - 1)}{p - 1} - h \right\} + 3n - 3 \ . \qquad (9)$$

4. Comparison with Experimental Values

The numbers of key comparisons and record moves discussed above are the maximum values in the worst case. To compare these values with experimental averages, experiments were executed on a PDP-11/34 computer. Each value was the average of 20 times of sorting of computer generated uniform random sequences.

Fig. 4 shows the number of key comparisons of both theoretical maximums and experimental averages. These increase as p increases.

Fig. 5 shows the number of record moves of both theoretical maximums and experimental averages. Since the number of record moves decreases as p increases, if we increase p to its maximum n-1, the number of record moves becomes a minimum. This means that the Generalized Heapsort is reduced to a "simple selection sort".

---

* For instance, if the height of the remaining tree is 2, 5 moves are performed as follows:

```
temporary:=R[rightmost];
R[rightmost]:=R[1];
R[1]:=R[son];
R[son]:=R[grandson];
R[grandson]:=temporary;.
```

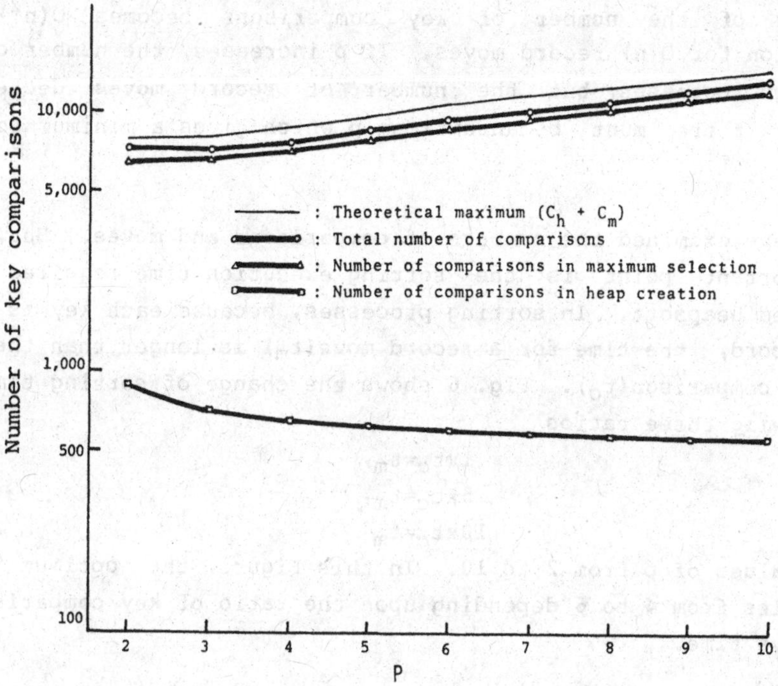

Fig. 4. Number of key comparisons for values of p

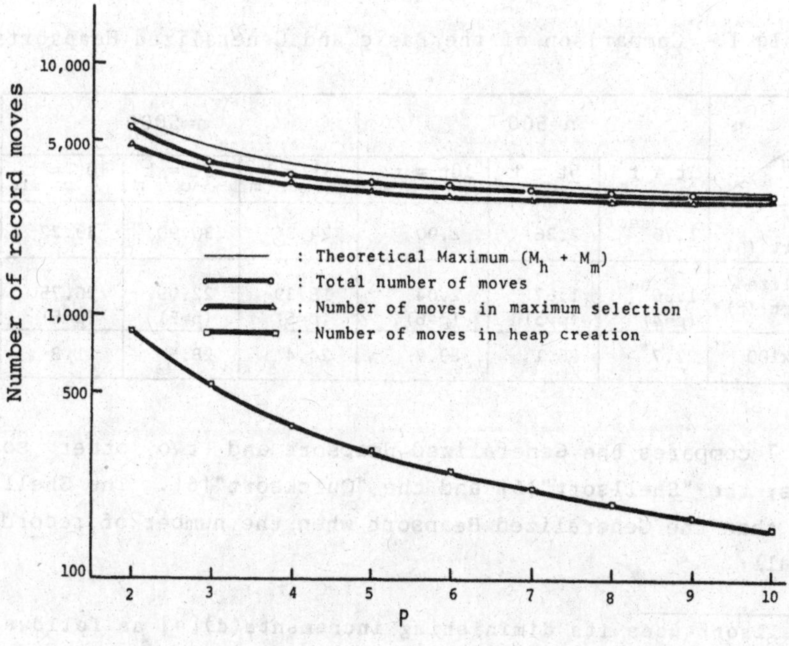

Fig. 5. Number of record moves for values of p

The order of the number of key comparisons becomes $O(n^2)$ in compensation for O(n) record moves. If p increases, the number of key comparisons increases, but the number of record moves decreases. Therefore, there must be an optimum p which gives a minimum sorting time.

We have examined the numbers of comparisons and moves. But, the most important point is the sorting execution time required for a Generalized Heapsort. In sorting processes, because each key is part of a record, the time for a record move(t_m) is longer than the time for a key comparison(t_c). Fig. 6 shows the change of sorting time for the following three ratios

$$1 \times t_c = t_m,$$
$$5 \times t_c = t_m,$$
$$10 \times t_c = t_m$$

and for values of p from 2 to 10. In this Figure, the optimum value of p varies from 4 to 6 depending upon the ratio of key comparison to record move time.

Table 1 shows the Generalized Heapsort compared with the Basic Heapsort. Approximately 20 to 30% of sorting time is saved if we choose an appropriate value of p.

Table 1. Comparison of the Basic and Generalized Heapsorts

Sorting Method \ n	n=500			n=5000		
	$1t_c = t_m$	$5t_c = t_m$	$10t_c = t_m$	$1t_c = t_m$	$5t_c = t_m$	$10t_c = t_m$
Basic Heapsort (α)	1.76 sec	2.26	2.90	24.34	30.90	39.22
Generalized Heapsort (β)	1.36 sec (p=4)	1.67 (p=5)	2.04 (p=6)	18.39 (p=5)	22.09 (p=5)	26.75 (p=5)
$(\frac{\alpha-\beta}{\alpha}) \times 100$	22.7 %	26.1	29.7	24.4	28.5	31.8

FiG. 7 compares the Generalized Heapsort and two other sorting algorithms; the "Shellsort"[5] and the "Quicksort"[6]. The Shellsort* is faster than the Generalized Heapsort when the number of records is fairly small.

* This Shellsort uses its diminishing increments(d)[4] as follows:

```
first,          d:= n div 3 + 1;
then,           d:= d div 3 + 1;.
```

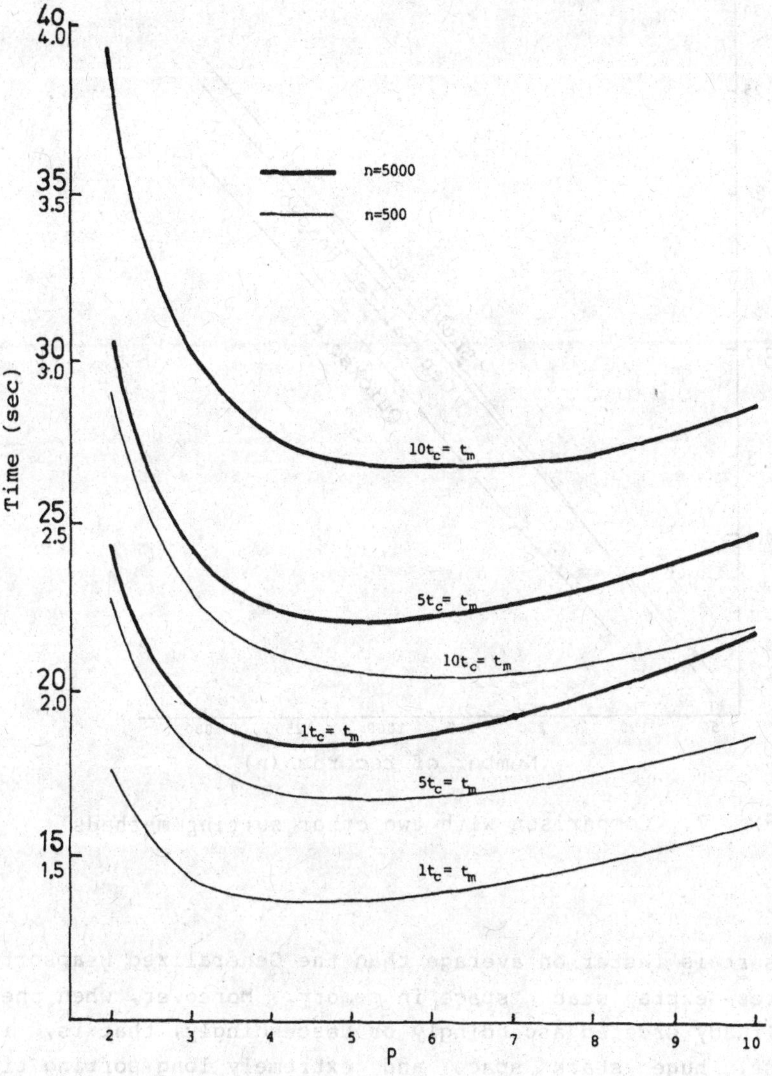

t_c: Comparison time

t_m: Move time

Fig. 6. Sorting time, with the ratio of comparison time to move time

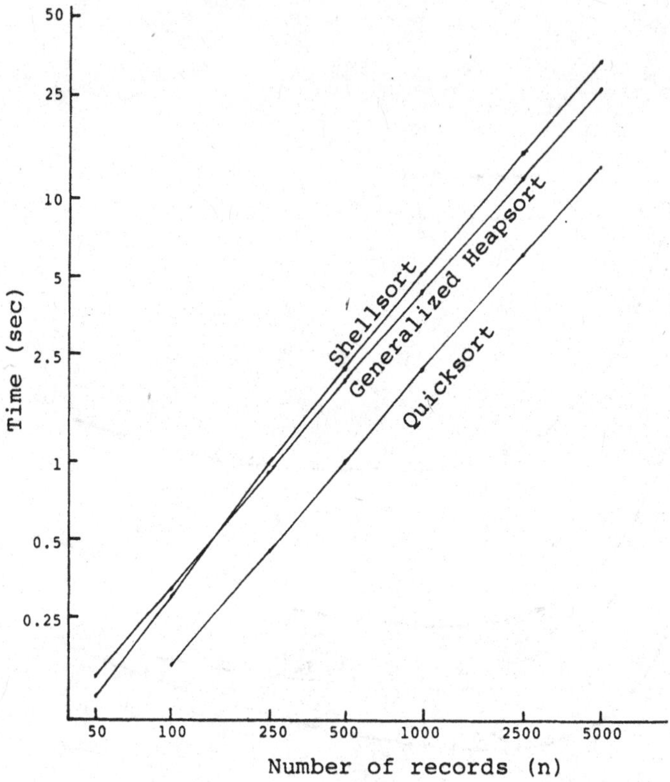

Fig. 7. Comparison with two other sorting methods

The Quicksort is faster on average than the Generalized Heapsort. But it requires extra stack space in memory. Moreover, when the given data is already ordered ascendingly or descendingly, that is, in the worst case, huge stack space and extremely long sorting time are required.

5. Conclusion

The efficiency and mathematical approach of the Generalized Heapsort have been described. If an appropriate value of p is chosen, which in most cases is $4 \leq p \leq 6$, the sorting time can be minimized.

The Generalized Heapsort, however, does not change the order of computing complexity of the Heapsort, which remains O(nlogn).

The algorithm of the Generalized Heapsort is not particularly complicated. It requires only a few modifications to the original algorithm. It is the fastest algorithm yet reported which does not require extra memory space. The Quicksort is faster on average than the Generalized Heapsort, but it has several demerits which have mentioned above. In general, the Heapsort, not only the Basic Heapsort but also the Generalized Heapsort shows a very stable response to any data condition, even data are sequentially or reversely ordered.

The numbers of key comparisons and record moves in the worst case have been described mathematically. However, the author has not yet succeeded in finding their mathematical averages. As stated above, the differences between the averages and maximum values are very small. Therefore, for examination or for comparison with other sorting algorithms, the maximum values are fairly useful.

The Generalized Heapsort algorithm is effective when data volumes are very large and also the ratio of comparison time to move time is large. However, if the move time is very much longer than the comparison time, another sorting algorithms, for instance the "key sort" should be used.

6. References

[1] Williams, J.W.J.: Algorithm 232: Heapsort.
Comm. ACM, Vol.7, No. 6, pp.347-348(1964).

[2] Floyd, R.W.: Algorithm 245: Treesort 3.
Comm. ACM, Vol.7, No.12, p.701(1964).

[3] Aho, A.V., Hopcroft, J.E. and Ullman, J.D.:
The Design and Analysis of Computer Algorithms.
Addison-Wesley Publishing Company, pp.87-92(1974).

[4] Knuth, D.E.: The Art of Computer Programming,
Vol.3/ Sorting and Searching.
Addison-Wesley Publishing Company, PP.145-147(1973).

[5] Shell, D.L.: A High-Speed Sorting Procedure.
Comm. ACM, Vol.2, No.7, PP.30-32(1959).

[6] Sedgewick, R.: Implementing Quicksort Programs.
Comm. ACM, Vol.21, No.10, PP.847-857(1978).

DECIDABILITY RESULTS ON A QUERY LANGUAGE FOR DATA BASES WITH INCOMPLETE INFORMATION

Hiroakira Ono

Faculty of Integrated Arts and Sciences
Hiroshima University, Hiroshima

Akira Nakamura

Department of Applied Mathematics
Hiroshima University, Hiroshima

Introduction

In [4], Lipski proposed a mathematical model of data bases with incomplete information and discussed some problems related to it. According to him, propositions which express queries to an information storage and retrieval system can be regarded as a special kind of formulas of the first-order predicate logic. So, in [3] he gave two way (i.e, *external* and *internal*) of interpreting formulas of the predicate logic, by using models of data bases with incomplete information. In regard to internal interpretations, some similarities to Kripke models for modal logics are known. In fact, certain relationships to the modal logic S4 were mentioned in [3].

In this paper, we will show some results on internal interpretations for a query language. In Section 2, a translation of formulas in a query language, called *extended formulas*, into formulas in the second-order language is introduced and then it will be shown that an extended formula is true in every internal interpretation if and only if the corresponding second-order formula is true in every second-order interpretation. By using this fact, we will prove in Section 3 recursive solvability of some decision problems related to a query language for data bases with incomplete information. As a corollary, we can answer affirmatively a conjecture proposed in [3], which says that internal equivalence of extended formulas containing only monadic predicate symbols is decidable.

1. Preliminaries

In the following, we will use almost the same terminology and notations as in [3]. Firstly, we will give a brief account of *internal interpretations* for a query language.

A first-order language L is a language which consists of a list of countable n-ary predicate symbols $P, Q, \ldots, P_1, P_2, \ldots,$ for each $n \geq 1$, a list of countable individual variables $x, y, \ldots, x_1, x_2, \ldots,$ the logical connectives $\neg$, $\wedge$ and the quantifier $\forall$. Other logical connectives $\vee$, $\supset$, $\equiv$, $\exists$ can be defined as abbreviations in the usual way. We suppose that L does not contain any function symbols and any individual or predicate constants. *First-order formulas* of L are defined in the usual way. Next, we will add a unary logical connective $\Box$ to L. The language thus obtained is denoted by L^*. (First-order) formulas of L^* are called *extended formulas*. In the following, formulas will be denoted by $\phi, \psi, \ldots,$ or $\phi(x_1, \ldots, x_n), \psi(x_1, \ldots, x_n), \ldots$. (Some of variables $x_1, \ldots, x_n$ may not occur in $\phi(x_1, \ldots, x_n)$ and other variables may occur in it.)

Following Lipski [3], we will introduce internal interpretations of extended formulas.

Definition 1.1. An *incomplete model* (or a *model* for short) is a triple $M = \langle X, u, U \rangle$, where X is a nonempty set called the individual domain of M, and u and U are mappings which associate some subsets $u(P) \subseteq U(P) \subseteq X^n$ for every n-ary predicate symbol P ($n \geq 1$).

If $u = U$ holds in an model $M = \langle X, u, U \rangle$, then M is said to be *complete*. Complete models are nothing but ordinary models for first-order formulas, as explained later.

Definition 1.2. Given two models $M_1 = \langle X, u_1, U_1 \rangle$ and $M_2 = \langle X, u_2, U_2 \rangle$ with the same individual domain X, M_2 is an *extension* of M_1 ($M_1 \preccurlyeq M_2$ or $M_2 \succcurlyeq M_1$, in symbol) if and only if for every predicate symbol P $u_1(P) \subseteq u_2(P) \subseteq U_2(P) \subseteq U_1(P)$.

Let $\phi(x_1, \ldots, x_n)$ be any extended formula with free variables $x_1, \ldots, x_n$. For any model $M = \langle X, u, U \rangle$ and $a_1, \ldots, a_n \in X$, we want to define the notion " *$\phi(x_1, \ldots, x_n)$ is satisfied in M when $x_1, \ldots, x_n$ are interpreted as $a_1, \ldots, a_n$, respectively* ", in symbol

$$M \models \phi(a_1, \ldots, a_n).$$

To do so, we first extend our language L^* by adding a new individual constant $\bar{a}$ for each $a \in X$. (By abuse of symbol, we will use the same letter a for $\bar{a}$, in the following.) The language thus obtained is denoted by $L^*[M]$.

Definition 1.3. Let $M = \langle X, u, U \rangle$ be any model. For each closed extended formula ϕ of $L^*[M]$, define $M \models \phi$ recursively as follows.

1) $M \models P(a_1, \ldots, a_n)$ iff $(a_1, \ldots, a_n) \in u(P)$,
   where P is an n-ary predicate symbol,

2) $M \models \neg\psi$ iff not $M \models \psi$,

3) $M \models \psi \wedge \theta$ iff $M \models \psi$ and $M \models \theta$,

3) $M \models \forall x\psi(x)$ iff for every $a \in X$ $M \models \psi(a)$,

5) $M \models \Box\psi$ iff for every $M' \succ M$ $M' \models \psi$.

Next, let $\phi(x_1,\ldots,x_n)$ be any extended formula of L^* with free variables $x_1,\ldots,x_n$. Then, define

$$M \models \phi(x_1,\ldots,x_n) \text{ iff } M \models \forall x_1\ldots\forall x_n\phi(x_1,\ldots,x_n).$$

Notice that $\forall x_1\ldots\forall x_n\phi(x_1,\ldots,x_n)$ is a closed formula of $L^*[M]$, in the above definition. By using the notation in [3], we can express the relation $\models$ as

$$M \models \phi(a_1,\ldots,a_n) \text{ iff } (a_1,\ldots,a_n) \in \|\phi(x_1,\ldots,x_n)\|_M$$

for any extended formula $\phi(x_1,\ldots,x_n)$ with free variables $x_1,\ldots,x_n$. When M is a complete model, the definition of $M \models \phi$ coincides with the ordinary one, for every first-order formula ϕ.

Definition 1.4. Let ϕ and ψ be arbitrary extended formulas.

1) ϕ is *internally valid* if and only if $M \models \phi$ holds for every model M.

2) ϕ and ψ are *internally equivalent* if and only if $\phi \equiv \psi$ is internally valid.

Let L' be arbitrary first-order language. Then, we will extend the language L' to a second-order language L'_2 by adding the second-order quantifier $\forall$. (For the notational convenience, we regard each predicate symbol of L' as a predicate variable of L'_2.) *Second-order formulas* can be defined also in the usual way. In this case, formulas of the form $\forall P\phi$ can be admitted. For each complete model $M = \langle X, u, u \rangle$, we can define a second-order interpretation of a given second-order formula in M. More precisely, we extend L'_2 by adding a new individual constant $\bar{a}$ for each $a \in X$ and a new n-ary predicate constant $\bar{A}$ for each $A \subseteq X^n$ ($n \geq 1$). (In this case, we will use also the same letter a for $\bar{a}$ and A for $\bar{A}$.) The language thus obtained is denoted by $L'_2[M]$.

Definition 1.5. For each formula ϕ of $L'_2[M]$ without free individual variables, define $M \models_2 \phi$ as follows.

1) $M \models_2 A(a_1,\ldots,a_n)$ iff $(a_1,\ldots,a_n) \in A$, where A is an n-ary predicate constant,

2) if ϕ is of the form $P(a_1,\ldots,a_m)$, $\neg\psi$, $\psi \wedge \theta$, $\forall x\psi(x)$, then $M \models_2 \phi$ is defined similarly as $M \models \phi$ (in Definition 1.3)

3) $M \models_2 \forall P\psi(P)$ iff for every $A \subseteq X^n$ $M \models_2 \psi(A)$, where P is an n-ary predicate symbol.

Next, for any formula $\phi(x_1,\ldots,x_n)$ of L'_2 with free individual variables $x_1,\ldots,x_n$, define

$$M \models_2 \phi(x_1,\ldots,x_n) \quad \text{iff} \quad M \models_2 \forall x_1 \ldots \forall x_n \phi(x_1,\ldots,x_n).$$

Clearly, our second-order interpretations are so-called *principal interpretations* for the second-order language. A second-order formula ϕ is *second-order valid* if and only if $M \models_2 \phi$ holds for every complete model M.

2. A translation of extended formulas into the second-order formulas

In this section, we will introduce a mapping which associates each extended formula ϕ of L^* with a formula ϕ^+ of a second-order language L'_2, so that ϕ is internally valid if and only if ϕ^+ is second-order valid. Thus, we can say that the internal validity of extended formulas is essentially a notion with the second-order character.

Suppose that L is a first-order language. For each m-ary predicate symbol P of L, we will introduce new m-ary predicate symbols $P^n{}_*$ and $P^n{}^*$ for each $n \geqq 0$. Then, the language L'_2 is a second-order language whose set of predicate symbols consists of $P^n{}_*$ and $P^n{}^*$ ($n \geqq 0$), corresponding to each P of L. Now, we will introduce some abridged notations. Let Ω and R be arbitrary n-ary predicate symbols of L'_2. Then, $\Omega \preccurlyeq R$ is the abbreviation of

$$\forall x_1 \ldots \forall x_n (\Omega(x_1,\ldots,x_n) \supset R(x_1,\ldots,x_n)).$$

Next, let $Q = (\Omega_1,\ldots,\Omega_m)$ and $R = (R_1,\ldots,R_m)$ be m-tuples of predicate symbols such that Q_i and R_i have the same arity for each $i = 1,\ldots,m$. Then, $\forall Q\phi(Q)$ and $Q \preccurlyeq R$ are abbreviations of $\forall\Omega_1 \ldots \forall\Omega_m \phi(\Omega_1,\ldots,\Omega_m)$ and $\Omega_1 \preccurlyeq R_1 \wedge \ldots \wedge \Omega_m \preccurlyeq R_m$, respectively. Furthermore, $Q_1 \preccurlyeq Q_2 \preccurlyeq \ldots \preccurlyeq Q_s$ is the abbreviation of $Q_1 \preccurlyeq Q_2 \wedge \ldots \wedge Q_{s-1} \preccurlyeq Q_s$. Define a transformation τ on the set of formulas of L'_2, as follows; $\tau(\phi)$ is a formula obtained from ϕ by replacing each $P^n{}_*$ and $P^n{}^*$ (irrespective of *free* or *bounded*) by $P^{n+1}{}_*$ and $P^{n+1}{}^*$, respectively, for each P and each $n \geqq 0$.

Definition 2.1. For each extended formula ϕ of L^*, define a second-order formula ϕ^* of L'_2 recursively as follows:

1) If $\phi = P(x_1,\ldots,x_n)$ then $\phi^* = P^0{}_*(x_1,\ldots,x_n)$.
2) If $\phi = \neg\psi$ then $\phi^* = \neg\psi^*$.
3) If $\phi = \psi \wedge \theta$ then $\phi^* = \psi^* \wedge \theta^*$.
4) If $\phi = \forall x\psi$ then $\phi^* = \forall x\psi^*$.
5) Let $\phi = \Box\psi$ and $P_1,\ldots,P_k$ be all predicate symbols appearing in ϕ. Then,

$$\phi^* = \forall P^1{}_* \forall P^1{}^* (P^0{}_* \preccurlyeq P^1{}_* \preccurlyeq P^1{}^* \preccurlyeq P^0{}^* \supset \tau(\psi^*)),$$

where $P^i{}_* = ((P_1)^i{}_*,\ldots,(P_k)^i{}_*)$ and $P^i{}^* = ((P_1)^i{}^*,\ldots,(P_k)^i{}^*)$

for i = 0, 1.

Clearly, if $P_1,\dots,P_k$ are all predicate symbols appearing in a formula ϕ then ϕ^* contains $(P_1)^0{}_*,(P_1)^0{}^*,\dots,(P_k)^0{}_*,(P_k)^0{}^*$ as *free* predicate symbols. The mapping ϕ^* can be extended naturally to the set of extended formulas of $L^*[M]$ for a fixed model M.

Lemma 2.1. Let $M = \langle X, u, U \rangle$ and $M^* = \langle X, v, v \rangle$ be a model for L^* and a complete model for L'_2, respectively. Let m be a non-negative integer. Moreover, suppose that for every predicate symbol P of L^*,

$$u(P) = v(P^m{}_*) \quad \text{and} \quad U(P) = v(P^m{}^*)$$

holds. Then, for any closed extended formula ϕ of $L^*[M]$

$$M \models \phi \quad \text{iff} \quad M^* \models_2 \tau^m(\phi^*)$$

holds, where τ^m is the composition of τ by m times.

Proof. We will show our lemma for every M, M* and m, by the induction on the number of logical connectives in ϕ.

(1) The case where ϕ is $P(a_1,\dots,a_n)$ for some $a_1,\dots,a_n \in X$. Then, $\tau^m(\phi^*) = P^m{}_*(a_1,\dots,a_n)$. So,

$$M \models P(a_1,\dots,a_n) \quad \text{iff} \quad (a_1,\dots,a_n) \in u(P) = v(P^m{}_*)$$
$$\text{iff} \quad M^* \models_2 P^m{}_*(a_1,\dots,a_n) .$$

(2) Induction step.

We will prove our lemma only for the case where ϕ is of the form $\Box\psi$. Other case can be verified easily. For the sake of brevity, we suppose that predicate symbols appearing in ϕ is only P and that P is k-ary. By the definition,

$$M \models \phi \quad \text{iff} \quad \text{for every } M' \succcurlyeq M \quad M' \models \psi.$$

So, it suffices to show that

(2.1) for every $M' \succcurlyeq M$ $M' \models \psi$

if and only if

(2.2) $M^* \models_2 \tau^m(\phi^*)$.

We remark here that

$$\tau^m(\phi^*) = \forall P^{m+1}{}_* \forall P^{m+1}{}^*(\, P^m{}_* \preccurlyeq P^{m+1}{}_* \preccurlyeq P^{m+1}{}^* \preccurlyeq P^m{}^* \supset \tau^{m+1}(\psi^*)\ ).$$

First, we suppose that (2.1) holds. Let A and B be arbitrary subsets of X^k such that

(2.3) $M^* \models_2 P^m{}_* \preccurlyeq A \preccurlyeq B \preccurlyeq P^m{}^*$.

Now, let us define a model $M' = \langle X, u', U' \rangle$ by $u'(P) = A$ and $U'(P) = B$. Since $M \preccurlyeq M'$ holds, $M' \models \psi$. By the hypothesis of induction,

(2.4) $M^* \models_2 (\tau^{m+1}(\psi^*))^+$

holds, where $(\tau^{m+1}(\psi^*))^+$ denotes the formula obtained from $\tau^{m+I}(\psi^*)$ by replacing each occurrence of $P^{m+1}{}_*$ and $P^{m+1}{}^*$ by predicate constants A and B, respectively. Since (2.4) follows from (2.3) for every A and B, (2.2) holds. Conversely, suppose that (2.2) holds. Let $M' = \langle X, u', U' \rangle$ be any model such that $M \preccurlyeq M'$. Define subsets A and B of X^k by $A = u'(P)$ and $B = U'(P)$. It holds that

$$M^* \models_2 P^m{}_* \preccurlyeq A \preccurlyeq B \preccurlyeq P^m{}^*,$$

since $M \preccurlyeq M'$. So, $M^* \models_2 (\tau^{m+1}(\psi^*))^+$ holds also, where $(\tau^{m+1}(\psi^*))^+$ is the formula defined above. By the hypothesis of induction, $M' \models \psi$. Thus, $M \models \phi$.

<u>Definition 2.2</u>. Let ϕ be an extended formula of L^* in which only predicate symbols $P_1,\dots,P_k$ appear. Then, define

$$\phi^+ = ((P_1)^0{}_* \preccurlyeq (P_1)^0{}^* \wedge \dots \wedge (P_k)^0{}_* \preccurlyeq (P_k)^0{}^*) \supset \phi^*.$$

<u>Theorem 2.2</u>. For any extended formula ϕ of L^*, ϕ is internally valid if and only if ϕ^+ is second-order valid.

<u>Proof</u>. Let $P_1,\dots,P_k$ be all predicate symbols appearing in ϕ. Suppose first that ϕ is not internally valid. Then, there exists a model $M = \langle X, u, U \rangle$ such that $M \models \phi$ does not hold. Let $M^* = \langle X, v, v \rangle$ be a complete model such that $v((P_i)^0{}_*) = u(P_i)$ and $v((P_i)^0{}^*) = U(P_i)$ for $i = 1,\dots,k$. Clearly,

$$M^* \models_2 (P_1)^0{}_* \preccurlyeq (P_1)^0{}^* \wedge \dots \wedge (P_k)^0{}_* \preccurlyeq (P_k)^0{}^*$$

holds. On the other hand, $M^* \models_2 \phi^*$ does not hold by Lemma 2.1. Thus, $M^* \models_2 \phi^+$ does not hold. Hence, ϕ^+ is not second-order valid. Conversely, suppose that $M'^* \models_2 \phi^+$ does not hold for some complete model $M'^* = \langle X', v', v' \rangle$. Define $M' = \langle X', u', U' \rangle$ by $u'(P_i) = v'((P_i)^0{}_*)$ and $U'(P_i) = v'((P_i)^0{}^*)$ for $i = 1,\dots,k$. Since

$$M'^* \models_2 (P_1)^0{}_* \preccurlyeq (P_1)^0{}^* \wedge \dots \wedge (P_k)^0{}_* \preccurlyeq (P_k)^0{}^*$$

holds, M' is really an incomplete model. Moreover, by Lemma 2.1 $M' \models \phi$ does not hold since $M'^* \models_2 \phi^*$ does not hold. Thus, ϕ is not internally valid.

Lipski introduced another kind of interpretations, i.e, *external interpretations*, for a query language for data bases with incomplete information in [3] and [4]. By Theorem 1.4 in [3], each external interpretation of first-order formulas can be represented by an internal interpretation of extended formulas. By using the above results, it can be said that various notions concerning external interpretations can be also treated within the second-order logic.

3. <u>Recursive solvability of some decision problems on a query language</u>

As an application of results in Section 2, we will show that two decision problems on a query language for data bases with incomplete information are recursively solvable. The *internal validity problem* for a class Φ of extended formulas is a problem of deciding whether a given formula in Φ is internally valid or not. The *internal equivalence problem* for a class Φ of extended formulas is a problem of deciding whether given two formulas in Φ are internally equivalent or not. It is easy to see that recursive solvability of the internal validity problem for Φ implies that of the internal equivalence problem and vice versa, if Φ is closed under the construction of formulas.

Theorem 3.1. The internal validity problem, and hence the internal equivalence problem, for the class of extended formulas containing only monadic predicate symbols are recursively solvable.

Proof. Let ϕ be arbitrary extended formulas containing only monadic predicate symbols. Then ϕ^+ introduced in Definition 2.2 is a second-order formula also containing only monadic predicate symbols. But, by Skolem - Behmann's result (see e.g. [1]), the decision problem for the second-order monadic predicate logic is recursively solvable. Therefore, whether ϕ^+ is second-order valid or not is decidable. Hence whether ϕ is internally valid or not is also decidable, by Theorem 2.2.

This result gives us an affirmative answer to the conjecture proposed by Lipski in [3]. On the other hand, this fact forms a remarkable contrast to the undecidability of the modal monadic predicate logics by Kripke [2].

Theorem 3.2. The internal validity problem, and hence the internal equivalence problem, for the class of open extended formulas are recursively solvable.

Proof. First, we remark that if ϕ is internally valid and if ϕ and ψ are internally equivalent then ψ is also internally valid. By Lemma 1.5 of [3] and its proof, we can show that for any open extended formula ϕ there is an open extended formula ψ internally equivalent to ϕ such that ψ is of the form $\bigwedge_{i=1}^{k} \bigvee_{j=1}^{h} \psi_{ij}$, where every ψ_{ij} is of one of the following forms; θ, $\neg\theta$, $\Box\neg\theta$, $\neg\Box\neg\theta$ for some atomic formula θ. Moreover, we can verify that for any predicate symbol P,

$$(\Box\neg P(x_1,\ldots,x_n))^* \equiv \neg P^{0}{}^*(x_1,\ldots x_n)$$

is second-order valid. Thus, ψ^* is equivalent to an open first-order formula ψ', which is obtained from ψ by first deleting all $\Box$ and replacing each occurrence of an atomic formula $P(x_1,\ldots,x_n)$ by $P^0{*}(x_1,\ldots,x_n)$ if it occurs in a scope of some $\Box$ in ψ, and by $P^0{}_*(x_1,\ldots,x_n)$, otherwise. Now, let $P_1,\ldots,P_k$ be all predicate symbols appearing in ϕ. Then, ψ^+ is shown to be equivalent to a first-order formula ψ'', where

$$\psi'' = ((P_1)^0{}_* \prec (P_1)^{0*} \wedge \ldots \wedge (P_k)^0{}_* \prec (P_k)^{0*}) \supset \psi'.$$

Thus, ϕ is internally valid if and only if ψ'' is (first-order) valid, by using Theorem 2.2. On the other hand, it can be seen that the universal closure of ψ'' can be transformed into a formula in a prenex normal form of the form $\forall x_1 \ldots \forall x_s \exists y_1 \ldots \exists y_t\ \zeta$, where ζ is an open formula. By the result of Bernays and Schönfinkel (see e.g. [1]), the validity problem for the class of first-order formulas of the above form is recursively solvable. Therefore, whether ψ'' is valid or not is decidable and hence whether ϕ is internally valid or not is also decidable.

It seems to be an interesting problem to research the lower or the upper bound of the computational complexity of these classes of extended formulas.

References

[1] A. Church, Introduction to mathematical logic I, Princeton Univ. Press, Princeton, New Jersey, 1956.

[2] S.A. Kripke, The undecidability of monadic modal quantification theory, *Zeitschr. f. math. Logik*, 8 (1962) 113-116.

[3] W. Lipski, Jr, On the logic of incomplete information, *Proc. 6th International Symposium on Mathematical Foundations of Computer Science*, Tatranska Lomnica, 1977, *Lecture Note in Computer Science 55*, Springer-Verlag, Berlin, (1977) 374-381.

[4] W. Lipski, Jr, On semantic issues connected with incomplete information data bases, to appear in *ACM Transactions on Database Systems*.

NEW RESULTS ON COMPLETENESS AND CONSISTENCY OF ABSTRACT DATA TYPES

Peter Padawitz

Technische Universität Berlin,F.R.G.

ABSTRACT

If an algebraic specification is designed in a structured way, a small specification is stepwise enriched by more complex operations and their defining equations. Based on normalization properties of term reductions we present sufficient "local" conditions for the completeness and consistency of enrichment steps, which can be efficiently verified in many cases where other attempts to prove the enrichment property "syntactically" have failed so far.

1. INTRODUCTION

Given an algebraic specification SPEC0 in the sense of /GTW 78/, additional operations Σ and additional equations E, the extended specification SPEC1 is called enrichment of SPEC0 if E defines Σ completely and consistently on SPEC0. That means that the data type given by SPEC0 coincides with the data type of SPEC1 restricted to SPEC0-operations. Enrichments were introduced in /GTW 78/. That paper also provides sufficient enrichment conditions, which are based on "canonical term algebra" representations of data types. Nourani (/Nou 79/) further investigated this approach (see also /Pad 79/). Completeness and consistency of algebraic specifications relative to a kind of final algebra semantics have been studied by Guttag (/Gut 75/).

Enrichments can be characterized both "syntactically" and "semantically". The syntactical characterization exclusively refers to the term equivalence relations generated by SPEC0 and SPEC1. The semantical characterization depends on the interpretation of Σ on some representation of the data type given by SPEC0. To use this characterization for enrichment proofs is convenient if one already knows a "mathematical model" of SPEC0, e.g. a canonical term algebra (see above).

In this paper we start from the syntactical characterization in order to infer sufficient enrichment conditions. Previous results mainly concerning completeness conditions are given in /EKP 78/ and /EKP 80/. Although term equivalence is in general undecidable, this approach is suggested by considering E as a term rewriting system: If term reductions via E are finitely and uniquely terminating (here called strongly resp. uniquely normalizing), then term equivalence is decidable. Hence, in order to attain "local" enrichment conditions we study normalization properties of term reductions. Tackling enrichments from this point of view we make the following obser-

vations:
Firstly, the equations of SPECO, say EO, mostly have another form than the "new" equations E. Roughly spoken, EO defines the data of SPECO-type while E specifies Σ on these data. Therefore, EO often describes interactive relationships between "constructors" while E represents "recursive" function definitions. Hence, E-reductions may be assumed to be strongly normalizing but EO-reductions should not. Facing this problem Huet has generalized the well-known Knuth-Bendix result (/KB 70/, Theor.5) by proving that unique normalization of E-reductions "modulo EO-equivalence" is decidable if E-reductions are strongly normalizing modulo EO-equivalence. We shall point out that the latter property is too strong to be satisfied by many data type specifications. Instead we show that strong and unique normalization of E-reductions and "preservation of EO-reductions" are sufficient for the enrichment property. Preservation of EO-reductions is a weak property because in a single EO-reduction step starting from some term t equations may be applied in parallel as far as their left sides do not overlap in t.
The second observation concerns the definition of a data type as an initial algebra: All terms representing data are ground terms, i.e. have no variables. But if term reductions are restricted to those of ground terms, the Knuth-Bendix result mentioned above does not hold any more: Unique normalization does not imply that there are confluent reduction sequences for "critical pairs" of nonground terms. Therefore, we introduce "ground term critical pairs" and prove that unique normalization of (ground term) E-reductions and preservation of (ground term) EO-reductions are also characterized by "local"confluence properties. Since only ground terms are reduced, confluence may be achieved by using auxiliary equations IO, which are not derivable but provable by induction on the structure of ground terms.
Chapter 2 presents preliminaries on relations, algebraic specifications, term orderings and term reductions. In chapter 3 we show how unique normalization of E-reductions and preservation of EO-reductions are characterized by local confluence conditions using the ground term critical pairs mentioned above. In chapter 4 we introduce the notion of strong enrichment in order to summarize the normalization properties of E-reductions which imply the enrichment property. Sufficient "local" conditions for strong enrichments are given in our main theorem (4.7) that refers to the results of chapters 2 and 3. Based on the recursive path ordering of terms (cf. /Der 79b/) path-decreasing specifications, which have strongly normalizing term reductions, are defined in chapter 5. Moreover, we demonstrate the application of our main theorem at a specification of finite sets enriched by a delete-operation and the member-predicate. ω denotes the set of natural numbers. If $n \in \omega$, then $[n] = \{i \in \omega | i \leq n\}$. ε denotes the empty word over ω, and for all $v,w \in \omega^*$ $v \leq w$ means that there is $u \in \omega^*$ with $vu = w$.

2. PRELIMINARIES

2.1 DEFINITION

Let T be a set and R,S binary relations on T. R·S denotes the product of R and S and R^{Δ}, R^{+} and R^{*} are the reflexive, transitive and reflexive-transitive closures of R, respectively. We write tRt' for (t,t') ∈ R.
Let t ∈ T and $D(t,R) = \{t' \in T \mid tRt'\}$. $NF(R) = \{t \in T \mid D(t,R) = \emptyset\}$ is the set of R-normal forms, and $NF(t,R) = NF(R) \cap D(t,R^{*})$ denotes the set of R-normal forms of t.
R is uniquely normalizing for t if $|NF(t,R)| \leq 1$. R is uniquely normalizing if R is uniquely normalizing for all t ∈ T.
A sequence $\{ti \mid i \in \omega\}$ is an ω-chain of R if ti R t(i+1) for all $i \in \omega$. R is strongly normalizing if R^{+} is irreflexive and R has no ω-chains.
R is weakly confluent for t if for all u,v ∈ D(t,R) $D(u,R^{*}) \cap D(v,R^{*}) \neq \emptyset$. R is weakly confluent if R is weakly confluent for all t ∈ T. □

2.2 PROPOSITION (noetherian induction w.r.t. R)

Let R be a strongly normalizing relation on T, and let P be a predicate on T. P is true for all t ∈ T if each t ∈ T satisfies the following implication:

$$(\forall t' \in D(t,R^{+}) : P(t')) \Longrightarrow P(t). \quad \square$$

One easily proves by noetherian induction:

2.3 PROPOSITION

Let R be a strongly normalizing relation on T, and let t ∈ T. R is uniquely normalizing for all t' ∈ $D(R^{*},t)$ iff R is weakly confluent for all t' ∈ $D(R^{*},t)$. □

2.4 PROPOSITION (multiset ordering, cf. /DM 79/)

Let R be a strongly normalizing relation on T, and let $\mathcal{M}(T)$ be the set of all finite multisets with elements taken from T. Then $\mathcal{R} \subseteq \mathcal{M}(T)^2$ is defined by

$$M \mathcal{R} N$$

iff M ≠ N and $\forall u \in N-M \; \exists t \in M-N$: tRu

is strongly normalizing, too. □

SPECIFICATIONS

We assume that the reader is familiar with the basic notions of many-sorted universal algebra used in the algebraic approach to data type specifications (cf. /GTW 78/).
Here we add some notational conventions:
Let S be a set of sorts, Σ a finite set of S-sorted operation symbols and X a set of S-sorted variables. The elements of the free S-sorted Σ-algebra over X, $T_{\Sigma}(X)$, are called Σ-terms over X. If X = $\emptyset$, we write T_{Σ} for $T_{\Sigma}(X)$ and call the elements of T_{Σ} simply Σ-terms. $subst_{\Sigma}$ is the set of Σ-term substitutions, i.e. the S-sorted functions $f: X \longrightarrow T_{\Sigma}$. The unique extension of f to a Σ-homomorphism from $T_{\Sigma}(X)$ to T_{Σ} is also denoted by f.

2.5 DEFINITION

For all $t \in T_\Sigma(X)$ var(t) is the set of variables occurring in t. A pair (L,R) of Σ-terms over X is called a Σ-equation if $L \notin X$ and $var(R) \subseteq var(L)$. If E is a set of Σ-equations, then $\langle S,\Sigma,E\rangle$ is called a specification. □

TERM ORDERINGS

Let S be a set of sorts and Σ a finite set of S-sorted operation symbols.

2.6 DEFINITION

The Σ-subterm relation is given by all pairs (t,t') of Σ-terms such that t' is a proper subterm of t. A binary relation > on T_Σ is Σ-compatible if for all $n \in \omega$, $s1,\dots,sn,s \in S$, $\sigma \in \Sigma_{s1\dots sn,s}$ and $ti,ti' \in T_{\Sigma,si}$, $i \in [n]$, $ti \geq ti'$ for all $i \in [n]$ and $tk > tk'$ for some $k \in [n]$ implies

$$\sigma(t1,\dots,tn) > \sigma(t1',\dots,tn').$$

An irreflexive, transitive and Σ-compatible relation, which contains the Σ-subterm relation, is called a Σ-simplification ordering. □

2.7 THEOREM (cf. /Der 79a/)

Σ-simplification orderings are strongly normalizing. □

TERM REDUCTIONS

Let $\langle S,\Sigma,E\rangle$ be a specification.

2.8 DEFINITION

A pair (l,r) of Σ-terms is called an E-production if $l = fL$ and $r = fR$ for some $f \in subst_\Sigma$ and $(L,R) \in E$. $P_\Sigma(E)$ denotes the set of E-productions. A Σ-compatible relation that contains $P_\Sigma(E)$ is called SPEC-compatible. A Σ-compatible relation > is recursively SPEC-compatible if for all $f,g \in subst_\Sigma$ and $(L,R) \in E$ $fx \geq gx$ for all $x \in var(R)$ implies $fL > gR$. □

2.9 DEFINITION (E-reductions)

$\xrightarrow[E]{}$ resp. $\overset{}{\underset{E}{\Longrightarrow}}$ denotes the least SPEC-compatible resp. recursively SPEC-compatible relation. The elements of $\xrightarrow[E]{}$ and $\underset{E}{\Longrightarrow}$ are called simple resp. recursive E-reductions. (Note that $\xrightarrow[E]{+} = \overset{+}{\underset{E}{\Longrightarrow}}$.) $\xrightarrow[E]{}$-normal forms are called SPEC-normal forms. If $\xrightarrow[E]{}$ is strongly (resp. uniquely) normalizing, then SPEC is called strongly (resp. uniquely) normalizing. SPEC is weakly confluent if $\xrightarrow[E]{}$ is weakly confluent. □

2.10 PROPOSITION

If there is a strongly normalizing and SPEC-compatible relation, then SPEC is strongly normalizing. □

3. CONFLUENCE OF TERM REDUCTIONS

Let SPEC = $\langle S,\Sigma,E\rangle$ be a specification and EO be a set of Σ-equations.

3.1 DEFINITION

Let $t \in T_\Sigma$. SPEC-normalization preserves recursive EO-reductions of t if for all $u \in T_\Sigma$ and all SPEC-normal forms t' resp. u' of t resp. u

$$t \xRightarrow[EO]{} u \text{ implies } t' \xRightarrow[EO]{\Delta} \cdot \xrightarrow[E]{*} u'.$$

SPEC commutes with recursive EO-reductions of t if for all $t0, t1 \in T_\Sigma$ there are $t2, t3, t4 \in T_\Sigma$ such that

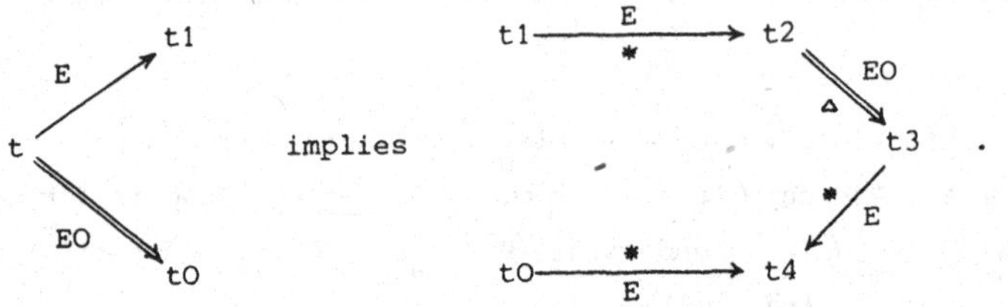

. □

3.2 LEMMA

Assume that SPEC is strongly normalizing and $\xrightarrow[E]{}$ is weakly confluent. Let $t \in T_\Sigma$. SPEC-normalization preserves recursive EO-reductions of all $u \in D(t, \xrightarrow[E]{*})$ iff SPEC commutes with recursive EO-reductions of all $u \in D(t, \xrightarrow[E]{*})$.

Proof: Since SPEC is strongly normalizing, the "only if"-direction follows immediately. By Proposition 2.3, each Σ-term t has a unique SPEC-normal form nf(t). Suppose that SPEC commutes with recursive EO-reductions of all $u \in D(t, \xrightarrow[E]{*})$. We prove by noetherian induction on t1 w.r.t. $\xrightarrow[E]{}$ that for all $t1, t2, t3 \in D(t, \xrightarrow[E]{*})$

$$t1 \xRightarrow[EO]{\Delta} t2 \xrightarrow[E]{*} t3 \text{ implies } nf(t1) \xRightarrow[EO]{\Delta} \cdot \xrightarrow[E]{*} nf(t3).$$

If t1 is SPEC-normal, then

$$nf(t1) = t1 \xRightarrow[EO]{\Delta} t2 \xrightarrow[E]{*} t3 \xrightarrow[E]{*} nf(t3).$$

Otherwise $t1 \xrightarrow[E]{} t4$ for some $t4 \in T_\Sigma$. Hence, by commutativity of SPEC with EO-reductions, we get

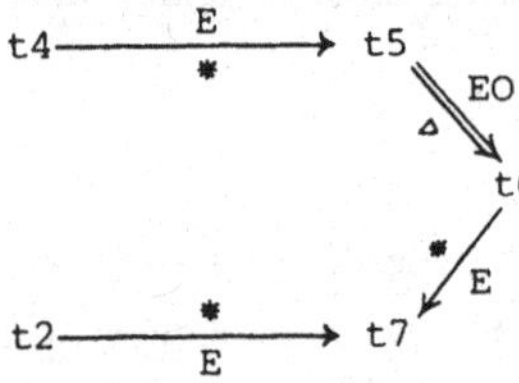

for some $t5, t6, t7 \in T_\Sigma$. By induction hypothesis,

$$nf(t5) \xRightarrow[EO]{\Delta} \cdot \xrightarrow[E]{*} nf(t7).$$

Since nf(t1) = nf(t4) = nf(t5) and nf(t3) = nf(t2) = nf(t7), we are done. □

While Proposition 2.3 stated that unique normalization of SPEC can be reduced to weak confluence of SPEC, Lemma 3.2 is the corresponding result concerning preservation of EO-reductions by SPEC-normalization.

In the rest of this chapter we show that the proof of weak confluence and commutativity with EO-reductions can be confined to the consideration of "ground term critical pairs" (see introduction).

3.3 DEFINITION

A *Σ-term* over X is *linear* if each variable occurs at most once in t. A set E of *Σ-equations* is *linear* if for all $(L,R) \in E$ L is linear. For all linear Σ-terms over X and all $x \in var(t)$ the *occurrence $O(x,t) \in \omega^*$ of x in t* is inductively defined by

$$O(x,x) = \varepsilon$$

and
$$O(x,\sigma(t1,\dots,tn)) = i\cdot O(x,ti) \text{ if } x \in var(ti). \quad \square$$

3.4 DEFINITION

Given $t \xrightarrow[E]{} t'$, the greatest linear Σ-term u over X such that $t = fu$ and $t' = f'u$ for some $f,f' \in subst_\Sigma$ and $(fx,f'x) \in P_\Sigma(E)$ for all $x \in var(u)$ is denoted by *com(t,E,t')*. For $t \xRightarrow[E]{} t'$ com(t,E,t') is defined the same except that "$(fx,f'x) \in P_\Sigma(E)$" is replaced by "$fx = gL \xRightarrow[E]{} g'R = f'x$ for some $g,g' \in subst_\Sigma$ and $(L,R) \in E$ ". $\square$

3.5 DEFINITION (critical pairs)

Given $(L,R) \in E$, $f \in subst_\Sigma$ and $fL \xrightarrow[EO]{} t$ (resp. $fL \xRightarrow[EO]{} t$), let $u = com(fL,EO,t)$. (fR,t) is called a *simple* (resp. *recursive*) *critical pair of (E,EO) for fL* if there is $x \in var(u)$ such that all occurrences w of variables in L satisfy $w \nleq O(x,u)$. *EO overlaps E* if critical pairs of (E,EO) exist. $\square$

3.6 LEMMA

Let $(L,R) \in E$ be linear, $f \in subst_\Sigma$ and $fL \xrightarrow[EO]{} t$ (resp. $fL \xRightarrow[EO]{} t$) such that (fR,t) is not a critical pair of (E,EO) for fL. Then there is $f' \in subst_\Sigma$ with $f'L = t$ and $fz \xrightarrow[EO]{\triangle} f'z$ (resp. $fz \xRightarrow[EO]{\triangle} f'z$) for all $z \in var(L)$.

Proof: Let $u = com(fL,EO,t)$. There are $g,g' \in subst_\Sigma$ such that $gu = fL$ and $g'u = t$. By assumption, for all $x \in var(u)$ there is $z \in var(L)$ with $O(z,L) \leq O(x,u)$. For all $z \in var(L)$ let $Vz = \{x \in var(u) \mid O(z,L) \leq O(x,u)\}$. Thus we have $sz \in subst_\Sigma$ and $tz \in T_\Sigma(Vz)$ such that $fz = sz(tz)$ and $sz(x) = gx$ for all $x \in Vz$. Define $sz', f' \in subst_\Sigma$ by $sz'(x) = g'x$ for all $x \in Vz$ and $f'z = sz'(tz)$, respectively. Since $(gx,g'x) \in P_\Sigma(EO)$ (resp. $gx \xRightarrow[EO]{} g'x$) for all $x \in var(u)$, we obtain $fz \xrightarrow[EO]{\triangle} f'z$ (resp. $fz \xRightarrow[EO]{\triangle} f'z$) for all $z \in var(L)$. $fL = gu$ implies $f'L = g'u$ and thus $f'L = t$. $\square$

3.7 THEOREM

Assume that $E \cup EO$ is linear, and let $t \in T_\Sigma$. For all subterms u of t, $u \xrightarrow[E]{} u1$ and $u \xrightarrow[EO]{} u0$ there is $u2 \in T_\Sigma$ with

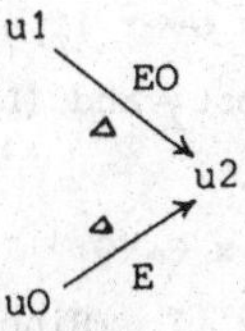

(*)

iff for all subterms u of t each simple critical pair (u1,u0) of (E,EO) for u and each simple critical pair (u0,u1) of (EO,E) for u satisfies (*) for some $u2 \in T_\Sigma$.

<u>Proof:</u> The "only-if"-part follows immediately. Let $t \xrightarrow[E]{} t1$, $t \xrightarrow[EO]{} t0$, $c1 = com(t,E,t1)$, $c0 = com(t,EO,t0)$,

$$V1 = \{x \in var(c1) \mid O(z,c0) \nless O(x,c1) \text{ for all } z \in var(c0)\}$$

and

$$V0 = \{x \in var(c0) \mid O(z,c1) \nleq O(x,c0) \text{ for all } z \in var(c1)\}.$$

Thus we have $c \in T_\Sigma(V0 \cup V1)$ and $f, f0, f1 \in subst_\Sigma$ such that $fc = t$, $f0(c) = t0$, $f1(c) = t1$ and

1. for all $x \in V1$ there are $g \in subst_\Sigma$ and $(L,R) \in E$ with $gL = fx \xrightarrow[EO]{\Delta} f0(x)$ and $gR = f1(x)$,
2. for all $x \in V0$ there are $g \in subst_\Sigma$ and $(L,R) \in EO$ with $gL = fx \xrightarrow[E]{\Delta} f1(x)$ and $gR = f0(x)$.

Hence, if there is $f2 \in subst_\Sigma$ with

$$f1(x) \xrightarrow[EO]{\Delta} f2(x) \xleftarrow[E]{\Delta} f0(x) \qquad \text{(a)}$$

for all $x \in V0 \cup V1$, then Σ-compatibility of $\xrightarrow[E]{}$ and $\xrightarrow[EO]{}$ implies

$$t1 \xrightarrow[EO]{\Delta} f2(c). \xleftarrow[E]{\Delta} t0 \qquad \text{(b)}$$

W.l.o.g. let $x \in V1$. If $fx = f0(x)$, define $f2(x) = f1(x)$, and (a) follows from $fx \xrightarrow[E]{} f1(x)$ (see 1.). Otherwise we may assume that $(f1(x),f0(x))$ is not a (simple) critical pair of (E,EO) for fx. By Lemma 3.6, there is $h \in subst_\Sigma$ with $hL = f0(x)$ and $gz \xrightarrow[EO]{\Delta} hz$ for all $z \in var(L)$ where (L,R) and g are given by 1. Hence $f2(x) = hR$ satisfies (a). □

3.8 <u>THEOREM</u>

Assume that $E \cup EO$ is linear and E does not overlap EO. Then the assertion of Theorem 3.7 remains valid if simple EO-reductions and simple critical pairs of (E,EO) are replaced by recursive EO-reductions resp. recursive critical pairs of (E,EO).

<u>Proof:</u> The proof of Theorem 3.7 carries over if assertion 3.7.2 is replaced by

2'. For all $x \in V0$ there are $g, g' \in subst_\Sigma$ and $(L,R) \in EO$ with $gL = fx \xrightarrow[E]{\Delta} f1(x)$ and $gR \overset{\Delta}{\underset{EO}{\Longrightarrow}} g'R = f0(x)$.

In addition, we must verify (a) for all $x \in V0$. If $fx = f1(x)$, define $f2(x) = f0(x)$, and (a) follows from $fx \underset{EO}{\Longrightarrow} f0(x)$ (see 2'.). Since E does not overlap EO, $(f0(x), f1(x))$ is not a (recursive) critical pair of (EO,E) for fx. Using Lemma 3.6 with E and EO interchanged, we obtain $h \in subst_\Sigma$ with $hL = f1(x)$ and $gz \xrightarrow[E]{\Delta} hz$ for all $z \in var(L)$. By definition of $c0$ and assertion 2'., we also have $gz \overset{\Delta}{\underset{EO}{\Longrightarrow}} g'z$ for all

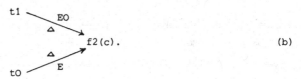

$z \in var(R)$. If there is $h' \in subst_{\Sigma}$ with

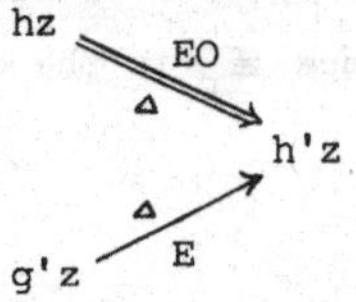

(c)

for all $z \in var(R)$, then $f2(x) = h'R$ satisfies (a) because $f1(x) = hL$ and $f0(x) = g'R$. We prove (b) by induction on the "size" of t. Suppose that t is of minimal size such that $t \xrightarrow[E]{} t1$ and $t \overset{}{\underset{EO}{\Longrightarrow}} t0$ for some $t1, t0 \in T_{\Sigma}$. Since for all $z \in var(L)$ gz is a proper subterm of t, we have gz = hz or gz = g'z (see above). Defining h'z = g'z resp. h'z = hz, (c) follows immediately. If t is not minimal, then for all $z \in var(R)$ with $hz \neq gz \neq g'z$ h'z satisfying (c) exists by induction hypothesis. Hence the preceding part of this proof implies (b). □

The following two theorems are provable analogous to Theorem 3.7 resp. 3.8.

3.9 THEOREM

Assume that E is linear, and let $t \in T_{\Sigma}$. SPEC is weakly confluent for all subterms of t iff for each subterm u of t and each simple critical pair (u1,u0) of (E,E) for u there is $u2 \in T_{\Sigma}$ with

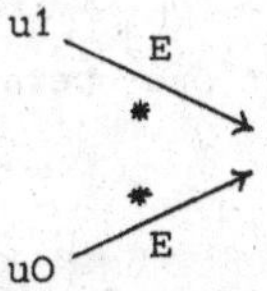

□

3.10 THEOREM

Assume that $E \cup EO$ is linear and E does not overlap EO. Let $t \in T_{\Sigma}$. SPEC commutes with recursive EO-reductions of all subterms of t iff for each subterm u of t and each recursive critical pair (u1,u0) of (E,EO) for u there are $u2, u3, u4 \in T_{\Sigma}$ with

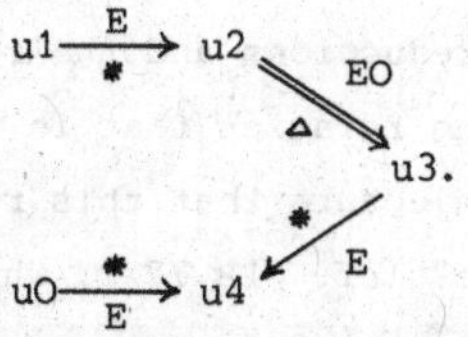

□

4. ENRICHMENTS OF SPECIFICATIONS

Given a specification SPEC = $\langle S, \Sigma, E \rangle$, the least Σ-congruence on T_{Σ} that contains $P_{\Sigma}(E)$ is usually called <u>SPEC-equivalence</u> and denoted by $\equiv_E$. According to the initial algebra approach to abstract data types the class of all Σ-algebras isomorphic to the quotient $T_{SPEC} = T_{\Sigma}/\equiv_E$ is called <u>semantics</u> or <u>abstract data type of SPEC.</u> The name SPEC-equivalence is also used for the property of two terms t,t' to be <u>SPEC-</u>

equivalent, i.e. to satisfy $t \equiv_E t'$. Moreover, let Induce(SPEC) be the set of all "theorems provable by induction on T_Σ", i.e. the set of all Σ-equations e such that each $(l,r) \in P_\Sigma(\{e\})$ satisfies $l \equiv_E r$. Since $\equiv_E$ is the equivalence closure of $\xrightarrow[E]{}$, we immediately obtain

4.1 PROPOSITION

If SPEC is strongly and uniquely normalizing, then SPEC-equivalence is decidable. □

For the rest of this chapter suppose that we are given two specifications $SPEC0 = \langle S,\Sigma0,E0\rangle$ and $SPEC1 = \langle S,\Sigma1,E1\rangle$ with $\Sigma0 \subseteq \Sigma1$ and $E0 \subseteq E1$.

4.2 DEFINITION

SPEC1 is an enrichment of SPEC0 if T_{SPEC0} and T_{SPEC1} are $\Sigma0$-isomorphic. SPEC1 is complete w.r.t. SPEC0 if for all $t1 \in T_{\Sigma1}$ there is $t0 \in T_{\Sigma0}$ with $t1 \equiv_{E1} t0$. SPEC1 is consistent w.r.t. SPEC0 if for all $t0,t0' \in T_{\Sigma0}$ $t0 \equiv_{E1} t0'$ implies $t0 \equiv_{E0} t0'$. □

4.3 LEMMA (cf. /EKP 78/)

SPEC1 is an enrichment of SPEC0 iff SPEC1 is complete and consistent w.r.t. SPEC0. □

4.4 DEFINITION

Let $I0 \subseteq$ Induce(SPEC0), $E = (E1 - E0) \cup I0$ and $SPEC = \langle S,\Sigma1,E\rangle$. SPEC1 is called a strong enrichment of SPEC0 if

1. for all $(L,R) \in E1 - E0$ L contains at least one operation symbol of $\Sigma1 - \Sigma0$,
2. all SPEC-normal forms are $\Sigma0$-terms,
3. SPEC is strongly normalizing,
4. SPEC is uniquely normalizing,
5. SPEC-normalization preserves recursive $(E0 - I0)$-reductions. □

Another notion of strong enrichment may be derived from G. Huet's results on the confluence of reductions modulo an equivalence relation (cf. /Huet 77/). Using his approach, 4.4.4/5 can be weakened, but, on the other hand, the corresponding conditions involve the consideration of inverse $(E0 - I0)$-reductions. Moreover, SPEC must be strongly normalizing modulo $(E0 - I0)$-reductions and their inverses, i.e. we need a SPEC-compatible and strongly normalizing relation that is closed under multiplication with $\xrightarrow[E0 - I0]{}$ and its inverse. We conjecture that this requirement forces all equations of $E0 - I0$ to be "permutative" (cf. /LB 77/), which is a property many actual enrichments do not have, e.g. example 5.4.

4.5 LEMMA

Let SPEC1 be a strong enrichment of SPEC0. Then SPEC1 is an enrichment of SPEC0. Moreover, if SPEC0-equivalence is decidable, then SPEC1-equivalence is decidable, too.

Proof: By 4.4.2/3/4, each $\Sigma 1$-term t has a unique SPEC-normal form nf(t), and nf(t) is a ΣO-term. Hence SPEC1 is complete w.r.t. SPECO. Furthermore, we show that for all $t,t' \in T_{\Sigma 1}$

$$t \equiv_{E1} t' \quad \text{iff} \quad nf(t) \equiv_{EO} nf(t'). \qquad \text{(a)}$$

From (a) we can conclude consistency of SPEC1 w.r.t. SPECO because 4.4.1 implies $t \equiv_{EO} nf(t)$ for all $t \in T_{\Sigma O}$. The assertion that SPEC1-equivalence is reducible to SPECO-equivalence also follows from (a). Since $E, EO \subseteq E1$, the "if"-part of (a) holds true. By 4.4.5, for all $t,t' \in T_{\Sigma 1}$

$$t \xRightarrow[EO - IO]{} t' \text{ implies } nf(t) \xRightarrow[EO - IO]{\Delta} \cdot \xrightarrow[E]{*} nf(t').$$

Thus, by 4.4.1,

$$t \xRightarrow[EO - IO]{} t' \text{ implies } nf(t) \equiv_{EO} nf(t').$$

Clearly,

$$t \xrightarrow[E]{} t' \text{ implies } nf(t) = nf(t').$$

But $E1 \subseteq (EO - IO) \cup E$ so that the "only-if"-part of (a) is valid. □

4.6 DEFINITION

A $\Sigma 1$-term $t = \sigma(t1,\dots,tn)$ is <u>ΣO-normal</u> if $\sigma \in \Sigma 1 - \Sigma O$ and $ti \in T_{\Sigma O}$ for all $i \in [n]$. □

4.7 MAIN THEOREM

Let IO, E and SPEC be as in Definition 4.4. SPEC1 is a strong enrichment of SPECO if the following conditions hold true:

1. For all $(L,R) \in E1 - EO$ L contains at least one operation symbol of $\Sigma 1 - \Sigma O$.
2. ΣO-normal $\Sigma 1$-terms are not SPEC-normal.
3. There is a SPEC-compatible $\Sigma 1$-simplification ordering.
4. $E \cup EO$ is linear.
5. E does not overlap EO - IO.
6. Let $u \in T_{\Sigma 1}$ and assume that SPEC is uniquely normalizing for all proper subterms of u. Then each simple critical pair (u1,uO) of (E,E) for u satisfies

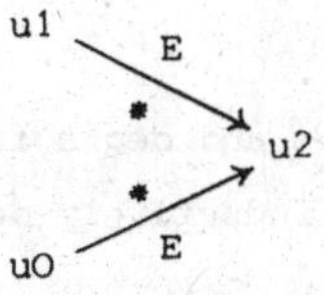

for some $u2 \in T_{\Sigma 1}$.

7. Let $u \in T_{\Sigma 1}$ and assume that SPEC-normalization preserves (EO - IO)-reductions of all proper subterms of u. Then each recursive critical pair (u1,uO) of (E,EO - IO) for u satisfies

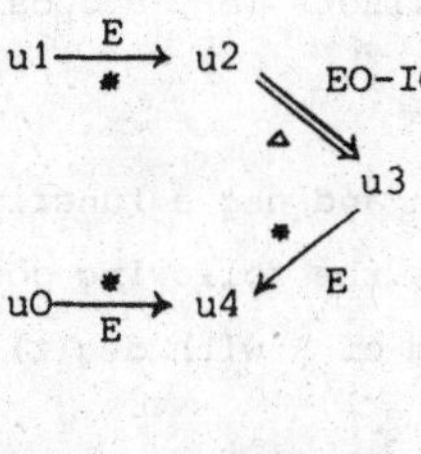

for some u2,u3,u4 $\in T_{\Sigma 1}$.

Proof: Clearly, 4.4.2 and 4.7.2 are equivalent. By Theorem 2.7 and Proposition 2.10, 4.7.3 implies 4.4.3. Let $>$ be the SPEC-compatible Σ1-simplification ordering required by 4.7.3, and let $t \in T_{\Sigma 1}$. Supposing 4.7.4 - 7 we get by noetherian induction on t w.r.t. $>$:

a) SPEC is uniquely normalizing for t,

b) SPEC-normalization preserves recursive (EO - IO)-reductions of t.

If t is $>$-normal, then t is SPEC-normal because $>$ is SPEC-compatible. Hence a) holds true, and $t \xRightarrow[EO\,-\,IO]{} u$ implies $t \xRightarrow[EO\,-\,IO]{} \cdot \xrightarrow[E]{*} u'$ for all SPEC-normal forms u' of u. Thus b) is satisfied, too. Now let t be not $>$-normal. By Proposition 2.3 and Theorem 3.9, a) is valid if the conclusion of 4.7.6 holds true for all $u \in T_{\Sigma 1}$ with $t \xrightarrow[E]{*} \cdot \trianglerighteq u$ where $\triangleright$ denotes the Σ1-subterm relation. But the assumption of 4.7.6 is true for such u by induction hypothesis because a proper subterm u' of u satisfies $u > u'$ and thus $t > u'$. Analogously, Lemma 3.2 and Theorem 3.10 imply that b) is valid if the conclusion of 4.7.7 holds true for all $u \in T_{\Sigma 1}$ with $t \xrightarrow[E]{*} \cdot \trianglerighteq u$. That the assumption of 4.7.7 is true for such u again follows by induction hypothesis. □

At first sight conditions 4.7.6 and 4.7.7 look somewhat complicated, but in fact they provide induction schemes for proving unique normalization of SPEC resp. preservation of (EO - IO)-reductions by SPEC-normalization. The proof of Theorem 4.7 points out that these induction schemes are only valid if 4.7.3 is satisfied.

5. HOW TO USE THEOREM 4.7

Let SPEC = $\langle S,\Sigma,E\rangle$ be a specification. There are several ways to construct a Σ-simplification ordering $>$. One way is to induce $>$ by a relation on some set S via a monotone function $\tau: T_\Sigma \longrightarrow S$ (cf. /Der 79a/). Here we use a special case of the recursive path ordering on T_Σ (Σ-rpo), which was shown to be a Σ-simplification ordering by /Der 79b/, and present a class of specifications SPEC such that the Σ-rpo is SPEC-compatible.

5.1 DEFINITION (cf. /Der 79b/)

Let Σ be a finite set of operation symbols and deg a function from Σ to ω. The recursive path ordering $>$ on T_Σ (Σ-rpo) is inductively defined as follows:

$$t = \sigma(t1,\dots,tn) > \tau(u1,\dots,um) = u$$

iff $deg(\sigma) > deg(\tau)$ and $t > ui$ for all $i \in [n]$

or $deg(\sigma) = deg(\tau)$ and $\{t1,\dots,tn\} \gg \{u1,\dots,um\}$

or $deg(\sigma) < deg(\tau)$ and $ti \geq u$ for some $i \in [m]$

where $\gg$ is the extension of $>$ to multisets (cf. Proposition 2.4). □

5.2 DEFINITION

Let SPEC = $\langle S,\Sigma,E\rangle$ be a specification and deg a function from Σ to ω. SPEC is path-decreasing if each $(L,R) \in E$ satisfies the following condition: If $L = \sigma(t1,\dots,tn)$ and $\tau(u1,\dots,um)$ is a maximal subterm of R with $deg(\tau) \geq deg(\sigma)$, then $deg(\tau) = deg(\sigma)$

and $\{t1,\dots,tn\} \supset\supset \{u1,\dots,um\}$ where $\supset\supset$ is the extension of the Σ-subterm relation to multisets. □

One easily verifies

5.3 LEMMA

If SPEC = $\langle S,\Sigma,E\rangle$ is path-decreasing, then the Σ-rpo is SPEC-compatible. □

Now we apply Theorem 4.7 to a specification of finite sets. For the syntactical schema we use to write down specifications we refer to /GTW 78/, /EKP 78/ et al. + denotes the disjoint union of a specification with new sorts, operation symbols or equations.

5.4 EXAMPLE

Let element be a specification that contains the sorts bool and element and the operations T,F:⟶ bool and EQ:element element ⟶ bool.

SPEC0 = element +
  sorts: set
  opns: ∅:⟶ set
    INS: set element ⟶ set
    IF: bool set set ⟶ set
  eqns: INS(INS(s,x),y) = IF(EQ(x,y),INS(s,y),INS(INS(s,y),x))
    IF(T,s,s') = s
    IF(F,s,s') = s'

Assume that

1. each $t \in T_{\Sigma 0,bool}$ satisfies either $t \equiv_{E0} T$ or $t \equiv_{E0} F$,
2. for all $t, u \in T_{\Sigma 0,element}$
   $t \equiv_{E0} u$ implies $EQ(t,u) \equiv_{E0} T$,
   $t \not\equiv_{E0} u$ implies $EQ(t,u) \equiv_{E0} F$.

Furthermore,

SPEC1 = SPEC0 +
  opns: DEL: set element ⟶ set
    HAS: set element ⟶ bool
  eqns: DEL(∅,x) = ∅
    DEL(INS(s,x),y) = IF(EQ(x,y),DEL(s,y),INS(DEL(s,y),x))
    HAS(∅,x) = F
    HAS(INS(s,x),y) = IF(EQ(x,y),T,HAS(s,y))

Let s,s' be two different set-variables and I0 be given by the set of all equations

IF(t,s,s') = s   and   IF(u,s,s') = s'

where t,u are $\Sigma 0$-terms of sort bool such that $t \equiv_{E0} T$ and $u \equiv_{E0} F$. Clearly, $I0 \subseteq$ Induce(SPEC0). Let E and SPEC be as in Definition 4.4. Using Theorem 4.7 we show that SPEC1 is a strong enrichment of SPEC0. 4.7.1,2,4 and 5 are immediately verified. Define deg: $\Sigma 1 \longrightarrow \omega$ by $deg^{-1}(0) = \Sigma 0 - \{IF\}, deg^{-1}(1) = \{IF\}$ and $deg^{-1}(2) = \{DEL,HAS\}$. Then SPEC is path-decreasing, and thus 4.7.3 holds true. If (u1,u0) is a simple critical pair of (E,E) for some $u \in T_{\Sigma 1}$, then u1 = u0 or there are $t,v,w \in T_{\Sigma 1}$ such that u = IF(t,v,w). In the latter case we have $t' \in T_{\Sigma 0}$ and $v',w' \in T_{\Sigma 1}$ such that u0 = IF(t',v',w'), $t \xrightarrow[IO]{} t'$, $v \xrightarrow[E]{\Delta} v'$ and $w \xrightarrow[E]{\Delta} w'$. If $t \equiv_{EO} T$, then u1 = v and $t' \equiv_{EO} T$, which implies $u1 \xrightarrow[E]{\Delta} v'$ and $u0 \xrightarrow[IO]{} v'$. Analogously, $t \equiv_{EO} F$ yields $u1 \xrightarrow[E]{\Delta} w'$ and $u0 \xrightarrow[IO]{} w'$. It remains to prove 4.7.7.

Let (u1,u0) be a recursive critical pair of (E,E1 - EO) for some $u \in T_{\Sigma 1}$. Then there are $t,v,w,z \in T_{\Sigma 1}$ such that (a) u = IF(t,v,w) or (b) u = DEL(INS(INS(t,v),w),z) or (c) u = HAS(INS(INS(t,v),w),z). We have $t',v',w',z' \in T_{\Sigma 1}$ such that (t,t'), (v,v'), (w,w'), $(z,z') \in \xRightarrow[EO\,-\,IO]{\Delta}$, u0 = IF(t',v',w') in case (a),
u0 = DEL(IF(EQ(v',w'),INS(t',w'),INS(INS(t',w'),v')),z') in case (b) and
u0 = HAS(IF(EQ(v',w'),INS(t',w'),INS(INS(t',w'),v')),z') in case (c).
In case (a) we can conclude as above that either
$u1 \xRightarrow[EO\,-\,IO]{\Delta} v'$ and $u0 \xrightarrow[IO]{} v'$ or $u1 \xRightarrow[EO\,-\,IO]{\Delta} w'$ and $u0 \xrightarrow[IO]{} w'$.
For all $x \in \{v,w,z\}$ there are SPEC-normal forms $x1, x0 \in T_{\Sigma 0}$ of x resp. x'. Since x is a proper subterm of u, we may assume

$$x1 \xRightarrow[EO\,-\,IO]{\Delta} x2 \xrightarrow[E]{*} x0 \qquad (1)$$

for some $x2 \in T_{\Sigma 0}$ (cf. 4.7.7).
In case (b) we have
u1 = IF(EQ(w,z),DEL(INS(t,v),z),INS(DEL(INS(t,v),z),w))
so that $u1 \xrightarrow[E]{*} t1$ and $u0 \xrightarrow[E]{*} t0$ where
t1 = IF(EQ(w1,z1),DEL(INS(t,v1),z1),INS(DEL(INS(t,v1),z1),w1)) and
t0 = DEL(IF(EQ(v0,w0),INS(t',w0),INS(INS(t',w0),v0)),z0).
Let $\equiv \; = \; \equiv_{EO}$. There are five cases:

$$v1 \equiv w1 \equiv z1,$$
$$v1 \equiv w1 \not\equiv z1 \not\equiv v1,$$
$$v1 \not\equiv w1 \equiv z1 \not\equiv v1,$$
$$v1 \not\equiv w1 \not\equiv z1 \equiv v1,$$
$$v1 \not\equiv w1 \not\equiv z1 \not\equiv v1.$$

Using (1) and the fact that for all $x,y \in \{v,w,z\}$ $x1 \equiv y1$ iff $x0 \equiv y0$, it is straightforward to show that in all these cases there are $t2,t3,t4 \in T_{\Sigma 1}$ with

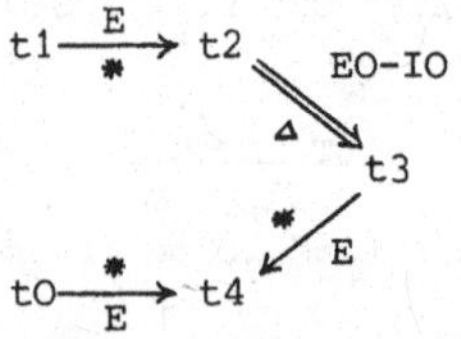

Note that the equations of IO are applicable because EQ(w1,z1),EQ(v0,w0) etc. are $\Sigma 0$-terms. In case (c) 4.7.7 is verified analogously. □

REFERENCES

/Der 79a/ Dershowitz, N.: A Note on Simplification Orderings, Inform. Process. Letters 9, No. 5, 1979, 212-215

/Der 79b/ --: Orderings for Term-Rewriting Systems, Proc. 20th IEEE Symp. on FOCS, 1979, 123-131

/DM 79/ Dershowitz, N., Manna, Z.: Proving Termination With Multiset Orderings, Comm. ACM, Vol. 22, No. 8, 1979, 465-476

/EKP 78/ Ehrig, H., Kreowski, H.-J., Padawitz, P.: Stepwise Specification and Implementation of Abstract Data Types, Proc. 5th ICALP, Udine, 1978, Springer Lect. Not. in Comp. Sci. 62, 205-226

/EKP 80/ --: Completeness in Algebraic Specifications, to appear in Bull. EATCS, No. 11, 1980

/Gut 75/ Guttag, J.V.: The Specification and Application to Programming of Abstract Data Types, Ph.D.Thesis, University of Toronto,1975

/GTW 78/ Goguen, J.A., Thatcher, J.W., Wagner, E.G.: An Initial Algebra Approach to the Specification, Correctness and Implementation of Abstract Data Types, in: Current Trends in Programming Methodology, IV: Data Structuring (R.Yeh Ed.), Prentice Hall, New Jersey, 1978, 80-144

/Huet 77/ Huet, G.: Confluent Reductions: Abstract Properties and Applications to Term Rewriting Systems, Proc. 18th IEEE Symp. on FOCS, Providence, RI., 1977, 30-45

/KB 70/ Knuth, D., Bendix, P.: Simple Word Problems in Universal Algebras, in: Computational Problems in Abstract Algebra (J. Leech Ed.), Pergamon Press, Oxford, 1970, 263-297

/LB 77/ Lankford, D.S., Ballantyne, A.M.: Decision Procedures for Simple Equational Theories with Permutative Axioms: Complete Sets of Permutative Reductions, Report ATP-3: Dept. of Math. and Comp. Sci., University of Texas at Austin, 1977

/Nou 79/ Nourani, F.: Constructive Extension and Implementation of Abstract Data Types and Algorithms, Ph.D.Thesis, University of California at LA, 1979

/Pad 79/ Padawitz, P.: Proving the Correctness of Implementations by Exclusive Use of Term Algebras, Forschungsbericht Nr. 79-8, TU Berlin, FB 20, 1979

ASYMPTOTIC COMPLEXITY OF GAME-SEARCHING PROCEDURES

Judea Pearl
Cognitive Systems Laboratory
School of Engineering and Applied Science
University of California, Los Angeles
Los Angeles, California 90024 USA

1. INTRODUCTION

We consider a class of two-person perfect-information games in which two players, called MAX and MIN, take alternate turns in selecting one out of d legal moves. We assume that the game is searched to a depth h, at which point the terminal positions are assigned a static evaluation function V_0. The task is to evaluate the minimax value, V_h, of the root node by examining, on the average, the least number of terminal nodes.

The most commonly used procedure for searching such game-trees is the α-β pruning algorithm [1]. Yet although the exponential growth of game-tree searching is slowed significantly by that algorithm, quantitative analyses of its effectiveness have been frustrated for over a decade. Of major concern are the problems of determining the optimal expected complexity of game-searching tasks and deciding whether the α-β procedure achieves this optimal performance.

The number of terminal nodes examined by α-β was shown by Slagle and Dixon (1969) to be lower bounded by $d^{\lceil h/2 \rceil} + d^{\lfloor h/2 \rfloor} - 1$ but may, in the worst case, reach the entire set of d^h terminal nodes [2]. The analysis of expected performance using uniform trees with random terminal values had begun with Fuller, Gaschnig, and Gillogly [3] who obtained formulas by which the average number of terminal examinations, $N_{d,h}$, can be computed. Unfortunately, the formula would not facilitate asymptotic analysis; simulation studies led to the following approximation for the branching factor: $r_{\alpha-\beta} = \lim_{h\to\infty} (N_{d,h})^{1/h} \approx (d)^{0.72}$.

Knuth and Moore [1] have analyzed a less powerful but simpler version of the α-β procedure by ignoring deep cutoffs. They have shown that the branching factor of this simplified model is O(d/log d) and speculated that the inclusion of deep cutoffs would not alter this behavior substantially. A more recent study by Baudet [4] confirmed this conjecture by deriving an integral formula for $N_{d,h}$ (deep cutoffs included) from which the branching factor can be estimated. In particular, Baudet shows that for continuous-valued trees $r_{\alpha-\beta}$ is bounded by $\xi/1-\xi \le r_{\alpha-\beta} \le M^{1/2}$ where ξ is the positive root of $x^d+x-1 = 0$ and M is the maximal value of the polynomial $(\sum_{k=0}^{d-1} x^k) \cdot (\sum_{k=0}^{d-1} (1-x^d)^k$ in the range $0 \le x \le 1$.

This paper highlights some curious properties of tall game-trees with random terminal values and examines their implications on the complexity of various game-searching methods. In particular, we show that for continuous-valued games, the quantity $\xi/1-\xi$ lower bounds the branching factor of every directional search algorithm and that an algorithm exists (called SCOUT) which actually achieves this bound. Games with discrete terminal values can, in almost all cases, be evaluated by examining an average of $O[(d)^{h/2}]$ terminal positions. This performance is optimal and is also achieved by the ALPHA-BETA procedure.

2. GAME TREES WITH AN ARBITRARY DISTRIBUTION OF TERMINAL VALUES

Consider a uniform tree (constant d) where the terminal nodes are assigned numerical values, $V_0(S_1), V_0(S_2), \dots V_0(S_{2^h})$, and assume the latter to be independent identically distributed random variables, drawn from a common distribution function $F_0(v) = P(V_0 \leq v)$. We shall refer to a tree drawn from such an ensemble as a (h,d,F_0)-tree and calculate the distribution of the minimax value of the root node. Without loss of generality we shall also assume that h is an even integer, h=2n, and that the root node always represents a MAX move.

Denoting the minimax value of the root node by $V_n(S)$, it is easy to show that its distribution function $F_n(v) = P[V_n(S) \leq v]$ is governed by the recursive relation:

$$F_n(v) = g[F_{n-1}(v)] \tag{1}$$

where

$$g(x) = [1-(1-x)^d]^d \tag{2}$$

The function g(x) is monotonic increasing over [0, 1] with a fixed point at $x = 1-\xi$ where ξ is the unique positive root of the equation $x^d+x-1 = 0$. Consequently, $F_n(v)$ satisfies:

$$\lim_{n\to\infty} F_n(v) = \begin{cases} 0 & F_0(v) < 1-\xi \\ 1-\xi & F_0(v) = 1-\xi \\ 1 & F_0(v) > 1-\xi \end{cases} \tag{3}$$

Equation (3) implies that when the game tree is sufficiently tall, the density of $V_n(S)$, $f_n(v)$, becomes highly concentrated around those values v^* satisfying:

$$F_0(v^*) = 1-\xi \tag{4}$$

<u>Theorem 1</u>: a) The root value of a (h, d, F_0)-tree with continuous strictly increasing terminal distribution F_0 converges, as $h \to \infty$ (in probability) to the $(1-\xi)$-quantile of F_0, where ξ is the solution of $x^d+x-1 = 0$.

b) If the terminal values are discrete: $v_1 < v_2 < \dots < v_M$, then the root value converges to a definite limit iff $1-\xi \neq F_0(v_i)$ for all i, in which case the limit is the smallest v_i satisfying $F_0(v_i) > 1-\xi$.

c) If one of the discrete values satisfies $F_0(v_i) = 1-\xi$ then $V_n(S)$ converges to a bi-valued random variable:

$$\lim_{n\to\infty} P[V_n(S)=v] = \begin{cases} 1-\xi & v = v_i \\ \xi & v = v_{i+1} \\ 0 & \text{otherwise} \end{cases} \tag{5}$$

□

One practical application of Theorem 1 is that game-searching algorithms can be effective in estimating the quantiles of an unknown distribution [5].

An important corollary of Theorem 1 is that when the terminal positions are assigned a WIN-LOSS status (i.e., $v_1=0$, $v_2=1$) with the probabilities P_0 and $1-P_0$, respectively, then the root node is almost a sure WIN or a sure LOSS, depending on whether P_0 is higher or lower than some fixed-point probability $P^*=\xi$. Denoting by P_n the probability that the root node is a WIN, it is possible to show that the slope of $P_n(P_0)$ at the transition point $P_0=P^*$ increases exponentially with n:

$$\frac{d}{dP_0}(P_n)\Bigg|_{P_0=P^*} = \frac{d(1-P^*)}{P^*}^{2n}, \text{ and } \frac{d(1-P^*)}{P^*} > 1 \text{ for } d > 1 \tag{6}$$

Also, a more detailed analysis shows that for sufficiently large n, P_n converges toward its asymptotic values at a super-exponential rate, i.e., for every $0 < \delta < 1$ we can find two integers n_1 and n_2, such that:

$$\begin{aligned} P_n &\le (\delta)^{d^{(n-n_1)}} && \text{for all } n > n_1 \text{ and } P_0 < P^* \\ 1-P_n &\le (\delta)^{d^{(n-n_2)}} && \text{for all } n > n_2 \text{ and } P_0 > P^* \end{aligned} \tag{7}$$

where n_1 and n_2 are functions of δ and P^*-P_0.

3. THE MEAN COMPLEXITY OF SOLVING A STANDARD (h, d, P_0)-GAME

Solving a game tree means deciding whether MAX can force a win given the WIN-LOSS status of the terminal positions. An absolute lower bound on the number of terminal node examinations needed for establishing the status of the root-node is given by the following argument. If the root node is a WIN, then there exists a subtree (called a solution tree) consisting of one branch emanating from each MAX node and all branches emanating from each MIN node, terminating at a set of WIN terminal positions. Similarly, if the game is a LOSS, such a solution tree exists for the opponent, terminating at all LOSS nodes. In either case, the number of terminal positions in a solution tree is d^n or $d^{h/2}$. The number of terminal node examinations required to solve the game must exceed $d^{h/2}$ since, regardless of how the solution tree was discovered, one must still ascertain that all its $d^{h/2}$ terminal nodes are WIN in order to defend the proposition "root is a WIN". Thus, $d^{h/2}$ represents the number of terminal nodes inspected by a non-deterministic algorithm which solves the (h, d, P_0)-game and is, therefore, a lower bound for all deterministic algorithms.

It is not hard to show that any algorithm solving the (h, d, P_0)-game would, in the worst case, inspect all d^h terminal positions. This can be done by cleverly arranging the terminal assignments in such a way that a decision could not be reached until the last node is inspected. Since the difference between $d^{h/2}$ and d^h may be quite substantial, it is interesting to evaluate the expected number of terminal examinations where the expectation is taken with respect to all possible WIN-LOSS assignments to the terminal nodes.

Definition: Let A be a deterministic algorithm which solves the (h, d, P_0)-game and let $I_A(h, d, P_0)$ denote the expected number of terminal positions examined by A. The quantity:

$$r_A(d, P_0) = \lim_{h\to\infty} [I_A(h, d, P_0)]^{1/h}$$

is called the branching factor corresponding to the algorithm A.

Definition: Let C be a class of algorithms capable of solving a general (h, d, P_0)-tree. An algorithm A is said to be asymptotically optimal over C if for some P_0 and all d:

$$r_A(d, P_0) \leq r_B(d, P_0) \qquad \forall B \varepsilon C$$

Definition: An algorithm A is said to be directional if for some linear arrangement of the terminal nodes it never selects for examination a node situated to the left of a previously examined node.

Simply stated, an algorithm is directional if it always examines nodes from left to right, regardless of the content of the nodes examined.

We now compute the branching factor of a simple directional algorithm, called SOLVE, given by the following informal description:

Algorithm SOLVE(S): To solve S, start solving its successors from left to right.

If S is MAX, return a WIN as soon as one successor is found to be a WIN; return a LOSS if all successors of S are found to be a LOSS.

If S is MIN, return a LOSS as soon as one successor is found to be a LOSS; return a WIN if all successors of S are found to be a WIN.

To compute $I_{SOLVE}(h, d, P_0)$ we consider the nth cycle preceding the terminal positions. Let x_n stand for the expected number of terminal nodes inspected in solving the root S of an n-cycle tree, and y_n the expected number of inspections used for solving any of the successors of S.

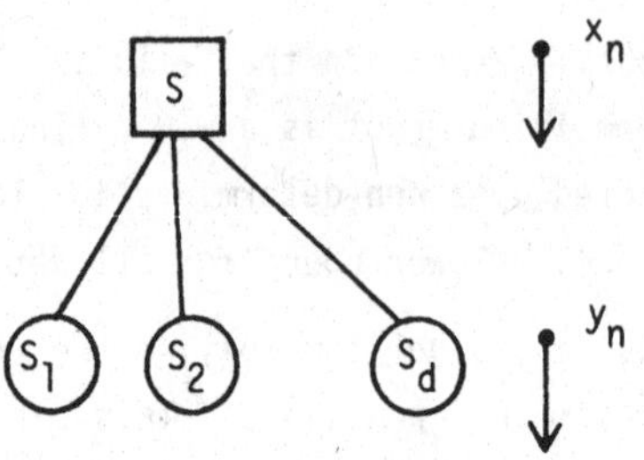

The probability of issuing a WIN after solving the kth successor is $(1-Q_n)^{k-1}\,Q_n$ where $Q_n = P^d_{n-1}$ is the probability that S_1 is a WIN. Such an event requires an average of $(k-1)y_n^- + y_n^+$ terminal inspections, where y_n^- and y_n^+ stand for the mean number of inspections required for establishing a LOSS or a WIN, respectively. Also, the event of issuing a LOSS for S carries a probability $(1-Q_n)^d$ and a mean expenditure of dy_n^- inspections. Therefore:

$$x_n = \sum_{k=1}^{d} Q_n(1-Q_n)^{k-1}\,[(k-1)y_n^- + y_n^+] + d(1-Q_n)^d\,y_n^-$$

$$= y_n^+\,Q_n\,\frac{1-(1-Q_n)^d}{Q_n} + y_n^-\,(1-Q_n)\,\frac{1-(1-Q_n)^d}{Q_n}$$

$$= [y_n^+\,Q_n + y_n^-\,(1-Q_n)]\,\frac{[1-(1-Q_n)^d]}{Q_n}$$

$$= y_n\,\frac{P_n}{P^d_{n-1}} \tag{8}$$

Using a similar analysis for any successor of S gives:

$$y_n = x_{n-1}\,\frac{1-P^d_{n-1}}{1-P_{n-1}} \tag{9}$$

Combining (8) and (9) we obtain:

$$\frac{x_n}{x_{n-1}} = \frac{P_n \cdot (1-P^d_{n-1})}{P^d_{n-1} \cdot (1-P_{n-1})} \tag{10}$$

Since x_n is equivalent to $I_{SOLVE}(2n, d, P_0)$ and $x_0 = 1$, we can state:

Theorem 2: The expected number of terminal positions in a (h, d, P_0)-tree examined by the SOLVE algorithm is given by:

$$I_{SOLVE}(h, d, P_0) = \prod_{i=1}^{h/2} \frac{P_i(1-P^d_{i-1})}{P^d_{i-1}(1-P_{i-1})} \tag{11}$$

where P_i, $i = 1, 2, \ldots h/2$, is related to P_0 by the recursion:

$$P_i = 1 - (1-P_{i-1}^d)^d \qquad (12) \; \square$$

Theorem 2 permits an easy calculation of $I_{SOLVE}(h, d, P_0)$ for wide ranges of d and h. In the special case where $P_0 = P^* = \xi$ all terms in the product of (11) are equal and, using $\xi^d = 1-\xi$, (11) reduces to:

$$I_{SOLVE}(h, d, P^*) = \left(\frac{\xi}{1-\xi}\right)^h \qquad (13)$$

Note that $\lim_{P_{n-1}\to 0} \frac{x_n}{x_{n-1}} = \lim_{P_{n-1}\to 1} \frac{x_n}{x_{n-1}} = d$ which, combined with the very rapid convergence of P_n (see equation (7)), leads directly to the asymptotic branching factor of SOLVE:

Corollary 1: The branching factor of the SOLVE algorithm is given by:

$$r_{SOLVE}(d, P_0) = \begin{cases} d^{1/2} & P_0 \neq \xi \\ \frac{\xi}{1-\xi} & P_0 = \xi \end{cases} \qquad (14)$$

where ξ is the positive solution of $x^d+x-1 = 0$. $\square$

Recalling that $d^{1/2}$ is an absolute lower bound for the branching factor of any tree solving algorithm, we conclude:

Corollary 2: SOLVE is asymptotically optimal for $P_0 \neq \xi$. $\square$

For finite values of h or for $P_0 = \xi$ we have no guarantee that SOLVE is optimal. Non-directional algorithms, such as that proposed by Stockman [6] may outperform SOLVE. However, Corollary 2 states that for very deep trees the savings could not be substantial in all cases where $P_0 \neq \xi$.

Any directional algorithm which is governed by a successor-ordering scheme identical to that of SOLVE must examine all the nodes examined by SOLVE. This is so because if some left-to-right algorithm B skips a node visited by SOLVE, a WIN-LOSS assignment can be found which would render the conclusion of SOLVE contrary to that of B. Thus B could not be a general algorithm for solving all (h, d, P_0)-trees. Now, since $I_{SOLVE}(h, d, P_0)$ is independent on the particular choice of ordering scheme, we may conclude that SOLVE is optimal over the class of directional game-solving algorithms. This leads to:

Corollary 3: The optimal branching factor of any directional algorithm which solves a general (h, d, P_0)-tree is given by (14). $\square$

The case $P_0 = \xi$ deserves special attention. Although it is not very likely to occur in practical WIN-LOSS games, it plays an important role in the analysis of continuous-valued games.

It can be shown [4] that, for large values of d, the asymptotic behavior of $r_{SOLVE}(d, P^*)$ becomes:

$$r_{SOLVE}(d, P^*) = \frac{\xi}{1-\xi} = \frac{d}{\log d}\left[1 + 0\left(\frac{\log \log d}{\log d}\right)\right] \qquad (15)$$

However for the range $2 \leq d \leq 5{,}000$, $\xi/1-\xi$ can be better approximated by the formula $(0.925)d^{0.74741}$ [7].

4. SOLVING, TESTING, AND EVALUATING GAME TREES

When the terminal positions are assigned real values, the root node must be evaluated rather than solved. The SOLVE algorithm discussed in Section 3 is insufficient to fully evaluate a (h, d, F_0)-game tree, but may be used to test the proposition "$V(S) > v$," where v is any fixed reference value chosen for the test. We simply interpret any terminal node t for which $V_0(t) > v$ as a WIN position (otherwise it is a LOSS), and apply SOLVE directly. If it issues a WIN, the proposition "$V(S) > v$" is proven, otherwise we deduce "$V(S) \leq v$." We call this procedure TEST(S, v, >), or TEST(S, v, ≥) if equality is permitted.

From the structural identity of SOLVE and TEST, it is clear that the expected number of nodes inspected by TEST is equal to that inspected by SOLVE if the terminal WIN labels are assigned with probability $P_0 = P[V_0(t) > v] = 1-F_0(v)$. Therefore:

$$I_{TEST}(h, d, F_0, v) = I_{SOLVE}(h, d, 1-F_0(v)) \qquad (16)$$

Equation (16), combined with (14), yields:

Theorem 3: The expected number of terminal positions examined by the TEST algorithm in testing the proposition "$V(S) > v$" for the root of a (h, d, F_0)-tree, has branching factor:

$$r_{TEST}(d, F_0, v) = \begin{cases} d^{1/2} & \text{if } v \neq v^* \\ \frac{\xi}{1-\xi} & \text{if } v = v^* \end{cases} \qquad (17)$$

where v^* satisfies $F_0(v^*) = 1-\xi$. □

From the fact that TEST is directional and SOLVE is optimal we can also conclude:

Corollary 4: The optimal branching factor of any directional algorithm which tests whether the root node of a (h, d, F_0)-tree exceeds a specified reference v is given by $r_{TEST}(d, F_0, v)$ in equation (17). □

When the terminal positions are assigned discrete values then unless $1-\xi$ coincides with one of the plateaus of F_0, the equation $F_0(v^*) = 1-\xi$ would not have a solution, and the limiting root value would converge to the smallest v' satisfying $F_0(v') > 1-\xi$. Thus all inequality propositions could be tested with a branching factor $d^{1/2}$.

Consider now the minimum number of terminal node examinations required to eval-uate a game tree. At the best possible case, even if somesome hands us for free the true value of S, any evaluation algorithm should be able to defend the proposition "$V(S) = v$", i.e., to defend the pair of propositions "$V(S) \geq v$" and "$V(S) \leq v$." Since the solution tree required for the verification of an inquality proposition contains $d^{h/2}$ terminal positions and since the sets of terminal positions partici-pating in the defense of each of these inequalities are mutually exclusive, save for the one position satisfying $V_0(t) = V(S)$, we have:

Corollary 5: Any procedure which evaluates a (h, d, F_0)-tree must examine at least $2d^{h/2}-1$ nodes. □

We assumed, of course, that the probability of two or more terminal nodes satisfying $V_0(t) = V(S)$ is zero, and that h is even. This result (in a slightly different form) was also proven by Knuth and Moore [1].

Let us consider now the more interesting question of estimating $I(h, d, F_0)$, the expected number of terminal examinations required for evaluating (h, d, F_0)-game trees. Let $I_D(h, d)$ be the minimal value of $I(h, d, F_0)$ achieved by any directional algorithm under the worst-case F_0. Every algorithm which evaluates a game tree must examine at least as many nodes as that required for testing whether the root value is greater than some reference v. This is so because one can always use the value V(S) to deduce all inequality propositions regarding V(S). This fact combined with the optimality of TEST over the class of directional algorithms (see Corollary 4) leads to $I_D(h, d) \geq (\xi/1-\xi)^h$, and:

Theorem 4: The expected number of terminal positions examined by any directional algorithm which evaluates a (h, d)-game tree with continuous terminal values must have a branching factor greater or equal to $\xi/1-\xi$. □

The quantity $\xi/1-\xi$ was shown by Baudet [4] to be a lower bound for the branching factor of the α-β procedure. Theorem 4 extends the bound to all directional game-evaluating algorithms.

In the next section we will present a straightforward evaluation algorithm called SCOUT which actually achieves the branching factor $\xi/1-\xi$, thus establishing the asymptotic optimality of SCOUT over the class of directional algorithms, includ-ing the α-β procedure.

5. TEST AND, IF NECESSARY, EVALUATE - THE SCOUT ALGORITHM

SCOUT evaluates a MAX position S by first evaluating its left most successor S_1, then 'scouting' the remaining successors, from left to right, to determine if any meets the condition $V(S_k) > V(S_1)$. If the inequality is found to hold for S_k, this node is then evaluated exactly and its value $V(S_k)$ is used for subsequent 'scoutings' tests. Otherwise S_k is exempted from evaluation and S_{k+1} selected for a test. When all successors have been either evaluated or tested and found unworthy of evaluation, the last value obtained is issued as V(S). An identical procedure is used for evaluating a MIN position S, save for the fact that the event $V(S_k) \geq V(S_1)$ now constitutes grounds for exempting S_k from evaluation.

At first glance it appears that SCOUT is very wasteful, any node S_k which is found to fail a test criterion is submitted back for evaluation. The terminal nodes inspected during such a test may (and in fact will) be revisited during the evaluation phase. An exact mathematical analysis, however, reveals that the amount of waste is not substantial and that SCOUT, in spite of some duplicated effort, still achieves the optimal branching factor $\xi/1-\xi$.

Two factors work in favor of SCOUT: (1) Most tests would result in exempting the tested node (and all its descendents) from further evaluation, and (2) testing for inequality using the TEST(S, v) procedure is relatively speedy. The speed of TEST stems from the fact that it induces many cutoffs not necessarily permitted by EVAL or any other evaluation scheme. As soon as one successor of a MAX node meets the criterion $V(S_k) > v$, all other successors can be ignored. EVAL, by contrast, would necessitate a further examination of the remaining successors to determine if any would possess a value higher than $V(S_k)$.

6. ANALYSIS OF SCOUT'S EXPECTED PERFORMANCE

Let S be a MAX node rooting an n-cycle tree (h = 2n) with a uniform branching degree d. Let z_n denote the expected number of terminal examinations undertaken by SCOUT. These examinations consist of those performed during the EVAL(S_k) phases (k = 1, ... d) plus those performed during the TEST(S_k, v, >) phases (k = 2, ... d). Since the subtrees emanating from the successors of S

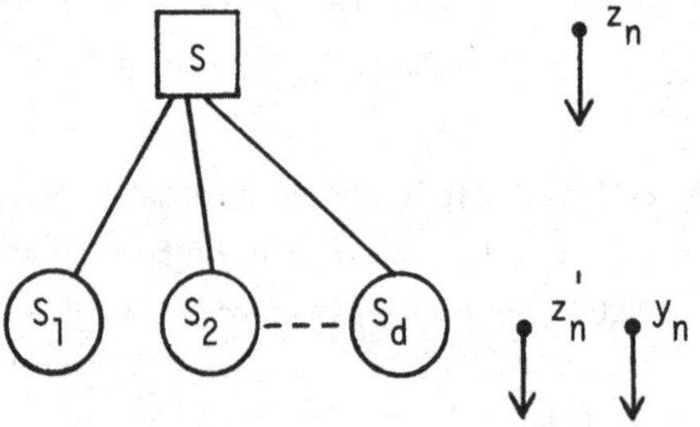

all have identically distributed terminal values, the number of positions examined in each EVAL(S_k) phase have identical expectations, called z_n'. Let v_k be the test criterion during the TEST(S_k, v, >) phase, and let $y_n^+(k)$ and $y_n^-(k)$ have the same interpretations as in Section 3. The event that S_k is found to satisfy the criterion $V(S_k) > v_k$ would consume a mean expenditure of $y_n^+(k) + z_n'$ inspections while a successor found to refute this test would consume, on the average, only $y_n^-(k)$

inspections. Thus, if q_k stands for the probability that successor S_k would require an evaluation, we have:

$$z_n = z_n' + \sum_{k=2}^{d} q_k(z_n' + y_n^+(k)) + \sum_{k=2}^{d} (1-q_k)\, y_n^-(k)$$

$$= z_n'[1 + \sum_{k=2}^{d} q_k] + \sum_{k=2}^{d} [q_k\, y_n^+(k) + (1-q_k)\, y_n^-(k)]$$

$$= z_n'[1 + \sum_{k=2}^{d} q_k] + \sum_{k=2}^{d} y_n(k) \tag{18}$$

Since S_k would require an evaluation iff $V(S_k) > \max\,[V(S_1), V(S_2), \ldots V(S_{k-1})]$ and all the node-values at any given level are independent, identically distributed and continuous random variables, we have:

$$q_k = \frac{1}{k} \qquad k = 2, \ldots d \tag{19}$$

Moreover, since we are interested in a worst case analysis, each $y_n(k)$ can be replaced by its highest possible value which, for large n, would be given by $(\xi/1-\xi)^{2n-1}$ (see equation (17)). Thus:

$$z_n \le z_n'\zeta(d) + (\xi/1-\xi)^{2n-1}\ (d-1) \tag{20}$$

where:

$$\zeta(d) = \sum_{k=1}^{d} \frac{1}{k} \tag{21}$$

Note that this approximation is not too pessimistic in light of the fact that for large n the values of all nodes converge rapidly toward the limiting value v*, and therefore, most tests would employ a threshold level v_k from the neighborhood of v*.

A similar argument applied to any successor of S gives:

$$z_n' \le z_{n-1}\ \zeta(d) + (\xi/1-\xi)^{2n-2}\ (d-1) \tag{22}$$

Combining (20) and (22) yields:

$$z_n \le z_{n-1}\ \zeta^2(d) + (d-1)\ (\xi/1-\xi)^{2n-2}\ [\zeta(d) + (\xi/1-\xi)] \tag{23}$$

(23) is a linear difference equation with $z_0 = 1$. Its asymptotic solution is determined by the relative size of $\xi/1-\xi$ and $\zeta(d)$. However, since for all d we have $\xi(d)/1-\xi(d) > \zeta(d)$, (23) becomes:

$$z_n = I_{SCOUT}(h, d, F) \sim \frac{(d-1)\ (1-\xi)^2}{\frac{\xi}{1-\xi} - \zeta(d)} \left(\frac{\xi}{1-\xi}\right)^h \tag{24}$$

<u>Theorem 5</u>: The expected number of terminal examinations performed by SCOUT in the evaluation of (h, d)-game trees with continuous terminal values has a branching factor:

$$r_{SCOUT} = \xi/1-\xi \qquad (25) \square$$

So far, our analysis was based on the assumption that the terminal nodes are assigned continuous values. We will now demonstrate that I_{SCOUT} is substantially reduced if the terminal nodes are assigned only discrete values.

Let's ignore the rare case where one of the discrete values coincides with v*. Under such conditions, Theorem 2(b) states that the values of all nodes at sufficiently high levels converge to the same limit, given by the lowest terminal value v' satisfying $F_0(v') > 1-\xi$. This convergence has two effects on the complexity of SCOUT as analyzed in equation (18): First, q_k is no longer equal to 1/k but rather, converges to zero at high n for all k > 1. The reason for this is that in order for $V(S_k)$ to be greater than $V(S_1)$ (which is most probably equal to v') it must exceed $V(S_1)$ by a finite positive quantity and, at a very high h, finite differences between any two nodes are extremely rare. Second, the threshold levels v_k against which the TEST(S_k, v, >) procedures are performed are no longer close to v* but differ from it by finite amounts. Under such conditions the proposition "$V(S_k) > v_k$" can be tested more efficiently since $r_{TEST} = d^{1/2}$ (see equation (17)).

Applying these considerations to the analysis of z_n in (18) gives:

<u>Theorem 6</u>: The expected number of terminal examinations performed by the SCOUT procedure in evaluating a (h, d, F_{V_0})-game with discrete terminal values has a branching factor:

$$r_{SCOUT} = d^{1/2} \qquad (26)$$

with exceptions only when one of the discrete values, v*, satisfies $F_0(v^*) = 1-\xi$. □

<u>Corollary 6</u>: For games with discrete terminal values satisfying the conditions of Theorem 6, the SCOUT procedure is asymptotically optimal over all evaluation algorithms. □

Of course, the transition from $r_{SOLVE} = \xi/1-\xi$ in the continuous case to $r_{SOLVE} = d^{1/2}$ in the discrete case does not occur abruptly. When the quantization levels are very close to each other it takes many more levels before SCOUT begins to acquire the lower branching factor of $d^{1/2}$. In fact, using the discussion of Section 1, it is possible to estimate the critical height, h_0, above which SCOUT would expand only $d^{1/2}$ nodes per level. For example, if the terminal values are integers, uniformly distributed from 1 to M, it can be shown [7] that $h_0(M, d)$ is approximately given by:

$$h_0(M, d) \cong \frac{\log M}{\log d(1-\xi)/\xi} \qquad (27)$$

Several improvements could be applied to the SCOUT algorithm to render it more efficient. For example, when a TEST procedure issues a non-exempt verdict, it could also return a new reference value and some information regarding how the decision was obtained in order to minimize the number of nodes to be inspected by EVAL. The main reasons for introducing SCOUT have been its conceptual and analytic simplicity and the fact that at the time of its inception it possessed the lowest branching factor of any known algorithm. However, the potential of SCOUT as a practical game-searching procedure should not be dismissed altogether. Recent simulation studies using the game of Kalah show [8] that the efficiency of SCOUT, even in its unpolished version, compares favorable with that of the α-β procedure.

Recently, Stockman [6] has also introduced an algorithm which examines fewer nodes than α-β. However, Stockman's algorithm requires an enormous storage space for tracing back a large number of potential strategies. SCOUT, by contrast, has storage requirements similar to those of α-β; at any point in time it only maintains pointers along one single path connecting the root to the currently expanded node.

7. ON THE OPTIMALITY OF THE ALPHA-BETA PROCEDURE

The branching factor of α-β is less tractable than that of SCOUT. Until very recently the tightest estimate of $r_{\alpha-\beta}$ has been that derived by Baudet [4], giving the lower bound $r_{\alpha-\beta} \geq \xi/1-\xi$ (a special case of Corollary 2) and an upper bound which is about 20 percent higher over the range $2 \leq d \leq 32$. Moreover, it can be shown that neither SCOUT nor α-β dominate one another on a node-by-node basis; i.e., nodes examined by SCOUT may be skipped by α-β and vice versa [7]. Hence, the enigma of whether α-β is optimal remained contingent upon determining the exact magnitude of $r_{\alpha-\beta}$ within the range delineated by Baudet.

This enigma has recently been resolved by Pearl [9] who demonstrated that the branching factor of α-β coincides indeed with the lower bound $\xi/1-\xi$, thus establishing the optimality of α-β over the class of directional search algorithms.

However, the difficulty of determining the branching factor of the α-β procedure only pertains to continuous-valued trees. If the terminal nodes are assigned discrete values, it is easy to show [7] that the α-β procedure, like SCOUT, attains the absolute minimal branching factor of $d^{1/2}$. The fact that at high levels almost all nodes attain the same minimax value, v^*, makes it increasingly probable that the α-β cutoff conditions are met successfully at all nodes where they are applicable and this, in turn, gives rise to a branching factor of $d^{1/2}$ as was demonstrated for SCOUT (Theorem 6). These results are summarized by Theorem 7:

<u>Theorem 7</u>: (a) For games with continuous terminal values, the α-β procedure is asymptotically optimal over directional search algorithms, and it achieves the branching factor $r_{\alpha-\beta} = \xi/1-\xi$, where ξ is the solution of $x^d+x-1 = 0$.

(b) For games with discrete terminal values satisfying the condition of Theorem 1(b), the α-β procedure is asymptotically optimal over all evaluation algorithms, attaining the branching factor $r_{\alpha-\beta} = d^{1/2}$. □

Paralleling SCOUT, the improvement of α-β's efficiency due to the discrete nature of the terminal values manifests itself only when the search depth h is larger than $h_0 = \log M/\log \frac{d(1-\xi)}{\xi}$, where M is the quantization density in the neighborhood of $V_0 = v^*$.

The establishment of the precise value of $r_{\alpha-\beta}$ for continuous-valued trees, together with our previous result that $r_{\alpha-\beta} = d^{1/2}$ for almost all discrete-valued trees, resolve two major uncertainties regarding the asymptotic behavior of α-β. However, the global optimality of α-β remains an unresolved issue. Naturally, the focus of attention now turns to non-directional algorithms, raising the question whether any such algorithm exists which exhibits a branching factor lower than $\xi/1-\xi$.

Indeed, Stockman [6] has introduced a non-directional algorithm which can be shown to examine fewer nodes than α-β. However, the magnitude of this improvement has not been evaluated yet, and it is not clear whether the superiority of Stockman's algorithm reflects a reduced branching factor, or merely a marginal improvement at low h's which disappears on taller trees. The latter seems more likely.

Notably, the problem of determining the existence of an algorithm superior to α-β can be reduced to the simpler problem of determining whether any non-directional algorithm can solve a bi-valued (h, d, P*)-game with a branching factor lower than $\xi/1-\xi$. For, if such an algorithm exists, it could be incorporated into SCOUT (replacing TEST) and thus enabling it to evaluate continuous-valued game trees with a branching factor lower than $\xi/1-\xi$. Unfortunately, even this reduced problem currently seems far from solution.

ACKNOWLEDGEMENT

This work was supported in part by the National Science Foundation Grants MCS 78-07468 and MCS 78-18924.

REFERENCES

[1] Knuth, D. E., and Moore, R. N. An analysis of alpha-beta pruning. Artificial Intelligence 6 (1975), 293-326.

[2] Slagle, J. R., and Dixon, J. K. Experiments with some programs that search game trees. Journal of the ACM 2 (1969), 189-207.

[3] Fuller, S. H., Gaschnig, J. G., and Gillogly, J. J. An analysis of the alpha-beta pruning algorithm. Department of Computer Science Report, Carnegie-Mellon University (1973).

[4] Baudet, G. M. On the branching factor of the alpha-beta pruning algorithm. Artificial Intelligence 10 (1978), 173-199.

[5] Pearl, J. An economical method of updating quantile estimates. UCLA-ENG-CSL-8018, University of California, Los Angeles (1980).

[6] Stockman, G. A minimax algorithm better than alpha-beta? Artificial Intelligence 12 (1979), 179-196.

[7] Pearl, J. Asymptotic properties of minimax trees and game-searching procedures. UCLA-ENG-CSL-7981, University of Los Angeles (1980). To appear in Artificial Intelligence.

[8] Noe, T. A comparison of the alpha-beta and SCOUT algorithms using the game of Kalah. UCLA-ENG-CSL-8017, University of California, Los Angeles (1980).

[9] Pearl, J. The solution for the branching factor of the alpha-beta pruning algorithm. UCLA-ENG-CSL-8019, University of California, Los Angeles (1980).

COMPLETENESS IN CLASSICAL LOGIC OF COMPLEX ALGORITHMS

Helena Rasiowa
Institute of Mathematics
University of Warsaw
PKiN, IX p., 00-901 Warsaw, Poland

Recently a considerable progress has been made in logical approaches to the theory of programs. Several logics of programs on the propositional level as well as on the first order level have been constructed, examined and applied to investigations in various directions, e.g. algorithmic logic of while...do... programs as initiated by Salwicki [13], algorithmic logic with nondeterministic programs as discussed by Mirkowska [6], extended algorithmic logic EAL dealing with recursive procedures and applying ω^+-valued logic Rasiowa ([9], [10], [11]), logic of complex algorithms LCA ([12]), dynamic logic as initiated by Pratt [7] (see also D.Harel, Lectures Notes in Computer Science 68, 1979), logic of effective definitions LED dealing with effective Friedman's schemes, as constructed by Tiuryn [14]. Those examples do not exhaust all known logics of programs, based on first order predicate logics.

Classical logic of complex algorithms, to be denoted by CLCA, is one of first order like logics of programs. It formalizes algorithmic properties of a class of deterministic programs called complex recursive ones or interacting stacks-programs, for which complex algorithms (see Janicki [4]) constitute mathematical models. Since certain complex algorithms may be considered to be mathematical models of recursive coroutines, it follows that CLCA deals in particular with algorithmic properties of programs with recursive coroutines and hence also with recursive procedures. It is in a sense an extension of algorithmic logic. CLCA is a modification of LCA, as presented in [12], eliminating the use of ω^+-valued logic from the construction of control systems occurring in complex algorithms and in pushdown algorithms. An idea of a modification was suggested to the author by Dimiter Skordev from the University of Sofia. The author is indepted to professor Skordev for his valuable conjecture.

In this paper a syntax and a semantics of formalized languages of CLCA is given and a complete axiomatization with a completeness theorem is presented.

1. Deterministic complex algorithms. Complex algorithms as introduced by Janicki [4] are certain Mazurkiewicz's algorithms (see [1], [5]).

The notion of a complex algorithm is connected with an algebraic approach to the theory of recursive coroutines, which following Conway [2] are program components able to interact in a symmetric way. A starting point of that approach was to represent each program component as an algebraic system like Mazurkiewicz's pushdown algorithm being an algebraic model of a recursive procedure. These systems have some additional instructions which make an interaction possible. Resulting algebraic systems which are models of recursive coroutines are defined as vectors of pushdown coroutines. They are in a sense equivalent to certain complex algorithms (see Janicki [4]). Pushdown algorithms use stacks. In vectors of coroutines a mechanism making possible an interaction of component systems applies an interaction of stacks which can be implemented in complex algorithms.

By a deterministic complex algorithm we shall mean a system

(1) $$Al = (W, L^*, \iota, \mathcal{J})$$

where W is a set (of objects),

L^* is the set of all words (stacks) including the empty word e_0 over a finite set L (of labels),

ι is an initial label of Al,

$\mathcal{J}$ is a finite set of instructions.

Each instruction I is an ordered pair $I = (f_I, r_I)$ of partial functions

(2) $f_I \subset L^* \times L^*$ a control function, $r_I \subset W \times W$ an action.

With every instruction I there is associated an initial word (stack) u_I in LL^* and two words (stacks) u_1, u_2 in L^* such that the following conditions are satisfied:

(3) $\operatorname{dom} f_I = \{u_I w \mid w \in L^*\}$,

(4) $f_I(u_I w) = u_1 w u_2$ for each word (stack) w in L^*,

(5) exactly one of the instructions has as the initial word the initial label ι of Al and any two instructions have either disjoint domains of actions or no of their initial words is an initial part of another.

A control function f_I defined by means of (3) and (4) will also be denoted in a suggestive way as follows

(6) $$u_I w \longmapsto u_1 w u_2 \quad \text{for each word } w \text{ in } L^* .$$

Thus instead of (f_I, r_I) we shall also write

(7) $$(u_I w \longmapsto u_1 w u_2 ,\ r_I) .$$

If for each instruction I of Al, u_I is a label and u_2 is the empty word e_o, then the algorithm Al is said to be a pushdown algorithm. If moreover u_1 is either a label or the empty word, then Al is said to be a finite-control algorithm, i.e. a mathematical model of programs described by flow-diagrams.

The ordered pairs (w,v) in $L^* \times W$ are called states.

By a finite computation of Al we shall mean any finite sequence of states

(8) $(w_o,v_o),\ldots,(w_n,v_n)$

satisfying the conditions: $w_o = \iota$, for each $i = 0,\ldots,n-1$,

$(w_{i+1},v_{i+1}) = (f_I(w_i), r_I(v_i))$ for some instruction I ,

$w_n = e_o$.

It follows from the conditions concerning the instructions of deterministic complex algorithms that for any state (w,v) at most one instruction I can be executed. Consequently for any initial state (ι, v) there exists at most one finite computation.

2. Formalized languages of CLCA and their realizations. Let $\mathcal{L}_o = (A_o, T, F_o)$ be a countable first order predicate language without quantifiers, A_o , T and F_o being the alphabet, the set of terms and the set of formulas over A_o, respectively. Assume that V, V_o, Φ and Π are: the set of individual variables, the set of propositional variables, the set of functors (i.e. of symbols for functions) and the set of predicates (i.e. of symbols for characteristic functions of relations), respectively. Assume also that the propositional constants $\mathbb{O}$ and $\mathbb{1}$, corresponding to any false statement and to any true statement occur in A_o.

The following terminology and notation will be used in the sequel. Let N and N_o be the set of all positive integers and the set of all non-negative integers, respectively. Let R be a realization of $\mathcal{L}_o$ in a set $U \neq \emptyset$, i.e. a mapping assigning to each n-argument functor φ a function $\varphi_R: U^n \rightarrow U$ and to each n-ary predicate ρ a function $\rho_R: U^n \rightarrow \{\wedge, \vee\}$, where $\wedge, \vee$ are the zero element and the unit element in the two-element Boolean algebra $B_o = (\{\wedge, \vee\}, \cup, \cap, \Rightarrow, \neg)$. Clearly ρ_R may be treated as the characterisic function of a relation $\rho^*_R \subset U^n$ such that $\rho^*_R(u_1,\ldots,u_n)$ holds if and only if $\rho_R(u_1,\ldots,u_n) = \vee$. Thus $\mathcal{L}_o$ and R determine an algebraic structure

$$\mathfrak{A}(\mathcal{L}_o, R) = (U, (\varphi_R)_{\varphi \in \Phi}, (\rho^*_R)_{\rho \in \Pi}).$$

Let W_U be the set of all valuations (state vectors) in U, i.e. mappings v assigning to each $x \in V$ an element v(x) in U and to each p in V_o an element v(p) of the two-element Boolean algebra B_o. Realization R associates with each term $\tau \in T$ a function $\tau_R: W_U \rightarrow U$

(a realization of τ) and with each formula $\alpha \in F_o$ a function $\alpha_R : W_U \to \{\wedge, \vee\}$ (realization of α), the propositional connective being realized as corresponding Boolean operations in B_o. In particular $\mathbf{O}_R(v) = \wedge$ and $\mathbf{I}_R(v) = \vee$ for each v in W_U.

Extend A_o to an alphabet A by adjoining a set $V_L = \{a_n \mid n \in N\}$ of label variables, a set $E = \{e_n \mid n \in N_o\}$ of label constants, a binary predicate $\triangleq$, three program operations signs $:o$ (composition sign), $\veebar$ (branching sign), c^* (complex iteration sign), infinite disjunction sign $\bigvee$, infinite conjunction sign $\bigwedge$ and auxiliary signs [,] ,/, sc , ad .

By a formalized language of CLCA (based on initial language $\mathcal{L}_o$) we shall understand a system

(1) $\qquad \mathcal{L} = (A, T, F_o, P, F)$

where T and F_o are the set of terms and the set of open formulas in $\mathcal{L}_o$, respectively, and P, F are sets of new well-formed expressions over A. The elements in P will be said to be programs and the elements in F will be called formulas. Definitions of programs and of formulas will be given simultaneously with definitions of their realizations.

By a label valuation or a label vector we shall mean any $v_L : V_L \to E$ satisfying the following conditions:

(v_L1) $\qquad$ there is $n \in N$ such that $v_L(a_n) = e_o$,

(v_L2) $\qquad$ for each $n \in N$, if $v_L(a_n) = e_o$, then $v_L(a_{n+1}) = e_o$.

The set of all label vectors will be denoted by W_L. We shall often identify any v_L in W_L with the sequence $(v_L(a_1), v_L(a_2), \ldots)$. It follows from ($v_L$1) and ($v_L$2) that any label vector v_L is either $(e_o, e_o, \ldots)$ or $(e_{k_1}, \ldots, e_{k_n}, e_o, \ldots)$, where $k_i \neq 0$ for $i = 1, \ldots, n$. The first sequence will be interpreted as the empty word (stack) over $\{e_n \mid n \in N\}$ and the second one as the word (stack) $e_{k_1} \ldots e_{k_n}$.

Any pair $(v_L, v) \in W_L \times W_U$ will be said to be a state (in $W_L \times W_U$). Each well-formed expression in $\mathcal{L}$ will be realized as a function or as a partial function on the set of states with values in one of the sets: U , $W_L \times W_U$, $\{\wedge, \vee\}$. More exactly, terms will be realized as functions $\tau_R : W_L \times W_U \to U$, programs as partial functions H_R from $W_L \times W_U$ into $W_L \times W_U$ and formulas as functions $\alpha_R : W_L \times W_U \to \{\wedge, \vee\}$.

We adopt for all terms $\tau \in T$ and for all formulas $\alpha \in F_o$

(2) $\qquad \tau_R(v_L, v) = \tau_R(v) \qquad$ and $\qquad \alpha_R(v_L, v) = \alpha_R(v)$.

Four kinds of atomic programs in P are adopted: substitutions (assignment programs), schedulings, label adjoinings and label supervisors.

Substitutions are expressions

(3) $[x_1/\tau_1 \ldots x_n/\tau_n\ p_1/\alpha_1 \ldots p_m/\alpha_m]$, $n,m \in N_0$,

where $x_1,\ldots,x_n$ are different individual variables, $\tau_1,\ldots,\tau_n \in T$, $p_1,\ldots,p_m$ are different propositional variables, $\alpha_1,\ldots,\alpha_m \in F_0$. The set of all substitutions will be denoted by S. If $s \in S$ and has form (3), then its realization for a state (v_L,v) is defined as follows:

$s_R(v_L,v) = (v_L,v')$, where $v'(x_i) = \tau_{iR}(v)$ for $i=1,\ldots,n$, $v'(p_i) = \alpha_{iR}(v)$ for $i = 1,\ldots,m$, and $v'(x)=v(x)$ for $x \neq x_1,\ldots,x_n$, $x \in V$, $v'(p) = v(p)$ for $p \neq p_1,\ldots,p_m$, $p \in V_0$.

We shall also use the notation $s_R(v) = v'$, where v' is defined above.

The following expressions are said to be schedulings:

(4) $sc[e_{k_1} \ldots e_{k_n} a_q]$, $n,q,k_1,\ldots,k_n \in N$,

(5) $sc[a_n]$, $n \in N$,

(6) $sc[e_0]$.

The set of all schedulings will be denoted by S_L^0. The set $S_L = S_L^0 - \{sc\,[e_0]\}$.

In order to extend realization R to S_L^0 we adopt for each $s^* \in S_L^0$

(7) $s^*_R(v_L,v) = (v'_L,v)$, where

$v'_L = (e_{k_1},\ldots,e_{k_n},v_L(a_q),v_L(a_{q+1}),\ldots)$ in the case (4),

$v'_L = (v_L(a_n),v_L(a_{n+1}),\ldots)$ in the case (5),

$v'_L = (e_0,e_0,\ldots)$ in the case (6).

The following expressions are called label adjoinings :

(8) $ad[e_{i_1} \ldots e_{i_m}]$, $m,i_1,\ldots,i_m \in N$.

The set of all label adjoinings will be denoted by Adj. In order to extend realization R to Adj we adopt the following definition: for each state (v_L,v), if $v_L = (e_{k_1},\ldots,e_{k_n},e_0,\ldots)$, $k_1,\ldots,k_n \in N$, then

(9) $ad[e_{i_1} \ldots e_{i_m}]_R(v_L,v) = ((e_{k_1},\ldots,e_{k_n},e_{i_1},\ldots,e_{i_m},e_0,\ldots),v)$.

The set Sp of label supervisors consists of the expressions

$[a_n \doteq e_k]$, $n \in N$, $k \in N_0$.

The following definition is adopted in order to extend R to the set Sp of label supervisors.

(10) $$[a_n \doteq e_k]_R(v_L,v) = \begin{cases} (v_L,v) & \text{if } v_L(a_n) = e_k \\ \text{undefined otherwise} & \end{cases}.$$

The role of atomic programs is determined by their realizations .

In particular schedulings transform label vectors into label vectors as follows:

$(v_L(a_1),\ldots,v_L(a_{q-1}),\ldots)\longmapsto(e_{k_1},\ldots,e_{k_n},v_L(a_q),v_L(a_{q+1}),\ldots)$

in the case (4) and $q>1$,

$(v_L(a_1),\ldots)\longmapsto(e_{k_1},\ldots,e_{k_n},v_L(a_1),\ldots)$ in the case (4) and $q=1$,

$(v_L(a_1),\ldots,v_L(a_{n-1}),v_L(a_n),\ldots)\longmapsto(v_L(a_n),\ldots)$ in the case (5), and

$v_L\mapsto(e_o,\ldots)$ in the case (6).

Label adjoinings are realized as concatenations, more precisely,

$(e_{k_1},\ldots,e_{k_n},e_o,\ldots)\longmapsto(e_{k_1},\ldots,e_{k_n},e_{i_1},\ldots,e_{i_m},e_o,\ldots)$ in the case of (8).

Label supervisors test whether the n-th coordinate of v_L is equal e_q or not for $[a_n \doteq e_k]_R(v_L,v)$, $n\in N$, $k\in N_o$.

The set P of programs has also the following properties:

(11) if $H_1,\ldots,H_n$ are in P, then $o[H_1\ldots H_n]$ is in P,

(12) if H_1,H_2 are in P and $\gamma\in F_o$, then $\curlyvee[\gamma\ H_1H_2]\in P$.

Realization R is extended to compositions and branchings of programs by adopting

$$(13)\quad o[H_1\ldots H_n]_R(v_L,v)=\begin{cases}H_{nR}(\ldots(H_{1R}(v_L,v)\ldots) & \text{if this is defined}\\ \text{undefined otherwise}\end{cases}$$

$$(14)\quad \curlyvee[\gamma\ H_1H_2]_R(v_L,v)=\begin{cases}H_{1R}(v_L,v) & \text{if this is defined and } \gamma_R(v)=\vee\\ H_{2R}(v_L,v) & \text{if this is defined and } \gamma_R(v)=\wedge\\ \text{undefined otherwise}\end{cases}$$

The following expressions are said to be instructions with an initial word $e_{k_1}\ldots e_{k_n}$

(15) $o[[a_1\doteq e_{k_1}]\ldots[a_n\doteq e_{k_n}]\ sc[e_{i_1}\ldots e_{i_m}a_{n+1}]\ \sigma\ s]$,

(16) $o[[a_1\doteq e_{k_1}]\ldots[a_n\doteq e_{k_n}]\ sc[a_{n+1}]\ \sigma\ s]$,

(17) $o[[a_1\doteq e_{k_1}]\ldots[a_n\doteq e_{k_n}]\curlyvee[\gamma\ o[s_1^*\ \sigma_1\ s_1]o[s_2^*\ \sigma_2 s_2]]]$,

where $n,m,k_1,\ldots,k_n,i_1,\ldots,i_m$ are in N, $\sigma\in Adj$ or is the empty expression, σ_1,σ_2 are in Adj or are empty expressions, $s,s_1,s_2\in S$ and s_1^*, s_2^* are schedulings in forms occurring in (15), (16). The set of all instructions will be denoted by $\mathfrak{J}$. Realization R is extended to $\mathfrak{J}$ by applying the definitions of realizations of atomic programs and (13), (14). It follows that each instruction I in $\mathfrak{J}$ is realized as an instruction (7) in Sec.1 of a complex algorithm, i.e. it has form $(u_I w \longmapsto u_1 w u_2, r_I)$, or as a pair of instructions with the same initial word but with the disjoint domains of actions. More exactly, in case (15) and $\sigma = \mathrm{ad}[e_{q_1}\ldots e_{q_p}]$ we obtain $(e_{k_1}\ldots e_{k_n} w \longmapsto e_{i_1}\ldots e_{i_m} w e_{q_1}\ldots e_{q_p}, s_R)$; in case (16) and the same form of σ we obtain $(e_{k_1}\ldots e_{k_n} w \longmapsto w e_{q_1}\ldots e_{q_p}, s_R)$; case (17) gives a pair of instructions

$$I_{1R} | \{(v_L, v) | \gamma_R(v) = \vee\} \qquad \text{and} \qquad I_{2R} | \{(v_L, v) | \gamma_R(v) = \wedge\}$$

where $I_i = o[[a_1 \doteq e_{k_1}]\ldots[a_n \doteq e_{k_n}]\, s_i^* \sigma_i s_i]$, $i = 1,2$.

If in instructions (15), (16), (17) σ, σ_1 and σ_2 are empty expressions and $n = 1$, then we obtain instructions of pushdown algorithms. If moreover $m=1$, then the instructions under consideration correspond to instructions in finite-control algorithms.

Now we are going to define new well-formed expressions in $\mathcal{L}$ which will be realized as complex algorithms. These expressions will be called complex recursive programs (cr-programs) or interacting stacks programs. The set of all cr-programs will be denoted by CR.

The set CR consists of the following expressions

(18) $c^*[H_\iota H_1 \ldots H_n H_t]$, where

1° $H_1, \ldots, H_n$ are instructions in $\mathfrak{J}$ with some initial words $u_1, \ldots, u_n$ such that no of them is an initial part of another;

2° $H_\iota = o[[a_1 \doteq e_\iota]\, sc[e_o]\, sc[e_\iota a_2]]$,

3° $H_t = [a_1 \doteq e_o]$.

In order to extend realization R to CR a notion of a finite computation of H in CR by realization R for a state (v_L, v) will be introduced. This is a finite sequence of states

(19) $(v_L, v), (v_L^o, v^o), \ldots, (v_L^{m+1}, v^{m+1})$

satisfying the following conditions:

$(v_L^o, v^o) = H_{\iota R}(v_L, v)$; for each $i=0,\ldots,m-1$ there is $j=1,\ldots,n$ such that $(v_L^{i+1}, v^{i+1}) = H_{jR}(v_L^i, v^i)$; $(v_L^{m+1}, v^{m+1}) = H_{tR}(v_L^m, v^m)$

and all states in (19) are defined.

Observe that at most one instruction H_j, $j=1,\ldots,n,t$ may be applied to (v_L^i, v^i) for $i=0,1,\ldots$. Moreover, (v_L^o, v^o) is defined if and only if $v_L(a_1) = e_\iota$. If this holds, then we have $(v_L^o, v^o) = ((e_o, \ldots), v)$. The label e_ι is said to be the initial label of H in form (18). Note also, that if a computation (19) of H by R for (v_L, v) exists, then

$v_L^{m+1} = (e_o, \dots)$

For any cr-program H in form (18) we define

(20) $H_R(v_L, v) = \begin{cases} (v_L^{m+1}, v^{m+1}) \text{ if (19) is a finite computation of H by R for } (v_L, v); \\ \text{undefined if a finite computation of H by R for } (v_L, v) \text{ does not exist.} \end{cases}$

The set P of all programs is the least set of expressions over A such that

(21) $S \cup S_L^o \cup Adj \cup Sp \cup CR \subset P$

and the conditions (11), (12) are satisfied.

It is worth mentioning that any cr-program and a realization R in $U \neq \emptyset$ determine a complex algorithm Al_{HR}. Indeed, for H in form (18), $Al_{HR} = (W_U, \tilde{L}_H, e_\iota, \mathfrak{J}_{HR})$, where L_H is the set of all e_k, $k \in N$, such that e_k occurs in some H_i for $i=1,\dots,n$, and $\mathfrak{J}_{HR}$ consists of H_{iR} for $i=1,\dots,n$, is a complex algorithm determined by H and realization R. If (19) is a computation of H by R for (v_L, v), then $(v_L^o, v^o), \dots, (v_L^m, v^m)$ is a computation of the algorithm Al_{HR} and conversely.

By atomic formulas we shall mean: formulas $a_n \doteq e_k$, $n \in N, k \in N_o$, and atomic formulas in F_o, i.e. $\rho(\tau_1 \dots \tau_n)$ for any n-ary predicate ρ in $\mathfrak{I}$ and terms $\tau_1, \dots, \tau_n \in T$, propositional constants $\mathbb{O}$, $\mathbb{1}$ and propositional variables in V_o. The set of all atomic formulas will be denoted by F_{at}.

The set F of all formulas in $\mathcal{L}$ is the least set of expressions over A containing F_{at} and satisfying the conditions:

(f1) if α, β are in F, then $(\alpha \vee \beta)$, $(\alpha \wedge \beta)$, $(\alpha \rightarrow \beta)$, $\sim\alpha$ are in F,

(f2) if α is in F and H is a program in P, then $H\alpha$ is a formula in F,

(f3) if $\alpha_i \in F$ for $i \in N$ and the set of individual variables and of propositional variables occurring in these formulas is finite, then $\bigvee(\alpha_1 \alpha_2 \dots)$ and $\bigwedge(\alpha_1 \alpha_2 \dots)$ are in F.

To simplify the notation we shall omit parentheses if this would not cause any ambiguity in reading formulas and we shall write $\alpha \leftrightarrow \beta$ instead of $(\alpha \rightarrow \beta) \wedge (\beta \rightarrow \alpha)$.

In order to extend realization R to F we adopt additionally the following definitions.

(22) $(a_n \doteq e_k)_R(v_L, v) = \begin{cases} \vee \text{ if } v_L(a_n) = e_k \\ \wedge \text{ otherwise} \end{cases}$

(23) $\bigvee(\alpha_1 \alpha_2 \dots)_R(v_L, v) = \bigcup_{i \in N} \alpha_{iR}(v_L, v)$,

(24) $\bigwedge(\alpha_1 \alpha_2 \dots)_R(v_L, v) = \bigcap_{i \in N} \alpha_{iR}(v_L, v)$,

$$(25)\quad H\alpha_R(v_L,v)=\begin{cases}\alpha_R(H_R(v_L,v)) & \text{if } H_R(v_L,v) \text{ is defined}\\ \wedge & \text{otherwise}\end{cases}$$

where operations $\bigcup, \bigcap$ are infinite joins and meets in the two-element Boolean algebra composed of $\vee$ and $\wedge$.

A formula α in F is said to be valid in a realization R if $\alpha_R(v_L,v)=\vee$ for every state (v_L,v). A formula α in F is said to be a tautology of CLCA if α is valid in each realization R. A realization R is called a model of α if α is valid in R. A realization R is called a model of a set $\mathcal{A}\subset F$ if R is a model of each formula α in $\mathcal{A}$.

For each $\mathcal{A}\subset F$ and $\alpha\in F$, α will be said to be a semantic consequence of $\mathcal{A}$ if each model of $\mathcal{A}$ is a model of α. This will be written thus $\mathcal{A}\models\alpha$. We set $Cn(\mathcal{A})=\{\alpha\in F\mid \mathcal{A}\models\alpha\}$. Any system $\mathcal{S}=(\mathcal{L},Cn)$, where Cn is defined by means of the above equations, is said to be a system of CLCA, and for every set $\mathcal{A}\subset F$, the system $\mathcal{S}(\mathcal{A})=(\mathcal{L},Cn,\mathcal{A})$ will be said to be an algorithmic theory based on CLCA. Any formula α such that $\mathcal{A}\models\alpha$ is said to be a theorem of $\mathcal{S}(\mathcal{A})$.

3. <u>Formalized theories based on CLCA.</u> The aim of this section is to formulate a formal consequence operation C in any formalized language $\mathcal{L}$ of CLCA by adopting a recursive set of logical axioms and certain rules of inference. We shall prove in Section 5, that for any $\mathcal{A}\subset F$, such that the set of all individual variables and of all propositional variables occurring in formula belonging to $\mathcal{A}$ is finite, and to any $\mathcal{A}\subset F_0$, $Cn(\mathcal{A})=C(\mathcal{A})$.

First of all certain auxiliary notions will be introduced.

Every substitution $s\in S$ of form (3) in Sec. 2 determines uniquely a mapping $\bar{s}: V\cup V_0\to T\cup F_0$ defined thus:

(1) $\bar{s}(x_i)=\tau_i$, $i=1,\dots,n$; $\bar{s}(p_i)=\alpha_i$, $i=1,\dots,m$;

$\bar{s}\mid(V-\{x_1,\dots,x_n\})\cup(V_0-\{p_1,\dots,p_m\})$ is the identity mapping.

For each expression θ in $\mathcal{L}$, $\bar{s}\theta$ will denote the expression obtained from θ by the simultaneous replacement of each $x\in V$ occurring in θ by $\bar{s}(x)$ and of $p\in V_0$ in θ by $\bar{s}(p)$. Clearly, $\bar{s}\tau\in T$ for each $\tau\in T$ and $\bar{s}(\alpha)\in F_0$ for $\alpha\in F_0$.

On the other hand each mapping $\bar{s}: V\cup V_0\to T\cup F_0$ satisfying the conditions

(i) $\bar{s}(x)\in T$ for $x\in V$, (ii) $\bar{s}(p)\in F_0$ for $p\in V_0$ and
(iii) $\{x\in V\mid \bar{s}(x)\neq x\}\cup\{p\in V_0\mid \bar{s}(p)\neq p\}$ is finite,

determines uniquely a substitution $s\in S$ in the obvious way.

Given any two substitutions $s_1,s_2\in S$, let $s_1 o s_2$ be a new substitution defined thus:

(2) $\overline{s_1 o s_2}(x) = \bar{s}_1(\bar{s}_2(x))$, for $x \in V$ and $\overline{s_1 o s_2}(p) = \bar{s}_1(\bar{s}_2(p))$, for $p \in V_o$.
The following statement is easy to prove.

3.1. For any $s_1, s_2 \in S$, each realization R and each state (v_L, v)

(3) $(s_1 o s_2)_R(v_L, v) = o[s_1 s_2]_R(v_L, v)$,

(4) $(s_1 o s_2)\alpha_R(v_L, v) = o[s_1 s_2]\alpha_R(v_L, v)$ for each $\alpha \in F$.

Analogously to substitutions any label scheduling $s^* \in S_L^o$ determines uniquely a mapping $\bar{s}^*: V_L \longrightarrow V_L \cup E$, which is defined as follows: if $s^* = sc[e_{k_1} \ldots e_{k_n} a_q]$, $n, q, k_1, \ldots, k_n \in N$, then $\bar{s}^*(a_i) = e_{k_i}$ for $i = 1, \ldots, n$, and $\bar{s}^*(a_{n+i}) = a_{q+i-1}$ for $i \in N$; if $s^* = sc[a_n]$, $n \in N$, then $\bar{s}^*(a_i) = a_{i+n-1}$ for $i \in N$; if $s^* = sc[e_o]$, then $\bar{s}^*(a_i) = e_o$ for $i \in N$.

On the other hand each mapping $\bar{s}^x: V_L \rightarrow V_L \cup E$ satisfying one of the conditions occurring in the definitions of mappings determined by label substitutions determines uniquely a label scheduling s^* in the obvious way .

Let s_1^* , s_2^* be any schedulings satisfying the condition

(5) if $s_2^* = sc[e_{k_1} \ldots e_{k_n} a_q]$, $n, q, k_1, \ldots, k_n \in N$, then $s_1^* \neq sc[e_o]$.

If (5) holds, then the equations

$$\overline{(s_1^* o\ s_2^*)}(a_i) = \bar{s}_1^*(s_2^*(a_i)) \quad \text{for } i \in N$$

determine a new scheduling $s_1^* o s_2^*$ in S_L^o and the following lemma can easily be proved.

3.2. For any schedulings s_1^* , s_2^* in S_L^o satisfying (5) , for each realization R in any $U \neq \emptyset$ and for each state (v_L, v) in $W_L \times W_U$ and each formula $\alpha \in F$

(6) $s_1^*\ o\ sc[e_o] = sc[e_o]$,

(7) $sc[e_o]\ o\ sc[a_n] = sc[e_o]$,

(8) $(s_1^*\ o\ s_2^*)_R(v_L, v) = o[s_1^*\ s_2^*]_R(v_L, v)$,

(9) $(s_1^*\ o\ s_2^*)\alpha_R(v_L, v) = o[s_1^*\ s_2^*]\alpha_R(v_L, v)$.

Given any two programs H_1, H_2 in Adj we form a new program $H_1 o H_2$ in Adj defined thus

(10) $ad[e_{k_1} \ldots e_{k_n}]\ o\ ad[e_{i_1} \ldots e_{i_m}] = ad[e_{k_1} \ldots e_{k_n} e_{i_1} \ldots e_{i_m}]$.

Note that the following statement holds

3.3. For any two label adjoings $H_1, H_2 \in$ Adj, each realization R in $U \neq \emptyset$, each state $(v_L, v) \in W_L \times W_U$ and each formula $\alpha \in F$

(11) $(H_1 o H_2)_R(v_L, v) = o[H_1 H_2]_R(v_L, v)$,

(12) $(H_1 o H_2)\alpha_R(v_L, v) = o[H_1 H_2]\alpha_R(v_L, v)$.

In order to introduce a formal consequence operation in any language $\mathcal{L}$ of CLCA three groups of axiom schemes will be adopted.

<u>Group A</u> (axiom schemes for classical logic)

$(A_1) \vdash \alpha \rightarrow (\beta \rightarrow \alpha)$, $(A_2) \vdash (\alpha \rightarrow (\beta \rightarrow \gamma)) \rightarrow ((\alpha \rightarrow \beta) \rightarrow (\alpha \rightarrow \gamma))$,

$(A_3) \vdash \alpha \rightarrow (\alpha \vee \beta)$, $(A_4) \vdash \beta \rightarrow (\alpha \vee \beta)$, $(A_5) \vdash (\alpha \rightarrow \gamma) \rightarrow ((\beta \rightarrow \gamma) \rightarrow ((\alpha \vee \beta) \rightarrow \gamma))$,

$(A_6) \vdash (\alpha \wedge \beta) \rightarrow \alpha$, $(A_7) \vdash (\alpha \wedge \beta) \rightarrow \beta$, $(A_8) \vdash (\alpha \rightarrow \beta) \rightarrow ((\alpha \rightarrow \gamma) \rightarrow (\alpha \rightarrow (\beta \wedge \gamma)))$,

$(A_9) \vdash (\alpha \rightarrow \beta) \rightarrow (\sim\beta \rightarrow \sim\alpha)$, $(A_{10}) \vdash \sim(\alpha \rightarrow \alpha) \rightarrow \beta$, $(A_{11}) \vdash \alpha \vee \sim\alpha$,

$(A_{12}) \vdash \mathbb{1}$, $(A_{13}) \vdash \sim \mathbb{O}$.

<u>Group B</u> (additional axiom schemes for infinite disjunctions and infinite conjunctions)

$(B_1) \vdash \alpha_i \rightarrow \bigvee(\alpha_1 \alpha_2 \ldots)$, $i \in N$, $(B_2) \vdash \bigwedge(\alpha_1 \alpha_2 \ldots) \rightarrow \alpha_i$, $i \in N$,

$(B_3) \vdash ((\alpha_1 \rightarrow \beta)(\alpha_2 \rightarrow \beta) \ldots) \rightarrow (\bigvee(\alpha_1 \alpha_2 \ldots) \rightarrow \beta)$,

$(B_4) \vdash ((\alpha \rightarrow \beta_1)(\alpha \rightarrow \beta_2) \ldots) \rightarrow (\alpha \rightarrow \bigwedge(\beta_1 \beta_2 \ldots))$.

<u>Group C</u> (additional axiom schemes for CLCA)

$(C_1) \vdash \sim((a_m \doteq e_k) \wedge (a_m \doteq e_n))$, $k, n \in N_o$, $k \neq n$, $m \in N$,

$(C_2) \vdash \bigvee((a_m \doteq e_o)(a_m \doteq e_1)(a_m \doteq e_2) \ldots)$, $m \in N$,

$(C_3) \vdash \bigvee((a_1 \doteq e_o)(a_2 \doteq e_o) \ldots)$, $(C_4) \vdash (a_m \doteq e_o) \rightarrow (a_{m+1} \doteq e_o)$, $m \in N$,

$(C_5) \vdash s\alpha \leftrightarrow \bar{s}\alpha$, $s \in S$, $\alpha \in F_{at}$, $(C_6) \vdash s^*\alpha \leftrightarrow \bar{s}^*\alpha$, $s^* \in S_L^o$, $\alpha \in F_{at}$,

$(C_7) \vdash s^*s\alpha \leftrightarrow ss^*\alpha$, $s^* \in S_L^o$, $s \in S$, $(C_8) \vdash (s_1 o s_2)\alpha \leftrightarrow o[s_1 s_2]\alpha$, $s_1, s_2 \in S$,

$(C_9) \vdash (s_1^* \, o \, s_2^*)\alpha \leftrightarrow o[s_1^* \, s_2^*]\alpha$, for s_1^* , $s_2^* \in S_L^o$ and satisfying (5) ,

$(C_{10}) \vdash H(sc[e_o]\alpha) \leftrightarrow sc[e_o]\alpha$, $H \in Adj$, $(C_{11}) \vdash H\alpha \leftrightarrow \alpha$, $H \in Adj$, $\alpha \in F_{at} \cap F_o$,

$(C_{12}) \vdash o[sH]\alpha \leftrightarrow o[Hs]\alpha$, $s \in S$, $H \in Adj$, $(C_{13}) \vdash (H_1 o H_2)\alpha \leftrightarrow o[H_1 H_2]\alpha$, H_1, H_2 are in Adj,

$(C_{14}) \vdash [\;]\alpha \leftrightarrow \alpha$, where $[\;]$ is the empty substitution or an identity substitution $[x_1/x_1 \ldots x_n/x_n \; p_1/p_1 \ldots p_m/p_m]$ or $sc[a_1]$,

$(C_{15}) \vdash [a_n \doteq e_k]\alpha \leftrightarrow ((a_n \doteq e_k) \wedge \alpha)$, $n \in N$, $k \in N_o$,

$(C_{16}) \vdash ((a_1 \doteq e_{k_1}) \wedge \ldots \wedge (a_n \doteq e_{k_n}) \wedge (a_{n+1} \doteq e_o)) \rightarrow$

$ad[e_{i_1} \ldots e_{i_m}]((a_1 \doteq e_{k_1}) \wedge \ldots \wedge (a_n \doteq e_{k_n}) \wedge (a_{n+1} \doteq e_{i_1}) \wedge \ldots \wedge$

$(a_{n+m} \doteq e_{i_m}) \wedge (a_{n+m+1} \doteq e_o))$, $n, m, k_1, \ldots, k_n, i_1, \ldots, i_m \in N$,

$(C_{17}) \vdash \bigwedge((H_1\alpha_1 \leftrightarrow H_2\alpha_1)(H_1\alpha_2 \leftrightarrow H_2\alpha_2)(H_1\alpha_3 \leftrightarrow H_2\alpha_3) \ldots) \rightarrow (H_1 H\alpha_i \leftrightarrow H_2 H\alpha_i)$,

$i \in N$, where H_1, H_2, H are compositions of finite sequences of programs in $S_L^o \cup Adj$ and $\alpha_1, \alpha_2, \ldots$ is an effective sequence of all $(a_i \doteq e_j)$, $i \in N$, $j \in N_o$,

$(C_{18}) \vdash H(\alpha\vee\beta)\leftrightarrow(H\alpha\vee H\beta)$, $(C_{19}) \vdash H(\alpha\wedge\beta)\leftrightarrow(H\alpha\wedge H\beta)$,

$(C_{20}) \vdash H\sim\alpha\rightarrow\sim H\alpha$, $(C_{21}) \vdash H\mathbb{1}\rightarrow(\sim H\alpha\rightarrow H\sim\alpha)$,

$(C_{22}) \vdash H(\alpha\rightarrow\beta)\rightarrow(H\alpha\rightarrow H\beta)$, $(C_{23}) \vdash H\mathbb{1}\rightarrow((H\alpha\rightarrow H\beta)\rightarrow H(\alpha\rightarrow\beta))$,

$(C_{24}) \vdash H\bigvee(\alpha_1\alpha_2\ldots)\leftrightarrow\bigvee(H\alpha_1 H\alpha_2\ldots)$,

$(C_{25}) \vdash H\bigwedge(\alpha_1\alpha_2\ldots)\leftrightarrow\bigwedge(H\alpha_1 H\alpha_2\ldots)$,

$(C_{26}) \vdash o[H_1H_2]\alpha\leftrightarrow H_1(H_2\alpha))$,

$(C_{27}) \vdash \veebar[\gamma\, H_1H_2]\alpha\leftrightarrow((\gamma\wedge H_1\alpha)\vee(\sim\gamma\wedge H_2\alpha))$,

$(C_{28}) \vdash c^*[H_\iota H_1\ldots H_nH_t]\alpha\leftrightarrow\bigvee(o[H_\iota H_1H_t]\alpha\ldots o[H_\iota H_1H_{i_1}\ldots H_{i_m}H_t]\alpha\ldots)$

$i_1,\ldots,i_m\in\{1,\ldots,n\}, m\in N$.

Let $\mathcal{A}_1$ be the set of all $\alpha\in F$ which are axioms, i.e.are of forms $(A_1)-(A_{13})$, $(B_1)-(B_4)$, $(C_1)-(C_{28})$. For each $\mathcal{A}\subset F$ we set $C(\mathcal{A})$ equal the least set of formulas containing $\mathcal{A}_1\cup\mathcal{A}$ and closed with respect to the following rules of inference:

$$(r_1)\ \frac{\alpha,\ \alpha\rightarrow\beta}{\beta}\ ,\qquad (r_2)\ \frac{\alpha,\ H\mathbb{1}}{H\alpha}\ ,\qquad (r_3)\ \frac{\alpha_n,\ n\in N}{\bigwedge(\alpha_1\ \alpha_2\ \ldots)}\ .$$

We shall write $\mathcal{A}\vdash\alpha$ instead of $\alpha\in C(\mathcal{A})$ and $\vdash\alpha$ instead of $\alpha\in C(\emptyset)$. The systems $\mathcal{S}=(\mathcal{L}, C)$ will be said to be formalized systems of CLCA and $\mathcal{S}(\mathcal{A})=(\mathcal{L},C,\mathcal{A})$ formalized theories based on CLCA.

Let us note the following statement

3.4. For any $H\in S\cup S^o_L\cup \mathrm{Adj}$ we have $\vdash H\mathbb{1}$.

It follows from (C_5), (C_6), (C_{11}), (A_7) , (A_{12}). Indeed we get $\vdash\Lambda\rightarrow H\mathbb{1}$ and hence (13) holds.

By an easy verification it may be proved that all logical exioms are tautologies of CLCA and that rules of inference have the property that if all premisses are satisfied by a realization R for a state (v_L,v), then the same holds for the conlusion. This yields

3.5 For every set $\mathcal{A}\subset F$, $C(\mathcal{A})\subset Cn(\mathcal{A})$.

Thus every formula provable in a formalized theory $\mathcal{S}(\mathcal{A})$ is a semantic consequence of $\mathcal{A}$.

4. __Algebras of formalized theories based on CLCA.__ Given a formalized theory $\mathcal{S}(\mathcal{A})=(\mathcal{L},C,\mathcal{A})$ consider the algebra of formulas

(1) $\mathcal{F}=(F\ ,\mathbb{1},\vee,\wedge,\rightarrow,\sim,(H)_{H\in P})$

and the relation $\approx$ on F defined thus

(2) $\alpha\approx\beta$ if and only if $\mathcal{A}\vdash(\alpha\rightarrow\beta)$ and $\mathcal{A}\vdash(\beta\rightarrow\alpha)$.

Axioms in Group A and (r_1) yield that $\approx$ is an equivalence relation preserving $\vee$, $\wedge$, $\rightarrow$, $\sim$. Applying also axioms in Group B and (r_3) we prove that

4.1.For any two sequences of formulas $(\alpha_n)_{n\in N}, (\beta_n)_{n\in N}$ such that their infinite disjunctions and infinite conjunctions are in F,

$\alpha_n \approx \beta_n$ for all $n\in N$ implies that

$\bigvee(\alpha_1\alpha_2\ldots) \approx \bigvee(\beta_1\beta_2\ldots)$ and $\bigwedge(\alpha_1\alpha_2\ldots) \approx \bigwedge(\beta_1\beta_2\ldots)$.

On applying the inductive argument with respect to the length of a program H in P we prove the following lemma.

4.2.For any α, β in F and every $H\in P$

(3) if $\alpha \approx \beta$, then $H\alpha \approx H\beta$.

For $H\in S \cup S_L^o \cup Adj$ this follows from 4.4,(C_{22}),(C_{23}).For H in Sp a proof applies (C_{15}). For programs in forms $o[H_1H_2]$ and $\ast[\gamma\, H_1H_2]$ a use is made of (C_{26}), (C_{27}), respectively.The cases just considered and forms of instructions yield (3) for all instructions.A proof for cr-programs applies (C_{28}) and 4.1.

Thus we proved that $\approx$ is a congruence on $\mathcal{F}$. Let

(4) $\mathcal{F}(\mathcal{A}) = (F/_{\approx}, V, \cup, \cap, \Rightarrow, \neg, (H)_{H\in P})$

be the quotient algebra $\mathcal{F}/_{\approx}$ formed of all equivalence classes $|\alpha|$ for α in F. Thus

(5) $V=|1|, |\alpha|\cup|\beta|=|\alpha\vee\beta|, |\alpha|\cap|\beta|=|\alpha\wedge\beta|, |\alpha|\Rightarrow|\beta|=|\alpha\to\beta|, \neg|\alpha|=|\sim\alpha|$,

(6) $H|\alpha|=|H\alpha|$ for every $H\in P$.

Axioms in Group A, in Group B, (r_1) and (r_3) yield

4.3.The reduct $\mathcal{F}_o(\mathcal{A}) = (F/_{\approx}, V, \cup, \cap, \Rightarrow, \neg)$ is a Boolean algebra in which

(7) $|\alpha|=V$ if and only if $\mathcal{A}\vdash\alpha$, for each $\alpha\in F$,

(8) $|\alpha|\leq|\beta|$ if and only if $\mathcal{A}\vdash\alpha\to\beta$,

(9) $|\bigvee(\alpha_1\alpha_2\ldots)| = \bigcup_{n\in N}|\alpha_n|$,

(10) $|\bigwedge(\alpha_1\alpha_2\ldots)| = \bigcap_{n\in N}|\alpha_n|$,where $\bigcup$, $\bigcap$ denote infinite joins and meets.

Moreover,it follows from (9),(10),(C_{24}), (C_{25}),(7),(8) and (5) that

(11) $|H\bigvee(\alpha_1\alpha_2\ldots)| = \bigcup_{n\in N}|H\alpha_n| = \bigcup_{n\in N}H|\alpha_n|$,

(12) $|H\bigwedge(\alpha_1\alpha_2\ldots)| = \bigcap_{n\in N}|H\alpha_n| = \bigcap_{n\in N}H|\alpha_n|$.

5.Model existence theorem. Let $\mathcal{S}(\mathcal{A}) = (\mathcal{L}, C, \mathcal{A})$ be a formalized theory based on CLCA.Assume in this section that either $\mathcal{A}\subset F_o$,i.e. $\mathcal{A}$ is a set of formulas in the initial language for $\mathcal{L}$, or $\mathcal{A}=\{\alpha_n\}_{n\in N}$ and the set of all individual variables and of all propositional variables in formulas belonging to $\mathcal{A}$ is finite. Then $\bigwedge(\alpha_1\alpha_2\ldots)$ is in F. Let α denote this infinite conjunction.

Under the above assumptions the following theorem holds.

5.1. If non $\mathcal{A}\vdash\alpha_0$, then there exists a model R of $\mathcal{A}$ in the set T of terms and a state $(v_L,v)\in W_L\times W_T$ such that $\alpha_{0R}(v_L,v)=\wedge$.

Sketch of a proof. A decomposition relation $>$ on F is introduced in such a way, that it holds for some formulas $\beta_1>\beta_i$, $i\in I$, if β_i are obtained of β_1 by a decomposition or by a simplification. This relation is an ordering with the minimality property. Let $F(\alpha_0)$ and $F(\alpha)$ be the sets of formulas in F defined thus:

(1) $F(\alpha_0)=\{\beta\in F\mid\alpha_0>\beta\}$, $F(\alpha)=\{\beta\in F\mid\alpha>\beta\}$.

It is easy to prove that $F(\alpha_0)\cup F(\alpha)$ is denumerable.

The assumption that non $\mathcal{A}\vdash\alpha_0$ and (7) in Sec.4 yield

(2) $|\alpha_0|\neq\vee$.

It follows from well known lemma on Boolean algebras (see [8], p.87) that there exists a prime filter ∇ in $\mathcal{F}(\mathcal{A})$ which satisfies the following conditions:

(i) $|\alpha_0|\notin\nabla$,

(ii) ∇ preserves infinite joins determined in $\mathcal{F}(\mathcal{A})$ by axioms (C_2), (C_3) and infinite meets determined by infinite conjunctions occurring in (C_{17}),

(iii) if $\bigvee(\beta_1\beta_2\ldots)\in F(\alpha_0)\cup F(\alpha)$, then ∇ preserves $|H_1\ldots H_n s\bigvee(\beta_1\beta_2\ldots)|=\bigcup_{i\in N}|H_1\ldots H_n s\beta_i|$ for all $H_1,\ldots,H_n\in S^0_L\cup Adj$ and $s\in S$, and analogously for infinite conjunctions and corresponding infinite meets.

The quotient algebra $\mathcal{F}_0(\mathcal{A})/\nabla$ is the two-element Boolean algebra. For any $\beta\in F$, let $\|\beta\|$ be the element of this algebra determined by $|\beta|$. From (i),

(3) $\|\alpha_0\|=\wedge$.

Let us set

(4) $v^0_L(a_m)=e_i$ if and only if $\|a_m\doteq e_i\|=\vee$.

This definition is correct. Indeed, by (C_2), (ii) and (7) in Sec.4, $\bigcup_{i\in N}\|a_m\doteq e_i\|=\vee$. Hence for each $m\in N$ there is $i\in N_0$ such that $\|a_m\doteq e_i\|$ is equal $\vee$. On the other hand it follows from (C_1) and (7) in Sec.4 that for each $m\in N$ there is exactly one i such that $\|a_m\doteq e_i\|=\vee$. Analogously (C_3), (ii), and (7) in Sec.4 yield $v^0_L(a_m)=e_0$ for some $m\in N$ and by (C_4), $v^0_L(a_m)=e_0$ implies that $v^0_L(a_{m+1})=e_0$. Thus v^0_L is a label vector.

The following mapping R

(5)
$$\varphi_R(\tau_1,\ldots,\tau_k)=\varphi(\tau_1\ldots\tau_k) \text{ for any k-argument functor } \varphi\in\Phi,$$
$$\rho_R(\tau_1,\ldots,\tau_k)=\|\rho(\tau_1\ldots\tau_k)\| \text{ for any k-ary predicate } \rho\in\Pi,$$

and $\tau_1,\ldots,\tau_k\in T$, is a realization of $\mathcal{L}$ in the set T of terms. We shall prove that R is a model of $\mathcal{A}$ but it is not a model of α_0.

Each valuation v in W_T determines uniquely for any $\bar{V}=\{x_1,\dots,x_n\} \cup \{p_1,\dots,p_m\} \subset V \cup V_0$ a substitution s_v defined thus:

$$s_v=[x_1/\tau_1 \dots x_n/\tau_n \ p_1/\gamma_1 \dots p_m/\gamma_m], \text{ where } \tau_i=v(x_i) \text{ for } i=1,\dots,n$$

(6) $\gamma_i=p_i$ if $v(p_i)=\| p_i\|$, $\gamma_i=\mathbb{1}$ if $v(p_i)=\vee \neq \| p_i\|$, $\gamma_i=\mathbb{0}$ if $v(p_i)=\wedge \neq \| p_i\|$, $i=1,\dots,m$

In particular v_0 such that $v_0(x)=x$ for $x\in V$ and $v_0(p)=p$ for $p\in V_0$ determines [ ]. Note that

(7) $s_{vR}(v_0)(x)=v(x)$ and $s_{vR}(v_0)(p)=v(p)$ for $x,p\in \bar{V}$.

Each label vector v_L determines the composition of two schedulings $o[sc[e_0]sc[e_{k_1}\dots e_{k_n}a_2]]$ for $v_L=(e_{k_1},\dots,e_{k_n},e_0,\dots)$ and $o[sc[e_0]sc[e_0]]$ for $v_L=(e_0,\dots)$.

Let $s^*_{v_L}$ be the second of schedulings determined by a given v_L. Then

(8) $o[sc[e_0]s^*_{v_L}]_R(v^0_L)=v_L$.

The following lemma 5.2 yields theorem 5.1.

5.2. If $\beta\in F(\alpha_0)\cup F(\alpha)$ or $\beta\in F_0$, then for every finite sequence of programs $H_1,\dots,H_n\in S^0_L\cup Adj$ and for every $s\in S$

(9) $H_1\dots H_n\, s\, \beta_R(v^0_L,v_0)=\| H_1\dots H_n s\beta\|$.

In particular

$$\alpha_{0R}(v^0_L,v_0)=\|\alpha_0\|=\wedge .$$

On the other hand, for any state (v_L,v), we have by (7) and (8)

$$sc[e_0]\, s^*_{v_L} s_v\, \beta_R(v^0_L,v_0)=\beta_R(v_L,v) .$$

That equation and (9) yield

(10) $\alpha_R(v_L,v)=\| sc[e_0]\, s^*_{v_L}\, s_v\, \alpha\|$.

Since $\alpha=\bigwedge(\alpha_1\alpha_2\dots)$ and $\alpha_i\in\mathcal{A}$, by (r_3), $\mathcal{A}\vdash\alpha$. On applying 3.4 and (r_2), we infer that $sc[e_0]s^*_{v_L}\, s_v\,\alpha\in C(\mathcal{A})$. Hence, by (7) in Sec 4 and (10), $\alpha_R(v_L,v)=\vee$ and consequently $\alpha_{nR}(v_L,v)=\vee$ for all $n\in N$.

Thus R is a model of $\mathcal{A}$. If $\mathcal{A}\subset F_0$, then 5.1 follows from the fact that (9) holds for each $\beta\in F_0$.

It follows from 5.1 and 3.5 that

5.3. Under the assumptions adopted in this section $C(\mathcal{A})=Cn(\mathcal{A})$. In particular $C(\emptyset)=Cn(\emptyset)$, i.e. the set of tautologies coincides with the set of formulas deducible from logical axioms. More generally, the set of formulas valid in all algebraic structures (data bases) being models of $\mathcal{A}$ coincides with the set of formulas deducible from logical axioms and formulas in $\mathcal{A}$ by means of adopted rules.

References

[1] Blikle A.,Mazurkiewicz A., An algebraic approach to the theory of programs,algorithms,languages and recursiveness,Proc.Intern.Symp. and Summer School on MFCS,1972,CCPAS Reports 1972

[2] Conway M.E.,Design of a separable-transition diagram compliler, Comm.ACM 6,July 1963,396-408

[3] Harel D.,Meyer A.R.,Pratt V.R.,Computability,and Completeness in Logics of programs,Proc. 9th Annual ACM Symposium on Theory of Computing,Boulder,Colorado,May 1977,261-268

[4] Janicki R.,An algebraic approach to the theory of recursive coroutines,Fundamenta Informaticae 1,No 1 (1977),131-145

[5] Mazurkiewicz A.,Recursive algorithms and formal languages,Bull.Ac. Pol.Sci.,Ser.Sci.Math.Astron.Phys.,20(1972),799-809

[6] Mirkowska G.,Algorithmic logic with nondeterministic programs,ICS PAS Reports 343 (1979),17

[7] Pratt V.R.,Semantical considerations in Floyd-Hoare Logic,Proc. 17th IEEE Symp. on FCS,1976

[8] Rasiowa H.,Sikorski R.,The Mathematics of Metamathematics,Warsaw, 3rd ed.1970

[9] Rasiowa H., ω^+-valued algorithmic logic as a tool to investigate procedures,Proc.MFCS'74,Lecture Notes in Computer Sci 28(1974) Springer Verlag

[10] Rasiowa H.,Completeness theorem for extended algorithmic logic, Proc.Vth Int.Congress of Logic Methodology and Philosophy of Science,1975 III,13-15

[11] Rasiowa H.,Algorithmic Logic.Multiple-valued extensions.Studia Logica,XXXVIII 4(1979),317-335

[12] Rasiowa H., Logic of complex algorithms,Proc.FCT'79,Berlin,ed.by L.Budach,Mathematische Forschung,2 (1979),Akademie Verlag,370-381

[13] Salwicki A.,Formalized algorithmic languages,Bull.Ac.Pol.Sci.,Ser. Math.Astron.Phys.18 (1970),227-232

[14] Tiuryn J.,Logic of effective definitions,RWTH Aachen Schriften zur Informatik und Angewndten Mathematik,55,juli 1979; Fundamenta Informaticae,to appear

INITIALLY - RESTRICTING ALGEBRAIC THEORIES

by H.Reichel
TH "Otto von Guericke"
Sektion Mathematik/Physik
DDR-301 Magdeburg
Boleslaw Bierut Platz 5

1. Motivation

In the last years considerable effort has been done to develop so-called 'specification languages' for data types, parameterized data types, and algorithms. Examples are CLEAR by Burstall and Goguen /BG 77/, OBJ by Goguen and Tardo /GT 77+79/, and the specification language in the AFFIRM-system by Musser /Mus 79/.

With respect to the definition of a mathematically exact semantics the initial approach of algebraic specifications /ADJ 75, BG 77, Ehr 78, EKP 78, KR 71/ seems to be the most successful one.

Since every algebraic theory uniquely up to isomorphisms determines the initial algebra the concept of an algebraic theory is used in defining semantics of specification languages as far as the specification of data types only is considered.

If we have to define the semantics of a specification language that allows the specification of parameterized data types and algorithms a much more general concept as that of algebraic theories is needed. In /TWW 78/ the expressive power is generalized using negation and implications. But an analysis of practical problems shows that first order theories are not general enough. We will illustrate this assertion by an example. Let's assume, we want to specify the well known algorithm of Ford-Fulkerson /FF 56/ wich produces a maximal flow for every finite transport net. For this task we have to specify firstly the class of all finite transport nets, and secondly the algorithm of Ford-Fulkerson itself. But the class of all finite transport nets is not a model class of a finite many-sorted first order theory. For the description of transport nets with finite node sets and finite arc sets we need the set of natural numbers as possible values of the 'capacity function' of the transport net. Thus, every transport net has the set of natural numbers as a semantically fixed component such that every transport net itself is an infinite but countable structure. From the cardinality theorem of Tarski it follows that the class of all finite transport nets is not a model class of a finite first order theory.

This example, motivated by practical problems, shows that any calculus to define semantics of specification languages for parameterized data types and algorithms should be able to describe more general model classes as parameter classes than first order classes.

In the sequel we shall develop the calculus of 'initially-restricting algebraic theories' which seems to satisfy all theoretical and practical requirements stated up to now. This concept results from cooperative work with U.L. Hupbach and H.Kaphengst both from VEB Robotron, Centre of Research and Development, Dresden.

2. Initially restricting algebraic theories - Canons

At the beginning we recall that a heterogeneous theory $\underline{T}$ is given by a set S of sort names, by a family $(\Sigma_{w,s})_{w\in S^*, s\in S}$ of operators, where S^* denotes the set of all finite words over S, and by a set $\mathfrak{A}$ of axioms. A $\underline{T}$-algebra $A = ((A_s)_{s\in S}, (\sigma_A)_{\sigma\in\Sigma})$ consists of a family $(A_s)_{s\in S}$ of carrier sets, and of a family $(\sigma_A)_{\sigma\in\Sigma}$, $\Sigma = \{\sigma\in\Sigma_{w,s} \mid w\in S^*, s\in S\}$, of operations.

We speak of an equational theory, if every axiom has the form of a term equation. A theory is said to be implicational, if every axiom is an implication where premise and conclusion are sets of term equations.

In some papers this notion of an algebraic theory is called a representation of an algebraic theory and an algebraic theory itself is given by a special kind of categories /Law 63, KR 72/.

The basic idea of the calculus is to mark some parts of an algebraic theory that are subject to a relatively-free interpretation, i.e., interpretation according to the initial approach.

Before we are able to give a defininition of an initially restricting algebraic theory we have to make more precise the notion of a relatively-free interpretation.

Definition 1. Let $\underline{T}_1$ and $\underline{T}_2$ be heterogeneous algebraic theories so that $\underline{T}_2$ is an enlargement of $\underline{T}_1$. This means that every sort name s of $\underline{T}_1$ is also a sort name of $\underline{T}_2$, every operator o of

$\underline{T}_1$ is also an operator of $\underline{T}_2$ with the same arity, and every axiom of $\underline{T}_1$ is satisfied in $\underline{T}_2$.

Let A be a $\underline{T}_2$-algebra. Then we can derive a $\underline{T}_1$-algebra $A{\downarrow}\underline{T}_1$ from A by forgetting all those carrier sets A_s and operations σ_A of A where s and σ are not contained in $\underline{T}_1$. The $\underline{T}_1$-algebra $A{\downarrow}\underline{T}_1$ is called the $\underline{T}_1$-part of A with respect to the theory enlargement $\underline{T}_1 \subseteq \underline{T}_2$.

A $\underline{T}_2$-algebra F is called <u>freely generated</u> by the $\underline{T}_1$-algebra B if there is a $\underline{T}_1$-homomorphism $j: B \longrightarrow F{\downarrow}\underline{T}_1$ such that for every $\underline{T}_2$-algebra M and every $\underline{T}_1$-homomorphism $f: B \longrightarrow M{\downarrow}\underline{T}_1$ there is one and only one $\underline{T}_2$-homomorphism $\bar{f}: F \longrightarrow M$ with $j \cdot (\bar{f}{\downarrow}\underline{T}_1) = f$ where $\bar{f}{\downarrow}\underline{T}_1 : F{\downarrow}\underline{T}_1 \longrightarrow M{\downarrow}\underline{T}_1$ denotes the $\underline{T}_1$-part of the $\underline{T}_2$-homomorphism with respect to the theory extension $\underline{T}_1 \subseteq \underline{T}_2$.

A $\underline{T}_2$-algebra E is called a free $\underline{T}_2$-extension of the $\underline{T}_1$-algebra B if E is freely generated by B such that $j: B \longrightarrow E{\downarrow}\underline{T}_1$ is the identity morphism of B . ∎

If $\underline{\emptyset}$ denotes the empty theory than $\underline{\emptyset} \subseteq \underline{T}$ is a theory enlargement and the initial $\underline{T}$-algebra is a free $\underline{T}$-extension of the unique $\underline{\emptyset}$-algebra consisting of the empty family of carrier sets and of the empty family of operations.

If F is freely generated by B then we can understand F as a semantically weakest completion of B to a $\underline{T}_2$-algebra.

It is clear that not for every theory enlargement $\underline{T}_1 \subseteq \underline{T}_2$ and any $\underline{T}_1$-algebra B a free $\underline{T}_2$-extension exists. In the case of homogeneous theories the concept of free extensions is not so powerfull since for most theory enlargements of homogeneous theories free $\underline{T}_2$-extensions of $\underline{T}_1$-algebras do not exist. But in the case of heterogeneous theories the concept of free extensions becomes the base for the specification of parameterized data types.

We will make this remark more intelligible by the example of the '<u>F</u>inite-<u>P</u>ower-<u>S</u>et-Construction' /Hup 79, KR 71, TWW 78/.

Let <u>FPS</u> be the following heterogeneous implicational theory:

<u>FPS</u> = <u>sorts</u> Bool; Elements; Sets
<u>oprs</u> true, false : $\longrightarrow$ Bool

```
oprs     _eq_: Elements,Elements ⟶ Bool  1)
         _∈_: Elements,Sets ⟶ Bool  1)
         ∅ : ⟶ Sets
         adjoin: Elements,Sets ⟶ Sets
axioms for all  e,e1,e2 ∈ Elements,  m ∈ Sets  let
     e1 eq e1 = true
     if (e1 eq e2) = true then  e1 = e2  fi
     adjoin(e,adjoin(e,m)) = adjoin(e,m)
     adjoin(e1,adjoin(e2,m)) = adjoin(e2,adjoin(e1,m))
     (e ∈ ∅) = false
     (e ∈ adjoin(e,m)) = true
     if (e1 ∈ m) = false then (e1 ∈ adjoin(e2,m))=(e1 eq e2) fi
end FPS
```

Obviously, there are FPS-algebras that have nothing to do with a Finite-Power-Set-Construction. If we restrict the class $\mathfrak{M}$(FPS) of all FPS-algebras to those FPS-algebras $M = ((M_s)_{s \in S}, (\sigma_M)_{\sigma \in \Sigma})$ such that

$M_{Bool} = \{true, false\}$;

M_{Sets} = set of all finite subsets of $M_{Elements}$;

$M_{Elements}$ = any set ;

$true_M = true$; $false_M = false$;

$eq_M : M_{Elements} \times M_{Elements} \longrightarrow \{true, false\}$ is the identity relation

$\emptyset_M$ is the empty subset of $M_{Elements}$;

$adjoin_M : M_{Elements} \times M_{Sets} \longrightarrow M_{Sets}$ associates with every element e of $M_{Elements}$ and every finite subset m of $M_{Elements}$ the finite subset $adjoin_M(e,m) = m \cup \{e\}$;

$\in_M : M_{Elements} \times M_{Sets} \longrightarrow$ true,false is the element relation.

By this semantical restriction of $\mathfrak{M}$(FPS) to $\mathfrak{M}^*$(FPS) we get an algebraic description of the wanted Finite-Power-Set-Construction.

---

1) The denotation _eq_ and _∈_ indicates that these both operators are used in infix notation within the formulation of the heterogeneous implicational theory.

By the concept of inital restrictions in an algebraic theory we introduce a general tool for such kinds of semantical restrictions of a model class $\mathfrak{M}(\underline{T})$ of an algebraic theory $\underline{T}$. In this approach an algebraic theory may be a usual homogeneous theory but it may be a heterogeneous theory, a heterogeneous implicational theory /TWW 78/ or an equationally-partial heterogeneous implicational theory as introduced in /KR 71, Rei 79/.

In the context of equationally-partial implicational heterogeneous theories the concept of initial restrictions is powerful enough to specify all partially recursive functions and all recursively enumerable sets.

Definition 2. Let $\underline{T}$ be any algebraic theory. An ordered pair $\underline{R} \lhd \underline{S}$ of subtheories $\underline{R} \subseteq \underline{S} \subseteq \underline{T}$ is called an initial restriction in $\underline{T}$. A $\underline{T}$-algebra M satisfies the initial restriction $\underline{R} \lhd \underline{S}$ if the $\underline{S}$-part $M{\downarrow}\underline{S}$ is a free $\underline{S}$-extension of the $\underline{R}$-part $M{\downarrow}\underline{R}$ of the $\underline{T}$-algebra M .

An ordered pair $\underline{\underline{T}} = (\underline{T}, \Delta)$ consisting of a finitary algebraic theory $\underline{T}$ and of a finite set $\Delta = \{ \underline{R}_j \lhd \underline{S}_j \mid j \in J \}$ of initial restrictions in $\underline{T}$ is called a 'canon', or in more detail an 'initially restricting algebraic theory'.

$\underline{\underline{T}} = (\underline{T}, \Delta)$ is called totally restricted if every sort name $s \in S$ and every operator $\sigma \in \Sigma$ is subject to an initial restriction.

$\mathfrak{M}(\underline{\underline{T}})$ denotes the class of all $\underline{T}$-algebras satisfying all initial restrictions out of Δ . ∎

Let $\underline{S}$ = sorts Bool
  oprs true, false : ⟶ Bool
  end $\underline{S}$

and $\underline{B}$ = sorts Bool; Elements
  oprs true, false : ⟶ Bool
    _eq_: Elements,Elements ⟶ Bool
  axioms for all e_1, e_2 Elements let
    $(e_1 \text{ eq } e_1) = \text{true}$
    if $(e_1 \text{ eq } e_2) = \text{true}$ then $e_1 = e_2$ fi
  end $\underline{B}$

Then $\underline{\underline{FPS}} = (\underline{FPS}, \{ \emptyset \lhd \underline{S}, \underline{B} \lhd \underline{FPS} \})$ is a canon with $\mathfrak{M}(\underline{\underline{FPS}}) \equiv \mathfrak{M}^*(\underline{FPS})$.

Here $\cong$ means that every $M \in \mathcal{M}(\underline{\underline{FPS}})$ is isomorphic to an $M' \in \mathcal{M}(\underline{FPS})$.

3. Applications

Using the introduced notions it is possible to define a canon $\underline{\underline{\text{Transport-nets}}}$ /Rei 79/ such that $\mathcal{M}(\underline{\underline{\text{Transport-nets}}})$ is the class of all transport nets as sketched above.

Benecke /Ben 79/ has proved a 'downward Löwenheim-Skolem Theorem' for model classes of canons (more precisely for signatur chains which are a not too restrictive special case of canons where the set of initial restrictions forms a chain $\ldots \underline{R}_i \lhd \underline{S}_i \subseteq \underline{R}_{i+1} \lhd \underline{S}_{i+1} \ldots$). Using this theorem he was able to prove that the usual infinite power set construction can not be described by a canon.

The example $\underline{\underline{FPS}}$ makes clear how canons can be used for the description of parameterized data types. The subcanon

$$\underline{\underline{B}} = (\underline{B}, \{\emptyset \lhd \underline{S}\}) \quad \underline{\underline{FPS}}$$

describes the parameter class for the Finite-Power-Set-Construction.

The notion of a 'parameter substitution' can now be defined by means of 'canon morphisms'.

Definition 3. Let $\underline{T}_1, \underline{T}_2$ be algebraic theories. A theory morphism $f: \underline{T}_1 \longrightarrow \underline{T}_2$ associates with every sort name s of $\underline{T}_1$ a sort name $f(s)$ of $\underline{T}_2$ and with every operator σ of $\underline{T}_1$ an operator $f(\sigma)$ of $\underline{T}_2$ so that

(1) $f: \underline{T}_1 \longrightarrow \underline{T}_2$ is compatible with the arity of every operator σ of $\underline{T}_1$, i.e., if the arity of σ is $\sigma : s_1,\ldots,s_n \longrightarrow s$ then the arity of $f(\sigma)$ is $f(\sigma): f(s_1),\ldots,f(s_n) \longrightarrow f(s)$;

(2) the 'f-image' of every axiom of $\underline{T}_1$ holds in $\underline{T}_2$.

For a given theory morphism $f: \underline{T}_1 \longrightarrow \underline{T}_2$ we can derive from every $\underline{T}_2$-algebra $M = ((M_s)_{s \in S_2}, (\sigma_M)_{\sigma \in \Sigma_2})$ a $\underline{T}_1$-algebra $f \bullet M$ by setting

$(f \bullet M)_s = M_{f(s)}$ for every sort name s of $\underline{T}_1$ and

$\sigma_{(f \bullet M)} = f(\sigma)_M$ for every operator σ of $\underline{T}_1$.

A canon morphism $f: (\underline{T}_1, \Delta_1) \longrightarrow (\underline{T}_2, \Delta_2)$ is a theory morphism $f: \underline{T}_1 \longrightarrow \underline{T}_2$ such that $f \circ M \in \mathcal{M}(\underline{T}_1, \Delta_1)$ holds for every $M \in \mathcal{M}(\underline{T}_2, \Delta_2)$. ∎

Obviously, the inclusion $i: \underline{B} \longrightarrow \underline{FPS}$ is a canon morphism $i: \underline{\underline{B}} \longrightarrow \underline{\underline{FPS}}$.

If we identify corresponding to the initial approach abstract data types with totally restricted canons then a correct parameter substitution would be a canon morphism $p: \underline{\underline{B}} \longrightarrow \underline{\underline{D}}$ where $\underline{\underline{D}}$ is a totally restricted canon. The data type resulting from the substitution $p: \underline{\underline{B}} \longrightarrow \underline{\underline{D}}$ in $\underline{\underline{FPS}}$ is then given by a pushout construction corresponding to the following diagram Dg1 in the category of canons.

Dg1:

$$\begin{array}{ccc} \underline{\underline{B}} & \xrightarrow{\quad p \quad} & \underline{\underline{D}} \\ \subseteq \downarrow & & \downarrow q_2 \\ \underline{\underline{FPS}} & \xrightarrow[\quad q_1 \quad]{} & \underline{\underline{R}} \end{array}$$

Unfortunatly, the pushout construction does not exist for all possible canon morphisms $\underline{\underline{B}} \xleftarrow{g} \underline{\underline{A}} \xrightarrow{h} \underline{\underline{C}}$.

But, if the pushout corresponding to Dg1 exists, then $q_2: \underline{\underline{D}} \longrightarrow \underline{\underline{R}}$ is again an inclusion and $\underline{\underline{R}}$ is a totally restricted canon.

To overcome this lack of the non-existence of general pushouts in the category of canons H. Kaphengst proposed the following generalisation of the notion of an initial restriction in an algebraic theory.

Definition 2 . Let $\underline{T}$ be any algebraic theory. An ordered pair $\underline{R} \lhd \underline{S}$ of theories with $\underline{R} \subseteq \underline{S}$, i.e., $\underline{R}$ is a subtheory of $\underline{S}$, together with a theory morphism $h: \underline{S} \longrightarrow \underline{T}$ is called an initial restriction in $\underline{T}$ and denoted by $(\underline{R} \lhd \underline{S}, h)$. A $\underline{T}$-algebra M satisfies $(\underline{R} \lhd \underline{S}, h)$ if $h \circ M$ is a free $\underline{S}$-extension of the $\underline{R}$-part $(h \circ M) \downarrow \underline{R}$.

As before, a canon $\underline{\underline{T}} = (\underline{T}, \Delta)$ is again a finitary algebraic theory $\underline{T}$ accompanied by a set Δ of initial restrictions in $\underline{T}$. ∎

The old notion $\underline{R} \lhd \underline{S}$ of an initial restriction is the special case given by the fact that $h: \underline{S} \longrightarrow \underline{T}$ is the inclusion of a subtheory $\underline{S} \subseteq \underline{T}$.

It is interesting that all known practical examples can be comprehended by the first version of a canon. But a suitable mathematical foundation requires the more general concept.

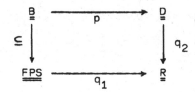

With respect to Definition 2 the category of canons is closed under pushouts. Let $f: \underline{\underline{A}} \longrightarrow \underline{\underline{C}}$, $g: \underline{\underline{A}} \longrightarrow \underline{\underline{B}}$ be any canon morphisms and

<u>Dg2</u>

$$\begin{array}{ccc} \underline{A} & \xrightarrow{\quad f \quad} & \underline{C} \\ {\scriptstyle g}\downarrow & & \downarrow{\scriptstyle q} \\ \underline{B} & \xrightarrow[\quad p \quad]{} & \underline{Q} \end{array}$$

a pushout diagram in the category of algebraic theories. If we set

$$\Delta_{\underline{\underline{Q}}} = \left\{ (\underline{R} \lhd \underline{S}, h\circ p) \mid (\underline{R} \lhd \underline{S}, h) \in \Delta_{\underline{\underline{B}}} \right\} \cup \left\{ (\underline{R} \lhd \underline{S}, h\circ q) \mid (\underline{R} \lhd \underline{S}, h) \in \Delta_{\underline{\underline{C}}} \right\}$$

we get a canon $\underline{\underline{Q}} = (\underline{Q}, \Delta_{\underline{\underline{Q}}})$ such that $p: \underline{\underline{B}} \longrightarrow \underline{\underline{Q}}$, $q: \underline{\underline{C}} \longrightarrow \underline{\underline{Q}}$ are canon morphisms and

<u>Dg3</u>

$$\begin{array}{ccc} \underline{\underline{A}} & \xrightarrow{\quad f \quad} & \underline{\underline{C}} \\ {\scriptstyle g}\downarrow & & \downarrow{\scriptstyle q} \\ \underline{\underline{B}} & \xrightarrow[\quad p \quad]{} & \underline{\underline{Q}} \end{array}$$

is a pushout diagram in the category of canons.

More generally, every subcanon $\underline{\underline{B}}$ of a canon $\underline{\underline{C}}$ can be interpreted as a parameter description. Let $p_1: \underline{\underline{B}} \longrightarrow \underline{\underline{D}}_1$ be any canon morphism where $\underline{\underline{D}}_1$ is not totally restricted. Then we may also interpret this canon morphism as a correct parameter substitution. The result of the parameter substitution is again described by a pushout construction. This kind of parameter substitution can be interpreted as a partial substitution, because a second non trivial substitution $p_2: \underline{\underline{D}}_1 \longrightarrow \underline{\underline{D}}_2$ of the subcanon $\underline{\underline{D}}_1$ of the canon $\underline{\underline{R}}_1$ can be given. See <u>Dg4</u>:

$$\begin{array}{ccccc} \underline{\underline{B}} & \xrightarrow{\quad p_1 \quad} & \underline{\underline{D}}_1 & \xrightarrow{\quad p_2 \quad} & \underline{\underline{D}}_2 \\ \downarrow{\scriptstyle \subseteq} & & \downarrow{\scriptstyle \subseteq} & & \downarrow{\scriptstyle \subseteq} \\ \underline{\underline{C}} & \xrightarrow[\quad p_1 \quad]{} & \underline{\underline{R}}_1 & \xrightarrow[\quad p_2 \quad]{} & \underline{\underline{R}}_2 \end{array}$$

The diagram Dg4 shows that the calculus of canons allows stepwise parameter substitutions.

There is an other more general way to use canons in the methodology of program design.

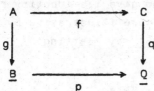

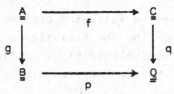

We can understand a canon $\underline{\underline{C}}$ which is not totally restricted as a description of a problem. For this kind of application the canon $\underline{\underline{FPS}}$ is not a good example because the problem described by $\underline{\underline{FPS}}$ would only be: "find any set and give its identity relation". We can make this example a little bit more illustrative by extending the theory FPS to the theory FPS' by setting

FPS' = FPS extended by
    oprs class: Elements ⟶ Sets
    axioms for all $e_1, e_2 \in$ Elements let
        $(e_1 \in class(e_1))$ = true
        if $(e_1 \in class(e_2))$ = true then $class(e_1) = class(e_2)$ fi
    end FPS'

and by forming the canon $\underline{\underline{FPS'}} = (FPS', \{\emptyset \lhd S, B \lhd FPS\})$.

Now, the canon $\underline{\underline{FPS'}}$ describes the following problem: "find any set M , give its identity relation, find any equivalence relation in the chosen set M , so that every equivalence class is finite, and associate with every element from M the corresponding equivalence class".

A subcanon $\underline{\underline{B}} \subseteq \underline{\underline{C}}$ can now be understood as a description of a subproblem and a canon morphism $p_1 : \underline{\underline{B}} \longrightarrow \underline{\underline{D}}_1$ as a solution of the subproblem, if $\underline{\underline{D}}_1$ is totally restricted, and as a partial solution, if $\underline{\underline{D}}_1$ is not totally restricted. From this point of view the diagram Dg4 describes the stepwise solution (in two steps) of the subproblem $\underline{\underline{B}}$ of $\underline{\underline{C}}$, if we assume that $\underline{\underline{D}}_2$ is totally restricted. The canon $\underline{\underline{R}}_2$ describes then the new version of the problem $\underline{\underline{C}}$ which arises from the solution of the subproblem described by $\underline{\underline{B}}$ $\underline{\underline{C}}$. If $\underline{\underline{R}}_2$ is totally restricted then the whole problem is solved. If not, then there exists at least one subcanon $\underline{\underline{B}}'$ of $\underline{\underline{R}}_2$ which is not totally restricted. A next step in solving the problem described by $\underline{\underline{C}}$ can be done by giving (may be partial) a solution $p' : \underline{\underline{B}}' \longrightarrow \underline{\underline{D}}'$ of the subproblem $\underline{\underline{B}}'$.

Problem classes characterized by the pattern "For any ... find a ... such that ..." can be described by an ordered pair $(\underline{\underline{C}}, \underline{\underline{B}})$ of canons where $\underline{\underline{B}}$ is a subcanon of $\underline{\underline{C}}$ which describes the 'for any - part'. The pair $(\underline{\underline{FPS'}}, (B, \{\emptyset \lhd S\}))$ describes the problem: "For any set M with given identity relation find an equivalence relation ϱ such that every equivalence class is finite and associate with every element from M the corresponding equivalence class".

On the base of canons, where the algebraic theories are assumed to be equationally-partial implicational heterogeneous theories, a specification language for specifications of data types, parameterized data types, and algorithms has been designed /HKR 80/.

REFERENCES

/ADJ 75/ Goguen,J.A., Thatcher,J.W., Wagner,E.G., Wright,J.B.: Abstract Data Types as Initial Algebras and the Correctness of Data Representations, in Proc. Confr. on Computer Graphics, Pattern Recognition, and Data Structure (Beverly Hills, CA.) 1975, pp. 89-93

/Ben 79/ Benecke,K.: Signaturketten und Operations- und Mengenformen über Signaturketten, Dissertation A, TH 'Otto von Guericke' Magdeburg, 1979

/BG 77/ Burstall,R.M., Goguen,J.A.,: Putting theories together to make specifications, Proc. Fifth Int. Joint Comp. on Artificial Intelligence, MIT (Cambridge,Mass)

/Ehr 78/ Ehrich,H.-D.: On the Theory of Specification, Implementation and Parameterization of Abstract Data Types, Forschungsbericht Dortmund, 1978

/EKP 78/ Ehrig,H., Kreowski,H.-J., Padawitz,P.: Stepwise Specification and Implementation of Abstract Data Types, Proc. 5. Int. Colloq. on Automata, Languages and Programming, Udine, 1978

/FF 56/ Ford,L.R., Fulkerson,D.R.: Maximal flow through a network, Canadian J. of Math., 8 (1956), pp. 399

/GT 77/ Goguen,J.A., Tardo,J.: OBJ-O Preliminary Users Manual, UCLA, Semantics and Theory of Computation Report, No. 10, 1977

/GT 79/ Goguen,J.A., Tardo,J.: An Introduction to OBJ: A Language for Writing and Testing Formal Algebraic Program Specifications, UCLA, Los Angeles, 1979

/HKR 80/ Hupbach,U., Kaphengst,H., Reichel,H.: Initiale algebraische Spezifikation von Datentypen, parameterisierten Datentypen und Algorithmen, VEB Robotron, Zentrum für Forschung und Technik, Dresden, WIB, 1980

/Hup 79/ Hupbach,U.: A Uniform Mathematical Framwork for Initial Algebraic Specifications, VEB Robotron, Zentrum für Forschung und Technik, Dresden, Preprint, 1979

/KR 71/ Kaphengst,H., Reichel,H.: Algebraische Algorithmentheorie, VEB Robotron, Zentrum für Forschung und Technik,Dresden, WIB Nr.1, 1971

/KR 72/ Kaphengst,H., Reichel,H.: Operative Theorien und Kategorien von operativen Systemen, in Studien zur Algebra und ihren Anwendungen, Akademie Verlag, Berlin, 1972

/Law 63/ Lawvere,F.W.: Functorial semantics of algebraic theories, Proc. Nat. Acad. Sci. U.S.A.,50,1963, pp. 869-872

/Mus 79/ Musser,D.R.: Abstract Data Types in the AFFIRM System, Proc. IEEE Conf. on Specification of Reliable Software, Cambridge, Mass., April 1979

/Rei 79/ Reichel,H.: Theorie der Äquoide, Dissertation B, Humboldt Universität, Berlin, 1979

/TWW 78/ Thatcher,J.W., Wagner,E.G., Wright,J.B.: Data Type Specification: Parameterization and the Power of Specification Techniques, Proc. SIGACT 10th Symp. on Theory of Computing, San Diego, May 1978

SCHEMES FOR
NONSEQUENTIAL PROCESSING SYSTEMS

Wolfgang Reisig
Lehrstuhl für Informatik II, RWTH Aachen
Büchel 29-31, D-5100 Aachen

Introduction

In this paper we shall consider schemes for systems which are composed of synchronization units and processing units. The processing units are considered to be elementary (not decomposable) with respect to the given scope of concern. A state of such a system is given by the subset of synchronization units which possess "control", i.e. which are capable of activating processing units. If a processing unit works, control is moved from one set of synchronization units to another. Two processing units may work concurrently iff their associated sets of synchronization units are disjoint.

Examples of such systems can be found in the field of nonsequential programming, operation systems or industrial production systems.

Consecutive activities of processing units amount to a nonsequential process. The set of processes which are capable of running on a system determine its behaviour.

For systems of the above described type, we shall define schemes in terms of labelled Petri nets: processing units and synchronization units are represented by transitions and places respectively. A state of the system is represented by a marking of the net. The performance of a processing unit is modelled by the firing of its corresponding transition. If it is irrelevant which of various synchronization units is involved in a given process, or if we want to express that different processing units cause the same effect, the corresponding places or transitions are labelled by the same symbol. In terms of net theory, our model is on a higher level than the condition-event interpretation since we can indicate different elements to posses equal properties. But we are far below the level of program schemes. We do not demand that processing units compute output values with respect to given input values. We do not know any notion of value in our model. The semantics of an interpreted scheme is not a function or a relation, but a set of processes (possible processing histories).

The aims of this paper are

- to introduce and characterize the set of processes of a scheme
- to give a notion of equivalence of schemes
- to transform the problem of whether or not schemes are equivalent to the problem of equality of formal regular languages.

This paper may be considered as an attempt to combine Petri net theory with tools of "classical" theories as schematology and formal languages.

1. Basic Notions

In this chapter we shall introduce nets and markings of nets as basic notions of net theory in the form of [2]. Furthermore, we define labelled nets which will be used later to define schemes and their processes.

1.1 Definition A triple $N = (S,T;F)$ is a net iff

(i) S and T are disjoint, finite sets

(ii) $F \subseteq (S\times T) \cup (T\times S)$ is a relation, the flow relation of N.

For each element $x \in S\cup T$ of N we define its

pre-set $^{\bullet}x := \{y \mid yFx\}$ (*) and its

post-set $x^{\bullet} := \{y \mid xFy\}$.

If there is no other specification, we call the elements of S and T places and transitions respectively.

We shall apply the usual graphical representation for nets: places and transitions are represented as circles and boxes respectively. The flow relation is represented by arrows between the corresponding circles and boxes.

1.2 Definition Let $N = (S,T;F)$ be a net.

A subset $M \subseteq S$ of places is called a case or a marking of N. A transition $t \in T$ is M-activated iff $^{\bullet}t \subseteq M$ and $t^{\bullet} \subseteq S \setminus M$. An M-activated transition t determines a followermarking M' of M by $M' := (M \setminus {}^{\bullet}t) \cup t^{\bullet}$. We then say: M fires with t to M' and we shall write $M[t>M'$. In this way, we obtain the relation $r \subseteq P(S)\times P(S)$ by $MrM' :\Leftrightarrow \exists t \in T \; M[t>M'$.

Given a distinguished case M, we define $[M] := \{M' \mid M(r \cup r^{-1})^{*}M'\}$.

A case M of N is contact-free iff for each transition t and each $M' \in [M]$ holds: $^{\bullet}t \subseteq M' \Rightarrow t^{\bullet} \subseteq S \setminus M'$.
(in this case, t is M'-activated iff $^{\bullet}t \subseteq M'$).

In the graphical representation of nets a case M is indicated by dots (tokens) inside the places of M.

It is well known [6] that each marked net N can be completed to a contact-free marked net without change in its behaviour:

construct to each place s a new place $\bar{s}$ such that $^{\bullet}\bar{s} = s^{\bullet}$ and $\bar{s}^{\bullet} = {}^{\bullet}s$. $\bar{s}$ obtains a token iff s has no token.

---

* We use the infix notation xFy for $(x,y) \in F$

1.3 As pointed out in the introduction, we use labelled nets in order to represent processing systems. Therefore we define nets, each element of which possesses as one component a symbol of some given alphabet.

<u>Definition</u> Let Σ and Π be disjunct alphabets, let A and B be disjunct finite sets and let $S : A \to \Sigma$ and $T : B \to \Pi$ be mappings.

Then a net $N = (S,T;F)$ is <u>labelled over Σ and Π</u> .

For elements $x \in A \cup B$, $\overline{x} := f_i(x)$ $(i \in \{1,2\})$ is the <u>label</u> of x .
For subsets $X \subseteq A \cup B$ of elements, let $\overline{X} := \{\overline{x} \mid x \in X\}$.

In general, we are not interested in the objects of labelled nets themselves but only in their labels. Therefore we shall consider labelled nets to be identical iff they are different only with respect to their labels (i.e. iff there exists an isomorphism between their objects which respects the flow relation and the labels).

In the graphical representation we write the label into the corresponding box or circle.

1.4 We now introduce schemes for nonsequential processing systems to be marked, labelled nets which fulfil some additional requirements:

<u>Definition</u> Let $N = (S,T;F)$ be a labelled net and let M be a contact-free case of N . Let furthermore for each $M' \in [M]$ and each $t \in T$ and each two different places $s_1 \neq s_2 \in S$ hold:

$(s_1,s_2 \in M' \vee s_1,s_2 \in {}^{\bullet}t \cup t^{\bullet}) \Rightarrow \overline{s}_1 \neq \overline{s}_2$.

Then $S = (S,T;F,M)$ is a <u>nonsequential processing scheme</u>.

The restrictions for the labels of schemes are reasonable if we consider their application: Different cases will be called equivalent iff the label sets of their elements are equal. We will presuppose a unique relationship between cases and their labels. Furthermore, the performance of a transition will be established by the labels of the places involved.

We shall use labelled nets not only for the construction of schemes but also for the representation of single processes (histories) which can run on such schemes. In this case, labelled elements are interpreted as occurrences of system elements with corresponding properties.

The next two chapters deal with nets which are capable of representing histories of schemes. Following this, the relationship between schemes and history nets will be discussed.

As an example of a scheme, consider Fig. 1. Fig. 2 shows a process of this scheme.

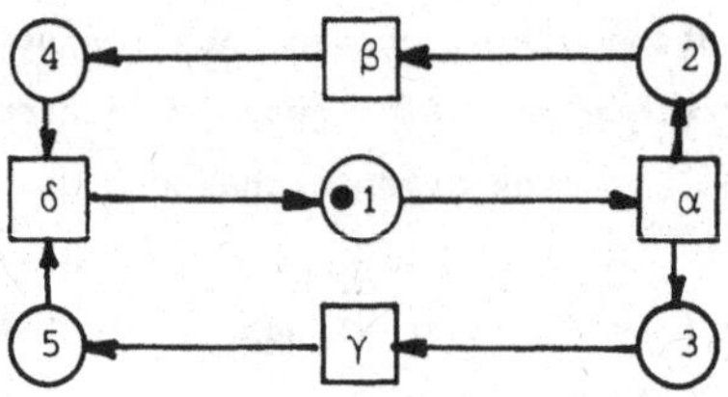

The scheme S_1

<u>*Fig. 1*</u> *Example of a nonsequential processing scheme*

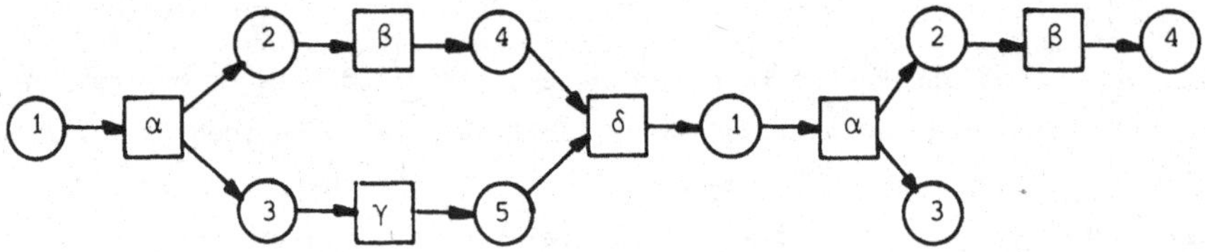

A history of S_1

<u>*Fig. 2*</u> *Example of a history*

2. <u>History Nets</u>

We now start the investigation of our model with a discussion of properties of nets which can represent histories of schemes.

In the introduction we described nonsequential processing systems as nets of synchronization units and processing units . For such a system, the notion of a process is intuitively quite clear: it is an "unfolding" of the system, whereby conflicts (mutual exclusion of processing units which are capable of working) are nondeterministically solved. The effect of such a process is a set·of mutually dependent activities of processing units and changes of control. This can again be represented by a net. Such a net is acyclic (because it is an "unfolding" of a system) , unmarked (because each instance of state which is reached during the process is represented by a set of places) and its places are not branched (because conflicts are solved).
A process is fully specified if in addition the relationship between an unfolded net and the system is given.
In order to characterize such processes in our model we shall define <u>history nets</u> as being unlabelled, acyclic nets with unbranched places. The elements of history nets obtain the labels of the corresponding elements in a scheme.

2.1 <u>Definition</u> A net $N = (S,T;F)$ is <u>acyclic</u> iff the transitive closure F^+ of F is irreflexive (i.e. $xF^+y \Rightarrow x \neq y$). For such a net it is worthwhile to define:

Two elements $x,y \in S \cup T$ are <u>concurrent</u> iff $\{(x,y),(y,x)\} \cap F^{+} = \emptyset$.
A maximal set of concurrent places is called a <u>slice</u>.
${}^{\bullet}N := \{s \in S \mid {}^{\bullet}s = \emptyset\}$ and $N^{\bullet} := \{s \in S \mid s^{\bullet} = \emptyset\}$ are the <u>initial</u> and the <u>final slice</u> of N respectively.

A labelled net $H = (S,T;F)$ is a <u>history net</u> iff

(i) H is acyclic

(ii) $s \in S \Rightarrow |{}^{\bullet}s| \leq 1 \wedge |s^{\bullet}| \leq 1$ (places are not branched)

(iii) $t \in T \Rightarrow |{}^{\bullet}t| \geq 1 \wedge |t^{\bullet}| \geq 1$

(iv) for each slice M and each transition $t \in T$:
$(\{s,s'\} \subseteq M \vee \{s,s'\} \subseteq {}^{\bullet}t \cup t^{\bullet}) \Rightarrow \overline{s} \neq \overline{s'}$.

H is <u>elementary</u> iff $|T| = 1$. H is <u>empty</u> iff $T = \emptyset$.

The requirement (iv) in the definition of history nets is no limitation in practice: each history of a scheme fulfils this property, as we shall see later on. A consequence of this property is the observation that an elementary history net is uniquely determined by the labels of its objects:

2.2 <u>Lemma</u> An elementary history net H is completely determined if the labels of ${}^{\bullet}H$, $H^{\bullet}$ and of its transition are given.

<u>Proof</u> Let $H = (S,\{t\};F)$. Different elements of H possess different labels because
$\{s,s'\} \subseteq S \Rightarrow (\{s,s'\} \subseteq {}^{\bullet}H \vee \{s,s'\} \subseteq H^{\bullet} \vee \{s,s'\} \subseteq {}^{\bullet}t \cup t^{\bullet})$.
F is determined by ${}^{\bullet}t$ and $t^{\bullet}$. These two sets are given by
${}^{\bullet}t = {}^{\bullet}H \setminus H^{\bullet}$ and $t^{\bullet} = H^{\bullet} \setminus {}^{\bullet}H$.

Examples of elementary history nets are given in Figs. 3 and 4 (i).

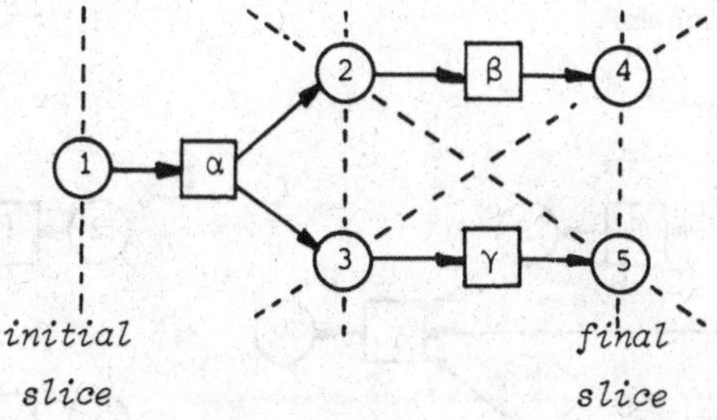

each dotted line meets the places of one slice

<u>*Figl 3.*</u> *A history net and its slices*

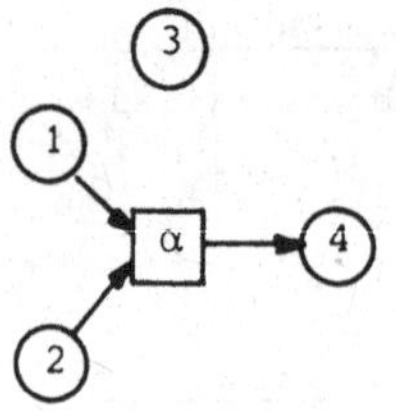

≡ 123 α 34

(i) the net representation *(ii) the string representation*

Fig. 4 *Example of an elementary history net and an elementary history string*

2.3 In order to process history nets we must be able to compose and decompose them. The idea of composing two history nets is intuitively quite simple: let the final slice of the first net be identical to the initial slice of the second one. Then the nets are composed by merging both slices mentioned:

Definition Let $H_i = (S_i, T_i; F_i)$ (i=1,2) be two history nets such that $\overline{H_1^{\bullet}} = \overline{{}^{\bullet}H_2}$. We presuppose without loss of generality that $H_1^{\bullet} = {}^{\bullet}H_2$ and that $(S_1 \cup T_1) \cap (S_2 \cup T_2) = H_1^{\bullet} = {}^{\bullet}H_2$.

Then the net $H_1 \cdot H_2$ is defined by

$H_1 \cdot H_2 = (S_1 \cup S_2 , T_1 \cup T_2 ; F_1 \cup F_2)$.

Fig. 5 (i) shows an example of the composition of history nets.

Notice that the product of history nets is not necessarily a history net again. The composition may yield new slices, the elements of which are possibly equally labelled. As an example, replace in Fig. 5 the label "5" by the label "1". However, situations of this kind will not occur if we compose history nets which represent histories of a scheme.

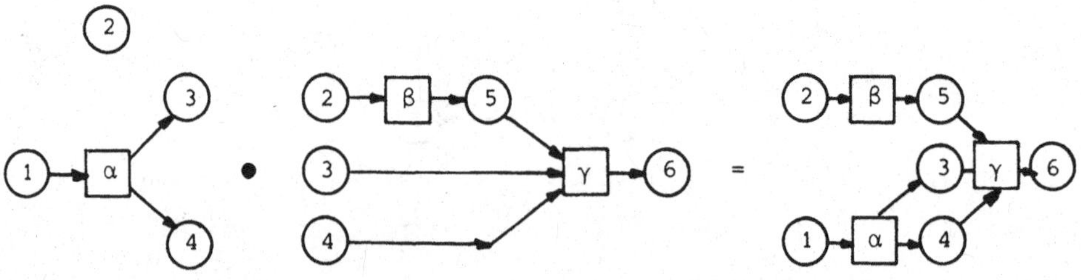

(i) the net representation

12α234 · 234β345γ6 = 12α234β345γ6

(ii) a string representation

Fig. 5 *Example of the composition of processes*

Two properties of history nets are important:

(a) The composition is a (partial) associative operation and (b) each history net is decomposable into elementary history nets.

2.4 Lemma Let H_1, H_2 and H_3 be history nets.

$H = H_1 \cdot (H_2 \cdot H_3)$ is defined iff $H' = (H_1 \cdot H_2) \cdot H_3$ is defined. Furthermore, $H = H'$ if they are defined.

2.5 Lemma Let H be a non-empty history net. Then there exist elementary history nets $H_1, \ldots, H_k$ such that $H = H_1 \cdot \ldots \cdot H_k$.

The decomposition of an arbitrary history net into elementary history nets is in general not unique.

3. History Strings

If we try to characterize sets of history nets of if we want to derive properties of such sets, their (S,T;F)-representation is not very handy. Therefore we develop a formal language representation which is mainly based on Lemma 2.2 .

3.1 Definition Let Σ and Π be disjoint, finite alphabets. We represent non-empty subsets of Σ by words $\sigma_1 \ldots \sigma_k \in \Sigma^*$ such that $1 \leq i < j \leq k \Rightarrow \sigma_i < \sigma_j$ with respect to an arbitrarily given order < on Σ. A word with this property is called a Σ-set. Let set_Σ be the set of all Σ-sets.

In the following we shall not distinguish between a set $\{\sigma_1, \ldots, \sigma_k\} \subseteq \Sigma$ and its correpsonding word $\sigma_{i_1} \ldots \sigma_{i_k} \in \Sigma^*$.

Let $A, B \in set_\Sigma$ and let $\pi \in \Pi$. The word $w = A \pi B \in set_\Sigma \, \Pi \, set_\Sigma$ is called an elementary history string. Its corresponding history net $H = \underline{net}(w)$ is defined by $^{\bullet}\overline{H} = A$, $\overline{H}^{\bullet} = B$, $\overline{t} = \pi$ (whereby t is the transition of H). According to Lemma 2.2, this definition is unique.

3.2 Lemma For each elementary history net H there exists exactly one elementary history string w such that $\underline{net}(w) = H$.

An example is shown in Fig. 4. .

3.3 We generalize the notion of elementary history strings in order to represent arbitrary history nets:

Definition Let Σ and Π be disjoint, finite alphabets. Then $set_\Sigma(\Pi set_\Sigma)^*$ is the set of history strings over Σ and Π .

For each history string w we define the net of w by

(i) the empty net $(\{a_1,\dots,a_k\},\emptyset,\emptyset)$ iff $w = \overline{a_1}\dots\overline{a_k} \in set_\Sigma$

(ii) the net $\underline{net}(A_o\pi_1A_1)\cdot\dots\cdot\underline{net}(A_{r-1}\pi_rA_r)$ iff

$A_o,\dots,A_r \in set_\Sigma;\ \pi_1,\dots,\Pi_r \in \Pi\ ;\quad w = A_o\pi_1A_1\dots A_{r-1}\pi_rA_r$.

3.4 We can now simply talk about histories; they may be represented as nets or as strings (examples are shown in Figs. 4 and 5) .

In order to unify both representations of histories, we shall use the dot-notations and set-theoretical operations in connection with the string representation. Their meaning is canonically defined by the corresponding operations of the corresponding nets.

In general, a history can be represented by more than one string of elementary histories. As an example, the composed net of Fig. 5 can be represented as $12\beta12\alpha345\gamma6$.

Lemma Let $xu\alpha v\beta wy$ $(\alpha,\beta \in \Pi;\ u,v,w \in set_\Sigma;\ x,y \in (\Sigma \cup \Pi)\ )$ be a history string. α and β are concurrent transitions in the corresponding net iff $v \subseteq u \cup w$. In this case, the same history is represented by the string $xu\beta v'\alpha wy$ whereby $v' = (u \cup w) \setminus v$.

4. History of schemes

In the last two chapters we have developed tools for the characterization of histories. In this chapter we will discover the connection between histories and schemes.

4.1 We will start with the consideration of the class of those histories which can run on a given scheme, starting with the distinguished case of the scheme.

Definition Let $S = (S,T;F,M_o)$ be a scheme. A history $H = A_o\pi_1A_1\dots\pi_rA_r$ is a starting history of S iff there are cases $M_1,\dots,M_r \in [M_o]$ and transitions $t_1,\dots,t_r \in T$ such that

$M_{i-1}\ [t_i\rangle\ M_i \quad (i = 1,\dots r)$

$\overline{M_i} = A_i \quad (i = 0,\dots,r)$

$\overline{t_i} = \pi_i \quad (i = 1,\dots,r)$.

An example of a starting history is given in Fig. 2 .

4.2 Theorem Let $S = (S,T;F,M_o)$ be a scheme over Σ and Π .
Let $\{M_o,\dots,M_n\} = \{M' \mid M_o\ r^*\ M'\}$ and let $X = \{x_o,\dots,x_n\}$ be a set of variables. For $i = o,\dots,n$ we define a set A_i of atomic terms by

$A_i = \{x_j\ \overline{t}\ \overline{M_i} \in X\Pi set_\Sigma \mid \exists\ t \in T\ \exists\ o \leq j \leq n \quad M_j[t\rangle M_i\}$.

Now let $(L_o,...,L_n)$ be the solution of

$eq((x_o, A_o \cup \overline{M_o}) , (x_1,A_1),...,(x_n,A_n))$. (*)

Then it holds: $H \in L_i \Leftrightarrow H$ is a starting history of S and $H^{\cdot} = M_i$.

As a consequence , $L(S) := \bigcup_{i=0}^{n} L_i$ is the set of all starting histories of S .

As an example we obtain for the scheme S_1 of Fig. 1:

(i) the markings

$M_o = \{s_1\}$
$M_1 = \{s_2,s_3\}$
$M_2 = \{s_3,s_4\}$
$M_3 = \{s_2,s_5\}$
$M_4 = \{s_4,s_5\}$

(ii) the equations

$x_o = \{x_4\delta 1, 1\}$
$x_1 = \{x_o\alpha 23\}$
$x_2 = \{x_1\beta 34\}$
$x_3 = \{x_1\gamma 25\}$
$x_4 = \{x_2\gamma 45 , x_3\beta 45\}$

In section 3.4 we remarked that in general different strings may represent equal histories. In the equations of the above defined type, all those strings are produced.

4.3 Definition Two schemes are equivalent iff the sets of their starting histories are equal.

Examples of equivalent schemes are shown in Figs. 6 and 8 .

From Theorem 4.2 follows immediately:

Corollary Two schemes S and S' are equivalent iff the languages $L(S)$ and $L(S')$ are equal.

We have now reduced the problem of whether or not two schemes are equivalent to the problem of the equality of formal languages.

From well knwon considerations of automata theory (*) follows:

Corollary The language $L(S)$ of a scheme S is regular.

There are reasonable algorithms for the decision of the equality of regular languages [1] .

What does the above notion of equivalence mean with respect to interpretations of schemes? An interpretation associates processing systems to schemes in such a way that equally labelled elements of schemes are replaced by operation- or synchronization units with equal properties. (One label may be considered to represent a property of operation- or synchronization units). It is obvious that each interpretation of equivalent schemes yields identical classes of processes.

* c.f. Appendix

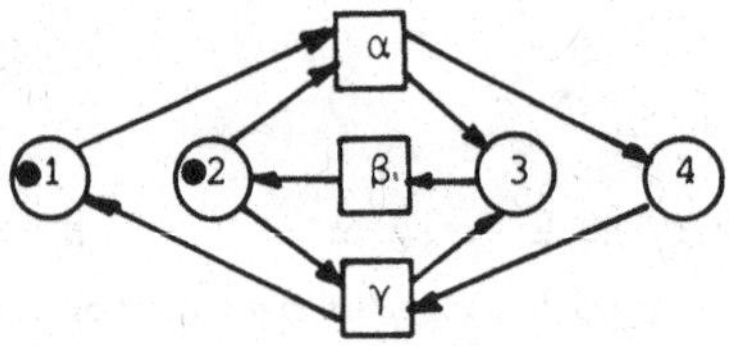

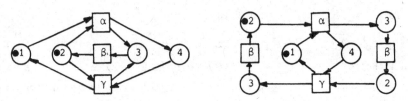

Fig. 6 *Equivalent schemes*

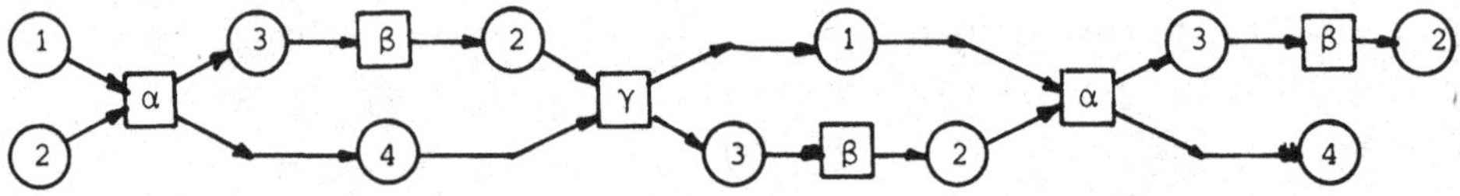

Fig. 7 *A process of the schemes of Fig. 6*

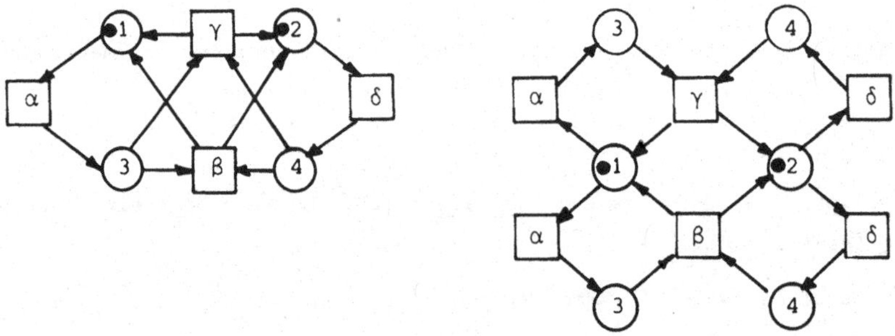

Fig. 8 *Equivalent schemes*

4.4 The distinguished case M of a scheme (S,T;F,M) is not necessarily to be considered as an initial case for histories. It may also be considered as a final case or as an indication of histories which could have happened in its past or could possibly happen in its future. The most general class of histories is the set of the "possible" histories of a schemes [2] .

We shall characterize these different classes of histories as solutions of different equational systems which can be derived from a given scheme. With respect to these considerations we define:

Definition Let S = (S,T;F,M) be a scheme. A history $H = A_o \pi_1 A_1 \ldots \pi_r A_r$ is a <u>(possible) history</u> of S iff there are markings $M_o, \ldots, M_r \in [M]$ and transitions $t_o, \ldots, t_r \in T$ such that

$M_{i-1} [t_i\rangle M_i \quad (i=1,\ldots,r)$

$\overline{M}_i = A_i \quad (i=o,\ldots,r)$

$\overline{t}_i = \pi_i \quad (i=1,\ldots,r)$

H is <u>visible</u> iff $M_o,\dots,M_r \in \{M' \mid M(r^* \cup (r^{-1})^*)\ M'\}$

H is <u>ending</u> iff $M_r = M$.

It is obvious that each ending and each starting history is visible and that each visible history is possible. The differences of these types of histories are sketched in Fig. 9 .

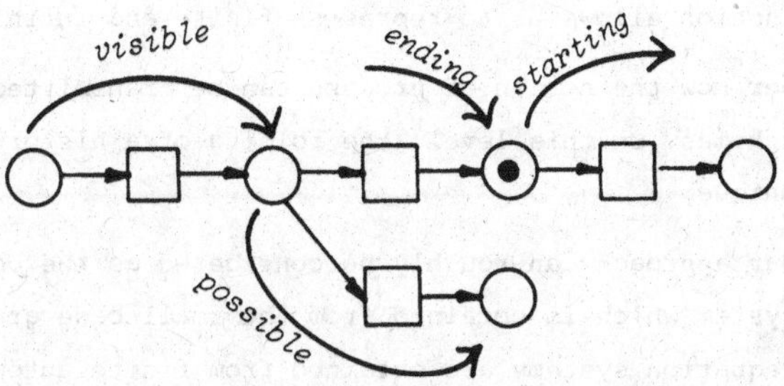

Fig. 9 *Outline of different types of histories*

4.5 A characterization of the ending histories of a scheme is obtained as follows:

<u>Theorem</u>: Let $S = (S,T;F,M_o)$ be a scheme over Σ and Π.

Let $\{M_o,\dots,M_n\} = \{M' \mid M_o\ (r^{-1})\ M'\}$, let $X = \{x_o,\dots,x_n\}$ and let

for $i = o,\dots,n$

$A_i = \{\overline{M}_i \overline{t} x_j \in set_\Sigma\ \Pi X \mid \exists\ t \in T\ \ \exists\ o \leq j \leq n\ :\ M_i\ [t\rangle\ M_j\}$

Finally, let $(L_o,\dots,L_n)$ be the solution of

<u>eq</u>$((x_o,A_o \cup \overline{M}_o)\ ,\ (x_1,A_1),\dots,(x_n,A_n))$.

Then it holds: $H \in L_i \Leftrightarrow H$ is an ending history of S and $H = M_i$.

As a consequence $\biguplus_{i=o}^{n} L_i$ is the set of all ending histories of S .

4.6 The visible and the possible histories of a scheme can be characterized as follows:

<u>Corollary</u> Replace in Theorem 4.2 the relation r^* by $r^* \cup (r^{-1})^*$ (by $[M_o]$ respectively) and consider the solution $(L_o,\dots,L_n)$ of the system

<u>eq</u>$((x_o,A_o \cup \overline{M}_o),\dots,(x_n,A_n \cup \overline{M}_n))$.

Then it holds: $H \in L_i \Leftrightarrow H$ is visible (possible respectively) and $H^{\bullet} = M_i$.

A similar construction with respect to Theorem 4.5 yields sets L_i with the property $H \in L_i \Leftrightarrow H$ is visible (possible respectively) and $\acute{H} = M_i$.

The solutions to the equational systems which were constructed in 4.5 and 4.6 are regular languages. If we introduce corresponding notions of equivalence, the considerations of 4.3 can be applied again.

Conclusion

There is a net morphism which relates processing schemes to (unlabelled) condition-event systems. For transition labels in [7] this morphism is denoted as "Aufrufbeschriftung". A similar construction is applicable to the labels of places.

Processes of condition-event systems are characterized in [5] and in [2] in terms of "net morphisms". This notion allows us to represent finite and infinite processes.

We have shown in this paper how the notion of process can be transmitted from condition-event systems to schemes. On this level, the folding of a history to a scheme is in general no longer unique.

In terms of net theory, our approach can roughly be considered as the construction of a recursive equation system which is obtained from the small case graph in a similar way as recursive equation systems are obtained from finite automata [3] .

Mazurkiewicz [4] and Winkowski [8] derive fiexedpoint representations of processes for condition-event systems (different elements are to be labelled differently). Unfolded nets are represented only by their transition [4] or by their places [8] . The representation of history nets by their places <u>and</u> their transitions in our approach allowed for the step from condition-event systems to processing schemes and thus for a notion of equivalence.

References

[1] Aho, Hopcroft, Ullmann: The Design and Analysis of Computer Algorithms. - Addison-Wesley Publishing Co., 1974

[2] Genrich, Lautenbach, Thiagarajan: An Overview of Net Theory.- Advanced Course on General Net Theory of Processes and Systems. Hamburg, 1979

[3] Hopcroft, Ullmann: Formal Languages and their Relation to Automata.- Addison-Wesley Publishing Co., 1969

[4] A. Mazurkiewicz: Concurrent Program Schemes and their Interpretation.- University of Aarhus, DAIMI PB-78 .

[5] C.A. Petri: Nichtsequentielle Prozesse.- GMD-ISF interner Bericht 76-6, Juni 1976 .

[6] C.A. Petri: General Net Theory.- Proceedings of the Joint IBM/University of Newcastle-upon-Tyne Seminar. B. Shaw (Ed.), 1976 .

[7] W. Reisig: Zur Verwendung von Petrinetż-Morphismen bei der Systemkonstruktion. - GI-Fachtagung "Formale Modelle für Informationssysteme", Informatik Fachbericht Nr. 21 . Springer Verlag 1979

[8] J. Winkowski: An Algebraic Approach to Concurrency.- 8th Symposium on Mathematical Foundations of Computer Science (MFCS), Lecture Notes in Computer Science 74, Springer Verlag, 1979 .

Appendix: Basic Notions and Results on Recursive Equations

(i) Let Φ and $X = \{x_1,\ldots,x_n\}$ be disjoint, finite sets (of symbols and variables). $Te := (\Phi \cup X)^*$ is the set of terms (over Φ and X).

The semantics of terms is defined by the recursive function

$$\underline{sem}: Te \times (P(\Phi^*))^n \longrightarrow P(\Phi^*)$$

$$(\varepsilon, L_1,\ldots,L_n) \mapsto \{\varepsilon\}$$

$$(w\varphi, L_1,\ldots,L_n) \mapsto \underline{sem}(w,L_1,\ldots,L_n)\cdot\{\varphi\} \quad \text{iff} \quad w \in (\Phi \cup X)^*,\ \varphi \in \Phi$$

$$(wx_i, L_1,\ldots,L_n) \mapsto \underline{sem}(w,L_1,\ldots,L_n)\cdot L_i \quad \text{iff} \quad w \in (\Phi \cup X)^*,\ x_i \in X$$

For a set $A \subseteq Te$ of terms we extend the function sem to

$$\underline{sem}(A,L_1,\ldots,L_n) := \bigcup_{w \in A} \underline{sem}(w,L_1,\ldots,L_n) .$$

(ii) Let $A_1,\ldots,A_n \subseteq Te$. A system of equations

$$\xi : \quad x_1 = A_1$$
$$\vdots$$
$$x_n = A_n$$

is an equational system over Φ and X . We also write

$$\xi = \underline{eq}((x_1,A_1),\ldots,(x_n,A_n)) .$$

(iii) The solution of ξ is the smallest n-tuple $(L_1,\ldots,L_n)$ of languages $L_i \subseteq \Phi^*$ such that $L_i = \underline{sem}(A_i,L_1,\ldots,L_n)\ (i=1,\ldots,n)$.

(iv) An equational system is right linear (left linear respectively) iff its terms are elements of $(X \cup \{\varepsilon\})\Phi^*$ $(\Phi^*(X \cup \{\varepsilon\})$ respectively). The components of the solution of each left linear and each right linear system are regular languages [3] .

DYNAMIC ALGEBRAS WHICH ARE NOT KRIPKE STRUCTURES

Jan Reiterman, Věra Trnková

Faculty of Nuclear Science and Technical Engineering, Technical University of Prague

Prague, Czechoslovakia

Faculty of Mathematics and Physics, Charles University, Prague

Prague, Czechoslovakia

Abstract: The first example of a dynamic algebra which is not isomorphic to any Kripke structure was given by Kozen [8]. We analyze properties of dynamic algebras to get general arguments making it possible to construct a lot of other examples.

Dynamic algebras were introduced by Kozen [6] and Pratt [12] to provide models of propositional dynamic logic (PDL); see [12] for motivation, examples and relation to computer science problems. Dynamic algebras include (standard) Kripke structures, the traditional models of PDL. They are axiomatized in a purely algebraic way in [12] and in a nearly algebraic way in [6], in contrary to Kripke structures which are a kind of relational structures. A relation between abstract dynamic algebras and Kripke structures was investigated by Kozen; he proved [6] that every separable dynamic algebra can be represented as a possibly non-standard Kripke structure and found [8] an example of a separable dynamic algebra which is isomorphic to no (standard) Kripke structure.

The aim of the current paper is to present other examples of that kind. In fact, we show that many Boolean algebras are Boolean parts of separable dynamic algebras which are not isomorphic to any Kripke structure.

The paper has five sections. Preliminaries are contained in sections 1 and 2. In section 3 we prove that every Kripke structure fulfils a condition, called relative σ-continuity. By means of this result, we show that every Boolean algebra, in which the zero is an infimum of a strictly decreasing sequence, is a Boolean part of a dynamic algebra which is not relatively σ-continuous (and hence not isomorphic to any Kripke structure) and the regular part of which has one generator. We also bring examples showing that the Kozen's axiomatization [6] of dynamic algebras is actually stronger than that of Pratt [12]. In section 4, we show that, on the other hand, the σ-continuity (and even complete continuity) of a dynamic algebra is not sufficient for it to be isomorphic to a Kripke structure. Section 5 contains remarks concerning dynamic algebras with reversion.

1. Axioms for dynamic algebras

1.1. Following Pratt [12], a dynamic algebra is a two-sorted algebra $(\mathcal{B},\mathcal{R},\langle\ \rangle)$ consisting of two one-sorted algebras

$$\mathcal{B} = (B,\vee,\ -\ ,0),\quad \mathcal{R} = (R,\cup\ ,\ ;\ ,{}^*)$$

(where $\vee$, $\cup$ and ; are binary operations, - and * unary operations, 0 a nullary operation) and an inter-sort operation $\langle\ \rangle : R\times B \longrightarrow B$, subject to the following axioms where $\langle\ \rangle$ and ; are ommited for brevity:

1. $\mathcal{B}$ is a Boolean algebra,

2 a. $a0 = 0 \quad (a\in R)$,

2 b. $a(p\vee q) = ap\vee aq \quad (a\in R, p,q\in B)$,

3. $(a\cup b)p = ap\vee bp \quad (a,b\in R, p\in B)$,

4. $(ab)p = a(bp) \quad (a,b\in R, p\in B)$,

5. $p\vee aa^*p \leq a^*p \leq p\vee a^*(-p\wedge ap) \quad (a\in R, p\in B)$.

It is shown in [12] that 5 is equivalent to

5'. For every $a\in R$, $p\in B$,

$$a^*p = \min\{q\in B; p\leq q \text{ and } aq\leq q\}$$

1.2. A dynamic algebra $(\mathcal{B},\mathcal{R},\langle\ \rangle)$ is *-continuous [12] if for every $a\in R$ and $p\in B$,

$$a^*p = \bigvee_{i=0}^{\infty} a^i p.$$

1.3. A dynamic algebra $(\mathcal{B},\mathcal{R},\langle\ \rangle)$ is separable [12] if distinct elements of R induce, via $\langle\ \rangle$, distinct actions on B, that is, if $a,b\in R$, $a\neq b$ implies $ap\neq bp$ for some $p\in B$.

If a dynamic algebra $(\mathcal{B},\mathcal{R},\langle\ \rangle)$ is separable then elements of R can be identified with functions they induce. In the sense of this identification, we get:

A separable dynamic algebra is a pair $(\mathcal{B},\mathcal{R})$ where

(i) $\mathcal{B}$ is a Boolean algebra,

(ii) $\mathcal{R}$ is a set of additive functions from $\mathcal{B}$ to $\mathcal{B}$,

(iii) $\mathcal{R}$ is closed under the composition and under the forming of pointwise joins of pairs of functions (that is, if $a,b\in\mathcal{R}$ then the function c defined by $cp = ap\vee bp$ belongs to $\mathcal{R}$),

(iv) For every $a\in\mathcal{R}$, the function

$$a^*p = \min\{q\in\mathcal{B}\ ;\ p\leq q \text{ and } aq\leq q\}$$

is well-defined and belongs to $\mathcal{R}$.

1.4. Dynamic algebras were introduced also by Kozen [6] who used a different set of axioms. For separable dynamic algebras, in reformulation à la 1.3, we have: a separable dynamic algebra in the sense of Kozen is a pair $(\mathcal{B},\mathcal{R})$ satisfying (i)-(iv) above and

(v) $\mathcal{R}$ contains the zero function and the identity function,

(vi) $(\mathcal{B},\mathcal{R})$ is $*$-continuous and

$$ab^*c = \bigvee_{i=0}^{\infty} ab^i c \text{ for all } a,b,c \in \mathcal{R}$$

where the join is with respect to the pointwise order in $\mathcal{R}$.

The difference arizing from (v) is, of course, not principal. On the other hand, we shall show (see 3.4) that (vi) is actually stronger than $*$-continuity. Dynamic algebras satisfying (vi) will be called strongly $*$-continuous.

We shall adopt the Pratt's axiomatization. However, all our examples of dynamic algebras will (or will be modified to) satisfy (v), (vi), too.

2. Kripke structures

2.1. The most simple example of a dynamic algebra is the separable dynamic algebra (exp Z, $K_{\exp Z}$) where Z is a set, exp Z is the Boolean algebra of all subsets of Z (with the usual set theoretical operations) and $K_{\exp Z}$ is the set of all completely additive functions on exp Z. Notice that completely additive functions can be identified with binary relations on Z; then composition and union of functions exp Z $\longrightarrow$ exp Z coincides with the usual set-theoretical composition and union respectively of relations. The operation $*$ corresponds to the forming of the reflective-and-transitive closure, that is

$$a^* = \bigcup_{i=0}^{\infty} a^i$$

The dynamic algebra (exp Z, $K_{\exp Z}$) is called the <u>full Kripke structure</u> [12] and subalgebras of (exp Z, $K_{\exp Z}$) are called <u>Kripke structures</u> [12]. Thus a Kripke structure consists of a subalgebra $\mathcal{B}$ of exp Z for some set Z and of a family $\mathcal{R}$ of binary relations on Z such that $\mathcal{R}$ is closed under composition and union of pairs of relations and under forming of reflective-and-transitive closure, and such that, for every set $Y \in \mathcal{B}$ and every relation $A \in \mathcal{R}$, the image AY of Y under A belongs to $\mathcal{B}$.

2.2. In [12] (see also [6]), there is proved that each separable dynamic algebra $(\mathcal{B},\mathcal{R})$ with $\mathcal{B}$ and $\mathcal{R}$ finite is isomorphic to a Kripke structure. The proof of the following generalization is implicitly contained in [7].

Proposition. Let $(\mathcal{B},\mathcal{R})$ be a separable dynamic algebra with $\mathcal{R}$ finite. Then $(\mathcal{B},\mathcal{R})$ is isomorphic to a Kripke structure.

Proof. It is shown in Kozen [6] that the classical Stone representation $h_{\mathcal{B}}: \mathcal{B} \longrightarrow \exp Z$, where Z is the set of all ultrafilters on $\mathcal{B}$,

$$h_{\mathcal{B}}p = \{f \in Z;\ p \in f\},$$

can be extended by putting

$$h_{\mathcal{R}}a = \{(f,g);\ \{ap;\ p \in f\} \subset g\}$$

to a couple $(h_{\mathcal{B}},h_{\mathcal{R}}):(\mathcal{B},\mathcal{R}) \longrightarrow (\exp Z, K_{\exp Z})$ which preserves all operations of dynamic algebras, except possibly $*$. We shall prove that it preserves $*$, too, if $\mathcal{R}$ is finite.

Let $a \in \mathcal{R}$. As $\mathcal{R}$ is finite, there is m such that $\bigcup_{i=0}^{m} a^i = \bigcup_{i=0}^{n} a^i$ for every $n \geq m$. Given $p \in \mathcal{B}$, put $q_0 = \bigvee_{i=0}^{m} a^i p$. We shall show that $q_0 = a^* p$. We have $aq_0 = a(\bigvee_{i=0}^{m} a^i p) = \bigvee_{i=0}^{m} a^{i+1} p \leq \bigvee_{i=0}^{m+1} a^i p = q_0$, and, of course, $p \leq q_0$. On the other hand, if $aq \leq q$ and $p \leq q$ then, by induction, $\bigvee_{i=0}^{n} a^i p \leq \bigcup_{i=0}^{n} a^i q \leq q$ for every n and so $q_0 \leq q$. So $q_0 = a^* p$ by 1.3 (iv). We have proved $a^* = \bigcup_{i=0}^{m} a^i$. Then $h_{\mathcal{R}}(a^*) = h_{\mathcal{R}}(\bigcup_{i=0}^{m} a^i) = h_{\mathcal{R}}(\bigcup_{i=0}^{n} a^i) = \bigcup_{i=0}^{n} (h_{\mathcal{R}}a)^i$ for every $n \geq m$. Hence $h_{\mathcal{R}}(a^*) = \bigcup_{i=0}^{\infty} (h_{\mathcal{R}}a)^i = [h_{\mathcal{R}}a]^*$.

3. Relative σ-continuity

Pratt and Kozen, observing that every Kripke structure is $*$-continuous [12] and strongly $*$-continuous [6] put the question whether each $*$-continuous (strongly $*$-continuous) dynamic algebra is isomorphic to a Kripke structure. A negative answer was given by Kozen [8]. In the current section, we prove that each Kripke structure fulfils a continuity condition which is not implied by (strong) $*$-continuity. This enables us to construct a plenty of counterexamples.

3.1. Let $(\mathcal{B},\mathcal{R})$ be a separable dynamic algebra. A sequence $\{c_i\}_{i\in\omega}$ in $\mathcal{B}$ is *$*$-generated* if

$$c_i = a^i p - \bigvee_{j=0}^{i-1} a^j p \quad (i = 1,2,\ldots)$$

for some $a \in \mathcal{R}$ and $p \in \mathcal{B}$.

A separable dynamic algebra $(\mathcal{B},\mathcal{R})$ is *relatively σ-continuous* if every $b \in \mathcal{R}$ is σ-additive on every $*$-generated sequence $\{c_i\}_{i\in\omega}$ in $(\mathcal{B},\mathcal{R})$, that is,

$$b \bigvee_{i\in I} c_i = \bigvee_{i\in I} b\, c_i$$

for every set $I \subset \omega$ such that $\bigvee_{i \in I} c_i$ exists in $\mathcal{B}$.

3.2. Theorem. Let a separable dynamic algebra $(\mathcal{B},\mathcal{R})$ be isomorphic to a Kripke structure. Then it is relatively σ-continuous.

Proof. We may suppose that $(\mathcal{B},\mathcal{R})$ is a Kripke structure. Let $\{c_i\}_{i \in \omega}$ be a $*$-generated sequence in $(\mathcal{B},\mathcal{R})$, $c_i = a^i p - \bigvee_{j=0}^{i-1} a^j p$ $(i = 1,2,\ldots)$. First,

(a) $\bigvee_{i=0}^{\infty} c_i$ exists in $\mathcal{B}$ and equals to $\bigcup_{i=0}^{\infty} c_i$

Indeed, $\bigcup_{i=0}^{\infty} c_i = \bigcup_{i=0}^{\infty} a^i p = a^* p$ because $(\mathcal{B},\mathcal{R})$ is a Kripke structure, see 2.1. So $\bigcup_{i=0}^{\infty} a^i p \in \mathcal{B}$. This is sufficient for (a) to hold. Second,

(b) if $\bigvee_{i \in I} c_i$ exists in $\mathcal{B}$ then $\bigvee_{i \in I} c_i = \bigcup_{i \in I} c_i$

Indeed, we have $\bigcup_{j \in I} c_j \subset \bigvee_{i \in I} c_i \subset \bigvee_{i \in \omega} c_i = \bigcup_{i \in \omega} c_i$

and so, to prove (b), it suffices to show that $c_j \cap (\bigvee_{i \in I} c_i) = \emptyset$ for all $j \in (\omega - I)$. But by the distributivity of operations in Boolean algebras, $c_j \cap (\bigvee_{i \in I} c_i) = c_j \wedge (\bigvee_{i \in I} c_i) = \bigvee_{i \in I} (c_j \wedge c_i) = \emptyset$.

Now, the theorem follows immediately from (b): if $b \in \mathcal{R}$ then $b(\bigvee_{i \in I} c_i) = b(\bigcup_{i \in I} c_i) = \bigcup_{i \in I} b\, c_i$. Hence $\bigcup_{i \in I} b\, c_i \in \mathcal{B}$ and then $\bigcup_{i \in I} b\, c_i = \bigvee_{i \in I} b\, c_i$ in $\mathcal{B}$. The proof is finished.

3.3. Theorem. Let $\mathcal{B}$ be a Boolean algebra which admits a strictly decreasing sequence $\{d_i\}_{i \in \omega}$ with $\bigwedge_{i=0}^{\infty} d_i = 0$. Then there exists a separable dynamic algebra $(\mathcal{B},\mathcal{R})$ such that

(i) $(\mathcal{B},\mathcal{R})$ is strongly $*$-continuous,

(ii) $(\mathcal{B},\mathcal{R})$ is not relatively σ-continuous and hence it is not isomorphic to any Kripke structure,

(iii) $\mathcal{R}$ has one generator.

Proof. Let $\{d_i\}_{i \in \omega}$ be as above. Then $\{-d_i\}_{i \in \omega}$ is a strictly increasing sequence with $\bigvee_{i=0}^{\infty} -d_i = 1$. Put $c_i = (-d_i) - \bigvee_{j=0}^{i-1} (-d_j)$ for $i \in \omega$. Then the c_i's are pairwise disjoint and $\bigvee_{i=0}^{\infty} c_i = 1$. Define an additive function $a: \mathcal{B} \longrightarrow \mathcal{B}$ as follows. Given $p \in \mathcal{B}$, denote

$$I_p = \{i \in \omega \ ; \ c_i \wedge p \neq 0\}$$

and put

$ap = \bigvee_{i \in I_p} (c_{i-1} \vee c_i \vee c_{i+1})$ (where $c_{-1} = 0$) if I_p is finite,

$ap = 1$ otherwise.

Denote $a^{\infty}: \mathcal{B} \longrightarrow \mathcal{B}$ the additive function defined by $a^{\infty} p = 1$ for

$p \neq 0$ and $a^{\infty} 0 = 0$.

Let $\mathcal{R}$ consist of all powers a^i ($i \in \omega$) and of a^{∞}. It is easy to see that $(\mathcal{B},\mathcal{R})$ satisfies (i)-(iv) of 1.3; in particular, $b^* = a^{\infty}$ for every $b \in \mathcal{R}$. Then also the strong $*$-continuity of $(\mathcal{B},\mathcal{R})$ follows easily. If we want (v) of 1.4 to be satisfied we simply add the zero function to $\mathcal{R}$.

But $(\mathcal{B},\mathcal{R})$ is not relatively σ-continuous. Indeed, $\bigvee_{i=2}^{\infty} c_i$ exists in $\mathcal{B}$ (viz $\bigvee_{i=2}^{\infty} c_i = 1 - (c_0 \vee c_1)$) and $a(\bigvee_{i=2}^{\infty} c_i) = 1$ by the definition of a. On the other hand $\bigvee_{i=2}^{\infty} ac_i = \bigvee_{i=2}^{\infty} (c_{i-1} \vee c_i \vee c_{i+1}) = \bigvee_{i=1}^{\infty} c_i = -c_0 \neq 1$, a contradiction.

3.4. Remark. The above dynamic algebra $(\mathcal{B},\mathcal{R})$ can be extended to obtain a dynamic algebra $(\mathcal{B},\mathcal{R}')$ which is $*$-continuous but not strongly $*$-continuous.

Indeed, let us add a new function $b: \mathcal{B} \longrightarrow \mathcal{B}$ to $\mathcal{R}$ where $bp = 0$ if I_p is finite and $bp = 1$ otherwise. Then $(\mathcal{B},\mathcal{R}')$ where $\mathcal{R}' = \mathcal{R} \cup \{b\}$ is a separable dynamic algebra which is $*$-continuous (we have $b^* p = bp = \bigvee_{i=0}^{\infty} b^i p$ for all $p \in \mathcal{B}$) but not strongly $*$-continuous because $ba^* a = a^{\infty}$ while $\bigvee_{i=0}^{\infty} ba^i a = b$.

3.5. In [8], in context with dynamic algebras with reversion, Kozen put the problem of the existence of a countable dynamic algebra which is isomorphic to no Kripke structure. For dynamic algebras without reversion a solution is as follows.

Corollary. For every infinite countable Boolean algebra $\mathcal{B}$ there exists a strongly $*$-continuous dynamic algebra $(\mathcal{B},\mathcal{R})$ with $\mathcal{R}$ countable, such that $(\mathcal{B},\mathcal{R})$ is not isomorphic to any Kripke structure.

Proof. According to 3.3, it is sufficient to prove that $\mathcal{B}$ admits a sequence $\{d_i\}_{i \in \omega}$ which is strictly decreasing and $\bigwedge_{i=0}^{\infty} d_i = 0$. If $\mathcal{B}$ is atomic, then the set A of atoms in $\mathcal{B}$ is countable, $A = \{a_i\}_{i \in \omega}$, and the sequence $\{d_i\}_{i \in \omega}$, $d_i = -(a_0 \vee a_1 \vee \ldots \vee a_i)$ has desired properties. If $\mathcal{B}$ is not atomic, there is $d_0 \in \mathcal{B}$ such that there exists no atom a with $d_0 > a$. In particular, d_0 is not an atom and we can find $d_1 \in \mathcal{B}$ with $0 \neq d_1 \lneqq d_0$. Analogously, we find $d_2 \in \mathcal{B}$ with $0 \neq d_2 \lneqq d_1$ and so on. In this way we find a chain $\{d_i\}_{i \in \sigma}$ which is strictly decreasing such that $\bigwedge_{i \in \sigma} d_i = 0$ where σ is an ordinal. As $\mathcal{B}$ is countable, the ordinal σ is countable so that the chain contains a cofinal sequence $\{d_{n_i}\}_{i \in \omega}$ with desired properties.

4. σ-continuous dynamic algebras

Examples of the preceding section were constructed not to be relatively σ-continuous. In this section we shall deal with dynamic algebras which are not isomorphic to Kripke structures in spite of being σ-continuous (completely continuous): a separable dynamic algebra $(\mathcal{B},\mathcal{R})$ is <u>σ-continuous</u> (<u>completely continuous</u>) if every $a \in \mathcal{R}$ is σ-additive (completely additive).

4.1. <u>Lemma.</u> Let $(h_{\mathcal{B}},h_{\mathcal{R}}):(\mathcal{B},\mathcal{R}) \longrightarrow (\mathcal{B}',\mathcal{R}')$ be a homomorphism of $*$-continuous dynamic algebras. Then $h_{\mathcal{B}}$ is relatively σ-additive in the sense that for every $*$-generated sequence $\{c_i\}_{i\in\omega}$ in $\mathcal{B}$,

$$h_{\mathcal{B}}(\bigvee_{i\in I} c_i) = \bigvee_{i\in I} h_{\mathcal{B}}c_i$$

whenever I is a subset of ω such that $\bigvee_{i\in I} c_i$ exists in $\mathcal{B}$.

<u>Proof.</u> Let $\{c_i\}$ be $*$-generated, $c_i = a^i p - \bigvee_{j=0}^{i} a^j p$ $(i = 1,2,\dots)$. Then $\bigvee_{i=0}^{\infty} c_i$ exists in $\mathcal{B}$ and equals to $a^* p$. Moreover,

(a) $\bigvee_{i=0}^{\infty} h_{\mathcal{B}}c_i = h_{\mathcal{B}} \bigvee_{i=0}^{\infty} c_i$

because $h_{\mathcal{B}}(\bigvee_{i=0}^{\infty} c_i) = h_{\mathcal{B}}(a^*p) = [h_{\mathcal{R}} a]^* h_{\mathcal{B}} p = \bigvee_{i=0}^{\infty} (h_{\mathcal{R}} a)^i h_{\mathcal{B}} p =$
$= \bigvee_{i=0}^{\infty} h_{\mathcal{B}}(a^i p) = \bigvee_{i=0}^{\infty} h_{\mathcal{B}}c_i$.

Let $\bigvee_{i\in I} c_i$ exist in $\mathcal{B}$. Then put $s = h_{\mathcal{B}}(\bigvee_{i\in I} c_i)$. Of course, $s \geq h_{\mathcal{B}} c_i$ for every $i \in I$. Let $s' \in \mathcal{B}$, $s' \geq h_{\mathcal{B}}(c_i)$ for all $i \in I$. Then

(b) $s - s' \wedge h_{\mathcal{B}} c_i = 0$ $(i \in I)$.

On the other hand, $c_j \wedge (\bigvee_{i\in I} c_i) = 0$ for all $j \in \omega - I$, hence $s \wedge h_{\mathcal{B}}(c_j) = 0$ and so

(c) $(s - s')\wedge h_{\mathcal{B}}(c_j) = 0$ $(j \in \omega - I)$.

By virtue of (b) and (c), and according to (a),

$$(s - s')\wedge h_{\mathcal{B}}(\bigvee_{i=0}^{\infty} c_i) = 0.$$

As $s - s' \leq h_{\mathcal{B}}(\bigvee_{i=0}^{\infty} c_i)$, we get $s - s' = 0$, so $s \leq s'$. The proof is finished.

4.2. <u>Lemma.</u> Let $(\mathcal{B},\mathcal{R})$ be a dynamic algebra such that $\mathcal{B}$ is a σ-algebra and $\mathcal{R}$ contains all completely additive functions on $\mathcal{B}$. Then each sequence $\{c_i\}_{i\in\omega}$ of pairwise disjoint non-zero elements of $\mathcal{B}$ is $*$-generated.

<u>Proof.</u> Put $p = c_0$ and define a completely additive function $a: \mathcal{B} \longrightarrow \mathcal{B}$ by

$$ap = \bigvee_{i\in I_p} c_{i+1} \text{ where } I_p = \{i \in \omega,\ p\wedge c_i \neq 0\}.$$

Then $c_i = a^i p - \bigvee_{i=0}^{i} a^j p$ for all i.

4.3. <u>Corollary.</u> Let $(\mathcal{B},\mathcal{R})$ be a separable $*$-continuous dynamic algebra such that $\mathcal{B}$ is a σ-algebra and $\mathcal{R}$ contains all completely additive functions on $\mathcal{B}$. If $(h_{\mathcal{B}},h_{\mathcal{R}})$ is a homomorphism from $(\mathcal{B},\mathcal{R})$ to any Kripke structure then $h_{\mathcal{B}}$ is σ-additive.

4.4. <u>Example.</u> For any Boolean algebra $\mathcal{B}$, let $K_{\mathcal{B}}$ denote the set of all completely additive functions from $\mathcal{B}$ to $\mathcal{B}$. Let $\mathcal{B}$ be a σ-algebra admitting no σ-additive embedding to any exp Z, e.g., $\mathcal{B}$ = the (complete) Boolean algebra of all regularly closed subsets of the Cantor discontinuum. Then the dynamic algebra $(\mathcal{B},K_{\mathcal{B}})$ is isomorphic to no Kripke structure.

4.5. <u>Remark.</u> Let $h:\exp K \longrightarrow \exp Z$ be a σ-additive homomorphism of Boolean algebra where X is a set of non-measurable cardinality. Then h is completely additive.

Indeed, for every $z \in Z$, the ultrafilter

$$\{Y \subset X;\ z \in hY\}$$

is closed under countable intersections. As K has non-measurable cardinality, it is closed under all intersections which, in turn, implies that h is completely additive.

4.6. <u>Example.</u> Let X be an uncountable set of non-measurable cardinality, say $\aleph_1$, $2^{\aleph_0}$ etc., and let $(\exp X,\mathcal{R})$ be a dynamic algebra such that $\mathcal{R}$ contains the set of all completely additive functions as a proper subset. Then $(\exp X,\mathcal{R})$ is not isomorphic to any Kripke structure.

Proof. Suppose the contrary. Then there exists an embedding $(h_{\exp X},h_{\mathcal{R}})$ of $(\exp X,\mathcal{R})$ into a full Kripke structure $(\exp Z, K_{\exp Z})$. By 4.3 and 4.5, $h_{\exp X}$ is completely additive. Choose $a \in \mathcal{R}$ which is not completely additive. So $a(\bigcup_{i\in I} P_i) \neq \bigcup_{i\in I} a\,P_i$ for some collection $\{P_i\}_{i\in I}$ of subsets of X. But then

$$h_{\mathcal{R}}(a)(\bigcup_{i\in I} h_{\exp X}(P_i)) = h_{\mathcal{R}}(a)(h_{\exp X}(\bigcup_{i\in I} P_i)) =$$

$$= h_{\exp X}\, a(\bigcup_{i\in I} P_i) \neq h_{\exp X}(\bigcup_{i\in I} a\,P_i) = \bigcup_{i\in I} h_{\exp X}(a\,P_i) =$$

$$= \bigcup_{i\in I} h_{\mathcal{R}}(a)\, h_{\exp X}(P_i).$$ Thus $h_{\mathcal{R}}(a) \notin K_{\exp Z}$, a contradiction.

4.7. <u>Theorem.</u> Let $\mathcal{B}$ be a complete Boolean algebra which does not satisfy the CCC, e.g. $\mathcal{B}$ = exp Z for an uncountable set Z. Let $\mathcal{R}$ be the set of all σ-additive functions on $\mathcal{B}$. Then $(\mathcal{B},\mathcal{R})$ is not isomorphic to any Kripke structure, in fact, it admits no homomorphism to any Kripke structure.

Proof. Remember that a Boolean algebra $\mathfrak{B}$ satisfies the CCC (countable chain condition) if every family of pairwise disjoint non-zero elements of $\mathfrak{B}$ is at most countable. Thus if $\mathfrak{B}$ does not satisfy the CCC then there exists a set $\{c_i; i \in X\}$ such that the c_i's are pairwise disjoint and non-zero, and such that X has an uncountable and non-measurable cardinality, say card $X = \aleph_1$. We may suppose $\bigvee_{i \in X} c_i = 1$. Consider the separable dynamic algebra $(\exp X, \mathfrak{R}')$ where $\mathfrak{R}'$ is the set of all σ'-additive functions on exp X and define an embedding $(j_{\mathfrak{B}}, j_{\mathfrak{R}'}) : (\exp X, \mathfrak{R}') \longrightarrow (\mathfrak{B}, \mathfrak{R})$ by

$$j_{\mathfrak{B}} Y = \bigvee_{i \in Y} c_i,$$

$$j_{\mathfrak{R}'}(a)(p) = \vee \{c_j;\ j \in a(\{i \in X;\ c_i \wedge p \neq 0\})\}$$

Now suppose that $(\mathfrak{B},\mathfrak{R})$ admits a homomorphism to a Kripke structure. Then $(\exp K, \mathfrak{R}')$ admits a homomorphism $(h_{\mathfrak{B}}, h_{\mathfrak{R}'})$ to a full Kripke structure $(\exp Z, K_{\exp Z})$ for some set Z. By 4.3 and 4.5, $h_{\mathfrak{B}}$ is completely additive. Consider the σ-additive function b:exp X $\longrightarrow$ exp X defined by

$bY = \emptyset$ if Y is countable, $bY = X$ otherwise.

Then $h_{\mathfrak{B}}(X) = h_{\mathfrak{B}}(bX) = h_{\mathfrak{R}'}(b)h_{\mathfrak{B}}(X) = h_{\mathfrak{R}'}(b)\,[\bigcup_{x \in X} h_{\mathfrak{B}}\{x\}] =$
$= \bigcup_{x \in X} h_{\mathfrak{R}'}(b)\, h_{\mathfrak{B}}\{x\} = \bigcup_{x \in X} h_{\mathfrak{B}}(b\{x\}) = \bigcup_{x \in X} h_{\mathfrak{B}}\emptyset = 0$ - a contradiction because $h(X) = Z$ for every homomorphism h:exp X $\longrightarrow$ exp Z of Boolean algebras.

5. Remarks to reversion

Sometimes, dynamic algebras with one more operation - reversion - are considered ([6],[7],[8]). A dynamic algebra with reversion is a dynamic algebra $(\mathfrak{B},\mathfrak{R},\langle\ \rangle)$ equipped with a unary operation $(\ )^- : \mathfrak{R} \longrightarrow \mathfrak{R}$ satisfying

6. $(ab)^- = b^- a^-$,
7. $(a \cup b)^- = a^- \cup b^-$,
8. $a^{--} = a$,
9. $p \leq -a(-a^- p)$.

Dynamic algebras with reversion will be investigated in a subsequent paper. It appears that the new operation forces very strong properties of dynamic algebras. E.g., for separable dynamic algebras with reversion, 6 and 7 are derivable from the other axioms and $*$-continuity implies strong $*$-continuity. Even, a separable dynamic algebra with reversion is completely continuous. It follows that our examples, except 4.4, cannot be modified to have reversion. As for 4.4, the corresponding modification is obtained by replacing the set of all completely additive functions by the set of all reversible completely additive functions.

References

[1] Banachowski, L., A. Kreczmar, G. Mirkowska, H. Rasiowa, and A. Salwicki: "An introduction to algorithmic Logic", in: Mazurkiewicz and Pawlak, eds., Math. Found. of Comp. Sci., Banach Center Publications, Warszaw, 1977.

[2] Berman, F.: A completeness technique for D-axiomatizable semantics, Proc. 11th ACM Symp. on Theory of Comp. (May 1979), 160 - 166.

[3] Fischer, M.J. and R.E. Ladner: Propositional modal logic of programs, Proc. 9th ACM Symp. on Theory of Comp. (May 197), 286 - 294.

[4] Halmos, P.R.: Algebraic Logic, Chelsea, New York 1962.

[5] Harel, D.: First Order Dynamic Logic, Lecture Notes in Comp. Sci 68, Springer Verlag, Berlin 1979.

[6] Kozen, D.: A representation theorem for models of *-free PDL, manuscript, July 1979.

[7] Kozen, D.: On the duality of dynamic algebras and Kripke models, manuscript, May 1979.

[8] Kozen, D.: On the representation of dynamic algebras, manuscript, October 1979.

[9] Parikh, R.: A completeness result for PDL, Symp. on Math. Found. of Comp. Sci., Warszawa, Springer Verlag 1978.

[10] Pratt, V.R.: A practical decision method for Propositional Dynamic Logic, Proc. 10th ACM Symp. on Theory of Comp. (May 1978), 326-337.

[11] Pratt, V.R.: Models of program logics, Proc. 20th IEEE Symp. on Foundations of Comp. Sci. (October 1979), to appear.

[12] Pratt, V.R.: Dynamic algebras: examples, constructions, applications, manuscript, July 1979.

[13] Salwicki, A.: Formalized Algorithmic Languages, Bull. Acad. Pol. Sci., Sér. Sci. Math. Astr. Phys. Vol. 18 No 5, 1970.

[14] Segerberg, K.: A completeness theorem in the modal logic of programs, Not. AMS 24:6(1977), A-552.

[15] Sikorski, R.: Boolean algebras, Springer Verlag 1964.

TIME AND SPACE BOUNDS IN PRODUCING CERTAIN PARTIAL ORDERS

Peter Ružička
Computing Research Center
Dúbravská 3 , 885 31 Bratislava
Czechoslovakia

1. INTRODUCTION

In this paper we deal with a problem of producing a partial order S_{n-k}^{k-1} from n singletons (drawn from a totally ordered set) , where S_m^k denotes a partial order on k+m+1 elements with one particular element, called the center (center(S_m^k)) , which is smaller than k other elements and greater than each of the remaining m elements. Many of the well known selection problems can be understood as the task of producing partial orders with the center.

Our major goal here is to investigate time-space trade off for this problem. We say a time-space trade off exists for a problem if there does not exist any algorithm solving the problem simultaneously in minimal time and in minimal space. Our interest lies in answering the following question : If there exists a time-space trade off for the considered problem, then

what is the minimal space required by a time optimal algorithm;
and alternatively, what is the minimal number of comparisons required by algorithms using absolutely minimal space ?

If these two "endpoints" are known, then we investigate a continuous time-space trade off for the problem by inspecting

the effect of space limitations on the time complexity;
or alternatively, the effect of time limitations on the space complexity.

We show that $\frac{1}{2}\log^2 n + \Theta(\log n)$ is the minimal space required by the time optimal algorithm producing S_{n-2}^1 and that 2n - 3 comparisons are necessary and sufficient to compute S_{n-2}^1 in the absolutely minimal space. Furthermore, it is shown that given an arbitrary space constraint S from the interval

$\langle 4, \frac{1}{2}\log^2 n + \frac{1}{2}\log n + 1 \rangle$ it is sufficient to produce S^1_{n-2} in $n + \frac{n}{f(k-1,S-1)} + k - O(1)$ binary comparisons, where $f(m,n)$ is the solution of the recurrent equation $f(m,n) = f(m-1,n) + f(m-1,n-k)$ for $m \geqslant 1$, $f(m,n) = 0$ for $m \leqslant 0$, $f(1,n) = 1$ for $n \geqslant 1$, $f(1,n) = 0$ for $n \leqslant 0$ and k is the minimal index such that $f(k,S) = \max_t \{f(t,S)\}$. We note that $f(m,m)$ is the number of partitions of an integer m into nonequal integer summands. Results of the same kind are also presented for the problem of producing S^2_{n-3}.

Further, we investigate the time complexity of on-line algorithms producing S^{k-1}_{n-k}. These are algorithms which produce S^{k-1}_{N-k} over all N processed elements at every step of computation (i.e. after reading each element from the input). Our main result is that there is a linear time on-line algorithm producing S^{k-1}_{n-k} iff k is the constant.

2. PROBLEM AND MODEL OF COMPUTATION

Assume we are given a totally ordered finite set X, the reservoir. The order is not known initially and can only be determined by performing successive binary comparisons between elements of X. In this paper we shall investigate the problem of producing the partial order S^k_m on n singletons.

Algorithms solving our problem can be represented as a finite comparison tree, data are stored in a finite number of internal memory cells (so called working space) and the input data are stored as a sequence of n distinct elements on a one-way read-only input tape. Inputs, i.e. elements of the reservoir, are read from the input tape into specified memory cells. Comparisons may be made between the contents of any pair of memory cells. In a comparison computation tree each interior node is associated with an operation and the output takes place at the leaves of the tree. A comparison operation have either two branches ($\leqslant, >$ comparisons) or three branches ($<, =, >$ comparisons); an input operation has one branch. A problem is described relative to a size parameter n (which is, in our case, the number of elements to be processed). For each n there is a finite comparison tree with a finite number of memory cells to describe the computation. Computation obviously begins at the root of the tree and proceeds from node to node until a leaf is reached. The path of the greatest length (more precisely, having maximum number of comparisons) indicates the worst-case time complexity of an algorithm and the number of memory cells used indicates the space complexity of an algorithm. Time (space) complexity of a problem is minimum time (space) complexity over all algorithms solving this problem.

3. MINIMAL SPACE ALGORITHMS

The widely used algorithm producing the partial order S^0_{n-1} is optimal simultaneously according to the space and time requirements. That yields a non-existence of a time-space trade off for this problem. Furthermore, $n - 1$ memory transfers are necessary for each algorithm using implicit data structures (i.e. data structure without any explicit indices or pointers) and producing S^0_{n-1} simultaneously in minimal time and in minimal space.

It is fairly easy to find an algorithm producing a partial order S^1_{n-2} and making $2n - 3$ binary comparisons in minimal space. Furthermore, each algorithm producing S^1_{n-2} in minimal space requires at least $2n - 3$ binary comparisons. To prove this it is sufficient to construct the following adversary strategy :

```
procedure ADVERSARY ( comparison  a : b ) ;
begin
   comment  c  is the third element in the working space together with
            a , b ;
   select
      no relationship between  a,b,c  is known : return ( a > b );
      a > c  or  b < c  is known : return ( a < b ) ;
      a < c  or  b > c  is known : return ( a < b ) ;
      a < c , b < c  is known : return ( a > b )
   end ;
   if  some element of  {a,b,c}  is lower than the rest of the set
   then  it is deleted from the working space
end
```

It can be observed that at least two comparisons are made with each of $n - 2$ elements deleted in the *if* statement. Inspecting the adversary more carefully with respect to the number of memory transfers the following lower bound can be obtained.

CLAIM 1
Each space optimal algorithm producing a partial order S^1_{n-2} from n singletons makes at least $2n - 3$ binary comparisons and $\Omega(n)$ memory transfers.

Consider now the class of algorithms producing S^1_{n-2} in the optimal number of comparisons. In order to obtain minimal space required by the time optimal algorithm producing S^1_{n-2} we start from Schreier's algorithm which was proved by Kislitsyn to be time optimal. Time optimal algorithm can be exhibited as follows :

<u>procedure</u> SECMINTIME (n) ;
<u>begin</u>
1. Set up a balanced binary tree for a knock-out tournament for a set of n elements ; the winner of the tournament is denoted as FIRST ;
2. SECOND $\longleftarrow$ MAXIMUM $\{$the set of all elements directly compared with FIRST in step 1$\}$;
3. <u>return</u> (FIRST , SECOND)

<u>end</u>

This algorithm makes $n + \lceil \log n \rceil - 2$ binary comparisons and the straightforward implementation by means of trees requires $O(n)$ memory cells. We show how the problem of producing S^1_{n-2} can be computed simultaneously in $n + \lceil \log n \rceil - 2$ binary comparisons and in $\frac{1}{2}\log^2 n + \Theta(\log n)$ memory cells. The existence of such an algorithm together with claim 1 implies a time-space trade off for this problem.

THEOREM 1
The minimal space required to produce S^1_{n-2} in $n + \lceil \log n \rceil - 2$ binary comparisons is $\frac{1}{2}\log^2 n + \Theta(\log n)$.

To prove theorem 1 we first show that for each comparison optimal algorithm $\frac{1}{2}\log^2 n + O(\log n)$ memory cells are sufficient. We assume without loss of generality that $n = 2^k$ for some $k \geqslant 1$; other cases follow easily by extending the original set by the appropriate number of $-\infty$ to fit the condition about the number of elements.

Consider the following space efficient modification of the SECMINTIME algorithm. This modification uses an implicit data structure based on the binomial trees T_k which are defined inductively as follows : a single node forms T_0 and two copies of a T_k with an additional edge between roots form a T_{k+1}. An alternative and very useful representation of a binomial tree T_{k+1} can be viewed as a root of $k+1$ sons being roots of $T_k, T_{k-1}, \ldots, T_0$, respectively. Our algorithm needs to save only two upper levels of each binomial tree. Therefore it is sufficient to consider only two level binomial trees which have the form S^0_i for $i = 0, 1, \ldots, \log n$. Initially this algorithm contains n singletons on the input tape. At each step of computation two elements of the input are read into the working space and, whenever possible, two copies of S_i^0 are used to construct S_{i+1}^0 .

```
procedure  SEGMINTS (n)  ;
begin
  repeat
    read  two elements from the input tape into the working space ;
    c ←— 0 ;
    while  there are two copies  A , B  of  S_c^0  in the working space
    do
       begin
         if  center(A) > center(B)
         then
            replace A  and  B  by  S_{c+1}^0  in which  center(S_{c+1}^0) is
            center(A)  and  c+1  elements less than  center(S_{c+1}^0)
            are  c  elements less than  center(A)  plus  center(B)
         else
            replace  A  and  B  by  S_{c+1}^0  in which  center(S_{c+1}^0)
            is  center(B)  and  c+1 elements less than  center(S_{c+1}^0)
            are  c  elements less than  center(B)  plus  center(A) ;
         c ←— c + 1
       end
  until  the input tape is empty ;
  return ( center(S_c^0) , MAXIMUM {c elements less than  center(S_c^0)})
end
```

To bound the number of space cells required by this algorithm it may be observed that

LEMMA 1

In SEGMINTS algorithm

a. the number of elements used is $\frac{1}{2}\log^2 n + O(\log n)$;

b. no additional space is needed to maintain these elements.

The proof follows from the fact that the only space consuming step is while cycle which requires at most $M(n)$ elements, where M is the solution of $M(4) = 4$, $M(2^k) = k + M(2^{k-1})$ for $k \geqslant 3$ and these elements can be represented compactly in an array using implicit implementation of the forest of two-level binomial trees.

Hence, an upper bound on space for computing S_{n-2}^1 in the minimal number of comparisons given in theorem 1 immediately follows from lemma 1. To show that the upper bound is optimal to within a constant factor of the lower ordered term we present here the corresponding lower bounds.

The lower estimation proof uses the idea of the adversary who, knowing comparisons of our algorithm, devises an ordering of the input which forces a comparison optimal algorithm to perform comparisons of a certain form only. We say that an algorithm producing S^1_{n-2} is in C-normal form, if it performs comparisons of two types only : either comparisons between centers of partial orders S^0_k for $k = 0, 1, \ldots, \lfloor \log n \rfloor - 1$ or comparisons between elements less than the center of the partial orders $S^0_{\lfloor \log n \rfloor}$. The rest of the proof of theorem 1 follows at once from the following lemma. For simplicity and clarity of the argument used we assume that $n = 2^k$ for some $k \geqslant 1$.

LEMMA 2

Each comparison optimal algorithm producing S^1_{n-2} for $n = 2^s$, $s \geqslant 1$, is in C-normal form.

To prove this we observe that for each algorithm producing S^1_{n-2} it is sufficient to maintain only these elements which are known not to be smaller than two other elements of the inspected set. Thus, each algorithm producing S^1_{n-2} can make comparisons only of the type :

(A) between center(S^0_u) and center(S^0_v) for $u \geqslant v \geqslant 0$;

(B) between center(S^0_v) , $v \geqslant 0$, and a noncenter element of S^0_u , $u \geqslant 1$;

(C) between a noncenter element a of S^0_u , $u \geqslant 1$, and a noncenter element b of S^0_v , $v \geqslant 1$, $u \geqslant v$;

(D) between two various noncenter elements a , b of S^0_u , $u \geqslant 2$.

Assume an adversary based on the following responding strategy :

```
procedure ADVERSARY ( comparison CMP ) ;
begin
   select
      CMP of type (A) : return ( center(S_u^0) > center(S_v^0) ) ;
      CMP of type (B) : return ( a < center(S_v^0) ) ;
      CMP of type (C) or (D) : return ( a > b )
   end
end
```

We see that comparisons of the type (B) and (C) lead to comparison non-optimal computations. A comparison of the type (A) for $u \neq v$ yields time non-optimal computation as well as comparisons of the type (D) for $u \neq s$ (by the assumption $n = 2^s$) . Thus, an adversary is constructed which forces each comparison optimal algorithm producing S^1_{n-2} for $n = 2^s$, $s \geqslant 1$, either to perform comparisons of the type (A) for $u = v$ and of the type (D) for $u = s$ or yield the contradiction with the comparison optimality condition.

Now let us turn our attention to the proof of space optimality. The case $n = 2^s$ for $s \geqslant 1$ follows from the previous observation about comparison optimal algorithms. The extention for the case $n \neq 2^s$, $s \geqslant 1$, follows directly from the observation that the space required by a comparison optimal space minimal algorithm producing S^1_{n-2} is lower bounded by the amount of space needed by a comparison optimal space minimal algorithm producing $S^1_{2^t-2}$ for $t = \lfloor \log n \rfloor$. This concludes the proof of theorem 1 .

Now consider a problem of memory transfer complexity for time optimal space minimal algorithms producing S^1_{n-2}. By the careful implementation of the SEGMINTS algorithm one can obtain an algorithm which uses only $O(n)$ memory transfers, but two indices to the working space. Thus this modified algorithm uses a non-implicit data structure. The algorithm is described in detail in [4]. As to the lower bounds on the number of memory transfers for time optimal space minimal algorithms producing S^1_{n-2}, we have a definite result only for the case of compact implementation (i.e. when a consecutive memory cells are used).

THEOREM 2
Any time optimal space minimal algorithm producing S^1_{n-2} from n singletons using the compact implementation of each two-level binomial tree and the compact implementation of the forest of all two-level binomial trees requires $\Omega(n)$ memory transfers.

The proof of this theorem is again in [4]. We note that there remains an unsolved problem to determine the number of memory transfers for time optimal space minimal algorithms producing S^1_{n-2} for the case in which binomial trees are not necessarily compactly implemented and in which the forest of all two-level binomial trees in the working space has to be implemented compactly only if the minimum space is overloaded. Another unsolved problem is to prove whether there exists an effective implementation of comparison optimal algorithms "in situ" using only $o(n)$ memory transfers. Note that our upper bound gives the $O(n)$ solution to the "in situ" problem and that theorem 2 answers only a special case of the lower bound problem for the time optimal space minimal algorithms.

Next we review some other results from [4] for the problem of producing a partial order S^k_m without proofs :

- Each algorithm producing S^2_{n-3} in minimal space needs at least $2n - 4$ binary comparisons.
- The minimal space required to produce S^1_{n-3} in optimal time is

$\frac{1}{3}\log^3 n + O(\log^2 n)$.

- For any rational $p \in (0, \frac{1}{2})$ there is an integer $c_p > 0$ such that for producing the partial order $S^{pn}_{(1-p)n}$ in minimal space $c_p.n.\log n - O(n)$ binary comparisons and $\Omega(n)$ memory transfers are necessary simultaneously.
- There is an algorithm producing $S^{n/2}_{n/2}$ in minimal space, linear time and linear number of memory transfers simultaneously.

4. TIME EFFICIENT ALGORITHMS IN RESTRICTED SPACE

This section is devoted to the solution of the following question : what is the time complexity of the problem under some space restriction ? Such a time characterization of the problem for each space constraint is called continuous time-space trade. The results presented in this section concern the time-space trade off in producing partial orders S^1_{n-2} and S^2_{n-3} . These problems were not considered by Munro and Dobkin in [1] .

The first problem we are to deal with is the producing a partial order S^1_{n-2} . In the previous section we have determined the space interval $\langle 3, \frac{1}{2}\log^2 n + \Theta(\log n)\rangle$ from which it is sufficient to take space constraints for specifying the continuous time-space trade off. The space optimal algorithm makes $2n - 3$ binary comparisons and the time optimal algorithm is SEGMINTS . Following the technique used by Tompa [5] or by Galil and Seiferas [2] the whole spectrum of algorithms can be obtained by combining these two algorithms. Such a combined algorithm can work as a time optimal algorithm in space S and it makes approximately $n.[1 + (\log N - 1)/(N - 1)]$ binary comparisons for $N = 2^{(\sqrt{8.S - 15} - 1)/2}$, $S \geq 3$. We present a new technique for obtaining an upper bound for the time-space trade off which is not based on the idea of combined time optimal and space optimal algorithms.

THEOREM 3

Let S be an integer, $S \geq 4$. Then there is an algorithm producing S^1_{n-2} in $n.\left[1 + \frac{1}{f(k-1,S-1)}\right] + k - O(1)$ binary comparisons in space S, where $f(m,n)$ is the solution of the recurrent equation

$$(4.1)\quad \begin{array}{ll} f(m,n) = f(m-1,n) + f(m-1,n-m) & \text{for } m \geq 1 \\ f(m,n) = 0 & \text{for } m \leq 0 \\ f(1,n) = 1 & \text{for } n \geq 1 \\ f(1,n) = 0 & \text{for } n \leq 0 \end{array}$$

$k = k(S)$ is the minimal index such that $f(k,S) = \max_t \{f(t,S)\}$.

Proof:

Consider the following algorithm producing S^1_{n-2} in space $A[1..S]$:

```
procedure  SECTRADECFF ( S,n ) ;
begin
   comment  let  n = f(k-1,S ) + c.f(k-1,S-k )   for some  c ≥ 1  and let
            k = k(S)  is the minimal index satisfying the condition
            f(k,S ) = max { f(t,S)} ;
                       t
   1. Create a partial order  S^0_{k-1}  using  A [1..S]  memory cells in the
      same way as in the  SECMINTS  algorithm and place it into consec-
      utive memory cells  A [1..k], with the center in  A [1] ;
      repeat
         i.  Create a partial order  S^0_{k-1}  using  A[k+1..S]  memory cells
             in the same way as in the  SECMINTS  algorithm and place it
             into memory cells  A[k+1..2k], with the center in  A [k+1] ;
        ii.  if  A [1] < A [k+2]
             then
                for  j ← 1  to  k+1  do
                   exchange ( A [j], A [j+k+1] ) ;
             if  A [k+1]  <  A [k+2]
             then  exchange ( A [k+1] , A [k+2] )
      until  the input tape is empty ;
   2. return ( A [1] , MAXIMUM { A [2], ... , A [i+1] } )
end
```

This algorithm uses S memory cells. The total number of comparisons performed by the algorithm can be achieved as the sum of $f(k-1,S)$ comparisons made in step 1 , $[n - f(k-1,S)].[f(k-1,S-k) + 1]/f(k-1,S-k)$ binary comparisons made in the repeat cycle and $k - 1$ binary comparisons made in step 2 . Hence we can obtain

$$f(k-1,S) + n.\left[1 + \frac{1}{f(k-1,S-k)}\right] - f(k-1,S) - \frac{f(k-1,S)}{f(k-1,S-k)} + k - 1 =$$

$$= n.\left[1 + \frac{1}{f(k-1,S-k)}\right] + k - O(1) .$$

Now we express the solution of the recurrent equation (4.1) in the analytical form. The sequence $f(1,1)$, $f(2,2)$, ... can be represented by means of the generating function $\frac{1}{1-x} \cdot \prod_{i=1}^{\infty} (1 + x^i)$. The solution $f(m,n)$ of the recurrent equation (4.1) can be expressed as a function of parameters m , n and coefficients of the generating function.

LEMMA 3

The solution of the recurrent equation (4.1) can be expressed in the form

$$f(m,n) = \begin{cases} f(n,n) & \text{for } 1 \leqslant n \leqslant m \\ 2^m & \text{for } \binom{m+1}{2} < n \\ 2^s + f(n,n) - f(n+s-m, n+s-m) & \text{for } m < n \leqslant \binom{m+1}{2} \end{cases}$$

where

$$s = \lfloor (\sqrt{8.n - 8.m - 15} - 1)/2 \rfloor .$$

Another time-space trade off result for producing S^2_{n-3} is presented without proof. The proof is contained in [4].

THEOREM 4

Let S be an integer, $S \geqslant 5$. Then there exists an algorithm producing S^2_{n-3} performing $n.\left[1 + \frac{k+2}{f(k-1,S-k-2)}\right] + O(k)$ binary comparisons in space S, where

$f(m,n)$ is the solution of the recurrent equation

$$f(m,n) = f(m-1,n) + f(m-1, S - \binom{m}{2} - 1) + 1 \qquad \text{for } n \geqslant 2,\ m > 1$$

$$f(1,n) = 1 \qquad \text{for } n \geqslant 2$$

$$f(m,n) = 0 \qquad \text{for } n \leqslant 1$$

$k = k(S)$ is the minimal index such that $f(k,S) = \max_t \{ f(t,S) \}$.

5. ON-LINE ALGORITHMS

The purpose of this section is to establish the following theorem :

THEOREM 5

1. Any on-line algorithm producing S^{k-1}_{n-k} must perform at least $\lceil \log(k+1) \rceil .n - O(k)$ binary comparisons.
2. For any $p : 0 < p \leqslant \frac{1}{2}$ there exists a constant $c_p > 0$ such that each on-line algorithm producing $S^{pn-1}_{(1-p)n}$ must perform at least $c_p.n.\log n - O(n)$ binary comparisons.

Let us consider these lower bounds in the connection with the following upper bound results. The trivial insertion algorithm for the problem of producing S^{k-1}_{n-k} makes $\lceil \log(k+1) \rceil .n - O(k)$ binary comparisons, while for the problem of producing $S^{pn-1}_{(1-p)n}$, $0 < p \leqslant \frac{1}{2}$, it performs $n.\log n - O(n)$ binary comparisons.

Here we present only a sketch of the proof of theorem 5. To prove the first part of this theorem, we show how to construct an adversary responding strategy by means of which each eliminated element is compared with at least $\lceil \log (k+1) \rceil$ other elements from the working space. Consider a comparison $a : b$ of the algorithm. Let T_a be a subtree with the root a taken from the partial order over elements in the working space. This subtree is constructed in such a way that all comparisons not made as comparisons between roots of such constructed subtrees are eliminated. Then the answer is $a > b$ if and only if the number of leaves of T_a is greater than the number of leaves of T_b.

To prove the second part of the theorem 5 we first consider the case $0 < p < \frac{1}{2}$. We show an idea how an adversary strategy can be constructed such that each of the first $\min (p,(1-p)).n$ eliminated elements is forced to be compared with at least $\log n + O(\log p)$ other elements from the working space. Given a comparison $a : b$ of the selection algorithm, the answer is $a > b$ if and only if either b is among the first $p.n$ elements read from the input tape and a is not or a, b are both among the first $p.n$ elements read from the input tape and a is known to be lower than x elements and b is known to be lower than y elements for $x \geqslant y$. In the case where a and b are not from the first $p.n$ elements read from the input tape the answer is arbitrary but cannot be in contradiction with the transitivity.

Now it is sufficient to sketch the proof for the case $p = \frac{1}{2}$. An optimal on-line algorithm producing $S_{n/2}^{n/2}$ in space $\frac{n}{2} + 2$ eliminates the elements which are known to be lower or greater than $\frac{n}{2} + 1$ elements. Consider that the computation is in the state when h elements greater and d elements lower than the median element have been eliminated. For the next eliminated element only two possibilities can occur. Either the algorithm computes an element lower than the median or the algorithm computes an element which is greater than the median element. Following a similar argument as it was used in the previous case $0 < p < \frac{1}{2}$, we obtain the following : If the eliminated element is lower than the median, then it is compared with at least $\lceil \log (\frac{n}{2} - h) \rceil$ other elements from the working space ; otherwise it is compared with at least $\lceil \log (\frac{n}{2} - d) \rceil$ other elements from the working space.

It is interesting that the time optimal on-line algorithms producing S_{n-k}^{k-1} have similar time complexity as the time optimal algorithm producing $\{S_{n-i}^{i-1}\}_{i=1}^{k}$ in space $k+1$. If k is the constant, then the optimal on-line time complexity is $\lceil \log(k+1) \rceil .n - O(k)$, while optimal time complexity for $\{S_{n-i}^{i-1}\}_{i=1}^{k}$ is $(\lfloor \log k \rfloor + 1).n - O(k)$. For $S_{(1-p)n}^{pn-1}$, $0 < p \leqslant \frac{1}{2}$, optimal on-line time complexity is $\Theta(n.\log n)$ as well as optimal time complexity for $\{S_{n-i}^{i-1}\}_{i=1}^{pn}$.

For small constants k we have obtained the exact lower bounds of the following form :

- Each on-line algorithm producing S_{n-2}^{1} must perform at least $2n - 3$ binary comparisons.
- Each on-line algorithm producing S_{n-3}^{2} must perform at least $2n - 4$ binary comparisons.

6. CONCLUSIONS

We have investigated time-space trade offs in producing certain partial orders with center. We have completed results of Dobkin and Munro [1] by solving the case $k = 2$, 3 in producing S_{n-k}^{k-1} . Furthermore, the efficiency of time optimal algorithms in limited space has been discussed for these problems by determining their memory transfer complexity. Among other results, we have shown that the number of comparisons is a relevant criterion for time complexity of problems producing partial orders with center even in the limited space.

Other computational models have been considered relative to producing partial orders with center in limited space. We have not discussed multipass algorithms of Paterson and Munro [3] , where they studied the trade off between the amount of internal space available and the number of passes over the input tape required. In this paper we have focussed our attention upon the on-line algorithms, in which a partial order with center over all processed elements is produced at each step of computation. It is shown that while we consider producing S_m^k for some constant k , $\lceil \log k \rceil .m + O(k)$ binary comparisons are sufficient and necessary. Otherwise $\Omega(n.\log n)$ binary comparisons are necessary to produce $S_{(1-p)n}^{pn}$ for some $0 < p \leqslant \frac{1}{2}$ by an on-line algorithm.

7. REFERENCES

1. Dobkin, D.P., Munro, J.I.: Time and Space Bounds for Selection Problems. Lecture Notes in Computer Science 62. Springer-Verlag, 1978
2. Galil, Z., Seiferas, J.: Saving Space in Fast String-Matching. 18th Symposium on Foundation of Computer Science, Providence, 1977
3. Paterson, M.S., Munro, J.I.: Selection and Sorting with Limited Storage. Report No. 24, University of Warwick, July 1978
4. Ružička, P.: Time-Space Trade Offs in Selection Problem. Thesis. 1980 (in Slovak)
5. Tompa, M.: Time-Space Tradeoffs for Straight-Line and Branching Programs. Technical Report No. 122 - 78 , Departement of Computer Science, University of Toronto, July 1978

AXIOMS OF ALGORITHMIC LOGIC UNIVOCALLY DETERMINE SEMANTICS OF PROGRAMS

Andrzej Salwicki
Mathematical Institute
Polish Academy of Sciences
Sniadeckich 8,P.O.Box 137
00-950 Warsaw

Abstract

Among many execution methods for programs that can be conceived of, only the standard notion of computation satisfies axioms of algorithmic logic AL and makes inference rules of AL sound. In this sense the axiomatic system of algorithmic logic specifies the semantics of programs. Next, we shall prove that by the relaxing of requirements , e.g. by the rejection of an axiom or an inference rule we shall create a liberal axiomatic system which allows nonstandard (i.e. transfinite and successful) runs of programs.

§1. INTRODUCTION

The problem whether the chosen semantics of a programming language can be defined axiomatically has been raised by many authors [cf. 1,2,4,5,6,7,8,9,12,11,22,16,19] . Here we shall make an attempt to clarify some technical details since ,it is our belief that in numerous cases either the reasoning was based on misunderstanding (it is easy to mistake the notion of semantics with the inequivalence of programs) or the axiomatic specification of semantics has not been a complete one and in effect it allowed nonstandard runs.
R e m a r k . A system of axioms should be complete in order to describe a reality (here: a semantics of a programming language).

Systems which are not complete can not be candidates for a categorical definition of semantics and on the other hand they are not sufficiently rich in order to ensure that every semantically valid sentence has a formal proof. □

In this paper we shall limit ourselves to the simple case of the programming language of while-programs. In the concluding remarks we shall return to this point.

What does it mean to define axiomatically the semantics of a programming language ? At least three different approaches can be met in the literature :

(i) a complete axiomatization of the logic of programs,
(ii) a relatively complete axiomatization of the logic of programs,
(iii) an axiomatization of inequivalence relation of programs .

The philosophy connected with algorithmic logic [cf. also 7] is based on the belief that our knowledge about a semantics of a programming language is sufficiently complete if there is a proof of every algorithmic property which is semantically valid. Hence the completeness of an axiomatic system with respect to a given class of semantics is a natural criterion to accept it as a proper definition of semantics. By the completeness we understand the coincidence of syntactical (axiomatically defined) and semantical operations of consequence [17]. The model existence theorem of metatheory of the logical system we have constructed ,assures us, that there exist an execution method which satisfies axioms . Hence the question of existence of an appropriate execution method is solved by the completeness property of our axiomatic system. As we can see the completeness theorem says even more : any formula valid in every data structure posseses a formal proof in the axiomatic system of AL [17]. However, it does not answer the question of the uniqueness of semantics. The natural question arises : are there different execution methods which satisfy axioms of AL? Can we treat an axiomatic system S for a logic of programs as a criterion of correctness of implementations ? The criterion accepts an automatic implementation of a programming language iff all axioms of the system S are valid and all inference rules are sound in this implementation . An implementation will be rejected if it does not satisfy the conditions quoted above .

We are convinced that the problem of axiomatic definition of a programming language should be studied in the way which enables separation of the specification of the semantics of program connectives from the specification of data structure upon which the programming language is based.

R e m a r k . In other places [3,14,15,23,24] we have proved that many important data structures can be given complete and categorical specification in the form of a set of algorithmic axioms. These works made use of completeness theorem and of standard semantics of program connectives. In this way we were able to prove in numerous cases that a data structure in question can be described categorically (i.e. up to isomorphism) . □

In this way we approached the second view toward the question : what does it mean to define semantics axiomatically? The first approach is to supply definition of program connectives which is valid under all possible data structures taken as realizations. The second approach is to treat the language as a whole, do not separate axioms of data structures that are used in the language of programs from the others which express properties of program connectives. This approach is presented in numerous papers [cf.2,5,11] . The first paper in which a result of relative completeness has been proved was of L. Banachowski [2] for the deterministic while programs. Independently the similar result has been found by S.Cook [5] for programs with procedures. Both papers bring results about language of partial correctness. In the work of D.Harel [11] we can find an axiomatic system in which every algorithmic property of a program can be expressed and studied. The assumption is made that the universe of semantics must be an extension of arithmetic.

We should also mention papers in which authors assume that an axiomatic system defines semantics if for every pair of inequivalent programs K and M there exists a proof of their inequivalence. In this papers an execution method is assumed and fixed. The results of this type are interesting,however we can not treat them as a contribution to our question.

From the works of hungarian colleagues (Andreka,Nemeti, Csirmaz et al.) we learned that the axiomatization of partial correctness known as Floyd-Hoare logic is complete with regard to standard as well as nonstandard computations. It means that F-H logic can not exclude nonstandard computations (runs) of programs. In order to do so we have to exclude the cases in which the set of formulas

$$\{(\text{if } \alpha \text{ then } K \text{ fi})^i \alpha\}_{i\in\omega} \cup \{(\text{while } \alpha \text{ do } K) \text{ true}\}$$

is consistent. A formula of the form $(\text{if } \alpha \text{ then } K \text{ fi})^n \alpha$ asserts that a computation of (while α do K) has at least n iterations of K, when the last formula (while α do K) true asserts that the computation has a result. The only way in which we can assure inconsistency of this set of formulas is by admitting the inference rule

$$\frac{\{(\text{if } \alpha \text{ then } K \text{ fi})^{i}(\neg\alpha \wedge \beta) \Rightarrow \gamma\}_{i \in \omega}}{(\text{while } \alpha \text{ do } K)\,\beta \Rightarrow \gamma}$$

In the section 2 we are proving that the system with ω-rule excludes nonstandard runs. In the section 3 we provide an argument showing that in in absence of ω-rule one can invent an execution method which satisfies all axioms of AL and the induction scheme and simultaneously it accepts nonstandard runs.

§2. THE STANDARD EXECUTION METHOD IS DEFINED IMPLICITLY BY THE AXIOMATIZATION OF ALGORITHMIC LOGIC

We shall prove the sentence stated above. First, we need some definitions in order to give a precise wording of this sentence. We shall assume a notion of configuration(also called state) of computation and all further considerations will use the notion of binary relation of immediate successing of states. The latter shall be also named the execution method. Most of the definitions that follow are known [2.5,17,19] Hence certain longer definitions will not be repeated here in full.

An algorithmic language is determined by its alphabet and the grammar which is the same for the whole class of algorithmic languages. One language of the class can differ from another by the set of functional and relational symbols when program connectives are the same. Here we shall work with deterministic while ... programs [17]. We assume the reader needs not definitions of terms, formulas and programs [17].

Given a language L we shall say that the mapping R is its realization in a nonempty set domain J if Rassociates with every functional symbol of L an operation $\varphi_R : J^n \rightarrow J$ of corresponding arity, and similarly, for every relational symbol ς of L,R associates with it a characteristic function of a relation of the same arity as

$$\varsigma_R : J^m \rightarrow \{0,1\}$$

By a valuation we shall mean a mapping $v: V \rightarrow J$ from the set of variables into the domain J [cf. 17].

DEF. 1. Any ordered pair of the form $(v, I_1; \ldots ;I_n)$

where v is a valuation of variables and $I_1, \ldots, I_n$ is afinite list of programs will be called a configuration (or a state).

DEF.2. A binary relation $\mapsto$ in the set of configurations will be called an execution method (also a relation of immediate successing) provided that every configuration $(v,\emptyset)$ with the empty list of programs has no successor.

EXAMPLE

The relation $\mapsto$ is called a standard execucion method if it satisfies the following conditions:

$(v, x:=\tau ; \hat{R}) \longmapsto (v', \hat{R})$ where $v'(z) = v(z)$ for $z \neq x$, $v'(x) = \tau(v)$, value of τ at v

$\hat{R}$ stands for the remainder of the list of programs

$(v,$ begin K ; M end ; $\hat{R}) \longmapsto (v,$ K ; M; $\hat{R})$

$(v,$ if γ then K else M ;$\hat{R}) \longmapsto (v,$ K;$\hat{R})$ if $\alpha(v) =$ true

$(v,$ if γ then K else M ;$\hat{R}) \longmapsto (v,$ M;$\hat{R})$ if $\alpha(v) =$ false

$(v,$ while γ do K;$\hat{R}) \longmapsto (v,$ K;while γ do K;$\hat{R})$ if $\alpha(v) =$ true

$(v,$ while γ do K;$\hat{R}) \longmapsto (v, \hat{R})$ if $\alpha(v) =$ false

DEF.3. By computation of a program K at a given valuation v we shall mean a maximal chain of configurations such that its minimal element is (v,K) and any two consecutive elements are in the relation of immediate successing.

DEF.4. Let o be a computation. The result of o is defined if o is ordered by $\longmapsto$ in a nonlimit ordinal and the last configuration of o is of the form $(v', \emptyset)$. The valuation v′ is then called the result of computation o.

DEF.5. A computation o is called standard iff it is finite or of type ω , otherwise we shall call it a nonstandard one.

DEF.6. We define the value of a formula of the form $K\alpha$ in a realization R and an execution method m at a valuation v in the following manner:

$$(K\alpha)_{R,m}(v) = \begin{cases} \alpha_R(v') & \text{if the computation starting with } (v,K) \text{ has a result } v' \\ \text{false} & \text{in the opposite case} \end{cases}$$

For the formulas of remaining forms the method of evaluation of their logical values is as usual [17].

DEF.7. By the algorithmic logic of deterministic while programs we shall mean here the system consisting of axioms and inference rules.

Schemes of axioms by an axiom we shall mean any formula of one of the following schemes

A1. All schemes of propositional tautologies.

A2. $(x := \tau)\alpha \Leftrightarrow \alpha(x/\tau)$

A3. $K(\alpha \wedge \beta) \Leftrightarrow K\alpha \wedge K\beta$

A4. $K(\alpha \vee \beta) \Leftrightarrow K\alpha \vee K\beta$

A5. $K \neg \alpha \Rightarrow \neg K\alpha$

A6. $K\ \mathrm{true} \Rightarrow (\neg K\alpha \Rightarrow K\neg\alpha)$

A7. $(\mathrm{begin}\ K\ ;\ M\ \mathrm{end})\alpha \Leftrightarrow KM\alpha$

A8. $(\mathrm{if}\ \gamma\ \mathrm{then}\ K\ \mathrm{else}\ M\ \mathrm{fi})\alpha \Leftrightarrow (\gamma \wedge K\alpha) \vee (\neg\gamma \wedge M\alpha)$

A9. $(\mathrm{while}\ \gamma\ \mathrm{do}\ K)\alpha = (\mathrm{if}\ \gamma\ \mathrm{then\ begin}\ K\ ;\ \mathrm{while}\ \gamma\ \mathrm{do}\ K\ \mathrm{end}\ \mathrm{fi})\alpha$

Inference rules

$$\mathrm{MP}\quad \frac{\alpha,\ (\alpha \Rightarrow \beta)}{\beta} \qquad\qquad \mathrm{N}\quad \frac{\alpha \Rightarrow \beta}{K\alpha \Rightarrow K\beta}$$

$$\frac{\{(\mathrm{if}\ \gamma\ \mathrm{then}\ K\ \mathrm{fi})^{i}(\neg\gamma \wedge \alpha) \Rightarrow \beta\}_{i \in \omega}}{(\mathrm{while}\ \gamma\ \mathrm{do}\ K)\ \alpha \Rightarrow \beta}$$

In the schemes and rules above α, β denote any formulas of algorithmic language, γ denotes a quantifier free formula, K,M denote programs x - a variable and τ - aterm.

DEF.8. An execution method is proper for a logic LOG iff for every realization R every axiom α of LOG is valid in R and m and every inference rule of LOG is sound in R and m.

In order to facilitate the proof of the following statement we are assuming that the algorithmic language L contains enough individual constants to name every element of the domain J.

THEOREM 1. Every execution method m proper for algorithmic logic AL is "similar" to the standard execution method $\mapsto$ in this sense that for every program K and for every realization R both methods define the same input-output relation between data and results of the program K.

LEMMA 2. With the assumptions of theorem 1 the execution method m is a deterministic one.

P R O O F of the lemma follows from the fact that the execution method satisfies all axioms of the form A3, A4. □

P r o o f of the theorem 1 is by induction on the length of program. For atomic programs of the form $x := \tau$ we observe the following facts

f1/ every computation beginning with $(v, x := \tau)$ has a result since

$$(x := \tau)\ \text{true} \Leftrightarrow \text{true}$$

Let v′ denotes this result.

f2/ Let v″ denotes the result of the standard computation with the same starting configuration (v,K) . Let c denotes the value $\tau_R(v)$ of the term τ at the valuation v. Since

$$(x := \tau)\ (x = c) \Leftrightarrow (\tau = c)$$

then both valuations v′ and v″ are equal at x, similarly we prove that $v'(z) = v''(z)$ for all $z \neq x$.

The cases of programs of the forms

begin K ; M end and if γ then K else M fi

are easy to treat with the help of axioms A7 and A8 of DEF.7.

For every program of the form

while γ do K

we wish to prove that if a computation of the program in the standard execution method is finite then it is also finite in the method m. This can be easily proved since it means that there exists a finite iteration of the simpler program if γ then K fi such that after say n, iterations we reach a state falsfying γ . By the inductive assumption the same phenomenon can be observed in the second computation. It is not difficult to argue that the results of both computations are equal. Suppose that the standard computation is infinite, can it be the case that the second computation has a result? The answer is no, since the ω-rule excludes the possibility that all iterations of if γ then K fi bring about γ and simultaneously

(while γ do K) true

holds.

§3. PSEUDOALGORITHMIC LOGIC ACCEPTS EXECUTION METHODS WITH NONSTANDARD RUNS OF PROGRAMS

DEF.8. By pseudoalgorithmic logic pAL we shall mean the axiomatic system resulting from AL by deleting the ω-rule and admitting the scheme of induction. Below we shall write the scheme using iteration quantifiers [17] because of its simplicity.

$$\{\alpha \wedge \bigcap K(\alpha \Rightarrow K\alpha)\} \Rightarrow \bigcap K\alpha$$

We have to remark that a form withot iteration quantifiers exists too, however it is of much more obscure form. Trying to translate it we obtain an expression

(while α do K)true $\Rightarrow \neg\alpha \vee$(while($\alpha \Rightarrow K\alpha$) do K)true

which is not a formula of algorithmic logic, however its semantical content can be expressed by the following formula where K′ and α' arise from K and α by simultaneous replacement of all variables by their primed counterparts, by s we denote the program

begin x := x′; y:= y′; ... end

and by s′ we denote its inverse; with these denotations we can express the scheme of induction as the following formula

```
(begin
     b1:= α ; s ; K′; b2:= α ; b:= b1 = b2: s ′;
     while b do
          begin b1:= α ; K; b2:= α ; b:= b1 ⇒b2 end
  end)true
  ∨¬α ∨ ¬(while α do K ) true .
```

From this example we shall learn whether it would be not useful to modify the algorithmic language in order to admit tests beeing the boolean combinations of quantifier free formulas as well as formulas of the form Kα . As an open question we leave the hypothesis that the above ugly formula is equivalent to the axiom A9 of DEF 7.

THEOREM 3 There exist an execution method proper for pseudoalgorithmic logic pAL which accepts nonstandard runs of programs.

Sketch of the proof. Consider the following set of formulas

$$(*)\{((x:=0;(\text{if}\neg\ x=e+1 \text{ then } x:=s(x) \text{ fi})^{i})\ \neg\ x=e+1)\}_{i\in\omega}$$

$$\cup\{(x:=0\ ;\text{while}\neg\ x=e+1 \text{ do } x:=s(x))\text{true}\}.$$

It is well known [10] that there exists a nonstandard model of Peano arithmetic which satisfies besides axioms of Peano also the formualas

$\neg(\underline{0} = e+1)$, $\neg(\underline{1} = e+1)$,..., $\neg(\underline{n} = e+1)$, ...

One can verify that any such a model will satisfy all axioms of pAL and the set (*) of formulas. □

FINAL REMARKS

We proposed here a view that one can treat an axiomatic system ofa logic of programs as an criterion deciding about appropriateness of an execution method semantics . We have proved that algorithmic lOgic implicitly defines the standard execution method. In this way we strengthened the previously proved completeness theorem about AL [17]. From the results of preceding section follows that relative or aritmetical completeness results about a logic of programs can not be treated as a proof of the unique definability of a semantics (execution method) by the axiomatic system in question.

In a separated paper we shall prove that NAL - algorithmic logic with nondeterministic programs [19] and also the algorithmic logic with recursive procedures [20] can be treated as implicit definitions of semantics.

The similar questions can be stated for PDL [13,21] and PAL [18], it is our hope that the analogous statemants can be formulated and proved for propositional logics of programs.

It is also interesting to study similar questions for the case of formal computations in which states are defined in a different way and computations are proof- like [25].

REFERENCES

[1] Andreka H.. Nemeti.I.. Completeness of Floyd logic, Bulletin of section of logic vol.7 (1978)

[2] Banachowski,L., Modular approach to the logical theory of programs Proc. MFCS'74 Symp. A.Blikle ed. Lecture Notes Comp. Sci. 28

[3] Bartol,W..M., On configurations of objects in LOGLAN computations Institute of Informatics, University of Warsaw, manuscript, 1980

[4] Blikle,A.. A survey of input-output semantics and program verification, ICS PAS Reports 344, Warsaw 1979

[5] Cook, S.A., Soundness and completeness of an axiom system for program verification, SIAM Journal on Computing, 7(1978) no 1

[6] Csirmaz, L., Programs and program verifications in a general setting, Preprint 4 of the Mathematical Institute of the Hungarian Academy of Sciences, Budapest 1980

[7] Dijkstra, E.W., A discipline of programming, Prentice Hall, 1976

[8] Floyd, R.W.. Assigning meaning to programs in Mathematical ASpects of Computer Science Proc. of Symp. in Applied Mathematics .AMS Providence, Rhode Island 1967

[9] Greif,I., Meyer,A.R., Specifying the semantics of while programs, M.I.T. Lab. for Comp. Sci. TM-130, MIT,Cambridge ,Mass. April 79

[10] Grzegorczyk, A., An outline of mathematical logic, Polish Scientific Publishers and North- Holland, Warsaw,1977

[11] Harel,D., First-Order dynamic logic in Lecture notes Comp. Sci. vol.68, Springer Vlg, 1979, Berlin

[12] Hoare, C.A., Wirth,N., An axiomatic definition of the programming language PASCAL, Acta Informatica 2(1973)335-355

[13] Kozen, D., On the duality between dynamic algebras and Kripke models, IBM research report RC 7893, Oct. 1979

[14] Kreczmar, A., Programmability in fields, Fundamenta Informaticae 1(1977)195-230

[15] Oktaba,H., On algorithmic theory of reference, Institite of Informatics, University of Warsaw, manuscript, 1980

[16] Meyer,A.R., Halpern,J.Y., Axiomatic definitions of programming languages, A theoretical assessment, Proc. 7-th POPL Symp. Las Vegas 1980 203-212

[17] Mirkowska,G., Algorithmic logic and its appliactions in programs Fundamenta Informaticae 1(1977)1-17, 147-165

[18] Mirkowska,G., Complete axiomatization of algorithmic properties of program schemes with bounded nondeterministic interpretations. Proc 12-th STOC symp. Los Angeles, April 1980,21-32

[19] Mirkowska,G., Model existence theorem for algorithmic logic of nondeterministic programs, 1978, to appear in Fundamenta Inform.

[20] Mirkowska,G., Salwicki,A., A complete axiomatic characterization of algorithmic properties of block-structured programs with procedures in Proc. MFCS'76 A.Mazurkiewicz ed. Lecture Notes Comp. Sci. vol.45 pp602-603, Springer Vlg.1976, Berlin

[21] Reiterman,J., Trnkova, V., Dynamic algebras which are not Kripke structures, this volume

[22] Salwicki,A., On the predicate calculi with iteration quantifiers, Bull. Pol. Acad. Sci. Ser. Math. 18(1970)278-282

[23] Salwicki,A., On algorithmic theory of stacks, in Proc MFCS'78 Zakopane J.Winkowski ed. Lecture Notes Comp. Scie. vol 64, Springer 1978 Berlin

[24] Salwicki, A., On algorithmic theory of dictionaries, to appear in Proc. Alg. Logic Seminar, Zürich 1979 E.Engeler ed. Lecture Notes Comp. Sci.

[25] Salwicki,A., Programmability and recursiveness, to appear

A LOGICAL APPROACH TO THE PROBLEM "P=NP?"

V.Yu.Sazonov

Institute of Mathematics, 630090, Novosibirsk, USSR

INTRODUCTION. A possible approach to the problem "P=NP?" or to the problem of exponential lower time complexity bound for NP-complete sets or, more generally and informally, to the so called enumeration problem [1, 8] *) consists in the analysis of those logical means and principles that the problem depends on. This may be 1) a technical analysis of logical and mathematical means and 2) an analysis of mathematical abstractions connected with the problem.

The first attempt of such a technical logical analysis concerned with "P=NP?" was undertaken by J.Hartmanis and J.E.Hopcroft [6]. They proved that in any sufficiently strong axiomatic system Ax some version $(P=NP)_{Ax}$ of P=NP is independent of Ax. Note that the original assertion P=NP may also be written down in the language Ax, and in the formulation of $(P=NP)_{Ax}$ the provability predicate Prf_{Ax} is used in some way. From an external point of view both assertions are equivalent, and if this equivalence were provable in Ax, then we should have the independence of P=NP itself in the ordinary sense. However, this, obviously, cannot be made for all Ax. There is also no hope to prove such equivalence for some fixed Ax. So, independence of the original problem is not proved.

The Main Result of this paper states, for some natural theory T, unprovability of the assertion on exponential lower time complexity bound of accepting NP-sets (Theorems 1.1, 1.3; the result announced in [13]). But, as opposed to [6] a direct formulation of the problem is used. Since the theory T is rather weak, this result may only be considered as a partial solution of the problem in terms of axiomatic independence. However, the difficulty of proving the Main Result (§5; compare with 3.8, 3.9 and §6) says that T is strong enough.

---

*) Unfortunately, the author knows no short, adequate and non-occupied English term for such an important and rather informal problem. It is written in Russian as "проблема перебора". Other English equivalents may be "exhaustive searching problem" or "trial problem". Note that a broader (and earlier) understanding of this problem also arises from [3,16,18]. In this paper the term "enumeration problem" will be appropriately specified.

Questions of technical logical analysis concerned with the complexity theory have also been considered recently by R.J.Lipton, R.A. De Millo, M.O'Donnell [9 - 11]. Besides other facts they obtained only conditional independence results for the enumeration problem.

As to the analysis of abstractions, it seems very important that some specific kind of mathematical abstraction is really and essentially connected with the enumeration problem (and with the computer practice too). § 7 is devoted to this question. There, in particular, the enumeration problem is stated as the problem of "constructive" understanding the sense of bounded quantifiers on finite binary strings. Such an approach to this problem is basic for all this work.

More generally, the main idea of this paper consists in replacing complexity restrictions by logical ones. Note that first steps in this direction were taken evidently by J.H.Bennett (see [5]), N.D.Jones, A.L.Selman and R.Fagin [5,7]. They reformulated polynomial time computability in logical terms. And we do this too (see 7.2). The main novelty of our approach is in attracting appropriate deductive apparatus (theories T, BA, UBA) and finitary mathematical considerations (§ 7).

For the lack of space, many proofs are omitted.

I wish to express gratitude to prof. B.A.Trakhtenbrot, M.K.Valiev, M.I.Dekhtjar' and N.V.Beljakin for discussion and valuable remarks.

§1. THEORIES T AND BA.

Let $p_1, p_2, \ldots$ be all polynomial time computable functions and predicates (or shortly P-functions and P-predicates) on the set $\{0,1\}^*$ of finite binary strings. For example:

$x = y$ - equality of binary strings;

Λ - the empty string constant;

$\sigma_0(x)$, $\sigma_1(x)$ - functions of concatenating zero and unit to x;

$Un(x)$ - x is unary string;

$|x|$, $|x|^2$ - the length and the square of the length of the string x;

Note, that here unary strings play the role of natural numbers. So, $\forall x(Un(|x|) \& Un(|x|^2))$ is true. The ordinary binary coding of natural numbers (by the function $B(i)$ below) is nonadequate for this paper because of exponential complexity of decoding.

x', $x<y$ - lexicographical successor and order ($\Lambda < 0 < 1 < 00 < 01 \ldots$);

$B(i)$ - the $|i|$-th binary string in the lexicographical ordering;

$x \prec y$ - x is an initial part of y;

$\langle x,y \rangle$, $\langle\langle i,j \rangle\rangle$ - binary and unary codes of ordered pairs of binary and unary strings, respectively;

$x[y]$ - the value of the propositional formula x on the string y;

EXP(x,y) - the predicate $2^{|x|} < |y|$;

M(z,x,t), M_2(z,x,y,t) - functions denoting the results of computations of Turing mashine (T.M.) z with inputs x and x,y, respectively, within $\leqslant |t|$ steps, the result being Λ if z does not halt in $|t|$ steps.

Below we also introduce notations for other P-functions and predicates. But for their termal representation those given above are sufficient.

Let also $\mathbb{P}$ denote the model $(\{0,1\}^*, p_1, p_2, \ldots)$;

Δ - the set of all first-order formulas with bounded quantifiers $\forall x < a$, $\exists x < a$ only, x does not occur in P-term a. Δ-formulas, of course, may contain free variables ;

$T \rightleftharpoons \{A \in \Delta \mid \mathbb{P} \models A\}$;

$T_0 = \{A \in T \mid A$ contains no qantifiers$\}$.

Let us show by examples the expressive power of the language. So the predicate SAT(x) = $\exists y. x[y]$ represents the set of satisfiable propositional formulas. For any P-function q(x) we denote by $(P = NP)_q$ the sentence $\forall x\,(q(x) \leftrightarrow \mathrm{SAT}(x))$. By virtue of NP-completeness of SAT the proposition P = NP is true iff for some q $\mathbb{P} \models (P = NP)_q$. In this very sense the proposition P = NP is expressible in our language. The formula ACCEPT(z) $\rightleftharpoons \forall x(\exists t M(z,x,t) \neq \Lambda \leftrightarrow \mathrm{SAT}(x))$ means obviously, that T.M. z accepts SAT. The following proposition ELB asserts the existence of exponential lower time complexity bound for any algorithm accepting SAT :

ELB $\rightleftharpoons \forall z\{\mathrm{ACCEPT}(z) \rightarrow \forall x \exists y > x[\mathrm{SAT}(y) \,\&\, \forall t(M(z,y,t) \neq \Lambda \rightarrow \mathrm{EXP}(y,t))]\}$.

Now we can formulate the Main Result of the paper. Let EXP be $\forall x \exists y\, \mathrm{EXP}(x,y)$ and ACCEPT be $\exists z\, \mathrm{ACCEPT}(z)$, both being true in $\mathbb{P}$.

1.1. MAIN RESULT. T + ACCEPT $\nvdash$ EXP. (In particular, T $\nvdash$ EXP.)

Using the following easy

1.2. PROPOSITION. T_0 + ELB + ACCEPT $\vdash$ EXP (see Appendix)

we immediately obtain a weakened form of the Main Result :

1.3. THEOREM. T $\nvdash$ ELB, i.e. the lower exponential time complexity bound for accepting SAT is not provable in T.

Note that the Main Result may be trivially strengthened by replacing EXP e.g. by EXP' = $\forall x \exists y\,(2^{\sqrt{|x|}} < |y|)$ because $T_0 \vdash (\mathrm{EXP} \leftrightarrow \mathrm{EXP}')$ (see also 6.3).

As the proof method of the Main Result (§ 5) is rather finitary and is applied to suitable axiomatic fragments of T, we introduce here one such important fragment BA (Bounded Arithmetic). Fix its non-logical axioms (below a, b, c are arbitrary terms):

$a = b \,\&\, a = c \rightarrow b = c$, $a = a$, $\sigma_i a = \sigma_i b \rightarrow a = b$ $(i \in \{0,1\})$,

$$\sigma_0 a \neq \sigma_1 b,$$

$$|a| \begin{cases} |\Lambda| = \Lambda, \\ |\sigma_0 a| = |\sigma_1 a| = \sigma_1 |a|, \end{cases} \qquad a' \begin{cases} \Lambda' = 0, \\ (\sigma_1 a)' = \sigma_0(a'), \\ (\sigma_0 a)' = \sigma_1 a, \end{cases}$$

$$\dots$$

$$M(a,b,c) \quad \{ \quad \dots$$

Lex. Ind. $A(\Lambda) \ \& \ \forall x < a[A(x) \to A(x')] \to A(a) \quad (A \in \Delta\ ,\ x \notin a).$

It is clear that for giving functions and predicates enumerated at the begining of the paragraph it suffices to have a finite number of recursive descriptions containing P-functions and P-predicates only. We do not write out them completely as it would be rather cumbersome.

Thus, BA means <u>a sufficiently strong system containing a finite number of obvious quantifier-free axioms and also the lexicographical induction</u>. And a hope is connected with BA that all or most of "obvious" Δ-propositions are provable in BA (see § 7 where a finitary-mathematical content of the theory BA is discussed).

The schema of lexicographical induction may be proved to be equivalent in BA to the following two ones:

$$A(\Lambda) \ \& \ \forall x[A(x) \to A(x')] \to A(y) \qquad (A \in \Delta),$$

Lin. Ind. $\quad A(\Lambda) \ \& \ \forall x[A(x) \to A(\sigma_0 x) \ \& \ A(\sigma_1 x)] \to A(y) \quad (A \in \Delta).$

Note, that the last principle of <u>linear induction</u>, if taken <u>on quantifier-free</u> A, is easily provable in the quantifier-free theory T_0. Such a variant of induction is strong enough to prove the most of (if not all) "obvious" quantifier-free formulas. But this principle is probably weaker than that of lexicographical induction even on quantifier-free formulas. The reason consists essentially in the fact that we can not arrive at a good constructive (see 7.4) understanding of lexicographical induction as opposite to the linear one on quantifier-free formulas.

To obtain in § 5 the proof of the Main Result 1.1 and discuss in § 7 the finitary-mathematical content of the theory BA we need

1.4. THEOREM. Let Ax be a set of Δ-formulas closed under substitution of terms. Then any proof of a Δ-formula A from axioms Ax (in particular, from BA or T) may be reconstructed into a proof containing Δ-formulas only (Δ-<u>proof</u> $Ax \vdash A$ written also as $Ax \rhd A$).

PROOF is based on a suitable generalization of the Cut-elimination theorem for the Gentzen sequent calculus LK [17](see Appendix).

§2. OPTIMAL CODING OF BINARY STRINGS

In theories, in which feasibility of exponentiation is not provable (e.g. in T), binary strings can not be identified with unary ones by the usual coding B(i) (see § 1). This follows from

2.1. PROPOSITION. $T_0 \vdash (EXP \leftrightarrow \forall x \exists i\ (x = B(i)))$ □

Nevertheless, such economical coding is possible which is exponentialless in a definite sense (see §§ 3,5).

2.2. DEFINITION. P-function ξ_j^x of unary argument j ($\xi_j^x = \xi_{|j|}^x$) and of binary - x is called polynomially optimal sequence (p.o.s. $\xi_\Lambda^x, \xi_1^x, \xi_{11}^x, \xi_{111}^x, \ldots$) if for any sequence α_j^x computable (by a T.M.) in a time $t(j,x)$ there exists a P-function $p(j,x,t)$ with unary values and arguments j and t such that for any j,x

$$\alpha_j^x = \xi_{p(j,x,t(j,x))}^x.$$

If, in particular, α_j^x does not depend on x or j, then, respectively,

2.2.1. (a) $\alpha_j = \alpha_j^x = \xi_{p_1(j,t_1(j))}$, where $\xi_j = \xi_j^0$, or

(b) $\alpha^x = \alpha_j^x = \xi_{p_2(x,t_2(x))}^x$ hold for suitable p_1 and p_2.

If α_j^x is P-function, then we obtain respectively

2.2.2. $\alpha_j^x = \xi_{q(j,x)}^x$, $\alpha_j = \xi_{q_1(j)}$, $\alpha^x = \xi_{q_2(x)}^x$.

So, p.o.s. ξ_j^x gives the "quickest" up to polynomials, enumeration of binary strings. It catches up with any α_i^x, if the time $t_\alpha(i,x)$ is taken into account.

2.3. THEOREM. There exists p.o.s. ξ_j^x which may be chosen even injective (i.e. such that $T_0 \vdash |i| \neq |j| \rightarrow \xi_i^x \neq \xi_j^x$). Moreover, if α_j^x is a P-sequence (or a P-term), then equalities 2.2.2 are in T_0.

PROOF. Let us first define a sequence $\tilde{\xi}_n^x$ by $\tilde{\xi}_{\langle\langle i,j,t\rangle\rangle}^x \rightleftharpoons \tilde{\xi}(i,j,t,x) \rightleftharpoons M_2(B(i),j,x,t)$. Let $B(i_0)$ be a program for α_j^x with sutable unary i_0. Then, $\alpha_j^x = M_2(B(i_0),j,x,t(j,x)) = \tilde{\xi}(i_0,j,t(j,x),x) = \tilde{\xi}_{\langle\langle i_0,j,t(j,x)\rangle\rangle}^x = \tilde{\xi}_{\tilde{p}(j,t(j,x))}^x$ where $\tilde{p}(j,t) \rightleftharpoons \langle\langle i_0,j,t\rangle\rangle$ is P-function.The required injective sequence ξ_n^x may be trivially extracted as subsequence of $\tilde{\xi}_n^x$ so that $\tilde{\xi}_n^x = \xi_{q(n,x)}^x$ holds for some P-function q. Hence, $\alpha_j^x = \tilde{\xi}_{\tilde{p}(j,t(j,x))}^x = \xi_{q(\tilde{p}(j,t(j,x)),x)}^x$. If $t(j,x)$ is a polynomial of $|j|$ and $|x|$ then, these equalities are true in $\mathbb{P}$ and lie in T_0 □

2.4. PROPOSITION. $T_0 + EXP \vdash \forall x \exists i (x = \xi_i)$, $\mathbb{P} \models \forall x\, \exists i (x = \xi i)$.

PROOF follows from 2.1 and from optimality of ξ_i: $T_0 \vdash B(i) = \xi_{p(i)}$

So, feasibility of exponentiation implies a possibility of optimal coding ξ_i of <u>all</u> binary strings by unary ones. And, what is more interesting, from §§ 3,5 it follows that this possibility is also compatible with the assumption $\neg$EXP.

§ 3. DETERMINISTIC AND RANDOM FINITE STRINGS

In any theory where EXP is not provable the following abbreviations may be reasonably introduced (cf. 2.4).

3.1. DEFINITION. "x is deterministic string" $\rightleftharpoons$ $DET(x) \rightleftharpoons \exists i(x= \xi_i)$, $DET^z(x) \rightleftharpoons \exists i(x= \xi_i^z)$ (relativization), $DET \rightleftharpoons \forall x DET(x)$, $DET^z \rightleftharpoons \forall x DET^z(x)$, "x is random string" $\rightleftharpoons$ $RAND(x) \rightleftharpoons \neg DET(x)$.

This definition may be considered as a formalization of the informal notion of a <u>very complex</u> finite binary string by A.N.Kolmogorov. The following simple facts show that $DET^z(x)$ is very natural notion.

3.2. PROPOSITION. $T_0 \vdash Un(i) \,\&\, Un(j) \,\&\, M(B(i),j,z,t)=x \rightarrow DET^z(x)$ □

3.3. COROLLARY. $T_0 \vdash DET^z(z)$, $T_0 \vdash Un(j) \rightarrow DET(j)$ □

3.4. PROPOSITION. $T_0 \vdash DET^z(x) \,\&\, Un(i) \rightarrow DET^{\langle z,y\rangle}(p(i,x,y))$, where p is any term of i,x,y □

3.5. COROLLARY. $T_0 \vdash x \prec y \,\&\, DET^z(y) \rightarrow DET^z(x)$ □

3.6. REMARK. Corollary 3.5 fails if in its formulation $\prec$ is replaced by the lexicographical order $<$.

In § 4 we will show how the hypothesis DET is connected with the possibility of optimal accepting of SAT. We have alredy shown that DET follows from EXP (2.4). But the nonexponential case is more interesting. We will prove in § 5 "nonexponentialness" of the coding ξ_i:

3.7. THEOREM. $T + DET \nvdash EXP$.

But a weaker result may be alredy proved.

3.8. THEOREM. $T_0 + DET \nvdash EXP$.

PROOF. Let $\mathbb{M}$ be an arbitrary nonstandard (i.e. $\neq \mathbb{P}$) model of T_0, and let $n \in \mathbb{M}$ be a nonstandard unary string (i.e. $\mathbb{M} \models Un(n)$, $n > \Lambda$, $n > 1$, $n > 11, \ldots$). Consider the submodel $\mathbb{D}$ of $\mathbb{M}$ with the carrier $\{x \in \mathbb{M} \mid \mathbb{M} \models \exists i(Un(i) \,\&\, x = \xi_i \,\&\, i < |n|^k)$ for some $k = 0,1,2,\ldots\}$. As follows from 3.4, $\mathbb{D}$, indeed, is closed under operatios of the model $\mathbb{M}$. Obviously T_0, DET and $\forall y \neg EXP(n,y)$ hold in $\mathbb{D}$ □

3.9. REMARK. The model-theoretic proof given above also does for stronger variants of Theorem 3.8 such as $T_0 + DET \nvdash \forall x \exists y(|x|^{\log|x|} < |y|)$ and so on, but not for the case with 3.7 (we can not prove $\mathbb{D} \models T$; cf. 3.6). The latter case forces us to make use of §5 proof-theoretic methods.

The following theorem is also proved model-theoretically.

3.10. THEREM. The theories $T + \neg\exists z DET^z$ $(+\neg EXP)$ and $T_0 + \exists z(RAND(z) \,\&\, DET^z)$ $(+\neg EXP)$ are both consistent □

3.11. OPEN QUESTION. Whether $T + \exists z(RAND(z) \,\&\, DET^z)$ or, equivalently, $T + \neg DET + \exists z DET^z$ is consistent? (See also the end of 7.3)

§ 4. OPTIMAL ALGORITHM ACCEPTING SAT

We take p.o.s. ξ_i of § 2 as the main part of the optimal algorithm accepting SAT. Below we will make use of the symbol Pol for polynomials with natural coefficients.

4.1. Note first, that if for $x \in SAT$ we can deterministically compute in a time $t(x)$ a "correct guess", i.e. such a word $g(x)$ for which $\mathbb{P} \models x[g(x)]$, then by 2.2.1 (b) and 2.4 we find some "correct guess" (which may be $\neq g(x)$) also by means of enumeration ξ^x_Λ, ξ^x_1, $\xi^x_{11}, \ldots$ in the time $Pol(|x|, t(x))$ (or $Pol(t(x))$, if we consider $t(x) > |x|$). An analogous result was given earlier by L.A.Levin in [8], but without explicit indicating optimal algorithm and also without any definition of optimal coding.

Let us pass from search algorithms of "correct guess" to the ones accepting SAT. Fix any computable total function α^x_i. Let $\mathfrak{A}_\alpha$ denote the binary code of the algorithm, which, for any given propositional formula x, computes in turn its values on the strings α^x_Λ, α^x_1, $\alpha^x_{11}, \ldots$ and stops iff the true value $x[\alpha^x_i]$ is obtained.

Let $\mathfrak{A}$ and $\mathfrak{A}_0$ be $\mathfrak{A}_\alpha$ for $\alpha = \xi^x_i$ and ξ_i respectively. By 2.4 it obviously follows that $\mathbb{P} \models ACCEPT(\mathfrak{A})$ & $ACCEPT(\mathfrak{A}_0)$. Consider running times for just described algorithms: $\tau_\alpha(x)$, $\tau(x)$, $\tau_0(x)$. The following simple fact was drawn to the author's attention by R.Fiby (Bratislava).

4.2. PROPOSITION. If α^x_i does not depend on x and enumerates all binary strings (which is equivalent to acceptance SAT by $\mathfrak{A}_\alpha$), then a lower exponential bound for τ_α takes place:

$$\exists k \, \exists^\infty x \quad 2^{\sqrt[k]{|x|}} \leqslant \tau_\alpha(x).$$

in particular, it holds for $\tau_0(x)$ □

Optimality of ξ easily implies $\mathfrak{A}$ to be the "best" algorithm accepting SAT, if compared with algorithms $\mathfrak{A}_\alpha$:

4.3. PROPOSITION. $\tau(x) \leqslant Pol_\alpha(\tau_\alpha(x))$ □

And this result may be strengthened to absolute optimality of $\mathfrak{A}$:

4.4. THEOREM. If SAT is deterministically accepted (by a T.M.) in a time $t(|x|)$ (for $x \in SAT$), then SAT is accepted by $\mathfrak{A}$ in the time $\tau(x) \leqslant Pol(t(|x|))$ □

In spite of 4.2 we can say that the running time $\tau_0(x)$ of $\mathfrak{A}_0$ is in some sense less than the exponentiation:

4.5. THEOREM. $T + ACCEPT(\mathfrak{A}_0) \nvdash EXP$.

This follows from the Theorem 3.7 and from the obvious

4.6. PROPOSITION. $T_0 + DET \vdash ACCEPT(\mathfrak{A}_0)$ □

So, we conclude, that unprovability in T of the lower exponential time complexity bound for accepting SAT (or ELB; see 1.1-1.3) may be obtained from 3.7.

§ 5. PROOF OUTLINE OF THEOREM 3.7: T + DET $\nvdash$ EXP.

In this paragraph we consider terms and formulas solely from the first-order language L_ν which only contains finite number of nonlogical symbols for sufficiently many P-functions and P-predicates $p_1, \ldots, p_k, \Lambda, \sigma_0, \sigma_1, =, <$ (e.g. as for BA) and for new (non-P-) function ν inverse to the P-function ξ_i. We relativize the notions Δ and $\rhd$ (cf. 1.4) to L_ν with the following restriction (without which 5.1 fails): in Δ-formulas variables in the scope of any ν must be free. Let $\mathbb{P}_\nu$ be $(\mathbb{P}, \nu)$ and T_ν be $\{A \in L_\nu \mid A \in \Delta$ and $\mathbb{P}_\nu \models A\}$. Theorem 3.7 in question then follows from the next one becouse $T \subseteq T_\nu \vdash$ DET.

5.1. THEOREM. $T_\nu \nvdash$ EXP.

PROOF. The idea is simple. EXP implies deductive consistency of some subsets $\widetilde{Ax}$ of T_ν, T_ν being the union of these $\widetilde{Ax}$'s. So, $T_\nu \vdash$ EXP would give $\widetilde{Ax} \vdash \mathrm{Consis}_{\widetilde{Ax}}$ for some $\widetilde{Ax}$, which is impossible (Gödel theorem; see e.g. [17], §10). Note that such an idea requires to state a relation between proofs and truthness of the proved theorems. But we can do this for Δ-proofs (with the restriction above) only, which in fact turns out to be quite sufficient. This idea is realized in the formal proof outlined below.

5.2. LEMMA. The fuhction $a \mapsto \mathrm{value}(a)$ naturally defined on the set of all closed terms a (from L_ν) is elementary.

PROOF is based on polynomial optimality of ξ_i (see Appendix).

5.3. DEFINITIONS. Fix some natural encoding for Δ-proofs U (and for Δ-formulas A, being the trivial proofs) by closed terms in the signature $\{\Lambda, \sigma_0, \sigma_1\}$. The code of U (A) will be written as $\ulcorner U \urcorner$ ($\ulcorner A \urcorner$). P-decidable sets S of formulas will be identified with the corresponding open formulas S(w) of one free variable. Introduce several notions which are evidently expressible in L_ν by open formulas or terms (without ν):

1°. $\mathrm{Prf}_S(u,v) \rightleftharpoons$ "u is a Δ-proof $S \rhd v$", the formula S being suitably inserted in that for Prf_S;

2°. $\mathrm{PC}(w,v) \rightleftharpoons$ the formula w is a partial case of the formula v";

3°. $\mathrm{True}(u,x,t) \rightleftharpoons$ "the value of Δ-formula u on argument(s) x is true and this fact is verified within $\leqslant |t|$ steps by an appropriate T.M. $\mathfrak{M}(u,x)$ evaluating Δ-formulas";

4°. $\mathrm{Ref}_v(u,x,t) \rightleftharpoons \mathrm{Ref}(v,u,x,t) \rightleftharpoons$ "the result (if any) of the following computation within $\leqslant |t|$ steps by an appropriate T.M. $\mathfrak{N}(v,u,x)$:

BEGIN given Δ-proof u, compute truth value of its final formula with argument evaluation x;

IF this value is true THEN let RESULT be Λ ELSE seek Refutation to certain preceeding formulas of the proof u following the proof rules in u in the inverse direction up to some axiom w of u is refuted;

IF PC(w,v) THEN let RESULT be such an argument evaluation (obtained from the Refutation to w) for which the formula v is false ELSE let RESULT be Λ END";

5°. Halt(u,x,t) and $Halt_v(u,x,t)$ mean that T.M. $\mathcal{M}(u,x)$ and $\mathcal{M}(v, \mathcal{N}(v,u,x))$, respectively, halt in $\leq |t|$ steps.

5.4. LEMMA. There exists P-decidable set $Ax_o \subseteq T_\nu$ such that for any P-decidable S and any B in Δ the following five conditions there hold:

(1) $Ax_o \triangleright (B(x) \mathbin{\&} Halt(\ulcorner B \urcorner, x, t) \leftrightarrow True(\ulcorner B \urcorner, x, t))$ $(B \rightleftharpoons B(x))$;

(2) $Ax_o \triangleright (Halt_v(u,x,t) \rightarrow Halt(v, Ref_v(u,x,t), t))$;

(3) if D is proof $S \triangleright B$ then $Ax_o \triangleright Prf_S(\ulcorner D \urcorner, \ulcorner B \urcorner)$;

(4) $Ax_o + EXP \vdash \forall vux \exists t(Halt_v(u,x,t) \mathbin{\&} Halt(u,x,t))$;

(5) given $B \rightleftharpoons B(\bar{x},y)$ such $E \rightleftharpoons E_B(\bar{x})$ in Δ may be constructed that
$$Ax_o \triangleright (E(\bar{x}) \leftrightarrow B(\bar{x}, \ulcorner E \urcorner)).$$

PROOF. Conditions (1) - (3) are rather trivial. (4) actually follows for sufficiently strong Ax_o from 5.2. Here the above restriction on Δ is used. (5) is the well-known Gödel diagonal trick (see e.g. [17], §10) and uses several true axioms in T_o □

Let Ax be arbitrary P-decidable and closed under term substitutions extension of Ax_o such that $Ax \subseteq T_\nu$. (5) gives for some F and G

(6) $Ax_o \triangleright (F(x) \leftrightarrow \neg Prf_{\widetilde{Ax}}(x, \ulcorner F \urcorner))$ and

(7) $Ax_o \triangleright (G(\langle u,v,x,t \rangle) \leftrightarrow (Prf_{\widetilde{Ax}}(u,v) \mathbin{\&} Halt_{\ulcorner G \urcorner}(u,x,t) \mathbin{\&}$
$\mathbin{\&} True(\ulcorner G \urcorner, Ref_{\ulcorner G \urcorner}(u,x,t),t) \rightarrow True(v,x,t)))$,

where $\widetilde{Ax}(w) \rightleftharpoons Ax(w) \vee PC(w, \ulcorner G \urcorner)$. Let us prove also that:

(8) $\widetilde{Ax}$ is closed under term substitutions; (9) $\mathbb{P} \models G$ and $\widetilde{Ax} \subseteq T_\nu$;

(10) $\widetilde{Ax} \triangleright (Prf_{\widetilde{Ax}}(u,v) \mathbin{\&} Halt_{\ulcorner G \urcorner}(u,x,t) \rightarrow True(v,x,t))$;

(11) $\widetilde{Ax} \not\triangleright F$; (12) $\widetilde{Ax} + EXP \vdash F$.

So, (8) is trivial. (9) is directly verified from (7) and truthness of Ax ($\subseteq T_\nu$). (10) easily follows from (2), from (1), with G in place of B and $Ref_{\ulcorner G \urcorner}(u,x,t)$ in place of x, axiom G of $\widetilde{Ax}$ and (7). (11): Suppose, otherwise, $\widetilde{Ax} \triangleright F$. Then by (3) $Ax_o \triangleright Prf_{\widetilde{Ax}}(\ulcorner D \urcorner, \ulcorner F \urcorner)$. But by (6) and the assumption we obtain $\widetilde{Ax} \triangleright \neg Prf_{\widetilde{Ax}}(\ulcorner D \urcorner, \ulcorner F \urcorner)$ which give the contradiction with (9). (12): Let, on the contrary, $\neg F(x)$ holds for some x. Then, by (6), $Prf_{\widetilde{Ax}}(x, \ulcorner F \urcorner)$ holds, too. From EXP, (4) and (10) there follows $\exists t True(\ulcorner F \urcorner, x, t)$. But (1), with $B \rightleftharpoons F$, gives F(x). The obtained contradiction proves F □

To complete the proof of 5.1, suppose $T_\nu \vdash EXP$. Then (12) implies $\widetilde{Ax} \vdash F$ for some $\widetilde{Ax}$ described above. But 1.4 (true for our Δ) and (8) give $\widetilde{Ax} \triangleright F$ which contradicts (11). So, theorem 5.1 is proved □

§ 6. ON STRENGTHENING THE MAIN RESULT

In spite of our theory T being rather weak, according to generally accepted canons, the proof of the Main Result uses rather involved technique (Cut elimination, Gödel diagonal trick and the notion of optimal sequence). If we didn't achieve a deadlock here then further steps may probably require some considerable efforts.

Let us only indicate three possible directions of strengthening the Main Result $T \nvdash ELB$ (or $T + ACCEPT \nvdash EXP$, or $T + DET \nvdash EXP$):

6.1. Add new axioms (e.g. Collection principle $\forall x < a \exists y A \rightarrow \rightarrow \exists b \forall x < a \exists y < b A$ from 7.3 or $\neg DET$ as in 3.11) to the theory T.

6.2. Replace accepting SAT by its recognizing (at least for T_o).

6.3. Lower the exponential bound (say, up to $n^{\log n}$; cf. 3.9 and the remark to 1.3)

In the meantime our attempts to do this give no result. This may mean that the theory T is still strong enough for the axiomatic investigation of the enumeration problem.

However, we would like to have confidence in that we don't simply replace the enumeration problem by other difficult ones, but investigate the essence of the problem. What does this essence mean? The next paragraph outlines an approach to this question by considering the finitary nature of theory BA. (What the theory T presents itself is rather unclear from the finitary point of view.)

§ 7. FINITARY-MATHEMATICAL CONTENT OF THEORY BA

7.1. Mathematics is not thinkable without abstractions. So, the most important abstraction of constructive mathematics is that of potential feasibility. It consists in the possibility to distract ourselves from any finite bounds (more generally, it would be - from any bounds). However, we assert that there is an axiomatic theory, namely BA, rather rich in content, which may be intuitively interpreted without this abstraction. Some other kind of abstraction is used here, call it abstraction of bounded feasibility. Being a kind of potential feasibility negation */, this absraction consists in the possibility to carry reasonings and conceive constructions

---

*/ A negation of potential feasibility was considered earlier by A.S.Yessenin-Volpin [4] (ultraintuitionism). However, the connection of the present considerations (which also may be characterised as "ultra") with those of [4] is not clear. It would be more appropriate to compare our approach with that of S.Cook [2], just in connection with 7.3 below, and with that of R.Parikh [12].

> if they are (or may be) relativized to some parameter bounds (in our case - to finite bounds).

This formulation requires some detailed discussion both on informal and formal levels. Here we only outline such a discussion.

It is clear, that the point of view of "relativization to bounds" (or the abstraction of bounded feasibility) corresponds better to the real computer practice than abstractions of potential feasibility or actual infinity. We always deal with some bounds, e.g. in space (memory overfilling), in time, in resources and in many cases these bounds should be rather taken into consideration, and we must not distract ourselves from them. These bounds may be, of course, rather arbitrary. So, we consider them as parametric. (Note, that infinite bounds are often considered as fixed. E.g. such is the set of natural numbers.)

7.2. Consider first <u>what constructions and computations are relativized to (parametric) bounds</u>. The simplest example is a notion of "primitive recursive" functions f over a parametric finite segment $\omega_n = \{0,\dots,n\}$ ($\bar{x} \leqslant n \Rightarrow f(n;\bar{x}) \leqslant n$, $\bar{x} \rightleftharpoons x_1,\dots,x_k$, k is fixed for f). The definition of such recursive functions differs from the ordinary one in: 1) the basic successor function x + 1 is replaced by the successor function modulo n + 1 (so n + 1 = 0; one may also take n + 1 = n) and 2) the bound n is considered as an additional argument. In passing from primitive recursive descriptions to arbitrary recursive ones relativized to some total functions $g_j: \omega^{k_j} \to \omega$ (in the ordinary case) or $g_j: \omega_n^{k_j} \to \omega_n$ (in our case) we just obtain ordinary partial recursive functions $f(\bar{x},\bar{g})$ relative to $\bar{g}$ or just all polynomial time computablr functions of the kind $\bar{g} \longmapsto \lambda\bar{x}\leqslant n.f(n;\bar{x},\bar{g})$, respectively. But this very naturally leads to the following <u>analogue of Church's thesis</u>:

> the polynomial time computability proves to be just the computability uniformly relativized (or relativizable) to finite parametric bounds.

It seems to the author that an appropriate thesis is necessary for good understanding the real nature of the polynomial time computability (and of the enumeration problem, too). Note that the above representation of P-functions (obtained by the author in 1976 [14]) resembles the known B.A.Trakhtenbrot's representation of computations in finite models [15] and R.Fagin's spectral representation of NP-sets [5].

7.3. Let us pass to discussion of <u>reasonings relativized to bounds</u>. It is probably most natural to formalize them in the ordinary language of second-order arithmetic, but interpreted in the finite parametric domain $\{o, \ldots n\}$. So, quantifiers are taken both on elements and on many place predicates over the domain. Let us dwell on the axiom system UBA (Uniformly Bounded Arithmetic), consisting of several quantifier-free properties of o,n, =, +1, $<$ ($o \leqslant x \leqslant n$, $n+1=0$ and so on), extensionality axioms, induction and comprehension schemes (possibly with a restriction on using predicate quantifiers). There may be some doubts on what logic should be used in carrying out proofs in UBA. But even if in spite of these doubts the classical logic is chosen, it may be asserted that in a reasonable sense the proofs in UBA are uniformly relativized to finite bounds (o and n). Moreover, we advance the hypothesis that

> the system UBA, and the system BA together with it, adequately formalizes the intuitive notion of reasoning uniformly relativized to finite parametric bounds.

We may be convinced in the fact on the ground of the experience in working with the systems UBA and BA. Let us explain why these systems are intuitively equivalent. (It would be better to say that BA is "conservative extension" of UBA). Naturally, only bounded formulas are of our interest. In UBA they are bounded yet and may be easily represented by bounded BA-formulas. By 1.4 unbounded quantifiers in proofs from BA of Δ-formulas may be eliminated. Hence, we may confine ourselves to the provability notion $\triangleright$ from 1.4. Taking into account considerations of 7.2 (Fagin's or our representation result) we get intuitive equivalence of the notions "BA$\triangleright$" and "UBA$\vdash$" and hence, equivalence of BA and UBA. By the way, remember that naturally arising here provability notion $\triangleright$ plays an essential role in the proof of the Main Result. So, our informal considerations are, indeed, helpful. (Note that more general notion of reasonings relativized to bounds is possible. So, there is an essentially new "tautology" - the Collection principle:

$$\forall x \leqslant a \, \exists y \, A \longrightarrow \exists b \, \forall x \leqslant a \, \exists y \leqslant b \, A .$$

If every "truth" is relativized to a bound b, then "b-truthness" of the antecedent should naturally mean just "b-truthness" of $\forall x \leqslant a \, \exists y \leqslant b \, A$, so the consequent is also "b-true" together with the antecedent. A formalization of this idea in terms of Kripke truthness will be published elsewhere. The corresponding logical sequent calculus is also obtained for which an analogue of Harrop theorem holds:

$$\vdash \exists x A \implies \vdash \exists x < b \, A \quad \text{for some term } b.$$

This confirms the proofs in such a calculus are, indeed, relativized to bounds. Let Δ-Coll mean Collection principle with A bounded. Then the theorem also holds for T + Δ-Coll with classical logic (cf. [12] where a weaker result is stated). In particular, T + $+\Delta$-Coll $\nvdash$ EXP. Compare also this and

7.3.1. THEOREM. $T_0 + \Delta$-Coll + $\exists z DET^z \vdash$ EXP, T_0 + Coll $\vdash$ EXP

with 3.7, 3.10, 3.11 and 4.2 (7.3.1 having been obtained before 4.2)).

7.4. Intuitively, the enumeration problem is the problem of constructive (in a new sense) understanding of bounded quantifiers on binary strings (or on predicates over the domain $\{0,\ldots, n\}$. A direct interpretation of bounded quantifiers uses actual enumeration of binary strings, say, in lexicographical order. But we can imagine no uniform (on n) determenistic process of enumeration of all binary strings of the length n, so that this process, as finite discrete object, could be described, say, as a k-dimensional $n \times \ldots \times n$-matrix with k independent of n. I.e., we can not relativize such a process to the bound n. That is why bounded quantifiers on binary strings in BA (or in UBA) are used rather formally as opposite to bounded quantifiers on unary strings (see also the discussion on lexicographical and linear inductions in § 1). This leads to the question: what is an arbitrary binary string? (For example, it is rather unclear what is an arbitrary binary string of a thousand of signs). It is worth comparing it with analogous problem of an arbitrary set of natural numbers, i.e. essentially with the continuum problem.

In this paper we have stated that several different answers to the above question are consistent with the theory T+$\neg$EXP (see 3.7, 3.10) all being in terms of determinisity (or constructivity) of finite binary strings (see also the Open Question 3.11).

APPENDIX

PROOF OF THEOREM 1.2. Let x be arbitrary. Suppose ACCEPT(z_0) holds for some z_0. Then ELB implies SAT(y) and $\forall t(M(z_0,y,t) \neq \Lambda \rightarrow$ EXP(y,t)) for some $y > x$. SAT(y) and ACCEPT(z_0) give $M(z_0,y,t) \neq \Lambda$ and, therefore, EXP(y,t) for some t. Finally, EXP(x,t) is obtained from the evident fact $T_0 \vdash$ EXP(y,t) & $x < y \rightarrow$ EXP(x,t) (the only axiom of T_0 needed for this proof). As x is arbitrary, this proves $\forall x \exists t$EXP(x,t) □

PROOF OF LEMMA 5.2. Let $\tilde f$ denote the superposition $\lambda i.\nu(f(\xi_i))$ and $\tilde c$ denote $\nu(c)$ for any function f and any constant c. Polynomial optimality of ξ_i easily implies that $\tilde f$ is P-function, if f is. Also such is $\tilde \nu$ (which coincides with ν on unary arguments). Replace our term a by $\xi_{\tilde a}$, where $\tilde a$ is the result of replacing in a any symbol for function or constant f by that for $\tilde f$. Note that value(a) = = value($\xi_{\tilde a}$), becouse of the identity $\xi_{\nu(x)} = x$, and the process of evaluating non P-term a is contained in that of evaluating

P-term $\xi_{\tilde{a}}$. But for P-terms of sufficiently large length n (and a fixed finite signature) the time of this evaluation is $\leqslant n^{k^n}$ for some constant number k. So, the evaluating function in question is elementary □

1.4'. THEOREM. Let Ax be a set of sequents closed under term substitutions. Then Cuts by formulas, which do not belong to sequents of Ax, can be eliminated from any LK_{Ax}-proof □

REFERENCES

1. Cook, S.A., The Complexity of Theorem Proving Procedures, Conf.Record of 3rd ACM Symposium on Theory of Computing, 1971, 151-158.
2. Cook, S.A., Feasibly Constructive Proofs and the Propositional Calculus, 17th Ann.Symp. on Theory of Computing, Conf.Record, May 1975, 83-97.
3. Dekhtjar', M.I., On the impossibility to eliminate the complete enumeration under the computation of functions relatively to their graphs, Doklady Akad.Nauk SSSR, v. 189, 1969, 748-751 (in Russian).
4. Yesenin-Volpin, A.S., An analysis of potential feasibility, Logiceskije issledovanija, Akad.Nauk SSSR, Moscow, 1959, 218-262 (in Russian).
5. Fagin, R., Generalized First-Order Spectra and Polynomial Time Recognizable sets, Complexity of Computations, SIAM-AMS Proc., vol.7, 1974, 43-73.
6. Hartmanis, J., Hopcroft, J.E., Independence Result in Computer Science, ACM SIGACT News, 8 (1976), № 4, 3-24.
7. Jones, N.D., Selman, A.L., Turing Machines and the Spectra of First-Order Formulas with Equality, Proc. 4th ACM Symp. on Theory of Computing, 1972, 157-167.
8. Levin, L.A., Universal Enumeration Tasks, Problemy Peredaci Informacii, IX, 3, 1973, 115-116 (in Russian).
9. Lipton, R., Model Theoretic Aspects of Computational Complexity, Proc. of the 1978 FOCS Symposium, 193-200 (1978).
10. De Millo, R.A., Lipton, R.J., Some connections between mathematical Logic and Complexity Theory, Proc. of the 1979 STOC, 153-159 (1979).
11. O'Donnell, M., A Programming Language Theorem which is Independent of Peano Arithmetic, Proc. of the 1979 STOC, 176-188 (1979).
12. Parikh, K., Existence and Feasibility in Arithmetic, the Journal of Symbolic Logic, vol. 36, № 3, 1971, 494-508.
13. Sazonov, V.Yu., Theory in which lower exponential complexity bound for NP complete tasks is unprovable, 5th All-Union Conf.on math. logic, Institute of Mathem., Novosibirsk, 1979, p. 133 (in Russian).
14. Sazonov, V.Yu., Polynomial computability and recursivity in finite domains, to be published.
15. Trakhtenbrot, B.A., The impossibility of an algorithm for the decidability problem on finite classes, Doklady AN SSSR, 70, № 4(1950), 569-572 (in Russian).
16. Trakhtenbrot, B.A., The formalization of some notions in terms of the complexity of computations, P.Suppes et al., eds., Logic, Methodology and Philosophy of Sciences IV, North-Holl., 1973, 205-213 (in Russian).
17. Takeuti, G., Proof Theory, North-Holland, 1975.
18. Yablonsky, S.V., On the algorithmic difficulties of minimal schemes synthesis, Problemy Kybernetiki, 2, 1959, Moscow, 75-121 (in Russian).

Verifying Concurrent System Specifications in COSY

M.W. Shields and P.E. Lauer
Computing Laboratory
University of Newcastle upon Tyne

Abstract

In this paper we illustrate the use of the COSY formalism [LTS79] for specifying, analysing and verifying highly parallel and distributed systems. We shall do this through a non-trivial example, the concurrent resource release mechanism which forms the central part of a novel, non-computational, concurrent and distributed solution to the problem of allocating reusable resources from a limited pool among a large number of concurrent users, the so-called COSY banker [LTD80]. After a brief overview of the COSY approach, we formally define a behavioural semantics for COSY programs in terms of vectors of strings - the vector firing sequences - which generalise the well-known notion of firing sequence to permit the explicit representation of concurrency in an algebraic manner and which may be manipulated in the same manner as strings except in cases where strings are inappropriate for the modelling of concurrent behaviour. Behavioural properties may be formally defined in terms of vector firing sequences. In particular, an analysis of the vector firing sequences of a given program allows one to determine whether a system specified by the program possesses desirable properties, whether these be general such as absense of deadlock or starvation, or specific, that is relating to particular properties required of a particular mechanism. We shall mainly be concerned with the latter form of analysis in our investigation of the concurrent resource release mechanism. More precisely, we demonstrate: firstly, a full characterisation of the behaviours of the mechanism; secondly, the correctness of the mechanism with respect to its desired properties and a functional interpretation of the operations it involves and thirdly, as a consequence of these, its absense of partial system deadlock. Full references to the copious work on other aspects of the notation are given in a conclusion.

1. Introduction to COSY

The COSY approach leads us to regard a system as characterisable by the set of (notionally indivisible) operations (actions) it executes (performs) together with a collection of constraints which specify how executions of these operations are to be (partially) ordered. A COSY program R thus determines a set, which we call VFS(R), of objects, actually vectors of strings, representing the possible histories of executions of its operations which obey its constraints. The formal theory associated with the notation is concerned with understanding the relationships between a specification object R and the behaviours it defines, VFS(R). Section 4 illustrates this.

The nature of the constraints is as follows. A constraint will prescribe that the elements of some particular subset of the set of operations of the system execute sequentially, that is, no more than one at a time, and only in certain orders. Thus, a constraint defines a set of strings composed of operations belonging to its corresponding subset. It is well known how to represent the set of histories of operation executions of a finite nondeterministic system by means of a regular expression. Briefly, COSY incorporates such regular expressions, called path expressions [CH74]. A single constraint is thus expressed by using a single path expression P; P constrains the operations it mentions to execute in some sequence. The set of all such sequences is called the set of firing sequences of P and denoted FS(P) (see section 2).

We may now see how a system may be described by a collection of paths. The operations of the system are those mentioned in at least one path in the collection. Roughly, a partial order of executions of these operations will be a permitted behaviour of the system if its restriction to the operations of any constituent path of the collection is a total order corresponding to a firing sequence of that path.

To give the reader some idea of the approach, consider the following example;
P = P1P2, where

P1 = path a;b end   and   P2 = path a;c end.

Here, the outermost path and end indicate looping forever, while the semicolon denotes sequentialization. The operations of P are given by Ops(P) = {a,b,c}. Thus the sequences permitted by P1 are given by

FS(P1) = {ε, a, ab, aba, abab, ababa, ababab, abababa,...}

where ε denotes the null string. Similarly, we have

FS(P2) = {ε, a, ac, aca, acac, acaca, acacac, acacaca,...}.

Now, the behaviour "execution of a followed by the concurrent executions of b and c" is a behaviour of P, since its restriction to P1 is "execution of a followed by execution of b", or ab∈FS(P1), and its restriction to P2 is ac∈FS(P2). We remark, in view of what is to come later, that this behaviour may be completely represented by a vector composed of these restrictions, namely (ab, ac), which is in fact a member of VFS(P), the set of vector firing sequences of P.

The COSY notation also incorporates generators (replicators) for economically defining regular expressions of arbitrary size and structure in terms of regular expression schemata. We shall see examples of replicators in section 3. Paths together with replicators constitute a subset of the full notation, further details of which may be found in [LTS79, LSB79].

We conclude this section with some remarks on the approach we are taking. The notation was developed with a view to encouraging the programmer to break free from the over-centralizing and over-sequentializing tendencies of conventional programming notations and to arrive at specifications of more concurrent and distributed systems. Hence COSY does not contain such constructs as assignment statements, conditional statements, block structures, or any specific synchronization primitives, such as semaphores or monitors. This means, a programmer who knows how to write a centralized and sequential program which is a solution for some general problem will have to relearn how to program the solution from the standpoint of obtaining maximal concurrency and distribution of control. To a certain extent this means he has to unlearn certain programming skills and acquire a new set of programming skills before he will be able to program with the same proficiency as in the sequential case. Similar remarks also apply in the case of programming by means of guarded commands [D76] and CSP s [H78]. There is some evidence that such a relearning process is worth while, since it has led to a number of programs which express interesting highly concurrent and distributed systems in an economical and informative way [LTS79, LTD80].

2. Formal aspects of COSY: Syntax and Semantics

2.1 In this section we formally define the language of path expressions and give a semantics for this language by means of a mapping which associates with each path expression P a set VFS(P) consisting of vectors whose coordinates are strings made up of operation names belonging to P. The elements of VFS(P) are interpreted as modelling possible discrete, asynchronous behaviours of a system satisfying the constraints defined in P.

2.2 Individual (R*-) Paths

An individual or R*-path is a string derived from the non-terminal "path" by the following production rules

```
path      = path sequence end
sequence  = {orelement @; }+
orelement = {element @, }+
element   = operation/element*/(sequence)
```

where non-underlined lower case words denote non-terminal symbols; the words "path" and "end", the comma, the semicolon, the star and the right and left parentheses are terminal symbols. The expression {nonterminal @ &}$^+$ indicates expressions of the form "nonterminal" or "nonterminal&...&nonterminal", and "/" indicates alternative substrings. Finally, the non-terminal "operation" may be replaced by any suitable operation name, usually an ALGOL-like identifier.

With each R*-path P, we associate its set of operations, Ops(P), and its set of cycles, Cyc(P). In the definition of Cyc(P) that follows, "seq" (respectively "orel" "elem" "op"), denotes any string derivable from a non-terminal "sequence" (respectively "orelement" "element" and "operation").

$$\begin{aligned}
&Cyc(\underline{path}\ seq\ \underline{end}) = Cyc((seq)) = Cyc(seq)\\
&Cyc(orel_1;\ldots;orel_n) = Cyc\ (orel_1).\ \ldots\ .Cyc(orel_n)\\
&Cyc(elem_1,\ldots,elem_n) = Cyc\ (elem_1) \cup \ldots \cup Cyc\ (elem_n)\\
&Cyc(elem^*) = Cyc(elem)^*\\
&Cyc(op) = \{op\}.
\end{aligned}$$

Here "." denotes string concatenation (except where it is used as ellipses or full stop), where if X,Y are sets of strings $X.Y = \{x.y \mid x \in X \wedge y \in Y\}$. "*" has its usual meaning. To each R*-path P, we associate its set FS(P) of firing sequences.

$FS(P) = Pref\ (Cyc(P)^*)$, where for any set X of strings, $Pref(X) = \{x \mid x.y \in X, \text{ some } y\}$.

We allow x or y, in the above, to be the null string ε. Thus $X \subseteq Pref(X)$ and $\varepsilon \in Pref(X)$. Recall that FS(P) denotes the set of sequences of operation executions permitted by P.

2.3 General (GR*-) paths

A general, or GR*-path is a string of the form $P = P_1 \ldots P_n$, where P_i is an R*-path, for each i. In future, when we write "$P = P_1 \ldots P_n$ is a GR*-path", the P_i will be understood to be R*-paths.

With each GR*-path, $P = P_1 \ldots P_n$, we associate a set of operations, $Ops(P) = Ops\ (P_1) \cup \ldots \cup Ops(P_n)$, and a set VFS(P), its set of permitted histories. We now introduce and motivate the definition of VFS(P).

Suppose $P = P_1 \ldots P_n$ is a GR*-path. Let us consider a period of activity of a system S obeying the constraint P. Let us suppose that we have a set of string variables $x_1, \ldots, x_n$. Initially, all of them are null ($x_i = \varepsilon$, each i). Whenever some operation a executes, x_i is reset to $x_i.a$ if $a \in Ops(P_i)$; in other words, each x_i contains a record of these operations in $Ops(P_i)$ which have executed, written in order of execution. Note that this action on the x_i's is well defined, since:-

(1) If a and b execute concurrently, then the system contains no constraints relating to the order of execution of a and b, whence, a fortiori, there is no i such that $a,b \in Ops(P_i)$.

Let us consider S as having run for a while and then having halted. It will have generated strings $x_i \in Ops(P_i)^*$. What can we say about these x_i? Well first, from the desideratum that the order of executions of operations must obey the constraints of all R*-paths in question, we must have (2) $x_i \in FS(P_i)$ each i.

Next, consider what happens if we restart S; suppose it executes exactly one operation a, and then halts again. Writing x_i' for the new value of x_i, we see that

$$(3)\qquad x_i' = \begin{cases} x_i.a & \text{if } a \in Ops(P_i) \\ x_i & \text{otherwise.} \end{cases}$$

We can express the above observations more concisely by going to <u>vectors of strings</u>. To backtrack slightly, let us consider a family of sets $A_1, \ldots, A_n$ and the corresponding family of string sets $A_1^*, \ldots, A_n^*$. We may form the Cartesian product of the A_i^*, $\underline{A} = A_1^* \times \ldots \times A_n^* = \{(y_1, \ldots, y_n) \mid y_i \in A_i^*\}$ and define a concatenation operation on $\underline{A}$ by

$$(x_1, \ldots, x_n).(y_1, \ldots, y_n) = (x_1.y_1, \ldots, x_n.y_n).$$

In particular our strings x_i of (3) may be made into a vector $\underline{x} = (x_1, \ldots, x_n)$.

If we let $\underline{a}_P = (a_1, \ldots, a_n)$, where

$$a_i = \begin{cases} a & \text{if } a \in Ops(P_i) \\ \varepsilon & \text{otherwise,} \end{cases}$$

then we see that (3) may be expressed

(4) $\underline{x}' = \underline{x}.\underline{a}_P$.

Here, we may say that a has <u>executed</u> at $\underline{x}$ extending it to the history $\underline{x}'$.

Let us denote by VFS(P), the set of all vectors $(x_1,\dots,x_n)$ that might be produced by our system S. Let us denote by Vops(P), the set of vectors $\underline{a}_P$, $a \in$ Ops(P). We denote by Vops(P)* the closure of Vops(P) in $\mathrm{Ops}(P_1)^* \times \dots \times \mathrm{Ops}(P_n)^*$ with respect to vector concatenation. Note that Vops(P)* contains a null element $\underline{\varepsilon} = (\varepsilon,\dots,\varepsilon)$. Now we have

(5) $\underline{\varepsilon} \in \mathrm{VFS}(P) \cap \mathrm{Vops}(P)^* \cap (\mathrm{FS}(P_1) \times \dots \times \mathrm{FS}(P_n))$

(6) Suppose $\underline{x} \in \mathrm{VFS}(P) \cap \mathrm{Vops}(P)^* \cap (\mathrm{FS}(P_1) \times \dots \times \mathrm{FS}(P_n))$ and $a \in \mathrm{Ops}(P)$, then $\underline{x} \cdot \underline{a}_P \in \mathrm{VFS}(P) \Leftrightarrow \underline{x} \cdot \underline{a}_P \in \mathrm{Vops}(P)^* \cap (\mathrm{FS}(P_1) \times \dots \times \mathrm{FS}(P_n))$.

From (5) and (6), we conclude that

$$\mathrm{VFS}(P) = \mathrm{Vops}(P)^* \cap (\mathrm{FS}(P_1) \times \dots \times \mathrm{FS}(P_n)).$$

which shall serve as a formal definition for VFS(P).

Let us pause briefly and look at this object VFS(P). We know that we may write

$$\underline{x} = \underline{a}_1 \cdot \underline{a}_2 \cdot \dots \cdot \underline{a}_m \quad , \underline{a}_i \in \mathrm{Vops}(P).$$

In fact possibly $\underline{x}$ may possibly be written in several ways. Writing $[\underline{y}]_i$ for the ith coordinate of a vector $\underline{y}$, let us consider a situation in which

$$\forall i \in \{1,\dots,n\}: [\underline{a}_1]_i \neq \varepsilon \Rightarrow [\underline{a}_2]_i = \varepsilon.$$

In this case $\underline{a}_1 \cdot \underline{a}_2 = \underline{a}_2 \cdot \underline{a}_1$ and $\underline{x} = \underline{a}_2 \cdot \underline{a}_1 \cdot \dots \cdot \underline{a}_m$

A glance at the definition of the vector operations $\underline{a}_P$, shows that if $a \neq b$ then

$$\underline{a}_P \cdot \underline{b}_P = \underline{b}_P \cdot \underline{a}_P \Leftrightarrow \forall i \in \{1,\dots,n\}: a \in \mathrm{Ops}(P_i) \Rightarrow b \notin \mathrm{Ops}(P_i)$$

that is that no single path constrains the operations a and b to execute in any sequence. We conclude that the following interpretation may be made. Let $\underline{x} \in \mathrm{VFS}(P)$ and let $a,b \in \mathrm{Ops}(P)$ with $a \neq b$. Then $\underline{x} \cdot \underline{a}_P$, $\underline{x} \cdot \underline{b}_P \in \mathrm{VFS}(P)$ and $\underline{a}_P \cdot \underline{b}_P = \underline{b}_P \cdot \underline{a}_P$ may be interpreted as follows: in the system state determined by $\underline{x}$, the operations a and b may execute <u>concurrently</u>.

Thus the elements VFS(P) model concurrent (or asynchronous) behaviours of a system obeying precisely the constraint P.

Let us fix a GR*-path $P = P_1 \dots P_n$. We have already defined concatenation in Vops(P)*. It is clear that Vops(P)* is a monoid with identity $\underline{\varepsilon}$ with respect to concatenation. If $X,Y \subseteq \mathrm{Vops}(P)^*$, we define

$$X.Y = \{\underline{x}.\underline{y} \mid \underline{x} \in X \wedge \underline{y} \in Y\}.$$

and

$$X^0 = \{\varepsilon\}; \quad X^n = X.X^{n-1}; \quad X^* = X^0 \cup X^1 \cup X^2 \cup \dots .$$

We may also define a relation '≤' (vector prefix) on Vops(P)* by

$$\underline{x} \leq \underline{y} \Leftrightarrow \exists \underline{z} \in \mathrm{Vops}(P)^*: \underline{x}.\underline{z} = \underline{y}$$

(Vops(P)*,≤) is obviously a partially ordered set.

If $X \subseteq \mathrm{Vops}(P)^*$, then we define $\mathrm{Pref}(X) = \{\underline{x} \in \mathrm{Vops}(P)^* \mid \underline{x} \leq \underline{y}, \text{ some } \underline{y} \in X\}$.

We observe that Pref(VFS(P)) = VFS(P); the beginning of a behaviour is a behaviour.

Finally, we shall find it convenient to define, for $\underline{x} \in \mathrm{Vops}(P)^*$ and $a \in \mathrm{Ops}(P)$, the expression $I_a(\underline{x})$, which denotes the number of occurrences of $\underline{a}_P$ in $\underline{x}$. Formally, if $b \in \mathrm{Ops}(P)$ and $\underline{x},\underline{y} \in \mathrm{Vops}(P)^*$

$$I_a(\underline{x}.\underline{y}) = I_a(\underline{x}) + I_a(\underline{y})$$

$$I_a(\underline{b}_P) = \begin{cases} 1 & \text{if } a=b \\ 0 & \text{otherwise} \end{cases}$$

2.4 <u>Verification of path programs</u>

The semantic mapping P → VFS(P) now permits us to speak formally of dynamic properties of a system specified by a path expression; properties of its set of possible behaviours that is of VFS(P). We may speak here of two types of properties, which we might call <u>general</u> and <u>specific</u>.

General properties are those which, as the name suggests, apply in general to pairs (P,VFS(P)) as abstract objects, where, roughly, one is not considering P in relation to any specific interpretation. Among such properties are freedom from deadlock and adequacy.

P is <u>deadlock-free</u> if and only if $\forall \underline{x} \in$ VFS(P) $\exists a \in$ Ops(P): $\underline{x}.\underline{a}_P \in$ VFS(P)

P is <u>adequate</u> if and only if $\forall \underline{x} \in$ VFS(P) $\forall$ a$\in$Ops(P) $\exists \underline{y} \in$ Vops(P)*: $\underline{x}.\underline{y}.\underline{a}_P \in$ VFS(P).

Adequacy is a property akin to absence of partial systems deadlock. Results have been obtained to assist the analysis of a path expression to detect their presence or absence [SL78, S79].

Specific properties, on the other hand, are to do with a path expression or class of path expressions as a description of some actual or projected mechanism. Thus, in the example in the next section, the operations are intended to denote actions of a mechanism on a pool of resources. The problem of verifying such a program is specific in that it applies only to that class and its interpretation and to no other.

Verification thus involves establishing that VFS(P) obeys some predicate which formally expresses the designer's intentions.

3. A resource releasing mechanism

3.1 The problem

We consider the following situation. We have a pool of N (reusable) resources $R_1,\ldots,R_N$ (they could be pages or buffer frames or devices). We wish to describe/specify a mechanism which is such that

(a) free resources are made available in parallel
(b) resources which have been borrowed may be replaced in parallel
(c) (a) and (b) may proceed in parallel.

3.2 A solution

To each resource R_i are associated 3 operations; GET(i), signifying that R_i is secured by some user of the mechanism; SKIP(i), signifying that an available resource R_i has not been taken by any user of the mechanism and PUT(i), signifying that a borrowed R_i is replaced by a user of the mechanism.

After any period of activity of the mechanism (or to every vector firing sequence corresponding to such a period), the pool will be in any one of 2^N states, corresponding to the 2^N subsets of $\{R_1,\ldots,R_N\}$. If $C \subseteq \{R_1,\ldots,R_N\}$ then its corresponding states S(C) will be that in which the free resources are precisely those belonging to C.C will be called a configuration (of free resources). We will represent each state S(C) by an integer c = c(C), $0 \leq c \leq 2^N-1$ such that if bin(c) = $a_N \ldots a_1$ is its binary representation then $a_i = 1 \Leftrightarrow R_i \in C$. c thus represents the characteristic function of the set C. To each integer $0 \leq c \leq 2^N-1$ and integer $1 \leq r \leq N$ we define bit(c,r) to be the rth bit in its binary representation i.e.

bin(c) = bit(c,N)...bit(c,1).

Let C(c) = $\{R_i \mid$bit(c,i) = 1$\}$. Clearly c(C(c)) = c.

We now define operations CONF(c),PGETB(c), PGETE(c); CONF(c) signifying that a configuration of free frames C(c) has been detected; PGETB(c) signifying that the resources R_i belonging to C(c) are being made available and PGETE(c), signifying the end of a block of acquisitions in parallel of the resources in C(c).

The mechanism proceeds in cycles or blocks of activity; each cycle begins with a CONF test followed by the execution of the corresponding PGET, which releases the appropriate free resources, to be either taken (via GET operations) or ignored (SKIP). The cycle concludes with a corresponding PGETE.

Let us begin with the configuration test and parallel releases. We have

```
(3.1)   path (CONF(0);PGETB(0);PGETE(0)),
             (CONF(1);PGETB(1);PGETE(1)),
               .          .          .
             (CONF(2^N-1);PGETB(2^N-1);PGETE(2^N-1)) end
```

The comma entails exclusive choice between the cycles; configuration test - parallel release begin - parallel release end.

Next we look at the parallel GET, SKIP mechanism. The solution requires that GET(r) or SKIP(r) may only execute if the precedingly executed operation was a parallel release begin corresponding to a configuration c in which R_r is free, that is, such that bit(c,r) = 1. Further, the GET or SKIP must be immediately followed by the corresponding release end. The following path, one for each resource R_r, is intended to express this:

(3.2r) path PGETB(c_1),...,PGETB(c_m);GET(r),SKIP(r);
PGETE(c_1),...,PGETE(c_m) end
where $\{c_1,...,c_m\} = \{c \mid bit(c,r) = 1\}$.

Finally we add paths which express the manner in which configurations are modified by GETs and PUTs (SKIPs have no effect on configurations, of course). We sketch the idea behind the path. Suppose R_r is available, then until R_r is taken (i.e. before execution of GET(r)) the system should be able to make any number of configuration tests showing R_r to be available i.e.

(3.3r) ("configuration tests showing R_r available")*; GET(r)

or

(3.4r) (CONF(c_1),...,CONF(c_m))*;GET(r)
where the c_i are as in (3.2r).

Of course no further GET(r) should be executed until PUT(r) has been executed. Before the execution of a PUT(r), the system should be able to make any number of configuration tests showing R_r to be taken, or

(3.5r) (CONF(c_1'),...,CONF(c_n'))*;PUT(r)
where $\{c_1',...,c_n'\} = \{c \mid bit(c,r) = 0\}$.

Since GET's and PUT's should, of course, strictly alternate, and since initially all resources are available, our path for R_r may be obtained by sequentially combining 3.4r and 3.5r using a semicolon, as:

(3.6r) path (CONF(c_1),...,CONF(c_m))*;GET(r);
(CONF(c_1'),...,CONF(c_n'))*;PUT(r) end

The complete solution is obtained by combining the above paths

(3.1)(3.21)...(3.2N)(3.61)...(3.6N).

We shall give the program in a concise form using replicators in the next subsection.

3.3 Some replicator notation

As we remarked in section 1, the full COSY notation contains facilities for the economical representation of paths of arbitrary size and structure, the replicator. We have not the space to go into great detail here, but we shall introduce enough of the replicator notation to give a concise statement of the program constructed in the previous subsection. Further details may be found in [LTS79, LTD80].

First, we introduce the collectivisor. This is a statement declaring an array of subscripted operations. For example, the statement

array GET, PUT, SKIP (1: N);

declares 3N operations, GET(1), GET(2),...,GET(N),...,PUT(N),...,SKIP(N).

Next, we introduce one form of the replicator. Suppose we have declared a collectivisor, array A (j: k). Suppose we also have a predicate P_r defined on the integers. Define

$$\{i_1,...,i_m\} = \{i \in \{j,j+1,...,k\} \mid P_r(i)\}.$$

If "&" denotes one of the separators "," or ";", then the replicator expression

```
[A(i) @&   |i || Pr(i)|   ]
```

expands to $A(i_1)$ & $A(i_2)$ & ... & $A(i_m)$.

Thus, for (3.2r), we require a predicate F(c,r) for each resource R_r; F(c,r) is true if R_r is available in configuration c, or formally F(c,r) ≡ (bit(c,r) = 1). We also require a collectivisor <u>array</u> PGETB,PGETE(0: 2^N-1). Given this the path may be written

```
(3.7) path [PGETB(c)@,  |c || F(c,r)|  ];GET(r),SKIP(r);[PGETE(c)@,  |c || F(c,r)|  ] end.
```

The replicator is not used only for individual collective names. On the same principle, one can replicate whole subexpressions and even paths. For example (3.1) may be expressed:

```
    path [(CONF(c);PGETB(c);PGETE(c))@,  |c ||  true|   ] end
```

where <u>true</u> denotes the predicate that is identically true. In practice, we would not bother to write the predicate in such a case. Finally, as an example of a replicator applied to an entire path, consider

```
(3.8) [path [PGETB(c)@,   |c || F(c,r)|  ]; GET(r),SKIP(r) ;
            [PGETE(c)@,   |c || F(c,r)|  ] end   |r:1,N,1|  ]
```

which defines N paths in each of which r is replaced by an integer from 1 to N.

Hopefully, this somewhat informal exposition of the replicator notation is sufficient to make understandable the following version of the concurrent resource releasing mechanism:

```
      program
         array GET, PUT, SKIP (1: N);
         array CONF, PGETB, PGETE (0: 2^N -1);
         predicate F(c,r) ≡ (bit(c,r) = 1);
(3.9)    predicate U(c,r) ≡ (bit(c,r) = 0);
         path [(CONF(c);PGETB(c);PGETE(c))@, |c| ] end
         [path [PGETB(c)@,  |c || F(c,r)|  ];GET(r), SKIP(r);
               [PGETE(c)@,  |c || F(c,r)|  ]end  |r: 1,N,1|  ]
         [path ([CONF(c)@,  |c || F(c,r)|  ])*; GET(r);
               ([CONF(c)@,  |c || U(c,r)|  ])*; PUT(r) end  |r: 1,N,1|  ]
      end program
```

In the next section we shall characterise the behaviour and properties of this system.

4. <u>Analysis of the resource releasing program</u>

In constructing the program (3.9) we made certain statements in justification of the various constructions introduced. For example, we assumed, in building it, that the CONF test was actually meaningful as an indication of the instantaneous configuration of free resources. Making such assumptions is part of the business of writing programs. That one has made them does not guarantee their accuracy, however.

In this section we are going to sketch a formal proof that (3.9) does what it is supposed to do, and without deadlocking. We call (3.9) RRM(N). One of our tasks will be to characterise the possible behaviours of RRM(N), that is, the set VFS(RRM(N)). Proofs have been omitted from consideration of space. They may be found in [SL80].

To begin with, let us express RRM(N) as a concatenation of its individual paths RRM(N) = SEL(N)PG(1)...PG(N)RP(1)...RP(N) where we are using the mnemonic names SEL (select configuration), PG(i) (ith parallel get) and RP(i) (i^{th} resource pool path) for the corresponding paths in 3.9 written in that order.

We shall find it useful to write out the Cycle sets of these individual paths, which are as follows

$$Cyc(SEL(N)) = \{CONF(0).PGETB(0).PGETE(0),\ldots,CONF(2^N-1).PGETB(2^N-1).PGETE(2^N-1)\}$$

$$Cyc(PG(r)) = \{PGETB(c).GET(r).PGETE(c')\,|\,F(c,r)\wedge F(c',r)\}\cup \{PGETB(c).SKIP(r).PGETE(c')\,|\,F(c,r)\wedge F(c',r)\}$$

where F(c,r) is the predicate defined in (3.7).

$$Cyc(RP(r)) = \cup\{CONF(c)^*.GET(c).CONF(c')^*.PUT(c')\,|\,F(c,r)\wedge U(c',r)\}$$

In section 3, we explained that the system was intended to operate in a sequence of 'blocks' of activity, beginning with a configuration test CONF(c), for some c. We shall state this in our first lemma, in which we begin the characterisation of VFS(RRM(N)). We now define the blocks in question. First redefining C from section 3, if $c\in\{0,\ldots,2^N-1\}$, then $C(c) = \{r\in\{1,\ldots,N\}\,|\,F(c,r)\}$; C(c) indicates the set of resources in a given configuration c. Likewise we define E(c) to be the corresponding set of empty resources

$$E(c) = \{1,\ldots,N\} - C(c).$$

If RRM(N) is working properly, it should be the case that in configuration c, the only GET(i)'s and SKIP(i)'s that may execute must satisfy $i \in C(c)$ and the only PUT(i)'s that may execute must satisfy either $i \in E(c)$ or GET(i) must just have executed. A block should therefore be of the form

$$x(c,X,Y) = CONF(c).PGETB(c).y(c,X,Y).PGETE(c)$$

where y(c,X,Y) is of the form

$$GET(r_1).\ \ldots\ .GET(r_l).SKIP(r_{l+1}).\ \ldots\ .SKIP(r_m).PUT(r_{m+1}).\ \ldots\ .PUT(r_n)$$

where $\{r_1,\ldots,r_l\} = X \subseteq C(c)$, $\{r_{l+1},\ldots,r_m\} = C(c) - X$ and $\{r_{m+1},\ldots,r_n\} = Y \subseteq E(c)\cup X$

Here all operations denote their corresponding vectors; underlining and subscripts have been omitted for the sake of typographical convenience.

Finally, we let

$$Block\ (N) = \{x(c,X,Y)\,|\,0\le c\le 2^N-1 \wedge X\subseteq C(c) \wedge Y\subseteq E(c)\cup X\}$$

<u>Lemma 1</u>

$$VFS(RRM(N)) \subseteq Pref(Block(N)^*).$$

In order to continue and complete our characterisation, we shall find it convenient to draw attention to a special set of vector firing sequences of RRM(N), those consisting of a full set of blocks:

$$FB(N) = VFS(RRM(N)) \cap Block\ (N)^*.$$

Suppose $x\in VFS(RRM(N))-\{\varepsilon\}$, then $x=x'.CONF(c).y$, $x'\in FB(N)$ and $CONF(c).y\in Pref\ (Block(N))$. We may define sets $X = \{r\,|\,GET(r) \text{ is in } y\}$, $Y = \{r\,|\,PUT(r) \text{ is in } y\}$ and $Z = \{r\,|\,SKIP(r) \text{ is in } y\}$. It may be shown that $CONF(c).y \le x(c,X,Y)$. In fact, more than this is true.

<u>Lemma 2</u>

(1) With the above notation, for any set X', $X\subseteq X'\subseteq C(c) - Z$, and for any set Y', $Y\subseteq Y' \subseteq E(c)\cup X'$, we have $x\le x'.x(c,X',Y')\in FB(N)$ and in particular

(2) If $x.CONF(c)\in VFS(RRM(N))$, then $\forall X\subseteq C(c)\ \forall Y\subseteq E(c)\cup X$: $x.x(c,X,Y)\in FB(N)$ whence

(3) $VFS(RRM(N)) = Pref(FB(N))$.

We must now characterise FB(N). We know that its elements are of the form $x(c_1,X_1,Y_1).\ \ldots\ .x(c_l,X_l,Y_l)$, and we know how the X_i and Y_i are constrained by the c_i. Hopefully, c_{i+1} will be determined by the previous configuration c_i and what has been done to it (by X_i and Y_i). With this in mind, we define, for every x(c,X,Y) in Block (N):

Next(c,X,Y) = c', where $C(c') = (C(c) - X) \cup Y$.

Clearly Next(c,X,Y) $\in \{0,\ldots,2^N-1\}$.

Our next lemma shows the "feed back" effects of GET's and PUT's on configuration tests.

Lemma 3

Suppose x, x.x(c,X,Y) $\in$ FB(N). Let a $\in$ Vops(RRM(N)), then x.x(c,X,Y).a $\in$ VFS(RRM(N)) $\Leftrightarrow$ a = CONF(Next(c,X,Y)).

From lemmas 1, 2 and 3 and induction, we have finally:-

Proposition 1

(1) $x \in FB(N) \Rightarrow \exists l, c_1,\ldots,c_l, X_1,\ldots,X_l, Y_1,\ldots,Y_l$:

(a) $x = x(c_1,X_1,Y_1). \ldots .x(c_l,X_l,Y_l)$

(b) $\forall i \in \{1,\ldots,l\}: X_i \subseteq C(c_i) \wedge Y_i \subseteq E(c_i) \cup X_i$.

(c) $\forall i \in \{1,\ldots,l-1\}: c_{i+1} = Next(c_i,X_i,Y_i)$

(d) $c_1 = 2^N-1$.

(2) VFS(RRM(N)) = Pref(FB(N)).

Now that we have fully characterised the behaviour of RRM(N), we may ask ourselves whether it does what it's supposed to. We define a function $f: VFS(RRM(N)) \rightarrow \mathbb{Z}^N$, where f(x) will be designed to represent the content of the resource pool after x has happened: for $x \in$ VFS(RRM(N)) define $f(x) = g(x) + \underline{1}$ where $\underline{1} = (1,\ldots,1)$ and

$$[g(x)]_i = I_{PUT(i)}(x) - I_{GET(i)}(x), \; i \in \{1,\ldots,N\}.$$

Consideration of Cyc(RP(i)), $i \in \{1,\ldots,N\}$, shows that $[f(x)]_i \in \{0,1\}$ for each $x \in$ VFS(RRM(N)). Clearly $[f(x)]_i = 1$ if and only if R_i is free. f(x) thus represents the configuration of free resources consequent on history x of RRM(N). Our program will thus be doing its job correctly if the configuration tests CONF(c) test f(x) correctly. We shall now show that they do. First a simple lemma.

Lemma 4

(1) $f(\varepsilon) = 2^N-1$

(2) $\forall x,y \in$ Vops(RRM(N))*: $g(x.y) = g(x) + g(y)$

We now tie the CONF(c)'s and f(x)'s together. First, for integers c, define v(c) = (bit(c,1),bit(c,2),...,bit(c,N)).

Lemma 5

Let x(c,X,Y) $\in$ Block(N), then v(Next(c,X,Y)) = v(c) + g(x(c,X,Y)).

From this, we may deduce

Proposition 2

Let $x \in$ FB(N) then x.CONF(c) $\in$ VFS(RRM(N)) $\Rightarrow$ v(c) = f(x).

From proposition3, we now have the proof of correctness of RRM(N), as follows.

(1) If x is a history of the system, then a configuration test applied at this point correctly identifies the configuration [Proposition 2].

(2) GET's can only execute on free resources and PUT's can only execute on borrowed resources [from Proposition 1, the definition of x(c,X,Y) and Proposition 2].

(3) In any block all GETs PUTs and SKIPs may execute in parallel. [because the corresponding vector operations commute] apart from those GET(i) and PUT(i) that occur in the same block.

We conclude this section with a sketch of a proof of adequacy. Adequacy, which implies freedom from deadlock, follows from the next lemma.

Lemma 6

(1) $\forall z \in \{0,1\}^N \forall c \in \{0,\ldots,2^N-1\} \exists X \subseteq C(c) \; \exists Y \subseteq E(c): \; z = g(x(c,X,Y,)) + v(c)$

(2) $\forall a \in Vops(RRM(N)) \exists x \in Block\ (N): I_a(x) = 1.$

Proposition 3

For all N>0 RRM(N) is adequate.

We have now established that RRM(N) performs as required.

We remark that the program RRM(N) is actually part of a rather larger program specifying a highly concurrent and distributed COSY solution to the Banker's Problem [Dij68], given in [LTD80]. This larger program contains, as well as RRM(N), which acts as a 'kernel' of it, the specification of access to the kernel by customers, a specific resource-to-customer allocation mechanism, various devices, based on counters, which ensure fairness and absense of starvation and a specification of customer structure. A proof of the correctness of the banker program, in a style similar to the above, has been sketched.

Conclusion

We have attempted to give the reader an idea of the potentials of COSY, both as a precise means for expressing a solution to an asynchronous design problem and also as a formalism in which such solutions may be analysed to any desired depth of rigour.

This paper does not cover the full range of our present understanding of the notation, nor has it spoken of the relationships between the work presented here and related work in the field.

We have not here presented the full COSY notation as presently developed; for example we have avoided the topic of processes, distributors or multiply nested distributors. Details of these language features may be found in [LTS79].

There also exist a number of results concerning the problem of deducing the adequacy properties of a system defined by a path from the syntactic structure of that path. Some of these may be found in [S79].

Finally, there has always been a strong connection between the COSY notation and Net Theory. The original formal semantics for the basic COSY notation was given in terms of a mapping from programs to nets [LC75] and this was developed further in [LSB79] and [LSB79a]. A relationship between paths and nets on both the system (path to net) and process (vector firing sequence to causal net) levels is given in [S79].

Acknowledgements

The research reported in this paper has been encouraged and supported by the Science Research Council of Great Britain. Some of the examples in this paper were developed in collaboration with P.R. Torrigiani and R. Devillers [LTD80]. Thanks to Mrs. Joan Armstrong for her excellent typing on such short notice.

Bibliography

[LC75] Lauer, P.E., Campbell, R.H.: Formal Semantics for a Class of High Level Primitives for Coordinating Concurrent Processes. Acta Informatica 5, pp. 247-332, 1975.

[LTS79] Lauer, P.E., Torrigiani, P.R., Shields, M.W.: COSY: a system specification language based on paths and processes. Acta Informatica, Vol. 12, pp. 109-158, 1979.

[D76] Dijkstra, E.W: A discipline of programming. Prentice Hall, 1976.

[H78] Hoare, C.A.R.: Communicating sequential processes. CACM Vol. 21, No. 8, August, 1978.

[CH74] Cambell, R.H., Habermann, A.H.: The specification of process synchronization by path expressions. Lecture Notes in Computer Science Vol. 16 Springer Verlag, pp. 89-102.

[LSB79] Lauer, P.E., Shields, M.W., Best, E.: The design and certification of asynchronous systems of processes. Proc. of EEC Advanced Course on Abstract Software Specification, Lyngby, Jan. 22 - Feb. 2, 1979. Lecture Notes in Computer Science (to appear).

[S79] Shields, M.W.: Adequate path expressions. Proc. Symp. on the Semantics of concurrent computation, Evian-les-Bains, July 2-4, 1979. Springer Lecture Notes in Computer Science Vol. 70, 1979.

[SL78] Shields, M.W., Lauer, P.E.: On the abstract specification and formal analysis of synchronization properties of concurrent systems. Proc. of Int. Conf. on Mathematical Studies of Information Processing, Aug. 23-26, Kyoto, 1978. Lecture Notes in Computer Science 75, Springer Verlag 1979, pp. 1-32.

[Dij68] Dijkstra, E.W.: Co-operating sequential processes. In: Programming Languages, ed. Genuys, Academic Press 1968.

[LTD80] Lauer, P.E., Torrigiani, P.R., Devillers, R.: A COSY Banker: Specification of highly parallel and distributed resource management. Proc. 4th International Symposium on Programming, Paris April 22-24, 1980 Lecture Notes in Computer Science Vol. 83 (ed. B. Robinet), Springer Verlag, 1980.

[LSB79a] Lauer, P.E., Shields, M.W., Best, E.: Formal Theory of the Basic COSY Notation. The Computing Laboratory, University of Newcastle upon Tyne, Technical Report Series No. 143, Nov. 1979.

[SL80] Shields, M.W., Lauer, P.E.: Programming and verifying concurrent systems in COSY. University of Newcastle upon Tyne, Computing Laboratory, ASM/68, January 1980.

DEADLOCKS AND LIVELOCKS IN TRANSITION SYSTEMS

Joseph Sifakis
Laboratoire IMAG
B.P. 53X, 38041 GRENOBLE Cedex, FRANCE

INTRODUCTION

In this paper we study the concepts of deadlock and livelock and give a method for proving the system properties related to these concepts.

The model used, transition systems, is a highly abstract relational model with a few primitive notions such as those of state and transition (action) which are at the base of any discrete model. The advantage of using such a primitive model, as far as the clarity of presentation and the generality of the results are concerned, is now widely recognized especially when studying the properties of parallel systems [KEL72][KEL76][KWO77][KWO79][ROS76].

The properties of "absence of deadlock" and "absence of livelock" are important correctness criteria for parallel systems ; thus, good understanding of the underlying concepts and of the related properties should contribute to a more thorough comprehension of the notion of system correctness. The literature dealing with the formal definition of these concepts is rather poor :

- Deadlock phenomena, the problem of their detection and protection methods against them, have very often been studied in a particular context, this of a set of processes sharing a set of common resources (for example [COF71][HOL72]). We think that the concept of deadlock must be introduced in terms of more primitive notions, independently of any context of use. Also, while no foundamental difference exists between the situation of total blocking and partial blocking in a system (a total blocking in a system S can imply the partial blocking in a system S' if S is a sub-system of S'), the term "deadlock" usually denotes total blocking. Finally, some confusion subsists yet between the very notion of deadlock and the properties expressing the eventuality for a system to reach a "sink" state. For example, the statement "a system S has a deadlock" can be given the three following meanings : 1) "there exists a set of states at which the system S is blocked forever", 2) "it is possible that the system S reaches a state at which it is blocked forever", 3) "the system S will certainly reach a state at which it is blocked forever".
- The concept of livelock is much less well explored and all the aforementioned remarks concerning deadlocks can be set in again for livelocks. It has been introduced in the literature through examples [KNU66][HOL71][DIJ71][ASH75] while formal definitions can be found in [LAM76] and [KWO79].

In this work we dissociate the study of the concepts (deadlock or livelock) from the study of the related properties. The concepts are defined with respect to a given transition (action) of a system ; their definition can be extended for a set of transitions or for a system (the set of all its transitions). We consider that a deadlock (respectively, a livelock) with respect to a transition t is a set of states such that if the system is initialized at a state of this set then it is impossible to enable (respectively, it is possible to evitate ad aeternam) the transition t.

In order to study the properties relative to the presence of deadlocks or livelocks, we adopt the general approach introduced in [SIF79] : it is supposed that a system property can be expressed by giving a "target" set of states and a "type of reachability" ; different types of reachability of the target set from the set of the initial states are defined. By appropriately choosing the target set, a family of properties corresponding to the different reachability types is generated. The main result is that the reachability types, and consequently system properties, can be characterized by simple relations involving the set of the initial states and fixed points of given continuous predicate transformers. The application of this general approach yields two families of properties by considering as target sets deadlocks or livelocks.

This paper is organized in four parts. The first part presents transition systems and introduces the concepts studied in terms of relations involving a basic predicate transformer. In part II it is shown that deadlocks and livelocks can be computed iteratively as fixed points of continuous functions. The families of deadlockability and livelockability properties are presented in part III as well as the methods for proving these properties. In the last part we show applications of the presented results.

I - TRANSITION SYSTEMS

A <u>transition system</u> [KEL72] is defined by a triplet $S = (Q,T,Rel)$ where

Q is a set of <u>states</u>

T is a finite set of <u>transitions</u>

$Rel \subseteq Q \times T \times Q$ is a relation.

The notation $q\text{-}t\!\to\! q'$ is used in the place of $(q,t,q') \in Rel$ and $q \to q'$ represents the fact that there exists $t \in T$ such that $q\text{-}t\!\to\! q'$. A transition t is said to be <u>enabled</u> by $q \in Q$ iff there exists $q' \in Q$ such that $q\text{-}t\!\to\! q'$; q' is the state <u>reached</u> from q after the <u>activation</u> of t.

These notations can be extended for any finite sequence $\sigma = t_{j1}\, t_{j2} \dots t_{js}$ over T ($\sigma \in T^*$) : $q\text{-}\sigma\!\to\! q'$ expresses the fact that there exists a sequence of states $q_0 = q, q_1, q_2, \dots, q_s = q'$, such that $q_{i-1}\text{-}t_{ji}\!\to\! q_i$ for $1 \le i \le s$. Furthermore, for $\sigma \in T^*$, $q\text{-}\sigma\!\to$ means that $\exists q' \in Q \;\; q\text{-}\sigma\!\to\! q'$; if σ is an infinite sequence over T we also use $q\text{-}\sigma\!\to$ for denoting that for every prefix σ_1 of σ we have $q\text{-}\sigma_1\!\to$.

With a transition system can be associated a digraph whose vertices are the elements of Q and the edges are labeled by T : there is an edge from q to q' labeled by t iff $q \text{-} t \rightarrow q'$.

Giving Rel is equivalent to giving a set of binary relations $\{R_i\}_{i=1}^m$, $m = |T|$, on Q,

$$R_i = \{(q,q') \in Q \times Q \mid q \text{-} t_i \rightarrow q'\}$$

i.e. R_i is the projection of Rel with respect to the transition t_i.

The <u>inverse</u> of a transition system $S = (Q,T,\{R_i\}_{i=1}^m)$ is the transition system $S^{-1} = (Q,T,\{R_i^{-1}\}_{i=1}^m)$ where R_i^{-1} represents the inverse of R_i.

Let Q be a set and P the set of unary predicates on Q :

$$P \in P \iff P : Q \rightarrow \{\underline{\text{true}},\underline{\text{false}}\}.$$

We represent by $L = (P,\vee,\wedge,\neg,\top,\bot)$ the complete lattice on P with respectively $\vee,\wedge,\neg,\top,\bot$ the operations of disjunction, conjunction, complementation, the "always true" predicate ($\vee P$), the "always false" predicate ($\wedge P$). L is isomorphic to the complete lattice of subsets of Q, $L' = (2^Q,\cup,\cap,\sim,Q,\emptyset)$; with every $P \in P$ can be associated its characteristic set $\underline{P} = \{q \in Q \mid P(q) = \underline{\text{true}}\}$. We use $\sqsubseteq$ and $\subseteq$ in order to represent the order relation on L and L' respectively :

$$(\forall P_1,P_2 \in P)\ (P_1 \sqsubseteq P_2 \overset{\text{def}}{\iff} \underline{P_1} \subseteq \underline{P_2}).$$

Definitions 1 : Given a transition system $S = (Q,T,\{R_i\}_{i=1}^m)$, we represent by c_i, $1 \le i \le m$, the predicate having as characteristic set $\underline{c_i} = \{q \mid \exists q'\ (q,q') \in R_i\}$.

1a/ An <u>invariant</u> J of S is a predicate J on Q such that $\forall (q,q') \in Q \times Q$,

$$J(q) = \underline{\text{true}} \text{ and } q \rightarrow q' \Rightarrow J(q') = \underline{\text{true}}.$$

An invariant of S^{-1} is called <u>inverse invariant</u> of S.

1b/ A <u>computation</u> of S [KWO79] <u>from</u> a given state $q_0 \in Q$ is a finite or infinite sequence σ over T such that $q_0 \text{-} \sigma \rightarrow$ and if σ is finite then $(\wedge_{i=1}^m \neg c_i)(q) = \underline{\text{true}}$ for every q such that $q_0 \text{-} \sigma \rightarrow q$.

A computation is said to be <u>non-terminating</u> if it is an infinite sequence.

1c/ A <u>trajectory</u> of S is a predicate W representing a set of states visited by S when a computation is executed i.e. W is a predicate such that $\forall q \in Q$

$$W(q) = \underline{\text{true}} \Rightarrow (\bigwedge_{i=1}^m \neg c_i)(q) = \underline{\text{true}} \text{ or } \exists q' (q \rightarrow q' \text{ and } W(q') = \underline{\text{true}}).$$

A <u>non-terminating trajectory</u> is a trajectory corresponding to a non-terminating computation i.e. a predicate W such that $\forall q \in Q$,

$$W(q) = \underline{\text{true}} \Rightarrow \exists q'\ (q \rightarrow q' \text{ and } W(q') = \underline{\text{true}}).$$

1d/ A <u>deadlock</u> <u>for</u> a transition t_1 in a transition system S is an invariant D of S that $D \sqsubseteq \neg c_1$.

1e/ A <u>livelock</u> <u>for</u> a transition t_1 in a transition system S is a non-terminating trajectory L of S such that $L \sqsubseteq \neg c_1$.

1f/ A <u>weak</u> <u>livelock</u> <u>for</u> a transition t_1 in a transition system $S = (Q,T,\{R_i\}_{i=1}^m)$ is a non-terminating trajectory of $S' = (Q,T-\{t_1\},\{R_i\}_{i=2}^{m})$.

1g/ A transition t has the <u>finite delay property</u> from $q_0 \in Q$ in S if for every non-terminating computation σ of S from $q_0 : \sigma_1$ is a prefix of σ with the property that for every x such that $\sigma_1 x$ is a prefix of σ, $q_0 - \sigma_1 x t \rightarrow$, implies that there exists some x' such that $\sigma_1 x' t$ is a prefix of σ.

A system has the finite delay property from q_0 if all its transitions have the finite delay property from q_0.

Observations 1 :

1a/ The notion of invariant introduced here corresponds to the notion of q_0-inductive in [KEL76] with the difference that the predicate J is not attached to any particular state q_0. To our knowledge, the notion of trajectory have never been identified explicitely in the literature and the distinction between the two types of livelock has first been pointed out in [KWO79].

1b/ The definitions of deadlock and livelock can be extended for a set of transitions $\{t_i\}_{i \in k}$, $k \subseteq \{1,2,...,m\}$, $k \neq \emptyset$. For this, it is sufficient to take $D \sqsubseteq \bigwedge_{i \in k} \neg c_i$, $L \sqsubseteq \bigwedge_{i \in k} \neg c_i$, and $S' = (Q,T-\{t_i\}_{i \in k}, \{R\}_{i=1}^{m} - \{R_i\}_{i \in k})$ in the definitions 1d/, 1e/ and 1f/ respectively.

A deadlock for all the transitions of S is a <u>total deadlock</u> of S. Formally, a total deadlock is a predicate D such that $D \sqsubseteq \bigwedge_{i=1}^{m} \neg c_i$, $m = |T|$.

1c/ Remark that a transition t_i has not the finite delay property from q_0 iff there exists a weak livelock L for t_i such that $L \sqsubseteq c_i$ and $\exists\, q \in Q\ \exists \sigma \in T^*$ such that $q_0 - \sigma \rightarrow q$ and $L(q) =$ <u>true</u>. That is, if t_i has not the finite delay property then there exists a non-terminating computation which does not contain t_i and such that for every state of the corresponding non-terminating trajectory, t_i is enabled.

Example 1 : Consider the transition system of figure 1. There is no deadlock for its transitions other than the total deadlock corresponding to the state (1,1). The reader can verify by simple observation the following statements : there is no livelock for t_1 ; there is a weak livelock for t_1 ; there is a livelock for t_2 ; there is a livelock for t_3 ; this system has the finite delay property from every possible initial state.

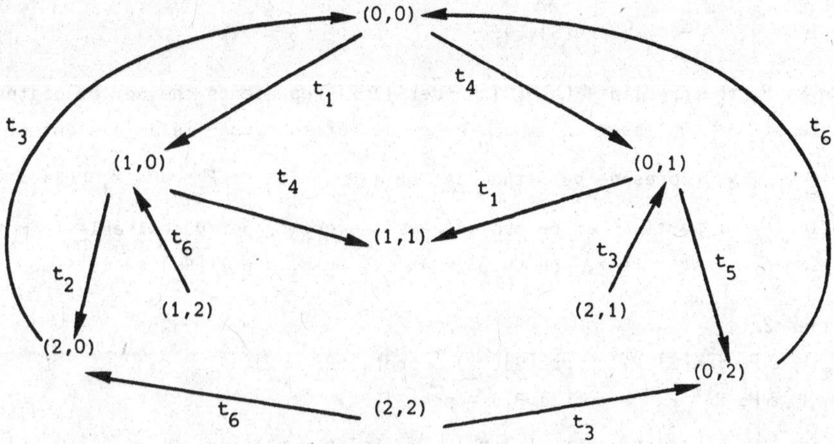

Figure 1

II - DEADLOCKS AND LIVELOCKS AS FIXED POINTS OF MONOTONIC FUNCTIONS

II.1 - Predicate transformers associated with a transition system

Let $S = (Q,T,\{R_i\}_{i=1}^{m})$ be a transition system, $\mathcal{R}$ the set of the binary relations on Q and $\mathcal{F}$ the set of unary functions on $\mathcal{P}$.

With every relation R of $\mathcal{R}$, we associate a function pre[R] of $\mathcal{F}$ such that $\forall P \in \mathcal{P}$

$$pre[R](P) = W \text{ where}$$

$$(\forall q \in Q)\ (W(q) = \underline{true} \iff \exists q'(P(q') = \underline{true} \text{ and } (q,q') \in R)).$$

Furthermore, for a given transition system S, we represent by pre[S] and post[S] the functions

$$pre[S] = pre[\bigcup_{i=1}^{m} R_i] = \bigvee_{i=1}^{m} pre[R_i],\quad post[S] = pre[S^{-1}].$$

Properties 1 :

1a/ $P \in \mathcal{P}$, $pre[0_R](P) = \perp$ where 0_R is the empty relation.

1b/ $P \in \mathcal{P}$, $pre[1_R](P) = P$ where $1_R = \{(q,q') \in Q^2 \mid q=q'\}$.

1c/ $P \in \mathcal{P}$, $P \neq \perp$, $pre[Q \times Q](P) = \top$.

1d/ $R_1,R_2 \in \mathcal{R}$, $P \in \mathcal{P}$, $pre[R_1 \cup R_2](P) = pre[R_1](P) \vee pre[R_2](P)$.

1e/ $P_1,P_2 \in \mathcal{P}$, $R \in \mathcal{R}$, $pre[R](P_1 \vee P_2) = pre[R](P_1) \vee pre[R](P_2)$.

1f/ $P_1,P_2 \in \mathcal{P}$, $R \in \mathcal{R}$, $P_1 \sqsubseteq P_2 \Rightarrow pre[R](P_1) \sqsubseteq pre[R](P_2)$.

1g/ $P_1,P_2 \in \mathcal{P}$, $R \in \mathcal{R}$, $pre[R](P_1 \wedge P_2) \sqsubseteq pre[R](P_1) \wedge pre[R](P_2)$.

Observations 2 : Let S be a transition system,

2a/ For $P \in \mathcal{P}$, the predicate pre[S](P) represents the set of all the possible direct predecessors of P i.e. all the states from which P can be reached by activating one transition of S. Also, post[S](P) represents the set of all the possible direct successors of P.

2b/ For $P \in \mathcal{P}$, the predicate $\widetilde{pre}[S](P) = \neg\, pre[S](\neg P)$ represents the set of states from which it is not possible to reach $\neg P$ by activating one transition in S.

Obviously, $\bigwedge_{i=1}^{m} \neg c_i \subseteq \widetilde{pre}[S](P)$.

2c/ For $P \in \mathcal{P}$, the predicate $(pre[S] \wedge \widetilde{pre}[S])(P)$ represents the set of states having at least one successor and whose every direct successor is an element of $\underline{P}$.

In the sequel we represent by $\tilde{F}$ the <u>dual</u> of a function $F \in \mathcal{F}$: $\forall P \in \mathcal{P}$, $\tilde{F}(P) = \neg F(\neg P)$.

The following properties can be proved. Also, every property derivable from these properties by substituting, pre by post and c_i by $k_i = post[R_i](\top)$ is true.

Properties 2 :

2a/ $\forall P_1, P_2 \in \mathcal{P}$, $\widetilde{pre}[S](P_1) \vee \widetilde{pre}[S](P_2) \subseteq \widetilde{pre}[S](P_1 \vee P_2)$.

2b/ $\forall P_1, P_2 \in \mathcal{P}$, $P_1 \subseteq P_2 \Rightarrow \widetilde{pre}[S](P_1) \subseteq \widetilde{pre}[S](P_2)$.

2c/ $\forall P_1, P_2 \in \mathcal{P}$, $\widetilde{pre}[S](P_1) \wedge \widetilde{pre}[S](P_2) = \widetilde{pre}[S](P_1 \wedge P_2)$.

2d/ $\forall P \in \mathcal{P}$, $pre[S](P) \vee pre[S](\neg P) \vee (\bigwedge_{i=1}^{m} \neg c_i) = \top$.

2e/ $\forall P \in \mathcal{P}$, $(pre[S] \circ \widetilde{post}[S])(P) \subseteq P$.

2f/ $\forall P \in \mathcal{P}$, $P \subseteq (\widetilde{pre}[S] \circ post[S])(P)$.

Proposition 1 : Let S be a transition system. The following statements are equivalent

a) J is an invariant of S

b) $post[S](J) \subseteq J$

c) $J \subseteq \widetilde{pre}[S](J)$.

Proof : a) and b) are obviously equivalent.

Suppose that $post[S](J) \subseteq J$. Then, $\widetilde{pre}[S]$ being monotonic we have, $(\widetilde{pre}[S] \circ post[S])(J) \subseteq \widetilde{pre}[S](J)$ and by property 2f, $J \subseteq \widetilde{pre}[S](J)$.

Conversely, suppose that $J \subseteq \widetilde{pre}[S](J)$. This implies $post[S](J) \subseteq (post[S] \circ \widetilde{pre}[S])(J)$ and by property 2e (after interchanging pre and post) we have $post[S](J) \subseteq J$. □

A similar proof can be carried out for proposition 2.

Proposition 2 : Let S be a transition system. The following propositions are equivalent.

a) J is an inverse invariant of S

b) $pre[S](J) \subseteq J$

c) $J \subseteq \widetilde{post}[S](J)$.

Proposition 3 : J is an invariant of a transition system S iff $\neg J$ is an inverse invariant of S.

Proof : Direct consequence of the propositions 1 and 2. □

Proposition 4 : Let S be a transition system.

a/ W is a trajectory of S iff W is a solution of $P \subseteq pre[S](P) \vee \bigwedge_{i=1}^{m} \neg c_i$ iff $\neg W$ is a solution of $(pre[S] \wedge \widetilde{pre}[S])(P) \subseteq P$.

b/ W is a non-terminating trajectory of S iff W is a solution of $P \subseteq pre[S](P)$ iff

$\neg W$ is a solution of $\widetilde{pre}[S](P) \subseteq P$.

Proof : The relations $P \subseteq pre[S](P) \vee \bigwedge_{i=1}^{m} \neg c_i$ and $P \subseteq pre[S](P)$ express directly the definitions of trajectory and non-terminating trajectory respectively. The proof can be completed by taking the dual of these relations (notice that by property 2d, $pre[S](P) \vee \bigwedge_{i=1}^{m} \neg c_i = pre[S](P) \vee \widetilde{pre}[S](P))$. □

II.2 - Recall of results on the fixed points of monotonic functions

In this paragraph, we recall some well-known results [TAR55][PAR69] on the fixed points of monotonic functions which are used later on.

Definition 2 : Let $F \in \mathcal{F}$ a monotonic function.

. F is <u>continuous from below</u> or <u>b-continuous</u> iff for every increasing sequence of predicates $\{P_i\}_i$, $P_i \subseteq P_{i+1}$, $i=0,1,2,\ldots$: $F(\bigvee_i P_i) = \bigvee_i F(P_i)$.

. F is <u>continuous from above</u> or <u>a-continuous</u> iff for every decreasing sequence of predicates $\{P_i\}_i$, $P_{i+1} \subseteq P_i$, $i=0,1,2,\ldots$: $F(\bigwedge_i P_i) = \bigwedge_i F(P_i)$.

Notation : Being given $F \in \mathcal{F}$ we represent by F^* and $F^\times$ the functions

$$F^* = I \vee F \vee F^2 \vee \ldots = \bigvee_i F^i \quad \text{(I is the identity function)}$$

$$F^\times = I \wedge F \wedge F^2 \wedge \ldots = \bigwedge_i F^i.$$

The unary operations * and x are called respectively <u>starring</u> and <u>crossing</u>.

Proposition 5 :

a/ Let F a monotonic function of $\mathcal{F}$, P_1 a predicate such that $P_1 \subseteq F(P_1)$ and P_0 the least fixed point of F which is greater than or equal to P_1

(i) $F^*(P_1) = \bigvee_{i=0}^{\infty} F^i(P_1) \subseteq P_0$

(ii) If F is b-continuous then, $F^*(P_1) = P_0$.

b/ Let F a monotonic function of $\mathcal{F}$, P_1 a predicate such that $F(P_1) \subseteq P_1$ and P_0 the greatest fixed point of F which is less than or equal to P_1.

(i) $P_0 \subseteq F^\times(P_1) = \bigwedge_{i=0}^{\infty} F^i(P_1)$

(ii) If F is a-continuous then, $F^\times(P_1) = P_0$.

Proposition 6 : Let F a monotonic function of $\mathcal{F}$.

a/ F is a b-continuous iff $\tilde{F}$ is a-continuous.

b/ For every predicate P of $\mathcal{P}$, if P_0 is the least fixed point of F which is greater than or equal to P, then $\neg P_0$ is the greatest fixed point of $\tilde{F}$ less than or equal to $\neg P$ (and conversely). Furthermore, if F is b-continuous then $F^*(P) = \neg(\tilde{F}^\times(\neg P))$.

The following theorem proved in [SIF79] guarantees that all the functions built from pre[S], for $S = (Q,T,\{R_i\}_{i=1}^m)$, are both a-continuous and b-continuous provided that the "non-determinacy" of S be bounded, [DIJ66] chapter 9, [ROE76], [HOA78], [GUE79].

Theorem 1 :

Let $\mathcal{R}_b = \{R \subset \mathcal{R} \mid \forall q \in Q\ \exists k \in \mathbb{N},\ |\{q' \mid (q,q') \in R\}| \leq k\}$ and $\mathcal{R}_b(P) = \{pre[R] \mid R \in \mathcal{R}_b\}$.

Every function constructed from elements of $\mathcal{R}_b(P)$ and constants by effectuating a finite number of times the operations of conjunction, disjunction, dualization, composition, starring and crossing, is both a-continuous and b-continuous.

In the sequel we suppose that the transition systems studied are such that the relations R_i belong to $\mathcal{R}_b$. This hypothesis allows a more elegant presentation of the results without being of any importance as far as their practical usage is concerned.

II.3 - Computing deadlocks and livelocks

Solving inequalities of the type $P \sqsubseteq G(P)$ or $G(P) \sqsubseteq P$ amounts to computing fixed points of $I \wedge G$ and $I \vee G$ where I is the identity function :

$$P \sqsubseteq G(P) \iff P = P \wedge G(P) \iff P = (I \wedge G)(P)$$

$$G(P) \sqsubseteq P \iff P = P \vee G(P) \iff P = (I \vee G)(P).$$

Furthermore, for every predicate P_1 of $\mathcal{P}$ we have : $(I \wedge G)(P_1) \sqsubseteq P_1$ and $P_1 \sqsubseteq (I \vee G)(P_1)$.
By proposition 6 :

- if G is a-continuous then $(I \wedge G)^{\times}(P_1)$ is the greatest solution of $P \sqsubseteq G(P)$ which is less than or equal to P_1 ;
- if G is b-continuous then $(I \vee G)^{*}(P_1)$ is the least solution of $G(P) \sqsubseteq P$ which is greater than or equal to P_1.

Proposition 7 : Let S be a transition system and P_1 a predicate on Q,
a/ $\widetilde{pre}[S]^{\times}(P_1)$ is the greatest invariant of S less than or equal to P_1,
b/ $post[S]^{*}(P_1)$ is the least invariant of S greater or equal to P_1,
c/ $\widetilde{post}[S]^{\times}(P_1)$ is the greatest inverse invariant of S less than or equal to P_1,
d/ $pre[S]^{*}(P_1)$ is the least inverse invariant of S greater than or equal to P_1.

Proof : This proposition is a direct consequence of the results of the preceding paragraph if it is taken into account the fact that $(I \vee F)^{*}(P) = F^{*}(P)$ if F is distributive with respect to the disjunction and $(I \wedge F)^{\times}(P) = F^{\times}(P)$ if F is distributive with respect to the conjunction. $\square$

Observation 3 : $post[S]^{*}(P_1)$ and $pre[S]^{*}(P_1)$ represent respectively the set of the <u>possible successors</u> and the set of the <u>possible predecessors</u> of the states verifying P_1.

Proposition 8 : Let S be a transition system and P_1 a predicate on Q,
a/ $(I \wedge (pre[S] \vee \widetilde{pre}[S]))^{\times}(P_1)$ is the greatest trajectory of S contained in P_1,
b/ $(I \wedge pre[S])^{\times}(P_1)$ is the greatest non-terminating trajectory contained in P_1,
c/ $(I \vee pre[S] \wedge \widetilde{pre}[S])^{*}(P_1)$ is the complement of the greatest trajectory of S contained in $\neg P_1$,
d/ $(I \vee \widetilde{pre}[S])^{*}(P_1)$ is the complement of the greatest non-terminating trajectory of

S contained in $\neg P_1$.

Proof : By combining the results of propositions 4 and 6. □

A consequence of propositions 7 and 8 is that :

Proposition 9 : For a transition t_1 of a transition system $S = (Q,T,\{R_i\}_{i=1}^m)$

a/ The greatest deadlock for t_1 is equal to
$D = \widetilde{pre}[S]^{\times}(\neg c_1) = \neg\, pre[S]^{*}(c_1)$.

b/ The greatest livelock for t_1 is equal to
$L = (I \wedge pre[S])^{\times}(\neg c_1) = \neg\, (I \vee \widetilde{pre}[S])^{*}(c_1)$.

c/ The greatest weak livelock for t_1 is equal to
$L' = (I \wedge pre[S_1])^{\times}(\top) = \neg\, (I \vee \widetilde{pre}[S_1])^{*}(\bot)$ where $S_1 = (Q,T-\{t_1\},\{R_i\}_{i=2}^m)$.

III - DEADLOCKABILITY AND LIVELOCKABILITY PROPERTIES

In [SIF79] a general approach for studying the properties of parallel systems is suggested. According to this approach those properties can be expressed by giving

a/ a set of target states characterized by a predicate P_2,

b/ a type of reachability of P_2 from the set of the initial states of the system.

The set of the different properties obtained for the same target predicate, when the different types of reachability are considered, constitutes a family of properties of the same type. For example, if P_2 is taken to be HALT (HALT contains all the termination states), the family of termination properties is obtained by considering the different ways of reaching some state of HALT from a possible initial state. Also, if we consider $P_2 = c_i$, we obtain the family of the activability properties for a transition t_i expressing the possibility for this transition to be enabled. The families of deadlockability and livelockability properties are obtained in this way by considering respectively that P_2 is a deadlock or a livelock. Nine different reachability types have been defined in [SIF79]. As an illustration of this approach, we consider here 3 different reachability types corresponding to these deadlockability and livelockability properties which seem to be the most interesting in practice.

Definition 3 : Let $S = (Q,T,\{R_i\}_{i=1}^m)$ be a transition system and $P_1, P_2 \in P$,

3a/ P_2 is 1-reachable or potentially reachable from P_1 iff $\forall q \in Q$, $P_1(q) = \underline{true}$, $\exists q' \in Q\ \exists \sigma \in T^*$ such that $P_2(q') = \underline{true}$ and $q\text{-}\sigma\!\to q'$ i.e. $P_1 \sqsubseteq pre[S]^{*}(P_2)$.

3b/ P_2 is 3-reachable or inevitably-reachable from P_1 iff $\forall q \in Q$, $P_1(q) = \underline{true}$, every trajectory from q has a state q' such that $P_2(q') = \underline{true}$ i.e. for every evolution of S from any initial state q verifying P_1, S will certainly pass through a state verifying P_2.
Obviously, 3-reachability can be simply expressed by the relation,
$P_1 \sqsubseteq (I \vee pre[S] \wedge \widetilde{pre}[S])^{*}(P_2)$.

3c/ P_2 is <u>1-s-reachable</u> or <u>potentially systematically reachable</u> form P_2 iff $post[S]^*(P_1)$ is 1-reachable from P_2 i.e. $post[S]^*(P_1) \sqsubseteq pre[S]^*(P_2)$.

Proposition 10 : For a given transition system S, $P_1, P_2 \in \mathcal{P}$,

a/ P_2 is 1-reachable from P_1 in S iff for every invariant J of S less than or equal to $\neg P_2, P_1 \wedge J = \bot$.

b/ P_2 is 3-reachable from P_1 in S iff for every trajectory W of S less than or equal to $\neg P_2,\ P_1 \wedge W = \bot$.

Proof : a/ P_2 is 1-reachable from $P_1 \iff P_1 \wedge \neg pre[S]^*(P_2) = \bot$. According to proposition 6b $\neg pre[S]^*(P_2) = \widetilde{pre}[S]^\times(\neg P_2)$ is the greatest invariant less than or equal to $\neg P_2$.

For b/ a similar proof can be carried out. □

Proposition 11 : For a given transition system S, $P_1, P_2 \in \mathcal{P}$, the following expressions are equivalent.

a/ P_2 is 1-s-reachable from P_1 in S,

b/ For every invariant J of S, $J \sqsubseteq \neg P_2$, $post[S]^*(P_1) \wedge J = \bot$,

c/ $P_1 \sqsubseteq \widetilde{pre}[S]^\times(pre[S]^*(P_2))$.

Proof : By the proposition 10a/ and the definition of 1-s-reachability, a/ is equivalent to b/.

$post[S]^*(P_1) \sqsubseteq pre[S]^*(P_2) \Rightarrow \widetilde{pre}[S]^\times \circ post[S]^*(P_1) \sqsubseteq \widetilde{pre}[S]^\times \circ pre[S]^*(P_2)$
$\Rightarrow post[S]^*(P_1) \sqsubseteq \widetilde{pre}[S]^\times \circ pre[S]^*(P_2) \Rightarrow P_1 \sqsubseteq \widetilde{pre}[S]^\times \circ pre[S]^*(P_2)$.

Conversely, $P_1 \sqsubseteq \widetilde{pre}[S]^\times \circ pre[S]^*(P_2) \Rightarrow post[S]^*(P_1) \sqsubseteq \widetilde{pre}[S]^\times \circ pre[S]^*(P_2)$
$\Rightarrow post[S]^*(P_1) \sqsubseteq pre[S]^*(P_2)$. □

Observation 4 : According to proposition 10 if P_2 is such that $\widetilde{pre}[S]^\times(\neg P_2) = \bot$ (respectively, $(I \wedge (pre[S] \vee \widetilde{pre}[S]))^\times(\neg P_2) = \bot$), then P_2 is 1-reachable (respectively, 3-reachable) from $\top$ (every possible initial state).

Definition 4 : A transition t of a transition system S is said to be <u>**-deadlockable</u> (respectively, <u>**-livelockable</u>, <u>**-weakly livelockable</u>) from P_1 if there exists a deadlock (respectively livelock, weak livelock) for t which is **-reachable from P_1, where ** stands for one of the prefixes "1", "3" and "1-s".

Remark that the statement "there exists a deadlock (respectively, livelock, weak livelock) for t which is **-reachable from P_1" of the preceding definition is equivalent to the statement "the greatest deadlock (respectively, livelock, weak livelock) for t is reachable from P_1". Thus, propositions 10 and 11 can be directly applied for proving deadlockability and livelockability properties by taking P_2 = the greatest deadlock or livelock or weak livelock for a given transition. In the next page we summarize the results of this paragraph (table 1).

Finally, a consequence of the observation 1c/ is the following proposition.

Proposition 12 : A transition t_1 of a transition system $S = (Q,T,\{R_i\}_{i=1}^{m})$ has the finite delay property from $q_0 \in Q$ iff $pre[S]^* \circ (I \wedge pre[S_1])^x(c_1)(q_0)$ = <u>false</u> where, $S_1 = (Q,T-\{t_1\}, \{R_i\}_{i=2}^{m})$.

<u>Table 1</u>

1	$P_1 \sqsubseteq pre[S]^*(P_2) \iff P_1 \wedge \widetilde{pre}[S]^x(\neg P_2) = \bot$ <u>P_2 is 1-reachable from P_1</u>
3	$P_1 \sqsubseteq (I \vee \widetilde{pre}[S] \wedge pre[S])^*(P_2) \iff P_1 \wedge (I \wedge (pre[S] \vee \widetilde{pre}[S]))^x(\neg P_2) = \bot$ <u>P_2 is 3-reachable from P_1</u>
1-s	$post[S]^*(P_1) \sqsubseteq pre[S]^*(P_2) \iff post[S]^*(P_1) \wedge \widetilde{pre}[S]^x(\neg P_2) = \bot$ $\Updownarrow$ $\qquad\qquad$ $\Updownarrow$ $P_1 \sqsubseteq \widetilde{pre}[S]^x \circ pre[S]^*(P_2) \iff P_1 \wedge pre[S]^* \circ \widetilde{pre}[S]^x(\neg P_2) = \bot$ <u>P_2 is 1-s-reachable from P_1</u>

$$t_1 \text{ is } \left\{\begin{array}{l} \text{**-deadlockable} \\ \text{**-livelockable} \\ \text{**-weakly livelockable} \end{array}\right\} \text{ from } P_1 \text{ when } P_2 = \left\{\begin{array}{l} D_1 \\ L_1 \\ L_1' \end{array}\right\}, \text{ where}$$

$D_1 = \widetilde{pre}[S]^x(\neg c_1) = \neg\, pre[S]^*(c_1)$ = the greatest deadlock for t_1

$L_1 = (I \wedge pre[S])^x(\neg c_1) = \neg\, (I \vee \widetilde{pre}[S])^*(c_1)$ = the greatest livelock for t_1

$L_1' = (I \wedge pre[S_1])^x(\top) = \neg\, (I \vee \widetilde{pre}[S_1])^*(\bot)$ = the greatest weak livelock for t_1

$S = (Q,T,\{R_i\}_{i=1}^{m})$ and $S_1 = (Q,T-\{t_1\},\{R_i\}_{i=2}^{m})$.

IV - APPLICATIONS

The presented results can be applied for the verification of systems described in different discrete models provided that, at a certain level of abstraction, these models can be considered as transition systems. In this case, it is necessary to give, for each particular model a method for computing the function <u>pre</u>. The systems studied in this paragraph are described in a model for which the function <u>pre</u> can be obtained in a direct manner.

Definition 5 : A CA-system is a triplet $S = (X,C,A)$ where :

- $X = \{x_1,x_2,\dots,x_n\}$ is a set of state variables with domains represented by $D_1,D_2,\dots,D_n$.
- $C = \{c_1,c_2,\dots,c_m\}$ is a set of conditions, each condition being a computable predicate on X.
- $A = \{a_1,a_2,\dots,a_m\}$ is a set of actions in bijection with the conditions. Each action a_i is an assignment $X := \alpha_i(X)$ where α_i is an arbitrary computable function representing an internal mapping of $\times_{i=1}^{n} D_i$.

A CA-system is considered as a transition system $S = (Q,T,\{R_i\}_{i=1}^{m})$ such that $Q \subseteq \times_{i=1}^{n} D_i$ and the relations R_i are defined by

$$(q,q') \in R_i \iff c_i(q) = \underline{\text{true}} \text{ and } \alpha_i(q) = q'.$$

Obviously, if P is predicate and S a CA-system then $\text{pre}[S](P) = \bigvee_{i=1}^{m} c_i \wedge P\alpha_i$.

CA-systems are at the base of many models, mechanisms or constructs used for representing non-deterministic systems. It is the underlying model of the class of programs with guarded commands [DIJ75] of the type

$$S = \underline{\text{do}}\ c_1 \to a_1 \,[\!]\, c_2 \to a_2 \,[\!]\, \dots \,[\!]\, c_m \to a_m\ \underline{\text{od}}$$

Remark that for every serial flowchart program (deterministic or not), an equivalent CA-system can be obtained. Furthermore, the properties of parallel systems can be studied on non-deterministic models "representing" them and CA-systems have been used for this purpose [LAM76][FLO78][SIF79].

Also, many models used for representing parallel systems such as vector replacement systems [KEL72], PT-nets [ACG79], parallel programs in [KEL76], can be considered as CA-systems. Thus, the presented results are directly applicable to systems described in these models. The reader can find examples of applications in [SIF79] and [SIF80].

V - CONCLUDING REMARKS

The main results of this paper can be summarized as follows :

a) The concepts of deadlock and livelock are introduced in terms of primitive notions, such as those of state and transition, independently of any particular context of using a system.

b) The related properties are defined, according to a general approach suggested in [SIF79], by considering different reachability types of deadlocks and livelocks. This approach yields a great number of properties ; which one is of interest depends on what is supposed to be a "good" functioning of the system under study. Moreover, contrary to [LAM76] and [KWO79], livelockability properties are defined independently of the finite delay property and of the possibility for a system to have total deadlocks.

c) Proving deadlockability and livelockability properties amounts to computing iteratively least or greatest fixed points of continuous predicate transformers. From this point of view this work is inspired in the work of A. van Lamsweerde and M. Sintzoff [LAM76] relative to the derivation of strongly correct parallel programs.

d) This work constitutes a basis for the study of livelock and deadlock phenomena in less primitive models. Obviously, these results can be applied to every model which can be considered as a transition system provided that a method for computing the basic predicate transformer pre from a description in this model is given.

REFERENCES

[ACG79] Advanced Course on general net theory of processes and systems. Hamburg University, October 1979 (to be published by Springer Verlag).

[ASH75] E.A. ASHCROFT : "Proving assertions about parallel programs". Journal of Comp. and Syst. Science, 10, 1975, pp. 110-135.

[COF71] E.G. COFFMAN, JR., M.J. ELPHICK, A. SHOSHANI : "System Deadlocks". Comp. Surveys, ACM, Vol.3, n°2, June 1971, pp.67-78.

[DIJ71] E.W. DIJKSTRA : "Hierarchical ordering of sequential processes". Acta Informatica, 1, 2, October 1971, pp. 115-138.

[DIJ75] E.W. DIJKSTRA : "Guarded commands, non determinacy and formal derivation of programs". Comm. ACM, vol.18, n°8, August 1975, pp. 453-457.

[DIJ76] E.W. DIJKSTRA : "A discipline of programming". Prentice Hall Inc., 1976.

[FLO78] L. FLON & N. SUZUKI : "Non determinism and the correctness of parallel programs" in "Formal description of programming concepts". North Holland Publ. Co., 1978, pp. 589-608.

[GUE79] P. GUERREIRO : "Un modèle relationnel pour les programmes non-déterministes". DEA report, IMAG, Grenoble, June 1979.

[HOA78] C.A.R. HOARE : "Some properties of predicate transformers". J.A.C.M., vol.25, n°3, July 1978, pp. 461-480.

[HOL71] R.C. HOLT : "Comments on prevention of system deadlocks". Comm. ACM, vol.14, n°1, January 1971, pp. 36-38.

[HOL72] R.C. HOLT : "Some deadlock properties of computer systems". Comp. Surveys, ACM, vol.4, n°2, September 1972, pp.179-196.

[KEL72] R.M. KELLER : "Vector replacement systems : a formalism modeling asynchronous systems". Princeton University, Technical report n° 117, December 1972.

[KEL76] R.M. KELLER : "Formal verification of parallel programs". Comm. ACM, vol.19, n°7, July 1976, pp. 371-384.

[KNU66] D.E. KNUTH : "Additional comments on a problem in concurrent programming control". Comm. ACM, vol.9, n°9, May 1966, pp. 321-322.

[KWO77] Y.S. KWONG : "On reduction of asynchronous systems". Theoretical Comp. Science, 5, 1977, pp. 25-50.

[KWO79] Y.S. KWONG : "On the absence of livelocks in parallel programs", in Springer Lecture notes in Computer science n° 70, Semantics of concurrent computation, July 1979, pp. 172-190.

[LAM76] A. van LAMSWEERDE and M. SINTZOFF : "Formal derivation of strongly correct parallel programs". MBLE Research Lab., report R338, October 1976, and Acta Informatica 12, fasc. 1, 1979, pp. 1-31.

[PAR69] D. PARK : "Fixpoint induction and proofs of program properties" in Machine Intelligence 5, 1969, pp. 59-78.

[ROE76] W.P. de ROEVER : "Dijkstra's predicate transformer, non determinism, recursion and termination". Springer Lecture notes in Computer science n° 45, MFCS, 1976, pp. 472-481.

[ROS76] B.K. ROSEN : "Correctness of parallel programs : the Church-Rosser approach". Theoretical Comp. Science, 2, 1976, pp. 183-207.

[SIF79] J. SIFAKIS : "A unified approach for studying the properties of transition systems". IMAG, report RR 179, December 1979.

[SIF80] J. SIFAKIS : "Deadlocks and livelocks in transition systems". IMAG, report RR 185, January 1980.

[TAR55] A. TARSKI : "A lattice-theoretical fixpoint theorem and its applications". Pacific Journal of Mathematics, 5, 1955, pp. 285-309.

DESCRIPTIONAL COMPLEXITY OF CONCURRENT PROCESSES

(preliminary version)

Giora Slutzki
Department of Mathematics and Computer Science
Clarkson College of Technology
Potsdam, New York 13676/USA

Abstract

This paper compares several algebraic software description techniques which were proposed recently. Using language theoretic tools we show that some of the most handy concurrent behavior descriptors (inverse shuffle and cancellation) when combined with the operations of shuffle, shuffle iteration and the regular operations yield the full power of Turing Machines. Specifically, the flow expressions of Shaw and Kimura's D-and E-expressions are all universal in this sense.

1. Introduction

Currently there is quite a confusing variety of methods and techniques to describe the behavior of a concurrent society of communicating (sequential) processes. The syntactical differences between these approaches are mainly two: (i) the way in which communication between the processes is achieved, and (ii) the amount of expressivity that one is willing to introduce into his syntax. For instance, in the semaphore discipline [3] and the parallel programs of [18] communication is achieved through shared locations. In [9,4,22] processes communicate by sending and recieving messages. Some of the methods are more procedure oriented than other; some are more suitable for proving properties of parallel programs while other might be more appropriate for concurrent software description.

In this paper we will discuss and compare algebraic, nonprocedural software description schemes. In this approach we abstract from the meaning of the operations by considering a finite set of symbols Σ (event types). In addition, we have a set of operation symbols Ω. Processes may be represented by <u>expressions</u> over Σ and Ω. By giving the operations in Ω (familiar) interpretations the set of possible executions (behaviors) of a process can be defined. Parallelism is modelled by special "concurrent" operations. Thus, the set of possible executions of a process is a formal language. We will compare and investigate the complexity of these languages.

Algebraic description techniques may be used to describe a variety of computer-based phenomena: program structures (sequential or parallel, synchronised or nonsynchronised), operating systems, problems related to distributed computing, resource management in multiprogramming environment, etc.

For instance, while designing a large and involved software system one of the main activities is producing successive, more and more procedure-oriented descriptions of the intended behavior of the system. This process winds up with the generation of a collection of software programs written in some particular computer language. During this process it might be helpful to have available an algebraic description of the system, expressing, at an appropriate level of abstraction, the sequences of events which are admissible in the system, but which for obvious reasons of manageability, supresses the large amount of detail inherent in any real system. Several such algebraic description techniques of software specification, tailored especially to suit concurrent environment, were proposed: (i) the path expressions [2,8] (ii) event expressions [23,24,21] (iii) flow expressions [25] and (iv) C- D-, and E-expressions [14,15,16]. Ideally, such a description language should be powerful enough to describe the intricacies of concurrent behavior, but at the same time we would prefer it to be less than universal (i.e., less powerful than a Turing Machine) to make itself amenable to formal (or automatic) analysis. Numerous examples of the use of the various types of expressions are given by their inventors in [2,8,23,24,25,14,15,16]. Semantical issues are discussed in [19,21].

In this paper path expressions will not be discussed because they specify regular behavior and because our present interest is in assessing bounds on the complexity of the more involved types of expressions. The paper is divided into five parts of which this is the first. The second section gives the basic definitions and a short survey. In the third section, using simulation technique of Rounds [21] we show some of the description schemes to be universal. We also compare the classes of languages resulting from the various types of expressions. Jantzen [13] communicated independent proofs of some of the results of section 3 using AFL techniques. Section 4 is a short section which using results of [12,20,27] indicated that the operations used to model concurrency and synchronisation introduce a very significant complexity into the description languages. In fact, exponential lower bounds seem to be pervasive, see also [17]. Last section is a brief summary.

2. Preliminaries and Brief Survey.

We assume the reader is familiar with rudiments of formal language theory [5,10] and in particular with regular languages (REG) and regular expressions (with $\cdot$, $\cup$ and * denoting respectively the operations of concatenation, union and Kleen star). Let Σ be an alphabet. The empty word will be denoted by λ and $\Lambda=\{\lambda\}$. We now define the operations of shuffle [5,6] and its Kleene closure [23,24,14,25].

2.1 Definition. (shuffle, notation Δ). Let $w,v \in \Sigma^*$ and $a,b \in \Sigma$. Then $w\Delta\lambda=\lambda\Delta w=w$ and $aw\Delta bv=a(w\Delta bv)\cup b(aw\Delta v)$. For $R,S \subseteq \Sigma^*, R\Delta S= \{r\Delta s \mid r\in R$ and $s\in S\}$. []

Note that the shuffle operation should be interpreted as a "concurrent operation" in the sense that in the combined process $\alpha\Delta\beta$ events generated by α and β can occur concurrently. Also, for words u and v, $u\Delta v$ may be viewed as a nondeterministic choice of one execution $w \in u\Delta v$.

2.2 Definition. (dagger, shuffle iteration, notation †). Let $R \subseteq \Sigma^*$. Then $R^\dagger=\cup\Delta^n R$ where union is over $n\geq 0$ and $\Delta^0 R=\Lambda$, $\Delta^{n+1}R=(\Delta^n R)\Delta R$. □

Basic to all the others is the following class of languages and the corresponding expressions defined by Kimura [14].

2.3 Definition. The class C is the smallest class of languages satisfying the following conditions: (i) REG $\subseteq C$ and (ii) for $R,S \in C$ all the sets $R\cdot S$, $R\cup S$, R^*, $R\Delta S$, $R^\dagger$ are in C.

The set of C-expressions is the smallest set of expressions such that: (i) all regular expressions are C-expressions, and (ii) if α and β are C-expressions then so are $(\alpha\cdot\beta)$, $(\alpha\cup\beta)$, $(\alpha)^*$, $(\alpha\Delta\beta)$, $(\alpha)^\dagger$. □

C-expressions were used in [14] to model the behavior of a community of noncommunicating sequential processes. Note that concurrency is indicated by the occurrence of Δ in the expression and not by all the possible interweavings (of events) resulting from its application (cf. remarks in [7]).

It is clear that the class of languages definable by C-expressions is precisely C. In [14] it was shown that $(abc)^\dagger \in C$-CF (context-free languages). In [26] we have shown that $\{a^n b^n \mid n\geq 0\}$ is not in C. It was also shown in [26] that languages in C have the IRS property (if infinite then containing an infinite regular subset) and the semilinear property. Results of essentially similar nature were obtained independently in [11].

We now present several extensions of C-expressions and C which introduce the capability of synchronisation into the description languages. The operation of cancellation [23,24,21,15] using Kimura's notation for it is defined as follows. Let $R \subseteq \Sigma_R^*$ and $Q \subseteq \Sigma_Q^*$. Then

$$R\%Q = \{x_0x_1\ldots x_n \varepsilon (\Sigma_R - \Sigma_Q)^* \mid \exists y_1, y_2, \ldots, y_n \varepsilon Q \text{ s.t. } x_0y_1x_1\ldots y_nx_n \varepsilon R\} \quad \ldots(1)$$

Intuitively, words of Q are striked out from words of R; if the resulting word has no letters from Σ_Q it is made an element of R%Q. The set of E-expressions is just the set of C-expressions augmented with %. *E* is the class of the corresponding languages. E_{REG} results from *E* by restricting Q in (1) to be regular.

Let A be an alphabet and $\bar{A}=\{\bar{a} \mid a\varepsilon A\}$. The full Dyck set over A is denoted by D(A) and it is the set of all words over $A\cup\bar{A}$ which cancel to λ under the rules $\bar{a}a \to \lambda$ and $a\bar{a} \to \lambda$. Event expressions [23,24] are essentially E-expressions in which the cancellation operator % has always D(A) (for some A) as its right operand; that is, always subwords of a Dyck language are cancelled (actually, the definition in [23,24] is more restrictive, but equivalent to ours). It should be observed that REG is closed under % [24] but obviously not under % with Dyck sets. Let L_E be the class of languages definable by event expressions. Rounds proved that L_E=RE (recursively enumerable sets) [21]. It was contemplated [16] that the power of L_E comes (partly) from the involvement of Dyck sets in their definition. It will follow from our results that this is not the case. Namely, we show that $L_E = E_{REG}$=RE which means that no expressivity is lost by giving up the Dyck sets and using cancellation with only regular sets.

Next we define the operation of inverse shuffle[5,6]. We use a slightly different version as given in [15]. Let $R \subseteq \Sigma_R^*$ and $Q \subseteq \Sigma_Q^*$. Then

$$R\sim Q = \{x_0x_1\ldots x_n \varepsilon (\Sigma_R - \Sigma_Q)^* \mid \exists\, y_1y_2\ldots y_n \varepsilon Q \text{ s.t. } x_0y_1x_1\ldots y_nx_n \varepsilon R\} \quad \ldots(2)$$

Intuitively, $w\varepsilon R\sim Q$ if there exist words $x\varepsilon R$ and $y\varepsilon Q$ such that $x\varepsilon w\Delta y$. The set of D-expressions is defined by augmenting C-expressions with the operator ~. *D* denotes the class of languages definable by D-expressions. D_{REG} results from *D* by restricting the application of ~ in (2) such that Q is regular. It was hoped [16] that D-expressions are not universal, i.e., $D \subsetneq$ RE. Again, however we show that D_{REG}=RE. Note that REG is closed under ~.

Shaw [25] defined a language of flow expressions. By dropping his infinite flows we are left with (what we call) F-expressions which are essentially C-expressions. Shaw defines the class of flow languages, we denote it by *F*, by applying a single inverse shuffle operation to a language of *C*. Moreover, the inverse shuffle is performed with a regular language of a fixed type (which is intended to simulate the semaphore synchronisation mechanism). Thus every flow language is of the form $L \sim W_S$ where $L \in C$ and $W_S \in REG$ is a set of the form $W_S = \Delta(s \cup s\bar{s})^*$ where the shuffle is over all $s \in S$, S and $\bar{S} = \{\bar{s} | s \in S\}$ are the alphabets of signals and waits respectively, and L is a language over some terminal alphabet and $S \cup \bar{S}$. Shaw [25] conjectured that F is a subclass of CS and incomparable with CF. Jantzen disproved this conjecture by using AFL techniques and in the next section we prove the same result by providing a direct simulation of universal computations.

Note that in event expressions (as defined originally in [23,24]) and in flow expressions [25], the operations of cancellation and inverse shuffle are implicit (in the semantic mechanism which takes the expression into the language it defines). On the other hand, D- and E-expressions introduce these operations in the syntactic level.

3. Comparison and Universality Results.

From the practical point of view it would be very desirable to have the various description schemes presented in the previous section be all less than universal. Unfortunately, as we have mentioned, this is not the case. It turns out that F, D and E (and even D_{REG} and F_{REG}) are all universal. The proofs of these facts use a simple simulation technique along the lines of [21] (although for F the construction becomes quite cumbersome).

3.1 Theorem. $D_{REG} = RE = F_{REG}$.

Proof. We show how to construct D- and E-expressions (with appropriate restrictions on ~ and % respectively) which simulate the computation of a 2-counter machine (2CM). Since the latter is universal the theorem follows. A 2-counter machine M is a program over a set of instructions of the following form:

$$\left.\begin{array}{l} q_i\text{: IF counter=0 THEN } \underline{\text{goto}}\ q_j \text{ ELSE } \underline{\text{goto}}\ q_k \\ q_i\text{: write}(\sigma)\text{; } \underline{\text{goto}}\ q_j \\ q_i\text{: counter} \leftarrow \text{counter} \pm 1\text{; } \underline{\text{goto}}\ q_j \end{array}\right\} (*)$$

$$q_i\text{: HALT}$$

The machine has two counters to operate on, C_A and C_B, and it is initialized in a distinguished starting state q_0, with some initial counter values. We assume that each machine has a unique HALTing state q_h. The sequence of symbols output during a complete computation of M (for some initial counter values) is the output string, and the set of all output strings is the language defined by M, L(M). A configuration of

M is a triple (r,s,q) where r and s are the values of counters C_A and C_B respectively and q is a state of M. In expressions which we shall write this configuration will be represented by the string $a^r b^s q$ (roughly). Let Q be the set of states of M; $q_0, q_h \varepsilon Q$ the starting and halting states respectively. Let Σ be the output alphabet of M. We will need several auxiliary symbols (disjoint from Σ).

$\{a,b,\bar{a},\bar{b}\}$ - for counter values; $\{\bar{q}|q\varepsilon Q\}$ - to match the "real" states $\{[,],¢\}$ - to keep things in "order"; and $\{\alpha,\beta,\gamma,\delta,\bar{\alpha},\bar{\beta},\bar{\gamma},\bar{\delta}\}$ - for counting in the expressions.

(I) <u>the case of E_{REG}</u>.

For each state of M write an E-expression which describes the set of all possible configuration changes at that state. Let

$$N = (\bar{\alpha}\bar{\gamma})^{\dagger} \ \Delta \ (\bar{\beta}\bar{\delta})^{\dagger} \quad \text{and } K = \lambda \cup \alpha\bar{\alpha} \cup \beta\bar{\beta} \cup \gamma\bar{\gamma} \cup \delta\bar{\delta}$$

Observe that N introduces an equal number of $\bar{\alpha}$'s and $\bar{\gamma}$'s and similarly an equal number of $\bar{\beta}$'s and $\bar{\delta}$'s; also note that K is finite and hence regular.

There are four different types of instructions;

(i) $q_i : C_A \leftarrow C_A + 1$; <u>goto</u> q_j

$$e_i = ¢((((\bar{a}\alpha)^*(\bar{b}\beta)^*\bar{q}_i][a(a\gamma)^*(b\delta)^*q_j)\Delta N)\%K)$$

The reader should be able to see that the language defined by e_i is:

$$L(e_i) = \{¢\bar{a}^n\bar{b}^m\bar{q}_i][a^{n+1}b^m q_j|n,m\geq 0\}$$

(ii) $q_i : C_A \leftarrow C_A - 1$; <u>goto</u> q_j

$$e_i = ¢(((\bar{a}(\bar{a}\alpha)^*(\bar{b}\beta)^*\bar{q}_i][(a\gamma)^*(b\delta)^*q_j)\Delta N)\%K)$$

$$L(e_i) = \{¢\bar{a}^{n+1}\bar{b}^m\bar{q}_i][a^n b^m q_j|n,m\geq 0\}$$

(iii) q_i : write(σ); <u>goto</u> q_j

$$e_i = ¢((((\bar{a}\alpha)^*(\bar{b}\beta)^*\bar{q}_i]\sigma[(a\gamma)^*(b\delta)^*q_j)\Delta N)\%K)$$

$$L(e_i) = \{¢\bar{a}^n\bar{b}^m\bar{q}_i]\sigma[a^n b^m q_j|n,m\geq 0,\sigma\varepsilon\Sigma\}$$

(iv) q_i : IF C_A=0 THEN <u>goto</u> q_j ELSE <u>goto</u> q_k

$$e_i = ¢((((\bar{b}\beta)^*\bar{q}_i][(b\delta)^*q_j)\Delta N)\%K) \quad \cup$$

$$¢((((\bar{a}\alpha)^*\bar{a}(\bar{b}\beta)^*\bar{q}_i][(a\gamma)^*a(b\delta)^*q_k)\Delta N)\%K)$$

$$L(e_i) = \{¢\bar{b}^m\bar{q}_i][b^m q_j|m\geq 0\} \cup \{¢\bar{a}^{n+1}\bar{b}^m\bar{q}_i][a^{n+1}b^m q_k|n,m\geq 0\}$$

Similar expressions are derived for instructions involving the counter C_B. Now let

$$\text{START} = [a^*b^*q_0 \qquad \text{and} \qquad \text{HALT} = ¢\bar{a}^*\bar{b}^*\bar{q}_h]$$

$$\tilde{Q} = \{q\bar{q} \mid q \in Q\} \qquad \text{and} \qquad \mathrm{COMP} = (\bigcup_{i \neq h} e_i)^{\dagger}$$

then the final expression is

$$e_{final} = (\mathrm{START} \Delta \mathrm{COMP} \Delta \mathrm{HALT}) \;\; \% \;\; ([\text{¢}(a\bar{a})^*(b\bar{b})^*\tilde{Q}])^*$$

which clearly defines a language in $\mathcal{E}_{REG}$. The proof that $L(e_{final})$ is equal to $L(M)$ is omitted.

(II) <u>the case of $\mathcal{D}_{REG}$</u>.

The D-expressions for each state of M are constructed as in (I) except that we write ~K' instead of %K where $K' = (\alpha\bar{\alpha})^*(\beta\bar{\beta})^*(\gamma\bar{\gamma})^*(\delta\bar{\delta})^*$. The languages defined by the expressions remain the same. The rest of the construction is precisely the same with % replaced by ~. Alternatively, the universality of $\mathcal{D}_{REG}$ follows from the next theorem. □

The next theorem was proved by Jantzen [13] using AFL theory. We prove it using simulation, as in the proof of theorem 3.1.

3.2 <u>Theorem.</u> $\mathcal{F}$ = RE.

<u>Proof</u>. (Outline) We will slightly restrict the operation of the 2-counter machine so that in (*) for each type of instruction $i \neq j$ and $i \neq k$ holds. No generality is lost by this assumption. Let M be any such machine, $Q = \{q_0, q_1, \ldots, q_h\}$ its states, q_0 the starting state, q_h the unique halting state and Σ its output alphabet. As in the proof of Theorem 3.1 we need auxiliary symbols to force the simulation, now however, we have to organize them into signal/wait discipline, see [25]. Thus in general, $\bar{s}$ "will wait" for the signal s, etc.

For each i ($0 \leq i \leq h$) and j ($1 \leq j \leq h-1$) we will have the following signal symbols: $\{a_i, \alpha_i, b_i, \beta_i\}$, $\{\tau_{j1}, \tau_{j2}, \tau_{j3}, \tau_{j4}, \tau_{j5}, \tau_{j6}, \tau_{j7}, \tau_{j8}\}$ and the corresponding wait symbols: $\{\bar{a}_i, \bar{\alpha}_i, \bar{b}_i, \bar{\beta}_i\}$ and $\{\bar{\tau}_{j1}, \bar{\tau}_{j2}, \bar{\tau}_{j3}, \bar{\tau}_{j4}, \bar{\tau}_{j5}, \bar{\tau}_{j6}, \bar{\tau}_{j7}, \bar{\tau}_{j8}\}$. In addition we will have $\{\text{¢}, \bar{\text{¢}}, \$, \bar{\$}\}$. First define the following expressions for $i = 1, 2, \ldots, h-1$.

$$d_i = (\tau_{i1} \cup \tau_{i1}\bar{\tau}_{i1})^* \Delta \ldots \Delta (\tau_{i8} \cup \tau_{i8}\bar{\tau}_{i8})^* \text{ and } N_i = (\bar{\tau}_{i1}\tau_{i2}\bar{\tau}_{i5}\tau_{i6})^{\dagger} \Delta (\bar{\tau}_{i3}\tau_{i4}\bar{\tau}_{i7}\tau_{i8})^{\dagger}.$$

We now construct an F-expression for each instruction of M($1 \leq i \leq h-1$).

(i) q_i: $C_A \leftarrow C_A + 1$; <u>goto</u> q_j

$$e_i = ((\bar{\text{¢}}(\tau_{i1}\bar{a}_i\alpha_i\bar{\tau}_{i2})^*(\tau_{i3}\bar{b}_i\beta_i\bar{\tau}_{i4})^*\bar{\$}\$\text{¢}a_j\bar{\alpha}_j(\tau_{i5}a_j\bar{\alpha}_j\bar{\tau}_{i6})^*(\tau_{i7}b_j\bar{\beta}_j\bar{\tau}_{i8})^*)\Delta N_i)$$

Note that $L(e_i^* \sim d_i) = \{\bar{\text{¢}}(\bar{a}_i\alpha_i)^n(\bar{b}_i\beta_i)^m\bar{\$}\$\text{¢}(a_j\bar{\alpha}_j)^{n+1}(b_j\bar{\beta}_j)^m \mid n, m \geq 0\}^*$

which can be seen by looking just at the pattern and the number of occurrences of the different τ_{ij}'s in e_i.

(ii) q_i: $C_A \leftarrow C_A - 1$; goto q_j

$$e_i=((\bar{¢}\bar{a}_i\alpha_i(\tau_{i1}\bar{a}_i\alpha_i\bar{\tau}_{i2})^*(\tau_{i3}\bar{b}_i\beta_i\bar{\tau}_{i4})^*\bar{\$}\$¢(\tau_{i5}a_j\bar{\alpha}_j\bar{\tau}_{i6})^*(\tau_{i7}b_j\bar{\beta}_j\tau_{i8})^*)\Delta N_i)$$

(iii) q_i: write(σ); goto q_j

$$e_i=((\bar{¢}(\tau_{i1}\bar{a}_i\alpha_i\bar{\tau}_{i2})^*(\tau_{i3}\bar{b}_i\beta_i\bar{\tau}_{i4})^*\bar{\$}\sigma\$¢(\tau_{i5}a_j\bar{\alpha}_j\bar{\tau}_{i6})^*(\tau_{i7}b_j\bar{\beta}_j\bar{\tau}_{i8})^*)\Delta N_i)$$

$$L(e_i^*\sim d_i) = \{\bar{¢}(\bar{a}_i\alpha_i)^n(\bar{b}_i\beta_i)^m\bar{\$}\sigma\$¢(a_j\bar{\alpha}_j)^n(b_j\bar{\beta}_j)^m \mid n,m\geq 0,\sigma\in\Sigma\}^*$$

(iv) q_i: IF $C_A=0$ THEN goto q_j ELSE goto q_k

$$e_i=\bar{¢}(\tau_{i3}\bar{b}_i\beta_i\bar{\tau}_{i4})^*\bar{\$}\$¢(\tau_{i7}b_j\bar{\beta}_j\bar{\tau}_{i8})^*\Delta(\bar{\tau}_{i3}\tau_{i4}\bar{\tau}_{i7}\tau_{i8})^{\dagger} \cup$$

$$(¢(\tau_{i1}\bar{a}_i\alpha_i\bar{\tau}_{i2})^*(\tau_{i3}\bar{b}_i\beta_i\bar{\tau}_{i4})^*\bar{\$}\$¢(\tau_{i5}a_k\bar{\alpha}_k\bar{\tau}_{i6})^*(\tau_{i7}b_k\bar{\beta}_k\bar{\tau}_{i8})\Delta N_i)$$

$$L(e_i^* \sim d_i)=\{\bar{¢}(\bar{b}_i\beta_i)^m\bar{\$}\$¢(b_j\bar{\beta}_j)^m \mid m\geq 0\}^* \cup$$

$$\{¢(\bar{a}_i\alpha_i)^{n+1}(\bar{b}_i\beta_i)^m\bar{\$}\$¢(a_k\bar{\alpha}_k)^{n+1}(b_k\bar{\beta}_k)^m \mid n,m\geq 0\}.$$

Expressions for instructions involving the counter C_B are derived similarly. Observe that we use the wait symbol $\bar{a}_i$ and the signal symbol α_i in conjunction in the "left part" of e_i while a_j and $\bar{\alpha}_j$ in the "right part". Similarly with b's and β's. This is to ensure that the values of the counters in two "consecutive expressions" (which should represent two consecutive instructions) fit together. Now let

$\text{START}=\$¢(a_0\bar{\alpha}_0)^*(b_0\bar{\beta}_0)^*$, $\quad \text{HALT}=\bar{¢}(\bar{a}_h\alpha_h)^*(\bar{b}_h\beta_h)^*\bar{\$}$ and define

$$\text{COMP} = \text{START}\ \Delta\ (e_1^*\Delta e_2^*\Delta\ldots\Delta e_{h-1}^*)\Delta\ \text{HALT}.$$

Clearly COMP is a C-expression. Now we construct the signal/wait expression W.

$$W = (d_1\Delta d_2\Delta\ldots\Delta d_{h-1})\ \Delta\ (a_0\cup a_0\bar{a}_0)^*\Delta\ldots\Delta(a_h\cup a_h\bar{a}_h)^*\Delta$$

$$(\alpha_0\cup\alpha_0\bar{\alpha}_0)^*\Delta\ldots\Delta(\alpha_h\cup\alpha_h\bar{\alpha}_h)^*\ \Delta\ (b_0\cup b_0\bar{b}_0)^*\Delta\ldots\Delta(b_h\cup b_h\bar{b}_h)^*\Delta$$

$$(\beta_0\cup\beta_0\bar{\beta}_0)^*\Delta\ldots\Delta(\beta_h\cup\beta_h\bar{\beta}_h)^*\ \Delta\ (¢\cup¢\bar{¢})^*\ \Delta\ (\$\cup\$\bar{\$})^*$$

The proof that L(COMP~W)=L(M) can now be broken into a sequence of straightforward but cumbersome manipulations which involve a controlled "moving" of parts of W into COMP. We will omit this part of the proof. [

The diagram of Figure 2 summerizes the inclusion relationships between the classes of languages (or equivalently, expressions) discussed above.

4. Remarks on the Complexity of Concurrent Operations.

We have used four concurrent operations in previous sections Δ, †, % and ~. The operations of cancellation and inverse shuffle also involve a good deal of "controlled" erasing with some flavor of intersection. One should not therefore be too surprised at the universality results of the previous section. It is also obvious that shuffle and dagger are respectively more difficult than concatenation and Kleene star.

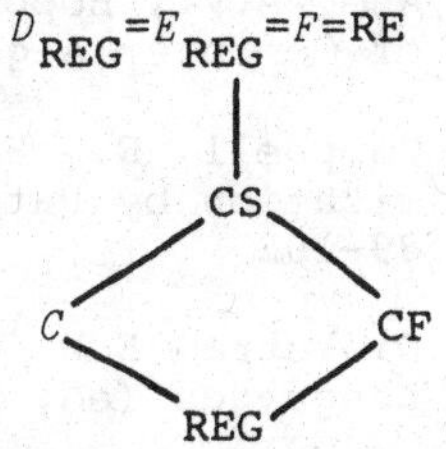

Figure 2

It follows therfore that all the complexity and completeness results concerning pure (or restricted) regular expressions [12,1,20,27] trivially translate into (most probably improvable) lower bounds when in addition the operations Δ and † (or even just Δ) are used. For instance, nonequivalence of star-free regular expressions is NP-complete [27]; nonuniversality of regular expressions (or equivalently, nonempty-complement) is PSPACE-complete [20,1].

It should be observed that properties like equivalence, emptiness and universality (i.e. being equal to Σ^*) in the description languages are connected to issues of correctness and deadlock on the behavioral level, see [25].

Finally we observe that the operation of squaring [20] which can exponentially reduce the length of some regular expressions can be replaced by the inverse shuffle operation with only linear length increase: $R^2=(R\#)^*\sim(\#\#)$ where # does not occur in R. Thus each "square" costs 8 additional symbols. It follows that expressions with $\{\cup,.,*,\sim\}$ have exponential (time and space) lower bounds [20,27].

5. Summary.

In this paper we have discussed several algebraic approaches to software description. We have compared their expressivity by looking at the classes of formal languages which result from such descriptions in a natural fashion. It turns out that the handy operations like inverse shuffle [12] and cancellation [23,24] are such not without a cause. Only by severely restricting their application can we get a description language which leaves some hope of being analyzable.

REFERENCES

[1] Aho, A.V., Hopcroft, J.E. and Ullman, J.D. - The Design and Analysis of Computer Algorithms; Addison-Wesley, 1974.

[2] Campbell, R., Habermann, A.N. - The Specification of Process Synchronization by Path Expressions; Springer Verlag, LNCS 16, 1974, pp. 89-102.

[3] Dijkstra, E.W. - Cooperating Sequential Processes; Programming Languages (ed. F. Genuys), Academic Press.

[4] Feldman, J.A. - A Programming Methodology for Distributed Computing (among other things); TR-9, Dept. of CS, Univ. of Rochester, 1976.

[5] Ginsburg, S. - The Mathematical Theory of Context-free Languages; McGraw-Hill, 1966.

[6] Ginsburg, S. and Spanier, E.H. - Mappings of Languages by Two-Tape Devices; JACM 12,3 (1965), pp. 423-434.

[7] Greif, I. - A Language for Formal Problem Specification; CACM 20, 12 (1977), pp. 931-935.

[8] Haberman, A.N. - Path Expressions; CS Dept., Carnegie-Mellon, June 1975.

[9] Hoare, C.A.R. - Communicating Sequential Processes; CACM 21, 8 (1978), pp. 666-677.

[10] Hopcroft, J.E. and Ullman, J.D. - Formal Languages and their Relation to Automata; Addison-Wesley, 1969.

[11] Höpner, M. and Opp, M. - About three Equational Classes of Languages built by shuffle Operations; Springer Verlag, LNCS 45, 1976, pp. 337-344.

[12] Hunt, H.B. III - On Time and Tape Complexity of Languages; Ph.D. Dissertation, Cornell Univ., 1973.

[13] Jantzen, M. - private communication.

[14] Kimura, T. - An Algebraic System for Process Structuring and Interprocess Communication; 8th ACM STOC, Hershey, Penn., 1976, pp. 92-100.

[15] Kimura, T. - Formal Description of Communication Behaviour; John Hopkins Conference on Information Sciences and Systems, Baltimore 1979.

[16] Kimura, T. - Algebraic Study of Concurrent System Behaviour; Working Note #43, Dept. of CS, Washington Univ., 1979.

[17] Ladner, R.E. - The Complexity of Problems in Systems of Communicati Sequential Processes; 11th ACM STOC, Atlanta, Georgia, 1979, pp. 214-223.

[18] Lipton, R.J. - The Reachability Problem Requires Exponential Space; Yale Research Report #6, 1976.

[19] Mazurkiewicz, A. - Parallel Recursive Program Schemes; 4th Symposiu

MFCS, Springer Verlag, LNCS 32, 1975, pp. 75-87.

[20] Meyer, A.R. and Stockmeyer, L.J. - The Equivalence Problem for Regular Expressions with Squaring Requires Exponential Space; 13th SWAT, 1972, pp. 125-129.

[21] Ogden, W.F., Riddle, W.E. and Rounds, W.C. - Complexity of Expressions Allowing Concurrency; 5th ACM POPL, Tucson, Arizona, 1978, pp. 185-194.

[22] Reif, J.H. - Analysis of Communicating Processes; TR-30, Dept. of CS, Univ. of Rochester, 1978.

[23] Riddle, W.E. - Modelling and Analysis of Supervisory Systems; Ph.D. Dissertation, Stanford Univ., March 1972.

[24] Riddle, W.E. - An Approach to Software System Modelling, Behavior, Specification and Analysis; RSSM/25, Dept. of CCS, Univ. of Michigan, July, 1976.

[25] Shaw, A.C. - Software Descriptions with Flow Expressions; IEEE Trans. on SE, 3, 1978, pp. 242-254.

[26] Slutzki, G. - Non-Synchronizing Concurrent Processes and their Languages; Dept. of CIS, Univ. of Delaware, April, 1979.

[27] Stockmeyer, L.J. - The Complexity of Decision Problems in Automata Theory and Logic; Project MAC, TR-133, MIT, 1974.

A UNIFORM APPROACH TO APPLICATIVE AND IMPERATIVE FEATURES IN PROGRAMMING LANGUAGES

Stefan Sokołowski
Institute of Mathematics, University of Gdańsk
ul. Wita Stwosza 57, 80-952 Gdańsk, Poland

Abstract:

We call "applicative" such features of programming languages as functional procedures or recursion inside arithmetical expressions. We call "imperative" such features as local variables, states, assignments, loops or parameters called by reference. We give a uniform input/output semantics and proof rules for a toy programming language that includes both. The semantics is nice in that it does not introduce explicitly anything that programmer chooses to leave implicit (e.g. stacks for recursion). The proof rules do not involve complicated variable- and parameter- replacements as is customary for procedures with parameters.

The paper is an informal bird's eye view rather than a formal exposition and the Reader is referred to other papers for technicalities of the approach. Several examples are given.

1. Motivations.

By a <u>state</u> we mean a valuation of a certain set of named variables. By a <u>statement</u> we mean a fragment of a program with the intended meaning to alter states. This can be easily made precise and there is no point going into details now.

An approach to description of semantics is <u>imperative</u> if it involves considerations of states and statements; otherwise it is <u>applicative</u> (compare [1],[2],[16]).

For example the meaning of the ALGOL 60 functional procedure

```
integer procedure newton(n,k); value n,k; integer n,k;
  newton := if k=0 ∨ k=n
              then 1
              else newton(n-1,k-1) + newton(n-1,k) ;
```

may be given in the applicative form as the least fixed point of the functional

$$F : (\mathrm{IntInt} \rightarrow \mathrm{Int}) \rightarrow (\mathrm{IntInt} \rightarrow \mathrm{Int}) \qquad (\mathrm{Int} - \text{integers})$$

defined by

$$F(f) = \lambda nk.(k=0 \vee k=n \rightarrow 1, \\ f(n-1,k-1) + f(n-1,k)\ ) .$$

The above functional procedure may be also given meaning in the imperative way, however much more clumsily. This would involve a study of stacks and auxiliary variables inaccessible for the programmer - and would in fact follow compiler's way around. For higher level reasoning about programs this is very unconvenient.

On the other hand the applicative approach alone is too far away from most present day programming languages to be accepted as the last word in the problem. What we need for today is a uniform description of semantics and uniform proof rules that would deal as nicely with the applicative features such as values, terms, functional procedures, composition of functions, parameters called by value etc., as with the imperative ones: states, statements, succession of statements, loops, procedures, local variables, parameters called by reference etc. The applicative and imperative features in programs may be mixed up, e.g. a functional procedure f (applicative) might be defined by a loop (imperative) with an occurrence of an assignment (imperative) whose right hand part calls recursively f (applicative).

In this paper we give a uniform semantics for a toy language that incorporates all features mentioned above. This semantics gives rise to verification methods. Both - semantics and verification - are higher-level, i.e. they do not introduce explicit stacks for recursion, nor new variables, for purposes of proofs. The essential restriction on generality is in accordance with tendencies to structure programs: the total ban on side effects. No procedure may alter the values of variables that are not quoted on its actual parameter list.

2. Main ideas.

In our approach a program is a set of procedure definitions together with an instruction to activate one of them. These procedures may call one another and every procedure called has to be defined in the set. To every procedure we attach a different world (data field) which is the set of all valuations of the procedure's private variables. Data fields for different procedures are assumed to have nothing in common and computations inside procedure's body do not affect anything from outside its field. By this approach there is no trouble in describing local variables: every variable is local to its data field. The procedures are thus separate modules whose only communications are the transfers of parameters at the entrance and at the exit.

We study now these transfers.

The semantical meaning of a procedure as a whole is, in the deterministic case, a partial function that transforms the input parameters to the output parameters. E.g. the semantical meaning of procedure "newton" from Section 1 is a function

$$[newton] : IntInt \rightarrow Int$$

(by brackets [...] we denote the meaning of a syntactical object, by arrow $\rightarrow$ a partial function). All procedures are thus treated applicatively.

At the call of a procedure a valuation in its data field is generated under which formal parameters take on corresponding actual ones as their values and local variables remain undefined. Therefore after the entrance to the procedure we are in an imperative position. Now the body of the procedure is executed to determine the output. This will be made precise further on.

A procedure may be called in a functional way, i.e. applied to some actual input parameters which are terms to form a more complex term. Its semantical meaning is a function over the data field. It can be also called in a procedural way, i.e. applied to some actual input parameters which are terms and to some actual output parameters which are variables, to form a statement. Its semantical meaning is a function from the data field to itself. Given a valuation v this function yields a new valuation v' that differs from v only over the variables from the actual output parameter list, namely the computed output is assigned to those variables.

Section 3 deals with the problems of semantics.

In Section 5 we study the partial correctness with respect to assertions and the partial correctness with respect to terms. The latter does not involve the notion of state and hence can be used to investigate applicative features where the former inevitably fails.

We say that an S (either a statement or a term) is partially correct with respect to terms t and u iff the value of u after S is, if defined, equal to the value of t before S. An errorless program that computes the factorial of n and assigns the computed value to variable s is therefore partially correct with respect to terms "n!" and "s". The "newton" from Section 1 is partially correct wrt terms $\lambda nk.\binom{n}{k}$ and Id. The two notions of partial correctness can be within a limited scope transformed one into the other. In program verification it is advisable to use them alternately since each has its advantages over the other. The calculus of partial correctness is developped within the calculus of relations (see [3],[4],[7],[9],[10]).

Section 7 is dedicated to termination.

3. Draft syntax and semantics.

For a precise description of syntax and semantics the Reader is referred to [15]. For the purposes of this presentation we offer a rather self-explanatory notations and explanations in the natural language backed up with a couple of examples.

In our toy language <u>statements</u> are structured in the usual way, using ";", "<u>if</u> ... <u>then</u> ... <u>else</u> ... <u>fi</u>" and "<u>while</u> ... <u>do</u> ... <u>od</u>". In the calculus of relations the semantics of such compound statements can be easily expressed in terms of primitive ones.

Primitive statements are either simultaneous assignments <u>si</u> x1:=t1 &...& xn:=tn <u>is</u> (comp. [6]), where x1,...,xn are distinct variables and t1,...,tn are terms, or procedure calls. The latter will be dealt with further on.

The trouble with the semantics of assignments is that the terms t1 through tn may be fairly complicated, for instance they may involve recursion, and hence an assignment cannot be treated as a simple indivisible action. Thus the semantics of assignment is given in two steps: first compute the values of t1 through tn and only afterwards perform the proper assignment:

(1) $[\underline{si}\ x1{:=}t1\ \&\ldots\&\ xn{:=}tn\ \underline{is}] = ([t1]\otimes\ldots\otimes[tn]\otimes Id)\cdot[x1,\ldots,xn :=]$.

Symbol ⊗ not occuring in the usual calculus of relations is the splitting of computations (see [13] or [15]). Its formal definition for relations is

$$R\otimes S = \{(x,yz):\ (x,y)\in R,\ (x,z)\in S\} \subseteq X\times YZ$$
$$\text{for } R\subseteq X\times Y \text{ and } S\subseteq X\times Z$$

(YZ is the set of two-element sequences over Y and Z resp.); and it reduces for functions to

$$f\otimes g : X\to YZ \quad \text{for } f:X\to Y \ \text{ and } \ g:X\to Z$$
$$(f\otimes g)(x) = f(x)g(x).$$

As usual Id is the identity relation (function) and • is the composition of relations. If terms t1,...,tn evaluate into types T1,...,Tn respectively then the first step of (1) leads from a set V of valuations to the set T1...TnV. For any v∈V, it yields the sequence of values of t1,...,tn under valuation v followed by v iself. The second step is the function

$$[x1,\ldots,xn :=] : T1\ldots TnV\to V$$

defined by

$$[x1,\ldots,xn :=](X1\ldots Xn\ v) = v1$$

where

$$v1(z) = \begin{cases} Xi & \text{if } z=xi \text{ for some } i=1,\ldots,n, \\ v(z) & \text{otherwise.} \end{cases}$$

Now in turn we have to study terms. Besides the conventional term formation rules we assume:

<u>Succession</u>:
If s is a statement and t is a term then s;t is a term and [s;t] = [s]•[t] ;

<u>Tupling</u>:
If t1,...,tn are terms then (t1,...,tn) is a term and [(t1,...,tn)] = [t1]⊗...⊗[tn] ;

<u>Functional calls</u>:
If p is a procedure name and t is a term then p(t) is a term and [p(t)] = [t]•[p] .

It is a high time now to take care of procedures. The syntactical shape of a procedure definition is

```
(2)     proc p(in x1:S1,...,xn:Sn)(out Q1,...,Qk);
          var y1:U1,...,ym:Um;
          t
        corp
```

where

p is the procedure's <u>name</u> ;
x1,...,xn are the <u>formal input parameters</u> and S1,...,Sn are their respective types ;
Q1,...,Qk are the names of types that provide the <u>output specification</u> ;

y1,...,ym are the *local variables* and U1,...,Um are their respective types ;

t is the procedure's *body* - a term, not a statement .

To describe semantics we define the *data field* attached to procedure p as the set V_p of all valuations of variables x1,...,xn,y1,...,ym , i.e. the set of all partial functions v such that v(xi) is, if defined, in Si for i=1,...,n and v(yi) is, if defined, in Ui for i=1,...,m. An essential restriction is that term t may not involve any other variables than x1,...,xn,y1,...,ym . Thus it can be fully evaluated over a $v \in V$. Another restriction is that the obtained value has to be a sequence from Q1...Qk.

Therefore $[t]: V \rightarrow Q1...Qk$. In the non-recursive case the meaning of the procedure, $[p]: S1...Sn \rightarrow Q1...Qk$, is given by

$$[p] = In_p \circ [x1,...,xn :=] \circ [t]$$

where In_p assigns to any sequence s1...sn the sequence $s1...sn\bot$ with $\bot$ - the nowhere defined valuation in V .

In the recursive case the least fixed point pattern has to be used to define [p] (see [15]).

A procedure defined as in (2) may be called either in the applicative way: p(t) is a term for any term t, or in the imperative one: p(*in* t1,...,tn)(*out* z1,...,zk) is a statement for any terms t1,...,tn and any distinct variables z1,...,zk. Here t1,...,tn are the *actual input parameters* and z1,...,zk are the *actual output parameters*. Variables z1,...,zk belong to the data field of the call and are of types Q1,...,Qk respectively.

The semantics of such a call is given by

$$[p(\underline{in}\ t1,...,tn)(\underline{out}\ z1,...,zk)] = ([p(t1,...,tn)] \otimes Id) \circ [z1,...,zk :=] .$$

In words: the functional call p(t1,...,tn) is executed while simultaneously the original valuation is retained and the output of the functional call is assigned to the variables z1,...,zk.

Note that the pushdown store for recursion is implicit in the splitting operation, and that the above mechanism for procedure calls excludes any possibility that a procedure call affect any variables not quoted on its output parameter list.

By a **program** we mean a set of procedure definitions closed under mutual calls, together with a statement that calls one of them. It is obvious what is meant by the meaning of a program.

An abstract "implementation" of the above semantics has been given in [12] in terms of recursive algorithms to show that this semantics although abstract is not surrealistic.

4. Simple examples.

For some more complicated examples the Reader is referred to [15]. We investigate there the semantics and correctness of a list processing program, of a syntax analyser, and of a quick sorting procedure - all of them recursive and rather complex.

Example 1: Integer division.

```
proc divide(in x:Int,y:Int)(out Int,Int);
  var p:Int,r:Int;
  if x<y
    then (0,x)
    else divide(in x-y,y)(out p,r); (p+1,r)
  fi
corp .
```

The data field of the above procedure consists of all valuations of variables x,y,p,r. The resulting meaning of the procedure is

$$[\text{divide}] = [\div] \otimes [\underline{\text{mod}}] : \text{IntInt} \rightarrow \text{IntInt}$$

(where ÷ is the truncated quotient of two integers and **mod** is the remainder operator)

$$[\text{divide}](X,Y) = (X \div Y)(X\ \underline{\text{mod}}\ Y) .$$

Example 2: Newton's coefficient.

```
proc newt(in n:Int,k:Int)(out Int);
  var ;
  if k=0 V k=n
    then 1
    else newt(n-1,k-1) + newt(n-1,k)
  fi
corp .
```

The resulting meaning is

$$[newt]: IntInt \rightarrow Int ,$$
$$[newt](N,K) = \binom{N}{K} .$$

Note that there are recursive calls inside term. The meaning of the expression after else is

$$[newt(n-1,k-1) + newt(n-1,k)] =$$
$$= ([(n-1,k-1)] \circ [newt] \otimes [(n-1,k)] \circ [newt]) \circ [+] .$$

5. Calculus of partial correctness.

Let $R \subseteq V \times V$; $b,c \subseteq V \times Bool$; $f,g \subseteq V \times Z$ where Z is a non-empty set. We call R partially correct wrt assertions b and c if

$$\langle b \rangle \circ R \subseteq R \circ \langle c \rangle$$

where $\langle b \rangle = \{(v,v): (v,true) \in b\} \subseteq V \times V$ (this definition comes from [3]). We call R partially correct wrt terms f and g if

$$R \circ g \subseteq f .$$

This definition comes from [13]. It can be read as "the value of g after R is equal to that of f before R". The Reader should be aware that for $b,c \subseteq V \times Bool$, the partial correctness wrt assertions b and c is in general __not__ equivalent to the partial correctness wrt terms b and c. The most we can state on that is:

__Theorem 1__ (on transitions)

If $b,c \subseteq V\times Bool$ are total functions then

$$R\circ c\subseteq b \iff \langle b\rangle\circ R \subseteq R\circ\langle c\rangle \text{ and } \langle\neg b\rangle\circ R \subseteq R\circ\langle\neg c\rangle .$$

In order to make the calculus of partial correctness into a part of the calculus of relations, note that:

__Theorem 2__

(a) $[x1,\ldots,xn :=]\circ[xi] = P^{i}_{n+1}$ (projection of an (n+1)-sequence into the i-th axis);

(b) $[x1,\ldots,xn :=]\circ[y] = P^{n+1}_{n+1}\circ[y]$ for $y\notin\{x1,\ldots,xn\}$;

(c) $T\circ(R\otimes S)\subseteq(T\circ R)\otimes(T\circ S)$, and if T is a function then $T\circ(R\otimes S) = (T\circ R)\otimes(T\circ S)$;

(d) $\langle b\rangle\circ R\subseteq R$ and $R\circ\langle b\rangle\subseteq R$;

(e) if R is a function then $\langle b\rangle\subseteq\langle(R\otimes S)\circ[=]\rangle$ implies $\langle b\rangle\circ R\subseteq S$;

(f) $\langle b\rangle\circ R\subseteq R\circ\langle b\rangle$ implies $\langle b\rangle\circ R^{*}\subseteq R^{*}\circ\langle c\rangle$;

(g) $R\circ f\subseteq f$ implies $R^{*}\circ f\subseteq f$.

By means of the above theorem we may show that program

```
P:  s:=1;
    while n>0 do
      si s:=s·n & n:=n-1 is
    od
```

is partially correct wrt terms n! and s. First check that term s·n! is an invariant for the __while__-loop:

$$\langle n>0\rangle\circ[\underline{si}\ s:=s\cdot n \ \&\ n:=n-1\ \underline{is}]\circ[s\cdot n!] =$$
$$= \langle n>0\rangle\circ([s\cdot n]\otimes[n-1]\otimes Id)\circ[s,n :=]\circ([s]\otimes[n]\circ[!])\circ[\cdot] =$$
(by th.2(c) and (a))
$$= \langle n>0\rangle\circ([s\cdot n]\otimes[n-1]\otimes Id)\circ(P^{1}_{3}\otimes P^{2}_{3}\circ[!])\circ[\cdot] =$$
$$= \langle n>0\rangle\circ([s\cdot n]\otimes[n-1]\circ[!])\circ[\cdot] =$$

$= \langle n>0\rangle \circ [(s\cdot n)\cdot(n-1)!] \subseteq$

(by th.2(e) and $\langle n>0\rangle \subseteq \langle (s\cdot n)\cdot(n-1)! = s\cdot n!\rangle$)

$\subseteq [s\cdot n!]$.

Now by th.2(e) and $\langle n=0\rangle \subseteq \langle s=s\cdot n!\rangle$ we have

$$\langle n=0\rangle \circ [s] \subseteq [s\cdot n!] .$$

Therefore

$[P]\circ[s] = [s:=1]\circ[$<u>while</u> $n>0$ <u>do</u> <u>si</u> $s:=s\cdot n$ & $n:=n-1$ <u>is</u> <u>od</u>$]\circ[s] \subseteq$
$\subseteq [s:=1]\circ(\langle n>0\rangle\circ[$<u>si</u> $s:=s\cdot n$ & $n:=n-1$ <u>is</u>$])^{*}\circ[s\cdot n!] \subseteq$ (th.2(g))
$\subseteq [s:=1]\circ[s\cdot n!] = [n!]$.

Note that all considered operations on relations ($\cup, \circ, {}^{*}, \otimes, \langle\ldots\rangle$) are continuous wrt $\subseteq$, hence following theorem can serve as a basis to deal with recursion:

<u>Theorem 3</u> (on recursion)

Let F be a continuous function $F: Rel(V) \to Rel(V)$ (Rel(V) - the set of relations on V) and let RO be its least fixed point. Then

(a) if for certain $b, c \subseteq V\times Bool$ and all $R \subseteq V\times V$, $\langle b\rangle\circ R \subseteq R\circ\langle c\rangle$ implies $\langle b\rangle\circ F(R) \subseteq F(R)\circ\langle c\rangle$, then $\langle b\rangle\circ RO \subseteq RO\circ\langle c\rangle$;

(b) if for certain $f, g \subseteq V\times Z$ and $b \subseteq V\times Bool$ and for all $R \subseteq V\times V$, $\langle b\rangle\circ R\circ g \subseteq f$ implies $\langle b\rangle\circ F(R)\circ g \subseteq f$, then $\langle b\rangle\circ RO\circ g \subseteq f$.

6. Examples (continued).

<u>Example 1</u>

We show that

$$\langle P_2^1 \geq 0 \wedge P_2^2 \geq 0\rangle\circ[divide]\circ P_2^1 \subseteq [\div] .$$

The induction hypothesis is

(1) $\langle P_2^1 \geq 0 \wedge P_2^2 \geq 0\rangle \circ R \circ P_2^1 \subseteq [\div]$,

and it has to be proved that

(2) $\langle P_2^1 \geq 0 \wedge P_2^2 \geq 0\rangle \circ In_{divide} \circ [x,y :=] \circ G(R) \circ P_2^1 \subseteq [\div]$,

where

$$G(R) = \langle x<y\rangle \circ ([0] \otimes [x]) \cup$$
$$\cup \langle x \geq y\rangle \circ ([(x-y,y)] \circ R \otimes Id) \circ [p,r :=] \circ [(p+1,r)] .$$

By Th.1

(3) $\langle x-y \geq 0 \wedge y \geq 0\rangle \circ ([x-y] \otimes [y]) \subseteq ([x-y] \otimes [y]) \circ \langle P_2^1 \geq 0 \wedge P_2^2 \geq 0\rangle$.

Hence

(4)
$$\begin{aligned}
&\langle x \geq 0 \wedge y \geq 0\rangle \circ G(R) \circ P_2^1 = \\
&= \langle x \geq 0 \wedge y \geq 0\rangle \circ \langle x<y\rangle \circ [0] \cup \\
&\quad \cup \langle x \geq 0 \wedge y \geq 0\rangle \circ \langle x \geq y\rangle \circ (([x-y] \otimes [y]) \circ R \otimes Id) \circ [p,r :=] \circ [p+1] = \\
&= \langle 0 \leq x<y\rangle \circ [0] \cup \\
&\quad \cup \langle x-y \geq 0 \wedge y \geq 0\rangle \circ ([x-y] \otimes [y]) \circ R \circ P_2^1 \circ [+1] \subseteq \quad \text{(by (3))} \\
&\subseteq \langle 0 \leq x<y\rangle \circ [0] \cup \\
&\quad \cup ([x-y] \otimes [y]) \circ \langle P_2^1 \geq 0 \wedge P_2^2 \geq 0\rangle \circ R \circ P_2^1 \circ [+1] \subseteq \quad \text{(by (1))} \\
&\subseteq \langle 0 \leq x<y\rangle \circ [0] \cup \\
&\quad \cup ([x-y] \otimes [y]) \circ [\div] \circ [+1] \subseteq \quad (\text{since } \langle 0 \leq x<y\rangle \subseteq \langle 0=x \div y\rangle) \\
&\subseteq [x \div y] \cup [(x-y) \div y+1] = [x \div y] .
\end{aligned}$$

Now we prove that

$$In_{divide} \circ [x,y :=] \circ [x \geq 0 \wedge y \geq 0] = [P_2^1 \geq 0 \wedge P_2^2 \geq 0]$$

and hence derive by Th.1:

(5)
$$\begin{aligned}
&\langle P_2^1 \geq 0 \wedge P_2^2 \geq 0\rangle \circ In_{divide} \circ [x,y :=] \subseteq \\
&\qquad \subseteq In_{divide} \circ [x,y :=] \circ \langle x \geq 0 \wedge y \geq 0\rangle .
\end{aligned}$$

By (4) and (5):

$$\langle P_2^1 \geq 0 \wedge P_2^2 \geq 0\rangle \circ In_{divide} \circ [x,y :=] \circ G(R) \circ P_2^1 \subseteq$$
$$\subseteq In_{divide} \circ [x,y :=] \circ [x \div y] =$$
$$= In_{divide} \circ [P_3^1 \div P_3^2] =$$
$$= [P_2^1 \div P_2^2] = [\div] .$$

Example 2

Apply Theorem 3 to $f=\binom{P_2^1}{P_2^2}$, $g=Id$, $b=\langle 0 \leq P_2^2 \leq P_2^1 \rangle$ and

$$F(R) = In_{newt} \circ [n,k :=] \circ$$
$$\circ(\langle k=0 \vee k=n\rangle \circ [1] \cup$$
$$\cup \langle k \neq 0 \wedge k \neq n\rangle \circ ([(n-1,k-1)] \circ R \otimes [(n-1,k)] \circ R) \circ [+]) .$$

The details are left to the Reader.

7. Termination.

A relation $R \subseteq V \times V$ is said to terminate properly over a set $A \subseteq V$ if $A \subseteq \text{dom } R = \{v: (\exists v')((v,v') \in R)\}$. Intuitively the proper termination is the non-abortion and finiteness of computations. More on that is given in [13] and [16].

The vulnerable points in termination proving are loops and recursion.

Theorem 1 (on loop-counters)

Let $R,S \subseteq V \times V$, $b \subseteq V \times Bool$. Then in order to prove that $\{b\} \subseteq \text{dom } R^*S$ (i.e. that R^*S properly terminates over $\{b\}$) it suffices to find a relation $g \subseteq V \times Nat$ ($Nat = \{0,1,2,\ldots\}$ is the set of natural numbers) such that

(a) $\{b\} \subseteq \text{dom } g$;

(b) $\{g=0\} \subseteq \text{dom } S$;

(c) $\{g>0\} \subseteq \text{dom } R$;

(d) $\langle g>0\rangle \circ R \subseteq R \circ \langle b\rangle$;

(e) $(R \circ g \otimes g) \circ [<] \subseteq [true]$.

-- For the idea of loop-counters the Reader is referred e.g. to [8], [11], [13]. Theorem 1 reduces the problem of termination of R^*S over {b} to the termination of g, S, R over {b}, {g=0}, {g>0} respectively, to the partial correctness of R wrt assertions g>0 and b, and to the partial correctness of R∘g ⊗ g wrt terms true and <.

Theorem 2 (on recursion-level counters)

Let F:Rel(V)→Rel(V) be continuous and b0,b1,b2,... ⊆ V×Bool be a sequence of terms with {b0} = ∅ (empty set). If for any i = 0,1,2,... and any R ⊆ V×V

$$\{bi\} \subseteq \text{dom } R \quad \text{implies} \quad \{b(i+1)\} \subseteq \text{dom } F(R)$$

then

$$\{(\exists i \in Nat)(bi)\} \subseteq \text{dom } R0$$

where R0 is the least fixed point of F.

(Compare with [15]).

The factorial example from Section 5 terminates properly over the set {n≥0}, which is easy to show with [n] for the loop-counter.

Procedure "divide" terminates over the set

$$\{P_2^1 \geq 0 \wedge P_2^2 > 0\} = \{(\exists i \in Nat)(i \cdot P_2^2 > P_2^1 \geq 0)\} .$$

Procedure "newt" terminates over the set

$$\{0 \leq P_2^2 \leq P_2^1\} = \{(\exists i \in Nat)(0 \leq P_2^2 \leq P_2^1 \leq i-1)\} .$$

References:

[1] Backus, J. "Can programming be liberated from the von Neumann style ? A functional programming style and its algebra of programs" Comm. ACM 21, 8, 1978

[2] Backus, J. "Programming language semantics and closed applicative languages" Proc. ACM Symp. on Principles of Programming Languages 1973, 71-86

[3] de Bakker, J. "The fixed point approach in semantics: theory and applications" Foundations of Computer Science, Mathematical Centre Tracts 63, 3-53, Amsterdam 1975

[4] Blikle, A. "An analysis of programs by algebraic means" Banach Center Publications, Vol. 2, 167-213, Warsaw 1977

[5] Blikle, A. "A survey of input-output semantics and program verification" ICS PAS Report 344, Warsaw 1979

[6] Blikle, A. "Specified programming" ICS PAS Report 333, Warsaw 1978

[7] Blikle, A.; Mazurkiewicz, A. "An algebraic approach to the theory of programs, algorithms, languages and recursiveness" MFCS 72, Proc. Symp. Jablonna 1972

[8] Katz, S.; Manna, Z. "A closer look at termination" Acta Informatica 5, 333-352, 1975

[9] Mazurkiewicz, A. "Foundations of theory of programming" (in Polish) Problemy przetwarzania informacji, 39-93, Warsaw 1974

[10] Mazurkiewicz, A. "Proving properties of processes" Algorytmy XI, 5-22, 1974

[11] Sokołowski, S. "Axioms for total correctness" Acta Informatica 9, 61-71, 1977

[12] Sokołowski, S. "Procedures and functions with parameters in the calculus of relations" Univ. of Gdańsk, Inst. of Math., Preprint No. 17, 1979

[13] Sokołowski, S. "Programs as term transformers" to appear in Fundamenta Informaticae

[14] Sokołowski, S. "Total correctness for procedures" MFCS 77, Lecture Notes in Computer Science Vol. 53, 475-483, 1977

[15] Sokołowski, S. "Term transformations and their role in investigating properties of programs" (in Polish) in preparation

[16] Tennent, R.D. "The denotational semantics of programming languages" Comm. ACM, Vol. 19, No. 8, 437-453, 1976

A RESOURCE ALLOCATION PROBLEM

Zbigniew Suraj
Department of Mathematics
Pedagogical College
35-310 RZESZOW, POLAND

Abstract. This paper deals with the following problems; we have a set of cyclic, deterministic processes, which progress by taking and later releasing a number of various kinds of resources, the system being represented by a place/transition net. We are given a technique for putting additional constraints on the system which, given certain assumptions about the pattern of resource usage by the processes, causes the system to execute only those of its original behaviours which do not lead to deadlock. The technique involves the introduction of additional places which have the effect of regulating the progression of the processes in relation to each other. These places act like semaphores.

Introduction

Let's consider the very simple example of Petri net (see Fig.3). It represents a system of three cyclic processes. The marking of the process equals one for some place and zero for others. This processes execute independently, it means that the executing of any process has no influences on executing other processes. Starting from a given marking (see Fig.3) any movement of any token is possible. But if processes use the resources (see Fig.2) (like common memory) it is necessary to consider in our system some constraints.

The number of the tokens in the additional place r represents the number of units of resources. The arrows from the place r to the transitions of the processes represent demands, and the arrows from the transitions of the processes to the place r represent releases of the resources.

The initial marking is given as in Fig.2. Then it is possible to fire, for example, the following sequences of transitions: $t_{01}t_{02}$, $t_{03}t_{13}t_{02}t_{23}$. If we fire the sequence of transitions $t_{03}t_{13}t_{01}t_{02}$ then we obtain a deadlock. But of course it is also possible in our net to execute all processes cyclicly. For example: $t_{01}t_{02}t_{11}t_{21}t_{31}t_{12}t_{03}t_{22}t_{32}t_{13}t_{23}t_{33}t_{43}$.

Our goal is to extend the given net S to the net S' in such a way that the following conditions will be satisfied:

1/ S' is deadlockfree,

2/ S' realizes all the "safe" executions allowed by S and only these executions (i.e. S' is "optimal").

This paper is based on the paper by Lautenbach and Thiagarajan [5]. A small subclass of concurrent systems processes, i.e. linear systems of concurrent copies of a cyclic process in [5] is considered.

We extend the result of Lautenbach and Thiagarajan to the case of cyclic linear systems with cycles of an arbitrary length and different maximal demands.

In this paper the technique of an extension of the linear system is presented. The properties 1/ and 2/ are proved. The most difficult part of the proof concerns the "optimal" property.

The paper contains five sections.

In the first section there are some basic notions of the theory of Petri nets. The second one deals with a certain subclass of the linear systems. The third one contains the properties of linear systems. In the fourth one an extension of the linear systems are considered. The basic properties of the linear system extension and the proof for the linear system extension to be deadlockfree and optimal are given in the fifth section.

1. Basic notions of Petri nets

In this section we adopt some basic notions of Petri nets theory from ([5],[9]).

A triple $N = (P,T,F)$ is a Petri net iff a/ P and T are finite disjoint sets of places and transitions, respectively, b/ $P \cup T \neq \emptyset$, c/ $F \subseteq (P\times T) \cup (T\times P)$ is the flow relation.

For each element $x \in P \cup T$, $x^{\bullet} = \{y: xFy\}$ is the post-set of x and ${}^{\bullet}x = \{\bar{y}: \bar{y}Fx\}$ is the pre-set of x.

A generalized Petri net is a quadruple $N = (P,T,F,W)$, where: a/ (P,T,F) is a Petri net, b/ $W: F \longrightarrow \mathbb{N}^{+} = \{1,2,\ldots\}$ is a weighting function.

In the remaining part of this section we will refer to this generalized Petri net as a Petri net.

Let $N = (P,T,F,W)$ be a Petri net and $A \subseteq F$. Then $W(A) = \sum_{a \in A} W(a)$. If $A = \emptyset$ then $W(A) = 0$ by convention.

A marking of N is a mapping $\mu : P \longrightarrow \mathbb{N} = \{0,1,\ldots\}$. By a marked net we mean a pair $S = (N,\mu)$, where: a/ N is a Petri net, b/ μ is a marking of N.

Instead of a marked net we shall write a net.

Let $S = (N,\mu)$ be a net, where $N = (P,T,F,W)$. Then N is said to be pure if for each $x \in P \cup T$, $^{\bullet}x \cap x^{\bullet} = \emptyset$. In this paper we shall consider only pure nets.

Let $S_1 = (N_1,\mu_1)$ and $S_2 = (N_2,\mu_2)$ be nets, where: $N_1 = (P_1,T_1,F_1,W_1)$, $N_2 = (P_2,T_2,F_2,W_2)$ and $P_1 \cap P_2 = \emptyset$. We say that $S = (N,\mu)$ is a union of S_1 and S_2 iff a/ $N = (P_1 \cup P_2, T_1 \cup T_2, F_1 \cup F_2, W_1 \cup W_2)$, b/ $\mu = \mu_1 \cup \mu_2$. Let's denote this union of nets S_1 and S_2 by $S_1 \cup S_2$.

Let $S = (N,\mu')$ be a net, T^* denotes the set of all strings composed of symbols of T including the empty string ε and $x \in T^*$. The reachability relation from μ' a marking μ'' is defined as usual (see I5I,I9I). If μ'' is reachable from μ', then we write $\mu' \xrightarrow[S]{x} \mu''$. A word x is called a trace of S. By $L(S)$ we denote the set of all finite traces in a net S. $L(S)$ is called the language of finite traces of a net S. An infinite sequence $x_0, x_1, \ldots$ is called an infinite trace in S if there is an infinite sequence of markings $\mu_0, \mu_1, \ldots$ such that, for all $i \in IN$ $\mu_i \xrightarrow[S]{x_i} \mu_{i+1}$, where $\mu_0 = \mu'$. A set of all infinity traces of S is called the language of infinite traces of S and we shall denote it by $L^{\infty}(S)$. By $L_B(S)$ we denote the set of all finite initial segments of infinite traces in S. $L_B(S)$ is called the language of safe traces of S. The set $L(S) - L_B(S)$ is called the language of unsafe traces and we shall denote it by $L_{NB}(S)$.

We say that a net S is deadlockfree (d-free) if $L(S) = L_B(S)$.

Let $S = (N,\mu)$ be a net. Then $[\mu\rangle_S$ is the set of markings reachable from μ defined as usual (see I5I,I9I).

In this work we shall use four concepte of liveness which are defined below.

Let $S = (N,\mu)$ be a net, where $N = (P,T,F,W)$ and $t \in T$. We say that

1/ t is live at μ if for all $x \in L(S)$ there is $y \in T^*$ such that $xyt \in L(S)$;

2/ t is conditionally-live (c-live) at μ if there is $x \in L^{\infty}(S)$ such that $\#(x,t) = \infty$ [1];

3/ t is eventually-dead (e-dead) at μ if there is $k(t) \in IN$ such that for all $x \in L(S)$ $\#(x,t) \leq k(t)$;

4/ t is dead at μ if for all $x \in L(S)$ $\#(x,t) = 0$.

We say that a net S is live (c-live, e-dead, dead) at μ if an arbitrary transition in S is live (c-live, e-dead, dead) at μ.

1/ Let x be a sequence of symbols and y be a symbol. Then $\#(x,y)$ is the number of times y appears in x.

2. Linear systems

A model of linear systems in this section is defined. Before we introduce some notions.

Definition 1. Let $S = (N,\mu)$ be a net. The net S is called 1-linear if

1/ for each $p \in P$ $|{}^{\bullet}p| = |p^{\bullet}| = 1$,

2/ for each $t \in T$ $|{}^{\bullet}t| = |t^{\bullet}| = 1$,

3/ for exactly one $p \in P$ $\mu(p) = 1$, otherwise $\mu(p) = 0$.

An example of the 1-linear net is shown in Fig.1.

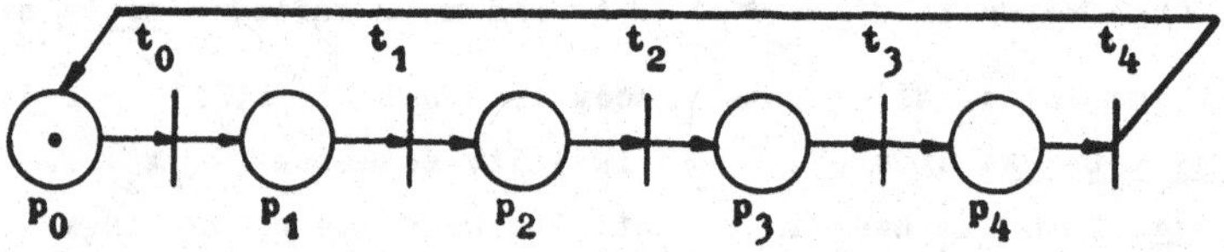

Fig.1

The place p such that $\mu(p) = 1$ is called the initial place and is denoted by p_0.

Let $S = (N,\mu)$ be a 1-linear net, where $N = (P,T,F,W)$. Let $p_i, p_j \in P$. We define in P a relation $<$ ($\leq$) as follows:

$$p_i < p_j \quad (p_i \leq p_j) \quad \text{iff} \quad i < j \quad (i \leq j).$$

It is easy to see that $\leq$ is an order on P. Later when we write $P = \{p_0, \ldots, p_n\}$ it means that $p_0 < \ldots < p_n$. In a similar way we define an order on T.

If $S = (N,\mu)$ is a 1-linear net, then a sequence $t_0, t_1, \ldots, t_n$ such that

$$\mu_i \xrightarrow[S]{t_i} \mu_{i+1} \quad (i = 0,1,\ldots,n),$$

where: $\mu_0 = \mu_{n+1} = \mu$ and $\mu_i \neq \mu$ for $i = 1,2,\ldots,n-1$ is called a process which is defined by S.

The number $n+1$ will be called a length of cycle $t_0,\ldots,t_n$. t_i is the i-th step and p_i i-th stage of process.

<u>Definition</u> 2. A pair (S,P_z) is a <u>m-linear system of concurrent processes</u> with resources P_z iff

1/ $S = (N,\mu)$ has m 1-linear connected components, where $N = (P,T,F,W)$,

2/ $P_z \subset P$,

3/ each connected component of net S obtained from N by delating P_z and the arrows to or from P_z with marking μ restricted to places appearing in this component make the d-free net,

4/ for each $r \in P_z$ there is at least one input arrow to r and at least one output arrow from r.

The set P_z is called the <u>set of resources</u>. In a graph of net the places $r \in P_z$ will be denoted as circles (see Fig.2). At each place which is a resource there is a label denoting a name of this resource. The marking of r is shown by placing $\mu(r)$ tokens into the circle representing r. The tokens of r represent the units of r.

By a <u>fragment</u> of (S,P_z) we shall mean a connected net composed of a 1-linear component, marked places P_z and arrows to and from transitions of 1-linear component.

In the sequel by linear system we shall understand a m-linear system of concurrent processes.

If (S,P_z) is a linear system, $S_1,\dots,S_m$ are its fragments, then union of nets $S_1,\dots,S_m$ uniquely defines S and we shall write $S = S_1 \cup \dots \cup S_m$. The marking μ of S is union of markings $\mu_1,\dots,\mu_m$ of $S_1,\dots,S_m$. We shall write $\mu_1 \cup \dots \cup \mu_m$ instead of μ. The marking μ is called <u>initial marking</u> of S.

An example of 3-linear system with $P_z = \{r\}$ is shown in Fig.2.

Let's note that the net S (Fig.2) is not d-free, since, for example, $t_{01}t_{03}$ do not belong to $L_B(S)$.

If $P_z = \emptyset$ then the linear system $(S,\emptyset)$ is called an <u>independent one</u>.

Let $T_1,\dots,T_m$ be sets of transitions corresponding to linear components $S_1,\dots,S_m$ of the system S. The order relation on set T_j is defined by $\leq$ in the 1-linear net S_j. t_{ij} is the i-th transition in T_j (with respect to the order $\leq$).

By a <u>length</u> of the linear component we shall understand a number of transitions in this component.

In the sequel by the independent system we shall understand the independent linear system and instead of $(S,\emptyset)$ we shall write S.

Let S be an independent system, μ' be a marking such that $\mu' = \mu_1' \cup \dots \cup \mu_m'$ and $\mu_j' \in [\mu_j\rangle S_j$ for $j = 1,\dots,m$, where $S_1,\dots,S_m$ are linear components of S.

Let $k_1,\ldots,k_m$ denote a length of corresponding linear components of S.

If $\mu'(p_{ij}) = 1$, where $i > 0$ then we say that j-th process is <u>active</u> at μ' (the i-th stage is reached). If $\mu'(p_{0j}) = 1$ then j-th process is <u>unactive</u> at μ'.

In Fig.3 is shown an independent system in which all the processes are unactive.

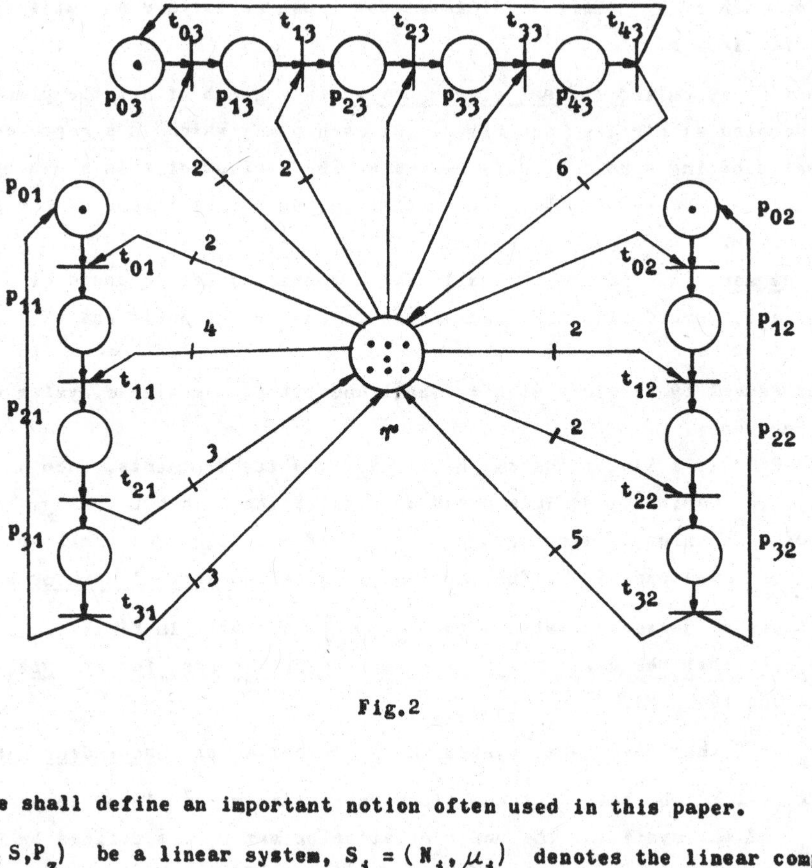

Fig.2

Now we shall define an important notion often used in this paper.

Let (S,P_z) be a linear system, $S_j = (N_j,\mu_j)$ denotes the linear component of S and its length is k_j, where $N_j = (P_j,T_j,F_j,W_j)$. Now let $r \in P_z$.

By $Z_r(i,j)$ we denote the number $W_j(\{(r,t)\in F_j:\ t \geqslant t_{ij}\})$. $Z_r(i,j)$ is called <u>global i-demand</u> of process which is defined by component S_j. This process is at i-th stage and its demands concern resource of type r (shortly: resource r).

If a process defined by corresponding component is at i-th stage then it will take $Z_r(i,j)$ units of resource r to the end of the cycle.

<u>Definition</u> 3. By a <u>maximal demand</u> concerning a resource r at the i-th stage we shall understand the number defined as follows:

$$Max(i,r) = \max_{1 \leq j \leq m} \{Z_r(i,j)\} ,$$

where: $0 \leq i < \max_{1 \leq j \leq m} \{ k_j \}$.

For example, in the linear system (Fig.2) we have: $Z_r(2,1) = 0$, $Z_r(2,2) = 2$, $Max(0,r) = 6$ and $Max(3,r) = 1$.

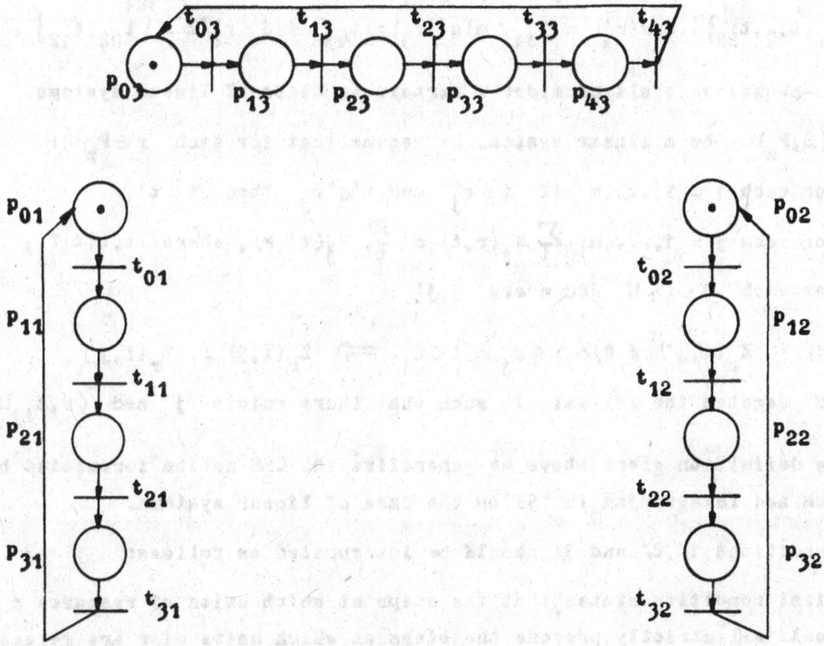

Fig.3

Let (S,P_z) be a linear system, $S_1,\dots,S_m$ its components and $k_1,\dots,k_m$ are their lengths. Let $r \in P_z$ and the component $S_j = (N_j, \mu_j)$, where $N_j=(P_j,T_j,F_j,W_j)$.

A set $r_j^{\bullet} = \{ t \in T_j : rF_j t\}$ is called the <u>set of transitions using</u> a resource r in S_j.

By $^{\bullet}r_j$ we denote the <u>set of transitions sending</u> resources r to S_j. This set can be described as follows:

$$^{\bullet}r_j = \{ t \in T_j : tF_j r\} .$$

By $max(r_j^\bullet)$ we denote the transition $t \in r_j^\bullet$ which has the maximal index. t is called the <u>maximal transition using</u> a resource r in S_j.

By $max(^\bullet r_j)$ we mean the transition $t \in {^\bullet r_j}$ which has the maximal index. The transition t is called the <u>maximal transition sending</u> resources to S_j.

$min(r_j^\bullet)$ and $min(^\bullet r_j)$ are defined in the similar way.

By $r_j^\bullet/l$ we denote the set consisting of l initial transitions of $r_j^\bullet$, where $0 \leq l \leq |r_j^\bullet|$. The set $r_j^\bullet/l$ is called a <u>segment</u> of $r_j^\bullet$ of length l.

For example, in a linear system (Fig.2) we have: $^\bullet r_2 = \{t_{32}\}$, $r_2^\bullet = \{t_{02}, t_{12}, t_{22}\}$, $max(r_1^\bullet) = t_{11}$, $min(^\bullet r_3) = t_{43}$ and $r_2^\bullet/2 = \{t_{02}, t_{12}\}$.

In the sequel we shall consider a certain subclass of linear systems.

Let (S, P_z) be a linear system. We assume that for each $r \in P_z$:

1/ for each $j = 1, \ldots, m$ if $t \in r_j^\bullet$ and $t' \in {^\bullet r_j}$ then $t < t'$,

2/ for each $j = 1, \ldots, m$ $\sum_t W_j(r,t) = \sum_{t'} W_j(t',r)$, where $t, t' \in T_j$,

3/ for each $0 < i \leq M$ and every j, j'

$$(Z_r(i,j) \cdot Z_r(i,j') \neq 0) \wedge i < k_j \wedge i < k_{j'} \Longrightarrow Z_r(i,j) = Z_r(i,j'),$$

where: M denotes the maximal i such that there exists j and $(r, t_{ij}) \in F_j$.

In the definition given above we generalize the CSS notion formulated by Lautenbach and Thiagarajan in I5I on the case of linear systems.

The conditions 1/,2/ and 3/ should be interpreted as follows:

The first condition states that the steps at which units of resource r are taken should (all) strictly precede the steps at which units of r are released.

The second condition demands that at the end of each run the total number of units of r that have been taken should exactly equal the total number of units of r that have been released.

At last the third condition means that every two processes whose demands have not been satisfied yet have the same global demands at an arbitrary stage of execution from the first up to the M-th stage.

Let's note that in a linear system shown in Fig.2 the above conditions are satisfied. In the sequel the linear systems satisfying the above conditions are called the linear systems.

3. The properties of linear systems

In this section we investigate the properties of linear systems. It is useful to observe that in the linear systems some properties of liveness of the whole system depend on properties of liveness of all single fragments of the system. More precisely,

Theorem 1. Let (S,P_z) be a linear system, μ is a initial marking of S, S_j denotes a fragment of S and $\mu' \in [\mu]_S$. Then

1/ if each fragment S_j is c-live at μ'/S_j then S is c-live at μ'.

2/ S is e-dead at μ' iff each fragment S_j is e-dead at μ'/S_j.

The proof is given in I9I.

The next theorem states a necessary and sufficient condition for a linear system to be c-live at its initial marking.

Theorem 2. Let (S,P_z) be a linear system and μ its initial marking. Then S is c-live at μ iff

$$\text{for each } r \in P_z \quad \mu(r) \geqslant \text{Max}(0,r).$$

The proof is given in I9I.

If not states otherwise, each linear system that we consider will be assumed to be c-live at its initial marking.

4. An extension of linear system

We have noticed earlier that in the linear system some unsafe traces can be generated. For example, for the linear system (Fig.2) the following traces are unsafe: $t_{01}t_{03}$, $t_{02}t_{03}t_{12}t_{13}$. If we fire these traces then we obtain a deadlock. Our goal is to extend the given linear system (S,P_z) to the system (S',P_z') in such a way that the following conditions will be satisfied:

1/ $L(S') = L_B(S')$,

2/ $L(S') = L_B(S)$.

The first condition states that S' is a deadlockfree (d-free). The second one means that the system S' executes only those original behaviours S which do not lead to deadlock.

We shall realize our goal through the aid of some new places which are added to a given linear system. Those additional places have prevented making unsafe traces in the linear system. The structure and the initial marking of these places is given below.

Let's take a linear system (S,P_z) and resource $r \in P_z$. We construct the sets of transitions using a resource r in components of S. By $r_i^{\bullet}$ we denote the set of transitions using a resource r corresponding to the i-th component. Let us assume that the number of such sets equals s $(1 \leqslant s \leqslant m)$, and $\alpha = \max_{1 \leqslant i \leqslant s}\{\alpha_i\}$, where $\alpha_i = |r_i^{\bullet}|$.

In the case of linear system (S,P_z) there can be generated unsafe traces corresponding to a resource r. The set of all unsafe traces corresponding to a resource r can be partioned into $\alpha - 1$ equivalent classes, where $\alpha = \max_{1 \leqslant i \leqslant s}\{\alpha_i\}$. The unsafe traces of type l belong to the class of type l $(1 \leqslant l \leqslant \alpha - 1)$.

Let $x \in T^{+} (= T^{*} - \{\varepsilon\})$. We say that x is an unsafe trace of type l corresponding to the i-th component $(1 \leqslant l \leqslant \alpha_i - 1)$ if

1/ there is $x' \in T^{*}$ such that $x = x't_{\beta}$, and $x \in L(S)$, where $t_{\beta} = \max(r_i^{\bullet}/l)$

2/ for each $y \in T^{*}$ $xyt_k \notin L(S)$, where $t_k = \max(r_i^{\bullet})$.

An example of unsafe trace of the type 1 corresponding to the first component for a linear system of Fig.2 is $t_{03}t_{01}$. $t_{02}t_{12}t_{03}t_{13}$ is unsafe trace of the type 2 for the third component.

We say that x is a unsafe trace of type l in S if there is i $(1 \leqslant i \leqslant s)$ and l such that x is unsafe trace of type l for the i-th component.

To make a system S a d-free one we add to the system $\alpha - 1$ new places corresponding to a resource r. Those places shall be called the control places and they will be denoted by $\bar{r}_l$ $(1 \leqslant l \leqslant \alpha - 1)$. The control places in a graph are described by ⊜. Each control place is labeled a name of resource with a proper index. By $A(r)$ we denote the set of control places corresponding to a resource r, so $A(r) = \{\bar{r}_1, \ldots, \bar{r}_{\alpha-1}\}$.

By adding $A(r) = \{\bar{r}_1, \bar{r}_2, \bar{r}_3\}$ to the linear system (Fig.2) we obtain an extension of linear system. It will be shown that an extension of linear system is d-free.

The control place $\bar{r}_1$ does not allow unsafe traces of the type 1 to generate. $t_{03}t_{01}$ will not be permitted due to $\bar{r}_1$.

Now we shall give the formal description of an extension of linear system (S,P_z) for a resource $r \in P_z$.

<u>Definition</u> 4. Let (S,P_z) be a linear system, $r \in P_z$ and $\alpha = \max_{1 \le i \le s}\{\alpha_i\}$, where $\alpha_i = |r_i^{\bullet}|$. Then the system $(S',\bar{P}_z)$ is <u>r-extension</u> of (S,P_z) if

1/ $\bar{P}_z = P_z \cup A(r)$, where $A(r) = \{\bar{r}_1,\dots,\bar{r}_{\alpha-1}\}$,

2/ a system obtained from $(S',\bar{P}_z)$ by delating of $A(r)$ and arrows to or from $A(r)$ with the restricted marking to P_z is the linear system (S,P_z),

3/ for every place $\bar{r}_l \in A(r)$ there is :

a/ l arrows from $\bar{r}_l$ to the consecutive transitions of the set $r_i^{\bullet}$ $(1 \le i \le s)$ with the weights equal to the weights of arrows which connect a place r with those transitions, if $l < \alpha_i$;

b/ $\alpha_i - 1$ arrows from $\bar{r}_l$ to the consecutive transitions of the set $r_i^{\bullet}$ with the weights equal to the weights of arrows which connect a place r with those transitions, if $l \geqslant \alpha_i$,

4/ for every place $\bar{r}_l \in A(r)$ there is exactly one arrow from the maximal transition, using a resource r, of each component. The weight of this arrow is equal to the sum of the weights of arrows which connect the place $\bar{r}_l$ with every transition uses resource r except the maximal transition of this component using of resource r,

5/ the initial marking of the place $\bar{r}_l (1 \le l \le \alpha - 1)$ equals $\mu(r) - \mathrm{Max}(\beta'+1,r)$ where β' is the index of the maximal transition of a segment of $r_i^{\bullet}$ with a length l in any component and such that in this component unsafe traces of a type l may be generated.

If we assume that every component of the linear system (S,P_z) is identical to each other then we shall obtain the definition the r-extension of CSS given in I5I.

Now by using this notion of r-extension the P_z-extension of S is defined in the natural way. We simply make r-extension of S for every $r \in P_z$. By (S',P_z') we shall denote P_z-extension of S.

An example of the $\{r\}$-extension of the linear system of Fig.2 is shown in Fig.4.

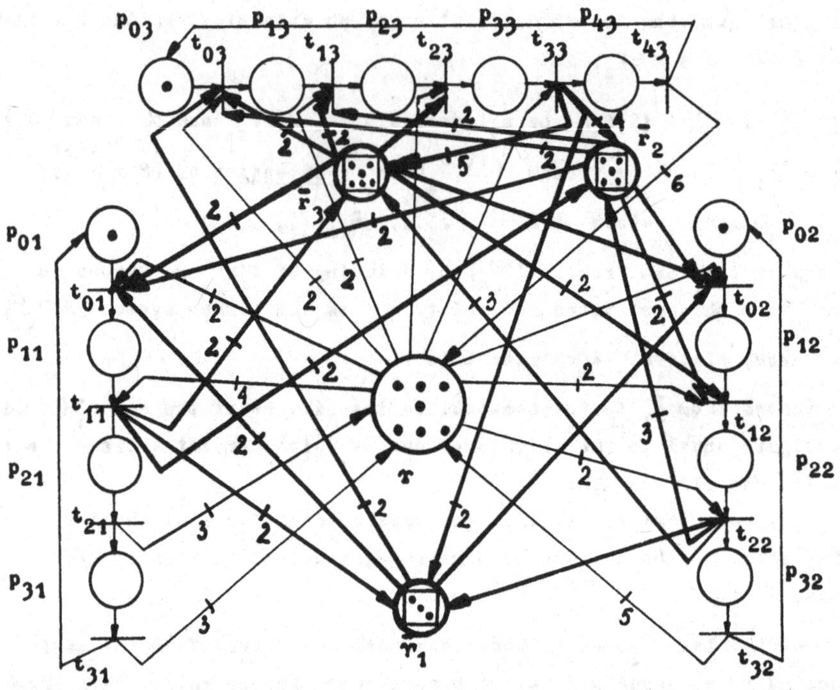

Fig.4

5. The properties of the linear system (S',P'_z)

Now we shall investigate some important properties of the linear system (S',P'_z).

Property 1. Let (S,P_z) be a linear system and (S',P'_z) its P_z-extension. Then (S',P'_z) is also a linear system.

Property 2. Let (S,P_z) be a linear system and (S',P'_z) its P_z-extension, $\mu 1$ denotes the initial marking S'. Then S' is c-live at $\mu 1$.

Those two simple properties are derived from the properties of the linear system (S,P_z) and the definition of P_z-extension of S.

Let (S,P_z) be a linear system, μ denotes the initial marking of S and $\mu' \in [\mu]_S$. Let $p_i \in P_j$, where P_j is a set of places of the j-th component. If $\mu'(p_i) = 1$ then p_i is called the <u>i-th stage of process</u> of the j-th component. By P' we note the set of all places representing the i-th stage of process of the j-th component. We say that p_β is the <u>stage of the most advanced process</u> of S at μ' if

β is the maximal index of the places of P'.

The following lemma states a simple sufficient condition for the most advanced process at a marking of a linear system to complete.

Lemma 1. Let (S,P_z) be a linear system, μ denotes the initial marking of S and $\mu' \in [\mu]_S$. Let p_β be the stage of the most advanced process of S at μ', k_j denotes the length of a component which contains the place p_β. Then $t_\beta t_{\beta+1} \dots t_{k_j-1}$ is firable at μ' iff for each $r \in P_z$ $\mu'(r) \geq Z_r(\beta,j)$, where t_β is in the j-th component.

The proof is analogous as for the Theorem 2.

Now we shall show that a net S' is live at the initial marking of S'.

Theorem 3. Let (S,P_z) be a linear system and (S',P'_z) its P_z-extension, μ and $\mu 1$ are the initial markings of S and S', respectively. Then S' is live at $\mu 1$.

Proof. Let $\mu 1' \in [\mu 1]_{S'}$. By Property 2 S' is c-live at $\mu 1$. Hence it is sufficient to show that $\mu 1 \in [\mu 1']_{S'}$. Let $r \in P_z$. Let's assume that at $\mu 1'$ the most advanced process of S' is in p_β stage and S_i is a component containing p_β. Now we shall prove that this process can execute one complete cycle in S' independently from a value of β. Let's consider the following cases: 1/ $t_\beta \leq t_{k'}$ where $t_{k'} = \min(r_i^\bullet)$. Then at $\mu 1'$ even the most advanced process would not yet have taken any units of r. It means that $\mu 1'(r) = \mu 1(r)$. Now $\mu 1(r) \geq Max(0,r)$ (Property 2 and Theorem 2). Furthermore $\mu 1(r) \geq Z_r(\beta,i)$. Hence $\mu 1'(r) \geq Z_r(\beta,i)$. 2/ $t_\beta > t_k$ where $t_k = \max(r_i^\bullet)$ Then $Z_r(\beta,i) = 0$. Thus $\mu 1'(r) \geq Z_r(\beta,i)$. 3/ p_β lies between $\max(r_i^\bullet/1)$ and $\max(r_i^\bullet/1+1)$. Consider $\bar{r}_1$ corresponding to a resource r. By definition of the initial marking $\bar{r}_1$ it follows $\mu 1(r) - \mu 1(\bar{r}_1) = \mu 1'(r) - \mu 1'(\bar{r}_1)$. Let $t_{\beta'} = \max(r_i^\bullet/1)$. Then $\mu 1(r) - \mu 1(\bar{r}_1) = Max(\beta'+1,r)$ and $Max(\beta'+1,r) \geq Z_r(\beta,i)$. Since $\mu 1'(\bar{r}_1) \geq 0$ it follows that $\mu 1'(r) \geq Z_r(\beta,i)$. Because we have considered now all the cases we conclude that for each $r \in P_z$ $\mu 1'(r) \geq Z_r(\beta,i)$. We can similarly show that for each $\bar{r}_1 \in A(r)$ $\mu 1'(\bar{r}_1) \geq Z_{\bar{r}_1}(\beta,i)$. By Lemma 1 it follows that at $\mu 1'$ the word $x = t_\beta t_{\beta+1} \dots t_{k_i-1}$ is firable. Let $n = \sum_{j=1} \sum_{k=1}^{k_j-1} \mu 1'(p_{kj})$ denote a number of all active processes at $\mu 1'$. If n=1 then we have managed to show that $\mu 1 \in [\mu 1']_{S'}$. To prove the theorem for n>1 we can repeat the above arguments at $\mu 1''$ where $\mu 1' \xrightarrow[S']{x} \mu 1''$. In other words, the theorem can be easily proved by induction on n.

Corollary 1. Let (S,P_z) be a linear system and (S',P'_z) its P_z-extension. Then $L(S') = L_B(S')$.

Proof. Directly from Theorem 3.

By Corollary 1 it follows that S' is d-free. We prove that S' is "optimal".

<u>Corollary</u> 2. Let (S,P_z) be a linear system and (S',P_z') its P_z-extension, μ and $\mu 1$ are the initial markings of S and S', respectively. Then $L(S') \subseteq L_B(S)$.

The proof is given in I9I.

It still remains to prove that $L_B(S) \subseteq L(S')$. To prove this theorem we need some auxiliary notions.

Let (S,P_z) be a linear system, (S',P_z') its P_z-extension and $\mu 1$ denote the initial marking of S'. Let $r \in P_z$ and $\bar{r}_1$ be a control place corresponding to a resource r. By $t_{\beta'}$ we denote the maximal transition at an arbitrary component S using $\bar{r}_1$. Let t_k be the maximal transition of an arbitrary component S using a resource r. By r_p and r_s we denote "dummy resources" which will simulate the behaviour of r in reference to $\bar{r}_1$. Precisely, $Max(\beta'+1,r)$ units of r are allocated to the resource r_s. r_p will "follow" $\bar{r}_1$ as closely as possible. We assume that this simulation satisfies the following condition: for each $\mu 1' \in [\mu 1]_S$,

$\mu 1'(r_p) + \mu 1'(r_s) = \mu 1'(r)$. The simulation is defined iteratively as follows: 1/ $\mu 1(r_p) = \mu 1(\bar{r}_1)$ and $\mu 1(r_s) = Max(\beta'+1,r)$, 2/ Let $\mu 1' \in [\mu 1]_S$, with $\mu 1'(r_p)$ and $\mu 1'(r_s)$ defined. Let $t \in T$ such that $\mu 1' \xrightarrow[S']{t} \mu 1''$. Then $\mu 1''(r_p)$ and $\mu 1''(r_s)$ are given by:

<u>Case</u> 1. t is a transition using a resource $\bar{r}_1$ in an arbitrary component S'. Choose $k_1,k_2 \in IN$ such that $k_1+k_2 = W(\bar{r}_1,t)$ and $k_1 = \max_k \{k: \mu 1'(r_p) - k \geq 0\}$. Then $\mu 1''(r_p) = \mu 1'(r_p) - k_1$ and $\mu 1''(r_s) = \mu 1'(r_s) - k_2$.

<u>Case</u> 2. t is a transition of an arbitrary component S', using a resource of type r and at the same time this transition does not use $\bar{r}_1$.
Choose $k_1,k_2 \in IN$ such that $k_1+k_2 = W(r,t)$ and $k_2 = \max_k \{k: \mu 1'(r_s) - k \geq 0\}$. Then $\mu 1''(r_p) = \mu 1'(r_p) - k_1$ and $\mu 1''(r_s) = \mu 1'(r_s) - k_2$.

<u>Case</u> 3. t is a transition of an arbitrary component S', sending a resource r. Choose $k_1,k_2 \in IN$ such that $k_1 + k_2 = W(t,r)$ and $k_1 = \max_k \{k: \mu 1'(r_p) + k \leq \mu 1''(\bar{r}_1)\}$. Then $\mu 1''(r_p) = \mu 1'(r_p) + k_1$ and $\mu 1''(r_s) = \mu 1'(r_s) + k_2$.

<u>Case</u> 4. t is a transition of an arbitrary component S' and it does not use a resource r. In this case $\mu 1''(r_p) = \mu 1'(r_p)$ and $\mu 1''(r_s) = \mu 1'(r_s)$.

The next lemma states the basic properties of the simulation.

<u>Lemma</u> 2. Let (S,P_z) be a linear system and (S',P_z') its P_z-extension. Let $r \in P_z$ and $\bar{r}_1$ denote a control place corresponding to the resource r, $\mu 1$ is the initial marking S' and $\mu 1' \in [\mu 1]_{S'}$. Then 1/ $\mu 1'(r) = \mu 1'(r_p) + \mu 1'(r_s)$, 2/ $\mu 1'(r_p) \leq \mu 1'(\bar{r}_1)$ 3/ if $\mu 1'(r_p) < \mu 1'(\bar{r}_1)$ then $\mu 1'(r_s) = 0$.

The proof is given in I9I.

Let (S,P_z) be a linear system, (S',P'_z) its P_z-extension, $r \in P_z$ and $\bar{r}_1 \in A(r)$. Suppose that $\mu 1' \in [\mu 1]_{S'}$, $t_{\beta'}$ denotes the maximal transition in an arbitrary component S' using $\bar{r}_1$, t_k is the maximal transition of an arbitrary component S' using a resource r. By $K_1(\mu 1')$ and $K_2(\mu 1')$ we denote the parameters which depend on the actual marking $\mu 1'$. The parameters are defined as follows:

$$K_1(\mu 1') = \sum_{j=1}^{s} \Big(\sum_{i=\beta'+2}^{k} \mu 1'(p_{ij}) \Big(\sum_{t_{\beta'+1}}^{t_{i-1}} W(r,t) \Big) \Big) \text{ and } K_2(\mu 1') = \sum_{j=1}^{s} \Big(\sum_{i=k+1}^{k_j-1} \mu 1'(p_{ij}) \Big(\sum_{t_i}^{t_{k_j-1}} W(t,r) \Big) \Big).$$

<u>Lemma</u> 3. Let (S,P_z) be a linear system and (S',P'_z) its P_z-extension. Let $r \in P_z$ and $\bar{r}_1 \in A(r)$. If $\mu 1' \in [\mu 1]_S$, and $\mu 1'(r_p) = \mu 1'(\bar{r}_1)$ then

$$\mu 1'(r_s) = \mathrm{Max}(\beta'+1,r) - K_1(\mu 1') - K_2(\mu 1').$$

The proof is given in I9I.

<u>Lemma</u> 4. Let (S,P_z) be a linear system, (S',P'_z) its P_z-extension, μ and $\mu 1$ are the initial markings of S and S', respectively. Then $L_B(S) \subseteq L(S')$.

<u>Proof</u>. Assume that the lemma is false. Then there exists $x \in L_B(S)$ and $t \in T$ such that $\mu \xrightarrow[S]{x} \mu'$ and $\mu 1 \xrightarrow[S']{x} \mu 1'$, t is firable at μ' and t is not firable at $\mu 1'$. This implies that for certain $r \in P_z$ and $\bar{r}_1 \in A(r)$ $\mu'(r) = \mu 1'(r) \geq W(r,t)$ and $\mu 1'(\bar{r}_1) < W(\bar{r}_1,t)$. Let $\mu' \xrightarrow[S]{t} \mu''$. By the condition 1 of Lemma 2 it follows that $\mu 1'(r) = \mu 1'(r_p) + \mu 1'(r_s)$, where r_p and r_s are the "dummy resources" simulating a behaviour of the resources r in reference to $\bar{r}_1$. Since $W(r,t) = W(\bar{r}_1,t)$ and thus $\mu 1'(r) > \mu 1'(\bar{r}_1)$. Besides by the condition 3 of Lemma 2 it follows that $\mu 1'(r_p) = \mu 1'(\bar{r}_1)$. Applying now Lemma 3 we obtain $\mu 1'(r_s) = \mathrm{Max}(\beta'+1,r) - K_1(\mu 1') - K_2(\mu 1')$ where β' is the index of the maximal transition in an arbitrary component S' using $\bar{r}_1$. Since $\mu''(r) = \mu'(r) - W(r,t)$, so by suitable substitutions we can get $\mu'(r) = \mathrm{Max}(\beta'+1,r) - K_1(\mu 1') - K_2(\mu 1') + \mu 1'(\bar{r}_1) - W(r,t)$. Let $d = W(r,t) - \mu 1'(\bar{r}_1)$. Clearly $d > 0$. Rewriting the expression for $\mu''(r)$ we get $\mu''(r) = \mathrm{Max}(\beta'+1,r) - K_1(\mu 1') - K_2(\mu 1') - d$. Let t_k denote the maximal transition in an arbitrary component S'_j, using a resource r and let t be from S_j. We shall argue (informally) that t_k is dead at μ''. To see this, let us assume that t_k is firable at μ''. Then $\mu''(p_k) = \mu 1'(p_k) > 0$. But this implies that $K_1(\mu 1') \geq \mathrm{Max}(\beta'+1,r) - W(r,t_k)$ which in turn means that $\mu''(r) < W(r,t_k)$. This is a contradiction. From the definition of $K_2(\mu 1')$, it follows that starting from μ'' the token count on r can be incremented by at most $K_2(\mu 1')$. Thus at this loading, the above argument would apply to establish the non-firability of t_k. Hence by induction on the length of firing sequences that are firable at μ'', we can prove that t_k is dead at μ''. But then $xt \notin L_B(S)$. Thus the transition t is firable at $\mu 1'$ in S'.

By the Corollary 2 and the Lemma 4 we get

<u>Theorem</u> 4. Let (S,P_z) be a linear system and (S',P'_z) its P_z-extension. Then $L(S') = L_B(S)$.

It means that an extension of the linear system is "optimal".

<u>Acknowledgment</u>. I wish to thank very much Professor A.Skowron for his constant encouragement and inspiration during the preparation of this paper and many helpful suggestions.

References

I1I Coffman E.G., Denning P.J., Operating systems theory, Prentice-Hall 1973.

I2I Haberman A.N., Prevention of system deadlocks, Comm.ACM 12,7(1969),373-387.

I3I Haberman A.N., Synchronization of communikating processes,Comm.ACM 15, 3(1972), 177-184.

I4I Hack M., Analysis of production schemata by Petri nets, MAC TR-94,Project MAC, M.I.T. Cambridge, MA(1972).

I5I Lautenbach K., Thiagarajan P.S., Analysis of resource allocation problem using Petri nets, 1st Europ.Confer. on Paral. and Distrib. Proc.,Toulouse, (1979).

I6I Peterson J.L., Petri nets, ACM Computing Surveys 9,(1977), 223-252.

I7I Skowron A., Teoria procesów współbieżnych, w przygotowaniu .

I8I Skowron A., O efektywności w systemach iteracyjnych, PWN, Warszawa 1979.

I9I Suraj Z., A resource allocation problem, ICS PAS REPORTS 404(1980).

AN $O(n^2 logn loglogn)$ EXPECTED TIME ALGORITHM FOR THE ALL SHORTEST DISTANCE PROBLEM

Tadao Takaoka* and Alistair Moffat
Department of Computer Science
University of Canterbury
Christchurch, New Zealand

Abstract: In the present paper we improve Spira's algorithm for the all shortest distance problem and reduce the expected computing time from $O(n^2 log^2 n)$ to $O(n^2 logn loglogn)$ where n is the number of vertices in a graph. We also give an algorithm for distance matrix multiplication with $O(n^2 logn)$ comparisons and additions between distances where n is the dimension of matrices.

1. Introduction

Dijkstra [1] gave an $O(n^2)$ algorithm for the single source problem for a graph with n vertices and non-negative distances between them. If we apply his algorithm n times changing sources, we have an $O(n^3)$ algorithm for the all shortest distance problem.

Spira [2] improved this n- source version and obtained an algorithm of $O(n^2 log^2 n)$ expected time for the all shortest distance problem. Carson and Law [3] tested Spira's method on a computer and confirmed that Spira's method overcame Dijkstra's method at n =120.

In the present paper we improve Spira's method further and give an algorithm for the all shortest distance problem with $O(n^2 logn loglogn)$ expected time. By experiment we see that our method overcomes Dijkstra's method at n=60 and is always better than Spira's method.

We also give an algorithm for distance matrix multiplication with $O(n^2 logn)$ comparisons and additions between distances and $O(n^{2.5})$ expected computing time where n is the dimension of matrices.

---

* On leave from Ibaraki University, Hitachi, Japan

2. Description of Spira's method

Here we desribe Spira's method

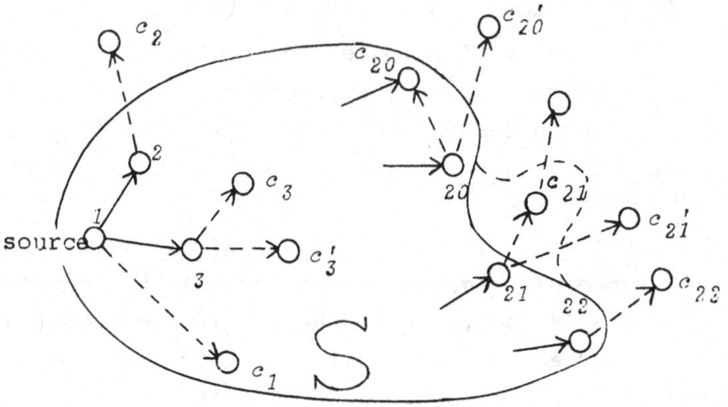

Fig. 1. Illustration for Spira's method

In Fig. 1, S is the solution set of vertices to which the shortest distances from source have been determined. Vertices in S are numbered in the order in which they are explored and called by those numbers for convenience. For vertex i, c_i is the candidate to be explored. Edges from each vertex are sorted and we maintain a pointer to determine the next available edge (i,c_i) from a vertex i. First pointers are set to indicate the shortest edges and S includes nothing but source, that is 1. Then we gradually enlarge S and if S becomes the whole set of vertices we halt.

Now how can we enlarge S? The shortest distance from source to vertex i is denoted $D(i)$, which has been determined. The distance of edge (i, j) is expressed by $d(i, j)$. The distances

$$\{D(i)+d(i, C_i) \mid i=1,2,\cdots\}$$

are maintained in a heap with the smallest at root. At first the heap contains distance $d(1,c_1)$ only. The vertices already in S are labelled. At j-th stage, that is, when $|S|=j$, we pick up the root of the heap. Let the picked-up distance be $D(i)+d(i,c_i)$. If vertex c_i is labelled we increase the pointer for vertex i by one, choose the next candidate $c_i{}'$ and put the distance $D(i)+d(i, c_i{}')$ on to the root of the heap and heapify it in $O(\log n)$ time. We repeat this process until we find an unlabelled candidate.

In our example in Fig. 1, suppose the increasing order of distances is

$D(3)+d(3,c_3)$, $D(20)+d(20, c_{20})$, $D(21)+d(21,c_{21})$,
$D(22) + d(22,C_{22})$, $\cdots$.

We pick up the first distance and see that c_3 is labelled. Hence, we choose the next shortest edge $(3, c_3')$ and put the distance $D(3) + d(3, c_3')$ back to the heap. We do the same thing for the distance $D(20) + d(20, c_{20})$. For the distance $D(21) + d(21, c_{21})$ we know that c_{21} is not labelled. Consequently, c_{21} is now labelled and numbered with 23. The new candidate c_{21}' for vertex 21 is chosen and the distance $D(21) + d(21, c_{21}')$ is put to the heap. The candidate for vertex 23 (previously c_{21}) c_{23} is chosen and the distance $D(23)+d(23, c_{23})$ is put to the heap. In this way we enlarge the set S $n-1$ times. We summarize this method in the following:

Additional notations

- p_k: Pointer for the sorted list of edges from vertex k.
- $I(k,\ell)$: The vertex such that the edge $(k, I(k, \ell))$ has ℓ-th rank in the sorted list of edges emitting from k.
- $N(k)$: Vertex k is included in S at the $N(k)$-th stage of the while-loop.

Vertices are expressed by integers.

Further explanations

Lines $2 \sim 8$: Initialization
i is the source

Lines $11 \sim 16$: Enlargement of S with k added
The new distance is put on the HEAP

Lines $17 \sim 24$: We search for a suitable candidate

At lines 16 and 23 we include heapifications. At line 16 we heapify HEAP by adding a new element. At line 23 we replace the root of HEAP and heapify it. Both lines take $O(\log n)$ comparisons or $O(\log n)$ time at most.

Algorithm (Spira, single source)

```
1     begin
2         LABEL(k) ← NO for k=1, ···, n ;
3         p_k ← 1 for k=1, ···, n ;
4         HEAP ← ∅ ;
5         S ← ∅ ;
6         k ← i ;
7         D(k) ← 0 ;
8         j ← 1 ;
9         while j < n do
10          begin
11              LABEL(k) ← YES ;
12              S ← S ∪ {k} ;
13              N(k) ← j ;
14              c_k ← I (k, p_k) ;
15              S_k ← D(k)+d(k, c_k) ;
16              HEAP ← HEAP ∪ {S_k} ; (heapification)
17              repeat
18                  let S_t be at the root of HEAP ;
19                  c ← c_t ;
20                  p_t ← p_t + 1 ;
21                  c_t ← I(t, p_t) ;
22                  S_t ← D(t)+d(t, c_t) ;
23                  replace the root of HEAP by S_t
                    and heapify the HEAP ;
24              until LABEL(c) = NO ;
25              j ← j + 1 ;
26              D(c) ← D(t)+d(t, c) ;
27              k ← c
28          end
29      end
```

3. Improvement

First we recall the analysis of Spira's algorithm. The while-loop is executed exactly $n-1$ times. The probability p_j of $LABEL = NO$ at line 24 is given by

$$p_j = (n-j)/n$$

Hence the repeat-loop is executed not more than f_j times expectedly where

$$f_j = 1/p_j = n/(n-j).$$

The total frequency of the repeat-loop execution is

$$\sum_{j=1}^{n-1} f_j = n\sum_{j=1}^{n-1} 1/(n-j) = O(n\log n)$$

At line 23 in the repeat-loop we have a heapification so that the expected running time is $O(n\log^2 n)$ in total. If we change source n times, the total running time would be $O(n^2\log^2 n)$. The time for presort is $O(n^2\log n)$ and is absorbed in $O(n^2\log^2 n)$.

Now we aim at keeping the probability p_j larger. The inefficiency of Spira's algorithm comes from the fact that we put new distances on to HEAP regardless of whether the candidates are labelled or not. If possible, we want to put the distance for a good candidate on to the HEAP. To do this, line 14 is replaced by

```
14.1    c_k ← I(k, p_k) ;
14.2    while LABEL(c_k) = YES do
14.3    begin
14.4        p_k ← p_k + 1 ;
14.5        c_k ← I(k, p_k)
14.6    end
```

The above while-loop is executed expectedly as many times as the repeat-loop in the original program, that is $O(n\log n)$ times. This will not affect the total running time in terms of functional order.

We can not do the same thing for lines 20 and 21 because it would increase the functional order of expected running time. Instead we search for a good candidate for a limited number of times and increase the probability of $LABEL = NO$ at line 24. Lines 20 and 21 are replaced by

```
20.1    count ← 0 ;
20.2    repeat
20.3        count ← count + 1 ;
20.4        p_t ← p_t + 1 ;
20.5        c_t ← I(t, p_t)
20.6    until LABEL(c_t) = NO or count > ⌈n/(n-N(t))⌉
```

With this modified version we claim that the probability p_j of $LABEL = N($ at line 24 is given by

$$p_j \geq \frac{1}{2j}\left(\frac{n-j}{n-1} + \frac{n-j}{n-2} + \cdots + \frac{n-j}{n-i} + \cdots + \frac{n-j}{n-j}\right)$$

The proof is briefly sketched as follows. Suppose j vertices are labelled. The vertex labelled at j-th stage has an unlabelled candidat with probability 1, that is, $(n-j)/(n-j)$, guaranteed by the first modification. Next suppose that $N(t) = i$ at line 20.5. Namely vertex t was labelled at i-th stage. If we simply increased p_t by one, the new candidate would have the probability $(n-j)/n$ that it is not labelled. By testing $n/(n-i)$ times, this probability is increased to be at least $\frac{1}{2}(n-j)/(n-i)$. (By lemma A). If vertex t such that $N(t) = i$ is not picked up from the heap, the probability that t is not labelled remains to be $(n-j)/(n-i)$. Finally we observe that vertex t is chosen from j vertices with probability $1/_j$. (Precise proof would be found by mathematical induction.)

4. <u>Analysis of the Improved version</u>

Obviously we have

$$p_j \geq \frac{n-j}{2j} \log \frac{n}{n-j}$$

The frequency f_j of the repeat-loop from line 17 to 24 is given by

$$f_j = 1/p_j$$

Hence the repeat-loop from line 20.2 to 20.6 is executed at most g_j times for a particular j where

$$g_j = (1/p_j) \cdot \sum_{i=1}^{j} \frac{1}{j} \cdot \frac{n}{n-i}$$

$$= 2n/(n-j)$$

because t is any integer from 1 to j with probability $1/j$.

Accordingly this repeat-loop is executed g times where

$$g = \sum_{j=1}^{n-1} g_j = O(n \log n) \quad (\textit{absorbed in } f \log n).$$

The repeat-loop from line 17 to line 24 is executed f times where

$$f = \sum_{j=1}^{n-1} f_j \leq \sum_{j=1}^{n-1} \frac{2j}{n-j} \frac{1}{\log \frac{n}{n-j}}$$

$$= 2n \int_{\varepsilon}^{1-\varepsilon} \frac{-x}{(1-x)\log e(1-x)} \, dx \quad (\varepsilon = \frac{1}{n})$$

$$= 2n \int_{\varepsilon}^{1-\varepsilon} \frac{y-1}{y \log_e y} \, dy$$

$= 2n\log_e\log_e n + const$ (by lemma B)

The overall time spent for the heapification at line 23 is therefore at most $f\log_2 n = O(n\log n\log\log n)$, which is the most dominant part.

Finally, for the all shortest distance problem we have the expected running time $O(n^2\log n\log\log n)$ because we can use our algorithm n times by changing sources. Note that the presort takes $O(n^2\log n)$ time, which is absorbed in $O(n^2\log n\log\log n)$.

Lemma A. If $(m-1)p \leq 1$ and $0 \leq p \leq 1$ then $1-(1-p)^m \geq \frac{1}{2}mp$

Proof. By induction on m, assuming for $k \leq m$, $(k-1)p \leq 1$.

Basis. Set $m=1$, then

$$1 - (1-p)^1 = p \geq \tfrac{1}{2}mp.$$

Inductive step. Assume true for $m-1$. Then

$$\begin{aligned}
1 - (1-p)^{m-1} &\geq \tfrac{1}{2}(m-1)p \\
- (1-p)^{m-1} &\geq \tfrac{1}{2}(m-1)p-1 \\
- (1-p)^{m} &\geq (\tfrac{1}{2}(m-1)p-1)(1-p) \quad \text{since } 1-p>0 \\
&= \tfrac{1}{2}(m-1)p-1-\tfrac{1}{2}(m-1)p^2+p \\
1 - (1-p)^{m} &\geq \tfrac{1}{2}mp + \tfrac{1}{2}p - \tfrac{1}{2}(m-1)p^2 \\
&\geq \tfrac{1}{2}mp \quad \text{since } \tfrac{1}{2}p(1-(m-1)p) > 0
\end{aligned}$$

(Q.E.D.)

To apply lemma A to our analysis, we set

$$p = \frac{n-j}{n} \qquad m = \left\lceil \frac{n}{n-i} \right\rceil$$

Then obviously $(m-1)p \leq 1$, $\frac{1}{2}mp \geq \frac{1}{2}(n-j)/(n-i)$.

Lemma B. If $\varepsilon = 1/n$ and

$$f(y) = \frac{y-1}{y\log y},$$

then

$$\int_{\varepsilon}^{1-\varepsilon} f(y)dy \leq \log_e\log_e n + const$$

Proof. Consider $f(y)$ as shown in Fig. 2.

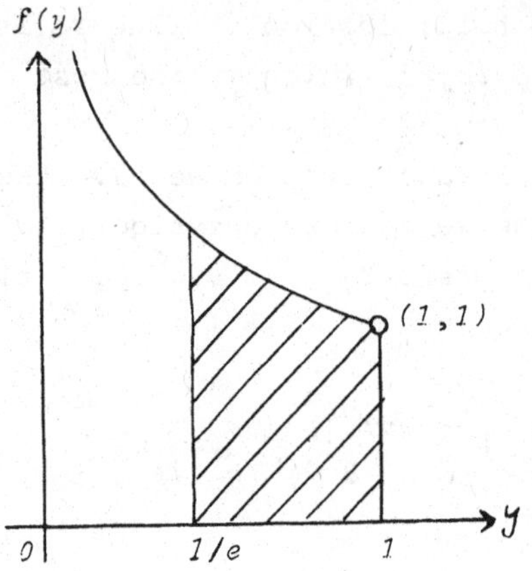

Hatched area = const

Fig. 2 Function $f(y)$

If we define $f(1) = 1$, then by L'Hospital's theorem, f is continuous to 1. Then

$$\int_{\varepsilon}^{1-\varepsilon} f(y)\,dy \leqslant \int_{\varepsilon}^{1/e} f(y)\,dy + \int_{1/e}^{1} f(y)\,dy$$

Clearly the second term is constant. The first term is evaluated as follows

$$\int_{\varepsilon}^{1/e} f(y)\,dy = \int_{e}^{n} -\frac{\frac{1}{x}-1}{\frac{1}{x}\log_e x}\cdot\frac{1}{x^2}\,dx \qquad (y = 1/_x)$$

$$= \int_{e}^{n} \frac{x-1}{x^2\log_e x}\,dx$$

$$\leqslant \int_{e}^{n} \frac{1}{x\log_e x}\,dx$$

$$= \Big[\log_e \log_e x\Big]_{x=e}^{x=n}$$

$$= \log_e \log_e n$$

(Q.E.D.)

5. Distance Matrix Multiplication

Let A and B be distance matrices whose components are non-negative real numbers regarded as distances. The product of A and B, C = A.B, is defined by

$$c_{ij} = \min_{1\leqslant k\leqslant n} \{a_{ik} + b_{kj}\} \qquad (1)$$

where a_{ij}, b_{ij} and c_{ij} are the (i,j) - component of matrices A, B and C. The problem here is to compute C efficiently.

Let $\boldsymbol{a} = (a_1, \cdots, a_n)$ and $\boldsymbol{b} = (b_1, \cdots, b_n)$ be two distance vectors whose components a_i and b_i are non-negative real numbers. The inner product of $\boldsymbol{a}$ and $\boldsymbol{b}$, $\boldsymbol{a}\cdot\boldsymbol{b}$ is defined by

$$\boldsymbol{a}\cdot\boldsymbol{b} = \min_{1\leqslant i\leqslant n} (a_i + b_i) \qquad (2)$$

To compute the product C is to compute n^2 inner products. It requires $O(n)$ time to compute $\boldsymbol{a}\cdot\boldsymbol{b}$. If $\boldsymbol{a}$ and $\boldsymbol{b}$ are sorted in increasing order, however, we can compute $\boldsymbol{a}\cdot\boldsymbol{b}$ faster.

Let $\boldsymbol{\alpha} = (\alpha_1, \cdots, \alpha_n)$ and $\boldsymbol{\beta} = (\beta_1, \cdots, \beta_n)$ be sorted vectors of $\boldsymbol{a}$ and $\boldsymbol{b}$, that is, $\alpha_1 < \alpha_2 \cdots < \alpha_n$ and $\beta_1 < \beta_2 < \cdots < \beta_n$. The index vectors I and J are defined by

$$I = (i_1, i_2, \cdots, i_n) \text{ where } \alpha_k = a_{i_k} \quad (k=1, \cdots, n)$$

$$J = (j_1, j_2, \cdots, j_n) \text{ where } \beta_\ell = b_{j_\ell} \quad (\ell=1, \cdots, n)$$

That is, i_k's and j_ℓ's are the indices of $\boldsymbol{a}$ and $\boldsymbol{b}$ after sorting has been done. It is obvious that I and J are computed in the same computational complexity as that for sorting. We can regard the index vectors I and J as permutations P and Q respectively on the index list $N = (1, 2, \cdots, n)$. That is,

$$i_k = P(k)\ ,\ k = P^{-1}(i_k) \quad for \quad k=1, \cdots, n$$

$$j_\ell = Q(\ell)\ ,\ \ell = Q^{-1}(j_\ell) \quad for \quad \ell=1, \cdots, n.$$

The value $k = P^{-1}(i_k)$ means the rank of the element a_{i_k} in the sorted vector. We establish the following lemma.

Lemma: If the index which gives the minimum value for the form (2) is not found from the first to the k-th component of I or from the first to the ℓ-th of J, then the wanted index will be found in the interval from the $(k+1)$-th to the $(P^{-1}(j_\ell)-1)$-th of I and in the interval from the $(\ell+1)$-th to the $(Q^{-1}(i_k)-1)$-th of J.

Proof: In Fig. 3, we suppose that $i_k = j_{Q^{-1}(i_k)}$ and $j_\ell = i_{P^{-1}(j_\ell)}$. These pairs of some indices are connected by straight lines.

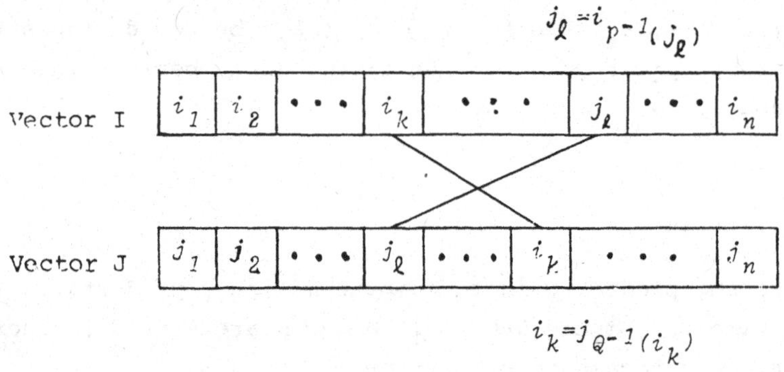

Fig. 3 Index vectors I and J

Let a_m+b_m be the minimum for (2) with m such that $\ell \leq m \leq n$. If m were found in I between $P^{-1}(j_\ell)$-th position and n-th position, the partner would be found in J between $(\ell+1)$-th and n-th position by the hypothesis of the lemma, and hence a_m+b_m would not be the minimum because $a_{j_\ell}<a_m$ and $b_{j_\ell}<b_m$. Likewise, if we suppose that m were not found in J between $Q^{-1}(i_k)$-th position and n-th position, a_m+b_m would not give the minumum for the form (2).

From this we see that m should be found in I between $(k+1)$-th position and $(P^{-1}(j_\ell)$-th position and in J between $(\ell+1)$-th position and $(Q^{-1}(i_k))$-th position if m has not been found in I from the first position to k-th position or in J from the first position to ℓ-th position.

Using this lemma, we can narrow the possible domain for m such that a_m+b_m is the minimum for (2). Let $I = (i_1,\cdots i_n)$ and $J = (j_1,\cdots,j_n)$ and we suppose

I means the permutation $\begin{pmatrix} 1,2,\cdots, & n \\ i_1,i_2,\cdots,i_n \end{pmatrix}$ and

J means the permutation $\begin{pmatrix} 1,2,\cdots, & n \\ j_1,j_2,\cdots,j_n \end{pmatrix}$.

Their inverse permutations are expressed by

$$\begin{pmatrix} 1,2,\cdots, & n \\ i'_1, i'_2, \cdots, i'_n \end{pmatrix} \quad \text{and} \quad \begin{pmatrix} 1,2,\cdots, & n \\ j'_1, j'_2, \cdots, j'_n \end{pmatrix}$$

Let $I^{-1} = (i'_1, \cdots, i'_n)$ and $J^{-1} = (j'_1, \cdots, j'_n)$. Using these notations we have the following algorithm for obtaining the minimum for (2).

Algorithm   (Inner product)

```
1    procedure MINSUM(a,b,I,I⁻¹,J,J⁻¹);
     begin
2        k:=1; ℓ:=1, u:=n; v:=n;
3        min:= + ∞ {a large number};
4        while k ≤ u and ℓ ≤ v do
           begin
5              if J⁻¹(I(k)) ≤ v do
                 begin
6                    v:= J⁻¹(I(k));
7                    if aᵢₖ +bᵢₖ < min
8                      then begin min:=aᵢₖ+bᵢₖ ; m:=iₖ end
                   end;
9              if I⁻¹(J(ℓ)) ≤ u then
                 begin
10                   u:= I⁻¹(J(ℓ));
11                   if aⱼℓ+bⱼℓ < min
12                     then begin min:= aⱼℓ+bⱼℓ ; m:= jℓ end

                 end;
13             k:= k+1; ℓ:=ℓ+1
           end;
14        MINSUM:= min
      end;
     begin    {main program}
15     sort a, sort b and make I,I⁻¹,J and J⁻¹;
16     c: = MINSUM(a,b,I,I⁻¹,J,J⁻¹)
     end
```

6. Analysis of algorithm for distance-matrix multiplication

First we analyse the algorithm for inner product. We recall the informal description of the algorithm. We scan indices in the index vector I from left to right and locate the same indices in the vector J. We do the same thing for J and I. Suppose we scatter i points at random on a line of length n. Then the expected length of intervals between two points is $n/(i-1)$. Suppose that we examine i indices from the left end of I and J. Then we have the following equation for the expected value of i.

$$i = n/(i-1), \quad \text{that is} \quad i = O(n^{\frac{1}{2}}).$$

Scanning indices is the most time-consuming part. Next we examine the expected value of the number of comparisons and additions between distances. Those operations are performed only when the possible intervals for m are narrowed. The intervals are expectedly reduced to half if they are narrowed. Hence the operations of comparisons and additions between distances are performed $O(\log n)$ times expectedly.

To compute C = A·B where A and B are distance matrices, we perform the computation of inner product n^2 times where we suppose A has n row vectors and B has n column vectors. The presort require $O(n^2 \log n)$ comparisons and computing time. Hence we can compute C in $O(n^{2.5})$ computing time and $O(n^2 \log n)$ comparisons and additions.

7. Summary

It is known that the computational complexities of the all shortest distance problem and distance matrix multiplication have the same functional order for worst case time and expected time. Therefore we can compare two algorithms in the present paper in the same table shown below

		additions	comparisons	computing time
Spira	average	$O(n^2 logn)$	$O(n^2 log^2 n)$	$O(n^2 log^2 n)$
	worst	$O(n^3)$	$O(n^3 logn)$	$O(n^3 logn)$
Improved Spira	average	$O(n^2 logloglogn)$	$(n^2 lognloglogn)$	$O(n^2 lognloglogn)$
	worst	$O(n^3)$	$O(n^3 logn)$	$O(n^3 logn)$
Distance Matrix	average	$O(n^2 logn)$	$O(n^2 logn)$	$O(n^{2.5})$
Multiplication	worst	$O(n^3)$	$O(n^3)$	$O(n^3)$

TABLE 1 Complexities of three methods

Improved Spira is better than Spira in every aspect. The algorithm for distance matrix multiplication is better than the other two in terms of comparisons and worst case computing time.

If we look at $kn/(n-i)$ candidates at the lines 14 and 20 in the improved version where k is a constant, then we can improve the constant factor of the complexity, but we can not change the functional order. If we look at an unlimited number of candidates, we may reduce the numbers of additions and comparisons but increase the number of label looks.

The algorithm for distance matrix multiplication may suggest that there could be an $O(n^2 logn)$ expected time algorithm for the all shortest distance problem.

References

(1) E.W. Dijkstra, "A note on two problems in connection with graphs," Numer. Math. 1, pp 269-271, (1959).

(2) P.M. Spira, "A new algorithm for finding all shortest paths in a graph of positive arcs in average time $O(n^2 log^2 n)$," SIAM Journal, Computing 2, pp 28-32, (1973).

(3) J.S. Carson and A.M. Law, "A note on Spira's algorithm for the all pairs shortest path problem," SIAM Journal, Computing 6, pp 696-699, (1977).

DECISION COMPLEXITY OF VARIANTS OF PROPOSITIONAL DYNAMIC LOGIC

M.K.Valiev
Institute of Mathematics
Novosibirsk 90, USSR

1. Propositional dynamic logic (PDL) was defined in [1] by Fischer and Ladner. They proved that satisfiability problem for PDL is decidable in nondeterministic exponential time. Pratt [2] constructed more effective algorithm deciding this problem in deterministic exponential time. In [1] exponential lower bound of complexity of this problem is also established. We show here that analogous results hold for deterministic variant of PDL (DPDL) which we considered in [3]. The same results hold for some other variants of PDL as well. Decidability of DPDL was proved earlier by Parikh [4], however, his algorithm has no elementary bounds of complexity. The proof given here is constructed so that on its way we also obtain the corrected proof of completeness of axiom system AxD for DPDL from [3] (the proof in [3] contains some flaws), though we also have the more direct proof, without any reference to AxD. In the exposition of decidability proof we use notations and some results of [3] extensively. Decidability of propositional variant of algorithmic logic of Salwicki [5] (without formulas of the form $\bigcap K\varphi$) follows from the decidability of DPDL. The problem of possibility of exponential lower bound in this case is open. We sketch further the proof of the result announced in [3] that an extension of PDL by some asynchronous programming constructs is not decidable, and, moreover, is not recursively enumerable.

2. Let us sketch briefly syntax and semantics of PDL. PDL has two sorts of variables: program variables A,B,... and propositional variables P,Q,... . Notions of program and formula are defined by simultaneous recursion; 1) A,B,... - (elementary) programs, P,Q,... - (elementary) formulas; 2) if a,b are programs, p is a formula, then $a \cup b$, a;b, a^*, p? are programs, $\neg p$, [a]p are formulas. Model of PDL is triple $\langle S, \tau, \pi \rangle$, where S is a set (of states), τ is a function which binds to every elementary program a binary relation on S, π is a function which binds to any s in S a set of elementary formulas true in s ($s \models p$ is the abbreviation for $p \in \pi(s)$). τ and π are extended to all the

programs and formulas in the following way: $\tau(a \cup b) = \tau(a) \cup \tau(b)$, $\tau(a;b)$ is the composition of $\tau(a)$, $\tau(b)$, $\tau(a^*)$ is the reflexive and transitive closure of $\tau(a)$, $\tau(p?) = \{\langle s,s\rangle : s \models p\}$; $s \models \neg p$ iff $s \not\models p$, $s \models [a]p$ iff $\forall t, (s\,\tau(a)\,t \supset t \models p)$. It easily follows from these definitions that $[p?]q$ expresses $p \supset q$.

DPDL differs from PDL by a restriction on the model notion only, namely, for any elementary program A $\tau(A)$ should be a partial function on S. The results given below for DPDL also hold (with slight modification of the proofs) for variants when elementary programs are interpreted as total functions or total relations. Complete axiomatizations for these variants can also be given on this base.

3. We obtain the proof of decidability of DPDL by applying the idea of filtered marking procedure from [2] to Lemma 6 of [3] which we formulate here as

LEMMA 1. p has a DPDL model iff there exists a good fat path in T(p) (for definitions of the tree T(p) and a fat path in T(p) see [3]).

The implication right to left in the lemma follows from Lemma 2 of [6] (in fact, the proof is simpler than that for Lemma 2 of [6]). The implication left to right follows from the fact that satisfiability of p implies non-provability of $\neg p$ in axiomatic system AxD for DPDL [3], and the assertion of Section 12 of [3]: (*) if $\neg p$ is not provable then T(p) contains a good fat path. However, the proof of the last assertion in [3] contains some flows. The most essential one is in the proof of assertion 4) of Lemma 8 whose correction needs some significant changes in the whole proof.

4. First we introduce some stronger notion of provability in AxD. More exactly, for any i we define a notion $\vdash_i$ of provability of the rank i. Σ_i denotes $\{p : \mathrm{AxD} \vdash_i p\}$, $\Sigma = \bigcup_i \Sigma_i$.

Then we reformulate Lemma 8 of [3] and assertion (*) above as

LEMMA 2. If $W \to [a]q \notin \Sigma$ then a full node s exists in $T(W, \neg[a]q)$ with the following properties: 1) s is reachable from the root by a word w in a, 2) L(s) has the form $\{V, \neg q\}$, 3) $V \to q \notin \Sigma$, 4) for any s' on the path leading from the root to s $\neg L(s') \notin \Sigma$.

LEMMA 3. If $\neg p \notin \Sigma$ then T(p) contains a good fat path.

Implication left to right of Lemma 1 follows from Lemma 3 together with easily provable fact of admissibility of the rule $\neg p \to \ \vdash\ \to p$ and the fact that if p is satisfiable then $\neg p \notin \Sigma$. (Notice that this shows that Σ coincides with the set of tautologies of DPDL and with the set of formulas provable in AxD).

Before the proof of Lemma 2 we give in the next two sections the proof of Lemma 3 using Lemma 2 and sketch the proof of decidability of DPDL using Lemma 1.

5. For the proof of Lemma 3 we describe the following inductive process of constructing a subtree D in T(p).

At the first stage we include in D an edge from the root to a node s with non-disprovable L(s) (i.e., $\neg L(s) \notin \Sigma$) (such a node exists) and all the edges leaving s. Define a queue N of all the statements of the form $s \models \neg[a]q$, and go to the next stage.

Let a finite subtree F of T(p) and a queue N of statements of the form $s \models \neg[a]q$, $s \in F$, be constructed up to the end of some stage. Describe the procedure Π executed at the next stage. Let $x \models \neg[a]q$ be the first element of N. If F contains a node y such that y is reachable from x by an a-path in F and $\neg q \in L(y)$ then exclude the first element from N, apply procedure of the first stage to all partial leaves of F and go to the next stage. Otherwise, F contains a leaf y such that L(y) contains a formula of the form $\neg[c]q$ and y is reachable from x by a word w such that $w;c \subseteq a$ (this assertion can easily be proved by induction on the number of nodes which are over x in F, using the fact: if s is full, L(s) contains $\neg[a]q$ and does not contain $\neg q$, then L(s) contains a formula of the form $\neg[A][c]q$ and $A;c \subseteq a$). Then, by Lemma 2 above there exists a node z in T(p) such that L(z) contains $\neg q$, z is reachable from y by a c-path α, i.e. z is reachable from x by an a-path, and for any s in α L(s) is not disprovable. Then Π adds the path α to F with all the (immediate) successors of full nodes in α , excludes the first element from N, applies procedure of the first stage to all the partial leaves of the subtree obtained (we denote this subtree by F'), adds the new statements of the form $s \models \neg[a]q$, $s \in F' \setminus F$, to N and goes to the next stage.

It is easy to verify that the subtree D obtained as the limit of this process is a good fat path. This proves Lemma 3, and, therefore, Lemma 1.

6. Lemma 1 gives the possibility to prove the finite model property for DPDL (we omit here the details of this proof) and to apply the algorithm described by Pratt [2] for PDL in our case (our Lemma 1 plays the role of Corollary 3.6 in [2]). To describe shortly this algorithm we note first that the graph G(p) obtained from T(p) by identification of nodes with identical labellings contains $\leq 2^{|p|}$ nodes . Then the first stage of the algorithm consists in constructing G(p) (it can be executed in exponential time). The second stage (which is executed in exponential time, too) consists in iterated applying to G(p) the procedure of deleting of nodes such that L(s) contains a formula of the form $\neg[a]q$ and any node s' reachable from s by an a-path

does not contain $\neg q$. Though notions of a tableau for p and a fat path in a tableau used in [2] differ from our notions T(p) and a fat path it is easy to verify that the latter notions have all the properties of Pratt's notions needed to prove that T(p) has a good fat path iff the above algorithm does not delete from G(p) a node which contains p. This gives

Theorem 1. Satisfiability problem for DPDL can be decided in deterministic exponential time.

7. We get now to the definition of Σ and the proof of Lemma 2.

Definition of Σ_i is conducted by simultaneous recursion together with the definition of a subtree $T_i(p)$ of T(p) for any formula p of the form $q \ \& \ \neg [a] R$ where R occurs neither in q nor in (tests of) a. Namely, $T_o(p) = T(p)$ and $T_{i+1}(p)$ is obtained from T(p) by deleting all the nodes s (with all the successors of them) such that $\neg L(s) \in \Sigma_i$.

By $M_i(q,a)$ we denote the set of all the full nodes s in $T_i(p)$ with the following properties: 1) L(s) contains $\neg R$, 2) any predecessor of s does not contain $\neg R$ (it follows that if $s \in M_i(q,a)$ then s is reachable from the root by a word w in a). For any s in T(p) q(a,s) denotes (as in [3]) the conjunction of all the formulas of L(s) except for the ones containing R, and $D_i(q,a)$ denotes the disjunction of all the formulas q(a,s), s in $M_i(q,a)$. (We shall also use the shorter notation $q_i(a)$ for $D_i(q,a)$).

Further we consider that AxD contains the rule

$$\rightarrow * \quad \frac{\rightarrow p \qquad \rightarrow [a]\,[a^*]\,p}{\rightarrow [a^*]\,p}$$

(this rule is admissible in AxD, as it is noted in [3]).

Then we say that $r \in \Sigma_i$ iff r has an inference in AxD such that in any application of the rule (Ind) of the form

$$\frac{U \rightarrow p,\ V \qquad p \rightarrow [a]\ p \qquad p \rightarrow q}{U \rightarrow [a^*]\ q,\ V}$$

p has the form $D_j(U \ \& \ \neg V,\ a^*)$, $j \leq i$.

8. The proof of the following lemma coincides (with minor changes) with the proof of Lemma 7 of [3].

Lemma 4. a) If $p_j(a) \rightarrow q$ belongs to Σ_i then $p \rightarrow [a]\, q$ belongs to Σ_i, $j \leq i$.

b) $p_j(a^*) \rightarrow [a]\ p_j(a^*)$ belongs to Σ_i, $j \leq i$.

The following Lemmas 5, 6 are needed for the proof of assertion 4) of Lemma 2 (for definitions of a clean conjunction U, formulas U_o and U_A see [3], section 8).

Lemma 5. If U is a clean conjunction then the sequent $U \rightarrow$ belongs to Σ_i iff $U_o \rightarrow$ belongs to Σ_i or $U_A \rightarrow$ belongs to Σ_i for some elementary program A.

We omit the easy proof of this lemma.

Lemma 6. Any rule Δ of AxD $\setminus \{$Ind, MD$\}$ (including $\rightarrow *$) is reversible, i.e. if the lower sequent of Δ belongs to Σ_i then the upper sequents also belong to Σ_i.

PROOF (Sketch). Here we consider the most difficult case of the rule $\rightarrow *$ only (notice that most of changes of the proof comparatively with that of [3] are caused by difficulties with the proof of reversibility of this rule).

So, let the sequent $U \rightarrow [a^*]\, q,\ V$ belong to Σ_i, and J be an inference for it. Then we show that $U \rightarrow [a]\,[a^*]\, q,\ V$ belongs to Σ_i (the case $U \rightarrow q,\ V$ is similar). If the last rule lr of J is different from (Ind) then the proof is easily conducted by induction on the height of J.

Consider the case when lr is $(\mathrm{Ind})_j$, $j \leq i$, applied to $[a^*]\, q$ (the case when $(\mathrm{Ind})_j$ is applied to another formula of the form $[b^*]q$ is similar and simpler). First we show that sequent $W \rightarrow [a^*]\, q$, where $W = D_j(U \& \neg V, a)$ belongs to Σ_i. Apply to this sequent the rule $(\mathrm{Ind})_j$. The first premise $W \rightarrow W_j(a^*)$ can be proved in propositional logic, the second one $W_j(a^*) \rightarrow [a]\ W_j(a^*)$ belongs to Σ_i by assertion b) of Lemma 4, and the third premise $W_j(a^*) \rightarrow q$ belongs to Σ_i because $D_j(U \& \neg V, a^*) \rightarrow q$ belongs to Σ_i, by assumption, and any disjunctive member of $W_j(a^*)$ is also a disjunctive member of $D_j(U \& \neg V, a^*$ Then, by assertion a) of Lemma 4 we obtain that $U \& \neg V \rightarrow [a]\ [a^*]q \in \Sigma_i$, and $U \rightarrow [a]\ [a^*]\ q,\ V \in \Sigma_i$, by the rule $\neg p \rightarrow \vdash \rightarrow p$.

9. Now we get to the last point of the proof of Lemma 2.

The proof proceeds by induction on complexity of a. The cases when a = A, p?, $b \cup c$, b;c are simple, and we consider the case $a = b^*$ only. Below we use the shorter notations T^R, T^R_i and T^q for $T(W, \neg[b^*]R$

$T_i(W, \neg[b^*]R)$ and $T(W, \neg[b^*]q)$, respectively.

Let i be a number such that for any $j \geq i$ $T_j^R = T_i^R$ (i exists because of finiteness of the set of formulas occuring in T^R).

Let $W \to [b^*]q \notin \Sigma$. Apply to this sequent the rule $(\mathrm{Ind})_i$. The first two premises of the rule belong to Σ_i. Therefore, the third premise $W(b^*) \to q$ does not belong to Σ, and a node s^R exists in $M_i(W, b^*)$ such that $W(b^*, s^R) \to q \notin \Sigma$. Comparison of trees T^R and T^q shows that a node s^q in T^q corresponds to the node s^R of T^R such that $L(s^q) = \{W(b^*, s^R), \neg q\}$, i.e. s^q satisfies property 2) from Lemma 2. s^q satisfies properties 1), 3), too. Then for the proof of Lemma 2 it is sufficient to show that s^q satisfies property 4), i.e. for any s' under s^q $\neg L(s') \notin \Sigma$.

Assume that t^q is the highest node under s^q such that $\neg L(t^q) \in \Sigma$. From Lemma 6 it follows that t^q cannot be partial. Let t^q be full. Notice that $\neg L(t^q) \in \Sigma$ iff $\neg K \in \Sigma$, where K is a clean part of $L(t^q)$.

Let t^R be the node of T^R lying on the path from the root to s^R on the same level as t^q. Notice that K is equal to clean part K' of $W(b^*, t^R)$ complemented by a formula of the form $\neg[A][c]q$ corresponding to the formula $\neg[A][c]R$ of $L(t^R)$. From the definition of the number i it follows that T_i^R does not contain nodes s such that $\neg L(s) \in \Sigma$. Hence we obtain that $\neg K' \notin \Sigma$. Since we assumed that $\neg K \in \Sigma$ we obtain by Lemma 5 that $\neg K_A \in \Sigma$. But the labelling of the next node above t^q on the path to s^q is K_A. This contradiction to the assumption on t^q proves Lemma 2, and, therefore, Theorem 1.

10. The lower bound of complexity of PDL established in [1] holds for DPDL, too.

Theorem 2. There is a constant c such that the satisfiability problem for DPDL cannot be decided in deterministic time $c^{n/\log n}$.

The proof of this theorem is almost identical to the proof in [1] (program $\vdash$ of [1] should be replaced by the program $A \cup B$).

11. We get to the second part of our paper. We consider here an extension of PDL (we denote it as APDL) with programming constructs $\|$, $^\#$, i.e. we add to the definition of syntax of PDL the condition: if a, b are programs, then $a \| b$, $a^\#$ are programs. Operations $\|$, $^\#$ were used in [7, 8] for describing asynchronous programs (strictly speaking, [8] does not contain $^\#$, however, $^\#$ may be expressed in the language of [8]). One of possible meanings of $a \| b$ is that programs a and b are executed over common memory in parallel and asynchronously (elementary programs are considered as indivisible). This supposes the following semantics of APDL: a language C(a) of strings (computation sequences)

of elementary programs is connected with any program a, operations $\cup$, ;, * have the usual meaning as operations over languages, $C(a//b) = \{\alpha_1\beta_1\alpha_2\beta_2\ldots\alpha_k\beta_k : \alpha_1\alpha_2\ldots\alpha_k \in C(a),\ \beta_1\ldots\beta_k \in C(b),$ α_i, β_i are words in the alphabet of elementary programs$\}$, $C(a^{\#}) = \{\Lambda\} \cup C(a) \cup C(a//a) \cup C(a//a//a) \cup \ldots$, and $\tau(a) = \bigcup_{w \in C(a)} \tau(w)$. (It is easy to see that this definition of semantics for PDL coincides with the given previously).

12. The following lemma can easily be proved ($\mathfrak{A}$ denotes the set of test-free program expressions of APDL).

Lemma 2. If a, b $\in \mathfrak{A}$ then formula $[a]\,q \equiv [b]\,q$ is a tautology of APDL iff a and b are equivalent (i.e., C(a) = C(b)).

We sketch below the proof of the following

Theorem 3. The equivalence problem for $\mathfrak{A}$ is Π_1-universal.

This theorem and Lemma 2 imply

Corollary. APDL is not axiomatizable.

13. The proof of Theorem 3 is based on the fact (which is proved below) that for any one-counter machine (CM) $\mathfrak{M}$ there exist expressions a_1, a_2, a_3 such that the set of finite computations of $\mathfrak{M}$ can be described as $\bigcap C(a_i)$.

Let us recall briefly the definition of CM. Any CM has a counter N which can store any positive integer. CM can execute instructions: Mult j, j =2,3,5,7 (multiply content S(N) of N by j and go to the next instruction), Div j,I (divide S(N) by j, if possible, and go to the next instruction; otherwise, go to instruction I).

Let Δ be a set of CM which do not halt on inputs of the form 2^n, n = 0,1,... . It is known that Δ is Π_1-universal. Hence, for the proof of Theorem 3 it is sufficient to prove the following

Lemma 3. Δ is reducible to the set of pairs of equivalent expressions from $\mathfrak{A}$.

14. To prove Lemma 3 we need some notation. Let $\mathfrak{M}$ be a CM with alphabet of instructions $G = \{g_0, \ldots, g_f\}$ where g_0, g_f are initial and final instructions, respectively. With any configuration $K=\langle g,n\rangle$ of $\mathfrak{M}$ we connect a string (code of K) $\sigma(K) = gA^nB^nC^ng$, and with any sequence of configurations $K_1, \ldots, K_m$, where $K_1 = \langle g_0, 2^n\rangle$ a string $ABCA^2B^2C^2\ldots A^{2^n}B^{2^n}C^{2^n}\ \sigma(K_1)\ \sigma(K_2)\ \ldots\ \sigma(K_m)$. By $L(\mathfrak{M})$ we denote the set of codes of (finite) computation sequences of $\mathfrak{M}$.

Then we have: $\mathcal{M} \in \Delta$ iff $L(\mathcal{M}) = \emptyset$, and, hence, iff $\Sigma^* \setminus L(\mathcal{M}) = \Sigma^*$, where $\Sigma = \{A,B,C\} \cup G$.

Therefore, for the proof of Lemma 3 it is sufficient to prove the

Lemma 4. For any $\mathcal{M}$ there exist expressions a_1, a_2, a_3 in $\mathfrak{A}$ such that 1) $L(\mathcal{M}) = C(a_1) \cap C(a_2) \cap C(a_3)$; 2) there exist expressions $\bar{a}_1$, $\bar{a}_2$, $\bar{a}_3$ in $\mathfrak{A}$ such that $C(\bar{a}_i) = \Sigma^* \setminus C(a_i)$.

Proof of this lemma is tedious, and we give here explicitly definitions of a_1, a_2 only, and some example explaining the meaning of a_3.

a_1 and a_2 we define as

$$((AB)^{\#}C^*)^*\{g_0(AB)^{\#}C^*g_0 \cup \ldots \cup g_f(AB)^{\#}C^*g_f\}^*,$$

$$(A^*(BC)^{\#})^*\{g_0A^*(BC)^{\#}g_0 \cup \ldots \cup g_fA^*(BC)^{\#}g_f\}^*,$$

respectively.

It is easy to verify that

$$a_1 \cap a_2 = \{A^nB^nC^n\}^*\{g_0A^nB^nC^ng_0 \cup \ldots \cup g_fA^nB^nC^ng_f\ ,\ n = 1,2,\ldots\}^*.$$

It is clear now that the role of a_3 is to coordinate consecutive blocks. For example, let first instruction of $\mathcal{M}$ be $g_0 \rightarrow$ Div 2;g_2. Then if we coose a_3' as

$$(A \cup B \cup C)^*g_0A^*B^*(((g_0g_1)\|(C^2A)^{\#})B^*C^*g_1 \cup ((g_0g_2)\|CA\|(C^2A^2)^{\#})B^*C^*g_2)\Sigma^*,$$

then we have that blocks corresponding to K_1, K_2 in all the strings of $a_1 \cap a_2 \cap a_3'$ have needed correspondence. a_3 is defined similar to a_3' but more involved.

We also omit the simple but tedious proof of assertion 2 of lemma 3, and indicate here the useful for this proof equality $(A \cup B)^* \setminus (AB)^{\#} = (AB)^{\#}B(A \cup B)^* \cup (A \cup B)^*A(AB)^{\#}$ only.

Notice that for the proof of theorem 3 it is sufficient to have expressions with $\#$-depth 1.

15. In [7] Kimura gives an axiom system for $\mathfrak{A}$ and poses a question of its completeness. Theorem 3 shows that this system (and any finitary system, too) cannot be complete.

Let $\mathfrak{A}'$ denote the set of $\#$-free expressions of $\mathfrak{A}$ (including tests). In [9] Abrahamson considers a logic L for programs in $\mathfrak{A}'$ whose syntax and semantics are essentially more rich than those of APDL (without $\#$). Many strong properties of asynchronous programs (as deadlock freeness and so on) which cannot be described in APDL can be described in L. It is shown that a subset L_0 of L is decidable (it is also true for APDL without $\#$ since any expression of $\mathfrak{A}'$ is equivalent to a regular expression, see Ginsburg [10]). The enrichment of L by $\#$ is not axiomatizable, too.

REFERENCES

1. Fischer M.J., Ladner R.E. Propositional modal logic of programs. Proc. 9th ACM Symp. on Theory of Computing, 1977, 286-294.
2. Pratt V.R. A near-optimal method for reasoning about action. MIT/LCS/TM-113, 1978.
3. Valiev M.K. On axiomatization of deterministic propositional dynamic logic. Lecture Notes in Computer Science, 74, 1979, 482-491.
4. Parikh R. A decidability result for a second order process logic. Proc. 19th Symp. on Found. of Computer Science, 1978, 177-183.
5. Salwicki A. Formalized algorithmic languages. Bull.Acad.Pol.Sci., 18 (1970), № 5, 227-232.
6. Pratt V.R. A practical decision method for propositional dynamic logic. Proc. 10th ACM Symp. on Theory of Computing, 1978, 326-337.
7. Kimura T. An algebraic system for process structuring and interprocess communication. Proc. 8th ACM Symp. on Theory of Computing, 1976, 92-100.
8. Mazurkiewicz A. Parallel recursive program schemes. Lecture Notes in Computer Science, 32 (1975), 75-87.
9. Abrahamson K. Modal logic of concurrent nondeterministic programs. Lecture Notes in COmputer Science, 70, 1979, 21-33.
10. Ginsburg S. The mathematical theory of context-free languages. Mc Graw-Hill, New York, 1966.

RELATIVIZED OBLIVIOUSNESS*)

(Extended abstract)

Paul M.B. Vitányi

Mathematisch Centrum

Amsterdam, The Netherlands

ABSTRACT

Relativized obliviousness is introduced to capture the intuitive idea, that some problems allow fastest computations which are more oblivious than do other problems, without any of such computations being oblivious in the standard sense. It is shown that each increase in the obliviousness of an algorithm (in several different well-defined meanings), for the solution of some problems, may necessarily require an increase in computation time from T(n) steps to T(n) log T(n) steps. There is, however, no problem for which a total oblivious algorithm requires more than order T(n) log T(n) steps, if the best algorithm for it runs in T(n) steps. We use on-line Turing machines as model of computation.

1. INTRODUCTION

An oblivious on-line Turing machine is one whose head movements are fixed functions of time, independent of the actual inputs to the machine. In this paper we introduce the notion of relativized obliviousness, to capture the nature of algorithms (and problems) which seem partly oblivious and partly not. The results show that a small difference in obliviousness between algorithms used for the solution of a given problem may incur an increase in running time which is as great as the penalty for using a completely oblivious algorithm.

The concept of an oblivious algorithm is interesting for several reasons. Just as a machine model provides a certain formalization of the idea of an algorithm, so does the notion of an oblivious machine provide a certain formalization for the notion of an oblivious algorithm. Apparently, the concept was first introduced by PATERSON, M. FISCHER and MEYER [1974] to capture the notion of an algorithm being independent of the actual data. For instance, a table look-up by sequential search can be programmed obliviously (reading to the end-of-table after having found the looked-for item), while a binary search cannot be, since the number of items examined is small compared to the entire table and which items are examined depend on the item sought. Oblivious algorithms have been considered in a growing number of papers, since they allow us easier to derive lower bounds on time complexity of such computations, or time-space trade-offs, for concrete problems like sorting, searching, multiplication

---

*) This paper is registered at the Mathematical Centre as report IW 137/80

of binary numbers, matrix inversion and so on. (See the recent conference proceedings of e.g. FOCS and STOC meetings.) However, there are, for non-oblivious algorithms, very often but a few places in the computation where nonoblivious behaviour is required; but inbetween these places the computation proceeds obliviously. Hence the machine performing the computation (and the nature of the problem it solves) is oblivious to certain parts or aspects of the problem presented. In the sequel we select from the possiblities which suggest themselves, to make the idea of relativized (or partial) obliviousness concrete, the following: obliviousness relative to a subset of Σ^*, where Σ is the input alphabet; obliviousness relative to a subset of Σ (throughout the input-string, in a sense to be defined); the degree k of nonobliviousness, where k is the least number of disjoint subsets in which Σ can be partitioned so that the computation proceeds oblivious relative to each such subalphabet; and finally a finite bound on the total number of nonoblivious moves the machine can make during the processing of the input. We indicate how these different notions of relativized obliviousness and degrees of nonobliviousness are related and derive the following main results.

For each $k > 1$ there is language O_k which can be recognized in real-time by a k-nonoblivious on-line Turing machine, but for any $k' < k$ the fastest on-line k'-nonoblivious Turing machine recognizes O_k in time $\Theta(n \log n)$.

For each $k > 0$ there is a language N_k which can be recognized in real-time by an on-line Turing machine which makes at most k nonoblivious moves during the processing of an input, but for any $k' < k$ the fastest on-line Turing machine making at most k' nonoblivious moves during the processing of an input recognizing N uses time $\Theta(n \log n)$.

This paper is an extended abstract of a preliminary investigation; complete proofs, additional results as well as justification of the naturalness of the chosen concepts by illustrating them in relation to some storage-retrieval problems will be given in a final version to appear elsewhere.

2. RELATIVIZED OBLIVIOUSNESS

We assume the reader to be familiar with the concepts of k-tape on-line deterministic Turing machines, real-time computations on such machines etc., as used by e.g. P. FISHER, MEYER and ROSENBERG [1972]. Recall, that such machines have a separate one-way read-only input tape, and a one-way write-only output tape, apart from the k storage tapes. This is the model of computation we shall use throughout the paper, and is intended by the unqualified use of the term "Turing machine", although the definitions and results below hold also for more sophisticated models such as multihead Turing machines with jumps. We say that a Turing machine is *oblivious* if the movement of head i at step t, $i = 1,2,\ldots,k$ when we talk about a k-tape machine, depends only on i and t, for each storage tape head i. Likewise, the movements of the input tape head and output tape head at step t depend on t only. One may think of the head movements as being controlled by a second autonomous machine which has storage tapes but no input or output tapes. In the introduction we mentioned some grounds to refine the notion of nonobliviousness by identifying large oblivious parts of a computation which is not oblivious altogether. Below we define several concepts of relativized obliviousness, and of measures of degrees of nonobliviousness, all of which definitions hold for each model of computation for which obliviousness is defined.

Let M be a Turing machine with input alphabet Σ. By grouping together equal length input words, which cause M to execute identical sequences of head movements (taking into consideration the movements of the input tape head, the storage tape heads, and the output tape head), M induces an equivalence relation $\equiv_M$ on Σ^*.

<u>DEFINITION 1</u>.

(i) $\varepsilon \equiv_M \varepsilon$.

(ii) $xa \equiv_M yb$, $x,y \in \Sigma^*$ and $a,b \in \Sigma$, if $x \equiv_M y$ and M makes exactly the same sequence of head movements from shifting its input tape head to a till just before it shifts its input tape head to the right of a, on an input word starting with xa, as it does from shifting its input tape head to b till just before it shifts its input tape head to the right of b, on an input word starting with yb.

(iii) For no $x,y \in \Sigma^*$ it holds that $x \equiv_M y$ if not by (i)-(ii).

It is easy to see that $\equiv_M$ is an equivalence relation on Σ^*, and that it can only hold between equal length words. In this paper we consider *on-line* computations only. In defining a similar notion for *off-line* computations, or to capture some more aspects of relativized obliviousness of on-line computations, we may need to add the following requirement to (ii):

(*) $\qquad x \equiv_M y$ iff for all $z \in \Sigma^*$ holds $xz \equiv_M yz$.

This has the effect of turning $\equiv_M$ into a right congruence relation, and means that if $x \equiv_M y$ then the future head movements of M do not depend on whether M first processes x or y. Our main results, however, do not depend on whether or not restriction (*) is included in (ii), since they deal with the notion introduced in definition 3 below, which essentially is concerned with infinite words, and therefore is invariant under this restriction.

<u>DEFINITION 2</u>. A Turing machine M with input alphabet Σ is *oblivious relative to* W, $W \subseteq \Sigma^*$, if for all words $x,y \in W$, $|x| = |y|$, holds $x \equiv_M y$. For short we call such an M: W-*oblivious*.

<u>DEFINITION 3</u>. A Turing machine M with input alphabet Σ is *oblivious relative to the alphabet* Δ, $\Delta \subseteq \Sigma$, if

(i) h is a homomorphism $h\colon \Sigma^* \to (\{¢\} \cup (\Sigma-\Delta))^*$ defined by $h(a) = ¢$ for all $a \in \Delta$ and $h(a) = a$ for all $a \in \Sigma-\Delta$;

(ii) for all $w \in \Sigma^*$, M is $h^{-1}h(w)$-oblivious.

For short we call such an M: Δ-*alphabet-oblivious*.

Note that alphabet-obliviousness is a weaker notion than the corresponding monoid obliviousness. Thus, if M is Δ-alphabet-oblivious, then M is also Δ^*-oblivious. But M may very well be Δ^*-oblivious without being also Δ-alphabet-oblivious for $\Delta \subset \Sigma$. We now relate the above defined relativized obliviousness to the earlier concepts.

- M is oblivious iff M is Σ-alphabet-oblivious iff M is Σ^*-oblivious, for Σ the input alphabet of M.
- If $\{a\}$ is a singleton subset of the input alphabet of M, then M is both $\{a\}$-alphabet-oblivious and $\{a\}^*$-oblivious.
- The input monoid Σ^* can contain infinitely many distinct subsets W_i, $i \in \mathbb{N}$, such that a given machine is W_i-oblivious for each $i \in \mathbb{N}$, but not W-oblivious for any $W \subset \Sigma^*$ such that $W_i \subset W$ for some $i \in \mathbb{N}$.
- The input alphabet Σ can contain at most $\#\Sigma$ subalphabets Δ_i such that a given machine is Δ_i-oblivious for each i, $1 \le i \le \#\Sigma$. This fact will form the basis for measuring degree of nonobliviousness below.

DEFINITION 4. A Turing machine M with input alphabet Σ has *degree of nonobliviousness* k, or is k-*nonoblivious*, if

(i) Σ can be partitioned into k disjoint nonempty subsets $\Delta_1, \Delta_2, \ldots, \Delta_k$, such that M is Δ_i-alphabet-oblivious for each i, $1 \le i \le k$;

(ii) Σ cannot be partitioned into $k' < k$ disjoint nonempty subsets $\Delta'_1, \Delta'_2, \ldots, \Delta'_{k'}$, such that M is Δ'_i-alphabet-oblivious for all i, $1 \le i \le k'$.

Hence every Turing machine M with input alphabet Σ has a degree of nonobliviousness between 1 (M is oblivious) and $\#\Sigma$ (that is, M is totally nonoblivious). PIPPENGER and M. FISCHER [1979] showed that any multitape Turing machine can be simulated on-line by an oblivious 2-tape Turing machine in time $O(n \log n)$ for n steps. They showed that this result cannot be improved in general, since there is a language L which is recognized by a 1-tape real-time Turing machine M, and any oblivious Turing machine M' recognizing L must use at least order $n \log n$ steps. Below we refine this result by showing that it holds for arbitrary small differences in degree of nonobliviousness. (The time complexity expressed is the *worst-case complexity*.)

THEOREM 1. *For each* $k > 1$ *there is a language* O_k *which can be recognized in real-time by a Turing machine* M_k *which is* k-*nonoblivious; any* k'-*nonoblivious Turing machine recognizing* O_k *has to use at least order* $n \log n$ *steps to do so in case* $k' < k$. *Moreover, for each* $k' < k$ *there are* k'-*nonoblivious Turing machine which recognize* O_k *in time* $O(n \log n)$.

PROOF SKETCH. First we define O_k. O_k is over the alphabet $\Sigma_k = \bigcup_{i=1}^{k} \Delta_i$ where $\Delta_i = \{a_i, \bar{a}_i\}$ for all i, $1 \le i \le k$.

O_k is defined in terms of a k-nonoblivious machine M_k which recognizes it in real-time using k stacks in which each cell may contain a 0 or a 1. Initialize all k stacks to empty and the finite control to the start state. Start reading, one symbol at a step, the input word $s_1s_2...s_i...s_n$. At each step M_k processes the read input symbol as follows: (at the ith step M_k reads s_i)

(i) Say that the input symbol s_i M_k reads at the ith step is in Δ_j $(1 \leq i \leq n, 1 \leq j \leq k)$, then this symbol s_i is pushed on all stacks h, $1 \leq h < j$ and $j < h \leq k$, as a 0 or a 1 subject to the following interpretation. The first symbol s_1 of the current input word $s_1s_2...s_n$ is in this computation henceforth interpreted as a 1, and its counterpart in the subalphabet is hails from, say Δ_ℓ, is henceforth interpreted as 0. The first symbol M_k meets, subsequent to processing s_1 in the process of recognizing $s_1s_2...s_n$, which is unequal to s_1, say $s \in \Delta_{\ell'}$, is henceforth interpreted as a 0 while its counterpart in $\Delta_{\ell'}$ is interpreted as a 1. For the remaining symbols in $\Sigma_k-(\Delta_\ell \cup \Delta_{\ell'})$ the unbarred symbols are interpreted as a 1 and the barred symbols as a 0.

(ii) M_k pops stack j. If the popped symbol was a 0 then M_k outputs a 0; if the popped symbol was a 1 then M_k outputs a 1; if the stack is empty then M_k outputs a 0.

The language O_k consists of those words $w \in \Sigma_k^*$, for which M_k outputs a 1 when it processes the last symbol of w.

<u>CLAIM 1</u>. M_k is k-nonoblivious, i.e., by the partition of Σ_k into $\Delta_1,\Delta_2,...,\Delta_k$.

<u>CLAIM 2</u>. O_k is not recognized by any k'-nonoblivious Turing machine with k' < k in time less than order n log n.

<u>PROOF SKETCH OF CLAIM 2</u>. Assume that O_k is recognized by a k'-nonoblivious Turing machine M with k' < k. Then there is a partition of Σ_k into disjoint nonempty subsets $\Gamma_1,\Gamma_2,...,\Gamma_{k'}$, such that M is Γ_i-alphabet-oblivious for i = 1,2,...,k'. Since Σ_k contains 2k elements, there must be a subset, say Γ_j $(1 \leq j \leq k')$, which contains at least 3 distinct letters, say s_1, s_2 and s_3. Now change M into a machine M^* recognizing $O_k \cap \{s_1s_2s_3s_3\}\{s_1,s_2,s_3\}^*$ by checking for inclusion in $S = \{s_1s_2s_3s_3\}\{s_1,s_2,s_3\}^*$ with the finite control. Since $k \geq 2$, either two out of s_1,s_2,s_3 hail from the same subalphabet $\Delta \in \{\Delta_i \mid 1 \leq i \leq k\}$ while the third comes from $\Sigma-\Delta$, or all 3 of s_1,s_2,s_3 come from distinct subalphabets $\Delta,\Delta',\Delta'' \in \{\Delta_i \mid 1 \leq i \leq k\}$. Hence we can select two elements, say s_1,s_2, which represent a push 1 and push 0 respectively on some stack in M_k, while the remaining s_3 represents a pop from that stack. Since M is by assumption $\{s_1,s_2,s_3\}$-alphabet-oblivious, on the input ensemble $\{s_1,s_2,s_3\}^*$ its head movements are independent of the received input symbols, but according to the pushing and popping regime of s_1,s_2 and s_3 it receives, it must store and retrieve information in an arbitrary and continuous manner. Using an elegant counting argument introduced by COOK and AANDERAA [1969], called an *overlap* argument, applicable to computations where heavy use is made continuously of previously read-in information, we can

prove that M^*, and hence M, must spend at least order n log n steps on inputs of length n in S.
END of Proof sketch of Claim 2.

Since PIPPENGER and FISCHER [1979] showed that each on-line Turing machine can be simulated on-line by a 2-tape oblivious Turing machine in time $O(n \log n)$, their result proves the last sentence of Theorem 1; and Claims 1 and 2 prove the first sentence. □

The reader will notice that we actually showed that no k'-nonoblivious Turing machine can on-line simulate certain aspects of k pushdown stores in less than order n log n time for $k' < k$. The whole result is perhaps more elegantly worded in terms of transducers or abstract storage units instead of on-line language recognizers. It would then read something like:
" There is an abstract storage unit consisting of k pushdown stores with a restricted set of possible commands, viz., pop stack j and push all other stacks $(1 \le j \le k)$, which is k-nonoblivious. Each k'-nonoblivious abstract storage unit (Turing machine-like) which simulates it on-line must use at least order n log n time to do so in case $k' < k$ ".

<u>COROLLARY 2</u>. *For each* $k > 1$ *and each* i $(1 \le i < k)$ *there is a* k*-nonoblivious Turing machine such that any* (k-i)*-nonoblivious Turing machine simulating it on-line must use at least order* n log n *steps for* n *steps of the former.*

<u>COROLLARY 3</u>. *Let* T(n) *be any time bound* $n \le T(n) = o(n \log n)$ *(*$f = o(g)$ *means* $\lim_{n\to\infty} \frac{f(n)}{g(n)} = 0$*). The class of languages recognized in* DTIME(T(n)), *by multitape on-line Turing machines, contains an infinite proper hierarchy of language families, according to increasing degree of nonobliviousness of the fastest Turing machines accepting them.*

Another measure of degree of nonobliviousness is formed by bounds on the number of nonoblivious moves a machine is allowed to make during a computation. We may think of a machine which keeps count of the number of nonoblivious moves it makes, and, when that count exceeds a certain threshold, becomes oblivious. This measure of degree of nonobliviousness, although totally different from the preceding one, yields analog results, as shown below. One might therefore conjecture that such results hold for each (or many) meaningful measures of degree of nonobliviousness.

<u>THEOREM 4</u>. *For each integer* $k \ge 1$ *there is a language* N_k *which can be recognized by a* k*-tape real-time Turing machine* $\mathcal{N}_k$ *which makes* k *or less nonoblivious moves during each computation; any Turing machine which expends at most* k-1 *nonoblivious moves during each computation and recognizes* N_k *has to use at least order* n log n *time. Moreover, there is an oblivious Turing machine recognizing* N_k *in time* $O(n \log n)$.

<u>PROOF SKETCH</u>. We first define N_k over the alphabet {0,1,2}.

N_k consists of all strings xay2za such that $a \in \{0,1\}$, $xy \in \{0,1,2\}^*$, $z \in \{0,1\}^*$ and the following 2 conditions hold:

(i) The letter 2 appears in xay2 at most k times.

(ii) The length of z is equal to the length of y minus the number of occurrences of the letter 2 in y.

$\mathcal{N}_k$ is defined as follows:

$\mathcal{N}_k$ records the incoming bit-stream on all of its k stacks until the first 2 arrives. Then on the first stack $\mathcal{N}_k$ starts to pop and compare the popped symbol against the incoming symbol. If they are equal $\mathcal{N}_k$ outputs 1 otherwise 0. If the stack is empty $\mathcal{N}_k$ outputs 0. Meanwhile, on all remaining stacks $\mathcal{N}_k$ continues to push the incoming bits. When the second 2 arrives $\mathcal{N}_k$ starts similarly popping the second stack and comparing the popped symbol against the incoming symbol; meanwhile ignoring stack 1 and continueing the head movement there, and pushing all incoming bits on stacks 3 to k. And so on, for the 3rd to k^{th} arriving letter 2. Therefore, $\mathcal{N}_k$ need make at most k nonoblivious moves in its computation, since it always rejects when it has seen k+1 letters 2.

The fact that the recognition of N_k by a Turing machine spending at most k-1 nonoblivious moves during its computation takes at least n log n steps is proven by induction on k. For k = 1 the theorem can be proved by applying an overlap argument similar to the one hinted at in the proof sketch of the previous theorem. For k = j > 1 we can show that we can reduce the problem either to the truth of the theorem for k = 1 or the truth of the theorem for the case k = j-1, both of which are true by induction assumption. The last sentence of the theorem follows as before. □

Because of the above Theorem 4, Corollaries 2 and 3 also hold with the concept of "k-nonobliviousness" replaced by "number of nonoblivious steps k" for each k. By the nature of the concept of k-nonobliviousness, a language over a finite alphabet cannot be inherently ∞-nonoblivious. However, no such natural restriction holds for the measure of the number of nonoblivious steps in a computation.

THEOREM 5. *There is a language* N *which is recognizable by a real-time Turing machine but which, for each* $T(n) = o(n \log n)$, $n \le T(n)$, *cannot be recognized by a* T(n)-*time bounded Turing machine with a finite bound on the number of nonoblivious steps it may make during a computation. However,* N *can be recognized by an oblivious Turing machine in time* $\mathcal{O}(n \log n)$.

PROOF SKETCH. Define N as N_k without restriction (i), i.e., there is no restriction on the number of times 2 may appear in the xay-part of a word. It is easy to see that N can be recognized by a multihead real-time Turing machine with head-to-head jumps; SAVITCH and VITÁNYI [1977]. KOSARAJU [1979] has shown that these devices can be simulated on-line in real-time by multitape Turing machines. Hence N is recognizable by a real-time Turing machine. By PIPPENGER and FISCHER's [1979] result it is recognizable by an $\mathcal{O}(n \log n)$ time bounded oblivious Turing machine. Since $\bigcup_{k=1}^{\infty} N_k = N$, it follows from Theorem 4 that any Turing machine which is allowed but a finitely bounded number of nonoblivious steps, need use at least order n log n time to recognize N. □

Since N_k is 2-nonoblivious for each k, and also N is 2-nonoblivious, we have that already each class of languages recognized by 2-nonoblivious Turing machines in time $T(n) = o(n \log n)$, $T(n) \geq n$, contains a whole infinite hierarchy as discussed, with respect the number of allowed nonoblivious steps, of T(n)-time-bounded Turing machine accepted language classes.

Yet another measure of bounded nonobliviousness to bound the number of nonoblivious steps as a function f(n) of the input length n.

REFERENCES

[1] COOK, S.A. & S.O. AANDERAA [1969], *On the minimum computation time of functions*, Trans. AMS 142, 291-314.

[2] FISCHER, P.C., A.R. MEYER & A.L. ROSENBERG [1972], *Real-time simulation of multihead tape units*, JACM 14, 590-607.

[3] KOSARAJU, R. [1979], *Real-time simulation of concatenable double-ended queues by double-ended queues*, Proceedings 11th ACM-STOC, 346-351.

[4] PATERSON, M.S., M.J. FISCHER & A.R. MEYER [1974], *An improved overlap argument for on-line multiplication*, SIAM-AMS Proceedings, Vol. 7, (Complexity of Computation), 97-112.

[5] PIPPENGER, N. & M.J. FISCHER [1979], *Relations among complexity measures*, JACM 26, 361-381.

[6] SAVITCH, W.J. & P.M.B. VITÁNYI [1977], *Linear time simulation of multihead Turing machines with head-to-head jumps*, Springer Lecture Notes in Computer Science (ICALP 4) 52, 453-464.

Abstract Data Types as Lattices of Finitely Generated Models [1])

M. Wirsing, M. Broy
Technische Universität München, Institut für Informatik
Postfach 20 24 20, D-8000 München 2

Abstract

For abstract data types with arbitrary first order formulas properties of the equations in the axioms are studied which allow to decide whether an abstract type has initial or terminal algebras or whether it forms a complete lattice. An example of an equationally defined abstract type forming a complete lattice with nonrecursive initial and terminal models is given.

1. Introduction

There exist several approaches to the semantics of abstract data types: initial algebras in /ADJ 78a/, isoinitial algebras in /Bertoni, Mauri, Miglioli 79/, terminal (final) algebras in /Wand 77/ or even the class of all finitely generated models (cf. /Broy et al. 79/, /Bauer, Wössner 80/, /Lescanne 79/ and also the "F-magmas" in e.g. /Courcelle, Guessarian 79/). Every finitely generated algebra can be represented by a quotient structure (i.e. a congruence relation) on the term algebra. As it is well-known (cf. /Birkhoff,Lipson 70/) the set of all quotient structures of a term algebra forms a complete lattice with the initial algebra as greatest and the terminal algebra as least element. The same holds if all laws are universally quantified equations. For data type extensions the situation becomes more complicated (cf. /Giarratana et al. 76/, /Wand 77/) since the requirement of initiality for the primitive type is equivalent to adding an infinite set of inequations.

But what happens if we allow besides universally quantified equations (/Guttag 75/, /ADJ 78a/) positive conditional formulas (/ADJ 77/), positive formulas (/Broy et al. 79/), or arbitrary first order formulas (/Bertoni, Mauri, Miglioli 79/) ? In this paper we study criteria under which the finitely generated models of a type with arbitrary formulas form a complete lattice. We establish sufficient conditions for the non-existence of initial or terminal models of a type (prop. 1,3,6) and for the property of forming a semilattice (prop. 2,4) or even a complete lattice (prop. 5) and thus in particular give criteria for the existence both of initial and terminal models of a type. These criteria include the theorems of /Giarratana et al. 76/, /ADJ 77/, /Broy et al. 79/ and /Wand 77/. Prop. 5 assures that a type forms a complete sublattice of the class $Gen(\Sigma)$ of all finitely generated Σ-algebras. Prop. 7 allows even to prove the existence of a complete lattice structure for types not forming sublattices of $Gen(\Sigma)$. Finally an example of a type with only two axioms is given which forms a complete lattice and has non-recursive initial and terminal models.

---

[1])This research was partially sponsored by the Sonderforschungsbereich 49 - Programmiertechnik - Munich

2. Basic Definitions and Results

We review briefly the basic notions concerning heterogeneous algebras and their connection to abstract data types:

A heterogeneous algebra $A = ((s^A)_{s\in S}, (f^A)_{f\in F})$ consists of a family of carrier sets s^A and of a family of total operations (functions) f^A on these carrier sets. Each function $f^A: s1^A \times \ldots \times sn^A \to s^A$ has a functionality $s1 \times \ldots \times sn \to s'$ ($si, s' \in S$, $n \geq 0$). For $n = 0$ f^A is a nullary function or constant. The index sets S of sorts s and F of function symbols f define the signature $\Sigma = (S,F)$. So $A = (S^A, F^A)$ becomes a Σ-algebra, where S^A (resp. F^A) abbreviates $(s^A)_{s\in S}$ (resp. $(f^A)_{f\in F}$).

A Σ-algebra A' is called Σ-subalgebra of a Σ-algebra A, if for all $s \in S: s^{A'} \subseteq s^A$ for all $f \in F$, $f^{A'}$ is the restriction of f^A to A' and A' is closed under all the operations of A.

For every Σ-algebra A there exists a least Σ-subalgebra $Sub(A)$ of A (with respect to the set inclusion). A is called finitely generated if $Sub(A) = A$.

From the function symbols itself we obtain particular Σ-algebras: Let $x1,\ldots,xk$ be (free) variables of the sorts $s1,\ldots,sk \in S$. Then $W(\Sigma;x1,\ldots,xk)$ is the least set (with respect to set inclusion) M such that $x1,\ldots,xk$ and every constant $f \in F$ belong to the appropriate sorts of M and, whenever $f: s1 \times \ldots \times sn \to s' \in F$ and $t1,\ldots,tn$ of sort $s1,\ldots,sn$ are in M, then the term $f(t1,\ldots,tn)$ belongs to the sort s of M. The elements of $W(\Sigma;x1,\ldots,xk)$ are called polynomials. $W(\Sigma;x1,\ldots,xk)$ is made into a Σ-algebra by defining

$$f^W(t1,\ldots,tn) =_{def} f(t1,\ldots,tn) \qquad \text{for} \qquad ti \in si^W.$$

This algebra is denoted by $W(\Sigma;x1,\ldots,xk)$. If $k = 0$ we write $W(\Sigma)$ and call it the term-algebra of Σ. Clearly, $W(\Sigma)$ is finitely generated and Σ-subalgebra of all $W(\Sigma;x1,\ldots,xk)$. The elements of $W(\Sigma)$ are called terms.

For two Σ-algebras A and B a family $\varphi = (\varphi_s)_{s\in S}$ of mappings $\varphi_s : s^A \to s^B$ is called Σ-homomorphism if for all $f: s1 \times \ldots \times sn \to s'$ and elements $a1 \in s1^A,\ldots,an \in sn^A$:

$$\varphi_{s'}(f^A(a1,\ldots,an)) = f^B(\varphi_{s1}(a1),\ldots,\varphi_{sn}(an)) .$$

Then every finitely generated Σ-algebra is homomorphic image of $W(\Sigma)$; there exists at most one homomorphism between two finitely generated Σ-algebras and this homomorphism, if it exists, is mono, epi and surjective (for the definition of mono, epi and surjective cf. /McLane 71/).

Properties of Σ-algebras are expressed by formulas which are built over equations $t =_s t'$ (where t, t' are polynomials of sort $s \in S$) using $\neg, \wedge, \vee, \to, \leftrightarrow, \forall, \exists$.
A formula without free identifiers is called sentence. For our propositions we always consider sentences in the following prenex normal form:

$$\text{(NF)} \quad Q_1 s_1 x_1 \ldots Q_n s_n x_n : \bigwedge_{1\leq i\leq k} \Big(\bigvee_{1\leq j\leq m} p_{ij} \neq q_{ij} \vee \bigvee_{m+1\leq j\leq r} u_{ij} = v_{ij} \Big) \quad \text{where } Q_i \in \{\forall,\exists\}$$

The interpretation of a formula in a Σ-algebra is defined as usual in a classical two-valued first-order logic. Truth of G in A is denoted by $A \models G$. In particular (for terms t_1, t_2 of sort s) we have $A \models t_1 =_s t_2$ iff $t_1^A = t_2^A$ in A and $A \models \forall s\, x : G$ iff for all $a \in s^A : A \models G[a/x]$.

The only predicate symbols occurring in formulas are the identity symbols $=_s$ for every sort s. Since we are working with heterogeneous algebras this is not an essential restriction: A predicate $p \subseteq s1 \times \ldots \times sn$ may be seen as boolean function $p': s1 \times \ldots \times sn \rightarrow$ bool where bool denotes the sort {true, false} of the truth values.

An abstract (data) type $T = (\Sigma, E)$ consists of a signature Σ and a (countable) set E of sentences, called axioms. A Σ-algebra A is called (fg-model) of type T, if A is finitely generated and $A \models G$ for all $G \in E$. The class of all fg-models of a type T is denoted by Gen(T). If $E = \emptyset$ we write Gen(Σ) instead of Gen($\Sigma,\emptyset$). We say that a sentence G is fg-valid in T if for all $A \in$ Gen(T) $A \models G$. T is fg-satisfiable if Gen(T) $\neq \emptyset$ and T is called monomorphic if all elements of Gen(T) are isomorphic.

Of course, the usual logical axioms and rules of inference (see e.g. /Chang, Keisler 74/) as well as a structural induction (cf. /Guttag 75/) hold for types. We call a sentence G provable in T if G can be deduced from the laws of T and from the logical axioms and rules including induction. Then provability implies fg-validity. But the completeness theorem of first-order logic does not hold for all types. If we consider, for instance, a type NAT of natural numbers (cf. /ADJ 78a/) with addition and multiplication then due to the restriction to finitely generated models Gödel's incompleteness theorem applies to NAT i.e. there exists a sentence $\forall$ nat x : G such that

- for all natural numbers n G[n/x] is provable,
- $\forall$ nat x : G is fg-valid, but not provable.

3. The Lattice of Models of an Abstract Type

In the following let a type $T = (\Sigma, E)$ be given. Due to their uniqueness property the homomorphisms induce a quasi ordering on the class Gen(T). For Σ-algebras A, B $\in$ Gen(T) we define

$A \leq B$ iff there exists a Σ-homomorphism $\varphi : B \rightarrow A$,

$A \cong B$ iff $A \leq B$ and $B \leq A$,

$|\text{Gen}(T)| =_{def} \text{Gen}(T)/\cong$.

Then $\leq$ is reflexive and transitive on Gen(T) and antisymmetric on |Gen(T)|. Thus $\leq$ is a partial ordering on |Gen(T)|. Upper bound, least upper bound (denoted by lub(T,H) for $H \subseteq$ |Gen(T)|), lower bound and greatest lower bound (denoted by glb(T,H)) are defined as usual. For A, B $\in$ |Gen(T)| we define

$A \sqcup B =_{def} \text{lub}(T,\{A,B\})$ and $A \sqcap B =_{def} \text{glb}(T,\{A,B\})$.

Then T is called a lattice if T is fg-satisfiable and $A \sqcup B$, $A \sqcap B$ exist for all A, B $\in$ |Gen(T)|. A lattice is called complete, if lub(T,H) and glb(T,H) exist for all H $\in$ |Gen(T)|. Complete upper and complete lower semilattices are defined as usual, too. A fg-model of T is called

initial if A = lub(T,|Gen(T)|) and terminal if A = glb(T,|Gen(T)|)

Then if T is a complete lattice it always has a terminal fg-model and an initial fg-model. Obviously, every monomorphic type forms a complete lattice. Initial and terminal fg-models in our sense are the extremal elements of Gen(T) or equivalently (since there exists at most one homomorphism between two fg-models) they are initial and final in the category Gen(T) (together with the Σ-homomorphisms). The initial (terminal/ final) models of Gen(T) and Alg(T), i.e. the category of all models of a type, coincide e.g. for equationally defined data type extensions.

In the rest of the paper we identify elements of Gen(T) with quotient structures of W( )

For the class $Gen(\Sigma)$ of all finitely generated Σ-algebras least upper bounds and greatest lower bounds may be characterized as follows:

Proposition 0

Let $H \subseteq |Gen(\Sigma)|$.

(1) $lub(\Sigma,H)$ is isomorphic to $W(\Sigma)/\sim$, where for all $t, t' \in W(\Sigma)$ of sort s $\sim$ is defined as follows:

$$t \sim_s t' \text{ iff } A \models t =_s t' \text{ for all } A \in H.$$

(2) $glb(\Sigma,H)$ is isomorphic to $W(\Sigma)/\approx$ where for all $t, t' \in W(\Sigma)$ of sort s $\approx$ is defined as follows:

$t \approx_s t'$ iff there exists a finite sequence $t_0,\ldots,t_n \in W(\Sigma)$ of sort s where t is t_0 and t' is t_n such that for all $1 \leq j \leq n$ there exists $B_j \in H$ with $B_j \models t_j =_s t_{j-1}$

The proof is a slight generalization of /Grätzer 67, p. 18/.

But even for types with very simple axioms least upper bounds may not always exist. To show this we consider two particular semantic properties of the axioms:

A formula G with at most the free identifiers $x1,\ldots,xn$ of sort $s1,\ldots,sn$ is called maximal iff for all $t1,\ldots,tn \in W(\Sigma)$ of sort $s1,\ldots,sn$

either $G[t1/x1,\ldots,tn/xn]$ is fg-valid in T,
or $\neg G[t1/x1,\ldots,tn/xn]$ is fg-valid in T.

This notion is similar to the notion of "maximal theory" of /Rasiowa, Sikorski 70/.

Uniform formulas are defined inductively:

every quantifier-free formula is uniform,
- $\forall sx: G$ is uniform iff G is uniform,
- $\exists sx: G$ with at most the free variables $y1,\ldots,yn$ is uniform iff for all terms $t1,\ldots,tn$ there exists a term t of sort s with
  (1) $G[t1/y1,\ldots,tn/yn, t/x]$ is uniform and
  (2) $\exists sx: G[t1/y1,\ldots,tn/yn]$ is fg-valid in T iff $G[t1/y1,\ldots,tn/yn,t/x]$ is fg-valid in T.

In particular uniform means that in a sentence $\exists\, s\, y : G$ the quantifier y may be represented in all models by the same term. Now we can formulate a (simple) proposition:

Proposition 1 (Nonexistence of initial algebras)

Let T be a fg-satisfiable type.

(1) If T contains an axiom of the form

$$u_1 = v_1 \vee u_2 = v_2$$

where none of the two equations is maximal, or

(2) if T contains an axiom of the form

$$\forall s\ x\ \exists s'\ y : u = v$$

which is not uniform,

then T does not have an initial algebra.

Proof by showing that the algebra $W(\Sigma)/\sim$ defined in prop. 0 does not satisfy the axioms.

Prop. 1(1) is a specialization of a theorem on the non-existence of free algebras; using the general theorem one can e.g. prove that there exist no free fields over a nonempty set of generators (cf. /Osswald 66/). Furthermore, one can easily prove that in the case of prop. 1(1) the type T does not form an (upper semi-)lattice. On the other side non-uniformity of an axiom does not exclude that T forms a lattice, but there is a close connection to the failure of the compactness theorem for first-order logic in the framework of abstract data types:

Example: type FINNAT ≡

sorts: fin, nat ,

functions: zero : → nat ,
succ : nat → nat ,
add : nat x nat → nat ,
make : nat → fin ,

laws:

$\forall$ nat m : zero $\neq$ succ(m) $\wedge$
(succ(m) = succ(n) → m = n) $\wedge$
add(m, zero) = m $\wedge$
add(m, succ(n)) = succ(add(m, n)) ,

(*) $\exists$ nat m $\forall$ nat n : make(add(n, m)) = make(n) $\wedge$ m $\neq$ zero

endoftype

Every fg-model of FINNAT may be described by a direct product

$$M(m) =_{def} \{0,\dots,m-1\} \times \mathbb{N}$$

where $\mathbb{N}$ denotes the standard model of the natural numbers and where the operation make is defined by

$$\text{make}(n) =_{def} n \text{ modulo } m .$$

$|\text{Gen(FINNAT)}| = \{ M(m) : m \in \mathbb{N}\setminus\{0\}\}$ forms a lattice with

$M(m) \sqcup M(m') = M(\text{lcm}(m,m'))$ and $M(m) \sqcap M(m') = M(\text{gcd}(m,m'))$

and with M(1) as 0-element. Hence every finite initial segment of $\mathbb{N}$ determines a model of FINNAT, but $\mathbb{N} \times \mathbb{N}$, the union of all "finite" models, is not a model of FINNAT. FINNAT forms a lattice but does not have any initial fg-model.

The term $\text{succ}^{k'}(\text{zero})$ with $k' =_{def} \text{lcm}(m_1,\dots,m_k)$ satisfies the axiom (*) in all $M(m_1),\dots,M(m_k)$ for arbitrary $m_1,\dots,m_k \in \mathbb{N}$. But for $|\text{Gen(FINNAT)}|$ itself no term $t \in W(\underline{nat})$ can uniformly satisfy the axiom (*).

If we apply maximality and uniformity to more general axioms we obtain sufficient conditions for the existence of arbitrary lub's.

Proposition 2 (Complete upper semilattice)

Let T be a fg-satisfiable type with uniform axioms in normal form (NF).

If for every $i=1,\dots,k$ there exists at most one $j \in \{l+1,\dots,r\}$ such that the equation $u_{ij}=v_{ij}$ is not maximal, then for every nonvoid set $H \subsetneq |Gen(T)|$ lub(T,H) exists (i.e. T forms a complete upper semilattice).
In particular, T has an initial fg-model.

Sketch of the proof

For technical simplicity we consider axioms of the form

$$(NF') \qquad \forall sx \exists s'y: \bigvee_{1\le j\le m} p_j \neq q_j \vee \bigvee_{1<k\le r} u_k=v_k$$

The uniformity implies that for all $w \in W(\Sigma)$ there exists $w' \in W(\Sigma)$ such that

$$(*) \qquad \left(\bigvee_j p_j \neq q_j \vee \bigvee_k u_k=v_k \right)[w/x,w'/y]$$

is fg-valid in T . On the other hand let $\emptyset \neq H \subseteq |Gen(T)|$ and suppose that lub(T,H) $=_{def} W(\Sigma)/\sim$, where (see prop. 0)

$$t \sim t' \quad \text{iff} \quad A \models t = t' \quad \text{for all} \quad A \in |Gen(T)|$$

is not a fg-model of T . Then in particular one of the sentences (*) must be false in lub(T,H). Therefore

$$(**) \qquad \left(\bigwedge_j p_j=q_j \wedge \bigwedge_k u_k \neq v_k \right)[w/x,w'/y]$$

must be true in lub(T,H). Using the maximality condition for $u_k=v_k$ we can find an element $A \in H$ satisfying (**) and hence contradicting (*) . Therefore A cannot be in $|Gen(T)|$ - contradiction to $H \subseteq |Gen(T)|$. □

If a type T has only universally quantified positive conditional axioms i.e.

$$\forall s_1x_1 \dots \forall s_nx_n: u_1=v_1 \rightarrow \dots \rightarrow u_n=v_n \qquad (n\ge 1)$$

then these axioms are first-order equivalent to

$$\forall s_1x_1 \dots \forall s_nx_n: u_1 \neq v_1 \vee \dots \vee u_{n-1} \neq v_{n-1} \vee u_n=v_n \; .$$

Furthermore the trivial Σ-algebra (all carrier sets of which are void or consist of only one element depending on the existence of constants with range s or of function symbols with range s and nonvoid domain) is a fg-model of T . Therefore according to prop. 2 every type T with positive conditional axioms forms a complete upper semilattice and we obtain in particular the result of /ADJ 77/ that T has an initial algebra.

For the existence of greatest lower bounds inequations cause problems:

Proposition 3 (Nonexistence of lower bounds)

Let T be a fg-satisfiable type containing an axiom of the form $p \neq p'$.

If there exists a term $t \in W(\Sigma)$ such that none of the equations $p = t$ and $p' = t$ is maximal, then there exist $A, B \in |Gen(T)|$ which have no lower bound in $|Gen(T)|$. In particular T has no terminal algebra.

Proof: Lower bounds of fg-models A and A' with $A \not\models p = t$ and $A' \models p' = t$ do not satisfy $p \neq p'$. □

By generalizing this condition we can show a theorem converse to proposition 3:

Proposition 4 (Complete lower semilattice)

Let T be a fg-satisfiable type with axioms in normal form (NF).
If for all $i=1,\dots,k$, $j=1,\dots,m$ the equation $p_{ij}=y$ (for new y) is maximal, then for every nonempty set $H \subseteq |Gen(T)|$ glb(T,H) exists (i.e. T forms a complete lower semilattice). In particular T has a terminal fg-model.

Sketch of the Proof

As in prop. 2 we consider only axioms of the form (NF').
Let $\emptyset \neq H \subseteq |Gen(T)|$. Then as in prop. 0 we define glb(T,H) by $W(\Sigma)/\approx$.
Suppose that glb(T,H) is not a fg-model of T. Then some axiom of T is false in glb(T,H). Thus there exists a term $t \in W(\Sigma)$ such that for all $t' \in W(\Sigma)$

$$(\bigvee_j p_j \neq q_j \vee \bigvee_k u_k = v_k)[t/x, t'/y]$$

is false in glb(T,H) and hence equivalently for all $t' \in W(\Sigma)$

$$(*) \qquad (\bigwedge_j p_j = q_j \wedge \bigwedge_k u_k \neq v_k)[t/x, t'/y]$$

is true in glb(T,H). Then according to the definition of

(i) $\bigwedge_k u_k \neq v_k [t/x, t'/y]$ holds in all $C \in H$ and

(ii) for all $j=1,\dots,m$ there exist terms $a_o,\dots,a_w$ and fg-models $A_1,\dots,A_w$ in H such that p_j is a_o, q_j is a_w and for all $i'=1,\dots,w$ $a_{i'-1} = a_{i'}$ holds in $A_{i'}$.

Using the maximality of $p_j=z$ we can prove that $p_j=q_j$ holds in all $A \in H$.
Thus (*) is true and some axiom is false in all $A \in H$ - contradiction to $H \subseteq |Gen(T)|$. □

In order to apply Wand's Main Theorem (/Wand 77/) in our framework we define:

A type $T' = (\Sigma', E')$ is called <u>algebra extension</u> of the Σ-algebra A of type $T = (\Sigma, E)$ if

(1) $\Sigma \subseteq \Sigma'$, $E \subseteq E'$ and for

$$E'' =_{def} E' \cup \{t =_s t' : t,t' \text{ of sort } s \in S \text{ and } t = t' \text{ holds in } A\}$$
$$\{t \neq_s t' : t,t' \text{ of sort } s \in S \text{ and } t \neq t' \text{ holds in } A\}$$

(2) (Σ, E'') is fg-satisfiable ("$\wedge$-faithfullness") and

(3) for all $t \in W(\Sigma')$ of sort $s \in S$ there exists $u \in W(\Sigma)$ such that $t =_s u$ is fg-valid in T ("$\wedge$-fullness").

Data type extensions in the sense of Wand (cf. also /Ehrig et al. 78/) correspond to algebra extensions for initial algebras (the former are more general but the difference is only of technical nature) of types all axioms of which are universally quantified equations. The conditions (2) and (3) ensure the maximality of the equations $t = y$ for $t \neq t' \in E'' \setminus E'$. Therefore prop. 4 guarantees the existence of a terminal fg-model for $|Gen(T)|$ being the result of Wand's Main Theorem.

Furthermore, prop. 4 assures the existence of a terminal element for $|\mathrm{Gen}(\Sigma,E")|$ if the axioms of $E'\setminus E$ are positive sentences, i.e. if they are built by $=_s, \wedge, \vee, \forall, \exists$ without any negation symbols. Guttag's sufficient completeness (for the definition see e.g. /Guttag, Horning 78/) implies condition (3) and the monomorphicity of T implies $\mathrm{Gen}(\Sigma,E') = \mathrm{Gen}(\Sigma,E")$. Therefore according to prop. 4 sufficient complete types with monomorphic primitive types and only positive axioms have a terminal fg-model. Thus we have obtained the result of /Broy et al. 79/.

Combining the propositions 2 and 4 we obtain a sufficient condition for proving that the fg-models of a type form a complete lattice:

Proposition 5 (Complete lattices)

Let T be a fg-satisfiable type with uniform axioms in normal form (NF).

If

(5.1) for every $i=1, \ldots, k$ there exists a most one $j \in \{m+1,\ldots,r\}$ such that $u_{ij} = v_{ij}$ is not maximal,

(5.2) for every $i=1,\ldots,k$, $j=1,\ldots,m$ the equation $p_{ij} = y$ (for new y) is maximal,

then the fg-models of T form a complete lattice.

Initial algebra extensions with universally quantified axioms satisfy prop. 5 and hence form a complete lattice. A "complete specification" H of / Giarratana et al. 76/ may be seen als algebra extension (Σ', E') of an initial Σ-algebra of type (Σ, E) where all axioms of $E'\setminus E$ have the form $f(t1, \ldots, tn) = t$ with $f \in F'\setminus F$ and $t \in W(\Sigma)$ (and pairwise different left-hand sides). The completeness in the sense of / Giarratana et al. 76/ assures the Λ-fullness; the Λ-faithfullness follows from the consistency conditions of the specification $_H H$. Then the class of all fg-models of the algebra extension is exactly the class R_t^H of "total representation algebras" satisfying H . Therefore according to prop. 5 $_H R_t^H$ forms a complete lattice being the theorem 4.6 of / Giarratana et al. 76/.

Examples for non-monomorphic types forming complete lattices are the types T(ARR) (in /Wand 77/, /Ehrich, Lohberger 78/), SET, BAG in /Guttag 79/ or the types SIEVE, GRAPH containing existential quantifiers in /Broy et al. 79/. All these types have uncountably many non-isomorphic fg-models.

Condition 5.2 is a straightforward generalization of prop. 3. Looking at positive conditional formulas instead of inequations prop. 3 implies another condition:

Proposition 6 (Nonexistence of lower bounds)

Let T be a fg-satisfiable type containing an axiom of the form $\forall sx: p = q \rightarrow u = v$

If there exists a term $w \in W(\Sigma)$ such that

- $(u \neq v)\,[w/x]$ is fg-valid in T and
- both, $p[w/x] = t$ and $q[w/x] = t$, are not maximal for some term t ,

then there exist A, B $\in$ Gen(T) which have no lower bound in Gen(T) . In particular T has not terminal algebra.

Proof: Using $(p = q \rightarrow u = v)\,[w/x] \Leftrightarrow (p \neq q)\,[w/x]$ we apply prop. 3.

□

As an example we consider the type SEMIGROUP based on a type ALPHABET which is supposed to be monomorphic :

```
type SEMIGROUP  ≡
     primitive : ALPHABET ,
     sort      :  sgroup,
     functions : widen : alphabet → sgroup ,
                 conc  : sgroup × sgroup → sgroup ,
     laws      :
      ∀ sgroup a,b,c : conc(a,conc(b,c)) = conc(conc(a,b),c) ,
      ∀ alphabet m,n : widen(m) = widen(n)  →  m = n
                                                        endoftype
```

If the carrier set of alphabet consists of at least two different elements m', n' then $m' \neq n'$ is fg-valid; clearly, neither widen(m) [m'/m, n'/n] = t nor widen(n) [m'/m, n'/n] = t are maximal for e.g. t = conc(widen(m'), widen(n')). Thus from prop. 5 we obtain that SEMIGROUP cannot form a lattice nor have any terminal element.

Therefore often injectivity axioms destroy the presence of terminal algebras (cf. also the types WORD and GENGROUP in /Bauer, Wössner 80/). On the other hand the satisfiability of u = v in p = w → u = v leads to complete lattices. Consider e.g. the type REDUCE(P) defined in /ADJ 78b/ to show the power of conditional axioms. With the help of the following proposition 7 one can prove that REDUCE(P) forms a complete lattice.

Proposition 7 (Complete lattices by nonmaximal conditionals)

Let $T = (\Sigma, E_1 \cup E_2)$ be a fg-satisfiable type such that

- E_1 satisfies the conditions 5.1, 5.2, and
- all axioms of E_2 are universally quantified, satisfy the conditions 5.1 and

(5.2') for every i=1, ..., k and for all terms $t_1, \ldots, t_n$ of sort $s_1, \ldots, s_n$ there exists $j \in \{m+1, \ldots, r\}$ such that $u_{ij} = v_{ij}\, [t_1/x_1, \ldots, t_n/x_n]$ is fg-satisfiable.

Then the fg-models of T form a complete lattice.

Sketch of the proof

T satisfies condition 5.1. Thus according to prop. 2 for every nonvoid set $B \subseteq |Gen(T)|$ lub(T,B) exists. We have to show that glb(T,B) exists:

Prop. 5 implies that the type $T' =_{def} (\Sigma, E_1)$ forms a complete lattice.

Let M be the set of all $M_t \in |Gen(T)|$ which satisfy the equations of (5.2'). Then

(1) glb(T', B ∪ M) is a fg-model of T' and due to (5.2') of M_t it is a fg-model of T, too. Clearly, glb(T', B ∪ M) ≤ glb(T', B); i.e. glb(T', B ∪ M) is lower bound of B in T'.

Due to the universal quantification we may assume that E_2 consists of axioms

$\forall sx{:}E$ of the form $\forall sx{:}\ \bigvee_j p_j \neq q_j \ \vee \ \bigvee_k u_k = v_k$.

We define

$$N_o =_{def} \ glb(T', B),$$

$$N_{n+1} =_{def} N_n / < u_{k'} = v_{k'}\,[t/x] \mid N_n \not\models E[t/x] \text{ and } M_t \models u_{k'} = v_{k'}\,[t/x] >$$

By induction on n one can prove $N_n \geq \mathrm{glb}(T', B \cup M)$. Thus using (1), $B' \geq N_n$ (for $B' \in B$) and the conditions 5.1, 5.2 we conclude that $N_n \in \mathrm{Gen}(T')$ holds. Furthermore using the maximality of $u_k = v_k$ for $k \neq k'$ (which follows from the definition of N_n) and 5.1, 5.2' we see that $N_n \geq C$ for every lower bound C of B in T. Define $N_\infty = \mathrm{glb}(T', N_n)$. N_∞ satisfies E_1 and E_2 by construction. Hence $N_\infty \in \mathrm{Gen}(T)$. $N_n \geq C$ for every lower bound C of B implies $N_\infty = \mathrm{glb}(T, B)$. □

4. Example: Primitive Recursive Functions

The type PREK of primitive recursive functions (cf. the difference to the type of all partial recursive functions in /Broy, Wirsing 80/ which does not form a lattice nor has initial (as data type extension) or terminal fg-models) has two sorts: the sort fun for the (primitive recursive) functionals and the sort nat for the values of the functionals. The connection between both sorts is defined by an "eval"-operator which applies a n-ary functional to a n-tuple of natural numbers. (For simplicity the arity of functionals is omitted. The formalization of a function arity : fun → nat as well as of $\leq$: nat x nat → bool is obvious).

type PREK ≡

sorts: nat, fun,

functions : zero : → nat
- succ : nat → nat
- zero' : → fun — "zero-functional"
- succ' : → fun — "successsor-functional"
- p_i^n : → fun, $1 \leq i \leq n$ — "i-th projection"
- comp^n: $(\mathrm{fun})^{m+1}$ → fun, $1 \leq m$, $0 \leq n$ — "composition"
- R : fun × fun → fun — "primitive recursion"
- eval : fun × $(\mathrm{nat})^n$ → nat, $n \geq 0$

laws: ∀ nat d', d", nat^n d, fun g, $g_1, \ldots, g_m$, f, h :

$$\mathrm{zero} \neq \mathrm{succ}(d') \wedge (\mathrm{succ}(d') = \mathrm{succ}(d'') \rightarrow d' = d'') \wedge$$
$$\mathrm{eval}(\mathrm{zero}') = \mathrm{zero} \wedge \mathrm{eval}(\mathrm{succ}', d') = \mathrm{succ}(d') \wedge$$
$$\mathrm{eval}(p_i^n, d) = d_i \wedge$$
$$\mathrm{eval}(\mathrm{comp}^n(g, g_1, \ldots, g_m), d) = \mathrm{eval}(g, \mathrm{eval}(g_1, d), \ldots, \mathrm{eval}(g_m, d)) \wedge$$
$$\mathrm{eval}(R(f, h), d, \mathrm{zero}) = \mathrm{eval}(f, d) \wedge$$
$$\mathrm{eval}(R(f,h), d, \mathrm{succ}(d')) = \mathrm{eval}(h, \mathrm{eval}(R(f,h), d, d'), d, d')$$

end of type

Due to the monomorphicity of nat all equations of sort nat are maximal. Every primitive recursive functional is terminating for all arguments. Thus, eval(f,d) = d' is maximal, too. The syntactic equality for objects of fun leads to an (initial) fg-model of PREK . Therefore according to prop. 5 PREK forms a complete lattice. For the terminal fg-models Z the equality in fun is defined by

$$Z \models f = g \text{ iff } \forall\, \mathrm{nat}^n\, d : \mathrm{eval}(f, d) = \mathrm{eval}(g,d) \text{ is fg - valid}$$

i.e. two functionals are equal in Z if they are extensionally equivalent. As well-known the (extensional) equality between primitive recursive functionals is not recursively enumerable and thus not decidable. Therefore the terminal fg-models of PREK are not "recursive" in the sense of /Bertoni et al. 79/, not "semi computable" in the sense of /Bergstra, Tucker 79/ and no "data types" in the sense of /Majster 79

The initial fg-models of PREK are recursive (if the carrier sets are recursively presented), computable and "data types". Now let us consider a type T_0 with universally quantified equations as axioms such that its initial fg-models are not recursive (cf. e.g. /Bertoni et al. 79/) whereas its terminal fg-models (being finite) are recursive. Then by taking the disjoint union of T_0 and PREK we obtain:

Proposition 8 :

There exists a type T such that T forms a complete lattice and the initial and terminal fg-models are not recursive.

In particular T has uncountably many non-isomorphic non-recursive fg-models as well as infinitely many non-isomorphic recursive models. Furthermore, if we consider PREK as algebra extension of the initial models of < nat, zero, succ, "no laws" > then PREK has only universally quantified equations as axioms. Therefore the following holds:

Corollary

There exists an equationally defined initial algebra extension T' such that

- T' forms a complete lattice and
- the initial and terminal fg-models of T' are not recursive.

Let us conclude this section with a remark on the form of the axioms:

If one applies the (tricky) encoding method of /Wirsing 77, 78/ (which we cannot present here for the lack of space) to the type T of prop. 8 then one obtains two one-sorted abstract types T", T"' such that both types form complete lattices with non-recursive initial and terminal fg-models and

- the signature of T" consists of one constant and one binary function symbol; the only axiom of T" has the form $\forall x_1 \ldots \forall x_6 : u = v \wedge u' \neq v'$,
- the signature of T"' consists of one constant and two unary function symbols, the only axiom of T"' has the form $\forall x : u_1 = v_1 \wedge u_2 = v_2 \wedge u_3 = v_3 \wedge u_4 \neq v_4$

5. Concluding Remarks

Restricting the class of models of a type to the class of finitely generated models suggests to consider the subset of the congruence relations on the term algebra of the type instead of the category of all models. Thus we may use naive set theory to talk about the (classes of isomorphic) finitely generated models of a type. This approach naturally leads to the question, whether the subset of congruence relations forms a (complete) sublattice of the well-known lattice of congruence relations on the "anarchic" term algebra or whether it forms a (complete) lattice at all.

Answering this question not only gives hints for the existence of maximal or minimal elements, but also a theory-oriented development of implementations by adding (consistent) further axioms and such reducing the set of compatible congruence relations until uniqueness is reached (cf. "abstract computation structure" in /Bauer, Wössner 80/).

Acknowledgment

We are indebted to Prof. F. L. Bauer for encouraging us to study the lattice structure of abstract types. We thank our colleagues W. Dosch, H. Partsch and P. Pepper for many interesting discussions.

References

/ADJ 77/
J.W. Thatcher, E.G. Wagner, J.B. Wright: Specification of abstract data types using conditional axioms. IBM Research Report RC-6214, 1977

/ADJ 78a/
J.A. Goguen, J.W. Thatcher, E.G. Wagner: An initial algebra approach to the specification, correctness and implementation of abstract data types. In: R.T. Yeh (ed.): Current Trends in Programming Methodology, Vol. 3, Data Structuring , N.J.: Prentice Hall, 1978

/ADJ 78b/
J.W. Thatcher, E.G. Wagner, J.B. Wright: Data type specification: Parameterization and the power of specification techniques. Proc. SIGACT 10th Annual Symposion on the Theory of Computing, 1978

/Bauer, Wössner 80/
F. L. Bauer, H. Wössner: Algorithmic language and program development. (to appear)

/Bergstra, Tucker 79/
J.A. Bergstra, J.V. Tucker: Algebraic specifications of computable and semicomputable data structures. Afdeling Informatice Amsterdam, IW 115/79

/Bertoni, Mauri, Miglioli 79/
A. Bertoni, G. Mauri, P.A. Miglioli: A characterization of abstract data as model-theoretic invariants. In : H.A. Maurer (ed.): Proc. 6th ICALP, Graz, LNCS 71 , 26-38 (1979)

/Bertoni et al. 79/
A. Bertoni, G. Mauri, P.A. Miglioli, M. Wirsing: On different approaches to abstract data types and the existence of recursive models. Bulletin of EATCS 9, 47-57 (1979)

/Birkhoff, Lipson 70/
G. Birkhoff, J.D. Lipson: Heterogeneous algebras. J. of Combinatorial Theory 8, 115-133 (1970)

/Broy et al. 79/
M. Broy, W. Dosch, H. Partsch, P. Pepper, M. Wirsing: Existential quantifiers in abstract data types. In: H.A. Maurer (ed.): Proc. 6th ICALP, Graz, LNCS 71 , 73-87 (1979)

/Broy, Wirsing 80/
M. Broy, M. Wirsing: Programming languages as abstract data types. In : M. Dauchet (ed.): Proc. 5th Colloquium on "Arbres en Algèbre et en Programmation", Lille, 1980

/Chang, Keisler 74/
C.C. Chang, H.J. Keisler: Model theory, Studies in Logic and Foundations of Mathematics Vol. 73, North-Holland

/Courcelle, Guessarian 78/
B. Courcelle, I. Guessarian: On some classes of interpretations. JCSS 17 : 3, 388-413 (1978)

/Ehrich, Lohberger 78/
H.D. Ehrich, V.G. Lohberger: Parametric specification of abstract data types, parameter substitution and graph replacements. Proc. Workshop "Graphentheoretische Konzepte in der Informatik", München: Hanser-Verlag (1978)

/Ehrig et al. 78/
H. Ehrig, H.J. Kreowski, P. Padawitz: Stepwise specification and implementation of abstract data types. Proc. 5th ICALP, Udine, LNCS 62, 205-226, 1978

/Giarratana et al. 76/
V. Giarratana, F. Gimona, U. Montanari: Observability concepts in abstract data type specification. Proc. of the 5th MFCS Symposium, LNCS 45 , 576-587 (1976)

/Grätzer 68/
G. Grätzer: Universal Algebra. Princeton, N.J.: van Nostrand, 1968

/Guttag 75/
J.V. Guttag: The specification and application to programming of abstract data types. Ph. D. Thesis, Univ. of Toronto, Dept. of Comp. Science, Rep. CSRG-59, 1975

/Guttag, Horning 78/
J.V. Guttag, J.J. Horning: The algebraic specification of abstract data types. Acta Informatica 10, 27-52 (1978)

/Guttag 79/
J.V. Guttag: Notes on type abstraction. In: F.L. Bauer, M. Broy (eds.): Program Construction, LNCS 69, 593-616 (1979)

/Lescanne 79/
P. Lescanne: Etude algêbrique et relationelle des types abstraits et de leurs representations. Dissertation, Nancy, September 1979, Rapport de Recherches 79-T-059 (1979)

/Majster 79/
M. Majster: Data types, abstract data types and their specification problem. TCS 8, 89-127 (1979)

/Milner 77/
R. Milner: Fully abstract models of typed lambda calculi. TCS 4, 1-22 (1977)

/McLane 71/
S. McLane: Categories for the working mathematician. Berlin: Springer, 1971

/Osswald 66/
H. Osswald: Freie Strukturen. Zulassungsarbeit, Universität Hannover, 1966

/Rasiowa, Sikorski 70/
H. Rasiowa, R. Sikorski: The mathematics of metamathematics. Monografie Matematyczne, Warszawa 1970

/Wand 77/
M. Wand: Final algebra semantics and data type extensions. Indiana University, Comp. Science Department, Technical Report No. 65, 1978

/Wirsing 77/
M. Wirsing: Das Entscheidungsproblem der Klasse von Formeln, die höchstens zwei Primformeln enthalten. Manuscripta Mathematica 22, 13-25 (1977)

/Wirsing 78/
M. Wirsing: Kleine unentscheidbare Klassen der Prädikatenlogik mit Identität und Funktionszeichen. Archiv für math. Logik und Grundlagenforschung 19, 97-109 (1978)

/Wirsing et al. 80/
M. Wirsing, P. Pepper, H. Partsch, W. Dosch, M. Broy: On hierarchies of abstract types. Technische Universität München, TUM-I 8007, May 1980

THE LR(k) PARSER

Jacek Witaszek
Institute of Mathematical Machines
Krzywickiego 34
02-078 Warsaw, Poland

Introduction

The problem of LR(k) parsing introduced by D.Knuth [7] has been discussed by many authors. As the parser built according to the Knuth's method is rather large (in the sense of the size of its tables) the main concern was to find out another method, which would result in a smaller one. The most notable results are due to Korenjak [8], DeRemer [3] , Anderson [2] , Aho and Ullman [1] and Pager [9] .

The paper presents yet another approach to LR(k) parsing. It resembles to some extent that of Aho and Ullman. In particular, in both cases the parser is built in two steps: first, the rather large, so called canonical LR(k) parser is constructed, and then it is reduced in size by the application of some transformations. From the practical point of view the main difference between these two approaches lies in the efficiency of computing the optimum transformations for a given parser i.e. those transformations which transform it into the smallest one . For the Aho - Ullman's transformations there is no efficient method of computing the optimum ones while this is not the case when ours are used.

We begin our presentation with the formal definition of the LR(k) parser. Then we sketch the way in which the canonical parser for a given grammar can be built. Next we define three classes of transformations on LR(k) parsers and prove that the property of being a valid parser for a given grammar is invariant under those transformations. Finaly we show on a simple example, how the theory developed in previous sections can be used to build a "small" LR(k) parser.

1. Notation

The notation used throughout this paper is actually based on that given in [5]. In particular ϵ denotes the empty string, ϕ - the empty set, and Ω - a special symbol not in any alphabet. If α is a string then $|\alpha|$ denotes its length, $j:\alpha$ the j-th symbol of α - if $1 \leq j \leq |\alpha|$ or

Ω otherwise, and $[\alpha]_j^i$ the substring formed of symbols: j through i - provided $1 \leq j \leq i \leq |\alpha|$. The following abbreviation will be used: $[\alpha]^i = [\alpha]_1^i$ and $[\alpha]_j = [\alpha]_j^d$ where $d = |\alpha|$. A context-free grammar is the four-tuple $G = \langle V,T,S,P \rangle$, where V and T are finite alphabets, $T \subseteq V$, called the grammar and terminal alphabets, respectively. Symbols in T will be called terminals, and symbols in V-T nonterminals. S is a distinct nonterminal called the start symbol, P is a finite set of productions of the form $A \rightarrow \alpha$, where $A \in V-T$, and α is a string over V. If $p \in P$ then LHS(p) denotes the left-hand side of p, and RHS(p) - its right-hande side. Customarily a, b, c will stand for terminal symbols, A, B, C - for nonterminal symbols, X, Y, Z - for grammar symbols $\alpha, \beta, \gamma, \delta, \eta,$ - for strings over V, and v, w, x, y, z for strings over T. We will write $\alpha \underset{G}{\Rightarrow} \beta$ to denote that α derives directly β in G, and $\alpha \underset{G}{\Rightarrow}_R \beta$ to denote that α derives β directly by rightmost derivation. Transitive and reflexive closures of $\Rightarrow_R$ and $\Rightarrow$ will be denoted by $\overset{*}{\Rightarrow}_R$ and $\overset{*}{\Rightarrow}$, respectively. We shall drop the subscript G, when it is clear what grammar we are talking about. We define $FIRST_k^G(\alpha) = \{v \mid \exists w: \alpha \underset{G}{\overset{*}{\Rightarrow}} vw, |v| = k \cup \cup |v| < k \,\&\, w = \varepsilon\}$. The grammar G is said to be LR(k) if 1° $S \overset{*}{\Rightarrow}_R \alpha Aw \Rightarrow_R \alpha\beta w$ 2° $S \overset{*}{\Rightarrow}_R \gamma Bx \Rightarrow_R \alpha\beta\delta$ and 3° $FIRST_k(w) = FIRST_k(\delta)$ imply $\alpha = \gamma$ A=B and $\delta = x$.

A deterministic finite state automaton (DFSA) is the fivetuple $N = \langle Q, q_1, F, V, \lambda \rangle$ where Q is a finite set of states (states will be denoted by q) $q_1 \in Q$ is the initial state, $F \subseteq Q$ is the set of final states, V is a finite set of input symbols, and $\lambda: Q \times V^* \rightarrow Q$ is the transition function.

2. The LR(k) parser

Definition 1. A LR(k) parser is the 6-tuple $M = \langle N,T,S,P,\varrho,\omega \rangle$, where $N = \langle Q, q_1, F, V, \lambda \rangle$ is a DFSA and is called the parsers control (states of N will be also refered to as states of the parser), T is a finite alphabet $T \subseteq V$, $S \in V-T$, P is a finite set of productions of the form $A \rightarrow \alpha$, and ϱ and ω are mapings $\varrho: F \rightarrow P$, $\omega: F \rightarrow \{1,2,\ldots,k\}$ where k is the LR-constant of the parser. We shall use the same notational conventions for elements of and strings over V, T and V-T as in the case of grammars. Additionally we will always assume that Q contains a distinct error state q_e such that for any $q \in F \cup \{q_e\}$ and any X: $\lambda(q,X) = q_e$.

The LR(k)parser will be interpreted as a machine equiped with a baloon memory able to hold strings over V (at the beginning this is the string to be parsed) and an output device. That type of memory has been employed here only for conceptual simplicity; as shown in [6] or [10] it might be replaced in a trivial way by a stack, a k-symbol input buffer and an input tape. The behavior of this machine describes the following algorithm, where η denotes the current content of the memory, and q the current state:

Algorithm 1

```
begin
    η:=string to be parsed;
  a:while η ≠ S do begin
        q:=q1; m:=0;
        while q ∉ F do begin
          m:=m+1;   X:=m:η ;
          if X =Ω then signal error and stop;
          q:=λ(q,X);
          if q=qe then signal error and stop
        end;
        p:=ϱ(q);   r:= ω(q);   A:=LHS(p);
        d:=|RHS(p)| ; γ':=[α]^(m-r-d);   γ'':= [α]_(m-r+1);
        output(p);
        η:= γ'Aγ''
      end;
      accept and stop
end
```

As only LR(k)parsers will be considered in this paper, parser instead of LR(k)parser will be used throughout the whole text.

The activities the parser performs in the course of one cycle of the while-loop labeled by "a" (see the algorithm above) will be refered to as a step of the parsing process. We will write $\eta \vdash_M \eta'(p)$ to denote that the parser M in one step transforms the content η of its memory to η' outputing the production p. Similary $\eta \vdash^n_M \eta'(p_1,p_2,\dots,p_n)$ denotes that M in n steps transforms the content η of its memory to η' outputing $p_1,p_2,\dots,p_n$. If the output is of no interest we will simply write $\eta \vdash_M \eta'$ or $\eta \vdash^n_M \eta'$. Reflexive and transitive closure of $\vdash_M$ will be denoted by $\vdash^*_M$.

Definition 2. The language accepted by the parser M is the set $L(M)=\{x \mid x \in T^*,\ x \vdash^*_M S\}$.

Definition 3. A parser is said to be well formed if 1° for any γ and β such that $\lambda(q_1,\gamma\beta)=q_f \in F, \omega(q_f)=|\beta|$ implies $\beta \in T^*$, 2° for any $q_f \in F$ $|RHS(\varrho(q_f))| + \omega(q_f) > 0$.

The following two theorems, given without proofs, express those properties of well formed parsers, which are essential for our further discussion.

Theorem 1. If M is well formed and for some γ, γ', β and β': $\gamma\beta \vdash_M \gamma'\beta'$, $\lambda(q_1,\gamma) \in F$ and $\lambda(q_1,\gamma') \in F$ then γ can not be an initial substring of γ' and vice versa.

Theorem 2. If M is well formed and for some γ, γ', β and x, some $n \geq 0$ and some $q_f \in F$: $\lambda(q_1,\gamma) \neq q_e$, $\gamma x \vdash_M^n \gamma'\beta$ and $\lambda(q_1,\gamma') = q_f$ then $\beta \in T^*$.

Definition 4. Let G be a LR(k)grammar. The parser $M=\langle N,T,S,P,\varrho,\omega\rangle$ is said to be a valid parser for G if 1° $G=\langle V,T,S,P\rangle$ where V is equal to the input alphabet of N, 2° M is well formed, 3° $L(G) \subseteq L(M)$ and 4° for any γ, α, v, A and $q_f \in F$ such that $\lambda(q_1,\gamma\alpha v) = q_f$, $\varrho(q_f) = A \rightarrow \alpha$, and $\omega(q_f) = |v|$, there exist such w, x and q_f' that $\gamma\alpha wx$ is a right sentential form, α is its handle, $A \rightarrow \alpha$ - the production which should be applied to reduce the handle, $\lambda(q_1,\gamma\alpha w) = q_f'$, $q_f' \in F$, $\varrho(q_f') = A \rightarrow \alpha$ and $\omega(q_f') = |w|$.

An obvious consequence of algorithm 1 and definition 4 is the following:

Proposition 1. Let M be a valid parser for grammar G. If γ, β, γ' and p are such that $\gamma\beta \vdash_M \gamma'\beta(p)$ and $\lambda(q_1,\gamma) \in F$ then $\gamma' \Rightarrow_R \gamma$ by production p.

The following theorems 3 and 4 show that the LR(k)parser as introduced in definition 4 actually does what intuitively we expect a parser should do, i.e. for any x it either produces the right parse of x - if x is in L(G) - or signals error otherwise.

Theorem 3. Let G be a LR(k)grammar and let M be a valid parser for this grammar. If for some $n > 0$, some $\gamma, x, \eta_0, \eta_1, \ldots, \eta_n$ and some $p_1, p_2, \ldots, p_n$: $\lambda(q_1,\gamma) \neq q_e$, $\eta_0 = \gamma x$ and $\eta_{i-1} \vdash_M \eta_i(p_i)$ for $i=1,2,\ldots,n$, then for $i=1,2,\ldots,n$: $\eta_i \Rightarrow_R \eta_{i-1}$ by production p_i.

Proof. Obviously there exist such v, x_1 and γ_1' that $x = vx_1$, $\lambda(q_1,\gamma v) \in F$ and $\eta_1 = \gamma_1' x_1$. But then (proposition 1) $\gamma_1' \Rightarrow_R \gamma v$ by production p_1 and thus $\eta_1 = \gamma_1' x_1 \Rightarrow_R \gamma v x_1 = \gamma x$ by the same production. This shows that the theorem is true for n=1.

Let us suppose now that $n \geq 2$ and that the theorem is true for n-1. As $\eta_{n-1} \vdash_M \eta_n(p_n)$ there must exist such initial substring γ_{n-1} of η_{n-1} that $\lambda(q_1,\gamma_{n-1}) \in F$. Moreover, according to theorem 2 there exists such x_{n-1} that $\eta_{n-1} = \gamma_{n-1}x_{n-1}$. Thus for some γ_n' : $\eta_n = \gamma_n' x_{n-1}$ and (proposition 1) $\gamma_n' \Rightarrow_R \gamma_{n-1}$ by production p_n. Hence, as x_{n-1} is in T^*, it must be $\eta_n = \gamma_n' x_{n-1} \Rightarrow_R \gamma_{n-1}x_{n-1} = \eta_{n-1}$ by the same production which completes the proof.

The most important consequence of theorem 3 is the following:

Proposition 2. If M is a valid parser for some LR(k)grammar G, and for some $\eta=\eta_0, \eta_1, \ldots, \eta_n=S$ and $p_1, p_2, \ldots, p_n$ we have $\eta_{i-1} \vdash_M \eta_i$, where $i=1,2,\ldots,n$, then η is a right sentential form in G, $S=\eta_n, \eta_{n-1}, \ldots, \eta_0=\eta$ is its rightmost derivation and $p_n, p_{n-1}, \ldots, p_1$ - its right parse.

Theorem 4. If M is a valid parser for a LR(k) grammar G then the parsing process of any η must end after a finite number of steps.

Proof. Note that as M is well formed it cannot scan in every step the same initial substring of η and put a nonterminal at its end. So, if the parsing process of η never ends, there must exist such γ_0, x, $|x| \leq k$, and β that $\eta \vdash_M^* \gamma_0 x$ and for any $i \geq 0$ there are such $q_{fi} \in F$, q_i, γ_i, v_i and x_i that: $\lambda(q_1, \gamma_i) = q_i$, $\lambda(q_1, \gamma_i v_i) = q_{fi}$, $x=v_i x_i$, $\omega(q_{fi}) = |v_i|$ and $\gamma_0 x \vdash_M^i \gamma_i x$. Define $Q' = \{q \mid \exists i: q=q_i\}$ and let $j>0$ be such that for any $q \in Q$ $q=q_i$ for some $i<j$. According to definition 4, p.4° for some z $\gamma_j z$ is a right sentential form and as for any i $\gamma_{i+1} \Rightarrow_R \gamma_i$ by production $\varrho(q_{fi})$, so for any $i<j$ $\gamma_{i+1} z \Rightarrow_R \gamma_i z$ by $\varrho(q_{fi})$. Note that $L(G) \subseteq L(M)$, hence for any $i<j$ there must exist such $q'_{fi} \in F$, w_i and z_i that: $z=w_i z_i$, $\lambda(q_i, w_i) = \lambda(q_1, \gamma_i w_i) = q'_{fi}$, $\varrho(q'_{fi}) = \varrho(q_{fi})$ and $\omega(q'_{fi}) = |w_i|$. This means that in the first j steps of our parsing process the actions the parser performs on γ_i $i=1,2,\ldots,n-1$ do not depend on whether $\gamma_i z$ or $\gamma_i x$ were considered. As in those j-1 steps M entered every state in Q', the above applies also to the j-th and next steps. Thus the parsing process of the right sentential form never ends, which contradicts our assumption that M is a valid parser for G (def.4 p.3°).

3. The canonical LR(k) parser

We will show now, how for a given grammar G, which is assumed to be LR(k), one can construct a special type of parser. This parser will be refered to as canonical parser for that grammar. The construction proceeds in the following 6 steps:

a/ Take the smallest integer $k \geq 0$ such that G is LR(k)

b/ Construct for G the so called k-characteristic grammar [5] [7] [10] $G'_k = \langle V', T', S', P' \rangle$ where 1° $V' = \{[A,v] \mid A \in V, |v| \leq k\} \cup V$, 2° $T' = V$, $S' = [S, \varepsilon]$, 4° $P' = \{ [A,v] \rightarrow X_1 X_2 \ldots X_{j-1} [X_j, w] \mid A \rightarrow X_1 X_2 \ldots X_n \in P, |v| \leq k, 1 \leq j \leq n, w \in FIRST_k^G(X_{j+1} \ldots X_n), X_j \in V-T \} \cup \{[A,v] \rightarrow X_1 X_2 \ldots X_n v \mid |v| \leq k, A \rightarrow X_1 X_2 \ldots X_n \in P\}$

c/ Remove from G'_k all useless symbols and useless productions

d/ Construct for G'_k the DFSA $N(G'_k)$ using the following algorithm. Note that the k-characteristic grammar is right linear, and the algorithm bellow actually computes a recognizer for this grammar.

Algorithm 2

begin

$V:=T'$: $q_e := \phi$;

$q_1 :=$ CLOSURE($\{\langle p,1\rangle \mid p \in P', \ LHS(p)=S'\}$) ;

$Q:=\{q_1, q_e\}$;

for each $q \in Q$ and $X \in V$ **do begin**

$q' := \{\langle p,j\rangle \mid \langle p,j\rangle \in q, \ j:RHS(p)=X\}$;

$q'' :=$ CLOSURE($\{\langle p,j+1\rangle \mid \langle p,j\rangle \in q'\}$) ;

$Q:=Q \cup \{q''\}$;

define $\lambda(q,X)=q''$

end

$F:=\{q \mid q \in Q, \exists \langle p,j\rangle : \langle p,j\rangle \in q, \ j=|RHS(p)|+1\}$;

define $N(G_k') = \langle Q, q_1, F, V, \lambda\rangle$

end

Note that every state of $N(G_k')$ is a set of items of the form $\langle p,j\rangle$, where $p \in P'$ and $1 \leq j \leq |RHS(p)|+1$. The function CLOSURE which maps sets of items into sets of items is defined as follows:

1^0 CLOSURE($\langle p,j\rangle$) =

$j:RHS(p) \in T' \rightarrow \langle p,j\rangle$

true $\rightarrow \{\langle p',1\rangle \mid j:RHS(p) \overset{*}{\underset{G_k'}{\Rightarrow}} LHS(p')\} \cup \{\langle p,j\rangle\}$

2^0 CLOSURE(ϕ) = ϕ

3^0 CLOSURE $(q) = \bigcup_{\langle p,j\rangle \in q}$ CLOSURE($\langle p,j\rangle$)

It has been shown [10] that G is LR(k) iff every final state of $N(G_k')$ contains exactly one item, which must be of the form $\langle [A,v] \rightarrow \alpha v, |\alpha v|+1\rangle$ for some $[A,v] \rightarrow \alpha v$ in P'.

e/ Define for G the canonical parser $M(G)=\langle N,T,S,P,\varrho,\omega\rangle$ as follows: $N=N(G_k')$, T,S,P are as in G, for any $q_f \in F$ if $\langle [A,v] \rightarrow \alpha v, |\alpha v|+1\rangle$ is the only item in q_f then $\omega(q_f)=|v|$ and $\varrho(q_f) = A \rightarrow \alpha$.

f/ Merge all those final states for which the values of both ϱ and ω are the same.

Theorem 5. The canonical parser for a given LR(k)grammar G is a valid parser for that grammar.

The proof of this theorem has been given in [10] and as it is rather complicated it will be omitted here.

4. Transformations on LR(k) parsers

Definition 5. Two states q and q' of a parser are said to be equivalent if for any α : 1^0 $\lambda(q,\alpha) \in F$ iff $\lambda(q',\alpha) \in F$, 2^0 if $\lambda(q,\alpha) = q_f$

and $\lambda(q_f',\alpha)=q_f$, $q_f,q_f' \in F$ then $\varrho(q_f)=\varrho(q_f')$ and $\omega(q_f)=\omega(q_f')$.

Obviously, this equivalence relation generates an unique partitioning of the set of states of any given parser M into equivalence classes, so M can be minimized in the usual way by merging states inside of any of the equivalence classes.

Definition 6. Let $M=\langle N,T,S,P,\varrho,\omega\rangle$, where $N=\langle Q,q_1,F,V,\lambda\rangle$, be a parser and let $[q]$ denotes the equivalence class containing q. Define a new parser $M'=\langle N',T,S,P,\varrho',\omega'\rangle$ where $N=\langle Q',q_1',F',V',\lambda'\rangle$ such that 1° Q'= paritioning of Q into equivalence classes, 2° $q_1'=[q_1]$ 3° F'= partitioning of F into equivalence classes, 4° for any q and α: $\lambda'([q],\alpha)=$ $=[\lambda(q,\alpha)]$ 5° for any $q_f \in F$:$\varrho'([q_f])=\varrho(q_f)$ and $\omega'([q_f])=\omega(q_f)$.

The transformation which transforms M to M', as described above, will be refered to as transformation μ.

From the above two definitions it follows immediately:

Theorem 6. If M is a valid parser for a given grammar G, then $\mu(M)$ is also a valid parser for this grammar.

The reason for introducing the two other transformations is to get rid off unnecessary context checking (transformation σ) and to increase the number of equivalent states (both σ and π).

Definition 7. Let $M=\langle N,T,S,P,\varrho,\omega\rangle$, where $N=\langle Q,q_1,F,V,\lambda\rangle$, be a parser, and q one of its states satisfying the following:

Condition 1. For q there exist such final state q_f and such terminal a that: 1° $\lambda(q,a)=q_f$, 2° for any X either $\lambda(q,X)=q_f$ or $\lambda(q,X)=q_e$, 3° $\omega(q_f)>0$, 4° $|RHS(\varrho(q_f))| + \omega(q_f) > 1$.

Define a new parser $M'=\langle N',T,S,P,\varrho',\omega'\rangle$, where $N'=\langle Q,q_1,F',V,\lambda'\rangle$, such that: 1° for any X and q' $\lambda'(q',X)=q_e$ - if q'=q - or $\lambda'(q,X)=\lambda(q,X)$ otherwise, 2° $F'=F\cup\{q\}$, 3° for any q_f' in F $\varrho'(q_f')=\varrho(q_f')$ and $\omega'(q_f')=$ $=\omega(q_f')$, 4° $\varrho'(q)=\varrho(q_f)$ and $\omega'(q)=\omega(q_f)-1$.

The transformation which transforms M to M' as described above will be refered to as transformation σ_q.

The intuitive explanation of the above definition is as follows. If checking of subsequent symbols right to the handle does not introduce any new information about the handle and the production which should be applied to reduce it, then the parser can give up that checking.

Theorem 7. Let M be a valid parser for a LR(k) grammar G, and q be a state satisfying cond.1. If $M'=\sigma_q(M)$ then M'is also a valid parser for G.

Proof. Obviously, p.1° of definition 4 must hold for M'. As $\omega'(q)=$ $=\omega(q_f)-1$ and at the same time $\omega(q_f)>0$ and $\omega(q_f)+|RHS\ (\varrho(q_f))|>1$, the well-formedness of M clearly implies the well-formedness of M'. Observe now that if for some η M finds the handle and reduces it, then M' does the same (that is M' finds the same handle and reduces it in the same way) except that M' possibly finds the handle after having scaned fewer symbols. Hence as p.3° and 4° hold for M they must also hold for M'.

Definition 8. The superposition of all possible - for a given parser - transformations $\mathfrak{G}_q$ will be refered to as transformation $\mathfrak{G}$. We will also write $M'=\mathfrak{G}(M)$ to denote that $M'$is the result of applying $\mathfrak{G}$ to M.

The transformation $\mathfrak{G}$ might be computed by the following algorithm, where M denotes the parser to be transformed.

Algorithm 3.

```
begin
    M' := M;
    while M' contains states satisfying cond.1 do
      begin
        q:=any state satisfying cond.1;
        M' := G_q(M')
      end
end
```

Observe that, as $\mathfrak{G}_q$ does not change the properties of any state but q, the outcome of this algorithm for a given parser M is unique. This justfies the validity of definition 8.

As one can see the transformation $\mathfrak{G}$ turns some nonfinal states of the parser into final ones possibly causing some other final states to become inaccessible. Obviously removing such states cuts down the number of states of the parser without changing any of its essential properties. Additionally this transformation may increase the number of equivalent states of the parser, which improves the result of its minimization.

Definition 9. Let $M=\langle N,T,S,P,\varrho,\omega\rangle$, where as usually $N=\langle Q,q_1,F,V,\lambda\rangle$, be a parser and let Δ be an arbitrary set of triplets of the form $\langle q,b,q_f\rangle$, where $q\in Q-F$, $b\in T$, $q_f\in F$, satisfying the following:

Condition 2. For any $\langle q,b,q_f\rangle$ in Δ: 1° $\omega(q_f)>0$, 2° $\lambda(q,b)=q_e$, 3° there exist such symbol a that $\lambda(q,a)=q_f$, 4° for any $q_f'\in F$ $\langle q,b,q_f'\rangle\in\Delta$ implies $q_f=q_f'$.

Define for M a new parser $M'=\langle N',T,S,P,\varrho,\omega\rangle$, where 1° $N'=\langle Q,q_1,F,V,\lambda'\rangle$, 2° for any q and X $\lambda'(q,X)=q_f$ if $\langle q,X,q_f\rangle$ is in Δ or $\lambda'(q,X)=\lambda(q,X)$ - otherwise.

The transformation which transforms M to M' as described above will be refered to as transformation π_Δ.

The intuitive explanation of the transformation π_Δ is as follows: if the parser has encountered the handle it can be reduced even though there are some incorrect symbols right to it. According to theorem 4 those symbols will be signalled as errors in one of the next steps. The reason for applying π_Δ is that this transformation turns unequivalent states of the parser into equivalent ones - provided the set Δ has been choosen properly.

The problem of finding the optimum Δ for a given parser M (i.e. such a Δ which would guarantie the best possible result of minimization of $\pi_\Delta(M)$) is obviously not a trivial one. Its complete discussion, omitted in this short paper, can be found in [10]. An algorithm has also been given in [10] which for a given parser computes in time proportional to $|V||Q|\log|Q|$ either the optimum Δ (this happens in most practical cases) or its reasonable good approximation.

<u>Theorem 8</u>. Let G be a LR(k) grammar, and M - a valid parser for G. If π_Δ is defined on M and $M'=\pi_\Delta(M)$ then M' is a valid parser for G.

<u>Proof</u>. We can prove that pp. 1°, 2°, and 3° of definition 4 hold for M' just in the same way as in the proof of theorem 7. To show that p.4° of this definition holds for M' we have to consider only those cases in which λ' and λ differ. According to definition 9 p.2° this may happen only for those q and b for which there exists such final state q_f that $\langle q,b,q_f\rangle\in\Delta$. Let for some γ : $\lambda'(q_1,\gamma)=\lambda(q_1,\gamma)=q$. We have then $\lambda'(q_1,\gamma b)=q_f$ while $\lambda(q_1,\gamma b)=q_e$. But according to cond.2 p.3° it must be $\lambda'(q_1,\gamma a)=\lambda(q_1,\gamma a)=q_f$ for some symbol a, thus as $\omega(q_f)>0$ (cond.2 p.1°), and as 4° holds for M it must also hold for M'.

5. <u>Example</u>

To show how the theory which was developed in previous sections can be employed to build a "small" parser, let us consider the following grammar G_E (E stands for example), $G_E=\langle\{S,A,E,T,\perp,+,(,),1\},\{\perp,+,(,),1\},S,P\rangle$ where $P=\{S\to A\perp,\ A\to E,\ E\to T+E,\ E\to T,\ T\to 1,\ T\to (E)\}$. As one can easely verify this grammar is LR(1) (in fact it is SLR(1)). Let M_E denotes the canonical parser for G_E. Tables representing functions: λ, ϱ and ω of M_E have been shown in figure 1. We have adopted there the following:

<u>Convention 1</u>. Final states are represented by negative integers. Non-final states are represented by unsigned integers, in particular the error state q_e is represented by 0, and the initial state q_1 - by 1. Rows of the λ-table corresponding to states in $F \cup \{q_e\}$ are omitted. For any pair of final states q_f, q_f' : $\varrho(q_f)=\varrho(q_f')$ and $\omega(q_f)=\omega(q_f')$ implies $q_f=q_f'$.

As one can see the states: 3, 6, 11, 12, 13, 16 and 17 satisfy condition 1 (see def.7), thus $\mathfrak{S}(M_E)= \mathfrak{S}_3(\mathfrak{S}_6(\mathfrak{S}_{11}(\mathfrak{S}_{12}(\mathfrak{S}_{13}(\mathfrak{S}_{16}(\mathfrak{S}_{17}(M_E)))))))$. Denote $M_E^1=\mathfrak{S}(M_E)$. Tables representing functions λ , ϱ and ω of M_E^1 have been shown in figure 2. After removing inaccessible final states (i. e. states -2, -4, -5 and -6) merging of equivalent final states (these are states 6 and 11, 12 and 16, 13 and 17) and renumbering states as to obey convention 1, the tables for M_E^1 become as shown in figure 3.

	⊥	+	(	)	1	S	A	E	T
1	0	0	5	0	6	0	2	3	4
2	-1	0	0	0	0	0	0	0	0
3	-2	0	0	0	0	0	0	0	0
4	-3	7	0	0	0	0	0	0	0
5	0	0	10	0	11	0	0	8	9
6	-4	-4	0	0	0	0	0	0	0
7	0	0	5	0	6	0	0	12	4
8	0	0	0	13	0	0	0	0	0
9	0	14	0	-3	0	0	0	0	0
10	0	0	10	0	11	0	0	15	9
11	0	-4	0	-4	0	0	0	0	0
12	-5	0	0	0	0	0	0	0	0
13	-6	-6	0	0	0	0	0	0	0
14	0	0	10	0	11	0	0	16	9
15	0	0	0	17	0	0	0	0	0
16	0	0	-5	0	0	0	0	0	0
17	0	-6	0	-6	0	0	0	0	0

λ- function

q_f	$\varrho(q_f)$	$\omega(q_f)$
-1	S → A⊥	0
-2	A → E	1
-3	E → T	1
-4	T → 1	1
-5	E → T+E	1
-6	T → (E)	1

Figure 1. Functions ϱ, ω and λ for M_E

	⊥	+	(	)	1	S	A	E	T
1	0	0	5	0	6	0	2	3	4
2	-1	0	0	0	0	0	0	0	0
4	-3	7	0	0	0	0	0	0	0
5	0	0	10	0	11	0	0	8	9
7	0	0	5	0	6	0	0	12	4
8	0	0	0	13	0	0	0	0	0
9	0	14	0	-3	0	0	0	0	0
10	0	0	10	0	11	0	0	0	0
14	0	0	10	0	11	0	0	16	9
15	0	0	0	17	0	0	0	0	0

λ - function

q_f	$\varrho(q_f)$	$\omega(q_f)$
-1	S → A⊥	0
-2	A → E	1
-3	E → T	1
-4	T → 1	1
-5	E → T+E	1
-6	T → (E)	1
3	A → E	0
6	T → 1	0
11	T → 1	0
12	E → T+E	0
13	T → (E)	0
16	E → T+E	0
17	T → (E)	0

Figure 2. Function ϱ , ω and λ for M_E^1

	$\perp$	+	(	)	1	S	A	E	T
1	0	0	4	0	-4	0	2	-2	3
2	-1	0	0	0	0	0	0	0	0
3	-3	5	0	0	0	0	0	0	0
4	0	0	8	0	-4	0	0	6	7
5	0	0	4	0	-4	0	0	-5	3
6	0	0	0	-6	0	0	0	0	0
7	0	9	0	-3	0	0	0	0	0
8	0	0	8	0	-4	0	0	10	7
9	0	0	8	0	-4	0	0	-5	7
10	0	0	0	-6	0	0	0	0	0

λ - function

q_f	$\varrho(q_f)$	$\omega(q_f)$
-1	$S \to A\perp$	0
-2	$A \to E$	0
-3	$E \to T$	1
-4	$T \to 1$	0
-5	$E \to T+E$	0
-6	$T \to (E)$	0

Figure 3. Functions λ, ϱ and ω for M_E^1 after merging of equivalent final states and renumbering of states

As one can observe M_E does not contain any equivalent states, while M_E^1 contains two pairs of equivalent states: 6 and 10, 4 and 8. As stated before the transformation π_Δ may also increase the number of equivalent states. Define $\Delta = \{<3,\perp,-3>, <7,),-3>\}$ (observe that this satisfies condition 2 - see def.9) and denote $M_E^2 = \pi_\Delta(M_E^1)$. Apart from those mentioned before, there are two other pairs of equivalent states in M_E^2 : 3 and 7, 5 and 9. Thus minimizing of M_E^2 cuts down the total number of states to six as shown in figure 4.

	$\perp$	+	(	)	1	S	A	E	T
1	0	0	4	0	-4	0	2	-2	3
2	-1	0	0	0	0	0	0	0	0
3	-3	5	0	-3	0	0	0	0	0
4	0	0	4	0	-4	0	0	6	3
5	0	0	4	0	-4	0	0	-5	3
6	0	0	0	-6	0	0	0	0	0

λ - function

q_f	$\varrho(q_f)$	$\omega(q_f)$
-1	$S \to A\perp$	0
-2	$A \to E$	0
-3	$E \to T$	1
-4	$T \to 1$	0
-5	$E \to T+E$	0
-6	$T \to (E)$	0

Figure 4. Functions λ, ϱ and ω for $\mu(M_E^2)$.

As mentioned in section 4 the best transformation π for a given parser can be computed in time $O(|V||Q| \log|Q|)$, ($|Q|$ and $|V|$ denote the cardinalities of the set of states of the parser and its alphabet, respectively). As one can easely see the time bound for the σ transformation is $O(k|V||Q|)$, and for the μ transformation - $O(|V||Q|\log|Q|)$ provided that the Hopcroft's algorithm has been used [4]. Thus the canonical parser can be transformed into the "small" one in time proportional to $|V||Q|\log|Q|$ (where $|Q|$ and $|V|$ are the corresponding values taken for the canonical parser).

The method as shown in this section has been used to generate parsers for various grammars, the result being similar or better than those yielded by other methods mentioned in the introduction.

References

1 Aho A.V., Ullman J.D.: Optimization of LR(k)parsers; Journal of Computer and System Science, vol.6, nr 6, 1972.

2 Anderson T., Eve J., Horning J.: Efficient LR(1)parsers; Acta Informatica, vol.2, nr 1, 1973.

3 DeRemer F.L.: Practical translators for LR(k)languages; Ph.D.Thesis, MIT Cambridge, Mass. Sept. 1969.

4 Gries D.: Describing an algorithm by Hopcroft; Acta Informatica, vol.2, nr 2, 1973.

5 Hopcroft J.E., Ullman J.E.: Formal languages and their relation to automata; Addison-Wesley, 1969.

6 McKeeman W.M., Horning J.J., Wortaman D.B.: A compiler generator; Prentice-Hall, 1970.

7 Knuth D.: On the translation of languages from left to right; Information and Control, vol.8, nr 6, 1965.

8 Korenjak A.J.: A practical method for constructing LR(k)processors; CACM, vol.12, nr 11, 1969.

9 Pager D.: A practical general method for constructing LR(k)parsers; Acta Informatica, vol.7, nr 2, 1977.

10 Witaszek J.: Construction and optimization of LR(k)parsers; (in polish), Prace IMM, 1979.

SUBSTITUTION SYSTEMS - A FAMILY OF SYSTEM MODELS BASED ON CONCURRENCY

H.J. Genrich, K. Lautenbach, P.S. Thiagarajan
Institut für Informationssystemforschung (ISF)
Gesellschaft für Mathematik und Datenverarbeitung
Schloss Birlinghoven, D-5205 St.Augustin 1

A general system model called substitution systems is presented with two purposes in mind. Firstly, we use this model as a vehicle for formalizing what we think are the basic aspects of systems that exhibit concurrency. Secondly, we propose substitution systems as a common framework for developing and comparing a class of system models. In support of this proposal, we present three known system models and show that they can be naturally viewed as substitution systems.

0. Introduction

In the recent past the study of systems and processes that exhibit concurrency has acquired a good deal of importance. Various, in fact a dizzying variety of, approaches have been proposed and are being pursued. Among these, one of the oldest and perhaps for this reason one of the more mature approaches is the one initiated by C. A. Petri in 1962 [13]. The theory which is emerging from this long and continuing effort goes under the name of net theory of systems and processes.

In this theory, both systems and processes are dealt with as mathematical objects called nets. The language of nets is sufficiently rich in that it permits one to attach a wide variety of useful interpretations to these objects. As a result, systems and processes can be studied at different modes of abstractions (software - hardware), with different purposes in mind (specification - implementation) and at different levels of detail (structure - behaviour). Yet another consequence of the generality of net theory is that it might be used to provide a common frame of reference; a frame of reference in which different system models that claim to represent concurrency can be compared and related to each other.

This paper reflects our first attempt to develop such a common reference point. It is neither possible nor fruitful to have a framework into which every approach to concurrency can be fitted. Hence we start with a particular and no doubt personal view of concurrency and what properties, at the very minimum, a formal model of a system ought to possess. Based on these considerations we introduce a system model called <u>substitution systems</u>.

In the second half of the paper we try to convince the reader that the substitution model, in a modest way, is an useful unifying concept. We do this by exhibiting three known system models called <u>assignment systems</u> , <u>loosely coupled systems</u> and <u>condition/event systems</u>. These models look very different on surface and represent three alternative ways of organizing systems. We show that, in spite of such differences, the three system models can be viewed in a natural fashion as specific instances of substitution systems.

The notion of a substitution system is due to Petri[14]. The three specific models mentioned above were also formulated by him to explore different ways of organizing systems.

In our formalism, we start with a transition scheme which captures our understanding of what states and changes in states should look like in the presence of concurrency. In the literature a number of such schemes have been proposed.(see for example [7], [16],[18]). However, as opposed to most such schemes, we do not equate concurrency with non-determinacy. We explicitly model those aspects of concurrency that are relevant for our current purposes through the notion of a <u>step</u> and some axioms concerning steps. Among the existing models of concurrent systems and processes, to mention just a few which are related to our approach:

At the process level, Hoare's communicating sequential processes [5] is certainly relevant. The line pursued by Milner [12] is even more relevant in that, it is, to our tastes, formally and conceptually much more appealing. The work of Lauer,Shields and Best[8], though in a different setting, reflects the same view of concurrency that is expressed in this paper. It is possible, at least in principle, to translate objects of their formalism into condition/ event system descriptions. At a more abstract level, Janicki has studied the mathematical properties of the concurrency relation [6]. Last but not least, Mazurkiewicz in his work [11] expresses his understanding of concurrent systems and processes which in essential details coincides with ours. As a result, this work and our subsequent interactions with him have been a source of encouragement and inspiration.

1. Substitution Schemes

When we consider the behaviour of a dynamic system, we have to interrelate the past, current, and future states-of-affairs in the system and in (a part of) its environment. Each possible state-of-affairs can be described in terms of the conditions concurrently holding in the case under consideration. E.g., for a single automaton, each case consists of two conditions, the state of the automaton, and an aspect of the environment representing the input symbol for the automaton. The transition to a new, different case is described on the one hand by a change in the holding of conditions, and on the other hand in terms of events which reflect the basic rules of change for the system.

Conditions and events cannot be chosen independently but the choice of conditions must be guided by the concept of event we choose. If, for example, 'events' should be infinitesimal changes, the class of conditions must be of such a cardinality that we are definitely unable to distinguish them by observation. Should event occurrences be synchronized by the ticks of a universal discrete clock? Such a clock, if it exists, is not accessible; it is only in small regions of space where a real clock is effectively usable. And the synchronization of many real clocks, even if they are not moving in relation to each other, is itself a problem of considerable practical and conceptual difficulty.

We now postulate that all changes which are possible in a system together with its environment are composed of definite indivisible elementary changes which we shall call events, and that the composition of event occurrences is by sequence and by concurrency. Thus, several independent elementary changes may occur concurrently, in one step.

Decomposing a system into conditions and elementary changes yields a kind of game board on which the system behaviour can be simulated playing the following 'token game': A current case, c, of the system is represented by putting a token on exactly those conditions which belong to that case. The rules of the game, namely the basic rules of change, tell us which new token distribution may be derived from c, or from which old token distribution, c may have been derived, in a sequence of moves (event occurrences).

It is often convenient to formulate the rules of change regarding all 'conceivable cases', i.e. arbitrary combinations of conditions. In general, it will then be possible to simulate several systems on the same game board. In this case we have to distinguish very clearly between different systems. We therefor postulate that the cases of different systems cannot be connected by applying the rules of the game; and on the other hand, that which can be connected belongs to the same system.

In the sequel, the game board together with the rules of the game is called a _transition scheme_, and a _transition system_ is one instance of that scheme. Since we wish to restrict the notion 'event' to those elementary changes which have an occurrence in the _system_ under consideration, we call the 'conceivable events' which may occur in some instance of the scheme simply _transitions_. For similar reasons, we call the 'conceivable cases', i.e. arbitrary collections of conditions, _constellations_.

Definition: A triple (S,T;r) is called a _transition scheme_, and a quadruple (S,T;r,C) a _transiton system_, iff

1) S is a non-empty, countable set of _conditions_ and $K := \wp(S)$ is the corresponding set of _constellations_;
2) T is a non-empty, countable set disjoint from S, the set of _transitions_ and $U := \wp(T)$ is the correponding set of conceivable steps;
3) $r \subseteq K \times U \times K$ is the _transition rule_ where $(k_1,u,k_2) \in r$ means that in constellation k_1, the elementary changes belonging to u may occur concurrently, in one step, yielding constellation k_2;
4) $C \subseteq K$ is a set of constellations belonging to one connected component of r; the elements of C are the _cases_ of the system. $E := \{t \mid \exists c_1,c_2 \in C: (c_1,\{t\},c_2) \in r\}$ is the set of (system) _events_, i.e. of those transitions which are possible in the system; correspondingly, $B := \bigcup c \mid c \in C$ is the set of _system conditions_.

Very often, it is convenient to make use of the pictorial interpretation of transition schemes which we get immediately from the following 'result': Any transition scheme (S,T;r) may be viewed as a directed graph whose arcs are labelled by sets of transitions. Formally:

Definition: A quadruple $(V,A;Q,Z)$ with $V \cap A = \emptyset$ and $Q,Z: A \rightarrow V$ is called a *directed graph*; the elements of V are called *vertices*, or *nodes*, the elements of A *arcs*, and the functions Q and Z assign to each arc its *initial* and its *final end point*, respectively.

Proposition 1: For a given transition scheme $(S,T;r)$, the quintuple $(K,r;Q,Z,L)$ with

$Q = \{(k_1,u,k_2) \mapsto k_1 \mid (k_1,u,k_2) \in r\}$

$Z = \{(k_1,u,k_2) \mapsto k_2 \mid (k_1,u,k_2) \in r\}$

$L = \{(k_1,u,k_2) \mapsto u \mid (k_1,u,k_2) \in r\}$

is a directed graph whose arcs are labelled by the labelling function $L: r \rightarrow U$.

Pictorially: $(k_1,u,k_2) \in r \iff \underset{k_1}{\bullet} \xrightarrow{u} \underset{k_2}{\bullet}$

Our definition of transition schemes is, of course, not yet complete. We now introduce some notation and then state the requirements to be met by transition schemes. Except for some technicalities, these postulates reflect our notion of concurrency, or causal independence, of elementary changes occurring in one step. Later we shall introduce a special class of transition schemes, namely *substitution schemes*, which will establish the bridge between the very general 'meta model' of transition systems and three concrete models of systems with non-sequential behaviour.

Notation: For a given transition scheme $(S,T;r)$, we write:

1) $k_1[u>k_2 \;:\iff (k_1,u,k_2) \in r$
In constellation k_1, the step u may occur leading to constellation k_2. For $t \in T$, we shall also write $k_1[t>k_2$ instead of $k_1[\{t\}>k_2$.

2) $concess(k,u) \;:\iff \exists k': k[u>k'$. If $u=\{t\}$ then we write $concess(k,t)$.
The step u has *concession* (may occur) in constellation k.

3) $\Delta(k_1,k_2) := (k_1-k_2, k_2-k_1)$
The 'difference' between two constellations k_1,k_2.

Axioms: Any given transition scheme $(S,T;r)$ has to fulfil the following requirements:

TS1 $k_1[u>k_2 \wedge k_3[u>k_4 \implies (k_1=k_3 \iff k_2=k_4)$
In any given context, the change effected by a step is uniquely determined by its extent.

TS2 $k_1[u>k_2 \implies (k_1=k_2 \iff u=\emptyset)$

The empty step is the only one effecting no change.

TS3 $k\in K \implies k[\emptyset>k$

(A mere technicality)

TS4 $k_1[u>k_2 \wedge t\in u \implies \neg concess\ (k_2,t)$

Through the occurrence of a step, all its elements lose concession.

TS5 $k_1[u>k_2 \implies \forall v,w\subseteq u\ \exists k_3,k_4 : (\ k_1[v>k_3 \wedge k_4[w>k_2 \wedge$
$(k_3=k_4 \iff w=u-v) \wedge$
$(v=w \iff \Delta(k_1,k_3)=\Delta(k_4,k_2))\ )$

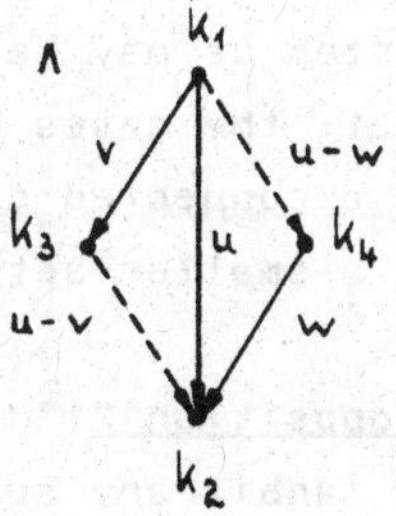

Each step can be arbitrarily divided into disjoint substeps, and within the context of one step, the change effected by a substep is fixed (see diagram on the right).

TS6 $k_1[u>k_2 \implies \forall x\in k_1-k_2\ \exists t\in u: x\notin k_t \quad \wedge \quad \forall x\in k_2-k_1\ \exists t\in u: x\in k_t$

(where $k[t>k_t$)

Conditions affected by a step are affected by one of its elementary changes.

These axioms yield immediately the following formulae:

Theorem 1: Let $k_1[u>k_2$, $k_1[v>k_3$ and $k_1[w>k_4$ with $v\subseteq u$ and $w=u-v$ (see the 'diamond' on the right). Then

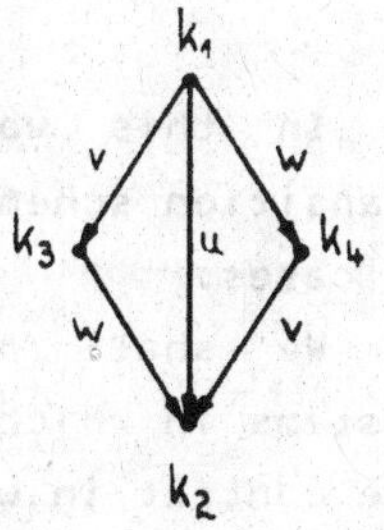

1) $k_3\cap k_4 = k_1\cap k_2$

2) $(k_1-k_i)\cap(k_i-k_2) = (k_i-k_1)\cap(k_2-k_i) = \emptyset \quad (i\in\{3,4\})$

3) $k_1-k_2 = \bigcup (k_1-k_t)\,|\,[t\in u\wedge k_1[t>k_t]$

4) $k_2-k_1 = \bigcup (k_t-k_1)\,|\,[t\in u\wedge k_1[t>k_t]$

Finally, we repeat in a more formal way that a transition system is a connected component of a transition scheme:

Defintion: For a transition scheme $(S,T;r)$, we define

1) $R1 := \{(k_1,k_2)\,|\,\exists u: (k_1,u,k_2)\in r\}$,
the binary relation of reachability-in-one-step between constellations;

2) $R := (R1 \cup R1^{-1})^*$,
the (equivalence) relation of full reachability.

Axiom: For a transition system $(S,T;r,C)$:

TS7 $\exists c\in K: C = \{k\,|\,cRk\}$ and $|C| > 1$

C is a non-trivial equivalence class of full reachability,

i.e. the set of constellations belonging to a connected component of r which does not consist of just one isolated constellation.

A constellation k which is connected to no other constellation is ruled out from being a case of any system. k might be called absurd, or inconsistent, or illegal. When modelling a system as a transition system we may have started with too many 'legal' constellations such that the cases of a given system cannot be determined as the elements of a connected component alone. Then we can restrict the given scheme to a smaller set of 'legal' constellations in the following way:

Proposition 2: Let (S,T;r) be a transition scheme, let $K' \subseteq K$ be an arbitrary subset of constellations, and let r' be derived from r as follows:

$(k_1,u,k_2) \in r' \iff (k_1,u,k_2) \in r \wedge \forall v \subseteq u \forall k_3 : [(k_1,v,k_3) \in r \implies k_3 \in K']$

(A step $(k_1,u,k_2) \in r$ belongs to r' iff k_1, k_2, and all intermediate constellations belong to K'.)

Then (S,T;r') is also a transition scheme in which all constellations in K-K' are isolated.

In this way we can treat every transition system as a special transition scheme by restricting the transition rule to the given set of cases.

We shall now define a special class of transition schemes and systems in which the change effected by a transition is independent of the context in which it may occur. We know that this is not the case in general but only within the range of the individual steps $(k_1,u,k_2) \in r$, as stated explicitly by axiom TS5.

Definition: A quadruple $(S,T;\varrho,r)$ is a substitution scheme iff

1) the triple (S,T;r) is a transition scheme;
2) $\varrho: T \to K \times K$ is a function which assigns to each transition t a pair of constellations. We denote $\varrho(t)$ by $(\bullet t, t\bullet)$ and extend this dot notation to subsets of T: $\bullet u := \bigcup \bullet t \mid t \in u$ and $u\bullet := \bigcup t\bullet \mid t \in u$. $\bullet t$ is called the set of preconditions, and $t\bullet$ the set of post conditions, of t.
3) For all steps $(k_1,u,k_2) \in r$, $k_1 - k_2 = \bullet u$ and $k_2 - k_1 = u\bullet$.

Definition: A quintuple $(S,T;\varrho,r,C)$ is called a substitution system iff $(S,T;\varrho,r)$ is a substitution scheme and (S,T;r,C) a transition system.

The term substitution is illustrated by the following trivial consequence of our definition:

<u>Proposition 3</u>: If $(S,T;\varrho,r)$ is a substitution scheme, then
$k_1[u>k_2 \implies k_2=(k_1-{\bullet}u)\cup u{\bullet}$

In fact, we have introduced a very strong form of substitution, namely:

<u>Proposition 4</u>: Substitution schemes are 1) <u>pure</u> and 2) <u>strict</u>:
1) $t\in T \implies {\bullet}t\cap t{\bullet}=\emptyset$
2) $\text{concess}(k,u) \implies {\bullet}u\subseteq k \wedge u{\bullet}\cap k=\emptyset$

Thus, in a substitution system, a transition cannot have concession in a given constellation in which the preconditions hold (are present) but a postcondition also holds. Such a situation in which pre- and postconditions of a transition get 'too close' to each other is called a <u>contact</u>. The absence of contacts is an important system property which can be met under names like <u>safety</u> or <u>persistence</u>.

If the necessary condition for transitions to have concession (see proposition 4) is also sufficient, concession <u>and</u> effect are fully determined by ϱ. In this case, the notion of change is strictly extensional.

<u>Definition</u>: A substitution scheme $(S,T;\varrho,r)$ satisfies the <u>extensionality principle</u>, iff
1) $\text{concess}(k,t) \iff {\bullet}t\subseteq k \wedge t{\bullet}\cap k=\emptyset$
2) $\text{concess}(k,u) \iff {\bullet}u\subseteq k \wedge u{\bullet}\cap k=\emptyset \wedge$
$\forall t_1,t_2\in u:[t_1\neq t_2 \implies {\bullet}t_1\cap{\bullet}t_2=t_1{\bullet}\cap t_2{\bullet}=\emptyset]$

A transition t has concession iff all its preconditions and none of its postcondition holds, and a step has concession iff all its elements have concession and no two of them are in 'conflict' because of sharing a pre- or postcondition.

Although our substitution schemes employ that rather strong form of substitution (propos. 4), they possess the same modelling power as transition schemes in general. To show this, we associate with every transition scheme a substitution scheme and then argue that the two schemes show the <u>same behaviour</u>. The construction we use is rather straight forward. We leave S unchanged but refine T such that we can distinguish several instances of a transition $t \in T$ according to the different changes it may effect in different contexts.

Theorem 2: Let $(S,T;r)$ be a transition scheme, and let $\hat{T}$, ϱ, and $\hat{r}$ be derived in the following way:

1) $\hat{T} := \{(t,\Delta(k_1,k_2)) \mid (k_1,t,k_2) \in r\}$
2) $\varrho : \hat{T} \to K \times K$ such that $\varrho : (t,(k,k')) \mapsto (k,k')$
3) $(k_1,\hat{u},k_2) \in \hat{r} \iff \exists u: [(k_1,u,k_2) \in r \wedge$
$$\hat{u} = \{(t,\Delta(k_1,k_t)) \mid t \in u \wedge (k_1,t,k_t) \in r\}]$$

Then $(S,\hat{T};\varrho,\hat{r})$ is a substitution scheme.

For a given transition scheme $(S,T;r)$, we call $(S,\hat{T};\varrho,\hat{r})$ its associated substitution scheme, or its substitution scheme representation, since the two look very similar in the following sense:

Proposition 5: Let $(S,T;r)$ and $(S,\hat{T};\varrho,\hat{r})$ be as in theorem 2, and let $(K,r;Q,Z,L)$ and $(K,\hat{r};\hat{Q},\hat{Z},\hat{L})$ be the corresponding labelled graphs (see proposition 1). Then

1) The two directed graphs are isomorphic by virtue of the identity function between constellations and the bijection between r and $\hat{r}$ established by theorem 2(3).
2) The labels of any two corresponding arcs are of equal cardinality.

From an abstract point of view, this result would probably justify already the statement that the two transition schemes show the same behaviour, that they are behaviourally equivalent. However, we can say, and intend to say, more about this similarity before we call it behavioural equivalence.

The transformation of a transition scheme into the associated substitution scheme preserves a set of fundamental (behavioural) patterns, or fundamental situations as they were called by Petri [15] for the condition/event-system model. Fundamental patterns are small substructures of a transition scheme, involving one, two, or three elementary changes whose interpretation will enable us to distinguish and classify several basic phenomena in the behaviour of systems.

We do not claim that the list of fundamental patterns we are going to show is complete. Rather, we define fundamental patterns to be those patterns in transitional schemes which, by our understanding of behaviour, must be preserved by behavioural equivalence transformations. Thus, behavioural equivalence depends on the notion of fundamental patterns being preserved.

In displaying these patterns it is essential that we be able to express both the presence and the absence of certain elements in a given transition rule r. In the following pictorial list, we use solid arrows for representing the presence, and dotted arrows for representing the absence, of an element. With each pattern we associate a corresponding notion known from the theory and practice of systems organization.

<u>Theorem 3</u>: The substitution scheme representation of a transition scheme preserves the following fundamental behavioural patterns:

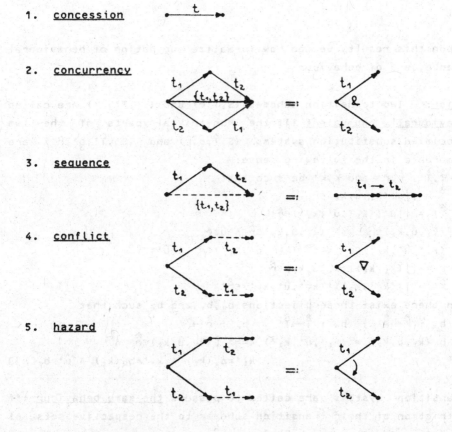

1. <u>concession</u>

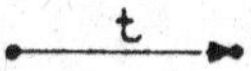

2. <u>concurrency</u>

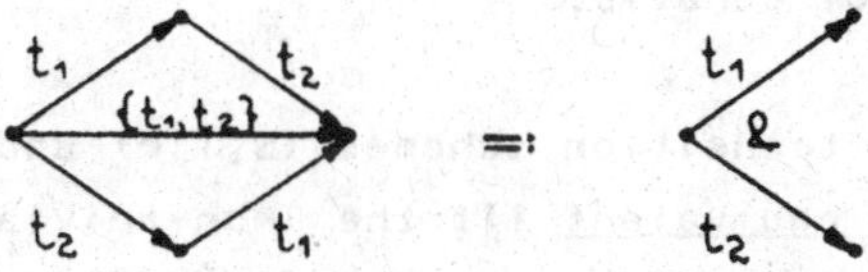

3. <u>sequence</u>

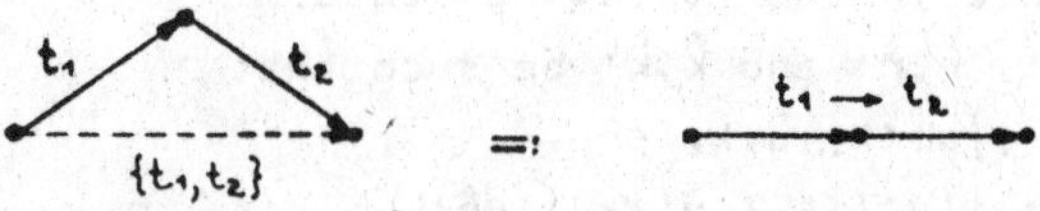

4. <u>conflict</u>

5. <u>hazard</u>

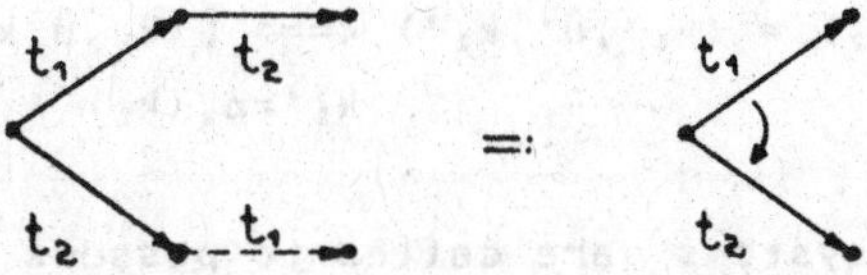

6. funnel

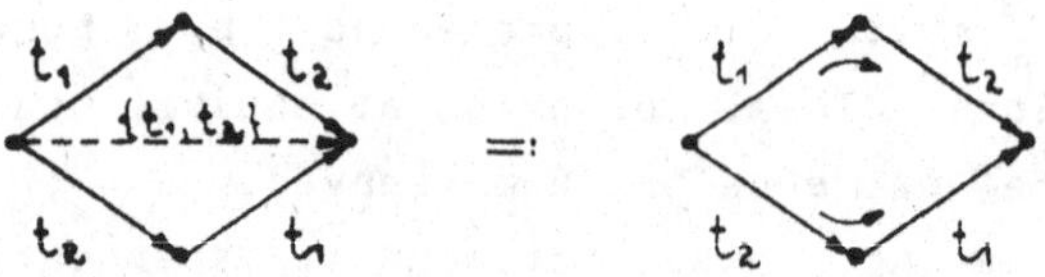

7. confusion (of concurrency with conflict or hazard)

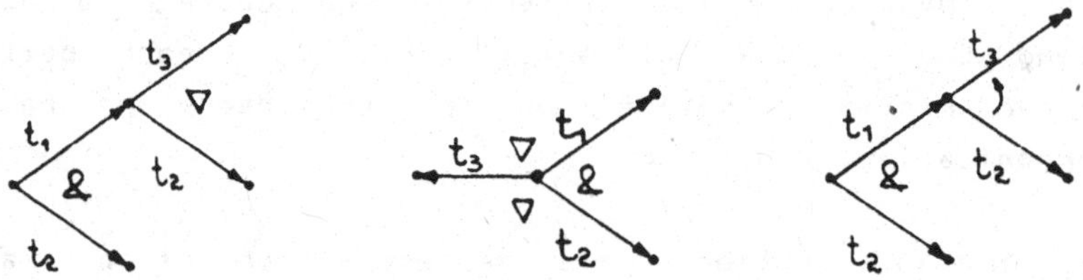

Based upon this result, we can now formalize our notion of behavioural equivalence, and of behaviour:

Definition: Two transition schemes $(S,T;r)$ and $(S',T';r')$ are called behaviourally equivalent iff the non-trivial parts of the two associated substitution systems $(S,\hat{T};\varrho,\hat{r})$ and $(S',\hat{T}';\varrho',\hat{r}')$ are isomorphic in the following sense:

Let $\hat{\hat{T}},\hat{\hat{T}}'$, $\hat{\hat{r}},\hat{\hat{r}}'$ and $\hat{\hat{K}},\hat{\hat{K}}'$ be such that

1) $\hat{\hat{T}} = \bigcup u \mid (k_1,u,k_2)\in\hat{r}$

$\hat{\hat{T}}' = \bigcup u' \mid (k_1',u',k_2')\in\hat{r}'$

$(k_1,\hat{u},k_2)\in\hat{\hat{r}} \iff (k_1,\hat{u},k_2)\in\hat{r} \wedge \hat{u}\neq\emptyset$

$(k_1',\hat{u}',k_2')\in\hat{\hat{r}}' \iff (k_1',\hat{u}',k_2')\in\hat{r}' \wedge \hat{u}'\neq\emptyset$

$\hat{\hat{K}} = \bigcup \{k_1,k_2\} \mid (k_1,\hat{u},k_2)\in\hat{\hat{r}}$

$\hat{\hat{K}}' = \bigcup \{k_1',k_2'\} \mid (k_1',\hat{u}',k_2')\in\hat{\hat{r}}'$

Then there exist three bijections b_K, b_T, and b_r such that

2) $b_K : \hat{\hat{K}}\rightarrow\hat{\hat{K}}'$; $b_T : \hat{\hat{T}}\rightarrow\hat{\hat{T}}'$; $b_r : \hat{\hat{r}}\rightarrow\hat{\hat{r}}'$

3) $b_r(k_1,\hat{u},k_2) = (k_1',\hat{u}',k_2') \iff [(k_1,\hat{u},k_2)\in\hat{\hat{r}} \wedge$

$k_1'=b_K(k_1) \wedge k_2'=b_K(k_2) \wedge \hat{u}'=b_T[\hat{u}]]$

Two transition systems are called to possess the same behaviour iff the restriction of their transition schemes to the respective sets of cases (cf. prop. 2) are behaviourally equivalent. We call the behaviour of a system, i.e. the class of all systems with the same behaviour, sequential iff there is no step $(k_1,u,k_2)\in r$ with $|u|>1$, and non-sequential otherwise.

2. Substitution Systems

So far we have stated the minimal requirements to be fulfilled by the basic rules of change in any model of systems with concurrency. We have shown some immediate logical consequences of these requirements and have arrived at a point where we can claim that there is a simple (meta) model, called substitution systems, which is sufficiently general and powerful.

However, without exhibiting additional properties or incorporating some concrete ideas about systems organization, our substitution systems may be viewed as being too general to be of any real use. And we expect, indeed, that a concrete system model gives an answer to questions like the following ones:

- Is there a particular concept of event being employed by the model?
- How is the concession of an event determined by a system which does not satisfy the extensionality principle?
- Can the cardinality of the set of conditions effected by an event be limited independent of the size of cases without limiting the modelling power?
- What are the system invariants which characterize the behaviour of a system?
- Do the systems obey certain conservation laws?
- ...

We are now going to present three different examples ('implementations') of substitution systems each answering such questions in an essentially different way. Two of the models, the condition/event Systems and the loosely coupled systems, are well known from literature. Therefore they will be dealt with only in a rather sketchy manner. The third example, called the assignment system model, is not nearly as well known and we will deal with it first.

2.1. Assignment Systems

In an assignment system the occurrence of an event e affects the holding of exactly one condition b. If e occurs at c and leads to c' then either $b \notin c$ and $c' = c \cup \dot{b}$ or $b \in c$ and $c' = c - \dot{b}$ ($\dot{x}$ denotes the singelton set {x}). The term 'assignment' is motivated by the following observation: A case c can be viewed as specifying the value 1 ($b \in c$) or the value 0 ($b \notin c$) for each condition b. Now assume that the event e occurs at c and leads to c' and that $c' = c \dot{\cup} b$ (hence $b \notin c$). The occurrence of e can then be looked upon as an assignment. It _assigns_ the new value 1 (c') to the (boolean) variable b whose current value is 0 (c).

We note that in this model, the occurrence of an event causes the least amount of change imanigable in condition holdings, due to axiom TS2. As a result, the mere applicability of the assignment associated with an event can not completely determine its concession at a case. If it does, then we will have a degenerate system of independent assigners. Consequently, our system model will be organized around the principle of coordinating a set of assigners of a very primitive kind where the desired coordination is achieved through _side-conditions_ and _side-effects_ alone (no flow). These remarks will sound less cryptic once we have defined the model. To do this we begin by recalling the notion of a directed graph.

Definition: A _directed graph_ is a quadruple $G = (V,A;Q,Z)$ where,

1) $V \cup A \neq \emptyset$ and $V \cap A = \emptyset$.
2) $Q,Z \in [A \rightarrow V]$ are the _source_ and _target_ functions respectively (let $[X \rightarrow Y]$ denote, for sets X and Y, the set of all functions from X into Y).

   V is the set of nodes and A is the set of arcs. For an arc $a \in A$, $I(a) := \{a' | Z(a') = Q(a)\}$ shall denote the set of arcs _preceding_ a.

Definition: An _assignment system_ is a 6-tuple $S = (P,X;Q,Z,F,C)$ where:

1) $(P,X;Q,Z)$ is a directed graph.
2) $F : X \rightarrow \bigcup [\mathcal{P}(I(x)) \rightarrow \{\emptyset, \dot{x}\}] | x \in X$, such that

$$\forall x \in X : F(x) \in [\mathcal{P}(I(x)) \rightarrow \{\emptyset, \dot{x}\}]$$

   (by $\dot{x}$ we denote the singleton $\{x\}$)
3) $C \subseteq \mathcal{P}(X)$.

P is the set of _preservers_. X, the set of arcs, will be often referred to as (system) _variables_ and sometimes as _conditions_. From the context, it will be clear whether we are dealing with $x \in X$ as a two-valued variable or as an arc of a directed graph or as a condition. Considering F, we note that the codomain of F is a set of functions. Hence $\forall x \in X$, we will denote F(x) as f_x . By definition,

$$f_x : \mathcal{P}(I(x)) \rightarrow \{\emptyset, \dot{x}\} .$$

C is the set of <u>cases</u> where a case is a set of conditions (that hold concurrently). C will have to satisfy an important requirement. Roughly speaking, C should be connected w.r.t. the operation of case-to-case transformation through the occurrence of a <u>step</u>. In what follows immediately however, we will concentrate on first bringing out very quickly the salient features of the model. Towards the end of the section we will define the notion of a step and complete our definition of the model.

Every arc x is accompanied by a function f_x. We shall view the ordered pair (x, f_x) as representing the left hand and right hand side of an assignment. We will, in fact call (x, f_x) an <u>assigner</u> and write for the sake of convenience a_x instead of (x, f_x).

Let $c \in C$ and $x \in X$. We say that a_x is <u>excited</u> at c if $f_x(c \cap I(x)) \neq c \cap \dot{x}$. In other words, $x \in c$ and $f_x(c \cap I(x)) = \emptyset$ or $x \notin c$ and $f_x(c \cap I(x)) = \dot{x}$. An excited assigner a_x may <u>fire</u> at c and when it fires it leads to a new c' given by $c' = (c - \dot{x}) \cup f_x(c \cap I(x))$. We can equivalently write,

$$c' = \begin{cases} c - \dot{x}, & \text{if } f_x(c \cap I(x)) = \emptyset \\ c \cup \dot{x}, & \text{if } f_x(c \cap I(x)) = \dot{x} . \end{cases}$$

We note that a_x is excited at c implies, $f_x(c \cap I(x)) = \emptyset$ iff $x \in c$. Hence the effect of a_x firing at c is to either remove x from c (if $x \in c$) or to add x to c (if $x \notin c$). To interpret this as an assignment we just need to observe that c may be viewed as specifying a boolean value for every variable. Let $c \in C$.

$\forall x \in X$:

$$c(x) = \begin{cases} 1, & \text{if } x \in c \\ 0, & \text{otherwise.} \end{cases}$$

In the same spirit, corresponding to every f_x we can construct a boolean function $g_x : \{0,1\}^n \rightarrow \{0,1\}$ where $n = |I(x)|$. To sketch this idea, given $n = |I(x)|$, we start with the natural 1-1 correspondence $h : \mathcal{P}(I(x)) \rightarrow \{0,1\}^n$ where $h(y) = z$ such that, $\forall b \in I(x)$, the bth component of Z denoted as Z(b) is given by:

$$Z(b) = \begin{cases} 1, & \text{if } b \in y \\ 0, & \text{if } b \notin y. \end{cases}$$

We now define g_x as follows:

$$g_x(z) = \begin{cases} 0, & f_x(h^{-1}(z)) = \emptyset \\ 1, & f_x(h^{-1}(z)) = \dot{x} \end{cases}$$

Now let $c \in C$ and $x \in X$ such that a_x is excited (has concession) at c. When a_x fires at c, the effect is to assign the new value as specified $g_x(h(c \cap I(x)))$ to the current value of x.

$$x \Leftarrow= g_x(h(c \cap I(x)))$$

In fig. 1 an example of an assignment system is shown. Here we have indicated a member of C by the value it assigns to the various variables. Instead of indicating f_x, we have specified a boolean expression denoting the corresponding g_x.

$C = \{x_5, x_6, x_7\}$. In other words, $x_i=0$ for $1 \le i \le 4$, and $x_j=1$ for $5 \le j \le 7$.

$g_1 = \overline{x_6}$

$g_2 = \overline{x_7}$

$g_3 = x_4$

$g_4 = x_1 x_2 + x_2 x_3 + x_3 x_1$

$g_5 = x_3 \quad g_6 = g_7 = x_5$

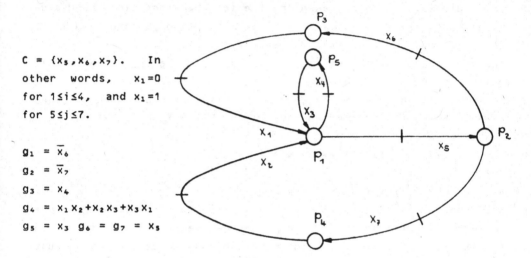

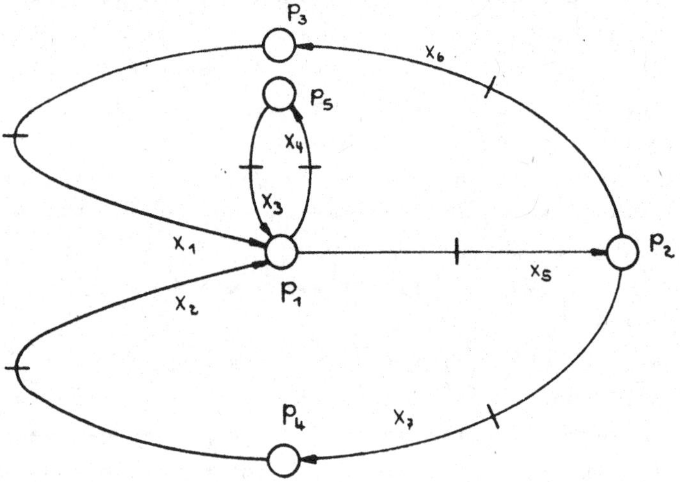

Fig. 1

A vertical bar on an arc indicates the assigner which separates the current value from the new value. Starting from the case indicated, <u>some</u> of the case transformations that can occur are shown in fig. 2. At $c=\{x_5, x_6, x_7\}$, a_5 is excited because $I(x_5)=\{x_1, x_2, x_3\}$, $I(x_5) \cap c = \emptyset$, $f_5(\emptyset)=\emptyset$, due to $g_5(0)=0$. But then, at c, $x_5=1$ and hence a_5 is excited at c. The labels on the arcs in fig. 2 indicate the set of arcs that can fire concurrently.

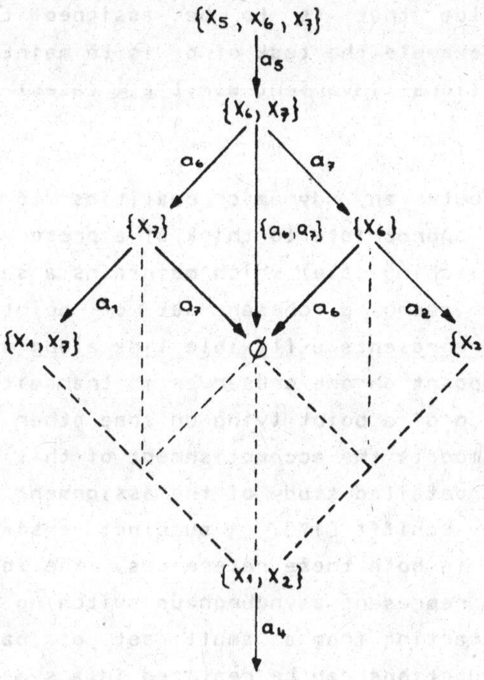

Fig. 2

As this example indicates, assigners may fire concurrently. In general, the behaviour of an assignment system can exhibit hazards. For example, in fig. 1, if we consider a case c' at which both a_3 and a_5 are excited then the firing of a_3 will remove the concession of a_5 but not vice versa.

To bring out our view of the roles played by the preservers, we consider p_1 of fig. 1, shown again below.

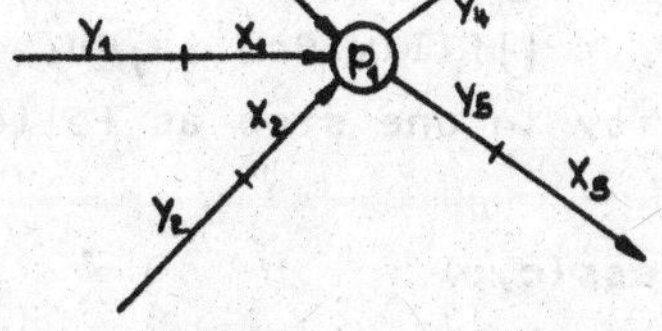

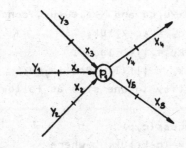

fig. 3

Suppose for each variable we introduce a corresponding y-variable.

y_i carries the new value that is to be assigned to x_i whenever a_i fires. Then in our example the task of p_1 is to maintain (preserve) the two invariant relations (invarient w.r.t all cases)

$y_4 = x_1x_2+x_2x_3+x_3x_1$

$y_5 = x_3$

We do not attribute any dynamic qualities to the role of a preserver. It is more appropriate to think of a preserver as a rigid body (rather than a switching gate) which maintains a set of invariant geometrical relations among a chosen set of points lying on its surface. An arc then represents a flexible link along which a change in the position of a point on one preserver is transmitted to produce a change in the position of a point lying on some other preserver. The firing of an assigner models the accomplishment of this propagation.

To date, the most detailed study of the assignment system model has been carried out by Schiffl [17]. A succinct version of this work may be found in [19]. In both these references, the focus is on ways of using the model to represent asynchronous switching circuits. The major result is that starting from a small set of basic elements, arbitrary switching functions can be realized in a systematic fashion in the form of a hazard-free assignment system.

To conclude this section, we will introduce the notion of a step and complete the formal definitions of the model. We will then be able to show that assignment systems belong to the family of substitution systems. Let $S = (P,X;Q,Z,F,C)$ be an assignment system. Let $A = \{a_x \mid x \in X\}$ be the set of assigners. Let $x \in X$ and $c \in C$. Then,

$$\text{concess}(c,a_x) :\Longleftrightarrow f_x(I(x)\cap c) \neq \dot{x}\cap c \; .$$

Let $u \subseteq X$ and $c \in C$. Then,

$$\text{concess}(c,u) :\Longleftrightarrow \begin{array}{l} 1)\ \forall a_x \in u,\ \text{concess}(c,a_x) \\ 2)\ \forall u_1 \subseteq u \text{ and } \forall a_x \in u-u_1,\ \text{concess}(c_1,a_x) \text{ where,} \\ \quad c_1 = (c-k_1)\cup k_2 \\ \quad k_1 = \bigcup \dot{y} \ \mid a_y \in u_1 \\ \quad k_2 = \bigcup f_y(I(y)\cap c) \mid a_y \in u_1 . \end{array}$$

We can now define reachability in one step as follows:

$\hat{r} \subseteq C \times \mathcal{P}(A) \times C$ is given by

$$(c,u,c') \in \hat{r} \Longleftrightarrow \begin{array}{l} 1)\ \text{concess}(c,u) \\ 2)\ c' = (c-k_1)\cup k_2 \quad \text{where} \\ \quad k_1 = \bigcup \dot{x} \mid a_x \in u, \quad k_2 = \bigcup f_x(I(x)\cap c) \mid a_x \in u \end{array}$$

We demand that every assignment system satisfy:

<u>Axiom</u>

<u>ASG1</u>: Let $\Sigma = (P,X;Q,Z,F,C)$ be an assignment system. Then $\forall c,c' \in C$, $\exists c_1,c_2,\dots,c_n \in C$ and $u_1,u_2,\dots,u_{n-1} \subseteq A$ such that,

1) $c=c_1$ and $c_n=c'$
2) For $1 \le i < n$, $(c_i,u_i,c_{i+1}) \in \hat{r}$ or $(c_{i+1},u_i,c_i) \in \hat{r}$.

Thus the set of cases is required to be connected under $\hat{r}$. To see that this model may be viewed as a substitution system, we first extend the notion of concession to the set of configurations, $K=\mathcal{P}(X)$. In other words, for $k \in K$ and $u \subseteq A$, we talk about concess(k,u). Using this notion we extend $\hat{r}$ to yield r' where $r' \subseteq K \times \mathcal{P}(A) \times K$. The details are straightforward and we shall omit them.

We then set $S=X$ and obtain T as follows:

$$T = \{a_x^+, a_x^- \mid a_x \in A\}$$

Next we specify $\varrho : T \to K \times K$ $(K=\mathcal{P}(S))$ to be:

$$\forall a_x \in A: \ \varrho(a_x^+) = (\emptyset,\dot{x}) \text{ and } \varrho(a_x^-) = (\dot{x},\emptyset).$$

An assigner a_x can fire in two different contexts. In one kind of firing modelled by a_x^+, the condition x is added to the constellation at which it fires. In the second context, modelled by a_x^-, the condition x is removed from the constellation at which a fires.

r, the required step relation is derived from r' as follows: $r \subseteq K \times \mathcal{P}(T) \times K$ where,

$$(k,u,k') \in r \iff 1)\ \forall a_x \in A : \{a_x^+, a_x^-\} \not\subseteq u$$
$$2)\ (k,v,k') \in r' \text{ where } v = \{a_x \in A \mid \{a_x^+,a_x^-\} \cap u \neq \emptyset\}.$$

It is straight forward to verify the following result.

<u>Theorem 4</u>: $(S,T;\varrho,r,C)$ as defined above is a substitution system.

2.2. <u>Loosely Coupled Systems</u>

The next example of a concrete system model implementing a particular class of substitution systems was introduced in order to study the consequences of mutual-exclusion-like couplings between components of dynamic systems. This model has been studied in detail by H. Wedde, and the interested reader is referred to [9],[10] and [20].

There are not many assumptions made on the structure and the behaviour of the system components. So it is possible to focus the attention on the effects caused by the coupling. The coupling itself is called loose because no finite synchronic distance is imposed on any two events belonging to different system components.

The only assumption about the system components called <u>parts</u> will be that every component is in any state-of-affairs in exactly one phase. A consequence of this assumption is that the events of a component are changes between single phases within that component. This implies that, in terms of conditions, each event has exactly one pre- and exactly one postcondition. Moreover, for every permitted change (event) is the reverse change also an event.

Another consequence of our assumption is that concurrency is 'expelled' from the components. It rather turns out to be a relation (of causal independence) between events of different components. The mutual exclusion relation then is introduced to indicate which phases are incompatible with each other.

<u>Definition</u>: A quintuple $(S;P,T,M,C)$ is called a <u>loosely coupled system</u>, iff

1) S is a set of <u>phases</u>, $K := \wp(S)$ is the corresponding set of <u>constellations</u>.

2) $P = \{p_1,\ldots,p_n\}$ is a finite set of <u>parts</u> partitioning S:
$\bigcup p \mid p \in P = S$ <u>and</u> $\forall p \in P : p \neq \emptyset$ <u>and</u> $\forall p,p' \in P : p \neq p' \Longrightarrow p \cap p' = \emptyset$

3) T is the set of <u>transitions</u> with
$T = \bigcup T_i \mid 1 \leq i \leq n$ where
$T_i := \{(b,b') \mid b,b' \in p_i \wedge b \neq b'\}$ for $1 \leq i \leq n$
For a given $t \in T$ we set $t =: ({}^\bullet t, t^\bullet)$, and accordingly for $u \subseteq T$:
${}^\bullet u := \bigcup {}^\bullet t \mid t \in u$ and $u^\bullet := \bigcup t^\bullet \mid t \in u$.

4) $M \subseteq S \times S - id$ is the <u>coupling relation</u> with
$M = \bigcup M\langle p,p'\rangle \mid p,p' \in P \wedge p \neq p'$ where
$\forall p,p' \in P, p \neq p' : M\langle p,p'\rangle \subseteq p \times p'$
$\forall p,p' \in P, p \neq p' : M\langle p,p'\rangle = M\langle p',p\rangle^{-1}$

5) C is the set of <u>cases</u> with $C \subseteq K' \subseteq K$ where
$K' := \{k \in K \mid \forall p \in P : |k \cap p| = 1 \wedge \forall b,b' \in k : (b,b') \notin M\}$
is the set of constellations which consist of n uncoupled phases, one from each part.

6) C is connected with respect to the <u>transition rule</u> $r \subseteq K' \times \wp(T) \times K'$ which is defined in the following way. For $t \in T$ and $u \subseteq T$,
$concess(k,t) :\Longleftrightarrow k \in K' \wedge {}^\bullet t \subseteq k \wedge t^\bullet \cap k = \emptyset \wedge ((k - {}^\bullet t) \cup t^\bullet) \in K'$
$concess(k,u) :\Longleftrightarrow k \in K' \wedge \forall t \in u : concess(k,t) \wedge$
$\neg \exists b,b' \in u^\bullet : (b \neq b' \wedge (b,b') \in M)$
$(k,u,k') \in r :\Longleftrightarrow concess(k,u) \wedge k' = (k - {}^\bullet u) \cup u^\bullet$

An immediate consequence of our definition is the following property of loosely coupled systems:

<u>Proposition 6</u>: The transition rule r of a loosely coupled system (S;P,T,M,C) is <u>symmetrical</u>, i.e. for every $(k,u,k')\in r$ there exists a $v\subseteq T$ with $(k',v,k)\in r$.

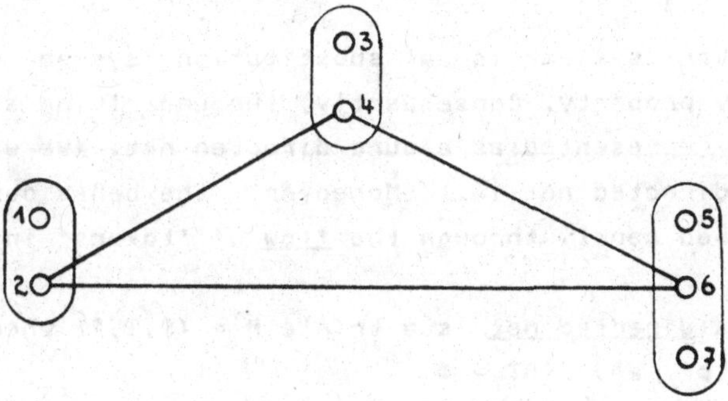

Fig. 4

In fig. 4 a loosely coupled system is shown that consists of three parts $p_1 = \{1,2\}$, $p_2 = \{3,4\}$, $p_3 = \{5,6,7\}$. The coupling relation (mutual exclusion) between different parts is represented by undirected arcs between phases.

The corresponding case graph is shown in fig. 5. There the nodes are representing the cases, every edge represents an event and its reverse, and thus the connectedness of the graph reflects the connectedness of C w.r.t. the relation r.

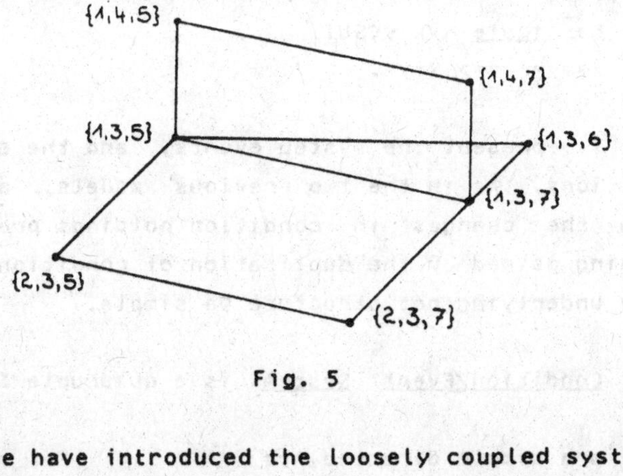

Fig. 5

From the way we have introduced the loosely coupled system model it is now quite easy to get its substitution system representation.

<u>Theorem 5</u>: Let $(S;P,T,M,C)$ be a loosely coupled system, r its transition rule, and $\rho : T \to K \times K$ the identity on T. Then $(S,T;\rho,r,C)$ is a substitution system.

2.3. <u>Condition/Event Systems</u>

A condition/event system is a substitution system which has the extensionality property. Consequently, the underlying structure of the system can be represented as a pure directed net. (We will soon define what a pure directed net is.) Moreover, the behaviour of the system can be described merely through the <u>flow</u> of 'tokens' in such a net.

<u>Definition</u>: A <u>directed net</u> is a triple $N = (S,T;F)$ where:

1) $S \cup T \neq \emptyset$ and $S \cap T = \emptyset$
2) $F \subseteq (S \cup T) \cup (T \times S)$ where $\forall x \in S \cup T : \exists y \in S \cup T$ such that $(x,y) \in F$ or $(y,x) \in F$.

Pictorially, S-elements are drawnn as circles and the T-elements as boxes. Representing the ordered pairs in F as directed arcs leads to a directed bipartite graph.

Let $N = (S,T;F)$ be a directed net. N is said to be <u>pure</u> if $\forall x,y \in S \cup T$, $(x,y) \in F \Rightarrow (y,x) \notin F$. The following notation is basic to the study of CE-systems.

$\forall x \in S \cup T$:

$\bullet x = \{y \mid (y,x) \in F\}$

$x \bullet = \{y \mid (x,y) \in F\}$

N is said to be <u>simple</u> $\forall x,y \in S \cup T$:

$(\bullet x = \bullet y \text{ and } x \bullet = y \bullet) \Rightarrow x = y$.

The elements of T represent the system events, and the elements of S the system conditions. As in the two previous models, an event is identified with the changes in condition holdings produced by its occurrence. Nothing gained by the duplication of conditions. Hence we shall demand the underlying net structure be simple.

<u>Definition</u>: A <u>Condition/Event System</u> is a quadruple $\Sigma = (B,E;F,C)$ where,

1) $(B,E;F)$ is a simple directed net
2) $C \subseteq K(=\mathcal{P}(B))$ is the set of <u>cases</u> .

B is the set of <u>conditions</u> and E is the set of <u>events</u>. An example of a CE-system is shown in fig. 6.

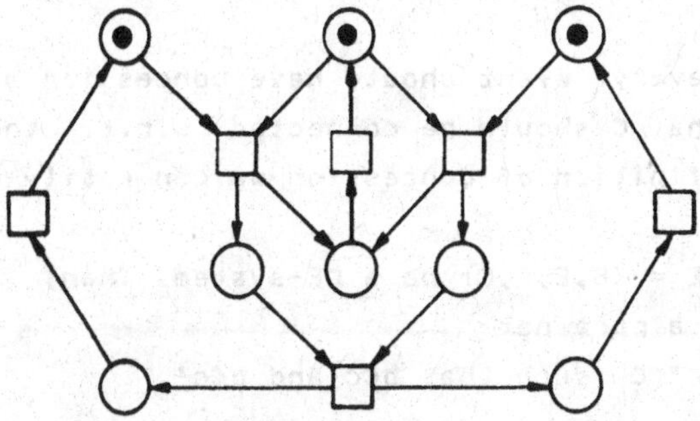

fig. 6

A CE-system will have to meet two additional requirements. To state these, we need the notion of concession and that of a step. Let $\Sigma = (B,E;F,C)$ be a CE-system, $c \in C$ and $e \in E$. Then,

$$\text{concess}(c,e) :\Longleftrightarrow {}^\bullet e \subseteq c \quad \text{and} \quad e^\bullet \cap c = \emptyset$$

Let $c \in C$ and $u \subseteq E$. Then,

$$\text{concess}(c,u) :\Longleftrightarrow 1)\ \forall e \in u : \text{concess}(c,e)$$
$$2)\ \forall e_1, e_2 \in u : {}^\bullet e_1 \cap {}^\bullet e_2 = \emptyset = e_1^\bullet \cap e_2^\bullet$$

The second part of the above definition says that two events e_1 and e_2 which both have concession at a case c are in <u>conflict</u> if they have a pre-condition in common $({}^\bullet e_1 \cap {}^\bullet e_1 \neq \emptyset)$ or a post condition in common $(e_1^\bullet \cap e_2^\bullet \neq \emptyset)$. They can not occur <u>concurrently</u> at c. When an event e occurs, then its pre-conditions $({}^\bullet e)$ cease to hold and its post conditions $(e^\bullet)$ begin to hold. We can now derive the reachability-in-one-step relation.

$\hat{r} \subseteq C \times \mathcal{P}(E) \times C$ is given by:

$$(c,u,c') \in \hat{r} \Longleftrightarrow 1)\ \text{concess}(c,u)$$
$$2)\ c' = (c - {}^\bullet u) \cup u^\bullet \text{ where}$$
$${}^\bullet u = \bigcup {}^\bullet e \mid e \in u \text{ and } u^\bullet = \bigcup e^\bullet \mid e \in u$$

The two requirements that a CE-system should meet are:

<u>Axioms</u>

<u>CE1</u> Let $\Sigma = (B,E;F,C)$ be a CE-system. Then $\forall e \in E : \exists c \in C$ such that concess(c,e).

<u>CE2</u> Let $\Sigma = (B,E;F,C)$ be a CE-system. Then $\forall c,c' \in C : \exists c_1, c_2, \ldots, c_n \in C$

and $u_1, u_2, \ldots, u_{n-1} \subseteq E$ such that:

1) $c=c_1$ and $c_n=c'$
2) $\forall 1 \leq i<n$, $(c_i, u_i, c_{i+1}) \in \hat{r}$ or $(c_{i+1}, u_i, c_i) \in \hat{r}$.

CE1 states that every event should have concession at at least one case. CE2 states that C should be connected w.r.t. the $\hat{r}$ relation. From CE1 and the definition of concession we can easily derive:

Proposition 7: Let $\Sigma = (B,E;F,C)$ be a CE-system. Then,

1) $(B,E;F)$ is a pure net
2) $\forall b \in B$: $\exists c,c' \in C$ such that $b \in c$ and $b \notin c'$.

To bring out the fact that a CE-system is a substitution system which has the extensionality property, we first extend the notion of concession. Let $\Sigma = (B,E;F,C)$ be a CE-system, $k \in K = \mathcal{P}(B)$ and $u \subseteq E$. Then,

concess(k,u) :<==> 1) $\forall e \in u$: $\bullet e \subseteq k$ and $e\bullet \cap k = \emptyset$

2) $\forall e_1, e_2 \in u$: $\bullet e_1 \cap \bullet e_2 = \emptyset = e_1 \bullet \cap e_2 \bullet$

$\hat{r}$ is then extended to $r \subseteq K \times \mathcal{P}(E) \times K$ in the obvious way. Now set S=B, T=E and define $\varrho : E \longrightarrow K \times K$ as:

$$\forall e \in T: \quad \varrho(e) = (\bullet e, e\bullet) \ .$$

Here the dot relation is the one we have defined w.r.t the net (B,E;F). It is straightforward to verify:

Theorem 6: $(S,T;r,\varrho,C)$ as defined above is a substitution sytem which has the extensionality property.

Among the three system models we have outlined, historically, the CE-systems are the earliest [13]. It also the most extensively studied model. Indeed, at the system level of representation, CE-systems provide the foundations for the net theory of systems and processes. A detailed study of the model from this stand point can be found in [3]. The CE-system model has been chosen to play the central role in our theory for many reasons. To list the important ones:

1) The CE-system model is a pure, combinatorial flow model which is free of side-conditions and side-effects. The fundamental situations are easy to depict graphically and to deal with.
2) A system and the processes it supports can be talked about in the same language; namely, the language of nets.

3) CE-systems naturally open up three avenues for enriching the (fomrmal) "flow" language that we start with for talking about systems. These three avenues called "completions" enable us to establish
   a) a solid link to static propositional and predicate logic.
   b) a metric which more than adequately compensates for the absence of a universal sequential time scale.
   c) a conservation principle using which one can begin to study information flow within CE-systems.
4) A clear understanding of the model leads to the formulation of a family of higher level net models which can be used for studying different principles of systems organization at different levels of detail. Place-Transition Systems [1], Bipolar Synchronization Systems [4] and Predicate-Transition Systems [2] are examples of such higher level net models.

3. Conclusion

In this paper we have presented a system model called substitution systems. This model reflects our deeply held belief that concurrency is a basic and not a derived notion. As a result,in our formalism,both the concept of a state(case) and that of a change-in-state(step) have the flavor of concurrency inseperably associated with them. Once this committment is made our axioms concerning concurrency and their consequences (TS5,TS6,theorem 1) are more or less inevitable. The second aspect of this model is that the the changes produced by a step are tied to the well-known mathematical notion of substitution. This simplifies matters considerably and fortunately does not involve any loss of generality (theorem 3). Our notion of behavioural equivalence might appear to be very restrictive. It is restrictive. The point is,starting with this notion,one can arrive at weaker notions of equivalence depending on the context in which one wishes to study equivalence problems.

Turning now to the three 'concrete' models, we have only indicated how they might all be viewed as substitution systems. Due to lack of space we have not been able to exploit this fact to carry out detailed comparisons and transformations. We can however make one little observation already. For an event e,in an assignment system |•eUe•|=1,in a loosely coupled system |•eUe•|=2 and in a condition/event system,in general,|•eUe•|>2. In our future work we hope to offer a richer collection such facts concerniing these three system models.

References

1. Genrich, H.J.; Lautenbach, K.: Facts in Place/Transition-Nets. In: Mathematical Foundations of Computer Science, Ed. Winkowski, J., Lecture Notes in Computer Science 64, pp. 213-231, Berlin, Heidelberg, New York : Springer, 1978
2. Genrich, H.J.; Lautenbach, K.: The Analysis of Distributed Systems by means of Predicate/Transition-Nets. In: Semantics of Concurrent Computation, Ed. Kahn, G., Lecture Notes in Computer Science 70, pp.109-122, Berlin, Heidelberg, New York: Springer, 1979.
3. Genrich, H.J.; Lautenbach, K.: Thiagarajan, P.S.: Elements of General Net Theory. In: Net Theory and Practice, Ed. Brauer, W., Lecture Notes in Computer Science, Berlin, Heidelberg, New York : Springer, 1979.
4. Genrich, H.J.; Thiagarajan, P.S.: Bipolar Synchronization Systems. In: Seventh International Symposium on Automata, Languages, and Programming, Lecture Notes in Computer Science, Berlin, Heidelberg, New York : Springer, 1980
5. Hoare, C.A.R.: Communicating Sequential Processes. CACM, 21, no.8, pp. 666-677, 1978
6. Janicki, R.: A Characterization of Concurrency-like Relations. In: Semantics of Concurrent Computation, Ed. Kahn, G., Lecture Notes in Computer Science 70, pp.109-122, Berlin, Heidelberg, New York : Springer, 1979.
7. Keller, R.M.: Formal Verification of Concurrent Programs. CACM, 19, no.7, pp.371-384, 1976.
8. Lauer, P.E.; Shields, M.W; Best, E.: On the Design and Certification of Asynchronous Systems of Processes. Part 1: COSY - A System Specification Language Based on Paths and Processes, Report ASM 49; Part 2: Formal Theory of the Basic COSY Notation, Report 45, The University of Newcastle upon Tyne, Newcastle, 1978.
9. Lautenbach, K; Wedde, H.: Generating Control Mechanisms by Restrictions. In Mathematical Foundations of Computer Science, ed. Mazurkiewicz, A, Lecture Notes in Computer Science 45, pp. 416-422, Berlin, Heidelberg, New York : Springer, 1976

10. Maggiolo-Schettini, A.; Wedde, H.; Winkowski, J.: Modeling a Solution for a Control Problem in Distributed Systems by Restrictions. In: Semantics of Concurrent Computation, Ed. Kahn, G., Lecture Notes in Computer Science 70, Berlin, Heidelberg, New York: Springer, 1979.

11. Mazurkiewicz, A.: Concurrent Program Schemes and their Interpretation. DAIMI PB-78, Aarhus University, Aarhus, 1977.

12. Milner, R.: Algebraic Concurrency. Notes of a Course given at Aarhus University, 1979.

13. Petri, C.A.: Kommunikation mit Automaten. Bonn : Institut für Instrumentelle Mathematik, Schriften des IIM Nr. 2, 1962

14. Petri, C.A.: Concepts of Net Theory. Mathematical Foundations of Computer Science, Math. Institute of the Slovak Ac. of Sciences, 1973

15. Petri, C.A.: Interpretations of Net Theory. St.Augustin : Gesellschaft für Mathematik und Datenverarbeitung Bonn, Interner Bericht ISF-75-07 (1975)

16. Pnueli, A.: The Temporal Semantics of Concurrent Programs. In: Semantics of Concurrent Computation, Ed. Kahn, G., Lecture Notes in Computer Science 70, pp. 1-20, Berlin, Heidelberg, New York: Springer, 1979.

17. Schiffl, H.: Zuordnungsgraphen. Diplomarbeit, Universität Bonn, Bonn, 1974 (in German)

18. Sifakis, J.: Deadlocks and Livelocks in Transition Systems. In: Mathematical Foundations of Computer Science, Ed. Dembinski, P., Lecture Notes in Computer Science, Berlin, Heidelberg, New York : Springer, 1980 (this volume).

19. Thiagarajan, P.S.: Genrich, H.J.: Assignment Systems - A Model for Asynchronous Computations. ISF-Report 76.10, St.Augustin : Gesellschaft für Mathematik und Datenverarbeitung, 1976

20. Wedde, H.: Lose Kopplung von Systemkomponenten. Bericht der GMD 96, St.Augustin : Gesellschaft für Mathematik und Datenverarbeitung, 1975

Vol. 49: Interactive Systems. Proceedings 1976. Edited by A. Blaser and C. Hackl. VI, 380 pages. 1976.

Vol. 50: A. C. Hartmann, A Concurrent Pascal Compiler for Minicomputers. VI, 119 pages. 1977.

Vol. 51: B. S. Garbow, Matrix Eigensystem Routines – Eispack Guide Extension. VIII, 343 pages. 1977.

Vol. 52: Automata, Languages and Programming. Fourth Colloquium, University of Turku, July 1977. Edited by A. Salomaa and M. Steinby. X, 569 pages. 1977.

Vol. 53: Mathematical Foundations of Computer Science. Proceedings 1977. Edited by J. Gruska. XII, 608 pages. 1977.

Vol. 54: Design and Implementation of Programming Languages. Proceedings 1976. Edited by J. H. Williams and D. A. Fisher. X, 496 pages. 1977.

Vol. 55: A. Gerbier, Mes premières constructions de programmes. XII, 256 pages. 1977.

Vol. 56: Fundamentals of Computation Theory. Proceedings 1977. Edited by M. Karpiński. XII, 542 pages. 1977.

Vol. 57: Portability of Numerical Software. Proceedings 1976. Edited by W. Cowell. VIII, 539 pages. 1977.

Vol. 58: M. J. O'Donnell, Computing in Systems Described by Equations. XIV, 111 pages. 1977.

Vol. 59: E. Hill, Jr., A Comparative Study of Very Large Data Bases. X, 140 pages. 1978.

Vol. 60: Operating Systems, An Advanced Course. Edited by R. Bayer, R. M. Graham, and G. Seegmüller. X, 593 pages. 1978.

Vol. 61: The Vienna Development Method: The Meta-Language. Edited by D. Bjørner and C. B. Jones. XVIII, 382 pages. 1978.

Vol. 62: Automata, Languages and Programming. Proceedings 1978. Edited by G. Ausiello and C. Böhm. VIII, 508 pages. 1978.

Vol. 63: Natural Language Communication with Computers. Edited by Leonard Bolc. VI, 292 pages. 1978.

Vol. 64: Mathematical Foundations of Computer Science. Proceedings 1978. Edited by J. Winkowski. X, 551 pages. 1978.

Vol. 65: Information Systems Methodology, Proceedings, 1978. Edited by G. Bracchi and P. C. Lockemann. XII, 696 pages. 1978.

Vol. 66: N. D. Jones and S. S. Muchnick, TEMPO: A Unified Treatment of Binding Time and Parameter Passing Concepts in Programming Languages. IX, 118 pages. 1978.

Vol. 67: Theoretical Computer Science, 4th GI Conference, Aachen, March 1979. Edited by K. Weihrauch. VII, 324 pages. 1979.

Vol. 68: D. Harel, First-Order Dynamic Logic. X, 133 pages. 1979.

Vol. 69: Program Construction. International Summer School. Edited by F. L. Bauer and M. Broy. VII, 651 pages. 1979.

Vol. 70: Semantics of Concurrent Computation. Proceedings 1979. Edited by G. Kahn. VI, 368 pages. 1979.

Vol. 71: Automata, Languages and Programming. Proceedings 1979. Edited by H. A. Maurer. IX, 684 pages. 1979.

Vol. 72: Symbolic and Algebraic Computation. Proceedings 1979. Edited by E. W. Ng. XV, 557 pages. 1979.

Vol. 73: Graph-Grammars and Their Application to Computer Science and Biology. Proceedings 1978. Edited by V. Claus, H. Ehrig and G. Rozenberg. VII, 477 pages. 1979.

Vol. 74: Mathematical Foundations of Computer Science. Proceedings 1979. Edited by J. Bečvář. IX, 580 pages. 1979.

Vol. 75: Mathematical Studies of Information Processing. Proceedings 1978. Edited by E. K. Blum, M. Paul and S. Takasu. VIII, 629 pages. 1979.

Vol. 76: Codes for Boundary-Value Problems in Ordinary Differential Equations. Proceedings 1978. Edited by B. Childs et al. VIII, 388 pages. 1979.

Vol. 77: G. V. Bochmann, Architecture of Distributed Computer Systems. VIII, 238 pages. 1979.

Vol. 78: M. Gordon, R. Milner and C. Wadsworth, Edinburgh LCF. VIII, 159 pages. 1979.

Vol. 79: Language Design and Programming Methodology. Proceedings, 1979. Edited by J. Tobias. IX, 255 pages. 1980.

Vol. 80: Pictorial Information Systems. Edited by S. K. Chang and K. S. Fu. IX, 445 pages. 1980.

Vol. 81: Data Base Techniques for Pictorial Applications. Proceedings, 1979. Edited by A. Blaser. XI, 599 pages. 1980.

Vol. 82: J. G. Sanderson, A Relational Theory of Computing. VI, 147 pages. 1980.

Vol. 83: International Symposium Programming. Proceedings, 1980. Edited by B. Robinet. VII, 341 pages. 1980.

Vol. 84: Net Theory and Applications. Proceedings, 1979. Edited by W. Brauer. XIII, 537 Seiten. 1980.

Vol. 85: Automata, Languages and Programming. Proceedings, 1980. Edited by J. de Bakker and J. van Leeuwen. VIII, 671 pages. 1980.

Vol. 86: Abstract Software Specifications. Proceedings, 1979. Edited by D. Bjørner. XIII, 567 pages. 1980

Vol. 87: 5th Conference on Automated Deduction. Proceedings, 1980. Edited by W. Bibel and R. Kowalski. VII, 385 pages. 1980.

Vol. 88: Mathematical Foundations of Computer Science 1980. Proceedings, 1980. Edited by P. Dembiński. VIII, 723 pages. 1980.

This series reports new developments in computer science research and teaching – quickly, informally and at a high level. The type of material considered for publication includes:

1. Preliminary drafts of original papers and monographs
2. Lectures on a new field or presentations of a new angle in a classical field
3. Seminar work-outs
4. Reports of meetings, provided they are
   a) of exceptional interest and
   b) devoted to a single topic.

Texts which are out of print but still in demand may also be considered if they fall within these categories.

The timeliness of a manuscript is more important than its form, which may be unfinished or tentative. Thus, in some instances, proofs may be merely outlined and results presented which have been or will later be published elsewhere. If possible, a subject index should be included. Publication of Lecture Notes is intended as a service to the international computer science community, in that a commercial publisher, Springer-Verlag, can offer a wide distribution of documents which would otherwise have a restricted readership. Once published and copyrighted, they can be documented in the scientific literature.

Manuscripts

Manuscripts should be no less than 100 and preferably no more than 500 pages in length.
They are reproduced by a photographic process and therefore must be typed with extreme care. Symbols not on the typewriter should be inserted by hand in indelible black ink. Corrections to the typescript should be made by pasting in the new text or painting out errors with white correction fluid. Authors receive 75 free copies and are free to use the material in other publications. The typescript is reduced slightly in size during reproduction; best results will not be obtained unless the text on any one page is kept within the overall limit of 18 x 26.5 cm (7 x 10½ inches). On request, the publisher will supply special paper with the typing area outlined.
Manuscripts should be sent to Prof. G. Goos, Institut für Informatik, Universität Karlsruhe, Zirkel 2, 7500 Karlsruhe/Germany, Prof. J. Hartmanis, Cornell University, Dept. of Computer-Science, Ithaca, NY/USA 14850, or directly to Springer-Verlag Heidelberg.

Springer-Verlag, Heidelberger Platz 3, D-1000 Berlin 33
Springer-Verlag, Neuenheimer Landstraße 28–30, D-6900 Heidelberg 1
Springer-Verlag, 175 Fifth Avenue, New York, NY 10010/USA

ISBN 3-540-10027-X
ISBN 0-387-10027-X